CASES AND MATERIALS ON
CRIMINAL LAW

Sixth Edition

By

Joshua Dressler

Frank R. Strong Chair in Law
Michael E. Moritz College of Law
The Ohio State University

Stephen P. Garvey

Professor of Law
Cornell Law School

AMERICAN CASEBOOK SERIES®

WEST®

A Thomson Reuters business

Mat #41237935

American Casebook Series is a trademark registered in the U.S. Patent and Trademark Office.

© West, a Thomson business, 1999, 2003, 2007
© 2009 Thomson Reuters
© 2012 Thomson Reuters

    610 Opperman Drive
    St. Paul, MN 55123
    1–800–313–9378

Printed in the United States of America

ISBN: 978–0–314–27982–8

To Maya Shoshana Dressler, for her courage and tenacity
To Lucy Belle Dressler, for her kindness and vivacity

— J.D.

To Carolyn, for her patience
To Liam, for his spirit
To Amon, for his joy

— S.P.G.

Preface to the Sixth Edition

Comments of Joshua Dressler

The response to the first five editions of this casebook has been gratifying. I thank all of you who have used the casebook, and in particular I appreciate the many adopters who have provided feedback on the earlier editions. I urge new adopters to look at the Preface to the First Edition, which follows *this* Preface, to get a sense of the pedagogical goals of this casebook.

Preparing a new edition of a casebook is always a bit troubling. I want to make it better, of course, but I have also always followed the wise but grammatically poor adage, "if it ain't (too) broke, don't fix it (too much)." When I come across a case that I believe might teach a topic better than the current one, the initial and obvious reaction is to change to the new case. But, as you might expect, when I do make such a change, some users love the new case while others are disappointed because they have lost "an old favorite." One might think that updating the Notes and Questions after a case is uncontroversial, but it isn't. Some people are unhappy when an old Note, which worked so well in class, is deleted to make room for a new one. So, I find the job of revising the casebook an ever-present adventure! There are, of course, changes to this edition—some new cases and Notes—all chosen after careful consideration; and I have tried to improve old Notes where I have received useful criticism. For new users (welcome and thanks!), I hope you will be happy with the product. For long-time users, I trust you will find the casebook remains familiar and comfortable.

There is, however, one fairly obvious change from the first five editions: I now have a co-author, Cornell Professor Stephen Garvey. I am honored he has agreed to join the casebook. I have long been an admirer of his scholarship and, luckily for me, he has been a long-time user of the casebook. He is also a wonderful person with whom to work. Most importantly for *your* purposes, we come to the issue of how to teach Criminal Law—what a casebook ought to offer the students—from a largely similar perspective.

Outside reading materials. My recommendations from the first edition, found in the Preface for the First Edition, remain valid today. Two of the texts mentioned there are now in newer editions: my own treatise, Understanding Criminal Law (6th ed. 2012); and Wayne LaFave, Criminal Law (5th ed. 2010).

Personal acknowledgements. I had a lot of help on the new edition. Many users of the casebook (including students) provided advice and suggestions. Many of those suggestions found their way into the new edition. Even where they did not, I benefitted from the comments. Happily for me, I have received help from so many people that I cannot list them all here, but please know that I appreciate—and need—the advice I receive.

Three students helped me prepare the sixth edition of the casebook: Dan Anderson (Moritz '12), Kailee Goold (Moritz '12), and Clara Levrault (Moritz '13). I thank them for their excellent assistance.

As before, my inspiration in life comes from my wife, Dottie.

Comments of Stephen Garvey

I began teaching criminal law over ten years ago using Professor Dressler's casebook. Having grown up, so to speak, on the book, you can well imagine my sense of privilege when asked to help continue its tradition. Professor Dressler, the consummate scholar, has been a patient mentor and wonderful friend and colleague over the years, as he has been for and to countless others. I will do my best to keep the book firmly on the course its principal author, with his characteristic insight and skill, charted nearly twenty years ago. Thanks, too, to you who use the book in your classrooms. The book is all the better for your helpful advice and suggestions. Indeed, my main hope for the future is that you will continue to keep them coming!

September 2012

PREFACE TO THE FIRST EDITION

This casebook was prepared for use in a basic course on criminal law. Although it is designed for a three- or four-unit semester-long class, the casebook will also work well in a shorter course, with deletions, some lecturing, and/or use of outside readings.

As its "author" I bring to this casebook my own experiences and philosophies, but ultimately the book is intended for *your* use, and not simply to please me. Therefore, the cases and readings were selected, the Notes and Questions formulated, and the casebook organized, so that it can comfortably be used by teachers who do not share all, or even most, of my pedagogical goals.

My goals in teaching criminal law. I have taught Criminal Law for nearly twenty years, in five different law schools, to students with widely varied academic backgrounds and capacities, life experiences, and levels of interest in the subject. But, I have always been guided in my teaching by certain general principles:

—Doctrine matters. I use the term "doctrine" here broadly to mean that students ought to leave a course in Criminal Law with a substantial body of knowledge. In the context of this casebook, this means that students will become familiar with the general and the specific: primary attention is directed to the "general part" of the criminal law, i.e., the common law principles of criminal responsibility that serve even today as the core of Anglo–American criminal law; but, as the general cannot be understood except in the context of the specific, some of the most important crimes against persons and property are covered in detail, both in their common law and modern statutory forms.

—In understanding doctrine, penal theory matters. A course in Criminal Law offers students an opportunity to consider jurisprudential concerns more forthrightly than in other first-year courses. Therefore, I want students to put the criminal law in its philosophical context, in particular, to test the rules of criminal responsibility by the standards of retributivism and utilitarianism, in order to see if the criminal law is fair, rational, or even intellectually consistent. I teach my class, and this casebook is written, with the view that these principles of punishment can inform our understanding of the law and guide us in our efforts to reform it.

—In understanding doctrine, other things matter, too. Since the criminal law seeks to affect and to render judgments about human behavior, it seems prudent to take some note of the findings of the behavioral sciences, e.g., psychology, anthropology, and sociology. Students should also see that social, economic, and political forces inevitably shape the law. Often these forces are noncontroversial, but not always. Therefore, the materials in the casebook invite discussion regarding social attitudes about such matters as race, gender, and sexual orientation, where they may have had a substantial impact on the development or application of the criminal law (e.g., rape law, self-defense, provocation, the death penalty).

—Statutes matter. Students start law school bewildered by the case method of study, yet they so quickly grow accustomed to it that many of them lose interest in statutes, even when good lawyering requires their attention. Consequently, I have selected materials that help students understand the rules of statutory construction and appreciate the lawyering skills relating to statutory interpretation. Also, the casebook emphasizes the Model Penal Code, in part so that students have ample opportunity to work with an integrated criminal code.

—Professional ethics matter. Even before they take courses on criminal procedure and professional responsibility, students should be sensitized to some of the ethical issues confronting criminal defense lawyers and prosecutors. I have selected various cases in part because they lend themselves to discussion of professional ethics, to the extent that the teacher wishes to follow this route.

—Controversy in the classroom is good if discussion of it is thoughtful, wide-open, and relevant. I want students to be angry—or pleased—with where the law may be going, because this means that they understand that the criminal law matters deeply in everyone's lives. Consequently, I want students to be aware of the "cutting edge" controversies in the criminal law. In support of this, the casebook is attentive to the Model Penal Code, since virtually all recently drafted penal codes are based, at least in part, on it, and because it provides a thoughtful alternative to the common law. The casebook also brings to the forefront—it does not shy away from—many present-day controversies, such as the death penalty, subjectivization of the objective "reasonable man" standard, "battered woman/child self-defense," suicide assistance and euthanasia, and acquaintance rape.

As I stated earlier, although this casebook is shaped by the preceding principles, it was prepared for use by teachers whose pedagogical goals may differ from mine. I do expect, however, that there will be at least one common link among adopters of this book: A belief that Criminal Law is an exciting subject to teach, in large part because it allows students to confront some of the Big Questions—questions about human nature, personal and social responsibility, and "right and wrong"—which philosophers, theologians, scientists, and poets, as well as lawyers, have grappled with for centuries.

Editing policies. I prefer students to read judicial opinions in largely intact form. Nonetheless, deletions are necessary. Because this book is intended for pedagogical use, rather than for serious scholarly pursuits, I have not followed all scholarly conventions in identifying omissions from the extracted materials. Therefore, users of the book should not quote directly from the extracts in legal or scholarly documents, but should instead go to the primary sources. Specifically, I have applied the following rules of thumb to extracted materials:

1.   Footnotes and citations have been omitted, unless there was a sound pedagogical reason for their retention. Neither ellipses nor other signals have been used to indicate their omission. Asterisks or brackets have been used, however, to indicate deletions of other textual material.

2.   Numbered footnotes are from the original materials and retain their original numbering. My own footnotes are designated by letters.

Outside reading materials. Students who wish to go beyond the casebook for additional study will find excellent references in various forms. Among "hornbooks," I recommend the following, in alphabetical order:

Joshua Dressler, Understanding Criminal Law (Matthew Bender & Co. 1987). This book, addressed to law students, focuses on the issues most commonly covered in criminal law casebooks. Obviously, it is especially suited for use with this casebook. A second edition will be published in the near future.

Wayne LaFave and Austin Scott, Jr., Criminal Law (West Publishing Co. 2d ed. 1986). The student edition is an abridgement of the authors' two-volume lawyers' treatise. Widely cited by courts and lucidly written, it emphasizes modern law and the Model Penal Code.

Rollin M. Perkins and Ronald N. Boyce, Criminal Law (Foundation Press 3d ed. 1982). The late Professor Perkins, one of the foremost scholars of the common law of crimes, originated this treatise. It remains strong in setting out the common law definitions of crimes. There is no special student edition.

Glanville Williams, Criminal Law : The General Part (Stevens & Sons 2d ed. 1961). Written by one of England's paramount scholars, this is the classic English treatise on the general principles of the criminal law.

By far the best reference source regarding the Model Penal Code is:

American Law Institute, Model Penal Code and Commentaries (1980 and 1985). This six-volume reference contains all of the sections of the Model Penal Code and their supporting Commentaries. The Commentaries are exceedingly helpful in explaining pre-Code law and the method and rationale of Code provisions.

Among the best books dealing with the underlying theories of the criminal law are:

George P. Fletcher, Rethinking Criminal Law (Little Brown & Co. 1978). Building heavily on common law traditions and the views of Continental, especially German, legal theorists, the author has written "neither a hornbook nor a treatise, but a reformist, critical work." (Preface, xxiii.) This book has deservedly received substantial scholarly attention since its publication.

Jerome Hall, General Principles of Criminal Law (Bobbs Merrill 2d ed. 1960). Now a classic in the field, the author states as his goal, "to elucidate the basic ideas of criminal law in light of current knowledge and to organize the law in terms of definite theory." (Preface, v.) The book centers on the general part of the criminal law.

H.L.A. Hart, Punishment and Responsibility (Oxford University Press 1968). This book contains previously published essays by the author, then Professor of Jurisprudence at Oxford University, regarding theories of punishment and legal standards of responsibility. These writings have greatly influenced thinking on the subjects.

Leo Katz, Bad Acts and Guilty Minds: Conundrums of the Criminal Law (University of Chicago Press 1987). Katz draws on insights from philosophy, psychology, and anthropology, as well as on well-known fictional incidents, to reflect on the basic concepts of the criminal law. Written for a general audience, the book provides considerable "food for thought."

Personal acknowledgements.[1] Many people assisted me in producing this book. Various colleagues offered useful advice and specific suggestions (many of which found their way into the book), including: Peter Arenella (UCLA); Pamela Bucy (Alabama); Linda Carter (McGeorge); Deborah Denno (Fordham); Catherine Hancock (Tulane); Yale Kamisar (Michigan); Leo Katz (Pennsylvania); Larry Levine (McGeorge); Fred Lawrence (Boston University); Steve Morse (Pennsylvania); Michael Perlin (New York); Michael Vitiello (McGeorge); and David Yellen (Hofstra). Especially generous with their time were two of my colleagues from Wayne State University: Lee Lamborn, who gave me many leads on materials to include in the text; and Jessica Litman, who was amazingly patient as I hounded her with copyright law questions.

My student research assistants helped me search for cases, commented on early drafts of the manuscript, and did critical cite checking. From Wayne State, I thank Joseph Hart, Sarah Resnick, Ted Tow and Mark Zousmer; from McGeorge, my thanks go to Sidonie Christian, Debra Larson, and Barry deWalt.

Thanks also go to June Frierson (Wayne State), on whom I called often for assistance in typing and reproduction of the manuscript. She did this work for me promptly, well, and with good humor.

I must also mention a few people who have helped me in very special ways. John Dolan and Lee Lamborn (Wayne State) are, quite simply, mensches. No matter how busy they were, their office doors were open to me when my work on the casebook—or life in general—temporarily got me down. They were and are true friends.

Nobody has provided me with greater support and love over the years than my partner in life, Dottie Kridler Dressler. I am not exaggerating when I say that this casebook would not have been born without her presence by my side.

Finally, I want to acknowledge two other persons who have influenced me. The first is David Dressler, who during his too-short life was Chief of Parole for New York State, a professor of both sociology and criminology, a

---

1. Copyright acknowledgements are separately listed.

scholar and talented writer (many of us are the former, but few are the latter), and, most importantly, my father. He never said, "Be as I am" or "Look at me," but nobody has been a more powerful role model in my life than he.

The other person whose influence cannot be understated is Sandy Kadish, one of this country's most thoughtful criminal law scholars and legal educators. Nobody can look at this casebook without realizing his influence on it. And, how could it be otherwise? I studied criminal law from his casebook (Paulsen and Kadish; and then Kadish and Paulsen) and, for fifteen years, I taught the subject from his book (now, Kadish and Schulhofer). With the publication of my own casebook comes my professional bar mitzvah, but I can think of no higher accolade than if someone were to say of this book, "Why, it is a son-of-Kadish (and Schulhofer)."

JOSHUA DRESSLER

April 1994

COPYRIGHT ACKNOWLEDGEMENTS

David P. Bruden & Sonja Lengnick, *Rape in the Criminal Justice System*, 87 Journal of Criminal Law and Criminology 1194 (1997). Copyright © 1997, Northwestern University, School of Law. Reprinted by special permission of Northwestern University School of Law, *Journal of Criminal Law and Criminology*, vol. 87, issue 4, 1997.

Pamela H. Bucy, *Corporate Ethos: A Standard for Imposing Corporate Criminal Liability*, 75 Minnesota Law Review 1095 (1991). Copyright © 1991, Minnesota Law Review Foundation. Reprinted by permission.

Peter Buscemi, Note, *Conspiracy: Statutory Reform Since the Model Penal Code*, 75 Columbia Law Review 1122 (1975). Copyright © 1975 by the Directors of the Columbia Law Review Association, Inc. All Rights Reserved. This article originally appeared at 75 Colum. L. Rev. 1122 (1975). Reprinted by permission.

Paul D. Butler, *Race–Based Jury Nullification: Case-in-Chief*, 30 John Marshall Law Review 911 (1997). Copyright © 1997, John Marshall Law Review. Reprinted by permission.

Stephen L. Carter, *When Victims Happen to be Black*, 97 Yale Law Journal 420 (1988). Copyright © 1988, Stephen L. Carter. Reprinted by permission.

John C. Coffee, Jr., *"No Soul to Damn: No Body to Kick": An Unscandalized Inquiry Into the Problem of Corporate Punishment*, 79 Michigan Law Review 386 (1981). Copyright © 1981, John C. Coffee, Jr. Reprinted by permission.

Richard Cohen, "Closing the Door on Crime," *Washington Post Magazine*, September 7, 1986, at W13. Copyright © 1986, Washington Post Writers Group. Reprinted with permission.

Doriane Lambelet Coleman, *Individualizing Justice Through Multiculturalism: The Liberals' Dilemma*, 96 Columbia Law Review 1093 (1996). Copyright © 1996, Directors of the Columbia Law Review Association, Inc. All Rights Reserved. This article originally appeared at 96 Colum.L.Rev. 1093 (1996). Reprinted by permission.

Anne M. Coughlin, *Sex and Guilt*, 84 Virginia Law Review 1 (1998). Copyright © 1998, Virginia Law Review Association. Reprinted with permission of the Virginia Law Review Association, William S. Hein, Co., successor to Fred B. Rothman & Co., and the author.

David Crump & Susan Waite Crump, *In Defense of the Felony Murder Doctrine*, 8 Harvard Journal of Law & Public Policy 359 (1985). Copyright © 1985 by the Harvard Society for Law & Public Policy Inc. Reprinted with permission of the *Harvard Journal of Law and Public Policy*.

The Cultural Defense in the Criminal Law, 99 Harvard Law Review 1293 (1986). Copyright © 1986 by the Harvard Law Review Association. Reprinted by permission.

Richard Delgado, *"Rotten Social Background": Should the Criminal Law Recognize a Defense of Severe Environmental Deprivation?*, 3 Law &

Summary of Contents

TABLE OF CONTENTS

———————

TABLE OF CASES

The principal cases are in bold type. Cases cited or discussed in the text are in roman type. References are to pages. Cases cited in principal cases and within other quoted materials are not included.

TABLE OF MODEL PENAL CODE SECTIONS

CASES AND MATERIALS ON
CRIMINAL LAW

Sixth Edition

CHAPTER 1

INTRODUCTION: SETTING THE STAGE

■ ■ ■

A. NATURE, SOURCES, AND LIMITS OF THE CRIMINAL LAW

HENRY M. HART, JR.—THE AIMS OF THE CRIMINAL LAW

23 Law and Contemporary Problems 401 (1958), 402–406

* * * What do we mean by "crime" and "criminal"? Or, put more accurately, what should we understand to be "the method of the criminal law," the use of which is in question? This latter way of formulating the preliminary inquiry is more accurate, because it pictures the criminal law as a process, a way of doing something, which is what it is. * * *

What then are the characteristics of this method?

1. The method operates by means of a series of directions, or commands, formulated in general terms, telling people what they must or must not do. Mostly, the commands of the criminal law are "must-nots," or prohibitions, which can be satisfied by inaction. "Do not murder, rape, or rob." But some of them are "musts," or affirmative requirements, which can be satisfied only by taking a specifically, or relatively specifically, described kind of action. "Support your wife and children," and "File your income tax return."

2. The commands are taken as valid and binding upon all those who fall within their terms when the time comes for complying with them, whether or not they have been formulated in advance in a single authoritative set of words. They speak to members of the community, in other words, in the community's behalf, with all the power and prestige of the community behind them.

3. The commands are subject to one or more sanctions for disobedience which the community is prepared to enforce.

Thus far, it will be noticed, nothing has been said about the criminal law which is not true also of a large part of the noncriminal, or civil, law. The law of torts, the law of contracts, and almost every other branch of private law that can be mentioned operate, too, with general directions prohibiting or requiring described types of conduct, and the community's tribunals enforce these commands. What, then, is distinctive about the method of the criminal law?

Can crimes be distinguished from civil wrongs on the ground that they constitute injuries to society generally which society is interested in preventing? The difficulty is that society is interested also in the due fulfillment of contracts and the avoidance of traffic accidents and most of the other stuff of civil litigation. The civil law is framed and interpreted and enforced with a constant eye to these social interests. Does the distinction lie in the fact that proceedings to enforce the criminal law are instituted by public officials rather than private complainants? The difficulty is that public officers may also bring many kinds of "civil" enforcement actions—for an injunction, for the recovery of a "civil" penalty, or even for the detention of the defendant by public authority. Is the distinction, then, in the peculiar character of what is done to people who are adjudged to be criminals? The difficulty is that, with the possible exception of death, exactly the same kinds of unpleasant consequences, objectively considered, can be and are visited upon unsuccessful defendants in civil proceedings.

If one were to judge from the notions apparently underlying many judicial opinions, and the overt language even of some of them, the solution of the puzzle is simply that a crime is anything which is *called* a crime, and a criminal penalty is simply the penalty provided for doing anything which has been given that name. So vacant a concept is a betrayal of intellectual bankruptcy. * * * [A] conviction for crime is a distinctive and serious matter—a something, and not a nothing. What is that something?

4. What distinguishes a criminal from a civil sanction and all that distinguishes it, it is ventured, is the judgment of community condemnation which accompanies and justifies its imposition. As Professor Gardner wrote not long ago, in a distinct but cognate connection:[13]

> The essence of punishment for moral delinquency lies in the criminal conviction itself. One may lose more money on the stock market than in a court-room; a prisoner of war camp may well provide a harsher environment than a state prison; death on the field of battle has the same physical characteristics as death by sentence of law. It is the expression of the community's hatred, fear, or contempt for the convict which alone characterizes physical hardship as punishment.

If this is what a "criminal" penalty is, then we can say readily enough what a "crime" is. It is not simply anything which a legislature chooses to call a "crime." It is not simply antisocial conduct which public officers are given a responsibility to suppress. It is not simply any conduct to which a legislature chooses to attach a "criminal" penalty. It is conduct which, if

---

13. Gardner, *Bailey v. Richardson and the Constitution of the United States,* 33 B.U.L.Rev. 176, 193 (1953). * * *

duly shown to have taken place, will incur a formal and solemn pronouncement of the moral condemnation of the community.

5. The method of the criminal law, of course, involves something more than the threat (and, on due occasion, the expression) of community condemnation of antisocial conduct. It involves, in addition, the threat (and, on due occasion, the imposition) of unpleasant physical consequences, commonly called punishment. But if Professor Gardner is right, these added consequences take their character as punishment from the condemnation which precedes them and serves as the warrant for their infliction. Indeed, the condemnation plus the added consequences may well be considered, compendiously, as constituting the punishment. Otherwise, it would be necessary to think of a convicted criminal as going unpunished if the imposition or execution of his sentence is suspended.

In traditional thought and speech, the ideas of crime and punishment have been inseparable; the consequences of conviction for crime have been described as a matter of course as "punishment." The Constitution of the United States and its amendments, for example, use this word or its verb form in relation to criminal offenses no less than six times. Today, "treatment" has become a fashionable euphemism for the older, ugly word. * * * [T]o the extent that it dissociates the treatment of criminals from the social condemnation of their conduct which is implicit in their conviction, there is danger that it will confuse thought and do a disservice.

At least under existing law, there is a vital difference between the situation of a patient who has been committed to a mental hospital and the situation of an inmate of a state penitentiary. The core of the difference is precisely that the patient has not incurred the moral condemnation of his community, whereas the convict has.

NOTES AND QUESTIONS

1. Two scholars have defined a crime as "any social harm defined and made punishable by law." Rollin M. Perkins & Ronald N. Boyce, Criminal Law 12 (3d ed. 1982). Is this definition helpful? Why, or why not? What do you think Professor Hart, supra, would say about this definition?

2. *The increasingly thin line between the "criminal" and "civil" methods of the law.* According to the preceding extract from Professor Hart's article, what is it that distinguishes a crime and the criminal process, on the one hand, from other legal directives and the civil process, on the other hand?

The criminal/civil divide has narrowed in the years since Hart's article was published. The civil law has taken on characteristics of the criminal law, and vice-versa. As you proceed with your studies, you should take note of those features of the law that seem to have blurred the criminal/civil distinction. Ask yourself whether there is good reason to preserve the distinct nature of criminal liability as it is described by Hart.

3. *Sources of American criminal law: the common law beginning.* The roots of American criminal law are found in English soil. The early colonists

brought to this country, and in large part accepted as their own, the judge-made law, i.e., common law, of England. Over time, however, the American common law of crimes diverged in key respects from the English version.

Beginning in the late nineteenth century, many state legislatures asserted authority to enact criminal statutes. At first, they used their power to supplement the common law, but eventually they replaced it by legislation. Today, in every state and in the federal system, legislators, rather than judges, exercise primary responsibility for defining criminal conduct and for devising the rules of criminal responsibility.

4. *The legislature's role.* Professor Hart, supra, at 412, has explained the legislature's perspective in criminal lawmaking as follows:

> A legislature deals with crimes always in advance of their commission * * *. It deals with them not by condemnation and punishment, but only by threat of condemnation and punishment, *to be imposed always by other agencies*. It deals with them always by directions formulated in *general terms*. The primary parts of the directions have always to be interpreted and applied by the private persons—the potential offenders—to whom they are initially addressed. In the event of a breach or claim of breach, both the primary and the remedial parts must be interpreted and applied by various officials—police, prosecuting attorneys, trial judges and jurors, appellate judges, and probation, prison, and parole authorities—responsible for their enforcement. The attitudes, capacities, and practical conditions of work of these officials often put severe limits upon the ability of the legislature to accomplish what it sets out to accomplish.

> If the primary parts of a general direction are to work successfully in any particular instance, otherwise than by fortunate accident, four conditions have always to be satisfied: (1) the primary addressee who is supposed to conform his conduct to the direction must know (a) of its existence, and (b) of its content in relevant respects; (2) he must know about the circumstances of fact which make the abstract terms of the direction applicable in the particular instance; (3) he must be able to comply with it; and (4) he must be willing to do so.

Beyond the matter of efficacy, is it *fair* to convict a person if one or more of these conditions are not satisfied? Why, or why not?

5. *Limits on legislative lawmaking: the Constitution.* Legislators do not have unlimited lawmaking power. Their actions are subject to federal and state constitutional law. For example, the United States Constitution prohibits *ex post facto* legislation (Article 1, §§ 9 and 10) and cruel and unusual punishment (Eighth Amendment), and provides that persons may not be deprived of life, liberty or property without due process of law (Fifth and Fourteenth Amendments). The study of the criminal law, therefore, necessarily includes consideration of these and other constitutional provisions.

Constitutional issues raise competing policy concerns. On the one hand, the doctrine of federalism teaches that each State has sovereign authority to promulgate and enforce its own criminal laws; and, pursuant to the doctrine of separation of powers, the legislative branch of government, rather than the judiciary, is now considered the appropriate lawmaking body. Therefore, when a *federal* court declares that a *state* statute is unconstitutional, it runs the risk of violating principles of federalism and of usurping legislative authority. On the other hand, President (later Chief Justice) William Howard Taft once pointed out that "[c]onstitutions are checks upon the hasty action of the majority. They are self-imposed restraints of a whole people upon a majority of them to secure sober action and a respect for the rights of the minority." H.R.J.Res. 4, 62nd Cong., 1st Sess., 47 Cong.Rec. 4 (1911). Since legislative bodies typically represent the will of the majority, it is usually the responsibility of the judiciary to ensure that the rights of the minority are respected. Therefore, if courts defer too readily to legislatures, they run the risk of abdicating their responsibility for enforcing the Constitution.

6. *The present-day role of the judiciary.* Modern courts do not simply pass upon the constitutionality of legislation. They also play a vital role in the ascertainment of guilt in individual cases by interpreting criminal statutes. This role comes into play when a legislature has drafted a statute that is subject to reasonable dispute as to its meaning. In such circumstances there have developed a number of "presumptions with which courts approach debatable issues of interpretation." Hart, supra, at 435. As you proceed through this coursebook you will become familiar with some of these "presumptions."

7. *Model Penal Code.* Until relatively recently, most state "criminal codes" were little more than collections of statutes, enacted by legislators in piecemeal fashion over many decades, defining various crimes and the punishments therefor.

These penal codes left much to be desired. First, not all common law crimes and defenses were codified, which meant that courts had to determine whether these gaps were intended or inadvertent. Second, many statutory systems were silent regarding essential penal doctrines, such as accomplice liability. Third, criminal codes typically included overlapping, even conflicting, penal statutes. Fourth, many codes applied internally inconsistent penological principles.

In order to bring coherence to the criminal law, the American Law Institute, an organization composed of eminent judges, lawyers, and law professors, set out in 1952 to develop a model code. A decade later, the Institute adopted and published the Model Penal Code and Commentaries thereto. Key portions of the Code (including some recent amendments, thereto) are set out in the appendix to this casebook.

The Model Penal Code has greatly influenced criminal law reform. Some states have adopted major portions of the Code. In other jurisdictions, courts look to it for guidance to fill holes in their own statutory systems. Perhaps most usefully, the Commentaries to the specific provisions of the Model Penal Code have shaped the reform debate in many state legislatures. For a fuller discussion of the status of the criminal law before the adoption of the Model Penal Code, see Sanford H. Kadish, *The Model Penal Code's Historical Antecedents,* 19 Rutgers L.J. 521 (1988). For a critical analysis of modern criminal codes, including an effort to rank them in terms of effectiveness, see Paul H. Robinson, Michael T. Cahill, & Usman Mohammad, *The Five Worst (and Five Best) American Criminal Codes,* 95 Nw. U. L. Rev. 1 (2000).

B. CRIMINAL LAW IN A PROCEDURAL CONTEXT: PRE–TRIAL

Criminal law casebooks use judicial opinions, mainly those of appellate courts, as the primary tool for exposing students to the general principles of the criminal law. This process can be misleading. It is easy to think that the commission of a crime inevitably results in a prosecution, culminating in a trial, conviction, and appeal of the conviction by the defendant. In fact, however, trials are the exception rather than the rule in the justice system. A great deal of the criminal process is barely visible in a criminal law course, although it is the focus of attention in courses relating to criminal procedure.

The criminal process begins, of course, when an alleged crime is reported to the police. According to the National Crime Victimization Survey (NCVS), an estimated 18.7 million persons, age 12 or older, were victims of violent or property crimes in the year 2010. Persons of ages 12 through 24 and African–Americans were victims of violent crimes at rates higher than older persons, and Hispanics and whites, respectively. However, only about 50 percent of all the violent victimizations and 40 percent of property crimes were reported to law enforcement agencies. U.S. Dept. of Justice, Bureau of Justice Statistics, Criminal Victimization 2010 (Sept. 2011, NCJ 235508).

The fact that a crime is reported does not ensure that an arrest will be made. The police might not investigate the report with vigor because they doubt (rightly or wrongly) the authenticity of the claim. Or, they may give the investigation low priority, because police departments have inadequate resources to investigate every reported offense. Unfortunately, as well, improper factors may affect criminal investigations. For example, the police may work hard to investigate a crime against a prominent individual, and yet do little to find the perpetrator of an offense against a homeless person. At times, some police departments have been accused of treating "black on black" crime—where the probable perpetrator and the victim are African–American—less seriously than offenses involving white victims. And, until relatively recently, some police departments treated domestic violence as more of a "family matter" than a public offense.

Even if the police investigate a crime report thoroughly, insufficient evidence may exist to make an arrest. The United States Constitution prohibits the police from arresting a suspect unless they have probable cause to believe that the individual committed an offense. The concept of "probable cause" is a fluid one, not quantified in percentage terms, but which requires that there be a substantial chance that the suspect committed the offense under investigation.

If a suspect *is* arrested, the prosecutor must overcome various hurdles before a trial may be held. In many states, the arrestee is entitled to a preliminary hearing within two weeks after arrest, at which proceeding a judge must determine whether the arrest was justified. If the judge determines that there is probable cause to proceed with the prosecution, the prosecutor is permitted in some states to file an "information" in the trial court and to proceed to trial. An "information" is a document that sets out the formal charges against the accused and the basic facts relating to them.

In many states and in the federal system, however, the accused may not be brought to trial unless she is indicted by a grand jury. A grand jury consists of lay members of the community who consider evidence presented to them by a prosecutor, after which they deliberate privately, and determine whether adequate evidence exists to prosecute the accused. If there is sufficient evidence, the grand jury issues an "indictment," a document similar to an information.

Even if an indictment is issued or an information is filed, a trial might still not be held. First, the accused is entitled to make various pretrial motions which, if successful, sometimes require the dismissal of charges. For example, if evidence to be used by the Government was secured in violation of the Constitution, it may not be introduced at trial. On occasion, suppression of such evidence so weakens the prosecutor's case that charges must be dismissed.

Far more often, a defendant may plead guilty rather than proceed to trial. Nearly always, a guilty plea is the result of bargaining between the prosecutor and the defendant's lawyer. Typically, in exchange for a guilty plea, a prosecutor agrees to dismiss certain charges, reduce the severity of a charge, or agrees to recommend a more lenient sentence upon conviction. Guilty plea rates vary by jurisdiction, by offense, and by year, but the conviction rate obtained by guilty pleas typically nears or exceeds ninety percent.

Thus, in short, many crimes go unreported, many reported crimes do not result in arrest, and where arrests occur, the great majority of prosecutions are disposed of prior to trial, largely by guilty pleas.

C. CRIMINAL LAW IN A PROCEDURAL CONTEXT: TRIAL BY JURY

The Sixth Amendment to the United States Constitution provides that "in all criminal prosecutions, the accused shall enjoy the right to a speedy and public trial, by an impartial jury." The right to trial by jury includes, "as its most important element, the right to have the jury, rather than the judge, reach the requisite finding of 'guilty'" in all prosecutions for which the maximum potential punishment exceeds incarceration of six months. Sullivan v. Louisiana, 508 U.S. 275, 113 S.Ct. 2078, 124 L.Ed.2d 182 (1993).

In Duncan v. Louisiana, 391 U.S. 145, 88 S.Ct. 1444, 20 L.Ed.2d 491 (1968), the Supreme Court explained the history and rationale of the right to trial by jury this way:

The guarantees of jury trial in the Federal and State Constitutions reflect a profound judgment about the way in which law should be enforced and justice administered. A right to jury trial is granted to criminal defendants in order to prevent oppression by the Government. Those who wrote our constitutions knew from history and experience that it was necessary to protect against unfounded criminal charges brought to eliminate enemies and against judges too responsive to the voice of higher authority. * * * Providing an accused with the right to be tried by a jury of his peers gave him an inestimable safeguard against the corrupt or overzealous prosecutor and against the compliant, biased, or eccentric judge. If the defendant preferred the common-sense judgment of a jury to the more tutored but perhaps less sympathetic reaction of the single judge, he was to have it.

In the federal system and in most states, a jury in a criminal trial is composed of twelve persons, who must reach a unanimous verdict to acquit or to convict. However, juries as small as six in number are constitutionally permissible. Williams v. Florida, 399 U.S. 78, 90 S.Ct. 1893, 26 L.Ed.2d 446 (1970) (jury of six is allowed); Ballew v. Georgia, 435 U.S. 223, 98 S.Ct. 1029, 55 L.Ed.2d 234 (1978) (jury of five is disallowed). Furthermore, state laws permitting non-unanimous verdicts by twelve-person juries are permissible, as long as the vote to convict constitutes a "substantial majority" of the jurors. Johnson v. Louisiana, 406 U.S. 356, 92 S.Ct. 1620, 32 L.Ed.2d 152 (1972) (upholding a 9–3 guilty verdict).

The Sixth Amendment provides that "the accused shall enjoy the right to * * * an impartial jury * * *." A juror is not impartial if her state of mind in reference to the issues or parties involved in the case would substantially impair her performance as a juror in accordance with the court's instructions on the law. In order to discover possible bias prior to trial, the judge and the attorneys examine prospective jurors ("venirepersons") regarding their attitudes and beliefs. The examination is called a *"voir dire."* If a venireperson's responses demonstrate partiality, the juror is excused "for cause."

The defense and the prosecutor are also entitled to exercise a limited number of "peremptory" challenges, i.e., challenges not based on cause. The primary purpose of peremptory challenges is to allow the parties to exclude persons from the jury whom they believe (often intuitively or as the result of such intangibles as "body language") are biased, but whose partiality was not adequately proven through the *voir dire*. Although the tradition of peremptory challenges is a venerable one, the Fourteenth Amendment Equal Protection Clause is violated if a prosecutor or defense lawyer exercises such a challenge solely on the basis of the venireperson's race or gender.

Because the purpose of the jury system is to defend against exercises of arbitrary power by the Government and to make available to defendants the common-sense judgment of the community, the accused is entitled to a jury drawn from a pool of persons constituting a fair cross-section of the community. This right is violated if large distinctive groups of persons, such as women or members of a racial or religious group, are systematically excluded from the jury pool for illegitimate reasons.

D. PROOF OF GUILT AT TRIAL

1. "PROOF BEYOND A REASONABLE DOUBT"

The Supreme Court ruled in In re Winship, 397 U.S. 358, 90 S.Ct. 1068, 25 L.Ed.2d 368 (1970), that in order to provide "concrete substance for the presumption of innocence—that bedrock 'axiomatic and elementary' principle whose 'enforcement lies at the foundation of our criminal law' "—the Due Process Clause of the United States Constitution requires the prosecutor to persuade the factfinder "beyond a reasonable doubt of every fact necessary to constitute the crime charged." The *Winship* Court justified the reasonable-doubt standard this way:

> The reasonable-doubt standard plays a vital role in the American scheme of criminal procedure. It is a prime instrument for reducing the risk of convictions resting on factual error. * * *

> * * * The accused during a criminal prosecution has at stake interests of immense importance, both because of the possibility that he may lose his liberty upon conviction and because of the certainty that he would be stigmatized by the conviction. Accordingly, a society that values the good name and freedom of every individual should not condemn a man for commission of a crime when there is reasonable doubt about his guilt. * * *

> Moreover, use of the reasonable-doubt standard is indispensable to command the respect and confidence of the community in applications of the criminal law. It is critical that the moral force of the criminal law not be diluted by a standard of proof that leaves people in doubt whether innocent men are being condemned.

Justice Harlan, who concurred in *Winship,* conceded that the practical effect of the reasonable-doubt standard is to enhance the risk that factually guilty people will be set free. But, he explained:

> In a criminal case, * * * we do not view the social disutility of convicting an innocent man as equivalent to the disutility of acquitting someone who is guilty. * * * In this context, I view the requirement of proof beyond a reasonable doubt in a criminal case as bottomed on the fundamental value determination of our society that it is far worse to convict an innocent man than to let a guilty man go free.

NOTES AND QUESTIONS

1. Do you agree with Justice Harlan that it *is* better to let a guilty person go free than to convict an innocent individual? If so, why? What if the guilty person who is freed because of the presumption-of-innocence and reasonable-doubt requirements is a serial murderer or rapist? If you still believe that Harlan is correct, how far would you take this principle? Do you agree with Blackstone that "it is better that *ten* guilty persons escape, than that one innocent suffer"? 4 Blackstone, Commentaries on the Laws of England *352 (1765) (emphasis added). See Jeffrey Reiman & Ernest van den Haag, *On the Common Saying that it is Better that Ten Guilty Persons Escape than that One Innocent Suffer: Pro and Con*, 7 Soc. Phil. & Policy 226 (Spring 1990).

In this regard, consider the following defense of the heavy burden of proof imposed on the Government by the Constitution, expressed by a jury foreperson to his fellow jurors during deliberations in a New York criminal case:

> * * * I think that we all understand why [the burden of proof is so great]: to protect citizens from the power of the state, from the tremendous power of the state.
>
> We understand that power much better after the last four days [of deliberation]. We discovered that it is, fundamentally, an absolute power, and a frightening one. We discovered that a man in a chair and a robe [the judge] could tell us we couldn't go home, that we couldn't talk to our families * * *. He could send us to jail.[a] * * * We discovered that, in the end, there seemed to be no limit to the power of the state over us, once we fell into its hands.
>
> * * * Knowing what we know now, imagine that we had a chance to set up our own state, to make a government, the twelve of us. What kind of protections would we try to offer to the citizens? I think, after what we've learned over the last few days, we would put the heaviest possible burden on the state before we would let it take away a person's liberty, and we would do that because we've learned the secret of government: that the state, any state, is, in the end, like a monster, more powerful than everything else. * * *
>
> Yesterday, in a moment I will never forget [two jurors] Dean and Felipe reminded us of a transcendent idea: that true justice, final justice, absolute justice, belongs to God; human justice can only be cautious, not perfect. For this reason the burden is so heavy.

D. Graham Burnett, A Trial by Jury 163–164 (2001). Are you persuaded?

2. *Defining "beyond a reasonable doubt."* How onerous a burden is "proof beyond a reasonable doubt"? The Supreme Court has said that the standard requires that a juror's mind be in a "subjective state of near

---

a. The judge ordered the jurors sequestered during deliberation, i.e., they were not permitted to go home, and were not permitted to talk to family members without permission and supervision. The jurors learned that if they violated the judge's orders, they could be held in contempt of court and jailed. In a couple of circumstances, the jurors felt that the judge acted officiously in dealing with jurors' requests.—Ed.

certitude'' of guilt. Jackson v. Virginia, 443 U.S. 307, 99 S.Ct. 2781, 61 L.Ed.2d 560 (1979).

Can "near certitude" be quantified? One Nevada trial judge tried to do so by distinguishing the burden required in a criminal case from those required to arrest a suspect (probable cause) and to obtain a civil judgment (preponderance of the evidence). He told jurors that on a scale of zero to ten, "the standard of probable cause [is] about one, and the burden of persuasion in civil trials [is] at just over five." As for reasonable doubt it is about "seven and a half, if you had to put it on a scale." Do you believe that if a juror feels that there is a 75% chance that the defendant is guilty that she is in a "subjective state of near certitude" of guilt?

The Nevada Supreme Court ruled that the judge's explanation was improper, without deciding whether the particular number—seven and a half—was too low. It stated, as have nearly all courts when confronted with the issue, that "[t]he concept of reasonable doubt is inherently qualitative. Any attempt to quantify it may impermissibly lower the prosecution's burden of proof, and is likely to confuse rather than clarify." McCullough v. State, 99 Nev. 72, 657 P.2d 1157 (Nev. 1983).

3. If "reasonable doubt" is not quantifiable, how *should* jurors be instructed on the concept? According to some observers, "the meaning of reasonable doubt is self-evident and * * * efforts to define it lead only to confusion or even dilution of the state's burden of proof." State v. Portillo, 182 Ariz. 592, 898 P.2d 970 (1995). According to the Supreme Court, "the Constitution neither prohibits trial courts from defining reasonable doubt nor requires them to do so as a matter of course." Victor v. Nebraska, 511 U.S. 1, 114 S.Ct. 1239, 127 L.Ed.2d 583 (1994). Furthermore, if a court *does* choose to define the concept, the Constitution does not require any particular form or words be used, as long as there is no reasonable likelihood that the definition, taken as a whole, would allow a conviction insufficient to meet the constitutional standard.

4. *A thought experiment.* Pretend you are on a jury in a criminal case. The judge will instruct you on the meaning of "reasonable doubt" in one of the following ways. Which one of the instructions below do you find most helpful as a juror? As a separate thought experiment, if you were the defendant's attorney, which instruction would you prefer?

The "Moral Certainty" Instruction

[Reasonable doubt] is not merely possible doubt; because every thing relating to human affairs, and depending on moral evidence, is open to some possible or imaginary doubt. It is that state of the case, which, after the entire comparison and consideration of all the evidence, leaves the minds of jurors in that condition that they cannot say they feel an abiding conviction, to a moral certainty, of the truth of the charge. (Based on Commonwealth v. Webster, 59 Mass. (5 Cush.) 295 (1850).)

The "Firmly Convinced" Instruction

The state has the burden of proving the defendant guilty beyond a reasonable doubt. In civil cases, it is only necessary to prove that a fact is more likely true than not or that its truth is highly probable. In criminal cases such as this, the State's proof must be more powerful than that. It must be beyond a reasonable doubt.

Proof beyond a reasonable doubt is proof that leaves you firmly convinced of the defendant's guilt. There are very few things in this world that we know with absolute certainty, and in criminal cases the law does not require proof that overcomes every doubt. If, based on your consideration of the evidence, you are firmly convinced that the defendant is guilty of the crime charged, you must find him/her guilty. If, on the other hand, you think there is a real possibility that he/she is not guilty, you must give him/her the benefit of the doubt and find him/her not guilty. (State v. Portillo, 182 Ariz. 592, 898 P.2d 970 (1995) [based on Federal Judicial Center, Pattern Criminal Jury Instructions 17–18 (Instruction 21) (1987)].)

The "No Waver or Vacillation" Instruction

A reasonable doubt is not a mere possible doubt, a speculative, imaginary or forced doubt. Such a doubt must not influence you to return a verdict of not guilty if you have an abiding conviction of guilt. On the other hand, if, after carefully considering, comparing and weighing all the evidence, there is not an abiding conviction of guilt, or, if, having a conviction, it is one which is not stable but one which wavers or vacillates, then the charge is not proved beyond every reasonable doubt and you must find the defendant not guilty because the doubt is reasonable. (Standard Jury Instructions in Criminal Cases (97–1), 697 So.2d 84 (Fla.1997).)

The "No Real Doubt" Instruction

It is the Government that has the burden of proving a defendant guilty beyond a reasonable doubt. If it fails to do so, you must, under your oath, find the defendant not guilty.

But while the Government's burden of proof is a strict or heavy burden, it is not necessary that the defendant's guilt be proved beyond all possible doubt. The law does not require mathematical certainty, because that is generally impossible. What is required is that the Government's proof exclude any reasonable doubt concerning the defendant's guilt.

A reasonable doubt is just precisely what it says. It is a real doubt based upon reason and common sense after a careful and impartial consideration of all of the evidence in the case. Proof beyond a reasonable doubt, stated a little bit differently, is proof of such a convincing character that you would be willing to rely and act upon it without hesitation in the most important of your own affairs. (United States v. Daniels, 986 F.2d 451, opinion withdrawn and superseded in part on rehearing, 5 F.3d 495 (11th Cir.1993).)

The "Thoroughly Convinced" Instruction

The law does not ask an accounting from [jurors] on the grounds by which they became convinced; it does not prescribe for them rules on which they must make the fullness and sufficiency of a proof particularly depend; it requires of them that they ask themselves, in silence and reflection to seek out, in the sincerity of their conscience, what impression the evidence reported against the accused and the ground of his defense have made on their reason. The law asks them only the single question, which encompasses the full measure of their duties: "Are you thoroughly convinced?" Article 353, French Rules of Procedure (as translated).

5. *The truth and nothing but the truth?* What if a judge tells a jury that "you are guided solely by the evidence in the case and the crucial, hard-core question you must ask yourselves ... is, where do you find the truth? The only triumph in any case, whether it be civil or criminal, is whether or not the truth has triumphed." United States v. Shamsideen, 511 F.3d 340 (2nd Cir. 2008). If you represented the defendant, would you have a legitimate basis for objecting to this instruction?

2. ENFORCING THE PRESUMPTION OF INNOCENCE

OWENS v. STATE

Court of Special Appeals of Maryland, 1992.
93 Md.App. 162, 611 A.2d 1043.

MOYLAN, JUDGE.

This appeal presents us with a small gem of a problem from the borderland of legal sufficiency. It is one of those few occasions when some frequently invoked but rarely appropriate language is actually pertinent. Ironically, in this case it was not invoked. The language is, "[A] conviction upon circumstantial evidence *alone* is not to be sustained unless the circumstances are inconsistent with any reasonable hypothesis of innocence."

We have here a conviction based upon circumstantial evidence alone. The circumstance is that a suspect was found behind the wheel of an automobile parked on a private driveway at night with the lights on and with the motor running. Although there are many far-fetched and speculative hypotheses that might be conjured up (but which require no affirmative elimination), there are only two unstrained and likely inferences that could reasonably arise. One is that the vehicle and its driver had arrived at the driveway from somewhere else. The other is that the driver had gotten into and started up the vehicle and was about to depart for somewhere else.

The first hypothesis, combined with the added factor that the likely driver was intoxicated, is consistent with guilt. The second hypothesis, because the law intervened before the forbidden deed could be done, is consistent with innocence. With either inference equally likely, a fact finder could not fairly draw the guilty inference and reject the innocent with the requisite certainty beyond a reasonable doubt. We are called upon, therefore, to examine the circumstantial predicate more closely and to ascertain whether there were any attendant and ancillary circumstances to render less likely, and therefore less reasonable, the hypothesis of innocence. Thereon hangs the decision.

The appellant, Christopher Columbus Owens, Jr., was convicted * * * by Judge D. William Simpson, sitting without a jury, of driving while intoxicated. Upon this appeal, he raises the single contention that Judge Simpson was clearly erroneous in finding him guilty because the evidence was not legally sufficient to support such finding.

The evidence, to be sure, was meager. The State's only witness was Trooper Samuel Cottman, who testified that at approximately 11 P.M. on March 17, 1991, he drove to the area of Sackertown Road in Crisfield in response to a complaint that had been called in about a suspicious vehicle. He spotted a truck matching the description of the "suspicious vehicle." It was parked in the driveway of a private residence.

The truck's engine was running and its lights were on. The appellant was asleep in the driver's seat, with an open can of Budweiser clasped between his legs. Two more empty beer cans were inside the vehicle. As Trooper Cottman awakened him, the appellant appeared confused and did not know where he was. He stumbled out of the vehicle. There was a strong odor of alcohol on his breath. His face was flushed and his eyes were red. When asked to recite the alphabet, the appellant "mumbled through the letters, didn't state any of the letters clearly and failed to say them in the correct order." His speech generally was "slurred and very unclear." * * * A check with the Motor Vehicles Administration revealed, moreover, that the appellant had an alcohol restriction on his license. The appellant declined to submit to a blood test for alcohol.

After the brief direct examination of Trooper Cottman (consuming but 3½ pages of transcript), defense counsel asked only two questions, establishing that the driveway was private property and that the vehicle was sitting on that private driveway. The appellant did not take the stand and no defense witnesses were called. The appellant's argument as to legal insufficiency is clever. He chooses to fight not over the fact of drunkenness but over the place of drunkenness. He points out that his conviction was under the Transportation Article, which is limited in its coverage to the driving of vehicles on "highways" and does not extend to driving on a "private road or driveway."

We agree with the appellant that he could not properly have been convicted for driving, no matter how intoxicated, back and forth along the short span of a private driveway. The theory of the State's case, however, rests upon the almost Newtonian principle that present stasis on the driveway implies earlier motion on the highway. The appellant was not convicted of drunken driving on the private driveway, but of drunken driving on the public highway before coming to rest on the private driveway.

It is a classic case of circumstantial evidence. From his presence behind the wheel of a vehicle on a private driveway with the lights on and the motor running, it can reasonably be inferred that such individual either 1) had just arrived by way of the public highway or 2) was just about to set forth upon the public highway. The binary nature of the probabilities—that a vehicular odyssey had just concluded or was just about to begin—is strengthened by the lack of evidence of any third reasonable explanation, such as the presence beside him of an inamorata or of a baseball game blaring forth on the car radio. Either he was coming or he was going.

The first inference would render the appellant guilty; the second would not. * * * For the State to prevail, there has to be some other factor to enhance the likelihood of the first inference and to diminish the likelihood of the second. We must look for a tiebreaker. * * *

In trying to resolve whether the appellant 1) had just been driving or 2) was just about to drive, it would have been helpful to know whether the driveway in which he was found was that of his own residence or that of some other residence. If he were parked in someone else's driveway with the motor still running, it would be more likely that he had just driven there a short time before. If parked in his own driveway at home, on the other hand, the relative strength of the inbound inference over the outbound inference would diminish.

The driveway where the arrest took place was on Sackertown Road. The charging document (which, of course, is not evidence) listed the appellant's address as 112 Cove Second Street. When the appellant was arrested, presumably his driver's license was taken from him. Since one of the charges against the appellant was that of driving in violation of an alcohol restriction on his license, it would have been routine procedure to have offered the license, showing the restriction, into evidence. In terms of our present legal sufficiency exercise, the license would fortuitously have shown the appellant's residence as well. Because of the summary nature of the trial, however, the license was never offered in evidence. For purposes of the present analysis, therefore, the appellant's home address is not in the case. We must continue to look for a tiebreaker elsewhere.

Three beer cans were in evidence. The presence of a partially con-sumed can of beer between the appellant's legs and two other empty cans in the back seat would give rise to a reasonable inference that the appellant's drinking spree was on the downslope rather than at an early stage. At least a partial venue of the spree, moreover, would reasonably appear to have been the automobile. One does not typically drink in the house and then carry the empties out to the car. Some significant drinking, it may be inferred, had taken place while the appellant was in the car. The appellant's state of unconsciousness, moreover, enforces that inference. One passes out on the steering wheel after one has been drinking for some time, not as one only begins to drink. It is not a reasonable hypothesis that one would leave the house, get in the car, turn on the lights, turn on the motor, and then, before putting the car in gear and driving off, consume enough alcohol to pass out on the steering wheel. Whatever had been going on (driving and drinking) would seem more likely to have been at a terminal stage than at an incipient one.

Yet another factor would have sufficed, we conclude, to break the tie between whether the appellant had not yet left home or was already abroad upon the town. Without anything further as to its contents being revealed, it was nonetheless in evidence that the thing that had brought Trooper Cottman to the scene was a complaint about a suspicious vehicle. The inference is reasonable that the vehicle had been observed driving in some sort of erratic fashion. Had the appellant simply been sitting, with his motor idling, on the driveway of his own residence, it is not likely that someone from the immediate vicinity would have found suspicious the presence of a familiar neighbor in a familiar car sitting in his own driveway. The call to the police, even without more being shown, inferentially augurs more than that. It does not prove guilt in and of itself. It simply makes one of two alternative inferences less reasonable and its alternative inference thereby more reasonable.

The totality of the circumstances are, in the last analysis, inconsistent with a *reasonable* hypothesis of innocence. They do not, of course, foreclose the hypothesis but such has never been required. They do make the hypothesis more strained and less likely. By an inverse proportion, the diminishing force of one inference enhances the force of its alternative. It makes the drawing of the inference of guilt more than a mere flip of a coin between guilt and innocence. It makes it rational and therefore within the proper purview of the factfinder. We affirm.

NOTES AND QUESTIONS

1. In *Owens,* the trial judge served as trier of fact, the role ordinarily reserved for a jury. If you had been a juror hearing this case, would you have voted to convict Owens? Look again at the jury instructions on burden of proof set out in the Note 4 "thought experiment" immediately preceding *Owens.* Based on any of these instructions (for example, focus on the "Firmly Convinced" instruction), are you convinced of Owens's guilt beyond a reasonable doubt?

2. At the conclusion of the opinion, the Court of Special Appeals stated that drawing an inference of guilt in this case involved "more than a flip of a coin between guilt and innocence," and that a finding of guilt was "rational and therefore within the proper purview of the factfinder." Is that enough to meet the proof-beyond-a-reasonable-doubt standard? Why did the court apply this test?

3. *The role of the trial judge in enforcing the presumption of innocence.* In a criminal trial, the prosecutor ordinarily makes an opening statement to the trier of fact, which is typically the jury, in which she outlines the evidence she plans to present at trial. The defense may also make an opening statement now, or may wait and give it when it presents its own case.

After opening statements, the prosecutor calls her witnesses. Upon completion of the State's case, the defense may make a motion for directed verdict of acquittal. In doing so, the defense asserts the presumption of innocence and claims thereby that the Government failed to overcome the presumption in its presentation of its case. The effect of such a motion, if granted, is the immediate termination of the trial in defendant's favor.

If the motion for directed verdict is denied, the defense presents its case, after which the prosecutor is permitted to introduce rebuttal testimony. At the conclusion, the defense may again move for a directed verdict of acquittal. If the motion is denied (or is not made), the parties make closing arguments to the jury, after which the judge (upon consultation with the parties) instructs the jury on the principles of law relevant to the case, including the constitutional presumption of innocence.

On what basis does a judge decide whether to grant a motion for directed verdict and, thereby, strip the jury of its factfinding role?[b] The following explanation is helpful:

> The functions of the jury include the determination of the credibility of witnesses, the weighing of the evidence, and the drawing of justifiable inferences of fact from proven facts. It is the function of the judge to deny the jury any opportunity to operate beyond its province. The jury may not be permitted to conjecture merely, or to conclude upon pure speculation or from passion, prejudice or sympathy. The critical point in this boundary is the existence or non-existence of a reasonable doubt as to guilt. If the evidence is such that reasonable jurymen *must* necessarily have such a doubt, the judge *must* require acquittal, because no other result is permissible within the fixed bounds of jury consideration. But if a reasonable mind *might* fairly have a reasonable doubt or *might* fairly *not* have one, the case is for the jury, and the decision is for the jurors to make. * * * Both innocence and guilt beyond reasonable doubt may lie fairly within the limits of reasonable conclusion from given facts. The judge's function is exhausted when he determines that the evidence does or does not permit the conclusion of guilt beyond reasonable doubt within the fair operation of a reasonable mind.

> The true rule, therefore, is that a trial judge, in passing upon a motion for directed verdict of acquittal, must determine whether upon the evidence, giving full play to the right of the jury to determine credibility, weigh the evidence, and draw justifiable inferences of fact, a reasonable mind might fairly conclude guilt beyond a reasonable doubt. If he concludes that upon the evidence there *must* be such a doubt in a reasonable mind, he *must* grant the motion; or, to state it another way, if there is no evidence upon which a reasonable mind might fairly conclude guilt beyond reasonable doubt, the motion must be granted. If he con-

---

b. Because a defendant has a constitutional right to trial by jury, which includes the right to have the jury reach the requisite finding of guilt, a trial judge may not direct a verdict for conviction, no matter how overwhelming the evidence of guilt. Sullivan v. Louisiana, 508 U.S. 275, 113 S.Ct. 2078, 124 L.Ed.2d 182 (1993).

cludes that either of the two results, a reasonable doubt or no reasonable doubt, is fairly possible, he *must* let the jury decide the matter.

Curley v. United States, 160 F.2d 229 (D.C.Cir.1947) (emphasis added).

4. *The presumption of innocence on appeal.* In *Owens*, the defendant appealed his conviction on the ground of "insufficiency of evidence," a shorthand way of claiming that the prosecutor did not overcome the presumption of innocence.

How should an appellate court resolve an insufficiency-of-evidence claim? Keep in mind that an appellate court is not the factfinder in a criminal case. That is the jury's role. The jury is ordinarily in a better position than an appellate court to resolve conflicting factual claims because it sees all of the evidence and, more importantly, is able to evaluate the credibility of the witnesses. Consequently, many jurisdictions provide, in essence, that when jurors are confronted with a record of historical facts that could support conflicting inferences, an appellate court should assume that the jury resolved those factual conflicts in favor of the prosecution. The relevant inquiry, then, is whether, after viewing the evidence in the light most favorable to the prosecution, any rational trier of fact *could* have found the essential elements of the crime proven beyond a reasonable doubt. See People v. Carter, 36 Cal.4th 1215, 32 Cal.Rptr.3d 838, 117 P.3d 544 (2005); Jackson v. Virginia, 443 U.S. 307, 99 S.Ct. 2781, 61 L.Ed.2d 560 (1979). If you were an appellate court judge and applied this standard in *Owens*, would you have affirmed the conviction?

E. JURY NULLIFICATION

INTRODUCTORY COMMENT

Suppose that a prosecutor proves beyond a reasonable doubt every fact necessary to constitute the crime charged, but the jury—the community's representative—does not want to convict the defendant. Perhaps the jurors believe that the defendant's conduct should not constitute a crime, although it does. Or, perhaps the jury feels that the police mistreated the defendant and it wants to acquit to send a message of its displeasure. Or, perhaps, the jurors simply feel compassion for the accused. In such circumstances, may the jury ignore the facts and the judge's instructions on the law and acquit the defendant? If it does so, this is called "jury nullification."

The Fifth Amendment Double Jeopardy Clause ("No person shall * * * be subject for the same offense to be twice put in jeopardy") bars the Government from reprosecuting a defendant after a jury acquittal. Therefore, ultimately, a jury has the raw power to acquit for any reason whatsoever. But, *should* juries nullify the law? And, since they have the power to do so, should they be informed of their power of nullification? These questions are considered in the next case.

STATE v. RAGLAND

Supreme Court of New Jersey, 1986.
105 N.J. 189, 519 A.2d 1361.

WILENTZ, C.J. * * *

[Defendant Ragland, a previously convicted felon, was prosecuted for various offenses, including armed robbery and possession of a weapon by a convicted felon. At the conclusion of the trial of the latter offense, the judge instructed the jury that if it found that the defendant was in possession of a weapon during the commission of the robbery, "you must find him guilty of the [possession] charge."

On appeal, the defendant argued that the judge's use of the word "must" in the instruction conflicted with the jury's nullification power, which he claimed was an essential attribute of his constitutional right to a jury trial. He also contended that the judge should have informed the jury regarding its power of nullification, as follows:

"You are here as representatives of your community. Accordingly you are entitled to act upon your conscientious feeling about what is a fair result in this case and acquit the defendant, even if the State has proven its case, if you believe that justice requires such a result."]

The defendant would require a charge that states, in effect, that if the jury does not find a, b and c beyond a reasonable doubt, it must find defendant not guilty, but that if it does find a, b and c beyond a reasonable doubt, then it may find defendant guilty. In support of this change in present practice, defendant contends that the jury's power of nullification—the unquestioned power of the jury to acquit with finality no matter how overwhelming the proof of guilt—is an essential attribute of a defendant's right to trial by jury; that use of the word "must" conflicts with that attribute, for it incorrectly advises the jury that if it finds the proof of guilt beyond a reasonable doubt it *must* convict, whereas the truth is that it need not do so, it may, in fact, acquit; that "must" convict, therefore, should never be used. * * *

While defendant's arguments suggest that the ultimate object is to assure that the jury is not impeded by this coercive language from performing its proper role, the effect of the change is somewhat different. Its only effect, its only tendency, is to make it more likely that juries will nullify the law, more likely, in other words, that no matter how overwhelming the proof of guilt, no matter how convinced the jury is beyond any reasonable doubt of defendant's guilt, despite the law, it will acquit. Even without an explicit charge on the power of nullification, the jury must understand from this contrasting language (*must* acquit but *may* convict) that it is quite properly free, and quite legally free (since it is the court who is telling it "may") to acquit even if it is convinced beyond a reasonable doubt of defendant's guilt. * * *

* * * We have been able to find but one federal case that supports the defendant's argument, *United States v. Hayward,* 420 F.2d 142 (D.C.Cir.

1969). This seventeen-year-old case has not been followed in other federal courts on this proposition. The overwhelming weight of authority is to the contrary, namely, even in those cases where the use of the word "must" is discouraged, it is not as a result of a constitutional command. * * *

We conclude that the power of the jury to acquit despite not only overwhelming proof of guilt but despite the jury's belief, beyond a reasonable doubt, in guilt, is not one of the precious attributes of the right to trial by jury. It is nothing more than a power. By virtue of the finality of a verdict of acquittal, the jury simply has the *power* to nullify the law by acquitting those believed by the jury to be guilty. We believe that the exercise of that power, while unavoidable, is undesirable and that judicial attempts to strengthen the power of nullification are not only contrary to settled practice in this state, but unwise both as a matter of governmental policy and as a matter of sound administration of criminal justice.

It is only relatively recently that some scholars have characterized this power as part of defendant's right to trial by jury and have defended it as sound policy. Like defendant, they take the position that the exercise of the power is essential to preserve the jury's role as the "conscience of the community."

There are various elements in this view of the jury as the "conscience of the community." Some laws are said to be unfair. Only the jury, it is thought, is capable of correcting that unfairness—through its nullification power. Other laws, necessarily general, have the capacity of doing injustice in specific applications. Again, only the jury can evaluate these specific applications and thereby prevent injustice through its nullification power. Cast aside is our basic belief that only our elected representatives may determine what is a crime and what is not, and only they may revise that law if it is found to be unfair or imprecise; only they and not twelve people whose names are picked at random from the box.

Finally, there is an almost mystical element to this contention about the "conscience of the community": before anyone is imprisoned, that person is entitled to *more* than a fair trial even when such a trial is pursuant to a fair law. He is entitled to the benefit of the wisdom and compassion of his peers, entitled to the right to have them conclude that he is guilty beyond any doubt, but that he shall be acquitted and go free because of some irrational, inarticulable instinct, some belief, some observation, some value, or some other notion of that jury.

If the argument is that jury nullification has proven to serve society well, that proof has been kept a deep secret. It is no answer to point to the occasions when laws that are deemed unjust have, in effect, been nullified by the jury. That proves only that the power may have done justice in those limited instances, without reflecting on whether, even in those instances, the cost of that justice exceeded its benefit, or whether in other instances it has done more harm, on balance, than the good. We know so little about this power that it is impossible to evaluate it in terms of results.

Since there is neither constitutional nor other legal authority mandating the proposed change in jury instructions, its ultimate justification must be that this new formulation of the proper charge is desirable; desirable that a jury should *not* be compelled to follow the law, for compulsion to follow the law is the natural tendency of the use of the word "must"; desirable that a jury should be left free to ignore the law, for that is the obvious tendency of telling the jury simply that it "may," or is "authorized" to, bring in a verdict of guilty, after saying it "must" find defendant not guilty. If indeed this is a desirable state of affairs, then the jury should be told of its power, so as to leave no doubt that the jury *knows* it is not compelled to bring back a guilty verdict despite its finding beyond a reasonable doubt that the defendant has committed the crime. The point here is different from that of those who say they are not sure whether the nullification power is desirable or undesirable, but since it exists, the jury should be told about it * * *. Defendant's position is that the nullification power is one of the essential attributes of his right to trial by jury, and that it is desirable. Given that premise, the conclusion is inescapable—the jury should be told.

Other consequences should follow a conclusion that the nullification power is desirable. Counsel should be told that they may address that point in summation, that defense counsel should be allowed to argue to the jury that it should *not* apply the law given by the court, but rather should follow its own conscience, along with whatever argument counsel deems persuasive, and the prosecutor similarly should address these otherwise irrelevant issues, presumably including an encomium on law and order. If the court makes introductory remarks to give the jury some idea of its role (as is customary), it should add to the usual explanation— that the jury is the finder of the facts and the judge is the finder of the law—the qualification that ultimately, regardless of the facts and regardless of the law, the jury, and only the jury, will determine guilt or innocence. On voir dire, potential jurors, in addition to being asked whether they believe they will be able to obey the court's charge, should also be asked if they believe they will be able to ignore the court's charge. If the nullification power is desirable, then, obviously, juries should include only those people who are capable of exercising it.[7]

If we are correct, that is, if such a change in the charge given to the jury is not compelled either by constitution, by statute, or by common law, then the question boils down to one of policy and the power of this Court. In deciding that question, it is essential to recognize precisely what we are talking about. There is no mystery about the power of nullification. It is the power to act against the law, against the Legislature and the Governor who made the law. In its immediate application, it transforms the jury, the body thought to provide the ultimate assurance of fairness, into the

---

7. Our review of recent jury instructions in criminal cases shows that the trial court invariably instructs the jury that it, and not the judge, is the final arbiter of the facts but that the judge determines the law, and that the jury is controlled by that law and *must* follow it. Defendant claims that this settled charge is also impermissible. * * *

only element of the system that is permissibly arbitrary. And in its immediate application, it would confuse any conscientious citizen serving on a jury by advising that person, after the meticulous definition of the elements of the crime, the careful description of the burden of proof, and the importance of the conscientious discharge of that person's duties, that, after all is said and done, he can do whatever he pleases. Spectators, formerly amazed at verdicts that clearly violated the law (namely, verdicts that suggested that the jury had nullified the law), will be comforted to know that there is nothing to be amazed about, that juries are not required to follow the law, that they are advised that one of their important functions is *not* to follow the law, and that this advice is given by the ultimate symbol of lawfulness, the judge. It is difficult to imagine a system more likely to lead to cynicism. * * *

The fundamental defect in jury nullification is obvious. It is a power that is absolutely inconsistent with the most important value of Western democracy, that we should live under a government of laws and not of men. * * *

Jury nullification is an unfortunate but unavoidable power. It should not be advertised, and, to the extent constitutionally permissible, it should be limited. Efforts to protect and expand it are inconsistent with the real values of our system of criminal justice. * * *

[The conviction was reversed, and a new trial ordered, on other grounds.]

NOTES AND QUESTIONS

1. Is jury nullification as bad as *Ragland* suggests? Consider these observations by District Judge Thomas A. Wiseman, Jr., in United States v. Datcher, 830 F.Supp. 411 (M.D.Tenn.1993):

> The drafters of the Constitution "clearly intended [the right of trial by jury] to protect the accused from oppression by the Government." Part of this protection is embodied in the concept of jury nullification: "In criminal cases, a jury is entitled to acquit the defendant because it has no sympathy for the government's position." "The Founding Fathers knew that, absent jury nullification, judicial tyranny not only was a possibility, but was a reality in the colonial experience." Although we may view ourselves as living in more civilized times, there is obviously no reason to believe the need for this protection has been eliminated. Judicial and prosecutorial excesses still occur, and Congress is not yet an infallible body incapable of making tyrannical laws.

> The power of a jury to nullify extends back to seventeenth century England. In *Bushell's Case*, Vaughn. 135, 124 Eng.Rep. 1006 (C.P. 1670), William Penn was acquitted of unlawful assembly notwithstanding damning facts * * *. The roots of jury nullification in this country reach back to 1735 and the prosecution of Peter Zenger for seditious libel. There the defendant admitted the facts charged but pleaded non-culpability, and the jury acquitted. "In the century following the Zenger case, it was generally

recognized in American jurisprudence that the jury, agent of the sovereign people, had a right to acquit those whom it felt it unjust to call criminal." * * *

This respect for nullification flows from the role of the jury as the "conscience of the community" in our criminal justice system. As Justice White wrote in *Williams v. Florida*, 399 U.S. 78, 90 S.Ct. 1893, 26 L.Ed.2d 446 (1970), "the essential feature of a jury obviously lies in the interposition between the accused and his accuser of the commonsense judgment of a group of laymen, and in the community participation and shared responsibility that results from that group's determination of guilt or innocence." This interposition serves the essential purpose of the jury trial, which is "to prevent oppression by the Government." * * *

When measured by this standard, a defendant's right to inform the jury of that information essential "to prevent oppression by the Government" is clearly of constitutional magnitude. That is, if community oversight of a criminal prosecution is the primary purpose of a jury trial, then to deny a jury information necessary to such oversight is to deny a defendant the full protection to be afforded by jury trial. Indeed, to deny a defendant the possibility of jury nullification would be to defeat the central purpose of the jury system.

Argument against allowing the jury to hear information that might lead to nullification evinces a fear that the jury might actually serve its primary purpose, that is, it evinces a fear that the community might in fact think a law unjust. The government, whose duty it is to seek justice and not merely conviction, should not shy away from having a jury know the full facts and law of a case. Argument equating jury nullification with anarchy misses the point that in our criminal justice system the law as stated by a judge is secondary to the justice as meted out by a jury of the defendant's peers. We have established the jury as the final arbiter of truth *and* justice in our criminal justice system; this court must grant the defendant's motion if the jury is to fulfill this duty.

On the other hand, consider United States v. Luisi, 568 F.Supp.2d 106 (D. Mass. 2008):

History has not vindicated nullification. To be sure, there have been isolated instances of "benevolent" nullification that "some may regard as tolerable." Proponents of nullification often cite the acquittal of William Penn [and Peter Zenger] * * * But these examples, culled from bygone centuries, are exceptions to an otherwise abhorrent strain of lawlessness.

By and large, when juries have felt free to apply their own law the result was what Professor Randall Kennedy has described as a "sabotage of justice." "Consider, for example, the two hung juries in the 1964 trials of Byron De La Beckwith in Mississippi for the murder of NAACP field secretary Medgar Evers, or the 1955 acquittal of J.W. Millam and Roy Bryant for the murder of fourteen-year-old [African–American] Emmett Till." History is replete with such "shameful examples of how nullification has been used to sanction murder and lynching." * * *

Nullification frustrates the sole purpose of the jury. As this Court has instructed juries for some thirty years now, the word verdict comes from two Latin words meaning roughly "to speak the truth." Nullifiers, however, would render verdicts without regard to the truth. Once juries begin to deviate from this core function, our justice system has no more legitimacy than a Kangaroo court. * * * There are undoubtedly well-intentioned would-be nullifiers who believe that they are aiding the cause of justice. In fact, they are undermining the jury's core function. By adding fuel to the flames of anti-jury sentiment, nullification threatens to erode the jury system and along with it the rule of law and the independent judiciary.

2. In People v. Williams, 25 Cal.4th 441, 106 Cal.Rptr.2d 295, 21 P.3d 1209 (2001), the defendant, 18 years of age, had sexual intercourse, arguably consensually, with his 16–year–old girl friend. Among the charges brought against Williams was the misdemeanor offense of unlawful sexual intercourse with a minor, so-called "statutory rape." In this regard, consider the following events, as recounted by the California Supreme Court:

During the first day of deliberations, the trial court received a message from the jury foreperson indicating that Juror No. 10 "refuses to adhere to Judge's instruction to uphold the law in regard to * * * statutory rape * * *. He believes the law is wrong and, therefore, will not hear any discussions." In response, the trial court questioned Juror No. 10 outside the presence of the other jurors:

"THE COURT: [I]t's been reported to me that you refuse to follow my instructions on the law in regard to * * * unlawful sexual intercourse, that you believe the law to be wrong and, therefore, you will not hear any discussion on that subject. Is that correct?

"[JUROR]: Pretty much, yes. * * *

"THE COURT: All right. Well, * * * I would remind you * * * that you took an oath at the outset of the case in the following language: 'Do you and each of you understand and agree that you will well and truly try the cause now pending before this Court and a true verdict render according only to the evidence presented to you and to the instructions of the Court.' You understand that if you would not follow the instructions that have been given to you by the court that you would be violating that oath? Do you understand that?

"[JUROR]: I understand that.

"THE COURT: Are you willing to abide by the requirements of your oath?

"[JUROR]: I simply cannot see staining a man, a young man, for the rest of his life for what I believe to be a wrong reason.

"THE COURT: Well, you understand that statutory rape or unlawful sexual intercourse has been described to you as a misdemeanor? Did you follow that in the instructions?

"[JUROR]: I've been told it is a misdemeanor. I still don't see—if it were a $10 fine, I just don't see convicting a man and staining his record for the rest of his life. I think that is wrong. I'm sorry, Judge.

"THE COURT: What you're saying is not the law either concerning that particular aspect.

"[JUROR]: I'm trying as best I can, Judge. And I'm willing to follow all the rules and regulations on the entire rest of the charges, but on that particular charge, I just feel duty-bound to object.

"THE COURT: So you're not willing then to follow your oath?

"[JUROR]: That is correct."

The trial court, over defendant's objection, excused Juror No. 10, replaced him with an alternate juror, and instructed the jury to begin its deliberations anew. The next day, the jury convicted defendant of the above described charges, including unlawful sexual intercourse with a minor.

If you were a juror and believed that it was unjust to convict the defendant notwithstanding the law, would you refuse to vote to convict? Why, or why not?

3. Although jurors are almost never informed of the nullification power before they begin deliberating, what should a trial judge do if the jury asks the judge directly during deliberations whether it has the power to nullify? See People v. Dillon, 34 Cal.3d 441, 194 Cal.Rptr. 390, 668 P.2d 697 (1983).

4. In their classic study of American jury behavior, Harry Kalven, Jr. and Hans Zeisel observed that "[i]n many ways the jury is the law's most interesting critic." Harry Kalven, Jr. & Hans Zeisel, The American Jury 219 (1966). Among the factors jurors consider in determining whether to acquit a defendant are: (1) the personal characteristics of the defendant; (2) the degree of harm caused by the defendant; (3) the jurors' belief that the victim was partially at fault for the offense; (4) their view of the morality or wisdom of the law that the defendant violated; (5) their belief that the defendant has been punished enough or that violation of the offense carries too harsh a penalty; and (6) their perception that the police or prosecutor acted improperly in bringing the case.

To the extent that the Kalven & Zeisel study might suggest that juries are more likely than judges to acquit defendants (whether on nullification or other grounds), this may be an outdated assumption. At least in federal courts, the average conviction rate of juries between 1946 and 2002 was 75%; judges convicted at roughly the same rate (73%). In the last decade of this period, however, judges have proven considerably more lenient: Juries have convicted 86% of the time, compared to 54% of the time by judges. Andrew D. Leipold, *Why Are Federal Judges So Acquittal Prone?*, 83 Wash. U.L.Q. 151, 164 (2005).

5. *Race-based jury nullification.* Consider Paul Butler, *Racially Based Jury Nullification: Black Power in the Criminal Justice System*, 105 Yale L.J. 677, 715 (1995), in which the author, a former federal prosecutor and now law professor, advocates race-based jury nullification. According to Butler, Afri-

can–American jurors should *not* nullify the law in cases involving black defendants charged with violent crimes, such as murder, rape, and assault. However, in prosecutions of African–Americans for nonviolent offenses, such as theft,

> nullification is an option that the juror should consider, although there should be no presumption in favor of it. A jury might vote for acquittal, for example, when a poor woman steals from Tiffany's, but not when the same woman steals from her next-door neighbor. Finally, in * * * "victimless" crimes likes narcotics offenses, there should be a presumption in favor of nullification.

In an address published in *Race–Based Jury Nullification: Case-in-Chief*, 30 J. Marshall L. Rev. 911, 912–13, 918–21 (1997), Professor Butler defended his proposal this way:

> I teach criminal law. My students learned that prison is for people who are the most dangerous and the most immoral in our society. Is there anyone here who really believes that over half of the most immoral and dangerous people in the United States are African–American when they constitute only 12 percent of the population? When I look at those statistics, I think that punishment, prison, and criminal law have become the way that we treat the problems of the poor, especially poor African–American people. I think that is immoral. I am confident that one day we, as a society, will understand that, but African–American people cannot afford to wait that long. * * *

> Now, to prevent that kind of "just us" justice, I advocate a program of black self-help outside and inside the courtroom. Outside the courtroom self-help includes the kind of community-building efforts that many of us are already engaged in: mentoring, tutoring, after-school programs, providing legal and medical care to the poor, working with inmates, and taking better care of our families. * * * Inside the courtroom self-help includes the responsible use of prosecutorial discretion, especially by black prosecutors. It also includes selective jury nullification for victimless crimes. * * *

> Now, I am a former prosecutor. Nullification is a partial cure that I come to reluctantly and for moral reasons. To me it is not enough to say that there is a power to nullify; there also has to be some moral basis for this power. In the [*Yale*] article I make several moral claims as to the power. I am going to quickly tell you about two.

> One is this phenomenon of democratic domination. * * * The reason why I believe that African–American jurors have a moral claim to selective nullification is based on this idea that they do not effectively have a say; they do not have the say that they should in the making of the law. They are the victims of the tyranny of the majority. * * * Let me tell you how it works in the context of the criminal justice system. With every crime bill, the Black Political Caucus—the national one or the one in the state—will make the argument, "Hey, guys, instead of spending all this money building prisons, let's spend some money on rehabilitation, on job training, on education. Those are the root causes of crime." In the Black Political Caucus' belief, the white majority will just say no. * * *

The second most powerful way to stop crime is parental training, teaching some of these kids who are having babies how to be good parents. Studies show that such training prevents more crime than the deterrent effect of prison. Now, that does not shock a lot of you. It does not shock a lot of legislators either, but, unfortunately, the majority seems to prefer the punishment regime. * * *

* * * "Democratic domination" is [the] name for it, and for me it is a moral reason as to why nullification is appropriate.

The [other] moral claim African–Americans have to the power of jury nullification is what I call the symbolic role of black jurors. If you look at Supreme Court cases, they often have the occasion to discuss black jurors. They do so because of our country's sad history of excluding black people from juries. The Court said that is a bad thing because black jurors serve this symbolic function. Essentially they symbolize the fairness and the impartiality of the law. The Court says that excluding black jurors undermines public confidence in the criminal justice system. * * *

* * * What about an African–American juror who * * * does not hold any confidence in the integrity of the system. So if she is aware of the implicit message that the Supreme Court says her presence sends, maybe she does not want to be the vehicle for that message. * * *

The political protest part is to encourage an end to this madness of locking up African–Americans when white people do not get locked up for the identical crimes.

Professor Andrew D. Leipold replied to Butler's comments in *Race–Based Jury Nullification: Rebuttal (Part A)*, 30 J. Marshall L. Rev. 923, 923–26 (1997):

Let me briefly outline a few of my concerns about Professor Butler's plan. * * *

My * * * technical argument is that juries are incapable of making reasoned nullification decisions, because at trial they will not be given the information they need. At the heart of Professor Butler's plan is the notion that juries should engage in a cost-benefit analysis when deciding whether to convict. Jurors are supposed to look at the defendant and ask, "Even if this defendant committed the crime charged, what are the rewards of keeping this person out of jail, and what are the risks to the community of letting this person stay free?" The problem is that juries will never hear the evidence that would help them answer this question.

Consider the problem in the context of a simple drug possession case. If we were sitting on a jury, what would we like to know about the defendant before we decided whether to nullify his conviction? We would probably want to know whether the defendant is contrite. We would want to know whether he had a criminal record, and if so, how serious were his prior crimes. We might want to know whether there was anyone else involved in the crime who is more blameworthy. We might wonder how the prosecution enforces this crime against others: are African–Americans disproportionately targeted or arrested for this type of crime? We might also want to know about the potential sentences the defendant would face if convicted; under our cost-benefit analysis, we might be more willing to nullify if the defendant faced a stiff, mandatory sentence.

The problem is that almost none of this information is admissible at trial. * * *

My philosophical concerns begin with the idea of legitimizing and institutionalizing a cost-benefit analysis as a method of jury decision-making. * * * Once we have agreed that jurors can legitimately decide the outcome of cases by a cost-benefit analysis rather than by applying the law as written to the evidence presented, we have started down a dangerous road. Is there any doubt that many other groups will also be drawn to the cost-benefit analysis? * * *

Assume that a jury nullifies in the case of a young African–American defendant who has been charged with simple [drug] possession. Maybe this is a good result: maybe in that specific case, society is better off keeping another African–American kid out of jail, away from a very harsh sentence. But now assume that the next jury comes back and says, "Yes, we think this defendant battered his wife, but you know, she decided to stay in the marriage rather than get a divorce, it looks like she provoked him by spending too much time at her job, she was nagging him, *et cetera*, and we are not going to send this guy to jail." * * * We might be repelled by this reasoning, but we do not have any standing to complain about the process by which the outcome was reached. Those juries also engaged in a cost-benefit analysis, the same process approved of by the Butler plan. * * *

The final concern I have is at the broadest philosophical level. It is a comment that makes me very sad to have to raise at all: whether you go to jail or get set free should not depend on the color of your skin. Using race as the reason for acquitting or convicting is a bad idea, and no matter how strategic the reasoning and no matter how good our intentions, it is still wrong. It is wrong because it encourages the kind of stereotyping that had led to problems in the first place. It is wrong because we are telling people that they will never get equal justice in the courts and so you should take whatever you can get, however you can get it, and be satisfied with that. In short, the plan raises the flag of surrender in the fight for equal justice under the law.

Whose arguments do you find more persuasive?

6. *Going too far?* What if a citizen stands in front of a courthouse and hands out pro-nullification leaflets, encouraging prospective jurors to ignore the law if they disagree with it, and to render verdicts based on conscience. Should this person be subject to criminal prosecution? Yes, according to a federal prosecutor. Julian Heicklen, a 78–year–old retired chemistry professor, was charged in 2011 with jury tampering for his leafletting efforts. Benjamin Weiser, *At the Border of Free Speech and Jury Tampering*, New York Times, February 26, 2011.

CHAPTER 2

PRINCIPLES OF PUNISHMENT

■ ■ ■

INTRODUCTION: INITIAL THOUGHTS
AND HARD STATISTICS

This chapter focuses on punishment, more specifically, on the justifications for punishment, sentencing decisions, and the goal of proportionality of punishment.

In the United States today, the word "punishment" typically evokes the thought of imprisonment, yet it need not. Other modes of punishment, some traditional (e.g., fines, community service, etc.) and some not so traditional (e.g., shaming, discussed at p. 61), are available in lieu of incarceration. Nonetheless, incarceration is the typical form of punishment meted out today in the United States for serious crimes.

Indeed, according to the Bureau of Justice Statistics, nearly 2.3 million persons were incarcerated in federal or state prisons or in local jails on December 31, 2010. See Bureau of Justice Statistics, Sourcebook of Criminal Justice Statistics, http://www.albany.edu/sourcebook/pdf/t612010.pdf (last visited May 14, 2012). According to the International Centre for Prison Studies, the United State has the highest incarceration rate in the world (743 per 100,000 population as of June 2011), followed by Rwanda (approximately 595 per 100,000 population).[a]

American incarceration rates disguise significant differences: Male prisoners made up 93.2% of all sentenced prisoners in 2009, while female prisoners made up 6.8%. Bureau of Justice Statistics, Prisoners in 2009, 20 tbl.5 (Dec. 2010, NCJ 231675). The incarceration rate for African–American males was 6.4 time that of white males and 2.6 times that of Hispanic males. Id. at 22 tbl.22. The rate for African–American females was 2.8 times that of white females and 1.9 times that of Hispanic females. Id. at 28 tbl.15.

The incarceration figures raise important moral and public policy questions about our punishment system. Two of the most important questions are: "Who should be punished?" and "Of those whom we

---

a. World Prison Brief, Entire World—Prison Population Rates per 100,000 of the National Population, http://www.prisonstudies.org/info/worldbrief/wpb_stats.php?area=all&category=wb_poprate.

punish, how much punishment is appropriate?" Another question is "Should we use more non-incarcerative methods of punishment?" In order to think sensibly about these and other penological questions, however, one must decide *why* we punish at all. That is the subject of Part A. of this chapter.

A. THEORIES OF PUNISHMENT

1. IN GENERAL

KENT GREENAWALT—PUNISHMENT

3 Encyclopedia of Crime and Justice 1282 (Joshua Dressler,
Editor-in-Chief, 2d ed. 2002), 1282–1284

Although punishment has been a crucial feature of every legal system, widespread disagreement exists over the moral principles that can justify its imposition. One fundamental question is why (and whether) the social institution of punishment is warranted. A second question concerns the necessary conditions for criminal liability and punishment in particular cases. A third relates to the form and severity of punishment that is appropriate for particular offenses and offenders. * * *

Since punishment involves pain or deprivation that people wish to avoid, its intentional imposition by the state requires justification. The difficulties of justification cannot be avoided by the view that punishment is an inevitable adjunct of a system of criminal law. If criminal law is defined to include punishment, the central question remains whether society should have a system of mandatory rules enforced by penalties. Relatively small associations of like-minded people may be able to operate with rules that are not backed by sanctions, and a choice by the larger society against authorizing legal punishment is at least theoretically possible. Moreover, actual infliction of penalties is not inextricably tied to authorization. A father who has threatened punishment if two daughters do not stop fighting must decide whether to follow through if the fight continues. Congruence between threat and actual performance on the scene does constitute one good reason for punishing. Future threats will be taken less seriously if past threats are not fulfilled, and parents usually wish to avoid the impression that they will not do what they say. Nevertheless, because he now sees that the punishment threatened is too severe, or understands better the children's reasons for fighting, the father may fail to carry out his threat.

In the broader society also, threatened punishments are not always inflicted on persons who have unquestionably committed crimes. The police or prosecutor may decide not to proceed, a jury may acquit in the face of unmistakable evidence of guilt, or a judge may decide after conviction not to impose punishment. A judge with legal authority to make such a decision must determine if punishment is appropriate; even if he is legally required to inflict it, he may find the countervailing reasons so powerful that he will not do so.

Threat of punishment must be real—need follow through

If actual punishment never or very rarely followed threatened punishment, the threat would lose significance. Thus, punishment in some cases is a practical necessity for any system in which threats of punishment are to be taken seriously; and to that extent, the justification of punishment is inseparable from the justification of threats of punishment.

The dominant approaches to justification are retributive and utilitarian. Briefly stated, a retributivist claims that punishment is justified because people deserve it; a utilitarian believes that justification lies in the useful purposes that punishment serves (the latter approach is sometimes also referred to as "consequentialist," or "instrumentalist"). Many actual theories of punishment do not fit unambiguously and exclusively into one of these two categories. Satisfying both retributive and utilitarian criteria may be thought necessary to warrant punishment; or utilitarian criteria may be thought crucial for one question (for example, whether there should be a system of punishment) and retributive criteria for another (for example, who should be punished); or the use of retributive sorts of approaches may be thought appropriate on utilitarian grounds. Beginning from rather straightforward versions of retributive and utilitarian theory, the analysis proceeds to positions that are more complex.

NOTES AND QUESTIONS

1. Professor Greenawalt notes three "punishment" questions that retributivists and utilitarians seek to answer. As explained more fully in H.L.A. Hart, Punishment and Responsibility 1–27 (1968), these three questions can be organized into two. The first question may be stated as follows: "What is the general justifying aim of the criminal justice system?" That is, why do we enact laws that define specified conduct as criminal and impose punishment for violation of those laws?

(1) What is general justific. for punishment

The remaining issues involve the distribution of punishment: "To whom may punishment be applied and in what manner and amount?" Some scholars and lawmakers would apply one penal theory—retribution or utilitarianism—to answer both of Hart's questions, while others would invoke one principle to answer the "general justifying aim" question and the other penal theory (or, perhaps, both) to resolve "distribution" problems. As you study criminal law this semester, consider whether you believe one principle more satisfactorily answers both questions, or whether a mixed ("hybrid") approach is preferable.

(2) To whom may punish. apply & (3) how much?

2. What is "punishment"? The answer is not as obvious as it seems. For example, is a physician convicted of Medicare fraud being "punished" if she is ordered by the sentencing court to perform community service by working in a medical "free clinic"?

What is punishment?

Or, consider "sexual predator" laws. Such laws establish procedures for the commitment of persons who, due to a mental abnormality or a personality disorder not amounting to a mental illness, are likely to engage in predatory acts of sexual violence. Commitment of a predator may occur after he has completed a prison sentence for a sex offense, or might even occur after an acquittal for a criminal offense. A person determined by a court to be a sexual predator is held in custody until he is no longer considered a threat to the community. Since the prognosis for rehabilitation of sexual predators is often poor, a predator might never be released. Is such commitment a form of "punishment"? If so, a person who has already served a prison sentence for a sex offense might legitimately claim that he is being punished twice for the same crime, and a person who is "punished" as a sexual predator after an acquittal could legitimately claim that his constitutional right to be free from "double jeopardy" has been violated.

Greenawalt, supra at 1282–83, has identified the following characteristics of punishment. First, "it is performed by, and directed at, agents who are responsible in some sense. God and humans can punish; hurricanes cannot. People, but not faulty television sets, are fit subjects of punishment." Second, it involves "designedly" harmful or unpleasant consequences. Third, the unpleasant consequences *usually* are "preceded by a judgment of condemnation; the subject of punishment is explicitly blamed for committing a wrong." Fourth, it is imposed by one who has authority to do so. Fifth, it is imposed for a breach of some established rule of behavior. And, finally, it is imposed on an actual or supposed violator of the rule of behavior. Based on *this* definition, is a person committed to a penal institution as a sexual predator the subject of "punishment"? See Kansas v. Hendricks, 521 U.S. 346, 117 S.Ct. 2072, 138 L.Ed.2d 501 (1997); see also Smith v. Doe, 538 U.S. 84, 123 S.Ct. 1140, 155 L.Ed.2d 164 (2003) (discussing what constitutes "punishment" from a constitutional law perspective).

3. Retributivism is based on the principle that people who commit crimes deserve punishment. In that sense, the theory is backward looking: the justification for punishment is found in the prior wrongdoing. In contrast, utilitarianism is forward looking in the sense that punishment is justified on the basis of the supposed benefits that will accrue from its imposition. In the materials that follow, these two philosophies are considered in greater depth.

2. UTILITARIAN JUSTIFICATIONS

JEREMY BENTHAM—AN INTRODUCTION TO THE PRINCIPLES OF MORALS AND LEGISLATION

(John Bowring ed., 1843), 1, 15–16, 83–84

[Chapter 1] I. Nature has placed mankind under the governance of two sovereign masters, *pain* and *pleasure*. It is for them alone to point out what we ought to do, as well as to determine what we shall do. * * * They govern us in all we do, in all we say, in all we think: every effort we can make to throw off our subjection, will serve but to demonstrate and confirm it. In words a man may pretend to abjure their empire: but in reality he will remain subject to it all the while. The *principle of utility* recognises this subjection, and assumes it for the foundation of that system, the object of which is to rear the fabric of felicity by the hands of reason and of law. Systems which attempt to question it, deal in sounds instead of sense, in caprice instead of reason, in darkness instead of light. * * *

II. * * * By the principle of utility is meant that principle which approves or disapproves of every action whatsoever, according to the tendency which it appears to have to augment or diminish the happiness of the party whose interest is in question: or, what is the same thing in other words, to promote or to oppose that happiness. I say of every action whatsoever; and therefore not only of every action of a private individual, but of every measure of government. * * *

[Chapter IV] I. Pleasures then, and the avoidance of pains, are the *ends* which the legislator has in view: it behoves him therefore to understand their *value*. Pleasures and pains are the *instruments* he has to work with: it behoves him therefore to understand their force, which is again, in other words, their value.

II. To a person considered *by himself,* the value of a pleasure or pain considered *by itself,* will be greater or less, according to the four following circumstances:

1. Its *intensity.*

2. Its *duration.*

3. Its *certainty or uncertainty.*

4. Its *propinquity or remoteness.* * * *

[Chapter XV] I. The general object which all laws have, or ought to have, in common, is to augment the total happiness of the community; and therefore, in the first place, to exclude, as far as may be, every thing that tends to subtract from the happiness: in other words, to exclude mischief.

II. But all punishment is mischief: all punishment in itself is evil. Upon the principle of utility, if it ought at all to be admitted, it ought only to be admitted in as far as it promises to exclude some greater evil.

III. It is plain, therefore, that in the following cases punishment ought not to be inflicted.

1. Where it is *groundless:* where there is no mischief for it to prevent; the act not being mischievous upon the whole.

2. Where it must be *inefficacious:* where it cannot act so as to prevent the mischief.

3. Where it is *unprofitable,* or too *expensive:* where the mischief it would produce would be greater than what it prevented.

4. Where it is *needless:* where the mischief may be prevented, or cease of itself, without it: that is, at a cheaper rate.

NOTES AND QUESTIONS

1. *Law and Economics.* Bentham's approach to the justification of punishment finds expression today in the economic analysis of law. According to Richard Posner, the "economic character of [Bentham's] analysis of crime and punishment is unmistakable despite the slightly archaic vocabulary * * *." Richard A. Posner, *Bentham's Influence on the Law and Economics Movement*, 51 Current Legal Probs. 425, 431 (1998). For example:

> Bentham * * * made a number of important economic points in the *Introduction [to the Principles of Morals and Legislation]*: a person commits a crime only if the pleasure he anticipates from the crime exceeds the anticipated pain, or in other words only if the expected benefit exceeds the expected cost; to deter crime, therefore, the punishment must impose sufficient pain that, when added to any other pain anticipated by the criminal, it will exceed the pleasure that he anticipates from the crime; a punishment greater than this should not be imposed, because the result would be to create pain (to the undeterrable criminal) not offset by pleasure (benefits) to the potential victims of crime; the schedule of punishment must be calibrated in such a way that if the criminal has a choice of crimes, he commits the least serious; fines are a better method of punishment than imprisonment, because they confer a benefit as well as impose a detriment; the less likely the criminal is to be caught, the heavier the punishment must be, to maintain an expected cost great enough to deter. * * *

Id.

KENT GREENAWALT—PUNISHMENT

3 Encyclopedia of Crime and Justice 1282 (Joshua Dressler, Editor-in-Chief, 2d ed. 2002), 1286–1287

Utilitarian theories of punishment have dominated American jurisprudence during most of the twentieth century. According to Jeremy Bentham's classical utilitarianism, whether an act or social practice is morally desirable depends upon whether it promotes human happiness better than possible alternatives. Since punishment involves pain, it can be justified only if it accomplishes enough good consequences to outweigh this harm. A theory of punishment may make the balance of likely consequences central to justification without asserting, as Bentham did, that all relevant consequences are reducible to happiness and unhappiness. It may even claim that reducing future instances of immoral violations of right is itself an appropriate goal independent of the effect of those violations on the people involved. In modern usage, *utilitarianism* is often employed to refer broadly to theories that likely consequences determine the morality of action, and this usage is followed here.

The catalogs of beneficial consequences that utilitarians have thought can be realized by punishment have varied, but the following have generally been regarded as most important.

1. *General deterrence.* Knowledge that punishment will follow crime deters people from committing crimes, thus reducing future violations of right and the unhappiness and insecurity they would cause. The person who has already committed a crime cannot, of course, be deterred from committing that crime, but his punishment may help to deter others. In Bentham's view, general deterrence was very much a matter of affording rational self-interested persons good reasons not to commit crimes. With a properly developed penal code, the benefits to be gained from criminal activity would be outweighed by the harms of punishment, even when those harms were discounted by the probability of avoiding detection. Accordingly, the greater the temptation to commit a particular crime and the smaller the chance of detection, the more severe the penalty should be.

general deterrence

Punishment can also deter in ways more subtle than adding a relevant negative factor for cool calculation. Seeing others punished for certain behavior can create in people a sense of association between punishment and act that may constrain them even when they are sure they will not get caught. Adults, as well as children, may subconsciously fear punishment even though rationally they are confident it will not occur. * * *

[2.] *Individual deterrence.* The actual imposition of punishment creates fear in the offender that if he repeats his act, he will be punished again. Adults are more able than small children to draw conclusions from the punishment of others, but having a harm befall oneself is almost always a sharper lesson than seeing the same harm occur to others. To deter an offender from repeating his actions, a penalty should be severe enough to outweigh in his mind the benefits of the crime. For the utilitarian, more severe punishment of repeat offenders is warranted partly because the first penalty has shown itself ineffective from the standpoint of individual deterrence.

specific deterrence

[3.] *Incapacitation and other forms of risk management.* Imprisonment temporarily puts convicted criminals out of general circulation, and the death penalty does so permanently. These punishments physically prevent persons of dangerous disposition from acting upon their destructive tendencies. Less drastic forms of risk management include probationary or parole supervision, and accompanying requirements (for example, random urine tests to detect use of illegal drugs) and prohibitions (use of alcohol or firearms, association with certain persons, contact with the victim, and so on). * * *

incapacitation

[4.] *Reform.* Punishment may help to reform the criminal so that his wish to commit crimes will be lessened, and perhaps so that he can be a happier, more useful person. Conviction and simple imposition of a penalty might themselves be thought to contribute to reform if they help an offender become aware that he has acted wrongly. * * * However, reform is usually conceived as involving more positive steps to make offenders less antisocial by altering their basic character, improving their skills, or teaching them how to control their crime-producing urges * * *. Various

reform

psychological therapies, medications, and even drastic interventions such as psychosurgery, are designed to curb destructive tendencies. Educational and training programs can render legitimate employment a more attractive alternative to criminal endeavors. These may indirectly help enhance self-respect, but their primary purpose is to alter the options that the released convict will face.

NOTES AND QUESTIONS

1. *Deterrence.* Does punishment deter? Does it deter effectively? These simple questions do not yield simple answers. Regarding the general deterrent value of punishment, research indicates that the benefit of punishment depends on various factors, including: the nature of the offense; the type of offender involved; the perceived risk of detection, arrest, and conviction; the nature and severity of the penalties threatened or imposed; and the temporal proximity (or celerity) between the crime and the imposition of punishment. According to one recent survey, we have "no real knowledge base about the celerity of punishment," but "there does seem to be a modest inverse relationship between the perceived certainty of punishment and crime" and "no real evidence of a deterrent effect for severity." Raymond Paternoster, *How Much Do We Really Know About Criminal Deterrence?*, 100 J. Crim. L. & Criminology 765, 818 (2010). For example, assume for a moment that the penalty for the offense of burglary is five years' imprisonment. Further assume that a would-be burglar of a home in a wealthy part of town perceives that the chances of being caught, tried, and convicted are only five percent. A rational burglar expecting to steal a great deal of valuable property might believe that a 5% chance of being caught, convicted, and sentenced to five years in prison is worth the risk. Suppose, however, that he thought there was a 95% chance of being arrested, convicted, and sentenced to *one* year in prison. He might be deterred more in the latter case, although the statutory punishment is less.

As for incapacitation, imprisonment has preventive value in the straightforward sense that, while jailed, an inmate cannot commit an offense in the outside society. However, because utilitarians believe that punishment is a mischief that should not be imposed unless it will result in a net benefit to society, punishment based on this principle is only justifiable to the extent that the sentencing authority can reliably predict the future dangerousness of offenders (and, then, only if the predicted reduction in crime from incapacitation outweighs the hardships that will be imposed on those incarcerated and the economic costs of their incarceration). Various techniques or methodologies are used to predict the risk that a particular individual will commit an act of violence in the future. A distinction is commonly drawn between clinical and actuarial techniques. Clinical approaches rely on "whatever information the individual clinician deem[s] relevant." Christopher Slobogin, *Dangerousness and Expertise Redux*, 56 Emory L.J. 275, 283 (2006). Actuarial approaches rely, "like insurance actuaries do, on a finite number of pre-identified variables that statistically correlate to risk and that produce a definitive probability or probability range of risk." Id. How successful are these techniques? Most researchers agree that actuarial methodologies are superior to clinical ones. As for the accuracy of actuarial methodologies, if a methodology that perfectly predicted future violence scored 1.0, and if one that predicted future violence no better than chance scored .50, then existing actuarial methodologies generally score between .65 and .71.[b] Jennifer L. Skeem & John Monahan, *Current Directions in Violence Risk Assessment*, 20 Current Directions in Psychol. Sci. 38, 40 (2011). Using the best prediction methodologies under ideal circumstances, probably more than 15% of those identified as high risk for violence would not commit another crime if left at large. Christopher Slobogin, *Risk Assessment*, in The Oxford Handbook of Sentencing and Corrections 196, 200-201 (Joan Petersilia & Kevin Reitz eds., 2012). See generally John Monahan, *Prediction of Crime and Recidivism*, in 3 Encyclopedia of Crime and Justice 1125 (Joshua Dressler, editor-in-chief, 2d ed. 2002).

The current strategy of incarcerating more persons and for longer terms is sometimes justified on dual grounds: first, that incarcerated criminals cannot commit more crimes while imprisoned (prevention by incapacitation); and second, the increased likelihood of long prison sentences will dissuade *others* from committing crimes (general deterrence). Studies of the effectiveness of this strategy in reducing homicides "have produced wildly divergent results." Thomas B. Marvell & Carlisle E. Moody, *The Impact of Prison Growth on Homicide*, 1 Homicide Stud. 205, 205 (1997) (summarizing the results). Some studies of "three strikes" laws that mandate increasingly long prison terms for repeat offenders suggest that they have not reduced crime rates to the extent predicted. James Austin et al., *The Impact of "Three Strikes and You're Out,"* 1 Punishment & Soc'y 131 (1999); see Michael Vitiello, *Punishment and Democracy: A Hard Look at Three Strikes' Overblown Promises*, 90 Cal. L. Rev. 257 (2002) (reviewing Franklin E. Zimring, Gordon Hawkins, & Sam Kamin, Punishment and Democracy: Three Strikes and You're Out in California (2001)).

2. *Rehabilitation*. Incarceration rarely is imposed today for rehabilitative (reform) purposes. The conventional wisdom is that past efforts to rehabilitate convicted offenders were mostly unsuccessful. Advocates of rehabilitation initially responded that adequate funds for reform measures were never appropriated and, therefore, the "failures" really represented a failure of will by legislators hesitant to appropriate large sums of money for what some taxpayers considered "coddling" of criminals.

Rehabilitation

Recent studies of rehabilitative efforts have called into question some of the earlier assumptions of failure. According to a meta-analysis—essentially, a computation of the "batting average" across all studies of rehabilitative efforts—"the existing research, which now involves hundreds of evaluation studies, shows that rehabilitation programs reduce recidivism about 10 percentage points." Francis T. Cullen & Shannon A. Santana, *Rehabilitation*, in 3 Encyclopedia of Crime and Justice 1314, 1324 (Joshua Dressler, editor-in-chief, 2d ed. 2002). It is also claimed that if principles of effective intervention

---

b. A score of .71 means that a 71% chance exists using the assessment instrument in question that a recidivist will receive a higher rating on the instrument than a non-recidivist.

are applied—targeting the proper persons, use of treatment techniques that reinforce societal values, etc.—the recidivism rate may be reduced about 25 percent. Id. Nonetheless, according to one pair of researchers, the "greatest obstacle to using rehabilitation treatment effectively to reduce criminal behavior is not a nothing-works research literature but, rather, a correctional system that does not use the research available and has no history of doing so." Mark W. Lipsey & Francis T. Cullen, *The Effectiveness of Correctional Rehabilitation: A Review of Systematic Reviews*, 3 Ann. Rev. L. & Soc. Sci. 297, 315 (2007). For a survey of the philosophical attacks on rehabilitation as a justification for punishment and efforts to "rehabilitate rehabilitation," see Michael Vitiello, *Reconsidering Rehabilitation,* 65 Tul. L. Rev. 1011 (1991).

[margin note: moral objection to rehab.]

Even assuming that rehabilitative measures work, can you think of any moral objection to rehabilitation as a justification for imposing punishment? Consider the following assertion: "[W]hen we cease to consider what the criminal deserves and consider only what will cure him * * *, we have tacitly removed him from the sphere of justice altogether." C.S. Lewis, *The Humanitarian Theory of Punishment*, in Contemporary Punishment: Views, Explanations, and Justifications 194 (Rudolph J. Gerber & Patrick D. McAnany eds., 1972). What do you think Lewis is getting at?

[margin note: Kant using man as means to an end immoral]

3. *Utilitarianism and punishment of the innocent.* Immanuel Kant, infra, has expressed the most common moral criticism of deterrence theory: even if general deterrence works (an empirical question), "one man ought never to be dealt with merely as a means subservient to the purpose of another." In what way does utilitarianism propose to use a person as a means to an end? Why, if at all, is that objectionable?

[margin note: Utilitarian may punish innocent?]

Applying utilitarian theory, is punishment of an innocent person ever justifiable? Consider the following scenario: An especially violent murder occurs in a small, racially divided community. The victim is white and, although there is no hard evidence to prove it, a rumor quickly spreads that the killer was black. As the result of racist activity by white supremacist groups, a white mob threatens to enter the community and kill innocent African–Americans and burn down their homes in order to exact vengeance. The town sheriff realizes that she lacks adequate personnel to stop the mob. She is convinced, however, that if she arrests an African–American for the crime and promises a quick trial, the mob will be satisfied. Therefore, she arrests and frames a homeless black man with a prior record of violent criminal activity. As predicted, the mob is satisfied; the man is subsequently tried, convicted, and punished for the crime.

Could a utilitarian justify the sheriff's actions? Why or why not? See Guyora Binder & Nicholas J. Smith, *Framed: Utilitarianism and Punishment of the Innocent*, 32 Rutgers L.J. 115 (2000); H.J. McCloskey, *A Non–Utilitarian Approach to Punishment*, in Contemporary Utilitarianism 239 (Michael D. Bayles ed., 1968); T.L.S. Sprigge, *A Utilitarian Reply to Dr. McCloskey,* in id. at 261.

3.   RETRIBUTIVE JUSTIFICATIONS

MICHAEL S. MOORE—THE MORAL WORTH OF RETRIBUTION

Responsibility, Character, and the Emotions: New Essays in Moral
Psychology (Ferdinand Schoeman ed., 1987), 179–182

[R]etributivism is sometimes identified with a particular measure of punishment such as *lex talionis*, an eye for an eye, or with a kind of punishment such as the death penalty. Yet retributivism answers a question prior to the questions to which these could be answers. True enough, retributivists at some point have to answer the "how much" and "what type" questions for specific offenses, and they are committed to the principle that punishment should be graded in proportion to desert; but they are not committed to any particular penalty scheme nor to any particular penalty as being deserved. Separate argument is needed to answer these "how much" and "what type" questions, *after* one has decided why one is punishing at all. It is quite possible to be a retributivist and to be against both the death penalty and *lex talionis*, the idea that crimes should be punished by like acts being done to the criminal.

Contrary to [the statements of some scholars], retributivism is *not* "the view that only the guilty are to be punished." A retributivist will subscribe to such a view, but that is not what is distinctive about retributivism. The distinctive aspect of retributivism is that the moral desert of an offender is a *sufficient* reason to punish him or her; the principle [quoted above] make[s] such moral desert only a *necessary* condition of punishment. Other reasons—typically, crime prevention reasons—must be added to moral desert, in this view, for punishment to be justified. Retributivism has no room for such additional reasons. That future crime might also be prevented by punishment is a happy surplus for a retributivist, but no part of the justification for punishing. * * *

[R]etributivism should not be confused with a theory of formal justice (the treating of like cases alike). Retributivism is not * * * "a particular application of a general principle of justice, namely, that equals should be treated equally and unequals unequally." True, a retributivist who also subscribes to the principle of formal justice is committed to punishing equally those persons who are equally deserving. However, the principle of formal justice says nothing about punishing anybody for anything; such a principle only dictates that, *if* we punish anyone, we must do so equally. Why we should punish anyone is the question retributivism purports to answer * * *.

Retributivism is a very straightforward theory of punishment: We are justified in punishing because and only because offenders deserve it. Moral culpability ("desert") is in such a view both a sufficient as well as a necessary condition of liability to punitive sanctions. Such justification gives society more than merely a right to punish culpable offenders. It does this, making it not unfair to punish them, but retributivism justifies more than this. For a retributivist, the moral culpability of the offender also gives society the *duty* to punish. Retributivism, in other words, is truly a theory of justice such that, if it is true, we have an obligation to set up institutions so that retribution is achieved.

NOTES AND QUESTIONS

1. *"Negative" versus "positive" retribution.* Moore writes that "retributivism is *not* 'the view that only the guilty are to be punished.'" *This* view—that the innocent should never be punished, i.e., that guilt is a *necessary* condition of punishment—has been characterized by some as "negative retributivism." E.g., J.L. Mackie, *Morality and Retributive Emotions*, Crim. Just. Ethics, Winter/Spring 1982, at 3, 4. Some utilitarians accept this retributive limitation on their theory.

In contrast, Moore is espousing what might be characterized as "positive retribution," the view that desert is both a necessary *and* sufficient condition for punishment. According to Moore, to a full-blooded retributivist, a wrongdoer *must* be punished for his culpable wrongdoing, even if it deters no future crime. But, what is the basis for what Moore describes as this "straightforward" theory? The materials that follow wrestle with this question.

IMMANUEL KANT—THE PHILOSOPHY OF LAW

(W. Hastie trans., 1887), 194–198

The right of administering punishment is the right of the sovereign as the supreme power to inflict pain upon a subject on account of a crime committed by him. * * *

Judicial or juridical punishment (*poena forensis*) is to be distinguished from natural punishment (*poena naturalis*), in which crime as vice punishes itself, and does not as such come within the cognizance of the legislator. Juridical punishment can never be administered merely as a means for promoting another good either with regard to the criminal himself or to civil society, but must in all cases be imposed only because the individual on whom it is inflicted *has committed a crime.* For one man ought never to be dealt with merely as a means subservient to the purpose of another, nor be mixed up with the subjects of real right. Against such treatment his inborn personality has a right to protect him, even although he may be condemned to lose his civil personality. He must first be found guilty and *punishable,* before there can be any thought of drawing from his punishment any benefit for himself or his fellow-citizens. The penal law is a categorical imperative; and woe to him who creeps through the serpent-windings of utilitarianism to discover some advantage that may discharge him from the justice of punishment, or even from the due measure of it, according to the Pharisaic maxim: "It is better that *one* man should die than that the whole people should perish." For if justice and righteousness perish, human life would no longer have any value in the world. What, then, is to be said of such a proposal as to keep a criminal alive who has been condemned to death, on his being given to understand that, if he agreed to certain dangerous experiments being performed upon him, he would be allowed to survive if he came happily through them? It is argued that physicians might thus obtain new information that would be of value to the commonweal. But a court of justice would repudiate with scorn any proposal of this kind if made to it by the medical faculty; for justice would cease to be justice, if it were bartered away for any consideration whatever.

* * * Even if a civil society resolved to dissolve itself with the consent of all its members—as might be supposed in the case of a people inhabiting an island resolving to separate and scatter themselves throughout the whole world—the last murderer lying in the prison ought to be executed before the resolution was carried out. This ought to be done in order that every one may realize the desert of his deeds, and that blood-guiltiness may not remain upon the people; for otherwise they might all be regarded as participators in the murder as a public violation of justice.

Kant is cruel?

Notes and Questions

1. Is Kant defending positive or negative retribution as those terms are defined on page 40, Note 1?

2. Death penalty controversies aside, what do you think of Kant's assertion that "the last murderer lying in the prison ought to be executed" before a society dissolves itself? Is this anything more than cruel infliction of needless pain?

2 JAMES FITZJAMES STEPHEN—A HISTORY OF THE CRIMINAL LAW OF ENGLAND

(1883), 80–82

Assaultive Retributiv.

* * * Whatever may be the nature or extent of the differences which exist as to the nature of morals, no one in this country regards murder, rape, arson, robbery, theft, or the like, with any feeling but detestation. I do not think it admits of any doubt that law and morals powerfully support and greatly intensify each other in this matter. Everything which is regarded as enhancing the moral guilt of a particular offence is recognised as a reason for increasing the severity of the punishment awarded to it. On the other hand, the sentence of the law is to the moral sentiment of the public in relation to any offence what a seal is to hot wax. It converts into a permanent final judgment what might otherwise be a transient sentiment. The mere general suspicion or knowledge that a man has done something dishonest may never be brought to a point, and the disapprobation excited by it may in time pass away, but the fact that he has been convicted and punished as a thief stamps a mark upon him for life. In short, the infliction of punishment by law gives definite expression and a solemn ratification and justification to the hatred which is excited by the commission of the offence, and which constitutes the moral or

popular as distinguished from the conscientious sanction of that part of morality which is also sanctioned by the criminal law. The criminal law thus proceeds upon the principle that it is morally right to hate criminals, and it confirms and justifies that sentiment by inflicting upon criminals punishments which express it.

* * * I am * * * of opinion that this close alliance between criminal law and moral sentiment is in all ways healthy and advantageous to the community. I think it highly desirable that criminals should be hated, that the punishments inflicted upon them should be so contrived as to give expression to that hatred, and to justify it so far as the public provision of means for expressing and gratifying a healthy natural sentiment can justify and encourage it.

These views are regarded by many persons as being wicked, because it is supposed that we never ought to hate, or wish to be revenged upon, any one. The doctrine that hatred and vengeance are wicked in themselves appears to me to contradict plain facts, and to be unsupported by any argument deserving of attention. Love and hatred, gratitude for benefits, and the desire of vengeance for injuries, imply each other as much as convex and concave.

NOTES AND QUESTIONS

1. What do you think of Stephen's views? Whatever you think of them, *must* a retributivist think this way? Indeed, are Stephen's ideas *really* retributive in nature? Consider these observations by Professor Michael Moore:

[R]etributivism is not the view that the preference of all citizens * * * should be satisfied. A * * * utilitarian might well believe, as did * * * Stephen that punishment should be exacted "for the sake of gratifying the feeling of hatred * * *," or that "the feeling of hatred and the desire of vengeance * * * are important elements of human nature which ought * * * to be satisfied in a regular public and legal manner." Yet a retributivist need not believe such things, but only that morally culpable persons should be punished, irrespective of what other persons feel, desire, or prefer.

Relatedly, retributivism is not the view that punishment is justified because without it vengeful citizens would take the law into their own hands. Usually it is those who are hostile to retributivism * * * who link it to this indefensible idea. Punishment for a retributivist is not justified by the need to prevent private violence, which is an essentially utilitarian justification. * * *

Nor is retributivism to be confused with denunciatory theories of punishment. In this latter view, punishment is justified because punishment is the vehicle through which society can express its condemnation of the criminal's behavior. This is a utilitarian theory, not a retributive one, for punishment is in this view to be justified by the good consequences it achieves—either the psychological satisfactions denunciation achieves, or

[handwritten margin note: Stephen a utilitarian? Punishment as means to an end]

the prevention of private violence, or the prevention of future crimes through the education benefits of such denunciation. A retributivist justifies punishment by none of these supposed good consequences of punishing.

Michael S. Moore, *The Moral Worth of Retribution*, in Responsibility, Character, and the Emotions: New Essays in Moral Psychology 180–181 (Ferdinand Schoeman ed., 1987).

2. In the passage quoted above, Moore suggests that retribution justifies punishment without reference to any good that might come from punishing an offender. Is that true? If not, if retribution justifies punishment because punishment achieves some good, what might that good be, and what difference would there then be between a retributive justification for punishment and a utilitarian one? See Mitchell N. Berman, *Two Kinds of Retributivism*, in Philosophical Foundations of Criminal Law 433 (R.A. Duff & Stuart P. Green eds., 2011).

[handwritten margin note: just deserts is true good — punishment aims to achieve]

[handwritten margin note: Protective / retributiv.]

HERBERT MORRIS—PERSONS AND PUNISHMENT

52 Monist 475 (1968), 476–479

My aim is to argue for four propositions concerning rights that will certainly strike some as not only false but preposterous: first, that we have a right to punishment; second, that this right derives from a fundamental human right to be treated as a person; third, that this fundamental right is a natural, inalienable, and absolute right; and, fourth, that the denial of this right implies the denial of all moral rights and duties. Showing the truth of one, let alone all, of these large and questionable claims, is a tall order. The attempt or, more properly speaking, the first steps in an attempt, follow. * * *

Let us first turn attention to the institutions in which punishment is involved. The institutions I describe will resemble those we ordinarily think of as institutions of punishment; they will have, however, additional features we associate with a system of just punishment.

[handwritten margin note: why just deserts is an intrinsic moral good — restores moral balance]

Let us suppose that men are constituted roughly as they now are, with a rough equivalence in strength and abilities, a capacity to be injured by each other and to make judgments that such injury is undesirable, a limited strength of will, and a capacity to reason and to conform conduct to rules. Applying to the conduct of these men are a group of rules, ones I shall label "primary," which closely resemble the core rules of our criminal law, rules that prohibit violence and deception and compliance with which provides benefits for all persons. These benefits consist of noninterference by others with what each person values, such matters as continuance of life and bodily security. The rules define a sphere for each person then, which is immune from interference by others. Making possible this mutual benefit is the assumption by individuals of a burden. The burden consists in the exercise of self-restraint by individuals over inclinations that would, if satisfied, directly interfere or create a substantial risk of interference with others in proscribed ways. If a person fails to exercise self-restraint even though he might have and gives in to such inclinations, he renounces a burden which others have voluntarily assumed and thus gains an advantage which others, who have restrained themselves, do not possess. This system, then, is one in which the rules establish a mutuality of benefit and burden and in which the benefits of noninterference are conditional upon the assumption of burdens.

Connecting punishment with the violation of these primary rules, and making public the provision for punishment, is both reasonable and just. First, it is only reasonable that those who voluntarily comply with the rules be provided some assurance that they will not be assuming burdens which others are unprepared to assume. * * * Second, fairness dictates that a system in which benefits and burdens are equally distributed have a mechanism designed to prevent a maldistribution in the benefits and burdens. * * *

Third, it is just to punish those who have violated the rules and caused the unfair distribution of benefits and burdens. A person who violates the rules has something others have—the benefits of the system—but by renouncing what others have assumed, the burdens of self-restraint, he has acquired an unfair advantage. Matters are not even until this advantage is in some way erased. Another way of putting it is that he owes something to others, for he has something that does not rightfully belong to him. Justice—that is punishing such individuals—restores the equilibrium of benefits and burdens by taking from the individual what he owes, that is, exacting the debt. * * *

There are also in this system we are considering a variety of operative principles compliance with which provides some guarantee that the system of punishment does not itself promote an unfair distribution of benefits and burdens. For one thing, provision is made for a variety of defenses, each one of which can be said to have as its object diminishing the chances of forcibly depriving a person of benefits others have if that person has not derived an unfair advantage. A person has not derived an unfair advantage if he could not have restrained himself or if it is unreasonable to expect him to behave otherwise than he did. Sometimes the rules preclude punishment of classes of persons such as children. Sometimes they provide a defense if on a particular occasion a person lacked the capacity to conform his conduct to the rules. Thus, someone who in an epileptic seizure strikes another is excused. Punishment in these cases would be punishment of the innocent, punishment of those who do not voluntarily renounce a burden others have assumed. Punishment in such cases, then, would not equalize but rather cause an unfair distribution in benefits and burdens.

NOTES AND QUESTIONS

1. According to Morris, criminals have a right to be punished. Punishment demonstrates respect for the offender by paying "deference to an individual's free choice by connecting punishment to a freely chosen act

violative of the rules" (id. at 485), an attitude one would not express regarding a noxious insect or, for that matter, a "sick" person incapable of rational choice. Punishment of a truly culpable individual, therefore, is seen as a way of respecting the wrongdoer's personhood ("you made a free choice, now you must live with the consequences"); it is also a way for the wrongdoer to pay his debt to the community and return to it in moral equilibrium.

2. Morris presents an account of retribution that emphasizes the respect punishment pays to a wrongdoer and portrays punishment as a way for a wrongdoer to repay his debt to society. The thoughts of murderer Gary Gilmore, written in a letter to his friend, Nicole, as he awaited execution on Utah's Death Row, give voice to Morris' account:

> Recently it has begun to make a little sense. I owe a debt, from a long time ago. * * * I'm on the verge of knowing something very personal, something about myself. Something that somehow wasn't completed and made me different. Something I owe, I guess. Wish I knew.
>
> Once you asked me if I was the devil, remember? I'm not. The devil would be far more clever than I, would operate on a much larger scale and of course would feel no remorse. * * * And I know the devil can't feel love. But I might be further from God than I am from the devil. Which is not a good thing. It seems that I know evil more intimately than I know goodness and that's not a good thing either. I want to get even, to be made even, whole, my debts paid (whatever it may take!) to have no blemish, no reason to feel guilt or fears. I hope this ain't corny, but I'd like to stand in the sight of God. To know that I'm just and right and clean.

Norman Mailer, The Executioner's Song 305–306 (1979).

But making a retributive judgment that a wrongdoer *deserves* to be punished is a dangerous undertaking, for dark emotions—hatred, anger, revenge, resentment, fear, sadism, and so forth—can all-too-easily accompany such a judgment. Consider the purported remarks of federal judge Kirby Benedict in the New Mexico Territory at the sentencing of a malefactor.[c]

> Jose Manuel Miguel Xavier Gonzales, in a few short weeks it will be spring. The snows of winter will flee away, the ice will vanish, and the air will become soft and balmy. In short, Jose Manuel Miguel Xavier Gonzales, the annual miracle of the years will awaken and come to pass, but you won't be there.
>
> The rivulet will run its soaring course to the sea, the timid desert flowers will put forth their tender shoots, the glorious valleys of this imperial domain will blossom as the rose. Still, you won't be here to see.

---

c. It is unclear when Judge Benedict sentenced the defendant. It may have been as early as 1864. Unfortunately, the records of the speech were burned in a fire at the Taos, New Mexico courthouse. The name of the accused is also in question, and may not have been as stated in the text. Some reports suggest that the name was Jesus Maria Martinez or Jose Maria Martin. An excerpt of the remarks may be found in Jack Smith, *Page Out of the Old West and a Poetic Hanging Judge,* L.A. Times, Oct. 18, 1990, at E1. For another version of the speech and more information about Judge Benedict, see Aurora Hunt, Kirby Benedict: Frontier Federal Judge 78–81 (1961).

From every treetop some wild woods songster will carol his mating song; butterflies will sport in the sunshine, the busy bee will hum happy as it pursues its accustomed vocation; the gentle breeze will tease the tassels of the wild grasses, and all nature will be glad, but you. You won't be here to enjoy it because I command the sheriff or some other officers of the country [sic] to lead you out to some remote spot, swing you by the neck from a knotting bough of some sturdy oak, and let you hang until you are dead.

And then, Jose Manuel Miguel Xavier Gonzales, I further command that such officer or officers retire quickly from your dangling corpse, so that vultures may descend from the heavens upon your filthy body until nothing shall remain but bare, bleached bones of a cold-blooded, blood-thirsty, throat-cutting, chili-eating, sheep-herding, murdering son of a bitch.[d]

Recall that Stephen believed it was "highly desirable that criminals should be hated." Do you agree? How might a retributivist respond to the ever-present risk of these dark emotions?

JEFFRIE G. MURPHY & JEAN HAMPTON— FORGIVENESS AND MERCY

(1988), 124–128, 130[e]

Retributive idea 1: punishment as a defeat. Those who wrong others * * * objectively demean them. They incorrectly believe or else fail to realize that others' value rules out the treatment their actions have accorded the others, and they incorrectly believe or implicitly assume that their own value is high enough to make this treatment permissible. So, implicit in their wrongdoings is a message about their value relative to that of their victims. * * *

* * * A retributivist's commitment to punishment is not merely a commitment to taking hubristic wrongdoers down a peg or two; it is also a commitment to asserting moral truth in the face of its denial. If I have value equal to that of my assailant, then that must be made manifest after I have been victimized. By victimizing me, the wrongdoer has declared

---

d. *Shades of Judge Benedict?* More recently, Zacarias Moussaoui, who pled guilty to participating in the planning of the September 11 attacks on the Twin Towers in New York City, was spared his life by a jury, after which he delivered a speech to the court, concluding with the statement: "God curse America and save Osama bin Laden. * * * America, you lost. I won." According to a *New York Times* account, a "clearly angered" sentencing judge, Leonia Brinkema, said:

Well, Mr. Moussaoui, if you look around this courtroom today, every person in this room when this proceeding is over will leave this courtroom, and they are free to go any place they want. They can go outside, they can feel the sun, they can smell fresh air. [In contrast,] [y]ou will spend the rest of your life in a super-maximum security facility. In terms of winners and losers, it's quite clear who won and who lost. * * * As for you, Mr. Moussaoui, you came here to be a martyr and to die in a great big bang of glory, but to paraphrase the poet T.S. Eliot, instead you will die with a whimper.

Neil A. Lewis, *A Last Moment In the Spotlight For Moussaoui*, N.Y. Times, May 5, 2006, at A1.

e. The book, *Forgiveness and Mercy*, was written in the form of a dialogue between the two authors. Professor Jean Hampton wrote this excerpt.

himself elevated with respect to me, acting as a superior who is permitted to use me for his purposes. A false moral claim has been made. Moral reality has been denied. The retributivist demands that the false claim be corrected. The lord must be humbled to show that he isn't the lord of the victim. If I cause the wrongdoer to suffer in proportion to my suffering at his hands, his elevation over me is denied, and moral reality is reaffirmed. I master the purported master, showing that he is my peer.

So I am proposing that retributive punishment is the defeat of the wrongdoer at the hands of the victim (either directly or indirectly through an agent of the victim's, e.g., the state) that symbolizes the correct relative value of wrongdoer and victim. It is a symbol that is conceptually required to reaffirm a victim's equal worth in the face of a challenge to it. * * *

But exactly how does punishment make this assertion? Consider that retributivists typically endorse the *lex talionis* as a punishment formula, or (as I would reinterpret it) as a formula for determining the extent to which the wrongdoer must be mastered. That formula calls for a wrongdoer to suffer something like what his victim suffered * * *. * * * To inflict on a wrongdoer something comparable to what he inflicted on the victim is to master him in the way that he mastered the victim. The score is even. Whatever mastery he can claim, she can also claim. If her victimization is taken as evidence of her inferiority relative to the wrongdoer, then his defeat at her hands negates that evidence. Hence the *lex talionis* calls for a wrongdoer to be subjugated in a way that symbolizes his being the victim's equal. The punishment is a second act of mastery that denies the lordship asserted in the first act of mastery. * * *

* * * [T]he *retributive* motive for inflicting suffering is to annul or counter the appearance of the wrongdoer's superiority and thus affirm the victim's real value. So even in a situation where neither the wrongdoer nor society will either listen to or believe the message about the victim's worth which the "punitive defeat" is meant to carry, and where the victim doesn't need to hear (or will not believe) that message in order to allay any personal fears of diminishment, the retributivist will insist on the infliction of punishment insofar as it is a way of "striking a blow for morality" or (to use a phrase of C.S. Lewis's) a way to "plant the flag" of morality.

NOTES AND QUESTIONS

1. How does Professor Hampton's view of retribution differ from Morris's? How does it differ from Stephen's?

2. Do you find retributivists persuasive in defending the principle that it is morally just to punish a wrongdoer, even if that punishment will not result in future societal benefit? Or, instead, do you believe that "the retributivist's 'respect for persons' merely cloaks a desire to inflict suffering on criminals with a clear conscience and a minimum of concern with their backgrounds or capacities"? David Dolinko, *Three Mistakes of Retributivism*, 39 UCLA L. Rev. 1623, 1650 (1992).

3. *A thought experiment.* It is alleged that Thomas Atkinson brutally murdered Joyce Paneck–Saglimbene, a 27–year–old New Jersey woman, in 1976. At the time, Atkinson was thirteen years old. The crime became a "cold case" until 2006 when Atkinson was arrested for the crime. Alan Feuer, *Arrest in a 30–Year–Old Murder Case Reignites the Pain of a Victim's Family,* N.Y. Times, Aug. 23, 2006, at C10. For current purposes, assume that the allegation is correct.

Atkinson is now forty-three years old. He is married, goes with his son to barbecues and ballgames, is described by neighbors as pleasant, a family man, never angry, helpful to those around him. Assume the following additional information (as a thought experiment you must accept the hypothesized facts): Atkinson is totally rehabilitated; he no longer represents a threat to the community; he is an active and positive member of his local community; he has felt deep remorse for the murder for many years and even sent an anonymous letter to the victim's family years ago begging forgiveness.

Now, with this information, do you believe Atkinson should be punished? Why, or why not? Are there any additional facts that would cause you to change your mind? If so, what are those facts? If you would punish Atkinson, does this demonstrate that you are a retributivist rather than a utilitarian?

4. *Must you choose one theory over the other?* We have seen that there are some critical differences between utilitarianism and retributivism. As a result, retributivists and utilitarians will often provide different answers to the questions that these theories of punishment seek to answer: what is the general justifying aim of the criminal law; whom should we punish in the criminal justice system; and how much and in what manner should we punish them? (See again p. 31, Note 1.)

Must one choose one of these theories at the exclusion of the other? Although some persons, including some lawmakers, *do* answer these questions with a single theory, many people (and lawmakers) see benefits—and weaknesses—in both theories of punishment. As a consequence, many people answer the first question—why did we develop a criminal justice system?—with a utilitarian explanation (e.g., "We wrote criminal laws and set up potential penalties for their violation in the hope of preventing harmful conduct."), and yet they provide retributive answers to the other questions (e.g., "We should punish, but only punish, guilty people because they deserve it, and they should be punished to the extent that they deserve it."). However, is such a mixed system intellectually coherent? How about the reverse—a retributive answer to the "general justifying aim" question and utilitarianism to resolve the other questions? Do you find yourself answering all of the questions with one theory?

Especially when one turns to the third question—how much punishment should be inflicted?—some legislators favor a mixture of retributivism and utilitarianism. The question is whether there is a sensible way to mix these theories. We come back to this question shortly (p. 58, Note 5).

B.   THE PENAL THEORIES IN ACTION

1.   WHO SHOULD BE PUNISHED?

THE QUEEN v. DUDLEY AND STEPHENS

Queen's Bench Division, 1884.
14 Q.B.D. 273.

Lord Coleridge, C.J. The two prisoners, Thomas Dudley and Edwin Stephens, were indicted for the murder of Richard Parker on the high seas on the 25th day of July in the present year. They were tried before my Brother Huddleston at Exeter on the 6th of November, and, under the direction of my learned Brother, the jury returned a special verdict, the legal effect of which has been argued before us, and on which we are now to pronounce judgment.

The special verdict as * * * it is finally settled before us is as follows.

[T]hat on July 5, 1884, the prisoners, Thomas Dudley and Edward Stephens, with one Brooks, all able-bodied English seamen, and the deceased also an English boy, between seventeen and eighteen years of age, the crew of an English yacht, a registered English vessel, were cast away in a storm on the high seas 1600 miles from the Cape of Good Hope, and were compelled to put into an open boat belonging to the said yacht. That in this boat they had no supply of water and no supply of food, except two 1lb. tins of turnips, and for three days they had nothing else to subsist upon. That on the fourth day they caught a small turtle, upon which they subsisted for a few days, and this was the only food they had up to the twentieth day when the act now in question was committed. That on the twelfth day the remains of the turtle were entirely consumed, and for the next eight days they had nothing to eat. That they had no fresh water, except such rain as they from time to time caught in their oilskin capes. That the boat was drifting on the ocean, and was probably more than 1000 miles away from land. That on the eighteenth day, when they had been seven days without food and five without water, the prisoners spoke to Brooks as to what should be done if no succour came, and suggested that some one should be sacrificed to save the rest, but Brooks dissented, and the boy, to whom they were understood to refer, was not consulted. That on the 24th of July, the day before the act now in question, the prisoner Dudley proposed to Stephens and Brooks that lots should be cast who should be put to death to save the rest, but Brooks refused to consent, and it was not put to the boy, and in point of fact there was no drawing of lots. That on that day the prisoners spoke of their having families, and suggested it would be better to kill the boy that their lives should be saved, and Dudley proposed that if there was no vessel in sight by the morrow morning the boy should be killed. That next day, the 25th of July, no vessel appearing, Dudley told Brooks that he had better go and have a sleep, and made signs to Stephens and Brooks that the boy had better be killed. The prisoner Stephens agreed to the act, but Brooks dissented from it. That the boy was then lying at the bottom of the boat quite helpless, and extremely weakened by famine and by drinking sea water, and unable to make any resistance, nor did he ever assent to his being killed. The prisoner Dudley offered a prayer asking forgiveness for them all if either of them should be tempted to commit a rash act, and that their souls might be saved. That Dudley, with the assent of Stephens, went to the boy, and telling him that his time was come, put a knife into his throat and killed him then and there; that the three men fed upon the body and blood of the boy for four days; that on the fourth day after the act had been committed the boat was picked up by a passing vessel, and the prisoners were rescued, still alive, but in the lowest state of prostration. That they were carried to the port of Falmouth, and committed for trial at Exeter. That if the men had not fed upon the body of the boy they would probably not have survived to be so picked up and rescued, but would within the four days have died of famine. That the boy, being in a much weaker condition, was likely to have died before them. That at the time of the act in question there was no sail in sight, nor any reasonable prospect of relief. That under these circumstances there appeared to the prisoners every probability that unless they then fed or very soon fed upon the boy or one of themselves they would die of starvation. That there was no appreciable chance of saving life except by killing some one for the others to eat. That assuming any necessity to kill anybody, there was no greater necessity for killing the boy than any of the other three men. But whether upon the whole matter by the jurors found the killing of Richard Parker by Dudley and Stephens be felony and murder the jurors are ignorant, and pray the advice of the Court thereupon, and if upon the whole matter the Court shall be of opinion that the killing of Richard Parker be felony and murder, then the jurors say that Dudley and Stephens were each guilty of felony and murder as alleged in the indictment.

NOTES AND QUESTIONS

1. Should Dudley and Stephens have been punished for their conduct? Why, or why not? Are your reasons based on retributive or utilitarian principles, or both?

2. Assume for a moment that a legislature concludes that someone in the defendants' predicament should be acquitted of criminal homicide. What should lawmakers do in such circumstances to protect a future Dudley or Stephens?

3. A fuller picture of the events relating to the *Dudley and Stephens* affair is set out brilliantly in A.W. Brian Simpson, Cannibalism and the Common Law (1984). Dudley, captain of the ill-fated Mignonette, was an

experienced yachtsman. He was married and the father of three children. Devoutly religious, he took prayer books to sea and conducted regular religious services on board. Dudley acted decisively and courageously throughout the crisis and was primarily responsible for the seamen's survival during the early period in the dinghy.

Stephens was a devoted husband, father of five, and respected local figure. His impeccable career as a seaman had been sullied as the result of an earlier wreck of a vessel of which he had been junior officer. Although he was not culpable for the latter loss, Stephens found it difficult to find employment until Dudley hired him to serve on the Mignonette.

Brooks's background is less clear. He claimed to be a bachelor, but there is evidence to suggest that he may have been married, deserted his wife, and accepted a position on the Mignonette in order to escape his wife, who may have been on his trail.

Parker was a wild-living illiterate youth. He signed on to the Mignonette in order to travel abroad, as a rite of passage into manhood.

Does any of this information change your answers to the questions raised in Note 1?

2.   HOW MUCH (AND WHAT) PUNISHMENT SHOULD BE IMPOSED?

PEOPLE v. SUPERIOR COURT (Du)

California Court of Appeal, Second District, 1992.
5 Cal.App.4th 822, 7 Cal.Rptr.2d 177.

ASHBY, ACTING PRESIDING JUSTICE. * * *

FACTS

The crime giving rise to defendant's [Soon Ja Du's] conviction [of voluntary manslaughter] occurred on the morning of March 16, 1991, at the Empire Liquor Market, one of two liquor stores owned and operated by defendant and her family. Although Empire Liquor was normally staffed by defendant's husband and son while defendant worked at the family's other store in Saugus, defendant worked at Empire on the morning of March 16 so that her son, who had been threatened by local gang members, could work at the Saugus store instead. Defendant's husband, Billy Du, was present at the Empire Liquor Market that morning, but at defendant's urging he went outside to sleep in the family van because he had worked late the night before.

Defendant was waiting on two customers at the counter when the victim, 15-year-old Latasha Harlins, entered the store. Latasha proceeded to the section where the juice was kept, selected a bottle of orange juice, put it in her backpack, and proceeded toward the counter.

Defendant had observed many shoplifters in the store,[3] and it was her experience that people who were shoplifting would take the merchandise,

---

3. Defendant's son, Joseph Du, testified that there were at least 40 shoplifting incidents a week at the store.

"place it inside the bra or anyplace where the owner would not notice," and then approach the counter, buy some small items and leave. Defendant saw Latasha enter the store, take a bottle of orange juice from the refrigerator, place it in her backpack and proceed to the counter. Although the orange juice was in the backpack, it was partially visible. Defendant testified that she was suspicious because she expected if the victim were going to pay for the orange juice, she would have had it in her hand.

Thirteen-year-old Lakeshia Combs and her brother, nine-year-old Ismail Ali, testified that Latasha approached the counter with money ("about two or three dollars") in her hand. According to these witnesses, defendant confronted Latasha, called her a "bitch" and accused her of trying to steal the orange juice; Latasha stated she intended to pay for it. According to defendant, she asked Latasha to pay for the orange juice and Latasha replied, "What orange juice?" Defendant concluded that Latasha was trying to steal the juice.[4]

Defendant began pulling on Latasha's sweater in an attempt to retrieve the orange juice from the backpack. Latasha resisted and the two struggled. Latasha hit defendant in the eye with her fist twice. With the second blow, defendant fell to the floor behind the counter, taking the backpack with her. During the scuffle, the orange juice fell out of the backpack and onto the floor in front of the counter. Defendant testified that she thought if she were hit one more time, she would die. Defendant also testified that Latasha threatened to kill her. Defendant picked up a stool from behind the counter and threw it at Latasha, but it did not hit her.

After throwing the stool, defendant reached under the counter, pulled out a holstered .38–caliber revolver, and, with some difficulty, removed the gun from the holster. As defendant was removing the gun from the holster, Latasha picked up the orange juice and put it back on the counter, but defendant knocked it away. As Latasha turned to leave defendant shot her in the back of the head from a distance of approximately three feet, killing her instantly. Latasha had $2 in her hand when she died.

Defendant's husband entered the store upon hearing defendant's calls for help and saw Latasha lying on the floor. Defendant leaned over the counter and asked, "Where is that girl who hit me?" Defendant then passed out behind the counter. Defendant's husband attempted to revive her and also dialed 911 and reported a holdup. Defendant, still unconscious, was transported to the hospital by ambulance, where she was treated for facial bruises and evaluated for possible neurological damage.

---

4. Defendant testified that it was Latasha's statement, "What orange juice?" which changed defendant's attitude toward the situation, since prior to that time defendant was not afraid of Latasha. Defendant also thought Latasha might be a gang member. Defendant had asked her son, Joseph Du, what gang members in America look like, and he replied "either they wear some pants and some jackets, and they wear light sneakers, and they either wear a cap or a hairband, headband. And they either have some kind of satchel, and there were some thick jackets. And he told me to be careful with those jackets sticking out." Latasha was wearing a sweater and a "Bruins" baseball cap.

prejudice

At defendant's trial, she testified that she had never held a gun before, did not know how it worked, did not remember firing the gun and did not intend to kill Latasha.

Defendant's husband testified that he had purchased the .38–caliber handgun from a friend in 1981 for self-protection. He had never fired the gun, however, and had never taught defendant how to use it. In 1988, the gun was stolen during a robbery of the family's store in Saugus. Defendant's husband took the gun to the Empire store after he got it back from the police in 1990.

hair trigger altered by thief

David Butler, a Los Angeles Police Department ballistics expert, testified extensively about the gun, a Smith & Wesson .38–caliber revolver with a two-inch barrel. In summary, he testified that the gun had been altered crudely and that the trigger pull necessary to fire the gun had been drastically reduced. Also, both the locking mechanism of the hammer and the main spring tension screw of the gun had been altered so that the hammer could be released without putting much pressure on the trigger. In addition, the safety mechanism did not function properly. * * *

The jury found defendant guilty of voluntary manslaughter * * *. By convicting defendant of voluntary manslaughter, the jury impliedly found that defendant had the intent to kill and that the killing was unlawful, *i.e.*, that it was neither justifiable nor excusable. Thus, the jury rejected the defenses that the killing was unintentional and that defendant killed in self-defense.

jury findings preclude self-defense

PROBATION REPORT

After defendant's conviction, the case was evaluated by a Los Angeles County Probation Officer, who prepared a presentence probation report. That report reveals the following about defendant:

At the time the report was prepared, defendant was a 51–year–old Korean-born naturalized American citizen, having arrived in the United States in 1976. For the first ten years of their residence in the United States, defendant worked in a garment factory and her husband worked as a repairman. Eventually, the couple saved enough to purchase their first liquor store in San Fernando. They sold this store and purchased the one in Saugus. In 1989, they purchased the Empire Liquor Market, despite being warned by friends that it was in a "bad area."

These warnings proved prophetic, as the store was plagued with problems from the beginning. The area surrounding the store was frequented by narcotics dealers and gang members, specifically the Main Street Crips. Defendant's son, Joseph Du, described the situation as "having to conduct business in a war zone." In December 1990, defendant's son was robbed while working at the store and he incurred the wrath of local gang members when he agreed to testify against one of their number who he believed had committed the robbery.[5] Soon thereafter, the

criminal activity @ store

---

5. * * * The store was burglarized over 30 times and shoplifting incidents occurred approximately 40 times per week. If Joseph tried to stop the shoplifters, "they show me their guns."

family closed the store for two weeks while defendant's husband formulated a plan (which he later realized was "naive") to meet with gang members and achieve a form of truce. The store had only recently been reopened when the incident giving rise to this case occurred.

The probation officer concluded "it is true that this defendant would be most unlikely to repeat this or any other crime if she were allowed to remain free. She is not a person who would actively seek to harm another * * *." However, she went on to state that although defendant expressed concern for the victim[6] and her family, this remorse was centered largely on the effect of the incident on defendant and her own family.[7] * * *

PEOPLE v. DU

Superior Court, Los Angeles County, 1991.
No. BA037738.

trial court decision

JUDGE JOYCE A. KARLIN:

[Judge Karlin sentenced Du to ten years in state prison (six years for voluntary manslaughter, and four years for use of a gun in the commission of a felony, a separate allegation), but then suspended the sentence and placed Du on probation. The following are the judge's remarks at sentencing.]

Statements by the district attorney, (which) suggest that imposing less than the maximum sentence will send a message that a black child's life is not worthy of protection, (are) dangerous rhetoric, which serves no purpose other than to pour gasoline on a fire. This is not a time for revenge, and my job is not to exact revenge for those who demand it.

There are those in this community who have publicly demanded in the name of justice that the maximum sentence be imposed in this case. But it is my opinion that justice is never served when public opinion, prejudice, revenge or unwarranted sympathy are considered by a sentencing court in resolving a case.

sentencing objectives

In imposing sentence I must first consider the objectives of sentencing a defendant: 1) to protect society; 2) to punish the defendant for committing a crime; 3) to encourage the defendant to lead a law-abiding life; 4) to

Joseph further testified that his life had been threatened over 30 times, and more than 20 times people had come into the store and threatened to burn it down. Joseph told his mother about these threats every day because he wanted to emphasize how dangerous the area was, and that he could not do business there much longer.

info @ Latasha

6. The probation report also reveals that Latasha had suffered many painful experiences during her life, including the violent death of her mother. Latasha lived with her extended family (her grandmother, younger brother and sister, aunt, uncle and niece) in what the probation officer described as "a clean, attractively furnished three-bedroom apartment" in South Central Los Angeles. Latasha had been an honor student at Bret Hart Junior High School, from which she had graduated the previous spring. Although she was making only average grades in high school, she had promised that she would bring her grades up to her former standard. Latasha was involved in activities at a youth center as an assistant cheerleader, member of the drill team and a summer junior camp counselor. She was a good athlete and an active church member.

7. The probation officer's ultimate conclusion and recommendation was that probation be denied and defendant sentenced to state prison.

P.O.'s rec. – prison

deter others; 5) to isolate the defendant so she can't commit other crimes; 6) to secure restitution for the victim; [and] 7) to seek uniformity in sentencing.

[margin: sentencing objectives]

The question becomes, are any of these sentencing objectives achieved by Mrs. Du being remanded to state prison? Let us start with the last objective first: uniformity in sentencing. According to statistics gathered for the Superior Courts of California, sentences imposed on defendants convicted of voluntary manslaughter last year ranged from probation with no jail time to incarceration in state prison for several years. Because of the unique nature of each crime of voluntary manslaughter, and by that I mean the uniquely different factual situations resulting in that crime, uniformity in sentencing is virtually impossible to achieve.

[margin: #1 uniformity in sentencing]

Which, then, of the other sentencing objectives lead to the conclusion that state prison is warranted?

Does society need Mrs. Du to be incarcerated in order to be protected? I think not.

[margin: #2 prot. of society]

Is state prison needed in order to encourage the defendant to lead a law-abiding life or isolate her so she cannot commit other crimes? I think not.

[margin: #3 encourage D to lead law-abiding life] [margin: #4 isolate D]

Is state prison needed to punish Mrs. Du? Perhaps.

[margin: #5 punish D]

There is, in this case, a presumption against probation because a firearm was used.[f] In order to overcome that presumption, the court must find this to be an unusual case, as that term is defined by law. There are three reasons that I find this is an unusual case:

[margin: unusual: #a]

First, * * * [t]he statute is aimed at criminals who arm themselves when they go out and commit other crimes. It is not aimed at shopkeepers who lawfully possess firearms for their own protection. Second, the defendant has no recent record, in fact, no record at any time of committing similar crimes or crimes of violence. Third, the defendant participated in the crime under circumstances of great provocation, coercion and duress. Therefore, this is, in my opinion, an unusual case that overcomes the statutory presumption against probation.

[margin: #b] [margin: #c]

Should the defendant be placed on probation?

One of the questions a sentencing court is required [by statute] to ask in answering that question is "whether the crime was committed because of unusual circumstances, such as great provocation." I find that it was.

[margin: Du was provoked]

I must also determine the vulnerability of the victim in deciding whether probation is appropriate. Although Latasha Harlins was not armed with a weapon at the time of her death, she had used her fists as weapons just seconds before she was shot.

[margin: victim used fists]

---

f. California Penal Code § 1203(e) provided: "Except in unusual cases where the interests of justice would best be served if the person is granted probation, probation shall not be granted to any of the following persons: * * * (2) Any person who used, or attempted to use, a deadly weapon upon a human being in connection with the perpetration of the crime of which he or she has been convicted."

The district attorney argues that Latasha was justified in her assault on Mrs. Du. Our courts are filled with cases which suggest otherwise. * * * Had Latasha Harlins not been shot and had the incident which preceded the shooting been reported, it is my opinion that the district attorney would have relied on the [store security] videotape and Mrs. Du's testimony to make a determination whether to file charges against Latasha.

Other questions I am required to address in determining whether probation is appropriate are "whether the carrying out of the crime suggested criminal sophistication and whether the defendant will be a danger to others if she is not imprisoned." Having observed Mrs. Du on videotape at the time the crime was committed and having observed Mrs. Du during this trial, I cannot conclude that there was any degree of criminal sophistication in her offense. Nor can I conclude that she is a danger to others if she is not incarcerated.

Mrs. Du is a 51–year–old woman with no criminal history and no history of violence. But for the unusual circumstances in this case, including the Du family's history of being victimized and terrorized by gang members, Mrs. Du would not be here today. Nor do I believe Mrs. Du would be here today if the gun she grabbed for protection had not been altered. This was a gun that had been stolen from the Du family and returned to them shortly before the shooting. The court has been presented with no evidence, and I have no reason to believe that Mrs. Du knew that the gun had been altered in such a way as to-in effect-make it an automatic weapon with a hairpin trigger. * * *

The district attorney would have this court ignore the very real terror experienced by the Du family before the shooting, and the fear Mrs. Du experienced as she worked by herself the day of the shooting. But there are things I cannot ignore. And I cannot ignore the reason Mrs. Du was working at the store that day. She went to work that Saturday to save her son from having to work. Mrs. Du's son had begged his parents to close the store. He was afraid because he had been the victim of repeated robberies and terrorism in that same store.

On the day of the shooting Mrs. Du volunteered to cover for her son to save him one day of fear. Did Mrs. Du react inappropriately to Latasha? Absolutely. Was Mrs. Du's over-reaction understandable? I think so.

If probation is not appropriate, and state prison time is warranted, then a short prison term would be an injustice. If Mrs. Du should be sent to prison because she is a danger to others or is likely to re-offend, then I could not justify imposing a short prison term.

NOTES AND QUESTIONS

1. The California Court of Appeal ruled that Judge Karlin did not abuse her discretion in putting Du on probation.

2. At the time of sentencing, Judge Karlin could have sent Du to prison for three, six, or eleven years for voluntary manslaughter, rather than

suspend the sentence and place her on probation. Given the options, what sentence would *you* have imposed?

3. If you believe that Du deserves to be punished on retributive grounds, how do you tell *how much* punishment she deserves? As one scholar has noted, the "greatest" puzzle of retributivism "is whether it can defend, in any principled way, claims about the proportionality of particular punishment to the particular harms culpably caused by particular offenders." Heidi M. Hurd, *Expressing Doubts About Expressivism*, 2005 U. Chi. Legal F. 405, 415. In this connection, do the beliefs or intuitions of the members of the community as to the right amount of punishment matter? See Paul H. Robinson, *Competing Conceptions of Modern Desert: Vengeful, Deontological, and Empirical*, 67 Cambridge L.J. 145 (2008). What about the subjective experience of the person being punished? See Adam J. Kolber, *The Subjective Experience of Punishment*, 109 Colum. L. Rev. 182 (2009).

4. *More details*. The homicide, and particularly Judge Karlin's probationary sentence, aggravated already existing tensions between African–American residents of South Central Los Angeles and Korean–American merchants. Some persons claim that those tensions, in turn, were a significant catalyst in the 1992 Los Angeles riots that resulted in enormous property damage (including the destruction of nearly two thousand Korean businesses, including the Empire Liquor Market, which was burned to the ground) and loss of life. Tony Castro, *African–Americans, Koreans Try to Heal Deep Wounds*, L.A. Daily News, Apr. 29, 2007, at N21.

Here are some additional details, as laid out in Brenda E. Stevenson, *Latasha Harlins, Soon Ja Du, and Joyce Karlin: A Case Study of Multicultural Female Violence and Justice on the Urban Frontier*, 89 J. Afr. Am. Hist. 152 (2004):

Latasha Harlin's mother was shot to death when she was eight years old, and her father abandoned her. She lived with her maternal grandmother, a deeply religious, strong-willed woman from Tuscaloosa, Alabama. Latasha was a freshman in high school at the time of the incident. Although "street-wise," she regularly cried whenever she passed by the cemetery where her mother was buried. She hoped to go to law school.

Soon Ja Du graduated from Seoul University as a literature major before she and her family emigrated to Los Angeles when she was thirty-nine years old. The move was traumatic, as her identity shifted from well-to-do daughter of a doctor and educated wife of a Korean army officer to manual laborer. Over time she and her husband purchased a convenience store in the San Fernando Valley and, later, bought two more stores, including the one in South Central Los Angeles. At the time, Du was a deaconess in the Valley Korean Central Presbyterian Church.

Judge Joyce Karlin was born in Venezuela, the daughter of a wealthy Jewish–American film studio executive. After law school she worked briefly in criminal defense but then became a federal prosecutor and married another prosecutor. Defense lawyers considered her bright, principled, with "the right instincts." After fourteen years as a prosecutor, she was appointed to the bench by a Republican governor. The *Du* case was Karlin's first jury trial as a judge. When Karlin came up for election, she won with a bare 50.07% of the vote. She left the bench in 1997 to pursue a political career as Joyce Fahey (her husband's surname). She won election to the Manhattan Beach City Council and later because that city's Mayor. She is now in general legal practice. Her husband, William Fahey, has become a Superior Court judge in Los Angeles County.

5. *A mixed theory approach to sentencing?* You will notice that under California law Judge Karlin was required to consider seven objectives of sentencing set out by state legislators. Take a look at them on pages 54–55. Does California seem to want its judges to sentence convicted persons on the basis of retributive or utilitarian goals, or are both theories of punishment involved?

Do you like the idea of permitting judges to sentence wrongdoers on the basis of *both* retributive and utilitarian theories of punishment? If so, should they be given a laundry list of objectives, as in California, or is there a better way? Consider this mixed theory:

> Punishment's purpose is utilitarian: to reduce crime and thus protect the rights of all to be secure in their persons and property. But that purpose must be pursued within retribution's limits: the state cannot punish someone unless he commits a crime, nor can it punish him disproportionately in relation to the crime he commits. Moreover, it cannot punish someone if no discernible good would come of it, even if the offender is guilty as charged. Thus, * * * a person can legitimately be punished only if he committed a crime, only in proportion to that crime, and only if doing so would produce a world with less crime.

Stephen P. Garvey, *Lifting the Veil on Punishment*, 7 Buff. Crim. L. Rev. 443, 450 (2004). Notice that this theory never results in more punishment than is retributively deserved, even if utilitarian goals might justify it. But, this approach can result in less punishment of a wrongdoer than is retributively deserved (or, even, no punishment at all) if utilitarian goals would not be furthered by full punishment.

A different mixed-theory sentencing approach would set the maximum and minimum punishment for an offense on the basis of retributivism, whereas utilitarian goals would determine, *within those parameters*, the actual sentence. This mixed theory is posited on the view that "most people's moral sensibilities, concerning most crimes, will orient them toward a range of permissible sanctions that are 'not undeserved.' Outside the perimeters of the range, some punishments will appear clearly excessive to do justice, and some will appear clearly too lenient—but there will nearly always be a substantial gray area between the two extremes" where utilitarian purposes of punishment can fit in. American Law Institute, Model Penal Code: Sentencing 5 (Tentative Draft No. 1, Apr. 9, 2007) (approved May 16, 2007).

MPC

Take a look at Model Penal Code § 1.02(2) in the Appendix at p. 942. Can you determine whether the Code's sentencing provisions are utilitarian, retributive, or some coherent combination of them?

§ 1.02

6. *Sentencing procedures.* A brief understanding of sentencing procedures is useful here. First, it is valuable to distinguish between "indeterminate" and "determinate" sentencing systems. A sentencing system is some-

times described as "indeterminate" if trial judges have broad sentencing discretion. For example, a judge may have authority to incarcerate a robber, in the words of a hypothetical sentencing statute, to "a term of years not exceeding ten," or even to put the robber on probation (release her with no prison sentence, but impose certain conditions, such as not possessing a weapon, and regularly meeting with a probation officer, for a specified number of years). Thus, the judge may choose to impose a five-year prison sentence in one case, and ten in another, and order probation in a third, typically based on information provided to the judge in a presentencing report. Such a sentencing system is "indeterminate" in the sense that the judge, and not the legislature, sets the appropriate punishment for each offender within very broad legislative imposed parameters.

In the purest version of indeterminate sentencing, the judge herself *imposes* an indeterminate sentence. For example, Model Penal Code § 6.06, as originally adopted, provided that for serious felonies, the judge would impose "a term the minimum of which shall by fixed by the Court at not less than one year nor more than ten years, and the maximum of which shall be life imprisonment." Thus, in this system, as the defendant leaves for prison, he does not know precisely how long he will be incarcerated, except within the broad parameters of the indeterminate sentence. For example, under the quoted MPC section above, the judge might impose a sentence of "a term of no less than three years and no more than life imprisonment." The ultimate release decision—will the defendant get out in three years, spend his entire life in prison, or something in between?—would be determined by a parole board, based on the inmate's rehabilitative progress and other factors.

Indeterminate sentencing systems came into disfavor in the 1970s. Some persons felt that judges and parole boards were too lenient, that they "coddled" criminals. Others persons, concerned about equality, were upset that two persons who committed similar offenses often received very different sentences. Thus, most states and federal courts have shifted toward a more "determinate" sentencing system. Indeed, the American Law Institute has recently abandoned the indeterminate sentencing provisions of the original Model Penal Code.

In some determinate sentencing jurisdictions, the legislature sets a specific sentence for each crime, although often permitting (as in California in *Du*) a specified higher or lower sentence if specific aggravating or mitigating circumstances are proven. The convicted defendant goes to prison knowing exactly how long she will be incarcerated. Parole boards do not exist in these jurisdictions.

Many states and the federal system have enacted determinate sentencing programs through a system of sentencing guidelines. For example, the Model Penal Code's new sentencing provisions (Articles 6A and 6B of the Code) establish a permanent sentencing commission as an independent agency of state government (§ 6A.01), which has as its purpose to develop sentencing guidelines that set forth presumptive sentences for persons convicted of crimes (§ 6B.02). When imprisonment is involved, the guidelines specify a presumptive range of sentence lengths (§ 6B.04(3)(a)), for example, "sixteen to twenty-four months." Sentencing courts are permitted to go outside the presumptive range, however, on the basis of a finding of one or more aggravating or mitigating factors enumerated in the guidelines (§ 6B.04(4)).**g**

7. *Getting rid of punishment?* Some argue that a state that has "persistently excluded [a person] from the rights and benefits of citizenship" lacks the moral standing to call such a person to account for his or her criminal wrongdoing. See R.A. Duff, Punishment, Communication, and Community 197 (2001). Do you agree? Others argue that punishment only makes sense if people are responsible for what they do, and no one is ever responsible for what he or she does, because what anyone does is predetermined. See Stephen P. Garvey, *Alternatives to Punishment*, in Oxford Handbook of Philosophy of Criminal Law 493 (John Deigh & David Dolinko eds., 2011) (discussing such arguments). What do you think? If you believe punishment should be abolished, what, if anything, would you put in its place? What about a system of preventive detention?

Even if we don't get rid of punishment, should we be looking for alternatives to the our principal form of punishment: imprisonment?

8. *Alternatives to imprisonment: restorative justice.* Punishment in the United States typically involves imprisonment in a prison or jail. Is punishment by incarceration of most offenders, however, a good idea from a utilitarian perspective and/or does it result in retributively indecent treatment? Consider these observations by United States Supreme Court Justice Blackmun in *United States v. Bailey*, 444 U.S. 394, 100 S.Ct. 624, 62 L.Ed.2d 575 (1980):

> [W]e do not live in an ideal world "even" (to use a self-centered phrase) in America, so far as jail and prison conditions are concerned. The complaints that this Court, and every other American appellate court, receives almost daily from prisoners about conditions of incarceration, about filth, about homosexual rape, and about brutality are not always the mouthings of the purely malcontent. * * *

> The atrocities and inhuman conditions of prison life in America are almost unbelievable; surely they are nothing less than shocking. * * *

> A youthful inmate can expect to be subjected to homosexual gang rape his first night in jail, or, it has been said, even in the van on the way to jail. Weaker inmates become the property of stronger prisoners or gangs, who sell the sexual services of the victim. Prison officials either are disinterested in stopping abuse of prisoners by other prisoners or are incapable of doing so, given the limited resources society allocates to the prison system. Prison officials often are merely indifferent to serious health and safety needs of prisoners as well.

According to federal figures, 21,936 inmates (a rate of 251 per 100,000) died in state prisons in the years 2001–2007, from illness, suicide, homicide, drug or alcohol overdose, or (in a small number of cases) accident. See http://bjs.ojp.usdoj.gove/content/dcrp/tables/dcst07spt.2.pdf.

Disenchantment with prison conditions has resulted in an emerging social movement called "restorative justice":

---

g. In order to save space, Articles 6A and 6B have not been included in the Model Penal Code reproduced in the Appendix.

Restorative justice provides an entirely different way of thinking about crime and victimization. Under previous criminal justice paradigms the state was viewed as the primary victim of criminal acts, and victims and offenders played passive roles. Restorative justice recognizes crime as first and foremost being directed against individual people. It assumes that those most effected by crime should have the opportunity to become actively involved in resolving the conflict. The emphasis is on restoration of losses, allowing offenders to take direct responsibility for their actions, and assisting victims in moving beyond their sense of vulnerability and achieving some closure.

Mark Umbreit, *Restorative Justice*, in 3 Encyclopedia of Crime and Justice 1333, 1334 (Joshua Dressler, editor-in-chief, 2d ed. 2002).

Although there are many aspects to restorative justice, incarceration is not a primary feature. Instead, victim-offender mediation typically occurs, the goal of which is to foster interpersonal reconciliation between victim and wrongdoer, as well as to strengthen social reconciliation between the offender and the community. Trained facilitators meet with the crime victim, who is encouraged to express her feelings and to communicate directly with the wrongdoer regarding the effects of the crime on her. The facilitator, in turn, works with the criminal to express his feelings and, ideally, to secure expressions of genuine remorse or shame. The crime victim also suggests ways an offender might seek to repair the harm; and members of the community become involved in "reparative probation boards" or "peacemaking circles" to ensure that the offender take responsibility for his actions and in order to strengthen the bonds between him and the larger community.

Restorative justice techniques are more often used to deal with property offenders than violent criminals (but see p. 438, Note 7, and its possible use in acquaintance rape cases), and typically the system is only used if both the offender and victim choose this alternative to traditional punitive measures.

9. *Alternatives to imprisonment: shaming.* One judge has stated that "[we] need to quit doing things by rote. To get the point across, to be meaningful, sometimes you have to do creative things." Henry J. Reske, *Scarlet Letter Sentences*, A.B.A. J., Jan. 1996, at 16. One "creative" form of sentencing is shaming, or "scarlet letter sentences." In this regard consider the next case.

UNITED STATES v. GEMENTERA

United States Court of Appeals for the Ninth Circuit, 2004.
379 F.3d 596.

O'SCANNLAIN, CIRCUIT JUDGE:

We must decide the legality of a supervised release condition that requires a convicted mail thief to spend a day standing outside a post office wearing a signboard stating, "I stole mail. This is my punishment."

I

Shawn Gementera pilfered letters from several mailboxes along San Francisco's Fulton Street on May 21, 2001. A police officer who observed the episode immediately detained Gementera * * *. After indictment, Gementera * * * pled guilty to mail theft, and the government dismissed a second count of receiving a stolen U.S. Treasury check.

The offense was not Gementera's first encounter with the law. Though only twenty-four years old at the time, Gementera's criminal history was lengthy for a man of his relative youth, and it was growing steadily more serious. * * *

On February 25, 2003, Judge Vaughn Walker of the United States District Court for the Northern District of California sentenced Gementera. The U.S. Sentencing Guidelines range was two to eight months incarceration; Judge Walker sentenced Gementera to the lower bound of the range, imposing two months incarceration and three years supervised release.[1] He also imposed conditions of supervised release.

One such condition required Gementera to "perform 100 hours of community service," to consist of "standing in front of a postal facility in the city and county of San Francisco with a sandwich board which in large letters declares: 'I stole mail. This is my punishment.' "[2] Gementera later filed a motion to correct the sentence by removing the sandwich board condition.

Judge Walker modified the sentence after inviting both parties to present "an alternative form or forms of public service that would better comport with the aims of the court." In lieu of the 100–hour signboard requirement, the district court imposed a four-part special condition in its stead. Three new terms * * * mandated that the defendant observe postal patrons visiting the "lost or missing mail" window, write letters of apology to any identifiable victims of his crime, and deliver several lectures at a local school. It also included a scaled-down version of the signboard requirement:

> The defendant shall perform 1 day of 8 total hours of community service during which time he shall either (i) wear a two-sided sandwich board-style sign or (ii) carry a large two-sided sign stating, "I stole mail; this is my punishment," in front of a San Francisco postal facility identified by the probation officer. For the safety of defendant and general public, the postal facility designated shall be one that employs one or more security guards. Upon showing by defendant that this condition would likely impose upon defendant psychological harm or effect or result in unwarranted risk of harm to defendant, the public or postal employees, the probation officer may withdraw or

---

1. The court explained that * * * "given the unpromising road that the defendant has been following, that he needs to have a taste of federal custody, to be sure a brief one, but he needs to understand that if he continues on the course that he has set for himself at his age he's going to be facing a lot more serious charges in the future."

2. At sentencing, the judge addressed Gementera: "We've also discussed the fact that you need to be reminded in a very graphic way of exactly what the crime you committed means to society. That is, the idea of you standing out in front of a post office with a board labeling you as somebody who has stolen mail." * * *

modify this condition or apply to the court to withdraw or modify this condition.

II

We first address Gementera's argument that the eight-hour sandwich board condition violates the Sentencing Reform Act.

The Sentencing Reform Act affords district courts broad discretion in fashioning appropriate conditions of supervised release, while mandating that such conditions serve legitimate objectives. * * * [A]ny condition must be "reasonably related" to "the nature and circumstances of the offense and the history and characteristics of the defendant." Moreover, it must be both "reasonably related" to and "involve no greater deprivation of liberty than is reasonably necessary" to "afford adequate deterrence to criminal conduct," "protect the public from further crimes of the defendant," and "provide the defendant with needed educational or vocational training, medical care, or other correctional treatment in the most effective manner." Accordingly, the three legitimate statutory purposes of deterrence, protection of the public, and rehabilitation frame our analysis. * * *

Of course, the district court's discretion, while broad, is limited—most significantly here, by the statute's requirement that any condition reasonably relate to a legitimate statutory purpose. "This test is applied in a two-step process; first, this court must determine whether the sentencing judge imposed the conditions for permissible purposes, and then it must determine whether the conditions are reasonably related to the purposes." Gementera's appeal implicates both steps of the analysis.

A

Gementera first urges that the condition was imposed for an impermissible purpose of humiliation. He points to certain remarks of the district court at the first sentencing hearing:

> He needs to understand the disapproval that society has for this kind of conduct, and that's the idea behind the humiliation. And it should be humiliation of having to stand and be labeled in front of people coming and going from a post office as somebody who has stolen the mail.

According to Gementera, these remarks, among others, indicate that the district court viewed humiliation as an end in itself and the condition's purpose.

Reading the record in context, however, we cannot but conclude that the district court's stated rationale aligned with permissible statutory objectives. At the second sentencing hearing, when the sentence was amended to what is now before us, the court explained: "Ultimately, the objective here is, one, to deter criminal conduct, and, number two, to rehabilitate the offender so that after he has paid his punishment, he does not reoffend, and a public expiation of having offended is, or at least it should be, rehabilitating in its effect." Although, in general, criminal punishment "is or at least should be humiliating," the court emphasized that "humiliation is not the point." The court's written order similarly stresses that the court's goal was not "to subject defendant to humiliation for humiliation's sake, but rather to create a situation in which the public exposure of defendant's crime and the public exposure of defendant to the victims of his crime" will serve the purposes of "the rehabilitation of the defendant and the protection of the public."

The court expressed particular concern that the defendant did not fully understand the gravity of his offense. Mail theft is an anonymous crime and, by "bringing home to defendant that his conduct has palpable significance to real people within his community," the court aimed to break the defendant of the illusion that his theft was victimless or not serious. In short, it explained:

> While humiliation may well be—indeed likely will be—a feature of defendant's experience in standing before a post office with such a sign, the humiliation or shame he experiences should serve the salutary purpose of bringing defendant in close touch with the real significance of the crime he has acknowledged committing. Such an experience should have a specific rehabilitative effect on defendant that could not be accomplished by other means, certainly not by a more extended term of imprisonment.

Moreover, "it will also have a deterrent effect on both this defendant and others who might not otherwise have been made aware of the real legal consequences of engaging in mail theft."

Read in its entirety, the record unambiguously establishes that the district court imposed the condition for the stated and legitimate statutory purpose of rehabilitation and, to a lesser extent, for general deterrence and for the protection of the public. * * *

B

Assuming the court articulated a legitimate purpose, Gementera asserts, under the second prong of our test that humiliation or so-called "shaming" conditions are not "reasonably related" to rehabilitation. In support, he cites our general statements that conditions must be reasonably related to the statutory objectives, several state court decisions,[9] and several law review articles * * *.

---

9. In *People v. Hackler*, 13 Cal.App.4th 1049, 16 Cal. Rptr. 2d 681 (Cal. Ct. App. 1993), a California court vacated a condition requiring a defendant during his first year of probation to wear a t-shirt whenever he was outside his home. The t-shirt read, "My record plus two-six packs equal four years," and on the back, "I am on felony probation for theft." Noting with disapproval the trial court's stated intention of "going back to some extent to the era of stocks" and transforming the defendant into "a Hester Prin [sic]," the court held that the t-shirt could not serve the rehabilitative purpose because it would render the defendant unemployable. By contrast, Gementera's condition was sharply limited temporally (eight hours) and spatially (one post office in a large city), eliminating any risk that its effects would similarly spill over into all aspects of the defendant's life. * * *

1

In evaluating probation and supervised release conditions, we have *flexible* emphasized that the "reasonable relation" test is necessarily a "very *standard* flexible standard," and that such flexibility is necessary because of "our uncertainty about how rehabilitation is accomplished." While our knowledge of rehabilitation is limited, we have nonetheless explicitly held that "a public apology may serve a rehabilitative purpose." Of course, for Gementera to prevail, introducing mere uncertainty about whether the condition aids rehabilitation does not suffice; rather, he must persuade us that the condition's supposed relationship to rehabilitation is unreasonable. * * *

2 * * *

Gementera and amicus contend that shaming conditions cannot be *shaming* rehabilitative because such conditions necessarily cause the offender to *not* withdraw from society or otherwise inflict psychological damage, and they *beld* would erect a per se bar against such conditions. *See* Toni Massaro, *per se* *Shame, Culture, and American Criminal Law*, 89 Mich. L. Rev. 1880, 1920–21 (1991) ("When it works, it redefines a person in a negative, often irreversible way" and the "psychological core" it affects cannot thereafter be rebuilt.) Though the district court had no scientific evidence before it, as Gementera complains, we do not insist upon such evidence in our deferential review. Moreover, the fact is that a vigorous, multifaceted, scholarly debate on shaming sanctions' efficacy, desirability, and underlying rationales continues within the academy. *See, e.g.*, Dan M. Kahan & Eric A. Posner, *Shaming White–Collar Criminals: A Proposal for Reform of the Federal Sentencing Guidelines*, 42 J.L. & Econ. 365, 371 (1999) (urging use of stigmatic punishments for white-collar criminals); Stephen P. Garvey, *Can Shaming Punishments Educate?*, 65 U. Chi. L. Rev. 733, 738–39 (1998); Dan M. Kahan, *What Do Alternative Sanctions Mean?*, 63 U. Chi. L. Rev. 591 (1996) (arguing that shaming sanctions reinforce public norms against criminality). By no means is this conversation one-sided.

People v. Johnson, 174 Ill. App. 3d 812, 528 N.E.2d 1360, 124 Ill. Dec. 252 (Ill. App. Ct. 1988), *Johnson* involved a condition that a DWI offender publish a newspaper advertisement with apology and *newspaper* mug shot. * * * Relying on the fact that defendant was a young lady and a good student with no *ad* prior criminal record, had injured no one, and otherwise had no alcohol or drug problem, it found the condition impermissible, given the perceived mental health risk. By contrast, we have specifically held that mandatory public apology may be rehabilitative. Moreover, the condition specifically provided that the signboard requirement would be withdrawn if the defendant showed that the condition would inflict psychological harm.

The defendant's third case, *People v. Letterlough*, 86 N.Y.2d 259, 655 N.E.2d 146, 631 N.Y.S.2d *Letterlough* 105 (N.Y. 1995), also involved a probation condition imposed upon a DWI offender. If he regained *license* driving privileges, the offender was required to affix a fluorescent sign to his license plate, stating *plate* "CONVICTED DWI.". * * * Under the New York statute, rehabilitation * * * was the "singular focus of the statute." Because the condition's "true design was not to advance defendant's rehabilitation, but rather to 'warn the public' of the threat presented by his presence behind the wheel," the court voided the condition. In contrast to the New York scheme, the district court [here] made plain the rehabilitative purpose of the condition. * * *

Criminal offenses, and the penalties that accompany them, nearly always cause shame and embarrassment. Indeed, the mere fact of conviction, without which state-sponsored rehabilitation efforts do not commence, is stigmatic. The fact that a condition causes shame or embarrassment does not automatically render a condition objectionable; rather, such feelings generally signal the defendant's acknowledgment of his wrongdoing. * * *

3

While the district court's sandwich board condition was somewhat crude, and by itself could entail risk of social withdrawal and stigmatization, it was coupled with more socially useful provisions, including lecturing at a high school and writing apologies, that might loosely be understood to promote the offender's social reintegration. *See* Note, *Shame, Stigma, and Crime: Evaluating the Efficacy of Shaming Sanctions in Criminal Law*, 116 Harv. L. Rev. 2186 (2003) (proposing how shaming sanctions may be structured to promote social reintegration most effectively). We see this factor as highly significant. In short, here we consider not a stand-alone condition intended solely to humiliate, but rather a comprehensive set of provisions that expose the defendant to social disapprobation, but that also then provide an opportunity for Gementera to repair his relationship with society—first by seeking its forgiveness and then by making, as a member of the community, an independent contribution to the moral formation of its youth. These provisions, tailored to the specific needs of the offender, counsel in favor of concluding that the condition passes the threshold of being reasonably related to rehabilitation. * * *

Accordingly, we hold that the condition imposed upon Gementera reasonably related to the legitimate statutory objective of rehabilitation.[16] In so holding, we are careful not to articulate a principle broader than that presented by the facts of this case. With care and specificity, the district court outlined a sensible logic underlying its conclusion that a set of conditions, including the signboard provision, but also including reintegrative provisions, would better promote this defendant's rehabilitation and amendment of life than would a lengthier term of incarceration. By contrast, a per se rule that the mandatory public airing of one's offense can *never* assist an offender to reassume his duty of obedience to the law would impose a narrow penological orthodoxy not contemplated by the Guidelines' express approval of "any other condition [the district court] considers to be appropriate." * * *

Affirmed.

HAWKINS, CIRCUIT JUDGE, dissenting:

* * * Clearly, the shaming punishment[1] at issue in this case was intended to humiliate Gementera. And that is all it will do. * * * Because

---

16. In view of this holding, we do not reach the separate issue of whether the condition reasonably relates to the objectives of deterrence and protection of the public.

1. One scholar has defined a "shaming" punishment as "marked by two features: first, there is an attempt to debase, degrade, or humiliate the offender; and second, the degradation occurs

humiliation is not one of the three proper goals under the Sentencing Reform Act, I would hold that the district court abused its discretion in imposing the condition. * * *

* * * [T]he true intention in this case was to humiliate Gementera, not to rehabilitate him or to deter him from future wrongdoing. When the district court initially imposed the sandwich board condition, the judge explained that Gementera should have to suffer the "humiliation of having to stand and be labeled in front of people coming and going from a post office as somebody who has stolen the mail." * * * Only at the hearing on Gementera's motion [to amend the sentence] did the district court change its characterization of the shaming punishment, remarking that the punishment was one of deterrence and rehabilitation and not merely humiliation.

Although the majority opinion initially seems to accept the district court's retroactive justification for the punishment, it later as much as concedes that the sandwich board condition amounted to a shaming punishment. Admitting that the condition was "crude" and "could entail risk of social withdrawal and stigmatization," the majority nonetheless finds the condition acceptable because it was "coupled with more socially useful provisions." * * * But the majority cites to no provision in the Sentencing Reform Act and to no case law indicating that * * * humiliation somehow ceases to be humiliation when combined with other punishment. * * * When such a novel proposition is put forward and no case law is cited to support it, there is usually a reason.[h] At the end of the day, we *are* charged with evaluating a condition whose primary purpose is to humiliate, and that condition should simply not be upheld.

* * * I also believe that this is simply bad policy. A fair measure of a civilized society is how its institutions behave in the space between what it may have the power to do and what it should do. The shaming component of the sentence in this case fails that test. "When one shames another person, the goal is to degrade the object of shame, to place him lower in the chain of being, to dehumanize him."

To affirm the imposition of such punishments recalls a time in our history when pillories and stocks were the order of the day. To sanction

---

before the public eye, often but not always with the aid of the public." Dan Markel, *Are Shaming Punishments Beautifully Retributive? Retributivism and the Implications for the Alternative Sanctions Debate*, 54 Vand. L. Rev. 2157, 2178 (Nov. 2001). * * *

h. The majority opinion responded to this criticism as follows:

Our purpose is not, as the dissent characterizes it, to suggest that an improper condition may be cured merely by setting it alongside proper conditions. Rather, our obligation is to assess whether an individual provision reasonably relates to the purpose of rehabilitation. Where that provision is part of an integrated rehabilitative scheme, we see no bar to looking at other aspects of the scheme in evaluating the purpose and reasonableness of the individual provision at issue. * * * A boot camp, for example, that operates by "breaking participants down" before "building them up again" is not rendered impermissible merely because the first step, standing alone, might be impermissible. Similarly, a program that emphasizes an offenders' separation from the community of law-abiding citizens, in order to generate contrition and an authentic desire to rejoin that community, need not be evaluated without reference to the program's affirmative provisions to reconcile the offender with the community and eventually to reintegrate him into it.

such use of power runs the very great risk that by doing so we instill "a sense of disrespect for the criminal justice system" itself.

I would vacate the sentence and remand for re-sentencing, instructing the district court that public humiliation or shaming has no proper place in our system of justice.

NOTES AND QUESTIONS

1. Do you believe the "shaming" punishment here satisfies any of the federal sentencing objectives set out in the opinion? Why, or why not? Do you agree with the dissent that this form of punishment is bad public policy? (For thoughtful discussion of shaming sanctions—both pro and con—see the articles cited in *Gementera*.)

If you dislike shaming sanctions, how do you respond to the argument that punishment itself is intended to stigmatize the offender as a wrongdoer, and that the humiliation involved is certainly less than the conditions one experiences in jail or prison? If you favor shaming sanctions, how do you respond to the assertion that shaming "menaces certain ideals that any morally respectable mode of punishment should not [menace], not the least of which is human dignity." Stephen P. Garvey, *Can Shaming Punishments Educate?*, 65 U. Chi. L. Rev. 733, 739 (1998).

2. *When does shaming go too far?* Some shaming sanctions are set out in footnote 9 of the majority opinion in *Gementera*. Assuming that any shaming sanctions are permitted, do you find any of *these* objectionable?

How do you feel about the following sanctions? First, a judge ordered a woman placed on probation to place an advertisement in her local newspaper stating that she had bought drugs in front of her children. Jan Hoffman, *Crime and Punishment: Shame Gains Popularity*, N.Y. Times, Jan. 16, 1997, at A1. Second, a man convicted of battery was required to erect a sign at all entrances to his family farm reading "Warning! A violent felon lives here. Enter at your own risk!" People v. Meyer, 176 Ill.2d 372, 223 Ill.Dec. 582, 680 N.E.2d 315 (1997). Third, a woman twice convicted of driving while intoxicated was required to spend two four-hour days at a morgue in order to show drivers the "potentially fatal consequences of drinking and driving." (The woman was Lindsay Lohan.) Sara Hammel, *Next Stop for Lindsay Lohan: The Morgue*, People.com, Jan. 18, 2008, http://www.people.com/people/article/0,,20172513,00.html. Fourth, two men who had thrown beer bottles at a car and were rude to the woman driving the vehicle were given a choice: 60 days in jail or an hour long stroll down Main Street wearing dresses. (The offenders chose the latter sentence.) Tim Doulin, *Some Judges Fashion Punishment to Fit Crime*, Columbus Dispatch, Nov. 28, 2001, at C13.

3. *And then there is this punishment....* Nathan Mallett ran onto the field after a Cleveland Browns football game because he was upset at his beloved Browns' 41–0 humiliating loss to the hated Pittsburgh Steelers. (It probably didn't help that he had drunk approximately 20 bottles of beer during the game.) His run on the field ended when a Steeler linebacker body-slammed him to the ground and held him until the police arrived. Upon conviction of disorderly conduct, Judge Joan Synenberg sentenced Mallett to

three days in jail (he could have received a sentence up to 30 days) to begin immediately before the Super Bowl game (with an order that he not be allowed to watch or listen to the game), 150 hours of community service with Browns' charities, and—last but certainly not least—an order not to attend a Browns game in Cleveland or any other city for five years. Ryan Ernst, *What's Up with That?*, Cincinnati Enquirer, Jan 22. 2006, at 2C. (Ernst suggested that the last sanction was odd, "considering that watching the Browns seems like a much greater punishment.")

4. *And, finally (sigh), there is this follow-up.* One month after Shawn Gementera fulfilled Judge Walker's sentence, he committed another mail-related theft crime. This time Judge Walker sentenced Gementera to a year in prison. Pam Smith, *"Scarlet Letter" Mail Thief Gets Less Creative Sentence Second Time Around*, The Recorder, May 25, 2006.

C. PROPORTIONALITY OF PUNISHMENT

My object all sublime
I shall achieve in time—
To let the punishment fit the crime—
The punishment fit the crime[i]

1. GENERAL PRINCIPLES

IMMANUEL KANT—THE PHILOSOPHY OF LAW
(W. Hastie trans., 1887), 447–448

But what is the mode and measure of punishment which public justice takes as its principle and standard? It is just the principle of equality, by which the pointer of the scale of justice is made to incline no more to one side than the other. It may be rendered by saying that the undeserved evil which any one commits on another is to be regarded as perpetrated on himself. Hence it may be said: "If you slander another, you slander yourself; if you strike another, you strike yourself; if you kill another, you kill yourself." This is the right of retaliation (*jus talionis*); and, properly understood, it is the only principle which in regulating a public court, as distinguished from a private judgement, can definitely assign both the quality and the quantity of a just penalty. * * * But how then would we render the statement: "If you *steal* from another, you steal from your-self?" In this way, whoever steals anything makes the property of all insecure; he therefore robs himself of all security in property, according to the right of retaliation. Such a one has nothing, and can acquire nothing * * *. But whoever has committed murder, must *die*. There is, in this case, no juridical substitute or surrogate, that can be given or taken for the satisfaction of justice. There is no *likeness* or proportion between life, however painful, and death; and therefore there is no equality between

---

i. William G. Gilbert & Arthur S. Sullivan, *The Mikado*, Act 2 (1885) ("A More Humane Mikado Never Did in Japan Exist").

the crime of murder and the retaliation of it but what is judicially accomplished by the execution of the criminal. His death, however, must be kept free from all maltreatment that would make the humanity suffering in his person loathsome or abominable.

JEREMY BENTHAM—AN INTRODUCTION TO THE PRINCIPLES OF MORALS AND LEGISLATION

(John Bowring ed., 1843), 86–88

[Chapter XIV] I. We have seen that the general object of all laws is to prevent mischief; that is to say, when it is worth while; but that, where there are no other means of doing this than punishment, there are four cases in which it is not worth while.

II. When it *is* worth while, there are four subordinate designs or objects, which, in the course of his endeavours to compass, as far as may be, that one general object, a legislator, whose views are governed by the principle of utility, comes naturally to propose to himself.

III. 1. His first, most extensive, and most eligible object, is to prevent, in as far as it is possible, and worth while, all sorts of offences whatsoever: in other words, so to manage, that no offence whatsoever may be committed.

IV. 2. But if a man must needs commit an offence of some kind or other, the next object is to induce him to commit an offence *less* mischievous, *rather* than one *more* mischievous: in other words, to choose always the *least* mischievous, of two offences that will either of them suit his purpose.

V. 3. When a man has resolved upon a particular offence, the next object is to dispose him to do *no more* mischief than is *necessary* to his purpose: in other words, to do as little mischief as is consistent with the benefit he has in view.

VI. 4. The last object is, whatever the mischief be, which it is proposed to prevent, to prevent it at as *cheap* a rate as possible.

VII. Subservient to these four objects, or purposes, must be the rules or canons by which the proportion of punishments to offences is to be governed.

VIII. Rule 1. The first object, it has been seen, is to prevent, in as far as it is worth while, all sorts of offences: therefore,

The value of the punishment must not be less in any case than what is sufficient to outweigh that of the profit of the offence. * * *

X. Rule 2. But whether a given offence shall be prevented in a given degree by a given quantity of punishment, is never any thing better than a chance; for the purchasing of which, whatever punishment is employed, is so much expended in advance. However, for the sake of giving it the better chance of outweighing the profit of the offence,

The greater the mischief of the offence, the greater is the expense, which it may be worth while to be at, in the way of punishment.

XI.   Rule 3. The next object is, to induce a man to choose always the least mischievous of two offences: therefore

Where two offences come in competition, the punishment for the greater offence must be sufficient to induce a man to prefer the less.

XII.   Rule 4. When a man has resolved upon a particular offence, the next object is, to induce him to do no more mischief than what is necessary for his purpose: therefore

The punishment should be adjusted in such manner to each particular offence, that for every part of the mischief there may be a motive to restrain the offender from giving birth to it.

XIII.   Rule 5. The last object is, whatever mischief is guarded against, to guard against it at as cheap a rate as possible: therefore

The punishment ought in no case to be more than what is necessary to bring it into conformity with the rules here given. * * *

XV.   Of the above rules of proportion, the four first, we may perceive, serve to mark out the limits on the side of diminution; the limits *below* which a punishment ought not to be *diminished;* the fifth, the limits on the side of *increase;* the limits *above* which it ought not to be *increased.* The five * * * are calculated to serve as guides to the legislator * * *.

NOTES AND QUESTIONS

1.   *Problem.* You are a legislator. You want to ensure that the penalty set for the offense of "driving a motor vehicle under the influence of alcohol" is proportional to the crime. You ask your staff to provide you with information that will help you make that determination. What do you want to know in order to reach a proper utilitarian result? How do you think you would determine the appropriate punishment from a retributive perspective?

2.   CONSTITUTIONAL PRINCIPLES

The Eighth Amendment to the United States Constitution provides: "Excessive bail shall not be required, nor excessive fines imposed, nor cruel and unusual punishment inflicted." In 1910, the Supreme Court ruled that the cruel and unusual punishment clause "was directed, not only against punishments which inflict torture, 'but against all punishments which by their excessive length or severity are greatly disproportioned to the offense charged.'" Weems v. United States, 217 U.S. 349, 30 S.Ct. 544, 54 L.Ed. 793 (1910), quoting O'Neil v. Vermont, 144 U.S. 323, 12 S.Ct. 693, 36 L.Ed. 450 (1892) (Field, J., dissenting). The Supreme Court has developed two lines of cases dealing with what constitutes disproportionate punishment. As Justice Kennedy recently explained:

"The Court's cases addressing the proportionality of sentences fall within two general classifications. The first involves challenges to the length of term-of-years sentences given all the circumstances in a particular case. The second comprises cases in which the Court implements the proportionality standard by certain categorical restrictions on the death penalty." Graham v. Florida, 560 U.S. ___, ___, 130 S.Ct. 2011, 2021, 176 L.Ed.2d 825 (2010).

COKER v. GEORGIA

Supreme Court of the United States, 1977.
433 U.S. 584, 97 S.Ct. 2861, 53 L.Ed.2d 982.

MR. JUSTICE WHITE announced the judgment of the Court and filed an opinion in which MR. JUSTICE STEWART, MR. JUSTICE BLACKMUN, and MR. JUSTICE STEVENS, joined.

Georgia Code Ann. § 26–2001 (1972) provides that "[a] person convicted of rape shall be punished by death or by imprisonment for life, or by imprisonment for not less than one nor more than 20 years."[1] Punishment is determined by a jury in a separate sentencing proceeding in which at least one * * * statutory aggravating circumstances must be found before the death penalty may be imposed. Petitioner Coker was convicted of rape and sentenced to death. Both the conviction and the sentence were affirmed by the Georgia Supreme Court. Coker was granted a writ of certiorari, limited to the single claim, rejected by the Georgia court, that the punishment of death for rape violates the Eighth Amendment, which proscribes "cruel and unusual punishments" and which must be observed by the States as well as the Federal Government.

I

While serving various sentences for murder, rape, kidnaping, and aggravated assault, petitioner escaped from the Ware Correctional Institution near Waycross, Ga., on September 2, 1974. At approximately 11 o'clock that night, petitioner entered the house of Allen and Elnita Carver through an unlocked kitchen door. Threatening the couple with a "board," he tied up Mr. Carver in the bathroom, obtained a knife from the kitchen, and took Mr. Carver's money and the keys to the family car. Brandishing the knife and saying "you know what's going to happen to you if you try anything, don't you," Coker then raped Mrs. Carver. Soon thereafter, petitioner drove away in the Carver car, taking Mrs. Carver with him. Mr. Carver, freeing himself, notified the police; and not long thereafter petitioner was apprehended. Mrs. Carver was unharmed.

Petitioner was charged with escape, armed robbery, motor vehicle theft, kidnaping, and rape. * * * The jury returned a verdict of guilty, rejecting his general plea of insanity. A sentencing hearing was then

---

1. The section defines rape as having "carnal knowledge of a female, forcibly and against her will. Carnal knowledge in rape occurs when there is any penetration of the female sex organ by the male sex organ."

conducted. * * * The jury was instructed that it could consider as aggravating circumstances whether the rape had been committed by a person with a prior record of conviction for a capital felony and whether the rape had been committed in the course of committing another capital felony, namely, the armed robbery of Allen Carver. The court also instructed, pursuant to statute, that even if aggravating circumstances were present, the death penalty need not be imposed if the jury found they were outweighed by mitigating circumstances, that is, circumstances not constituting justification or excuse for the offense in question, "but which, in fairness and mercy, may be considered as extenuating or reducing the degree" of moral culpability or punishment. The jury's verdict on the rape count was death by electrocution. Both aggravating circumstances on which the court instructed were found to be present by the jury.

II

* * * It is now settled that the death penalty is not invariably cruel and unusual punishment within the meaning of the Eighth Amendment; it is not inherently barbaric or an unacceptable mode of punishment for crime; neither is it always disproportionate to the crime for which it is imposed. * * *

In sustaining the imposition of the death penalty * * *, however, the Court firmly embraced the holdings and dicta from prior cases to the effect that the Eighth Amendment bars not only those punishments that are "barbaric" but also those that are "excessive" in relation to the crime committed. * * * [A] punishment is "excessive" and unconstitutional if it (1) makes no measurable contribution to acceptable goals of punishment and hence is nothing more than the purposeless and needless imposition of pain and suffering; or (2) is grossly out of proportion to the severity of the crime. A punishment might fail the test on either ground. Furthermore, these Eighth Amendment judgments should not be, or appear to be, merely the subjective views of individual Justices; judgment should be informed by objective factors to the maximum possible extent. To this end, attention must be given to the public attitudes concerning a particular sentence—history and precedent, legislative attitudes, and the response of juries reflected in their sentencing decisions are to be consulted. * * *

III

That question, with respect to rape of an adult woman, is now before us. We have concluded that a sentence of death is grossly disproportionate and excessive punishment for the crime of rape and is therefore forbidden by the Eighth Amendment as cruel and unusual punishment.[4] * * *

---

4. Because the death sentence is a disproportionate punishment for rape, it is cruel and unusual punishment within the meaning of the Eighth Amendment even though it may measurably serve the legitimate ends of punishment and therefore is not invalid for its failure to do so. We observe that in the light of the legislative decisions in almost all of the States and in most of the countries around the world, it would be difficult to support a claim that the death penalty for rape is an indispensable part of the States' criminal justice system.

[Justice White surveyed objective indicia of public sentiment regarding the acceptability of the death penalty for the rape of an adult woman. He recounted that in 1925, 18 states, the District of Columbia, and the federal government authorized capital punishment in such circumstances. By 1977, however, Georgia was the sole jurisdiction authorizing death for the rape of an adult woman, and only two other states allowed capital punishment for the rape of a child.

Also, since 1973, Georgia juries had sentenced rapists to death only six times in 63 rape convictions appealed to the state supreme court. Justice White observed that "[t]his obviously is not a negligible number * * *. Nevertheless, it is true that in the vast majority of cases, at least 9 out of 10, juries have not imposed the death sentence."]

IV

These recent events evidencing the attitude of state legislatures and sentencing juries do not wholly determine this controversy, for the Constitution contemplates that in the end our own judgment will be brought to bear on the question of the acceptability of the death penalty under the Eighth Amendment. Nevertheless, the legislative rejection of capital punishment for rape strongly confirms our own judgment, which is that death is indeed a disproportionate penalty for the crime of raping an adult woman.

We do not discount the seriousness of rape as a crime. It is highly reprehensible, both in a moral sense and in its almost total contempt for the personal integrity and autonomy of the female victim and for the latter's privilege of choosing those with whom intimate relationships are to be established. Short of homicide, it is the "ultimate violation of self." It is also a violent crime because it normally involves force, or the threat of force or intimidation, to overcome the will and the capacity of the victim to resist. Rape is very often accompanied by physical injury to the female and can also inflict mental and psychological damage. Because it undermines the community's sense of security, there is public injury as well.

Rape is without doubt deserving of serious punishment; but in terms of moral depravity and of the injury to the person and to the public, it does not compare with murder, which does involve the unjustified taking of human life. Although it may be accompanied by another crime, rape by definition does not include the death of or even the serious injury to another person.[13] The murderer kills; the rapist, if no more than that, does not. Life is over for the victim of the murderer; for the rape victim, life may not be nearly so happy as it was, but it is not over and normally is not beyond repair. We have the abiding conviction that the death penalty, which "is unique in its severity and irrevocability," is an excessive penalty for the rapist who, as such, does not take human life.

---

13. See n. 1, *supra,* for the Georgia definition of rape.

This does not end the matter; for under Georgia law, death may not be imposed for any capital offense, including rape, unless the jury or judge finds one of the statutory aggravating circumstances and then elects to impose that sentence. For the rapist to be executed in Georgia, it must therefore be found not only that he committed rape but also that one or more of the following aggravating circumstances were present: (1) that the rape was committed by a person with a prior record of conviction for a capital felony; (2) that the rape was committed while the offender was engaged in the commission of another capital felony, or aggravated battery; or (3) the rape "was outrageously or wantonly vile, horrible or inhuman in that it involved torture, depravity of mind, or aggravated battery to the victim." Here, the first two of these aggravating circumstances were alleged and found by the jury.

Neither of these circumstances, nor both of them together, change our conclusion that the death sentence imposed on Coker is a disproportionate punishment for rape. Coker had prior convictions for capital felonies—rape, murder, and kidnaping—but these prior convictions do not change the fact that the instant crime being punished is a rape not involving the taking of life. * * *

* * * The judgment of the Georgia Supreme Court upholding the death sentence is reversed * * *.

[Justices Brennan and Marshall concurred in the judgment, based on their shared view that the death penalty, in *all* circumstances, constitutes cruel and unusual punishment.]

MR. JUSTICE POWELL, concurring in the judgment in part and dissenting in part.

I concur in the judgment of the Court on the facts of this case, and also in the plurality's reasoning supporting the view that ordinarily death is disproportionate punishment for the crime of raping an adult woman. Although rape invariably is a reprehensible crime, there is no indication that petitioner's offense was committed with excessive brutality or that the victim sustained serious or lasting injury. The plurality, however, does not limit its holding to the case before us or to similar cases. Rather, in an opinion that ranges well beyond what is necessary, it holds that capital punishment *always*—regardless of the circumstances—is a disproportionate penalty for the crime of rape.

* * * It is * * * quite unnecessary for the plurality to write in terms so sweeping as to foreclose each of the 50 state legislatures from creating a narrowly defined substantive crime of aggravated rape punishable by death.[1] * * *

MR. CHIEF JUSTICE BURGER, with whom MR. JUSTICE REHNQUIST joins, dissenting.

---

1. It is not this Court's function to formulate the relevant criteria that might distinguish aggravated rape from the more usual case, but perhaps a workable test would embrace the factors identified by Georgia: the cruelty or viciousness of the offender, the circumstances and manner in which the offense was committed, and the consequences suffered by the victim. * * *

* * * I accept that the Eighth Amendment's concept of disproportionality bars the death penalty for minor crimes. But rape is not a minor crime; hence the Cruel and Unusual Punishments Clause does not give the Members of this Court license to engraft their conceptions of proper public policy onto the considered legislative judgments of the States. Since I cannot agree that Georgia lacked the constitutional power to impose the penalty of death for rape, I dissent from the Court's judgment. * * *

Unlike the plurality, I would narrow the inquiry in this case to the question actually presented: Does the Eighth Amendment's ban against cruel and unusual punishment prohibit the State of Georgia from executing a person who has, within the space of three years, raped three separate women, killing one and attempting to kill another, who is serving prison terms exceeding his probable lifetime and who has not hesitated to escape confinement at the first available opportunity? Whatever one's view may be as to the State's constitutional power to impose the death penalty upon a rapist who stands before a court convicted for the first time, this case reveals a chronic rapist whose continuing danger to the community is abundantly clear. * * *

In my view, the Eighth Amendment does not prevent the State from taking an individual's "well-demonstrated propensity for life-endangering behavior" into account in devising punitive measures which will prevent inflicting further harm upon innocent victims. * * *

The plurality acknowledges the gross nature of the crime of rape. A rapist not only violates a victim's privacy and personal integrity, but inevitably causes serious psychological as well as physical harm in the process. The long-range effect upon the victim's life and health is likely to be irreparable; it is impossible to measure the harm which results. Volumes have been written by victims, physicians, and psychiatric specialists on the lasting injury suffered by rape victims. Rape is not a mere physical attack—it is destructive of the human personality. The remainder of the victim's life may be gravely affected, and this in turn may have a serious detrimental effect upon her husband and any children she may have. * * * Victims may recover from the physical damage of knife or bullet wounds, or a beating with fists or a club, but recovery from such a gross assault on the human personality is not healed by medicine or surgery. To speak blandly, as the plurality does, of rape victims who are "unharmed," * * * takes too little account of the profound suffering the crime imposes upon the victims and their loved ones. * * *

* * * The plurality's conclusion * * * is based upon the bare fact that murder necessarily results in the physical death of the victim, while rape does not. However, no Member of the Court explains why this distinction has relevance, much less constitutional significance. It is, after all, not irrational—nor constitutionally impermissible—for a legislature to make the penalty more severe than the criminal act it punishes[16] in the hope it would deter wrongdoing * * *.

---

16. For example, hardly any thief would be deterred from stealing if the only punishment upon being caught were return of the money stolen.

As a matter of constitutional principle, th[e] test cannot have the primitive simplicity of "life for life, eye for eye, tooth for tooth." Rather States must be permitted to engage in a more sophisticated weighing of values in dealing with criminal activity which consistently poses serious danger of death or grave bodily harm. If innocent life and limb are to be preserved I see no constitutional barrier in punishing by death all who engage in such activity, regardless of whether the risk comes to fruition in any particular instance. * * *

NOTES AND QUESTIONS

1. The dissent provided a fuller account of Coker's criminal history and of the rape for which he was sentenced to death than is set out in Justice White's opinion. In 1971, Coker raped and stabbed to death a young woman. Still free eight months later, he kidnaped and twice raped a second victim, sixteen years old, and then beat her severely with a club, after which he dragged her into a wooded area where he left her for dead. After the latter incident, Coker was arrested, prosecuted for his crimes, and sentenced to three life terms, two 20–year terms, and one eight-year term of imprisonment.

Less than two years later, Coker escaped from prison and raped the victim here, "Mrs. Carver," who was also sixteen years old. After the rape, Coker took the victim with him in the Carver family automobile. Before he left, the defendant told Mr. Carver, whom he had tied up and gagged, that he would kill his wife if the police caught him, because "[I] don't have nothing to lose—[I am in] prison for the rest of [my] life, anyway."

Do these additional facts change your view of the proper constitutional outcome?

2. Does Justice White's constitutional analysis conform to utilitarian or retributive concepts of proportionality? What about Chief Justice Burger's dissent?

3. *Coker and the matter of gender.* Do you believe that Justice White's opinion undervalued the harm caused by rape? If so, does this mean that the death penalty for rape is justified? No, according to an amicus brief filed on behalf of the American Civil Liberties Union and various women's groups. In a brief written by Ruth Bader Ginsburg, who now sits on the Supreme Court, the groups argued that "[t]he death penalty for rape should be rejected as a vestige of an ancient, patriarchal system in which women were viewed both as the property of men and as entitled to a crippling 'chivalric protection.' " Brief for American Civil Liberties Union et al. as Amici Curiae Supporting Petitioner, Coker v. Georgia, 433 U.S. 584, 97 S.Ct. 2861, 53 L.Ed.2d 982 (1977) (No. 75–5444), at 11.

In ancient time, rape was a crime against a man's property, more specifically, "the theft of virginity, an embezzlement of * * * [the woman's] fair price on the market." Susan Brownmiller, Against Our Will: Men, Women and Rape 18 (1975). According to the amicus brief, this ancient attitude was carried over into American rape law: "[t]he death penalty as a potential sanction for rape is part of the fabric of laws and enforcement patterns based on obsolete and demeaning notions about women which inevitably yields lack of enforcement of rape laws, rather than protection of women."

4. *Coker and the matter of race.* "The death penalty for rape has been reserved overwhelmingly for black defendants, especially those convicted of raping white woman." James R. Acker, *Social Science in Supreme Court Death Penalty Cases: Citation Practices and Their Implications,* 8 Just.Q. 421, 431 (1991). For example, of 455 persons executed for rape between 1930 and 1972, 89.5% were nonwhite. Marvin E. Wolfgang & Marc Riedel, *Racial Discrimination, Rape and the Death Penalty*, in The Death Penalty in America 194 (Hugo Bedau ed., 3d ed. 1982). And, in 1972, when the death penalty temporarily was declared unconstitutional, of eighty rapists awaiting execution, all were incarcerated in prisons in the South, and their victims "were overwhelmingly white." Michael Mello, *Executing Rapists: A Reluctant Essay on the Ethics of Legal Scholarship*, 4 Wm. & Mary J. Women & L. 129, 172 (1997). The briefs filed on behalf of Coker cited statistics informing the Supreme Court of the racial aspects of the issue. Although none of the Justices in *Coker* referred to the studies, their knowledge of the discriminatory application of the death penalty for this crime may have affected the outcome.

5. *The meaning of Coker.* Patrick Kennedy brutally raped his eight-year-old stepdaughter in 1998. He was sentenced to death pursuant to a Louisiana statute authorizing the death penalty for rape of a child under age of twelve. Is the Louisiana statute, enacted after *Coker*, constitutional? Consider, first, does the statute violate *Coker*'s *holding*? Look back, carefully, at the opinion to answer that question. Second, whatever *Coker* holds, does its *rationale* support a bar on the death penalty for child rape?

In Kennedy v. Louisiana, 554 U.S. 407, 128 S.Ct. 2641, 171 L.Ed.2d 525 (2008), the Supreme Court, per Justice Kennedy, concluded that *Coker*'s holding did not in itself bar the death penalty in child rape cases:

> *Coker*'s analysis of the Eighth Amendment is susceptible of a reading that would prohibit making child rape a capital offense. In context, however, *Coker*'s holding was narrower than some of its language read in isolation. The *Coker* plurality framed the question as whether, "with respect to rape of an adult woman," the death penalty is disproportionate punishment. And it repeated the phrase "an adult woman" or an "adult female" in discussing the act of rape or the victim of rape eight times in its opinion.

Does this mean that the death penalty for child rape is constitutional? No. By a 5–4 vote, the Supreme Court held that death is also a grossly disproportionate punishment for the crime of child rape:

> It must be acknowledged that there are moral grounds to question a rule barring capital punishment for a crime against an individual that did not result in death. These facts illustrate the point. Here the victim's fright, the sense of betrayal, and the nature of her injuries caused more prolonged physical and mental suffering than, say, a sudden killing by an unseen assassin. The attack was not just on her but on her childhood. For this reason, we should be most reluctant to rely upon the language of the plurality in *Coker,* which posited that, for the victim of rape, "life may

not be nearly so happy as it was" but it is not beyond repair. Rape has a permanent psychological, emotional, and sometimes physical impact on the child. We cannot dismiss the years of long anguish that must be endured by the victim of child rape.

It does not follow, though, that capital punishment is a proportionate penalty for the crime. * * * Evolving standards of decency that mark the progress of a maturing society counsel us to be most hesitant before interpreting the Eighth Amendment to allow the extension of the death penalty, a hesitation that has special force where no life was taken in the commission of the crime. * * *

Our concern here is limited to crimes against individual persons. We do not address, for example, crimes defining and punishing treason, espionage, terrorism, and drug kingpin activity, which are offenses against the State. As it relates to crimes against individuals, though, the death penalty should not be expanded to instances where the victim's life was not taken. * * *

Our decision is consistent with the justifications offered for the death penalty. * * *

The goal of retribution, which reflects society's and the victim's interests in seeing that the offender is repaid for the hurt he caused, does not justify the harshness of the death penalty here. In measuring retribution, as well as other objectives of criminal law, it is appropriate to distinguish between a particularly depraved murder that merits death as a form of retribution and the crime of child rape.

There is an additional reason for our conclusion that imposing the death penalty for child rape would not further retributive purposes. In considering whether retribution is served, among other factors we have looked to whether capital punishment "has the potential * * * to allow the community as a whole, including the surviving family and friends of the victim, to affirm its own judgment that the culpability of the prisoner is so serious that the ultimate penalty must be sought and imposed." In considering the death penalty for nonhomicide offenses this inquiry necessarily also must include the question whether the death penalty balances the wrong to the victim.

It is not at all evident that the child rape victim's hurt is lessened when the law permits the death of the perpetrator. Capital cases require a long-term commitment by those who testify for the prosecution * * *. In cases like this the key testimony is not just from the family but from the victim herself. During formative years of her adolescence, made all the more daunting for having to come to terms with the brutality of her experience, [victim] L.H. was required to discuss the case at length with law enforcement personnel. In a public trial she was required to recount once more all the details of the crime to a jury as the State pursued the death of her stepfather. * * *

Society's desire to inflict the death penalty for child rape by enlisting the child victim to assist it over the course of years in asking for capital punishment forces a moral choice on the child, who is not of mature age to make that choice. * * *

With respect to deterrence, * * * the death penalty * * * diminishes the penalty's objectives. Underreporting is a common problem with respect to child sexual abuse. Although we know little about what differentiates those who report from those who do not report, one of the most commonly cited reasons for nondisclosure is fear of negative consequences for the perpetrator, a concern that has special force where the abuser is a family member. The experience of [those] who work with child victims indicates that, when the punishment is death, both the victim and the victim's family members may be more likely to shield the perpetrator from discovery, thus increasing underreporting. As a result, punishment by death may not result in more deterrence or more effective enforcement.

In addition, by in effect making the punishment for child rape and murder equivalent, a State that punishes child rape by death may remove a strong incentive for the rapist not to kill the victim.

Justice Alito explained the views of the four dissenters:

A major theme of the Court's opinion is that permitting the death penalty in child-rape cases is not in the best interests of the victims of these crimes and society at large. In this vein, the Court suggests that it is more painful for child-rape victims to testify when the prosecution is seeking the death penalty. The Court also argues that "a State that punishes child rape by death may remove a strong incentive for the rapist not to kill the victim," and may discourage the reporting of child rape.

These policy arguments, whatever their merits, are simply not pertinent to the question whether the death penalty is "cruel and unusual" punishment. * * * The Court's policy arguments concern matters that legislators should—and presumably do—take into account in deciding whether to enact a capital child-rape statute, but these arguments are irrelevant to the [constitutional] question that is before us * * *. * * *

After * * * the arguments noted above are put aside, what is left? * * *

The Court's [principal justification for its holding] * * * is that murder * * * is unique in its moral depravity and in the severity of the injury that it inflicts on the victim and the public. But the Court makes little attempt to defend these conclusions.

With respect to the question of moral depravity, is it really true that every person who is convicted of capital murder and sentenced to death is more morally depraved than every child rapist? Consider the following two cases. In the first, a defendant robs a convenience store and watches as his accomplice shoots the store owner. The defendant acts recklessly, but was not the triggerman and did not intend the killing. In the second case, a previously convicted child rapist kidnaps, repeatedly rapes, and tortures multiple child victims. Is it clear that the first defendant is more morally depraved than the second? * * *

With respect to the question of the harm caused by the rape of child in relation to the harm caused by murder, it is certainly true that the loss of human life represents a unique harm, but that does not explain why other grievous harms are insufficient to permit a death sentence. And the Court does not take the position that no harm other than the loss of life is sufficient. The Court takes pains to limit its holding to "crimes against individual persons" and to exclude "offenses against the State," a category that the Court stretches—without explanation—to include "drug kingpin activity." But the Court makes no effort to explain why the harm caused by such crimes is necessarily greater than the harm caused by the rape of young children. This is puzzling in light of the Court's acknowledgment that "[r]ape has a permanent psychological, emotional, and sometimes physical impact on the child."

What do *you* think? Consider:

No matter how much life-long physical damage a man inflicts while raping a three-year old little girl, no matter how ritualistically he tortures her over hours or days, no matter how delicious he finds her sobbing agony and how coolly indifferent he is to her desperate need for subsequent care, no matter whether he has stolen her away from all she knows and kept her naked, starved, and terrorized in a pitch dark hole in the ground, no matter how many victims he has similarly brutalized or how often he repeats his cruelty with the same terrorized victim, so long as she survives the torment, he has a constitutional right to live out his natural life free of the threat that death will be visited upon him in punishment. In its rawest form, this is the Supreme Court's holding in *Kennedy v. Louisiana*. And the more raw it becomes as one contemplates the fiendish ways in which people can hurt others—particularly those who are vulnerable and helpless—in ways that leave them a hair's breadth from death. What could possibly make sense of continuing to permit the imposition of the death penalty [in general], while prohibiting it for "crimes against individuals" that do not result in death?

Heidi M. Hurd, *Death to Rapists: A Comment on* Kennedy v. Louisiana, 6 Ohio St. J. Crim. L. 351, 351 (2008).

EWING v. CALIFORNIA

Supreme Court of the United States, 2003.
538 U.S. 11, 123 S.Ct. 1179, 155 L.Ed.2d 108.

JUSTICE O'CONNOR announced the judgment of the Court and delivered an opinion in which THE CHIEF JUSTICE and JUSTICE KENNEDY join.

In this case, we decide whether the Eighth Amendment prohibits the State of California from sentencing a repeat felon to a prison term of 25 years to life under the State's "Three Strikes and You're Out" law.

I

A

California's three strikes law reflects a shift in the State's sentencing policies toward incapacitating and deterring repeat offenders who threaten the public safety. The law was designed "to ensure longer prison sentences and greater punishment for those who commit a felony and have been previously convicted of serious and/or violent felony offenses." * * *

* * * Though the three strikes laws vary from State to State, they share a common goal of protecting the public safety by providing lengthy prison terms for habitual felons.

B * * *

[Under California law, if] the defendant has one prior "serious" or "violent" felony conviction, he must be sentenced to "twice the term otherwise provided as punishment for the current felony conviction." If the defendant has two or more prior "serious" or "violent" felony convictions, he must receive "an indeterminate term of life imprisonment." Defendants sentenced to life under the three strikes law become eligible for parole on a date calculated by reference to a "minimum term," which is the greater of (a) three times the term otherwise provided for the current conviction, [or] (b) 25 years * * *. * * *

C

On parole from a 9–year prison term, petitioner Gary Ewing walked into the pro shop of the El Segundo Golf Course in Los Angeles County on March 12, 2000. He walked out with three golf clubs, priced at $399 apiece, concealed in his pants leg. * * * The police apprehended Ewing in the parking lot.

Ewing is no stranger to the criminal justice system. [Between 1984 and September 1993, Ewing pled guilty or was convicted of theft on three occasions, as well as battery, burglary, possession of drug paraphernalia, and unlawful possession of a firearm.]

In October and November 1993, Ewing committed three burglaries and one robbery at a Long Beach, California, apartment complex over a 5–week period. * * *

On December 9, 1993, Ewing was arrested on the premises of the apartment complex for trespassing and lying to a police officer. * * *A jury convicted Ewing of first-degree robbery and three counts of residential burglary. Sentenced to nine years and eight months in prison, Ewing was paroled in 1999.

Only 10 months later, Ewing stole the golf clubs at issue in this case. He was charged with, and ultimately convicted of, one count of felony grand theft of personal property in excess of $400. * * *

* * * Ewing was sentenced under the three strikes law to 25 years to life. * * *

II

A

The Eighth Amendment, which forbids cruel and unusual punishments, contains a "narrow proportionality principle" that "applies to noncapital sentences." We have most recently addressed the proportionality principle as applied to terms of years in a series of cases beginning with *Rummel v. Estelle,* [445 U.S. 263, 100 S.Ct. 1133, 63 L.Ed.2d 382 (1980)].

In *Rummel,* we held that it did not violate the Eighth Amendment for a State to sentence a three-time offender to life in prison with the possibility of parole. Like Ewing, Rummel was sentenced to a lengthy prison term under a recidivism statute. Rummel's two prior offenses were a 1964 felony for "fraudulent use of a credit card to obtain $80 worth of goods or services," and a 1969 felony conviction for "passing a forged check in the amount of $28.36." His triggering offense was a conviction for felony theft—"obtaining $120.75 by false pretenses."

This Court ruled that "[h]aving twice imprisoned him for felonies, Texas was entitled to place upon Rummel the onus of one who is simply unable to bring his conduct within the social norms prescribed by the criminal law of the State." * * * We noted that * * * "[o]utside the context of capital punishment, successful challenges to the proportionality of particular sentences have been exceedingly rare." Although we stated that the proportionality principle "would * * * come into play in the extreme example * * * if a legislature made overtime parking a felony punishable by life imprisonment," we held that "the mandatory life sentence imposed upon this petitioner does not constitute cruel and unusual punishment under the Eighth and Fourteenth Amendments." * * *

Three years after *Rummel,* in *Solem v. Helm,* 463 U.S. 277, 279, 103 S.Ct. 3001, 77 L.Ed.2d 637 (1983), we held that the Eighth Amendment prohibited "a life sentence without possibility of parole for a seventh nonviolent felony." The triggering offense in *Solem* was "uttering a 'no account' check for $100." We specifically stated that the Eighth Amendment's ban on cruel and unusual punishments "prohibits * * * sentences that are disproportionate to the crime committed" * * *. The *Solem* Court then explained that three factors may be relevant to a determination of whether a sentence is so disproportionate that it violates the Eighth Amendment: "(i) the gravity of the offense and the harshness of the penalty; (ii) the sentences imposed on other criminals in the same jurisdiction; and (iii) the sentences imposed for commission of the same crime in other jurisdictions."

Applying these factors in *Solem,* we struck down the defendant's sentence of life without parole. We specifically noted the contrast between that sentence and the sentence in *Rummel,* pursuant to which the defendant was eligible for parole. * * *

Eight years after *Solem,* we grappled with the proportionality issue again in *Harmelin* [*v. Michigan,* 501 U.S. 957, 111 S.Ct. 2680, 115 L.Ed.2d 836 (1991)]. Harmelin was not a recidivism case, but rather involved a first-time offender convicted of possessing 672 grams of cocaine. He was sentenced to life in prison without possibility of parole. A majority of the Court rejected Harmelin's claim that his sentence was so grossly disproportionate that it violated the Eighth Amendment. The Court, however, could not agree on why his proportionality argument failed. Justice Scalia, joined by The Chief Justice, * * * would * * * have declined to apply gross disproportionality principles except in reviewing capital sentences.

Justice Kennedy, joined by two other Members of the Court, * * * specifically recognized that "[t]he Eighth Amendment proportionality principle also applies to noncapital sentences." He then identified four principles of proportionality review—"the primacy of the legislature, the variety of legitimate penological schemes, the nature of our federal system, and the requirement that proportionality review be guided by objective factors"—that "inform the final one: The Eighth Amendment does not require strict proportionality between crime and sentence. Rather, it forbids only extreme sentences that are 'grossly disproportionate' to the crime." * * *

The proportionality principles in our cases distilled in Justice Kennedy's concurrence guide our application of the Eighth Amendment in the new context that we are called upon to consider.

B * * *

Throughout the States, legislatures enacting three strikes laws made a deliberate policy choice that individuals who have repeatedly engaged in serious or violent criminal behavior, and whose conduct has not been deterred by more conventional approaches to punishment, must be isolated from society in order to protect the public safety. * * *

Our traditional deference to legislative policy choices finds a corollary in the principle that the Constitution "does not mandate adoption of any one penological theory." A sentence can have a variety of justifications, such as incapacitation, deterrence, retribution, or rehabilitation. Some or all of these justifications may play a role in a State's sentencing scheme. Selecting the sentencing rationales is generally a policy choice to be made by state legislatures, not federal courts.

When the California Legislature enacted the three strikes law, it made a judgment that protecting the public safety requires incapacitating criminals who have already been convicted of at least one serious or violent crime. Nothing in the Eighth Amendment prohibits California from making that choice. * * *

The State's interest in deterring crime also lends some support to the three strikes law. * * * Four years after the passage of California's three strikes law, the recidivism rate of parolees returned to prison for the commission of a new crime dropped by nearly 25 percent. Even more dramatically:

> "[a]n unintended but positive consequence of 'Three Strikes' has been the impact on parolees leaving the state. More California parolees are now leaving the state than parolees from other jurisdictions entering California. This striking turnaround started in 1994. * * * "

To be sure, California's three strikes law has sparked controversy. Critics have doubted the law's wisdom, cost-efficiency, and effectiveness in reaching its goals. This criticism is appropriately directed at the legislature, which has primary responsibility for making the difficult policy choices that underlie any criminal sentencing scheme. We do not sit as a "superlegislature" to second-guess these policy choices. It is enough that the State of California has a reasonable basis for believing that dramatically enhanced sentences for habitual felons "advance[s] the goals of [its] criminal justice system in any substantial way."

III

Against this backdrop, we consider Ewing's claim that his three strikes sentence of 25 years to life is unconstitutionally disproportionate to his offense of "shoplifting three golf clubs." We first address the gravity of the offense compared to the harshness of the penalty. At the threshold, we note that Ewing incorrectly frames the issue. The gravity of his offense was not merely "shoplifting three golf clubs." Rather, Ewing was convicted of felony grand theft for stealing nearly $1,200 worth of merchandise after previously having been convicted of at least two "violent" or "serious" felonies. * * *

In weighing the gravity of Ewing's offense, we must place on the scales not only his current felony, but also his long history of felony recidivism. Any other approach would fail to accord proper deference to the policy judgments that find expression in the legislature's choice of sanctions. In imposing a three strikes sentence, the State's interest is not merely punishing the offense of conviction, or the "triggering" offense: "[I]t is in addition the interest * * * in dealing in a harsher manner with those who by repeated criminal acts have shown that they are simply incapable of conforming to the norms of society as established by its criminal law." To give full effect to the State's choice of this legitimate penological goal, our proportionality review of Ewing's sentence must take that goal into account.

Ewing's sentence is justified by the State's public-safety interest in incapacitating and deterring recidivist felons, and amply supported by his own long, serious criminal record. * * *

We hold that Ewing's sentence of 25 years to life in prison, imposed for the offense of felony grand theft under the three strikes law, is not grossly disproportionate and therefore does not violate the Eighth Amendment's prohibition on cruel and unusual punishments. * * *

JUSTICE SCALIA, concurring in the judgment.

* * * Out of respect for the principle of *stare decisis,* I might * * * accept the * * * holding of *Solem v. Helm*—that the Eighth Amendment contains a narrow proportionality principle—if I felt I could intelligently apply it. This case demonstrates why I cannot.

Proportionality—the notion that the punishment should fit the crime—is inherently a concept tied to the penological goal of retribution.

"[I]t becomes difficult even to speak intelligently of 'proportionality,' once deterrence and rehabilitation are given significant weight," not to mention giving weight to the purpose of California's three strikes law: incapacitation. In the present case, the game is up once the plurality has acknowledged that "the Constitution does not mandate adoption of any one penological theory," and that a "sentence can have a variety of justifications, such as incapacitation, deterrence, retribution, or rehabilitation." That acknowledgment having been made, it no longer suffices merely to assess "the gravity of the offense compared to the harshness of the penalty"; that classic description of the proportionality principle * * * now becomes merely the "first" step of the inquiry. Having completed that step (by a discussion which, in all fairness, does not convincingly establish that 25–years-to-life is a "proportionate" punishment for stealing three golf clubs), the plurality must then *add* an analysis to show that "Ewing's sentence is justified by the State's public-safety interest in incapacitating and deterring recidivist felons."

Which indeed it is—though why that has anything to do with the principle of proportionality is a mystery. Perhaps the plurality should revise its terminology, so that what it reads into the Eighth Amendment is not the unstated proposition that all punishment should be reasonably proportionate to the gravity of the offense, but rather the unstated proposition that all punishment should reasonably pursue the multiple purposes of the criminal law. That formulation would make it clearer than ever, of course, that the plurality is not applying [constitutional] law but evaluating policy. * * *

JUSTICE THOMAS, concurring in the judgment.

* * * In my view, the Cruel and Unusual Punishments Clause of the Eighth Amendment contains no proportionality principle. * * *

[The dissenting opinion of JUSTICE STEVENS, joined by JUSTICES SOUTER, GINSBURG, and BREYER, is omitted.]

JUSTICE BREYER, with whom JUSTICE STEVENS, JUSTICE SOUTER, and JUSTICE GINSBURG join, dissenting. * * *

I * * *

The plurality applies Justice Kennedy's analytical framework in *Harmelin, supra.* And, for present purposes, I will consider Ewing's Eighth Amendment claim on those terms. * * * To implement this approach, courts faced with a "gross disproportionality" claim must first make "a threshold comparison of the crime committed and the sentence imposed." If a [disproportionality] claim crosses that threshold—itself a *rare* occurrence—then the court should compare the sentence at issue to other sentences "imposed on other criminals" in the same, or in other, jurisdictions. The comparative analysis will "validate" or invalidate "an initial judgment that a sentence is grossly disproportionate to a crime."

I recognize the warnings implicit in the Court's frequent repetition of words such as "rare." Nonetheless I believe that the case before us is a "rare" case—one in which a court can say with reasonable confidence that the punishment is "grossly disproportionate" to the crime.

II

Ewing's claim crosses the gross disproportionality "threshold." First, precedent makes clear that Ewing's sentence raises a serious disproportionality question. Ewing is a recidivist. Hence the two cases most directly in point are those in which the Court considered the constitutionality of recidivist sentencing: *Rummel* and *Solem.* Ewing's claim falls between these two cases. It is stronger than the claim presented in *Rummel,* where the Court upheld a recidivist's sentence as constitutional. It is weaker than the claim presented in *Solem,* where the Court struck down a recidivist sentence as unconstitutional.

Three kinds of sentence-related characteristics define the relevant comparative spectrum: (a) the length of the prison term in real time, *i.e.,* the time that the offender is likely actually to spend in prison; (b) the sentence-triggering criminal conduct, *i.e.,* the offender's actual behavior or other offense-related circumstances; and (c) the offender's criminal history.

In *Rummel,* the Court held constitutional (a) a sentence of life imprisonment *with parole available within 10 to 12 years,* (b) for the offense of obtaining $120 by false pretenses, (c) committed by an offender with two prior felony convictions (involving small amounts of money). In *Solem,* the Court held unconstitutional (a) a sentence of life imprisonment *without parole,* (b) for the crime of writing a $100 check on a nonexistent bank account, (c) committed by an offender with six prior felony convictions (including three for burglary). Which of the three pertinent comparative factors made the constitutional difference?

The third factor, prior record, cannot explain the difference. The offender's prior record was *worse* in *Solem,* where the Court found the sentence too long, than in *Rummel,* where the Court upheld the sentence. The second factor, offense conduct, cannot explain the difference. The nature of the triggering offense—viewed in terms of the actual monetary loss—in the two cases was about the same. The one critical factor that explains the difference in the outcome is the length of the likely prison term measured in real time. In *Rummel,* where the Court upheld the sentence, the state sentencing statute authorized parole for the offender, Rummel, after 10 or 12 years. In *Solem,* where the Court struck down the sentence, the sentence required the offender, Helm, to spend the rest of his life in prison.

Now consider the present case. The third factor, *offender characteristics—i.e.,* prior record—does not differ significantly here from that in *Solem.* Ewing's prior record consists of four felony convictions (involving three burglaries, one with a knife) constrasted with Helm's six prior felony convictions (including three burglaries though none with weapons). The second factor, *offense behavior,* is worse than that in *Solem,* but only to a degree. It would be difficult to say that the actual behavior itself here (shoplifting) differs significantly from that at issue in *Solem* (passing a bad check) or in *Rummel* (obtaining money through false pretenses). Rather the difference lies in the *value* of the goods obtained. That difference, measured in terms of the most relevant feature (loss to the victim, *i.e.,* wholesale value) and adjusted for the irrelevant feature of inflation, comes down (in 1979 values) to about $379 here compared with $100 in *Solem,* or (in 1973 values) to $232 here compared with $120.75 in *Rummel.* Alternatively, if one measures the inflation-adjusted value difference in terms of the golf clubs' sticker price, it comes down to $505 here compared to $100 in *Solem,* or $309 here compared to $120.75 in *Rummel.*

The difference in *length* of the real prison term—the first, and critical, factor in *Solem* and *Rummel*—is considerably more important. Ewing's sentence here amounts, in real terms, to at least 25 years without parole or good-time credits. That sentence is considerably shorter than Helm's sentence in *Solem,* which amounted, in real terms, to life in prison. Nonetheless Ewing's real prison term is more than twice as long as the term at issue in *Rummel,* which amounted, in real terms, to at least 10 or 12 years. And, Ewing's sentence, unlike Rummel's (but like Helm's sentence in *Solem*), is long enough to consume the productive remainder of almost any offender's life. (It means that Ewing himself, seriously ill when sentenced at age 38, will likely die in prison.)

The upshot is that the length of the real prison term—the factor that explains the *Solem/Rummel* difference in outcome—places Ewing closer to *Solem* than to *Rummel,* though the greater value of the golf clubs that Ewing stole moves Ewing's case back slightly in *Rummel's* direction. Overall, the comparison places Ewing's sentence well within the twilight zone between *Solem* and Rummel—a zone where the argument for unconstitutionality is substantial, where the cases themselves cannot determine the constitutional outcome.

Second, Ewing's sentence on its face imposes one of the most severe punishments available upon a recidivist who subsequently engaged in one of the less serious forms of criminal conduct. I do not deny the seriousness of shoplifting, which * * * costs retailers in the range of $30 billion annually. But consider that conduct in terms of the factors that this Court mentioned in *Solem*—the "harm caused or threatened to the victim or society," the "absolute magnitude of the crime," and the offender's "culpability." In respect to all three criteria, the sentence-triggering behavior here ranks well toward the bottom of the criminal conduct scale. * * *

This case, of course, involves shoplifting engaged in by a *recidivist.* One might argue that *any* crime committed by a recidivist is a serious crime potentially warranting a 25–year sentence. But this Court rejected that view in *Solem,* and in *Harmelin,* with the recognition that "no penalty is *per se* constitutional." Our cases make clear that, in cases involving recidivist offenders, we must focus upon "the [offense] that triggers the life sentence," with recidivism playing a "relevant," but not necessarily determinative, role. And here, as I have said, that offense is among the less serious, while the punishment is among the most serious.

* * *

Taken together, these three circumstances make clear that Ewing's "gross disproportionality" argument is a strong one. That being so, his claim *must* pass the "threshold" test. * * *

III

Believing Ewing's argument a strong one, sufficient to pass the threshold, I turn to the comparative analysis. * * *

As to California itself, we know the following: First, between the end of World War II and 1994 (when California enacted the three strikes law), *no one* like Ewing could have served more than *10* years in prison. * * *

Second, statistics suggest that recidivists *of all sorts* convicted during that same time period in California served a small fraction of Ewing's real-time sentence. On average, recidivists served three to four additional (recidivist-related) years in prison, with 90 percent serving less than an additional real seven to eight years.

Third, we know that California has reserved, and still reserves, Ewing-type prison time, *i.e.,* at least 25 real years in prison, for criminals convicted of crimes far worse than was Ewing's. * * * It imposes, for example, upon nonrecidivists guilty of arson causing great bodily injury a maximum sentence of nine years in prison; it imposes upon those guilty of voluntary manslaughter a maximum sentence of 11 years. It reserves the sentence that it here imposes upon (former-burglar-now-golf-club-thief) Ewing, for nonrecidivist, first-degree murderers.

As to other jurisdictions, we know the following: The United States, bound by the federal Sentencing Guidelines, would impose upon a recidivist, such as Ewing, a sentence that, in any ordinary case, would not exceed 18 months in prison * * * [Justice Breyer then looked at how other states would punish Ewing.]

The upshot is that comparison of other sentencing practices, both in other jurisdictions and in California at other times (or in respect to other crimes), validates what an initial threshold examination suggested. * * * Outside the California three strikes context, Ewing's recidivist sentence is virtually unique in its harshness for his offense of conviction, and by a considerable degree.

IV

This is not the end of the matter. California sentenced Ewing pursuant to its "three strikes" law. That law represents a deliberate effort to provide stricter punishments for recidivists. And, it is important to consider whether special criminal justice concerns related to California's three strikes policy might justify including Ewing's theft within the class of triggering criminal conduct (thereby imposing a severe punishment), even if Ewing's sentence would otherwise seem disproportionately harsh.

I can find no such special criminal justice concerns that might justify this sentence. * * *

* * * One might argue that those who commit several *property* crimes should receive long terms of imprisonment in order to "incapacitate" them, *i.e.,* to prevent them from committing further crimes in the future. But that is not the object of this particular three strikes statute. Rather, as the plurality says, California seeks " 'to reduce *serious* and *violent* crime.' " The statute's definitions of both kinds of crime include crimes against the person, crimes that create danger of physical harm, and drug crimes. They do not include even serious crimes against property, such as obtaining large amounts of money, say, through theft, embezzlement, or fraud. * * *

Nor do the remaining criminal law objectives seem relevant. No one argues for Ewing's inclusion within the ambit of the three strikes statute on grounds of "retribution." For reasons previously discussed, in terms of "deterrence," Ewing's 25–year term amounts to overkill. And "rehabilitation" is obviously beside the point. The upshot is that, in my view, the State cannot find in its three strikes law a special criminal justice need sufficient to rescue a sentence that other relevant considerations indicate is unconstitutional. * * *

NOTES AND QUESTIONS

1. Justice O'Connor's opinion for the Court was joined by only two other justices, whereas there are *four* dissenters. In view of those numbers, why isn't Justice Breyer's opinion the "Court's opinion," and O'Connor's a dissent?

2. Do *you* believe that Ewing's sentence was excessive, i.e., disproportional? Defend your answer.

3. *The Canadian approach.* Section 12 of the Canadian Charter of Rights and Freedoms, like the Eighth Amendment to the United States Constitution, prohibits "cruel and unusual punishment," which has also been interpreted in Canada to include a proportionality component. But, here the similarity ends. For example, consider experienced drug smuggler Edward Dewey Smith, who was convicted of importing 7.5 ounces of cocaine into Canada from Bolivia. Pursuant to a statute that required the imposition of a minimum sentence of seven years' imprisonment for the importation of *any* illegal narcotic into the country, Smith was sentenced to seven years of incarceration.

The Supreme Court of Canada held that this sentence constituted grossly disproportionate punishment in violation of the Canadian Charter. R v. Smith, [1987] 1 S.C.R. 1045. In reaching this conclusion, the Court ignored Smith's experienced drug background and the nature of the drug imported, and instead evaluated the legitimacy of the punishment against a hypothetical of the most innocent possible offender. According to Justice Lamer:

[A] judge who would sentence to seven years in a penitentiary a young person who, while driving back into Canada from a winter break in the U.S.A. is caught with one, indeed, let's postulate, his or her first "joint of grass," would certainly be considered by most Canadians to be a cruel and, all would hope, a very unusual judge.

What do you think of this approach?

4. *Kennedy v. Louisiana* holds that death is an unconstitutional punishment for a juvenile who commits a homicide offense. The Supreme Court has also recently held that life without the possibility of parole is an unconstitutional punishment for a juvenile offender who commits a *non*homicide offense. Graham v. Florida, 560 U.S. ___, ___, 130 S.Ct. 2011, 2034, 176 L.Ed.2d 825 (2010). What about life imprisonment without the possibility of parole for a juvenile who commits a homicide offense? Is *that* an unconstitutional punishment?

CHAPTER 3

MODERN ROLE OF CRIMINAL STATUTES

■ ■ ■

A. PRINCIPLE OF LEGALITY

The American legal system espouses the principle *nullum crimen sine lege, nulla poena sine lege*, or "no crime without law, no punishment without law." In other words, a person may not be convicted and punished unless her conduct was defined as criminal (today, in the United States, by statute rather than by judges). This prohibition on retroactive criminal lawmaking constitutes the essence of the principle of legality, a principle that has been characterized as *the* first principle of American criminal law. Herbert L. Packer, The Limits of the Criminal sanction 79–80 (1968).

There are three interrelated corollaries to the legality principle that are also covered in this chapter section. First, criminal statutes should be understandable to reasonable law-abiding persons. Second, criminal statutes should be crafted so that they do not "delegate[] basic policy matters to policemen, judges, and juries for resolution on an *ad hoc* and subjective basis." Grayned v. City of Rockford, 408 U.S. 104, 92 S.Ct. 2294, 33 L.Ed.2d 222 (1972). Third, judicial interpretation of ambiguous statutes should "be biased in favor of the accused," a concept that has come to be known as the lenity doctrine.

1. THE REQUIREMENT OF PREVIOUSLY DEFINED CONDUCT

COMMONWEALTH v. MOCHAN

Superior Court of Pennsylvania, 1955.
177 Pa.Super. 454, 110 A.2d 788.

HIRT, JUDGE.

[Mochan was charged in separate indictments with intending "to debauch and corrupt, and further devising and intending to harass, embarrass and villify [sic] * * * one Louise Zivkovich and the members of [her] family" by telephoning her various times, during which he

> did wickedly and maliciously refer to the said Louise Zivkovich as a lewd, immoral and lascivious woman of an indecent and lewd charac-

92

ter, and [made] other scurrilous, opprobrious, filthy, disgusting, and indecent [comments] * * * intending as aforesaid to blacken the character and reputation of the said Louise Zivkovich * * * to the great damage, injury and oppression of the said Louise Zivkovich and other good citizens of this Commonwealth to the evil example of all other in like case offending, and against the peace and dignity of the Commonwealth of Pennsylvania.

The conduct alleged in the indictments was not prohibited by statute. However, Section 1101 of the Pennsylvania Penal Code of 1939 provided that "[e]very offense * * * punishable either by the statutes or common law of this Commonwealth and not specifically provided for by this Act, * * * shall continue to be an offense punishable as heretofore." The prosecutor contended that Mochan's conduct was unlawful under Pennsylvania common law.]

* * * Defendant was tried before a judge without a jury and was convicted on both charges and was sentenced. He has appealed * * * on the ground * * * that the conduct charged in the indictments, concededly not a criminal offense in this State by any statute, does not constitute a misdemeanor at common law. * * *

It is established by the testimony that the defendant * * * on numerous occasions and on the specific dates laid in the indictments, telephoned one Louise Zivkovich, a stranger to him and a married woman of the highest character and repute. He called as often as three times each week and at any hour of the day or night. His language on these calls was obscene, lewd and filthy. He not only suggested intercourse with her but talked of sodomy as well, in the loathsome language of that criminal act, on a number of occasions. * * *

It is of little importance that there is no precedent in our reports which decides the precise question here involved. The test is not whether precedents can be found in the books but whether the alleged crimes could have been prosecuted and the offenders punished under the common law. In Commonwealth v. Miller, 94 Pa.Super. 499, 507, the controlling principles are thus stated: "The common law is sufficiently broad to punish as a misdemeanor, although there may be no exact precedent, any act which directly injures or tends to injure the public to such an extent as to require the state to interfere and punish the wrongdoer, as in the case of acts which injuriously affect public morality, or obstruct, or pervert public justice, or the administration of government." Cf. Commonwealth of Pennsylvania v. DeGrange, 97 Pa.Super. 181, in which it is said: "Whatever openly outrages decency and is injurious to public morals is a misdemeanor at common law." Any act is indictable at common law which from its nature scandalously affects the morals or health of the community. * * * And as early as Updegraph v. Commonwealth, 11 Serg. & R. 394, it was held that Christianity is a part of the common law and maliciously to vilify the Christian religion is an indictable offense.

[handwritten margin notes: "Smith"; "criminal intent"; "injury to public morality"; "Dissent"; "invading legislative field"]

To endeavor merely to persuade a married woman to commit adultery is not indictable. Smith v. Commonwealth, 54 Pa. 209. The present defendant's criminal intent was evidenced by a number of overt acts beyond the mere oral solicitation of adultery. The vile and disgusting suggestions of sodomy alone and the otherwise persistent lewd, immoral and filthy language used by the defendant, take these cases out of the principle of the Smith case. Moreover potentially at least, defendant's acts injuriously affected public morality. The operator or any one on defendant's four-party telephone line could have listened in on the conversations, and at least two other persons in Mrs. Zivkovich's household heard some of defendant's immoral and obscene language over the telephone.

* * * [T]he factual charges in the body of the indictments identify the offense as a common law misdemeanor and the testimony established the guilt of the defendant.

Judgments and sentences affirmed.

WOODSIDE, JUDGE (dissenting).

Not unmindful of the reprehensible conduct of the appellant, I nevertheless cannot agree with the majority that what he did was a crime punishable under the laws of this Commonwealth.

The majority is declaring something to be a crime which was never before known to be a crime in this Commonwealth. They have done this by the application of such general principles as "it is a crime to do anything which injures or tends to injure the public to such an extent as to require the state to interfere and punish the wrongdoer;" and "whatever openly outrages decency and is injurious to public morals is a misdemeanor."

Not only have they declared it to be a crime to do an act "injuriously affecting public morality," but they have declared it to be a crime to do any act which has a "potentially" injurious effect on public morality.

Under the division of powers in our constitution it is for the legislature to determine what "injures or tends to injure the public."

One of the most important functions of a legislature is to determine what acts "require the state to interfere and punish the wrongdoer." There is no reason for the legislature to enact any criminal laws if the courts delegate to themselves the power to apply such general principles as are here applied to whatever conduct may seem to the courts to be injurious to the public.

There is no doubt that the common law is a part of the law of this Commonwealth, and we punish many acts under the common law. But after nearly two hundred years of constitutional government in which the legislature and not the courts have been charged by the people with the responsibility of deciding which acts do and which do not injure the public to the extent which requires punishment, it seems to me we are making an unwarranted invasion of the legislative field when we arrogate that responsibility to ourselves by declaring now, for the first time, that certain acts are a crime.

When the legislature invades either the judicial or the executive fields, or the executive invades either the judicial or legislative fields, the courts stand ready to stop them. But in matters of this type there is nothing to prevent our invasion of the legislative field except our own self restraint. * * *

Until the legislature says that what the defendant did is a crime, I think the courts should not declare it to be such.

I would therefore reverse the lower court and discharge the appellant.

NOTES AND QUESTIONS

1.   Does the decision in this case violate the legality principle, as that concept is explained in the text immediately preceding the case?

2.   What, if anything, troubles you about this case? Do you agree with the dissent that the court "invaded" the legislative province? If so, what is wrong with that? Aren't judges at least as qualified as legislators, many of whom are not lawyers, to formulate new criminal offenses?

Suppose that prior to Mochan's telephone calls the legislature had enacted a statute making it a crime "to do anything which injures or tends to injure the public or which openly outrages decency." Or, suppose for a moment that a legislature, contemplating the momentous problem of drafting a new criminal code, decided to solve its problem by a single grand enactment: "whoever does anything bad shall be punished as justice may require." Herbert L. Packer, The Limits of the Criminal Sanction 92 (1968). Would these solutions resolve your concerns about *Mochan?*

3.   The court said that "[t]o endeavor to persuade a married woman to commit adultery is not indictable," but "vile and disgusting suggestions of sodomy alone" *were* indictable acts. Why do you think the court drew this distinction? Can you think of any legitimate basis?

4.   Nearly all states have abolished common law offenses, including now Pennsylvania. 18 Pa.Cons.Stat.Ann. § 107(b) (2011) (but see R.I. Gen. Law. § 11–1–1 (2011), which authorizes the prosecution of common law offenses). Nonetheless, as the following materials suggest, even in states that have abolished common law offenses, common law doctrine retains significance.

KEELER v. SUPERIOR COURT

Supreme Court of California, 1970.
2 Cal.3d 619, 87 Cal.Rptr. 481, 470 P.2d 617.

MOSK, JUSTICE.

In this proceeding for writ of prohibition[a] we are called upon to decide whether an unborn but viable fetus is a "human being" within the

---

a.   A writ of prohibition "arrests the proceedings of any tribunal * * *, when such proceedings are without or in excess of the jurisdiction of such tribunal * * *." Cal. Code Civ. Proc. § 1102

meaning of the California statute defining murder (Pen.Code, § 187). We conclude that the Legislature did not intend such a meaning, and that for us to construe the statute to the contrary and apply it to this petitioner would exceed our judicial power and deny petitioner due process of law.

The evidence received at the preliminary examination may be summarized as follows: Petitioner and Teresa Keeler obtained an interlocutory decree of divorce on September 27, 1968. They had been married for 16 years. Unknown to petitioner, Mrs. Keeler was then pregnant by one Ernest Vogt, whom she had met earlier that summer. She subsequently began living with Vogt in Stockton, but concealed the fact from petitioner. * * *

On February 23, 1969, Mrs. Keeler was driving on a narrow mountain road * * *. She met petitioner driving in the opposite direction; he blocked the road with his car, and she pulled over to the side. He walked to her vehicle and began speaking to her. He seemed calm, and she rolled down her window to hear him. He said, "I hear you're pregnant. If you are you had better stay away * * * from here." She did not reply, and he opened the car door; as she later testified, "He assisted me out of the car. * * * [I]t wasn't roughly at this time." Petitioner then looked at her abdomen and became "extremely upset." He said, "You sure are. I'm going to stomp it out of you." He pushed her against the car, shoved his knee into her abdomen, and struck her in the face with several blows. She fainted, and when she regained consciousness petitioner had departed.

Mrs. Keeler drove back to Stockton, and the police and medical assistance were summoned. She had suffered substantial facial injuries, as well as extensive bruising of the abdominal wall. A Caesarian section was performed and the fetus was examined *in utero*. Its head was found to be severely fractured, and it was delivered stillborn. The pathologist gave as his opinion that the cause of death was skull fracture with consequent cerebral hemorrhaging, that death would have been immediate, and that the injury could have been the result of force applied to the mother's abdomen. There was no air in the fetus' lungs, and the umbilical cord was intact.

Upon delivery the fetus weighed five pounds and was 18 inches in length. Both Mrs. Keeler and her obstetrician testified that fetal movements had been observed prior to February 23, 1969. The evidence was in conflict as to the estimated age of the fetus; the expert testimony on the point, however, concluded "with reasonable medical certainty" that the fetus had developed to the stage of viability, i.e., that in the event of premature birth on the date in question it would have had a 75 percent to 96 percent chance of survival.

An information was filed charging petitioner, in Count I, with committing the crime of murder (Pen.Code, § 187) in that he did "unlawfully

---

(2011). In criminal proceedings, a defendant who has been committed for trial may petition to the superior court for a writ of prohibition, in this case on the ground that his conduct, even if proven, does not constitute the offense charged. See Cal. Pen. Code § 999a (2011).

kill a human being, to wit Baby Girl VOGT, with malice aforethought." In Count II petitioner was charged with wilful infliction of traumatic injury upon his wife, and in Count III, with assault on Mrs. Keeler by means of force likely to produce great bodily injury. * * * [O]nly the murder count is actually in issue.

I

Penal Code section 187 provides: "Murder is the unlawful killing of a human being, with malice aforethought." The dispositive question is whether the fetus which petitioner is accused of killing was, on February 23, 1969, a "human being" within the meaning of this statute. If it was not, petitioner cannot be charged with its "murder" * * *.

Def. of murder

Section 187 was enacted as part of the Penal Code of 1872. Inasmuch as the provision has not been amended since that date, we must determine the intent of the Legislature at the time of its enactment. But section 187 was, in turn, taken verbatim from the first California statute defining murder, part of the Crimes and Punishments Act of 1850. Penal Code section 5 (also enacted in 1872) declares: "The provisions of this Code, so far as they are substantially the same as existing statutes, must be construed as continuations thereof, and not as new enactments." We begin, accordingly, by inquiring into the intent of the Legislature in 1850 when it first defined murder as the unlawful and malicious killing of a "human being."

It will be presumed, of course, that in enacting a statute the Legislature was familiar with the relevant rules of the common law, and, when it couches its enactment in common law language, that its intent was to continue those rules in statutory form. * * *

We therefore undertake a brief review of the origins and development of the common law of abortional homicide. From that inquiry it appears that by the year 1850—the date with which we are concerned—an infant could not be the subject of homicide at common law *unless it had been born alive.* Perhaps the most influential statement of the "born alive" rule is that of Coke, in mid–17th century: "If a woman be quick with childe,[5] and by a potion or otherwise killeth it in her wombe, or if a man beat her, whereby the childe dyeth in her body, and she is delivered of a dead childe, this is a great misprision [i.e., misdemeanor], and no murder; but if the childe be born alive and dyeth of the potion, battery, or other cause, this is murder; for in law it is accounted a reasonable creature, *in rerum natura,* when it is born alive." (3 Coke, Institutes *58 (1648).) * * * In the 18th century * * * Coke's requirement that an infant be born alive in order to be the subject of homicide was reiterated * * * by both Blackstone and Hale. * * *

By the year 1850 this rule of the common law had long been accepted in the United States. As early as 1797 it was held that proof the child was

---

5. "Quickening" is said to occur when movements of the fetus are first sensed or observed, and ordinarily takes place between the 16th and 18th week of pregnancy. * * *

born alive is necessary to support an indictment for murder, and the same rule was reiterated on the eve of the first session of our Legislature. * * *

We conclude that in declaring murder to be the unlawful and malicious killing of a "human being" the Legislature of 1850 intended that term to have the settled common law meaning of a person who had been born alive, and did not intend the act of feticide * * * to be an offense under the laws of California.

Nothing occurred between the years 1850 and 1872 to suggest that in adopting the new Penal Code on the latter date the Legislature entertained any different intent. * * *

It is the policy of this state to construe a penal statute as favorably to the defendant as its language and the circumstances of its application may reasonably permit; just as in the case of a question of fact, the defendant is entitled to the benefit of every reasonable doubt as to the true interpretation of words or the construction of language used in a statute. We hold that in adopting the definition of murder in Penal Code section 187 the Legislature intended to exclude from its reach the act of killing an unborn fetus.

II

The People urge, however, that the sciences of obstetrics and pediatrics have greatly progressed since 1872, to the point where with proper medical care a normally developed fetus prematurely born at 28 weeks or more has an excellent chance of survival, i.e., is "viable"; that the common law requirement of live birth to prove the fetus had become a "human being" who may be the victim of murder is no longer in accord with scientific fact, since an unborn but viable fetus is now fully capable of independent life; and that one who unlawfully and maliciously terminates such a life should therefore be liable to prosecution for murder under section 187. We may grant the premises of this argument; indeed, we neither deny nor denigrate the vast progress of medicine in the century since the enactment of the Penal Code. But we cannot join in the conclusion sought to be deduced: we cannot hold this petitioner to answer for murder by reason of his alleged act of killing an unborn—even though viable—fetus. To such a charge there are two insuperable obstacles, one "jurisdictional" and the other constitutional.

Penal Code section 6 declares in relevant part that "No act or omission" accomplished after the code has taken effect "is criminal or punishable, except as prescribed or authorized by this Code, or by some of the statutes which it specifies as continuing in force and as not affected by its provisions, or by some ordinance, municipal, county, or township regulation * * *." This section embodies a fundamental principle of our tripartite form of government, i.e., that subject to the constitutional prohibition against cruel and unusual punishment, the power to define crimes and fix penalties is vested exclusively in the legislative branch. Stated differently, there are no common law crimes in California. * * *

Settled rules of construction implement this principle. Although the Penal Code commands us to construe its provisions "according to the fair import of their terms, with a view to effect its objects and to promote justice" (Pen.Code, § 4), it is clear the courts cannot go so far as to create an offense by enlarging a statute, by inserting or deleting words, or by giving the terms used false or unusual meanings. Penal statutes will not be made to reach beyond their plain intent; they include only those offenses coming clearly within the import of their language. * * *

Applying these rules to the case at bar, we would undoubtedly act in excess of the judicial power if we were to adopt the People's proposed construction of section 187. * * * We recognize that the killing of an unborn but viable fetus may be deemed by some to be an offense of similar nature and gravity; but as Chief Justice Marshall warned long ago, "It would be dangerous, indeed, to carry the principle, that a case which is within the reason or mischief of a statute, is within its provisions, so far as to punish a crime not enumerated in the statute, because it is of equal atrocity, or of kindred character, with those which are enumerated." (United States v. Wiltberger (1820) 18 U.S. (5 Wheat.) 76, 96, 5 L.Ed. 37.) Whether to thus extend liability for murder in California is a determination solely within the province of the Legislature. For a court to simply declare, by judicial fiat, that the time has now come to prosecute under section 187 one who kills an unborn but viable fetus would indeed be to rewrite the statute under the guise of construing it. Nor does a need to fill an asserted "gap" in the law * * * justify judicial legislation of this nature: to make it "a judicial function 'to explore such new fields of crime as they may appear from time to time' is wholly foreign to the American concept of criminal justice" and "raises very serious questions concerning the principle of separation of powers."

The second obstacle to the proposed judicial enlargement of section 187 is the guarantee of due process of law. Assuming *arguendo* that we have the power to adopt the new construction of this statute as the law of California, such a ruling, by constitutional command, could operate only prospectively, and thus could not in any event reach the conduct of petitioner on February 23, 1969.

The first essential of due process is fair warning of the act which is made punishable as a crime. "That the terms of a penal statute creating a new offense must be sufficiently explicit to inform those who are subject to it what conduct on their part will render them liable to its penalties, is a well-recognized requirement, consonant alike with ordinary notions of fair play and the settled rules of law." (Connally v. General Constr. Co. (1926) 269 U.S. 385, 391, 46 S.Ct. 126, 127, 70 L.Ed. 322.) "No one may be required at peril of life, liberty or property to speculate as to the meaning of penal statutes. All are entitled to be informed as to what the State commands or forbids." (Lanzetta v. New Jersey (1939) 306 U.S. 451, 453, 59 S.Ct. 618, 619, 83 L.Ed. 888.) * * *

This requirement of fair warning is reflected in the constitutional prohibition against the enactment of ex post facto laws (U.S. Const., art. I, §§ 9, 10; Cal. Const., art. I, § 16). When a new penal statute is applied retrospectively to make punishable an act which was not criminal at the time it was performed, the defendant has been given no advance notice consistent with due process. And precisely the same effect occurs when such an act is made punishable under a preexisting statute but by means of an unforeseeable *judicial* enlargement thereof. (Bouie v. City of Columbia (1964) 378 U.S. 347, 84 S.Ct. 1697, 12 L.Ed.2d 894.)

In *Bouie* two Negroes took seats in the restaurant section of a South Carolina drugstore; no notices were posted restricting the area to whites only. When the defendants refused to leave upon demand, they were arrested and convicted of violating a criminal trespass statute which prohibited entry on the property of another "after notice" forbidding such conduct. Prior South Carolina decisions had emphasized the necessity of proving such notice to support a conviction under the statute. The South Carolina Supreme Court nevertheless affirmed the convictions, construing the statute to prohibit not only the act of entering after notice not to do so but also the wholly different act of remaining on the property after receiving notice to leave.

The United States Supreme Court reversed the convictions, holding that the South Carolina court's ruling was "unforeseeable" and when an "unforeseeable state-court construction of a criminal statute is applied retroactively to subject a person to criminal liability for past conduct, the effect is to deprive him of due process of law in the sense of fair warning that his contemplated conduct constitutes a crime." Analogizing to the prohibition against retrospective penal legislation, the high court reasoned "Indeed, an unforeseeable judicial enlargement of a criminal statute, applied retroactively, operates precisely like an *ex post facto* law, such as Art. I, § 10, of the Constitution forbids. An *ex post facto* law has been defined by this Court as one 'that makes an action done before the passing of the law, and which was *innocent* when done, criminal; and punishes such action,' or 'that *aggravates* a *crime*, or makes it *greater* than it was, when committed.' Calder v. Bull, 3 Dall. 386, 390, 1 L.Ed. 648. If a state legislature is barred by the *Ex Post Facto* Clause from passing such a law, it must follow that a State Supreme Court is barred by the Due Process Clause from achieving precisely the same result by judicial construction. * * * If a judicial construction of a criminal statute is 'unexpected and indefensible by reference to the law which had been expressed prior to the conduct in issue,' it must not be given retroactive effect."

The court remarked in conclusion that "Application of this rule is particularly compelling where, as here, the petitioners' conduct cannot be deemed improper or immoral." In the case at bar the conduct with which petitioner is charged is certainly "improper" and "immoral," and it is not contended he was exercising a constitutionally favored right. But the matter is simply one of degree, and it cannot be denied that the guarantee of due process extends to violent as well as peaceful men. The issue remains, would the judicial enlargement of section 187 now proposed have been foreseeable to this petitioner? * * *

Turning to the case law, we find no reported decision of the California courts which should have given petitioner notice that the killing of an unborn but viable fetus was prohibited by section 187. * * * [Discussion omitted.]

Finally, although a defendant is not bound to know the decisional law of other states, * * * the cases decided in our sister states * * * are unanimous in requiring proof that the child was born alive before a charge of homicide can be sustained. And the text writers of the same period are no less unanimous on the point.

We conclude that the judicial enlargement of section 187 now urged upon us by the People would not have been foreseeable to this petitioner, and hence that its adoption at this time would deny him due process of law. * * *

BURKE, ACTING CHIEF JUSTICE (dissenting).   *Dissent*

The majority hold that "Baby Girl" Vogt, who, according to medical testimony, had reached the 35th week of development, had a 96 percent chance of survival, and was "definitely" alive and viable at the time of her death, nevertheless was not a "human being" under California's homicide statutes. In my view, in so holding, the majority ignore significant common law precedents, frustrate the express intent of the Legislature, and defy reason, logic and common sense.

Penal Code section 187 defines murder as "the unlawful killing of a human being, with malice aforethought." * * * The majority pursue the meaning of the term "human being" down the ancient hallways of the common law, citing Coke, Blackstone and Hale to the effect that the slaying of a "quickened" * * * child constituted "a great misprision," but not murder. * * *

The majority cast a passing glance at the common law concept of quickening, but fail to explain the significance of that concept: At common law, the quickened fetus *was* considered to be a human being, a second life separate and apart from its mother. As stated by Blackstone, * * * "Life is the immediate gift of God, a right inherent by nature in every individual; *and it begins in contemplation of law as soon as an infant is able to stir in the mother's womb.*" * * *

This reasoning explains why the killing of a quickened child was considered "a great misprision," although the killing of an unquickened child was no crime at all at common law. Moreover, although the common law did not apply the labels of "murder" or "manslaughter" to the killing of a quickened fetus, it appears that at common law this "great misprision" was severely punished. * * *

Thus, at common law, the killing of a quickened child was severely punished, since that child was considered to be a human being. The majority would have us assume that the Legislature in 1850 and 1872 simply overlooked this "great misprision" in codifying and classifying criminal offenses in California, or reduced that offense to the lesser offense of illegal abortion with its relatively lenient penalties. * * *

Of course, I do not suggest that we should interpret the term "human being" in our homicide statutes in terms of the common law concept of quickening. At one time, that concept had a value in differentiating, as accurately as was then scientifically possible, between life and nonlife. The analogous concept of viability is clearly more satisfactory, for it has a well defined and medically determinable meaning denoting the ability of the fetus to live or survive apart from its mother.

The majority opinion suggests that we are confined to common law concepts, and to the common law definition of murder or manslaughter. However, the Legislature, in Penal Code sections 187 and 192, has defined those offenses for us: homicide is the unlawful killing of a "human being." Those words need not be frozen in place as of any particular time, but must be fairly and reasonably interpreted by this court to promote justice and to carry out the evident purposes of the Legislature in adopting a homicide statute. * * *

We commonly conceive of human existence as a spectrum stretching from birth to death. However, if this court properly might expand the definition of "human being" at one end of that spectrum, we may do so at the other end. Consider the following example: All would agree that "Shooting or otherwise damaging a corpse is not homicide. * * * *" In other words, a corpse is not considered to be a "human being" and thus cannot be the subject of a "killing" as those terms are used in homicide statutes. However, it is readily apparent that our concepts of what constitutes a "corpse" have been and are being continually modified by advances in the field of medicine, including new techniques for life revival, restoration and resuscitation * * *. Would this court ignore these developments and exonerate the killer of an apparently "drowned" child merely because that child would have been pronounced dead in 1648 or 1850? Obviously not. Whether a homicide occurred in that case would be determined by medical testimony regarding the capability of the child to have survived prior to the defendant's act. And that is precisely the test which this court should adopt in the instant case.

The common law reluctance to characterize the killing of a quickened fetus as a homicide was based solely upon a presumption that the fetus would have been born dead. * * * Based upon the state of the medical art in the 17th, 18th and 19th centuries, that presumption may have been well-founded. However, as we approach the 21st century, it has become apparent that "This presumption is not only contrary to common experience and the ordinary course of nature, but it is contrary to the usual rule with respect to presumptions followed in this state." (People v. Chavez (1947) 77 Cal.App.2d 621, 626, 176 P.2d 92, 95.)

* * * If, as I have contended, the term "human being" in our homicide statutes is a fluid concept to be defined in accordance with

present conditions, then there can be no question that the term should include the fully viable fetus.

The majority suggest that to do so would improperly create some new offense. However, the offense of murder is no new offense. Contrary to the majority opinion, the Legislature has not "defined the crime of murder in California to apply only to the unlawful and malicious killing of one who has been born alive." Instead, the Legislature simply used the broad term "human being" and directed the courts to construe that term according to its "fair import" with a view to effect the objects of the homicide statutes and promote justice. What justice will be promoted, what objects effectuated, by construing "human being" as excluding Baby Girl Vogt and her unfortunate successors? Was defendant's brutal act of stomping her to death any less an act of homicide than the murder of a newly born baby? No one doubts that the term "human being" would include the elderly or dying persons whose potential for life has nearly lapsed; their proximity to death is deemed immaterial. There is no sound reason for denying the viable fetus, with its unbounded potential for life, the same status.

[handwritten margin note: Fetus never in class of living]

The majority also suggest that such an interpretation of our homicide statutes would deny defendant "fair warning" that his act was punishable as a crime. Aside from the absurdity of the underlying premise that defendant consulted Coke, Blackstone or Hale before kicking Baby Girl Vogt to death, it is clear that defendant had adequate notice that his act could constitute homicide. * * *

Our homicide statutes have been in effect in this state since 1850. The fact that the California courts have not been called upon to determine the precise question before us does not render "unforeseeable" a decision which determines that a viable fetus is a "human being" under those statutes. Can defendant really claim surprise that a 5–pound, 18–inch, 34–week–old, living, viable child is considered to be a human being? * * *

NOTES AND QUESTIONS

1. In response to *Keeler,* the California legislature amended its murder statute to read: "Murder is the unlawful killing of a human being, or a fetus, with malice aforethought." Cal. Penal Code § 187(a). (Therapeutic abortions, as defined by state law, are expressly excluded from the scope of the statute. Section 187(b).) Is the amended statute fully in accord with Justice Burke's dissent? If not, how might he have preferred that the legislature protect fetuses?

2. More than two decades before *Keeler*, an intermediate appellate court in California held that a viable fetus that dies during the birth process is a human being for purposes of the murder statute. People v. Chavez, 77 Cal.App.2d 621, 176 P.2d 92 (1947). Although it was not part of the holding, the *Chavez* court observed:

[handwritten margin note: Chavez]

> There is not much change in the child itself between a moment before and a moment after its expulsion from the body of its mother, and

normally, while still dependent upon its mother, the child for some time before it is born, has not only the possibility but a strong probability of an ability to live an independent life. * * * While before birth or removal it is in a sense dependent upon its mother for life, there is another sense in which it has started an independent existence after it has reached a state of development where it is capable of living and where it will, in the normal course of nature and with ordinary care, continue to live and grow as a separate being. While it may not be possible to draw an exact line applicable to all cases, the rules of law should recognize and make some attempt to follow the natural and scientific facts to which they relate. * * * [It] would be a mere fiction to hold that a child is not a human being because the process of birth has not been fully completed, when it has reached that state of viability when the destruction of the life of its mother would not end its existence and when, if separated from the mother naturally or by artificial means, it will live and grow in the normal manner.

According to dissenting Justice Burke, Keeler should have been on notice from the "strong dicta" in the *Chavez* quote above that the term "human being" might be interpreted twenty years after *Chavez* to include the viable fetus he killed.

To the extent that the outcome in *Keeler* is based on due process grounds (remember: there is the independent "jurisdictional" basis for the holding), do you think that *Chavez* undercuts the *Keeler* court's constitutional holding? The United States Supreme Court recently stated that "a judicial alteration of a common law doctrine of criminal law [only] violates the principle of fair warning * * * where it is 'unexpected and indefensible by reference to the law which had been expressed prior to the conduct in issue.'" Rogers v. Tennessee, 532 U.S. 451, 121 S.Ct. 1693, 149 L.Ed.2d 697 (2001). Applying *this* standard in light of *Chavez*, do you think the state supreme court could have properly applied the murder statute to Keeler?

3. *Ex post facto legislation and due process.* Both the *ex post facto* clause of the Constitution, which prohibits retroactive *legislation* and *legislative* expansion of existing statutes, and the due process clause, which concerns retroactive *judicial* lawmaking, "safeguard common interests—in particular, the interests in fundamental fairness (through notice and fair warning) and the prevention of the arbitrary and vindictive use of the laws." Rogers v. Tennessee, supra. As the Court observed in Lynce v. Mathis, 519 U.S. 433, 117 S.Ct. 891, 137 L.Ed.2d 63 (1997):

> The presumption against the retroactive application of new laws is an essential thread in the mantle of protection that the law affords the individual citizen. That presumption "is deeply rooted in our jurisprudence, and embodies a legal doctrine centuries older than our Republic." * * * In both the civil and the criminal context, the Constitution places limits on the sovereign's ability to use its law-making power to modify bargains it has made with its subjects. The basic principle is one that protects not only the rich and the powerful, but also the indigent defendant engaged in negotiations that may lead to an acknowledgment of guilt and a suitable punishment.

4. *Crimes by analogy.* Look again at the statement of Chief Justice Marshall quoted in *Keeler* at p. 99. This is an early expression of the legality principle and rejection of the principle of crime and punishment by analogy. The analogy principle, employed in the Soviet Union until 1958 and in the People's Republic of China until 1998, provides that a person may be convicted and punished "despite the absence of any defined criminal behavior. If the actions of the accused are perceived to be inimical to the socio-political order then he may be found guilty of a defined crime which prohibits analogous behavior." Dana Giovanetti, *The Principle of Analogy in Sino–Soviet Criminal Laws*, 8 Dalhousie L.J. 382, 382 (1984). Likewise, the Senate of the Free City of Danzig in 1935 promulgated a decree (later followed by Nazi Germany) that provided that "[a]ny person who commits an act which the law declares to be punishable or which is deserving of penalty according to the fundamental conceptions of a penal law and sound popular feeling, shall be punished." The decree further provided that if no penal law existed "directly covering an act, it should be punished under the law of which the fundamental conception applies most nearly to the said act." Advisory Opinion No. 65, Consistency of Certain Danzig Legislative Decrees with the Constitution of the Free City, 1935 P.C.I.J. (ser. A/B) No. 65, at 45 (Dec. 4).

2. THE VALUES OF STATUTORY CLARITY

IN RE BANKS

Supreme Court of North Carolina, 1978.
295 N.C. 236, 244 S.E.2d 386.

MOORE, JUSTICE.

The State argues that the trial court erred in ruling that G.S. 14–202, the so-called "Peeping Tom" statute, is unconstitutional. Respondent, however, contends that this statute is * * * unconstitutionally vague, because "men of common intelligence must necessarily guess at its meaning and differ as to its application * * *." *Connally v. General Construction Co.,* 269 U.S. 385, 46 S.Ct. 126, 70 L.Ed. 322 (1926).

G.S. 14–202 provides:

"*Secretly peeping into room occupied by female person.*—Any person who shall peep secretly into any room occupied by a female person shall be guilty of a misdemeanor and upon conviction shall be fined or imprisoned in the discretion of the court."

The requirement that a statute be couched in terms of appropriate definiteness has been referred to as a fundamental common law concept. * * *

This requirement of definiteness has in this century been declared an essential element of due process of law. *See Connally v. General Construction Co., supra.* Several United States Supreme Court cases indicate that the evils remedied by the definiteness requirement are the lack of fair notice of the conduct prohibited and the failure to define a reasonably ascertainable standard of guilt. In present case respondent does not advance a strict vagueness argument based on the lack of intelligibility of the terms employed in the challenged statute. Instead, he argues that the statute cannot mean what it says, since, if taken literally, it would prohibit much conduct which the legislature clearly did not intend to include. Its intended scope is therefore indefinite and reasonable men could differ as to its application. Thus, concludes defendant, the statute is unconstitutionally vague.

In passing upon the constitutionality of the statute, we begin with the presumption that it is constitutional and must be so held unless it is in conflict with some constitutional provision of the State or Federal Constitutions. A well recognized rule in this State is that, where a statute is susceptible to two interpretations—one constitutional and one unconstitutional—the Court should adopt the interpretation resulting in a finding of constitutionality.

Criminal statutes must be strictly construed. But, while a criminal statute must be strictly construed, the courts must nevertheless construe it with regard to the evil which it is intended to suppress. The intent of the legislature controls the interpretation of a statute. When the language of a statute is clear and unambiguous, there is no room for judicial construction and the courts must give the statute its plain and definite meaning, and are without power to interpolate, or superimpose, provisions and limitations not contained therein. But where a statute is ambiguous or unclear in its meaning, resort must be had to judicial construction to ascertain the legislative will, and the courts will interpret the language to give effect to the legislative intent. As this Court said in *State v. Partlow*, 91 N.C. 550 (1884), the legislative intent " * * * is to be ascertained by appropriate means and *indicia*, such as the purposes appearing from the statute taken as a whole, the phraseology, the words ordinary or technical, the law as it prevailed before the statute, the mischief to be remedied, the remedy, the end to be accomplished, statutes *in pari materia*, the preamble, the title, and other like means. * * * " Other *indicia* considered by this Court in determining legislative intent are the legislative history of an act and the circumstances surrounding its adoption; earlier statutes on the same subject; the common law as it was understood at the time of the enactment of the statute; and previous interpretations of the same or similar statutes, *cf. Wainwright v. Stone*, 414 U.S. 21, 94 S.Ct. 190, 38 L.Ed.2d 179 (1973). * * *

On the subject of the constitutional challenge of a statute for indefiniteness, the United States Supreme Court has said, in *Boyce Motor Lines v. United States,* 342 U.S. 337, 72 S.Ct. 329, 96 L.Ed. 367 (1952):

"A criminal statute must be sufficiently definite to give notice of the required conduct to one who would avoid its penalties, and to guide the judge in its application and the lawyer in defending one charged with its violation. But few words possess the precision of mathematical symbols, most statutes must deal with untold and unforeseen variations in factual situations, and the practical necessities of discharging the business of government inevitably limit the specificity with which legislators can spell out prohibitions. Consequently, no more than a reasonable degree of certainty can be demanded. Nor is it unfair to require that one who deliberately goes perilously close to an area of proscribed conduct shall take the risk that he may cross the line."[b]

In *Wainwright v. Stone, supra,* where defendant challenged the Florida "Crime Against Nature" statute on grounds of vagueness, the United States Supreme Court, in upholding the constitutionality of the statute, held that the judgment of federal courts as to the vagueness of a state statute must be made in the light of prior state constructions of the statute. This holding implies that a statute challenged on the grounds of impermissible vagueness should not be tested for constitutional specificity in a vacuum, but should be judged in the light of its common law meaning, its statutory history and the prior judicial interpretation of its particular terms.

Applying the foregoing principles, we now turn to an examination of G.S. 14–202, commonly known as the "Peeping Tom" statute. The statute apparently was derived from the common law crimes of common nuisance and eavesdropping. The words "Peeping Tom" have a commonly understood meaning in this country as being one who sneaks up to a window and peeps in for the purpose of spying on and invading the privacy of the inhabitants.

Our statute, passed by the General Assembly in 1923, makes it a crime to "peep secretly." This Court has had the occasion to deal with this statute in * * * prior cases: *State v. Banks,* 263 N.C. 784, 140 S.E.2d 318 (1965); *State v. Bivins,* 262 N.C. 93, 136 S.E.2d 250 (1964). * * * [T]hese cases involved conduct within the purview of the common usage of the term "Peeping Tom." In *State v. Bivins, supra,* the Court interpreted the word "peep" in a manner so as to convey the idea of a "Peeping Tom." The Court said that "to peep" means "to look cautiously or slyly—as if through a crevice—out from chinks and knotholes."

This Court has not expressly defined the word "secretly" as used in the statute. Respondent argues that the word adds nothing to the clarification of the meaning of the statute. In order to pass on his contention, we must resort to the rules of statutory construction set forth above, and to the additional rule that words of a statute are not to be deemed merely redundant if they can reasonably be construed so as to add something to the statute in harmony with its purpose.

In *State v. Banks, supra,* the Court * * * indicated that the word "secretly" as used in G.S. 14–202 conveys the definite idea of spying upon another with the intention of invading her privacy. Hence, giving the language of the statute its meaning as interpreted by this Court, G.S. 14–

b. "Those who skate on thin ice can hardly expect to find a sign which will denote the precise spot where they may fall in." Knuller v. Director of Public Prosecutions [1973] AC 435 (Lord Morris).

202 prohibits the wrongful spying into a room upon a female with the intent of violating the female's legitimate expectation of privacy. This is sufficient to inform a person of ordinary intelligence, with reasonable precision, of those acts the statute intends to prohibit, so that he may know what acts he should avoid in order that he may not bring himself within its provisions.

Defendant cites *Kahalley v. State,* 254 Ala. 482, 48 So.2d 794, to support his contention that G.S. 14–202 is unconstitutionally vague. In *Kahalley,* the Alabama Supreme Court held that the Alabama "Peeping Tom" statute was violative of the Fourteenth Amendment in that it was so vague and uncertain that it fixed no ascertainable standard whereby the public could be governed. The Alabama statute is, however, distinguishable from G.S. 14–202 in that the former statute contains no requirement that the peeping be done "secretly." Thus, this element of wrongful intent required by the North Carolina statute is missing in the Alabama statute.

We hold, therefore, that G.S. 14–202 is sufficiently definite to give an individual fair notice of the conduct prohibited, and to guide a judge in its application and a lawyer in defending one charged with its violation, and that this statute violates neither [the state constitution] nor the Due Process Clause of the Federal Constitution by reason of vagueness and uncertainty.

Respondent next argues that G.S. 14–202 is unconstitutional because it prohibits innocent conduct, and is therefore overly broad. In speaking to a similar contention, Mr. Justice Brennan, for the Supreme Court of the United States, in *Zwickler v. Koota,* 389 U.S. 241, 88 S.Ct. 391, 19 L.Ed.2d 444 (1967), stated:

"[H]is constitutional attack is that the statute, although lacking neither clarity nor precision, is void for 'overbreadth,' that is, that it offends the constitutional principle that 'a governmental purpose to control or prevent activities constitutionally subject to state regulation may not be achieved by means which sweep unnecessarily broadly and thereby invade the area of protected freedoms.' [Citations omitted.]" * * *

* * * [T]he Court indicated that the doctrine of overbreadth has not and will not be invoked when a limiting construction has been or could be placed on the challenged statute.

In *Lemon v. State,* 235 Ga. 74, 218 S.E.2d 818 (1975), the Supreme Court of Georgia upheld the validity of their "Peeping Tom" statute. There, as here, defendant argued that the Georgia statute was overbroad and hence unconstitutional. In answer to this argument, that court stated:

"[T]he statute is not so overbroad as to proscribe legitimate conduct. The statute is sufficiently narrowed by the requirement that the defendant act with wrongful intent, thereby omitting from its scope those persons who have a legitimate purpose upon another's property, or those who only inadvertently glance in the window of another.''

Likewise, our statute, G.S. 14–202, is sufficiently narrowed by judicial interpretation to require that the act condemned must be a spying for the wrongful purpose of invading the privacy of the female occupant of the room, thereby omitting from its scope those persons who have a legitimate purpose upon another's property and those who only inadvertently glance in the window of another. Thus, the statute is not so overbroad as to proscribe legitimate conduct. We hold, therefore, that the statute is not unconstitutional for overbreadth. * * *

NOTES AND QUESTIONS

As drafted, guilty but not as redrafted

1. Suppose that Banks had genuinely believed that the victim wanted to be spied upon. Would he be guilty of violation of Section 14–202, as drafted? Would he be guilty, as the court interpreted the statute?

2. Suppose that Banks had been spying on a *male*, unaware that a female was also in the room. Would he be guilty of violation of Section 14–202, as drafted? Would he be guilty, as the court interpreted the statute?

3. Why are unduly vague statutes unconstitutional? The Supreme Court has explained the requirement of fair notice this way:

fair notice

> Vague laws offend several important values. First, because we assume that man is free to steer between lawful and unlawful conduct, we insist that laws give the person of ordinary intelligence a reasonable opportunity to know what is prohibited, so that he may act accordingly. Vague laws may trap the innocent by not providing fair warning. Second, if arbitrary and discriminatory enforcement is to be prevented, laws must provide explicit standards for those who apply them. A vague law impermissibly delegates basic policy matters to policemen, judges, and juries for resolution on an *ad hoc* and subjective basis, with the attendant dangers of arbitrary and discriminatory application. Third, but related, where a vague statute "abut[s] upon sensitive areas of basic First Amendment freedoms," it "operates to inhibit the exercise of [those] freedoms." Uncertain meanings inevitably lead citizens to "steer far wider of the unlawful zone * * * than if the boundaries of the forbidden areas were clearly marked."

Grayned v. City of Rockford, 408 U.S. 104, 92 S.Ct. 2294, 33 L.Ed.2d 222 (1972).

Is the void-for-vagueness doctrine wise? After all, isn't it true that the clearer and more precise a statute is, the easier it will be for an enterprising wrongdoer to avoid the law by slipping through a gap in the penal code? Therefore, is the vagueness doctrine ultimately counter-utilitarian? For a review of how courts have evaluated vagueness claims, see Robert Batey, *Vagueness and the Construction of Criminal Statutes—Balancing Acts*, 5 Va. J. Soc. Pol'y & L. 1 (1997). As Batey's survey indicates, defendants rarely succeed with their due process vagueness claims.

4. In *Wainwright v. Stone,* cited in *Banks,* the Supreme Court upheld against a void-for-vagueness attack a Florida statute that prohibited, without defining, "the abominable and detestable crime against nature, either with mankind or beast * * *." As *Banks* indicated, however, statutes are not considered in a vacuum, but are judged on the basis of such factors as the common law meaning of terms, statutory history, and (as in *Stone*) any prior judicial interpretations of the state statute. As the Supreme Court emphasized in *Stone,* "[w]hen a state statute has been construed to forbid identifiable conduct so that 'interpretation by [the state court] puts these words in the statute as definitely as if it had been so amended by the legislature,' claims of impermissible vagueness must be judged in that light." Is it *really* reasonable to expect a law-abiding person not only to read the penal code before she acts, but also to research case law "redrafting" the statute?

[handwritten margin note: community's general understanding]

Beyond researching case law, are there other ways in which law-abiding persons might ascertain the meaning of the phrase "abominable and detestable crime against nature"?

5. *Banks* considered the issue of whether the "Peeping Tom" statute was vague or overbroad. What is the difference between these two objections? Do you see any vagueness or overbreadth problems with the following Missouri statutory provision: "Any person required to register as a sexual offender * * * shall be required on October thirty-first of each year to avoid all Halloween-related contact with children." R.S. Mo. 589.426(1) (2008).

6. *Problem.* Sabrina Poirer, a student at Pensacola Christian College, a 5000–student college in Pensacola, Florida, was disciplined for "optical intercourse" (what students sometimes referred to as "making eye babies"). This conduct was not defined. Thomas Bartlett, *A College That's Strictly Different,* Chronicle of Higher Learning, Mar. 24, 2006, at A40.

If you had been a student at the college, would you have known what conduct was barred? Putting aside your thoughts about the wisdom (or lack thereof) of this rule, try to draft a definition of the prohibited conduct.

7. *The lenity doctrine.* The lenity principle provides that if a statute can reasonably be interpreted favorably to the government and just as reasonably be interpreted favorably to the defendant's interests, it should be read in the light more favorable to the individual. In essence, the doctrine serves as a sort of tie-breaker: if all reasonable means of interpreting the statute leave us unable to determine its true meaning, it should be construed strictly *against* the government. The Supreme Court has explained the reason for the lenity doctrine this way:

[handwritten margin note: lenity doctrine]

> This venerable rule not only vindicates the fundamental principle that no citizen should be held accountable for a violation of a statute whose commands are uncertain, or subjected to punishment that is not clearly prescribed. It also places the weight of inertia upon the party that can best induce [the legislature] to speak more clearly and keep courts from making criminal law in [the legislature's] stead.

United States v. Santos, 553 U.S. 507, 128 S.Ct. 2020, 170 L.Ed.2d 912 (2008).

Today, the lenity doctrine often is not applied. For the Model Penal Code approach to the subject, see § 1.02(3).

8. *Selective enforcement.* It is Pittsburgh in 1948 in Pulitzer Prize playwright August Wilson's powerful play, Seven Guitars (1996). Canewell, a harmonica player, explains why he was once jailed:

> I ain't done nothing. Ask Floyd. Singing. That's all I did. I was right down there on Maxwell Street waiting on Floyd. I started fiddling with my harmonica. I said if I'm gonna stand here and play I may as well throw my hat down * * * somebody might put something in it. The police said I was disturbing the peace. * * * Loitering. * * * [D]isrespecting the Law. They rolled all that together and charged me with laziness and give me thirty days. (Act I, Scene 3.)

Later, Floyd, a guitarist, explains what a police officer told him when Floyd was arrested: "I'm arresting you in advance. You gonna do something." (Act I, Scene 4.)

This fictional dialogue gets at an important point: Vague and overbroad statutes not only are of constitutional concern because they fail to give the law-abiding individual adequate notice of prohibited conduct, but also because such laws can be applied in a selective or discriminatory manner by the police and other legal institutions. In particular, ordinances that prohibit "vagrancy" and "loitering" have been attacked on constitutional grounds.

Consider, for example, the following Jacksonville, Florida vagrancy ordinance:

> Rogues and vagabonds, or dissolute persons who go about begging, common gamblers, persons who use juggling or unlawful games or plays, common drunkards, common night walkers, thieves, pilferers or pickpockets, traders in stolen property, lewd, wanton and lascivious persons, keepers of gambling places, common railers and brawlers, persons wandering or strolling around from place to place without any lawful purpose or object, habitual loafers, disorderly persons, persons neglecting all lawful business and habitually spending their time by frequenting houses of ill fame, gaming houses, or places where alcoholic beverages are sold or served, persons able to work but habitually living upon the earnings of their wives or minor children shall be deemed vagrants and, upon conviction in the Municipal Court shall be punished as provided for Class D offenses.

The Supreme Court, in classic language written by Justice William Douglas, declared the ordinance unconstitutional in Papachristou v. City of Jacksonville, 405 U.S. 156, 92 S.Ct. 839, 31 L.Ed.2d 110 (1972). As you will see, the Court worried that such ordinances are overly broad—thus, they potentially punish "innocent" conduct—and, because their vagueness allows for arbitrary and discriminatory law enforcement. Here is a taste of the Court's reasoning:

> The Jacksonville ordinance makes criminal activities which by modern standards are normally innocent. "Nightwalking" is one. * * * We know * * * from experience that sleepless people often walk at night, perhaps hopeful that sleep-inducing relaxation will result. * * *
>
> "[P]ersons able to work but habitually living upon the earnings of their wives or minor children"—like habitually living "without visible

means of support"—might implicate unemployed pillars of the community who have married rich wives.

"[P]ersons able to work but habitually living upon the earnings of their wives or minor children" may also embrace unemployed people out of the labor market, by reason of a recession or disemployed by reason of technological or so-called structural displacements.

Persons "wandering or strolling" from place to place have been extolled by Walt Whitman and Vachel Lindsay. * * * Persons "neglecting all lawful business and habitually spending their time by frequenting * * * places where alcoholic beverages are sold or served" would literally embrace many members of golf clubs and city clubs.

Walkers and strollers and wanderers may be going to or coming from a burglary. Loafers or loiterers may be "casing" a place for a holdup. Letting one's wife support him is an intra-family matter, and normally of no concern to the police. Yet it may, of course, be the setting for numerous crimes.

The difficulty is that these activities are historically part of the amenities of life as we have known them. They are not mentioned in the Constitution or in the Bill of Rights. These unwritten amenities have been in part responsible for giving our people the feeling of independence and self-confidence, the feeling of creativity. These amenities have dignified the right of dissent and have honored the right to be nonconformists and the right to defy submissiveness. They have encouraged lives of high spirits rather than hushed, suffocating silence. * * *

Another aspect of the ordinance's vagueness appears when we focus, not on the lack of notice given a potential offender, but on the effect of the unfettered discretion it places in the hands of the Jacksonville police. * * *

Those generally implicated by the imprecise terms of the ordinance— poor people, nonconformists, dissenters, idlers—may be required to comport themselves according to the lifestyle deemed appropriate by the Jacksonville police and the courts. Where, as here, there are no standards governing the exercise of the discretion granted by the ordinance, the scheme permits and encourages an arbitrary and discriminatory enforcement of the law. It furnishes a convenient tool for "harsh and discriminatory enforcement by local prosecuting officials, against particular groups deemed to merit their displeasure." It results in a regime in which the poor and the unpopular are permitted to "stand on a public sidewalk * * * only at the whim of any police officer." * * *

A presumption that people who might walk or loaf or loiter or stroll or frequent houses where liquor is sold, or who are supported by their wives or who look suspicious to the police are to become future criminals is too precarious for a rule of law.

Papachristou effectively invalidated vagrancy and similar statutes. While the Court took an almost light-hearted view of the subject, cities in more recent times have encountered genuinely serious dangers, such as public "loitering" by gang members intent on causing future violent harm. Cities have encountered difficulties drafting legislation that conforms with constitutional demands. In this regard, consider the next case.

CITY OF CHICAGO v. MORALES

Supreme Court of the United States, 1999.
527 U.S. 41, 119 S.Ct. 1849, 144 L.Ed.2d 67.

JUSTICE STEVENS announced the judgment of the Court and delivered the opinion of the Court with respect to Parts I, II, and V [in which JUSTICES O'CONNOR, KENNEDY, SOUTER, GINSBURG, and BREYER join], and an opinion with respect to Parts III, IV, and VI, in which JUSTICE SOUTER and JUSTICE GINSBURG join.

In 1992, the Chicago City Council enacted the Gang Congregation Ordinance, which prohibits "criminal street gang members" from "loitering" with one another or with other persons in any public place. The question presented is whether the * * * ordinance violates the Due Process Clause of the Fourteenth Amendment to the Federal Constitution.

Due process violated?

I

Before the ordinance was adopted, the city council's Committee on Police and Fire conducted hearings to explore the problems created by the city's street gangs, and more particularly, the consequences of public loitering by gang members. Witnesses included residents of the neighborhoods where gang members are most active, as well as some of the aldermen who represent those areas. Based on that evidence, the council made a series of findings that are included in the text of the ordinance and explain the reasons for its enactment.

The council found that a continuing increase in criminal street gang activity was largely responsible for the city's rising murder rate, as well as an escalation of violent and drug related crimes. It noted that in many neighborhoods throughout the city, "the burgeoning presence of street gang members in public places has intimidated many law abiding citizens." Furthermore, the council stated that gang members "establish control over identifiable areas * * * by loitering in those areas and intimidating others from entering those areas; and * * * members of criminal street gangs avoid arrest by committing no offense punishable under existing laws when they know the police are present * * *." It further found that "loitering in public places by criminal street gang members creates a justifiable fear for the safety of persons and property in the area" and that "aggressive action is necessary to preserve the city's streets and other public places so that the public may use such places without fear." Moreover, the council concluded that the city "has an interest in discouraging all persons from loitering in public places with criminal gang members."

The ordinance creates a criminal offense punishable by a fine of up to $500, imprisonment for not more than six months, and a requirement to perform up to 120 hours of community service. Commission of the offense

penalty

involves four predicates. <u>First</u>, the police officer must reasonably believe that at least one of the two or more persons present in a "public place" is a "criminal street gang member." <u>Second</u>, the persons must be "loitering," which the ordinance defines as "remaining in any one place with no apparent purpose." <u>Third</u>, the officer must then order "all" of the persons to disperse and remove themselves "from the area." <u>Fourth</u>, a person must disobey the officer's order. If any person, whether a gang member or not, disobeys the officer's order, that person is guilty of violating the ordinance.[2] * * *

III * * *

Vagueness may invalidate a criminal law for either of two independent reasons. First, it may fail to provide the kind of notice that will enable ordinary people to understand what conduct it prohibits; second, it may authorize and even encourage arbitrary and discriminatory enforcement. Accordingly, we first consider whether the ordinance provides fair notice to the citizen and then discuss its potential for arbitrary enforcement.

IV

"It is established that a law fails to meet the requirements of the Due Process Clause if it is so vague and standardless that it leaves the public uncertain as to the conduct it prohibits * * *." The * * * term "loiter" may have a common and accepted meaning, but the definition of that term in this ordinance—"to remain in any one place with no apparent purpose" does not. It is difficult to imagine how any citizen of the city of Chicago standing in a public place with a group of people would know if he or she had an "apparent purpose." If she were talking to another person, would she have an apparent purpose? If she were frequently checking her watch

---

2. The ordinance states in pertinent part:

"(a) Whenever a police officer observes a person whom he reasonably believes to be a criminal street gang member loitering in any public place with one or more other persons, he shall order all such persons to disperse and remove themselves from the area. Any person who does not promptly obey such an order is in violation of this section.

"(b) It shall be an affirmative defense to an alleged violation of this section that no person who was observed loitering was in fact a member of a criminal street gang.

"(c) As used in this section:

"(1) 'Loiter' means to remain in any one place with no apparent purpose.

"(2) 'Criminal street gang' means any ongoing organization, association in fact or group of three or more persons, whether formal or informal, having as one of its substantial activities the commission of one or more of the criminal acts enumerated in paragraph (3), and whose members individually or collectively engage in or have engaged in a pattern of criminal gang activity. * * *

"(5) 'Public place' means the public way and any other location open to the public, whether publicly or privately owned. * * *

"(e) Any person who violates this Section is subject to a fine of not less than $100 and not more than $500 for each offense, or imprisonment for not more than six months, or both.

"In addition to or instead of the above penalties, any person who violates this section may be required to perform up to 120 hours of community service pursuant to section 1–4–120 of this Code."

and looking expectantly down the street, would she have an apparent purpose?

Since the city cannot conceivably have meant to criminalize each instance a citizen stands in public with a gang member, the vagueness that dooms this ordinance is not the product of uncertainty about the normal meaning of "loitering," but rather about what loitering is covered by the ordinance and what is not. * * *[24]

The city's principal response to this concern about adequate notice is that loiterers are not subject to sanction until after they have failed to comply with an officer's order to disperse. * * * We find this response unpersuasive for at least two reasons.

First, the purpose of the fair notice requirement is to enable the ordinary citizen to conform his or her conduct to the law. * * * Although it is true that a loiterer is not subject to criminal sanctions unless he or she disobeys a dispersal order, the loitering is the conduct that the ordinance is designed to prohibit. If the loitering is in fact harmless and innocent, the dispersal order itself is an unjustified impairment of liberty. * * * Because an officer may issue an order only after prohibited conduct has already occurred, it cannot provide the kind of advance notice that will protect the putative loiterer from being ordered to disperse. Such an order cannot retroactively give adequate warning of the boundary between the permissible and the impermissible applications of the law.

Second, the terms of the dispersal order compound the inadequacy of the notice afforded by the ordinance. It provides that the officer "shall order all such persons to disperse and remove themselves from the area." This vague phrasing raises a host of questions. After such an order issues, how long must the loiterers remain apart? How far must they move? If each loiterer walks around the block and they meet again at the same location, are they subject to arrest or merely to being ordered to disperse again? * * *

* * * This ordinance is therefore vague "not in the sense that it requires a person to conform his conduct to an imprecise but comprehensible normative standard, but rather in the sense that no standard of conduct is specified at all."

The broad sweep of the ordinance also violates " 'the requirement that a legislature establish minimal guidelines to govern law enforcement.' " There are no such guidelines in the ordinance. In any public place in the city of Chicago, persons who stand or sit in the company of a gang member may be ordered to disperse unless their purpose is apparent.

---

24. One of the trial courts that invalidated the ordinance gave the following illustration: "Suppose a group of gang members were playing basketball in the park, while waiting for a drug delivery. Their apparent purpose is that they are in the park to play ball. The actual purpose is that they are waiting for drugs. Under this definition of loitering, a group of people innocently sitting in a park discussing their futures would be arrested, while the 'basketball players' awaiting a drug delivery would be left alone."

The mandatory language in the enactment directs the police to issue an order without first making any inquiry about their possible purposes. It matters not whether the reason that a gang member and his father, for example, might loiter near Wrigley Field is to rob an unsuspecting fan or just to get a glimpse of Sammy Sosa leaving the ballpark; in either event, if their purpose is not apparent to a nearby police officer, she may—indeed, she "shall"—order them to disperse. * * *

Nevertheless, the city * * * [argues] that the text of the ordinance limits the officer's discretion in three ways. First, it does not permit the officer to issue a dispersal order to anyone who is moving along or who has an apparent purpose. Second, it does not permit an arrest if individuals obey a dispersal order. Third, no order can issue unless the officer reasonably believes that one of the loiterers is a member of a criminal street gang.

* * * [W]e find each of these limitations insufficient. That the ordinance does not apply to people who are moving * * * does not even address the question of how much discretion the police enjoy in deciding which stationary persons to disperse under the ordinance. Similarly, that the ordinance does not permit an arrest until after a dispersal order has been disobeyed does not provide any guidance to the officer deciding whether such an order should issue. The "no apparent purpose" standard for making that decision is inherently subjective because its application depends on whether some purpose is "apparent" to the officer on the scene.

Presumably an officer would have discretion to treat some purposes—perhaps a purpose to engage in idle conversation or simply to enjoy a cool breeze on a warm evening—as too frivolous to be apparent if he suspected a different ulterior motive. Moreover, an officer conscious of the city council's reasons for enacting the ordinance might well ignore its text and issue a dispersal order, even though an illicit purpose is actually apparent.

It is true, as the city argues, that the requirement that the officer reasonably believe that a group of loiterers contains a gang member does place a limit on the authority to order dispersal. That limitation would no doubt be sufficient if the ordinance only applied to loitering that had an apparently harmful purpose or effect, or possibly if it only applied to loitering by persons reasonably believed to be criminal gang members. But this ordinance, for reasons that are not explained in the findings of the city council, requires no harmful purpose and applies to non-gang members as well as suspected gang members. It applies to everyone in the city who may remain in one place with one suspected gang member as long as their purpose is not apparent to an officer observing them. Friends, relatives, teachers, counselors, or even total strangers might unwittingly engage in forbidden loitering if they happen to engage in idle conversation with a gang member.

Ironically, the definition of loitering in the Chicago ordinance not only extends its scope to encompass harmless conduct, but also has the perverse consequence of excluding from its coverage much of the intimidating conduct that motivated its enactment. As the city council's findings demonstrate, the most harmful gang loitering is motivated either by an apparent purpose to publicize the gang's dominance of certain territory, thereby intimidating nonmembers, or by an equally apparent purpose to conceal ongoing commerce in illegal drugs. * * * [W]e must assume that the ordinance means what it says and that it has no application to loiterers whose purpose is apparent. The relative importance of its application to harmless loitering is magnified by its inapplicability to loitering that has an obviously threatening or illicit purpose. * * *

VI

In our judgment, * * * the ordinance does not provide sufficiently specific limits on the enforcement discretion of the police "to meet constitutional standards for definiteness and clarity." We recognize the serious and difficult problems testified to by the citizens of Chicago that led to the enactment of this ordinance. "We are mindful that the preservation of liberty depends in part on the maintenance of social order." However, in this instance the city has enacted an ordinance that affords too much discretion to the police and too little notice to citizens who wish to use the public streets. * * *

JUSTICE O'CONNOR, with whom JUSTICE BREYER joins, concurring in part and concurring in the judgment. * * *   *Concurrence*

It is important to courts and legislatures alike that we characterize more clearly the narrow scope of today's holding. As the ordinance comes to this Court, it is unconstitutionally vague. Nevertheless, there remain open to Chicago reasonable alternatives to combat the very real threat posed by gang intimidation and violence. For example, the Court properly and expressly distinguishes the ordinance from laws that require loiterers to have a "harmful purpose," from laws that target only gang members, and from laws that incorporate limits on the area and manner in which the laws may be enforced. In addition, the ordinance here is unlike a law that "directly prohibits" the " 'presence of a large collection of obviously brazen, insistent, and lawless gang members and hangers-on on the public ways,' " that " 'intimidates residents.' " * * *

In my view, the gang loitering ordinance could have been construed [by the Illinois courts] more narrowly. The term "loiter" might possibly be construed in a more limited fashion to mean "to remain in any one place with no apparent purpose other than to establish control over identifiable areas, to intimidate others from entering those areas, or to conceal illegal activities." Such a definition would be consistent with the Chicago City Council's findings and would avoid the vagueness problems of the ordinance * * *. As noted above, so would limitations that restricted the ordinance's criminal penalties to gang members or that more carefully delineated the circumstances in which those penalties would apply to nongang members. * * *

JUSTICE SCALIA, dissenting.

The citizens of Chicago were once free to drive about the city at whatever speed they wished. At some point Chicagoans (or perhaps Illinoisans) decided this would not do, and imposed prophylactic speed limits designed to assure safe operation by the average (or perhaps even subaverage) driver with the average (or perhaps even subaverage) vehicle. This infringed upon the "freedom" of all citizens, but was not unconstitutional.

Similarly, the citizens of Chicago were once free to stand around and gawk at the scene of an accident. At some point Chicagoans discovered that this obstructed traffic and caused more accidents. They did not make the practice unlawful, but they did authorize police officers to order the crowd to disperse, and imposed penalties for refusal to obey such an order. Again, this prophylactic measure infringed upon the "freedom" of all citizens, but was not unconstitutional.

Until the ordinance that is before us today was adopted, the citizens of Chicago were free to stand about in public places with no apparent purpose—to engage, that is, in conduct that appeared to be loitering. In recent years, however, the city has been afflicted with criminal street gangs. As reflected in the record before us, these gangs congregated in public places to deal in drugs, and to terrorize the neighborhoods by demonstrating control over their "turf." Many residents of the inner city felt that they were prisoners in their own homes. Once again, Chicagoans decided that to eliminate the problem it was worth restricting some of the freedom that they once enjoyed. The means they took was similar to the second, and more mild, example given above rather than the first: Loitering was not made unlawful, but when a group of people occupied a public place without an apparent purpose and in the company of a known gang member, police officers were authorized to order them to disperse, and the failure to obey such an order was made unlawful. The minor limitation upon the free state of nature that this prophylactic arrangement imposed upon all Chicagoans seemed to them (and it seems to me) a small price to pay for liberation of their streets. * * *

V * * *

The fact is that the present ordinance is entirely clear in its application, cannot be violated except with full knowledge and intent, and vests no more discretion in the police than innumerable other measures authorizing police orders to preserve the public peace and safety. As suggested by their tortured analyses, and by their suggested solutions that bear no relation to the identified constitutional problem, the majority's real quarrel with the Chicago Ordinance is simply that it permits (or indeed requires) too much harmless conduct by innocent citizens to be proscribed. * * *

But in our democratic system, how much harmless conduct to proscribe is not a judgment to be made by the courts. So long as constitutionally guaranteed rights are not affected, and so long as the proscription has a rational basis, *all sorts* of perfectly harmless activity by millions of perfectly innocent people can be forbidden—riding a motorcycle without a safety helmet, for example, starting a campfire in a national forest, or selling a safe and effective drug not yet approved by the FDA. All of these acts are entirely innocent and harmless in themselves, but because of the *risk* of harm that they entail, the freedom to engage in them has been abridged. The citizens of Chicago have decided that depriving themselves of the freedom to "hang out" with a gang member is necessary to eliminate pervasive gang crime and intimidation—and that the elimination of the one is worth the deprivation of the other. This Court has no business second-guessing either the degree of necessity or the fairness of the trade.

NOTES AND QUESTIONS

1. Whose view of the ordinance do you find most persuasive? Justice Scalia writes that "[a]ll of these acts [prohibited by the ordinance] are entirely innocent and harmless in themselves, but because of the *risk* of harm that they entail, the freedom to engage in them has been abridged." Should lawmakers be permitted to punish people for "entirely innocent and harmless" conduct because of the risk that *non*-innocent and *non*-harmless conduct might ensue? We will return to this question in Chapter 10.

B. STATUTORY INTERPRETATION

Courts and practicing lawyers spend considerable time interpreting criminal statutes. Look again at *Banks*, p. 105, and note the various presumptions and rules of, and sources for, statutory interpretation. Issues of interpretation arise throughout the study and practice of criminal law and, therefore, throughout this casebook. The following case is an example of the United States Supreme Court's efforts to define a single word—"carries"—in a federal criminal statute.

MUSCARELLO v. UNITED STATES

Supreme Court of the United States, 1998.
524 U.S. 125, 118 S.Ct. 1911, 141 L.Ed.2d 111.

JUSTICE BREYER delivered the opinion of the Court.

A provision in the firearms chapter of the federal criminal code imposes a 5–year mandatory prison term upon a person who "uses or carries a firearm" "during and in relation to" a "drug trafficking crime." 18 U.S.C. § 924(c)(1). The question before us is whether the phrase "carries a firearm" is limited to the carrying of firearms on the person. We hold that it is not so limited. Rather, it also applies to a person who knowingly possesses and conveys firearms in a vehicle, including in the locked glove compartment or trunk of a car, which the person accompanies. * * *

A

We begin with the statute's language. The parties vigorously contest the ordinary English meaning of the phrase "carries a firearm." Because they essentially agree that Congress intended the phrase to convey its ordinary, and not some special legal, meaning, and because they argue the linguistic point at length, we too have looked into the matter in more than usual depth. Although the word "carry" has many different meanings, only two are relevant here. When one uses the word in the first, or primary, meaning, one can, as a matter of ordinary English, carry firearms in a wagon, car, truck, or other vehicle that one accompanies. When one uses the word in a different, rather special, way, to mean, for example, "bearing" or (in slang) "packing" (as in "packing a gun"), the matter is less clear. But, for reasons we shall set out below, we believe Congress intended to use the word in its primary sense and not in this latter, special way.

Consider first the word's primary meaning. The Oxford English Dictionary gives as its *first* definition "convey, originally by cart or wagon, hence in any vehicle, by ship, on horseback, etc."; see also Webster's Third New International Dictionary 343 (1986) (*first* definition: "move while supporting (*as in a vehicle* or in one's hands or arms)"); Random House Dictionary of the English Language Unabridged 319 (2d ed. 1987) (*first* definition: "to take or support from one place to another; convey; transport").

The origin of the word "carries" explains why the first, or basic, meaning of the word "carry" includes conveyance in a vehicle. See Barnhart Dictionary of Etymology 146 (1988) (tracing the word from Latin "carum", which means "car" or "cart"); 2 Oxford English Dictionary (tracing the word from Old French "carier" and the late Latin "carricare," which meant to "convey in a car") * * *.

The greatest of writers have used the word with this meaning. See, *e.g.*, The King James Bible, 2 Kings 9:28 ("[H]is servants carried him in a chariot to Jerusalem"); *id.*, Isaiah 30:6 ("[T]hey will carry their riches upon the shoulders of young asses"). Robinson Crusoe says, "[w]ith my boat, I carry'd away every Thing". D. Defoe, Robinson Crusoe 174 (J. Crowley ed. 1972). And the owners of Queequeg's ship, Melville writes, "had lent him a [wheelbarrow], in which to carry his heavy chest to his boarding-house." H. Melville, Moby Dick 43 (U. Chicago 1952). * * *

These examples do not speak directly about carrying guns. But there is nothing linguistically special about the fact that weapons, rather than drugs, are being carried. Robinson Crusoe might have carried a gun in his boat; Queequeg might have borrowed a wheelbarrow in which to carry not a chest, but a harpoon. And, to make certain that there is no special ordinary English restriction (unmentioned in dictionaries) upon the use of "carry" in respect to guns, we have surveyed modern press usage, albeit crudely, by searching computerized newspaper databases—both the New York Times data base in Lexis/Nexis, and the "US News" data base in

Westlaw. We looked for sentences in which the words "carry," "vehicle," and "weapon" (or variations thereof) all appear. We found thousands of such sentences, and random sampling suggests that many, perhaps more than one-third, are sentences used to convey the meaning at issue here, *i.e.*, the carrying of guns in a car. * * *

Now consider a different, somewhat special meaning of the word "carry"—a meaning upon which the linguistic arguments of petitioners and the dissent must rest. The Oxford English Dictionary's *twenty-sixth* definition of "carry" is "bear, wear, hold up, or sustain, as one moves about; habitually to bear about with one." Webster's defines "carry" as "to move while supporting," not just "in a vehicle, but also in one's hands or arms." * * *

These special definitions, however, do not purport to *limit* the "carrying of arms" to the circumstances they describe. No one doubts that one who bears arms on his person "carries a weapon." But to say that is not to deny that one may *also* "carry a weapon" tied to the saddle of a horse or placed in a bag in a car.

Nor is there any linguistic reason to think that Congress intended to limit the word "carries" in the statute to any of these special definitions. * * *

We recognize, as the dissent emphasizes, that the word "carry" has other meanings as well. But those other meanings, (*e.g.*, "carry all he knew," "carries no colours"), are not relevant here. * ** * The relevant linguistic facts are that the word "carry" in its ordinary sense includes carrying in a car and that the word, used in its ordinary sense, keeps the same meaning whether one carries a gun, a suitcase, or a banana. * * *

B

We now explore more deeply the purely legal question of whether Congress intended to use the word "carry" in its ordinary sense, or whether it intended to limit the scope of the phrase to instances in which a gun is carried "on the person." We conclude that neither the statute's basic purpose nor its legislative history support circumscribing the scope of the word "carry" by applying an "on the person" limitation.

This Court has described the statute's basic purpose broadly, as an effort to combat the "dangerous combination" of "drugs and guns." And the provision's chief legislative sponsor has said that the provision seeks "to persuade the man who is tempted to commit a Federal felony to leave his gun at home."

From the perspective of any such purpose (persuading a criminal "to leave his gun at home"), what sense would it make for this statute to penalize one who walks with a gun in a bag to the site of a drug sale, but to ignore a similar individual who * * * travels to a similar site with a similar gun in a similar bag, but instead of walking, drives there with the gun in his car? How persuasive is a punishment that is without effect until a drug dealer who has brought his gun to a sale (indeed has it available for use) actually takes it from the trunk (or unlocks the glove compartment) of his car? It is difficult to say that, considered as a class, those who prepare, say, to sell drugs by placing guns in their cars are less dangerous, or less deserving of punishment, than those who carry handguns on their person. * * *

C

We are not convinced by petitioners' remaining arguments to the contrary. First, they say that our definition of carry makes it the equivalent of "transport." Yet, Congress elsewhere in related statutes used the word "transport" deliberately to signify a different, and broader, statutory coverage. The immediately preceding statutory subsection, for example, imposes a different set of penalties on one who, with an intent to commit a crime, "ships, transports, or receives a firearm" in interstate commerce. 18 U.S.C. § 924(b). Moreover, § 926A specifically "entitle[s]" a person "not otherwise prohibited * * * from transporting, shipping, or receiving a firearm" to "transport a firearm * * * from any place where he may lawfully possess and carry it" to "any other place" where he may do so. Why, petitioners ask, would Congress have used the word transport, or used both "carry" and "transport" in the same provision, if it had intended to obliterate the distinction between the two?

The short answer is that our definition does not equate "carry" and "transport." "Carry" implies personal agency and some degree of possession, whereas "transport" does not have such a limited connotation and, in addition, implies the movement of goods in bulk over great distances. If Smith, for example, calls a parcel delivery service, which sends a truck to Smith's house to pick up Smith's package and take it to Los Angeles, one might say that Smith has shipped the package and the parcel delivery service has transported the package. But only the truck driver has "carried" the package in the sense of "carry" that we believe Congress intended. Therefore, "transport' is a broader category that includes "carry" but also encompasses other activity. * * *

Second, petitioners point out that, in *Bailey v. United States,* 516 U.S. 137, 116 S.Ct. 501, 133 L.Ed.2d 472 (1995), we considered the related phrase "uses * * * a firearm" found in the same statutory provision now before us. See 18 U.S.C. § 924(c)(1) ("uses or carries a firearm"). We construed the term "use" narrowly, limiting its application to the "active employment" of a firearm. Petitioners argue that it would be anomalous to construe broadly the word "carries," its statutory next-door neighbor.

In *Bailey,* however, we limited "use" of a firearm to "active employment" in part because we assumed "that Congress * * * intended each term to have a particular, nonsuperfluous meaning." A broader interpretation of "use," we said, would have swallowed up the term "carry." But "carry" as we interpret that word does not swallow up the term "use." "Use" retains the same independent meaning we found for it in *Bailey,* where we provided examples involving the displaying or the bartering of a gun. "Carry" also retains an independent meaning, for, under *Bailey,* carrying a gun in a car does not necessarily involve the gun's "active employment." More importantly, having construed "use" narrowly in *Bailey,* we cannot also construe "carry" narrowly without undercutting the statute's basic objective. For the narrow interpretation would remove the act of carrying a gun in a car entirely from the statute's reach, leaving a gap in coverage that we do not believe Congress intended.

Third, petitioners say that our reading of the statute would extend its coverage to passengers on buses, trains, or ships, who have placed a firearm, say, in checked luggage. To extend this statute so far, they argue, is unfair, going well beyond what Congress likely would have thought possible.* * *

In our view, this argument does not take adequate account of other limiting words in the statute—words that make the statute applicable only where a defendant "carries" a gun *both* "during *and* in relation to" a drug crime. * * *

Once one takes account of the words "during" and "in relation to," it no longer seems beyond Congress' likely intent, or otherwise unfair, to interpret the statute as we have done. * * *

At the same time, the narrow interpretation creates its own anomalies. The statute, for example, defines "firearm" to include a "bomb," "grenade," "rocket having a propellant charge of more than four ounces," or "missile having an explosive or incendiary charge of more than one-quarter ounce," where such device is "explosive," "incendiary," or delivers "poison gas." 18 U.S.C. § 921(a)(4)(A). On petitioners' reading, the "carry" provision would not apply to instances where drug lords, engaged in a major transaction, took with them "firearms" such as these, which most likely could not be carried on the person.

Fourth, petitioners argue that we should construe the word "carry" to mean "immediately accessible." * * * That interpretation, however, is difficult to square with the statute's language, for one "carries" a gun in the glove compartment whether or not that glove compartment is locked. Nothing in the statute's history suggests that Congress intended that limitation. * * *

Finally, petitioners and the dissent invoke the "rule of lenity." The simple existence of some statutory ambiguity, however, is not sufficient to warrant application of that rule, for most statutes are ambiguous to some degree. " 'The rule of lenity applies only if, "after seizing everything from which aid can be derived," ' * * * we can make "no more than a guess as to what Congress intended." ' " To invoke the rule, we must conclude that there is a " ' "grievous ambiguity or uncertainty" ' " in the statute." Certainly, our decision today is based on much more than "a guess as to what Congress intended," and there is no "grievous ambiguity" here. The problem of statutory interpretation in these cases is indeed no different from that in many of the criminal cases that confront us. Yet, this Court has never held that the rule of lenity automatically permits a defendant to win. * * *

For these reasons, we conclude that petitioners' conduct falls within the scope of the phrase "carries a firearm." * * *

JUSTICE GINSBURG, with whom THE CHIEF JUSTICE, JUSTICE SCALIA, and JUSTICE SOUTER join, dissenting. * * *

Without doubt, "carries" is a word of many meanings, definable to mean or include carting about in a vehicle. But that encompassing definition is not a ubiquitously necessary one. Nor, in my judgment, is it a proper construction of "carries" as the term appears in § 924(c)(1). In line with *Bailey* [*v. United States*] and the principle of lenity the Court has long followed, I would confine "carries a firearm," for § 924(c)(1) purposes, to the undoubted meaning of that expression in the relevant context. I would read the words to indicate not merely keeping arms on one's premises or in one's vehicle, but bearing them in such manner as to be ready for use as a weapon.

I * * *

Unlike the Court, I do not think dictionaries, surveys of press reports, or the Bible[4] tell us, dispositively, what "carries" means embedded in § 924(c)(1). On definitions, "carry" in legal formulations could mean, *inter alia,* transport, possess, have in stock, prolong (carry over), be infectious, or wear or bear on one's person. At issue here is not "carries" at large but "carries a firearm." The Court's computer search of newspapers is revealing in this light. Carrying guns in a car showed up as the meaning "perhaps more than one-third" of the time. One is left to wonder what meaning showed up some two-thirds of the time. * * *

On lessons from literature, a scan of Bartlett's and other quotation collections shows how highly selective the Court's choices are. If "[t]he greatest of writers" have used "carry" to mean convey or transport in a vehicle, so have they used the hydra-headed word to mean, *inter alia,* carry in one's hand, arms, head, heart, or soul, sans vehicle. Consider, among countless examples:

"[H]e shall gather the lambs with his arm, and carry them in his bosom." The King James Bible, Isaiah 40:11.

"And still they gaz'd, and still the wonder grew,
That one small head could carry all he knew."

O. Goldsmith, The Deserted Village, ll. 215–216, in The Poetical Works of Oliver Goldsmith 30 (A. Dobson ed. 1949).

"There's a Legion that never was 'listed,
That carries no colours or crest."

---

4. The translator of the Good Book, it appears, bore responsibility for determining whether the servants of Ahaziah "carried" his corpse to Jerusalem. Compare [the majority's quote] with, *e.g.,* The New English Bible, 2 Kings 9:28 (His servants *conveyed* his body to Jerusalem.); Saint Joseph Edition of the New American Bible ("His servants *brought* him in a chariot to Jerusalem."); Tanakh: The Holy Scriptures ("His servants *conveyed* him in a chariot to Jerusalem."); see also *id.,* Isaiah 30:6 ("They *convey* their wealth on the backs of asses."); The New Jerusalem Bible ("[T]hey *bear* their riches on donkeys' backs.") (emphasis added in all quotations).

R. Kipling, The Lost Legion, st. 1, in Rudyard Kipling's Verse, 1885–1918, p. 222 (1920). * * *[6]

These and the Court's lexicological sources demonstrate vividly that "carry" is a word commonly used to convey various messages. Such references, given their variety, are not reliable indicators of what Congress meant, in § 924(c)(1), by "carries a firearm." * * *

[The dissent argued further that it "is reasonable to comprehend Congress as having provided mandatory minimum [sentences, as required by Section 924(c)(1)] for the most life-jeopardizing gun-connection cases (guns in or at the defendant's hand when committing an offense) * * *."]

II

Section 924(c)(1), as the foregoing discussion details, is not decisively clear one way or another. The sharp division in the Court on the proper reading of the measure confirms, "[a]t the very least, * * * that the issue is subject to some doubt. Under these circumstances, we adhere to the familiar rule that, 'where there is ambiguity in a criminal statute, doubts are resolved in favor of the defendant.'" * * *

NOTES AND QUESTIONS

1. We are not done with 18 USC § 924(c)(1). You will remember that the statute sets out special punishment of a person who "uses or carries" a firearm during and in relation to a drug trafficking crime. Let's focus now on the word "uses." The Court above noted that *Bailey v. United States* interpreted "uses" narrowly to require "active employment" of a firearm.

Now, consider these two scenarios: Scenario 1: *S* sells his gun for narcotics. Smith v. United States, 508 U.S. 223, 113 S.Ct. 2050, 124 L.Ed.2d 138 (1993). Scenario 2: *W* receives a firearm in exchange for narcotics. Watson v. United States, 552 U.S. 74, 128 S.Ct. 579, 169 L.Ed.2d 472 (2007). In view of *Bailey* and *Muscarello*, do you believe either (or even both) of these cases involve "use" of a firearm? How would you develop your answer?

2. Kilmon v. State, 394 Md. 168, 905 A.2d 306 (2006):

Notwithstanding occasional flights of fancy that may test the proposition, the law necessarily and correctly presumes that Legislatures act reasonably, knowingly, and in pursuit of sensible public policy. Where there is a legitimate issue of interpretation, therefore, courts are required, to the extent possible, to avoid construing a statute in a manner that would

---

6. Popular films and television productions provide corroborative illustrations. * * * [I]n the television series "M*A*S*H," Hawkeye Pierce (played by Alan Alda) presciently proclaims: "I will not carry a gun. * * * I'll carry your books, I'll carry a torch, I'll carry a tune, I'll carry on, carry over, carry forward, Cary Grant, cash and carry, carry me back to Old Virginia, I'll even 'hari-kari' if you show me how, but I will not carry a gun!" See http:// www.geocities.com/Hollywood/ 8915/mashquotes.html.

produce farfetched, absurd, or illogical results which would not likely have been intended by the enacting body. Stated simply and in the affirmative, courts must attempt to construe statutes in a common sense manner.

Based on this standard, how did the United States Supreme Court do?

CHAPTER 4

ACTUS REUS

■ ■ ■

INTRODUCTORY COMMENT: DEFINING *"ACTUS REUS"*

In general, a crime contains two components: an *"actus reus"* and the *"mens rea."* The *"actus reus"* is the physical or external part of the crime; the *"mens rea"* is the mental or internal ingredient.

The term *"actus reus"* has no universally accepted definition. Courts and criminal lawyers use the term in various ways. Consider a hypothetical statutory offense of first-degree murder, defined as "killing another person by means of explosive device." Assume the following simple facts: *A* throws a hand grenade into *B*'s house, killing *B*. What is the *actus reus*—the physical component—of this offense? Some might say that the *actus reus* was *A*'s conduct (throwing the hand grenade into the house). Others would say that the *actus reus* was not the conduct, but was the result of *B*'s death. But, the most common definition of the term would include *both* the conduct *and* the harmful result:

> [A]*ctus reus* is to be interpreted as the comprehensive notion of act, harm, and its connecting link, causation, with *actus* expressing the voluntary physical movement in the sense of conduct and *reus* expressing the fact that this conduct results in a certain proscribed harm, i.e., that it "causes" an injury to the legal interest protected in that crime. Albin Eser, *The Principle of "Harm" in the Concept of Crime: A Comparative Analysis of the Criminally Protected Legal Interests*, 4 Duq.L.Rev. 345, 386 (1965).

Murder is a so-called "result crime": that is, its ultimate purpose is to prevent or punish a harmful result, namely, the death of another human being. Some offenses, however, are defined in terms of conduct, such as the crime of driving an automobile while intoxicated. No ultimate result—no death or injury to person or property—is required to be guilty of this offense. As you will see in Part C. of this chapter, however, the term "harm" may be defined broadly enough that lawyers can say, at least metaphorically, that every crime—including so-called conduct crimes—involves harm to others. Therefore, the Eser definition of *actus reus* provided above can apply to all offenses.

A. VOLUNTARY ACT

MARTIN v. STATE

Alabama Court of Appeals, 1944.
31 Ala.App. 334, 17 So.2d 427.

SIMPSON, JUDGE.

Appellant was convicted of being drunk on a public highway, and appeals. Officers of the law arrested him at his home and took him onto the highway, where he allegedly committed the proscribed acts, viz., manifested a drunken condition by using loud and profane language.

The pertinent provisions of our statute are: "Any person who, while intoxicated or drunk, appears in any public place where one or more persons are present, * * * and manifests a drunken condition by boisterous or indecent conduct, or loud and profane discourse, shall, on conviction, be fined", etc. Code 1940, Title 14, Section 120.

Under the plain terms of this statute, a voluntary appearance is presupposed. The rule has been declared, and we think it sound, that an accusation of drunkenness in a designated public place cannot be established by proof that the accused, while in an intoxicated condition, was involuntarily and forcibly carried to that place by the arresting officer.

Conviction of appellant was contrary to this announced principle and, in our view, erroneous. * * *

Reversed and rendered.

NOTES AND QUESTIONS

1. Federal law provides that it is offense for an alien to nonconsensually enter or "at any time [be] found in the United States." 8 U.S.C. § 1326(a) (2012). If an alien is kidnaped or brought to the United States in a catatonic state, is he guilty of the offense? *Should* he be? See United States v. Montague, 75 F.Supp.2d 670 (S.D.Tex.1999); United States v. Hernandez–Hernandez, 519 F.3d 1236 (10th Cir. 2008).

2. *Punishing thoughts, and the saga of "pre-cogs."* The often-stated "rule" is that the criminal law does not punish mere thoughts.[a] This has not always been, and is not everywhere, so. Long ago in England, "compassing the King's death"—contriving or even imagining his death—constituted treason. In 1995, a person was arrested in Kenya for "imagining the death" of its President. Donatella Lorch, *Is Kenya Sliding Back Toward Repression?*, New York Times, Oct. 1, 1995, at 3.

Is there *really* something wrong with punishing persons for their thoughts? Would it *really* be objectionable, for example, for Congress to make it a crime "to intend to assassinate the President of the United States"? Punishment for mere thoughts is condemned on various grounds:

---

a. "Keep violence in the mind where it belongs." Brian Aldiss, Barefoot in the Head (1969).

Rooted in skepticism about the ability either to know what passes through the minds of men or to predict whether antisocial behavior will follow from antisocial thoughts, the act requirement serves a number of closely-related objectives: it seeks to assure that the evil intent of the man branded a criminal has been expressed in a manner signifying harm to society; that there is no longer any substantial likelihood that he will be deterred by the threat of sanction; and that there has been an identifiable occurrence so that multiple prosecution and punishment may be minimized. Abraham S. Goldstein, *Conspiracy to Defraud the United States,* 68 Yale L.J. 405, 405–06 (1959).

Do some or all of these objections to punishing thoughts withstand scrutiny? Suppose that a person charged with "intending to assassinate the President" freely confesses to the crime? Would you still want to bar punishment? Why, or why not?

Suppose technology someday makes it possible to accurately read a person's thoughts. This may not be a far-fetched assumption. Two psychologists recently used electrodes to measure the brain waves of twenty-nine college students who had been instructed to plan a terrorist bombing in Houston, Texas or a vacation in another city—whichever they chose. You will need to read the study to understand the process the scientists used (it would take up too much space here), but watching for a particular brainwave (P300), the psychologists accurately identified ten out of twelve terrorists in the group, and correctly matched twenty of thirty terrorist-related details. See John B. Meixner & J. Peter Rosenfeld, *A Mock Terrorism Application of the P300–based Concealed Information Test*, 48 Psychophysiology 149 (2011).

Or, take it one step further back. Suppose we could predict future events, even before criminal thoughts are formed. Consider the 2002 movie, *Minority Report*. Set in the year 2054, the Washington D.C. police "Pre–Crime Unit" utilizes three psychic beings ("pre-cogs") who have visions of murders well before they are committed. These visions are used to justify arresting and convicting persons for pre-crime. Assuming that the pre-cogs' visions are reliable, is there any reason why a society should not use the criminal law in this manner? If "proof beyond a reasonable doubt" is sufficient to justify punishment after a crime has occurred, why isn't it enough to justify punishment for pre-crime? See Saul Smilansky, *Determinism and Prepunishment: The Radical Nature of Compatibilism*, 67 Analysis 347 (2007) (discussing the issue). Can you provide a utilitarian or retributive justification for the requirement of conduct?

3. *Voluntary versus involuntary actions.* Influenced by Model Penal Code § 2.01(1), many modern criminal codes expressly provide that, issues of "omission" aside (a matter taken up in Section B. infra), a person is not guilty of an offense unless his conduct includes a voluntary act. This provision not only excludes punishment for mere thoughts, but it also bars liability for purely involuntary conduct. Do you find the following justification for the latter principle persuasive?

It is fundamental that a civilized society does not punish for thoughts alone. Beyond this, the law cannot hope to deter involuntary movement * * *; the sense of personal security would be undermined in a society where such movement * * * could lead to formal social condemnation of the sort that a conviction necessarily entails. Persons whose involuntary movements threaten harm to others may present a public health or safety problem, calling for therapy or even for custodial commitment; they do not present a problem of correction.

American Law Institute, Model Penal Code and Commentaries, Comment to § 2.01 at 214–15 (1985).

4. What constitutes a "voluntary act"? In reading the remaining materials in this subsection, consider Michael S. Moore, *Responsibility and the Unconscious,* 53 S.Cal.L.Rev. 1563, 1567–68 (1980):

> In law, no less than in morals, the idea of human action lies at the heart of ascriptions of responsibility. One is responsible only for those consequences that are caused by his actions, and not for those things in which his body, but not his acting self, is causally implicated. One is responsible if he hits another with a stick, but is not responsible if his arm-with-stick is caused by the wind to strike another. On what basis does one distinguish those bodily motions that are actions from those that are not? * * *
>
> What one seeks is an answer to Wittgenstein's famous question, "[W]hat is left over if I subtract the fact that my arm goes up from the fact that I raise my arm?" Seemingly "something" is left over, as is shown by the relationship between the following statements:
>
> > (1) *X* raised his arm.
> >
> > (2) *X*'s arm went up.
>
> (1) implies (2), but (2) does not imply (1). *X*'s arm may go up because, for example, the wind blows it, someone grabs it, or a reflex occurs. Hence (1) and (2) are not equivalent statements. To say that *X* raised his arm is to say *more* than merely that certain motions of his body took place.

STATE v. UTTER

Court of Appeals of Washington, 1971.
4 Wash.App. 137, 479 P.2d 946.

Farris, Judge.

Claude Gilbert Utter was charged * * * with the crime of murder in the second degree. He was convicted by a jury of the crime of manslaughter. He appeals from that conviction.

Appellant and the decedent, his son, were living together at the time of the latter's death. The son was seen to enter his father's apartment and shortly after was heard to say, "Dad, don't." Shortly thereafter he was seen stumbling in the hallway of the apartment building where he collapsed, having been stabbed in the chest. He stated, "Dad stabbed me" and died before he could be moved or questioned further.

Mr. Utter entered the armed services in December of 1942 and was honorably discharged in October of 1946. He was a combat infantryman. As a result of his service, he was awarded a 60 per cent disability pension.

Appellant testified that on the date of his son's death he began drinking during the morning hours. He was at the liquor store at 9 a.m. and purchased a quart of Thunderbird wine and a quart of port wine and drank the bottle of port wine with the exception of two drinks. Mr. Utter went for more liquor around noon. At that time he purchased 2 quarts of whiskey and 4 quarts of wine. Upon his return from the liquor store, he and another resident of the apartment "sat around drinking whiskey out of water glasses." Appellant remembers drinking with his friend and the next thing he remembers was being in jail subsequent to the death of his son. He has no recollection of any intervening events.

Appellant introduced evidence on "conditioned response" during the trial. Conditioned response was defined by Dr. Jarvis, a psychiatrist, as "an act or a pattern of activity occurring so rapidly, so uniformly as to be automatic in response to a certain stimulus." Mr. Utter testified that as a result of his jungle warfare training and experiences in World War II, he had on two occasions in the 1950's reacted violently towards people approaching him unexpectedly from the rear.

The trial court ruled that conditioned response was not a defense in Washington and instructed the jury to disregard all evidence introduced on this subject. * * *

The major issue presented on appeal is whether it was error for the trial court to instruct the jury to disregard the evidence on conditioned response. The trial court held that the defendant was attempting to present a defense of irresistible impulse—a theory of criminal insanity that has consistently been rejected in this state. In so holding, the trial court considered the defense to be one of mental incapacity. This was not so.

There are two components of every crime. One is objective—the actus reus; the other subjective—the mens rea. The actus reus is the culpable act itself, the mens rea is the criminal intent with which one [commits the actus reus]. However, the mens rea does not encompass the entire mental process of one accused of a crime. There is a certain minimal mental element required in order to establish the actus reus itself. This is the element of volition.

In the present case, the appellant was charged with second degree murder and found guilty of manslaughter. The actus reus of both is the same—homicide. Thus, in order to establish either, the fact of homicide must first be established.

Appellant contends that his evidence was presented for the purpose of determining whether in fact a homicide had been committed. He argues that his evidence, if believed, establishes that no "act" was committed within the definition of homicide (RCW 9.48.010):

> Homicide is the killing of a human being by the act, procurement or omission of another and is either (1) murder, (2) manslaughter, (3) excusable homicide or (4) justifiable homicide.

What is the meaning of the word "act" as used in this statute?

> It is sometimes said that no crime has been committed unless the harmful result was brought about by a "voluntary act." Analysis of such a statement will disclose, however, that as so used the phrase "voluntary act" means no more than the mere word "act." An act must be a willed movement or the omission of a possible and legally-required performance. This is essential to the *actus reus* rather than to the mens rea. "A spasm is not an act."

R. Perkins, Criminal Law 660 (1957).

> [A]n "act" involves an exercise of the will. It signifies something done voluntarily. * * * We find these statements abundantly sustained by the text-writers and decisions of our courts.

Heiman v. Pan American Life Ins. Co., 183 La. 1045, 1061, 165 So. 195 (1935).

Thus, to invert the statement of Perkins, the word "act" technically means a "voluntary act."

It is the appellant's contention that any of the alleged "acts" he committed were not those which involved mental processes, but rather were learned physical reactions to external stimuli which operated automatically on his autonomic nervous system. Although the theory sought to be presented by appellant is similar to one of mental incapacity, it is nevertheless distinct from that concept. * * *

Appellant contends that a person in an automatistic[b] or unconscious state is incapable of committing a culpable act—in this case, a homicidal act.

The question is not one of mental incapacity. "Criminal responsibility must be judged at the level of the conscious." State v. Sikora, 44 N.J. 453, 470, 210 A.2d 193 (1965).

There is authority to support the proposition of the appellant. * * *

> If a person is in fact unconscious at the time he commits an act which would otherwise be criminal, he is not responsible therefor.

> The absence of consciousness not only precludes the existence of any specific mental state, but also excludes the possibility of a voluntary act without which there can be no criminal liability.

R. Anderson, 1 Wharton's Criminal Law and Procedure § 50 (1957). * * *

---

b. McClain v. State, 678 N.E.2d 104 (Ind.1997):

Automatism has been defined as "the existence in any person of behaviour of which he is unaware and over which he has no conscious control." A seminal British case concisely described automatism as "connoting the state of a person who, though capable of action, is not conscious of what he is doing." Automatism manifests itself in a range of conduct, including somnambulism (sleepwalking), hypnotic states, fugues, metabolic disorders, and epilepsy and other convulsions or reflexes.

Automatism

In State v. Strasburg, 60 Wash. 106, 110 P. 1020 (1910) the Washington Supreme Court * * * made an extensive review of basic tenets of criminal law and noted in part as follows:

"All of the several pleas and excuses which protect the committer of a forbidden act from the punishment which is otherwise annexed thereto may be reduced to this single consideration, the want or defect of *will*. An involuntary act, as it has no claim to merit, so neither can it induce any guilt; the concurrence of the will, when it has its choice either to do or to avoid the fact in question, being the only thing that renders human actions either praiseworthy or culpable. * * *

"Without the consent of the *will*, human actions cannot be considered as culpable; nor where there is no will to commit an offense is there any just reason why a party should incur the penalties of a law made for the punishment of crimes and offenses."

An "act" committed while one is unconscious is in reality no act at all. It is merely a physical event or occurrence for which there can be no criminal liability. However, unconsciousness does not, in all cases, provide a defense to a crime. When the state of unconsciousness is voluntarily induced through the use and consumption of alcohol or drugs, then that state of unconsciousness does not attain the stature of a complete defense. Thus, in a case such as the present one where there is evidence that the accused has consumed alcohol or drugs, the trial court should give a cautionary instruction with respect to voluntarily induced unconsciousness.

The issue of whether or not the appellant was in an unconscious or automatistic state at the time he allegedly committed the criminal acts charged is a question of fact. Appellant's theory of the case should have been presented to the jury if there was substantial evidence in the record to support it.

It is the function and province of the jury to weigh evidence and determine credibility of witnesses and decide disputed questions of fact. However, a court should not submit to the jury an issue of fact unless there is substantial evidence in the record to support it.

We find that the evidence presented was insufficient to present the issue of defendant's unconscious or automatistic state at the time of the act to the jury. There is no evidence, circumstantial or otherwise from which the jury could determine or reasonably infer what happened in the room at the time of the stabbing; the jury could only speculate on the existence of the triggering stimulus. * * *

NOTES AND QUESTIONS

1. What is the Wittgenstein/Moore "something" (p. 130, Note 4 supra) that distinguishes voluntary acts from involuntary ones? How does the Model Penal Code define "voluntary act"? Look at §§ 1.13 and 2.01.

2. Why did the court conclude that there was insufficient evidence here to raise the issue of unconsciousness or automatism? And, why does the court say that, even if the issue had been raised, the jury should have received a cautionary instruction "with respect to voluntarily induced unconsciousness."

3. *Automatism*. McClain v. State, 678 N.E.2d 104 (Ind.1997):

> In the states that have addressed the issue, it is well established that automatism can be asserted as a defense to a crime. * * * [T]he debate in these states has focused on the manner in which evidence of automatism can be presented. These jurisdictions are split between recognizing insanity and automatism as separate defenses and classifying automatism as a species of the insanity defense.

As a practical matter, why would a defendant prefer to seek acquittal on the basis of the "defense" of a lack of a voluntary act than on the ground of insanity? See State v. Deer, 158 Wash.App. 854, 244 P.3d 965 (2010).

4. *Different meanings of "involuntary."* You should be alert to the fact that the term "involuntary" has multiple meanings in the criminal law. For example, if Jill points a loaded gun at Jack's head and threatens to kill him immediately unless he helps her rob a bank, Jack's decision to accede to her threat is "involuntary" in the sense that his actions were coerced, but are his actions "involuntary" in the sense described in *Utter?*

5. *"Voluntary act" versus "mens rea."* It is important to distinguish between the *actus reus* and *mens rea* components of a crime. As *Utter* shows, although the doctrines of "voluntary act" and *"mens rea"* are related, they should not be confused. As developed more fully in the next chapter, the term *"mens rea"* signifies the actor's state of mind regarding the *social harm* of the offense, whereas the element of *voluntariness* applies to the *act* that caused the social harm. In this regard, keep this example in mind: Carl, standing on a target range, aims his gun at the target and pulls the trigger, at which instant Dorothy unforeseeably walks in front of the target, is struck by a bullet from Carl's gun, and dies as a result. On these facts, Carl lacks any blameworthy state of mind (*mens rea*) regarding Dorothy's death (the social harm of "criminal homicide"), i.e., Carl did not intentionally, recklessly, or negligently kill Dorothy. Nonetheless, Carl's act of pulling the trigger was voluntary.

Even when an offense does not contain a *mens rea* component, as occasionally is the case, a voluntary act is still required for conviction. See State v. Deer, 158 Wash.App. 854, 244 P.3d 965 (2010); but see Model Penal Code § 2.05.

6. *Problem*. In People v. Decina, 2 N.Y.2d 133, 157 N.Y.S.2d 558, 138 N.E.2d 799 (1956), the State of New York alleged in an indictment that *D*, who knew he was subject to epileptic seizures, suffered an attack while driving his car and, during the seizure, struck and killed four children. *D* was charged with "operating a vehicle in a reckless or culpably negligent manner, causing the death of four persons." The court denied *D*'s motion to quash (throw out) the indictment. Isn't conduct during an epileptic seizure "involuntary"? If so, was *Decina* wrongly decided? Would the prosecution have been permitted under Model Penal Code § 2.01(1)?

7. *Possession as an act.* Penal codes typically prohibit possession of specified substances or objects, e.g., heroin, burglar's tools, or obscene literature. But, it is possible for a person to come into possession of such matters involuntarily—even in the absence of any conduct at all—such as when *A* plants drugs in *B*'s purse in order to avoid detection during an airport security search. In light of the voluntary act requirement, how would the Model Penal Code deal with a prosecution of *B* for possession of the drugs?

Unwitting possession

Look at Model Penal Code Section 2.01(4) for the answer. As a separate matter, why might one scholar have observed that, *"[t]aken literally*, this provision is nonsense." Douglas Husak, *Rethinking the Act Requirement*, 28 Cardozo L. Rev. 2437, 2440 (2007) (emphasis added).

8. *Sleepwalking.* In Smith v. State, 284 Ga. 33, 663 S.E.2d 155 (2008), in a murder prosecution, *S* sought to introduce expert testimony that he shot his wife "while asleep or in a state of confusional arousal due to [a physiological sleep] disorder." On what legal theory would this evidence, if believed, assist *S* in his defense? Look at the Model Penal Code for a possible answer.

Sleepwalking

Such cases, although hardly common, are not as farfetched as one might think. In 2007, for example, a soldier had sex with a fifteen-year-old girl, but was acquitted of rape on the ground that he suffered from a rare condition ("sexsomnia") and, therefore, had intercourse with her while he was asleep. Luke Salkeld, *"Sexsomniac" RAF Man Sobs as he is Cleared of Raping a Girl in his Sleep*, Daily Mail (London), Aug. 7, 2007, at 27. See also *Set "Dream Killer" Free*, The Mirror, Nov. 19, 2009, at p.23 (a devoted husband who strangled his wife during a nightmare was acquitted of murder).

Sexsomnia

9. *What about "semi-voluntary"?* One issue that should be in the back—and, sometimes, in the forefront—of your mind as you study criminal law is whether the law that has developed over the centuries is consistent with modern scientific knowledge about human behavior. To the extent that it is not, should the law change to conform with scientific understanding, even though we realize that what we "know" today may again prove false in the future? In this regard, consider Deborah W. Denno, *Crime and Consciousness: Science and Involuntary Acts*, 87 Minn. L. Rev. 269, 271–72 (2002):

> Criminal law * * * presumes that most human behavior is voluntary and that individuals are consciously aware of their acts. On the other hand, it also presumes that individuals who act unconsciously * * * are not "acting" at all. * * *
>
> In contrast to these legal "dichotomies" (voluntary/involuntary, conscious/unconscious), most neuroscientific research has revealed a far more fluid and dynamic relationship between conscious and unconscious processes. * * * [H]uman behavior is not always conscious or voluntary in the "either/or" way that the voluntary act requirement presumes. Rather, consciousness manifests itself in degrees that represent varying levels of awareness.

In her *Minnesota Law Review* article, Professor Denno surveys modern scientific research on human consciousness, which she asserts has proven that the either/or dichotomy of the law—a "familiar way to view the world in the

1900s," id. at 388, based as it was on then-dominant Freudian psychoanalytic conceptions of consciousness—is false. She argues, therefore, that the law is both too harsh (treating some people as fully responsible for "voluntary" acts that are, in fact, only partially voluntary) and too lenient (requiring acquittal of persons for their "involuntary" conduct when they actually committed semi-voluntary acts).

If brain science *does* prove what Denno claims, how should the criminal law deal with people who commit "semi-voluntary" acts? Could it be that criminal law doctrine should *not* change? For another perspective, see Stephen J. Morse, *New Neuroscience, Old Problems: Legal Implications of Brain Science*, 6 Cerebrum 81 (2004).

B. OMISSIONS ("NEGATIVE ACTS")

1. GENERAL PRINCIPLES

PEOPLE v. BEARDSLEY

Supreme Court of Michigan, 1907.
150 Mich. 206, 113 N.W. 1128.

McALVAY, C.J. Respondent was convicted of manslaughter * * * and was sentenced to the state prison * * * for a minimum term of one year and a maximum term not to exceed five years.

He was a married man living at Pontiac, and at the time the facts herein narrated occurred, he was working as a bartender and clerk at the Columbia Hotel. He lived with his wife in Pontiac, occupying two rooms on the ground floor of a house. * * * His wife being temporarily absent from the city, respondent arranged with a woman named Blanche Burns, who at the time was working at another hotel, to go to his apartments with him. He had been acquainted with her for some time. They knew each other's habits and character. They had drunk liquor together, and had on two occasions been in Detroit and spent the night together in houses of assignation. On the evening of Saturday, March 18, 1905, he met her at the place where she worked, and they went together to his place of residence. They at once began to drink and continued to drink steadily, and remained together, day and night, from that time until the afternoon of the Monday following, except when respondent went to his work on Sunday afternoon. There was liquor at these rooms, and when it was all used they were served with bottles of whiskey and beer by a young man who worked at the Columbia Hotel * * *. He was the only person who saw them in the house during the time they were there together. Respondent gave orders for liquor by telephone. On Monday afternoon, about 1 o'clock, the young man went to the house to see if anything was wanted. At this time he heard respondent say they must fix up the rooms, and the woman must not be found there by his wife, who was likely to return at any time. During this visit to the house the woman sent the young man to a drug store to purchase, with money she gave him, camphor and morphine tablets. He procured both articles. There were six grains of morphine in quarter-grain tablets. She concealed the morphine from respondent's notice, and was discovered putting something into her mouth by him and the young man as they were returning from the other room after taking a drink of beer. She in fact was taking morphine. Respondent struck the box from her hand. Some of the tablets fell on the floor, and of these, respondent crushed several with his foot. She picked up and swallowed two of them, and the young man put two of them in the spittoon. Altogether it is probable she took from three to four grains of morphine. The young man went away soon after this. Respondent called him by telephone about an hour later, and after he came to the house requested him to take the woman into the room in the basement which was occupied by a Mr. Skoba. She was in a stupor, and did not rouse when spoken to. Respondent was too intoxicated to be of any assistance and the young man proceeded to take her downstairs. While doing this, Skoba arrived, and together they put her in his room on the bed. Respondent requested Skoba to look after her, and let her out the back way when she waked up. Between 9 and 10 o'clock in the evening, Skoba became alarmed at her condition. He at once called the city marshal and a doctor. An examination by them disclosed that she was dead.

* * * In the brief of the prosecutor, his position is stated as follows: "It is the theory of the prosecution that the facts and circumstances attending the death of Blanche Burns in the house of respondent were such as to lay upon him a duty to care for her, and the duty to take steps for her protection, the failure to take which, was sufficient to constitute such an omission as would render him legally responsible for her death. * * * There is no claim on the part of the people that the respondent was in any way an active agent in bringing about the death of Blanche Burns, but simply that he owed her a duty which he failed to perform, and that in consequence of such failure on his part she came to her death." Upon this theory a conviction was asked and secured.

The law recognizes that under some circumstances the omission of a duty owed by one individual to another, where such omission results in the death of the one to whom the duty is owing, will make the other chargeable with manslaughter. This rule of law is always based upon the proposition that the duty neglected must be a legal duty, and not a mere moral obligation. It must be a duty imposed by law or by contract, and the omission to perform the duty must be the immediate and direct cause of death. * * * One authority has briefly and correctly stated the rule, which the prosecution claims should be applied to the case at bar, as follows: "If a person who sustains to another the legal relation of protector, as husband to wife, parent to child, master to seaman, etc., knowing such person to be in peril of life, willfully or negligently fails to make such reasonable and proper efforts to rescue him as he might have done without jeopardizing his own life or the lives of others, he is guilty of manslaughter at least, if by reason of his omission of duty the dependent person dies." "So one who from domestic relationship, public duty, voluntary choice, or otherwise, has the custody and care of a human being, helpless either from imprisonment, infancy, sickness, age, imbecility, or other incapacity of mind or body, is bound to execute the charge with proper diligence and will be held guilty of manslaughter, if by culpable negligence he lets the helpless creature die." * * *

* * * Seeking for a proper determination of the case at bar by the application of the legal principles involved, we must eliminate from the case all consideration of mere moral obligation, and discover whether respondent was under a legal duty towards Blanche Burns at the time of her death, knowing her to be in peril of her life, which required him to make all reasonable and proper effort to save her, the omission to perform which duty would make him responsible for her death. This is the important and determining question in this case. * * * The record in this case discloses that the deceased was a woman past 30 years of age. She had been twice married. She was accustomed to visiting saloons and to the use of intoxicants. She previously had made assignations with this man in Detroit at least twice. There is no evidence or claim from this record that any duress, fraud, or deceit had been practiced upon her. On the contrary it appears that she went upon this carouse with respondent voluntarily and so continued to remain with him. Her entire conduct indicates that she had ample experience in such affairs.

It is urged by the prosecutor that the respondent "stood towards this woman for the time being in the place of her natural guardian and protector, and as such owed her a clear legal duty which he completely failed to perform." The cases * * * establish that no such legal duty is created based upon a mere moral obligation. The fact that this woman was in his house created no such legal duty as exists in law and is due from a husband towards his wife, as seems to be intimated by the prosecutor's brief. Such an inference would be very repugnant to our moral sense. Respondent had assumed either in fact or by implication no care or control over his companion. Had this been a case where two men under like circumstances had voluntarily gone on a debauch together and one had attempted suicide, no one would claim that this doctrine of legal duty could be invoked to hold the other criminally responsible for omitting to make effort to rescue his companion. How can the fact that in this case one of the parties was a woman change the principle of law applicable to it? * * * We find no more apt words to apply to this case than those used by Mr. Justice Field, in United States v. Knowles [4 Sawy. (U.S.) 517, Fed.Cas. No. 15,540]: "In the absence of such obligations, it is undoubtedly the moral duty of every person to extend to others assistance when in danger, * * * and, if such efforts should be omitted by any one when they could be made without imperiling his own life, he would by his conduct draw upon himself the just censure and reproach of good men; but this is the only punishment to which he would be subjected by society." * * *

The conviction is set aside, and respondent is ordered discharged.

NOTES AND QUESTIONS

1. Graham Hughes, *Criminal Omissions,* 67 Yale L.J. 590, 624 (1958):

To be temperate about such a decision is difficult. In its savage proclamation that the wages of sin is death, it ignores any impulse of charity and compassion. It proclaims a morality which is smug, ignorant and vindictive. In a civilized society, a man who finds himself with a helplessly ill person who has no other source of aid should be under a duty to summon help, whether the person is his wife, his mistress, a prostitute or a Chief Justice. The *Beardsley* decision deserves emphatic repudiation by the jurisdiction which was responsible.

Do you agree?

If Beardsley were held legally responsible for Blanche Burns's death, would he also have to be held accountable for failing to come to the aid of a *male* drinking partner who attempted to commit suicide?

2. Jones v. United States, 308 F.2d 307, 310 (D.C.Cir.1962):

There are at least four situations in which the failure to act may constitute breach of a legal duty. One can be held criminally liable: first, where a statute imposes a duty * * *; second, where one stands in a certain status relationship to another; third, where one has assumed a contractual duty to care for another; and fourth, where one has voluntarily assumed the care of another and so secluded the helpless person as to prevent others from rendering aid.

Failure to act may also constitute a breach of duty in a fifth situation: when a person creates a risk of harm to another. For example, if an automobile driver by negligence (or, perhaps, even innocently) strikes and injures a pedestrian, the driver has a legal duty to make sure that the victim receives medical care. If the driver fails to assist, he may be held criminally responsible for the additional harm resulting from his omission, such as the pedestrian's death.

3. *Problem.* Robert Hogans stole Pam Bandy's car, kidnaped Bandy, and placed her in the car trunk. For five days, he drove the car while Bandy pounded on the inside of the trunk and begged for help. During some of this time, Terressa Nix, Hogans's 25–year–old girlfriend, was a passenger in the stolen car, and once was in it alone for a few minutes. Nix did nothing to help Bandy, although she heard the cries for help. Bandy eventually died from drinking window washer fluid to quench her thirst. Nix was prosecuted for murder, based on her failure to act. (Hogans, too, was charged in the death.) Her lawyer moved for directed verdict of acquittal on the ground that Nix had no legal duty to aid the victim. Should the motion have been granted? People v. Nix, 208 Mich.App. 648, 528 N.W.2d 208 (1995) (decided on other grounds).

4. No discussion of the omission rule seems complete without mention of the infamous 1964 murder of Katherine ("Kitty") Genovese by Winston Moseley. The facts surrounding her death are now in some dispute. See Jim Rasenberger, *Kitty, 40 Years Later,* N.Y. Times, Feb. 8, 2004, Sect. 14, at 1. But, as the facts were first reported and repeated in contemporary books, e.g.,

Abraham M. Rosenthal, Thirty–Eight Witnesses (1964), Genovese was stabbed in the back by Moseley as she got out of her car in front of her apartment building in Queens, New York. She cried out for help ("Oh, my God, he stabbed me! Please help me! Please help me!"), a cry that was heard and ignored by as many as thirty-eight of her apartment neighbors. Despite Kitty's cries, her assailant stabbed her again, fled, and then returned and finally killed her when nobody came to her aid.

Why did none of her neighbors come to her aid, if only by calling the police? The usual answer is that her neighbors were guilty of urban indifference to the needs of others. But, this may not have been so. Intrigued by the Genovese case, social scientists conducted various studies of bystander behavior in emergency circumstances. In the first such examination, New York University undergraduates (the "subjects") were invited by the experimenters to participate in what the subjects were led to believe would be discussions of personal problems confronting college students. The subjects were told that they would be part of either two-person, three-person, or six-person discussion groups, in which each discussant would be placed alone in a cubicle where he or she could talk to the other discussion group member(s) by intercom, to avoid embarrassment. The experimenters then played a tape, in which it sounded as if another student (really, an experimenter feigning illness) was suffering a life-threatening epileptic seizure in another cubicle.

The results of the study, replicated in subsequent experiments, suggest the existence of "bystander effect." That is, in 81% of the cases in which a subject believed that he or she was the only person who could hear the victim suffering the attack, the seizure was reported in a timely manner. Only 31% of the subjects acted promptly, however, when they thought that four other persons had heard the attack. Bibb Latane & John M. Darley, The Unresponsive Bystander: Why Doesn't He Help? 90–96 (1970). As Professor Leo Katz has put it, "[i]f Kitty Genovese failed to receive help, it was because, being part of a large group, nobody felt responsible. For Kitty Genovese, then, there was no safety in numbers." Leo Katz, Bad Acts and Guilty Minds 150 (1987).

5. In May, 1997, David Cash, a high school senior, walked into a Las Vegas casino restroom and discovered his close friend, Jeremy Strohmeyer, struggling with a seven-year-old girl in a bathroom stall. Cash left without saying anything. Strohmeyer, who had dragged the girl into the restroom, raped and murdered the girl after Cash left. According to Cash, who was interviewed later:

> I have done nothing wrong. It's a very tragic event, okay? But the simple fact remains I do not know this little girl. I do not know starving children in Panama. I do not know people that die of disease in Egypt. The only person I knew in this event was Jeremy Strohmeyer, and I know as his best friend that he had potential. I'm sad that I lost a best friend. I'm not going to lose sleep over somebody else's problem.

Las Vegas police stated that Cash violated no state law by failing to stop the crime or report it to a nearby casino security guard. Lynda Gorov, *Outrage Follows Cold Reply to Killing*, Boston Globe, Aug. 7, 1998, at A1.

Why does the common law permit people like Cash callously to permit harm to come to others, even when they could prevent or mitigate the harm

Why no liability?

at no significant physical risk to themselves? Various justifications are offered for the common law rule. First, "non-doings" (omissions) are inherently more ambiguous than wrongdoings (acts). It is harder to determine the motives—and, thus, the culpability—of an omitter. If Alice puts a gun at Betty's head and voluntarily pulls the trigger, it is reasonable to infer that she intended to kill (or, at least, seriously injure) Betty. But, when Carole fails to help David, who is drowning in a pool, there are plausible exculpatory explanations for Carole's omission, e.g., she did not appreciate the seriousness of David's predicament or she was paralyzed with fear.

Second, difficult line-drawing problems arise in omission cases. For example, in the Kitty Genovese case (Note 4 supra), if criminal responsibility for omissions were appropriate, who besides the assailant would be responsible for Genovese's death? All thirty-eight persons who awakened to her cries for help? Only those who realized the seriousness of her plight? Only those whose inaction was the result of moral indifference?

Third, well-meaning bystanders often make matters worse by intervening in ongoing events. Therefore, to the extent that the criminal law is capable of compelling action, a rule requiring assistance might cause more harm than good in many cases.

Finally, there is an issue of freedom:

> A penal law that *prohibits* a person from doing X (e.g., unjustifiably killing another person) permits that individual to do anything other than X * * *. In contrast, a law that *requires* a person to do Y (e.g., to help a bystander) bars that person from doing anything other than Y. * * *

> What is the significance of this point? It is that the United States is a country that highly values individual liberty * * *. * * * [I]n a society that generally values personal autonomy, we need to be exceptionally cautious about [creating legal duties to act] that *compel* us to benefit others, rather than passing laws that simply require us not to harm others. The issue here, after all, is whether *criminal* law (as distinguished from tort law and religious, educational, and family institutions) should try to compel Good Samaritanism.

Joshua Dressler, *Some Brief Thoughts (Mostly Negative) About "Bad Samaritan" Laws*, 40 Santa Clara L. Rev. 971, 986–987 (2000). Traditionally, American criminal law sets only minimalist goals. It seeks to prevent people from causing positive harm to others; it does not compel individuals, upon the threat of criminal punishment, to be virtuous.

Are you persuaded by any of these arguments? For more on this subject, see Symposium, 40 Santa Clara L. Rev. 957–1103 (2000).

6. *Misprision of a felony*. Absent special circumstances, a person has no legal duty to inform the police of another person's plans to commit a criminal offense. Although the matter is not without doubt, the English common law apparently provided that failure to disclose information about a previously committed felony to proper authorities constituted the misdemeanor offense of misprision of a felony. Rollin M. Perkins & Ronald N. Boyce, Criminal Law 572–77 (3d ed. 1982).

In the United States, mere nondisclosure of knowledge of a crime committed by another does not constitute misprision. Typical of statutes in this country, the federal misprision statute requires proof of active concealment of a known felony, and not simple nondisclosure to proper authorities. 18 U.S.C. § 4 (2012). See generally Gabriel D. M. Ciociolo, *Misprision of Felony and its Progeny*, 41 Brandeis L.J. 697 (2002).

2. DISTINGUISHING ACTS FROM OMISSIONS

BARBER v. SUPERIOR COURT

California Court of Appeal, Second District, 1983.
147 Cal.App.3d 1006, 195 Cal.Rptr. 484.

COMPTON, ASSOCIATE JUSTICE.

In these * * * proceedings we consider petitions for writs of prohibition * * * filed by two medical doctors who are charged in a complaint, now pending before a magistrate in the Los Angeles judicial district, with the crimes of murder and conspiracy to commit murder * * *.

At the close of a lengthy preliminary hearing the magistrate ordered the complaint dismissed. On motion of the People, * * * the superior court ordered the magistrate to reinstate the complaint. * * *

Deceased Clarence Herbert underwent surgery for closure of an ileostomy. Petitioner Robert Nejdl, M.D., was Mr. Herbert's surgeon and petitioner Neil Barber, M.D. was his attending internist. Shortly after the successful completion of the surgery, and while in the recovery room, Mr. Herbert suffered a cardio-respiratory arrest. He was revived by a team of physicians and nurses and immediately placed on life support equipment.

Within the following three days, it was determined that Mr. Herbert was in a deeply comatose state from which he was not likely to recover. Tests and examinations performed by several physicians, including petitioners herein, each specializing in relevant fields of medicine indicated that Mr. Herbert had suffered severe brain damage, leaving him in a vegetative state, which was likely to be permanent.

At that time petitioners informed Mr. Herbert's family of their opinion as to his condition and chances for recovery. While there is some dispute as to the precise terminology used by the doctors, it is clear that they communicated to the family that the prognosis for recovery was extremely poor. At that point, the family convened and drafted a written request to the hospital personnel stating that they wanted "all machines taken off that are sustaining life" (sic). As a result, petitioners, either directly or as a result of orders given by them, caused the respirator and other life-sustaining equipment to be removed. Mr. Herbert continued to breathe without the equipment but showed no signs of improvement. * * *

After two more days had elapsed, petitioners, after consulting with the family, ordered removal of the intravenous tubes which provided hydration and nourishment. From that point until his death, Mr. Herbert received nursing care which preserved his dignity and provided a clean and hygienic environment.

The precise issue for determination by this court is whether the evidence presented before the magistrate was sufficient to support his determination that petitioners should not be held to answer to the charges of murder and conspiracy to commit murder. * * *

Murder is "the *unlawful* killing of a human being, * * * with malice aforethought." (Pen.Code, § 187, emphasis added.) Malice may be express or implied. It is express when there is an intent *unlawfully* to take any life. It is implied when the circumstances show an abandoned and malignant heart. (Pen.Code, § 188.) * * *

The use of the term "unlawful" in defining a criminal homicide is generally to distinguish a criminal homicide from those homicides which society has determined to be "justifiable" or "excusable." Euthanasia, of course, is neither justifiable nor excusable in California. * * *

Obviously the [legal doctrines relating to criminal homicide] evolved and were codified at a time well prior to the development of the modern medical technology which is involved here, which technology has caused our society to rethink its concepts of what constitutes "life" and "death."

This gap between the statutory law and recent medical developments has resulted in the instant prosecution and its attendant legal dispute. That dispute in order to be resolved within the framework of existing criminal law must be narrowed to a determination of whether petitioners' conduct was unlawful. * * *

Historically, death has been defined in terms of cessation of heart and respiratory function. Health and Safety Code section 7180(a)(2)[1] now provides for an alternative definition in terms of irreversible cessation of all brain function.

This is a clear recognition of the fact that the real seat of "life" is brain function rather than mere metabolic processes which result from respiration and circulation.

Of course it is conceded by all that at the time petitioners terminated further treatment, Mr. Herbert was not "dead" by either statutory or historical standards since there was still some minimal brain activity. If Mr. Herbert had in fact been "brain dead," this prosecution could not have been instituted because one cannot be charged with killing another person who is already dead.

---

1. Health and Safety Code section 7180 provides:

"(a) An individual who has sustained either (1) irreversible cessation of circulatory and respiratory functions, or (2) irreversible cessation of all functions of the entire brain, including the brain stem, is dead. A determination of death must be made in accordance with accepted medical standards. * * *." * * *

We deal here with the physician's responsibility in a case of a patient who, though not "brain dead," faces an indefinite vegetative existence without any of the higher cognitive brain functions. * * *

As a predicate to our analysis of whether the petitioners' conduct amounted to an "unlawful killing," we conclude that the cessation of "heroic" life support measures is not an affirmative act but rather a withdrawal or omission of further treatment.

Even though these life support devices are, to a degree, "self-propelled," each pulsation of the respirator or each drop of fluid introduced into the patient's body by intravenous feeding devices is comparable to a manually administered injection or item of medication. Hence "disconnecting" of the mechanical devices is comparable to withholding the manually administered injection or medication.

Further we view the use of an intravenous administration of nourishment and fluid, under the circumstances, as being the same as the use of the respirator or other form of life support equipment.

The prosecution would have us draw a distinction between the use of mechanical breathing devices such as respirators and mechanical feeding devices such as intravenous tubes. The distinction urged seems to be based more on the emotional symbolism of providing food and water to those incapable of providing for themselves rather than on any rational difference in cases such as the one at bench.

* * * Medical procedures to provide nutrition and hydration are more similar to other medical procedures than to typical human ways of providing nutrition and hydration. Their benefits and burdens ought to be evaluated in the same manner as any other medical procedure.

The authority cited by the People for the holding that a murder charge may be supported by the failure to feed an infant is easily distinguishable. The parent in that case had a clear duty to feed an otherwise healthy child. As we will discuss, *infra*, the duty of a physician under the circumstances of the case at bench is markedly different.

In the final analysis, since we view petitioners' conduct as that of omission rather than affirmative action, the resolution of this case turns on whether petitioners had a duty to continue to provide life sustaining treatment.

There is no criminal liability for failure to act unless there is a legal duty to act. Thus the critical issue becomes one of determining the duties owed by a physician to a patient who has been reliably diagnosed as in a comatose state from which any meaningful recovery of cognitive brain function is exceedingly unlikely. * * *

In examining this issue we must keep in mind that the life-sustaining technology involved in this case is not traditional treatment in that it is not being used to directly cure or even address the pathological condition. It merely sustains biological functions in order to gain time to permit other processes to address the pathology. * * *

A physician has no duty to continue treatment, once it has proved to be ineffective. Although there may be a duty to provide life-sustaining machinery in the *immediate* aftermath of a cardio-respiratory arrest, there is no duty to continue its use once it has become futile in the opinion of qualified medical personnel. * * *

Of course, the difficult determinations that must be made under these principles is the point at which further treatment will be of no reasonable benefit to the patient, who should have the power to make that decision and who should have the authority to direct termination of treatment.

No precise guidelines as to when or how these decisions should be made can be provided by this court since this determination is essentially a medical one to be made at a time and on the basis of facts which will be unique to each case. * * *

Several authorities have discussed the issue of which life-sustaining procedures must be used and for how long their use must be maintained in terms of "ordinary" and "extraordinary" means of treatment. The use of these terms begs the question. A more rational approach involves the determination of whether the proposed treatment is proportionate or disproportionate in terms of the benefits to be gained versus the burdens caused.

Under this approach, proportionate treatment is that which, in the view of the patient, has at least a reasonable chance of providing benefits to the patient, which benefits outweigh the burdens attendant to the treatment. Thus, even if a proposed course of treatment might be extremely painful or intrusive, it would still be proportionate treatment if the prognosis was for complete cure or significant improvement in the patient's condition. On the other hand, a treatment course which is only minimally painful or intrusive may nonetheless be considered disproportionate to the potential benefits if the prognosis is virtually hopeless for any significant improvement in condition. * * *

Of course the patient's interests and desires are the key ingredients of the decision making process. * * *

When the patient, however, is incapable of deciding for himself, because of his medical condition or for other reasons, there is no clear authority on the issue of who and under what procedure is to make the final decision. * * *

Under the circumstances of this case, the wife was the proper person to act as a surrogate for the patient with the authority to decide issues regarding further treatment, and would have so qualified had judicial approval been sought. There is no evidence that there was any disagreement among the wife and children. Nor was there any evidence that they were motivated in their decision by anything other than love and concern for the dignity of their husband and father.

Furthermore, in the absence of legislative guidance, we find no legal requirement that prior judicial approval is necessary before any decision to withdraw treatment can be made. * * *

In summary we conclude that the petitioners' omission to continue treatment under the circumstances, though intentional and with knowledge that the patient would die, was not an unlawful failure to perform a legal duty. In view of our decision on that issue, it becomes unnecessary to deal with the further issue of whether petitioners' conduct was in fact the proximate cause of Mr. Herbert's ultimate death.

* * * The superior court erred in determining that as a matter of law the evidence required the magistrate to hold petitioners to answer [to the charges of murder and conspiracy]. * * *

NOTES AND QUESTIONS

1. Arthur Leavens, *A Causation Approach to Criminal Omissions,* 76 Cal.L.Rev. 547, 586–87 (1988):

> Since the patient in *Barber,* even in his comatose state, was by California law alive and in no imminent danger of death when the doctors cut off his nutrition and hydration, it is difficult to avoid concluding that the doctors caused his death. Given that euthanasia is not legally justified in California, such intentional conduct seems unavoidably to constitute criminal homicide.

2. In 2000, California enacted "The Health Care Decisions Act," a complex sets of provisions that provides in part that "death resulting from withholding or withdrawing health care in accordance with this [Act] does not for any purpose constitute a suicide or homicide * * *." West Ann. Cal. Prob. Code § 4656 (2011). This provision is similar in substance to Section 13(b) of the Uniform Health Care Decision Act of 1993.

3. A child is chased down the street by a dangerous dog. She runs toward an open door of a stranger's house. The homeowner, aware of her plight, slams the door in the child's face. See Leo Katz, Bad Acts and Guilty Minds 140 (1987). In determining legal responsibility, should it matter whether the homeowner, aware of the child's situation, closes an open door or simply fails to open a closed one?

In this context, consider the following awful scenario: Evildoer develops a "human trash compacter" and places two small children, John and Mary, whom he has kidnaped, inside it. A button is attached to the machine. Evildoer tells you, "If you push the button, my machine will simultaneously release Mary unscathed and kill John by compacting him. If you do *not* push the button within five seconds, the opposite will occur: John will emerge unhurt, but Mary will be killed." See Michael Tooley, *An Irrelevant Consideration: Killing versus Letting Die,* in Killing and Letting Die 60 (Bonnie Steinbock ed. 1980). You are unrelated to either child. You are convinced you cannot disengage the machine. What would you do? If John's and Mary's separate parents observed you, would you have "more explaining" to do to

John's parents if you pushed the button than to Mary's family if you did not push the button?

C. SOCIAL HARM

As mentioned briefly in the Introductory Comment to this chapter, there are generally two types of offenses, "result crimes" and "conduct crimes." In the first case, the law punishes because of an unwanted outcome, such as the death of another person (criminal homicide) or the destruction of a dwelling house (arson). With conduct crimes, the law prohibits specific behavior, such as driving under the influence of alcohol or solicitation to commit murder.

It is easy to see with result crimes that the law is not punishing a person for his thoughts or even for his voluntary acts or omissions, but rather is punishing for the harm resulting from his acts or omissions. And, because the result is a crime, and not simply a tort, we can call the outcome "*social* harm." That is, the loss suffered from a murder or other violent crime is experienced not only by the immediate victim, but also by society. There is intangible harm resulting from any crime, including a community's loss of a sense of security.

Is there social harm, however, when a person commits a *conduct* crime, such as driving under the influence of alcohol? In a tangible sense, there may be no harm. Indeed, the reason why a legislature may prohibit drunk driving is precisely to *avoid* the harm that can result from such conduct if it is not deterred or terminated. But, in another sense, conduct crimes *do* involve social harm. According to one definition, social harm is the "negation, endangering, or destruction of an individual, group, or state interest, which [is] deemed socially valuable." Albin Eser, *The Principle of "Harm" in the Concept of Crime: A Comparative Analysis of the Criminally Protected Legal Interests,* 4 Duq.L.Rev. 345, 413 (1965). So defined, "social harm" occurs not only, for example, when A kills V, but also when A solicits B to kill V, or when C drives on a public road in an intoxicated condition, because in these latter circumstances an endangerment of a socially valuable interest occurs. In this sense, therefore, it may be said that social harm is "the very essence" of crime. Id. at 345.

The dichotomy between result and conduct crimes can be overstated. If you look at the *actus reus* elements of some criminal offenses, you will find both conduct (or "nature of conduct") elements, as well as result (or "result of conduct") elements. For example, in People v. Decina, 2 N.Y.2d 133, 157 N.Y.S.2d 558, 138 N.E.2d 799 (1956) (p. 134, Note 6 supra), *D* was charged with "operating a vehicle in a reckless or culpably negligent manner, causing the death of another person." Notice that the *actus reus* of this offense ("operating a vehicle in a * * * manner causing the death of another person") includes conduct ("operating a vehicle") and a result ("causing the death of another person"). A person is not guilty of this offense unless the prosecutor proves the specified conduct *and* result.

Offenses also contain "attendant circumstance" elements. *Such elements constitute a part of the* actus reus *of an offense.* An attendant circumstance is a condition that must be present, in conjunction with the prohibited conduct or result, in order to constitute the crime. For example, assume that a statute provides that "it is an offense to drive an automobile in an intoxicated condition." The words "in an intoxicated condition" represent an attendant circumstance: the *actus reus* of the offense does not occur unless the actor drives her car (the conduct) while intoxicated (the circumstance that must be present at the time of her conduct). "In an intoxicated condition" is not a conduct element because the offense, as defined, does not prohibit a person from *becoming* intoxicated, only that, in such condition, she must not drive her automobile.

NOTES AND QUESTIONS

1. Look again at the hypothetical driving-while-intoxicated statute immediately above. There is another "attendant circumstance" element in it. What is it?

2. It is sometimes necessary for a lawyer to be able to distinguish between the various components—conduct elements, result elements, and attendant circumstances—of the *actus reus* of a crime, so familiarity with the concepts is helpful. Consider, for example, Model Penal Code § 210.1, which provides that a person is guilty of criminal homicide if "he purposely, knowingly, recklessly, or negligently causes the death of another human being." What words represent the *actus reus* of this offense? Break down the *actus reus* into its nature-of-conduct, result and/or attendant circumstance elements.

Do the same with the common law offense of burglary: "Breaking and entering a dwelling house of another at nighttime with the intent to commit a felony therein."

CHAPTER 5

MENS REA

■ ■ ■

"Even a dog distinguishes between being stumbled over and being
kicked."
Oliver W. Holmes, Jr., The Common Law 3 (1881)

A. NATURE OF "MENS REA"

UNITED STATES v. CORDOBA–HINCAPIE

United States District Court, E.D. New York, 1993.
825 F.Supp. 485.

WEINSTEIN, SENIOR DISTRICT JUDGE. * * *

The term, "*mens rea*," meaning "a guilty mind; a guilty or wrongful
purpose; a criminal intent," is shorthand for a broad network of concepts
encompassing much of the relationship between the individual and the
criminal law. These doctrines of criminal responsibility and the theories
that support them are deeply rooted in our legal tradition as one of our
first principles of law. * * *

Western * * * nations have long looked to the wrongdoer's mind to
determine both the propriety and the grading of punishment. "For hundreds of years the books have repeated with unbroken cadence that *Actus
non facit reum nisi mens sit rea.*" [See] *Black's Law Dictionary* 55 (4th ed.
1968) (defining the *actus non* rule: "An act does not make [the doer of it]
guilty, unless the mind be guilty; that is, unless the intent be criminal.").
This is the criminal law's mantra. * * *

The ancient English law tended towards strict liability for acts. But-
for causation was considered the essential prerequisite to criminal fault.
* * *

Toward the end of the Middle Ages, the modern focus on the criminal's state of mind gradually began to evolve. "[T]he history of the
recognition of culpable states of mind should be viewed as a continuing
process of self-civilization." By the end of the twelfth century, the Roman
law, with its concept of *culpa*, and the canon law, with it[s] emphasis on
moral guilt, began to influence the development of doctrines of culpability.

149

* * * It was inevitable that the development of the criminal law, based as it is upon general and evolving societal mores, would track the development of prevailing views about moral wrongdoing. "The early felonies were roughly the external manifestations of the heinous sins of the day." The word "felon" itself is a derivative of a Latin term meaning one who is "full of bitterness or venom" and who is "cruel, fierce, wicked, base."

"[T]he requirement of a guilty state of mind (at least for the more serious crimes) had been developed by the time of Coke." * * *

Once the "exceedingly vague" concept of moral blameworthiness was recognized the law embarked upon the long journey of refinement and development of culpability distinctions that continues to this day. * * *

NOTES AND QUESTIONS

1. *The two usages of "mens rea."* Oliver Wendell Holmes observed that, "I have always thought that most of the difficulties as to the *mens rea* was due to having no precise understanding what the *mens rea* is." 1 Holmes–Laski Letters 4 (M. Wolfe, ed. 1953) (letter of July 14, 1916). Part of the difficulty in understanding "what the *mens rea* is" stems from the fact that the term has both a broad and a narrow meaning. The modern trend is to use the term in its narrow context, but both meanings retain significance.

Broadly speaking, *"mens rea"* means "guilty mind," "vicious will," "immorality of motive," or, simply, "morally culpable state of mind." This is the "culpability" meaning of *"mens rea."* In this sense, a defendant is guilty of a crime if she commits the social harm of the offense with *any* morally blameworthy state of mind; it is not significant whether she caused the social harm intentionally or, instead, with some other blameworthy mental state (e.g. recklessly).

More narrowly, *"mens rea"* refers to the mental state the defendant must have had with regard to the "social harm" elements set out in the definition of the offense. This is the "elemental" meaning of *mens rea.* Using this meaning, a defendant is not guilty of an offense, even if she has a culpable frame of mind, if she lacks the mental state specified in the definition of the crime. For example, an offense may be structured as follows:

"A person is guilty of [name of offense] if she *intentionally* does X [e.g., robs a bank, takes a human life, or injures another—the social harm element(s) of the offense]."

Here, a defendant is not guilty of the offense if she does X recklessly, even though recklessness is a morally blameworthy state of mind (and, thus, the defendant has a *"mens rea"* in the culpability sense of the term), because the defendant does not have the specific state of mind required for this offense ("to do X intentionally").

2. Why is a requirement of *mens rea*, in Judge Weinstein's words, "deeply rooted in our legal tradition as one of our first principles of law"? Is the requirement based on utilitarian or retributive principles, or both? Arguments for permitting criminal convictions in the absence of *mens rea*—strict liability—are considered in detail in Section C. of this chapter.

3. In Norval Morris's remarkable book, The Brothel Boy and Other Parables of the Law (1992), he tells the story of a teenage boy in Burma in the 1920s, possessed of extremely low intelligence, who raped and killed a girl. In the parable, the protagonist, Eric Blair (the birth name of George Orwell), was a magistrate forced to consider whether the boy should be executed. After discussing the matter with Dr. Veraswami, a man whom he respected, "Blair" observes, "I protested that we both knew the boy meant no harm, no evil. [Because of his low intelligence, he did not realize he was doing anything wrong.] The more I thought about him and his crime, the less wicked it seemed, though the injury to the girl and her family was obviously extreme; *but it was a tragedy, not a sin.*" Morris, supra, at 16 (emphasis added). What is Morris/Blair's point?

REGINA v. CUNNINGHAM

Court of Criminal Appeal, 1957.
41 Crim.App. 155, 2 Q.B. 396, 2 All Eng.Rep. 412.

BYRNE, J., read the judgment of the court: * * *

The appellant was convicted * * * upon an indictment framed under section 23 of the Offences against the Person Act, 1861, which charged that he unlawfully and maliciously caused to be taken by Sarah Wade a certain noxious thing, namely, coal gas, so as thereby to endanger the life of the said Sarah Wade.

The facts were that the appellant was engaged to be married and his prospective mother-in-law was the tenant of a house, No. 7A, Bakes Street, Bradford, which was unoccupied, but which was to be occupied by the appellant after his marriage. Mrs. Wade and her husband, an elderly couple, lived in the house next door. At one time the two houses had been one, but when the building was converted into two houses a wall had been erected to divide the cellars of the two houses, and that wall was composed of rubble loosely cemented.

On the evening of Jan. 17 last, the appellant went to the cellar of No. 7a, Bakes Street, wrenched the gas meter from the gas pipes and stole it, together with its contents.[a] * * *

The facts were not really in dispute, and in a statement to a police officer the appellant said: "All right I will tell you, I was short of money, I had been off work for three days, I got 8 shillings from the gas meter. I tore it off the wall and threw it away." Although there was a stop tap within two feet of the meter, the appellant did not turn off the gas, with the result that a very considerable volume of gas escaped, some of which seeped through the wall of the cellar and partially asphyxiated Mrs. Wade, who was asleep in her bedroom next door, with the result that her life was endangered.

At the close of the case for the prosecution counsel who appeared for the appellant at the trial and who has appeared for him again in this

---

a. At the time of these events, "pay" gas meters were common, i.e., users placed coins in a meter in order to obtain the desired gas heat.

court, submitted that there was no case to go to the jury, but the learned judge, quite rightly in our opinion, rejected this submission. * * *

The act of the appellant was clearly unlawful and, therefore, the real question for the jury was whether it was also malicious within the meaning of section 23 of the Offences against the Person Act, 1861.

* * * Section 23 provides as follows:

"Whosoever shall unlawfully and maliciously administer to or cause to be administered to or taken by any other person any poison or other destructive or noxious thing, so as thereby to endanger the life of such person, or so as thereby to inflict upon such person any grievous bodily harm, shall be guilty of felony * * *."

Counsel argued * * * that the learned judge misdirected the jury as to the meaning of the word "maliciously." * * *

* * * [T]he following principle * * * was propounded by the late Professor C. S. Kenny in the first edition of his Outlines of Criminal Law published in 1902 * * *: " * * * * in any statutory definition of a crime, 'malice' must be taken not in the old vague sense of 'wickedness' in general, but as requiring either (i) an actual intention to do the particular kind of harm that in fact was done, or (ii) recklessness as to whether such harm should occur or not (i.e. the accused has foreseen that the particular kind of harm might be done, and yet has gone on to take the risk of it). It is neither limited to, nor does it indeed require, any ill-will towards the person injured." * * *

In his summing-up, the learned judge directed the jury as follows: * * *

" 'Unlawful' does not need any definition. It is something forbidden by law. What about 'malicious'? 'Malicious' for this purpose means wicked—something which he has no business to do and perfectly well knows it. 'Wicked' is as good a definition as any other which you would get." * * *

With the utmost respect to the learned judge, we think it is incorrect to say that the word "malicious" in a statutory offence merely means wicked. We think the learned judge was, in effect, telling the jury that if they were satisfied that the appellant acted wickedly—and he had clearly acted wickedly in stealing the gas meter and its contents—they ought to find that he had acted maliciously in causing the gas to be taken by Mrs. Wade so as thereby to endanger her life. In our view, it should have been left to the jury to decide whether, even if the appellant did not intend the injury to Mrs. Wade, he foresaw that the removal of the gas meter might cause injury to someone but nevertheless removed it. We are unable to say that a reasonable jury, properly directed as to the meaning of the word "maliciously" in the context of section 23, would, without doubt, have convicted.

In these circumstances, this court has no alternative but to allow the appeal and quash the conviction.

NOTES AND QUESTIONS

1. Notice that to the trial court "malice" meant "wicked." In contrast, the appellate court treated "malice" as a shorthand for two distinguishable states of mind, either "intent" or "recklessness." More precisely, however, what must the defendant "intend" or be "reckless" about?

2. The trial court and the Court of Criminal Appeal both appreciated that Cunningham could not be convicted in the absence of *mens rea*. In this context, however, reconsider p. 150, Note 1 and the "culpability" and "elemental" meanings of the term "*mens rea*." Would you say that the trial court understood the *mens rea* requirement in the culpability or elemental sense? What about the appellate court?

3. The term "malice" is used in the definition of many common law and statutory offenses. For example, common law arson is defined as the "*malicious* burning of the dwelling house of another." As the Court of Criminal Appeal defined "malice," what must the Government prove to convict a person of arson?

4. "*Recklessness.*" According to the Court of Criminal Appeal, what is the definition of the *mens rea* term "recklessness"? Based on the facts set out in the opinion was Cunningham reckless?

B. GENERAL ISSUES IN PROVING CULPABILITY

1. "INTENT"

PEOPLE v. CONLEY

Illinois Appellate Court, 1989.
187 Ill.App.3d 234, 134 Ill.Dec. 855, 543 N.E.2d 138.

JUSTICE CERDA delivered the opinion of the court:

[Defendant William J. Conley was convicted of aggravated battery based on permanent disability. Section 12–4(a) of the Illinois Criminal Code of 1961 defined this offense as follows: "[a] person who, in committing a battery,[b] intentionally or knowingly causes great bodily harm, or permanent disability or disfigurement commits aggravated battery." This appeal followed.]

The defendant was charged with aggravated battery in connection with a fight which occurred at a party * * *. Approximately two hundred high school students attended the party and paid admission to drink unlimited beer. One of those students, Sean O'Connell, attended the party with several friends. At some point during the party, Sean's group was approached by a group of twenty boys who apparently thought that

---

b. Ill.Rev.Stat.1983, ch.38, par. 12–3(a): "A person commits battery if he intentionally or knowingly without legal justification and by any means, (1) causes bodily harm to an individual or (2) makes physical contact of an insulting or provoking nature with an individual." Battery is a misdemeanor under Illinois law.

someone in Sean's group had said something derogatory. Sean's group denied making a statement and said they did not want any trouble. Shortly thereafter, Sean and his friends decided to leave and began walking toward their car which was parked a half block south of the party.

A group of people were walking toward the party from across the street when someone from that group shouted "There's those guys from the party." Someone emerged from that group and approached Sean who had been walking with his friend Marty Carroll * * *. That individual demanded that Marty give him a can of beer from his six-pack. [Marty refused. The individual, later identified as defendant Conley, attempted to strike Marty with a wine bottle, but Marty ducked. The bottle struck Sean in the face, causing him to fall to the ground.—ed.] Sean * * * sustained broken upper and lower jaws and four broken bones in the area between the bridge of his nose and the lower left cheek. Sean lost one tooth and had root canal surgery to reposition ten teeth that had been damaged. Expert testimony revealed that Sean has a permanent condition called mucosal mouth[c] and permanent partial numbness in one lip. The expert also testified that the life expectancy of the damaged teeth might be diminished by a third or a half. * * *

The defendant initially contends on appeal that the State failed to prove beyond a reasonable doubt that Sean O'Connell incurred a permanent disability. * * * The defendant contends there must be some disabling effect for an aggravated battery conviction based on permanent disability. The defendant does not dispute that Sean lost a tooth or that surgery was required to repair damaged teeth. The defendant also does not dispute that Sean will have permanent partial numbness in one lip or suffer from a condition called mucosal mouth. The defendant maintains, however, that there is no evidence as to how these injuries are disabling because there was no testimony of any tasks that can no longer be performed as a result of these injuries. * * *

[The appellate court determined that "for an injury to be deemed disabling, all that must be shown is that the victim is no longer whole such that the injured bodily portion or part no longer serves the body in the same manner as it did before the injury." Applying this standard, the court stated that Sean's injuries were sufficient to constitute a permanent disability.—ed.]

The defendant further argues that the State failed to prove beyond a reasonable doubt that he intended to inflict any permanent disability. The thrust of defendant's argument is that under section 12–4(a), a person must intend to bring about the particular harm defined in the statute. The defendant asserts that while it may be inferred from his conduct that he intended to cause harm, it does not follow that he intended to cause permanent disability. The State contends it is not necessary that the defendant intended to bring about the particular injuries that resulted.

---

c. This condition was not defined in the trial record or court opinion.

The State maintains it met its burden by showing that the defendant intentionally struck Sean. * * *

For proper resolution of this issue, it is best to return to the statutory language. Section 12–4(a) employs the terms "intentionally or knowingly" to describe the required mental state. The relevant statutes state:

> "4–4. Intent. A person intends, or acts intentionally or with intent, to accomplish a result or engage in conduct described by the statute defining the offense, when his conscious objective or purpose is to accomplish that result or engage in that conduct."

> "4–5. Knowledge. A person knows or acts knowingly or with knowledge of: (b) The result of his conduct, described by the statute defining the offense, when he is consciously aware that such result is practically certain to be caused by his conduct."

Section 12–4(a) defines aggravated battery as the commission of a battery where the offender intentionally or knowingly causes great bodily harm, or permanent disability or disfigurement. Because the offense is defined in terms of result, the State has the burden of proving beyond a reasonable doubt that the defendant either had a "conscious objective" to achieve the harm defined, or that the defendant was "consciously aware" that the harm defined was "practically certain to be caused by his conduct." * * *

Although the State must establish the specific intent to bring about great bodily harm, or permanent disability or disfigurement under section 12–4(a), problems of proof are alleviated [by] the ordinary presumption that one intends the natural and probable consequences of his actions * * *. * * * Intent can be inferred from the surrounding circumstances, the offender's words, the weapon used, and the force of the blow. * * * [T]he surrounding circumstances, the use of a bottle, the absence of warning and the force of the blow are facts from which the jury could reasonably infer the intent to cause permanent disability. Therefore, we find the evidence sufficient to support a finding of intent to cause permanent disability beyond a reasonable doubt. * * *

NOTES AND QUESTIONS

1. *Battery.* Generally speaking, a criminal battery is an unlawful application of force to the person of another. Even the slightest unlawful touching, if offensive, satisfies the *actus reus* component of the offense. The requisite mental state is less clear. Some courts and statutes require that the unlawful touching be intentional, but there is support for the proposition that criminal negligence is sufficient. Rollin M. Perkins & Ronald N. Boyce, Criminal Law 156–57 (3d ed. 1982). Simple battery was a common law misdemeanor. As in *Conley*, aggravated battery is usually classified as a statutory felony.

2. *Common law "intent."* In the context of result crimes, e.g., battery and murder, the term "intent" ordinarily is defined to include not only those results that are the conscious object of the actor—what he wants to occur— but also those results that the actor knows are virtually certain to occur from his conduct, even if he does not want them to arise.

Guilty of 1 count intentional killing + 1 count knowing killing

For example, suppose that Roger wants to kill Zachary. Roger constructs a bomb of sufficient explosive capacity to destroy a building and almost certainly kill everyone inside it. Roger plants the bomb in Zachary's home, which he knows will be occupied by Zachary and his wife. Based on these facts, Roger "intends" two deaths: Zachary, because it is his conscious object to kill him; *and* Zachary's wife, because Roger knows that she will almost certainly die in the same explosion. Based on the *Conley* opinion, however, of how many counts of "intentional" killing is Roger guilty under Illinois law?

3. *Proving intent.* When a prosecutor alleges that a defendant intended certain harm, juries are being asked, in essence, to look into the mind of a person to determine (as the last Note teaches) his purpose for acting or, at least, to determine whether he knew that the result was virtually certain to occur. Short of a confession, how does a prosecutor prove this internal state of mind?

One (but not the only) answer to the question is one recently expressed in a fortune cookie received by an author of this casebook: "YOUR ACTIONS REVEAL YOUR THOUGHTS MORE THAN YOU REALIZE." The legalistic version of this message is the one set out in *Conley*: the "ordinary presumption" is that a person "intends the natural and probable consequences of his actions." This presumption is more accurately characterized as an inference. That is, it is reasonable for a juror, like anyone else, to infer that a person ordinarily intends the foreseeable consequences of his actions. For example, if Georgia places three bullets in a gun, walks over to Helen, who is asleep, puts the gun at Helen's head, and voluntarily fires the gun three times, killing Helen, a juror may properly infer from these external events that Georgia intended to kill Helen. In the absence of additional facts (for example, that Georgia was suffering from a delusionary belief that she was an actress on stage using a toy gun), wouldn't you probably infer such intent in these circumstances?

Sandstrom presumption unconstitutional

In Sandstrom v. Montana, 442 U.S. 510, 99 S.Ct. 2450, 61 L.Ed.2d 39 (1979), the Supreme Court ruled that it is unconstitutional for a judge to instruct the jury that "the law *presumes* that a person intends the ordinary consequences of his voluntary acts." As discussed at p. 467 infra, the prosecutor is required to prove every element of an offense beyond a reasonable doubt. The due process clause is violated, therefore, if the element of intent is presumed and the defendant is required to disprove that he intended the ordinary consequences of his voluntary acts. The Constitution is not violated, however, if the jury on its own applies its common sense in such circumstances; and a judge is allowed to inform the jurors that they may, but need not, draw such an inference.

transferred intent

4. *Transferred intent (the basics).* You will notice in *Conley* that the defendant attempted to hit one person (Marty) but instead struck another (Sean). Could Conley have argued successfully, "Yes, I intended to hurt Marty, but not Sean, so you cannot convict me"? The answer is no. When a defendant intends to cause harm to one person but accidentally causes it to another, courts typically assert what has come to be known as the "transferred intent" doctrine. People v. Scott, 14 Cal.4th 544, 59 Cal.Rptr.2d 178, 927 P.2d 288 (1996), explains:

The common law doctrine of transferred intent was applied in England as early as the 16th century. The doctrine became part of the common law in many American jurisdictions, * * * and is typically invoked in the criminal law context when assigning criminal liability to a defendant who attempts to kill one person but accidentally kills another instead. Under such circumstances, the accused is deemed as culpable, and society is harmed as much, as if the defendant had accomplished what he had initially intended, and justice is achieved by punishing the defendant for a crime of the same seriousness as the one he tried to commit against his intended victim. Under the classic formulation of the common law doctrine of transferred intent, the defendant's guilt is thus "exactly what it would have been had the blow fallen upon the intended victim instead of the bystander."

Does the law, however, *need* the transferred intent doctrine to reach such a fair and sensible result? The answer is no, as Justice Mosk, concurring in *Scott*, explains:

> The "transferred intent" rule, of course, does not literally "transfer" [intent] * * * *from* an intended victim *to* an unintended victim. It is nothing more, and nothing less, than a "legal fiction, used to reach what is regarded with virtual unanimity as a just result" * * *. * * *

> The "transferred intent" rule, however, is a peculiarly mischievous legal fiction. * * *

> Moreover, the "transferred intent" rule is an altogether unnecessary legal fiction. It is based on the assumption that, in its absence, the perpetrator could escape liability for murder if he unlawfully killed not his intended victim but rather some unintended victim. That assumption, in turn, is based on yet another, namely, that [mens rea] exists in the perpetrator only in relation to an intended victim. * * *

> It is * * * plain that [intent] does not exist in the perpetrator only in relation to an intended victim. True, an unlawful intent to kill almost always happens to be directed at an intended victim. The reports demonstrate that such an intent is rarely possessed as to everyone in general or no one in particular. But there is no requirement of an unlawful intent to kill *an intended victim.* The law speaks in terms of an unlawful intent to kill *a* person, not *the* person *intended to be killed.* ([A]ccord, Dressler, Understanding Criminal Law (2d ed. 1995) [speaking of Anglo–American law generally: "The social harm of murder is the 'killing of a human being by another human being.' The requisite intent, therefore, is the intent to kill *a,* not a specific, human being."].)

You will notice that Justice Mosk suggests not only that the transferred intent doctrine is unnecessary but that it is mischievous. This is because confusion can arise if a prosecutor seeks to "transfer" the intent to commit one type of social harm to a different type of harm, rather than merely to "transfer" the intent from one victim to another. For example, in Regina v. Pembliton, 12 Cox Crim.Cas. 607 (1874), *P* threw a rock at *X,* intending to strike him with it. Instead, the rock hit a window in a building behind *X.* If *P* were charged with the offense of "intentional injury to property," should the prosecutor be able to transfer P's intent to hit X to the window behind him? Do you see the potential problem?

What if Denise shoots to kill Charley, her Secret Service husband, but the bullet strikes and kills the President of the United States. May Denise be convicted of intentionally killing the President, a different and more serious offense than simple murder?

5. *Transferred intent (the advanced course).* In the classic "bad aim" case, an errant bullet from D's gun, intended to kill X, kills innocent bystander Y *instead*. The doctrine permits the prosecutor to charge D with intentionally killing Y. But may the prosecutor *also* charge D with *attempted* murder of X (an offense that requires an intention to kill)? Or, suppose that one bullet not only kills its intended victim, X, but also strikes and kills Y? May D be prosecuted for *two* counts of intent-to-kill murder for the actions of the one bullet?

Courts have wrestled with these and various other "transferred intent" scenarios, frequently, but not universally, applying the doctrine. Can you see the potential conceptual and policy problems with applying the doctrine universally in such circumstances? Consider just two potential scenarios. In the first, $D1$ intends to kill $Y1$, who is using $X1$ as a shield. $D1$ fires one bullet through $X1$, killing both. How many counts of intentional (as this term is defined in Note 2, supra) killings should be brought? In the second case, $D2$, intending to kill $Y2$, fires one bullet at $Y2$. As he does, $X2$ jumps in front of $Y2$. Both $X2$ and $Y2$ are killed. Of how many counts of intentional killing should be brought here? What seems like the just outcome in these cases?

For thoughtful discussion of the "transferred intent" doctrine generally, see Anthony M. Dillof, *Transferred Intent: An Inquiry into the Nature of Criminal Culpability*, 1 Buffalo Crim. L. Rev. 501 (1998); Douglas N. Husak, *Transferred Intent*, 10 Notre Dame J.L. Ethics & Pub Pol'y 65 (1996).

6. *"Specific intent" and "general intent" offenses.* Few distinctions in criminal law are more perplexing and difficult to draw than the one between so-called "specific intent" and "general intent" offenses. Indeed, these terms are so "notoriously difficult" to define and apply that "a number of text writers [have] recommended that they be abandoned altogether." People v. Hood, 1 Cal.3d 444, 82 Cal.Rptr. 618, 462 P.2d 370 (1969). The concepts *have* been abandoned in jurisdictions that apply the Model Penal Code, but other states persist in using the terms and often drawing critical legal distinctions between them. Familiarity, therefore, with the terms "general intent" and "specific intent" is essential.

You should start with the unpleasant understanding that the terms "specific intent" and "general intent" do not have universally accepted definitions. Therefore, you will often have to infer the meanings of the terms from their context. In some circumstances, a court may denominate an offense as "general intent" when no particular mental state is set out in the definition of the crime and, therefore, the prosecutor need only prove that the social harm of the offense was performed with a morally blameworthy state of mind. In contrast, "specific intent" is an offense in which a mental state *is* expressly set out in the definition of the crime. Thus, according to *this* version of the distinction, "general intent" and "specific intent" restate respectively the "culpability" and "elemental" definitions of *mens rea* set out earlier in this casebook (p. 150, Note 1).

Sometimes, however, the term "specific intent" is used to denote an offense that contains in its definition the *mens rea* element of "intent" or, perhaps, "knowledge"; "general intent" is then reserved for crimes that permit conviction on the basis of a less culpable mental state, such as "recklessness" or "negligence."

A third usage of the term "general intent"—perhaps the most common— is to designate as "general intent" *any* mental state, whether expressed or implied, in the definition of the offense that relates *solely* to the conduct and/or result that constitutes the social harm of the criminal offense. For example, if battery is defined by state law as "an intentional application of force upon another," this offense would be considered "general intent" because the mental state ("intentional") pertains exclusively to the state of mind the actor must possess regarding the social harm of the offense (the "application of force upon another").

In contrast, "specific intent" designates "a special mental element which is required above and beyond any mental state required with respect to the actus reus of the crime." State v. Bridgeforth, 156 Ariz. 60, 62, 750 P.2d 3, 5 (1988). One of three types of special mental elements is typically found in the definition of specific intent crimes. First, to be guilty of some offenses, the State must prove an intention by the actor to commit some future act, separate from the *actus reus* of the offense ("possession of marijuana *with intent to sell*"). Second, an offense may require proof of a special motive or purpose for committing the *actus reus* ("offensive contact upon another *with the intent to cause humiliation*"). Third, some offenses require proof of the actor's awareness of an attendant circumstance ("intentional sale of obscene literature to a person *known to be under the age of 18 years*"). If one of these special mental elements in found in the definition of an offense, the crime is characterized as "specific intent."

In view of the latter explanation, are the following offenses "general intent" or "specific intent"?

A. Common law larceny: "Trespassory taking and carrying away of the personal property of another with the intent to steal."

B. Common law rape: "Sexual intercourse by a male with a female not his wife, without her consent."

C. "Intentional receipt of stolen property, with knowledge that it is stolen."

D. Common law burglary: "Breaking and entering the dwelling house of another at night with the intent to commit a felony therein."

2. THE MODEL PENAL CODE APPROACH

INTRODUCTORY COMMENT

Section 2.02 of the Model Penal Code ("General Requirements of Culpability") is probably the most influential section of the Code. By statute or judicial action, many states have adopted this section's systematic approach to the issue of *mens rea.*

Section 2.02 is significant in various respects. First, the Code consistently applies an "elemental" approach (p. 150, Note 1) to the issue of *mens rea.* That is, the prosecutor must prove that the defendant committed each material element of the charged offense with the particular state of mind required in the definition of that crime. Guilt cannot be based simply on proof that the defendant committed the *actus reus* of an offense in a morally blameworthy manner.

Second, the Code abandons the countless common law and pre-Code statutory *mens rea* terms and replaces them with just four culpability terms, "purposely," "knowingly," "recklessly," and "negligently." Third, principles of statutory construction set out in Section 2.02 assist in resolving many of the *mens rea* issues that have plagued courts over the years.

You should read Section 2.02 (found in the appendix) with *great* care in conjunction with the following excerpt from the Commentary to it. For a thorough survey of the Code's approach to matters concerning culpability, see Paul H. Robinson & Jane A. Grall, *Element Analysis in Defining Criminal Liability: The Model Penal Code and Beyond,* 35 Stan.L.Rev. 681 (1983); see also Kenneth W. Simons, *Should the Model Penal Code's Mens Rea Provisions Be Amended?,* 1 Ohio St. J. Crim. L. 179 (2003); Ronald L. Gainer, *The Culpability Provisions of the Model Penal Code,* 19 Rutgers L.J. 575 (1988).

AMERICAN LAW INSTITUTE, MODEL PENAL CODE AND COMMENTARIES, COMMENT TO § 2.02

(1985), 229–30, 233–34, 236–38, 240–41, 244

1. *Objective.* This section expresses the Code's basic requirement that unless some element of mental culpability is proved with respect to each material element of the offense, no valid criminal conviction may be obtained. This requirement is subordinated only to the provision of Section 2.05 for a narrow class of strict liability offenses that are limited to those for which no severer sentence than a fine may be imposed.

The section further attempts the extremely difficult task of articulating the kinds of culpability that may be required for the establishment of liability. It delineates four levels of culpability: purpose, knowledge, recklessness and negligence. It requires that one of these levels of culpability must be proved with respect to each "material element" of the offense, which may involve (1) the nature of the forbidden conduct, (2) the attendant circumstances, or (3) the result of conduct.[1] The question of

---

1. * * * Section 1.13(10) defines the concept of "material element" to include all elements except those that relate exclusively to statutes of limitation, jurisdiction, venue, and the like. The "material elements" of offenses are thus those characteristics (conduct, circumstances, result) of the actor's behavior that, when combined with the appropriate level of culpability, will constitute the offense.

which level of culpability suffices to establish liability must be addressed separately with respect to each material element, and will be resolved either by the particular definition of the offense or the general provisions of this section.

The purpose of articulating these distinctions in detail is to advance the clarity of draftsmanship in the delineation of the definitions of specific crimes, to provide a distinct framework against which those definitions may be tested, and to dispel the obscurity with which the culpability requirement is often treated when such concepts as "general criminal intent," "mens rea," "presumed intent," "malice," "wilfulness," "scienter" and the like have been employed. What Justice Jackson called "the variety, disparity and confusion" of judicial definitions of "the requisite but elusive mental element"[2] in crime should, insofar as possible, be rationalized by a criminal code. * * *

2. *Purpose and Knowledge.* In defining the kinds of culpability, the Code draws a narrow distinction between acting purposely and knowingly, one of the elements of ambiguity in legal usage of the term "intent." Knowledge that the requisite external circumstances exist is a common element in both conceptions. But action is not purposive with respect to the nature or result of the actor's conduct unless it was his conscious object to perform an action of that nature or to cause such a result. It is meaningful to think of the actor's attitude as different if he is simply aware that his conduct is of the required nature or that the prohibited result is practically certain to follow from his conduct.

* * * Although in most instances either knowledge or purpose should suffice for criminal liability, articulating the distinction puts to the test the issue whether an actual purpose is required and enhances clarity in drafting. * * *

3. *Recklessness.* An important discrimination is drawn between acting either purposely or knowingly and acting recklessly. As the Code uses the term, recklessness involves conscious risk creation. It resembles acting knowingly in that a state of awareness is involved, but the awareness is of risk, that is of a probability less than substantial certainty; the matter is contingent from the actor's point of view. Whether the risk relates to the nature of the actor's conduct, or to the existence of the requisite attendant circumstances, or to the result that may ensue, is immaterial; the concept is the same, and is thus defined to apply to any material element.

The risk of which the actor is aware must of course be substantial in order for the recklessness judgment to be made. The risk must also be unjustifiable. Even substantial risks, it is clear, may be created without recklessness when the actor is seeking to serve a proper purpose, as when a surgeon performs an operation that he knows is very likely to be fatal but reasonably thinks to be necessary because the patient has no other, safer chance. Some principle must, therefore, be articulated to indicate the nature of the final judgment to be made after everything has been

---

2. Morissette v. United States, 342 U.S. 246, 252 (1952).

weighed. Describing the risk as "substantial" and "unjustifiable" is useful but not sufficient, for these are terms of degree, and the acceptability of a risk in a given case depends on a great many variables. Some standard is needed for determining *how* substantial and *how* unjustifiable the risk must be in order to warrant a finding of culpability. There is no way to state this value judgment that does not beg the question in the last analysis; the point is that the jury must evaluate the actor's conduct and determine whether it should be condemned. The Code proposes, therefore, that this difficulty be accepted frankly, and that the jury be asked to measure the substantiality and unjustifiability of the risk by asking whether its disregard, given the actor's perceptions, involved a gross deviation from the standard of conduct that a law-abiding person in the actor's situation would observe.

Ultimately, then, the jury is asked to perform two distinct functions. First, it is to examine the risk and the factors that are relevant to how substantial it was and to the justifications for taking it. In each instance, the question is asked from the point of view of the actor's perceptions, i.e., to what extent he was aware of risk, of factors relating to its substantiality and of factors relating to its unjustifiability. Second, the jury is to make the culpability judgment in terms of whether the defendant's conscious disregard of the risk justifies condemnation. Considering the nature and purpose of his conduct and the circumstances known to him, the question is whether the defendant's disregard of the risk involved a gross deviation from the standards of conduct that a law-abiding person would have observed in the actor's situation. * * *

4. *Negligence.* The fourth kind of culpability is negligence. It is distinguished from purposeful, knowing or reckless action in that it does not involve a state of awareness. A person acts negligently under this subsection when he inadvertently creates a substantial and unjustifiable risk of which he ought to be aware. He is liable if given the nature and degree of the risk, his failure to perceive it is, considering the nature and purpose of the actor's conduct and the circumstances known to him, a gross deviation from the care that would be exercised by a reasonable person in his situation. As in the case of recklessness, both the substantiality of the risk and the elements of justification in the situation form the relevant standards of judgment. And again it is quite impossible to avoid tautological articulation of the final question. The tribunal must evaluate the actor's failure of perception and determine whether, under all the circumstances, it was serious enough to be condemned. The jury must find fault, and must find that it was substantial and unjustified; that is the heart of what can be said in legislative terms.

As with recklessness, the jury is asked to perform two distinct functions. First, it is to examine the risk and the factors that are relevant to its substantiality and justifiability. In the case of negligence, these questions are asked not in terms of what the actor's perceptions actually were, but in terms of an objective view of the situation as it actually existed. Second, the jury is to make the culpability judgment, this time in terms of whether the failure of the defendant to perceive the risk justifies condemnation. * * *

5. *Offense Silent as to Culpability.* Subsection (3) provides that unless the kind of culpability sufficient to establish a material element of an offense has been prescribed by law, it is established if a person acted purposely, knowingly or recklessly with respect thereto. This accepts as the basic norm what usually is regarded as the common law position. More importantly, it represents the most convenient norm for drafting purposes. When purpose or knowledge is required, it is conventional to be explicit. And since negligence is an exceptional basis of liability, it should be excluded as a basis unless explicitly prescribed.

NOTES AND QUESTIONS

1. A. Jacob wanted to kill Vanessa, his wife. He drove his car at a very high rate of speed into Vanessa, who was holding Xavier, their infant son, in her arms. Jacob fervently hoped that Xavier would survive the collision. The car struck Vanessa and Xavier, killing both instantly. According to § 2.02 of the Model Penal Code, with what form of culpability ("purposely," "knowingly," "recklessly," or "negligently") did Jacob kill Vanessa? With what form of culpability did he kill Xavier?

B. Roberta despised modern architecture. Therefore, she decided to burn down Sam's "modern" residence. Roberta did not want Sam, who she knew was inside, to die, so she tossed salt over her left shoulder immediately before she torched the residence. Roberta was genuinely convinced that this would protect Sam from all harm. Much to her surprise, Sam was burned to death in the fire. With what M.P.C. form of culpability did Roberta kill Sam?

[handwritten margin notes: Negligent / Reckless / Risk-taking must be substantial and unjustifiable]

C. The same as B., but assume that Roberta was not sure if the salt-over-shoulder act would protect Sam, but she was optimistic that it would.

2. Section 2.02 of the Code defines the various culpability terms and provides rules for interpreting the *mens rea* elements of criminal statutes. It is sometimes necessary to consider Section 2.03, as well. Section 2.03(1) concerns issues of causation, a matter to which we turn in the next chapter. But, subsections (2)(a) and (3)(a) need to be considered if a result in a criminal case varies in some way from that which was desired, contemplated, or risked by the actor. Consider:

A. *A* fires a gun at *B*, intending to kill *B*, but instead killing *C*. Did *A* kill *C* purposely, knowingly, recklessly, or negligently?

[handwritten margin note: transferred intent]

B. Reconsider *Keeler v. Superior Court*, p. 95, supra, in which *K* stomped on his pregnant wife's abdomen in order to kill her fetus, which he did. Suppose, however, *K*'s wife had given birth to the fetus, which miraculously survived the attack, but the wife died. In light of § 2.03(2)(a), what is *K*'s level of culpability in regard to his wife's death?

3. Model Penal Code § 222.1(1) defines robbery, in part, as follows: "A person is guilty of robbery if, in the course of committing a theft, he: (a) inflicts serious bodily injury upon another * * *." Is Toby guilty of robbery if,

while committing a theft, he negligently inflicts serious bodily injury upon Ursula? Look carefully at all of § 2.02 for the answer.

3. "KNOWLEDGE" OF ATTENDANT CIRCUMSTANCES (THE "WILFUL BLINDNESS" PROBLEM)

STATE v. NATIONS

Missouri Court of Appeals, Eastern District, 1984.
676 S.W.2d 282.

SATZ, JUDGE.

Defendant, Sandra Nations, owns and operates the Main Street Disco, in which police officers found a scantily clad sixteen year old girl "dancing" for "tips." Consequently, defendant was charged with endangering the welfare of a child "less than seventeen years old," § 568.050 RSMo 1978. Defendant was convicted and fined $1,000.00. * * *

Specifically, defendant argues the state failed to show she knew the child was under seventeen and, therefore, failed to show she had the requisite intent to endanger the welfare of a child "less than seventeen years old." We agree.

The pertinent part of § 568.050 provides:

"1. A person commits the crime of endangering the welfare of a child if: * * *

(2) He knowingly encourages, aids or causes a child less than seventeen years old to engage in any conduct which causes or tends to cause the child to come within the provisions of subdivision (1)(c) * * * of section 211.031, RSMo * * *."

The reference to "subdivision (1)(c)" * * * vested in the juvenile court exclusive original jurisdiction of any proceeding in which a child is alleged to be in need of care and treatment because "[t]he behavior, environment or associations of the child are injurious to his welfare or to the welfare of others." Thus, § 568.050 requires the state to prove the defendant "knowingly" encouraged a child "less than seventeen years old" to engage in conduct tending to injure the child's welfare * * *.

"Knowingly" is a term of art, whose meaning is limited to the definition given to it by our present Criminal Code. Literally read, the Code defines "knowingly" as actual knowledge—"A person 'acts knowingly,' or with knowledge, (1) with respect * * * to attendant circumstances when he is aware * * * that those circumstances exist * * *." So read, this definition of "knowingly" or "knowledge" excludes those cases in which "the fact [in issue] would have been known had not the person wilfully 'shut his eyes' in order to avoid knowing." The Model Penal Code, the source of our Criminal Code, does not exclude these cases from its definition of "knowingly." Instead, the Model Penal Code proposes that "[w]hen knowledge of the *existence of a particular fact* is an element of an offense, such knowledge is established if a person is aware of a high probability of its existence [, unless he actually believes that it does not exist]." Model Penal Code § 2.02(7). This definition sounds more like a restatement of the definition of "recklessly"[d] than "knowingly." The similarity is intentional. The Model Penal Code simply proposes that wilful blindness to a fact "be viewed as one of acting knowingly when what is involved is a matter of existing fact, but not when what is involved is the result of the defendant's conduct, necessarily a matter of the future at the time of acting."[6] * * *

Our legislature, however, did not enact this proposed definition of "knowingly." Although the definitions of "knowingly" and "recklessly" in our Criminal Code are almost identical to the primary definitions of these terms as proposed in the Model Penal Code, the Model Penal Code's proposed expanded definition of "knowingly," encompassing wilful blindness of a fact, is absent from our Criminal Code. The sensible, if not compelling, inference is that our legislature rejected the expansion of the definition of "knowingly" to include wilful blindness of a fact and chose to limit the definition of "knowingly" to actual knowledge of the fact. Thus, in the instant case, the state's burden was to show defendant actually was aware the child was under seventeen, a heavier burden than showing there was a "high probability" that defendant was aware the child was under seventeen. In short, the state's burden was to prove defendant acted "knowingly," not just "recklessly." The state proved, however, that defendant acted "recklessly," not "knowingly." This we conclude from our review of the record. * * *

The record shows that, at the time of the incident, the child was sixteen years old. When the police arrived, the child was "dancing" on stage for "tips" with another female. The police watched her dance for some five to seven minutes before approaching defendant in the service area of the bar. Believing that one of the girls appeared to be "young," the police questioned defendant about the child's age. Defendant told them that both girls were of legal age and that she had checked the girls' identification when she hired them. When the police questioned the child,

---

d. For the definition of "recklessly," see Model Penal Code § 2.02(2)(c), in the Appendix.

6. The additional or expanded definition of "knowingly" proposed in § 2.02(7) of the Model Penal Code

"deals with the situation British commentators have denominated 'wilful blindness' or 'connivance,' the case of the actor who is aware of the probable existence of a material fact but does not satisfy himself that it does not in fact exist. * * * Whether such cases should be viewed as instances of acting recklessly or knowingly presents a subtle but important question.

"The draft proposes that the case be viewed as one of acting knowingly when what is involved is a matter of existing fact, but not when what is involved is the result of the defendant's conduct, necessarily a matter of the future at the time of acting. The position reflects what we believe to be the normal policy of criminal enactments which rest liability on acting 'knowingly,' as is so commonly done. The inference of 'knowledge' of an existing fact is usually drawn from proof of notice of substantial probability of its existence, unless the defendant establishes an honest, contrary belief. The draft solidifies this usual result and clarifies the terms in which the issue is submitted to the jury." Model Penal Code § 2.02(7) commentary at 129–30 (Tent. Draft No. 4, 1953).

she initially stated that she was eighteen but later admitted that she was only sixteen. She had no identification.

* * * The state also called the child as a witness. Her testimony was no help to the state. She testified the defendant asked her for identification just prior to the police arriving, and she was merely crossing the stage to get her identification when the police took her into custody. Nor can the state secure help from the defendant's testimony. She simply corroborated the child's testimony; i.e., she asked the child for her identification; the child replied she would "show it to [her] in a minute"; the police then took the child into custody.

These facts simply show defendant was untruthful. Defendant could not have checked the child's identification, because the child had no identification with her that day, the first day defendant "hired" the child. This does not prove that defendant knew the child was less than seventeen years old. At best, it proves defendant did not know or refused to learn the child's age. The latter is the best case for the state. But defendant's refusal to learn the age of this "young" child who was "dancing" "scantily clad" in her disco bar simply proves that defendant was "aware of a high probability" that the child was under seventeen, or, stated otherwise, in the definitional language of our Criminal Code, proves that defendant was conscious of "a substantial and unjustifiable risk" that the child was under seventeen and that defendant's disregard of the risk was a "gross deviation" from the norm. This, however, is not "knowledge" under our Criminal Code. It is "recklessness," nothing more. Having failed to prove defendant knew the child's age was less than seventeen, the state failed to make a submissible case.

Judgment reversed. * * *

NOTES AND QUESTIONS

1. *Sandra Nations: an update.* Sandra Nations would later become Sandra Nations Venezia, husband of Thomas Venezia. So, who is he and why should we care? It seems Venezia, son of a St. Louis tavern owner, graduated from an eighth-grade education to become leader of a gambling and strip-club empire valued at $48 million. Along the way, he assembled a crew of associates to assist in his criminal activities, including a mayor, his lawyer (who supposedly "owned" fifteen of seventeen county judges), an unindicted co-conspiring congressman (who, as of 2010, is still serving the people in the House of Representatives) and, oh yes, Sandra Nations. In fact, Sandra was so much a part of the empire that she agreed to divorce Venezia and accompany him to Nevada so he could marry another woman whom he feared might otherwise testify against him.

In 1995, Thomas Venezia, most of his associates, his new wife, and Sandra Nations were convicted in federal court of racketeering. Thomas spent seven years in prison; Sandra (who testified against her husband) received three years' probation. Thomas eventually ended up dead along with a young woman in a murder-suicide (not clear who killed whom) or outright murder by a third person. Malcolm Gay, *Win Lose Die*, Riverfront Times, Nov. 30, 2005 & Dec. 7, 2005.

2. The *Nations* court stated (p. 165) that, under Missouri law, "the state's burden was to show defendant was actually aware the child was under seventeen, a heavier burden than showing [under the MPC] there was a 'high probability' that defendant was aware the child was under seventeen." Did the court correctly state the burden under the Model Penal Code? Look again at Section 2.02(7).

3. *Nations* refused to recognize the doctrine of "willful blindness"? (It is also spelled "wilful blindness.") Why? As the court observes, the Model Penal Code *does* recognize it. Here is what the United States Supreme Court said about the doctrine in Global–Tech Appliances, Inc. v. SEB S.A., 563 U.S. ___, 131 S.Ct. 2060, 179 L.Ed.2d 1167 (2011):

> The doctrine of willful blindness is well established in criminal law. * * * [C]ourts applying the doctrine * * * hold that defendants cannot escape the reach of * * * statutes [that require knowledge of an attendant circumstance] by deliberately shielding themselves from clear evidence of critical facts that are strongly suggested by the circumstances. * * *

> While [courts] articulate the doctrine * * * in slightly different ways, all appear to agree on two basic requirements: (1) the defendant must subjectively believe there is a high probability that a fact exists and (2) the defendant must take deliberate actions to avoid learning of that fact. We think these requirements give willful blindness an appropriately limited scope that surpasses recklessness and negligence.

How does the Court's characterization of the doctrine differ, if at all, from that of the Model Penal Code?

Do you agree with the Supreme Court that the culpability of a person who is wilfully blind is greater than one who is reckless in regard to the attendant circumstance in question? If your answer is yes to that question, are you saying that such a defendant (for example, Nations) *really* "knows" the pertinent fact, or is the argument that "a willfully blind defendant * * * can *almost* be said to have actually known the critical facts," id. (emphasis added), and, therefore, "no legitimate interest of an accused is prejudiced by such a standard"? United States v. Jewell, 532 F.2d 697 (9th Cir. 1976). If you agree with the latter observation, why isn't a defendant such as Sandra Nations prejudiced when she is convicted for having knowledge of the minor's age, when all that can be said is that she "can *almost* be said to have actually known the critical facts"? For more on this subject, see David Luban, *Contrived Ignorance*, 87 Geo. L.J. 961 (1999); and Ira P. Robbins, *The Ostrich Instruction: Deliberate Ignorance as a Criminal Mens Rea*, 81 J. Crim. L. & Criminology 191 (1990).

4. The "wilful blindness" instruction is often called an "ostrich instruction." As one court explained:

> [This] is what * * * real ostriches do (or at least are popularly supposed to do). They do not just fail to follow through on suspicions of bad things. They are not merely *careless* birds. They bury their heads in

the sand so that they will not see or hear bad things. They *deliberately* avoid acquiring unpleasant knowledge. * * * A deliberate effort to avoid guilty knowledge is all the guilty knowledge the law requires.

United States v. Giovannetti, 919 F.2d 1223 (7th Cir. 1990) (but see United States v. Black, 530 F.3d 596 (7th Cir. 2008), vacated and remanded, 561 U.S. ___, 130 S.Ct. 2963, 177 L.Ed.2d 695 (2010) (observing that the reference to ostriches burying their head in the sand when frightened "is pure legend and a canard on a very distinguished bird," and bemoaning the fact that "[i]t is too late * * * to correct this injustice")).

5. *Criminal defense lawyers as culpable ostriches?: an ethics lesson.* The American Bar Association Model Rules of Professional Conduct prohibits lawyers from knowingly offering false evidence at trial. Thus, if a criminal defense lawyer knows that her client plans to testify falsely—to perjure himself—the lawyer may not permit her client to so testify. So, what if a criminal defense attorney states the following to her client:

> Before you tell me what happened [regarding the crime charged], I just want to let you know that I cannot put you on the stand if I *know* you are going to lie. While it is helpful for me to know everything that happened, and I am ethically required to keep what you say confidential, if I know that what you are about to say will be a lie, I cannot allow you to testify. If I know you have lied on the stand, I may even have to tell the judge. But if I only believe that you will lie (or have lied) but don't know for sure, I can continue to defend you as best I can. Do you understand what I am saying?

Deborah Hellman, *Willfully Blind for Good Reason*, 3 Crim. Law & Philos. 301, 306 (2009).

Assume that the client gets the hint and does not tell his lawyer facts regarding the crime, and then falsely testifies at trial. Is the defense lawyer wilfully blind? Should she be treated as having violated the professional code by "knowingly" introducing false evidence at trial? If not, why not? What distinguishes this case from *Nations* or other "wilful blindness" cases?

6. *"Wilful."* "Wilful" (or "willful") is a term frequently used in non-Model Penal Code statutes. "The word 'willfully' is sometimes said to be 'a word of many meanings' whose construction is often dependent on the context in which it appears." Bryan v. United States, 524 U.S. 184, 118 S.Ct. 1939, 141 L.Ed.2d 197 (1998).

Two common interpretations of the term have developed. First, "wilful" may merely mean that the actor intentionally committed the prohibited act. Alternatively, the term requires proof that the actor intentionally performed the prohibited act in bad faith, with a wrongful motive, or in violation of a known legal duty. See generally Michael Tigar, *"Willfulness" and "Ignorance" in Federal Criminal Law*, 37 Clev.St.L.Rev. 525 (1989). Because the term "wilful" is used in many statutes, the drafters of the Model Penal Code doubted that they could rid criminal codes of the term, so it included a provision relating to it. See Section 2.02(8).

4. PROBLEMS IN STATUTORY INTERPRETATION

FLORES–FIGUEROA v. UNITED STATES

Supreme Court of the United States, 2009.
556 U.S. 646, 129 S.Ct. 1886, 173 L.Ed.2d 853.

JUSTICE BREYER delivered the opinion of the Court.

A federal criminal statute forbidding "[a]ggravated identity theft" imposes a mandatory consecutive 2–year prison term upon individuals convicted of certain other crimes *if,* during (or in relation to) the commission of those other crimes, the offender *"knowingly* transfers, possesses, or uses, without lawful authority, *a means of identification of another person."* 18 U. S. C. § 1028A(a)(1) (emphasis added). The question is whether the statute requires the Government to show that the defendant *knew* that the means of identification he or she unlawfully transferred, possessed, or used, in fact, belonged to "another person." We conclude that it does.

I

A

The statutory provision in question references a set of predicate crimes, including, for example, theft of government property, fraud, or engaging in various unlawful activities related to passports, visas, and immigration. It then provides that if any person who commits any of those other crimes (in doing so) "knowingly transfers, possesses, or uses, without lawful authority, a means of identification of another person," the judge must add two years imprisonment to the offenders underlying sentence. § 1028A(a)(1). All parties agree that the provision applies only where the offender knows that he is transferring, possessing, or using *something.* And the Government reluctantly concedes that the offender likely must know that he is transferring, possessing, or using that *something* without lawful authority. But they do not agree whether the provision requires that a defendant also know that the *something* he has unlawfully transferred is, for example, a real ID belonging to another person rather than, say, a fake ID (*i.e.,* a group of numbers that does not correspond to any real Social Security number).

Petitioner Ignacio Flores–Figueroa argues that the statute requires that the Government prove that he *knew* that the "means of identification" belonged to someone else, *i.e.,* was "a means of identification *of another person.*" The Government argues that the statute does not impose this particular knowledge requirement. The Government [claims] * * * that word * * * does not modify the statutes last phrase ("a means of identification of another person") or, at the least, it does not modify the last three words of that phrase ("of another person").

B

The facts of this case illustrate the legal problem. Ignacio Flores–Figueroa is a citizen of Mexico. In 2000, to secure employment, Flores gave his employer a false name, birth date, and Social Security number, along with a counterfeit alien registration card. The Social Security number and the number on the alien registration card were not those of a real person. In 2006, Flores presented his employer with new counterfeit Social Security and alien registration cards; these cards (unlike Flores' old alien registration card) used his real name. But this time the numbers on both cards were in fact numbers assigned to other people.

Flores' employer reported his request to U.S. Immigration and Customs Enforcement. Customs discovered that the numbers on Flores' new documents belonged to other people. The United States then charged Flores with two predicate crimes, namely, entering the United States without inspection, and misusing immigration documents. And it charged him with aggravated identity theft, the crime at issue here.

* * * After a bench trial, the court found Flores guilty of the predicate crimes and aggravated identity theft. * * *

II

There are strong textual reasons for rejecting the Government's position. As a matter of ordinary English grammar, it seems natural to read the statute's word "knowingly" as applying to all the subsequently listed elements of the crime. The Government cannot easily claim that the word "knowingly" applies only to the statute's first four words, or even its first seven. It makes little sense to read the provisions language as heavily penalizing a person who "transfers, possesses, or uses, without lawful authority" a *something,* but does not know, at the very least, that the "something" (perhaps inside a box) is a "means of identification." Would we apply a statute that makes it unlawful *"knowingly* to possess drugs" to a person who steals a passengers bag without knowing that the bag has drugs inside?

The Government claims more forcefully that the word "knowingly" applies to all but the statutes last three words, *i.e.,* "of another person." The statute, the Government says, does not require a prosecutor to show that the defendant *knows* that the means of identification the defendant has unlawfully used in fact belongs to another person. But how are we to square this reading with the statute's language?

In ordinary English, where a transitive verb has an object, listeners in most contexts assume that an adverb (such as knowingly) that modifies the transitive verb tells the listener how the subject performed the entire action, including the object as set forth in the sentence. Thus, if a bank official says, "Smith knowingly transferred the funds to his brothers account," we would normally understand the bank officials statement as telling us that Smith knew the account was his brother's. * * *

Of course, a statement that does *not* use the word "knowingly" may be unclear about just what Smith knows. Suppose Smith mails his bank draft to Tegucigalpa, which (perhaps unbeknownst to Smith) is the capital of Honduras. If the bank official says, "Smith sent a bank draft to the capital of Honduras," he has expressed next to nothing about Smith's knowledge of that geographic identity. But if the official were to say, "Smith *knowingly* sent a bank draft to the capital of Honduras," then the official has suggested that Smith knows his geography.

Similar examples abound. * * * If we say that someone knowingly ate a sandwich with cheese, we normally assume that the person knew both that he was eating a sandwich and that it contained cheese. Or consider the Government's own example, " 'John knowingly discarded the homework of his sister.' " The Government rightly points out that this sentence "does not *necessarily*" imply that John knew whom the homework belonged to. But that is what the sentence, as *ordinarily* used, does imply.

At the same time, dissimilar examples are not easy to find. The Government says that "knowingly" modifies only the verbs in the statute, while remaining indifferent to the subject's knowledge of at least part of the transitive verbs object. In certain contexts, a listener might understand the word "knowingly" to be used in that way. But the Government has not provided us with a single example of a sentence that, when used in typical fashion, would lead the hearer to believe that the word "knowingly" modifies only a transitive verb without the full object, *i.e.*, that it leaves the hearer gravely uncertain about the subject's state of mind in respect to the full object of the transitive verb in the sentence. The likely reason is that such sentences typically involve special contexts * * *. * * * No special context is present here.

* * * [C]ourts [also] ordinarily read a phrase in a criminal statute that introduces the elements of a crime with the word "knowingly" as applying that word to each element. For example, in *Liparota* v. *United States*, 471 U. S. 419 (1985), this Court interpreted a federal food stamp statute that said, " 'whoever knowingly uses, transfers, acquires, alters, or possesses coupons or authorization cards *in any manner not authorized by [law]*' " is subject to imprisonment. The question was whether the word "knowingly" applied to the phrase "in any manner not authorized by [law]." The Court held that it did, despite the legal cliche "ignorance of the law is no excuse."

More recently, we had to interpret a statute that penalizes "[a]ny person who—(1) knowingly transports or ships using any means or facility of interstate or foreign commerce by any means including by computer or mails, any visual depiction, if—(A) the producing of such visual depiction involves the use of a minor engaging in sexually explicit conduct." 18 U. S. C. § 2252(a)(1)(A); [*United States v.*] *X–Citement Video*, [513 U.S. 64 (1994)]. In issue was whether the term "knowingly" in paragraph (1) modified the phrase "the use of a minor" in subparagraph (A). The language in issue in *X–Citement Video* (like the language in *Liparota*) was more ambiguous than the language here not only because the phrase the "use of a minor" was not the direct object of the verbs modified by "knowingly," but also because it appeared in a different subsection. Moreover, the fact that many sex crimes involving minors do not ordinarily require that a perpetrator know that his victim is a minor supported the Government's position. Nonetheless, we again found that the intent element applied to the "use of a minor." * * *

The Government correctly points out that in these cases more was at issue than proper use of the English language. But if more is at issue here, what is it? The Government makes a further textual argument, a complex argument based upon a related provision of the statute. That provision applies "[a]ggravated identity theft" where the predicate crime is terrorism. See § 1028A(a)(2). The provision uses the same language as the provision before us up to the end, where it adds the words "or a false identification document." Thus, it penalizes anyone who "knowingly transfers, possesses, or uses, without lawful authority, a means of identification of another person or a false identification document."

The Government's argument has four steps. Step One: We should not interpret a statute in a manner that makes some of its language superfluous. Step Two: A person who knows that he is transferring, possessing, or using a " 'means of identification' " " 'without lawful authority,' " must know that the document either (a) belongs " 'to another person' " or (b) is a " 'false identification document' " because " *there are no other choices.*' " Step Three: Requiring the offender to *know* that the "means of identification" belongs to another person would consequently be superfluous in this terrorism provision. Step Four: We should not interpret the same phrase ("of another person") in the two related sections differently.

If we understand the argument correctly, it seems to suffer two serious flaws. If the two listed circumstances (where the ID belongs to another person; where the ID is false) are the only two circumstances possibly present when a defendant (in this particular context) unlawfully uses a "means of identification," then why list them at all? Why not just stop after criminalizing the knowing unlawful use of a "means of identification"? (Why specify that Congress does not mean the statute to cover, say, the use of dog tags?) The fact is, however, that the Government's reasoning at Step Two is faulty. The two listed circumstances are *not* the only two circumstances possibly present when a defendant unlawfully uses a "means of identification." One could, for example, verbally provide a seller or an employer with a made-up Social Security number, not an "identification *document,*" and the number verbally transmitted to the seller or employer might, or might not, turn out to belong to another person. The word "knowingly" applied to the "other person" requirement (even in a statute that similarly penalizes use of a "false identification *document*") would not be surplus.

The Government also considers the statute's purpose to be a circumstance showing that the linguistic context here is special. It describes that purpose as "provid[ing] enhanced protection for individuals whose identifying information is used to facilitate the commission of crimes." And it points out that without the knowledge requirement, potential offenders will take great care to avoid wrongly using IDs that belong to others, thereby enhancing the protection that the statute offers.

The question, however, is whether Congress intended to achieve this enhanced protection by permitting conviction of those who do not *know* the ID they unlawfully use refers to a real person, *i.e.*, those who do not *intend* to cause this further harm. And, in respect to this latter point, the statute's history (outside of the statute's language) is inconclusive. [The Court looked at legislative history and cited conflicting evidence of Congress's intention. The Court then turned to the Government's last argument.]

Finally, and perhaps of greatest practical importance, there is the difficulty in many circumstances of proving beyond a reasonable doubt that a defendant has the necessary knowledge. Take an instance in which an alien who unlawfully entered the United States gives an employer identification documents that *in fact* belong to others. How is the Government to prove that the defendant *knew* that this was so? The Government may be able to show that such a defendant knew the papers were not his. But perhaps the defendant did not care whether the papers (1) were real papers belonging to another person or (2) were simply counterfeit papers. The difficulties of proof along with the defendant's necessary guilt of a predicate crime and the defendant's necessary knowledge that he has acted "without lawful authority," make it reasonable, in the Government's view, to read the statute's language as dispensing with the knowledge requirement.

We do not find this argument sufficient, however, to turn the tide in the Government's favor. For one thing, in the classic case of identity theft, intent is generally not difficult to prove. For example, where a defendant has used another person's identification information to get access to that person's bank account, the Government can prove knowledge with little difficulty. The same is true when the defendant has gone through someone else's trash to find discarded credit card and bank statements, or pretends to be from the victim's bank and requests personal identifying information. Indeed, the examples of identity theft in the legislative history (dumpster diving, computer hacking, and the like) are all examples of the types of classic identity theft where intent should be relatively easy to prove, and there will be no practical enforcement problem. For another thing, to the extent that Congress may have been concerned about criminalizing the conduct of a broader class of individuals, the concerns about practical enforceability are insufficient to outweigh the clarity of the text. * * * But had Congress placed conclusive weight upon practical enforcement, the statute would likely not read the way it now reads. Instead, Congress used the word knowingly followed by a list of offense elements. And we cannot find indications in statements of its purpose or in the practical problems of enforcement sufficient to overcome the ordinary meaning, in English or through ordinary interpretive practice, of the words that it wrote. * * *

[Justice Scalia filed an opinion concurring in part and concurring in the judgment, in which Justice Thomas joined. Justice Alito also filed an opinion concurring in part and concurring in the judgment.]

NOTES AND QUESTIONS

1. Consider this hypothetical drawn from Justice Alito's concurring opinion: "The mugger knowingly assaulted two people in the park, an employee of company X and a jogger from town Y." If you heard someone say this, would you assume that the mugger knew that his first victim was an employee of company X, and that he knew the home town of the second victim? If not, does this suggest that Justice Breyer is wrong in his reading of the statute?

2. The Model Penal Code § 2.02(4) addresses statutory interpretation problems of the sort involved here. How would *Flores–Figueroa* have been decided according to this provision?

3. *Problem.* Y, an employee of a company doing business with the federal government, supplied false information to his employer in connection with a Department of Defense security clearance questionnaire. *Y*'s employer routinely sent the questionnaire, containing *Y*'s false statements, to a federal agency concerned with security clearances. When the falsehoods were discovered, *Y* was prosecuted for violation of 18 U.S.C. § 1001, which provides in pertinent part:

> Whoever, in any matter within the jurisdiction of any department or agency of the United States, knowingly * * * makes any false, fictitious or fraudulent statements * * * [is guilty of a felony].

At trial, *Y* admitted that his statements were knowingly inaccurate, but he requested a jury instruction requiring the Government to prove not only that he had actual knowledge of their falsity, but also that he had knowledge that the statements were made in a matter within the jurisdiction of a federal agency. United States v. Yermian, 468 U.S. 63, 104 S.Ct. 2936, 82 L.Ed.2d 53 (1984). Should the trial court have instructed the jury as *Y* requested? Apply M.P.C. §§ 1.13(10) and 2.02.

C. STRICT LIABILITY OFFENSES

UNITED STATES v. CORDOBA–HINCAPIE

United States District Court, E.D. New York, 1993.
825 F.Supp. 485.

WEINSTEIN, SENIOR DISTRICT JUDGE. * * *

* * * [T]he *mens rea* principle remains, in the modern criminal law, a fundamental requirement. * * * Like most ancient doctrines, however, it has grown far more sophisticated and nuanced than it once was. It can no longer simply be invoked. Its application must be carefully explained and its many distinctions must be considered. Not only has the law developed an appreciation of gradations in mental states, but it now also openly

recognizes limited exceptions to a rule once characterized as admitting no compromise. * * *

Perhaps the most common exception to the *mens rea* principle has been in cases involving what are characterized as "public-welfare offenses." Criminal liability has been permitted to attach without regard to fault in instances in which the actor's conduct involves

> minor violations of the liquor laws, the pure food laws, the anti-narcotics laws, motor vehicle and traffic regulations, sanitary, building and factory laws and the like.

Francis Bowes Sayre, *Public Welfare Offenses*, 33 Colum.L.Rev. 55, 78 (1933).

Sayre dated the development of this welfare-exception doctrine to the middle of the nineteenth century. Emphasizing that he was speaking of "light" offenses, he explained it as follows:

> The decisions permitting convictions of light police offenses without proof of a guilty mind came just at the time when the demands of an increasingly complex social order required additional regulation of an administrative character unrelated to questions of personal guilt; the movement also synchronized with the trend of the day away from nineteenth century individualism toward a new sense of the importance of collective interests. * * *

Sayre was able to discern from the cases two principles identifying the contours of the public-welfare offense doctrine. First, if punishment of the wrongdoer far outweighs regulation of the social order as a purpose of the law in question, then *mens rea* is probably required. Second, if the penalty is light, involving a relatively small fine and not including imprisonment, then *mens rea* probably is not required. * * *

Strict liability has been permitted in the criminal law in a number of other instances. The most widely recognized form of strict liability outside the realm of public-welfare offenses probably is the doctrine, embodied in statute and upheld by courts in a majority of states, that the perpetrator of the crime of "statutory rape," that is, intercourse with a person below the age at which the law deems consent possible, cannot defend on the grounds that he did not know of or was mistaken as to the victim's age. * * *

NOTES AND QUESTIONS

1. The term "strict liability" is used in somewhat distinct circumstances. Some offenses, as defined, do not expressly possess any mental-state element—all that seemingly must be proven is the *actus reus*. Public-welfare offenses are the most common examples of such strict-liability offenses. As the next case suggests, however, a statute that is silent regarding *mens rea* may, nonetheless, be interpreted as requiring at least some minimal level of *mens rea* (and, thus, are not truly "strict liability" in nature).

Often, an offense will contain a *mens rea* requirement as to some, but not all, elements of the crime. Typically, the element that does *not* require proof of culpability will be an "attendant circumstance" element. For example, Judge Weinstein described statutory rape as strict liability in nature. Fairly obviously, it will be a rare case indeed in which the *act* of sexual intercourse itself will be other than intentional; what makes statutory rape "strict liability" in character (when it is) is the fact that the actor may be convicted although he believed, even reasonably, that the underage female with whom he had intercourse was old enough to consent to the act.

As the latter example and next case suggest, some "strict liability" cases involve mistake-of-fact or, less often, mistake-of-law claims. We leave the general thrust of the mistake doctrines for Parts D. and E. of this chapter. The essential point here, however, is that to the extent that one or more *actus reus* elements of an offense are strict liability in nature—if there is no *mens rea* to negate as to those elements—then there is no basis for acquittal on the ground of mistake of fact or law as to those strict liability elements.

STAPLES v. UNITED STATES

Supreme Court of the United States, 1994.
511 U.S. 600, 114 S.Ct. 1793, 128 L.Ed.2d 608.

JUSTICE THOMAS delivered the opinion of the Court. * * *

I

The National Firearms Act (Act), 26 U.S.C. §§ 5801–5872, imposes strict registration requirements on statutorily defined "firearms." The Act includes within the term "firearm" a machinegun, and further defines a machinegun as "any weapon which shoots, * * * or can be readily restored to shoot, automatically more than one shot, without manual reloading, by a single function of the trigger." Thus, any fully automatic weapon is a "firearm" within the meaning of the Act.[1] Under the Act, all firearms must be registered in the National Firearms Registration and Transfer Record maintained by the Secretary of the Treasury. Section 5861(d) makes it a crime, punishable by up to 10 years in prison, for any person to possess a firearm that is not properly registered.

Upon executing a search warrant at petitioner's home, local police and agents of the Bureau of Alcohol, Tobacco and Firearms (BATF) recovered, among other things, an AR–15 rifle. The AR–15 is the civilian version of the military's M–16 rifle, and is, unless modified, a semiautomatic weapon. The M–16, in contrast, is a selective fire rifle that allows the operator, by rotating a selector switch, to choose semiautomatic or automatic fire. Many M–16 parts are interchangeable with those in the AR–15 and can be used to convert the AR–15 into an automatic weapon. No doubt to inhibit such conversions, the AR–15 is manufactured with a

---

1. As used here, the terms "automatic" and "fully automatic" refer to a weapon that fires repeatedly with a single pull of the trigger. That is, once its trigger is depressed, the weapon will automatically continue to fire until its trigger is released or the ammunition is exhausted. Such weapons are "machineguns" within the meaning of the Act. We use the term "semiautomatic" to designate a weapon that fires only one shot with each pull of the trigger, and which requires no manual manipulation by the operator to place another round in the chamber after each round is fired.

metal stop on its receiver that will prevent an M–16 selector switch, if installed, from rotating to the fully automatic position. The metal stop on petitioner's rifle, however, had been filed away, and the rifle had been assembled with an M–16 selector switch and several other M–16 internal parts, including a hammer, disconnector, and trigger. Suspecting that the AR–15 had been modified to be capable of fully automatic fire, BATF agents seized the weapon. Petitioner subsequently was indicted for unlawful possession of an unregistered machinegun in violation of § 5861(d).

At trial, BATF agents testified that when the AR–15 was tested, it fired more than one shot with a single pull of the trigger. It was undisputed that the weapon was not registered as required by § 5861(d). Petitioner testified that the rifle had never fired automatically when it was in his possession. He insisted that the AR–15 had operated only semiautomatically, and even then imperfectly, often requiring manual ejection of the spent casing and chambering of the next round. According to petitioner, his alleged ignorance of any automatic firing capability should have shielded him from criminal liability for his failure to register the weapon. He requested the District Court to instruct the jury that, to establish a violation of § 5861(d), the Government must prove beyond a reasonable doubt that the defendant "knew that the gun would fire fully automatically."

The District Court rejected petitioner's proposed instruction * * *.

Petitioner was convicted and sentenced to five years' probation and a $5,000 fine.

The Court of Appeals affirmed. * * *

II

A

Whether or not § 5861(d) requires proof that a defendant knew of the characteristics of his weapon that made it a "firearm" under the Act is a question of statutory construction. As we observed in *Liparota v. United States*, 471 U.S. 419, 105 S.Ct. 2084, 85 L.Ed.2d 434 (1985), "[t]he definition of the elements of a criminal offense is entrusted to the legislature, particularly in the case of federal crimes, which are solely creatures of statute." Thus, we have long recognized that determining the mental state required for commission of a federal crime requires "construction of the statute and * * * inference of the intent of Congress." *United States v. Balint*, 258 U.S. 250, 253, 42 S.Ct. 301, 302, 66 L.Ed. 604 (1922).

The language of the statute, the starting place in our inquiry, provides little explicit guidance in this case. Section 5861(d) is silent concerning the *mens rea* required for a violation. It states simply that "[i]t shall be unlawful for any person * * * to receive or possess a firearm which is not registered to him in the National Firearms Registration and Transfer Record." Nevertheless, silence on this point by itself does not necessarily suggest that Congress intended to dispense with a conventional *mens rea* element, which would require that the defendant know the facts that make his conduct illegal. On the contrary, we must construe the statute in light of the background rules of the common law, in which the requirement of some *mens rea* for a crime is firmly embedded. As we have observed, "[t]he existence of a *mens rea* is the rule of, rather than the exception to, the principles of Anglo–American criminal jurisprudence." See also *Morissette v. United States*, 342 U.S. 246, 250, 72 S.Ct. 240, 243, 96 L.Ed. 288 (1952) ("The contention that an injury can amount to a crime only when inflicted by intention is no provincial or transient notion. It is as universal and persistent in mature systems of law as belief in freedom of the human will and a consequent ability and duty of the normal individual to choose between good and evil").

There can be no doubt that this established concept has influenced our interpretation of criminal statutes. Indeed, we have noted that the common-law rule requiring *mens rea* has been "followed in regard to statutory crimes even where the statutory definition did not in terms include it." Relying on the strength of the traditional rule, we have stated that offenses that require no *mens rea* generally are disfavored, and have suggested that some indication of congressional intent, express or implied, is required to dispense with *mens rea* as an element of a crime. *Morissette*, *supra*.

According to the Government, however, the nature and purpose of the Act suggest that the presumption favoring *mens rea* does not apply to this case. The Government argues that Congress intended the Act to regulate and restrict the circulation of dangerous weapons. Consequently, in the Government's view, this case fits in a line of precedent concerning what we have termed "public welfare" or "regulatory" offenses, in which we have understood Congress to impose a form of strict criminal liability through statutes that do not require the defendant to know the facts that make his conduct illegal. In construing such statutes, we have inferred from silence that Congress did not intend to require proof of *mens rea* to establish an offense. * * *

* * * Typically, our cases recognizing such offenses involve statutes that regulate potentially harmful or injurious items. In such situations, we have reasoned that as long as a defendant knows that he is dealing with a dangerous device of a character that places him "in responsible relation to a public danger," he should be alerted to the probability of strict regulation, and we have assumed that in such cases Congress intended to place the burden on the defendant to "ascertain at his peril whether [his conduct] comes within the inhibition of the statute." *Balint, supra*. Thus, we essentially have relied on the nature of the statute and the particular character of the items regulated to determine whether congressional silence concerning the mental element of the offense should be interpreted as dispensing with conventional *mens rea* requirements.

B

The Government argues that § 5861(d) defines precisely the sort of regulatory offense described in *Balint*.[e] In this view, all guns, whether or not they are statutory "firearms," are dangerous devices that put gun owners on notice that they must determine at their hazard whether their weapons come within the scope of the Act. * * *

The Government seeks support for its position from our decision in *United States v. Freed*, 401 U.S. 601, 91 S.Ct. 1112, 28 L.Ed.2d 356 (1971), which involved a prosecution for possession of unregistered grenades under § 5861(d). The defendant knew that the items in his possession were grenades, and we concluded that § 5861(d) did not require the Government to prove the defendant also knew that the grenades were unregistered. * * *

As the Government concedes, *Freed* did not address the issue presented here. * * * [O]ur analysis in *Freed* likening the Act to the public welfare statute in *Balint* rested entirely on the assumption that the defendant *knew* that he was dealing with hand grenades—that is, that he knew he possessed a particularly dangerous type of weapon * * *, possession of which was not entirely "innocent" in and of itself. The predicate for that analysis is eliminated when, as in this case, the very question to be decided is *whether* the defendant must know of the particular characteristics that make his weapon a statutory firearm.

* * * In glossing over the distinction between grenades and guns, the Government ignores the particular care we have taken to avoid construing a statute to dispense with *mens rea* where doing so would "criminalize a broad range of apparently innocent conduct." In *Liparota*, we considered a statute that made unlawful the unauthorized acquisition or possession of food stamps. * * * Our conclusion that the statute should not be treated as defining a public welfare offense rested on the commonsense distinction that a "food stamp can hardly be compared to a hand grenade."

Neither, in our view, can all guns be compared to hand grenades. Although the contrast is certainly not as stark as that presented in *Liparota*, the fact remains that there is a long tradition of widespread lawful gun ownership by private individuals in this country. * * * Here, the Government essentially suggests that we should interpret [§ 5861(d)] under the altogether different assumption that "one would hardly be surprised to learn that owning a gun is not an innocent act." That proposition is simply not supported by common experience. Guns in general are not "deleterious devices or products or obnoxious waste materials" that put their owners on notice that they stand "in responsible relation to a public danger."

The Government protests that guns, unlike food stamps, but like grenades and narcotics, are potentially harmful devices. * * * But that an

---

e. In *Balint*, the defendants were indicted for unlawfully selling derivatives of opium and cocoa leaves in the absence of valid prescription orders, in violation of the Narcotics Act. The defendants demurred to the indictment on the ground that it did not allege that they had sold the drugs knowing them to be such. The Court characterized the Act as a public welfare offense. It upheld the strict liability nature of the offense, despite the fact that it constituted a felony punishable by up to five years in prison.

item is "dangerous," in some general sense, does not necessarily suggest, as the Government seems to assume, that it is not also entirely innocent. Even dangerous items can, in some cases, be so commonplace and generally available that we would not consider them to alert individuals to the likelihood of strict regulation. * * *

* * * Roughly 50 percent of American homes contain at least one firearm of some sort, and in the vast majority of States, buying a shotgun or rifle is a simple transaction that would not alert a person to regulation any more than would buying a car.

If we were to accept as a general rule the Government's suggestion that dangerous and regulated items place their owners under an obligation to inquire at their peril into compliance with regulations, we would undoubtedly reach some untoward results. Automobiles, for example, might also be termed "dangerous" devices and are highly regulated at both the state and federal levels. Congress might see fit to criminalize the violation of certain regulations concerning automobiles, and thus might make it a crime to operate a vehicle without a properly functioning emission control system. But we probably would hesitate to conclude on the basis of silence that Congress intended a prison term to apply to a car owner whose vehicle's emissions levels, wholly unbeknownst to him, began to exceed legal limits between regular inspection dates. * * *

We concur in the Fifth Circuit's conclusion on this point: "It is unthinkable to us that Congress intended to subject such law-abiding, well-intentioned citizens to a possible ten-year term of imprisonment if * * * what they genuinely and reasonably believed was a conventional semi-automatic [weapon] turns out to have worn down into or been secretly modified to be a fully automatic weapon." As we noted in *Morissette*, the "purpose and obvious effect of doing away with the requirement of a guilty intent is to ease the prosecution's path to conviction." We are reluctant to impute that purpose to Congress where, as here, it would mean easing the path to convicting persons whose conduct would not even alert them to the probability of strict regulation in the form of a statute such as § 5861(d).

C

The potentially harsh penalty attached to violation of § 5861(d)—up to 10 years' imprisonment—confirms our reading of the Act. Historically, the penalty imposed under a statute has been a significant consideration in determining whether the statute should be construed as dispensing with *mens rea*. * * *

As commentators have pointed out, the small penalties attached to such offenses logically complemented the absence of a *mens rea* requirement: In a system that generally requires a "vicious will" to establish a crime, imposing severe punishments for offenses that require no *mens rea* would seem incongruous. * * * [C]ommentators collecting the early cases

have argued that offenses punishable by imprisonment cannot be understood to be public welfare offenses, but must require *mens rea*. * * *

* * * Close adherence to the early cases * * * might suggest that
punishing a violation as a felony is simply incompatible with the theory of
the public welfare offense. In this view, absent a clear statement from
Congress that *mens rea* is not required, we should not apply the public
welfare offense rationale to interpret any statute defining a felony offense
as dispensing with *mens rea*. But see *United States v. Balint*, [*supra*].

We need not adopt such a definitive rule of construction to decide this
case, however. Instead, we note only that where, as here, dispensing with
mens rea would require the defendant to have knowledge only of traditionally lawful conduct, a severe penalty is a further factor tending to suggest
that Congress did not intend to eliminate a *mens rea* requirement. In such
a case, the usual presumption that a defendant must know the facts that
make his conduct illegal should apply.

III * * *

We emphasize that our holding is a narrow one. * * * As we noted in
Morissette: "Neither this Court nor, so far as we are aware, any other has
undertaken to delineate a precise line or set forth comprehensive criteria
for distinguishing between crimes that require a mental element and
crimes that do not." We attempt no definition here, either. We note only
that our holding depends critically on our view that if Congress had
intended to make outlaws of gun owners who were wholly ignorant of the
offending characteristics of their weapons, and to subject them to lengthy
prison terms, it would have spoken more clearly to that effect.

For the foregoing reasons, the judgment of the Court of Appeals is
reversed, and the case is remanded for further proceedings consistent with
this opinion. * * *

[The concurring opinion of Justice Ginsburg, with whom Justice
O'Connor joined, is omitted.]

JUSTICE STEVENS, with whom JUSTICE BLACKMUN joins, dissenting. * * *

The Court is preoccupied with guns that "generally can be owned in
perfect innocence." This case, however, involves a semiautomatic weapon
that was readily convertible into a machinegun * * *. These are not guns
* * * that can be found in almost "50 percent of American homes." They
are particularly dangerous—indeed, a substantial percentage of the unregistered machineguns now in circulation are converted semiautomatic
weapons. * * *

I

Contrary to the assertion by the Court, the text of the statute does
provide "explicit guidance in this case." * * * Significantly, [§ 5861(d)]
contains no knowledge requirement, nor does it describe a common-law
crime.

The common law generally did not condemn acts as criminal unless the actor had "an evil purpose or mental culpability," and was aware of all the facts that made the conduct unlawful. In interpreting statutes that codified traditional common-law offenses, courts usually followed this rule, even when the text of the statute contained no such requirement. Because the offense involved in this case is entirely a creature of statute, however, "the background rules of the common law," do not require a particular construction, and critically different rules of construction apply. * * *

Although the lack of an express knowledge requirement in § 5861(d) is not dispositive, its absence suggests that Congress did not intend to require proof that the defendant knew all of the facts that made his conduct illegal. * * *

II

"Public welfare" offenses share certain characteristics: (1) they regulate "dangerous or deleterious devices or products or obnoxious waste materials"; (2) they "heighten the duties of those in control of particular industries, trades, properties or activities that affect public health, safety or welfare"; and (3) they "depend on no mental element but consist only of forbidden acts or omissions." Examples of such offenses include Congress' exertion of its power to keep dangerous narcotics, hazardous substances, and impure and adulterated foods and drugs out of the channels of commerce. * * *

The National Firearms Act unquestionably is a public welfare statute. * * *

NOTES AND QUESTIONS

1. *Morissette v. United States*, frequently quoted in *Staples* and a seminal case in the field, involved a junk dealer who entered a military bombing range and took spent bomb casings that had been lying around for years. He flattened them out and sold them for profit. Morissette was indicted and convicted of violating a federal statute that provided that "[w]hoever * * * steals, purloins, or knowingly converts to his use or the use of another, or without authority, sells, conveys or disposes of any * * * thing of value of the United States * * * shall be fined not more than $10,000 or imprisoned not more than ten years, or both * * *."

Morissette did not deny that he knowingly took the bomb casings, but he claimed that he thought that the casings had long ago been abandoned by the Government—they were free for the taking—and, therefore, he did not intend to steal the casings from the Government. The Government argued that unlike common law larceny, which required a specific intent to steal, the federal statute here did not expressly contain this *mens rea* element. The Court rejected the Government's argument, drawing a distinction between offenses drawn from the common law and entirely new statutory crimes, such as public welfare offenses:

> Congressional silence as to mental elements in an Act merely adopting into federal statutory law a concept of crime already so well defined in

common law and statutory interpretation by the states * * * warrant[s] quite contrary inferences than the same silence in creating an offense new to general law, for whose definition the courts have no guidance except the Act. * * *

* * * [W]here Congress borrows terms of art in which are accumulated the legal tradition and meaning of centuries of practice, it presumably knows and adopts the cluster of ideas that were attached to each borrowed word in the body of learning from which it was taken and the meaning its use will convey to the judicial mind unless otherwise instructed. In such case, absence of contrary direction may be taken as satisfaction with widely accepted definitions, not as a departure from them.

2. Strict liability is typically criticized on two grounds. First, strict liability legislation arguably does not deter, since the actor, by hypothesis, is unaware—and, as a reasonable person, would not be aware—of the facts that render his conduct dangerous. Second, it is unjust to condemn a person who is not morally culpable. But, are these claims accurate? Consider Richard A. Wasserstrom, *Strict Liability in the Criminal Law*, 12 Stan.L.Rev. 731, 736–37, 740–41 (1960):

> [On the issue of deterrence,] it might be the case that a person engaged in a certain kind of activity would be more careful precisely because he knew that this kind of activity was governed by a strict liability statute. It is at least plausible to suppose that the knowledge that certain criminal sanctions will be imposed if certain consequences ensue might induce a person to engage in that activity with much greater caution than would be the case if some lesser standard prevailed.

> In the second place * * *, it seems reasonable to believe that the presence of strict liability offenses might have the added effect of keeping a relatively large class of persons from engaging in certain kinds of activity. A person who did not regard himself as capable of conducting an enterprise in such a way so as not to produce the deleterious consequences proscribed by the statute might well refuse to engage in that activity at all. Of course, if the penalties for violation of the statute are minimal—if payment of fines is treated merely as a license to continue in operation—then unscrupulous persons will not be deterred by the imposition of this sanction. But this does not imply that unscrupulous persons would be quite so willing to engage in these activities if the penalties for violation were appreciably more severe. * * *

> * * * [T]he second of the two major kinds of criticism directed against strict criminal liability is that punishment of persons in accordance with the minimal requirements of strict liability—the punishment of persons in the absence of *mens rea*—is irreconcilable with those fundamental, long extant standards of criminal culpability which prevail in the community. * * *

> A * * * question is whether the proposition is presented as a *descriptive* or *prescriptive* assertion. It is not clear whether the imposition of strict liability is thought to be incompatible with the accepted values of society or whether the prevalence of strict liability is inconsistent with what ought to be accepted values.

As an empirical assertion the protest against strict liability on the grounds that it contravenes public sentiment is * * * at best an open hypothesis. Those who seek to substantiate its correctness turn to the fact that minimal penalties are often imposed. They construe this as indicative of the felt revulsion against the concept of strict criminal liability. That judges and juries often refuse to impose those sanctions which would be imposed in the comparable cases involving the presence of *mens rea,* is taken as additional evidence of community antipathy.

The evidence is, however, no less (and probably no more) persuasive on the other side. * * * While few persons would seriously wish to maintain that the legislature is either omniscient or a wholly adequate reflection of general or popular sentiment, the fact that so many legislatures have felt such apparently little compunction over enacting such statutes is surely indicative of the presence of a comparable community conviction. Strict liability offenses, as the critics so persistently note, are not mere sports, mere sporadic legislative oversights or anomalies. They are, again as the critics note, increasing in both number and scope. It may very well be the case that strict liability offenses ought to be condemned by the community; it is much more doubtful that they are presently held in such contumely.

3.   Do you believe the *Staples* Court reached the right result as a matter of precedent? As a matter of policy? Is your answer to the latter question based more on your feelings about guns and gun control, or regarding the concept of strict criminal liability?

4.   *Strict liability and the Constitution: the "constitutional innocence" principle. Staples* involved a statutory interpretation dispute. But, even if a legislature intends to enact a strict liability offense, there remains a fundamental question: is strict criminal liability constitutional? The Supreme Court has hardly been helpful in answering this question. On the one hand, per *Morissette,* it has intoned that *mens rea* is "no provincial or transient notion" and is "universal and persistent in mature systems of law." But, the Court has also warned that, although strict liability offenses have a "generally disfavored status," they "do not invariably offend constitutional requirements." United States v. United States Gypsum Co., 438 U.S. 422, 98 S.Ct. 2864, 57 L.Ed.2d 854 (1978). All of this has caused one scholar exasperatedly to describe the Court's *mens rea* jurisprudence this way: "*Mens rea* is an important requirement, but it is not a constitutional requirement, except sometimes." Herbert L. Packer, *Mens Rea and the Supreme Court,* 1962 Sup.Ct.Rev. 107, 107.

Professor Alan Michaels concludes, however, that a "balanced appraisal of the Supreme Court's strict liability decisions * * * reveals the Court's consistent adherence to an underlying principle that establishes the constitutional parameters of strict liability." Michaels describes the principle as "constitutional innocence":

According to [this] principle * * *, strict liability is constitutional when, but only when, the intentional conduct covered by the statute could be made criminal by the legislature. In other words, strict liability runs afoul of the Constitution [and violates the due process clause] if the other elements of the crime, with the strict liability element excluded, could not themselves be made a crime. Otherwise, strict liability is constitutional.

Alan C. Michaels, *Constitutional Innocence*, 112 Harv. L. Rev. 828, 834 (1999).

For example, consider the offense of bigamy, which frequently is a strict liability crime. It may be defined as possessing two *actus reus* elements: (1) marrying another person; and (2) while being married. The first element, of course, occurs intentionally. What makes the offense strict liability (when it is) is that a person may be convicted even if she reasonably but incorrectly believes that, for example, her first husband is deceased or that her first husband obtained a valid divorce. Applying the constitutional innocence principle, the issue is whether it would be constitutional for a legislature to punish a person simply for marrying another person (the non-strict liability element of bigamy). If it would be constitutional, then the addition of the second, strict-liability element does not render the statute unconstitutional. However, assuming that a hypothetical law prohibiting all marriages would be unconstitutional because it violates a person's fundamental right to marry, the bigamy law as drafted would violate due process under Michaels's analysis.

In view of the constitutional innocence principle, and assuming the dissent's statutory interpretation of the firearms law had prevailed, would this (now) strict liability firearms offense be constitutional?

GARNETT v. STATE

Court of Appeals of Maryland, 1993.
332 Md. 571, 632 A.2d 797.

MURPHY, CHIEF JUDGE.

Maryland's "statutory rape" law prohibiting sexual intercourse with an underage person is codified in Maryland Code (1957, 1992 Repl.Vol.) Art. 27, § 463, which reads in full:

"Second degree rape.

(a) *What constitutes.*—A person is guilty of rape in the second degree if the person engages in vaginal intercourse with another person:

(1) By force or threat of force against the will and without the consent of the other person; or

(2) Who is mentally defective, mentally incapacitated, or physically helpless, and the person performing the act knows or should reasonably know the other person is mentally defective, mentally incapacitated, or physically helpless; or

(3) Who is under 14 years of age and the person performing the act is at least four years older than the victim.

(b) *Penalty.*—Any person violating the provisions of this section is guilty of a felony and upon conviction is subject to imprisonment for a period of not more than 20 years."

Subsection (a)(3) represents the current version of a statutory provision dating back to the first comprehensive codification of the criminal law by the Legislature in 1809. * * *

I

Raymond Lennard Garnett is a young retarded man. At the time of the incident in question he was 20 years old. He has an I.Q. of 52. His guidance counselor from the Montgomery County public school system, Cynthia Parker, described him as a mildly retarded person who read on the third-grade level, did arithmetic on the 5th–grade level, and interacted with others socially at school at the level of someone 11 or 12 years of age. Ms. Parker added that Raymond attended special education classes and for at least one period of time was educated at home when he was afraid to return to school due to his classmates' taunting. Because he could not understand the duties of the jobs given him, he failed to complete vocational assignments; he sometimes lost his way to work. As Raymond was unable to pass any of the State's functional tests required for graduation, he received only a certificate of attendance rather than a high-school diploma.

In November or December 1990, a friend introduced Raymond to Erica Frazier, then aged 13; the two subsequently talked occasionally by telephone. On February 28, 1991, Raymond, apparently wishing to call for a ride home, approached the girl's house at about nine o'clock in the evening. Erica opened her bedroom window, through which Raymond entered; he testified that "she just told me to get a ladder and climb up her window." The two talked, and later engaged in sexual intercourse. Raymond left at about 4:30 a.m. the following morning. On November 19, 1991, Erica gave birth to a baby, of which Raymond is the biological father.

Raymond was tried * * * on one count of second degree rape under § 463(a)(3) proscribing sexual intercourse between a person under 14 and another at least four years older than the complainant. At trial, the defense twice proffered evidence to the effect that Erica herself and her friends had previously told Raymond that she was 16 years old, and that he had acted with that belief. The trial court excluded such evidence as immaterial, explaining:

> "Under 463, the only two requirements as relate to this case are that there was vaginal intercourse, [and] that * * * Ms. Frazier was under 14 years of age and that * * * Mr. Garnett was at least four years older than she. [* * *]

> "It is in the Court's opinion a strict liability offense."

The court found Raymond guilty. It sentenced him to a term of five years in prison, suspended the sentence and imposed five years of probation, and ordered that he pay restitution to Erica and the Frazier family. * * *

II * * *

Section 463(a)(3) does not expressly set forth a requirement that the accused have acted with a criminal state of mind, or *mens rea*. The State insists that the statute, by design, defines a strict liability offense, and that its essential elements were met in the instant case when Raymond, age 20, engaged in vaginal intercourse with Erica, a girl under 14 and more than 4 years his junior. Raymond replies that the criminal law exists to assess and punish morally culpable behavior. He says such culpability was absent here. He asks us to engraft onto subsection (a)(3) an implicit *mens rea* requirement * * *. Raymond argues that it is unjust, under the circumstances of this case which led him to think his conduct lawful, to brand him a felon and rapist.

III * * *

Modern scholars generally reject the concept of strict criminal liability. Professors LaFave and Scott summarize the consensus that punishing conduct without reference to the actor's state of mind fails to reach the desired end and is unjust:

> " 'It is inefficacious because conduct unaccompanied by an awareness of the factors making it criminal does not mark the actor as one who needs to be subjected to punishment in order to deter him or others from behaving similarly in the future, nor does it single him out as a socially dangerous individual who needs to be incapacitated or reformed. It is unjust because the actor is subjected to the stigma of a criminal conviction without being morally blameworthy. Consequently, on either a preventive or retributive theory of criminal punishment, the criminal sanction is inappropriate in the absence of mens rea.' "

LaFave & Scott, [*Criminal Law* (2d ed. 1986)], at 248, *quoting* Herbert L. Packer, Mens Rea *and the Supreme Court*, 1962 Sup.Ct.Rev. 107, 109.

Dean Singer has articulated other weaknesses of strict criminal liability theory: 1) extensive government civil regulations and strict liability in tort achieve the same deterrent effect; 2) the judicial efficiency of dispatching minor offenses without an inquiry into *mens rea* is attained equally by decriminalizing them, and hearing such cases in a regulatory or administrative forum; 3) the small penalties imposed for most strict liability offenses oblige the public to engage in a pernicious game of distinguishing "real" crime from some lesser form of crime; 4) some strict liability laws may result from careless drafting; and 5) strict liability dilutes the moral force that the criminal law has historically carried. Singer, [*The Resurgence of* Mens Rea: *III—The Rise and Fall of Strict Criminal* Liability, 30 B.C.L.Rev. 337, 389–397, 403–404 (1989)]. The author concludes that "the predicate for all criminal liability is blameworthiness; it is the social stigma which a finding of guilt carries that distinguishes the criminal [penalty] from all other sanctions. If the predicate is removed, the criminal law is set adrift."

[handwritten margin note: MPC approach]

Conscious of the disfavor in which strict criminal liability resides, the Model Penal Code states generally as a minimum requirement of culpability that a person is not guilty of a criminal offense unless he acts purposely, knowingly, recklessly, or negligently, *i.e.*, with some degree of *mens rea*. Model Penal Code § 2.02. The Code allows generally for a defense of ignorance or mistake of fact negating *mens rea*. § 2.04. The Model Penal Code generally recognizes strict liability for offenses deemed "violations," defined as wrongs subject only to a fine, forfeiture, or other civil penalty upon conviction, and not giving rise to any legal disability. *Id.* at §§ 1.04, 2.05.[2]

The commentators similarly disapprove of statutory rape as a strict liability crime. In addition to the arguments discussed above, they observe that statutory rape prosecutions often proceed even when the defendant's judgment as to the age of the complainant is warranted by her appearance, her sexual sophistication, her verbal misrepresentations, and the defendant's careful attempts to ascertain her true age. Voluntary intercourse with a sexually mature teen-ager lacks the features of psychic abnormality, exploitation, or physical danger that accompanies such conduct with children. *But see* Frances Olsen, *Statutory Rape: A Feminist Critique of Rights Analysis*, 63 Tex.L.Rev. 387, 401–413 (1984).

[handwritten margin note: moral wrong theory]

* * * Statutory rape laws are often justified on the * * * "moral wrong" theory;[f] by such reasoning, the defendant acting without *mens rea* nonetheless deserves punishment for having * * * violated moral teachings that prohibit sex outside of marriage. * * * We acknowledge here that it is uncertain to what extent Raymond's intellectual and social retardation may have impaired his ability to comprehend imperatives of sexual morality in any case.

IV

The legislatures of 17 states have enacted laws permitting a mistake of age defense in some form in cases of sexual offenses with underage persons. In Kentucky, the accused may prove in exculpation that he did not know the facts or conditions relevant to the complainant's age. In Washington, the defendant may assert that he reasonably believed the complainant to be of a certain age based on the alleged victim's own declarations. In some states, the defense is available in instances where the complainant's age rises above a statutorily prescribed level, but is not available when the complainant falls below the defining age. In other states, the availability of the defense depends on the severity of the sex offense charged to the accused.

In addition, the highest appellate courts of four states have determined that statutory rape laws by implication required an element of

[handwritten margin note: MPC stat. rape]

---

2. With respect to the law of statutory rape, the Model Penal Code strikes a compromise with its general policy against strict liability crimes. The Code prohibits the defense of ignorance or a reasonable mistake of age when the victim is below the age of ten, but allows it when the critical age stipulated in the offense is higher than ten. Model Penal Code, at §§ 213.1, 213.6(1). * * *

f. The "moral wrong" principle is described more fully at p. 196, Note 5.

mens rea as to the complainant's age. In the landmark case of *People v. Hernandez*, 61 Cal.2d 529, 39 Cal.Rptr. 361, 393 P.2d 673 (1964), the California Supreme Court * * * reversed the trial court's refusal to permit the defendant to present evidence of his good faith, reasonable belief that the complaining witness had reached the age of consent. * * *

V

We think it sufficiently clear, however, that Maryland's second degree rape statute defines a strict liability offense that does not require the State to prove *mens rea*; it makes no allowance for a mistake-of-age defense. The plain language of § 463, viewed in its entirety, and the legislative history of its creation lead to this conclusion. * * *

Section 463(a)(3) prohibiting sexual intercourse with underage persons makes no reference to the actor's knowledge, belief, or other state of mind. As we see it, this silence as to *mens rea* results from legislative design. First, subsection (a)(3) stands in stark contrast to the provision immediately before it, subsection (a)(2) prohibiting vaginal intercourse with incapacitated or helpless persons. In subsection (a)(2), the Legislature expressly provided as an element of the offense that "the person performing the act *knows or should reasonably know* the other person is mentally defective, mentally incapacitated, or physically helpless." In drafting this subsection, the Legislature showed itself perfectly capable of recognizing and allowing for a defense that obviates criminal intent * * *. That it chose not to include similar language in subsection (a)(3) indicates that the Legislature aimed to make statutory rape with underage persons a more severe prohibition based on strict criminal liability.

Second, an examination of the drafting history of § 463 during the 1976 revision of Maryland's sexual offense laws reveals that the statute was viewed as one of strict liability from its inception and throughout the amendment process. * * *

* * * [T]he Legislature explicitly raised, considered, and then explicitly jettisoned any notion of a *mens rea* element with respect to the complainant's age in enacting the law that formed the basis of current § 463(a)(3). In the light of such legislative action, we must inevitably conclude that the current law imposes strict liability on its violators.

This interpretation is consistent with the traditional view of statutory rape as a strict liability crime designed to protect young persons from the dangers of sexual exploitation by adults, loss of chastity, physical injury, and, in the case of girls, pregnancy. The majority of states retain statutes which impose strict liability for sexual acts with underage complainants. We observe again, as earlier, that even among those states providing for a mistake-of-age defense in some instances, the defense often is not available where the sex partner is 14 years old or less; the complaining witness in the instant case was only 13. * * *

VI

Maryland's second degree rape statute is by nature a creature of legislation. Any new provision introducing an element of *mens rea* * * * should properly result from an act of the Legislature itself, rather than judicial fiat. Until then, defendants in extraordinary cases, like Raymond, will rely upon the tempering discretion of the trial court at sentencing. * * *

ELDRIDGE, JUDGE, dissenting: * * *

The majority takes the position that the statute defines an entirely strict liability offense and has no *mens rea* requirement whatsoever. The majority indicates that the defendant's "knowledge, belief, or other state of mind" is wholly immaterial. The majority opinion at one point states: "We acknowledge here that it is uncertain to what extent Raymond's intellectual and social retardation may have impaired his ability to comprehend imperatives of sexual morality in any case." Nevertheless, according to the majority, it was permissible for the trial judge to have precluded exploration into Raymond's knowledge and comprehension because the offense is entirely one of strict liability. * * *

In my view, the issue concerning a *mens rea* requirement in § 463(a)(3) is not [so] limited * * *. I agree with the majority that an ordinary defendant's mistake about the age of his or her sexual partner is not a defense to a prosecution under § 463(a)(3). * * * This does not mean, however, that the statute contains no *mens rea* requirement at all. * * *

There are pure strict liability offenses where "the purpose of the penalty is to regulate rather than to punish behavior" and where criminal "liability is imposed regardless of the defendant's state of mind." These "offenses commonly involve light fines or penalties." There are other offenses (also unfortunately often called "strict liability" offenses) where the legislature has dispensed with a knowledge requirement in one respect but has not intended to impose criminal liability regardless of the defendant's state of mind. * * *

Neither the statutory language nor the legislative history of § 463(a)(3), or of the other provisions of the 1976 and 1977 sexual offense statutes, indicate that the General Assembly intended § 463(a)(3) to define a pure strict liability offense where criminal liability is imposed regardless of the defendant's mental state. The penalty provision for a violation of § 463(a)(3), namely making the offense a felony punishable by a maximum of 20 years imprisonment, is strong evidence that the General Assembly did not intend to create a pure strict liability offense.

In the typical situation involving an older person's engaging in consensual sexual activities with a teenager below the age of consent, and the scenario which the General Assembly likely contemplated when it enacted § 463(a)(3), * * * the defendant knows and intends that he or she is engaging in sexual activity with a young person. In addition, the defendant knows that the activity is regarded as immoral and/or improper by large segments of society. Moreover, the defendant is aware that "consent" by persons who are too young is ineffective. Although in a particular case the defendant may honestly but mistakenly believe, because of representations or appearances, that the other person is above the age of consent, the ordinary defendant in such case is or ought to be aware that there is a risk that the young person is not above the age of consent. As the majority opinion points out, "the traditional view [is] that those who engage in sex with young persons do so at their peril, assuming the risk that their partners are underage * * *." It seems to me that the above-mentioned knowledge factors, and particularly the mental ability to appreciate that one is taking a risk, constitute the *mens rea* of the offense[ ] defined by § 463(a)(3) * * *. * * * [T]he General Assembly assumed that a defendant is able to appreciate the risk involved by intentionally and knowingly engaging in sexual activities with a young person. There is no indication that the General Assembly intended that criminal liability attach to one who, because of his or her mental impairment, was unable to appreciate that risk.

* * * Under the view that § 463(a)(3) * * * define[s] pure strict liability offenses without any regard for the defendant's mental state, presumably a 20 year old, who passes out because of drinking too many alcoholic beverages, would be guilty of a sexual offense if a 13 year old engages in * * * sexual activities with the 20 year old while the latter is unconscious. I cannot imagine that the General Assembly intended any such result. * * *

ROBERT M. BELL, JUDGE, dissenting.

"It may be possible to conceive of legislation * * * so flagrantly in conflict with natural right, that the courts may set it aside as unwarranted, though no clause of the constitution can be found prohibiting it. But the cases must be rare indeed; and whenever they do occur the interposition of the judicial *veto* will rest upon such foundations of necessity that there can be little or no room for hesitation." [Singer, *supra.*]

Dissent

I do not dispute that the legislative history of * * * section 463 may be read to support the majority's interpretation that subsection (a)(3) was intended to be a strict liability statute. Nor do I disagree that it is in the public interest to protect the sexually naive child from the adverse physical, emotional, or psychological effects of sexual relations. I do not believe, however, that the General Assembly, in every case, whatever the nature of the crime and no matter how harsh the potential penalty, can subject a defendant to strict criminal liability. To hold, *as a matter of law*, that section 463(a)(3) does not require the State to prove that a defendant possessed the necessary mental state to commit the crime, *i.e.* knowingly engaged in sexual relations with a female under 14, or that the defendant may not litigate that issue in defense, "offends a principle of justice so rooted in the traditions of conscience of our people as to be ranked as fundamental" and is, therefore, inconsistent with due process. * * *

NOTES AND QUESTIONS

1. Does the outcome in *Garnett* bother you? If not, how do you justify imposition of punishment in this case? How much punishment would *you* impose? On the other hand, if the outcome in this case *does* bother you, why does it? Would you object to his conviction if Garnett was not mentally disabled? If his disability is important to your answer, why is it relevant? For an excellent discussion of the issues raised by *Garnett,* see Elizabeth Nevins–Saunders, *Incomprehensible Crimes: Defendants with Mental Retardation Charged with Statutory Rape*, 85 N.Y.U. L. Rev. 1067 (2010).

2. As *Garnett* noted, the Model Penal Code generally rejects strict criminal liability. The Commentary explains the American Law Institute's view on the subject:

> This section [§ 2.05] makes a frontal attack on absolute or strict liability in the penal law * * *. The method used is not to abrogate strict liability completely, but to provide that when conviction rests upon that basis the grade of the offense is reduced to a violation, which is not a "crime" [under Section 1.04] and under Sections 1.04(5) and 6.02(4) may result in no sentence other than a fine, or a fine and forfeiture or other authorized civil penalty. * * *

> * * * It has been argued, and the argument undoubtedly will be repeated, that strict liability is necessary for enforcement in a number of the areas where it obtains. But if practical enforcement precludes litigation of the culpability of alleged deviation from legal requirements, the enforcers cannot rightly demand the use of penal sanctions for the purpose. Crime does and should mean condemnation and no court should have to pass that judgment unless it can declare that the defendant's act was culpable. This is too fundamental to be compromised. American Law Institute, Model Penal Code and Commentaries, Comment to § 2.05 at 282–83 (1985).

3. According to Professor Catherine Carpenter's research reported in 2003, twenty-nine states and the District of Columbia apply strict liability principles to statutory rape. Eighteen states have a "hybrid" approach: A defendant may claim lack of *mens rea*—that he reasonably believed the female was old enough to consent to intercourse—in the ordinary statutory rape case, but strict liability principles apply when the underage female is very young. Only two states entirely reject strict liability for statutory rape. Catherine L. Carpenter, *On Statutory Rape, Strict Liability, and the Public Welfare Offense Model*, 53 Am. U. L. Rev. 313, 385–91 (2003).

4. Reconsider p. 184, Note 4. Is the Maryland statutory rape statute constitutional? Is it relevant to this question that the Supreme Court recently held that adults have a constitutional right to engage in homosexual sodomy? Lawrence v. Texas, 539 U.S. 558, 123 S.Ct. 2472, 156 L.Ed.2d 508 (2003). See Arnold H. Loewy, *Statutory Rape in a Post Lawrence v. Texas World*, 58 S.M.U. L. Rev. 77 (2005); State v. Holmes, 154 N.H. 723, 920 A.2d 632 (2007).

D. MISTAKE AND MENS REA

1. MISTAKE OF FACT

PEOPLE v. NAVARRO

Appellate Department, Los Angeles County Superior Court, 1979.
99 Cal.App.3d Supp. 1, 160 Cal.Rptr. 692.

DOWDS, JUDGE.

[Defendant was charged with violation of California Penal Code § 487.1, grand theft, and was convicted of petty theft, a lesser offense. Under state law, "[e]very person who shall feloniously steal * * * the personal property of another * * * is guilty of theft." Cal.Pen.Code § 484(a). This statute essentially codified the common law definition of larceny, i.e., "the trespassory taking and carrying away of the personal property of another with the intent to steal the property."]

* * * [Defendant's] contention on appeal is that the jury was improperly instructed. The only facts set forth in the record on appeal are that defendant was charged with stealing four wooden beams from a construction site and that the state of the evidence was such that the jury could have found that the defendant believed either (1) that the beams had been abandoned as worthless and the owner had no objection to his taking them or (2) that they had substantial value, had not been abandoned and he had no right to take them.

The court refused two jury instructions proposed by defendant reading as follows:

DEFENDANT'S A

"If one takes personal property with the good faith belief that the property has been abandoned or discarded by the true owner, he is not guilty of theft. This is the case even if such good faith belief is unreasonable.

The prosecutor must prove beyond a reasonable doubt that the defendant did not so believe for you to convict a defendant of theft."

DEFENDANT'S B

"If one takes personal property with the good faith belief that he has permission to take the property, he is not guilty of theft. This is the case even if such good faith belief is unreasonable.

The prosecutor must prove beyond a reasonable doubt that the defendant did not so believe for you to convict a defendant of theft."

Instead, the court instructed the jury in the words of the following modified instructions:

MODIFIED—DEFENDANT'S A

"If one takes personal property in the reasonable and good faith belief that the property has been abandoned or discarded by the true owner, he is not guilty of theft."

MODIFIED—DEFENDANT'S B

"If one takes personal property in the (reasonable) and good faith belief that he has the consent or permission of the owner to take the property, he is not guilty of theft.

If you have a reasonable doubt that the defendant had the required criminal intent as specified in these instructions, the defendant is entitled to an acquittal."

Accordingly, the question for determination on appeal is whether the defendant should be acquitted if there is a reasonable doubt that he had a good faith belief that the property had been abandoned or that he had the permission of the owner to take the property or whether that belief must be a reasonable one as well as being held in good faith.

A recent decision by the California Supreme Court throws light on this question. In *People v. Wetmore* (1978) 22 Cal.3d 318, 149 Cal.Rptr. 265, 583 P.2d 1308, defendant was charged with burglary, like theft a specific intent crime. The Supreme Court held that the trial court had erroneously refused to consider the * * * evidence that, because of mental illness, defendant was incapable of forming the specific intent required for conviction of the crime * * *. * * *

The instant case, does not, of course, involve evidence of mental illness. Evidence was presented, however, from which the jury could have concluded that defendant believed that the wooden beams had been abandoned and that the owner had no objection to his taking them, i.e., that he lacked the specific criminal intent required to commit the crime of theft (intent permanently to deprive an owner of his property). * * *

* * * In *People v. Devine* (1892) 95 Cal. 227, 30 P. 378, defendant's conviction of larceny was reversed. He had driven away in a wagon, without any attempt at secrecy, a number of hogs, his own and three bearing another's mark or brand. The Supreme Court pointed out: "There are cases in which all the knowledge which a person might have acquired by due diligence is to be imputed to him. But where a felonious intent must be proven it can be done only by proving what the accused knew. One cannot intend to steal property which he believes to be his own. He may be careless, and omit to make an effort to ascertain that the property which he thinks his own belongs to another; but so long as he believes it to be his own he cannot feloniously steal it * * *." * * *

Cases in other jurisdictions also hold that where the law requires a specific criminal intent, it is not enough merely to prove that a reasonable man would have had that intent, without meeting the burden of proof that the defendant himself also entertained it. * * *

* * * The proper rule, it seems to us, is set forth in Perkins on Criminal Law (2d ed. 1969) at pages 940–941: "If no specific intent or other special mental element is required for guilt of the offense charged, a mistake of fact will not be recognized as an excuse unless it was based upon reasonable grounds * * *. [On the other hand, b]ecause of the

requirement of a specific intent to steal there is no such thing as larceny by negligence. One does not commit this offense by carrying away the chattel of another in the mistaken belief that it is his own, no matter how great may have been the fault leading to this belief, if the belief itself is genuine.''

LaFave and Scott, Handbook on Criminal Law (1972) sets forth at page 357 what the authors call the " * * * rather simple rule that an honest mistake of fact or law is a defense when it negates a required mental element of the crime * * *.'' As an example they refer to the crime of receiving stolen property, stating " * * * if the defendant by a mistake of either fact or law did not know the goods were stolen, even though the circumstances would have led a prudent man to believe they were stolen, he does not have the required mental state and thus may not be convicted of the crime.''

In the instant case the trial court in effect instructed the jury that even though defendant in good faith believed he had the right to take the beams, and thus lacked the specific intent required for the crime of theft, he should be convicted unless such belief was reasonable. In doing so it erred. It is true that if the jury thought the defendant's belief to be unreasonable, it might infer that he did not in good faith hold such belief. If, however, it concluded that defendant in good faith believed that he had the right to take the beams, even though such belief was unreasonable as measured by the objective standard of a hypothetical reasonable man, defendant was entitled to an acquittal since the specific intent required to be proved as an element of the offense had not been established. * * *

The judgment is reversed.

NOTES AND QUESTIONS

1. If Navarro's belief that the beams were abandoned as worthless was unreasonable, doesn't this mean that he acted in a morally culpable manner? If so, why was his conviction reversed? To answer this question and better understand the common law approach to mistake-of-fact claims, it would be well to remember the distinction between the "culpability" and "elemental" meanings of the term *"mens rea"* (p. 150, Note 1), and the related distinction between "general intent" and "specific intent" crimes (p. 158, Note 6).

2. The rule set out by Professor Perkins in *Navarro* describes the common law approach to mistakes of fact. Perkins distinguishes between mistakes relating to specific intent crimes and those concerning general intent offenses. What is that distinction? Is Perkins's statement of the law consistent with the "rather simple rule" set forth by Professors LaFave and Scott, quoted immediately thereafter?

3. How would *Navarro* be analyzed under Model Penal Code § 2.04? For general discussion of the Code's treatment of mistake, see Peter W. Low, *The Model Penal Code, The Common Law, and Mistakes of Fact: Recklessness, Negligence, or Strict Liability?*, 19 Rutgers L.J. 539 (1988).

4. *Problem.* Here, really, are the facts, according to defendant *B*: *M* convinced *B* that *M* was a former Navy SEAL working for the CIA. *M* told *B* that the CIA wanted to recruit *B* as an agent to participate in a complicated CIA operation, "Double White." This operation required *B* to stage a robbery of the Wal–Mart at which *B* and *B*'s wife worked in order to "establish his outlaw status so that he could more easily infiltrate a drug cartel." *M* instructed *B* on how to conduct the robbery, including the requirement that *B* not wear a mask or gloves "and to make sure the cameras in the store caught the robbery on tape so the drug cartel would know that [*B*] robbed the store." *B* did as instructed, believing that the money he took would be immediately returned to Wal–Mart. State v. Blurton, 352 S.C. 203, 573 S.E.2d 802 (2002).

Assume that robbery is defined as "the forcible taking of the personal property of another with the intent to permanently deprive such person of the property." Based on the facts described here, is *B* entitled to a jury instruction on mistake-of-fact? If so, under what circumstances should *B* be acquitted of robbery?

5. *The "moral wrong" doctrine.* As *Navarro* teaches, at common law, a reasonable mistake of fact, but not an unreasonable one, ordinarily exculpates a defendant prosecuted for a general intent crime. The reasonableness of the mistake negates the culpability required for the offense. Infrequently, however, a court applying common law mistake doctrine will permit conviction of an actor whose mistake of fact was reasonable, if the defendant was culpable according to the "moral wrong" doctrine.

Consider Regina v. Prince, L.R. 2 Crim.Cas.Res. 154 (1875). *P* took an unmarried 14–year–old girl out of the possession and against the will of her parents, in violation of a statute that provided:

> Whosoever shall unlawfully take or cause to be taken an unmarried girl, being under the age of sixteen years, out of the possession and against the will of her father or mother * * * shall be guilty of a misdemeanor.

P testified that he believed that the female was eighteen years old. *P* was convicted, although *P*'s mistaken belief regarding the girl's age was deemed reasonable.

The Court for Crown Cases Reserved ruled that *P* was properly convicted. In an opinion that Baron Bramwell stated "gives full scope to the doctrine of the mens rea," the British court essentially invoked the moral wrong doctrine. According to the doctrine, even if an actor's mistake of fact is reasonable (and, thus, no moral culpability can be found on the basis of the mistaken belief), his intentional commission of an immoral act serves as the requisite blameworthiness to justify conviction (assuming, of course, that the *actus reus* of the offense was committed).

To apply the moral wrong doctrine, a court looks at the defendant's conduct through the accused's eyes, i.e., in *Prince*, we assume, as *P* believed, that he had taken an 18–year–old female (rather than a 14–year–old) out of the possession of her parents. If *that* conduct is immoral, the defendant assumes the risk that, unbeknownst to him, the attendant circumstances were not as he believed them to be and, therefore, that his conduct was not only immoral but also illegal. Bramwell explained:

[W]hat the statute contemplates, and what I say is wrong, is the taking of a female of such tender years that she is properly called a *girl*, can be said to be in another's *possession* * * *. No argument is necessary to prove this; it is enough to state the case. The legislature has enacted that if any one does this wrong act, he does it at the risk of her turning out to be under sixteen.

The moral wrong doctrine is highly controversial. What is troubling about its use?

6. *"Legal wrong" doctrine.* As an alternative to the moral wrong doctrine, some courts apply what may be characterized as a "legal wrong" doctrine. It works in the same manner, except that the term "illegal" substitutes for "immoral." That is, if a defendant's conduct, based on the facts as he believes them to be, constitutes a crime—not simply an immorality—he may be convicted of the *more serious* offense that his conduct establishes.

For example, assume that Statute 1 provides that it is a *felony* to furnish particular contraband (e.g., child pornography) to a person under the age of eighteen; Statute 2 provides that it is a *misdemeanor* to furnish the same contraband to a person age eighteen or older. If *D* furnishes the item to a seventeen-year-old (the *actus reus* of Statute 1) whom he reasonably believes is eighteen years old (the *mens rea* of Statute 2), the legal wrong doctrine provides that *D* may be convicted of the *felony*, and punished accordingly.

7. Consider again the facts set out in Note 6. Assume that the jurisdiction has a provision similar to Model Penal Code § 2.04. Of which offense, if any, would *D* be guilty?

2. MISTAKE (OR IGNORANCE) OF LAW

PEOPLE v. MARRERO

Court of Appeals of New York, 1987.
69 N.Y.2d 382, 515 N.Y.S.2d 212, 507 N.E.2d 1068.

BELLACOSA, JUDGE. * * *

[Julío Marrero, a guard at a federal prison in Danbury Connecticut, was arrested in a New York social club in possession of an unlicensed loaded .38 caliber automatic pistol, in alleged violation of New York Penal Law § 265.02.

Prior to trial, Marrero moved to dismiss his indictment on the ground that, under New York Penal Law § 265.20(a)(1), peace officers were exempt from criminal liability under the firearm possession statute. The term "peace officer," as defined by the interplay of Criminal Procedure Law (CPL) §§ 1.20 and 2.10, included any official or guard "of any state correctional facility or of any penal correctional institution." Marrero argued that as a guard in a Connecticut federal prison, he was a "peace officer" by virtue of the statutory language, "any penal correctional institution."

The trial judge agreed with Marrero's interpretation of the law, and granted the motion to dismiss the indictment. The State appealed, and by a 3–2 vote, an appellate court reversed the trial court's ruling and reinstated the indictment. It interpreted the language of the statutes to exempt only state guards. Consequently, at trial, Marrero could not argue that he was exempt from criminal liability. Marrero was convicted of violation of Penal Law § 265.02, from which this appeal followed.]

On the trial of the case, the court rejected the defendant's argument that his personal misunderstanding of the statutory definition of a peace officer is enough to excuse him from criminal liability under New York's mistake of law statute (Penal Law § 15.20). The court refused to charge the jury on this issue and defendant was convicted of criminal possession of a weapon in the third degree. We affirm the Appellate Division order upholding the conviction. * * *

The starting point for our analysis is the New York mistake statute as an outgrowth of the dogmatic common-law maxim that ignorance of the law is no excuse. The central issue is whether defendant's personal misreading or misunderstanding of a statute may excuse criminal conduct in the circumstances of this case.

The common-law rule on mistake of law was clearly articulated in *Gardner v. People,* (62 N.Y. 299). In *Gardner,* the defendants misread a statute and mistakenly believed that their conduct was legal. The court insisted, however, that the "mistake of law" did not relieve the defendants of criminal liability. * * *

* * * This is to be contrasted with *People v. Weiss,* 276 N.Y. 384, 12 N.E.2d 514 where, in a kidnapping case, the trial court precluded testimony that the defendants acted with the honest belief that seizing and confining the child was done with "authority of law." We held it was error to exclude such testimony since a good-faith belief in the legality of the conduct would negate an express and necessary element of the crime of kidnapping, i.e., intent, without authority of law, to confine or imprison another. Subject to the mistake statute, the instant case, of course, falls within the *Gardner* rationale because the weapons possession statute violated by this defendant imposes liability irrespective of one's intent.

The desirability of the *Gardner*-type outcome, which was to encourage the societal benefit of individuals' knowledge of and respect for the law, is underscored by Justice Holmes' statement: "It is no doubt true that there are many cases in which the criminal could not have known that he was breaking the law, but to admit the excuse at all would be to encourage ignorance where the law-maker has determined to make men know and obey, and justice to the individual is rightly outweighed by the larger interests on the other side of the scales" (Holmes, The Common Law, at 48 [1881]).

The revisors of New York's Penal Law intended no fundamental departure from this common-law rule in Penal Law § 15.20, which provides in pertinent part:

"§ 15.20.   *Effect of ignorance or mistake upon liability.* * * *

"2.   A person is not relieved of criminal liability for conduct because he engages in such conduct under a mistaken belief that it does not, as a matter of law, constitute an offense, unless such mistaken belief is founded upon an official statement of the law contained in (a) a statute or other enactment * * * (d) an interpretation of the statute or law relating to the offense, officially made or issued by a public servant, agency, or body legally charged or empowered with the responsibility or privilege of administering, enforcing or interpreting such statute or law." * * *

The defendant claims as a first prong of his defense that he is entitled to raise the defense of mistake of law under section 15.20(2)(a) because his mistaken belief that his conduct was legal was founded upon an official statement of the law contained in the statute itself. Defendant argues that his mistaken interpretation of the statute was reasonable in view of the alleged ambiguous wording of the peace officer exemption statute, and that his "reasonable" interpretation of an "official statement" is enough to satisfy the requirements of subdivision (2)(a). * * *

Δ argument

The prosecution * * * counters defendant's argument by asserting that one cannot claim the protection of mistake of law under section 15.20(2)(a) simply by misconstruing the meaning of a statute but must instead establish that the statute relied on actually permitted the conduct in question and was only later found to be erroneous. To buttress that argument, the People analogize New York's official statement defense to the approach taken by the Model Penal Code (MPC). Section 2.04 of the MPC provides:

The's argument

"Section 2.04.   *Ignorance or Mistake.* * * *

"(3) A belief that conduct does not legally constitute an offense is a defense to a prosecution for that offense based upon such conduct when * * * (b) he acts in reasonable reliance upon an official statement of the law, *afterward determined to be invalid or erroneous,* contained in (i) a statute or other enactment" (emphasis added).

MPC

Although the drafters of the New York statute did not adopt the precise language of the Model Penal Code provision with the emphasized clause, it is evident and has long been believed that the Legislature intended the New York statute to be similarly construed. In fact, the legislative history of section 15.20 is replete with references to the influence of the Model Penal Code provision. * * *

It was early recognized that the "official statement" mistake of law defense was a statutory protection against prosecution based on reliance of a statute that did *in fact* authorize certain conduct. "It seems obvious that society must rely on some statement of the law, and that conduct which *is in fact* 'authorized' * * * should not be subsequently condemned. The threat of punishment under these circumstances can have no deterrent effect unless the actor doubts the validity of the official pronounce-

Δ Conduct not authorized

ment—*a questioning of authority that is itself undesirable"* (Note, *Proposed Penal Law of New York,* 64 Colum.L.Rev. 1469, 1486 [emphasis added]). While providing a narrow escape hatch, the idea was simultaneously to encourage the public to read and rely on official statements of the law, not to have individuals conveniently and personally question the validity and interpretation of the law and act on that basis. If later the statute was invalidated, one who mistakenly acted in reliance on the authorizing statute would be relieved of criminal liability. That makes sense and is fair. To go further does not make sense and would create a legal chaos based on individual selectivity.

In the case before us, the underlying statute never *in fact authorized* the defendant's conduct; the defendant only thought that the statutory exemptions permitted his conduct when, in fact, the primary statute clearly forbade his conduct. * * *

We recognize that some legal scholars urge that the mistake of law defense should be available more broadly where a defendant misinterprets a potentially ambiguous statute not previously clarified by judicial decision and reasonably believes in good faith that the acts were legal. * * *

We conclude that the better and correctly construed view is that the defense should not be recognized, except where specific intent is an element of the offense or where the misrelied-upon law has later been properly adjudicated as wrong. Any broader view fosters lawlessness. * * *

* * * If defendant's argument were accepted, the exception would swallow the rule. Mistakes about the law would be encouraged, rather than respect for and adherence to law. There would be an infinite number of mistake of law defenses which could be devised from a good-faith, perhaps reasonable but mistaken, interpretation of criminal statutes, many of which are concededly complex. Even more troublesome are the opportunities for wrong-minded individuals to contrive in bad faith solely to get an exculpatory notion before the jury. These are not in terrorem arguments disrespectful of appropriate adjudicative procedures; rather, they are the realistic and practical consequences were the dissenters' views to prevail. Our holding comports with a statutory scheme which was not designed to allow false and diversionary stratagems to be provided for many more cases than the statutes contemplated. This would not serve the ends of justice but rather would serve game playing and evasion from properly imposed criminal responsibility.

Accordingly, the order of the Appellate Division should be affirmed.

[WACHTLER, CHIEF JUSTICE, and SIMONS and TITONE, JJ., concurred.]

HANCOCK, JUDGE (dissenting). * * *

The basic difference which divides the court may be simply put. Suppose the case of a man who has committed an act which is criminal not because it is inherently wrong or immoral but solely because it violates a criminal statute. He has committed the act in complete good faith under the mistaken but entirely reasonable assumption that the act does not constitute an offense because it is permitted by the wording of the statute. Does the law require that this man be punished? The majority says that it does and holds that (1) Penal Law § 15.20(2)(a) must be construed so that the man is precluded from offering a defense based on his mistake of law and (2) such construction is compelled by prevailing considerations of public policy and criminal jurisprudence. We take issue with the majority on both propositions.

There can be no question that under the view that the purpose of the criminal justice system is to punish blameworthiness or "choosing freely to do wrong," our supposed man who has acted innocently and without any intent to do wrong should not be punished. * * * Since he has not knowingly committed a wrong there can be no reason for society to exact retribution. Because the man is law-abiding and would not have acted but for his mistaken assumption as to the law, there is no need for punishment to deter him from further unlawful conduct. Traditionally, however, under the ancient rule of Anglo–American common law that ignorance or mistake of law is no excuse, our supposed man would be punished.

The maxim *"ignorantia legis neminem excusat"* finds its roots in Medieval law when the "actor's intent was irrelevant since the law punished the *act itself.*" * * * Although the common law has gradually evolved from its origins in Anglo–Germanic tribal law (adding the element of intent [*mens rea*] and recognizing defenses based on the actor's mental state * * *) the dogmatic rule that ignorance or mistake of law is no excuse has remained unaltered. Various justifications have been offered for the rule, but all are frankly pragmatic and utilitarian—preferring the interests of society (e.g., in deterring criminal conduct, fostering orderly judicial administration, and preserving the primacy of the rule of law) to the interest of the individual in being free from punishment except for intentionally engaging in conduct which he knows is criminal.

Today there is widespread criticism of the common-law rule mandating categorical preclusion of the mistake of law defense. The utilitarian arguments for retaining the rule have been drawn into serious question; but the fundamental objection is that it is simply wrong to punish someone who, in good-faith reliance on the wording of a statute, believed that what he was doing was lawful. It is contrary to "the notion that punishment should be conditioned on a showing of subjective moral blameworthiness." This basic objection to the maxim *"ignorantia legis neminem excusat"* may have had less force in ancient times when most crimes consisted of acts which by their very nature were recognized as evil *(malum in se)*. In modern times, however, with the profusion of legislation making otherwise lawful conduct criminal *(malum prohibitum)*, the "common law fiction that every man is presumed to know the law has become indefensible in fact or logic."

With this background we proceed to a discussion of our disagreement with the majority's construction of Penal Law § 15.20(2)(a) and the policy and jurisprudential arguments made in support of that construction. * * *

It is difficult to imagine a case more squarely within the wording of Penal Law § 15.20(2)(a) or one more fitted to what appears clearly to be the intended purpose of the statute than the one before us. * * *

Defendant's mistaken belief that, as a Federal corrections officer, he could legally carry a loaded weapon without a license was based on the express exemption from criminal liability under Penal Law § 265.02 accorded * * * to "peace officers" as defined in the Criminal Procedure Law and on his reading of the statutory definition for "peace officer" * * * as meaning a correction officer "of *any* penal correctional institution" (emphasis added), including an institution not operated by New York State. Thus, he concluded erroneously that, as a corrections officer in a Federal prison, he was a "peace officer" and, as such, exempt by the express terms of Penal Law § 265.–20(a)(1)(a). This mistaken belief, based in good faith on the statute defining "peace officer," is, defendant contends, the precise sort of "mistaken belief * * * founded upon an official statement of the law contained in * * * a statute or other enactment" which gives rise to a mistake of law defense under Penal Law § 15.20(2)(a). He points out, of course, that when he acted in reliance on his belief he had no way of foreseeing that a court would eventually resolve the question of the statute's meaning against him and rule that his belief had been mistaken, as three of the five-member panel at the Appellate Division ultimately did in the first appeal.

The majority, however, has accepted the People's argument that to have a defense under Penal Law § 15.20(2)(a) "a defendant must show that the statute *permitted his conduct,* not merely that he believed it did." * * *

Nothing in the statutory language suggests the interpretation urged by the People and adopted by the majority: that Penal Law § 15.20(2)(a) is available to a defendant *not* when he has mistakenly read a statute *but only* when he has correctly read and relied on a statute which is later invalidated. Such a construction contravenes the general rule that penal statutes should be construed against the State and in favor of the accused * * *.

More importantly, the construction leads to an anomaly: only a defendant who is *not mistaken* about the law when he acts has a mistake of law defense. * * * Such construction is obviously illogical; it strips the statute of the very effect intended by the Legislature in adopting the mistake of law defense. The statute is of no benefit to a defendant who has proceeded in good faith on an erroneous but concededly reasonable interpretation of a statute, as defendant presumably has. * * *

* * * It is self-evident that in enacting Penal Law § 15.20(2) as part of the revision and modernization of the Penal Law the Legislature intended to effect a needed reform by abolishing what had long been considered the unjust archaic common-law rule totally prohibiting mistake of law as a defense. * * *

The majority construes the statute, however, so as to rule out *any* defense based on mistake of law. In so doing, it defeats the only possible purpose for the statute's enactment and resurrects the very rule which the Legislature rejected in enacting Penal Law § 15.20(2)(a) as part of its modernization and reform of the Penal Law. * * *

Instead, the majority bases its decision on an analogous provision in the Model Penal Code and concludes that despite its totally different wording and meaning Penal Law § 15.20(2)(a) should be read as if it were Model Penal Code § 2.04(3)(b)(i). But New York in revising the Penal Law did not adopt the Model Penal Code. * * * New York followed parts of the Model Penal Code provisions and rejected others. * * *

While Penal Law § 15.20(2) and Model Penal Code § 2.04 are alike in their rejection of the strict common-law rule, they are not alike in wording and differ significantly in substance. * * *

Thus, the precise phrase in the Model Penal Code limiting the defense under section 2.04(3)(b)(i) to reliance on a statute "afterward determined to be invalid or erroneous" which, if present, would support the majority's narrow construction of the New York statute, is omitted from Penal Law § 15.20(2)(a). How the Legislature can be assumed to have enacted the very language which it has specifically rejected is not explained. * * *

Any fair reading of the majority opinion, we submit, demonstrates that the decision to reject a mistake of law defense is based on considerations of public policy and on the conviction that such a defense would be bad, rather than on an analysis of CPL 15.20(2)(a) under the usual principles of statutory construction. * * *

* * * [A] statute which recognizes a defense based on a man's good-faith mistaken belief founded on a well-grounded interpretation of an official statement of the law contained in a statute is a just law. The law embodies the ideal of contemporary criminal jurisprudence "that punishment should be conditioned on a showing of subjective moral blameworthiness." * * *

If defendant's offer of proof is true, his is not the case of a "free agent confronted with a choice between doing right and doing wrong and choosing freely to do wrong." He carried the gun in the good-faith belief that, as a Federal corrections officer, it was lawful for him to do so under the words of the statute. * * *

We do not believe that permitting a defense in this case will produce the grievous consequences the majority predicts. * * * Indeed, although the majority foresees "an infinite number of mistake of law defenses," New Jersey, which adopted a more liberal mistake of law statute in 1978,[g] has apparently experienced no such adversity * * *. Nor is there any

---

g. The New Jersey statute provides that a "belief that conduct does not legally constitute an offense is a defense to a prosecution for that offense * * * when * * * [t]he actor otherwise diligently pursues all means available to ascertain the meaning and application of the offense to his conduct and honestly and in good faith concludes his conduct is not an offense in circumstances in which a law-abiding and prudent person would also so conclude." N.J.S.A. 2C:2–4(c)(3).

reason to believe that courts will have more difficulty separating valid claims from "diversionary stratagem[s]" in making preliminary legal determinations as to the validity of the mistake of law defense than of justification or any other defense. * * *

There should be a reversal and defendant should have a new trial in which he is permitted to assert a defense of mistake of law under Penal Law § 15.20(2)(a).

[KAYE and ALEXANDER, JJ., concurred in the dissent.]

NOTES AND QUESTIONS

1. Who has the better side of the arguments regarding the meaning of Section 15.20(2), New York's mistake-of-law statute? Who has the better side of the underlying policy arguments? On the latter issue, consider Dan M. Kahan, *Ignorance of the Law* Is *an Excuse—but Only for the Virtuous*, 96 Mich. L. Rev. 127, 131, 133–34 (1997):

> The New York Court of Appeals's reason for denying a mistake of law defense was the Holmesian *utility of knowledge* principle. The point of punishing the legally mistaken, the court explained, is "to encourage the societal benefit of individuals' knowledge of and respect for the law." Were Marrero to be afforded a defense, "[m]istakes about the law would be encouraged."

> There's nothing persuasive in this account. The [Holmesian fear] of strategic heedlessness [namely, that "a person bent on violating the rights of others * * * could evade punishment by remaining studiously ignorant of his legal duties"] obviously rang false in Marrero's individual case. Marrero hadn't deliberately shielded himself from legal knowledge; rather he had tenaciously attempted to ferret it out,[h] displaying exactly the type of dedication to legal learning that the utility of knowledge purports to value.

> Nor would an excuse for Marrero have promoted strategic heedlessness in others. Marrero sought to present a *reasonable mistake of law* defense. Had the court sided with Marrero, it would have been establishing, in effect, a negligence standard with respect to the existence or meaning of the law defining who counts as a "peace officer" under the New York gun possession statute. Under such a standard, heedlessness would be a foolish strategy, for a lawbreaker who deliberately failed to take reasonable steps to learn the law would be deemed negligent and hence denied a defense.

> In fact, if the goal were truly to maximize private knowledge of law, a negligence standard would be unambiguously superior to a strict liability standard. This is so because the value of learning the law is always higher when the law excuses reasonable mistakes of law than when it doesn't.

---

h. Although it is not set out in the Court of Appeals opinion above, Marrero's understanding of the law was based not only on his own reading of the statute, but also on a statement of an instructor in a local criminal justice course. "[I]t was also how the statutes were understood by local gun dealers, who routinely sold weapons to federal prison guards without demanding proof that the guards were licensed to carry such weapons." Kahan, at 131.

[handwritten margin note: Marrero's reliance on instructor in course]

The preceding argument might suggest that the dissent was correct in *Marrero*—that a reasonable mistake of law should excuse. But, there is another way to look at the issue. Sometimes a person—perhaps Marrero—will believe that his conduct is wrongful and, therefore, investigate the law in order to see if he can find a loophole to fit through. If so, as Professor Stephen Garvey has put it, Marrero's "reason for looking so closely into the law was not so much to honor it, but to find a gap in it that he could exploit." If so, Garvey writes,

> one might say that the law should not tolerate, let alone encourage, the search for loopholes. Refusing to excuse an actor who believes, even reasonably, that the law permits him to engage in conduct he otherwise believes to be wrongful (or believes that most others believe to be wrongful), is one way to discourage it.

Stephen P. Garvey, *When Should a Mistake of Fact Excuse?*, 42 Texas Tech. L. Rev. 359, 366 (2009).

2. *An exception to the no-excuse rule: "entrapment by estoppel" or "reasonable reliance."* Commonwealth v. Twitchell, 416 Mass. 114, 617 N.E.2d 609 (1993):

> Although it has long been held that "ignorance of the law is no defence," there is substantial justification for treating as a defense the belief that conduct is not a violation of law when a defendant has reasonably relied on an official statement of the law, later determined to be wrong, contained in an official interpretation of the public official who is charged by law with the responsibility for the interpretation or enforcement of the law defining the offense. Federal courts have characterized an affirmative defense of this nature as "entrapment by estoppel."

This defense is sometimes codified by statute. Other courts rely on general "fairness" principles or on constitutional due process standards to recognize a defense.

Model Penal Code § 2.04(3)(b) codifies one version of this defense. In a jurisdiction applying the Code, could Marrero rely on his criminal justice instructor or the statements of gun dealers to avoid conviction?

What would the result be in the following case under the Model Penal Code? *H*, a minister, was convicted of violation of a statute making it unlawful to erect or maintain any sign intended to aid in the solicitation or performance of marriages. On appeal, *H* argued that his conviction was invalid because the court refused to permit him to introduce evidence that he did not erect the signs until the State's Attorney (the local prosecutor) advised him that his intended actions were lawful. Should *H* have been permitted to introduce this evidence? See Hopkins v. State, 193 Md. 489, 69 A.2d 456 (1949). What if, instead, *H* had contacted the state's most successful criminal defense lawyer for advice? Or your criminal law professor?

3. *A constitutional exception to the no-defense rule.* In *Marrero*, the defendant did not claim that he was unaware of the firearm possession statute at issue. Rather, he claimed to have been *mistaken* as to its meaning (and, perhaps, to have reasonably relied on others' interpretations of the statute). However, what if a person charged with an offense says, "I didn't even know

that the statute existed"? Does ignorance (as distinguished from mistake) of law *ever* excuse?

In Lambert v. California, 355 U.S. 225, 78 S.Ct. 240, 2 L.Ed.2d 228 (1957), a Los Angeles ordinance provided that it was unlawful for "any convicted person" to remain in the city for more than five days without registering as a convicted person. The ordinance defined "any convicted person" as follows:

> "Any person who * * * has been or hereafter is convicted of an offense punishable as a felony in the State of California, or who has been or who is hereafter convicted of any offense in any place other than the State of California, which offense, if committed in the State of California, would have been punishable as a felony."

At the time of her arrest, *L* had been a resident of Los Angeles for seven years. She previously had been convicted of forgery while she lived in the city, but she failed to register. She claimed that she did not do so because she was unaware of the ordinance. The Supreme Court held, 5–4, that *L*'s due process rights were violated:

> We must assume that appellant had no actual knowledge of the requirement that she register under this ordinance, as she offered proof of this defense which was refused. The question is whether a registration act of this character violates due process where it is applied to a person who has no actual knowledge of his duty to register, and where no showing is made of the probability of such knowledge.

> We do not go with Blackstone in saying that "a vicious will" is necessary to constitute a crime, for conduct alone without regard to the intent of the doer is often sufficient. There is wide latitude in the lawmakers to declare an offense and to exclude elements of knowledge and diligence from its definition. But we deal here with conduct that is wholly passive—mere failure to register. It is unlike the commission of acts, or the failure to act under circumstances that should alert the doer to the consequences of his deed. The rule that "ignorance of the law will not excuse" is deep in our law * * *. On the other hand, due process places some limits on its exercise. Engrained in our concept of due process is the requirement of notice. * * * Notice is required in a myriad of situations where a penalty or forfeiture might be suffered for mere failure to act. * * * [T]he principle is * * * appropriate where a person, wholly passive and unaware of any wrongdoing, is brought to the bar of justice for condemnation in a criminal case.

> Registration laws are common and their range is wide. Many such laws are akin to licensing statutes in that they pertain to the regulation of business activities. But the present ordinance is entirely different. Violation of its provisions is unaccompanied by any activity whatever, mere presence in the city being the test. Moreover, circumstances which might move one to inquire as to the necessity of registration are completely lacking. * * * We believe that actual knowledge of the duty to register or proof of the probability of such knowledge and subsequent failure to comply are necessary before a conviction under the ordinance can stand.

In light of *Lambert*, consider the following:

A.   The late Whitney Houston was once invited to sing the National Anthem at a Detroit Tigers baseball game. Assume she sung it as part of a medley of patriotic songs and is charged with violation of Mich.Comp.Laws Ann. § 750.542 (2002), which prohibits the singing of the National Anthem "in any public place * * * except as an entire and separate composition * * * and without embellishments of national or other melodies * * *." Does *Lambert* apply to these hypothetical facts?

B.   On July 1, a state law takes effect requiring pharmacists to compile records of the names and addresses of all purchasers of Viagra, a prescription drug for erectile dysfunction. A pharmacist, unaware of the law until July 8 (she was on an around-the-world vacation from January 1 until June 30), is prosecuted for her week-long recordkeeping omissions. Does *Lambert* protect her?

4.   *Culture and ignorance of law.* Assume the following: An Iraqi mother and father and their two daughters come to the United States to escape political repression and take residence in Nebraska. After being here for a year, the parents permit their daughters, ages 13 and 14 respectively, to marry two Iraqi men, ages 28 and 34 respectively. The practice of marrying girls of this age is customary in Iraq but illegal in Nebraska, where the minimum legal marital age is seventeen. The parents are charged with child abuse, on the ground that they permitted this underage marriage to occur. Should the parents' lack of knowledge of Nebraska law serve as an excuse? To what extent should a person's foreign cultural background be considered in determining culpability?

CHEEK v. UNITED STATES

Supreme Court of the United States, 1991.
498 U.S. 192, 111 S.Ct. 604, 112 L.Ed.2d 617.

JUSTICE WHITE delivered the opinion of the Court.

Title 26, § 7201 of the United States Code provides that any person "who willfully attempts in any manner to evade or defeat any tax imposed by this title or the payment thereof" shall be guilty of a felony. Under 26 U.S.C. § 7203, "[a]ny person required under this title * * * or by regulations made under authority thereof to make a return * * * who willfully fails to * * * make such return" shall be guilty of a misdemeanor. This case turns on the meaning of the word "willfully" as used in §§ 7201 and 7203.

I

Petitioner John L. Cheek has been a pilot for American Airlines since 1973. He filed federal income tax returns through 1979 but thereafter ceased to file returns. He also claimed an increasing number of withholding allowances—eventually claiming 60 allowances by mid–1980—and for the years 1981 to 1984 indicated on his W–4 forms that he was exempt from federal income taxes. In 1983, petitioner unsuccessfully sought a refund of all tax withheld by his employer in 1982. Petitioner's income during this period at all times far exceeded the minimum necessary to trigger the statutory filing requirement.

As a result of his activities, petitioner was indicted for 10 violations of federal law. He was charged with six counts of willfully failing to file a federal income tax return for the years 1980, 1981, and 1983 through 1986, in violation of 26 U.S.C. § 7203. He was further charged with three counts of willfully attempting to evade his income taxes for the years 1980, 1981, and 1983 in violation of 26 U.S.C. § 7201. In those years, American Airlines withheld substantially less than the amount of tax petitioner owed because of the numerous allowances and exempt status he claimed on his W–4 forms. The tax offenses with which petitioner was charged are specific intent crimes that require the defendant to have acted willfully.

At trial, the evidence established that between 1982 and 1986, petitioner was involved in at least four civil cases that challenged various aspects of the federal income tax system. In all four of those cases, the plaintiffs were informed by the courts that many of their arguments, including that they were not taxpayers within the meaning of the tax laws, that wages are not income, that the Sixteenth Amendment does not authorize the imposition of an income tax on individuals, and that the Sixteenth Amendment is unenforceable, were frivolous or had been repeatedly rejected by the courts. During this time period, petitioner also attended at least two criminal trials of persons charged with tax offenses. In addition, there was evidence that in 1980 or 1981 an attorney had advised Cheek that the courts had rejected as frivolous the claim that wages are not income.

Cheek represented himself at trial and testified in his defense. He admitted that he had not filed personal income tax returns during the years in question. He testified that as early as 1978, he had begun attending seminars sponsored by, and following the advice of, a group that believes, among other things, that the federal tax system is unconstitutional. Some of the speakers at these meetings were lawyers who purported to give professional opinions about the invalidity of the federal income tax laws. Cheek produced a letter from an attorney stating that the Sixteenth Amendment did not authorize a tax on wages and salaries but only on gain or profit. Petitioner's defense was that, based on the indoctrination he received from this group and from his own study, he sincerely believed that the tax laws were being unconstitutionally enforced and that his actions during the 1980–1986 period were lawful. He therefore argued that he had acted without the willfulness required for conviction of the various offenses with which he was charged.

In the course of its instructions, the trial court advised the jury that to prove "willfulness" the Government must prove the voluntary and intentional violation of a known legal duty, a burden that could not be proved by showing mistake, ignorance, or negligence. The court further advised the jury that an objectively reasonable good-faith misunderstanding of the law would negate willfulness but mere disagreement with the law would not. The court described Cheek's beliefs about the income tax system and instructed the jury that if it found that Cheek "honestly and reasonably believed that he was not required to pay income taxes or to file tax returns," a not guilty verdict should be returned. * * *

At the end of the first day of deliberation, the jury sent out [a] note saying that it * * * could not reach a verdict because " '[w]e are divided on the issue as to if Mr. Cheek honestly & reasonably believed that he was not required to pay income tax.' " When the jury resumed its deliberations, the District Judge gave the jury an additional instruction. This instruction stated in part that "[a]n honest but unreasonable belief is not a defense and does not negate willfulness." * * * Approximately two hours later, the jury returned a verdict finding petitioner guilty on all counts.

Petitioner appealed his convictions, arguing that the District Court erred by instructing the jury that only an objectively reasonable misunderstanding of the law negates the statutory willfulness requirement. The United States Court of Appeals for the Seventh Circuit rejected that contention and affirmed the convictions. * * *

II

The general rule that ignorance of the law or a mistake of law is no defense to criminal prosecution is deeply rooted in the American legal system. Based on the notion that the law is definite and knowable, the common law presumed that every person knew the law. This common-law rule has been applied by the Court in numerous cases construing criminal statutes.

The proliferation of statutes and regulations has sometimes made it difficult for the average citizen to know and comprehend the extent of the duties and obligations imposed by the tax laws. Congress has accordingly softened the impact of the common-law presumption by making specific intent to violate the law an element of certain federal criminal tax offenses. Thus, the Court almost 60 years ago interpreted the statutory term "willfully" as used in the federal criminal tax statutes as carving out an exception to the traditional rule. This special treatment of criminal tax offenses is largely due to the complexity of the tax laws. In *United States v. Murdock,* 290 U.S. 389, 54 S.Ct. 223, 78 L.Ed. 381 (1933), the Court recognized that:

> "Congress did not intend that a person, by reason of a bona fide misunderstanding as to his liability for the tax, as to his duty to make a return, or as to the adequacy of the records he maintained, should become a criminal by his mere failure to measure up to the prescribed standard of conduct."

The Court held that the defendant was entitled to an instruction with respect to whether he acted in good faith based on his actual belief. In

Murdock, the Court interpreted the term "willfully" as used in the criminal tax statutes generally to mean "an act done with a bad purpose," or with "an evil motive."

Subsequent decisions have refined this proposition. In *United States v. Bishop,* 412 U.S. 346, 93 S.Ct. 2008, 36 L.Ed.2d 941 (1973), we described the term "willfully" as connoting "a voluntary, intentional violation of a known legal duty," and did so with specific reference to the "bad faith or evil intent" language employed in *Murdock.* * * *

* * * Taken together, [these cases] conclusively establish that the standard for the statutory willfulness requirement is the "voluntary, intentional violation of a known legal duty." * * *

III * * *

Willfulness, as construed by our prior decisions in criminal tax cases, requires the Government to prove that the law imposed a duty on the defendant, that the defendant knew of this duty, and that he voluntarily and intentionally violated that duty. We deal * * * with the case where the issue is whether the defendant knew of the duty purportedly imposed by the provision of the statute or regulation he is accused of violating * * *. In such a case, if the Government proves actual knowledge of the pertinent legal duty, the prosecution, without more, has satisfied the knowledge component of the willfulness requirement. But carrying this burden requires negating a defendant's claim of ignorance of the law or a claim that because of a misunderstanding of the law, he had a good-faith belief that he was not violating any of the provisions of the tax laws. This is so because one cannot be aware that the law imposes a duty upon him and yet be ignorant of it, misunderstand the law, or believe that the duty does not exist. In the end, the issue is whether, based on all the evidence, the Government has proved that the defendant was aware of the duty at issue, which cannot be true if the jury credits a good-faith misunderstanding and belief submission, whether or not the claimed belief or misunderstanding is objectively reasonable.

In this case, if Cheek asserted that he truly believed that the Internal Revenue Code did not purport to treat wages as income, and the jury believed him, the Government would not have carried its burden to prove willfulness, however unreasonable a court might deem such a belief. Of course, in deciding whether to credit Cheek's good-faith belief claim, the jury would be free to consider any admissible evidence from any source showing that Cheek was aware of his duty to file a return and to treat wages as income, including evidence showing his awareness of the relevant provisions of the Code or regulations, of court decisions rejecting his interpretation of the tax law, of authoritative rulings of the Internal Revenue Service, or of any contents of the personal income tax return forms and accompanying instructions that made it plain that wages should be returned as income.

We thus disagree with the Court of Appeals' requirement that a claimed good-faith belief must be objectively reasonable if it is to be considered as possibly negating the Government's evidence purporting to show a defendant's awareness of the legal duty at issue. * * *

It was * * * error to instruct the jury to disregard evidence of Cheek's understanding that, within the meaning of the tax laws, he was not a person required to file a return or to pay income taxes and that wages are not taxable income, as incredible as such misunderstandings of and beliefs about the law might be. Of course, the more unreasonable the asserted beliefs or misunderstandings are, the more likely the jury will consider them to be nothing more than simple disagreement with known legal duties imposed by the tax laws and will find that the Government has carried its burden of proving knowledge. * * *

JUSTICE BLACKMUN, with whom JUSTICE MARSHALL joins, dissenting. * * *

This Court's opinion today, I fear, will encourage taxpayers to cling to frivolous views of the law in the hope of convincing a jury of their sincerity. If that ensues, I suspect we have gone beyond the limits of common sense. * * *

NOTES AND QUESTIONS

1. Based on the trial judge's instructional error discussed in Part III of the opinion, the case was remanded for retrial. On retrial with a correct jury instruction, Cheek was again convicted on all counts, sentenced to a year and a day in prison, and fined $62,000. His convictions were affirmed. United States v. Cheek, 3 F.3d 1057 (7th Cir.1993) (observing, "Like most of us, John Cheek, does not like to pay taxes. Unlike most of us, however, he has refused to pay them. As a result of his refusal to pay federal income taxes, Mr. Cheek has been a frequent visitor to our courts.").

2. In *Marrero* (p. 197), the defendant was not permitted to raise a claim of *reasonable* mistake of law. In *Cheek*, the defendant *was* permitted to claim a patently *unreasonable* mistake of law as a defense. What is going on here?

3. *Problem.* W was prosecuted pursuant to the following statute:

A person who wilfully: 1. seizes, confines, inveigles, or kidnaps another, with intent to cause him, without authority of law, to be confined or imprisoned within this state * * * against his will * * * is guilty of kidnapping * * *.

At trial, W was not permitted by the trial court to introduce evidence that X, a law enforcement officer, requested his assistance in arresting V, a suspect in a criminal investigation. In order to ensure W of X's authority to assist in the seizure (arrest), X supposedly "deputized" W by handing him a State Secret Service badge. (In actuality, this action did not provide W with the requisite legal authority for his actions.)

Based on what you learned in *Cheek*, should W have been permitted to introduce this evidence? See People v. Weiss, 276 N.Y. 384, 12 N.E.2d 514 (1938).

4. According to <http://nojusticeinamerica.weebly.com>:

If you extort a little bit of money they call you a thief. If you steal trillions of dollars they call you president. * * * In 1894 the U.S. Supreme Court ruled that there is no constitutional basis for the United States Government to collect taxes on the wages of working Americans and ordered them to stop. This ruling has never been overturned. Federal income tax is illegal or at best to be considered voluntary. If you don't file a tax form and you do not pay the tax you simply do not owe it.

Having read this on the Internet, are *you* going to stop paying your taxes?

CHAPTER 6

CAUSATION

■ ■ ■

A. ACTUAL CAUSE (CAUSE–IN–FACT)

VELAZQUEZ v. STATE

District Court of Appeal of Florida, 1990.
561 So.2d 347.

HUBBART, J. * * *

[The facts in this vehicular homicide prosecution are set out at p. 229, but are not relevant for current purposes.—Ed.]

* * * [V]ehicular homicide is no different than any other criminal offense in which the occurrence of a specified result, caused by a defendant's conduct, is an essential element of the offense—such as murder, manslaughter, aggravated battery, and arson. Clearly there can be no criminal liability for such result-type offenses unless it can be shown that the defendant's conduct was a cause-in-fact of the prohibited result, whether the result be the death of a human being, personal injury to another, or injury to another's property. * * *

Courts throughout the country have uniformly followed the traditional "but for" test in determining whether the defendant's conduct was a cause-in-fact of a prohibited consequence in result-type offenses such as vehicular homicide. Under this test, a defendant's conduct is a cause-in-fact of the prohibited result if the said result would *not* have occurred "but for" the defendant's conduct; stated differently, the defendant's conduct is a cause-in-fact of a particular result if the result would *not* have happened in the absence of the defendant's conduct. Thus, a defendant's reckless operation of a motor vehicle is a cause-in-fact of the death of a human being * * * if the subject death would *not* have occurred "but for" the defendant's reckless driving or would not have happened in the absence of such driving.

In relatively rare cases, however, the "but for" test for causation-in-fact fails and has been abandoned in favor of the "substantial factor" test. This anomaly occurs when two defendants, acting independently and not in concert with one another, commit two separate acts, each of which

213

substantial factor

alone is sufficient to bring about the prohibited result—as when two defendants concurrently inflict mortal wounds upon a human being, each of which is sufficient to cause death. In such case, each defendant's action was not a "but for" cause of death because the deceased would have died even in the absence of each defendant's conduct—although obviously not in the absence of both defendants' conduct considered together. In these rare cases, the courts have followed a "substantial factor" test, namely, the defendant's conduct is a cause-in-fact of a prohibited result if the subject conduct was a "substantial factor" in bringing about the said result. Thus, each defendant's conduct in independently and concurrently inflicting mortal wounds on a deceased clearly constitutes a "substantial factor" in bringing about the deceased's death, and, consequently, is a cause-in-fact of the deceased's death. * * *

OXENDINE v. STATE

Supreme Court of Delaware, 1987.
528 A.2d 870.

H<small>ORSEY</small>, J<small>USTICE</small>:

Defendant, Jeffrey Oxendine, Sr., appeals his conviction * * * of manslaughter (11 *Del.C.* § 632(1))[1] in the beating death of his six-year-old son, Jeffrey Oxendine, Jr. Oxendine was sentenced to twelve years' imprisonment.[2] On appeal, Oxendine's principal argument is that the Trial Court committed reversible error by denying his motion for a judgment of acquittal on the issue of causation. Specifically, he argues that the State's medical testimony, relating to which of the codefendants' admittedly repeated beatings of the child was the cause of death, was so vague and uncertain as to preclude his conviction of any criminal offense.

We conclude that the evidence upon causation was insufficient to sustain Oxendine's conviction of manslaughter, but that the evidence was sufficient to sustain his conviction of the lesser included offense of assault in the second degree (11 *Del.C.* § 612(1)).[3] * * *

The facts may be summarized as follows: On the morning of January 18, 1984, Leotha Tyree, Oxendine's girlfriend, who lived with him, pushed Jeffrey into the bathtub causing microscopic tears in his intestines which led to peritonitis. During a break at work that evening, Oxendine telephoned home and talked to Jeffrey, who complained of stomach pains.

---

1. 11 *Del.C.* § 632(1) states:

"A person is guilty of manslaughter when: (1) He recklessly causes the death of another person."

2. Codefendant, Leotha Tyree, was also convicted in the same trial of manslaughter in the death of Jeffrey Oxendine, Jr. and was sentenced to nine years' imprisonment. On direct appeal, this Court has affirmed her conviction.

3. 11 *Del.C.* § 612(1) states:

"A person is guilty of assault in the second degree when: (1) He intentionally causes serious physical injury to another person."

Assault in the Second Degree is a Class C felony for which the range of punishment is 2 to 20 years.

When Oxendine returned home from work, he saw bruises on Jeffrey and knew that Tyree had beaten the child during the day. * * *

The next morning at approximately 7:30 a.m., Oxendine went into Jeffrey's bedroom and began screaming at him to get up. A neighbor in the same apartment building testified to hearing sounds coming from the room of blows being struck, obscenities uttered by a male voice, and cries from a child saying, "Please stop, Daddy, it hurts." After hearing these sounds continue for what seemed like five to ten minutes, the witness heard a final noise consisting of a loud thump, as if someone had been kicked or punched "with a great blow."

Later that day, Jeffrey's abdomen became swollen. When Oxendine arrived home from work at about 5:00 p.m., Tyree told him of Jeffrey's condition and urged him to take Jeffrey to the hospital. Oxendine, apparently believing that Jeffrey was exaggerating his discomfort, went out, bought a newspaper, and returned home to read it. Upon his return, Tyree had prepared to take Jeffrey to the hospital. En route, Jeffrey stopped breathing; and was pronounced dead shortly after his arrival at the hospital.

I

In order to convict Oxendine of manslaughter, the State had to show that his conduct caused Jeffrey's death. 11 *Del.C.* § 261 defines causation as the "antecedent but for which the result in question would not have occurred." * * *

During its case-in-chief, the State called medical examiners Dr. Inguito and Dr. Hameli, who both testified that Jeffrey's death was caused by intra-abdominal hemorrhage and acute peritonitis, occurring as a result of blunt force trauma to the front of the abdomen. Similarly, each pathologist identified two distinct injuries, one caused more than twenty-four hours before death, and one inflicted less than twenty-four hours before death.

Dr. Inguito could not separate the effects of the two injuries. In his view, it was possible that both the older and more recent hemorrhage could have contributed to the death of the child, but he was unable to tell which of the hemorrhages caused the death of the child. Dr. Inguito could not place any quantitative value on either of the hemorrhages nor could he state whether the fresh hemorrhage or the older hemorrhage caused the death. The prosecutor never asked, nor did Dr. Inguito give, an opinion on whether the second hemorrhage accelerated Jeffrey's death.

Dr. Hameli, on the other hand, was of the opinion that the earlier injury was the underlying cause of death. According to him, the later injury, *i.e.,* the second hemorrhage, "was an aggravating, and probably some factors [sic] contributing," but it was the earlier injury that was the plain underlying cause of death.

The prosecutor, however, did explicitly ask Dr. Hameli if the second injury accelerated Jeffrey's death. The relevant portion of the testimony is as follows:

Prosecutor: Dr. Hameli, within a reasonable degree of medical certainty and in your expert opinion, did the second hemorrhage accelerate this child's death?

Hameli: I do not know. If you are talking about timewise—I assume that's what you are talking about, exploration.

Prosecutor: You cannot give an opinion of that area; is that correct?

Hameli: No.

Oxendine moved for judgment of acquittal at the end of the State's case-in-chief. The Trial Court, however, denied his motion.

As part of her case, codefendant Tyree called Dr. Hofman, a medical examiner, who disagreed about the number of injuries. He perceived only one injury inflicted about twelve hours before death. Subsequently, the prosecutor asked Hofman the following hypothetical question that assumed two blows when Hofman only testified as to one blow:

Prosecutor: In your expert medical opinion within a reasonable degree of medical certainty, if this child, given his weakened state as a result of the significant trauma to his abdominal cavity, suffered subsequently another blunt force trauma to the same area, would it accelerate this child's death? * * *

Hofman: My opinion, as in a general statement, not knowing this child, it certainly would have an impact on shortening this child's life.

Prosecutor: Is then, therefore, your answer yes?

Hofman: Yes.

At the end of trial, Oxendine again moved for judgment of acquittal. The Trial Court denied the motion and instructed the jury on the elements of recklessness, causation and on various lesser included offenses. The ultimate and only theory of causation on which the jury was charged was based on "acceleration." The Trial Court instructed the jury that "[a] defendant who causes the death of another * * * is not relieved of responsibility for causing the death if another later injury accelerates, that is, hastens the death of the other person. Contribution without acceleration is not sufficient." As previously noted, the jury returned verdicts of manslaughter against Oxendine and Tyree.

II

In this case, the evidence established that Oxendine inflicted a non-lethal injury upon Jeffrey after his son had, twenty-four hours earlier, sustained a lethal injury from a previous beating inflicted by Tyree. Thus, for Oxendine to be convicted of manslaughter in this factual context, the State was required to show for purposes of causation under 11 *Del.C.* § 261 that Oxendine's conduct hastened or accelerated the child's death.

[handwritten margin note: Aggravation or Contribution without acceleration is insufficient]

The Superior Court correctly instructed the jury that "[c]ontribution [or aggravation] without acceleration is insufficient to establish causation." We do not equate aggravation with acceleration. It is possible to make the victim's pain more intense, *i.e.,* aggravate the injury, without accelerating the time of the victim's death. Thus, in terms of section 261, and as applied to defendant, the relevant inquiry is: but for his infliction of the second injury, would the victim have died when he died? If the second injury caused his son to die *any* sooner, then defendant, who inflicted the second injury, would be deemed to have caused his son's death within the definition of section 261.

[handwritten margin note: Would the victim have died when he did?]

A finding of medical causation may not be based on speculation or conjecture. A doctor's testimony that a certain thing is possible is no evidence at all. His opinion as to what is possible is no more valid than the jury's own speculation as to what is or is not possible. Almost anything is possible, and it is improper to allow a jury to consider and base a verdict upon a "possible" cause of death. Therefore, a doctor's testimony can only be considered evidence when his conclusions are based on reasonable medical certainty that a fact is true or untrue.

The State's expert medical testimony, even when viewed in the light most favorable to the State, was * * * insufficient to sustain the State's ultimate theory of causation ("acceleration") on which the court instructed the jury. Both of the State's expert witnesses, Dr. Inguito and Dr. Hameli, were unable to state with any degree of medical certainty that the second injury contributed to the death of the child. Dr. Inguito could only testify that it was possible that both the older and more recent hemorrhage could have contributed to the death of the child. As for Dr. Hameli, he testified that the second injury independent of the first injury could have caused death but probably would not cause death. Furthermore, Dr. Hameli explicitly stated that he could not give an opinion as to whether the second injury accelerated Jeffrey's death. Similarly, Dr. Inguito was neither asked nor did he offer an opinion about acceleration.

The record establishes that the only theory of causation under which the State submitted the case to the jury was the acceleration theory. The State apparently abandoned its initial theories of causation and adopted the acceleration theory as the cause of death, based on the testimony of Dr. Hofman, a witness for co-defendant Tyree, recalled by the State on rebuttal. That was too late to sustain the State's case-in-chief for manslaughter.

The States concedes that when it closed its case-in-chief it did not have a prima facie case to support acceleration. Therefore, even though the State could, based on Dr. Hofman's testimony, establish a prima facie case of acceleration at the end of the trial, Oxendine's conviction of manslaughter must be set aside for insufficiency of the evidence to establish that his conduct accelerated Jeffrey's death. * * *

[handwritten margin note: Insufficient evidence at close of State's case]

It is extremely "difficult to be objective about the death of a child. * * * Those responsible ought to be punished. Nevertheless, there must

be proof as to who, if anyone, inflicted the injuries that resulted in death."
"Reprehensible and repulsive as the conduct of the defendant is, nevertheless it is not proof of manslaughter."

The Trial Court, however, properly denied Oxendine's motion for
judgment of acquittal at the close of the State's case because its medical
testimony was sufficient for a rational trier of fact to conclude beyond a
reasonable doubt that Oxendine was guilty of the lesser included offense
of assault in the second degree, 11 *Del.C.* § 612(1). Therefore, we reverse
Oxendine's conviction of manslaughter and remand the case to Superior
Court for entry of a judgment of conviction and resentence of defendant
for the lesser included offense of assault in the second degree.

NOTES AND QUESTIONS

1. The court observed that the prosecution abandoned its initial theories
of causation in favor of the acceleration theory. What other theories do you
think the prosecution might have had in mind?

2. Who is the actual cause of *V*'s death in the following hypotheticals?
(Assume that *D* and *X* did not act in concert.) How would these cases be
resolved under Model Penal Code § 2.03(1)?

A. *X* intentionally stabs *V* in the chest. *V* will die from loss of blood in 15
minutes. Simultaneously, *D* intentionally shoots *V* in the leg. *V* would not die
from this wound by itself. *V* dies in 10 minutes.

B. The same as A., except that *D* *un*intentionally shoots *V*.

C. The same as A., except that *V* dies in 15 minutes.

D. *X* stabs *V*. Simultaneously, *D* stabs *V*. Neither wound by itself would
kill *V*. *V* dies from loss of blood from the two wounds.

E. *X* shoots *V* in the heart. Simultaneously, *D* shoots *V* in the head. *V*
would die instantly from either wound. *V* dies instantly.

F. *X* stabs *V*. Five minutes later, *D* shoots *V* in the head. *V* would die
from the wound inflicted by *X* in 15 minutes. *V* would and does die instantly
from the wound inflicted by *D*.

3. Nancy, a hiker, enters the desert with a canteen filled with sufficient
water to survive. Unbeknownst to her, Oscar, intending to kill her, places a
fatal dose of a fast-acting poison in the canteen. While in the desert, Petunia
steals the canteen, believing that it contains pure water. Nancy, without
water, dies of thirst in the desert. Who caused her death? See H.L.A. Hart &
Tony Honoré, Causation in the Law 239–241 (2d ed. 1985).

4. If you assume that the defendant and Leotha Tyree were equally
culpable—that both were aware that their actions created a substantial and
unjustifiable risk of causing death to the defendant's son—why should it
matter in criminal law that one caused the harm and the other did not?

B. PROXIMATE CAUSE ("LEGAL" CAUSE)

The but-for test is too imprecise a standard for determining causal
accountability for harm because it fails to exclude remote candidates for

legal responsibility. "Mankind might still be in Eden, but for Adam's biting an apple." Welch v. State, 45 Ala.App. 657, 235 So.2d 906 (1970).[a] Although Adam's conduct satisfies the but-for test of responsibility for today's wrongdoing, we do not follow the causal chain as far back as it may lead us.

The doctrine of "proximate" or "legal" causation serves the purpose of determining who or what events among those that satisfy the but-for standard should be held accountable for the resulting harm. *Thus, it should be noticed, a person or event cannot be a proximate cause of harm unless she or it is an actual cause, but a person or event can be an actual cause without being the proximate cause.*

Issues of proximate causation generally arise when an intervening force exists, i.e., when some but-for causal agent comes into play *after* the defendant's voluntary act or omission and *before* the social harm occurs. Typically, an intervening cause will be: (1) "an act of God," i.e., an event that cannot be traced back to any human intermediary; (2) an act of an independent third party, which accelerates or aggravates the harm caused by the defendant, or which causes it to occur in an unexpected manner; or (3) an act or omission of the victim that assists in bringing about the outcome. An intervening cause that "breaks the causal chain" is sometimes described as a superceding cause or *novus actus interveniens* ("new intervening act").

A critical matter to keep in mind is this: Proximate causation analysis is not a matter of applying hard and fast rules leading to some scientifically "correct" outcome; instead, it is an effort by the factfinder to determine, *based on policy considerations or matters of fairness*, whether it is proper to hold the defendant(s) criminally responsible for a prohibited result. Consequently, although courts sometimes act as if there is a foolproof way of identifying the "proximate cause" of social harm, it is more accurate to think in terms of *factors* that potentially affect causal responsibility. The materials that follow relate to those factors.

As you work through the materials keep in mind, as one court "wryly put it, '[j]udges, even learned ones, attorneys, and law students have struggled with the concept [of proximate cause]. It has not been any easier for jurors although they usually have the advantage of common sense.'" People v. Talavera, 2011 WL 227694, at *6 (Cal.App. 2011) (quoting Maupin v. Widling, 192 Cal.App.3d 568, 573, 237 Cal.Rptr. 521, 524 (1987)).

---

a. In 1961, meteorologist and mathematician Edward Lorenz used a numerical computer model to rerun a weather prediction. However, when he inputted the number ".506" into the computer as a shorthand for the proper number (.506127), the result was an entirely different weather scenario. Two years later, Lorenz published a paper in which he wrote that perhaps "one flap of a seagull's wings could change the course of weather forever." Later, the seagull became a butterfly, and in 1972 he published another paper entitled, "Does the Flap of a Butterfly's Wings in Brazil Set Off a Tornado in Texas?" This has come to be known as the "butterfly effect"—the idea that the flapping of the wings of a single butterfly can have a far-reaching ripple effect on history. See also Ray Bradbury, A Sound of Thunder and Other Stories (2005) (in which a man travels back in time to the prehistoric era, accidentally steps on a butterfly, and as a result changes history, resulting in the election of a fascist president in the year 2055).

PEOPLE v. RIDEOUT

Court of Appeals of Michigan, 2006.
272 Mich.App. 602, 727 N.W.2d 630.

SAWYER, P.J.

Defendant was convicted, following a jury trial, of operating a motor vehicle while intoxicated (OWI) or while visibly impaired (OWVI) and thereby causing death. [MCL 257.625(4).] * * * He now appeals and we reverse and remand.

At 2:00 a.m. on November 23, 2003, defendant was driving his sport utility vehicle (SUV) east on 17 Mile Road in northern Kent County. He attempted to turn north onto Edgerton Avenue and drove into the path of an oncoming car driven by Jason Reichelt. Reichelt's car hit defendant's SUV and spun 180 degrees, coming to rest on the centerline of 17 Mile Road. The SUV came to rest on the side of the road. It was later determined that defendant had a blood alcohol concentration of 0.16, which is twice the legal limit.

Reichelt and his passenger, Jonathan Keiser, were not seriously injured, but Reichelt's car was severely damaged and the headlights stopped working. Both men left the car and walked to the SUV to determine if anyone was injured. After speaking briefly with defendant, the two men walked back to Reichelt's car. Reichelt indicated that he was aware that oncoming cars could hit his darkened car and that he wanted to determine if he could turn on the flashers. As Reichelt and Keiser stood by the car, an oncoming car driven by Tonya Welch hit Keiser, killing him.

At the center of this appeal is the issue of causation. Defendant argues that not only did the trial court improperly instruct the jury on causation, there was also insufficient evidence of causation to establish defendant's guilt. Because the two issues are intertwined with the question of what must be proven to establish causation in such a case, we shall analyze both issues together beginning with a determination of what the prosecutor must show to establish causation.

As the Supreme Court discussed in *People v. Schaefer,* [473 Mich. 418, 703 N.W.2d 774 (2005)] causation consists of two components:

In criminal jurisprudence, the causation element of an offense is generally comprised of two components: factual cause and proximate cause. The concept of factual causation is relatively straightforward.
* * *

The existence of factual causation alone, however, will not support the imposition of criminal liability. Proximate causation must also be established. As we noted in *[People v.] Tims*[, 449 Mich. 83, 96, 534 N.W.2d 675 (1995)], proximate causation is a legal colloquialism. It is a legal construct designed to prevent criminal liability from attaching when the result of the defendant's conduct is viewed as too remote or unnatural. Thus, a proximate cause is simply a factual cause "of which the law will take cognizance."

We initially note that there is no dispute at this point that defendant was intoxicated and that his driving was the cause of the initial accident. Furthermore, there is no argument that defendant's driving was the factual or "but-for" cause of the second accident. * * *

Of course, factual causation is relatively easy to establish. * * * But the question whether defendant is the proximate cause of the subsequent accident, and thus of the victim's death, is not so easily resolved. *Schaefer* discussed this requirement in further detail:

> For a defendant's conduct to be regarded as a proximate cause, the victim's injury must be a "direct and natural result" of the defendant's actions. In making this determination, it is necessary to examine whether there was an intervening cause that superseded the defendant's conduct such that the causal link between the defendant's conduct and the victim's injury was broken. If an intervening cause did indeed *supersede* the defendant's act as a legally significant causal factor, then the defendant's conduct will not be deemed a proximate cause of the victim's injury.

> The standard by which to gauge whether an intervening cause supersedes, and thus severs the causal link, is generally one of reasonable foreseeability. For example, suppose that a defendant stabs a victim and the victim is then taken to a nearby hospital for treatment. If the physician is negligent in providing medical care to the victim and the victim later dies, the defendant is still considered to have proximately caused the victim's death because it is reasonably foreseeable that negligent medical care might be provided. At the same time, *gross* negligence or intentional misconduct by a treating physician is not reasonably foreseeable, and would thus break the causal chain between the defendant and the victim.

> The linchpin in the superseding cause analysis, therefore, is whether the intervening cause was foreseeable based on an objective standard of reasonableness. * * *

With these basic principles in mind, we conclude that the trial court improperly instructed the jury on the issue of proximate cause. * * * The trial court is required to instruct jurors on all elements of the crime charged and must not exclude consideration of material issues, defenses, and theories for which there is supporting evidence. * * * "It is error for the trial court to give an erroneous or misleading jury instruction on an essential element of the offense."

The trial court gave detailed and extensive instructions on factual causation, including reinforcement of the concept that defendant had to be "a" cause of the accident, but not necessarily "the" cause of the accident. But the trial court's instructions on proximate cause and superseding intervening causes were virtually nonexistent. The trial court did implicitly touch on the issue of proximate cause when it instructed the jury that one of several causes "is a substantial factor in causing a death if, but for that cause's contribution, the death would not have occurred, unless the death was an utterly unnatural result of whatever happened." But the instructions also told the jury that another cause could be a superseding cause only if it was the sole cause * * *.

This is not a correct statement of the law. A superseding intervening cause does not need to be the only cause. * * * The effect of the trial court's instructions was that the jury could convict defendant if they found him to be a factual cause of the accident and that the jury could find the existence of a superseding intervening cause only if that superseding intervening cause was the only cause of the second accident. The jury was not adequately instructed on the issues of proximate and intervening causes.

This conclusion is enough to set aside defendant's conviction, with directions to the trial court to properly instruct the jury on the causation issue. But we agree with defendant that the problem in this case goes even deeper, because there was insufficient evidence to establish proximate cause at all. * * * We view the evidence in a light most favorable to the prosecution to determine if a rational trier of fact could find beyond a reasonable doubt that the essential elements of the crime were established.

The troubling aspect of this case is that the second accident only occurred after Keiser had reached a position of safety (the side of the road) and then chose to reenter the roadway with Reichelt to check on the car. While foreseeability is the linchpin of the superseding causation analysis, and it is at least arguably foreseeable that a person involved in an accident would check on his or her vehicle even if it remains on the road, the analysis does not end there. As Professor Dressler discusses in *Understanding Criminal Law* (3d ed.), there is no universal test for determining if an intervening cause is also a superseding cause:

> One early twentieth century scholar observed that all efforts to set down universal tests that explain the law of causation are "demonstrably erroneous." [Jeremiah Smith, *Legal Cause in Actions of Tort,* 25 Harv. L. R. 223, 317 (1912).] There are no hard-and-fast rules for determining when an intervening cause supersedes the defendant's conduct. However, there are various factors that assist the factfinder in the evaluative process.

Indeed, Dressler points out that to say that foreseeability is the "linchpin" is "a slight overstatement," though it is of great significance. Rather, Dressler discusses six factors to be considered in determining if an intervening cause is a superseding cause.

Of the six factors discussed by Dressler, three are not relevant here. They are the (1) *de minimis* contribution to social harm factor, (2) the intended-consequences doctrine, and (3) the omissions factor. The foreseeability factor is relevant here, but its application is less than clear. As

Dressler points out, a responsive intervening cause will establish proximate cause, while a coincidental intervening cause will not unless it was foreseeable.[b] In discussing responsive intervening causes, Dressler points to the example[] of a * * * wounded victim being negligently treated and dying. That is, the harm results from actions taken in response to the defendant's conduct. A coincidental intervening cause would exist * * * where the defendant's conduct put the victim in the "wrong place at the wrong time," such as an assault victim who is attacked by a "knife-wielding maniac" while waiting in the emergency room for treatment of the initial wounds.

Whether the intervening cause is responsive or coincidental in the case at bar is arguable at best. On the one hand, the victim reentering the roadway to check on the vehicle was in direct response to the accident, though not in direct response to defendant's having driven. On the other hand, Welch's driving down the road when she did was entirely coincidental.

In our view, Keiser's decision to reenter the roadway renders the foreseeability factor of little value to the analysis. Rather, that decision directly involves the two remaining factors identified by Dressler that are present here. Those two factors, we believe, compel the conclusion that the intervening cause of the second accident was also a superseding cause.

First, there is the apparent-safety doctrine, which Dressler describes as follows:

> One scholar has observed that when a "defendant's active force has come to rest in a position of apparent safety, the court will follow it no longer." [Joseph H. Beale, *The Proximate Consequences of an Act,* 33 Harv. L. R. 633, 651 (1920).] For example, consider a somewhat simplified version of the facts in *State v. Preslar* [48 N.C. 421 (1856)]: *D* threatened the life of *V,* his spouse. As a consequence, *V* was forced to leave the house on a freezing night in order to protect herself. *V* walked to within 200 yards of her father's home, where she would have been welcome, but she chose to spend the night in the extreme cold, rather than bother her father by entering the house. *V* froze to death during the night. Clearly, *D* was an actual cause of *V's* death: but for *D's* threatening conduct, *V* would not have gone out into the cold. But, *V's* decision to sleep outside was also a but-for cause of her own death. Is *D* the proximate cause of *V's* death? The court in *Preslar* answered this question in the negative.

> The result may be explained in terms of the apparent-safety doctrine. *D* did not follow *V* from their home. When *V* reached the vicinity of her father's house, she knew that she could enter and be free from immediate harm. Therefore, her decision to sleep outside constituted a superseding intervening cause.

[handwritten margin note: Preslar]

---

b.   See p. 225, Note 3, for greater detail.

Similarly, in the case at bar, Keiser had reached a position of apparent safety: he had gotten out of the vehicle and was alongside the road, off the pavement. Had the second accident occurred before Keiser could extricate himself from the Reichelt vehicle and get to the side of the road, then the causal chain would have been intact. But he was able to get out of harm's way and to a relatively safe position at the side of the road. He then made the choice to return to the roadway and place himself in a more dangerous position. Like the victim in *Preslar,* Keiser made a decision regarding his actions after the immediate danger was over. And that decision, like the decision in *Preslar,* ended the initial causal chain and started a new one, one for which defendant was not responsible.

The point of a person making a decision brings us to the remaining factor discussed in Dressler, that of voluntary human intervention:

> A defendant is far more apt to be relieved of criminal responsibility in the case of a "free, deliberate, and informed" [Hart & Honore, Causation in the Law (2d ed. 1985), p. 326]—a voluntary, knowing, and intelligent—human agent than in the case of an intervention of a natural force or the actions of a person whose conduct is not fully free. The result in the *Preslar* case, described [above], can be explained in terms of this factor. *V* chose to sleep in the cold rather than to enter her father's home. Her decision was free, deliberate, and with full knowledge of the fact that it was exceedingly cold outside. Under these circumstances, the responsibility for her death is shifted from *D* to *V.* This outcome is consistent with the retributive principle that accords special significance to the free-will actions of human agents.

Similarly, in the case at bar, Keiser made the voluntary decision to return to the vehicle on the roadway, despite the danger that it posed. He could have chosen to remain on the side of the road. He chose instead to reenter the roadway, with the danger of standing in the roadway next to an unlit vehicle in the middle of the night being readily apparent.

In sum, we conclude that the prosecution failed to present sufficient evidence to establish that defendant's actions were a proximate cause of Keiser's death. Therefore, we vacate defendant's conviction for OWI/OWVI causing death.

NOTES AND QUESTIONS

1. Do you agree with the Court of Appeals in *Rideout* that, *as a matter of law,* the "prosecution failed to present sufficient evidence to establish that [Rideout's] actions were a proximate cause of Keiser's death"? The Michigan Supreme Court disagreed on that score, partially reversing the Court of Appeals and stating that a "reasonable jury could find that the actions of the decedent were foreseeable based on an objective standard of reasonableness." People v. Rideout, 477 Mich. 1062, 728 N.W.2d 459, 460 (2007). How should the judge in *Rideout* have instructed the jury on proximate causation? Should the court have read to the jury, and explained, the six factors mentioned in

the case? If not, and you were the judge, how would *you* explain the doctrine of proximate causation to the jury?

2.   *Problem. D1* and *D2* met *V* at a bar. *V* had been drinking heavily. *V* began asking other patrons for a ride home around 9 p.m. *D1* and *D2*, who had decided to rob *V*, offered him a ride. *V* accepted. After robbing *V* in the car and forcing him to lower his trousers and remove his boots, *D1* and *D2* abandoned *V* by the side of an unlit, rural two-lane highway. They also left his boots and jacket on the shoulder, but not his eyeglasses, which remained in the car. The night was cold with blowing snow, but otherwise clear. The road was dry. *B* was driving a pickup truck at fifty miles an hour, ten miles in excess of the speed limit, in the northbound lane. A car in the southbound lane passed *B* and flashed its lights. Immediately thereafter *B* saw *V* siting in the middle of the northbound lane with his hands in the air. *B* "went into a kind of shock," failed to apply his brakes, and struck and killed *V. D1* and *D2* were charged with second-degree murder inasmuch as they were aware that their actions created an extreme risk of death to *V.* Did *D1* and *D2* proximately cause *V*'s death? Kibbe v. Henderson, 534 F.2d 493 (2d Cir. 1976), *rev'd*, 431 U.S. 145, 97 S.Ct. 1730, 52 L.Ed.2d 203 (1977).

3.   *Coincidental and responsive intervening causes.* As *Rideout* explained, it is often very useful to distinguish between coincidental and responsive intervening causes in proximate causation analysis. (In other words, this is one of the six factors that can help determine proximate causation.) Here is how Wayne R. LaFave, Criminal Law 344–345 (4th ed. 2003), explains these concepts and their legal effect:

> As might be expected, courts have tended to distinguish cases in which the intervening act was a *coincidence* from those in which it was a *response* to the defendant's prior actions. An intervening act is a *coincidence* when the defendant's act merely put the victim at a certain place at a certain time, and because the victim was so located it was possible for him to be acted upon by the intervening cause. * * * [I]t is important to note that there may be a coincidence even when the subsequent act is that of a human agency, as where A shoots B and leaves him lying in the roadway, resulting in B being struck by C's car; or where A shoots at B and causes him to take refuge in a park, where B is then attacked and killed by a gang of hoodlums.

> By contrast, an intervening act may be said to be a *response* to the prior actions of the defendant when it involves a reaction to the conditions created by the defendant. The most obvious illustrations are actions by the victim to avoid harm, actions of a bystander to rescue him, and actions by medical personnel in treating the victim. * * *

> * * * Thus—though the distinction is not carefully developed in many of the decided cases—it may be said that a coincidence will break the chain of legal cause unless it was foreseeable, while a response will do so only if it is abnormal (and, if abnormal, also unforeseeable).

In light of this explanation, how would *you* analyze the *Rideout* facts?

4.   *Contributory negligence of the victim.* Was Keiser contributorily negligent in his own death? If so, should this fact serve as a defense to Rideout's

prosecution? It is worth noting that tort concepts of "contributory negligence" and "comparative negligence" are not carried over directly to the
criminal law. Although similarities exist, "the rules of causation in criminal
cases are not tied to the rules of causation in civil cases." People v. Tims, 449
Mich. 83, 534 N.W.2d 675, 684 (1995). Specifically, "although a victim's
contributory negligence is a factor to consider in determining whether the
defendant's negligence caused the victim's death, it is not a defense." Id at
681.

5. *De minimis causes.* One of the proximate-causation factors listed but
not discussed in *Rideout* involves de *minimis* contributions to social harm.
Thus, even if butterflies affect our weather (see p. 219, footnote a), their
contribution is tiny compared to other meteorological factors that precede or
follow the butterfly. It follows, as well, that the law generally will not treat a
very minor but-for cause of harm legally responsible for the result when there
is a far more substantial cause to whom responsibility can be attached. For
example, if your friend is mortally wounded by a homicidal maniac, after
which you negligently cause trivial injury to your friend as you drive her to
the hospital, thereby accelerating her death by a few seconds, the law will
very likely ignore your *de minimis* contribution to your friend's death.

6. *Omissions.* Can an omission ever function as a superseding intervening cause? According to one treatise, Rollin M. Perkins & Ronald N. Boyce,
Criminal Law 819–821 (3d ed. 1982), the answer is no: No matter how
unforeseeable an omission may be, this "negative act" will not cut off liability
of an earlier "positive act." In essence, "nothing" does not supersede "something."

Should this be? For example, suppose that A picks up hitchiker V on a
terribly cold night, robs V, knocks him unconscious, and then abandons V on a
rural road. Suppose that the lone driver to observe V in that condition is
Brutus, V's brother, who recognizes V but chooses to let him lie there because
Brutus wants V to die so that he can inherit his brother's large estate. If V
freezes to death, should Brutus's criminal omission relieve A of liability for
the death? Why, or why not? Would you feel differently if A had not robbed V
but had knocked V unconscious and then abandoned him in that condition
because V had made improper sexual advances in the car? Should Brutus's
omission *now* relieve A of causal responsibility for V's death?

7. *The "intended consequences" doctrine.* One scholar has written that:

[S]ince the degree of moral obliquity exhibited by the act, and the extent
of the social menace involved[ ] are factors to be considered, the [proxi-
mate causation] result will not be the same for all offenses. In particular,
the legal eye reaches [back] further in the examination of intentional
crimes than in those in which this element is wanting. Rollin M. Perkins,
Criminal Law 693 (2d ed. 1969).

More recently, Perkins asserted that "any intended consequence of an act
is proximate." Rollin M. Perkins & Ronald N. Boyce, supra, at 818. More
specifically, this doctrine provides that if an intentional wrongdoer gets what
she wanted—she gets the result she wanted *in the general manner she wanted
it*—she should not escape criminal responsibility even if an unforeseeable
event intervened.

For example, in Regina v. Michael, 169 Eng. Rep. 48 (1840), *M* wanted the death of her young son, *V*. Therefore, *M* procured poison, which she furnished to *N*, *V*'s nurse, in the guise of medicine. *M* instructed *N* to give *V* a teaspoonful (a lethal dose) of the "medicine" later that day. *N* did not do so because she believed that the "medicine" was unnecessary, but she negligently left the potion nearby. A few days later, *Y*, a five-year-old youth, discovered the poison and innocently administered it to *V*, who died. According to the "intended consequences" doctrine, *M* was the proximate cause of *V*'s death, despite *N*'s negligence and *Y*'s unexpected intervention: *M* wanted her son dead by means of poison, and she got exactly that, albeit at the hands of *Y* and not *N*.

8. *"Apparent safety" doctrine.* Look again at the apparent safety doctrine, and the *Preslar* case in particular, discussed in *Rideout*. Do you agree with the outcome in *Preslar*? Should it matter to the outcome whether *D* was at home or was out searching for *V* at the time she reached her parents' residence? Should it matter whether he was a regular wife batterer?

9. *"Free, deliberate and informed human intervention."* As this doctrine is explained in *Rideout*, consider Regina v. Blaue, [1975] 1 W.L.R. 1411, [1975] 3 All Eng.Rep. 446 (C.A.): *B* stabs *V*, an eighteen-year-old Jehovah's Witness, after she refuses *B*'s sexual advances. *V*'s lung is pierced in the attack. She is taken to a hospital where a doctor determines that she needs a blood transfusion to survive. Although she realizes that she will die without the blood, *V* refuses to consent to the life-saving transfusion, based on her religious belief that accepting the transfusion would constitute a sin. Is *B* the proximate cause of *V*'s ensuing death? How would this case come out if you applied the other proximate causation factors?

10. *Model Penal Code: a better approach?* Section 2.03 of the Model Penal Code takes "a fresh approach" to the issues discussed in this chapter section:

> Subsections (2) and (3) are based on the theory that but-for causation is the only strictly causal requirement that should be imposed generally, and that the remaining issue is the proper scope of liability in light of the actor's culpability. These subsections assume that liability requires purpose, knowledge, recklessness, or negligence with respect to the result that is an element of the offense, and deal explicitly with variations between the actual result and the intended, contemplated or foreseeable result. Criteria are provided for determining the materiality or immateriality of such variations.

> Subsection (2) addresses cases in which the culpability requirement with respect to the result is purpose or knowledge, i.e., cases in which purposely or knowingly causing a specified result is a material element of the offense. If the actual result[13] is not within the purpose or contemplation of the actor, the culpability requirement is not satisfied, except in the circumstances set out in Subsections (2)(a) and (2)(b).

---

13. The term "actual result" is meant to be contrasted with the designed or contemplated (or, in the case of Subsection (3), the probable) result in terms of its specific character and manner of occurrence.

Subsection (2)(a) deals with situations in which the actual result differs from the result designed or contemplated only in that a different person or property was injured or affected,[14] or in that the injury or harm designed or contemplated would have been more serious or extensive than that which actually occurred.[15] Following existing law, the Code makes such differences immaterial.

Subsection (2)(b) deals with situations in which the actual result involves the same kind of injury or harm as that designed or contemplated, but in which the precise injury inflicted was different or occurred in a different way. Here the Code makes no attempt to catalogue the possibilities—intervening or concurrent causes, natural or human; unexpected physical conditions; distinctions between mortal and nonmortal wounds; and so on. It deals only with the ultimate criterion by which the significance of such factors ought to be judged—whether the actual result is too remote or accidental in its occurrence to have a [just][16] bearing on the actor's liability or the gravity of his offense. * * *

Subsection (3) deals with offenses in which recklessness or negligence is the required culpability and in which the actual result is not within the risk of which the actor was aware or, in the case of negligence, of which he should have been aware. The governing principles are the same as in the case of crimes requiring purpose or knowledge.

American Law Institute, Model Penal Code and Commentaries, Comment to § 2.03 at 260–261, 263 (1985).

In order to apply the MPC approach to "proximate cause," ask yourself the following questions (assuming the crime requires purpose with respect to the prohibited result): 1) What was the "actual result"? 2) Was the actual result "within the purpose of the actor"? If it was, then the actor's conduct is a "proximate cause." If it was not, 3) did the "actual result involve the same kind of injury or harm as that designed"? If it did not, then the actor's conduct is not a "proximate cause." If it did, 4) was the "actual result too remote or accidental in its occurrence to have a [just] bearing on the actor's

MPC analysis

14. For example, if a bullet misses its intended victim and kills an unseen bystander, the actor's lack of purpose to kill the bystander does not bar liability for murder under Section 210.2(1)(a) so long as there was an intention to kill the original target.

15. For example, a person would not escape liability for causing (nonfatal) bodily injury under Section 211.1(1)(a) [assault] on the grounds that he intended to cause death. If the reverse is true, and the harm caused is more extensive or serious than the harm designed or contemplated (or, in the case of Section 2.03(3), the probable harm), then liability for the excess would be prohibited by application of the normal principles of culpability stated in Section 2.02. E.g., an attack that results in death, though only intended to cause injury, would not support a conviction for murder under Section 210.2(1)(a) [murder]. The actor might well be liable, however, for recklessly or negligently causing death (Sections 210.2(1)(b), 210.3, and 210.4) if he intended to cause serious bodily harm.

16. The word "just" is in brackets because of disagreement within the Institute over whether it is wise to put undefined questions of justice to the jury. The inclusion of the term has the merit of putting it clearly to the jury that the issue it must decide is whether in light of the remoteness or accidental quality of the occurrence of the actual result, it would be just to accord it significance in determining the actor's liability or the gravity of his offense. Submitting explicit questions involving a broad moral concept like "justice" to the jury is not so different from submitting questions of "unjustifiable risk" and "gross deviation" required by the Code's definition of recklessness and negligence. Section 2.02. * * *

liability"? If it was, then the actor's conduct is not a "proximate cause." If it was not, then the actor's conduct is a "proximate cause."

VELAZQUEZ v. STATE

District Court of Appeal of Florida, 1990.
561 So.2d 347.

HUBBART, J. * * *

* * * The sole issue presented for review is whether a defendant driver of a motor vehicle who participates in a reckless and illegal "drag race" on a public road may be properly convicted of vehicular homicide for the death of one of the co-participant drivers suffered in the course of the "drag race"—when the sole basis for imposing liability is the defendant's participation in said race. * * *

I * * *

On April 23, 1988, at approximately 2:30 A.M., the defendant Velazquez met the deceased Adalberto Alvarez at a Hardee's restaurant in Hialeah, Florida. The two * * * agreed to race each other in a "drag race" with their respective automobiles. They, accordingly, left the restaurant and proceeded to set up a quarter-mile "drag race" course on a nearby public road which ran perpendicular to a canal alongside the Palmetto Expressway in Hialeah; a guardrail and a visible stop sign stood between the end of this road and the canal. The two men began their "drag race" at the end of this road and proceeded away from the canal in a westerly direction for one-quarter mile. Upon completing the course without incident, the deceased Alvarez suddenly turned his automobile 180 degrees around and proceeded east toward the starting line and the canal; the defendant Velazquez did the same and followed behind Alvarez. Alvarez proceeded in the lead and attained an estimated speed of 123 m.p.h.; he was not wearing a seat belt and subsequent investigation revealed that he had a blood alcohol level between .11 and .12. The defendant Velazquez, who had not been drinking, trailed Alvarez the entire distance back to the starting line and attained an estimated speed of 98 m.p.h. As both drivers approached the end of the road, they applied their brakes, but neither could stop. Alvarez * * * crashed through the guardrail first and was propelled over the entire canal, landing on its far bank; he was thrown from his car upon impact, was pinned under his vehicle when it landed on him, and died instantly from the resulting injuries. The defendant also crashed through the guardrail, but landed in the canal where he was able to escape from his vehicle and swim to safety uninjured. * * *

II * * *

* * * Even where a defendant's conduct is a cause-in-fact of a prohibited result, * * * Florida and other courts throughout the country have for good reason declined to impose criminal liability (1) where the prohibited result of the defendant's conduct is beyond the scope of any fair

assessment of the danger created by the defendant's conduct, or [(2)] where it would otherwise be unjust, based on fairness and policy considerations, to hold the defendant criminally responsible for the prohibited result. * * *

Where * * * a participant passenger in * * * an illegal "drag race" accidently grabs the steering wheel of a vehicle involved in the race, instead of the gear shift he was assigned to operate, causing the vehicle to go out of control, crash, and kill the passenger—this court has held that the defendant driver of the subject motor vehicle was improperly convicted of vehicular homicide. *J.A.C. v. State,* 374 So.2d 606 (Fla. 3d DCA 1979). The court reasoned that the passenger's reckless act of grabbing the steering wheel was an independent intervening act which superseded the respondent's wrongful conduct in participating in the "drag race." * * * [The] court implicitly concluded that it would be unjust to hold the defendant criminally responsible for the passenger's death because the passenger, in effect, killed himself by his own reckless conduct.* * *

III

Turning now to the instant case, it is clear that the defendant's reckless operation of a motor vehicle in participating in the "drag race" with the deceased was, technically speaking, *a* cause-in-fact of the deceased's death under the "but for" test. But for the defendant's participation in the subject race, the deceased would not have recklessly raced his vehicle at all and thus would not have been killed. However, under the authority of *J.A.C.* * * *, the defendant's participation in the subject "drag race" was not a proximate cause of the deceased's death because, simply put, the deceased, in effect, killed himself by his own volitional reckless driving—and, consequently, it would be unjust to hold the defendant criminally responsible for this death.

The undisputed facts in this case demonstrate that the "drag race" was, in effect, over when the defendant and the deceased had completed the agreed-upon one-quarter mile course and had crossed the finish line. * * * Clearly, the deceased was on a near-suicide mission when, on his own hook, he returned to the starting line of the race after the race was apparently over * * *. * * *

* * * No one forced this young man to participate in the subject "drag race"; no one forced him to whirl around and proceed back toward the canal after the race was apparently over; no one forced him to travel 123 m.p.h., vault a canal, and kill himself upon impact. He did all these things himself, and was, accordingly, the major cause of his own death. * * *

The final judgment of conviction and sentence under review is reversed, and the cause is remanded to the trial court with directions to grant the defendant's motion to dismiss [the prosecution]. * * *

NOTES AND QUESTIONS

1. What if an innocent bystander, standing on the far bank, had also been killed by Alvarez's car. Would Velazquez be the proximate cause of *that* death?

2. The *Velazquez* court said that the victim, in essence, committed suicide—there was no criminal homicide at all! From a causal perspective, do you agree? Why, or why not?

In this regard, consider these facts: Megan Meier, a thirteen-year-old girl, committed suicide after being tormented over the Internet by "Josh Evans," who sent her cruel messages ridiculing her, and finally sending a message stating that the world would be better off without her. Sobbing and deeply upset, Megan hanged herself in her bedroom closet. "Josh Evans" turned out to be Lori Drew, the forty-year-old mother of a girl who had been a long-time friend of Megan's before they had a falling out. Christopher Leonard, *Town Shuns Family Over Hoax, Suicide*, Associated Press, Dec. 7, 2007. From a proximate causation perspective, is this a stronger or weaker case for the argument that a homicide has occurred? Is it conceptually possible to say that a suicide is also a homicide?

3. *Update.* Isaac Velazquez turned his life around after the drag race. He now is an attorney and father of three boys. As he wrote the author of this casebook, "[o]bviously, it was one of the most difficult times in my life and I give God all of the credit for delivering me (physically and legally) from that situation."

4. *Problems.* In view of everything that you have read so far, how should the following cases be decided?

A. *B* shoots *V,* with the intent to kill. *V*'s wound is not mortal, but he requires hospitalization. In the hospital, *V* is treated by a physician who is recovering from scarlet fever. *V* contracts the disease from the doctor and dies from it. *B* is charged with murder, defined to require a mental state of intent with respect to *V*'s death. Is *B* the proximate cause of *V*'s death? Bush v. Commonwealth, 78 Ky. 268 (1880).

B. During a prison melee, *R* stabs *X* eleven times, drops the knife, and flees. *X,* mortally wounded, grabs the knife and staggers up a flight of stairs in search of *R.* On the second floor, *X* encounters *V,* an innocent party, who attempts to take the knife from him. *X* stabs and kills *V.* At the time of the latter stabbing, *X* was in a state of shock from a massive loss of blood from the initial wound. *R* is charged with murder, defined to require a mental state of extreme recklessness with respect to *V*'s death. Is *R* the proximate cause of *V*'s death? People v. Roberts, 2 Cal.4th 271, 6 Cal.Rptr.2d 276, 826 P.2d 274 (1992).

C. *D* is standing outside his car, parked on a public road, when *X* begins firing shots at him from a moving automobile. To protect himself, *D* runs 10 to 12 feet and picks up *V,* a two-year-old boy, and holds him in front of his face, as a shield. A bullet from *X*'s gun wounds *V. D* escapes unscathed. *X* is never found. *D* is prosecuted for aggravated battery, for intentionally or knowingly causing the gunshot wounds suffered by *V*. Is *D* the proximate cause of the harm? People v. Hall, 273 Ill.App.3d 838, 210 Ill.Dec. 290, 652 N.E.2d 1266 (1995).

D. *D* and an accomplice burglarize the home of *V* and her fiancé. While *D* sexually assaults *V* and stabs her repeatedly, *D*'s accomplice repeatedly stabs and kills *V*'s fiancé. *V's* wounds would have killed her if she had not received the prompt medical treatment she did in fact receive. Her wounds eventually healed, but *V's* physical and mental condition deteriorated. She became self-destructive and about fourteen months following the attack she became psychotic. She was involuntarily admitted to a psychiatric ward, where she inflicted wounds on herself that two days later caused her death. *D* is charged with murder, define to require a mental state of intent with respect to *V*'s death. Is *D* the proximate cause of *V*'s death? People v. Talavera, 2011 WL 227694, at *2–4 (Cal.App.2011). See also Stephenson v. State, 205 Ind. 141, 179 N.E. 633 (1932).

C. CONCURRENCE OF THE ELEMENTS

STATE v. ROSE

Supreme Court of Rhode Island, 1973.
112 R.I. 402, 311 A.2d 281.

ROBERTS, CHIEF JUSTICE.

These are two indictments, one (No. 70–573) charging the defendant, Henry Rose, with leaving the scene of an accident, death resulting, in violation of G.L.1956 § 31–26–1[1] and the other (No. 70–572) charging the defendant with [negligent] manslaughter. The defendant was tried on both indictments * * *, and a verdict of guilty was returned in each case. Thereafter the defendant's motions for a new trial were denied * * *.

These indictments followed the death of David J. McEnery, who was struck by defendant's motor vehicle at the intersection of Broad and Summer Streets in Providence at about 6:30 p.m. on April 1, 1970. According to the testimony of a bus driver, he had been operating his vehicle north on Broad Street and had stopped at a traffic light at the intersection of Summer Street. While the bus was standing there, he observed a pedestrian starting to cross Broad Street, and as the pedestrian reached the middle of the southbound lane he was struck by a "dirty, white station wagon" that was proceeding southerly on Broad Street. The pedestrian's body was thrown up on the hood of the car. The bus driver further testified that the station wagon stopped momentarily, the body of the pedestrian rolled off the hood, and the car immediately drove off along Broad Street in a southerly direction. The bus operator testified that he

---

1. General Laws 1956 § 31–26–1 reads, in part, as follows: "Duty to stop in accidents resulting in personal injury.—(a) The driver of any vehicle knowingly involved in an accident resulting in injury to or death of any person shall immediately stop such vehicle at the scene of such accident or as close thereto as possible but shall then forthwith return to and in every event shall remain at the scene of the accident until he has fulfilled the requirements of '31–26–3. Every such stop shall be made without obstructing traffic more than is necessary. * * * *'"

had alighted from his bus, intending to attempt to assist the victim, but was unable to locate the body.

Subsequently, it appears from the testimony of a police officer, about 6:40 p.m. the police located a white station wagon on Haskins Street, a distance of some 610 feet from the scene of the accident. The police further testified that a body later identified as that of David J. McEnery was wedged beneath the vehicle when it was found and that the vehicle had been registered to defendant. * * *

We turn, first, to defendant's contention that the trial court erred in denying his motion for a directed verdict of acquittal in each case. * * * In a criminal case the trial justice, in passing on such a motion, is required to give full credibility to the state's evidence, view it in a light most favorable to the state, and draw therefrom every reasonable inference consistent with guilt. However, where the evidence adduced by the state and the reasonable inferences to be drawn therefrom, even when viewed in a light most favorable to the state, are insufficient to establish guilt beyond a reasonable doubt, the court must grant the defendant's motion for a directed verdict. * * *

The defendant here argues that in neither case did the evidence exclude any reasonable hypothesis or theory of the innocence of defendant. In so arguing in case No. 70–572, charging defendant with manslaughter, defendant directs our attention to the fact that the court charged the jury that there was no evidence in the case of culpable negligence on the part of defendant up to and including the time at which Mr. McEnery was struck by the station wagon. He further charged the jury that, in order to find defendant guilty of manslaughter, it would be necessary to find that McEnery was alive immediately after the impact and that the conduct of defendant following the impact constituted culpable negligence.

The defendant is contending that if the evidence is susceptible of a finding that McEnery was killed upon impact, he was not alive at the time he was being dragged under defendant's vehicle and defendant could not be found guilty of manslaughter. An examination of the testimony of the only medical witness makes it clear that, in his opinion, death could have resulted immediately upon impact by reason of a massive fracture of the skull. The medical witness also testified that death could have resulted a few minutes after the impact but conceded that he was not sure when it did occur.

We are inclined to agree with defendant's contention in this respect. Obviously, the evidence is such that death could have occurred after defendant had driven away with McEnery's body lodged under his car and, therefore, be consistent with guilt. On the other hand, the medical testimony is equally consistent with a finding that McEnery could have died instantly upon impact and, therefore, be consistent with a reasonable conclusion other than the guilt of defendant. It is clear, then, that, the testimony of the medical examiner lacking any reasonable medical certainty as to the time of the death of McEnery, we are unable to conclude that on such evidence defendant was guilty of manslaughter beyond a reasonable doubt. Therefore, we conclude, with respect to Indictment No. 70–572, that it was error to deny defendant's motion for a directed verdict of acquittal.

We are unable, however, to reach the same conclusion concerning the denial of the motion for a directed verdict of acquittal with respect to Indictment No. 70–573, in which defendant was charged with leaving the scene of an accident. * * *

NOTES AND QUESTIONS

1. *Problem.* V, a police officer, wishing to question D-driver, directs D to park his car near the curb, where V is standing. D accidentally drives his car onto V's foot. After V repeatedly cries out, "Get off my foot," D says, "Fuck you, you can wait," and finally reverses the car off V's foot. D is charged with battery, defined in the jurisdiction as "any act that intentionally or recklessly causes harmful or offensive contact to another." Is D guilty? See Fagan v. Commissioner of Metropolitan Police, [1969] 1 Q.B. 439.

CHAPTER 7

CRIMINAL HOMICIDE

■ ■ ■

A. OVERVIEW

1. HOMICIDE STATISTICS

According to the United Nations Office on Drugs and Crime (UNODC), there were approximately 468,000 intentional homicides world-wide in 2010, or 6.9 homicides per 100,000 population. The highest homicide rates were in Africa and the Americas (17 and 16 per 100,000, respectively); the lowest rates were in Asia and Europe (3 and 4 per 100,000). UNODC, Global Study on Homicide 2011 (http://www.unodc.org/documents/data-and-analysis/statistics/Homicide/Globa_study_on_homicide_2011_web.pdf).

According to statistics compiled by the United States Department of Justice, the homicide rate in the United States reached its historic peak rate of 10.2 homicides per 100,000 population in 1980. Thereafter, the rate declined briefly, but rose again peaking anew at a 9.8–per–100,000 rate in 1991. From 1992 to 2000, the rate declined sharply, and since then has stabilized. During the years 1976–2005, the highest homicide rates for both victims and offenders were in the 18–24 year-old age group. James Alan Fox & Marianne W. Zawitz, Homicide Trends in the United States, available at http://www.bjs.ojp.usdoj.gov/content/pub/pdf/htius.pdf. (These figures do not include the homicides resulting from the September 11, 2001 terrorist attacks, and do not include accidental and negligent homicides.) In 2008, the homicide rate was nearly half its historic peak, namely, 5.4 victims per 100,000 persons. See http://www.census.gov/compendia/statab/2012/tables/12s0312.pdf.

2. COMMON LAW ORIGINS AND STATUTORY REFORM

AMERICAN LAW INSTITUTE, MODEL PENAL CODE AND COMMENTARIES, COMMENT TO § 210.2

(1980), 13–16

1. *Common–Law Background.* At common law, murder was defined as the unlawful killing of another human being with "malice afore-thought."[1] Whatever the original meaning of that phrase, it became over time an "arbitrary symbol" used by judges to signify any of a number of mental states deemed sufficient to support liability for murder. Successive generations added new content to "malice aforethought" until it encom-passed a variety of mental attitudes bearing no predictable relation to the ordinary sense of the two words. Even today, judges find in the elasticity of this ancient formula a convenient vehicle for announcing new depar-tures in the law of homicide.

Various authorities have given different summaries of the several meanings of "malice aforethought." Generally, these definitions converge on four constituent states of mind. First and foremost, there was intent to kill. Common-law authorities included in the notion of intent to kill awareness that the death of another would result from one's actions, even if the actor had no particular desire to achieve such a consequence. Thus, intentional or knowing homicide was murder unless the actor killed in the heat of passion engendered by adequate provocation, in which case the crime was manslaughter. A second species of murder involved intent to cause grievous bodily harm. Again, knowledge that conduct would cause serious bodily injury was generally assimilated to intent and was deemed sufficient for murder if death of another actually resulted. A third catego-ry of murder was sometimes called depraved-heart murder. This label derived from decisions and statutes condemning as murder unintentional homicide under circumstances evincing a "depraved mind" or an "aban-doned and malignant heart." Older authorities may have described such circumstances as giving rise to an "implied" or "presumed" intent to kill or injure, but the essential concept was one of extreme recklessness regarding homicidal risk. Thus, a person might be liable for murder absent any actual intent to kill or injure if he caused the death of another in a manner exhibiting a "wanton and wilful disregard of an unreasonable human risk" or, in confusing elaboration, a "wickedness of disposition, hardness of heart, cruelty, recklessness of consequences, and a mind regardless of social duty." The fourth kind of murder was based on intent to commit a felony. This is the origin of the felony-murder rule, which

---

1. The traditional definition of murder was given by Coke in the seventeenth century: "When a man of sound memory and of the age of discretion unlawfully kills any reasonable creature in being, and under the King's peace, with malice aforethought, either express or implied by the law, the death taking place within a year and a day." Quoted in Royal Comm'n on Capital Punishment, Report, CMD. No. 8932, at 26 (1953).

assigns strict liability for homicide committed during the commission of a felony. These four states of mind exhausted the meaning of "malice aforethought"; the phrase had no residual content.[13]

2. *Antecedent Statutory Variations.* Prior to the recodification effort begun by the Model Penal Code, most American jurisdictions maintained a law of murder built around these common-law classifications. The most significant departure was the division of murder into degrees, a change initiated by the Pennsylvania legislation of 1794. That statute provided that "all murder, which shall be perpetrated by means of poison, or by lying in wait, or by any other kind of willful, deliberate or premeditated killing, or which shall be committed in the perpetration, or attempt to perpetrate any arson, rape, robbery or burglary shall be deemed murder in the first degree; and all other kinds of murder shall be deemed murder in the second degree." The thrust of this reform was to confine the death penalty, which was then mandatory on conviction of any common-law murder, to homicides judged particularly heinous. Other states followed the Pennsylvania practice until at one time the vast majority of American jurisdictions differentiated degrees of murder and the term "first-degree murder" passed into common parlance.

Leaving the question of felony-murder aside, the extent to which the common law had been modified in other ways prior to the drafting of the Model Penal Code varied considerably from jurisdiction to jurisdiction.

AMERICAN LAW INSTITUTE, MODEL PENAL CODE AND COMMENTARIES, COMMENT TO § 210.3

(1980), 44–46

1. *Common–Law Background.* Initially, the common law did not distinguish murder from manslaughter. Early statutes, however, sought to differentiate among criminal homicides for the purpose of withdrawing benefit of clergy from the more heinous killings. This initiative led to the division of criminal homicides into murder, which retained its status as a capital crime, and the lesser offense of manslaughter. The courts defined murder in terms of the evolving concept of "malice aforethought" and treated manslaughter as a residual category for all other criminal homicides. Thus, in its classic formulation, manslaughter consisted of homicide without malice aforethought on the one hand and without justification or excuse on the other.

Traditional statements of the English law as it further evolved divided the offense into two types. First, homicide, even if intentional, was said to be without malice and hence manslaughter if committed in the heat of passion upon adequate provocation. Second, homicide was also manslaugh-

---

13. Some early writers asserted a fifth distinct species of "malice aforethought" based on intent to oppose lawful arrest. Under this rule, causing the death of another while resisting lawful arrest would be murder even if the facts did not show an intent to kill or injure or any form of extreme recklessness. Modern authorities agree, however, that resisting arrest is not an independently sufficient basis of liability for murder. * * *

ter if it resulted from an act that was regarded as unduly dangerous to life or limb or from an act that was otherwise unlawful. This category thus encompassed conduct that was insufficiently reckless or negligent to constitute "depraved-heart" murder but at the same time exhibited culpability greater than needed for ordinary conceptions of civil negligence. It also included cases where the actor caused the death of another in the commission of an unlawful act, sometimes described as the misdemeanor-manslaughter analogue to the felony-murder rule. Courts commonly referred to the first category as voluntary manslaughter and the second as involuntary manslaughter, although the distinction had no grading significance at common law.

2. *Antecedent Statutory Variations.* Virtually every state recognized the crime of manslaughter at the time the Model Penal Code was drafted. The largest number contained no explicit definition of the offense and hence determined its content by reference to the common law. There were also a few states, typified by Florida, that carried forward the substance of the common-law offense by defining manslaughter as "the killing of a human being by the act, procurement or culpable negligence of another where such killing shall not be justifiable or excusable homicide nor murder." A more common variation was reflected in the federal manslaughter provision:

> Manslaughter is the unlawful killing of a human being without malice. It is of two kinds:
>
> > Voluntary—Upon a sudden quarrel or heat of passion.
> >
> > Involuntary—In the commission of an unlawful act not amounting to a felony, or in the commission in an unlawful manner, or without due caution and circumspection, of a lawful act which might produce death.

Statutes that followed this pattern typically departed from the common law by providing a grading differential between voluntary and involuntary manslaughter.

3. VARIATIONS ON THE THEME: SOME HOMICIDE STATUTES*

CALIFORNIA PENAL CODE

§ 187. Murder defined; death of fetus

(a) Murder is the unlawful killing of a human being, or a fetus [except during a lawful abortion or when solicited, aided, abetted, or consented to by the mother], with malice aforethought. * * *

§ 188. Malice, express malice, and implied malice defined

Such malice may be express or implied. It is express when there is manifested a deliberate intention unlawfully to take away the life of a

---

* As of January, 2012.

fellow creature. It is implied, when no considerable provocation appears, or when the circumstances attending the killing show an abandoned and malignant heart.

When it is shown that the killing resulted from the intentional doing of an act with express or implied malice as defined above, no other mental state need be shown to establish the mental state of malice aforethought. Neither an awareness of the obligation to act within the general body of laws regulating society nor acting despite such awareness is included within the definition of malice.

§ 189. Murder; degrees

All murder which is perpetrated by means of a destructive device or explosive, a weapon of mass destruction, knowing use of ammunition designed primarily to penetrate metal or armor, poison, lying in wait, torture, or by any other kind of willful, deliberate, and premeditated killing, or which is committed in the perpetration of, or attempt to perpetrate, arson, rape, carjacking, robbery, burglary, mayhem, kidnapping, train wrecking, or any act punishable under [one of various enumerated penal codes sections relating to sexual offenses not including rape], or any murder which is perpetrated by means of discharging a firearm from a motor vehicle, intentionally at another person outside of the vehicle with the intent to inflict death, is murder in the first degree. [Punishable by death, life imprisonment without possibility of parole, or imprisonment for 25 years to life]. All other kinds of murders are of the second degree. [Punishable by imprisonment for a term of 15 years to life]. * * *

To prove the killing was "deliberate and premeditated," it shall not be necessary to prove the defendant maturely and meaningfully reflected upon the gravity of his or her act.

§ 192. Manslaughter

Manslaughter is the unlawful killing of a human being without malice. It is of three kinds:

(a) Voluntary—upon a sudden quarrel or heat of passion. [Punishable by imprisonment for 3, 6, or 11 years.]

(b) Involuntary—in the commission of an unlawful act, not amounting to felony; or in the commission of a lawful act which might produce death, in an unlawful manner, or without due caution and circumspection. This subdivision shall not apply to acts committed in the driving of a vehicle. [Punishable by imprisonment for 2, 3, or 4 years.]

(c) Vehicular—

(1) * * * driving a vehicle in the commission of an unlawful act, not amounting to a felony, and with gross negligence; or driving a vehicle in the commission of a lawful act which might produce death, in an unlawful manner, and with gross negligence. [Punishable by up to one year in county jail, or imprisonment for 2, 4, or 6 years.]

(2) * * * driving a vehicle in the commission of an unlawful act, not amounting to a felony, but without gross negligence, or driving a vehicle in the commission of a lawful act, which might produce death, in an unlawful manner, but without gross negligence. [Punishable by imprisonment in the county jail for not more than one year.] * * *

This section shall not be construed as making any homicide in the driving of a vehicle punishable which is not a proximate result of the commission of an unlawful act, not amounting to felony, or of the commission of a lawful act which might produce death, in an unlawful manner.

"Gross negligence," as used in this section, shall not be construed as prohibiting or precluding a charge of murder under Section 188 upon facts exhibiting wantonness and a conscious disregard for life to support a finding of implied malice * * *.

§ 194. Murder and manslaughter; time of death; computation

To make the killing either murder or manslaughter, it is not requisite that the party die within three years and a day after the stroke received or the cause of death administered. If death occurs beyond the time of three years and a day, there shall be a rebuttable presumption that the killing was not criminal. The prosecution shall bear the burden of overcoming this presumption. In the computation of time, the whole of the day on which the act was done shall be reckoned the first.

ILLINOIS CRIMINAL CODE

§ 9–1. First degree murder

(a) A person who kills an individual without lawful justification commits first degree murder [punishable by life imprisonment, or a term of not less than 20 years and not more than 60 years] if, in performing the acts which cause the death:

(1) he either intends to kill or do great bodily harm to that individual or another, or knows that such acts will cause death to that individual or another; or

(2) he knows that such acts create a strong probability of death or great bodily harm to that individual or another; or

(3) he is attempting or committing a forcible felony other than second degree murder. * * *

§ 9–1.2 Intentional Homicide of an Unborn Child

(a) A person commits the offense of intentional homicide of an unborn child if, in performing acts which cause the death of an unborn child, he without lawful justification:

(1) either intended to cause the death of or do great bodily harm to the pregnant woman or her unborn child or knew that such acts would

cause death or great bodily harm to the pregnant woman or her unborn child; or

(2) knew that his acts created a strong probability of death or great bodily harm to the pregnant woman or her unborn child; and

(3) knew that the woman was pregnant.

(b) For purposes of this Section, * * * "unborn child" shall mean any individual of the human species from fertilization until birth * * *.

(c) This Section shall not apply to acts which cause the death of an unborn child if those acts were committed during any abortion * * * to which the pregnant woman has consented. This Section shall not apply to acts which were committed pursuant to usual and customary standards of medical practice during diagnostic testing or therapeutic treatment.

(d) Penalty. The sentence for intentional homicide of an unborn child shall be the same as for first degree murder * * *.

§ 9–2. Second Degree Murder

(a) A person commits the offense of second degree murder when he or she commits the offense of first degree murder as defined in paragraph (1) or (2) of subsection (a) of Section 9–1 of this Code and either of the following mitigating factors are present:

(1) At the time of the killing he or she is acting under a sudden and intense passion resulting from serious provocation by the individual killed or another whom the offender endeavors to kill, but he or she negligently or accidentally causes the death of the individual killed; or

(2) At the time of the killing he or she believes the circumstances to be such that, if they existed, would justify or exonerate the killing under the principles stated in Article 7 of this Code, but his or her belief is unreasonable.

(b) Serious provocation is conduct sufficient to excite an intense passion in a reasonable person. * * *

(d) Sentence. [Second Degree Murder is a Class 1 felony, punishable by imprisonment of not less than 4 years and not more than 15 years.]

§ 9–2.1 Voluntary Manslaughter of an Unborn Child

(a) A person who kills an unborn child without lawful justification commits voluntary manslaughter of an unborn child if at the time of the killing he is acting under a sudden and intense passion resulting from serious provocation by another whom the offender endeavors to kill, but he negligently or accidentally causes the death of the unborn child.

Serious provocation is conduct sufficient to excite an intense passion in a reasonable person.

(b) A person who intentionally or knowingly kills an unborn child commits voluntary manslaughter of an unborn child if at the time of the killing he believes the circumstances to be such that, if they existed, would justify or exonerate the killing under the principles stated in Article 7 of this Code, but his belief is unreasonable.

(c) Sentence. [Voluntary Manslaughter of an unborn child is a Class 1 felony, punishable by imprisonment of not less than 4 years and not more than 15 years.]

§ 9–3. Involuntary Manslaughter and Reckless Homicide

(a) A person who unintentionally kills an individual without lawful justification commits involuntary manslaughter if his acts whether lawful or unlawful which cause the death are such as are likely to cause death or great bodily harm to some individual, and he performs them recklessly, except in cases in which the cause of the death consists of the driving of a motor vehicle, or operating a snowmobile, all-terrain vehicle, or watercraft, in which case the person commits reckless homicide. * * *

(d) Sentence. [Involuntary manslaughter and reckless homicide are Class 3 felonies, punishable by imprisonment of not less than 2 years and not more than 5 years.]

§ 9–3.2 Involuntary Manslaughter and Reckless Homicide of an Unborn Child

(a) A person who unintentionally kills an unborn child without lawful justification commits involuntary manslaughter of an unborn child if his acts whether lawful or unlawful which cause the death are such as are likely to cause death or great bodily harm to some individual, and he performs them recklessly, except in cases in which the cause of death consists of the driving of a motor vehicle, in which case the person commits reckless homicide of an unborn child.

(b) Sentence. [Involuntary manslaughter of an unborn child is a Class 3 felony, punishable by imprisonment of not less than 2 years and nor more than 5 years.]

MICHIGAN PENAL CODE

§ 750.316 First degree murder; definition

(1) A person who commits any of the following is guilty of first degree murder and shall be punished by imprisonment for life:

(a) Murder perpetrated by means of poison, lying in wait, or any other willful, deliberate, and premeditated killing.

(b) Murder committed in the perpetration, or attempt to perpetrate, arson, criminal sexual conduct in the first, second, or third degree, child abuse in the first degree, a major controlled substance offense, robbery, carjacking, breaking and entering of a dwelling, home invasion in the first or second degree, larceny of any kind, extortion, kidnapping, or vulnerable adult abuse in the first or second degree * * *.

(c) A murder of a peace officer or corrections officer committed while the peace officer or corrections officer is lawfully engaged in the performance of any of his or her duties as a peace officer or corrections officer, knowing that the peace officer or corrections officer is a peace officer or corrections officer engaged in the performance of his or her duty as a peace officer or corrections officer. * * *

§ 750.317   Second degree murder

All other kinds of murder shall be murder of the second degree, and shall be punished by imprisonment in the state prison for life, or any terms of years, in the discretion of the court trying the same.

§ 750.321   Manslaughter

Any person who shall commit the crime of manslaughter shall be guilty of a felony punishable by imprisonment in the state prison, not more than 15 years or by fine of not more than 7,500 dollars, or both, at the discretion of the court.

§ 750.322   Manslaughter; wilful killing of unborn quick child

The wilful killing of an unborn quick child by any injury to the mother of such child, which would be murder if it resulted in the death of such mother, shall be deemed manslaughter.

NEW YORK PENAL LAW

§ 125.05   * * * [D]efinition of terms

The following definitions are applicable to this article:

(1) "Person," when referring to the victim of a homicide, means a human being who has been born and is alive. * * *

§ 125.10   Criminally negligent homicide

A person is guilty of criminally negligent homicide [a Class E felony, punishable by imprisonment not exceeding four years] when, with criminal negligence, he causes the death of another person.

§ 125.15   Manslaughter in the second degree

A person is guilty of manslaughter in the second degree [a Class C felony, punishable by imprisonment not exceeding fifteen years] when:

(1) He recklessly causes the death of another person; or

(2) He commits upon a female an abortional act which causes her death, unless such abortional act is justifiable [under the state abortion law]; or

(3) He intentionally causes or aids another person to commit suicide.

§ 125.20   Manslaughter in the first degree

A person is guilty of manslaughter in the first degree [a Class B felony, punishable by imprisonment not exceeding 25 years] when:

(1) With intent to cause serious physical injury to another person, he causes the death of such person or of a third person; or

(2) With intent to cause the death of another person, he causes the death of such person or of a third person under circumstances which do not constitute murder because he acts under the influence of extreme emotional disturbance, as defined in paragraph (a) of subdivision one of section 125.25. The fact that homicide was committed under the influence of extreme emotional disturbance constitutes a mitigating circumstance reducing murder to manslaughter in the first degree and need not be proved in any prosecution initiated under this subdivision; or

(3) He commits upon a female pregnant for more than twenty-four weeks an abortional act which causes her death, unless such abortional act is justifiable [under the state abortion law]; or

(4) Being eighteen years old or more and with intent to cause physical injury to a person less than eleven years old, the defendant recklessly engages in conduct which creates a grave risk of a serious physical injury to such person and thereby causes the death of such person.

§ 125.25 Murder in the second degree

A person is guilty of murder in the second degree [a Class A–I felony, of which the punishment is imprisonment of 15–25 years] when:

(1) With intent to cause the death of another person, he causes the death of such person or of a third person; except that in any prosecution under this subdivision, it is an affirmative defense that:

> (a) The defendant acted under the influence of extreme emotional disturbance for which there was a reasonable explanation or excuse, the reasonableness of which is to be determined from the viewpoint of a person in the defendant's situation under the circumstances as the defendant believed them to be * * *; or

> (b) The defendant's conduct consisted of causing or aiding, without the use of duress or deception, another person to commit suicide * * *; or

(2) Under circumstances evincing a depraved indifference to human life, he recklessly engages in conduct which creates a grave risk of death to another person, and thereby causes the death of another person; or

(3) Acting either alone or with one or more other persons, he commits or attempts to commit robbery, burglary, kidnapping, arson, rape in the first degree, criminal sexual act in the first degree, sexual abuse in the first degree, aggravated sexual abuse, [or] escape * * *, and, in the course of and in furtherance of such crime or of immediate flight therefrom, he, or another participant, if there be any, causes the death of a person other than one of the participants except that in any prosecution under this subdivision, in which the defendant was not the only participant in the underlying crime, it is an affirmative defense that the defendant:

(a) Did not commit the homicidal act or in any way solicit, request, command, importune, cause or aid the commission thereof; and

(b) Was not armed with a deadly weapon, or any instrument, article or substance readily capable of causing death or serious physical injury and of a sort not ordinarily carried in public places by law-abiding persons; and

(c) Had no reasonable ground to believe that any other participant was armed with such a weapon, instrument, article or substance; and

(d) Had no reasonable ground to believe that any other participant intended to engage in conduct likely to result in death or serious physical injury; or

(4) Under circumstances evincing a depraved indifference to human life, and being eighteen years old or more the defendant recklessly engages in conduct which creates a grave risk of serious physical injury or death to another person less than eleven years old and thereby causes the death of such person.

(5) Being eighteen years old or more, while in the course of committing rape in the first, second or third degree, criminal sexual act in the first, second or third degree, sexual abuse in the first degree, aggravated sexual abuse in the first, second, third or fourth degree, or incest * * *, against a person less than fourteen years old, he or she intentionally causes the death of such person.

§ 125.27   Murder in the first degree

A person is guilty of murder in the first degree [a Class A–I felony, for which the penalty is life imprisonment without parole, or a term of imprisonment of 20–25 years] when:

(1) With intent to cause the death of another person, he causes the death of such person or of a third person; and either [the intended victim was a police or peace officer, or employee of state or local correctional facility, who was at the time of the killing engaged in the course of performing his official duties, and the defendant knew or reasonably should have known of the intended victim's identity as an officer or employee of the correctional facility; or was a judge, or a witness to a crime committed on a prior occasion; or the homicide was committed by a prisoner or escapee; or the victim was killed during the commission or attempted commission of one of the felonies enumerated in Section 125.25; or the death occurred in the furtherance of an act of terrorism as defined by statute; or the killing was committed in an especially cruel and wanton manner; or the defendant intentionally caused the death of two or more additional persons within the state in separate criminal transactions within a period of twenty-four months when committed in a similar fashion or pursuant to a common scheme or plan]; and [t]he defendant

was more than eighteen years of age at the time of the commissions of the crime. * * *

PENNSYLVANIA CONSOLIDATED STATUTES

§ 2501. Criminal homicide

(a) Offense defined.—A person is guilty of criminal homicide if he intentionally, knowingly, recklessly or negligently causes the death of another human being.

(b) Classification.—Criminal homicide shall be classified as murder, voluntary manslaughter, or involuntary manslaughter.[a]

§ 2502. Murder

(a) Murder of the first degree.—A criminal homicide constitutes murder of the first degree when it is committed by an intentional killing. [Punishable by death or life imprisonment.]

(b) Murder of the second degree.—A criminal homicide constitutes murder of the second degree when it is committed while defendant was engaged as a principal or an accomplice in the perpetration of a felony. [Punishable by life imprisonment.]

(c) Murder of the third degree.—All other kinds of murder shall be murder of the third degree. Murder of the third degree is a felony of the first degree. [Punishable by imprisonment of no more than 40 years.]

(d) Definitions.—As used in this section the following words and phrases shall have the meanings given to them in this subsection: * * *

"Intentional killing." Killing by means of poison, or by lying in wait, or by any other kind of willful, deliberate and premeditated killing.

"Perpetration of a felony." The act of the defendant in engaging in or being an accomplice in the commission of, or an attempt to commit, or flight after committing, or attempting to commit robbery, rape, or deviate sexual intercourse by force or threat of force, arson, burglary or kidnapping. * * *

§ 2503. Voluntary manslaughter

(a) General rule.—A person who kills an individual without lawful justification commits voluntary manslaughter if at the time of the killing he is acting under a sudden and intense passion resulting from serious provocation by:

(1) the individual killed; or

(2) another whom the actor endeavors to kill, but he negligently or accidentally causes the death of the individual killed.

---

a. Separate statutory provisions criminalize the "murder of unborn child" and the "voluntary manslaughter of unborn child." "Unborn child" is defined as "an individual organism of the species homo sapiens from fertilization until live birth." With minor exceptions and the exclusion of the death penalty, these offenses parallel the definitions of, and penalties for, the offenses of murder and voluntary manslaughter set out in this text.

(b) Unreasonable belief killing justifiable.—A person who intentionally or knowingly kills an individual commits voluntary manslaughter if at the time of the killing he believes the circumstances to be such that, if they existed, would justify the killing under Chapter 5 of this title, but his belief is unreasonable.

(c) Grading.—Voluntary manslaughter is a felony of the first degree. [Punishable by imprisonment of no more than 20 years.]

§ 2504. Involuntary manslaughter

(a) General rule.—A person is guilty of involuntary manslaughter when as a direct result of the doing of an unlawful act in a reckless or grossly negligent manner, or the doing of a lawful act in a reckless or grossly negligent manner, he causes the death of another person.

(b) Grading.—Involuntary manslaughter is a misdemeanor of the first degree. [Punishable by imprisonment of no more than 5 years.] Where the victim is under 12 years of age and is in the care, custody or control of the person who caused the death, involuntary manslaughter is a felony of the second degree. [Punishable by imprisonment of no more than 10 years.]

§ 2505. Causing or aiding suicide

(a) Causing suicide as criminal homicide.—A person may be convicted of criminal homicide for causing another to commit suicide only if he intentionally causes such suicide by force, duress or deception.

(b) Aiding or soliciting suicide as an independent offense.—A person who intentionally aids or solicits another to commit suicide is guilty of a felony of the second degree [10–year maximum] if his conduct causes such suicide or an attempted suicide, and otherwise of a misdemeanor of the second degree. [Punishable by imprisonment of no more than 2 years.]

NOTES AND QUESTIONS

1. Article 210 of the Model Penal Code divides criminal homicide into three categories—murder, manslaughter, and negligent homicide. These offenses differ in key respects from the common law and antecedent statutory law, as explained infra.

4. THE PROTECTED INTEREST: "HUMAN BEING"

PEOPLE v. EULO

Court of Appeals of New York, 1984.
63 N.Y.2d 341, 482 N.Y.S.2d 436, 472 N.E.2d 286.

COOKE, CHIEF JUDGE.

These appeals involve a question of criminal responsibility in which defendants, charged with homicide, contend that their conduct did not cause death. * * *

I

[In separate prosecutions, defendants Eulo and Bonilla were convicted of manslaughter. Their cases were similar: the accused shot his victim in the head; the victim was taken to a hospital in an unconscious state and placed on a respirator to enable breathing; upon later determination that the victim's brain had irreversibly ceased to function and with the consent of next of kin, the victim was declared dead, artificial respiration terminated, and bodily organs removed for transplantation purposes.]

II

Defendants' principal point in each of these appeals is that the respective Trial Judges failed to adequately instruct the juries as to what constitutes a person's death, the time at which criminal liability for a homicide would attach. It is claimed that in New York, the time of death has always been set by reference to the functioning of the heart and the lungs; that death does not occur until there has been an irreversible cessation of breathing and heartbeat.

There having been extensive testimony at both trials concerning each victim's diagnosis as "brain dead," defendants argue that, in the absence of clear instruction, the juries may have erroneously concluded that defendants would be guilty of homicide if their conduct was the legal cause of the victims' "brain death" rather than the victims' ultimate state of cardiorespiratory failure. In evaluating defendants' contentions, it is first necessary to review: how death has traditionally been determined by the law; how the principle of "brain death" is now sought to be infused into our jurisprudence; and, whether, if at all, this court may recognize a principle of "brain death" without infringing upon a legislative power or prerogative. * * *

A person's passing from life has long been an event marked with a variety of legal consequences. * * * [I]n recent times, death marks the point at which certain of the deceased's organs, intended to be donated upon death, may be transferred. In the immediate context, * * * determination of a person's "death" is relevant because our Penal Law defines homicide in terms of "conduct which causes the *death* of a person" (Penal Law, § 125.00 [emphasis added]).

Death has been conceptualized by the law as, simply, the absence of life: "Death is the opposite of life; it is the termination of life." But, while erecting death as a critical milepost in a person's legal life, the law has had little occasion to consider the precise point at which a person ceases to live. * * *

Within the past two decades, machines that artificially maintain cardiorespiratory functions have come into widespread use. This technical accomplishment has called into question the universal applicability of the traditional legal and medical criteria for determining when a person has died.

These criteria were cast into flux as the medical community gained a better understanding of human physiology. It is widely understood that the human brain may be anatomically divided, generally, into three parts: the cerebrum, the cerebellum, and the brain stem. The cerebrum, known also as the "higher brain," is deemed largely to control cognitive functions such as thought, memory, and consciousness. The cerebellum primarily controls motor coordination. The brain stem, or "lower brain," which itself has three parts known as the midbrain, pons, and medulla, controls reflexive or spontaneous functions such as breathing, swallowing, and "sleep-wake" cycles.

* * * Within a relatively short period after being deprived of oxygen, the brain will irreversibly stop functioning. With the suffocation of the higher brain all cognitive powers are lost and a cessation of lower brain functions will ultimately end all spontaneous bodily functions.

Notwithstanding a total irreversible loss of the entire brain's functioning, contemporary medical techniques can maintain, for a limited period, the operation of the heart and the lungs. Respirators or ventilators can substitute for the lower brain's failure to maintain breathing. This artificial respiration, when combined with a chemical regimen, can support the continued operation of the heart. This is so because, unlike respiration, the physical contracting or "beating" of the heart occurs independently of impulses from the brain: so long as blood containing oxygen circulates to the heart, it may continue to beat and medication can take over the lower brain's limited role in regulating the rate and force of the heartbeat.

It became clear in medical practice that the traditional "vital signs"—breathing and heartbeat—are not independent indicia of life, but are, instead, part of an integration of functions in which the brain is dominant. As a result, the medical community began to consider the cessation of brain activity as a measure of death.[15]

The movement in law towards recognizing cessation of brain functions as criteria for death followed this medical trend. The immediate motive for adopting this position was to ease and make more efficient the transfer of donated organs. Organ transfers, to be successful, require a

---

15. The initial problem for doctors was to devise a technical means of verifying when the entire brain ceases to function. Unlike tests for determining the cessation of breathing and heartbeat, more sophisticated means were necessary to measure the less obvious functioning of the brain. A seminal study was issued in 1968, under the auspices of Harvard Medical School, setting forth a multistep test designed to identify the existence of physical indicia of brain activity. Under it, responsiveness to painful stimuli is to be tested. The subject is also to be observed for any spontaneous movement or respiration and any operation of various bodily reflexes. The absence of brain activity, when demonstrated under these tests, is then sought to be confirmed by reapplication of the tests at least 24 hours later and through the reading of an EEG, which when "flat" has confirmatory value. This test has served as the foundation for currently applied tests for determining when the brain has ceased to function.

"viable, intact organ." Once all of a person's vital functions have ceased, transferable organs swiftly deteriorate and lose their transplant value. * * *

* * * [T]he first legal recognition of cessation of brain functions as a criterion for determining death came in the form of a Kansas statute enacted in 1970. Denominated "[a]n Act relating to and defining death," the statute states, in part, that death will be deemed to have occurred when a physician applying ordinary medical standards determines that there is an "absence of spontaneous respiratory and cardiac functions and * * * attempts at resuscitation are considered hopeless * * * *or* * * * there is the absence of spontaneous brain function."

In the years following enactment of this statute, a growing number of sister States enacted statutes of their own. Some opted for the Kansas approach. Others defined death solely in terms of brain-based criteria as determined by accepted methods of medical practice. And still others retain the cardiorespiratory yardstick, but provide that when artificial means of sustaining respiration and heartbeat preclude application of the traditional criteria, death may be determined according to brain-based criteria * * *. In the absence of any statute defining death, some jurisdictions have judicially adopted brain-based criteria for determining death. * * *

In New York, the term "death," although used in many statutes, has not been expressly defined by the Legislature. This raises the question of how this court may construe these expressions of the term "death" in the absence of clarification by the Legislature. When the Legislature has failed to assign definition to a statutory term, the courts will generally construe that term according to "its ordinary and accepted meaning as it was understood at the time." If the term at issue has been judicially defined prior to its use in a statute, however, that definition will be assigned to the term, absent contrary indications. In every case, of course, the term must be read in accordance with the apparent purpose of the statute in which it is found.

Bearing these principles in mind, it must be added that statutory construction is not "a ritual to be observed by unimaginative adherence to well-worn professional phrases." * * * This is particularly true when a "word must be applied under changed conditions." The guiding principle is that there must always be fidelity to the fair import of the term.

It has been called to this court's attention that the Legislature has, on a number of occasions, had bills before it that would expressly recognize brain-based criteria for determining death and has taken no affirmative action. This legislative void in no way impedes this court from fulfilling its obligation to construe laws of the State. Indeed, advances made in medical science have caused a focus on the issues of when a jury may find criminal responsibility for homicide, of when physicians may transfer donated organs, and of when a person's body may be accorded the dignity of final repose. It is incumbent upon this court to instill certainty and uniformity in these important areas.

We hold that a recognition of brain-based criteria for determining death is not unfaithful to prior judicial definitions of "death," as presumptively adopted in the many statutes using that term. Close examination of the common-law conception of death and the traditional criteria used to determine when death has occurred leads inexorably to this conclusion. * * *

* * * Ordinarily, death will be determined according to the traditional criteria of irreversible cardiorespiratory repose. When, however, the respiratory and circulatory functions are maintained by mechanical means, their significance, as signs of life, is at best ambiguous. Under such circumstances, death may nevertheless be deemed to occur when, according to accepted medical practice, it is determined that the entire brain's function has irreversibly ceased.

Death remains the single phenomenon identified at common law; the supplemental criteria are merely adapted to account for the "changed conditions" that a dead body may be attached to a machine so as to exhibit demonstrably false indicia of life. It reflects an improved understanding that in the complete and irreversible absence of a functioning brain, the traditional loci of life—the heart and lungs—function only as a result of stimuli originating from outside the body and will never again function as part of an integrated organism.[28]

This court searches in vain for evidence that * * * the Legislature intended to render immutable the criteria used to determine death. By extension, to hold to the contrary would be to say that the law could not recognize diagnostic equipment such as the stethoscope or more sensitive equipment even when it became clear that these instruments more accurately measured the presence of signs of life.

Moreover, the Legislature has consistently declared, from the time it adopted the * * * Penal Code in 1881 through several recodifications, that our Penal Law should be construed "according to the fair import of [its] terms to promote justice and effect the objects of the law" (Penal Law, § 5.00). It is the first object of our Penal Law "[to] proscribe conduct which unjustifiably and inexcusably causes or threatens substantial harm to individual or public interests" (Penal Law, § 1.05, subd. 1). Therefore, in the instant matters, to construe our homicide statute to provide for

---

28. In reaching this conclusion, this court is aware of the criticism from some quarters that the perceived motivation for the development and recognition of brain-based criteria for death renders these criteria "theoretically impure." This is asserted on the ground that the prospect of more easily accessible transplants serves to "adulterate the purity of [the] scientific case by baiting it with the prospect of this extraneous—though extremely appealing—gain." * * * [However,] [t]he Presidential Commission, charged with evaluating how death should be determined, cited studies reporting "that organs are procured in only a small percentage of cases in which brain-based criteria might be applied." The Commission itself found that the "medical concern over the determination of death rests much less with any wish to facilitate organ transplantation than with the need both to render appropriate care to patients and to replace artificial support with more fitting and respectful behavior when a patient has become a dead body."

criminal responsibility for homicide when a defendant's conduct causes injury leading to the victim's total loss of brain functions, is entirely consistent with the Legislature's concept of death. * * *

III

Each defendant correctly notes that the respective Trial Judges did not expressly instruct the juries concerning the criteria to be applied in determining when death occurred. Whether medically accepted brain-based criteria are legally cognizable became an issue in these cases when the respective juries heard testimony concerning the victims being pronounced medically dead while their hearts were beating and before artificial maintenance of the cardiorespiratory systems was discontinued. To properly evaluate whether these diagnoses of death were legally and medically premature and, therefore, whether the subsequent activities were possibly superseding causes of the deaths, the juries had to have been instructed as to the appropriate criteria for determining death: irreversible cessation of breathing and heartbeat or irreversible cessation of the entire brain's functioning.

The courts here adequately conveyed to the juries their obligation to determine the fact and causation of death. The courts defined the criteria of death in relation to the chain of causation. By specifically charging the juries that they might consider the surgical [transplantation] procedures as superseding causes of death, the courts made clear by ready implication that death should be deemed to have occurred after *all* medical procedures had ended.

The trial courts could have given express instructions that death may be deemed to have occurred when the victims' entire brain, including the brain stem, had irreversibly ceased to function. On the facts of these cases, that would have been the better practice. But, as mentioned, the brain-based criteria are supplemental to the traditional criteria, each describing the same phenomenon of death. In the context of a criminal case for homicide, there is no theoretical or practical impediment to the People's proceeding under a theory that the defendant "cause[d] the death" of a person, with death determined by either criteria.

Even though each of these cases was presented to a jury which had been charged that death should be deemed to have occurred after the medical intervention had ended, testimony concerning the attending physicians' diagnoses of the victims as dead, according to brain-based criteria, was nonetheless highly relevant. It was these medical pronouncements that caused the victims to be removed from the medical systems that maintained their breathing and heartbeat. If the victims were properly diagnosed as dead, of course, no subsequent medical procedure such as the organ removals would be deemed a cause of death. If victims' deaths were prematurely pronounced due to a doctor's negligence, the subsequent procedures may have been a cause of death, but that negligence would not constitute a superseding cause of death relieving defendants of liability. If, however, the pronouncements of death were premature due to the gross negligence or the intentional wrongdoing of doctors, as determined by a grave deviation from accepted medical practices or disregard for legally cognizable criteria for determining death, the intervening medical procedure would interrupt the chain of causation and become the legal cause of death. Thus, the propriety of the medical procedures is integral to the question of causation.

A review of the records, viewed in a light most favorable to the People, indicates that there was sufficient evidence for a rational juror to have concluded beyond a reasonable doubt that each defendant's conduct caused the victim's death and that the medical procedures were not superseding causes of death.

NOTES AND QUESTIONS

1. Did the court overstep its authority by recognizing brain-based criteria for determining "death" for criminal homicide purposes? Is this a matter properly left to the legislature?

2. *The other end of the continuum.* At common law, a live birth was a prerequisite to a criminal homicide prosecution; a fetus, even a viable one, was not considered a "human being." See p. 95, supra. Typically, a live birth is manifested when the child breathes spontaneously or has a heartbeat, even if only momentarily.

Should a live birth be a prerequisite to a criminal homicide prosecution? Take a look at the statutes set out on pp. 238–247. Does the killing of an embryo or fetus (not born alive) constitute some form of criminal homicide? What is the Model Penal Code answer to this question?

3. *"Year and a day rule."* At common law, a defendant could not be prosecuted for murder unless the victim died within a year and a day of the act inflicting injury. 4 Blackstone, Commentaries on the Law of England *197 (1769). In other words, if *D* shoots *V* on January 1, 2010, and *V* dies on January 1, 2011, a homicide has occurred; if *V* dies on January 2, 2011 or later, a criminal homicide prosecution is barred—the loss of life is not causally attributed to *D*'s actions—although *D* may be charged with a non-homicide offense (e.g. assault with intent to kill).

In light of advances in the medical field for prolonging life indefinitely on life support machinery, many legislatures and courts have concluded that the year-and-a-day rule is "an outdated relic of the common law." Rogers v. Tennessee, 532 U.S. 451, 121 S.Ct. 1693, 149 L.Ed.2d 697 (2001). A relatively recent survey indicated that almost half of the states no longer follow the rule. Commonwealth v. Casanova, 429 Mass. 293, 708 N.E.2d 86 (1999).

The potential legal effect of abandoning the rule may be seen in Pennsylvania. In 1966, William J. Barnes shot and partially paralyzed a Philadelphia police officer during a failed burglary. Barnes served twenty years in prison for his crimes. In prison and after release, he reportedly reformed himself and was living a lawful life. Forty-one years after the crime, the officer died from a urinary tract infection. In September 2007, asserting that she can prove a chain of causation from the 1966 shooting to the 2007 death, prosecutor

Lynne Abraham charged the frail 72–year–old Barnes with murder. Ian Urbina, *41 Years After Crime, Prosecutor Says Assault Victim is Now Murder Victim*, New York Times, Sept. 19, 2007. In the interim, Barnes was incarcerated because state law barred pre-trial release of persons charged with murder. Julie Shaw & Christine Olley, *Judge: No Bail for Shooter in 41–Year Delayed Death of Cop*, Philadelphia Daily News, April 10, 2009. He was acquitted in 2010.

B. INTENTIONAL KILLINGS

1. DEGREES OF MURDER: THE DELIBERATION–PREMEDITATION FORMULA

STATE v. GUTHRIE

Supreme Court of Appeals of West Virginia, 1995.
194 W.Va. 657, 461 S.E.2d 163.

CLECKLEY, JUSTICE:

The defendant, Dale Edward Guthrie, appeals the * * * jury verdict * * * finding him guilty of first degree murder.[b] In May of 1994, the defendant was sentenced to serve a life sentence * * *. * * *

I. * * *

It is undisputed that on the evening of February 12, 1993, the defendant removed a knife from his pocket and stabbed his co-worker, Steven Todd Farley, in the neck and killed him. The two men worked together as dishwashers * * * and got along well together before this incident. On the night of the killing, the victim * * * was poking fun at the defendant who appeared to be in a bad mood. He told the defendant to "lighten up" and snapped him with a dishtowel several times. * * * The dishtowel flipped the defendant on the nose and he became enraged.

The defendant removed his gloves and started toward the victim. * * * The defendant then pulled a knife from his pocket and stabbed the victim in the neck. * * *

It is * * * undisputed that the defendant suffers from a host of psychiatric problems. He experiences up to two panic attacks daily and had received treatment for them * * * for more than a year preceding the killing. He suffers from chronic depression (dysthymic disorder), an obsession with his nose (body dysmorphic disorder), and borderline personality disorder. * * *

The defendant testified he suffered a panic attack immediately preceding the stabbing. He described the attack as "intense"; he felt a lot of pressure and his heart beat rapidly. * * *

---

b. Under West Virginia law: "Murder by poison, lying in wait, imprisonment, starving, or by *any willful, deliberate and premeditated killing*, or in the commission of, or attempt to commit [specified felonies] is murder of the first degree. All other murder is murder of the second degree." (Emphasis added.)

II * * *

* * * [T]he defendant asserts the trial court's instructions regarding the elements of first degree murder were improper because the terms wilful, deliberate, and premeditated were equated with a mere intent to kill.

The jury was instructed that in order to find the defendant guilty of murder it had to find five elements beyond a reasonable doubt: "The Court further instructs the jury that murder in the first degree is when one person kills another person unlawfully, willfully, maliciously, deliberately and premeditatedly[.]" In its effort to define these terms, the trial court gave three instructions [previously authorized by this Court]. State's Instruction No. 8, commonly referred to as the *Clifford* instruction, stated:

> "The Court instructs the jury that to constitute a willful, deliberate and premeditated killing, it is not necessary that the intention to kill should exist for any particular length of time prior to the actual killing; it is only necessary that such intention should have come into existence for the first time at the time of such killing, or at any time previously."

See State v. Clifford, 59 W.Va. 1, 52 S.E. 981 (1906). State's Instruction No. 10 stated: "The Court instructs the jury that in order to constitute a 'premeditated' murder an intent to kill need exist only for an instant." State's Instruction No. 12 stated: "The Court instructs the jury that what is meant by the language willful, deliberate and premeditated is that the killing be intentional." State's Instruction Nos. 10 and 12 are commonly referred to as *Schrader* instructions. *See State v. Schrader,* 172 W.Va. 1, 302 S.E.2d 70 (1982).

The linchpin of the problems that flow from these instructions is the failure adequately to inform the jury of the difference between first and second degree murder. Of particular concern is the lack of guidance to the jury as to what constitutes premeditation and the manner in which the instructions infuse premeditation with the intent to kill.* * *

In addition to *Clifford,* there are several cases that have made specific attempts to further define premeditation. In *State v. Dodds,* 54 W.Va. 289, 297–98, 46 S.E. 228, 231 (1903), we said:

> "The next ingredient of the crime is that it must be deliberate. To deliberate is to reflect, with a view to make a choice. If a person reflects, though but for a moment before he acts, it is unquestionably a sufficient *deliberation* within the meaning of the statute. The last requisite is that the killing must be *premeditated. To premeditate is to think of a matter before it is executed. The word, premeditated, would seem to imply something more than deliberate, and may mean that the party not only deliberated, but had formed in his mind the plan of destruction.*" (Emphasis added to last sentence).

* * *

The source of the problem in the present case stems from language in *State v. Schrader,* 172 W.Va. 1, 302 S.E.2d 70 (1982). * * * [W]e gave it a different definition than that approved in *State v. Hatfield,* 169 W.Va. 191, 286 S.E.2d 402 (1982). * * * In *Schrader,* we stated:

> "Hence, when the West Virginia Legislature adopted the Virginia murder statute in 1868, the meaning of 'premeditated' as used in the statute was essentially 'knowing' and 'intentional.' Since then, courts have consistently recognized that the mental process necessary to constitute 'willful, deliberate and premeditated' murder can be accomplished very quickly or even in the proverbial 'twinkling of an eye.' * * * *The achievement of a mental state contemplated in a statute such as ours can immediately precede the act of killing. Hence, what is really meant by the language 'willful, deliberate and premeditated' * * * is that the killing be intentional.*" (Emphasis added).

The language emphasized above supplied the legal authority and basis for State's Instruction Nos. 10 and 12.

While many jurisdictions do not favor the distinction between first and second degree murder, given the doctrine of separation of powers, we do not have the judicial prerogative to abolish the distinction between first and second degree murder and rewrite the law of homicide for West Virginia * * *. On the other hand, we believe within the parameters of our current homicide statutes the *Schrader* definition of premeditation and deliberation is confusing, if not meaningless. To allow the State to prove premeditation and deliberation by only showing that the intention came "into existence for the first time at the time of such killing" completely eliminates the distinction between the two degrees of murder. Hence, we feel compelled in this case to attempt to make the dichotomy meaningful by making some modifications to our homicide common law.

Premeditation and deliberation should be defined in a more careful, but still general way to give juries both guidance and reasonable discretion. * * *

* * * To the extent that the *Schrader* opinion is inconsistent with our holding today, it is overruled. * * *

Finally we feel obligated to discuss what instruction defining premeditation is now acceptable. What came about as a mere suggestion in *Hatfield,* we now approve as a proper instruction under today's decision. * * *

new instruction

> "The jury is instructed that murder in the first degree consists of an intentional, deliberate and premeditated killing which means that the killing is done after a period of time for prior consideration. The duration of that period cannot be arbitrarily fixed. The time in which to form a deliberate and premeditated design varies as the minds and temperaments of people differ, and according to the circumstances in which they may be placed. Any interval of time between the forming of the intent to kill and the execution of that intent, which is of

sufficient duration for the accused to be fully conscious of what he intended, is sufficient to support a conviction for first degree murder.''

* * *

III

Based on the foregoing, the judgment of the [trial court] is reversed, and this case is remanded for a new trial. * * *

NOTES AND QUESTIONS

1. Based on the facts of this case, and the legal instruction laid out at the end of Part II of the opinion, do you believe Guthrie is guilty of first- or second-degree murder?

2. The overruled *Schrader* opinion, quoted in *Guthrie*, itself quoted a famous Virginia case to the effect that ''no time is too short for a wicked man to frame in his mind a scheme for murder, and to contrive the means of accomplishing it.'' King v. Commonwealth, 4 Va. 78, 2 Va.Cas. 78 (1817). Do you agree with this assertion?

3. According to the court here, the *Schrader* definition of premeditation and deliberation was ''confusing, if not meaningless.'' In what way was this so? Do you find the law set out in *this* case clear and meaningful? Is there now a sensible line in West Virginia between the two degrees of murder? In this regard, consider Michigan's approach in People v. Morrin, 31 Mich.App. 301, 187 N.W.2d 434 (1971):

Morin

> [T]he division of murder into degrees was prompted by a feeling that not all murders reflected the same quantum of culpability on the part of the wrongdoer. * * *

> A number of jurisdictions have all but obliterated this distinction by observing the rule that premeditation and deliberation need precede the homicidal act only momentarily. * * * The rule prevalent in those jurisdictions grants the jury an unstructured discretion to find [first-degree murder].

> Michigan adheres to a more meaningful standard. * * * To premeditate is to think about beforehand; to deliberate is to measure and evaluate the major facets of a choice or problem. As a number of courts have pointed out, premeditation and deliberation characterize a thought process undisturbed by hot blood. While the minimum time necessary to exercise this process is incapable of exact determination, the interval between initial thought and ultimate actions should be long enough to afford a reasonable man time to subject the nature of his response to a ''second look.''

Does the language in *Morrin* add anything to your understanding of the deliberation-premeditation formula? Based on *this* definition, would your answer to Note 1 change?

Using *Morrin* to understand the terms, can a person premeditate without deliberating? Can one deliberate without premeditating?

4. What does "wilful" mean in the "wilful, deliberate, premeditated" formula?

5. *A procedural excursus: the doctrine of "lesser included offenses."* Generally speaking, a defendant has the right to a jury instruction upon request (and, in some states, even in the absence of request, or upon request by the prosecutor) that he may be found guilty of an offense "included" within the offense charged, as long as the factfinder could reasonably conclude from the evidence introduced at trial that the defendant is guilty of the lesser, but not the greater, offense.

For example, look at the California or Michigan penal codes (pp. 238 and 242). A defendant in those states, if charged with first-degree "wilful, premeditated, deliberate" murder, is entitled to an instruction regarding, and may be convicted of, *second*-degree murder if evidence is introduced at trial from which the jury can rationally conclude that the defendant intended to kill the victim (thus, acted with the requisite malice to be convicted of murder), but that he committed the crime in an *un*premeditated or *non*-deliberate manner (thus, lowering the offense to "all other kinds of murder").

This doctrine is not limited to criminal homicide prosecutions. A person charged with "assault with intent to commit rape," as another example, is entitled to an instruction on simple assault, as long as a jury might reasonably find that he committed an assault *without* intending to rape.

Although a defendant may be convicted of a *lesser* offense than that charged pursuant to the lesser-included-offense doctrine, rules relating to fair notice provide that she may not be convicted of a *more serious* degree or offense than that charged.

6. As *Morrin* (Note 3) suggests (and other courts agree), the ostensible purpose of the wilful-deliberation-premeditation formula is to distinguish between more and less culpable intentional killings. In reading the next two cases, reflect on whether the formula properly separates the more culpable (or, for that matter, dangerous) killers from the lesser ones.

MIDGETT v. STATE

Supreme Court of Arkansas, 1987.
292 Ark. 278, 729 S.W.2d 410.

NEWBERN, JUSTICE.

This child abuse case resulted in the appellant's conviction of first degree murder. The sole issue on appeal is whether the state's evidence was sufficient to sustain the conviction. We hold there was no evidence of the " * * * premeditated and deliberated purpose of causing the death of another person * * *" required for conviction of first degree murder * * *. However, we find the evidence was sufficient to sustain a conviction of second degree murder, described in Ark.Stat.Ann. § 41–1503(1)(c) (Repl.1977), as the appellant was shown to have caused his son's death by delivering a blow to his abdomen or chest " * * * with the purpose of causing serious physical injury * * *." The conviction is thus modified from one of first degree murder to one of second degree murder and affirmed.

The facts of this case are as heart-rending as any we are likely to see. The appellant is six feet two inches tall and weighs 300 pounds. His son, Ronnie Midgett, Jr., was eight years old and weighed between thirty-eight and forty-five pounds. The evidence showed that Ronnie Jr. had been abused by brutal beatings over a substantial period of time. Typically, as in other child abuse cases, the bruises had been noticed by school personnel, and a school counselor * * * had gone to the Midgett home to inquire. Ronnie Jr. would not say how he had obtained the bruises or why he was so lethargic at school except to blame it all, vaguely, on a rough playing little brother. He did not even complain to his siblings about the treatment he was receiving from the appellant. His mother, the wife of the appellant, was not living in the home. The other children apparently were not being physically abused by the appellant.

Ronnie Jr.'s sister, Sherry, aged ten, testified that on the Saturday preceding the Wednesday of Ronnie Jr.'s death their father, the appellant, was drinking whiskey (two to three quarts that day) and beating on Ronnie Jr. She testified that the appellant would "bundle up his fist" and hit Ronnie Jr. in the stomach and in the back. On direct examination she said that she had not previously seen the appellant beat Ronnie Jr., but she had seen the appellant choke him for no particular reason on Sunday nights after she and Ronnie Jr. returned from church. * * * She said the bruises on Ronnie Jr.'s body noticed over the preceding six months had been caused by the appellant. She said the beating administered on the Saturday in question consisted of four blows, two to the stomach and two to the back.

On the Wednesday Ronnie Jr. died, the appellant appeared at a hospital carrying the body. He told hospital personnel something was wrong with the child. An autopsy was performed, and it showed Ronnie Jr. was a very poorly nourished and under-developed eight-year-old. There were recently caused bruises on the lips, center of the chest plate, and forehead as well as on the back part of the lateral chest wall, the soft tissue near the spine, and the buttocks. There was discoloration of the abdominal wall and prominent bruising on the palms of the hands. Older bruises were found on the right temple, under the chin, and on the left mandible. Recent as well as older, healed, rib fractures were found.

The conclusion of the medical examiner who performed the autopsy was that Ronnie Jr. died as the result of intra-abdominal hemorrhage caused by a blunt force trauma consistent with having been delivered by a human fist. The appellant argues that in spite of all this evidence of child abuse, there is no evidence that he killed Ronnie Jr. having premeditated and deliberated causing his death. We must agree. * * *

* * * The evidence in this case supports only the conclusion that the appellant intended not to kill his son but to further abuse him or that his

intent, if it was to kill the child, was developed in a drunken, heated, rage while disciplining the child. Neither of those supports a finding of premeditation or deliberation.

Perhaps because they wish to punish more severely child abusers who kill their children, other states' legislatures have created laws permitting them to go beyond second degree murder. For example, Illinois has made aggravated battery one of the felonies qualifying for "felony murder," and a child abuser can be convicted of murder if the child dies as a result of aggravated battery. * * * California has also adopted a murder by torture statute making the offense murder in the first degree without regard to the intent to kill. * * *

All of this goes to show that there remains a difference between first and second degree murder, not only under our statute, but generally. Unless our law is changed to permit conviction of first degree murder for something like child abuse or torture resulting in death, our duty is to give those accused of first degree murder the benefit of the requirement that they be shown by substantial evidence to have premeditated and deliberated the killing, no matter how heinous the facts may otherwise be. * * *

* * * The dissenting opinion's conclusion that the appellant starved Ronnie Jr., must be based solely on the child's underdeveloped condition which could, presumably, have been caused by any number of physical malfunctions. There is no evidence the appellant starved the child. The dissenting opinion says it is for the jury to determine the degree of murder of which the appellant is guilty. That is true so long as there is substantial evidence to support the jury's choice. The point of this opinion is to note that there was no evidence of premeditation or deliberation which are required elements of the crime of first degree murder. * * *

HICKMAN, JUSTICE, dissenting.

Simply put, if a parent deliberately starves and beats a child to death, he cannot be convicted of the child's murder. In reaching this decision, the majority * * * substitutes its judgment for that of the jury. The majority has decided it cannot come to grips with the question of the battered child who dies as a result of deliberate, methodical, intentional and severe abuse. A death caused by such acts is murder by any legal standard, and that fact cannot be changed—not even by the majority. The degree of murder committed is for the jury to decide—not us. * * *

In this case the majority, with clairvoyance, decides that this parent did not intend to kill his child, but rather to keep him alive for further abuse. This is not a child neglect case. The state proved Midgett starved the boy, choked him, and struck him several times in the stomach and back. The jury could easily conclude that such repeated treatment was intended to kill the child. * * *

I cannot fathom how this father could have done what he did; but it is not my place to sit in judgment of his mental state, nor allow my human feelings to color my judgment of his accountability to the law. The law has an objective standard of accountability for all who take human life. If one does certain acts and the result is murder, one must pay. The jury found Midgett guilty and, according to the law, there is substantial evidence to support that verdict. That should end the matter for us. He is guilty of first degree murder in the eyes of the law. His moral crime as a father is another matter, and it is not for us to speculate why he did it.

I would affirm the judgment.

NOTES AND QUESTIONS

1. *Aftermath.* Shortly after *Midgett* was decided, the Arkansas legislature responded by amending its criminal code to permit a verdict of first-degree capital murder when, "[u]nder circumstances manifesting extreme indifference to the value of human life," a person "knowingly causes the death of a person fourteen (14) years of age or younger." Ark. Code Ann. 5–10–101(a)(9).

STATE v. FORREST

Supreme Court of North Carolina, 1987.
321 N.C. 186, 362 S.E.2d 252.

MEYER, JUSTICE.

Defendant was convicted of the first-degree murder of his father, Clyde Forrest. * * * [T]he case was tried as a noncapital case, and defendant was sentenced accordingly to life imprisonment. * * *

The facts of this case are essentially uncontested, and the evidence presented at trial tended to show the following series of events. On 22 December 1985, defendant John Forrest admitted his critically ill father, Clyde Forrest, Sr., to Moore Memorial Hospital. Defendant's father, who had previously been hospitalized, was suffering from numerous serious ailments, including severe heart disease, hypertension, a thoracic aneurysm, numerous pulmonary emboli, and a peptic ulcer. By the morning of 23 December 1985, his medical condition was determined to be untreatable and terminal. Accordingly, he was classified as "No Code," meaning that no extraordinary measures would be used to save his life, and he was moved to a more comfortable room.

On 24 December 1985, defendant went to the hospital to visit his ailing father. No other family members were present in his father's room when he arrived. While one of the nurse's assistants was tending to his father, defendant told her, "There is no need in doing that. He's dying." She responded, "Well, I think he's better." The nurse's assistant noticed that defendant was sniffling as though crying and that he kept his hand in his pocket during their conversation. She subsequently went to get the nurse.

When the nurse's assistant returned with the nurse, defendant once again stated his belief that his father was dying. The nurse tried to comfort defendant, telling him, "I don't think your father is as sick as you think he is." Defendant, very upset, responded, "Go to hell. I've been taking care of him for years. I'll take care of him." Defendant was then left alone in the room with his father.

Alone at his father's bedside, defendant began to cry and to tell his father how much he loved him. His father began to cough, emitting a gurgling and rattling noise. Extremely upset, defendant pulled a small pistol from his pants pocket, put it to his father's temple, and fired. He subsequently fired three more times and walked out into the hospital corridor, dropping the gun to the floor just outside his father's room.

Following the shooting, defendant, who was crying and upset, neither ran nor threatened anyone. Moreover, he never denied shooting his father and talked openly with law enforcement officials. Specifically, defendant made the following oral statements: "You can't do anything to him now. He's out of his suffering." "I killed my daddy." "He won't have to suffer anymore." "I know they can burn me for it, but my dad will not have to suffer anymore." "I know the doctors couldn't do it, but I could." "I promised my dad I wouldn't let him suffer." * * *

* * * Though defendant's father had been near death as a result of his medical condition, the exact cause of the deceased's death was determined to be the four point-blank bullet wounds to his head. Defendant's pistol was a single-action .22–calibre five-shot revolver. The weapon, which had to be cocked each time it was fired, contained four empty shells and one live round.

At the close of the evidence, defendant's case was submitted to the jury for one of four possible verdicts: first-degree murder, second-degree murder, voluntary manslaughter, or not guilty. After a lengthy deliberation, the jury found defendant guilty of first-degree murder. * * *

In his * * * assignment of error, defendant asserts that the trial court committed reversible error in denying his motion for directed verdict as to the first-degree murder charge. Specifically, defendant argues that the trial court's submission of the first-degree murder charge was improper because there was insufficient evidence of premeditation and deliberation presented at trial. We do not agree * * *.

We recently addressed this very issue in the case of *State v. Jackson*, 317 N.C. 1, 343 S.E.2d 814 (1986). Our analysis of the relevant law in that case is instructive in the case at bar:

> Before the issue of a defendant's guilt may be submitted to the jury, the trial court must be satisfied that substantial evidence has been introduced tending to prove each essential element of the offense charged * * *.

> First-degree murder is the intentional and unlawful killing of a human being with malice and with premeditation and deliberation. * * *

Premeditation and deliberation relate to mental processes and ordinarily are not readily susceptible to proof by direct evidence. Instead, they usually must be proved by circumstantial evidence. Among other circumstances to be considered in determining whether a killing was with premeditation and deliberation are: (1) want of provocation on the part of the deceased; (2) the conduct and statements of the defendant before and after the killing; (3) threats and declarations of the defendant before and during the course of the occurrence giving rise to the death of the deceased; (4) ill-will or previous difficulty between the parties; (5) the dealing of lethal blows after the deceased has been felled and rendered helpless; and (6) evidence that the killing was done in a brutal manner. We have also held that the nature and number of the victim's wounds is a circumstance from which premeditation and deliberation can be inferred.

As in *Jackson,* we hold in the present case that there was substantial evidence that the killing was premeditated and deliberate * * *. Here, many of the circumstances that we have held to establish a factual basis for a finding of premeditation and deliberation are present. It is clear, for example, that the seriously ill deceased did nothing to provoke defendant's action. Moreover, the deceased was lying helpless in a hospital bed when defendant shot him four separate times. In addition, defendant's revolver was a five-shot single-action gun which had to be cocked each time before it could be fired. Interestingly, although defendant testified that he always carried the gun in his job as a truck driver, he was not working on the day in question but carried the gun to the hospital nonetheless.

Most persuasive of all on the issue of premeditation and deliberation, however, are defendant's own statements following the incident. Among other things, defendant stated that he had thought about putting his father out of his misery because he knew he was suffering. He stated further that he had promised his father that he would not let him suffer and that, though he did not think he could do it, he just could not stand to see his father suffer any more. These statements, together with the other circumstances mentioned above, make it clear that the trial court did not err in submitting to the jury the issue of first-degree murder based upon premeditation and deliberation. * * *

NOTES AND QUESTIONS

1. According to *Forrest,* proof of brutality, including the existence of many wounds on the victim, is circumstantial evidence of deliberation and premeditation. In People v. Anderson, 70 Cal.2d 15, 73 Cal.Rptr. 550, 447 P.2d 942 (1968), the California Supreme Court reached the opposite conclusion, suggesting that the inference of deliberation and premeditation is stronger when the actor inflicts a single, lethal wound. What would be the basis for the latter argument? Which approach makes more sense?

2. Consider this limerick written by a Santa Clara University law student after she had finished reading the *Midgett* and *Forrest* cases:

> The rulings, it's true, seem illogical.
> Midgett's actions, in deed, diabolical.
> But he didn't scheme or plot,
> While Forrest planned his shot.
> We are bound by the statutes we chronicle.

Or, consider this effort from Adam Garvin (University of Arizona):

> The *Midgett* and *Forrest* cases
> Bring many a scowl to students' faces.
> One beat his little boy for fun.
> The other lovingly employed a gun.
> Law metes out justice on a flawed basis.

Do you agree with the limerick writers? In *your* view, who was more culpable, Midgett or Forrest? Is your answer consistent with the results in these cases? If not, is it because one (or both) of the courts misapplied the law (i.e., did not properly apply the statutes they "chronicled")? Or, is the deliberation-premeditation distinction itself flawed? Do you agree with Professor David Crump that the standard is a "dysfunctional method of separating the most serious homicides from lesser ones"? David Crump, *"Murder, Pennsylvania Style": Comparing Traditional American Homicide Law to the Statutes of Model Penal Code Jurisdictions*, 109 W. Va. L. Rev. 257, 349 (2007). Consider:

> The *Forrest* case appears to indicate that the drafters of the Model Penal Code were right when they said that the premise underlying the premeditation formula, "that the person who plans ahead is worse than the person who kills on sudden impulse, * * * does not * * * survive analysis." * * *
>
> * * * [S]ome of the worst murders are not planned at all. James Stephen recognized that sudden, unpremeditated murder can be among the most heinous [3 *History of the Criminal Law of England* 94 (1883)]:
>
>> * * * [Imagine a man], passing along the road, sees a boy sitting on a bridge over a deep river and, out of mere wanton barbarity, pushes him into it and so drowns him. A man makes advances to a girl who repels him. He deliberately but instantly cuts her throat. * * * In none of these cases is there premeditation unless the word is used in a sense * * * unnatural * * *, but each represents even more diabolical cruelty and ferocity than that which is involved in murders premeditated in the natural sense of the word.
>
> The case of *Midgett v. State* confirms the accuracy of Stephen's observations.

Matthew A. Pauley, *Murder by Premeditation*, 36 Am. Crim. L. Rev. 145, 164–165 (1999).

In your view, should the deliberation-premeditation distinction be abandoned? If so, how would you draw the line between more and less culpable intentional killings, or would you treat them all alike?

3. Critics of the premeditation-deliberation formula (Note 2) usually reason that the distinction does not reliably distinguish between the more and

less culpable killers—or even between the more and less dangerous ones. But, might there be another justification for the traditional statutory line separating first- and second-degree murder, namely, general deterrence? So reasons Professor Michael Mannheimer:

> Whether or not intentional murderers who also premeditate and deliberate are the most dangerous and culpable killers, they are the most deterrable. * * * Where a murder is premeditated and deliberate, it is much more likely that the murderer has not only thought out the crime itself but has developed a plausible means of avoiding, or at least delaying, detection. The premeditation-deliberation formula thus seeks to identify those killers most likely to escape or significantly delay detection, apprehension, and punishment, requiring that punishment severity be maximized to offset the diminished certainty and swiftness of punishment for such culprits.

Michael J. Zydney Mannheimer, *Not the Crime but the Cover–Up: A Deterrence–Based Rationale for the Premeditation–Deliberation Formula*, 86 Indiana L.J. 879, 881 (2011).

2. MANSLAUGHTER: "HEAT OF PASSION" KILLINGS

a. Common Law Principles

GIROUARD v. STATE

Court of Appeals of Maryland, 1991.
321 Md. 532, 583 A.2d 718.

COLE, JUDGE.

In this case we are asked to reconsider whether the types of provocation sufficient to mitigate the crime of murder to manslaughter should be limited to the categories we have heretofore recognized, or whether the sufficiency of the provocation should be decided by the factfinder on a case-by-case basis. Specifically, we must determine whether words alone are provocation adequate to justify a conviction of manslaughter rather than one of second degree murder.

The Petitioner, Steven S. Girouard, and the deceased, Joyce M. Girouard, had been married for about two months on October 28, 1987, the night of Joyce's death. Both parties, who met while working in the same building, were in the army. They married after having known each other for approximately three months. The evidence at trial indicated that the marriage was often tense and strained, and there was some evidence that after marrying Steven, Joyce had resumed a relationship with her old boyfriend, Wayne.

On the night of Joyce's death, Steven overheard her talking on the telephone to her friend, whereupon she told the friend that she had asked her first sergeant for a hardship discharge because her husband did not love her anymore. Steven went into the living room where Joyce was on the phone and asked her what she meant by her comments; she responded, "nothing." Angered by her lack of response, Steven kicked away the plate of food Joyce had in front of her. He then went to lie down in the bedroom.

Joyce's taunting

Joyce followed him into the bedroom, stepped up onto the bed and onto Steven's back, pulled his hair and said, "What are you going to do, hit me?" She continued to taunt him by saying, "I never did want to marry you and you are a lousy fuck and you remind me of my dad."[1] The barrage of insults continued with her telling Steven that she wanted a divorce, that the marriage had been a mistake and that she had never wanted to marry him. She also told him she had seen his commanding officer and filed charges against him for abuse. She then asked Steven, "What are you going to do?" Receiving no response, she continued her verbal attack. She added that she had filed charges against him in the Judge Advocate General's Office (JAG) and that he would probably be court martialed.[2]

When she was through, Steven asked her if she had really done all those things, and she responded in the affirmative. He left the bedroom with his pillow in his arms and proceeded to the kitchen where he procured a long handled kitchen knife. He returned to Joyce in the bedroom with the knife behind the pillow. He testified that he was enraged and that he kept waiting for Joyce to say she was kidding, but Joyce continued talking. She said she had learned a lot from the marriage and that it had been a mistake. She also told him she would remain in their apartment after he moved out. When he questioned how she would afford it, she told him she would claim her brain-damaged sister as a dependent and have the sister move in. Joyce reiterated that the marriage was a big mistake, that she did not love him and that the divorce would be better for her.

After pausing for a moment, Joyce asked what Steven was going to do. What he did was lunge at her with the kitchen knife he had hidden behind the pillow and stab her 19 times. Realizing what he had done, he dropped the knife and went to the bathroom to shower off Joyce's blood. Feeling like he wanted to die, Steven went back to the kitchen and found two steak knives with which he slit his own wrists. He lay down on the bed waiting to die, but when he realized that he would not die from his self-inflicted wounds, he got up and called the police, telling the dispatcher that he had just murdered his wife.

When the police arrived they found Steven wandering around outside his apartment building. Steven was despondent and tearful and seemed detached, according to police officers who had been at the scene. He was unconcerned about his own wounds, talking only about how much he

---

1. There was some testimony presented at trial to the effect that Joyce had never gotten along with her father, at least in part because he had impregnated her when she was fourteen, the result of which was an abortion. Joyce's aunt, however, denied that Joyce's father was the father of Joyce's child.

2. Joyce lied about filing the charges against her husband.

loved his wife and how he could not believe what he had done. Joyce Girouard was pronounced dead at the scene.

At trial, defense witness, psychologist, Dr. William Stejskal, testified that Steven was out of touch with his own capacity to experience anger or express hostility. He stated that the events of October 28, 1987, were entirely consistent with Steven's personality, that Steven had "basically reach[ed] the limit of his ability to swallow his anger, to rationalize his wife's behavior, to tolerate, or actually to remain in a passive mode with that. He essentially went over the limit of his ability to bottle up those strong emotions. What ensued was a very extreme explosion of rage that was intermingled with a great deal of panic." Another defense witness, psychiatrist, Thomas Goldman, testified that Joyce had a "compulsive need to provoke jealousy so that she's always asking for love and at the same time destroying and undermining any chance that she really might have to establish any kind of mature love with anybody."

Steven Girouard was convicted, at a court trial * * *, of second degree murder and was sentenced to 22 years incarceration, 10 of which were suspended. * * *

Petitioner relies primarily on out of state cases to provide support for his argument that the provocation to mitigate murder to manslaughter should not be limited only to the traditional circumstances of: extreme assault or battery upon the defendant; mutual combat; defendant's illegal arrest; injury or serious abuse of a close relative of the defendant's; or the sudden discovery of a spouse's adultery. Petitioner argues that manslaughter is a catchall for homicides which are criminal but that lack the malice essential for a conviction of murder. Steven argues that the trial judge did find provocation (although he held it inadequate to mitigate murder) and that the categories of provocation adequate to mitigate should be broadened to include factual situations such as this one.

The State counters by stating that although there is no finite list of legally adequate provocations, the common law has developed to a point at which it may be said there are some concededly provocative acts that society is not prepared to recognize as reasonable. Words spoken by the victim, no matter how abusive or taunting, fall into a category society should not accept as adequate provocation. According to the State, if abusive words alone could mitigate murder to manslaughter, nearly every domestic argument ending in the death of one party could be mitigated to manslaughter. This, the State avers, is not an acceptable outcome. Thus, the State argues that the courts below were correct in holding that the taunting words by Joyce Girouard were not provocation adequate to reduce Steven's second degree murder charge to voluntary manslaughter.

Initially, we note that the difference between murder and manslaughter is the presence or absence of malice. Voluntary manslaughter has been defined as "an *intentional* homicide, done in a sudden heat of passion, caused by adequate provocation, before there has been a reasonable opportunity for the passion to cool" (Emphasis in original).

There are certain facts that may mitigate what would normally be murder to manslaughter. For example, we have recognized as falling into that group: (1) discovering one's spouse in the act of sexual intercourse with another; (2) mutual combat; (3) assault and battery. There is also authority recognizing injury to one of the defendant's relatives or to a third party, and death resulting from resistance of an illegal arrest as adequate provocation for mitigation to manslaughter. Those acts mitigate homicide to manslaughter because they create passion in the defendant and are not considered the product of free will.

In order to determine whether murder should be mitigated to manslaughter we look to the circumstances surrounding the homicide and try to discover if it was provoked by the victim. Over the facts of the case we lay the template of the so-called "Rule of Provocation." The courts of this State have repeatedly set forth the requirements of the Rule of Provocation:

1. There must have been adequate provocation;

2. The killing must have been in the heat of passion;

3. It must have been a sudden heat of passion—that is, the killing must have followed the provocation before there had been a reasonable opportunity for the passion to cool;

4. There must have been a causal connection between the provocation, the passion, and the fatal act.

We shall assume without deciding that the second, third, and fourth of the criteria listed above were met in this case. We focus our attention on an examination of the ultimate issue in this case, that is, whether the provocation of Steven by Joyce was enough in the eyes of the law so that the murder charge against Steven should have been mitigated to voluntary manslaughter. For provocation to be "adequate," it must be " 'calculated to inflame the passion of a reasonable man and tend to cause him to act for the moment from passion rather than reason.' " The issue we must resolve, then, is whether the taunting words uttered by Joyce were enough to inflame the passion of a *reasonable* man so that that man would be sufficiently infuriated so as to strike out in hot-blooded blind passion to kill her. Although we agree with the trial judge that there was needless provocation by Joyce, we also agree with him that the provocation was not adequate to mitigate second degree murder to voluntary manslaughter.

Although there are few Maryland cases discussing the issue at bar, those that do hold that words alone are not adequate provocation. * * *

* * * [W]ords can constitute adequate provocation if they are accompanied by conduct indicating a present intention and ability to cause the defendant bodily harm. Clearly, no such conduct was exhibited by Joyce in this case. While Joyce did step on Steven's back and pull his hair, he could not reasonably have feared bodily harm at her hands. This, to us, is certain based on Steven's testimony at trial that Joyce was about 5'1" tall and weighed 115 pounds, while he was 6'2" tall, weighing over 200

pounds. Joyce simply did not have the size or strength to cause Steven to fear for his bodily safety. Thus, since there was no ability on the part of Joyce to cause Steven harm, the words she hurled at him could not * * * constitute legally sufficient provocation.

Other jurisdictions overwhelmingly agree with our cases and hold that words alone are not adequate provocation. * * *

Thus, with no reservation, we hold that the provocation in this case was not enough to cause a reasonable man to stab his provoker 19 times. * * * The standard is one of reasonableness; it does not and should not focus on the peculiar frailties of mind of the Petitioner. That standard of reasonableness has not been met here. We cannot in good conscience countenance holding that a verbal domestic argument ending in the death of one spouse can result in a conviction of manslaughter. We agree with the trial judge that social necessity dictates our holding. Domestic arguments easily escalate into furious fights. We perceive no reason for a holding in favor of those who find the easiest way to end a domestic dispute is by killing the offending spouse. * * *

[handwritten margin note: Don't take into account D's frailties]

[handwritten margin note: policy]

NOTES AND COMMENTS

1. According to *Girouard,* what constitutes "adequate provocation"? Justice Christiancy of the Michigan Supreme Court explained the concept this way in the nineteenth century:

> The principle involved in the question [of what constitutes "adequate provocation"], and which I think clearly deducible from the majority of well considered cases, would seem to suggest as the true general rule, that reason should, at the time of the act, be disturbed or obscured by passion to an extent which *might render* ordinary men, of fair average disposition, *liable* to act rashly or without due deliberation or reflection, and from passion, rather than judgment. Maher v. People, 10 Mich. 212 (1862).

[handwritten margin note: Maher — adequate provocation defined in terms of ordinary person]

Girouard was a bench trial. Assume, however, that it had been a jury trial, that you had served on the jury, and that the judge had instructed you on "adequate provocation" in Justice Christiancy's language. Based on what you know from the case, would you have voted to convict the defendant of murder or of voluntary manslaughter?

2. *Words as provocation.* At common law, "words alone" do not constitute adequate provocation. Is the reason that, as an empirical matter, ordinary people do not act violently in response to verbal assaults? If that isn't the reason, what *is* the explanation for the rule?

Should the law distinguish between insulting words and informational ones (e.g., "Your husband is having an affair with Zelda")? Some courts consider informational words by their nature more provocative. See People v. Pouncey, 437 Mich. 382, 471 N.W.2d 346 (1991). Do you agree?

[handwritten margin note: Some courts find provocation in informational words]

3. Who decides what constitutes adequate provocation, courts or juries? The answer to this question has changed over time. Brown v. United States, 584 A.2d 537 (D.C.App.1990):

Under the common law, the doctrine of provocation developed along the lines of fixed categories of conduct by the victim, paradigms of misbehavior, which the law recognized as sufficiently provocative to mitigate what would otherwise be malicious conduct by the defendant. * * * Traditionally, a defendant seeking to negate the malice element * * * would have to present some evidence of provocative behavior by the victim. However, such evidence would not automatically entitle the defendant to an instruction on [voluntary manslaughter] * * *. First, the court would have to determine that the victim's conduct constituted legally adequate provocation, i.e., that it fit within one of the tried and true categories of provocative conduct like adultery or assault. Thus, in order to have the jury consider such evidence, the defendant either would have to present it in a form recognized as legally adequate by the court, or ask the court to recognize a new category of provocative conduct. * * *

Over the years this traditional view of provocation as a set of rigid categories of recognized conduct has been abandoned by a growing number of state legislatures, courts, and commentators, with the result that the emerging "modern" view of provocation * * * has now swung around to the view [that the issue should largely be left to the jury].

The rationale offered for the modern view is strikingly similar to that offered by Judge Christiancy, who, writing for the *Maher* court [10 Mich. 212 (1862)], said: "[t]he law can not with justice assume by the light of past decisions to catalogue all the various facts and combinations of facts which shall be held to constitute reasonable or adequate provocation." The Pennsylvania Supreme Court [Commonwealth v. Paese, 220 Pa. 371, 373, 69 A. 891, 892 (1908)] came to the same conclusion * * *: "What is sufficient provocation * * * has not been exactly defined, and is probably incapable of exact definition, for it must vary with the myriad shifting circumstances of men's temper and quarrels. It is a concession to the infirmity of human nature, not an excuse for undue or abnormal irascibility, and, therefore to be considered in view of all circumstances."

Is the shift to juries a good idea? Consider an assault case from Norway, in which a man beat his girlfriend because she constantly berated him. The case was heard by a three-judge panel, composed of two lay judges and a professional judge. The lay jurors voted to acquit, on the ground that the victim "did not get more than she had to expect based on her behavior." According to these jurors, the "beatings must be seen in light of [the woman's] more or less making a lifestyle out of provoking and irritating the accused so that he lost control." The professional judge dissented. *Acquittal in Beating Stirs Anger*, Sacramento Bee, Mar. 4, 1995.

Does the difference in response between the jurors and the professional judge suggest that the issue of adequate provocation in homicide cases should be kept from jurors? On the other hand, if the provocation defense is "a concession to the infirmity of human nature," shouldn't jurors—the community's representatives—be the ones to decide when the concession is proper?

4. *The role of the legislature.* The last Note asked you to consider whether a trial judge or a jury is better equipped to decide what constitutes adequate provocation. Sometimes, however, a legislature steps in. For exam-

ple, although *Girouard* accurately stated that the common law (and, at that time, Maryland law) treated discovery of one's spouse in the act of sexual intercourse with another person as "adequate provocation," the Maryland legislature has since amended its definition of manslaughter to provide that such discovery no longer constitutes "legally adequate provocation for the purpose of mitigating a killing from the crime of murder to voluntary manslaughter even though the killing was provoked by that discovery." Md. Code § 2–207(b) (2012).

Should legislatures enact such hard-and-fast provisions? As a separate matter, do you agree that visual discovery of adultery should *never* mitigate an intentional homicide to manslaughter? Why or why not?

5. *"Cooling off time."* The provocation defense is unavailable to a defendant who kills the victim after he has a "reasonable opportunity for the passion to cool," i.e., after a reasonable person in the defendant's situation would have calmed down. Originally, this element of the defense was determined by the judge, but it, too, is now ordinarily a question of fact for the jury.

Traditionally, the cooling-off requirement has meant that a defendant could not introduce evidence of provocative conduct that occurred well before the homicidal act in support of a manslaughter claim. Is that sensible? Don't emotions build over time? What if a man is forcibly sodomized and becomes outraged by taunts days or weeks later? State v. Gounagias, 88 Wash. 304, 153 P. 9 (1915) (not permitting the defense). What if a woman kills her former boyfriend and wishes to claim that her outrage and passion were the result of the decedent's abusive behavior over an extended period of time? Commonwealth v. Stonehouse, 521 Pa. 41, 555 A.2d 772 (1989) (permitting evidence of prior abuse).

6. Aaron is lawfully walking along the sidewalk with his daughter Sarah when a car recklessly driven by Ben runs over the curb, striking and killing Sarah. Ben's car hits a tree, immobilizing him. Aaron, emotionally over-wrought, pulls out a knife he is carrying and moves toward the car, intending to kill Ben. Ruth, an innocent bystander, intentionally blocks Aaron's homicidal path to the car. Aaron intentionally kills Ruth. See Regina v. Scriva (No. 2), [1951] Vict.L.R. 298.

Assume Aaron is prosecuted for Ruth's death. Aaron wants to claim provocation, but the prosecutor asserts that the jury should not be permitted to consider the claim. Should a jury instruction on manslaughter be given? If you were the prosecutor, how would you defend your no-instruction position? If you represented Aaron, how would you respond?

What would happen if Aaron were prosecuted in Pennsylvania? Consider P.C.S. § 2503(a), set out at p. 246. What do you think explains Pennsylvania law?

7. *Trying to make sense of the provocation doctrine.* In light of everything you have read so far, why *do* some intentional killings constitute voluntary manslaughter rather than murder? Put differently, what *is* the rationale of the provocation "defense"? Consider the following excerpts. The first excerpt explains the important distinction between "justification" and

"excuse" defenses, and describes the confusion in the law regarding whether to characterize the provocation defense as a partial justification defense ("partial" because the defendant is not acquitted, but is convicted of a lesser crime) or as a partial excuse. The second excerpt provides one potential solution to the "justification versus excuse" puzzle.

JOSHUA DRESSLER—RETHINKING HEAT OF PASSION: A DEFENSE IN SEARCH OF A RATIONALE

73 Journal of Criminal Law and Criminology 421 (1982), 436–43

Ordinarily, * * * a person is punishable for a crime if it is shown that the actor voluntarily caused the social harm with the * * * mental state, or mens rea, deemed serious enough to make the harm punishable. If the government proves beyond a reasonable doubt, for example, that the actor intentionally killed a human being by a voluntary act, the government has proven murder. * * *

Such proof only fulfills the prima facie case of the crime of murder. The defendant may raise a * * * defense. It is here that the concepts of "justification" and "excuse" materialize. * * * The theories underlying the two defenses differ substantially * * *. With a justification, society indicates its approval of the actor's conduct * * *. With homicide, for example, the existence of a justification [such as self-defense] implies that under the circumstances * * * society * * * does not believe that the death of the human being was undesirable, or that it at least represents a lesser harm than if the defendant had not acted as he did. * * *

A defendant asserting an excuse admits to wrongdoing, but asserts that he should not be punished because he is not morally blameworthy for the harm. Thus, [whereas justifications focus on the act,] excuses focus on the actor * * *. * * * The insane killer, for example, avoids punishment, not because there was no harm in the killing, but because his mental disease renders his conduct in some fashion morally blameless. * * *

A careful analysis of the language and of the results of common law heat of passion cases demonstrates that there is uncertainty whether the [provocation] defense is a sub-species of justification or of excuse. The uncertainty is well expressed by Austin.

> Is [the provoker] partly responsible because he roused a violent impulse or passion in me so that it wasn't truly or merely me "acting of my own accord" [excuse]? Or is it rather that he having done me such injury, I was entitled to retaliate [justification]?[157] * * *

Unfortunately, courts have often failed to coherently state which doctrinal path is involved; or worse, they have rationalized the doctrine under both theories. * * *

---

157. J.L. Austin, [A Plea for Excuses, "The Presidential Address to the Aristotelian Society, 1956," "Proceedings of the Aristotelian Society, 1956–1957," Vol. LVIV, *reprinted in* Ordinary Language 42 (V. Chappel ed. 1965)], at 43.

A reasonable interpretation of some common law precedent can support the thesis that heat of passion is a partial justification. All of the [traditional] common law forms of "adequate provocation" have one thing in common; they all involve unlawful conduct by the provoker. Lawful conduct, no matter how provocative, is never adequate provocation. It is possible, of course, to defend this rule with excusing language,[166] but it is far easier to explain it as justification based, by contending that it is the unlawfulness of the provocation which makes the response (killing) less socially undesirable. As Aristotle said, "it is apparent injustice that occasions rage." The typical victim in a heat of passion case is someone who has "asked for it." The attacker is, in a way, only "restor[ing] the balance of justice." * * *

Specifically, the [common law] "sight of adultery" cases add support to the justification thesis. * * * [A] married person who kills upon sight of adultery commits manslaughter, but an unmarried individual who kills upon sight of unfaithfulness by one's lover or fiancé is a murderer. Only a highly unrealistic belief about passion can explain this rule in terms of excusing conduct. It is implausible to believe that when an actor observes his or her loved one in an act of sexual disloyalty, that actor will suffer from less anger simply because the disloyal partner is not the actor's spouse. Instead, this rule is really a judgment by courts that adultery is a form of injustice perpetrated upon the killer which merits a violent response, whereas "mere" sexual unfaithfulness out of wedlock does not. Thus, it has been said that adultery is the "highest invasion of [a husband's] property," whereas in the unmarried situation the defendant "has no such control" over his faithless lover.

Another justification-oriented rule is the misdirected retaliation doctrine, wherein it is said that the defense is only applicable when it is an "act * * * by the dead man," not a third person, which provokes the accused. * * *

There is substantial basis, then, for the claim that heat of passion is, at least at times, viewed as a partial justification * * *.[c] There is also substantial support, however, for the assertion that the defense is based on a theory that the harm is the same as with murder, but that the accused's personal blameworthiness is less than that of the murderer. The language, if not always the result, in provocation cases is usually excuse oriented. The problem, however, is that court opinions vary in their excuse reasoning.

---

166. *E.g.,* reasonable, blameless actors never become enraged by lawful conduct.

c. For example, Professor Susan Rozelle argues that the provocation doctrine should rest "on the idea that the victim 'had it coming' "—that is, that the defendant was legally entitled to use moderate force in response to the decedent's provocation, but that the force used (deadly force) by the defendant was excessive. Susan. D. Rozelle, *He Had It Coming: Provocation as a Partial Justification*, in Criminal Law Conversations (Paul H. Robinson, Stephen P. Garvey, & Kimberly Kessler Ferzan, eds. 2009), at 326.

JOSHUA DRESSLER—WHY KEEP THE PROVOCATION DEFENSE?: SOME REFLECTIONS ON A DIFFICULT SUBJECT

86 Minnesota Law Review 959 (2002), 971–975

The provocation defense is an excuse defense, albeit a partial one, but one that may (but need not) have a justification-like component. My best effort to explain basic provocation law runs as follows: An intentional homicide is not mitigated to manslaughter unless certain conditions are met. First, there must be a provocative event that results in the actor feeling rage or some similar overwrought emotion. It is important here to understand why the provocation does—and does not—result in anger. It is not that the provocation "touches a nerve" as, for example, when a person drops a cup when he is stung on the hand by a wasp. The act of dropping the cup—the wasp almost literally hitting a nerve—is a physiological action (in legal terms, an involuntary act) and not one "mediated by judgment and reason." In the provocation context, however, anger is preceded by some judgment by the provoked party, even if it occurs instantly, that he or another to whom he feels an emotional attachment has been wronged in some manner by the provoker. In the ordinary provocation case, for example, when the provoker spits in another's face, uses insulting racial epithets, wrongs the individual by assaulting him, or commits some harm to a loved one, the provoker sends a disparaging message (or, at least, the provoked party reasonably interprets it this way) or commits a seeming injustice, which incites the victim of the provocation to fury.

Fury, however, is not enough to activate the defense. The law considers only some provocations "adequate" to reduce a homicide to manslaughter. If we believe that the provocation is the type that entitles a person to feel anger, or even more strongly, if we feel that the provocation should make a person feel anger or outrage, e.g., when a person is verbally insulted or spat upon, then we may characterize the emotion as, in some sense, "justifiable" or, if you will, appropriate. In this very limited way the heat-of-passion doctrine potentially contains a "justificatory" feature.

The basis for mitigation, however, does not require a finding that the provoked party's anger or outrage is one we find appropriate or of which we approve ("justifiable"). It is enough that we are prepared to "excuse" the actor for feeling as he does, or perhaps more precisely, we empathize with the actor's feelings. We must remember that the provocation defense is based to a considerable extent on the law's concession to ordinary human frailty;[d] the ultimate question, therefore, is whether we (or the jury) consider the provoked party's anger within the range of expected human responses to the provocative situation. Put somewhat differently, we must decide if the provocative event might cause an ordinary person—

---

d. So understood, the defense is a "recognition that the human courier is accompanied by the luggage of imperfection." Kevin Bennardo, *Of Ordinariness and Excuse: Heat-of-Passion and the Seven Deadly Sins*, 36 Capital U. L. Rev. 675, 678 (2008).

one of ordinary and neither short nor saintly temperament—to become enraged or otherwise emotionally overcome. * * *

One must keep in mind * * * that "justifying" or "excusing" the provoked party for his emotional upset does not in itself entitle the defendant to mitigation for a killing. * * * The modern defense is * * * about excusable loss of self-control. It is not enough simply to say that a defendant's anger, which was mediated by judgment and reason, was, in the sense I have explained, justifiable or excusable: The provocation must be so serious that we are prepared to say that an ordinary person in the actor's circumstances, even an ordinarily law-abiding person of reasonable temperament, might become sufficiently upset by the provocation [and suffer such an emotional outburst as] to experience substantial impairment of his capacity for self-control and, as a consequence, to act violently.

Under no circumstances is the provoked killing justifiable in the slightest; indeed, the actor's violent loss of self-control is unjustifiable. Moreover, the loss of self-control is not totally excusable, because the law's assumption is that the provoked party was not wholly incapable of controlling or channeling his anger. If he were totally incapable, a full excuse would be defensible. Instead the defense is based on our common experience that when we become exceptionally angry—remembering that we are not blaming the person for his anger—our ability to conform our conduct to the dictates of the law is seriously undermined, hence making law-abiding behavior far more difficult than in nonprovocative circumstances. It is this understandably greater difficulty to control conduct that appropriately mitigates a provoked actor's blameworthiness, and therefore, his responsibility for a homicide.

NOTES AND QUESTIONS

1. *Should* the provocation defense be considered a (partial) justification or a (partial) excuse? (For the view that the defense should only apply if the killing is *both* partially justified *and* partially excused, see Mitchell N. Berman & Ian P. Farrell, *Provocation Manslaughter as Partial Justification and Partial Excuse*, 52 Wm. & Mary L. Rev. 1027 (2011).)

Some scholars believe that the provocation doctrine might better be explained by means of the concept of *akrasia* (Greek for one who acts inconsistently with his or her own best judgment), rather than by consideration of the justification/excuse distinction. Professor Stephen Garvey, for example, distinguishes between a person who acts in *defiance* of law (and, thus, is guilty of murder when he intentionally kills) and one who, less culpably, *violates* the law (and, thus, is guilty of manslaughter when he kills intentionally):

[T]he provoked killer's culpability consists of failure to control the desire to kill, a desire resulting from provocation and heat of passion, such that at the moment he acts, his desire to kill leads him to believe (erroneously and unreasonably) that the law allows him to kill; or, knowing the law does not allow him to kill and believing he should [not kill] * * *, he nonetheless succumbs to his lethal desire.

Stephen P. Garvey, *Passion's Puzzle*, 90 Iowa L. Rev. 1677, 1684 (2005). According to this view, the person who is entitled to have his offense reduced to manslaughter is one who, although he has the capacity for self-control, tries to exercise it but ultimately succumbs to his passions. This person is less culpable than one who does not make the attempt at self-control.

2. Reconsider Note 6 (p. 271 supra): Is Aaron entitled to a jury instruction on manslaughter if the provocation defense is based on excuse principles? On justification principles?

3. *Problem*. In what a trial judge described as "a Shakespearean tragedy brought into the real world," a Connecticut lawyer stabbed to death his neighbor because he erroneously thought, based on information from the lawyer's wife, the man had just molested their two-year-old daughter. (Nobody had molested her.) Murder or manslaughter? Does it matter to the analysis whether the heat-of-passion defense is a partial justification or partial excuse?

b. The Objective Standard: Who Is the "Reasonable Man"?
INTRODUCTORY COMMENT

As developed in the preceding materials, in order for an intentional homicide to constitute manslaughter rather than murder, a defendant must have killed in response to provocation "calculated to inflame the passion of a *reasonable man*," or which "might render *ordinary men*, of fair average disposition, liable to act rashly or without due deliberation or reflection, and from passion, rather than judgment."

This "reasonable man" (or, occasionally, "ordinary man") shows up throughout the criminal law and represents an objective standard by which the defendant's conduct is measured. But, who *is* this "reasonable man"? What characteristics does he possess? (Indeed, is he really a "he," or is the word "man" meant to be used in the gender-neutral sense of "person"?).

In the provocation context, the question one must sometimes consider is this: *To what extent, if any, should the jury, in evaluating provocation, be instructed that the "reasonable man" possesses the defendant's own personal characteristics and personal prior experiences?* For various historical reasons, English courts have focused on this question more often than the American judiciary—although it is highly relevant here, too—so, we cross the Atlantic now to consider the question.

The starting point to understanding the issue in English law is Bedder v. Director of Public Prosecutions, [1954] 2 All E.R. 801, [1954] 1 W.L.R. 1119, in which it was decided that the "reasonable man" was a wholly impersonal figure to which no specific characteristics of the defendant were to be attributed. The accused in *Bedder* was a sexually impotent male who killed a prostitute after she taunted him with his failure to have intercourse. He grasped her, and in her efforts to get away, she slapped him in the face, punched him in the stomach, and kicked him in the groin. Bedder believed that the jury should be permitted to take into consideration his physical infirmity—sexual impotence—in evaluating the adequacy of the provocation. The judge, however, instructed the jury in strictly objective terms, and the House of Lords approved this approach. Lord Simonds observed that "[i]t would be plainly illogical not to recognise an unusually excitable or pugnacious temperament in the accused as a matter to be taken into account but yet to recognise for that purpose some unusual physical characteristic, be it impotence or another."

In response to *Bedder* and on recommendation of the Royal Commission on Capital Punishment, Parliament enacted the Homicide Act of 1957. Section 3 provided:

> Where on a charge of murder there is evidence on which the jury can find that the person charged was provoked (whether by things done or by things said or by both together) to lose his self-control, the question whether the provocation was enough to make a reasonable man do as he did shall be left to be determined by the jury; and in determining that question the jury shall take into account everything both done and said according to the effect which, in their opinion, it would have on a reasonable man.

This section of the Homicide Act plainly changed the law in two significant ways. First, if there was evidence that a defendant in fact was provoked to lose his self-control (the subjective element of the provocation doctrine), the question of whether the objective element was met—how the reasonable man would react—had to be left to the jury. No longer could a judge withdraw the issue from the jury. Second, in applying the objective standard, the jury could consider everything said and/or done to the defendant—in short, the common law rule that words alone were insufficient was abrogated.

This left one critical set of issues to be decided. That is, did the Homicide Act by implication abrogate the rule of *Bedder* that the "reasonable man" is devoid of any particular characteristics of the defendant? If *Bedder* is no longer good law, to what extent does (and should) the law authorize jurors to incorporate characteristics and experiences of the defendant into the "reasonable man"—are there limits to the "subjectivization" of the "reasonable man" standard?

The *Camplin* case, set out below, was the House of Lords first effort to answer some of these questions. In reading the case and thinking about the subject, you would do well to distinguish between two ways in which a defendant's characteristics might be considered in a provocation case: (1) in determining whether the *gravity of the provocation* would be sufficient to cause the "reasonable man" to lose self-control; and (2) in assessing the *level of self-control* to be expected of the "reasonable man."

(handwritten in left margin: The Objective Standard)

DIRECTOR OF PUBLIC PROSECUTIONS v. CAMPLIN

House of Lords, 1978.
2 All Eng.Rep. 168, 2 W.L.R. 679.

LORD DIPLOCK. * * * The respondent, Camplin, who was 15 years of age, killed a middle-aged Pakistani, Mohammed Lal Khan, by splitting his skull with a chapati pan, a heavy kitchen utensil like a rimless frying pan. At the time the two of them were alone together in Khan's flat. At Camplin's trial for murder * * * his only defence was that of provocation so as to reduce the offence to manslaughter. According to the story that he told in the witness box * * *, Khan had [sodomized] him in spite of his resistance and had then laughed at him, whereupon Camplin had lost his self-control and attacked Kahn fatally with the chapati pan.

In his address to the jury on the defence of provocation, counsel for Camplin had suggested to them that when they addressed their minds to the question whether the provocation relied on was enough to make a reasonable man do as Camplin had done, what they ought to consider was not the reaction of a reasonable adult but the reaction of a reasonable boy of Camplin's age. The judge thought that this was wrong in law. So in this summing-up he took pains to instruct the jury that they must consider whether—

> the provocation was sufficient to make a reasonable man in like circumstances act as the defendant did. Not a reasonable boy, as [counsel for Camplin] would have it, or a reasonable lad; it is an objective test—a reasonable man.

The jury found Camplin guilty of murder. On appeal the Court of Appeal, Criminal Division, allowed the appeal and substituted a conviction for manslaughter on the ground that the passage I have cited from the summing-up was a misdirection. The court held that

> the proper direction to the jury is to invite the jury to consider whether the provocation was enough to have made a reasonable person of the same age as the appellant in the same circumstances do as he did.

The point of law of general public importance involved in the case has been certified as being:

(handwritten in left margin: Issue)

> Whether, on the prosecution for murder of a boy of 15, where the issue of provocation arises, the jury should be directed to consider the question * * * whether the provocation was enough to make a reasonable man do as he did by reference to a "reasonable adult" or by reference to a "reasonable boy of 15." * * *

[Lord Diplock summarized the *Bedder* opinion and the changes in law brought by section 3 of the Homicide Act (see the Introductory Comment supra). He then proceeded:]

The public policy that underlay the adoption of the "reasonable man" test in the common law doctrine of provocation was to reduce the incidence of fatal violence by preventing a person relying on his own exceptional pugnacity or excitability as an excuse for loss of self-control. The rationale of the test may not be easy to reconcile in logic with more universal propositions as to the mental element in crime. Nevertheless it has been preserved by the 1957 Act but fails to be applied now in the context of a law of provocation that is significantly different from what it was before the Act was passed.

Although it is now for the jury to apply the "reasonable man" test, it still remains for the judge to direct them what, in the new context of the section, is the meaning of this apparently inapt expression * * *. * * *

As I have already pointed out, for the purposes of the law of provocation the "reasonable man" has never been confined to the adult male. It means an ordinary person of either sex, not exceptionally excitable or pugnacious, but possessed of such powers of self-control as everyone is entitled to expect that his fellow citizens will exercise in society as it is today. A crucial factor in the defence of provocation from earliest times has been the relationship between the gravity of provocation and the way in which the accused retaliated, both being judged by the social standards of the day. When Hale was writing in the 17th century pulling a man's nose was thought to justify retaliation with a sword; when *Mancini* [[1978] 1 All Eng.Rep. 1236] was decided by this House, a blow with a fist would not justify retaliation with a deadly weapon. But so long as words unaccompanied by violence could not in common law amount to provocation the relevant proportionality between provocation and retaliation was primarily one of degrees of violence. Words spoken to the accused before the violence started were not normally to be included in the proportion sum. But now that the law has been changed so as to permit of words being treated as provocation, even though unaccompanied by any other acts, the gravity of verbal provocation may well depend on the particular characteristics or circumstances of the person to whom a taunt or insult is addressed. To taunt a person because of his race, his physical infirmities or some shameful incident in his past may well be considered by the jury to be more offensive to the person addressed, however equable his temperament, if the facts on which the taunt is founded are true than it would be if they were not. It would stultify much of the mitigation of the previous harshness of the common law in ruling out verbal provocation as capable of reducing murder to manslaughter if the jury could not take into consideration all those factors which in their opinion would affect the gravity of taunts and insults when applied to the person to whom they are addressed. So to this extent at any rate the unqualified proposition accepted by this House in *Bedder* that for the purposes of the "reasonable man" test any unusual physical characteristics of the accused must be ignored requires revision as a result of the passing of the 1957 Act.

That he was only 15 years of age at the time of the killing is the relevant characteristic of the accused in the instant case. It is a characteristic which may have its effects on temperament as well as physique. If the jury think that the same power of self-control is not to be expected in an ordinary, average or normal boy of 15 as in an older person, are they to treat the lesser powers of self-control possessed by an ordinary, average or normal boy of 15 as the standard of self-control with which the conduct of the accused is to be compared?

It may be conceded that in strict logic there is a transition between treating age as a characteristic that may be taken into account in assessing the gravity of the provocation addressed to the accused and treating it as a characteristic to be taken into account in determining what is the degree of self-control to be expected of the ordinary person with whom the accused's conduct is to be compared. But to require old heads on young shoulders is inconsistent with the law's compassion of human infirmity to which Sir Michael Foster ascribed the doctrine of provocation more than two centuries ago. The distinction as to the purpose for which it is legitimate to take the age of the accused into account involves considerations of too great nicety to warrant a place in deciding a matter of opinion, which is no longer one to be decided by a judge trained in logical reasoning but by a jury drawing on their experience of how ordinary human beings behave in real life. * * *

In my opinion a proper direction to a jury on the question left to their exclusive determination by Section 3 of the 1957 Act would be on the following lines. The judge should state what the question is, using the very terms of the section. He should then explain to them that the reasonable man referred to in the question is a person having the power of self-control to be expected of an ordinary person of the sex and age of the accused, but in other respects sharing such of the accused's characteristics as they think would affect the gravity of the provocation to him, and that the question is not merely whether such a person would in like circumstances be provoked to lose his self-control but also would react to the provocation as the accused did.

I accordingly agree with the Court of Appeal that the judge ought not to have instructed the jury to pay no account to the age of the accused even though they themselves might be of opinion that the degree of self-control to be expected in a boy of that age was less than in an adult. * * *

I would dismiss the appeal.

LORD SIMON OF GLAISDALE. * * * [I]t is accepted that the phrase "reasonable man" really means "reasonable person," so as to extend to "reasonable woman." So, although this has never yet been a subject of decision, a jury could arguably * * * take the sex of the accused into account in assessing what might reasonably cause her to lose her self-control. * * * If so, this is already some qualification on the "reasonable person" as a pure abstraction devoid of any personal characteristics, even if such a concept were of any value to the law. This qualification might be crucial: take the insult "whore" addressed respectively to a reasonable man and a reasonable woman. Nevertheless, as counsel for the appellant sternly and cogently maintained, *Bedder* would preclude the jury from considering that the accused was, say, pregnant, or presumably undergoing menstruation or menopause. * * *

The original reasons in this branch of the law were largely reasons of the heart and of common sense, not the reasons of pure juristic logic. * * * But justice and common sense then demanded some limitation: it would be unjust that the drunk man or one exceptionally pugnacious or bad-tempered or over-sensitive should be able to claim that these matters rendered him peculiarly susceptible to the provocation offered, where the sober and even-tempered man would hang for his homicide. Hence, * * * the development of the concept of the reaction of a reasonable man to the provocation offered * * *. * * *

I think that the standard of self-control which the law requires before provocation is held to reduce murder to manslaughter is still that of the reasonable person (hence his invocation in Section 3 of the 1957 Act), but that, in determining whether a person of reasonable self-control would lose it in the circumstances, the entire factual situation, which includes the characteristics of the accused, must be considered. * * *

My Lords, for the foregoing reasons I would dismiss the appeal. * * *

[The statements of Lord Morris of Borth-y-Gest, Lord Fraser of Tullbelton and Lord Scarman, all of whom also voted to dismiss the appeal, are omitted.]

NOTES AND QUESTIONS

1. Look again at the last paragraph of the Introductory Comment on page 277. According to Lord Diplock, how should a jury be instructed regarding a defendant's category (1) characteristics? What about category (2)? As a matter of sound policy, do you agree with *Camplin*?

2. *V* taunts *M* for being addicted to glue sniffing. How would Lord Diplock want the jury instructed in this case? See Regina v. Morhall [1995] 3 All E.R. 659, [1996] 1 App.Cas. 90. Do you see a difficulty in instructing the jury in this case?

3. Consider the facts in Commonwealth v. Carr, 398 Pa.Super. 306, 580 A.2d 1362 (1990):

> On May 13, 1988, Claudia Brenner and Rebecca Wight were hiking along the Appalachian Trail in Adams County, when they found an appropriate campsite and stopped for the night. There, they were resting and engaging in lesbian lovemaking when Claudia Brenner was shot in the right arm. After a short pause, additional shots were fired, as a result of which Brenner was struck four additional times in and about her face, neck and head. Rebecca Wight ran for cover behind a tree and was shot in the head and back. Brenner attempted to help Wight, who was unable to walk, but was unable to rouse her. Brenner thereupon went for help, but by the time help arrived, Wight was dead. Suspicion subsequently focused on Stephen Roy Carr. * * * He was subsequently * * * found guilty of murder in the first degree.

Carr defended at trial on grounds, inter alia, that he had shot Brenner and Wight in the heat of passion caused by the serious provocation of their nude homosexual lovemaking. In support of this defense and to show the existence of passion, Carr offered to show a history of constant rejection by women, including his mother who may have been involved in a lesbian relationship, sexual abuse while in prison [on an earlier offense] in Florida, inability to hold a job, and retreat to the mountains to avoid further rejection. This was relevant, he contended, to show that he was impassioned when provoked by the "show" put on by the women, including their nakedness, their hugging and kissing and their oral sex. The trial court refused to allow evidence of Carr's psychosexual history, finding it irrelevant.

If Pennsylvania law followed the reasoning of *Camplin* in regard to the "reasonable man" standard, would some or all of Carr's proffered testimony have been admissible? In your view, *should* the evidence be admissible? If you would not permit Carr to introduce his evidence, would you feel differently if the case involved a battered woman who kills her husband after a trivial provocation and who wishes to have her actions in response to the provocation measured by the standards of the "reasonable battered woman with battered woman syndrome"?

4. What if scientific evidence on aggression were to show that "[s]ome men are highly vulnerable to stress, others are strikingly resistant to it. * * * It seems likely * * * that a number of factors, some genetic, others environmental, combine to produce the differences of susceptibility and response." Peter Brett, *The Physiology of Provocation*, 1970 Crim. L. Rev. 634, 637. See also Terrie E. Moffitt, *Genetic and Environmental Influences on Antisocial Behaviors: Evidence from Behavior–Genetic Research,* in 55 Advance in Genetics (Jeffrey C. Hall et al., eds. 2005), at 41 (appraising prior quantitative behavioral and genetic evidence, and concluding that genes influence approximately 50% of population variation in antisocial behavior, environmental factors shared by family members influence 20%, and environmental factors experienced uniquely by individuals influence 20–30% of population variation). If this is true, does this suggest that short-tempered persons may not be to blame for possessing a "short fuse" and, therefore, should not be held to the standard of a person of ordinary self-control?

5. *Culture, provocation, and the "reasonable man."* In South Australia, George Stewart, a member of an Aboriginal tribe, "talked man's talk," i.e., spoke about sacred tribal secrets which only initiated members of the tribe should know. Women and young men—the uninitiated—were present, so his statements constituted sacrilege. Harry Gibson tried to quiet Stewart, a fight ensued, and ultimately Gibson killed Stewart. See Regina v. Gibson, an unpublished opinion described in Robert L. Misner, *The Awkward Case of Harry Gibson*, 1986 Ariz.St.L.J. 691, 692–93. The judge told the non-Aboriginal jury, id. at 708–10:

It is true that a nun might be shocked more readily and more deeply than many members of the general public by a blaspheming of the Christian faith. And a tribesman would be more shocked, disturbed and aroused by an improper disclosure of the sacred mysteries of tribal lore than you or I would be. The law is not foolish. It takes account of these matters. * * *

Not every form of provocation is of effect in the criminal law. The provocation is usually said to be such as would cause a reasonable man to lose control of himself. Where tribal lore in a tribal setting is improperly referred to * * * it is useless to think of a reasonable white man. One must think of a reasonable man having the awareness, the timidity, the ordinary reactions of a Pitjantjajara tribesman, viewing the tribe as a social group and accused as a member of the group.

Do you agree with the jury instruction? Do you believe that a jury should measure the gravity of a provocation from the cultural perspective of the parties? If so, consider the case of a Pakistani man who, enraged, strangled to death his adult daughter because she wanted out of an arranged marriage. He sought to show that, in his culture, such disobedience by a woman or girl is highly provocative and brings shame upon family members. Dahleen Glaton & Antonio Oliva, *"Honor Killing" Alleged in Ga.; Pakistani Immigrant is Accused of Strangling Daughter Who Opposed Her Arranged Marriage*, Chicago Tribune, July 8, 2008, at C3. Is there a principled way to distinguish this case from the "tribal secrets" case?

Do you agree with Justice David Doherty of the Ontario Court of Appeal, [2006] O.J. No. 1507, who suggested:

In some situations, there can be no doubt that the accused's religious or cultural beliefs will be attributed to the ordinary person to properly apply the "ordinary person" test * * *. * * * [O]ne's religious and cultural beliefs can give a "special significance" to the acts or insult said to have constituted the provocation. * * *

* * * The difficult problem, as I see it, is [when] the alleged beliefs which give [an] insult added gravity are premised on the notion that women are inferior to men and that violence against women is in some circumstances accepted, if not encouraged. These beliefs are antithetical to fundamental Christian values, including gender equality. If it arguable that as a matter of criminal law policy, the "ordinary person" cannot be fixed with beliefs that are irreconcilable with fundamental Canadian values. Criminal law may simply not accept that a belief system which is contrary to those fundamental values should somehow provide the basis for a partial defence to murder.

In a liberal democracy, founded on equal rights, but also founded on cultural and religious diversity, is Justice Doherty's approach appropriate? Would you let the defendant in the Pakistani case introduce evidence regarding his culture? If you would, what do you think of the following jury instruction:

[T]here is one thing about the defendant you shall *not* take into account. You shall not consider his own personal views, or the particular views of his ethnic community, about what it is right to be extremely angry about. Rather, you shall judge the reasonableness of his anger by how angry you, as a representative of the people of the state, conclude an individual who is otherwise like him is *right* to feel or, at least, *not wrong to feel* in response to what actually upset him.

Peter Westen, *Individualizing the Reasonable Person in Criminal Trial*, 2 Crim. Law & Phil. 137, 158 (2008).

6. *The sex of the "reasonable person."* According to Lord Diplock, "the reasonable man referred to * * * is a person having the power of self-control to be expected of an ordinary person of the sex and age of the accused." It is easy to understand why the sex of the defendant might be relevant in some cases in measuring the gravity of a provocation (assume the defendant is called a "whore" or "slut"), but why is the sex of the defendant relevant on matters of "power of self-control"?

Is there any practical effect in taking into consideration the sex of the accused in determining the adequacy of provocation? Note the following:

> [T]he legal standards that define adequate provocation and passionate "human" weakness reflect a male view of understandable homicidal violence. Homicide is overwhelmingly a male act. In 1984, eighty-seven percent of those arrested in the United States for homicide * * * were male. * * *
>
> Women rarely kill. * * * Female homicide is so different from male homicide that women and men may be said to live in two different cultures, each with its own "subculture of violence."

Laurie J. Taylor, Comment, *Provoked Reason in Men and Women: Heat-of-Passion Manslaughter and Imperfect Self–Defense,* 33 UCLA L.Rev. 1679, 1679–81 (1986); see also Robbin S. Ogle et al., *A Theory of Homicidal Behavior Among Women*, 33 Criminology 173 (1995) (finding that women tend to respond to stressful events by feeling guilt and hurt rather than externalizing their feelings as anger directed at a target).

Is a woman who "acts like a man" by killing in response to infidelity or other provocative acts likely to be aided or hurt by an instruction that the jury evaluate her actions by the standards of the "reasonable woman"?

c. Model Penal Code and Beyond

PEOPLE v. CASASSA
Court of Appeals of New York, 1980.
49 N.Y.2d 668, 427 N.Y.S.2d 769, 404 N.E.2d 1310.

JASEN, JUDGE.

The significant issue on this appeal is whether the defendant, in a murder prosecution, established the affirmative defense of "extreme emotional disturbance" which would have reduced the crime to manslaughter in the first degree.

On February 28, 1977, Victoria Lo Consolo was brutally murdered. Defendant Victor Casassa and Miss Lo Consolo had been acquainted for some time prior to the latter's tragic death. They met in August, 1976 as a result of their residence in the same apartment complex. * * * The two apparently dated casually * * * until November, 1976 when Miss Lo Consolo informed defendant that she was not "falling in love" with him. Defendant claims that Miss Lo Consolo's candid statement of her feelings "devastated him."

Miss Lo Consolo's rejection of defendant's advances also precipitated a bizarre series of actions on the part of defendant which, he asserts, demonstrate the existence of extreme emotional disturbance upon which he predicates his affirmative defense. Defendant, aware that Miss Lo Consolo maintained social relationships with others, broke into the apartment below Miss Lo Consolo's on several occasions to eavesdrop. These eavesdropping sessions allegedly caused him to be under great emotional stress. Thereafter, on one occasion, he broke into Miss Lo Consolo's apartment while she was out. Defendant took nothing, but, instead, observed the apartment, disrobed and lay for a time in Miss Lo Consolo's bed. During this break-in, defendant was armed with a knife which, he later told police, he carried "because he knew that he was either going to hurt Victoria or Victoria was going to cause him to commit suicide."

Defendant's final visit to his victim's apartment occurred on February 28, 1977. Defendant brought several bottles of wine and liquor with him to offer as a gift. Upon Miss Lo Consolo's rejection of this offering, defendant produced a steak knife which he had brought with him, stabbed Miss Lo Consolo several times in the throat, dragged her body to the bathroom and submerged it in a bathtub full of water to "make sure she was dead." * * *

Defendant waived a jury and proceeded to trial before the County Court. * * * The defendant did not contest the underlying facts of the crime. Instead, the sole issue presented to the trial court was whether the defendant, at the time of the killing, had acted under the influence of "extreme emotional disturbance." (Penal Law, § 125.25, subd. 1, par. [a].) The defense presented only one witness, a psychiatrist, who testified, in essence, that the defendant had become obsessed with Miss Lo Consolo and that the course which their relationship had taken, combined with several personality attributes peculiar to defendant, caused him to be under the influence of extreme emotional disturbance at the time of the killing.

In rebuttal, the People produced several witnesses. Among these witnesses was a psychiatrist who testified that although the defendant was emotionally disturbed, he was not under the influence of "extreme emotional disturbance" * * * because his disturbed state was not the product of external factors but rather was "a stress he created from within himself, dealing mostly with a fantasy, a refusal to accept the reality of the situation."

The trial court in resolving this issue noted that the affirmative defense of extreme emotional disturbance may be based upon a series of events, rather than a single precipitating cause. In order to be entitled to the defense, the court held, a defendant must show that his reaction to such events was reasonable. In determining whether defendant's emotional reaction was reasonable, the court considered the appropriate test to be whether in the totality of the circumstances the finder of fact could understand how a person might have his reason overcome. Concluding that the test was not to be applied solely from the viewpoint of defendant, the court found that defendant's emotional reaction at the time of the commission of the crime was so peculiar to him that it could not be considered reasonable so as to reduce the conviction to manslaughter in the first degree. Accordingly, the trial court found defendant guilty of the crime of murder in the second degree. * * *

On this appeal defendant contends that the trial court erred in failing to afford him the benefit of the affirmative defense of "extreme emotional disturbance." It is argued that the defendant established that he suffered from a mental infirmity not arising to the level of insanity which disoriented his reason to the extent that his emotional reaction, from his own subjective point of view, was supported by a reasonable explanation or excuse. Defendant asserts that by refusing to apply a wholly subjective standard the trial court misconstrued section 125.25 of the Penal Law. We cannot agree.

Section 125.25 (subd. 1, par. [a]) of the Penal Law provides that it is an affirmative defense to the crime of murder in the second degree where "[t]he defendant acted under the influence of extreme emotional disturbance for which there was a reasonable explanation or excuse." This defense allows a defendant charged with the commission of acts which would otherwise constitute murder to demonstrate the existence of mitigating factors which indicate that, although he is not free from responsibility for his crime, he ought to be punished less severely by reducing the crime upon conviction to manslaughter in the first degree.

In enacting section 125.25, the Legislature adopted the language of the manslaughter provisions of the Model Penal Code. * * *

The "extreme emotional disturbance" defense is an outgrowth of the "heat of passion" doctrine which had for some time been recognized by New York as a distinguishing factor between the crimes of manslaughter and murder. However, the new formulation is significantly broader in scope than the "heat of passion" doctrine which it replaced.

For example, the "heat of passion" doctrine required that a defendant's action be undertaken as a response to some provocation which prevented him from reflecting upon his actions. Moreover, such reaction had to be immediate. The existence of a "cooling off" period completely negated any mitigating effect which the provocation might otherwise have had. In [People v.] Patterson[, 39 N.Y.2d 288, 383 N.Y.S.2d 573, 347 N.E.2d 898 (1976)], however, this court recognized that "[a]n action influenced by an extreme emotional disturbance is not one that is necessarily so spontaneously undertaken. Rather, it may be that a significant mental trauma has affected a defendant's mind for a substantial period of time, simmering in the unknowing subconscious and then inexplicably coming to the fore." * * *

The thrust of defendant's claim, however, concerns a question arising out of another perceived distinction between "heat of passion" and "extreme emotional disturbance" * * *, to wit: whether, assuming that the defense is applicable to a broader range of circumstances, the standard by which the reasonableness of defendant's emotional reaction is to be tested must be an entirely subjective one. * * *

Consideration of the Comments to the Model Penal Code, from which the New York statute was drawn, are instructive. The defense of "extreme emotional disturbance" has two principal components—(1) the particular defendant must have "acted under the influence of extreme emotional disturbance," and (2) there must have been "a reasonable explanation or excuse" for such extreme emotional disturbance, "the reasonableness of which is to be determined from the viewpoint of a person in the defendant's situation under the circumstances as the defendant believed them to be." The first requirement is wholly subjective—i.e., it involves a determination that the particular defendant did in fact act under extreme emotional disturbance, that the claimed explanation as to the cause of his action is not contrived or sham.

The second component is more difficult to describe—i.e., whether there was a reasonable explanation or excuse for the emotional disturbance. It was designed to sweep away "the rigid rules that have developed with respect to the sufficiency of particular types of provocation, such as the rule that words alone can never be enough," and "avoids a merely arbitrary limitation on the nature of the antecedent circumstances that may justify a mitigation." "The ultimate test, however, is objective; there must be 'reasonable' explanation or excuse for the actor's disturbance." In light of these comments and the necessity of articulating the defense in terms comprehensible to jurors, we conclude that the determination whether there was reasonable explanation or excuse for a particular emotional disturbance should be made by viewing the subjective, internal situation in which the defendant found himself and the external circumstances as he perceived them at the time, however inaccurate that perception may have been, and assessing from that standpoint whether the explanation or excuse for his emotional disturbance was reasonable, so as to entitle him to a reduction of the crime charged from murder in the second degree to manslaughter in the first degree.[2] We recognize that even such a description of the defense provides no precise guidelines and necessarily leaves room for the exercise of judgmental evaluation by the jury. This, however, appears to have been the intent of the draftsmen. "The purpose was explicitly to give full scope to what amounts to a plea in mitigation based upon a mental or emotional trauma of significant dimensions, with the jury asked to show whatever empathy it can." (Wechsler,

2. We emphasize that this test is to be applied to determine whether defendant's emotional disturbance, and not the act of killing, was supported by a reasonable explanation or excuse.

Codification of Criminal Law in the United States: The Model Penal Code, 68 Col.L.Rev. 1425, 1446.) * * *

* * * In the end, we believe that what the Legislature intended in enacting the statute was to allow the finder of fact the discretionary power to mitigate the penalty when presented with a situation which, under the circumstances, appears to them to have caused an understandable weakness in one of their fellows. Perhaps the chief virtue of the statute is that it allows such discretion without engaging in a detailed explanation of individual circumstances in which the statute would apply, thus avoiding the "mystifying cloud of words" which Mr. Justice Cardozo abhorred.

We conclude that the trial court, in this case, properly applied the statute. The court apparently accepted, as a factual matter, that defendant killed Miss Lo Consolo while under the influence of "extreme emotional disturbance," a threshold question which must be answered in the affirmative before any test of reasonableness is required. The court, however, also recognized that in exercising its function as trier of fact, it must make a further inquiry into the reasonableness of that disturbance. In this regard, the court considered each of the mitigating factors put forward by defendant, including his claimed mental disability, but found that the excuse offered by defendant was so peculiar to him that it was unworthy of mitigation. The court obviously made a sincere effort to understand defendant's "situation" and "the circumstances as defendant believed them to be," but concluded that the murder in this case was the result of defendant's malevolence rather than an understandable human response deserving of mercy. We cannot say, as a matter of law, that the court erred in so concluding. Indeed, to do so would subvert the purpose of the statute.

In our opinion, this statute would not require that the jury or the court as trier of fact find mitigation on any particular set of facts, but, rather, allows the finder of fact the opportunity to do so, such opportunity being conditional only upon a finding of extreme emotional disturbance in the first instance. * * *

NOTES AND QUESTIONS

1. In the following cases, is the defendant entitled to a jury instruction on manslaughter under the Model Penal Code?

A. Defendant Raguseo lived in an apartment building in which each tenant had an assigned parking space. He took meticulous care of his spot, painting the lines on either side of the space, sweeping it regularly, and clipping the shrubbery nearby. One night Raguseo found someone else's car in his space. He called the police, who informed him that they did not have authority to tow a vehicle parked on private property. Two hours later, when the owner of the car returned, Raguseo stabbed him repeatedly, killing him. State v. Raguseo, 225 Conn. 114, 622 A.2d 519 (1993).

B. In a fit of rage, the defendant strangled to death his wife on their honeymoon cruise because she refused to stop eating sweets and because she did not know how to use the "complex" silverware settings aboard the cruise ship. United States v. Roston, 986 F.2d 1287 (9th Cir.1993).

C.   Alice killed Gerald because he reminded her of her ex-husband.

D.   Franklin Crow bludgeoned his roommate to death with a sledgehammer and a clawhammer after an argument over an empty roll of toilet paper. Detroit Free Press, Feb. 24, 2006, at 2.

2.   *"Reasonable explanation or excuse."* The Commentary to the Model Penal Code explains this critical language:

> Of course, Section 210.3(1)(b) does require that the actor's emotional distress be based on "reasonable explanation or excuse." This language preserves the essentially objective character of the inquiry and erects a barrier against debilitating individualization of the legal standard. But the statute further provides that the "reasonableness of such explanation or excuse shall be determined from the viewpoint of a person in the actor's situation under the circumstances as he believes them to be." The last clause clarifies the role of mistake. The trier of fact must evaluate the actor's conduct under the circumstances that the actor believed to exist. Thus, for example, a man who reasonably but mistakenly identifies his wife's rapist and kills the wrong person may be eligible for mitigation if his extreme emotional disturbance were otherwise subject to reasonable explanation or excuse.
>
> The critical element in the Model Code formulation is the clause requiring that reasonableness be assessed "from the viewpoint of a person in the actor's situation." The word "situation" is designedly ambiguous. On the one hand, it is clear that personal handicaps and some external circumstances must be taken into account. Thus, blindness, shock from traumatic injury, and extreme grief are all easily read into the term "situation." This result is sound, for it would be morally obtuse to appraise a crime for mitigation of punishment without reference to these factors. On the other hand, it is equally plain that idiosyncratic moral values are not part of the actor's situation. An assassin who kills a political leader because he believes it is right to do so cannot ask that he be judged by the standard of a reasonable extremist. Any other result would undermine the normative message of the criminal law. In between these two extremes, however, there are matters neither as clearly distinct from individual blameworthiness as blindness or handicap nor as integral a part of moral depravity as a belief in the rightness of killing. Perhaps the classic illustration is the unusual sensitivity to the epithet "bastard" of a person born illegitimate. An exceptionally punctilious sense of personal honor or an abnormally fearful temperament may also serve to differentiate an individual actor from the hypothetical reasonable man, yet none of these factors is wholly irrelevant to the ultimate issue of culpability. The proper role of such factors cannot be resolved satisfactorily by abstract definition of what may constitute adequate provocation. The Model Code endorses a formulation that affords sufficient flexibility to differentiate in particular cases between those special aspects of the actor's situation that should be deemed material for purpose of grading and those that should be ignored. There thus will be room for interpreta-

essentially objective [handwritten margin note]

tion of the word "situation," and that is precisely the flexibility desired. * * * In the end, the question is whether the actor's loss of self-control can be understood in terms that arouse sympathy in the ordinary citizen. Section 210.3 faces this issue squarely and leaves the ultimate judgment to the ordinary citizen in the function of a juror assigned to resolve the specific case.

American Law Institute, Model Penal Code and Commentaries, Comment to § 210.3 at 62–63 (1980).

3. In light of Note 2, reconsider the facts in *Commonwealth v. Carr* (Note 3, p. 281). Under the Model Penal Code, was Carr entitled to have his "psychosexual history" considered by the fact-finder? Why, or why not? What if Carr had told the judge that he wished to introduce the evidence in order to show why he had come to believe that homosexuality was evil and, therefore, why he had become outraged when he saw evilness acted out in his presence. Would that change your answer as to the admissibility of the evidence?

4. *Diminished capacity and the Model Penal Code.* Unlike the common law, in which heat-of-passion and diminished capacity (or "diminished responsibility") are separate doctrines, Model Penal Code § 210.3(1)(b) not only is a broader version of the heat-of-passion doctrine, but is intended as well to "allow an inquiry into areas which have been treated as part of the law of diminished responsibility or the insanity defense." American Law Institute, Model Penal Code and Commentaries, Comment to § 210.3 at 54. Look again at *Casassa*: Is this simply a provocation case, or one that focuses at least as much on the defendant's possible impaired mental capacity to conform his conduct to the law?

5. *Does the MPC go too far?* According to the findings of Professor Victoria Nourse, who conducted a comparison of cases applying the "extreme mental or emotional disturbance" provision of the Model Penal Code to cases using common law standards, 26% of MPC claims that reached juries involved what she characterized as "departure" claims, whereas no departure claims reached juries in common law jurisdictions. Victoria Nourse, *Passion's Progress: Modern Law Reform and the Provocation Defense*, 106 Yale L.J. 1331, 1352 (1997). Departure claims "involve a wide range of situations inspiring rage, from divorce to rejection, from protective orders to broken engagements." Id. at 1353. In a majority of these cases, the precipitating factor was that the victim moved furniture out, announced her departure, or filed for divorce. Nourse also discovered that when a defendant in a criminal homicide case alleged infidelity *after the relationship had ended*, he had an 88% chance of reaching the jury in MPC states, whereas the success rate was only 39% in jurisdictions applying traditional standards. Id. at 1362. Overall, Professor Nourse concluded that the MPC results were "illiberal and often perverse." Id. at 1332.

6. *Beyond the M.P.C.* You may have noticed that the three main cases in the provocation section—*Girouard*, *Camplin*, and *Casassa*—involved angry males, and the victims in two of the cases were females. Indeed, it has been written that "voluntary manslaughter has never been a female-friendly doctrine." Emily L. Miller, *(Wo)manslaughter: Voluntary Manslaughter, Gender, and the Model Penal Code*, 50 Emory L.J. 665, 667 (2001). Consequently,

some scholars have called for outright abolition of the heat-of-passion defense. As one writer summarized the abolitionist argument:

> Provocation is a male-centered and male-dominated defense. Although the defense is supposedly founded on compassion for ordinary human infirmity, it is really a legal disguise to (partially) excuse male aggression by treating men "as natural aggressors, and in particular *women's* natural aggressors." Men who are provoked desire to inflict retaliatory suffering on those who have attacked their self-worth. More often than not, the self-worth "attackers" are women. In studies of battered women, for example, violence is prompted by male possessiveness and sexual jealousy; a male's feelings of self-worth require "absolute possession of a woman's sexual fidelity, or her labour, and of (on demand) her presence, love, and attention in general." In reality, therefore, the defense simply reinforces precisely what the law should seek to eradicate, namely, "men's violence against women, and their violence in general."

Joshua Dressler, Why Keep the Provocation Defense?: Some Reflections on a Difficult Subject, 86 Minn. L. Rev. 959, 975–976 (2002).

Do you agree with this criticism of the defense? Are there other reasons why you would abolish the defense? Or, would you retain the defense? If so, do you prefer the narrower common law heat-of-passion doctrine to the "extreme mental or emotional disturbance" provision of the MPC?

Professor Victoria Nourse favors retention of the defense, but in far fewer circumstances than it presently is available. She reasons that "the defendant's claim to our compassion must put him in a position of normative equality vis-à-vis his victim." This only exists, she argues, when society "shares" the defendant's rage, i.e., when the provoker's conduct would result in criminal punishment. Nourse, Note 5, supra, at 1396. Thus, for example, as adultery is no longer a crime in almost all jurisdictions, a defendant who kills because of another person's infidelity would not be entitled to a provocation instruction. He would be guilty of murder in the absence of any other defense claim.

3. MURDER VERSUS MANSLAUGHTER: A LITERARY PROBLEM

WILLA CATHER—O PIONEERS

(1913).

[The following excerpt is from Chapters 6 and 7 of Part IV ("The White Mulberry Tree") of O Pioneers.]

When Emil alighted at the Shabatas' gate, his horse was in a lather. He tied her in the stable and hurried to the house. It was empty. She might be at Mrs. Hiller's or with Alexandra. But anything that reminded him of her would be enough, the orchard, the mulberry tree ... When he reached the orchard the sun was hanging low over the wheatfield. Long fingers of light reached through the apple branches as through a net; the orchard was riddled and shot with gold; light was the reality, the trees were merely interferences that reflected and refracted light. Emil went softly down between the cherry trees toward the wheatfield. When he came to the corner, he stopped short and put his hand over his mouth. Marie was lying on her side under the white mulberry tree, her face half hidden in the grass, her eyes closed, her hands lying limply where they had happened to fall. She had lived a day of her new life of perfect love, and it had left her like this. Her breast rose and fell faintly, as if she were asleep. Emil threw himself down beside her and took her in his arms. The blood came back to her cheeks, her amber eyes opened slowly, and in them Emil saw his own face and the orchard and the sun. "I was dreaming this," she whispered, hiding her face against him, "don't take my dream away!"

When Frank Shabata got home that night, he found Emil's mare in his stable. Such an impertinence amazed him. Like everybody else, Frank had had an exciting day. Since noon he had been drinking too much, and he was in a bad temper. He talked bitterly to himself while he put his own horse away, and as he went up the path and saw that the house was dark he felt an added sense of injury. He approached quietly and listened on the doorstep. Hearing nothing, he opened the kitchen door and went softly from one room to another. Then he went through the house again, upstairs and down, with no better result. He sat down on the bottom step of the box stairway and tried to get his wits together. In that unnatural quiet there was no sound but his own heavy breathing. Suddenly an owl began to hoot out in the fields. Frank lifted his head. An idea flashed into his mind, and his sense of injury and outrage grew. He went into his bedroom and took his murderous 405 Winchester from the closet.

When Frank took up his gun and walked out of the house, he had not the faintest purpose of doing anything with it. He did not believe that he had any real grievance. But it gratified him to feel like a desperate man. He had got into the habit of seeing himself always in desperate straits. His unhappy temperament was like a cage; he could never get out of it; and he felt that other people, his wife in particular, must have put him there. It had never more than dimly occurred to Frank that he made his own unhappiness. Though he took up his gun with dark projects in his mind, he would have been paralyzed with fright had he known that there was the slightest probability of his ever carrying any of them out.

Frank went slowly down to the orchard gate, stopped and stood for a moment lost in thought. He retraced his steps and looked through the barn and the hayloft. Then he went out to the road, where he took the footpath along the outside of the orchard hedge. The hedge was twice as tall as Frank himself, and so dense that one could see through it only by peering closely between the leaves. He could see the empty path a long way in the moonlight. His mind traveled ahead to the stile, which he always thought of as haunted by Emil Bergson. But why had he left his horse?

At the wheatfield corner, where the orchard hedge ended and the path led across the pasture to the Bergsons', Frank stopped. In the warm, breathless night air he heard a murmuring sound, perfectly inarticulate, as low as the sound of water coming from a spring, where there is no fall, and where there are no stones to fret it. Frank strained his ears. It ceased. He held his breath and began to tremble. Resting the butt of his gun on the ground, he parted the mulberry leaves softly with his fingers and peered through the hedge at the dark figures on the grass, in the shadow of the mulberry tree. It seemed to him that they must feel his eyes, that they must hear him breathing. But they did not. Frank, who had always wanted to see things blacker than they were, for once wanted to believe less than he saw. The woman lying in the shadow might so easily be one of the Bergsons' farm-girls. . . . Again the murmur, like water welling out of the ground. This time he heard it more distinctly, and his blood was quicker than his brain. He began to act, just as a man who falls into the fire begins to act. The gun sprang to his shoulder, he sighted mechanically and fired three times without stopping, stopped without knowing why. Either he shut his eyes or he had vertigo. He did not see anything while he was firing. He thought he heard a cry simultaneous with the second report, but he was not sure. He peered again through the hedge, at the two dark figures under the tree. They had fallen a little apart from each other, and were perfectly still—No, not quite; in a white patch of light, where the moon shone through the branches, a man's hand was plucking spasmodically at the grass.

Suddenly the woman stirred and uttered a cry, then another, and another. She was living! She was dragging herself toward the hedge! Frank dropped his gun and ran back along the path, shaking, stumbling, gasping. He had never imagined such horror. The cries followed him. They grew fainter and thicker, as if she were choking. He dropped on his knees beside the hedge and crouched like a rabbit, listening; fainter, fainter; a sound like a whine; again—a moan—another—silence. Frank scrambled to his feet and ran on, groaning and praying. From habit he went toward the house, where he was used to being soothed when he had worked himself into a frenzy, but at the sight of the black, open door, he started back. He knew that he had murdered somebody, that a woman was bleeding and moaning in the orchard, but he had not realized before that it was his wife. The gate stared him in the face. He threw his hands over his head. Which way to turn? He lifted his tormented face and looked at the sky. "Holy Mother of God, not to suffer! She was a good girl—not to suffer!"

Frank had been wont to see himself in dramatic situations; but now, when he stood by the windmill, in the bright space between the barn and the house, facing his own black doorway, he did not see himself at all. He stood like the hare when the dogs are approaching from all sides. And he ran like a hare, back and forth about that moonlit space, before he could make up his mind to go into the dark stable for a horse. The thought of going into a doorway was terrible to him. He caught Emil's horse by the bit and led it out. He could not have buckled a bridle on his own. After two or three attempts, he lifted himself into the saddle and started for Hanover. If he could catch the one o'clock train, he had money enough to get as far as Omaha.

While he was thinking dully of this in some less sensitized part of his brain, his acuter faculties were going over and over the cries he had heard in the orchard. Terror was the only thing that kept him from going back to her, terror that she might still be she, that she might still be suffering. A woman, mutilated and bleeding in his orchard—it was because it was a woman that he was so afraid. It was inconceivable that he should have hurt a woman. He would rather be eaten by wild beasts than see her move on the ground as she had moved in the orchard. Why had she been so careless? She knew he was like a crazy man when he was angry. She had more than once taken that gun away from him and held it, when he was angry with other people. Once it had gone off while they were struggling over it. She was never afraid. But, when she knew him, why hadn't she been more careful? Didn't she have all summer before her to love Emil Bergson in, without taking such chances? Probably she had met the Smirka boy, too, down there in the orchard. He didn't care. She could have met all the men on the Divide there, and welcome, if only she hadn't brought this horror on him.

NOTES AND QUESTIONS

1.   Marie and Emil died. Based on what you have learned so far, of what common law crime is Frank guilty? Of what offense is he guilty under the Model Penal Code?

C.   UNINTENTIONAL KILLINGS: UNJUSTIFIED RISK–TAKING

INTRODUCTION: A ROAD MAP

The last chapter section considered intentional killings. As it turns out, as we saw, an intentional killing may constitute murder or manslaughter (typically, "voluntary manslaughter"). Now we turn to *unintentional* killings that are the result of unjustified risk-taking. As with intentional homicides, there are important murder/manslaughter lines to be drawn here. The common law approach to risk-taking was explained in Pagotto v. State, 127 Md.App. 271, 732 A.2d 920 (1999), as follows:

> At the bottom end of the culpability scale is mere civil liability for a wrongful death, where there may be uncontestable fault and perhaps heavy civil liability but still something less than criminality. * * *

> Higher up the ascending scale of blameworthy negligence are those more "gross deviations" from the standard of care used by an ordinary person where the negligent conduct can reasonably be said

to manifest "a wanton or reckless[e] disregard of human life." That level of fault constitutes involuntary manslaughter of the gross negligence variety. Yet higher still on the culpability ladder are those acts of a life-endangering nature so reckless that they manifest a wanton indifference to human life. That level of blameworthiness constitutes * * * murder of the depraved-heart variety. * * * "[O]ur cases have not drawn a precise line between depraved heart murder and involuntary manslaughter." As an abstract matter, however, we know that there is—somewhere—such a line. There must be or else there is no legally cognizable distinction between murder and manslaughter.

The next two cases focus on judicial and statutory efforts to draw the line between risk-taking that constitutes murder and that which amounts to manslaughter (typically called "involuntary manslaughter"). And, if you glance now at the Model Penal Code, you will see that the Code requires further line-drawing: lawyers and juries often must distinguish between risk-taking that constitutes murder from that which constitutes manslaughter or the non-common law offense of negligent homicide.

We start the process by looking at what the California Penal Code characterizes as "abandoned and malignant heart" murder, which is the equivalent of the "depraved heart" murder concept noted above in *Pagotto*. We do this by way of a Problem: the facts in one case (*Moore*) are set out; the relevant law is described in a second case (*Knoller*); and that leaves it to you to decide whether the defendant in *Moore* is (and should be) guilty of murder.

PEOPLE v. MOORE

California Court of Appeal, Second District, 2010.
187 Cal.App.4th 937, 114 Cal.Rptr.3d 540.

GILBERT, P.J. * * *

FACTS

On November 29, 2006, at about 6:30 p.m., [Hal] Moore was speeding through * * * Pasadena in his Nissan Pathfinder ("Pathfinder"). He was angry because someone had burglarized his apartment while he attended his bachelor party in Mexico. He blamed his fiancée for not being at the apartment to take care of his things.

Moore was driving northbound on Hill Avenue. The speed limit on Hill Avenue is 35 miles per hour. Moore passed Annemarie Phillips at a high rate of speed. Phillips estimated his speed at 80 to 90 miles per hour. In passing Phillips, Moore crossed over into the southbound lane. Moore also passed Yolanda Chan. As he passed, he straddled the double yellow line. Cars heading southbound moved out of his way.

---

e. Notice that the term "reckless" is used here to explain the heightened degree of negligence, commonly characterized as "criminal negligence," a degree of culpability that crosses the line from civil to criminal liability. This is an unfortunate use of words. Modern statutes, following the lead of the Model Penal Code, usually distinguish "criminal negligence" from "recklessness" rather than use the latter term to define the former. The common law was not always so precise.

As Moore approached the intersection of Hill Avenue and Washington Boulevard, he checked his speedometer. He was going about 70 miles per hour. A white Toyota Corolla was crossing the intersection on Washington Boulevard. Moore saw the car, and noticed that the traffic signal for Hill Avenue was red. Moore did not try to stop because he was going too fast.

Moore's Pathfinder struck the Toyota, causing the Toyota to strike a black "BMW" waiting in the left turn lane. A passenger in the Toyota, Bertha Vasquez Arias, was killed. The driver of the BMW, Zaruhi Ovesepyan, suffered a broken arm.

Moore did not get out of his Pathfinder to check on the victims. Instead, he continued to drive north on Hill Avenue.

Pasadena Police Department Officer, Victor Cass, saw Moore's Pathfinder on Allen Avenue. It was traveling about 40 to 45 miles per hour in a 25–mile–per–hour zone. It had smoke or steam pouring from under its front end, and major front end damage. Cass turned on his patrol car's lights and siren, and pursued Moore. Moore continued driving through intersections without stopping at stop signs. Multiple police cars arrived and followed Moore until he turned into the driveway of his residence.

When Moore got out of his car, Cass grabbed his arm. Moore attempted to pull his arm from the officer's grasp. Officers ordered him to stop resisting, but he did not comply. Eventually, three officers subdued him by taking him to the ground.

After waiving his *Miranda* rights (*Miranda v. Arizona* (1966) 384 U.S. 436, 86 S.Ct. 1602, 16 L.Ed.2d 694), Moore agreed to talk with Officer Luis Marquez. Moore said he did not intend to kill anyone, that he did not experience any mechanical failure, and that he was simply going too fast. Marquez asked if he knew anyone was dead after the crash. Moore replied, "Yeah man. I cut them in half, dude. It's a wonder I survived." Marquez asked about leaving the scene of the accident. Moore replied, "Leaving the scene wasn't really the problem. * * * [T]hey were dead." When asked where he was going after the accident, Moore said he was "going to clean up, probably have a beer, sit down, sit at home and watch television." Asked why he resisted arrest, Moore replied, "I don't know. I just went wacky from Tobacky."

[Moore was charged with second-degree murder (Cal. Pen. Code, §§ 187 and 189, as set out on pages 238–239 of the casebook) and other criminal offenses, including resisting a police officer, as well as the Vehicle Code offenses of leaving the scene of an accident, evading a peace officer, and reckless driving with bodily injury.]

PEOPLE v. KNOLLER

Supreme Court of California, 2007.
41 Cal.4th 139, 59 Cal.Rptr.3d 157, 158 P.3d 731.

KENNARD, J. * * *

II. THE ELEMENTS OF IMPLIED MALICE

Murder is the unlawful killing of a human being, or a fetus, with malice aforethought. (§ 187, subd. (a).) Malice may be express or implied. (§ 188.) At issue here is the definition of "implied malice."

* * * Second degree murder is the unlawful killing of a human being with malice aforethought but without the additional elements, such as willfulness, premeditation, and deliberation, that would support a conviction of first degree murder. Section 188 provides: "[M]alice may be either express or implied. It is express when there is manifested a deliberate intention to take away the life of a fellow creature. It is implied, when no considerable provocation appears, or when the circumstances attending the killing show an abandoned and malignant heart."

The statutory definition of implied malice, a killing by one with an "abandoned and malignant heart" (§ 188), is far from clear in its meaning. Indeed, an instruction in the statutory language could be misleading, for it "could lead the jury to equate the malignant heart with an evil disposition or a despicable character" instead of focusing on a defendant's awareness of the risk created by his or her behavior. "Two lines of decisions developed, reflecting judicial attempts 'to translate this amorphous anatomical characterization of implied malice into a tangible standard a jury can apply.'" Under both lines of decisions, implied malice requires a defendant's awareness of the risk of death to another.

The earlier of these two lines of decisions, * * * originated in * * * *People v. Thomas* (1953) 41 Cal.2d 470, 480, 261 P.2d 1, which stated that malice is implied when "the defendant for a base, antisocial motive and with wanton disregard for human life, does an act that involves a high degree of probability that it will result in death." * * * The later line dates from this court's 1966 decision in *People v. Phillips,* [64 Cal.2d 574, 51 Cal.Rptr. 225, 414 P.2d 353]: Malice is implied when the killing is proximately caused by " 'an act, the natural consequences of which are dangerous to life, which act was deliberately performed by a person who knows that his conduct endangers the life of another and who acts with conscious disregard for life.' " * * *

In *People v. Watson* (1981) 30 Cal.3d 290, 300, 179 Cal.Rptr. 43, 637 P.2d 279, we held that these two definitions of implied malice in essence articulated the same standard. Concerned, however, that juries might have difficulty understanding the *Thomas* test's concept of "wanton disregard for human life," we later emphasized that the "better practice in the future is to charge juries solely in the straightforward language of the conscious disregard for human life definition of implied malice," the definition articulated in the *Phillips* test. * * *

NOTES AND QUESTIONS

1. Based on the law set out in *Knoller*, would you convict Moore of second-degree murder if you were a juror? Be prepared to defend your

position. Assuming arguendo that Moore was *not* guilty of second-degree murder, i.e., that his conduct did not demonstrate that he possessed an "abandoned and malignant heart," of what homicide offense *would* he be guilty under California law? (Look at pp. 238–240, supra.) Look also at the quote from *Pagotto*, p. 294, that explains the common law in this regard.

2. In *Moore*, suppose the homicide had occurred exactly as it did, but that Moore's response thereafter had been very different—he immediately stopped his vehicle and called 911 on his cell phone, rushed over to the car to see if he could help and only then realized that the victim was dead, and then he remained at the scene to explain, remorsefully, his conduct to the police. With these different facts, would your verdict be different?

3. Four years before these events, Moore was convicted of driving under the influence of alcohol. Over the defendant's objection, the prosecutor sought to introduce evidence of the prior conviction. In your view, is this evidence relevant in determining whether Moore was guilty of second-degree murder?

4. *What makes a heart "depraved" or "abandoned and malignant"?* Many courts, like California, have struggled to translate the "amorphous anatomical characterization of implied malice" into a standard that adequately explains to juries the point at which hazardous conduct resulting in death—more precisely, the state of mind linked to the risky conduct—constitutes murder. The Utah Supreme Court has described the state of mind as "an utter callousness toward the value of human life and a complete and total indifference as to whether one's conduct will create the requisite risk of death * * * of another." State v. Standiford, 769 P.2d 254 (Utah 1988). An Alabama court stated that a person guilty of depraved indifference is one "bent on mischief" who "act[s] with a 'don't give a damn attitude,' in total disregard of the public safety." King v. State, 505 So.2d 403 (Ala.Cr.App.1987). New York's highest court, in People v. Suarez, 6 N.Y.3d 202, 811 N.Y.S.2d 267, 844 N.E.2d 721 (2005), stated that

> depraved indifference is best understood as an utter disregard for the value of human life—a willingness to act not because one intends harm, but because one simply doesn't care whether grievous harm results or not. Reflecting wickedness, evil or inhumanity, as manifested by brutal, heinous and despicable acts, depraved indifference is embodied in conduct that is "so wanton, so deficient in a moral sense of concern, so devoid of regard of the life or lives of others, and so blameworthy," as to render the actor as culpable as one whose conscious objective is to kill. Quintessential examples are firing into a crowd; * * * opening the lion's cage at the zoo; placing a time bomb in a public place [without the intent to kill]; poisoning a well from which people are accustomed to draw water; * * * and dropping stones from an overpass onto a busy highway.

Do you find the *Standiford*, *King*, or *Suarez* tests preferable to the *Thomas* or *Phillips* tests set out in *Knoller?* Why, or why not?

5. All human conduct involves risk-taking, so how risky must a person's conduct be in order to display an "abandoned and malignant heart"? What does *Knoller* say about this?

(justifiable) surgery vs.

Russian Roulette (not justifiable)

Suppose a doctor, with appropriate consent, performs very dangerous experimental surgery (let's say the chances of death are 75%) in order to save the life of her critically ill patient. If the patient dies during surgery, has the surgeon acted with an abandoned and malignant heart? If not, why not?

Compare the odds of death in that case to a person who, playing a game commonly called "Russian Roulette," puts a single bullet in a six-cylinder gun, spins the cylinder, and fires once at another person. Has *he* acted with a malignant heart? Or, what about a person who blindfolds herself and fires a loaded gun into an occupied room where, let's say, the chances of killing someone are five percent? If that five percent chance turns into reality, should this constitute murder? If so, what does this tell us about the answer to the question "how risky is too risky"?

6. Now, turn to the Model Penal Code. Of what homicide offense would Moore be guilty? To answer, look at the Code's definitions of murder (§ 210.2) and manslaughter (§ 210.3). Notice that the MPC does not describe murder in the common law's colorful "depraved heart" language, but rather with the colorless (and bloodless?) term of "recklessness," which in turn is defined in Section 2.02 of the Code. Do you prefer the Code's approach?

How would the Code resolve the two hypotheticals in Note 5?

Under the Model Code, how does the recklessness that constitutes murder differ from that of manslaughter? The Commentary explains:

> Ordinary recklessness * * * is made sufficient for a conviction of manslaughter under Section 210.3(1)(a). In a prosecution for murder, however, the Code calls for the further judgment whether the actor's conscious disregard of the risk, under the circumstances, manifests extreme indifference to the value of human life. * * * Whether recklessness is so extreme that it demonstrates [such] indifference is not a question, it is submitted, that can be further clarified. It must be left directly to the trier of fact under instructions which make it clear that recklessness that can fairly be assimilated to purpose or knowledge should be treated as murder and that less extreme recklessness should be punished as manslaughter.

implied malice

American Law Institute, Model Penal Code and Commentaries, Comment to § 210.2 at 21–22 (1980). Is this helpful?

7. *Intent to cause grievous bodily injury.* At common law, a person acts with malice aforethought—and, therefore, is guilty of murder—if, with the intent to cause grievous (or "serious") bodily injury, she accidentally kills another. Of what offense is such a person guilty under the Model Penal Code? The Commentary to the Code explains the drafters' views on this form of criminal homicide:

> Section 210.2 accords no special significance to an intent to cause grievous bodily harm, though such a purpose established malice aforethought at common law and thus sufficed for murder or, where murder was divided into degrees, for murder in the second degree under the usual formulation. The deletion of intent to injure as an independently sufficient culpability for murder rests on the judgment that it is preferable to handle such cases under the standards of extreme recklessness and

recklessness contained in Sections 210.2(1)(b) and 210.3(1)(a). That the actor intended to cause injury of a particular nature or gravity is, of course, a relevant consideration in determining whether he acted with "extreme indifference to the value of human life" under Section 210.2(1)(b) or "recklessly" with respect to death of another under Section 210.3(1). Most traditional illustrations of murder based on intent to injure will fall within the recklessness category as defined in the Model Code. In the rare case of purposeful infliction of serious injury not involving recklessness with respect to death, the actor should be prosecuted for some version of aggravated assault or, perhaps, for negligent homicide.

American Law Institute, Model Penal Code and Commentaries, Comment to § 210.2 at 28–29 (1980).

STATE v. WILLIAMS

Court of Appeals of Washington, 1971.
4 Wash.App. 908, 484 P.2d 1167.

HOROWITZ, CHIEF JUDGE.

Defendants, husband and wife, were charged * * * with the crime of manslaughter for negligently failing to supply their 17–month child with necessary medical attention, as a result of which he died on September 12, 1968. Upon entry of findings, conclusions and judgment of guilty, sentences were imposed * * *. Defendants appeal.

The defendant husband, Walter Williams, is a 24–year old full-blooded Sheshont Indian with a sixth-grade education. His sole occupation is that of laborer. The defendant wife, Bernice Williams, is a 20–year–old part Indian with an 11th grade education. At the time of the marriage, the wife had two children, the younger of whom was a 14–month son. Both parents worked and the children were cared for by the 85–year–old mother of the defendant husband. The defendant husband assumed parental responsibility with the defendant wife to provide clothing, care and medical attention for the child. Both defendants possessed a great deal of love and affection for the defendant wife's young son.

The court expressly found:

That both defendants were aware that William Joseph Tabafunda was ill during the period September 1, 1968 to September 12, 1968. The defendants were ignorant. They did not realize how sick the baby was. They thought that the baby had a toothache and no layman regards a toothache as dangerous to life. They loved the baby and gave it aspirin in hopes of improving its condition. They did not take the baby to a doctor because of fear that the Welfare Department would take the baby away from them. They knew that medical help was available because of previous experience. They had no excuse that the law will recognize for not taking the baby to a doctor.

The defendants Walter L. Williams and Bernice J. Williams were negligent in not seeking medical attention for William Joseph Tabafunda.

That as a proximate result of this negligence, William Joseph Tabafunda died.

From these and other findings, the court concluded that the defendants were each guilty of the crime of manslaughter as charged.

Defendants * * * contend that the findings do not support the conclusions that the defendants are guilty of manslaughter as charged. * * *

Parental duty to provide medical care for a dependent minor child was recognized at common law and characterized as a natural duty. * * * The existence of the duty also is assumed * * * in statutes that provide special criminal and civil sanctions for the performance of that duty. * * * On the question of the quality or seriousness of breach of the duty, at common law, in the case of involuntary manslaughter, the breach had to amount to more than mere ordinary or simple negligence—gross negligence was essential. In Washington, however, RCW 9.48.150[3] supersede[s] involuntary manslaughter as [it was] defined at common law. Under [this] statute[] the crime is deemed committed even though the death of the victim is the proximate result of only simple or ordinary negligence.

Simple Negligence enough

The concept of simple or ordinary negligence describes a failure to exercise the "ordinary caution" necessary to make out the defense of excusable homicide. RCW 9.48.150. Ordinary caution is the kind of caution that a man of reasonable prudence would exercise under the same or similar conditions. If, therefore, the conduct of a defendant, regardless of his ignorance, good intentions and good faith, fails to measure up to the conduct required of a man of reasonable prudence, he is guilty of ordinary negligence because of his failure to use "ordinary caution." If such negligence proximately causes the death of the victim, the defendant, as pointed out above, is guilty of statutory manslaughter. * * *

The * * * issue of proximate cause requires consideration of the question of when the duty to furnish medical care became activated. If the duty to furnish such care was not activated until after it was too late to save the life of the child, failure to furnish medical care could not be said to have proximately caused the child's death. Timeliness in the furnishing of medical care also must be considered in terms of "ordinary caution." The law does not mandatorily require that a doctor be called for a child at the first sign of any indisposition or illness. The indisposition or illness may appear to be of a minor or very temporary kind, such as a toothache or cold. If one in the exercise of ordinary caution fails to recognize that his child's symptoms require medical attention, it cannot be said that the failure to obtain such medical attention is a breach of the duty owed. * * *

---

3. RCW 9.48.150 provides:

"Homicide is excusable when committed by accident or misfortune in doing any lawful act by lawful means, with ordinary caution and without any unlawful intent."

It remains to apply the law discussed to the facts of the instant case.
* * *

Dr. Gale Wilson, the autopsy surgeon and chief pathologist for the King County Coroner, testified that the child died because an abscessed tooth had been allowed to develop into an infection of the mouth and cheeks, eventually becoming gangrenous. This condition, accompanied by the child's inability to eat, brought about malnutrition, lowering the child's resistance and eventually producing pneumonia, causing the death. Dr. Wilson testified that in his opinion the infection had lasted for approximately 2 weeks, and that the odor generally associated with gangrene would have been present for approximately 10 days before death. He also expressed the opinion that had medical care been first obtained in the last week before the baby's death, such care would have been obtained too late to have saved the baby's life. Accordingly, the baby's apparent condition between September 1 and September 5, 1968 became the critical period for the purpose of determining whether in the exercise of ordinary caution defendants should have provided medical care for the minor child.

The testimony concerning the child's apparent condition during the critical period is not crystal clear, but is sufficient to warrant the following statement of the matter. The defendant husband testified that he noticed the baby was sick about 2 weeks before the baby died. The defendant wife testified that she noticed the baby was ill about a week and a half or 2 weeks before the baby died. The evidence showed that in the critical period the baby was fussy; that he could not keep his food down; and that a cheek started swelling up. The swelling went up and down, but did not disappear. In that same period, the cheek turned "a bluish color like." The defendants, not realizing that the baby was as ill as it was or that the baby was in danger of dying, attempted to provide some relief to the baby by giving the baby aspirin during the critical period and continued to do so until the night before the baby died. The defendants thought the swelling would go down and were waiting for it to do so; and defendant husband testified, that from what he had heard, neither doctors nor dentists pull out a tooth "when it's all swollen up like that." There was an additional explanation for not calling a doctor given by each defendant. Defendant husband testified that "the way the cheek looked, * * * and that stuff on his hair, they would think we were neglecting him and take him away from us and not give him back." Defendant wife testified that the defendants were "waiting for the swelling to go down," and also that they were afraid to take the child to a doctor for fear that the doctor would report them to the welfare department, who, in turn, would take the child away. "It's just that I was so scared of losing him." They testified that they had heard that the defendant husband's cousin lost a child that way. The evidence showed that the defendants did not understand the significance or seriousness of the baby's symptoms. However, there is no evidence that the defendants were physically or financially unable to obtain a doctor, or that they did not know an available doctor, or that the symptoms did not continue to be a matter of concern during the critical period. Indeed, the evidence shows that in April 1968 defendant husband had taken the child to a doctor for medical attention.

In our opinion, there is sufficient evidence from which the court could find, as it necessarily did, that applying the standard of ordinary caution, * * * defendants were sufficiently put on notice concerning the symptoms of the baby's illness and lack of improvement in the baby's apparent condition in the period from September 1 to September 5, 1968 to have required them to have obtained medical care for the child. The failure so to do in this case is ordinary or simple negligence, and such negligence is sufficient to support a conviction of statutory manslaughter.

The judgment is affirmed.

NOTES AND QUESTIONS

1. This case involves linked issues of causation and *mens rea*. Can you see the linkage?

2. Do you believe the Williamses were guilty of negligence? Why, or why not? Does (and should) it matter that the defendants had little education? That they are Native Americans? That they were subject to a maximum prison sentence of twenty years?

3. Assuming that the Williamses were guilty of ordinary negligence in the death of their child, of what form of criminal homicide would they be guilty under the Model Penal Code?

4. *"Criminal" versus "civil" negligence.* Criminal homicide convictions on the basis of ordinary negligence are nearly non-existent today. Indeed, Washington redrafted its manslaughter statutes in 1975 to require a heightened level of negligence ("criminal negligence") to be convicted of manslaughter in the second degree, the least serious form of manslaughter in the state. Rev. Code Wash. § 9A.32.070. Criminal negligence "requires the jury to find negligence so gross as to merit not just damages but also punishment." State v. Hazelwood, 946 P.2d 875 (Alaska 1997).

5. "Negligence" is considered an "objective" form of fault because liability is based on the actor's failure to live up to the external—objective—standard of care of the "reasonable person." The harmdoer is guilty although—indeed, because—she did not subjectively appreciate the dangerousness of her conduct, assuming that a reasonable person in her situation would have foreseen the risk. Nonetheless, as Holmes has explained, "negligence" does contain one subjective component:

> The test of foresight is not what this very criminal foresaw, but what a man of reasonable prudence would have foreseen. [¶] On the other hand, there must be actual present knowledge of the present facts which make an act dangerous. The act is not enough by itself. * * *
>
> * * * It is enough that such circumstances were actually known as would have led a man of common understanding to infer from them the rest of the group making up the present state of things. For instance, if a workman on a house-top at mid-day knows that the space below him is a

street in a great city, he knows facts from which a man of common understanding would infer that there were people passing below. He is therefore bound to draw that inference, or, in other words, is chargeable with knowledge of that fact also, whether he draws the inference or not. If, then, he throws down a heavy beam into the street, he does an act which a person of ordinary prudence would foresee is likely to cause death, or grievous bodily harm, and he is dealt with as if he foresaw it, whether he does so in fact or not.

Oliver Wendell Holmes, The Common Law 53–55 (1881).

Look at the Model Penal Code definition of negligence in Section 2.02(2)(d). Does it contain a subjective component, as well?

6. *"Negligence": the debate. Should* persons be punished for negligently causing harm to others, even if that negligence is substantial? The drafters of the Model Penal Code wrestled with this issue.

It has been urged that inadvertent negligence is not a sufficient basis for criminal conviction, both on the utilitarian ground that threatened sanctions cannot influence the inadvertent actor and on the moral ground that criminal punishment should be reserved for cases involving conscious fault. The utilitarian argument is that the inadvertent actor by definition does not perceive the risks of his conduct, and thus cannot be deterred from risk creation. The moral argument is that the legitimacy of criminal condemnation is premised upon personal accountability of the sort that is usually and properly measured by an estimate of the actor's willingness consciously to violate clearly established societal norms. Those who hold this view argue that the actor who does not perceive the risks associated with his conduct presents a moral situation different in kind from that of the actor who knows exactly what he is doing and what risks he is running and who nevertheless makes a conscious choice condemned by the penal law.

American Law Institute, Model Penal Code and Commentaries, Comment to § 210.4 at 86 (1980).

Is the utilitarian argument against punishment for negligence persuasive? The drafters of the Code ultimately did not think so:

When people have knowledge that conviction and sentence, not to speak of punishment, may follow conduct that inadvertently creates improper risk, they are supplied with an additional motive to take care before acting, to use their faculties and draw on their experience in gauging the potentialities of completed conduct. To some extent, at least, this motive may promote awareness and thus be effective as a measure of control.

Id., Comment to § 2.02 at 243 (1985).

Are you persuaded? What if a person, as a result of physical or mental disability, lacks the capacity to act safely? Even if there are utilitarian justifications for punishment of such a person, is it morally just to hold a person to a standard of care he cannot satisfy?

Capacity issues aside, *is* a negligent party morally culpable and, therefore, deserving of censure? No, according to two legal scholars:

We are not morally culpable for taking risks of which we are unaware. At any point in time we are failing to notice a great many things, we have forgotten a great many things, and we are misinformed or uninformed about many things. An injunction to notice, remember, and be fully informed about anything that bears on risks to others is an injunction no human being can comply with, so violating this injunction reflects no moral defect. Even those most concerned with the well-being of others will violate this injunction constantly.

Larry Alexander & Kimberly Kessler Ferzan, Crime and Culpability 71 (2009).

Do you agree, or is there a way for a person to defend punishment of a negligent wrongdoer on "just desert" grounds? Assume a drunk driver causes an accident that results in the death of another person. You ask the driver, "what in the world were you thinking when you got into your car in an intoxicated condition?" He responds "I just didn't think." Would it be appropriate to suggest that one who "just didn't think" demonstrates an insensitivity to the protected interests of others and, therefore, deserves punishment? Or, consider this effort to defend retributive-based punishment for a negligently-caused death:

> An actor who creates a risk of causing death but who was unaware of that risk is fairly subject to retributive punishment if he was either *nonwillfully ignorant* or *self-deceived* with respect to the existence of the risk, and if such ignorance or self-deception was due to the causal influence of a desire he should have controlled. The culpability of such an actor does not consist in any choice to do wrong, but rather in the culpable failure to exercise *doxastic self-control*, i.e., control over desires that influence the formation and awareness of one's beliefs. An actor who is nonwillfully ignorant allows desire to preclude him from forming the belief that he is imposing a risk of death when the evidence available to him supports the formation of that belief, while an actor who is self-deceived forms that belief but allows desire to prevent him from becoming aware of it. In either case the actor could and should have controlled the wayward desire, thereby allowing the relevant belief to form and surface into awareness.

Stephen P. Garvey, *What's Wrong with Involuntary Manslaughter?*, 85 Tex. L. Rev. 333, 337–338 (2006). Thus, for example, if a drunk driver *really* failed to appreciate the risk of driving in an intoxicated condition, his ignorance or self-deception in that regard was the result of an inexcusable failure to control a "wayward desire" to drink before driving, which "preclude[d] him from forming the belief that he [was] imposing a risk of death" by driving in that condition.

Jerome Hall insists, however, that although *blame* may be appropriate in some cases of negligence, *punishment* for it is not:

> [A]lthough many [negligent] persons are frequently blamed, this does not warrant a leap from that commonplace fact to the conclusion that punishment for negligence is justified. "Blame" is a very wide notion and, like praise, it permeates all of daily life. Important differences exist between raising an eyebrow and putting a man in jail, between blame for not developing one's potentialities and blame for voluntarily harming a

human being, between blame that can be rejected or that leaves the censured person free to do as he pleases and the blame signified in the inexorable imposition of a major legal privation, and, finally, between the blame expressed in a judgment for damages and the blame implied in punishing a criminal.

Jerome Hall, *Negligent Behavior Should Be Excluded From Penal Liability,* 63 Colum.L.Rev. 632, 641 (1963).

7.   Sam and Tiffany are rich, well-educated social climbers. One weekend they become so preoccupied planning the "party of the decade" that they completely fail to notice the obvious fact that their infant child is growing mortally ill upstairs. See Larry Alexander, *Reconsidering the Relationship Among Voluntary Acts, Strict Liability, and Negligence in Criminal Law,* 7 Soc.Phil. & Policy (Spring 1990) at 84, 100. Are these parents more deserving of punishment than the Williamses? If so, why?

8.   *Prosecutions for negligence and scapegoating.* Is it possible that in some circumstances, especially when extraordinary or shocking harm occurs— e.g., many people die in plane crash or, as in *Williams,* a young, innocent child dies a slow death due to lack of medical attention—that there is a public need to affix blame and criminal responsibility when no blame is deserved (after all, harm *can* occur non-negligently), or to scapegoat by affixing blame on a few when there is lots of blame to go around?

For example, in 1942, approximately 500 patrons of a Boston nightclub were burned to death fleeing a fire in a popular Boston nightclub. See Commonwealth v. Welansky, 316 Mass. 383, 55 N.E.2d 902 (1944). An academic study of the public reaction to the terrible event is noteworthy:

> Frustrations and fears aroused by the * * * holocaust created a desperate desire on the part of the people of Boston to fix the blame and punish those responsible for the catastrophe. There resulted * * * accusations, if not unwarranted, at least out of proportion to the possible guilt of the accused. The scapegoating was most intense against the owners of the [nightclub] and against the public officials responsible for the safety of Boston's citizens. Officials and owners were especially satisfying scapegoats since the tragedy permitted the releasing of much latent aggression. It is when such latent hostility is present that scapegoating is most dangerous.

Helene R. Veltfort & George E. Lee, *The Cocoanut Grove Fire: A Study in Scapegoating,* 38 J. Abnormal & Soc. Psych. 138, 154 (No. 2 clinical supp. 1943).

9.   In Walker v. Superior Court, 47 Cal.3d 112, 253 Cal.Rptr. 1, 763 P.2d 852 (1988), *V, W*'s four-year-old daughter, experienced flu-like symptoms. Four days later, she complained of a stiff neck. Consistent with the tenets of *W*'s Christian Science faith, *W* treated *V*'s illness exclusively by prayer, even as *V* lost weight and became disoriented. After 17 days without medical treatment, *V* died of acute meningitis. Of what form of criminal homicide, if any, is *W* guilty?

In determining *W*'s culpability, should the jury evaluate her behavior from the perspective of a reasonable Christian Scientist? How would the

Model Penal Code answer this question? See Section 2.02(2)(d), and weigh this explanation of it:

> The standard for ultimate judgment invites consideration of the "care that a reasonable person would observe in the actor's situation." There is an inevitable ambiguity in "situation." If the actor were blind or if he had just suffered a blow or experienced a heart attack, these would certainly be facts to be considered in a judgment involving criminal liability, as they would be under traditional law. But the heredity, intelligence or temperament of the actor would not be held material in judging negligence, and could not be without depriving the criterion of all its objectivity. The Code is not intended to displace discriminations of this kind, but rather to leave the issue to the courts.[27]

American Law Institute, Model Penal Code and Commentaries, Comment to § 2.02 at 242 (1985).

10. *Problem.* On an exceedingly cold day in Detroit, Leroy Lyons lit a torch made up of rolled newspapers in order to thaw frozen water pipes beneath his kitchen floor. Shortly thereafter, two friends showed up and asked Lyons to repay them for money they had furnished him so that he could buy illegal drugs for personal use. While an unseen fire smoldered under the kitchen floor, Lyons and his wife left the house for an hour in order to obtain the money to pay off his debt. Their seven young children remained alone in the house. While the parents were away, the house was enveloped in flames. All of the children were killed when smoke trapped them in one room. Although there was a window in that room, it had bars on it to prevent burglaries. Jim Schaefer, Jeffrey S. Ghannam & Janet Wilson, *Father Started Tragic Blaze,* Detroit Free Press, Feb. 19, 1993, at A1.

If you were a prosecutor, what homicide charges would you bring against the parents? Apply Michigan law, p. 242 supra. What about under the Model Penal Code?

11. *And then there is this case.* While Maine dominatrix Barbara Asher was providing her services to a man strapped to a replica of a medieval torture device in her "chambers," the customer had a heart attack. She failed to do anything to help him for five minutes as he "flailed and died strapped to the rack." Ms. Asher then called her boyfriend who chopped up the body and dumped the remains behind a restaurant. She was prosecuted for involuntary manslaughter (and dismemberment of a corpse) . . . and acquitted—despite an appeal by the prosecutor, in closing arguments, wearing a leather bondage mask to make his points. Go figure. *Madam Beats Rap, Zip It, Prosecutor Told,* Herald Sun, Feb. 1, 2006, at 32.

---

27. There is a similar problem with recklessness. Though recklessness requires defendant's conscious disregard of risk, * * * Section 2.02(2)(c) * * * requires the same discriminations demanded by the standard of negligence.

D. UNINTENTIONAL KILLINGS: UNLAWFUL CONDUCT

1. THE FELONY–MURDER RULE

a. The Doctrine: In General

The felony-murder rule cannot help but fascinate. It has deep but terribly obscure roots. It is one of four traditional branches on the tree of murder, yet clearly the odd one out. It permits severe punishment for the most heinous of offenses in some cases that can appropriately be described as accidents. In its classic form, the operation of the rule follows a compellingly simply, almost mathematical, logic: a felony + a killing = a murder. Abandoned by its motherland [in England], the felony-murder rule, like so many outcasts, has found a niche in America.[f]

AMERICAN LAW INSTITUTE, MODEL PENAL CODE AND COMMENTARIES, COMMENT TO § 210.2

(1980), 30–32

The classic formulation of the felony-murder doctrine declares that one is guilty of murder if a death results from conduct during the commission or attempted commission of any felony. Some courts have made no effort to qualify the application of this doctrine, and a number of earlier English writers also articulated an unqualified rule. At the time the Model Code was drafted, a number of American legislatures, moreover, perpetuated the original statement of the rule by statute. As thus conceived, the rule operated to impose liability for murder based on the culpability required for the underlying felony without separate proof of any culpability with regard to the death. The homicide, as distinct from the underlying felony, was thus an offense of strict liability. This rule may have made sense under the conception of *mens rea* as something approaching a general criminal disposition rather than as a specific attitude of the defendant towards each element of a specific offense. Furthermore, it was hard to claim that the doctrine worked injustice in an age that recognized only a few felonies and that punished each as a capital offense.[74]

In modern times, however, legislatures have created a wide range of statutory felonies. Many of these crimes concern relatively minor misconduct not inherently dangerous to life and carry maximum penalties far less severe than those authorized for murder. Application of the ancient rigor of the felony-murder rule to such crimes will yield startling results.

---

f. James J. Tomkovicz, *The Endurance of the Felony–Murder Rule: A Study of the Forces that Shape Our Criminal Law*, 51 Wash. & Lee L. Rev. 1429, 1429–30 (1994).

74. At common law all felonies were punishable by death. In a felony-murder situation, it made little difference whether the actor was convicted of murder or of the underlying felony because the sanction was the same. The primary use of the felony-murder rule at common law therefore was to deal with a homicide that occurred in furtherance of an attempted felony that failed. Since attempts were punished as misdemeanors, * * * the use of the felony-murder rule allowed the courts to punish the actor in the same manner as if his attempt had succeeded. Thus, a conviction for attempted robbery was a misdemeanor, but a homicide committed in the attempt was murder and punishable by death.

For example, a seller of liquor in violation of a statutory felony becomes a murderer if his purchaser falls asleep on the way home and dies of exposure. And a person who communicates disease during felonious sexual intercourse is guilty of murder if his partner subsequently dies of the infection.

The prospect of such consequences has led to a demand for limitations on the felony-murder rule.

PEOPLE v. FULLER

California Court of Appeal, Fifth District, 1978.
86 Cal.App.3d 618, 150 Cal.Rptr. 515.

FRANSON, ACTING PRESIDING JUSTICE. * * *

This appeal challenges the California felony-murder rule as it applies to an unintentionally caused death during a high speed automobile chase following the commission of a nonviolent, daylight burglary of an unattended motor vehicle. Solely by force of precedent we hold that the felony-murder rule applies and respondents can be prosecuted for first degree murder. * * *

The pertinent facts are as follows: On Sunday, February 20, 1977, at about 8:30 a.m., uniformed Cadet Police Officer Guy Ballesteroz was on routine patrol in his vehicle * * *. As the officer approached the Fresno Dodge car lot, he saw an older model Plymouth parked in front of the lot. He also saw respondents rolling two tires apiece toward the Plymouth. His suspicions aroused, the officer radioed the dispatcher and requested that a police unit be sent.

* * * Ballesteroz made a U-turn and headed northbound on Blackstone. The respondents got into the Plymouth and drove away "really fast." Thereafter, a high speed chase ensued which eventually resulted in respondents' car running a red light * * * and striking another automobile which had entered the intersection. The driver of the other automobile was killed. Respondents were arrested at the scene. The chase from the car lot covered some seven miles and lasted approximately 10 to 12 minutes. * * *

Later investigation revealed that four locked Dodge vans at the car lot had been forcibly entered and the spare tires removed. Fingerprints from both of the respondents were found on the jack stands in some of the vans.

Penal Code section 189 provides, in pertinent part: "All murder * * * which is committed *in the perpetration of,* or attempt to perpetrate, arson, rape, robbery, *burglary,* mayhem, or [lewd acts with a minor], is murder of the first degree; * * *." (Emphasis added.) This statute imposes strict liability for deaths committed in the course of one of the enumerated felonies whether the killing was caused intentionally, negligently, or merely accidentally. * * *

Burglary falls expressly within the purview of California's first degree felony-murder rule. Any burglary within Penal Code section 459[g] is sufficient to invoke the rule.

---

g. "Every person who enters any house, room, apartment, tenement, shop, warehouse, store, mill, barn, stable, outhouse, or other building, tent, vessel, railroad car, trailer coach, * * * [or]

* * * Thus, the trial court erred in striking the murder count premised upon the felony-murder rule.

We deem it appropriate, however, to make a few observations concerning the irrationality of applying the felony-murder rule in the present case. * * *

If we were writing on a clean slate, we would hold that respondents should not be prosecuted for felony murder since * * * an automobile burglary is not dangerous to human life. The present case demonstrates why this is so. Respondents committed the burglary on vans parked in a dealer's lot on a Sunday morning. There were no people inside the vans or on the lot at the time. The respondents were not armed and presumably had no expectation of using violence during the burglary.

* * * [Under the felony-murder statute,] if a merchant in pursuit of a fleeing shoplifter is killed accidentally (by falling and striking his head on the curb or being hit by a passing automobile), the thief would be guilty of first degree felony murder assuming the requisite intent to steal at the time of the entry into the store. Such a harsh result destroys the symmetry of the law by equating an accidental killing resulting from a petty theft with a premeditated murder. In no sense can it be said that such a result furthers the ostensible purpose of the felony-murder rule which is to deter those engaged in felonies from killing negligently or accidentally. * * *

Notes and Questions

1. If the doors of the vans from which the tires were stolen had been shut but unlocked, would the defendants have been guilty of first-degree murder?

2. Could the court have avoided the outcome that it described as irrational? For example, could it have interpreted the statutory phrase "in the perpetration of" in a manner that would have taken this case outside the scope of the felony-murder rule? (See p. 331 infra.)

3. Another example of the felony-murder rule is People v. Stamp, 2 Cal.App.3d 203, 82 Cal.Rptr. 598 (1969): S and his armed accomplices entered an office, took cash, and ordered the occupants to lie on the floor for five minutes while they fled. One of the occupants, suffering from advanced heart disease, had a fright-induced lethal heart attack twenty minutes later. S and his cohorts were convicted of first-degree felony murder.

b. The Policy Debate

NELSON E. ROTH & SCOTT E. SUNDBY—THE FELONY–MURDER RULE: A DOCTRINE AT CONSTITUTIONAL CROSSROADS

70 Cornell Law Review 446 (1985), 446–55, 457–59

Few legal doctrines have been as maligned and yet have shown as great a resiliency as the felony-murder rule. Criticism of the rule consti-

---

vehicle * * * when the doors of such vehicles are locked, * * * with the intent to commit larceny or any felony is guilty of burglary."

tutes a lexicon of everything that scholars and jurists can find wrong with a legal doctrine: it has been described as "astonishing" and "monstrous," an unsupportable "legal fiction," "an unsightly wart on the skin of the criminal law," and as an "anachronistic remnant" that has " 'no logical or practical basis for existence in modern law.' "Perhaps the most that can be said for the rule is that it provides commentators with an extreme example that makes it easy to illustrate the injustice of various legal propositions.

Despite the widespread criticism, the felony-murder rule persists in the vast majority of states. Most states have attempted to limit the rule's potential harshness either by limiting the scope of its operation or by providing affirmative defenses. Such patchwork attempts to mitigate the rule's harshness, however, have been legitimately criticized because "they do not resolve [the rule's] essential illogic." * * * The United States thus remains virtually the only western country still recognizing a rule which makes it possible "that the most serious sanctions known to law might be imposed for accidental homicide."[12] * * *

I

THE CONCEPTUAL BASIS OF THE FELONY-MURDER RULE

A.   *The Rule's Historical Development* * * *

The purpose of the felony-murder rule at common law is * * * vague. It is frequently argued that the rule's purpose was not fully articulated because all felonies at common law were punished by death and, therefore, the rule had little practical impact. * * *

Whatever the felony-murder rule's justification at common law, courts have attempted to provide the rule with a contemporary rationale. These post hoc rationalizations fall into four general categories: deterrence, transferred intent, retribution, and general culpability.

B.   *Deterrence*

The deterrence rationale consists of two different strains. The first approach views the felony-murder rule as a doctrine intended to deter negligent and accidental killings during commission of felonies. Proponents argue that co-felons will dissuade each other from the use of violence if they may be liable for murder. Justice Holmes attempted to justify the rule on this basis by arguing that the rule would be justified if experience showed that death resulted disproportionately from the commission of felonies. Holmes added the caveat that "I do not * * *, however, mean to argue that the rules under discussion arose on the

---

12.   * * * England, where the doctrine originated, abolished the felony-murder rule in 1957. The Homicide Act, 1957, 5 & 6 Eliz. 2 ch. 11 § 1. The rule apparently never existed in France or Germany.

above reasoning, any more than that they are right, or would be generally applied in this country.''

The second view focuses not on the killing, but on the felony itself, and endorses the felony-murder rule as a deterrent to dangerous felonies. From this perspective, punishing both accidental and deliberate killings that result from the commission of a felony is "the strongest possible deterrent" to "undertaking inherently dangerous felonies."

Both of the deterrence justifications are logically flawed and neither has proven to have a basis in fact. The illogic of the felony-murder rule as a means of deterring killing is apparent when applied to accidental killings occurring during the commission of a felony. Quite simply, how does one deter an unintended act? * * * Moreover, any potential deterrence effect on unintentional killings is further reduced because few felons either will know that the felony-murder rule imposes strict liability for resulting deaths or will believe that harm will result from commission of the felony. Finally, statistical evidence has not borne out Holmes's proposed justification that a disproportionate number of killings occur during felonies.[34]

The purpose of deterring the commission of dangerous felonies through the felony-murder rule also lacks a legitimate basis. First, considerable doubt exists that serious crimes are deterred by varying the weight of the punishment. Second, the rule from this perspective uses the sanctions for murder to deter felonies, and "it is usually accepted as wiser to strike at the harm intended by the criminal rather than at the greater harm possibly flowing from his act which was neither intended nor desired by him." Where the killing is unintended, it would be far more sensible to enhance the sentence for conduct over which the felon had control, such as the carrying of a deadly weapon, rather than automatically to elevate the killing to murder. Finally, as with the other deterrence rationale, the felony-murder rule can have no deterrent effect if the felon either does not know how the rule works or does not believe a killing will actually result. * * *

C. Transferred Intent and Constructive Malice: The Felony–Murder Rule's Presumption of Culpability

The felony-murder rule may be conceptualized as a theory of "transferred or constructive intent." This theory posits that the intent to commit the felony is "transferred" to the act of killing in order to find culpability for the homicide. The rule thus serves "the purpose of * * * reliev[ing] the state of the burden of proving premeditation or malice."

Judges and commentators have criticized the transferred intent theory of felony murder as "an anachronistic remnant" that operates "fictitiously" to broaden unacceptably the scope of murder. The very concept of transferred intent has been criticized as having "no proper place in criminal law." * * *

---

34. For instance, only one-half of one percent of all robberies result in homicide. The statistical data is summarized in Enmund v. Florida, 458 U.S. 782, 799–800 nn. 23–24 (1982).

The inapplicability of transferred intent to felony murder becomes evident when the crime's two different mens rea elements are examined: the intent to commit the felony and the culpability for the killing. The mental patterns are thus distinct and separate; for example, the intent to burglarize cannot be equated with the malice aforethought required for murder. The non-transferability of culpability is even more evident where the felony-murder rule allows elevation of the killing to first degree murder. In such a situation, the rule equates the intent to commit the felony with premeditation and deliberation, specific mental states that require proof of particular acts and thoughts. * * *

D. Retribution and General Culpability: A Strict Liability View of the Felony–Murder Rule

* * * An alternative approach is to view the rule as not requiring a separate mens rea element for the homicide, but as justifying conviction for murder simply on the basis that the defendant committed a felony and a killing occurred.

* * * The justifications advanced for this conceptualization are deterrence of the underlying felony, and the notion that the felon has exhibited an "evil mind" justifying severe punishment.

The "evil mind" theory of felony murder finds its roots in seventeenth and eighteenth century English notions of criminology. Mens rea was a less developed concept and judges focused on the harm resulting from a defendant's illegal act, rather than the maliciousness of his intent. The felony-murder rule thus partly operated on an unarticulated rationale that one who does bad acts cannot complain about being punished for their consequences, no matter how unexpected. Moreover, the felony-murder rule conceived from an "evil mind" perspective comported with the retribution theory of punishment prevailing at the time of the rule's development, which focused on the resulting harm, not on the actor's mental state, in deciding the appropriate punishment. A convict, therefore, bore responsibility for his felony and for any harmful result arising from the crime regardless of his specific intentions.

Continued reliance on a general culpability theory to justify the felony-murder rule has been described as a rather "primitive rationale" and as "a tribute to the tenacity of legal conceptions rooted in simple moral attitudes." The "evil mind" theory conflicts with the basic premise that "the criminal law is concerned not only with guilt or innocence in the abstract but also with the degree of criminal liability." Although the general culpability rationale was perhaps sufficient as long as a general intent of wrongdoing established malice aforethought, it conflicts with the progressive trend of categorizing homicide according to the degree of culpability. Indeed, the felony-murder rule viewed from a general culpability perspective effectively eliminates a mens rea element in convicting a felon for a killing occurring during the commission of a felony, and results in the rule operating as a strict liability crime: the occurrence of a killing is punished as murder regardless of the defendant's culpability.

DAVID CRUMP & SUSAN WAITE CRUMP—IN DEFENSE OF THE FELONY MURDER DOCTRINE

8 Harvard Journal of Law & Public Policy 359 (1985), 361–63, 367–72, 374–76

I. THE POLICIES SUPPORTING THE FELONY MURDER RULE

A. *Rational Classification and Proportional Grading of Offenses: Actus Reus as an Element of Just Desert*

Classical theory divides the elements of crimes into two categories: mens rea and actus reus. Mens rea, or "guilty mind," is the mental state or states required to complete the offense. Actus reus may be translated literally as "the wrongful act," but it is better understood as referring to all of the physical elements of the crime, including the defendant's actions, the surrounding circumstances, and the consequences.

Differences in result must be taken into account as part of actus reus if classification and grading are to be rational. For example, murder and attempted murder may require similar mental states * * * but no common law jurisdiction treats the two offenses as one, and certainly none treats attempted murder more severely. The only difference justifying this classification is that death results in one offense but not in the other. Similarly, it is a misdemeanor for a person to operate a motor vehicle while impaired by drugs or alcohol, but if this conduct causes the death of a human being, the offense in some jurisdictions is elevated to the status of homicide. * * *

These classifications are the result of a concern for grading offenses so as to reflect societal notions of proportionality. * * *

The felony murder doctrine serves this goal, just as do the distinctions inherent in the separate offenses of attempted murder and murder, or impaired driving and vehicular homicide. Felony murder reflects a societal judgment that an intentionally committed robbery that causes the death of a human being is qualitatively more serious than an identical robbery that does not. Perhaps this judgment could have been embodied in a newly defined offense called "robbery-resulting-in-death"; but * * * such a proliferation of offense definitions is undesirable. Thus the felony murder doctrine reflects the conclusion that a robbery that causes death is more closely akin to murder than to robbery. If this conclusion accurately reflects societal attitudes, and if classification of crimes is to be influenced by such attitudes in order to avoid depreciation of the seriousness of the offense and to encourage respect for the law, then the felony murder doctrine is an appropriate classificatory device.

There is impressive empirical evidence that this classification does indeed reflect widely shared societal attitudes. * * *

B. *Condemnation: Reaffirming the Sanctity of Human Life*

A purpose of sentencing closely related to proportionality is that of condemnation. Some would regard proportional justice and condemnation as technically separate objectives, while others would view them as substantially equivalent. In any event, the purpose of condemnation or of expressing societal outrage deserves separate mention as a policy concern underlying the felony murder rule.

Condemnation itself is a multifaceted idea. It embodies the notion of reinforcement of societal norms and values as a guide to the conduct of upright persons, as opposed to less upright ones who presumably require the separate prod of "deterrence." The felony murder rule serves this purpose by distinguishing crimes that cause human deaths, thus reinforcing the reverence for human life. To put the argument differently, characterizing a robbery-homicide solely as robbery would have the undesirable effect of communicating to the citizenry that the law does not consider a crime that takes a human life to be different from one that does not—a message that would be indistinguishable, in the minds of many, from a devaluation of human life.

Another aspect of condemnation is the expression of solidarity with the victims of crime. If we as a society label a violent offense in a manner that depreciates its significance, we communicate to the victim by implication that we do not understand his suffering. * * * Felony murder is a useful doctrine because it reaffirms to the surviving family of a felony-homicide victim the kinship the society as a whole feels with him by denouncing in the strongest language of the law the intentional crime that produced the death.

Yet another facet of condemnation is expiation. A sound penal system attempts to provide the convicted defendant with a means by which he can "repay his debt to society" and thereby anticipate at least qualified readmittance—not only in the calculating eyes of the law as it measures his service of sentence, but in the hearts of fellow citizens, at least for crimes for which such repayment is possible. The felony murder rule may serve this purpose. * * *

C. Deterrence

Deterrence is often cited as one justification for the felony murder doctrine. * * * Deterrence is the policy most often recognized in the cases. Scholars, however, tend to dismiss this rationale, using such arguments as the improbability that felons will know the law, the unlikelihood that a criminal who has formed the intent to commit a felony will refrain from acts likely to cause death, or the assertedly small number of felony-homicides.

The trouble with these criticisms is that they underestimate the complexity of deterrence. There may be more than a grain of truth in the proposition that felons, if considered as a class, evaluate risks and benefits differently than members of other classes in society. The conclusion does not follow, however, that felons cannot be deterred, or that criminals are so different from other citizens that they are impervious to inducements or deterrents that would affect people in general. There is mounting evidence that serious crime is subject to deterrence if consequences are adequately communicated. The felony murder rule is just the sort of simple, commonsense, readily enforceable, and widely known principle that is likely to result in deterrence.

At the same time, the argument that felons may be ignorant of the law is unduly categorical. If it is meant to state that felons probably cannot quote the statutory language or cite the section number governing their actions contemporaneously with the event, the proposition is probably correct. Nevertheless, the general population, including felons, is probably more aware of the outlines of the felony murder doctrine than of many other, more common criminal concepts, if only because of the influence of television. * * *

The argument against deterrence often proceeds on the additional assumption that felony murder is addressed only to accidental killings and cannot result in their deterrence. By facilitating proof and simplifying the concept of liability, however, felony murder may deter intentional killings as well. The robber who kills intentionally, but who might claim under oath to have acted accidentally, is thus told that he will be deprived of the benefit of this claim. * * * The proposition that accidental killings cannot be deterred is inconsistent with the widespread belief that the penalizing of negligence, and even the imposition of strict liability, may have deterrent consequences.

D. Clear and Unambiguous Definition of Offenses and Sentence Consequences

Clear definition of crimes is advantageous. Imprecision in homicide definition is particularly prevalent and troublesome. Jury instructions on the presence or absence of premeditation, on conditions required for reduction to voluntary manslaughter, on the double misnomer embodied in "malice aforethought," and on the fine gradations between intent, knowledge, recklessness, and criminal negligence are typical sources of confusion. These concepts may be valuable because they relate to just desert and thus to proportionality, but the definitions of these terms, when given to lay jurors, may produce verdicts that differ more on account of jurors' understanding of words than on account of evidence of the crime. Hence unpredictable dispositions are a likely result.

If properly defined and applied, the felony murder doctrine sometimes provides the advantage of greater clarity. The mental state of intention to commit robbery, rape, or kidnapping is less ambiguous than the terms generally governing homicidal mental states. * * *

E. Optimal Allocation of Criminal Justice Resources

Another advantage of the felony murder rule * * * is that it may aid in the optimal allocation of criminal justice resources. * * * The efforts of judges, courtroom time, lawyering on both sides, and support services are all scarce resources. Although we resist thinking of criminal justice in these terms, and few would be willing to put a specific dollar price upon its proper function, the quality of our justice is limited by the scarcity of these resources and by the efficiency with which we allocate them. * * *

* * * The rule has beneficial allocative consequences because it clearly defines the offense, simplifies the task of the judge and jury with respect to questions of law and fact, and thereby promotes efficient administration of justice. Indeed, no less a tribunal than the California Supreme Court has stated this rationale:

> The Legislature has said in effect that this deterrent purpose [of the felony murder rule] outweighs the normal legislative policy of examining the individual state of mind of each person causing an unlawful killing to determine whether the killing was with or without malice, deliberate or accidental, and calibrating our treatment of the person accordingly. Once a person perpetrates or attempts to perpetrate one of the enumerated felonies, then in the judgment of the Legislature, he is no longer entitled to such fine judicial calibration, but will be deemed guilty of first degree murder for any homicide committed in the course thereof. * * *

F. *Minimization of the Utility of Perjury*

Many crimes are defined more broadly than their harmful consequences alone might justify. For example, there are prohibitions upon the possession of heroin or the carrying of certain kinds of weapons, even though these actions, without use of the contraband, are not intrinsically harmful. A person might attempt to defend his possession of heroin by stating that he did not intend to use or distribute it (for example, he might explain that he collects controlled substances as others collect coins or stamps). This explanation, even if true, would be regarded as irrelevant under most statutes.

Such a result may be justified by the concern that any other approach would unduly reward perjury. The denial of harmful intent in such a situation is too facile. Sources of contrary evidence persuasive beyond reasonable doubt are likely to be absent even if the defensive theory is perjurious. If lack of intent to use an illegally possessed machine gun vitiated the possessory offense, the crime would be far more difficult to prosecute, and the ultimate harm that is the real concern would become that much more difficult to control. A similar rationale may underlie the felony murder rule; thus * * * the Pennsylvania Supreme Court justified its application of the felony murder rule to the circumstances before it with the observation, "It is rare * * * that a criminal telephones or telegraphs his criminal intent * * *."

Scholars criticizing the felony murder rule sometimes argue or assume that juries will disbelieve false claims of accident. The criticism assumes too much: The accident claim need only rise to the level of reasonable doubt to be effective under conventional homicide law. Experienced trial lawyers would not deny the frequent occurrence of erroneous acquittals, given the standard of proof required. Moreover, the incentive to perjury is itself a liability. The law itself is brought into disrepute when it is defined so that perjury is frequent. Jurors might be induced to lose respect for the criminal justice system even as they acquit the defendant on his ambiguous claim of accident, which they disbelieve but cannot reject beyond a reasonable doubt.

NOTES AND QUESTIONS

1. Hawaii and Kentucky, by statute, do not recognize a felony-murder rule. In Michigan, there is no statutory strict-liability felony-murder rule, and the common law felony-murder rule was abolished by judicial authority. People v. Aaron, 409 Mich. 672, 299 N.W.2d 304 (1980). In New Mexico, the prosecutor must prove that the defendant had a culpable state of mind, independent of the mental state required for the underlying felony, that is sufficient to constitute second-degree murder. State v. Ortega, 112 N.M. 554, 817 P.2d 1196 (1991).

England abolished the felony-murder rule in the Homicide Act of 1957. The Canadian Supreme Court struck down that country's "constructive murder" rule on the ground that it is a principle of fundamental justice that a conviction for murder requires proof of subjective foresight of death. R v. Vaillancourt, [1987] 2 S.C.R. 636; R v. Martineau, [1990] 2 S.C.R. 633.

2. The Commentary to the Model Penal Code subjects the felony-murder doctrine to a thirteen page critique and concludes that the rule is "indefensible in principle." American Law Institute, Model Penal Code and Commentaries, Commentary to § 210.2, at 38–39 (1980).

What is left of the doctrine under the Code? Look carefully at § 210.2(1)(b). What would the result be if the events described in *Fuller* (p. 309 supra) occurred in a jurisdiction that adopted the Model Penal Code in its entirety?

c.   Limitations on the Rule

i.   Overview

JAMES J. TOMKOVICZ—THE ENDURANCE OF THE FELONY–MURDER RULE: A STUDY OF THE FORCES THAT SHAPE OUR CRIMINAL LAW

51 Washington and Lee Law Review 1429 (1994), 1465–67

The classic felony-murder rule held that a death caused during the commission of any felony constitutes murder. One not schooled in the intricacies of contemporary statutes and judge-made doctrines pertinent to felony-murder might assume that the broad, original version is still generally the law. That is far from the case. While the breadth of the doctrine varies from jurisdiction to jurisdiction, a number of restrictions limit most modern incarnations of felony-murder. This proclivity for confining the rule is often the product of hostility to the rule itself. Some maintain that the consistent determination to restrict felony-murder leads logically to the abolition of the doctrine. * * * As I see it, the limitations placed on felony-murder's operation are another reason for its survival.

An unlimited felony-murder rule could make us confront a number of unsettling outcomes in individual cases. Individuals engaged in felonies that are neither risky nor inherently immoral could be convicted of murder for consequential killings. Such convictions would probably not be frequent, but could occur often enough and would, by their nature, attract sufficient publicity to disconcert more than a few. The number of individuals punished without fault and the disparity between fault and the punishment imposed would both increase and, consequently, be harder to ignore. * * * The unfairness * * * could give felony-murder opponents the support that they lack and an impetus for abolition.

An unlimited felony-murder rule, however, is *not* the law of our land. In most places, the rule is cabined in a number of ways. A * * * review of typical restraints put upon the rule is in order.

ii. The "Inherently Dangerous Felony" Limitation

PEOPLE v. HOWARD

Supreme Court of California, 2005.
34 Cal.4th 1129, 23 Cal.Rptr.3d 306, 104 P.3d 107.

KENNARD, J.

Murder is the unlawful killing of a human being, with malice aforethought. But under the second degree felony-murder rule, the prosecution can obtain a conviction without showing malice if the killing occurred during the commission of an inherently dangerous felony. Is the crime of driving with a willful or wanton disregard for the safety of persons or property while fleeing from a pursuing police officer (Veh.Code, § 2800.2) an inherently dangerous felony for purposes of the second degree felony-murder rule? We conclude it is not.

I

At 12:40 a.m. on May 23, 2002, California Highway Patrol Officer Gary Stephany saw defendant driving a Chevrolet Tahoe (a sport utility vehicle) without a rear license plate, and signaled him to pull over. Defendant stopped on the side of the road. But when Officer Stephany and his partner * * * got out of their patrol car, defendant restarted the engine and sped to a nearby freeway. The officers gave chase at speeds of up to 90 miles per hour and radioed for assistance. Defendant left the freeway and drove onto a surface street, turning off his car's headlights. He ran two stop signs and a red light, and he drove on the wrong side of the road. His speed was 15 to 20 miles over the posted speed limit of 50 miles per hour. At some point, he made a sharp turn onto a small dirt road and escaped.

Minutes later, Officer Anthony Arcelus and his partner * * * saw the Tahoe with its headlights on again and took up the chase. Officer Arcelus * * * estimated the Tahoe's speed at more than 80 miles per hour, and he saw it run a stop sign and a traffic light. By then, the car's headlights were again turned off. Up to that point, the chase had taken place in rural parts of Fresno County. When the Tahoe started heading toward downtown Fresno, Officer Arcelus gave up the pursuit, fearing that the high-speed chase might cause an accident.

About a minute after Officer Arcelus stopped chasing the Tahoe, he saw it run a red light half a mile ahead of him and collide with a car driven by Jeanette Rodriguez. Rodriguez was killed * * *. It turned out that the Tahoe that defendant was driving had been stolen earlier that day. Defendant * * * was arrested and charged with murder * * * and with evading a police officer in willful or wanton disregard for the safety of persons or property (§ 2800.2). * * *

* * * The jury convicted defendant of [both] counts.

The Court of Appeal affirmed. As pertinent here, it rejected defendant's contention that he could not be convicted under the second degree felony-murder rule because section 2800.2 is not an inherently dangerous felony. * * *

II

Because the second degree felony-murder rule is a court-made rule, it has no statutory definition. This court has described it thusly: "A homicide that is a direct causal result of the commission of a felony *inherently dangerous to human life* (other than the * * * felonies enumerated in Pen.Code, § 189) constitutes at least second degree murder." The rule "eliminates the need for proof of malice in connection with a charge of murder." It is * * * a substantive rule * * * based on the theory that "when society has declared certain inherently dangerous conduct to be felonious, a defendant should not be allowed to excuse himself by saying he was unaware of the danger to life because, by declaring the conduct to be felonious, society has warned him of the risk involved."

Because the second degree felony-murder rule is "a judge-made doctrine without any express basis in the Penal Code," its constitutionality has been questioned. And, as we have noted in the past, legal scholars have criticized the rule for incorporating "an artificial concept of strict criminal liability that 'erodes the relationship between criminal liability and moral culpability.'" Therefore, we have repeatedly stressed that the rule " 'deserves no extension beyond its required application.' "

"In determining whether a felony is inherently dangerous [under the second degree felony-murder rule], the court looks to the elements of the felony *in the abstract,* 'not the "particular" facts of the case,' i.e., not to the defendant's specific conduct." That is, we determine whether the felony "by its very nature * * * cannot be committed without creating a substantial risk that someone will be killed * * *."

Felonies that have been held inherently dangerous to life include shooting at an inhabited dwelling, poisoning with intent to injure, arson of a motor vehicle, grossly negligent discharge of a firearm, manufacturing methamphetamine, kidnapping, and reckless or malicious possession of a destructive device.

Felonies that have been held *not* inherently dangerous to life include practicing medicine without a license under conditions creating a risk of great bodily harm, serious physical or mental illness, or death [*People v. Burroughs,* 35 Cal.3d 824, 201 Cal.Rptr. 319, 678 P.2d 894 (1984)]; false imprisonment by violence, menace, fraud, or deceit; possession of a concealable firearm by a convicted felon; possession of a sawed-off shotgun; [prison] escape; grand theft; conspiracy to possess methedrine; extortion; * * * and child endangerment or abuse.

III

In determining whether section 2800.2 is an offense inherently dangerous to life, we begin by reviewing the statutory scheme.* * *

Section 2800.2, which was the basis for defendant's conviction under the second degree felony-murder rule, provides:

> (a) If a person flees or attempts to elude a pursuing peace officer in violation of Section 2800.1 and the pursued vehicle is driven in a willful or wanton disregard for the safety of persons or property, the person driving the vehicle, upon conviction, shall be punished by imprisonment in the state prison, or by confinement in the county jail. * * * The court may also impose a fine * * * or may impose both that imprisonment or confinement and fine.

> (b) For purposes of this section, a willful or wanton disregard for the safety of persons or property includes, but is not limited to, driving while fleeing or attempting to elude a pursuing peace officer during which time either three or more violations that are assigned a traffic violation point count under Section 12810 occur, or damage to property occurs.

In concluding that section 2800.2 is an inherently dangerous felony, the Court of Appeal relied heavily on *People v. Johnson* (1993) 15 Cal.App.4th 169, 18 Cal.Rptr.2d 650. There the Court of Appeal, construing an earlier version of section 2800.2 that was essentially the same as what is now subdivision (a) of that section, held that driving with "willful or wanton disregard for the safety of persons or property" was inherently dangerous to life. We need not decide, however, whether *Johnson* was correct, because in 1996, three years after *Johnson* was decided, the Legislature amended section 2800.2 to add subdivision (b). Subdivision (b) very broadly defines the term "willful or wanton disregard for the safety of persons or property," as used in subdivision (a), to include *any* flight from an officer during which the motorist commits three traffic violations that are assigned a "point count" under section 12810, or which results in "damage to property."

Violations that are assigned points under section 12810 and can be committed without endangering human life include driving an unregistered vehicle owned by the driver, driving with a suspended license, driving on a highway at slightly more than 55 miles per hour when a higher speed limit has not been posted, failing to come to a complete stop at a stop sign, and making a right turn without signaling for 100 feet before turning.

The Court of Appeal * * * concluded that subdivision (b) "did not change the elements of the section 2800.2 offense, in the abstract, or its inherently dangerous nature." But, as we pointed out in the preceding paragraph, subdivision (b) greatly expanded the meaning of the quoted statutory phrase to include conduct that ordinarily would not be considered particularly dangerous.[2]

* * * In the absence of any evidence of legislative intent, we assume that the Legislature contemplated that we would determine the application of the second degree felony-murder rule to violations of section 2800.2 based on our long-established decisions holding that the rule applies only to felonies that are inherently dangerous in the *abstract.* As we have explained * * *, a violation of section 2800.2 is not, in the abstract, inherently dangerous to human life. Therefore, the second degree felony-murder rule does not apply when a killing occurs during a violation of section 2800.2.* * *

CONCLUSION

Nothing here should be read as saying that a motorist who kills an innocent person in a hazardous, high-speed flight from a police officer should *not* be convicted of murder. A jury may well find that the motorist has acted with malice by driving with conscious disregard for the lives of others, and thus is guilty of murder. But, * * * the prosecution may not (as it did here) resort to the second degree felony-murder rule to remove from the jury's consideration the question whether a killing that occurred during a violation of section 2800.2 was done with malice.

CONCURRING AND DISSENTING OPINION BY BROWN, J.

I concur with the majority's holding that the defendant's conviction for second degree felony murder must be reversed * * *. However, * * * I cannot countenance the majority's continued allegiance to this dubious doctrine.

Here, the defendant was convicted solely on a second degree felony-murder theory. The majority appears to acknowledge the rule is constitutionally and analytically suspect * * * I agree, but I would go farther and abrogate the rule entirely. As the facts of this case conclusively demon-

2. * * * The dissent * * * notes that "although the Legislature elected to include subdivision (b) as part of section 2800.2, it could just have easily have added a separate section, establishing a distinct felonious offense of committing three 'points' violations while driving to elude a police officer." True. But the Legislature did not do so. * * * [W]e must examine the law the Legislature *did* enact, not a hypothetical law the Legislature *could* have enacted.

strate, the application of the second degree felony-murder rule remains irredeemably arbitrary.

The majority concludes, based on a technical parsing of the provision's grammar, that a violation of Vehicle Code section 2800.2 is not an inherently dangerous felony for purposes of second degree felony murder. However, a commonsense construction of the statute's language leads to the opposite conclusion—a conclusion that is considerably less counterintuitive. As one lower court stated in addressing the same issue we review here, "It would seem clear as a matter of logic that any felony whose key element is 'wanton disregard' for human life necessarily falls within the scope of 'inherently dangerous' felonies. * * * [A]part from the 'wanton disregard' element, one must also be engaged in the act of fleeing from a pursuing peace officer whose vehicle is displaying lights and sirens. Any high-speed pursuit is inherently dangerous to the lives of the pursuing police officers. In even the most ethereal of abstractions, it is not possible to imagine that the 'wanton disregard' of the person fleeing does not encompass disregard for the safety of the pursuing officers." Unlike the majority, I find [this] statement * * * persuasive. * * *

Indeed, I agree with [dissenting] Justice Baxter that if any offense should easily qualify as inherently dangerous, Vehicle Code section 2800.2 certainly would. * * *

* * * I would abrogate the nonstatutory second degree felony-murder rule and leave it to the Legislature to define precisely what conduct subjects a defendant to strict criminal liability.

DISSENTING OPINION BY BAXTER, J. * * *

The majority focus upon subdivision (b) of section 2800.2, which was added in 1996. * * * The majority reason that, because some statutory "points" violations are not inherently dangerous, one can commit the unitary felony described in both subdivisions of section 2800.2 in a way that does not place human life at risk.

I am not persuaded. Subdivision (a) of section 2800.2 gives clear and specific notice that one who, in order to elude police pursuit, drives with reckless indifference to safety is guilty of a felony. Such reckless driving is, of course, inherently dangerous—by definition, it creates a substantial risk that someone will be killed. Moreover, there is no doubt that defendant committed exactly the reckless endangerment of human life forbidden by the statute. * * *

* * * [T]he principal reason for applying the felony-murder rule is present. The purpose of the felony-murder doctrine " 'is to deter those engaged in felonies from killing negligently or accidentally.' " Because the doctrine absolves the prosecution from proving malice, it properly applies when " 'the killer is engaged in a felony whose inherent danger to human life renders logical an imputation of malice on the part of all who commit it.' "

Those requirements are met here. It is appropriate to deter persons from killing negligently or accidentally—as did defendant—while engaged—as was defendant—in recklessly unsafe driving to elude police pursuit, a specific form of conduct made felonious by section 2800.2, subdivision (a). Moreover, the inherent danger such conduct poses to human life is so clear that it is logical to impute malice to anyone who commits it.

Under such circumstances, it perverts reason to refuse to apply the felony-murder rule simply because subdivision (b) of section 2800.2 may additionally describe a nondangerous felony. Where society has warned, in plain statutory words, that the particular conduct committed by the defendant is both dangerous and felonious, it should not matter that the statute may forbid nondangerous conduct as well.[2]

It is worth noting that, although the Legislature elected to include subdivision (b) as part of section 2800.2, it could just as easily have added a separate section, establishing a distinct felonious offense of committing three "points" violations while driving to elude a peace officer. This would equally have satisfied the apparent legislative purpose to deter flight from the police by expanding the circumstances under which driving to elude a pursuing police officer would constitute a felony.

* * * If subdivision (a) described an inherently dangerous felony before the addition of subdivision (b) in 1996, the unchanged words of that subdivision equally do so following the 1996 amendment.

NOTES AND QUESTIONS

1. The "inherently dangerous felony" limitation is by far the most common limitation placed on the felony-murder rule. Indeed, according to Guyora Binder, *The Origins of American Felony Murder Rules*, 57 Stan. L. Rev. 59, 64 (2004), by the time English courts first applied a felony-murder rule, "[i]t did not apply to all felonies, and it did not hold felons strictly liable for accidental deaths. Instead English law conditioned felony murder liability on causing death through an act of violence or an act manifestly dangerous to human life, in the perpetration or attempt of a felony." Thus, if Professor Binder's revisionist historical account of the development of the felony-murder rule is correct, any American jurisdiction that does *not* recognize an inherent-dangerous-felony "limitation" has actually *expanded* on the English common law rule!

2. Unlike California, some states define "inherently dangerous Felony" by considering the manner in which the felony was committed on the present occasion, in order to determine whether the felony is "inherently dangerous." Other states denominate a felony "inherently dangerous" if it is dangerous to

---

2.   * * * It has * * * been said that the statute must be examined in isolation from the facts of the case, so as to prevent the unfair possibility that the accused will be deemed to have committed an "inherently dangerous" felony simply because a death resulted. I find [this premise] questionable where, as here, it is clear that the accused committed a form of the felony which, by its terms, necessarily endangers life, and that his murder conviction is based on the inherently dangerous form of the felony.

human life under either the "abstract" or "facts-of-the-case" standard. Can you see any problem with the facts-of-the-case approach?

3. Why is there an "inherently dangerous felony" limitation on the felony-murder rule? What does the California court give for a reason?

4. As cited in *Howard*, the state supreme court ruled in *People v. Burroughs* that the felony of "practicing medicine without a license under conditions creating a risk of great bodily harm, serious physical or mental illness, or death" is not inherently dangerous.

In *Burroughs*, B, a 77–year–old "healer," was charged with second-degree felony murder because he convinced a terminally ill leukemia patient to read his book, *Healing and the Age of Enlightenment*, forego traditional cancer treatment, and undergo treatment consisting of lemonade, salt water, herb tea, use of a lamp to bathe the cancer victim in various tints of light, and deep abdominal massaging. The patient died shortly thereafter as a result of internal hemorrhaging brought on by the massages. Can you figure out why the court held that the *Burroughs* felony was not inherently dangerous? (By the way, Burroughs's book—a more recent edition—is still on the market. You can buy it on Amazon!)

5. *Depraved heart murder versus felony murder.* In light of the "inherently dangerous felony" limitation, consider People v. Sanchez, 86 Cal. App.4th 970, 103 Cal.Rptr.2d 809 (2001):

[T]he difference between implied [depraved heart] malice and felony murder is that, under the [former] theory, when the defendant kills a person while committing an act which, by its nature, poses a high probability that the act will result in death, the trier of fact *may infer* the defendant killed with malice aforethought; whereas, under the felony-murder theory, if the inherently dangerous act is a felony, the defendant is *deemed* to have killed with malice aforethought as a matter of law.

6. *Problem.* D gave birth to V. Shortly after birth, D went on drug binges, during which she ingested illegal narcotics for days on end. During these periods, she placed V in a walker and propped a bottle of formula up on the walker for the baby to feed itself. She did not hold the baby nor change its diaper or clothes for days. V lived only 52 days. D was charged with second-degree felony murder. State v. Stewart, 663 A.2d 912 (R.I.1995). The predicate felony provided:

Every person having the custody or control of any child under the age of eighteen (18) years who shall * * * cause or permit that child to be an habitual sufferer for want of food, clothing, proper care, or oversight, * * * or who shall cause or permit the home of that child to be the resort of lewd, drunken, wanton, or dissolute persons * * * shall be guilty of a felony.

Is the felony inherently dangerous "in the abstract"?

7. *Timing can matter.* Sometimes, timing—including timing by lawyers—can have a huge impact on the development of the law. For example, in 1984, in *People v. Burroughs* (it is cited in *Howard*, and summarized in Note 4) the California high court stated that it had "serious reservations" regarding the "rationality and moral vitality" of the felony-murder rule. However,

because the state legislature expressly enacted a first-degree felony-murder provision, the *Burroughs* court recognized that it lacked authority to abolish it, absent some constitutional violation. On the other hand, the court believed that it could abolish the *second*-degree felony-murder rule because it is not expressly included in the second-degree portion of the California murder statute. (Look again, if you need to, at pp. 238–240). The court said that because second-degree felony-murder is "a creature of judicial invention," it could be abolished, as well, by the judiciary and—drums rolling—the time "may be ripe to reconsider its continued vitality." But, the court passed on the opportunity. Why? Because the issue of the validity of the second-degree felony-murder rule was not "raised, briefed or argued" by the defendant's lawyer. In short: the court may have been prepared then and there to abolish second-degree felony-murder in the State of California, but the defense lawyer failed to make the argument. So, the opportunity was lost.

Time passed. All seven justices sitting on the court in *Burroughs* were replaced over time by new judges. A quarter century later, a defense lawyer finally made the claim invited by the *Burroughs* court. What happened? Contrary to the court's comments in *Burroughs* (and, for that matter, in *Howard*, see p. 319), the state supreme court ruled, by a vote of 6–1, that the second-degree felony-murder rule is *not* a "creature of judicial invention." In People v. Chun, 45 Cal.4th 1172, 203 P.3d 425, 91 Cal.Rptr.3d 106 (2009), the state high court concluded that the 1850 legislature, which adopted the state's first murder statute, intended to enact the common law felony-murder rule in its entirety. Therefore, *Chun* held, the court lacked authority to abolish the second-degree felony-murder doctrine.

The point of history—and message to you, as a future lawyer—is this: Timing can be critical, and what lawyers argue *or fail to argue* can have a long-term impact on the development of the law.

iii. The "Independent Felony" (or Merger) Limitation

PEOPLE v. SMITH

Supreme Court of California, 1984.
35 Cal.3d 798, 201 Cal.Rptr. 311, 678 P.2d 886.

MOSK, JUSTICE.

Defendant appeals from a judgment convicting her of second degree murder (Pen.Code, § 187), [and] felony child abuse (§ 273a, subd. (1)) * * *.

Defendant and her two daughters, three-and-a-half-year-old Bethany (Beth) and two-year-old Amy, lived with David Foster. On the day Amy died, she refused to sit on the couch instead of the floor to eat a snack. Defendant became angry, took Amy into the children's bedroom, spanked her and slapped her in the face. Amy then went towards the corner of the bedroom which was often used for discipline; defendant hit her repeatedly, knocking her to the floor. Foster then apparently joined defendant to "assist" in Amy's discipline. * * * Eventually, defendant knocked the child backwards and she fell, hitting her head on the closet door.

Amy stiffened and went into respiratory arrest. Defendant and Foster took her to the hospital * * *. Amy died that evening. * * *

Our opinions have repeatedly emphasized that felony murder, although the law of this state, is a disfavored doctrine * * *. * * * Accordingly, we have reiterated that this "highly artificial concept" "should not be extended beyond any rational function that it is designed to serve." "Applying this principle to various concrete factual circumstances, we have sought to insure that the [doctrine] * * * be given the narrowest possible application consistent with its ostensible purpose—which is to deter those engaged in felonies from killing negligently or accidentally."

In accord with this policy, we restricted the scope of the felony-murder rule in [*People v. Ireland* (1969) 70 Cal.2d 522, 538–540, 75 Cal.Rptr. 188, 450 P.2d 580] by holding it inapplicable to felonies that are an integral part of and included in fact within the homicide. In that case the defendant and his wife were experiencing serious marital difficulties which eventually culminated in defendant's drawing a gun and killing his wife. The jury was instructed that it could find the defendant guilty of second degree felony murder if it determined that the homicide occurred during the commission of the underlying felony of assault with a deadly weapon. * * * We reasoned that "the utilization of the felony-murder rule in circumstances such as those before us extends the operation of that rule 'beyond any rational function that it is designed to serve.' To allow such use of the felony-murder rule would effectively preclude the jury from considering the issue of malice aforethought in all cases wherein homicide has been committed as a result of a felonious assault—a category which includes the great majority of all homicides. This kind of bootstrapping finds support neither in logic nor in law. We therefore hold that *a second degree felony-murder instruction may not properly be given when it is based upon a felony which is an integral part of the homicide and which the evidence produced by the prosecution shows to be an offense included in fact within the offense charged*."

Very soon after *Ireland* we again had occasion to consider the question of merger in *People v. Wilson* (1969) 1 Cal.3d 431, 82 Cal.Rptr. 494, 462 P.2d 22. There the defendant forcibly entered his estranged wife's apartment carrying a shotgun. Once inside the apartment, he * * * proceeded to break into the bathroom where he killed his wife. * * *

* * * The jury was instructed on first degree felony murder on the theory that the homicide was committed in the course of a burglary because the defendant had entered the premises with intent to commit a felony, i.e., assault with a deadly weapon. We held that the felony-murder rule cannot apply to burglary-murder cases in which "the entry would be nonfelonious but for the intent to commit the assault, and the assault is an integral part of the homicide and is included in fact in the offense charged. * * *." Because under *Ireland* the "elements of the assault were necessary elements of the homicide," the felony of burglary based on an intent to commit assault was included in fact in the homicide. We

reasoned that "Where a person enters a building with an intent to assault his victim with a deadly weapon, he is not deterred by the felony-murder rule. That doctrine can serve its purpose only when applied to a felony independent of the homicide." * * *

In *People v. Sears* (1970) 2 Cal.3d 180, 84 Cal.Rptr. 711, 465 P.2d 847, we followed *Wilson* in a slightly different factual situation. There the defendant entered a cottage with the intent to assault his estranged wife. In the course of the assault, her daughter intervened and was killed by the defendant. The People argued that this situation was distinguishable on the ground that the felony of burglary with intent to assault the wife was "independent of the homicide" of the daughter and therefore the felony-murder rule could apply. We rejected the theory, holding that "It would be anomalous to place the person who intends to attack one person and in the course of the assault kills another inadvertently or in the heat of battle in a worse position than the person who from the outset intended to attack both persons and killed one or both." * * *

In addition to the offenses of assault with a deadly weapon and burglary with intent to assault, the felony of discharging a firearm at an inhabited dwelling has also been held to merge into a resulting homicide; thus, application of the felony-murder rule in this situation is similarly prohibited. * * *

Cases in which the second degree felony-murder doctrine has withstood an *Ireland* attack include those in which the underlying felony was furnishing narcotics; driving under the influence of narcotics; poisoning food, drink or medicine; armed robbery (*People v. Burton* (1971) 6 Cal.3d 375, 387 [99 Cal.Rptr. 1, 491 P.2d 793]); kidnaping; and finally, felony child abuse by malnutrition and dehydration * * *. * * * [N]one of these decisions involved an underlying felony that has as its principal purpose an assault on the person of the victim.

In *People v. Burton*, we refined the *Ireland* rule by adding the caveat that the felony-murder doctrine may nevertheless apply if the underlying offense was committed with an "independent felonious purpose." [In *Burton*, the underlying felony was armed robbery. The defendant asserted that the felony-murder rule did not apply because an armed robbery necessarily includes an assault with a deadly weapon. Therefore, he reasoned, the felony was an integral part of the homicide and included in fact within it.] Even if the felony was included within the facts of the homicide and was integral thereto, a further inquiry is required to determine if the homicide resulted "from conduct for an independent felonious purpose" as opposed to a "single course of conduct with a single purpose." In cases like *Ireland,* the "purpose of the conduct was the very assault which resulted in death"; on the other hand, "in the case of armed robbery, * * * there is an independent felonious purpose, namely * * * to acquire money or property belonging to another."

Our task is to apply the foregoing rules to the offense at issue here—felony child abuse defined by section 273a, subdivision (1).[4] * * *

The language of *Ireland, Wilson* and *Burton* bars the application of the felony-murder rule "where the purpose of the conduct was the very assault which resulted in death." In cases in which the violation of section 273a, subdivision (1), is a direct assault on a child that results in death * * *, it is plain that the purpose of the child abuse was the "very assault which resulted in death." It would be wholly illogical to allow this kind of assaultive child abuse to be bootstrapped into felony murder merely because the victim was a child rather than an adult, as in *Ireland*.

In the present case the homicide was the result of child abuse of the assaultive variety. Thus, the underlying felony was unquestionably an "integral part of" and "included in fact" in the homicide within the meaning of *Ireland*. Furthermore, we can conceive of no independent purpose for the conduct, and the People suggest none; just as in *Ireland*, the purpose here was the very assault that resulted in death. To apply the felony-murder rule in this situation would extend it "beyond any rational function that it is designed to serve." We reiterate that the ostensible purpose of the felony-murder rule is not to deter the underlying felony, but instead to deter negligent or accidental killings that may occur in the course of committing that felony. When a person *willfully* inflicts unjustifiable physical pain on a child under these circumstances, it is difficult to see how the assailant would be further deterred from killing negligently or accidentally in the course of that felony by application of the felony-murder rule. * * *[7]

NOTES AND QUESTIONS

1. *Smith* is not the California Supreme Court's last word on the merger doctrine. Subsequent cases took the court in a different direction, and then seemed to partially reverse course. In People v. Chun, 45 Cal.4th 1172, 91 Cal.Rptr.3d 106, 203 P.3d 425 (2009), the California high court conceded "that the current state of the law regarding merger is 'muddled.'" After an extensive historical review of California's merger jurisprudence, the *Chun* court announced California's current position:

When the underlying felony is assaultive in nature, such as a violation of [California Penal Code] section 246 [shooting at an occupied vehicle] * * *, we now conclude that the felony merges with the homicide and

---

4. Section 273a, subdivision (1), provided: "Any person who, under circumstances or conditions likely to produce great bodily harm or death, willfully causes or permits any child to suffer, or inflicts thereon unjustifiable physical pain or mental suffering, or having the care or custody of any child, willfully causes or permits the person or health of such child to be injured, or willfully causes or permits such child to be placed in such situation that its person or health is endangered, is punishable by imprisonment in the county jail not exceeding 1 year, or in the state prison for not less than 1 year nor more than 10 years."

7. [Because this case involves the assaultive version of child abuse], we need not address the question of whether the merger doctrine applies when the defendant is guilty of felony child abuse of the non-assaultive variety, e.g., by extreme neglect * * * or by failure to intervene when a child in his care or custody in placed in life-endangering situation.

[handwritten margin note: assaultive felonies excluded]

cannot be the basis of a felony-murder instruction. An "assaultive" felony is one that involves a threat of immediate violent injury. In determining whether a crime merges, the court looks to its elements and not the facts of the case. Accordingly, if the elements of the crime have an assaultive aspect, the crime merges with the underlying homicide even if the elements also include conduct that is not assaultive. For example, in *People v. Smith*, the court noted that child abuse under section 273a "includes both active and passive conduct, i.e., child abuse by direct assault and child endangering by extreme neglect." Looking to the facts before it, the court decided the offense was "of the assaultive variety," and therefore merged. It reserved the question whether the nonassaultive variety would merge. Under the approach we now adopt, both varieties would merge. This approach both avoids the necessity of consulting facts that might be disputed and extends the protection of the merger doctrine to the potentially less culpable defendant whose conduct is not assaultive.

This conclusion is also consistent with our repeatedly stated view that the felony-murder rule should not be extended beyond its required application. We do not have to decide at this point exactly what felonies are assaultive in nature, and hence may not form the basis of a felony-murder instruction, and which are inherently collateral to the resulting homicide and do not merge.

2. What is the rationale of the merger limitation on the felony-murder rule? *[handwritten: Deter accidental & negligent killings]*

3. According to the Tennessee Supreme Court:

[C]ourts have viewed the merger doctrine as a [non-constitutional] principle for discerning legislative intent and, more specifically, as a principle that preserves "some meaningful domain in which the Legislature's careful graduation of homicide offenses can be implemented." * * * The doctrine has largely been applied in those states where the felony murder statute fails to specifically list the felonies capable of supporting a felony murder conviction, Where a "legislature explicitly states that a particular felony is a predicate felony for felony-murder, no 'merger' occurs."

State v. Godsey, 60 S.W.3d 759 (Tenn. 2001).

[handwritten margin note: Godsey says that if legis has identified felonies that qualify no need for merger]

What is the *Godsey* court getting at?

4. *Smith* discussed *People v. Wilson* (p. 327), in which the court held that the felony burglary in that case (the defendant entered premises with intent to commit an assault) merged with the homicide. Therefore, the court ruled, the defendant could not be convicted of *first*-degree felony-murder. Now look at the California Penal Code (pp. 238–240), and reconsider Note 3. Why does *Wilson* seem wrongly decided? Why, indeed, did the California Supreme Court overrule *Wilson* in 2009? People v. Farley, 46 Cal.4th 1053, 96 Cal. Rptr.3d 191, 210 P.3d 361 (2009). Why is *Wilson* also wrongly decided in light of *Chun* (Note 1)?

[handwritten margin note: Burglary is a listed a felony for felony murder. So: Wilson wrong]

iv. Killings "in the Perpetration" or "in Furtherance" of a Felony

STATE v. SOPHOPHONE

Supreme Court of Kansas, 2001.
270 Kan. 703, 19 P.3d 70.

LARSON, J.:

This is Sanexay Sophophone's direct appeal of his felony-murder conviction for the death of his co-felon during flight from an aggravated burglary in which both men participated.

The facts are not in dispute. [Sophophone and three other individuals broke into a house in Emporia. The resident reported the break-in to the police. The police responded to the call, observed Sophophone and the others leaving the back of the house, and ordered them to stop. The individuals, one being Sophophone, started to run away. One officer ran down Sophophone, handcuffed him, and placed him in a police car. Meanwhile, another officer chased one of the intruders later identified as Somphone Sysoumphone. The officer ordered the suspect to the ground and not to move. Sysoumphone was lying face down but raised up and fired at the officer, who returned fire and killed him. It is not disputed that Sysoumphone was one of the individuals observed by the officers leaving the house that had been burglarized.]

Sophophone was charged with conspiracy to commit aggravated burglary, aggravated burglary, * * * and felony murder.

Sophophone moved to dismiss the felony-murder charges, contending the complaint was defective because * * * the police officer [and not he or one of his co-felons] * * * killed Sysoumphone and further because he was in custody and sitting in the police car when the deceased was killed and therefore not attempting to commit or even fleeing from an inherently dangerous felony. His motion to dismiss was denied by the trial court.

Sophophone was convicted by a jury of all counts. * * *

The applicable provisions of K.S.A. 21–3401 read as follows:

"Murder in the first degree is the killing of a human being committed: * * *

"(b) in the commission of, attempt to commit, or flight from an inherently dangerous felony as defined in K.S.A. 21–3436 and amendments thereto."

Aggravated burglary is one of the inherently dangerous felonies as enumerated by K.S.A. 21–3436(10).

Sophophone does not dispute that aggravated burglary is an inherently dangerous felony which given the right circumstances would support a felony-murder charge. His principal argument centers on his being in custody at the time his co-felon was killed by the lawful act of the officer which he contends was a "break in circumstances" sufficient to insulate him from further criminal responsibility.

This "intervening cause" or "break in circumstances" argument has no merit under the facts of this case. We have held in numerous cases that "time, distance, and the causal relationship between the underlying felony and a killing are factors to be considered in determining whether the killing occurs in the commission of the underlying felony and the defendant is therefore subject to the felony-murder rule." Based on the uncontroverted evidence in this case, the killing took place during flight from the aggravated burglary, and it is only because the act which resulted in the killing was a lawful one by a third party that a question of law exists as to whether Sophophone can be convicted of felony murder. * * *

* * * [W]e look to the prevailing views concerning the applicability of the felony-murder doctrine where the killing has been caused by the acts of a third party. * * *

In Dressler, Understanding Criminal Law, * * * the question is posed of whether the felony-murder rule should apply when the fatal act is performed by a non-felon. Dressler states:

"This issue has perplexed courts. Two approaches to the question have been considered and applied by the courts.

"[b] The 'Agency' Approach

"The majority rule is that the felony-murder doctrine does not apply if the person who directly causes the death is a non-felon.* * *

"The reasoning of this approach stems from accomplice liability theory. Generally speaking, the acts of the primary party (the person who directly commits the offense) are imputed to an accomplice on the basis of the agency doctrine. It is as if the accomplice says to the primary party: 'Your acts are my acts.' It follows that [a co-felon] cannot be convicted of the homicides because the primary party was not the person with whom she was an accomplice. It is not possible to impute the acts of the antagonistic party—[the non-felon or] the police officer—to [a co-felon] on the basis of agency.

"[c] The 'Proximate Causation' Approach

"An alternative theory, followed by a few courts for awhile, holds that a felon may be held responsible under the felony-murder rule for a killing committed by a non-felon if the felon set in motion the acts which resulted in the victim's death.

"Pursuant to this rule, the issue becomes one of proximate causation: if an act by one felon is the proximate cause of the homicidal conduct by [the non-felon] or the police officer, murder liability is permitted." * * *

The leading case adopting the agency approach is *Commonwealth v. Redline*, 391 Pa. 486, 495, 137 A.2d 472 (1958), where the underlying principle of the agency theory is described as follows:

"In adjudging a felony-murder, it is to be remembered at all times that the thing which is imputed to a felon for a killing incidental to his felony is malice and not the act of killing. The mere coincidence of homicide and felony is not enough to satisfy the felony-murder doctrine."

The following statement from *Redline* is more persuasive for Sophophone:

"In the present instance, the victim of the homicide was one of the robbers who, while resisting apprehension in his effort to escape, was shot and killed by a policeman in the performance of his duty. Thus, the homicide was justifiable and, obviously, could not be availed of, on any rational legal theory, to support a charge of murder. How can anyone, no matter how much of an outlaw he may be, have a criminal charge lodged against him for the consequences of the lawful conduct of another person? The mere question carries with it its own answer."
* * *

The minority of the states whose courts have adopted the proximate cause theory believe their legislatures intended that any person, co-felon, or accomplice who commits an inherently dangerous felony should be held responsible for any death which is a direct and foreseeable consequence of the actions of those committing the felony. These courts apply the civil law concept of proximate cause to felony-murder situations. * * *

It appears to the majority that to impute the act of killing to Sophophone when the act was the lawful and courageous one of a law enforcement officer acting in the line of his duties is contrary to the strict construction we are required to give criminal statutes. There is considerable doubt about the meaning of K.S.A. 21–3401(b) as applied to the facts of this case, and we believe that making one criminally responsible for the lawful acts of a law enforcement officer is not the intent of the felony-murder statute as it is currently written. * * *

We hold that under the facts of this case where the killing resulted from the lawful acts of a law enforcement officer in attempting to apprehend a co-felon, Sophophone is not criminally responsible for the resulting death of Somphone Sysoumphone, and his felony-murder conviction must be reversed. * * *

ABBOTT, J., dissenting: * * *

When an issue requires statutory analysis and the statute is unambiguous, we are limited by the wording chosen by the legislature. We are not free to alter the statutory language, regardless of the result. In the present case, the felony-murder statute does not require us to adopt the "agency" theory favored by the majority. Indeed, there is nothing in the statute which establishes an agency approach. The statute does not address the issue at all. The requirements, according to the statute, are: (1) there must be a killing, and (2) the killing must be committed in the commission, attempt to commit, or flight from an inherently dangerous felony. The statute simply does not contain the limitations discussed by the majority. * * * The facts in this case, in my opinion, satisfy all of the requirements set forth in K.S.A. 21–3401(b). * * *

Here, Sophophone set in motion acts which would have resulted in the death or serious injury of a law enforcement officer had it not been for the highly alert law enforcement officer. This set of events could have very easily resulted in the death of a law enforcement officer, and in my opinion this is exactly the type of case the legislature had in mind when it adopted the felony-murder rule. * * *

NOTES AND QUESTIONS

1. *The res gestae doctrine. Sophophone* considers two issues. The first is sometimes characterized as the "*res gestae*" issue. That is, the felony-murder rule applies when a killing occurs "during" the commission or attempted commission of a felony. Nearly all courts agree that the felony-murder doctrine still applies, however, *even after a felony is technically completed*, if the killing occurs during the escape from the scene of the crime, at least if it is part of one continuous transaction. For example, the felony-murder rule remains active if a robber flees to a rooftop, and a police officer in pursuit falls into an airshaft and dies. People v. Matos, 83 N.Y.2d 509, 611 N.Y.S.2d 785, 634 N.E.2d 157 (1994). It was also held to apply when the perpetrator of a home invasion, fleeing from a police vehicle, collided with a civilian car, killing its occupants, ten minutes and ten miles away from the scene of the felony. People v. Gillis, 474 Mich. 105, 712 N.W.2d 419 (2006).

As *Sophophone* points out, it is not enough to prove felony murder that the killing occurs, as a temporal matter, during the commission of the offense. There must also be a causal relationship between the felony and the killing. For example, the felony-murder rule should not apply if a customer in a grocery store, unaware that a robbery is underway, coincidentally dies of a heart attack. Or, suppose that Alice, in felonious possession of an unlicensed firearm, accidentally strikes and kills pedestrian Victor with her car. Although the death occurred *during* the commission of the felony (since possession of the firearm is a continuing offense), the felony-murder rule should not apply as there is no causal relationship between the felony and the death.

Presumably, as well, there must be more than a simple but-for causal connection between the felony and the death. That is, the death must be a proximate cause of the felony (or, as some courts might put it, there must be a *logical* nexus to the felony). One justice, in People v. Hudson, 222 Ill.2d 392, 305 Ill.Dec. 927, 856 N.E.2d 1078 (2006) (Freeman, J., specially concurring), has raised the issue with this hypothetical:

> Defendant X robs an individual at gunpoint. During the robbery, defendant X accidentally discharges the gun. At the forest preserve two blocks away, the victim is riding a horse. The horse bolts at the sound of the gunshot, crosses a busy street, and throws the victim to the ground. An oncoming car cannot stop in a timely fashion and runs over the victim, inflicting the injuries that result in the death.

Here, it will be noticed, X *is* the but-for cause of the death: but for firing the gun, the horse would not have bolted, and so on. But, X's responsibility for the victim's death *on the basis of felony-murder* should require a proximate causation analysis that considers the role of the intervening causes (the horse bolting and the oncoming car striking the victim).

For more on the *res gestae* principle and a controversial expansion of it, see Dana K. Cole, *Expanding Felony–Murder in Ohio: Felony–Murder or Murder–Felony?*, 63 Ohio St. L.J. 15 (2002).

2. Most felony-murder cases, of course, occur when a felon accidentally or with a culpable state of mind personally kills an innocent person. Sometimes, however, the scenario is as follows: Two (or more) persons attempt to perpetrate a felony, but the intended victim of the felony, a police officer, or another innocent party repels the felony by killing one of the co-felons (*Sophophone*) or accidentally kills an innocent bystander (e.g., People v. Lowery, 178 Ill.2d 462, 227 Ill.Dec. 491, 687 N.E.2d 973 (1997)). Does the holding and/or reasoning of *Sophophone* reach the death-of-innocent-person (*Lowery*) version of the scenario?

3. As a matter of policy, do you favor the majority or the dissent's approach in *Sophophone*? What about as a matter of statutory interpretation?

Some statutes are explicit in regard to the issues raised here. For example, New Jersey imposes felony-murder liability when "the actor, acting either alone or with one or more other persons, is engaged in the commission of [an enumerated felony] * * * and in the course of such crime or of immediate flight therefrom, *any person* causes the death *of a person other than one of the participants*." N.J.Stat.Ann. 2C–11–3 (2011).

4. In light of *Sophophone*, is there another way to hold a felon responsible for the killing of a co-felon at the hands of a third person? Yes, as seen in Taylor v. Superior Court, 3 Cal.3d 578, 91 Cal.Rptr. 275, 477 P.2d 131 (1970), overruled on other grounds in People v. Antick, 15 Cal.3d 79, 123 Cal.Rptr. 475, 539 P.2d 43 (1975).

In *Taylor,* robbers *A* and *B* entered a liquor store run by Mr. and Mrs. West. *C,* an accomplice in the robbery, remained outside in the getaway car. Inside, *A,* "chattering insanely," ordered Mr. West to put money in a bag, telling him repeatedly, "Don't move or I'll blow your head off. He's got a gun. He's got a gun." In response, Mrs. West picked up a gun and shot and killed *B. A* and *C* were prosecuted for *B*'s death.

The court refused to apply the felony-murder doctrine. It concluded, however, that *A*'s conduct in the store was malicious, i.e., extremely reckless, and that this behavior proximately caused the initiation of the gunfire by Mrs. West. Therefore, *A* could be convicted of murder for *B*'s death at Mrs. West's hands. *C,* sitting in the car, was also guilty, because *A*'s reckless conduct could be imputed to him under accomplice liability doctrine. As a practical matter, does it matter which theory—felony murder or recklessness—is used to convict *A* and *C*?

Suppose Mrs. West had killed *A* rather than *B*. Could *B* and *C* have been convicted of murder in *A*'s death? See *Antick,* supra.

2.   UNLAWFUL–ACT MANSLAUGHTER (THE "MISDEMEANOR MANSLAUGHTER" RULE)

An unintended homicide that occurs during the commission of an unlawful act not amounting to a felony constitutes common law involuntary manslaughter. As explained by the court in Comber v. United States, 584 A.2d 26 (D.C.App.1990):

> The doctrine became known as the "misdemeanor-manslaughter rule," something of an analogue to the felony-murder rule. * * * Where the * * * doctrine applies, involuntary manslaughter liability attaches even where the defendant does not act with the degree of [culpability] ordinarily required for involuntary manslaughter predicated on criminally negligent behavior. In effect, the defendant's intentional commission of a misdemeanor supplies the culpability required to impose homicide liability.

Criticism of the unlawful-act doctrine parallels that of the felony-murder rule:

> Unlawful-act involuntary manslaughter has been severely criticized. The flaw in the concept is that a person may be convicted of unlawful-act manslaughter even though the person's conduct does not create a perceptible risk of death. Thus, a person is punished for the fortuitous result, the death, although the jury never has to determine whether the person was at fault with respect to the death. The concept violates the important principle that a person's criminal liability for an act should be proportioned to his or her moral culpability for that act. The wrongdoer should be punished for the unlawful act and for homicide if he or she is at fault with respect to the death, but should not be punished for a fortuitous result merely because the act was unlawful. State v. Pray, 378 A.2d 1322 (Me.1977).

The extremity of the misdemeanor-manslaughter doctrine is evident from its application in real and hypothetical circumstances. For example, an automobile driver who non-negligently causes the death of a pedestrian due to the driver's failure to obey a stop sign, in violation of a traffic ordinance, is guilty of manslaughter. State v. Hupf, 48 Del. 254, 101 A.2d 355 (1953). A Michigan driver going one mile over the speed limit in a construction zone who kills a construction worker may be held strict liable for a 15–year manslaughter conviction. Mich. Comp. L. 257.601b(3) (2011). Similarly, an actor is guilty of manslaughter if he unjustifiably pushes the victim in the chest with his forearm (a criminal battery) and the victim, intoxicated, falls down, strikes the back of his head on the pavement, and dies. See *Pray,* supra.

Manslaughter convictions have been upheld for deaths arising from non-criminal, but morally wrongful, conduct. For example, in Commonwealth v. Mink, 123 Mass. 422 (1877), Lucy Mink attempted to kill herself with a gun in the presence of Charles Ricker. Ricker took hold of Mink in order to prevent her from shooting herself. A struggle ensued and Mink's pistol accidentally discharged, killing Ricker. Although attempted suicide was not a criminal offense, the court held that Mink was guilty of criminal homicide because her conduct was morally wrongful. But see Commonwealth v. Catalina, 407 Mass. 779, 556 N.E.2d 973 (1990) (now limiting the unlawful-act doctrine to deaths resulting from batteries).

Because of the rule's harshness, many courts limit the doctrine to deaths resulting from either *malum in se* misdemeanor conduct, Mills v. State, 13 Md.App. 196, 282 A.2d 147 (1971), or the commission of a "dangerous" misdemeanor, e.g., *Comber,* supra ("if the manner of its commission entails a reasonably foreseeable risk of appreciable physical injury"). Led by the Model Penal Code, other states have abolished the misdemeanor-manslaughter rule.

3. A BRAIN TEASER TO END ALL BRAIN TEASERS

At the 1994 annual awards dinner of the American Association for Forensic Science, Don Harper Mills, President of the Association, astounded the audience with the following story, which has since made its way to various Internet discussion groups:[h]

On 23 March, 1994, the medical examiner viewed the body of Ronald Opus and concluded that he died from a shotgun wound of the head. The decedent had jumped from the top of a ten-story building intending to commit suicide (he left a note indicating his despondency). As he fell past the ninth floor, his life was interrupted by a shotgun blast through a window, which killed him instantly. Neither the shooter nor the decedent was aware that a safety net had been erected at the eighth floor level to protect some window washers and that Opus would not have been able to complete his suicide anyway because of this.

* * * The room on the ninth floor whence the shotgun blast emanated was occupied by an elderly man and his wife. They were arguing and he was threatening her with the shotgun. He was so upset that, when he pulled the trigger, he completely missed his wife and the pellets went though the window striking Opus.

* * * When confronted with this charge, the old man * * * [was] adamant that [he did not know] that the shotgun was loaded. The old man said it was his long-standing habit to threaten his wife with the unloaded shotgun. He had no intention to [kill] her * * *. That is, the gun had been accidentally loaded.

The continuing investigation turned up a witness who saw the old couple's son loading the shotgun approximately six weeks prior to the fatal incident. It transpired that the old lady had cut off her son's

h. The story is published with the permission of Don Harper Mills, M.D., J.D.

financial support and the son, knowing the propensity of his father to use the shotgun threateningly, loaded the gun with the expectation that his father would shoot his mother. * * *

There was an exquisite twist. Further investigation revealed that the son had become increasingly despondent over the failure of his attempt to engineer his mother's [death]. This led him to jump off the ten-story building on March 23, only to be killed by a shotgun through a ninth-story window.

The medical examiner closed the case as a suicide.

NOTES AND QUESTIONS

1. Was the medical examiner correct in determining that no homicide occurred? Can you see any way that an ingenious prosecutor could successfully bring homicide charges against the old man under either common law or Model Penal Code principles?

E.   CAPITAL MURDER

1.   THE CONSTITUTIONAL AND POLICY DEBATE

INTRODUCTORY COMMENT

In Furman v. Georgia, 408 U.S. 238, 92 S.Ct. 2726, 33 L.Ed.2d 346 (1972), the Supreme Court set aside death sentences in four Georgia cases. Although the judgment was announced in a brief statement of the Court, all nine justices filed opinions, taking up more than 200 pages, explaining their reasoning.

Justices Brennan and Marshall concluded that capital punishment is unconstitutional in all circumstances, regardless of the procedures used to administer the penalty. Justices Douglas, Stewart, and White, also supporting the judgment, rejected this broad attack on capital punishment. They reasoned that because Georgia juries had unfettered discretion in determining who would be executed, there was too great a risk that the death penalty was being imposed arbitrarily, capriciously, or in a discriminatory manner. The four dissenters (Chief Justice Burger, and Justices Blackmun, Powell, and Rehnquist) rejected the *per se* and procedural attacks on the death penalty.

Although only two members of the Court took the abolitionist position, the effect of *Furman* was to end executions nationwide because all death penalty statutes were constitutionally infirm under the reasoning of the case. Thereafter, thirty–five states reformulated their sentencing provisions in an effort to overcome the Court's objections. In order to limit the discretion of the sentencing authority, as required by *Furman,* most states enacted death penalty laws based on Model Penal Code § 210.6, which provided for a post-conviction sentencing hearing at which the parties may introduce evidence of statutory aggravating and mitigating factors relating to the murder and the defendant.[i] The Supreme Court considered the constitutionality of such a statute in the next case.

GREGG v. GEORGIA

Supreme Court of the United States, 1976.
428 U.S. 153, 96 S.Ct. 2909, 49 L.Ed.2d 859.

Judgment of the Court, and opinion of MR. JUSTICE STEWART, MR. JUSTICE POWELL, and MR. JUSTICE STEVENS, announced by MR. JUSTICE STEWART.

The issue in this case is whether the imposition of the sentence of death for the crime of murder under the law of Georgia violates the Eighth and Fourteenth Amendments. * * *

I

[Gregg was convicted of intent-to-kill murder and armed robbery. At a post-conviction sentencing hearing, the jury imposed the death penalty after it found beyond a reasonable doubt that Gregg was guilty of two statutory aggravating circumstances.]

II

Before considering the issues presented it is necessary to understand the Georgia statutory scheme for the imposition of the death penalty. The Georgia statute * * * retains the death penalty for six categories of crime: murder, kidnaping for ransom or where the victim is harmed, armed robbery, rape, treason, and aircraft hijacking. The capital defendant's guilt or innocence is determined in the traditional manner, either by a trial judge or a jury, in the first stage of a bifurcated trial.

* * * After a verdict, finding, or plea of guilty to a capital crime, a presentence hearing is conducted before whoever made the determination of guilt. The sentencing procedures are essentially the same in both bench and jury trials. * * * The defendant is accorded substantial latitude as to the types of evidence that he may introduce. * * *.

In the assessment of the appropriate sentence to be imposed the judge is also required to consider or to include in his instructions to the jury "any mitigating circumstances or aggravating circumstances otherwise authorized by law and any of [10] statutory aggravating circumstances which may be supported by the evidence * * *." * * * Before a convicted defendant may be sentenced to death * * * the jury, or the trial judge in cases tried without a jury, must find beyond a reasonable doubt one of the

---

i. Section 210.6 was included in the Model Penal Code in 1962 over the objection of members of the American Law Institute (including Herbert Wechsler, Chief Reporter of the Model Penal Code) who opposed the death penalty. The section was included so that states that chose to impose capital punishment would apply the reform procedures set out therein. On October 23, 2009, the American Law Institute withdrew Section 210.6 from the Code, "in light of the current intractable institutional and structural obstacles to ensuring a minimally adequate system for administering capital punishment."

10 aggravating circumstances specified in the statute.[9] The sentence of death may be imposed only if the jury (or judge) finds one of the statutory aggravating circumstances and then elects to impose that sentence. If the verdict is death, the jury or judge must specify the aggravating circumstance(s) found. In jury cases, the trial judge is bound by the jury's recommended sentence. * * *

III

We address initially the basic contention that the punishment of death for the crime of murder is, under all circumstances, "cruel and unusual" in violation of the Eighth and Fourteenth Amendments of the Constitution. * * *

It is clear * * * that the Eighth Amendment has not been regarded as a static concept. As Mr. Chief Justice Warren said, in an often-quoted phrase, "[t]he Amendment must draw its meaning from the evolving standards of decency that mark the progress of a maturing society." *Trop v. Dulles,* [356 U.S. 86, 78 S.Ct. 590, 2 L.Ed.2d 630 (1958)]. Thus, an assessment of contemporary values concerning the infliction of a challenged sanction is relevant to the application of the Eighth Amendment. * * * [T]his assessment does not call for a subjective judgment. It requires, rather, that we look to objective indicia that reflect the public attitude toward a given sanction.

---

9. The statute provides in part: * * *

"(b) In all cases * * * for which the death penalty may be authorized, the judge shall consider, or he shall include in his instructions to the jury for it to consider, any mitigating circumstances or aggravating circumstances otherwise authorized by law and any of the following statutory aggravating circumstances which may be supported by the evidence:

"(1) The offense of murder, rape, armed robbery, or kidnapping was committed by a person with a prior record of conviction for a capital felony, or the offense of murder was committed by a person who has a substantial history of serious assaultive criminal convictions.

"(2) The offense of murder, rape, armed robbery, or kidnapping was committed while the offender was engaged in the commission of another capital felony, or aggravated battery, or the offense of murder was committed while the offender was engaged in the commission of burglary or arson in the first degree.

"(3) The offender by his act of murder, armed robbery, or kidnapping knowingly created a great risk of death to more than one person in a public place by means of a weapon or device which would normally be hazardous to the lives of more than one person.

"(4) The offender committed the offense of murder for himself or another, for the purpose of receiving money or any other thing of monetary value.

"(5) The murder of a judicial officer, former judicial officer, district attorney or solicitor or former district attorney or solicitor during or because of the exercise of his official duty.

"(6) The offender caused or directed another to commit murder or committed murder as an agent or employee of another person.

"(7) The offense of murder, rape, armed robbery, or kidnapping was outrageously or wantonly vile, horrible or inhuman in that it involved torture, depravity of mind, or an aggravated battery to the victim.

"(8) The offense of murder was committed against any peace officer, corrections employee or fireman while engaged in the performance of his official duties.

"(9) The offense of murder was committed by a person in, or who has escaped from, the lawful custody of a peace officer or place of lawful confinement.

"(10) The murder was committed for the purpose of avoiding, interfering with, or preventing a lawful arrest or custody in a place of lawful confinement, of himself or another. * * * "

But our cases also make clear that public perceptions of standards of decency with respect to criminal sanctions are not conclusive. A penalty also must accord with "the dignity of man," which is the "basic concept underlying the Eighth Amendment." This means, at least, that the punishment not be "excessive." When a form of punishment in the abstract (in this case, whether capital punishment may ever be imposed as a sanction for murder) rather than in the particular (the propriety of death as a penalty to be applied to a specific defendant for a specific crime) is under consideration, the inquiry into "excessiveness" has two aspects. First, the punishment must not involve the unnecessary and wanton infliction of pain. Second, the punishment must not be grossly out of proportion to the severity of the crime. * * *

* * * We now consider specifically whether the sentence of death for the crime of murder is a *per se* violation of the Eighth and Fourteenth Amendments to the Constitution. We note first that history and precedent strongly support a negative answer to this question.

The imposition of the death penalty for the crime of murder has a long history of acceptance both in the United States and in England. The common-law rule imposed a mandatory death sentence on all convicted murderers. * * *

It is apparent from the text of the Constitution itself that the existence of capital punishment was accepted by the Framers. At the time the Eighth Amendment was ratified, capital punishment was a common sanction in every State. * * *

For nearly two centuries, this Court, repeatedly and often expressly, has recognized that capital punishment is not invalid *per se*. * * *

The most marked indication of society's endorsement of the death penalty for murder is the legislative response to *Furman*. The legislatures of at least 35 States have enacted new statutes that provide for the death penalty for at least some crimes that result in the death of another person. And the Congress of the United States, in 1974, enacted a statute providing the death penalty for aircraft piracy that results in death. * * *

The jury also is a significant and reliable objective index of contemporary values because it is so directly involved. The Court has said that "one of the most important functions any jury can perform in making * * * a selection [between life imprisonment and death for a defendant convicted in a capital case] is to maintain a link between contemporary community values and the penal system." It may be true that evolving standards have influenced juries in recent decades to be more discriminating in imposing the sentence of death. But the relative infrequency of jury verdicts imposing the death sentence does not indicate rejection of capital punishment *per se*. Rather, the reluctance of juries in many cases to impose the sentence may well reflect the humane feeling that this most irrevocable of sanctions should be reserved for a small number of extreme cases. * * *

As we have seen, however, the Eighth Amendment demands more than that a challenged punishment be acceptable to contemporary society. The Court also must ask whether it comports with the basic concept of human dignity at the core of the Amendment. * * * [T]he sanction imposed cannot be so totally without penological justification that it results in the gratuitous infliction of suffering.

The death penalty is said to serve two principal social purposes: retribution and deterrence of capital crimes by prospective offenders.

In part, capital punishment is an expression of society's moral outrage at particularly offensive conduct. This function may be unappealing to many, but it is essential in an ordered society that asks its citizens to rely on legal processes rather than self-help to vindicate their wrongs. * * * "Retribution is no longer the dominant objective of the criminal law," but neither is it a forbidden objective nor one inconsistent with our respect for the dignity of men. Indeed, the decision that capital punishment may be the appropriate sanction in extreme cases is an expression of the community's belief that certain crimes are themselves so grievous an affront to humanity that the only adequate response may be the penalty of death.

Statistical attempts to evaluate the worth of the death penalty as a deterrent to crimes by potential offenders have occasioned a great deal of debate. The results simply have been inconclusive. * * *

Although some of the studies suggest that the death penalty may not function as a significantly greater deterrent than lesser penalties, there is no convincing empirical evidence either supporting or refuting this view. We may nevertheless assume safely that there are murderers, such as those who act in passion, for whom the threat of death has little or no deterrent effect. But for many others, the death penalty undoubtedly is a significant deterrent. There are carefully contemplated murders, such as murder for hire, where the possible penalty of death may well enter into the cold calculus that precedes the decision to act. And there are some categories of murder, such as murder by a life prisoner, where other sanctions may not be adequate.

The value of capital punishment as a deterrent of crime is a complex factual issue the resolution of which properly rests with the legislatures, which can evaluate the results of statistical studies in terms of their own local conditions and with a flexibility of approach that is not available to the courts. * * *

Finally, we must consider whether the punishment of death is disproportionate in relation to the crime for which it is imposed. There is no question that death as a punishment is unique in its severity and irrevocability. * * * But we are concerned here only with the imposition of capital punishment for the crime of murder, and when a life has been taken deliberately by the offender, we cannot say that the punishment is invariably disproportionate to the crime. It is an extreme sanction, suitable to the most extreme of crimes.

We hold that the death penalty is not a form of punishment that may never be imposed, regardless of the circumstances of the offense, regardless of the character of the offender, and regardless of the procedure followed in reaching the decision to impose it. * * *

IV

We now consider whether Georgia may impose the death penalty on the petitioner in this case. * * *

While *Furman* did not hold that the infliction of the death penalty *per se* violates the Constitution's ban on cruel and unusual punishments, it did recognize that the penalty of death is different in kind from any other punishment imposed under our system of criminal justice. Because of the uniqueness of the death penalty, *Furman* held that it could not be imposed under sentencing procedures that created a substantial risk that it would be inflicted in an arbitrary and capricious manner. * * *

* * * [T]he concerns expressed in *Furman* * * * can be met by a carefully drafted statute that ensures that the sentencing authority is given adequate information and guidance. As a general proposition these concerns are best met by a system that provides for a bifurcated proceeding at which the sentencing authority is apprised of the information relevant to the imposition of sentence and provided with standards to guide its use of the information. * * *

We * * * turn to consideration of the constitutionality of Georgia's capital-sentencing procedures. * * *

These procedures require the jury to consider the circumstances of the crime and the criminal before it recommends sentence. No longer can a Georgia jury do as *Furman's* jury did: reach a finding of the defendant's guilt and then, without guidance or direction, decide whether he should live or die. Instead, the jury's attention is directed to the specific circumstances of the crime * * *. In addition, the jury's attention is focused on the characteristics of the person who committed the crime * * *. As a result, while some jury discretion still exists, "the discretion to be exercised is controlled by clear and objective standards so as to produce nondiscriminatory application."

As an important additional safeguard against arbitrariness and caprice, the Georgia statutory scheme provides for automatic appeal of all death sentences to the State's Supreme Court. * * *

For the reasons expressed in this opinion, we hold that the statutory system under which Gregg was sentenced to death does not violate the Constitution. * * *

Mr. Justice White, with whom The Chief Justice and Mr. Justice Rehnquist join, concurring in the judgment.

* * * The issue in this case is whether the death penalty imposed for murder on petitioner Gregg under the new Georgia statutory scheme may constitutionally be carried out. I agree that it may. * * *

Petitioner's argument that there is an unconstitutional amount of discretion in the system which separates those suspects who receive the death penalty from those who receive life imprisonment, a lesser penalty, or are acquitted or never charged, seems to be in final analysis an indictment of our entire system of justice. Petitioner has argued, in effect, that no matter how effective the death penalty may be as a punishment, government, created and run as it must be by humans, is inevitably incompetent to administer it. This cannot be accepted as a proposition of constitutional law. Imposition of the death penalty is surely an awesome responsibility for any system of justice and those who participate in it. Mistakes will be made and discriminations will occur which will be difficult to explain. However, one of society's most basic tasks is that of protecting the lives of its citizens and one of the most basic ways in which it achieves the task is through criminal laws against murder. I decline to interfere with the manner in which Georgia has chosen to enforce such laws on what is simply an assertion of lack of faith in the ability of the system of justice to operate in a fundamentally fair manner. * * *

I therefore concur in the judgment of affirmance. * * *

MR. JUSTICE BLACKMUN, concurring in the judgment. * * *

MR. JUSTICE BRENNAN, dissenting.

The Cruel and Unusual Punishments Clause "must draw its meaning from the evolving standards of decency that mark the progress of a maturing society." * * *

* * * [T]he Clause forbidding cruel and unusual punishments under our constitutional system of government embodies in unique degree moral principles restraining the punishments that our civilized society may impose on those persons who transgress its laws. * * *

This Court inescapably has the duty, as the ultimate arbiter of the meaning of our Constitution, to say whether, when individuals condemned to death stand before our Bar, "moral concepts" require us to hold that the law has progressed to the point where we should declare that the punishment of death, like punishments on the rack, the screw, and the wheel, is no longer morally tolerable in our civilized society. My opinion in *Furman v. Georgia* concluded that our civilization and the law had progressed to this point and that therefore the punishment of death, for whatever crime and under all circumstances, is "cruel and unusual" in violation of the Eighth and Fourteenth Amendments of the Constitution. I shall not again canvass the reasons that led to that conclusion. I emphasize only that foremost among the "moral concepts" recognized in our cases and inherent in the Clause is the primary moral principle that the State, even as it punishes, must treat its citizens in a manner consistent with their intrinsic worth as human beings—a punishment must not be so severe as to be degrading to human dignity. * * *

The fatal constitutional infirmity in the punishment of death is that it treats "members of the human race as nonhumans, as objects to be toyed with and discarded. [It is] thus inconsistent with the fundamental premise of the Clause that even the vilest criminal remains a human being possessed of common human dignity." * * *

Mr. JUSTICE MARSHALL, dissenting. * * *

Since the decision in *Furman,* the legislatures of 35 States have enacted new statutes authorizing the imposition of the death sentence for certain crimes, and Congress has enacted a law providing the death penalty for air piracy resulting in death. I would be less than candid if I did not acknowledge that these developments have a significant bearing on a realistic assessment of the moral acceptability of the death penalty to the American people. But if the constitutionality of the death penalty turns, as I have urged, on the opinion of an *informed* citizenry, then even the enactment of new death statutes cannot be viewed as conclusive. In *Furman,* I observed that the American people are largely unaware of the information critical to a judgment on the morality of the death penalty, and concluded that if they were better informed they would consider it shocking, unjust, and unacceptable. A recent study, conducted after the enactment of the post-*Furman* statutes, has confirmed that the American people know little about the death penalty, and that the opinions of an informed public would differ significantly from those of a public unaware of the consequences and effects of the death penalty.[1]

Even assuming, however, that the post-*Furman* enactment of statutes authorizing the death penalty renders the prediction of the views of an informed citizenry an uncertain basis for a constitutional decision, the enactment of those statutes has no bearing whatsoever on the conclusion that the death penalty is unconstitutional because it is excessive. An excessive penalty is invalid under the Cruel and Unusual Punishments Clause "even though popular sentiment may favor" it. The inquiry here, then, is simply whether the death penalty is necessary to accomplish the legitimate legislative purposes in punishment, or whether a less severe penalty—life imprisonment—would do as well.

The two purposes that sustain the death penalty as nonexcessive in the Court's view are general deterrence and retribution. In *Furman,* I canvassed the relevant data on the deterrent effect of capital punishment. The state of knowledge at that point, after literally centuries of debate, was summarized as follows by a United Nations Committee:

> "It is generally agreed between the retentionists and abolitionists, whatever their opinions about the validity of comparative studies of deterrence, that the data which now exist show no correlation between the existence of capital punishment and lower rates of capital crime." * * *

The other principal purpose said to be served by the death penalty is retribution. The notion that retribution can serve as a moral justification

---

1. Sarat & Vidmar, Public Opinion, The Death Penalty, and the Eighth Amendment: Testing the Marshall Hypothesis, 1976 Wis. L. Rev. 171.

for the sanction of death * * * is * * * the most disturbing aspect of today's unfortunate decisions.

The concept of retribution is a multifaceted one, and any discussion of its role in the criminal law must be undertaken with caution. On one level, it can be said that the notion of retribution or reprobation is the basis of our insistence that only those who have broken the law be punished, and in this sense the notion is quite obviously central to a just system of criminal sanctions. But our recognition that retribution plays a crucial role in determining who may be punished by no means requires approval of retribution as a general justification for punishment. It is the question whether retribution can provide a moral justification for punishment—in particular, capital punishment—that we must consider. * * *

The [plurality's] contentions—that society's expression of moral outrage through the imposition of the death penalty preempts the citizenry from taking the law into its own hands and reinforces moral values—are not retributive in the purest sense. They are essentially utilitarian in that they portray the death penalty as valuable because of its beneficial results. These justifications for the death penalty are inadequate because the penalty is, quite clearly I think, not necessary to the accomplishment of those results.

There remains for consideration, however, what might be termed the purely retributive justification for the death penalty—that the death penalty is appropriate, not because of its beneficial effect on society, but because the taking of the murderer's life is itself morally good. * * *

* * * [T]he taking of life "because the wrongdoer deserves it" surely must fall, for such a punishment has as its very basis the total denial of the wrongdoer's dignity and worth.

The death penalty, unnecessary to promote the goal of deterrence or to further any legitimate notion of retribution, is an excessive penalty forbidden by the Eighth and Fourteenth Amendments. * * *

NOTES AND QUESTIONS

1. *Mandatory death-penalty statutes.* Some states responded to *Furman* by eliminating jury discretion altogether. For example, North Carolina redrafted its murder statute to impose the death penalty for all first-degree murder convictions. On the same day that *Gregg* was decided, the Supreme Court invalidated this statutory scheme. Woodson v. North Carolina, 428 U.S. 280, 96 S.Ct. 2978, 49 L.Ed.2d 944 (1976).

The *Woodson* Court stated that "there is general agreement that American juries have persistently refused to convict a significant portion of persons charged with first-degree murder * * * under mandatory death penalty statutes." The Court reasoned from this that, as a practical matter, North Carolina's system invited juries to determine which murderers would live (by convicting them of second-degree murder) and which would die, without standards to guide them.

The Court recognized another constitutional shortcoming of the North Carolina statute:

[The shortcoming] is its failure to allow the particularized consideration of relevant aspects of the character and record of each convicted defendant before the imposition upon him of a sentence of death. * * * A process that accords no significance to [such factors] excludes * * * the possibility of compassionate or mitigating factors stemming from the diverse frailties of humankind. It treats all persons convicted of a designated offense not as uniquely human beings, but as members of a faceless, undifferentiated mass to be subjected to the blind infliction of the penalty of death.

2. *Jury sentencing.* In Ring v. Arizona, 536 U.S. 584, 122 S.Ct. 2428, 153 L.Ed.2d 556 (2002), the Supreme Court ruled that a defendant's Sixth Amendment right to trial by jury requires that juries, rather than judges, make the critical factual determination of whether aggravating circumstances exist and, therefore, whether the defendant is eligible for the death penalty.

3. *Statistics.* As of April, 2012, thirty-three states and the federal government had valid statutes authorizing the imposition of the death penalty. In recent years, Connecticut, Illinois, New Jersey, and New Mexico repealed their death penalty statutes, and New York's statute has been declared unconstitutional and no new statute has been enacted.

There were 1,237 executions (1060 by lethal injection) between 1977 and the end of 2010. At year-end 2010, 3,158 inmates (all but 60 of whom were male) were under sentence of death. Four states—California (699), Florida (392), Texas (315), and Pennsylvania (215)—held more than half of all Death Row inmates.

During 2010, forty-six inmates were executed, another twenty died in prison, and fifty-three were removed from Death Row as a result of judicial reversal of the inmate's conviction or sentence, or due to executive commutation. U.S. Dep't of Justice, Capital Punishment, 2010—Statistical Tables (NCJ 236510, Dec. 2011). According to the Death Penalty Information Center, the racial composition of persons on Death Row as of April 1, 2011, was as follows: white (44%); African–American (42%); Hispanic (12%); Native American (1%); and Asian (1%). See http://www.deathpenaltyinfo.org/documents/DRUSASpring2011.pdf.

At year-end 2010, considering all sentences and executions between 1977 and 2010, the national average lag time between death sentence and execution was just short of fifteen years. Capital Punishment, 2010, *supra.* In California, the lag time was more than twenty-five years. Carol J. Williams, *Death Penalty Costs California $184 Million a Year, Study Says*, Los Angeles Times, June 20, 2011, available at http://articles.latimes.com/2011/jun/20/local/la-me-adv-death-penalty-costs–20110620. In Valle v. Florida, 564 U.S. ___, 132 S.Ct. 1, 180 L.Ed.2d 940 (2011), the Supreme Court denied an application for stay of execution of an inmate initially sentenced to death thirty-three years earlier. Justice Breyer was the sole dissenter, stating that he had "little doubt about the cruelty of so long a period of incarceration under sentence of death."

4. *Public opinion.* Support for the death penalty has shrunk in recent years, perhaps due to the risk of executing innocent persons, in light of exonerations of some inmates based on newly available DNA evidence casting doubt on their guilt. According to Gallup poll studies, in 2011, 61% of Americans approved of capital punishment, the lowest level of support since 1977 (49%), the year *Furman* invalidated the death penalty statutes in existence at that time (p. 338), and well below the 80% support reported by Gallup in 1994. Frank Newport, *In U.S. Support for Death penalty Falls to 39–Year Low*, available at http://www.gallup.com/poll/150089/Support–Death–Penalty–Falls–Year–Low.aspx.

5. *Whatever happened to the "Class of 1972"?* Before turning to the policy debate regarding the death penalty, it may be worth asking this question: Whatever happened to the persons on Death Row in 1972 when the United States Supreme Court ruled in *Furman v. Georgia* that the death penalty laws then in existence were unconstitutional?

The immediate effect of *Furman* was that the 589 persons awaiting execution around the country were saved from that fate. But, what happened to them after that? Their death sentences became "life imprisonment" sentences. In most states, by law, this meant that these former Death Row inmates, years later, became eligible for parole. According to Joan M. Cheever, Back From the Dead (2006), 322 of the 589 inmates were years later released from prison on parole. Of that number, 78 were re-incarcerated thereafter because they were convicted of a new crime. Of this number, 42 were convicted of drug or alcohol-rated offenses, burglary, or possession of a firearm; 29 were imprisoned for armed robbery or aggravated assault; two were convicted of attempted murder; two were guilty of manslaughter, and three committed new murders, one of whom would later be executed for *that* crime. Nine of the inmates who were never released killed persons in prison, two of whom were again sentenced to death for their new crimes. Ten of the "lifers" committed suicide in prison. And, overall, seven members of the Class of 1972 were later determined to be innocent of the crimes that sent them to Death Row.

6. *The policy debate: deterrence.* Perhaps the most frequently cited study supporting the view that capital punishment deters homicides is Isaac Ehrlich, *The Deterrent Effect of Capital Punishment: A Question of Life and Death,* 65 Am.Econ.Rev. 397 (June 1975). Professor Ehrlich concluded that for the period from 1933 to 1967, each additional execution in the United States might have saved eight lives. Many scholars, however, criticized the Ehrlich study as empirically flawed and other criminologists could not replicate Ehrlich's findings. See David C. Baldus & James W.L. Cole, *A Comparison of the Work of Thorsten Sellin & Isaac Ehrlich on the Deterrent Effect of Capital Punishment,* 85 Yale L.J. 170 (1975); William J. Bowers and Glenn L. Pierce, *The Illusion of Deterrence in Isaac Ehrlich's Research on Capital Punishment,* 85 Yale L.J. 187 (1975). By the late twentieth century it was accurate to state that "there is a wide consensus among America's top criminologists that scholarly research has demonstrated that the death penalty does, and can do, little to reduce rates of criminal violence." Michael L. Radelet & Ronald L. Akers, *Deterrence and the Death Penalty: The Views of the Experts,* 87 J.

Crim.L. & Criminology 1, 10 (1996). However, according to Professor Jeffrey Fagan:

> History is now repeating itself. In the past five years, a new wave of a dozen or more studies have appeared, reporting deterrent effects of capital punishment that go well beyond Ehrlich's findings. The new deterrence studies analyze data that spans the entire period since the resumption of executions in the U.S. [in] 1973 * * *. The new studies go further, though, claiming that exonerations cause murders to increase. Several claim that pardons, commutations, and exonerations cause murders to increase. Some say that even murders of passion, among the most irrational of lethal acts, can be deterred.

Jeffrey Fagan, *Death and Deterrence Redux: Science, Law and Causal Reasoning on Capital Punishment*, 4 Ohio St. J. Crim. L. 255, 257–58 (2006) (citing the new deterrence studies).

If these new deterrence studies are correct—one of which concluded that each execution deters eighteen murders on average!—then the argument for the death penalty is obviously enhanced. Indeed, according to two authors, if these studies are right, capital punishment is "morally obligatory, not just permissible * * * not for retributive reasons, but rather to prevent the taking of innocent lives." Cass R. Sunstein & Adrian Vermeule, *Is Capital Punishment Morally Required? Acts, Omissions, and the Life–Life Tradeoffs*, 58 Stan. L. Rev. 703, 705 (2005). That is, they argue, a state is responsible for the murders it fails to prevent as well as the killings it perpetrates through capital punishment. Therefore, even if one considers an execution a "murder," that "murder" is justifiable if it will prevent a greater number of murders by its citizens.

The preceding argument starts from the assumption that the new deterrence studies are accurate. However, they have been characterized by other researchers in the field as flawed. E.g., Fagan, supra; John J. Donahue & Justin Wolfers, *Uses and Abuses of Empirical Evidence in the Death Penalty Debate*, 58 Stan. L. Rev. 791 (2005). Today, it is probably fair to state that most criminologists are of the view that the "only scientifically and ethically acceptable conclusion from the complete body of existing social science literature on deterrence and the death penalty is that it is impossible to tell whether deterrent effects are strong or weak, or whether they exist at all." Fagan, supra, at 315.

    7. *Policy debate: retribution.* Is the death penalty justifiable on retributive grounds? Yes, according to Ernest van den Haag, *In Defense of the Death Penalty: A Legal–Practical–Moral Analysis,* 14 Crim.L.Bull. 51, 66–68 (1978):

> "The life of each man should be sacred to each other man," the ancients tell us. They unflinchingly executed murderers. They realized it is not enough to proclaim the sacredness and inviolability of human life. * * * Does it not cheapen human life to punish the murderer by incarcerating him as one does a pickpocket? Murder differs in quality from other crimes and deserves, therefore, a punishment that differs in quality from other punishments.

If it were shown that no punishment is more deterrent than a trivial fine, capital punishment for murder would remain just, even if not useful. For murder is not a trifling offense. Punishment must be proportioned to the gravity of the crime, if only to denounce it and to vindicate the importance of the norm violated. Thus, all penal systems proportion punishments to crimes. The worse the crime the higher the penalty deserved. Why not the highest penalty—death—for the worst crime— wanton murder? Those rejecting the death penalty have the burden of showing that no crime deserves capital punishment—a burden which they have not so far been willing to bear.

Abolitionists are wrong when they insist that we all have an equally inalienable right to live to our natural term—that if the victim deserved to live, so does the murderer. That takes egalitarianism too far for my taste: The crime sets victim and murderer apart; if the victim died, the murderer does not deserve to live.

Never to execute a wrongdoer, regardless of how depraved his acts, is to proclaim that no act can be so irredeemably vicious as to deserve death—that no human being can be wicked enough to be deprived of life. Who actually believes that? I find it easier to believe that those who affect such a view do so because of a failure of nerve. They do not think themselves—and therefore anyone else—competent to decide questions of life and death. Aware of human frailty they shudder at the gravity of the decision and refuse to make it. * * * Such an attitude may be proper for inquiring philosophers and scientists. But not for courts. They can evade decisions on life and death only by giving up their paramount duties: to do justice, to secure the lives of the citizens, and to vindicate the norms society holds inviolable.

Is there an adequate response to the view that the death penalty is morally required for heinous murders? Reflect on John Kaplan, *The Problem of Capital Punishment,* 1983 U. Ill. L. Rev. 555, 565–67, 569–70:

The view that we should impose capital punishment because it is morally right is often phrased as an assertion that the person who would commit murder—or, more likely, some especially aggravated form of murder—should properly forfeit his own life. One problem with this argument is that it is usually supported simply by its assertion as a moral principle, rather than by any reasoning.

Often this kind of argument is phrased in terms of the victim and draws its emotional force from a feeling that somehow, by placing the defendant in the position that his victim now occupies, we will right some moral balance. Of course this is not a pragmatic argument; obviously nothing that we do to the defendant will do the victim any good. * * *

It is probable that the great majority of those who are sentenced to capital punishment have committed horrible crimes of the kind that the majority of us would agree deserved capital punishment, based simply on reading about them in the newspapers. * * *

In general, the people who commit those especially vicious, baffling, senseless crimes which do result in death sentences, fall into one of three categories. First of all there are those in whom the cultural connection between male sexuality and aggression and the need to dominate becomes unbalanced. This type of personality unfortunately exists throughout our society in more or less attenuated form. In extreme cases, sexuality becomes so unbalanced—indeed it can only be described as "perverted"—that the individual has a kind of sexual need to kill. Whether one defines this as a kind of mental illness, the perpetrators are far from normal. The next major kind of aggravated murderer is the person who is infused with a hatred which surfaces either almost continuously or else explosively on random occasions in a way that is virtually inexplicable. Finally, there is the person whose values can only be called feral. He looks upon the world as we envision a wild animal would look from the jungle. He feels no moral reason not to injure anyone, just as he feels that those around him have no moral reason not to injure him.

The interesting thing about all three of these kinds of people is that the more closely one examines their backgrounds and what has happened to them as they were growing up, the less one feels that it is morally necessary to kill them, any more than one would feel it was morally necessary to kill an escaped leopard from the zoo. They may be very, very dangerous people, but when one sees the kinds of backgrounds that the overwhelming majority of them have come from, the moral argument for executing them grows weaker. Though we certainly do not want anything to do with them, there appears to be no moral requirement that we injure further one whose humanity has been so diluted over the years by past injuries. * * *

One does not have to go so far as to say, with the French, "To understand all is to forgive all" in order to recognize that a great part of the moral imperative behind executing someone * * * disappears when we know about the conditions in which he was raised and the forces that shaped him. They may be as dangerous as an escaped leopard, but there is no moral imperative to executing such an animal if the danger can be handled in other ways.

* * * If we believe that everyone is responsible for his own acts, it is harder to regard those who perpetrate the most vicious killings as an exception to this. But the fact is we do not regard everyone as responsible for his acts. The huge edifice of mens rea in criminal law, which requires that for all serious crimes some blameworthy state of mind exist, is testament to that. * * *

More important, we recognize that many different conditions which do not prevent some responsibility for one's actions may nonetheless lessen that responsibility. * * * Under some circumstances, even though by no means an excuse, youth, drunkenness, mental retardation, previous blameless life, or extreme emotion all can lessen what would otherwise be seen as the proper punishment. If all these things are properly seen as mitigating factors, does not the history of [the usual "heinous" murderer] lessen the moral imperative of executing him?

Or, consider:

The reason justice requires the categorical abolition of executions is because of the relationship between [retribution] and the enduring, albeit enigmatic, concept of human dignity. That dignity is the exalted moral status that all human life possesses by virtue of human existence himself. * * *

* * * As [Jeffrie] Murphy trenchantly observes, "[s]ending painful voltage through a man's testicles to which electrodes have been attached, or boiling him in oil * * * are not human ways of relating to another person. [* * *]" [Jeffrie Murphy, *Cruel and Unusual Punishments*, in Retribution, Justice and Therapy: Essays in the Philosophy of Law, 223, 233 (1979).]

That failure of respect for human dignity degrades the offender and the punishing agent.

Dan Markel, *State, Be Not Proud: A Retributivist Defense of the Commutation of Death Row and the Abolition of the Death Penalty*, 40 Harv. C.R–C.L. L. Rev. 407, 465, 467 (2005).

8. *Executing the innocent.* Due to the advent of DNA, there is "mounting evidence that innocent individuals have been sentenced to death, and undoubtedly executed, more often than previously understood." United States v. Sampson, 275 F. Supp.2d 49, 54 (D. Mass. 2003). For example, serious doubts have been cast—enough to trouble the prosecutor in the case—on the execution of Ruben Cantu, a Texas man convicted of murder, although the only witness to the crime recanted his confession and alleged that he was coerced by police to make the false accusation. *12 Years After Execution, Evidence of Innocence*, New York Times, Nov. 22, 2005, at A20. Controversy also built around the refusal of Texas Governor Rick Perry to grant a 30–day reprieve to Cameron Willingham, subsequently executed, although an arson expert concluded that the evidence that put the inmate on Death Row was seriously flawed. James C. McKinley, *Controversy Builds in Texas Over an Execution*, New York Times, Oct. 20, 2009, at A14 (National Edition).

Some apparently innocent persons were saved at nearly the last moment. On August 23, 2001, Charles Fain, an 18–year resident of Death Row in Idaho, was freed after DNA tests proved what he had long-ago claimed—that he was innocent of the rape and murder of a 9–year–old girl. Raymond Bonner, *Death Row Inmate Is Freed After DNA Test Clears Him*, New York Times, Aug. 24, 2001, at A10. Fain's situation is not unique. In Tennessee, a jury acquitted a man of a murder for which he had spent fifteen years on Death Row, after DNA demonstrated that he could not be the killer. Associated Press, December 6, 2007. Between 1976 and 1997, for every seven executions that occurred, one other Dear Row Inmate was released. Joseph P. Shapiro, *The Wrong Men on Death Row*, U.S. News & World Report, Nov. 9, 1998, at 22. And, in Illinois between 1977 and 2000, 12 men were executed and 13 other Death Row inmates were freed by the courts. Dirk Johnson, *Illinois, Citing Verdict Errors, Bars Executions*, New York Times, Feb. 1, 2000, at A1; Ken Armstrong & Steve Mills, *Death Row Justice Derailed*, Chicago Tribune, Nov. 14, 1999.

One must be careful in any discussion of this issue. The term "innocent person" is ambiguous. The cases just mentioned involved persons whom a court, jury (upon retrial after reversal of a death penalty conviction), or state executive determined did not factually commit the homicides for which they were convicted (or, at least, that there was reasonable doubt as to their guilt, which justified their acquittal). The term can also apply, however, to those who commit a homicide, but who should be convicted of a lesser degree of the crime—they are "innocent" of the grounds that would justify the special penalty of death. There will never be any way to measure with certainty the number of persons that fit either category, but the most far-reaching study of death penalty cases in the United States discovered that reversible error occurred in 68% of the capital sentences that were reviewed during the years 1973 through 1995. On retrial, 82% of the defendants who were originally sentenced to death were found deserving of a lesser penalty, and 7% were found to be innocent of the capital crime. James Liebman, et al., A Broken System: Error Rates in Capital Cases, 1973–1995 (2000).

There are various explanations for the errors that occur in the death penalty process, including poor representation by defense counsel, judicial error, and prosecutorial or police misconduct. But, in view of human fallibility, the risk of executing an innocent person reaches near certainty over time, even if every possible procedural reform could be implemented and human impropriety eliminated. Does this fact alone justify the abolition of the death penalty? After all, our society constructs highways with full knowledge that innocent lives will be lost as a result. The benefits of public roads are thought to outweigh the drawbacks. Should we apply the same calculus to the death penalty issue? If not, why not?

Alternatively, should the issue be resolved on non-consequentialist grounds? For example, is it morally preferable to abolish the death penalty, in order to guarantee that innocent persons will not be executed, even if the result is that many murderers do not get the punishment they (arguably) deserve according to retributivist standards? For example, suppose that among those presently awaiting execution, we are told that twenty of them—we do not know which ones—are definitely innocent. Is it morally preferable to execute all of them, including the innocent, since this means that more than 3000 murderers receive their (arguably) just deserts, or should all of the capital murderers be spared in order to protect the innocent lives? See Richard O. Lempert, *Desert and Deterrence: An Assessment of the Moral Bases of the Case for Capital Punishment,* 79 Mich.L.Rev. 1177, 1225–31 (1981).

Moral and policy issues aside, how may a person convicted of murder in a state court, and whose appeals have been exhausted, prove his actual innocence in a federal court? The Supreme Court ruled in House v. Bell, 547 U.S. 518, 126 S.Ct. 2064, 165 L.Ed.2d 1 (2006), that a prisoner must be able to present "new reliable evidence * * * not presented at trial," and such new evidence must establish that "it is more likely than not that no reasonable juror"—not a single one—"would have found [him] guilty beyond a reasonable doubt."

9. *Changes of judicial mind.* Sometimes justices change their mind. That has occurred on rare occasions with the death penalty: One justice who previously believed that capital punishment was constitutional changed his mind, largely because of concern about its fair application. Justice Lewis

Powell stated that, upon reflection after he left the Court, he had "come to think that capital punishment should be abolished." He did not believe that executions were inherently immoral, but rather concerned that it was enforced so rarely that it did not deter and could not fairly be enforced. John C. Jeffries, Justice Lewis F. Powell, Jr., 451–452 (1994).

Justice Harry Blackmun changed his mind near the conclusion of his service on the Court. In Callins v. Collins, 510 U.S. 1141, 114 S.Ct. 1127, 127 L.Ed.2d 435 (1994), he wrote:

> From this day forward, I no longer shall tinker with the machinery of death. For more than 20 years I have endeavored—indeed, I have struggled—along with a majority of this Court, to develop procedural and substantive rules that would lend more than the mere appearance of fairness to the death penalty endeavor. Rather than continue to coddle the Court's delusion that the desired level of fairness has been achieved and the need for regulation eviscerated, I feel morally and intellectually obligated simply to concede that the death penalty experiment has failed. It is virtually self-evident to me now that no combination of procedural rules or substantive regulations ever can save the death penalty from its inherent constitutional deficiencies. The basic question—does the system accurately and consistently determine which defendants "deserve" to die?—cannot be answered in the affirmative. * * * The problem is that the inevitability of factual, legal, and moral error gives us a system that we know must wrongly kill some defendants, a system that fails to deliver the fair, consistent, and reliable sentences of death required by the Constitution.

And, in 2008, Justice John Paul Stevens, since retired, wrote this:

> [I am persuaded] that current decisions by state legislatures, by the Congress of the United States, and by this Court to retain the death penalty as a part of our law are the product of habit and inattention rather than an acceptable deliberative process that weighs the costs and risks of administering that penalty against its identifiable benefits, and rest in part on a faulty assumption about the retributive force of the death penalty. * * *

> The legitimacy of deterrence as an acceptable justification for the death penalty is * * * questionable, at best. Despite 30 years of empirical research in the area, there remains no reliable statistical evidence that capital punishment in fact deters potential offenders.[13] In the absence of such evidence, deterrence cannot serve as a sufficient penological justification for this uniquely severe and irrevocable punishment.

> We are left, then, with retribution as the primary rationale for imposing the death penalty. And indeed, it is the retribution rationale that animates much of the remaining enthusiasm for the death penalty. * * *

---

13. Admittedly, there has been a recent surge in scholarship asserting the deterrent effect of the death penalty, but there has been an equal, if not greater, amount of scholarship criticizing the methodologies of those studies and questioning the results. [See Note 6, supra, in this casebook.—Ed.]

At the same time, however, * * * our society has moved away from public and painful retribution towards ever more humane forms of punishment. State-sanctioned killing is therefore becoming more and more anachronistic. In an attempt to bring executions in line with our evolving standards of decency, we have adopted increasingly less painful methods of execution, and then declared previous methods barbaric and archaic. But by requiring that an execution be relatively painless, we necessarily protect the inmate from enduring any punishment that is comparable to the suffering inflicted on his victim. This trend, while appropriate and required by the Eighth Amendment's prohibition on cruel and unusual punishment, actually undermines the very premise on which public approval of the retribution rationale is based.

* * * The time for a dispassionate, impartial comparison of the enormous costs that death penalty litigation imposes on society with the benefits that it produces has surely arrived.

Baze v. Rees, 553 U.S. 35, 128 S.Ct. 1520, 170 L.Ed.2d 420 (2008) (concurring in the judgment).

2. THE QUEST FOR RELIABLE PROCEDURES

INTRODUCTORY COMMENT

Furman v. Georgia (p. 338 supra) taught that juries may not be given unfettered discretion to make life-and-death sentencing decisions in capital cases. *Woodson v. North Carolina* (p. 346, Note 1) taught the opposite lesson: that juries must be provided *some* discretion, because the Constitution prohibits treating "uniquely human beings" as members of a "faceless, undifferentiated mass to be subjected to the blind infliction of the penalty of death." Together, these two lessons constitute "the yin and the yang of the eighth amendment," Scott E. Sundby, *The Lockett Paradox: Reconciling Guided Discretion and Unguided Mitigation in Capital Sentencing,* 38 UCLA L.Rev. 1147, 1148 (1991). According to Justice Scalia, the two injunctions, "like * * * the twin objectives of good and evil * * * cannot be reconciled." Walton v. Arizona, 497 U.S. 639, 110 S.Ct. 3047, 111 L.Ed.2d 511 (1990) (concurring opinion).

Does the current system of guided discretion coupled with individualized sentencing work reliably? The materials in this subsection look at this issue.

a. The Lingering Question of Racial Discrimination

McCLESKEY v. KEMP
Supreme Court of the United States, 1987.
481 U.S. 279, 107 S.Ct. 1756, 95 L.Ed.2d 262.

POWELL, J., delivered the opinion of the Court, in which REHNQUIST, C.J., and WHITE, O'CONNOR, and SCALIA, JJ., joined. * * *

This case presents the question whether a complex statistical study that indicates a risk that racial considerations enter into capital sentencing determinations proves that petitioner McCleskey's capital sentence is unconstitutional under the Eighth or Fourteenth Amendment.

I

[Warren McCleskey, a black man, was convicted of the murder of a white police officer during the course of a robbery. In the post-conviction sentencing hearing, the jury recommended the death penalty after it found beyond a reasonable doubt the existence of two statutory aggravating circumstances (that the killing occurred during the commission of a robbery, and that the victim was a peace officer engaged in the performance of his duties) and no mitigating factors. The judge followed the recommendation and sentenced McCleskey to death. On appeal, the state supreme court affirmed the conviction and sentence.]

McCleskey next filed a petition for a writ of habeas corpus in the Federal District Court for the Northern District of Georgia. His petition raised 18 claims, one of which was that the Georgia capital sentencing process is administered in a racially discriminatory manner in violation of the Eighth and Fourteenth Amendments to the United States Constitution. In support of his claim, McCleskey proffered a statistical study performed by Professors David C. Baldus, Charles Pulaski, and George Woodworth, and (the Baldus study) that purports to show a disparity in the imposition of the death sentence in Georgia based on the race of the murder victim and, to a lesser extent, the race of the defendant. The Baldus study is actually two sophisticated statistical studies that examine over 2,000 murder cases that occurred in Georgia during the 1970's. The raw numbers collected by Professor Baldus indicate that defendants charged with killing white persons received the death penalty in 11% of the cases, but defendants charged with killing blacks received the death penalty in only 1% of the cases. The raw numbers also indicate a reverse racial disparity according to the race of the defendant: 4% of the black defendants received the death penalty, as opposed to 7% of the white defendants.

Baldus also divided the cases according to the combination of the race of the defendant and the race of the victim. He found that the death penalty was assessed in 22% of the cases involving black defendants and white victims; 8% of the cases involving white defendants and white victims; 1% of the cases involving black defendants and black victims; and 3% of the cases involving white defendants and black victims. Similarly, Baldus found that prosecutors sought the death penalty in 70% of the cases involving black defendants and white victims; 32% of the cases involving white defendants and white victims; 15% of the cases involving black defendants and black victims; and 19% of the cases involving white defendants and black victims.

Baldus subjected his data to an extensive analysis, taking account of 230 variables that could have explained the disparities on nonracial grounds. One of his models concludes that, even after taking account of 39 nonracial variables, defendants charged with killing white victims were 4.3

times as likely to receive a death sentence as defendants charged with killing blacks. According to this model, black defendants were 1.1 times as likely to receive a death sentence as other defendants. Thus, the Baldus study indicates that black defendants, such as McCleskey, who kill white victims have the greatest likelihood of receiving the death penalty. * * *

II

McCleskey's first claim is that the Georgia capital punishment statute violates the Equal Protection Clause of the Fourteenth Amendment. He argues that race has infected the administration of Georgia's statute in two ways: persons who murder whites are more likely to be sentenced to death than persons who murder blacks, and black murderers are more likely to be sentenced to death than white murderers. As a black defendant who killed a white victim, McCleskey claims that the Baldus study demonstrates that he was discriminated against because of his race and because of the race of his victim. In its broadest form, McCleskey's claim of discrimination extends to every actor in the Georgia capital sentencing process, from the prosecutor who sought the death penalty and the jury that imposed the sentence, to the State itself that enacted the capital punishment statute and allows it to remain in effect despite its allegedly discriminatory application. We agree with the Court of Appeals, and every other court that has considered such a challenge, that this claim must fail.

Our analysis begins with the basic principle that a defendant who alleges an equal protection violation has the burden of proving "the existence of purposeful discrimination." A corollary to this principle is that a criminal defendant must prove that the purposeful discrimination "had a discriminatory effect" on him. Thus, to prevail under the Equal Protection Clause, McCleskey must prove that the decisionmakers in *his* case acted with discriminatory purpose. He offers no evidence specific to his own case that would support an inference that racial considerations played a part in his sentence. Instead, he relies solely on the Baldus study. McCleskey argues that the Baldus study compels an inference that his sentence rests on purposeful discrimination. McCleskey's claim that these statistics are sufficient proof of discrimination, without regard to the facts of a particular case, would extend to all capital cases in Georgia, at least where the victim was white and the defendant is black.

The Court has accepted statistics as proof of intent to discriminate in certain limited contexts. First, this Court has accepted statistical disparities as proof of an equal protection violation in the selection of the jury venire in a particular district. * * * Second, this Court has accepted statistics in the form of multiple-regression analysis to prove statutory violations under Title VII of the Civil Rights Act of 1964 [relating to employment discrimination].

But the nature of the capital sentencing decision, and the relationship of the statistics to that decision, are fundamentally different from the corresponding elements in the venire-selection or Title VII cases. Most importantly, each particular decision to impose the death penalty is made by a petit jury selected from a properly constituted venire. Each jury is unique in its composition, and the Constitution requires that its decision rest on consideration of innumerable factors that vary according to the characteristics of the individual defendant and the facts of the particular capital offense. Thus, the application of an inference drawn from the general statistics to a specific decision in a trial and sentencing simply is not comparable to the application of an inference drawn from general statistics to a specific venire-selection or Title VII case. In those cases, the statistics relate to fewer entities, and fewer variables are relevant to the challenged decisions. * * *

Finally, McCleskey's statistical proffer must be viewed in the context of his challenge. McCleskey challenges decisions at the heart of the State's criminal justice system. "[O]ne of society's most basic tasks is that of protecting the lives of its citizens and one of the most basic ways in which it achieves the task is through criminal laws against murder." *Gregg v. Georgia,* 428 U.S. 153, 226, 96 S.Ct. 2909, 2949, 49 L.Ed.2d 859 (1976) (WHITE, J., concurring). Implementation of these laws necessarily requires discretionary judgments. Because discretion is essential to the criminal justice process, we would demand exceptionally clear proof before we would infer that the discretion has been abused. * * * Accordingly, we hold that the Baldus study is clearly insufficient to support an inference that any of the decisionmakers in McCleskey's case acted with discriminatory purpose. * * *

* * * Accordingly, we reject McCleskey's equal protection claims. * * *

IV

[The court then turned to McCleskey's alternative argument that the Baldus study demonstrates that the Georgia capital sentencing system violates the Eighth Amendment.] * * *

To evaluate McCleskey's challenge, we must examine exactly what the Baldus study may show. Even Professor Baldus does not contend that his statistics *prove* that race enters into any capital sentencing decisions or that race was a factor in McCleskey's particular case. Statistics at most may show only a likelihood that a particular factor entered into some decisions. There is, of course, some risk of racial prejudice influencing a jury's decision in a criminal case. There are similar risks that other kinds of prejudice will influence other criminal trials. The question "is at what point that risk becomes constitutionally unacceptable." McCleskey asks us to accept the likelihood allegedly shown by the Baldus study as the constitutional measure of an unacceptable risk of racial prejudice influencing capital sentencing decisions. This we decline to do. * * *

Individual jurors bring to their deliberations "qualities of human nature and varieties of human experience, the range of which is unknown and perhaps unknowable." The capital sentencing decision requires the individual jurors to focus their collective judgment on the unique characteristics of a particular criminal defendant. It is not surprising that such collective judgments often are difficult to explain. But the inherent lack of predictability of jury decisions does not justify their condemnation. On the contrary, it is the jury's function to make the difficult and uniquely human judgments that defy codification and that "buil[d] discretion, equity, and flexibility into a legal system."

McCleskey's argument that the Constitution condemns the discretion allowed decisionmakers in the Georgia capital sentencing system is antithetical to the fundamental role of discretion in our criminal justice system. Discretion in the criminal justice system offers substantial benefits to the criminal defendant. Not only can a jury decline to impose the death sentence, it can decline to convict or choose to convict of a lesser offense. Whereas decisions against a defendant's interest may be reversed by the trial judge or on appeal, these discretionary exercises of leniency are final and unreviewable. * * *

At most, the Baldus study indicates a discrepancy that appears to correlate with race. Apparent disparities in sentencing are an inevitable part of our criminal justice system. * * * As this Court has recognized, any mode for determining guilt or punishment "has its weaknesses and the potential for misuse." Specifically, "there can be 'no perfect procedure for deciding in which cases governmental authority should be used to impose death.'" Despite these imperfections, our consistent rule has been that constitutional guarantees are met when "the mode [for determining guilt or punishment] itself has been surrounded with safeguards to make it as fair as possible." Where the discretion that is fundamental to our criminal process is involved, we decline to assume that what is unexplained is invidious. In light of the safeguards designed to minimize racial bias in the process, the fundamental value of jury trial in our criminal justice system, and the benefits that discretion provides to criminal defendants, we hold that the Baldus study does not demonstrate a constitutionally significant risk of racial bias affecting the Georgia capital sentencing process.

V

Two additional concerns inform our decision in this case. First, McCleskey's claim, taken to its logical conclusion, throws into serious question the principles that underlie our entire criminal justice system. The Eighth Amendment is not limited in application to capital punishment, but applies to all penalties. Thus, if we accepted McCleskey's claim that racial bias has impermissibly tainted the capital sentencing decision, we could soon be faced with similar claims as to other types of penalty.[38] Moreover, the claim that his sentence rests on the irrelevant factor of race easily could be extended to apply to claims based on unexplained discrep-

---

38. Studies already exist that allegedly demonstrate a racial disparity in the length of prison sentences. See, *e.g.*, Spohn, Gruhl, & Welch, The Effect of Race on Sentencing: A Reexamination of an Unsettled Question, 16 Law & Soc.Rev. 71 (1981–1982); Unnever, Frazier, & Henretta, Race Differences in Criminal Sentencing, 21 Sociological Q. 197 (1980).

ancies that correlate to membership in other minority groups, and even to gender.[40] * * * As these examples illustrate, there is no limiting principle to the type of challenge brought by McCleskey. The Constitution does not require that a State eliminate any demonstrable disparity that correlates with a potentially irrelevant factor in order to operate a criminal justice system that includes capital punishment. * * *

Second, McCleskey's arguments are best presented to the legislative bodies. * * * Legislatures * * * are better qualified to weigh and "evaluate the results of statistical studies in terms of their own local conditions and with a flexibility of approach that is not available to the courts." * * *

JUSTICE BRENNAN, with whom JUSTICE MARSHALL, * * * JUSTICE BLACKMUN and JUSTICE STEVENS join * * *, * * * dissenting. * * *

At some point in this case, Warren McCleskey doubtless asked his lawyer whether a jury was likely to sentence him to die. A candid reply to this question would have been disturbing. First, counsel would have to tell McCleskey that few of the details of the crime or of McCleskey's past criminal conduct were more important than the fact that his victim was white. Furthermore, counsel would feel bound to tell McCleskey that defendants charged with killing white victims in Georgia are 4.3 times as likely to be sentenced to death as defendants charged with killing blacks. In addition, frankness would compel the disclosure that it was more likely than not that the race of McCleskey's victim would determine whether he received a death sentence * * *. Finally, the assessment would not be complete without the information that cases involving black defendants and white victims are more likely to result in a death sentence than cases featuring any other racial combination of defendant and victim. The story could be told in a variety of ways, but McCleskey could not fail to grasp its essential narrative line: there was a significant chance that race would play a prominent role in determining if he lived or died.

The Court today holds that Warren McCleskey's sentence was constitutionally imposed. It finds no fault in a system in which lawyers must tell their clients that race casts a large shadow on the capital sentencing process. * * * The Court's evaluation of the significance of petitioner's evidence is fundamentally at odds with our consistent concern for rationality in capital sentencing * * *.

Considering the race of a defendant or victim in deciding if the death penalty should be imposed is completely at odds with [the] concern that an individual be evaluated as a unique human being. Decisions influenced by race rest in part on a categorical assessment of the worth of human beings according to color, insensitive to whatever qualities the individuals in question may possess. Enhanced willingness to impose the death sentence on black defendants, or diminished willingness to render such a sentence

---

40. See Chamblin, The Effect of Sex on the Imposition of the Death Penalty (speech given at a symposium of the American Psychological Association, entitled "Extra-legal Attributes Affecting Death Penalty Sentencing," New York City, Sept., 1979); Steffensmeier, Effects of Judge's and Defendant's Sex on the Sentencing of Offenders, 14 Psychology, Journal of Human Behavior, 3 (Aug. 1977).

when blacks are victims, reflects a devaluation of the lives of black persons. When confronted with evidence that race more likely than not plays such a role in a capital sentencing system, it is plainly insufficient to say that the importance of discretion demands that the risk be higher before we will act—for in such a case the very end that discretion is designed to serve is being undermined. * * *

In fairness, the Court's fear that McCleskey's claim is an invitation to descend a slippery slope also rests on the realization that any humanly imposed system of penalties will exhibit some imperfection. Yet to reject McCleskey's powerful evidence on this basis is to ignore both the qualitatively different character of the death penalty and the particular repugnance of racial discrimination, considerations which may properly be taken into account in determining whether various punishments are "cruel and unusual." Furthermore, it fails to take account of the unprecedented refinement and strength of the Baldus study. * * *

NOTES AND QUESTIONS

1.   After retirement from the Court, Justice Powell indicated that if he could change his vote in any case he heard while on the Court, it would be his vote in *McCleskey*. John C. Jeffries, Jr., Justice Lewis F. Powell, Jr. 451–52 (1994).

2.   Warren McCleskey died in Georgia's electric chair in September, 1991.

3.   A study commissioned by Maryland Governor Parris Glendening, a supporter of the death penalty, found that from 1978 through 1999, blacks who killed whites were significantly more likely to face the death penalty in Maryland than blacks who killed blacks or white killers (regardless of the race of the victim). Adam Liptak, *Death Penalty Found More Likely When Victim Is White*, New York Times, Jan. 8, 2003, at A12. The study also found that the disparities were almost entirely the result of decisions made by prosecutors in deciding whom to charge with capital murder. Later actions by prosecutors at trial, and by judges and juries, had little impact on the outcome.

Racial-disparity results have been reported in other studies. See generally, David C. Baldus & George Woodworth, *Racial Discrimination and the Death Penalty: An Empirical and Legal Overview*, in America's Experiment with Capital Punishment 601 (James R. Acker et al., 2d ed. 2003). And, according to a study of more than one hundred post-*Furman* executions arising from Harris County, Texas, which includes the City of Houston, the race of the defendant alone—even holding the race of the victim constant—played a significant role in explaining who was sentenced to death. According to the study, even controlling for the nature of the murders involved, "the bar appears to have been set lower for pursuing death against black defendants." Scott Phillips, *Racial Disparities in the Capital of Capital Punishment*, 45 Houston L. Rev. 807 (2008).

4.   Does the Baldus study in *McClesky* suggest that persons undeserving of death are sentenced to die due to racial discrimination, or rather that

persons deserving to die escape punishment due to racism, or both? Does this difference matter?

5. *Other disparities.* Lawyer-author Scott Turow, a member of the Illinois blue-ribbon commission formed to look at that state's capital punishment system observed,

> I was struck again and again by the wide variation in the seriousness of the crime. There were many monstrous offenses, but also a number of garden-variety murders. And the feeling that the system is an unguided ship is only heightened when one examines the first-degree homicides that have resulted in sentences other than death.

Scott Turow, *To Kill or Not to Kill*, The New Yorker, Jan. 6, 2003, at 44. A person who committed a "stickup gone bad" was on Death Row, Turow reported, whereas a man who had knocked a victim unconscious and then put him on railroad tracks in front of an oncoming train, and a woman who fed acid to her baby, avoided the death penalty. Turow's conclusion was that, for many persons on Death Row, they were essentially there "for the crime of having the wrong lawyers," id., in that they were defended by inexperienced attorneys and by lawyers paid so little by the state to represent indigents that they received inadequate representation.

Geography, as well, seems to have much to do with sentencing judgments. In Illinois, a person who commits first-degree murder in a rural area is five times more likely to receive a death sentence than one who murders in Chicago's Cook County. Id. In New York, murderers outside New York City and its suburbs are ten times more likely to face the death penalty than those inside the New York City region. Alan Finder, *New York's New Death Penalty: Most Defendants Are White, From Upstate*, New York Times, Jan. 21, 1999, at A23. Meanwhile, in Nebraska, prosecutors in urban counties were more likely to seek the death penalty than those in rural areas, but urban-area judges (until recently, state law provided for judicial, rather than jury, sentencing in death penalty cases) were less likely to impose the death penalty than those in rural communities. Pam Belluck, *Nebraska Is Said to Use Death Penalty Unequally*, New York Times, Aug. 2, 2001, at A13. See also Katherine Barnes, et al., *Place Matters (Most): An Empirical Study of Prosecutorial Decision–Making in Death–Eligible Cases*, 51 Arizona L. Rev. 305 (2009) (concluding, based on an empirical analysis of 1997–2001 Missouri homicide cases, that geographical and racial disparities existed in sentencing because of broad prosecutorial discretion).

b. Victim Impact Evidence

PAYNE v. TENNESSEE
Supreme Court of the United States, 1991.
501 U.S. 808, 111 S.Ct. 2597, 115 L.Ed.2d 720.

R**EHNQUIST**, C.J. delivered the opinion of the court, in which W**HITE**, O'C**ONNOR**, S**CALIA**, K**ENNEDY**, and S**OUTER**, JJ. joined. * * *

In this case we reconsider our holdings in *Booth v. Maryland*, 482 U.S. 496, 107 S.Ct. 2529, 96 L.Ed.2d 440 (1987), and *South Carolina v.*

Gathers, 490 U.S. 805, 109 S.Ct. 2207, 104 L.Ed.2d 876 (1989), that the Eighth Amendment bars the admission of victim impact evidence during the penalty phase of a capital trial.

The petitioner, Pervis Tyrone Payne, was convicted by a jury on two counts of first-degree murder and one count of assault with intent to commit murder in the first degree. He was sentenced to death for each of the murders, and to 30 years in prison for the assault.

The victims of Payne's offenses were 28–year–old Charisse Christopher, her 2–year–old daughter Lacie, and her 3–year–old son Nicholas. The three lived together in an apartment in Millington, Tennessee, across the hall from Payne's girlfriend, Bobbie Thomas. On Saturday, June 27, 1987, Payne * * * passed the morning and early afternoon injecting cocaine and drinking beer. * * * Sometime around 3 p.m., Payne * * * entered the Christophers' apartment, and began making sexual advances towards Charisse. Charisse resisted and Payne became violent. A neighbor who resided in the apartment directly beneath the Christophers * * * called the police after she heard a "blood curdling scream" from the Christopher apartment.

When the first police officer arrived at the scene, he immediately encountered Payne who was leaving the apartment building, so covered with blood that he appeared to be " 'sweating blood.' " * * *

Inside the apartment, the police encountered a horrifying scene. Blood covered the walls and floor throughout the unit. Charisse and her children were lying on the floor in the kitchen. Nicholas, despite several wounds inflicted by a butcher knife that completely penetrated through his body from front to back, was still breathing. Miraculously, he survived, but not until after undergoing seven hours of surgery and a transfusion of 1700 cc's of blood—400 to 500 cc's more than his estimated normal blood volume. Charisse and Lacie were dead.

Charisse's body was found on the kitchen floor on her back, her legs fully extended. She had sustained 42 direct knife wounds and 42 defensive wounds on her arms and hands. The wounds were caused by 41 separate thrusts of a butcher knife. None of the 84 wounds inflicted by Payne were individually fatal; rather, the cause of death was most likely bleeding from all of the wounds. * * *

During the sentencing phase of the trial, Payne presented the testimony of four witnesses: his mother and father, Bobbie Thomas, and * * * a clinical psychologist * * *. [Thomas and Payne's relatives testified that Payne attended church and was a person of good character. The psychologist testified that Payne scored low on an intelligence test and was "mentally handicapped."]

The State presented the testimony of Charisse's mother, Mary Zvolanek. When asked how Nicholas had been affected by the murders of his mother and sister, she responded:

"He cries for his mom. He doesn't seem to understand why she doesn't come home. And he cries for his sister Lacie. He comes to me many times during the week and asks me, Grandmama, do you miss my Lacie. And I tell him yes. He says, I'm worried about my Lacie."

In arguing for the death penalty during closing argument, the prosecutor commented on the continuing effects of Nicholas' experience, stating:

"But we do know that Nicholas was alive. And Nicholas was in the same room. Nicholas was still conscious. His eyes were open. He responded to the paramedics. He was able to follow their directions. He was able to hold his intestines in as he was carried to the ambulance. So he knew what happened to his mother and baby sister."

"There is nothing you can do to ease the pain of any of the families involved in this case. There is nothing you can do to ease the pain of Bernice or Carl Payne, and that's a tragedy. * * * There is obviously nothing you can do for Charisse and Lacie Jo. But there is something that you can do for Nicholas.

"Somewhere down the road Nicholas is going to grow up, hopefully. He's going to want to know what happened. And he is going to know what happened to his baby sister and his mother. He is going to want to know what type of justice was done. He is going to want to know what happened. With your verdict, you will provide the answer." * * *

The jury sentenced Payne to death on each of the murder counts. * * *

We granted certiorari, to reconsider our holdings in *Booth* and *Gathers* that the Eighth Amendment prohibits a capital sentencing jury from considering "victim impact" evidence relating to the personal characteristics of the victim and the emotional impact of the crimes on the victim's family.

In *Booth*, the defendant robbed and murdered an elderly couple. As required by a state statute, a victim impact statement was prepared based on interviews with the victims' son, daughter, son-in-law, and granddaughter. The statement, which described the personal characteristics of the victims, the emotional impact of the crimes on the family, and set forth the family members' opinions and characterizations of the crimes and the defendant, was submitted to the jury at sentencing. The jury imposed the death penalty. * * *

This Court held by a 5-to-4 vote that the Eighth Amendment prohibits a jury from considering a victim impact statement at the sentencing phase of a capital trial. The Court made clear that the admissibility of victim impact evidence was not to be determined on a case-by-case basis, but that such evidence was *per se* inadmissible in the sentencing phase of a capital case except to the extent that it "related directly to the circumstances of the crime." In *Gathers,* decided two years later, the Court extended the rule announced in *Booth* to statements made by a prosecutor to the sentencing jury regarding the personal qualities of the victim.

The *Booth* Court began its analysis with the observation that the capital defendant must be treated as a "uniquely individual human bein[g]," and therefore the Constitution requires the jury to make an individualized determination as to whether the defendant should be executed based on the "character of the individual and the circumstances of the crime." The Court concluded that while no prior decision of this Court had mandated that only the defendant's character and immediate characteristics of the crime may constitutionally be considered, other factors are irrelevant to the capital sentencing decision unless they have "some bearing on the defendant's 'personal responsibility and moral guilt.'" To the extent that victim impact evidence presents "factors about which the defendant was unaware, and that were irrelevant to the decision to kill," the Court concluded, it has nothing to do with the "blameworthiness of a particular defendant." Evidence of the victim's character, the Court observed, "could well distract the sentencing jury from its constitutionally required task [of] determining whether the death penalty is appropriate in light of the background and record of the accused and the particular circumstances of the crime." The Court concluded that, except to the extent that victim impact evidence relates "directly to the circumstances of the crime," the prosecution may not introduce such evidence at a capital sentencing hearing because "it creates an impermissible risk that the capital sentencing decision will be made in an arbitrary manner."

Booth and *Gathers* were based on two premises: that evidence relating to a particular victim or to the harm that a capital defendant causes a victim's family do not in general reflect on the defendant's "blameworthiness," and that only evidence relating to "blameworthiness" is relevant to the capital sentencing decision. However, the assessment of harm caused by the defendant as a result of the crime charged has understandably been an important concern of the criminal law, both in determining the elements of the offense and in determining the appropriate punishment. Thus, two equally blameworthy criminal defendants may be guilty of different offenses solely because their acts cause differing amounts of harm. "If a bank robber aims his gun at a guard, pulls the trigger, and kills his target, he may be put to death. If the gun unexpectedly misfires, he may not. His moral guilt in both cases is identical, but his responsibility in the former is greater." *Booth*, 482 U.S., at 519, 107 S.Ct., at 2541 (Scalia, J., dissenting). * * *

Wherever judges in recent years have had discretion to impose sentence, the consideration of the harm caused by the crime has been an important factor in the exercise of that discretion * * *. * * *

Payne echoes the concern voiced in *Booth*'s case that the admission of victim impact evidence permits a jury to find that defendants whose victims were assets to their community are more deserving of punishment that those whose victims are perceived to be less worthy. As a general matter, however, victim impact evidence is not offered to encourage comparative judgments of this kind—for instance, that the killer of a hardworking, devoted parent deserves the death penalty, but that the murderer of a reprobate does not. It is designed to show instead *each* victim's "uniqueness as an individual human being," whatever the jury might think the loss to the community resulting from his death might be. The facts of *Gathers* are an excellent illustration of this: the evidence showed that the victim was an out of work, mentally handicapped individual, perhaps not, in the eyes of most, a significant contributor to society, but nonetheless a murdered human being. * * *

We are now of the view that a State may properly conclude that for the jury to assess meaningfully the defendant's moral culpability and blameworthiness, it should have before it at the sentencing phase evidence of the specific harm caused by the defendant. "[T]he State has a legitimate interest in counteracting the mitigating evidence which the defendant is entitled to put in, by reminding the sentencer that just as the murderer should be considered as an individual, so too the victim is an individual whose death represents a unique loss to society and in particular to his family." *Booth*, 482 U.S., at 517, 107 S.Ct., at 2540 (White, J., dissenting). By turning the victim into a "faceless stranger at the penalty phase of a capital trial," *Booth* deprives the State of the full moral force of its evidence and may prevent the jury from having before it all the information necessary to determine the proper punishment for a first-degree murder. * * *

We thus hold that if the State chooses to permit the admission of victim impact evidence and prosecutorial argument on that subject, the Eighth Amendment erects no *per se* bar. A State may legitimately conclude that evidence about the victim and about the impact of the murder on the victim's family is relevant to the jury's decision as to whether or not the death penalty should be imposed. There is no reason to treat such evidence differently than other relevant evidence is treated. * * *

JUSTICE SOUTER, with whom JUSTICE KENNEDY joins, concurring. * * *

* * * Murder has foreseeable consequences. When it happens, it is always to distinct individuals, and after it happens other victims are left behind. Every defendant knows, if endowed with the mental competence for criminal responsibility, that the life he will take by his homicidal behavior is that of a unique person, like himself, and that the person to be killed probably has close associates, "survivors," who will suffer harms and deprivations from the victim's death. Just as defendants know that they are not faceless human ciphers, they know that their victims are not valueless fungibles, and just as defendants appreciate the web of relationships and dependencies in which they live, they know that their victims are not human islands, but individuals with parents or children, spouses or friends or dependents. Thus, when a defendant chooses to kill, or to raise the risk of a victim's death, this choice necessarily relates to a whole human being and threatens an association of others, who may be distinctly hurt. The fact that the defendant may not know the details of a victim's life and characteristics, or the exact identities and needs of those who may survive, should not in any way obscure the further facts that death is always to a "unique" individual, and harm to some group of survivors is a consequence of a successful homicidal act so foreseeable as to be virtually inevitable.

That foreseeability of the killing's consequences imbues them with direct moral relevance, and evidence of the specific harm caused when a homicidal risk is realized is nothing more than evidence of the risk that the defendant originally chose to run despite the kinds of consequences that were obviously foreseeable. It is morally both defensible and appropriate to consider such evidence when penalizing a murderer, like other criminals, in light of common knowledge and the moral responsibility that such knowledge entails. * * *

JUSTICE MARSHALL, with whom JUSTICE BLACKMUN joins, dissenting.

Power, not reason, is the new currency of this Court's decisionmaking. Four Terms ago, a five-Justice majority of this Court held that "victim impact" evidence of the type at issue in this case could not constitutionally be introduced during the penalty phase of a capital trial. *Booth v. Maryland.* By another 5–4 vote, a majority of this Court rebuffed an attack upon this ruling just two Terms ago. *South Carolina v. Gathers.* Nevertheless, today's majority overrules *Booth* and *Gathers* and credits the dissenting views expressed in those cases. Neither the law nor the facts supporting *Booth* and *Gathers* underwent any change in the last four years. Only the personnel of this Court did. * * *

JUSTICE STEVENS, with whom JUSTICE BLACKMUN joins, dissenting.

* * * Justice Marshall is properly concerned about the majority's trivialization of the doctrine of *stare decisis.* But even if *Booth* and *Gathers* had not been decided, today's decision would represent a sharp break with past decisions. Our cases provide no support whatsoever for the majority's conclusion that the prosecutor may introduce evidence that sheds no light on the defendant's guilt or moral culpability, and thus serves no purpose other than to encourage jurors to decide in favor of death rather than life on the basis of their emotions rather than their reason. * * *

* * * Evidence that serves no purpose other than to appeal to the sympathies or emotions of the jurors has never been considered admissible. Thus, if a defendant, who had murdered a convenience store clerk in cold blood in the course of an armed robbery, offered evidence unknown to him at the time of the crime about the immoral character of his victim, all would recognize immediately that the evidence was irrelevant and inadmissible. Evenhanded justice requires that the same constraint be imposed on the advocate of the death penalty. * * *

* * * [In] *Lockett v. Ohio,* 438 U.S. 586, 98 S.Ct. 2954, 57 L.Ed.2d 973 (1978), * * * Chief Justice Burger concluded that in a capital case, the

sentencer must not be prevented "from considering, as a mitigating factor, any aspect of a defendant's character or record and any of the circumstances of the offense that the defendant proffers as a basis for a sentence less than death." * * *

Today's majority has obviously been moved by an argument that has strong political appeal but no proper place in a reasoned judicial opinion. Because our decision in *Lockett* recognizes the defendant's right to introduce all mitigating evidence that may inform the jury about his character, the Court suggests that fairness requires that the State be allowed to respond with similar evidence about the *victim*. This argument is a classic *non sequitur:* The victim is not on trial; her character, whether good or bad, cannot therefore constitute either an aggravating or mitigating circumstance. * * *

The premise that a criminal prosecution requires an even-handed balance between the State and the defendant is also incorrect. The Constitution grants certain rights to the criminal defendant and imposes special limitations on the State designed to protect the individual from overreaching by the disproportionately powerful State. * * *

The majority attempts to justify the admission of victim impact evidence by arguing that "consideration of the harm caused by the crime has been an important factor in the exercise of [sentencing] discretion." This statement is misleading and inaccurate. It is misleading because it is not limited to harm that is foreseeable. It is inaccurate because it fails to differentiate between legislative determinations and judicial sentencing. It is true that an evaluation of the harm caused by different kinds of wrongful conduct is a critical aspect in legislative definitions of offenses and determinations concerning sentencing guidelines. * * * But the majority cites no authority for the suggestion that unforeseeable and indirect harms to a victim's family are properly considered as aggravating evidence on a case-by-case basis. * * *

The notion that the inability to produce an ideal system of justice in which every punishment is precisely married to the defendant's blameworthiness somehow justifies a rule that completely divorces some capital sentencing determinations from moral culpability is incomprehensible to me. Also incomprehensible is the argument that such a rule is required for the jury to take into account that each murder victim is a "unique" human being. The fact that each of us is unique is a proposition so obvious that it surely requires no evidentiary support. What is not obvious, however, is the way in which the character or reputation in one case may differ from that of other possible victims. Evidence offered to prove such differences can only be intended to identify some victims as more worthy of protection than others. Such proof risks decisions based on the same invidious motives as a prosecutor's decision to seek the death penalty if a victim is white but to accept a plea bargain if the victim is black.

Given the current popularity of capital punishment in a crime-ridden society, the political appeal of arguments that assume that increasing the severity of sentences is the best cure for the cancer of crime, and the political strength of the "victims' rights" movement, I recognize that today's decision will be greeted with enthusiasm by a large number of concerned and thoughtful citizens. The great tragedy of the decision, however, is the danger that the "hydraulic pressure" of public opinion that Justice Holmes once described—and that properly influences the deliberations of democratic legislatures—has played a role * * * in the Court's * * * resolution of the constitutional issue involved. Today is a sad day for a great institution.

NOTES AND QUESTIONS

1. Consider the following letter sent to one of the authors of this casebook from an attorney involved in the defense of a young man who, during a robbery at a park, pulled out a gun and shot a young man and woman who were in the park on a date, causing the death of the man. The defendant was convicted, after which the sentencing phase commenced. The lawyer wrote:

> During the penalty trial, the young brother of the deceased victim testified. The boy was 7 years old. He told of how he missed his brother and he was near tears in his testimony. This was near the end of the day, a long day of victim impact testimony. The judge was due to discharge the jury for the day when the young boy finished. But the judge was so visibly moved by this testimony that he turned toward the back wall, obviously in tears, and asked his clerk to discharge the jury. Prior to having the clerk take action, the judge had been turned away for almost a full minute. The jury clearly saw this happen.

The attorney moved for a mistrial and asked the judge to restart the penalty phase with a new jury. The motion was denied. The jury later returned a verdict of death. In interviews after the verdict, they cited the judge's reaction as having moved them and influenced their penalty decision.

Should the boy's testimony have been permitted? Should a new jury have been empaneled?

Do emotions have a legitimate role to play in capital sentencing hearings? To the extent that conceptions of deserved punishment are at issue, should feelings such as compassion for the defendant and, under *Payne,* compassion for the victim, count for anything? What about moral outrage at the criminal? Samuel H. Pillsbury, *Emotional Justice: Moralizing the Passions of Criminal Punishment,* 74 Cornell L.Rev. 655, 710 (1989), believes that the deliberative process in death penalty cases should not be wholly rationalistic:

> The language of law is the language of rationality, of the cool and the deliberative. While this insistence upon rationalistic expression has general merit in the elucidation of critical issues, in some instances it obscures more than it reveals. Where, as in criminal punishment, the influence of emotions is too fundamental to ignore or entirely condemn, the law's vocabulary requires expansion to permit emotive discourse. * * * The heart has its reasons, which reason knows not.

Professor Susan Bandes, in *Empathy, Narrative, and Victim Impact Statements*, 63 U.Chi.L.Rev. 361, 395, 401–03 (1996), however, worries about the effects of victim impact statements:

> Victim impact statements evoke not merely sympathy, pity, and compassion for the victim, but also a complex set of emotions directed toward the defendant, including hatred, fear, racial animus, vindictiveness, undifferentiated vengeance, and the desire to purge collective anger. These emotional reactions have a crucial common thread: they all deflect the jury from its duty to consider the individual defendant and his moral culpability. * * *

> * * * Contrary to Justice Steven's assertion in his dissent in *Payne*, the problem with victim impact statements is not that they evoke emotion rather than reason. Rather, it is that they evoke unreasoned, unreflective emotion that cannot be placed in any usable perspective. In evidentiary terms, victim impact statements are prejudicial and inflammatory. They overwhelm the jury with feelings of outrage toward the defendant and identification with the victim. Finally, victim impact statements diminish the jury's ability to process other relevant evidence, such as evidence in mitigation. * * * The admission of a victim impact statement does not simply expand the jury's empathetic horizons by making the victim more human. Instead, it interferes with—and indeed may completely block—the jury's ability to empathize with the defendant or comprehend his humanity.

In order to minimize the risk of "moral error," Professor Pillsbury, supra, would require judges to instruct jurors on the proper role of emotions. Judges should tell jurors that there is "nothing wrong" with feelings of anger regarding murder, but that "anger can overwhelm proper judgment." He proposes that, in determining what sentence to recommend or impose, jurors be told to consider the defendant, and also the victim, "as you might a neighbor * * * or social acquaintance, someone that you know and care about." Pillsbury, supra, at 704. Jurors should also be told "of their obligation to try to empathize with the offender as part of assessing deserved punishment." Id. at 703.

For recent empirical research that suggests that victim impact statements may reduce the reliability of the sentencing process, see Janice Nadler & Mary R. Rose, *Victim Impact Testimony and the Psychology of Punishment*, 88 Cornell L. Rev. 419 (2003); and Scott E. Sundby, *The Capital Jury and Empathy: The Problem of Worthy and Unworthy Victims*, 88 Cornell L. Rev. 343 (2003).

2. Victim-impact statements are growing more sophisticated. Consider this description from Kelly v. California, 555 U.S. 1020, 129 S.Ct. 564, 172 L.Ed.2d 445 (2008) (statement of Stevens, J., respecting the denial of the petition[ ] for writ[ ] of certiorari):

> The prosecution played a 20–minute video consisting of a montage of still photographs and video footage documenting [19–year–old Sara] Weir's life from her infancy until shortly before she was killed. The video was narrated by the victim's mother with soft music playing in the background, and it showed scenes of her swimming, horseback riding, and

attending school and social functions with her family and friends. The video ended with a view of her grave marker and footage of people riding horseback in Alberta, Canada—the " 'kind of heaven' " in which her mother said she belonged.

(If you would like to see the video, it is available on the United States Supreme Court website at http://www.supremecourtus.gov/opinions/video/ kelly_v_california.aspx.)

Do you believe such videos should be permitted? According to Justice Stevens, the "emotionally evocative" video was "not probative of the culpability or character of the offender or the circumstances of the offense. Nor was the evidence particularly probative of the impact of the crimes on the victims' family members. The * * * video footage * * * bore no direct relation to the effect of [the] crime on the victims' family members." But, wouldn't a video that *did* describe the effect of the murder on Sara Weir's family have been *more* "emotionally evocative" and, therefore, more harmful to the interests of the defendant whose life was in the hands of the jurors?

3. SUBSTANTIVE LIMITATIONS ON THE DEATH PENALTY

TISON v. ARIZONA

Supreme Court of the United States, 1987.
481 U.S. 137, 107 S.Ct. 1676, 95 L.Ed.2d 127.

O'CONNOR, J., delivered the opinion of the Court, in which REHNQUIST, C.J., and WHITE, POWELL, and SCALIA, JJ., joined. * * *

The question presented is whether the petitioners' participation in the events leading up to and following the murder of four members of a family makes the sentences of death imposed by the Arizona courts constitutionally permissible although neither petitioner specifically intended to kill the victims and neither inflicted the fatal gunshot wounds. * * *

I

Gary Tison was sentenced to life imprisonment as the result of a prison escape during the course of which he had killed a guard. After he had been in prison a number of years, Gary Tison's wife, their three sons Donald, Ricky, and Raymond, Gary's brother Joseph, and other relatives made plans to help Gary Tison escape again. The Tison family assembled a large arsenal of weapons for this purpose. Plans for escape were discussed with Gary Tison, who insisted that his cellmate, Randy Greenawalt, also a convicted murderer, be included in the prison break. * * *

On July 30, 1978, the three Tison brothers entered the Arizona State Prison at Florence carrying a large ice chest filled with guns. The Tisons armed Greenawalt and their father, and the group, brandishing their weapons, locked the prison guards and visitors present in a storage closet. The five men fled the prison grounds in the Tison's Ford Galaxy automobile. No shots were fired at the prison.

After leaving the prison, the men abandoned the Ford automobile and proceeded on to an isolated house in a white Lincoln automobile that the brothers had parked at a hospital near the prison. At the house, the Lincoln automobile had a flat tire * * *. The group decided to flag down a passing motorist and steal a car. Raymond stood out in front of the Lincoln; the other four armed themselves and lay in wait by the side of the road. One car passed by without stopping, but a second car, a Mazda occupied by John Lyons, his wife Donnelda, his 2–year–old son Christopher, and his 15–year–old niece, Theresa Tyson, pulled over to render aid.

[Shortly thereafter, Gary Tison and Greenawalt intentionally shot to death the Lyonses and Tyson. Ricky and Raymond Tison, the petitioners, were some distance away, filling a water jug, when the shootings occurred. They expressed surprise at the killings.]

The State then individually tried each of the petitioners for capital murder of the four victims as well as for the associated crimes of armed robbery, kidnaping, and car theft. The capital murder charges were based on Arizona felony-murder law providing that a killing occurring during the perpetration of robbery or kidnaping is capital murder, and that each participant in the kidnaping or robbery is legally responsible for the acts of his accomplices. Each of the petitioners was convicted of the four murders under these accomplice liability and felony-murder statutes. * * *

* * * [T]he judge sentenced both petitioners to death.

On direct appeal, the Arizona Supreme Court affirmed. The Court found:

"The record establishes that both Ricky and Raymond Tison were present when the homicides took place and that they occurred as part of and in the course of the escape and continuous attempt to prevent recapture. The deaths would not have occurred but for their assistance. That they did not specifically intend that the Lyonses and Theresa Tyson die, that they did not plot in advance that these homicides would take place, or that they did not actually pull the triggers on the guns which inflicted the fatal wounds is of little significance." * * *

* * * We granted certiorari in order to consider the Arizona Supreme Court's application of *Enmund* [*v. Florida,* 458 U.S. 782, 102 S.Ct. 3368, 73 L.Ed.2d 1140 (1982)].

II

In *Enmund v. Florida,* this Court reversed the death sentence of a defendant convicted under Florida's felony-murder rule. Enmund was the driver of the "getaway" car in an armed robbery of a dwelling. The occupants of the house, an elderly couple, resisted and Enmund's accomplices killed them. * * *

This Court, citing the weight of legislative and community opinion, found a broad societal consensus, with which it agreed, that the death penalty was disproportional to the crime of robbery-felony murder "in these circumstances." The Court noted that although 32 American jurisdictions permitted the imposition of the death penalty for felony murders under a variety of circumstances, Florida was 1 of only 8 jurisdictions that authorized the death penalty "solely for participation in a robbery in which another robber takes life." Enmund was, therefore, sentenced under a distinct minority regime, a regime that permitted the imposition of the death penalty for felony murder *simpliciter*. * * *

After surveying the States' felony-murder statutes, the *Enmund* Court next examined the behavior of juries in cases like Enmund's in its attempt to assess American attitudes toward capital punishment in felony-murder cases. * * * The Court found the fact that only 3 of 739 death row inmates had been sentenced to death absent an intent to kill, physical presence, or direct participation in the fatal assault persuasive evidence that American juries considered the death sentence disproportional to felony murder *simpliciter*.

Against this background, the Court undertook its own proportionality analysis. Armed robbery is a serious offense, but one for which the penalty of death is plainly excessive * * *. Furthermore, the Court found that Enmund's degree of participation in *the murders* was so tangential that it could not be said to justify a sentence of death. It found that neither the deterrent nor the retributive purposes of the death penalty were advanced by imposing the death penalty upon Enmund. The *Enmund* Court was unconvinced "that the threat that the death penalty will be imposed for murder will measurably deter one who does not kill and has no intention or purpose that life will be taken." In reaching this conclusion, the Court relied upon the fact that killing only rarely occurred during the course of robberies, and such killing as did occur even more rarely resulted in death sentences if the evidence did not support an inference that the defendant intended to kill. The Court acknowledged, however, that "[i]t would be very different if the likelihood of a killing in the course of a robbery were so substantial that one should share the blame for the killing if he somehow participated in the felony."

That difference was also related to the second purpose of capital punishment, retribution. The heart of the retribution rationale is that a criminal sentence must be directly related to the personal culpability of the criminal offender. * * * Thus, in Enmund's case, "the focus [had to] be on *his* culpability, not on that of those who committed the robbery and shot the victims, for we insist on 'individualized consideration as a constitutional requirement in imposing the death sentence.'" Since Enmund's own participation in the felony murder was so attenuated and since there was no proof that Enmund had any culpable mental state, the death penalty was excessive retribution for his crimes. * * *

Petitioners [here] argue strenuously that they did not "intend to kill" as that concept has been generally understood in the common law. We accept this as true. Traditionally, "one intends certain consequences when he desires that his acts cause those consequences or knows that those consequences are substantially certain to result from his acts." As petitioners point out, there is no evidence that either Ricky or Raymond Tison took any act which he desired to, or was substantially certain would, cause death. * * *

* * * [Therefore,] [p]etitioners do not fall within the "intent to kill" category of felony murderers for which *Enmund* explicitly finds the death penalty permissible under the Eighth Amendment.

On the other hand, it is equally clear that petitioners also fall outside the category of felony murderers for whom *Enmund* explicitly held the death penalty disproportional: their degree of participation in the crimes was major rather than minor, and the record would support a finding of the culpable mental state of reckless indifference to human life. * * *

Raymond Tison brought an arsenal of lethal weapons into the Arizona State Prison which he then handed over to two convicted murderers, one of whom he knew had killed a prison guard in the course of a previous escape attempt. By his own admission he was prepared to kill in furtherance of the prison break. He performed the crucial role of flagging down a passing car occupied by an innocent family whose fate was then entrusted to the known killers he had previously armed. He robbed these people at their direction and then guarded the victims at gunpoint while they considered what next to do. He stood by and watched the killing, making no effort to assist the victims before, during, or after the shooting. Instead, he chose to assist the killers in their continuing criminal endeavors, ending in a gun battle with the police in the final showdown.

Ricky Tison's behavior differs in slight details only. * * *

These facts not only indicate that the Tison brothers' participation in the crime was anything but minor; they also would clearly support a finding that they both subjectively appreciated that their acts were likely to result in the taking of innocent life. The issue raised by this case is whether the Eighth Amendment prohibits the death penalty in the intermediate case of the defendant whose participation is major and whose mental state is one of reckless indifference to the value of human life. *Enmund* does not specifically address this point. * * *

A critical facet of the individualized determination of culpability required in capital cases is the mental state with which the defendant commits the crime. Deeply ingrained in our legal tradition is the idea that the more purposeful is the criminal conduct, the more serious is the offense, and, therefore, the more severely it ought to be punished. The ancient concept of malice aforethought was an early attempt to focus on mental state in order to distinguish those who deserved death from those who through "Benefit of * * * Clergy" would be spared. * * * In *Enmund v. Florida*, the Court recognized again the importance of mental state, explicitly permitting the death penalty in at least those cases where the felony murderer intended to kill and forbidding it in the case of a minor actor not shown to have had any culpable mental state.

A narrow focus on the question of whether or not a given defendant "intended to kill," however, is a highly unsatisfactory means of definitively distinguishing the most culpable and dangerous of murderers. Many who intend to, and do, kill are not criminally liable at all—those who act in self-defense or with other justification or excuse. Other intentional homicides, though criminal, are often felt undeserving of the death penalty—those that are the result of provocation. On the other hand, some nonintentional murderers may be among the most dangerous and inhumane of all—the person who tortures another not caring whether the victim lives or dies, or the robber who shoots someone in the course of the robbery, utterly indifferent to the fact that the desire to rob may have the unintended consequence of killing the victim as well as taking the victim's property. This reckless indifference to the value of human life may be every bit as shocking to the moral sense as an "intent to kill." Indeed it is for this very reason that the common law and modern criminal codes alike have classified behavior such as occurred in this case along with intentional murders. * * * [W]e hold that the reckless disregard for human life implicit in knowingly engaging in criminal activities known to carry a grave risk of death represents a highly culpable mental state, a mental state that may be taken into account in making a capital sentencing judgment when that conduct causes its natural, though also not inevitable, lethal result.

The petitioners' own personal involvement in the crimes was not minor, but rather, as specifically found by the trial court, "substantial." Far from merely sitting in a car away from the actual scene of the murders acting as the getaway driver to a robbery, each petitioner was actively involved in every element of the kidnaping-robbery and was physically present during the entire sequence of criminal activity culminating in the murder of the Lyons family and the subsequent flight. The Tisons' high level of participation in these crimes further implicates them in the resulting deaths. * * *

* * * We will not attempt to precisely delineate the particular types of conduct and states of mind warranting imposition of the death penalty here. Rather, we simply hold that major participation in the felony committed, combined with reckless indifference to human life, is sufficient to satisfy the *Enmund* culpability requirement. * * *

JUSTICE BRENNAN, with whom JUSTICE MARSHALL * * *, JUSTICE BLACKMUN and JUSTICE STEVENS join * * * dissenting. * * *

Under the felony-murder doctrine, a person who commits a felony is liable for *any* murder that occurs during the commission of that felony, regardless of whether he or she commits, attempts to commit, or intended to commit that murder. The doctrine thus imposes liability on felons for killings committed by cofelons during a felony. This curious doctrine is a living fossil from a legal era in which all felonies were punishable by death; in those circumstances, the state of mind of the felon with respect to the murder was understandably superfluous, because he or she could be executed simply for intentionally committing the felony. Today, in most American jurisdictions and in virtually all European and Commonwealth countries, a felon cannot be executed for a murder that he or she did not commit or specifically intend or attempt to commit. In some American jurisdictions, however, the authority to impose death in such circumstances still persists. Arizona is such a jurisdiction. * * *

One reason the Court offers for its conclusion that death is proportionate punishment for persons falling within * * * [the recklessness] category is that limiting the death penalty to those who intend to kill "is a highly unsatisfactory means of definitively distinguishing the most culpable and dangerous of murderers." To illustrate that intention cannot be dispositive, the Court offers as examples "the person *who tortures* another not caring whether the victim lives or dies, or the robber *who shoots* someone in the course of the robbery, utterly indifferent to the fact that the desire to rob may have the unintended consequence of killing the victim as well as taking the victim's property." Influential commentators and some States have approved the use of the death penalty for persons, like those given in the Court's examples, *who kill* others in circumstances manifesting an extreme indifference to the value of human life. * * * But the constitutionality of the death penalty for those individuals is no more relevant to this case than it was to *Enmund,* because this case, like *Enmund,* involves accomplices *who did not kill.* Thus, although some of the "most culpable and dangerous of murderers" may be those who killed without specifically intending to kill, it is considerably more difficult to apply that rubric convincingly to those who not only did not intend to kill, but who also have not killed.

It is precisely in this context—where the defendant has not killed—that a finding that he or she nevertheless intended to kill seems indispensable to establishing capital culpability. It is important first to note that such a defendant has not committed an *act* for which he or she could be sentenced to death. The applicability of the death penalty therefore turns entirely on the defendant's mental state with regard to an act committed by another. Factors such as the defendant's major participation in the events surrounding the killing or the defendant's presence at the scene are relevant insofar as they illuminate the defendant's mental state with regard to the killings. They cannot serve, however, as independent grounds for imposing the death penalty.

Second, when evaluating such a defendant's mental state, a determination that the defendant acted with intent is qualitatively different from a determination that the defendant acted with reckless indifference to human life. The difference lies in the nature of the choice each has made. The reckless actor has not *chosen* to bring about the killing in the way the intentional actor has. The person who chooses to act recklessly and is indifferent to the possibility of fatal consequences often deserves serious punishment. But because that person has not chosen to kill, his or her moral and criminal culpability is of a different degree than that of one who killed or intended to kill.

The importance of distinguishing between these different choices is rooted in our belief in the "freedom of the human will and a consequent ability and duty of the normal individual to choose between good and evil." *Morissette v. United States,* 342 U.S. 246, 250, 72 S.Ct. 240, 243, 96 L.Ed. 288 (1952). To be faithful to this belief, which is "universal and persistent in mature systems of law," the criminal law must ensure that the punishment an individual receives conforms to the choices that individual has made. Differential punishment of reckless and intentional actions is therefore essential if we are to retain "the relation between criminal liability and moral culpability" on which criminal justice depends. The State's ultimate sanction—if it is ever to be used—must be reserved for those whose culpability is greatest. * * *

NOTES AND QUESTIONS

1. *Aftermath.* On subsequent state appeals, the death sentences of Ricky and Raymond Tison were reduced to life imprisonment. One of the two actual triggermen in the murders, Randy Greenawalt, was executed on January 23, 1997.

As for the second triggerman, Gary Tison—the recipient of the murderous activities intended to help him escape—the story is a little different: He fled into the Arizona desert after a half-hour gun battle between sheriff deputies and himself, his son Donald Tison (who was killed in the gunfire), and Donald's brothers and Greenawalt (who all surrendered). Three hundred law enforcement officers and hundreds of civilian volunteers unsuccessfully searched for Gary Tison in the desert, in 120–degree heat, near the small town of Chuichu, Arizona. Weeks later, a foul odor led a citizen to the bloated and decomposed body of Gary Tison. He was lying face up under a mesquite tree, unwounded, but dead from exposure to the desert heat. *Death in the Desert,* Time Magazine, September 4, 1978.

2. Accomplice law (Chapter 11 infra) provides that a person who intentionally assists in the commission of an offense is guilty of that crime, even if the perpetrator would have committed the offense without the accomplice's assistance. An accomplice whose assistance was unnecessary might be termed a "noncausal accessory." Various studies of actual jury behavior in death penalty cases and of mock juries suggest that "community sentiment discriminates between felony-murder triggermen and felony-murder non-causal accessories, with the latter being significantly less likely than the former to get the death penalty." Norman J. Finkel, *Capital Felony–Murder, Objective Indicia, and Community Sentiment,* 32 Ariz.L.Rev. 819, 888 (1990); see also Joshua Dressler, *The Jurisprudence of Death by Another: Accessories and Capital Punishment,* 51 U.Colo.L.Rev. 17 (1979) (reaching the same outcome).

Is this community sentiment justifiable? For example, in terms of the death penalty, would *you* distinguish as a juror between the following three persons charged in the death of the victim during a bank robbery: (1) the triggerman in the bank robbery, who personally killed the victim; (2) the person who solicited the robbery, but who was not present during the commission of the robbery or homicide; and (3) the unarmed accomplice to the robbery, whose assistance was limited to opening the door to the bank so that the triggerman could enter?

3. *Other substantive limitations.* The Supreme Court had ruled that the Eighth Amendment to the United States Constitution prohibits a state from carrying out a death sentence upon a prisoner who is currently insane (even if he was sane at the time of the murder). Ford v. Wainwright, 477 U.S. 399, 106 S.Ct. 2595, 91 L.Ed.2d 335 (1986).

Execution of "mentally retarded" murderers (a term not defined by the Supreme Court) is also unconstitutional. Atkins v. Virginia, 536 U.S. 304, 122 S.Ct. 2242, 153 L.Ed.2d 335 (2002). Although such persons frequently can distinguish right from wrong, the *Atkins* Court concluded that they have diminished capacity to understand and process information, to engage in logical reasoning, to control their impulses, and to understand others' reactions to their conduct. As a consequence, their retardation diminishes their personal culpability. Under retributive theory, *Atkins* suggests, the appropriate punishment must be mitigated due to their diminished culpability. The same factors that reduce the individual's moral culpability also make it less likely he is deterrable by the penalty of death. The Court also expressed concern that mentally retarded individuals are more apt to falsely confess, and they are less able to give meaningful assistance to their lawyers, and are "typically poor witnesses, [such that] their demeanor may create an unwarranted impression of lack of remorse for their crimes."

Current standards of decency also bar the execution of murderers who were under the age of 18 at the time of the homicide. Roper v. Simmons, 543 U.S. 551, 125 S.Ct. 1183, 161 L.Ed.2d 1 (2005). And, as noted earlier (p. 78, Note 5), the Constitution prohibits the execution of rapists.

CHAPTER 8

RAPE

■ ■ ■

A. OVERVIEW

1. RAPE (SEXUAL ASSAULT) STATISTICS

U.S. DEPT. OF JUSTICE, BUREAU OF JUSTICE STATISTICS—SEX OFFENSES AND OFFENDERS

February 1997, NCJ–163392, 1–7

Preliminary estimates for 1995 indicate that the public age 12 or older experienced 260,300 rapes and attempted rapes and nearly 95,000 other sexual assaults and threats of sexual assault.[1] * * *

- The nearly 355,000 rapes and sexual assaults reported by victims in the preliminary estimates for 1995 were significantly below the number of such offenses estimated for 1993. In a comparison of the two years, the number of offenses experienced by victims is estimated to have dropped by a quarter and the per capita rate of rape and sexual assault to have dropped 30%. The 1993 rate translates into about 1 rape/sexual assault victimization for every 435 persons age 12 or older, and the 1995 preliminary rate equals 1 offense for every 625 residents at least 12 years old.

- For both 1994 and 1995 the percentage of rape/sexual assault victimizations reported to a law enforcement agency was 32%. The most common reason given by victims of rape/sexual assault for reporting the crime to the police was to prevent further crimes by the offender against them. The most common reason cited by the victim for not reporting the crime to the police was that it was considered a personal matter. * * *

- Per capita rates of rape/sexual assault were found to be highest among residents age 16 to 19, low-income residents, and urban

---

1. In the National Crime Victimization Survey, rape is defined as forced sexual intercourse where the victim may be either male or female and the offender may be of the same sex or a different sex from the victim. Sexual assault includes a wide range of victimizations involving attacks in which unwanted sexual contact occurs between the victim and the offender. Threats and attempts to commit such offenses are included in the counts.

residents. There were no significant differences in the rate of rape/sexual assault among racial groups.

- Overall, an estimated 91% of the victims of rape and sexual assault were female. Nearly 99% of the offenders they described in single-victim incidents were male.

CHARACTERISTICS OF RAPE/SEXUAL ASSAULT INCIDENTS

- About two-thirds of rapes/sexual assaults were found to occur during the 12 hours from 6 p.m. to 6 a.m.

- Nearly 6 out of 10 rape/sexual assault incidents were reported by victims to have occurred in their own home or at the home of a friend, relative, or neighbor.

- More than half of rape/sexual assault incidents were reported by victims to have occurred within 1 mile of their home or at their home.

- About 1 of every 16 rape/sexual assault victims reported that a firearm was present during the commission of the offense. Most victims (84%), however, reported that no weapon was used by the offender.

CHARACTERISTICS OF RAPE/SEXUAL ASSAULT OFFENDERS AS DESCRIBED BY VICTIMS

- About 9 out of 10 rape/sexual assault victimizations involved a single offender, according to victims' reports.

- Three out of four rape/sexual assault victimizations involved offenders (both single-and multiple-offender incidents) with whom the victim had a prior relationship as a family member, intimate, or acquaintance. Strangers accounted for nearly 20% of the victimizations involving a single offender but 76% of the victimizations involving multiple offenders. About 7% of all rape/sexual assault victimizations involved multiple offenders who were strangers to the victim.

- About 4 in 10 rape/sexual assault incidents involved offenders who were age 30 or older, according to victims. About a quarter of the incidents involved offenders under age 21.

CONSEQUENCES OF THE RAPE/SEXUAL ASSAULT VICTIMIZATION

- About 7 out of 10 victims of rape/sexual assault reported that they took some form of self-protective action during the crime. The most common form of self-defense was to resist by struggling or to chase and try to hold the offender.

- Among victims who took a self-protective action, just over half felt that their actions helped the situation. About 1 in 5 victims felt that their actions either made the situation worse or simultaneously helped and worsened the situation. * * *

THE LAW ENFORCEMENT RESPONSE TO RAPE AND OTHER SEX OFFENSES * * *

- In 1995, 87% of recorded forcible rapes were completed crimes and the remainder were classified as attempts. Law enforcement agencies indicated that about 8% of forcible rapes reported to them were determined to be unfounded and were excluded from the count of crimes. * * *

- In 1995 law enforcement agencies reported to the FBI that about half of all reported forcible rapes were cleared by an arrest. Jurisdictions of varying size had little difference in the clearance rate.

NOTES AND QUESTIONS

1. *Interpreting rape statistics.* Two important matters need to be understood about the preceding data. First, the figures are based on an annual National Crime Victimization Survey (NCVS) conducted by the U.S. Department of Justice's Bureau of Justice Statistics. The NCVS collects information from a nationally representative sample of U.S. households regarding nonfatal crimes reported and unreported to the police, perpetrated against persons age 12 or older. The survey obviously can do nothing more than provide an estimate of criminal victimization.

Second, you should note the definition of rape set out in footnote 1 of the excerpt. As you will see in this chapter, the NCVS definition of rape is broader than the traditional legal definition, which focuses exclusively on forcible vaginal intercourse of females by males. It is also a broader definition than was used until 2012 by the Federal Bureau of Investigation, the other major source for national crime data. For years the FBI defined rape for reporting purposes as "carnal knowledge of a female, forcibly and against her will." This narrow definition, besides being limited to rapes reported to the police, inevitably omitted many sexual assaults, including those facilitated with drugs or alcohol rather than by force, sexual assaults of unconscious victims and those with disabilities, as well as all sexual violence against male victims. The FBI hereafter will use a far more expansive definition of rape: "penetration, no matter how slight, of the vagina or anus with any body part or object, or oral penetration by a sex organ of another person, without the consent of the victim."

2. *Same-sex rape.* Same-sex rape has been an under-discussed (indeed, sometimes *un*discussed) topic in criminal justice public policy conversation. Nearly all discussion of the topic has been limited to sexual assaults within jails and prisons. (One study of inmate violence indicated that more than 4% of inmates reported being sexually victimized in a 12–month period.) Nonetheless, same-sex rape outside prisons is not rare, as reported in the next Note. See generally Bennett Capers, *Real Rape Too*, 99 Cal. L. Rev. 1259, 1261–1262, 1266–1277, 1308 (2011) (reporting in-prison and outside-prison data regarding male-on-male sexual assault, and contending that "rape has been gendered too long" by legal definition and its application, and stating that "while rape is often done by men, it is also done to men").

3. *More recent survey data.* In 2010, there were an estimated 188,380 rapes in the United States of persons age 12 or older. Bureau of Justice

Statistics, Criminal Victimization, 2010 (Sept. 2011, NCJ 235508) (using the NCVS survey approach discussed in Note 1).

There are other, far more startling, reported data. A 2010 telephone survey of a nationally representative sample of 16,507 adults, conducted by the Center for Disease Control and Prevention, estimated a much higher number of sexual assaults. Among the reported findings were: nearly 18.3% of women and 1.4% of men in the United States have been raped at some time in their lives (defined broadly as completed forced penetration, attempted forced penetration, or alcohol/drug facilitated completed penetration); about 1% of women (thus, approximately 1.3 million) reported being raped in the 12–month period prior to the survey; 51.1% of female victims of rape reported being raped by an intimate partner and 40.8% by an acquaintance; for male victims, 52.4% reported being raped by an acquaintance and 15.1% by a stranger; an estimated 13% of women and 6% of men have experienced sexual coercion in their lifetime (i.e., unwanted sexual penetration after being pressured in a nonphysical way); 79.6% of female victims of a completed rape experienced their first rape before the age of 25; 42.2% of these women experienced their first completed rape before the age of 18 years, while 27.8% of male victims of completed rape experienced their first rape when they were 10 years of age or younger. The National Intimate Partner and Sexual Violence Survey: 2010 Summary Report (Executive Summary), available at http://www.cdc.gov/ViolencePrevention/pdf/NISVS_Executive_Summary-a.pdf.

4. *Sexual assault on college campuses.* The National College Women Sexual Victimization Study, jointly sponsored by the NIJ and Bureau of Justice Statistics, reported the results of a telephone survey of 4,446 women attending randomly selected 2– or 4–year colleges or universities (enrollments: 1,000 + students) during the academic year 1996–1997. Among those questioned, 2.8% provided information that the researchers categorized as either a completed or attempted rape during the preceding seven months. Specifically, the victimization rate was 27.7 rapes per 1,000 female students. Calculated on a calendar year basis, the data suggest that 4.9% of college women are victimized yearly on campus. Bonnie S. Fisher et al., The Sexual Victimization of College Women (NCJ 182369, Dec. 2000).

2. SOCIAL CONTEXT

SUSAN ESTRICH—RAPE

95 Yale Law Journal 1087 (1986), 1089–92

* * * The history of rape, as the law has been enforced in this country, is a history of both racism and sexism.[2] One could write an article of this length dealing only with the racism. * * * My focus is sexism.

---

2. The death penalty for rape in this country, now unconstitutional under Coker v. Georgia, 433 U.S. 584 (1977), was traditionally reserved for black men who raped white women. Between 1930 and 1967, 89% of the men executed for rape in this country were black. That figure includes 36% of the black men who were convicted of raping a white woman; only 2% of the defendants convicted of rape involving any other racial combination were executed. Professor Wolfgang, after a systematic analysis of 1,238 rape convictions between 1945 and 1965, concluded that race was the only factor that accounted for the disparities in the imposition of the death penalty. *See* Wolfgang, *Racial Discrimination in the Death Sentence for Rape,* in Executions in America 110–20

In recent years, rape has emerged as a topic of increasing research and attention among feminists, in both popular and scholarly journals. But much of the feminist writing is not focused on an analysis of the *law* of rape, and some that is so focused is not very firmly grounded in the criminal law. At the same time, much of the writing about rape in the more traditional criminal law literature, with the exception of some recent articles (primarily student notes), does little more than mirror the condescension and misunderstanding, if not outright hostility to women, that have made rape a central part of the feminist agenda. * * *

To examine rape within the criminal law tradition is to expose fully the sexism of the law. Much that is striking about the crime of rape—and revealing of the sexism of the system—emerges only when rape is examined relative to other crimes * * *. * * *

The study of rape * * * also raises broader questions about the way conceptions of gender and the different backgrounds and perspectives of men and women should be encompassed within the criminal law. In one of his most celebrated essays, Oliver Wendell Holmes explained that the law does not exist to tell the good man what to do, but to tell the bad man what not to do. Holmes was interested in the distinction between the good and bad man; I cannot help noticing that both are men. Most of the time, a criminal law that reflects male views and male standards imposes its judgment on men who have injured other men. It is "boys' rules" applied to a boys' fight.[9] In rape, the male standard defines a crime committed against women, and male standards are used not only to judge men, but also to judge the conduct of women victims. Moreover, because the crime involves sex itself, the law of rape inevitably treads on the explosive ground of sex roles, of male aggression and female passivity, of our understandings of sexuality—areas where differences between a male and a female perspective may be most pronounced. * * *

In considering [rape], my questions are * * *: How have the limits on the crime of rape been formulated? What do those limits signify? What makes it rape, as opposed to sex? In what ways is rape defined differently from other crimes? What do those differences tell us about the law's attitudes towards women, men, sex, and sexuality?

NOTES AND QUESTIONS

1. *Rape and racism.* It is difficult to understate the role of racism in the history of rape prosecutions. If sexism has resulted in the creation of "boys' rules," racism has resulted in "whites' rules" in the enforcement and punishment of rape laws. Footnote 2 of the Estrich excerpt points to some of the

(W. Bowers ed. 1974). Although the death penalty for rape is now prohibited, at least one study has found that black men convicted of raping white women continue to receive the harshest penalties.

9. In referring to "male" standards and "boys' rules," I do not mean to suggest that *every* man adheres to them. A "male view" is nonetheless distinct from a "female view" not only by the gender of most of those who adhere to it, but also by the character of the life experiences and socialization which tend to produce it.

disparate penalty figures. But, there is also the specter of false accusations of interracial rape—a white woman discovered in a socially unacceptable interracial sexual relationship accusing her black sexual partner of rape—that haunts U.S. history.

Perhaps the most infamous, but far from only, case of such racism is the story of the "Scottsboro boys." The case involved an alleged incident on a train from Chattanooga to Memphis, which passed through Alabama on the night of March 25, 1931. Nine black youths and several white youths were riding the freight train illegally. James Goodman, Stories of Scottsboro 3–4 (1995). The youths got into a fight, and the black youths "chased or threw" all but one of the whites from the train shortly after it pulled away from a station. Id. at 4. At the next stop, dozens of white men armed with pistols, rifles, and shotguns grabbed the blacks, "tied them to one another with a plow line," put them on a flatbed truck, and drove them to the jail in Scottsboro. They were originally charged with assault. But, shortly thereafter, the black youths learned that they were accused of rape of two white women:

> One of the women, Victoria Price, pointed to six of them. * * * [A] guard said that "If those six had Miss Price, it stands to reason that the others had Miss Bates." The boys protested, insisting they hadn't touched the women, hadn't even seen them before * * *. Clarence Norris called the women liars. One of the guards struck him with his bayonet, cutting to the bone the hand that Norris put up to shield his face. "Nigger," the guard hollered, "you know damn well how to talk about white women." Id. at 5.

The youths were charged with rape and brought to trial in a haste, and convicted and sentenced to death within days. Their convictions were overturned by the United States Supreme Court because they were denied counsel at trial. Powell v. Alabama, 287 U.S. 45, 53 S.Ct. 55, 77 L.Ed. 158 (1932). Many years later, one of the women who testified at trial that she had been raped by the black youths admitted that "those Negroes did not touch me * * *." Goodman, supra, at 195.

After *Powell*, Alabama dropped charges against four of the defendants. The other five were retried, convicted again, and received sentences of 20 years, 75 years (two defendants), 99 years, and death. The death sentence was commuted to life by Alabama Governor Bibb Graves. Three of the Scottsboro prisoners were paroled in 1943, 1946, and 1950. One escaped from prison in 1948 and was arrested in Detroit in 1950. Michigan Governor G. Mennen Williams refused Alabama's request for extradition, and Alabama abandoned extradition proceedings. In 1976, Governor George Wallace pardoned the last surviving Scottsboro defendant (the one who had been sentenced to death).

2. Why does the law prohibit rape? One view is that rape is a crime of violence. One scholar has gone so far as to suggest that rape be treated "as a variety of ordinary (simple or aggravated) battery because that is what rape is." Michael Davis, *Setting Penalties: What Does Rape Deserve?*, 3 Law & Phil. 61, 62–63 (1984). Does that seem right to you? Does this approach leave something important out of the concept of rape? If so, what?

Many feminists argue that rape laws are meant to safeguard sexual autonomy, *i.e.* the right of a person to choose with whom she or he will be sexually intimate. So understood, sexual autonomy is the right "to refuse to have sex with any person at any time, for any reason or for no reason." Stephen Schulhofer, *Unwanted Sex*, Atlantic Monthly, Oct. 1998, at 55, 62. Nancy Venable Raine, a survivor of a three-hour forcible rape by a home intruder, described her loss of autonomy this way:

> The rapist * * * violated my most basic human need—my bodyright. By destroying my ability to control my own body, he * * * made my body an object. I lost a sense of it as the boundary of self, the fundamental and most sacred of all borders. * * * [Only] touch that respects bodyright is healing; it restores the autonomy and authenticity of the self. * * *
>
> The most personal part of being raped had less to do with what happened to my body for three hours * * *, than with what happened to my spirit. The loss of faith that there is order and continuity of life—that life is meaningful—is the most personal of all losses. * * * To lose faith in life was, for me, the loss on connection with the intangible world—with soul, spirit, anima, essence, vital force, or whatever one chooses to call it.

Nancy Venable Raine, After Silence: Rape and My Journey Back 163, 206–207 (1998).

According to the "autonomy" perspective, traditional rape laws "correct the existing imbalance in sexual power: By punishing rape, the law seeks to constrain the exercise of male sexual autonomy to the extent necessary to secure the sexual autonomy of women." Anne M. Coughlin, *Sex and Guilt*, 84 Va.L.Rev. 1, 5 (1998). Under this view, should sexual penetration be essential to the crime?

Some feminists reject the idea that rape laws have a benevolent purpose, such as to protect a woman's autonomy. They reason that rape laws are a mechanism for sustaining male dominance of women. Catherine A. MacKinnon in *Feminism, Marxism, Method, and the State: Toward Feminist Jurisprudence*, 8 Signs 635, 644 (1983), asserts that the law "coercively and authoritatively constitutes the social order in the interest of men as a gender * * *. It achieves this through embodying and ensuring male control over women's sexuality at every level, occasionally cushioning, qualifying, or de jure prohibiting its excesses when necessary to its normalization." Viewed this way, no line may exist between voluntary sexual relations and coerced sex, with the effect that "rape is implicit in most heterosexual relationships." Schulhofer, supra, at 60 (explaining, but not defending, this proposition).

For a different and intriguing explanation of rape laws, see p. 412, Note 7.

JOSHUA DRESSLER—WHERE WE HAVE BEEN, AND WHERE WE MIGHT BE GOING: SOME CAUTIONARY REFLECTIONS ON RAPE LAW REFORM

46 Cleveland State Law Review 409 (1998), 410–413

* * * One does not have to accept the view that rape law was devised for the misogynistic purpose of "embodying and ensuring male control over women's sexuality" to agree with the assertion that the common law

approach to the offense—a crime which by definition deals with male conduct in relation to females—was male-centered. After all the law of rape developed during a time when women played no role in legal affairs, even as to offenses that affected them intimately.

Boys' rules have certainly not been eradicated everywhere and in every case, but feminists can take legitimate pride in the fact that rape law has undergone significant reform in just the past decade or two, largely as a result of their efforts. * * * [A]lthough additional legal reform is in order, the time may also be right for us to concern ourselves at least a little with the possibility that rape reform *could* go (or perhaps *is* going) down some other paths that fair-minded persons will later regret. Just a few decades ago, rape law was so irrational and insensitive to the legitimate interests of women that there was really no need to strike a balance: virtually any reform effort was likely to result in improvement. But, we are past that extreme stage. * * *

Is there really a risk that rape law reform will go too far? At first blush, my concern seems silly. After all, men still retain disproportionate lawmaking power * * *. In my view, however, there is not an insignificant risk of expanding rape law too far in certain regards.

Let me explain. Consider for a moment a political lesson from the Oklahoma City bombing case. After that horrendous incident, President Bill Clinton moved quickly to demand legislation expanding the Government's authority to monitor and infiltrate organizations it suspect[ed] of terrorism. The President took the position normally reserved for political conservatives who made similar * * * calls for expanded police powers during the McCarthy, civil rights, and Vietnam War eras. But, as Clinton sought to diminish citizens' civil liberties, lo and behold, opposition to the anti-terrorist measure came from not only an expected (but ordinarily politically weak) source, the American Civil Liberties Union, but also from an *unexpected* one—from conservative Republicans who warned about expanded federal police power. * * * [T]hese Republicans did not suddenly get "A.C.L.U. religion." Instead, conservatives * * * feared that if the Government were given a free rein to conduct surveillance of militia groups, they might also infiltrate the National Rifle Association and other political enemies of the left and friends of the right. So, in the Oklahoma City situation, although the political left and right traded sides, the political system has its usual "yin and yang," the usual competing, tugging forces. The adversarial system was at work in Congress.

One could naturally expect the same yin and yang in rape law reform. * * * [W]e still have Democrats and Republicans, liberals and conservatives, advocates of civil liberties and proponents of unfettered law enforcement, and men and women, all with potentially competing interests at stake. But, the rape reform movement has not followed the expected course. Many of the usual supporters of civil liberties and the rights of criminal suspects have been in the political bed with their usual enemies. Many feminists—who typically favor the interests of underdogs, which includes * * * people accused of crime—have allied themselves with political conservatives. Feminists seek to abolish "boys' rules" to sexual relations; political conservatives seek to strengthen the power of police and prosecutors and to increase the punishment of wrongdoers. Strange bedfellows like this can produce unwanted offspring. * * *

Therefore, * * * a thoughtful and reasoned look at where we have been in rape law and where we may be going [is justified]. The goal should ultimately be to strike a sensible balance. We should not give up the gains in rape reform and, indeed, should go further in some regards, but we should move with considerable caution.

NOTES AND QUESTIONS

1. *Feminist and civil libertarian: what should a person do?* Consider these personal observations by a then-recent law school graduate:

> Like many female civil libertarians, I often feel trapped in the feminist defense attorney dilemma. On the one hand, I am and always will be a woman. I have suffered through sexual harassment. I have been the recipient of unfair discrimination. I have carefully analyzed issues of social role and stereotype. Of course, I possess strong opinions on the subject of rape. I follow the feminist scholars. * * *

> I know that as a woman, I am to condemn rape as the most invidious of crimes. I also realize that rape, in particular, is a crime that cannot be analyzed outside a social context. As the literature expresses quite vehemently, rape is not as simple as an act done by one individual to another, whose criminality is determined by a fair trial. Rape laws and trials implicate extensive historical and social attitudes that reflect the existing patriarchy * * *.

> * * * Finally, I know the extent to which rape harms the victim. "Rape is one of the most brutal, invasive and degrading forms of criminal victimization. Researchers have thoroughly documented that victims of rape suffer intense trauma, and profound and lasting injury." I know this not just from reading, but also from personal experience. I am one of the millions of women that, according to statistics, have experienced such harm. This combination of knowledge and personal experience informs the feminist side of my dilemma.

> On the other hand, I am an aspiring defense attorney. I am a civil libertarian who sincerely believes in the rights of the criminal defendant. I think social reforms should not come at the expense of individual liberty. For example, I believe incriminating evidence should be excluded, even if true and highly relevant, if obtained in violation of a criminal defendant's constitutional rights. Additionally, a criminal defendant should be able to present any evidence that is probative of his innocence, unless its prejudicial effect substantially outweighs its probative value. Even then, in close cases, judges should err on the side of admitting exculpatory evidence.

In the same vein, I believe that the social goals of encouraging rape reporting and reforming the rape trial process should not outweigh the individual criminal defendant's rights. For example, the social goal of encouraging rape reporting should not compromise the defendant's fair trial guarantees. * * *

* * * While [recent rape reform laws] cause higher reporting and conviction rates, they inevitably cause more innocent people to be reported and convicted. Such reforms also risk infringing upon other constitutional guarantees. These considerations inform the civil libertarian side of my dilemma.

Aya Gruber, *Pink Elephants in the Rape Trial: The Problem of Tort–Type Defenses in the Criminal Law of Rape,* 4 Wm. & Mary J. Women & L. 203, 203, 205–06 (1997).

The tensions in this regard can be great. Professor and former Public Defender Cookie Ridolfi has told the story of representing a man she believed was innocent, charged with a brutal rape. She concludes her story this way:

After more than a week of trial where emotions ran high for everyone, the jury acquitted [my client]. Afterwards, I met with jurors. One woman told me that she believed in his innocence because she was certain that I could not have fought for him in the way that I did had he committed that crime. * * * I later learned that he was arrested and convicted in two new rape/assault cases similar to the one I had tried. * * * [T]hat trial and that complainant still haunt me. * * *

* * * I remain firm in my belief that every person, no matter what the charge or circumstances of the case, deserves dedicated and competent counsel. I also know that some men are victims of a woman's false charges of rape and agree strongly that this defense must be pursued when a defendant makes this claim. I am not critical of any other woman who chooses to defend a man charged with rape. But for all of the reasons I have given, I would find it difficult to again be in the position where I would have to challenge a woman's claim of rape knowing that what she claims may be true.

Cookie Ridolfi, *Statement on Representing Rape Defendants*, July 26, 1989 (unpublished manuscript, on file with author at Santa Clara Law School).

2. *Do words matter?* In a 2007 sexual assault prosecution in Lincoln, Nebraska, a trial judge ordered the prosecutor and witnesses (including the person who claimed to have been sexually assaulted) not to use the terms "rape" or "sexual assault" to describe what happened. Is there any justification for such an order? Would there be circumstances in which use of the term "victim" should also be barred? What problems do you see in such a judicial ban on these words? Associated Press, *Word "Rape" Banned in Court*, June18, 2007; Jon Ruhlen, *Latest Defense Trend Puts Words Like "Victim" on Trial*, The Hutchinson News, April 17, 2009.

3. *Rape law reform.* As the Dressler excerpt points out, the offense of rape in its traditional form is a crime that only a male can perpetrate (although a female might be an accomplice), and of which only a female can be a victim. Indeed, in its traditional form, the victim can only be a female *not*

the wife of the perpetrator. However, as a look at some of the statutes set out in the next chapter subsection will show you, and as the materials in this chapter will demonstrate, rape law has undergone significant changes in recent years.

Take a look at the statutes that follow to get a sense of how modern legislatures define various forms of sexual violence, and also notice the variations in punishment that may be imposed for the crimes. (What follows are not necessarily all of the sexual offenses in any given jurisdiction.) And, remember to look at Article 213 of the Model Penal Code.

3. VARIATIONS ON THE THEME: SOME SEXUAL OFFENSE STATUTES*

ALABAMA CRIMINAL CODE

§ 13A–6–60. Definitions

The following definitions apply in this article:

(1) Sexual intercourse. Such term has its ordinary meaning and occurs upon any penetration, however slight; emission is not required. * * *

(5) Mentally defective. Such term means that a person suffers from a mental disease or defect which renders him incapable of appraising the nature of his conduct.

(6) Mentally incapacitated. Such term means that a person is rendered temporarily incapable of appraising or controlling his conduct owing to the influence of a narcotic or intoxicating substance administered to him without his consent, or to any other incapacitating act committed upon him without his consent.

(7) Physically helpless. Such term means that a person is unconscious or for any other reason is physically unable to communicate unwillingness to an act.

(8) Forcible compulsion. Physical force that overcomes earnest resistance or a threat, express or implied, that places a person in fear of immediate death or serious physical injury to himself or another person.

§ 13A–6–61. Rape; first degree

(a) A person commits the crime of rape in the first degree [punishable by a term of imprisonment of not less than ten years and not more than 99 years or life]:

(1) He or she engages in sexual intercourse with a member of the opposite sex by forcible compulsion; or

---

* As of January 1, 2010.

(2) He or she engages in sexual intercourse with a member of the opposite sex who is incapable of consent by reason of being physically helpless or mentally incapacitated; or

(3) He or she, being 16 years or older, engages in sexual intercourse with a member of the opposite sex who is less than 12 years old. * * *

§ 13A–6–62.   Rape; second degree

(a) A person commits the crime of rape in the second degree [punishable by imprisonment of no less than two years and not more than twenty years] if:

(1) Being 16 years old or older, he or she engages in sexual intercourse with a member of the opposite sex less than 16 and more than 12 years old; provided, however, the actor is at least two years older than the member of the opposite sex.

(2) He or she engages in sexual intercourse with a member of the opposite sex who is incapable of consent by reason of being mentally defective.

CALIFORNIA PENAL CODE

§ 261.   Rape; "Duress"; "Menace"

(a) Rape [punishable by imprisonment in the state prison for three, six, or eight years] is an act of sexual intercourse accomplished with a person * * * under any of the following circumstances:

(1) Where a person is incapable, because of a mental disorder or developmental or physical disability, of giving legal consent, and this is known or reasonably should be known to the person committing the act.* * *

(2) Where it is accomplished against a person's will by means of force, violence, duress, menace, or fear of immediate and unlawful bodily injury on the person or another.

(3) Where a person is prevented from resisting by any intoxicating or anesthetic substance, or any controlled substance, and this condition was known, or reasonably should have been known by the accused.

(4) Where a person is at the time unconscious of the nature of the act, and this is known to the accused. As used in this paragraph, "unconscious of the nature of the act" means incapable of resisting because the victim meets one of the following conditions:

(A) Was unconscious or asleep.

(B) Was not aware, knowing, perceiving, or cognizant that the act occurred.

(C) Was not aware, knowing, perceiving, or cognizant of the essential characteristics of the act due to the perpetrator's fraud in fact.

(D) Was not aware, knowing, perceiving, or cognizant of the essential characteristics of the act due to the perpetrator's fraudulent representation that the sexual penetration served a professional purpose when it served no professional purpose.

(5) Where a person submits under the belief that the person committing the act is the victim's spouse, and this belief is induced by any artifice, pretense, or concealment practiced by the accused, with intent to induce the belief.

(6) Where the act is accomplished against the victim's will by threatening to retaliate in the future against the victim or any other person, and there is a reasonable possibility that the perpetrator will execute the threat. As used in this paragraph, "threatening to retaliate" means a threat to kidnap or falsely imprison, or to inflict extreme pain, serious bodily injury, or death.

(7) Where the act is accomplished against the victim's will by threatening to use the authority of a public official to incarcerate, arrest, or deport the victim or another, and the victim has a reasonable belief that the perpetrator is a public official. * * *

(b) As used in this section, "duress" means a direct or implied threat of force, violence, danger, or retribution sufficient to coerce a reasonable person of ordinary susceptibilities to perform an act which otherwise would not have been performed, or acquiesce in an act to which one otherwise would not have submitted. The total circumstances, including the age of the victim, and his or her relationship to the defendant, are factors to consider in appraising the existence of duress.

(c) As used in this section, "menace" means any threat, declaration, or act which shows an intention to inflict an injury upon another.

§ 261.5. Unlawful sexual intercourse with a minor * * *

(a) Unlawful sexual intercourse is an act of sexual intercourse accomplished with a person who is not the spouse of the perpetrator, if the person is a minor. For the purposes of this section, a "minor" is a person under the age of 18 years and an "adult" is a person who is at least 18 years of age.

(b) Any person who engages in an act of unlawful sexual intercourse with a minor who is not more than three years older or three years younger than the perpetrator, is guilty of a misdemeanor.

(c) Any person who engages in an act of unlawful sexual intercourse with a minor who is more than three years younger than the perpetrator is guilty of either a misdemeanor or a felony, and shall be punished by imprisonment in a county jail not exceeding one year, or by imprisonment * * *.

(d) Any person 21 years of age or older who engages in an act of unlawful sexual intercourse with a minor who is under 16 years of age is guilty of either a misdemeanor or a felony, and shall be punished by imprisonment in a county jail not exceeding one year, or by imprisonment * * * for two, three, or four years. * * *

§ 261.6. "Consent"; Effect of current or previous relationship

In prosecutions * * * in which consent is at issue, "consent" shall be defined to mean positive cooperation in act or attitude pursuant to an exercise of free will. The person must act freely and voluntarily and have knowledge of the nature of the act or transaction involved.

A current or previous dating or marital relationship shall not be sufficient to constitute consent where consent is at issue in a prosecution * * *.

§ 261.7. "Consent"; Communication to use condom or other birth control device

In prosecutions * * * in which consent is at issue, evidence that the victim suggested, requested, or otherwise communicated to the defendant that the defendant use a condom or other birth control device, without additional evidence of consent, is not sufficient to constitute consent.

§ 263. Penetration

The essential guilt of rape consists in the outrage to the person and feelings of the victim of the rape. Any sexual penetration, however slight, is sufficient to complete the crime.

§ 266c. Inducing consent to sexual act by fraud or fear

Every person who induces any other person to engage in sexual intercourse, sexual penetration, oral copulation, or sodomy when his or her consent is procured by false or fraudulent representation or pretense that is made with the intent to create fear, and which does induce fear, and that would cause a reasonable person in like circumstances to act contrary to the person's free will, and does cause the victim to so act, is punishable by imprisonment in a county jail for not more than one year or in the state prison for two, three, or four years.

As used in this section, "fear" means the fear of physical injury or death to the person or to any relative of the person or member of the person's family.

INDIANA CRIMINAL CODE

§ 35–42–4–1. Rape

(a) Except as provided in subsection (b), a person who knowingly or intentionally has sexual intercourse with a member of the opposite sex when:

(1) the other person is compelled by force or imminent threat of force;

(2) the other person is unaware that the sexual intercourse is occurring; or

(3) the other person is so mentally disabled or deficient that consent to sexual intercourse cannot be given;

commits rape, a Class B felony [subject to imprisonment of from 6 to 20 years, with the advisory sentence being 10 years].

(b) An offense described in subsection (a) is a Class A felony [subject to imprisonment of from 20 to 50 years, with the advisory sentence being 30 years] if:

(1) it is committed by using or threatening the use of deadly force;

(2) it is committed while armed with a deadly weapon;

(3) it results in serious bodily injury to a person other than a defendant; or

(4) the commission of the offense is facilitated by furnishing the victim, without the victim's knowledge, with a drug * * * or a controlled substance * * * or knowing that the victim was furnished with the drug or controlled substance without the victim's knowledge.

§ 35–42–4–8. Sexual battery

(a) A person who, with intent to arouse or satisfy the person's own sexual desires or the sexual desires of another person, touches another person when that person is:

(1) compelled to submit to the touching by force or the imminent threat of force; or

(2) so mentally disabled or deficient that consent to the touching cannot be given;

commits sexual battery, a Class D felony [subject to imprisonment of from 6 months to 3 years, with the advisory sentence being 1½ years].

(b) An offense described in subsection (a) is a Class C felony [subject to imprisonment of from 2 to 8 years, with the advisory sentence being 4 years] if:

(1) it is committed by using or threatening the use of deadly force

(2) it is committed while armed with a deadly weapon; or

(3) the commission of the offense is facilitated by furnishing the victim, without the victim's knowledge, with a drug or a controlled substance or knowing that the victim was furnished with the drug or controlled substance without the victim's knowledge.

NEW JERSEY CODE OF CRIMINAL JUSTICE

§ 2C:14–1. Definitions

The following definitions apply to this chapter: * * *

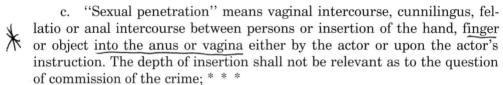

c. "Sexual penetration" means vaginal intercourse, cunnilingus, fellatio or anal intercourse between persons or insertion of the hand, finger or object into the anus or vagina either by the actor or upon the actor's instruction. The depth of insertion shall not be relevant as to the question of commission of the crime; * * *

f. "Severe personal injury" means severe bodily injury, disfigurement, disease, incapacitating mental anguish or chronic pain;

g. "Physically helpless" means that condition in which a person is unconscious or is physically unable to flee or is physically unable to communicate unwillingness to act;

h. "Mentally defective" means that condition in which a person suffers from a mental disease or defect which renders that person temporarily or permanently incapable of understanding the nature of his conduct, including, but not limited to, being incapable of providing consent;

i. "Mentally incapacitated" means that condition in which a person is rendered temporarily incapable of understanding or controlling his conduct due to the influence of a narcotic, anesthetic, intoxicant, or other substance administered to that person without his prior knowledge or consent, or due to any other act committed upon that person which rendered that person incapable of appraising or controlling his conduct * * *.

§ 2C:14–2. Sexual assault

a. An actor is guilty of aggravated sexual assault if he commits an act of sexual penetration with another person under any one of the following circumstances:

(1) The victim is less than 13 years old;

(2) The victim is at least 13 but less than 16 years old; and

(a) The actor is related to the victim by blood or affinity to the third degree, or

(b) The actor has supervisory or disciplinary power over the victim by virtue of the actor's legal, professional, or occupational status, or

(c) The actor is a resource family parent, a guardian, or stands in loco parentis within the household;

(3) The act is committed during the commission, or attempted commission, whether alone or with one or more other persons, of robbery, kidnapping, homicide, aggravated assault on another, burglary, arson or criminal escape;

(4) The actor is armed with a weapon or any object fashioned in such a manner as to lead the victim to reasonably believe it to be a weapon and threatens by word or gesture to use the weapon or object;

(5) The actor is aided or abetted by one or more other persons and the actor uses physical force or coercion;

(6) The actor uses physical force or coercion and severe personal injury is sustained by the victim;

(7) The victim is one whom the actor knew or should have known was physically helpless, mentally defective or mentally incapacitated.

Aggravated sexual assault is a crime of the first degree [punishable by imprisonment for a specific term, between 10 and 20 years].

b. An actor is guilty of sexual assault if he commits an act of sexual contact with a victim who is less than 13 years old and the actor is at least four years older than the victim.

c. An actor is guilty of sexual assault if he commits an act of sexual penetration with another person under any one of the following circumstances:

(1) The actor uses physical force or coercion, but the victim does not sustain severe personal injury;

(2) The victim is on probation or parole, or is detained in a hospital, prison or other institution and the actor has supervisory or disciplinary power over the victim by virtue of the actor's legal, professional or occupational status;

(3) The victim is at least 16 but less than 18 years old and:

(a) The actor is related to the victim by blood or affinity to the third degree; or

(b) The actor has supervisory or disciplinary power of any nature or in any capacity over the victim; or

(c) The actor is a family resource parent, a guardian, or stands in loco parentis within the household;

(4) The victim is at least 13 but less than 16 years old and the actor is at least four years older than the victim.

Sexual assault is a crime of the second degree [punishable by imprisonment for a specific term, between 5 and 10 years].

TITLE 18, PENNSYLVANIA CONSOLIDATED STATUTES

§ 3101. Definitions * * *

"Forcible compulsion." Compulsion by use of physical, intellectual, moral, emotional or psychological force, either express or implied. The term includes, but is not limited to, compulsion resulting in another person's death, whether the death occurred before, during or after sexual intercourse. * * *

"Sexual intercourse." In addition to its ordinary meaning, includes intercourse per os or per anus, with some penetration however slight; emission is not required.

§ 3105. Prompt complaint

Prompt reporting to public authority is not required in a prosecution under this chapter: Provided, however, That nothing in this section shall be construed to prohibit a defendant from introducing evidence of the complainant's failure to promptly report the crime if such evidence would be admissible pursuant to the rules of evidence.

§ 3106. Testimony of complainants

The credibility of a complainant of an offense under this chapter shall be determined by the same standard as is the credibility of a complainant of any other crime. The testimony of a complainant need not be corroborated in prosecutions under this chapter. No instructions shall be given cautioning the jury to view the complainant's testimony in any other way than that in which all complainants' testimony is viewed.

§ 3107. Resistance not required

The alleged victim need not resist the actor in prosecutions under this chapter: Provided, however, That nothing in this section shall be construed to prohibit a defendant from introducing evidence that the alleged victim consented to the conduct in question.

§ 3121. Rape

(a) Offense defined.—A person commits a felony of the first degree [punishable by a term of imprisonment not exceeding 20 years] when the person engages in sexual intercourse with a complainant:

(1) By forcible compulsion.

(2) By threat of forcible compulsion that would prevent resistance by a person of reasonable resolution.

(3) Who is unconscious or where the person knows that the complainant is unaware that the sexual intercourse is occurring.

(4) Where the person has substantially impaired the complainant's power to appraise or control his or her conduct by administering or employing, without the knowledge of the complainant, drugs, intoxicants or other means for the purpose of preventing resistance.

(5) Who suffers from a mental disability which renders the complainant incapable of consent.

(b) Additional Penalties.—In addition to the penalty provided for by subsection (a), a person may be sentenced to an additional term not to exceed ten years' confinement * * * where the person engages in sexual intercourse with a complainant and has substantially impaired the complainant's power to appraise or control his or her conduct by administering or employing, without the knowledge of the complainant, any substance for the purpose of preventing resistance through the inducement of euphoria, memory loss and any other effect of this substance.

(c) Rape of a Child.—A person commits the offense of rape of a child, a felony of the first degree [punishable by a term of imprisonment not exceeding 40 years], when the person engages in sexual intercourse with a complainant who is less than 13 years of age.

(d) Rape of a Child with Serious Bodily Injury.—A person commits the offense of rape of a child resulting in serious bodily injury, a felony of the first degree [punishable by a term of imprisonment not exceeding life imprisonment], when the person violates this section and the complainant is under 13 years of age and suffers serious bodily injury in the course of the offense.

§ 3124.1 Sexual assault

Except as provided in section 3121 * * * a person commit a felony of the second degree [punishable by a term of imprisonment not exceeding 10 years] when that person engages in sexual intercourse * * * with a complainant without the complainant's consent.

B. FORCIBLE RAPE

Rape is "the carnal knowledge of a woman forcibly and against her will." 4 Blackstone, Commentaries on the Law of England * 210 (1769).

1. IN GENERAL

STATE v. ALSTON

Supreme Court of North Carolina, 1984.
310 N.C. 399, 312 S.E.2d 470.

MITCHELL, JUSTICE.

The defendant raises on appeal the question whether the evidence of his guilt of * * * second degree rape was sufficient to * * * support his conviction * * *.

The State's evidence tended to show that at the time the incident occurred the defendant and the prosecuting witness in this case, Cottie Brown, had been involved for approximately six months in a consensual sexual relationship. During the six months the two had conflicts at times and Brown would leave the apartment she shared with the defendant to stay with her mother. She testified that she would return to the defendant and the apartment they shared when he called to tell her to return. Brown testified that she and the defendant had sexual relations throughout their relationship. Although she sometimes enjoyed their sexual relations, she often had sex with the defendant just to accommodate him. On those occasions, she would stand still and remain entirely passive while the defendant undressed her and had intercourse with her.

Brown testified that at times their consensual sexual relations involved some violence. The defendant had struck her several times throughout the relationship when she refused to give him money or refused to do what he wanted. Around May 15, 1981, the defendant struck her after asking her for money that she refused to give him. Brown left the apartment she shared with the defendant and moved in with her mother. She did not have intercourse with the defendant after May 15 until the alleged rape on June 15. After Brown left the defendant, he called her several times and visited her at Durham Technical Institute where she was enrolled in classes. When he visited her they talked about their relationship. Brown testified that she did not tell him she wanted to break off their relationship because she was afraid he would be angry.

On June 15, 1981, Brown arrived at Durham Technical Institute by taxicab to find the defendant standing close to the school door. The defendant blocked her path as she walked toward the door and asked her where she had moved. Brown refused to tell him, and the defendant grabbed her arm, saying that she was going with him. Brown testified that it would have taken some effort to pull away. The two walked toward the parking lot and Brown told the defendant she would walk with him if he let her go. The defendant then released her. She testified that she did not run away from him because she was afraid of him. She stated that other students were nearby.

Brown stated that she and the defendant then began a casually paced walk in the neighborhood around the school. They walked, sometimes side by side, sometimes with Brown slightly behind the defendant. As they walked they talked about their relationship. Brown said the defendant did not hold her or help her along in any way as they walked. The defendant talked about Brown's "dogging" him and making him seem a fool and about Brown's mother's interference in the relationship. When the defendant and Brown left the parking lot, the defendant threatened to "fix" her face so that her mother could see he was not playing. While they were walking out of the parking lot, Brown told the defendant she wanted to go to class. He replied that she was going to miss class that day.

The two continued to walk away from the school. Brown testified that the defendant continually talked about their relationship as they walked, but that she paid little attention to what he said because she was preoccupied with her own thoughts. They passed several people. They walked along several streets and went down a path close to a wooded area where they stopped to talk. The defendant asked again where Brown had moved. She asked him whether he would let her go if she told him her address. The defendant then asked whether the relationship was over and Brown told him it was. He then said that since everyone could see her but him he had a right to make love to her again. Brown said nothing.

The two turned around at that point and began walking towards a street they had walked down previously. Changing directions, they walked in the same fashion they had walked before—side by side with Brown sometimes slightly behind. The defendant did not hold or touch Brown as they walked. Brown testified that the defendant did not say where they were going but that, when he said he wanted to make love, she knew he was going to the house of a friend. She said they had gone to the house on prior occasions to have sex. The defendant and Brown passed the same group of men they had passed previously. Brown did not ask for assistance because some of the men were friends of the defendant, and she assumed they would not help. The defendant and Brown continued to walk to the house of one of the defendant's friends, Lawrence Taylor.

When they entered the house, Taylor was inside. Brown sat in the living room while the defendant and Taylor went to the back of the house and talked. When asked why she did not try to leave when the defendant and Taylor were in the back of the house, Brown replied, "It was nowhere to go. I don't know. I just didn't." The defendant returned to the living room area and turned on the television. He attempted to fix a broken fan. Brown asked Taylor for a cigarette, and he gave her one.

The defendant began talking to Brown about another man she had been seeing. By that time Taylor had gone out of the room and perhaps the house. The defendant asked if Brown was "ready." The evidence tended to show that she told him "no, that I wasn't going to bed with him." She testified that she did not want to have sex with the defendant and did not consent to do so at any time on June 15.

After Brown finished her cigarette, the defendant began kissing her neck. He pulled her up from the chair in which she had been sitting and started undressing her. * * * He told her to lay down on a bed which was in the living room. She complied and the defendant pushed apart her legs and had sexual intercourse with her. Brown testified that she did not try to push him away. She cried during the intercourse. Afterwards they talked. * * *

* * * Brown made a complaint to the police the same day.

The defendant continued to call Brown after June 15, but she refused to see him. One evening he called from a telephone booth and told her he had to talk. When he got to her apartment he threatened to kick her door down and Brown let him inside. Once inside he said he had intended merely to talk to her but that he wanted to make love again after seeing her. Brown said she sat and looked at him, and that he began kissing her. She pulled away and he picked her up and carried her to the bedroom. He performed oral sex on her and she testified that she did not try to fight him off because she found she enjoyed it. The two stayed together until morning and had sexual intercourse several times that night. * * *

In his * * * assignment of error the defendant contends there was no substantial evidence that the sexual intercourse between Brown and him was by force and against her will. He argues that the evidence was insufficient to allow the trial court to submit the issue of his guilt of second degree rape to the jury. After a review of the evidence, we find this argument to have merit.

Second degree rape involves vaginal intercourse with the victim both by force and against the victim's will. G.S. 14–27.3. Consent by the victim is a complete defense, but consent which is induced by fear of violence is void and is no legal consent.

A defendant can be guilty of raping even his mistress or a "common strumpet." This is so because consent to sexual intercourse freely given can be withdrawn at any time prior to penetration. If the particular act of intercourse for which the defendant is charged was both by force and against the victim's will, the offense is rape without regard to the victim's consent given to the defendant for prior acts of intercourse.

Where as here the victim has engaged in a prior continuing consensual sexual relationship with the defendant, however, determining the victim's state of mind at the time of the alleged rape obviously is made more difficult. Although inquiry in such cases still must be made into the victim's state of mind at the time of the alleged rape, the State ordinarily will be able to show the victim's lack of consent to the specific act charged only by evidence of statements or actions by the victim which were clearly communicated to the defendant and which expressly and unequivocally indicated the victim's withdrawal of any prior consent and lack of consent to the particular act of intercourse.

In the present case the State introduced such evidence. * * * Brown testified unequivocally that she did not consent to sexual intercourse with the defendant on June 15. She was equally unequivocal in testifying that she submitted to sexual intercourse with the defendant only because she was afraid of him. During their walk, she told the defendant that their relationship was at an end. When the defendant asked her if she was "ready" immediately prior to having sexual intercourse with her, she told him "no, that I wasn't going to bed with him." Even in the absence of physical resistance by Brown, such testimony by her provided substantial evidence that the act of sexual intercourse was against her will.

The State did not offer substantial evidence, however, of the element of force. As we have stated, actual physical force need not be shown in order to establish force sufficient to constitute an element of the crime of rape. Threats of serious bodily harm which reasonably induce fear thereof are sufficient. In the present case there was no substantial evidence of either actual or constructive force.

The evidence in the present case tended to show that, shortly after the defendant met Brown at the school, they walked out of the parking lot with the defendant in front. He stopped and told Brown he was going to "fix" her face so that her mother could see he was not "playing." This threat by the defendant and his act of grabbing Brown by the arm at the school, although they may have induced fear, appeared to have been unrelated to the act of sexual intercourse between Brown and the defendant. More important, the record is devoid of evidence that Brown was in any way intimidated into having sexual intercourse with the defendant by that threat or any other act of the defendant on June 15. * * *

We note that the absence of an explicit threat is not determinative in considering whether there was sufficient force in whatever form to overcome the will of the victim. It is enough if the totality of the circumstances gives rise to a reasonable inference that the unspoken purpose of the threat was to force the victim to submit to unwanted sexual intercourse. The evidence introduced in the present case, however, gave rise to no such inference. * * * Although Brown's general fear of the defendant may have been justified by his conduct on prior occasions, absent evidence that the defendant used force or threats to overcome the will of the victim *to resist the sexual intercourse alleged to have been rape,* such general fear was not sufficient to show that the defendant used the force required to support a conviction of rape. * * *

NOTES AND QUESTIONS

1. The court characterized Alston's and Brown's relationship as a "consensual sexual relationship." Is that how *you* would characterize it? Why, or why not?

2. According to the court, in a case involving a "continuing consensual sexual relationship," what must the prosecution generally show in order to meet its burden of proof that the sexual intercourse in question was nonconsensual? As a matter of public policy, do you agree with the rule announced?

3. *"Constructive force."* Modern statutes typically provide that nonconsensual intercourse obtained by *threat* of force (characterized that way or, perhaps, by a word such as "menace") constitutes forcible rape. At the time of *Alston*, the North Carolina rape statute did not include such a term, but that state's courts interpreted it to prohibit "constructive force," i.e., threats of force.

4. Suppose that Alston had called Brown on June 14 and told her, "The next time I see you, I intend to have sex with you, and if you don't cooperate, I'll kill you." If he did not repeat the threat on June 15—indeed, if he were outwardly pleasant—would this constitute forcible rape? Even in the absence of actual force, was Alston's conduct on June 15 sufficiently threatening to constitute rape?

As a matter of policy, should a male be convicted of rape, even in the absence of force or threatening words, solely because of his "threatening capacity," i.e., his greater size, strength, and fighting ability than the female? See Stephen J. Schulhofer, *Taking Sexual Autonomy Seriously: Rape Law and Beyond,* 11 Law & Phil. 35, 51 (1992).

5. Was *Alston* properly decided? Consider the following clashing remarks.

Susan Estrich, *Rape,* 95 Yale L.J. 1087, 1111–12 (1986):

Decisions such as * * * *Alston* are vulnerable to attack on traditional doctrinal grounds. The courts' unwillingness to credit the victim's past experience of violence at the hands of the defendant stands in sharp contrast to the black letter law that a defendant's knowledge of his attacker's reputation for violence or ownership of a gun is relevant to the reasonableness of his use of deadly force in self-defense.

That these decisions depart so straightforwardly from established criminal law doctrine is noteworthy but not unusual in the law of rape. More interesting is the apparent paradox that they create. In [*Alston*], the court says—and this is explicit, not implicit—that sex was without the woman's consent. It also says that there was no force. In other words, the woman was not forced to engage in sex, but the sex she engaged in was against her will.

Such a paradox is almost inevitable if one adopts, and then enforces, the most traditional male notion of a fight as the working definition of "force." In a fight, you hit your assailant with your fists or your elbows or your knees. In a fight, the one attacked fights back. In these terms, there was no fight in *Alston.* Therefore, there was no force.

I am not at all sure how the judges who decided *Alston* would explain the victim's simultaneous refusal to consent and failure to resist. For myself, it is not at all difficult to understand that a woman who had been repeatedly beaten, who had been a passive victim of both violence and sex during the "consensual" relationship, who had sought to escape from the man, who is confronted and threatened by him, who summons the courage to tell him their relationship is over only to be answered by his assertion of a "right" to sex—a woman in such a position would not fight. She wouldn't fight; she might cry. Hers is the reaction of "sissies" in playground fights. Hers is the reaction of people who have already been beaten, or who never had the power to fight in the first instance. Hers is, from my reading, the most common reaction of women to rape. * * *

To say that there is no "force" in such a situation is to create a gulf between power and force, and to define the latter solely in schoolboy terms. Mr. Alston did not beat his victim—at least not with his fists. He didn't have to. She had been beaten—physically and emotionally—long before. But that beating was one that the court was willing to go to great lengths to avoid recognizing.

That the law prohibiting forced sex understands force in such narrow terms is frustrating enough for its women victims. Worse, however, is the fact that the conclusion that no force is present may emerge as a judgment not that the man did not act unreasonably, but as a judgment that the woman victim did.

Vivian Berger, *Not So Simple Rape,* 7 Crim.Just. Ethics (Winter/Spring 1988) at 69, 75–76:

I'm certain that Alston is a terrible person and that Cottie [Brown] should be pitied rather than blamed. But did he *rape* her? I share the doubts of the appellate court that reversed his conviction. Estrich does not. She argues eloquently, indeed angrily, that *Alston* represents yet another instance of schoolboy rules regarding force unjustly applied to defenseless women. * * *

* * * If the author means only to say that women more often cry than physically resist when confronted with male sexual aggression, I imagine that she may well be right and, as I have said, I don't quarrel with her overall view that a "no" without an actual fight can turn intercourse into rape. Yet if she means, as the sentence on "beaten" people suggests, that Cottie's global "reaction" to a difficult situation, not just her tears and lack of resistance, is "common" and makes what occurred "rape," I find myself somewhat troubled. * * *

I worry that a *too* "understanding" attitude toward the Cotties of the world by the legal system may backfire and ultimately damage the cause of women in general. * * * [W]e don't want the law to patronize women; when it did in a vast number of areas, we fought it and won significant victories. To treat as victims in a legal sense all of the female victims of life is at some point to cheapen, not celebrate, the rights to self-determination, sexual autonomy, and self-and societal respect of women. Naturally, no bright line exists to make the border separating justified use of rape law to safeguard female personhood and choice * * * from abuse of this law to "defend" women who abdicate self and will entirely. Because overprotection risks enfeebling instead of empowering women, the tension between reformist goals * * * seems to me to make cases like *Alston* a close call, not a springboard for moral outrage.

Thus, as to Cottie, I think it acceptable if not ineluctable to regard her as a pitiable woman, involved with an utterly contemptible man in a sick relationship, whose sexual dynamics included a course of conduct involving passivity, submission, and inconsistent response on her part, dominance and occasional violence on his. Had she taken Alston to court when he beat her, he ought to have been convicted of battery: vindicating her right to be free of physical injury would scarcely have amounted to undue solicitude for a weakling or depreciation of women as a group. But "rape" strikes me at least arguably as a misnomer for the event at issue here. Her stated "no," while not a "yes," bore greater resemblance to a mental reservation or a "do what you will" than to a firm and clear rejection, when viewed against the totality of the couple's ongoing inter-actions.

6. *Problem.* V was a patient in a hospital. During the middle of the night, she was aroused from her sleep just enough to be aware that B was feeling the tubing being used to administer antibiotics to her intravenously. V incorrectly assumed that B was her nurse, and she did not open her eyes. B then pulled down her bed clothing, began to feel V's abdomen, pulled her underwear down, and then inserted his finger in V's vagina. Based solely on *Alston*, what difficulties would there be in convicting B of rape? See State v. Brown, 332 N.C. 262, 420 S.E.2d 147 (1992). How might this case be resolved in Alabama (see p. 389 for the statute)? What about New Jersey (see p. 394 supra)?

7. Michelle J. Anderson, *All–American Rape*, 79 St. John's L. Rev. 625, 628–632 (2005):

[T]he vast majority of state laws in the United States derive from the classic rape narrative: they basically require a defendant to exert force against the victim before the state may convict him of what is commonly thought of as rape. Putting aside those circumstances in which the victim *cannot* consent—such as when the victim is underage, mentally incapacitated, or physically helpless—in order to be convicted of a state's highest * * * sexual offense, statutes in forty-three states * * * require that the defendant use force against his victim. * * *

Sixteen states * * * do criminalize sexual penetration that is nonconsensual and without force. These states, however, impose less punishment upon non-consensual penetration, with greater than half of them categorizing these offenses as mere misdemeanors.

RUSK v. STATE

Court of Special Appeals of Maryland, 1979.
43 Md.App. 476, 406 A.2d 624.

THOMPSON, JUDGE.

We are called upon to review the sufficiency of the evidence to convict for rape. Whatever the law may have been before, it is now clear that our standard must be: Is the evidence sufficient for a finder of fact to conclude that the accused was guilty beyond a reasonable doubt? We hold that the evidence was not sufficient. In making this review we must look at the evidence in the light most favorable to the prosecution.

Edward Salvatore Rusk, the appellant, was convicted * * * of rape in the second degree and of assault. * * * The appellant does not challenge the conviction for assault * * *.

The prosecutrix was a twenty-one year old mother of a two-year-old son. She was separated from her husband but not yet divorced. Leaving her son with her mother, she attended a high school reunion after which she and a female friend, Terry, went bar hopping in the Fells Point area of Baltimore. They drove in separate cars. At the third bar the prosecutrix met appellant. * * * They had a five or ten minute conversation in the bar; at the end of which the prosecutrix said she was ready to leave. Appellant requested a ride home and she agreed. When they arrived at appellant's home, the prosecutrix parked at the curb on the side of the street opposite his rooming house but did not turn off the ignition. She put the car in park and appellant asked her to come up to his apartment. She refused. He continued to ask her to come up, and she testified she then became afraid. While trying to convince him that she didn't want to go to his apartment she mentioned that she was separated and if she did, it might cause her marital problems particularly if she were being followed by a detective. The appellant then took the keys out of the car and walked over to her side of the car, opened the door and said, "Now will you come up?" The prosecutrix then told him she would. She stated:

"At that point, because I was scared, because he had my car keys. I didn't know what to do. I was someplace I didn't even know where I was. It was in the city. I didn't know whether to run. I really didn't think, at that point, what to do. Now, I know that I should have blown the horn. I should have run. There were a million things I could have done. I was scared, at that point, and I didn't do any of them."

The prosecutrix followed appellant into the rowhouse, up the stairs, and into the apartment. When they got into appellant's room, he said that he had to go to the bathroom and left the room for a few minutes. [Although there was evidence of a telephone in the room, the prosecutrix testified that she did not notice one.—Ed.] The prosecutrix made no attempt to leave. When appellant came back, he sat on the bed while she sat on the chair next to the bed. He turned the light off and asked her to get on the bed with him. He started to pull her onto the bed and also began to remove her blouse. She stated she took off her slacks and removed his clothing because "he asked [her] to do it." After they both undressed, prosecutrix stated:

> "I was still begging him to please let, you know, let me leave. I said, 'you can get a lot of other girls down there, for what you want,' and he just kept saying, 'no,' and then I was really scared, because I can't describe, you know, what was said. It was more the look in his eyes; and I said, at that point—I didn't know what to say; and I said, 'If I do what you want, will you let me go without killing me?' Because I didn't know, at that point, what he was going to do; and I started to cry; and when I did, he put his hands on my throat, and started lightly to choke me; and I said, 'If I do what you want, will you let me go?' And he said, yes, and at that time, I proceeded to do what he wanted me to."

She stated that she performed oral sex and they then had sexual intercourse.[1] * * *

---

1. If we could say at this point that there is enough evidence for a reasonable fact finder to say such threat of force is solely that which overcame her will to resist, the conduct of both following intercourse would belie that conclusion:

> "A. All right. Now, after the sexual intercourse came to a conclusion, what is the very next thing that took place?
>
> A. I asked him if I could leave now, and he said, 'Yes;' and I got up and got dressed; and he got up and got dressed; and he walked me to my car, and asked if he could see me again; and I said, 'Yes;' and he asked me for my telephone number; and I said, 'No, I'll see you down Fell's Point sometime,' just so I could leave.
>
> Q. What is the reason that you said that you would meet him the next day?
>
> A. I didn't say the next day, and I just said I would see him down there only so I could leave. I didn't know what else to say. I had no intention of meeting him again."

After arriving home she said:

> "I sat in the car, thinking about it a while, and I thought I wondered what would happen if I hadn't of done what he wanted me to do. So I thought the right thing to do was to go report it, and I went from there to Hillendale to find a police car."

If, in quiet contemplation after the act, she had to wonder what would have happened, her submission on the side of prudence seems hardly justified. Indeed, if *she* had to wonder afterward, how can a fact finder reasonably conclude that she was justifiably in fear sufficient to overcome her will to resist, at the time.

The Court of Appeals of Maryland last spoke on the amount of force required to support a rape conviction in *Hazel v. State,* 221 Md. 464, 469, 157 A.2d 922, 925 (1960), when the Court said:

> "Force is an essential element of the crime and to justify a conviction, the evidence must warrant a conclusion either that the victim resisted and her resistance was overcome by force or that she was prevented from resisting by threats to her safety."[2]

In all of the victim's testimony we have been unable to see any resistance on her part to the sex acts and certainly can we see no fear as would overcome her attempt to resist or escape as required by *Hazel.* Possession of the keys by the accused may have deterred her vehicular escape but hardly a departure seeking help in the rooming house or in the street. We must say that "the way he looked" fails utterly to support the fear required by *Hazel.* * * *

Appellee argues * * * that the issue as to whether or not intercourse was accompanied by force or threats of force is one of credibility to be resolved by the triers of the fact. We cannot follow the argument. As we understand the law, the trial judge in ruling on a motion to acquit must first determine that there is legally sufficient evidence for the jury to find the victim was reasonably in fear. That is the rule set forth in *Hazel* * * *.

Cases from other jurisdictions have followed the rule that the victim's fear which overcomes her will to resist must be a reasonable fear. * * *

* * * [W]e find the evidence legally insufficient to warrant a conclusion that appellant's words or actions created in the mind of the victim a reasonable fear that if she resisted, he would have harmed her, or that faced with such resistance, he would have used force to overcome it. The prosecutrix stated that she was afraid, and submitted because of "the look in his eyes." After both were undressed and in the bed, and she pleaded to him that she wanted to leave, he started to lightly choke her. At oral argument it was brought out that the "lightly choking" could have been a heavy caress. We do not believe that "lightly choking" along with all the facts and circumstances in the case, were sufficient to cause a reasonable fear which overcame her ability to resist. In the absence of any other evidence showing force used by appellant, we find that the evidence was insufficient to convict appellant of rape.

WILNER, JUDGE, dissenting. * * *

The majority's error, in my judgment, is not in their exposition of the underlying principles of law that must govern this case, but rather in the

---

2. Since *Hazel,* the Maryland Legislature has codified extensively the law pertaining to sexual offenses providing in Md.Code, Art. 27, § 463 as follows:

> "(a) What constitutes.—A person is guilty of rape in the second degree if the person engages in vaginal intercourse with another person:
>
> (1) By force or threat of force against the will and without the consent of the other person.* * * "

The statute has made no change in the force as required by *Hazel.*

manner that they have applied those principles. * * * Under the guise of judging the sufficiency of the evidence presented against appellant, they have tacitly—perhaps unwittingly, but nonetheless effectively—substituted their own view of the evidence (and the inferences that may fairly be drawn from it) for that of the judge and jury. In so doing, they have not only improperly invaded the province allotted to those tribunals, but, at the same time, have perpetuated and given new life to myths about the crime of rape that have no place in our law today. * * *

Md.Annot.Code art. 27, § 463(a) considers three types of conduct as constituting second degree rape. We are concerned only with the first: a person is guilty of rape in the second degree if he (1) engages in vaginal intercourse with another person, (2) by force or threat of force, (3) against the will, and (4) without the consent of the other person. There is no real question here as to the first, third, or fourth elements of the crime. The evidence was certainly sufficient to show that appellant had vaginal intercourse with the victim, and that such act was against her will and without her consent. The point at issue is whether it was accomplished by force or threat of force; and I think that in viewing the evidence, that point should remain ever clear. *Consent is not the issue here, only whether there was sufficient evidence of force or the threat of force.*

statute

Unfortunately, courts, including in the present case a majority of this one, often tend to confuse these two elements—force and lack of consent—and to think of them as one. They are not. They mean, and require, different things. What seems to cause the confusion—what, indeed, has become a common denominator of both elements—is the notion that the victim must actively resist the attack upon her. If she fails to offer sufficient resistance (sufficient to the satisfaction of the judge), a court is entitled, or at least presumes the entitlement, to find that there was no force or threat of force, or that the act was not against her will, or that she actually consented to it, or some unarticulated combination or synthesis of these elements that leads to the ultimate conclusion that the victim was not raped. Thus it is that the focus is almost entirely on the extent of resistance—*the victim's acts, rather than those of her assailant.* Attention is directed not to the wrongful stimulus, but to the victim's reactions to it. Right or wrong, that seems to be the current state of the Maryland law; and, notwithstanding its uniqueness in the criminal law, and its illogic, until changed by statute or the Court of Appeals, I accept it as binding.

But what is required of a woman being attacked or in danger of attack? How much resistance must she offer? Where is that line to be drawn between requiring that she either risk serious physical harm, perhaps death, on the one hand, or be termed a willing partner on the other? * * *

From * * * pronouncements in *Hazel*, this Court has articulated what the majority refers to as a "rule of reason"—i.e., that "where the victim's story could not be corroborated by wounds, bruises or disordered clothing, the lack of consent could be shown by fear based upon reasonable apprehension." *Winegan v. State,* 10 Md.App. 196, 200, 268 A.2d 585, 588 (1970). As so phrased, I do not consider this to be a rule of reason at all; it is highly unreasonable, and again mixes the element of consent with that of force. But what I do accept is what the Court of Appeals said in *Hazel:* (1) if the acts and threats of the defendant were reasonably calculated to create in the mind of the victim—having regard to the circumstances in which she was placed—a real apprehension, due to fear, of imminent bodily harm, serious enough to impair or overcome her will to resist, then such acts and threats are the equivalent of force; (2) submission is not the equivalent of consent; and (3) the real test is whether the assault was committed without the consent and against the will of the prosecuting witness.

Upon this basis, the evidence against appellant must be considered. * * * The victim—I'll call her Pat—attended a high school reunion. * * *

* * * We know nothing about Pat and appellant. We don't know how big they are, what they look like, what their life experiences have been. We don't know if appellant is larger or smaller than she, stronger or weaker. We don't know what the inflection was in his voice as he dangled her car keys in front of her. We can't tell whether this was in a jocular vein or a truly threatening one. We have no idea what his mannerisms were. The trial judge and the jury could discern some of these things, of course, because they could observe the two people in court and could listen to what they said and how they said it. But all we know is that, between midnight and 1:00 a.m., in a neighborhood that was strange to Pat, appellant took her car keys, demanded that she accompany him, and most assuredly implied that unless she did so, at the very least, she might be stranded. * * *

How does the majority Opinion view these events? It starts by noting that Pat was a 21–year–old mother who was separated from her husband but not yet divorced, as though that had some significance. To me, it has none, except perhaps (when coupled with the further characterization that Pat and Terry had gone "bar hopping") to indicate an underlying suspicion, for which there is absolutely no support in the record, that Pat was somehow "on the make." Even more alarming, and unwarranted, however, is the majority's analysis [in footnote 1] of Pat's initial reflections on whether to report what had happened.

It is this type of reasoning—if indeed "reasoning" is the right word for it—that is particularly distressing. The concern expressed by Pat, made even more real by the majority Opinion of this Court, is one that is common among rape victims, and largely accounts for the fact that most incidents of forcible rape go unreported by the victim. If appellant had desired, and Pat had given, her wallet instead of her body, there would be no question about appellant's guilt of robbery. Taking the car keys under those circumstances would certainly have supplied the requisite threat of force or violence and negated the element of consent. No one would seriously contend that because she failed to raise a hue and cry she had consented to the theft of her money. Why then is such life-threatening action necessary when it is her personal dignity that is being stolen?

Rape has always been considered a most serious crime, one that traditionally carried the heaviest penalty. But until recently, it remained shrouded in the taboos and myths of a Victorian age, and little real attention was given to how rapes occur, how they may be prevented, and how a victim can best protect herself from injury when an attack appears inevitable. * * *

* * * As the result of the Battelle Study[8] we now know some things about this crime that we could only guess at before. * * *

Of particular significance is what was learned about resistance. The most common type of resistance offered by victims is verbal. Note: verbal resistance *is* resistance! In cases arising in the large cities, only 12.7% of the victims attempted flight, and only 12% offered physical resistance. The reason for this is apparent from the next thing learned: that *"[r]ape victims who resisted were more likely to be injured than ones who did not."* * * *

Where does this leave us but where we started? A judge and a jury, observing the witnesses and hearing their testimony, concluded without dissent that there was sufficient evidence to find beyond a reasonable doubt that appellant had sexual intercourse with Pat by force or threat of force against her will and without her consent; in other words, that the extent of her resistance and the reasons for her failure to resist further were reasonable. No claim is made here that the jury was misinstructed on the law of rape. Yet a majority of this Court, without the ability to see and hear the witnesses, has simply concluded that, in their judgment, Pat's fear was not a reasonable one, or that there was no fear at all * * *. * * * Brushing all of this aside, they have countermanded the judgment of the trial court and jury and declared Pat to have been, in effect, an adulteress.[17] * * *

STATE v. RUSK

Court of Appeals of Maryland, 1981.
289 Md. 230, 424 A.2d 720.

MURPHY, CHIEF JUDGE. * * *

We think the reversal of Rusk's conviction by the Court of Special Appeals was in error for the fundamental reason so well expressed in the dissenting opinion by Judge Wilner * * * that * * * the reasonableness of

---

8. This was a study conducted by the Battelle Memorial Institute Law and Justice Study Center under grant from the LEAA (National Institute of Law Enforcement and Criminal Justice). The Report of the study was published during 1977 and 1978. * * *

17. Interestingly, appellant was convicted of assault arising out of the same incident, but did not contest the sufficiency of the evidence supporting that conviction. It would seem that if there was not enough evidence of force, or lack of consent, to permit the rape conviction, there was an equal insufficiency to support the assault conviction. The majority is spared, in this case, the need to deal with that thorny dilemma.

Pat's apprehension of fear was plainly a question of fact for the jury to determine. * * *

Judgment of the Court of Special Appeals reversed; case remanded to that court with directions that it affirm the judgment of the Criminal Court of Baltimore * * *.

COLE, JUDGE, dissenting:

I agree with the Court of Special Appeals that the evidence adduced at the trial of Edward Salvatore Rusk was insufficient to convict him of rape. * * *

While courts no longer require a female to resist to the utmost or to resist where resistance would be foolhardy, they do require her acquiescence in the act of intercourse to stem from fear generated by something of substance. She may not simply say, "I was really scared," and thereby transform consent or mere unwillingness into submission by force. These words do not transform a seducer into a rapist. She must follow the natural instinct of every proud female to resist, by more than mere words, the violation of her person by a stranger or an unwelcomed friend. She must make it plain that she regards such sexual acts as abhorrent and repugnant to her natural sense of pride. She must resist unless the defendant has objectively manifested his intent to use physical force to accomplish his purpose. The law regards rape as a crime of violence. The majority today attenuates this proposition. It declares the innocence of an at best distraught young woman. It does not demonstrate the defendant's guilt of the crime of rape.

My examination of the evidence in a light most favorable to the State reveals no conduct by the defendant reasonably calculated to cause the prosecutrix to be so fearful that she should fail to resist and thus, the element of force is lacking in the State's proof. * * *

I find it incredible for the majority to conclude that on these facts, without more, a woman was forced to commit oral sex upon the defendant and then to engage in vaginal intercourse. In the absence of any verbal threat to do her grievous bodily harm or the display of any weapon and threat to use it, I find it difficult to understand how a victim could participate in these sexual activities and not be willing. * * *

NOTES AND QUESTIONS

1. Regarding the majority opinion of the Court of Special Appeals, Professor Susan Estrich observed:

> In a very real sense, the "reasonable" woman under the view of the * * * judges who would reverse Mr. Rusk's conviction is not a woman at all. Their version of a reasonable person is one who does not scare easily, one who does not feel vulnerability, one who is not passive, one who fights back, not cries. The reasonable woman, it seems, is not a schoolboy "sissy." She is a real man.

Susan Estrich, *Rape*, 95 Yale L.J. 1087, 1114 (1986).

2. Was Rusk guilty of rape because he used force to obtain intercourse or because he threatened it? If it is the former, what was the force? If he is guilty because he threatened Pat, was the threat expressed or implied? If it was the latter, how should the law deal with the possibility that a person might be convicted because his words or actions were misinterpreted?

[handwritten margin note: fear of force is not threat of force, against the will]

3. *Resistance (part 1)*. In light of Maryland's statutory definition of rape, what is the basis for the resistance requirement?

4. *Resistance (part 2)*. *Rusk* represents a much watered-down version of the original resistance rule. For an example of the undiluted version, consider *Brown v. State*, 127 Wis. 193, 106 N.W. 536 (1906). *Brown* involved a 20–year–old defendant who forced himself upon a 16–year–old girl recovering from a bout of the measles. The events occurred as she crossed along a rural path near the defendant's parent's farm, on her way to her grandmother's house. The court goes on:

[handwritten margin note: Resistance rule — original form]

> Her story is that he at once seized her, tripped her to the ground, placed himself in front and over her, unbuttoned her underclothing, then his own clothing, and had intercourse with her; that the only thing she said was to request him to let her go, and, throughout the description of the event, her only statement with reference to her own conduct was, repeatedly:
>
> > "I tried as hard as I could to get away. I was trying all the time to get away just as hard as I could, I was trying to get up; I pulled at the grass; I screamed as hard as I could, and he told me to shut up, and I didn't, and then he held his hand on my mouth until I was almost strangled."
>
> Also that at one time she got hold of the fence to try to pull herself away. Whenever he removed his hand from her mouth she repeated her screams. * * * She makes no mention of any use of her hands or her lower limbs. * * * [After the incident, she went to her grandmother's home. When she discovered a "flow of blood," she] was taken to the family physician for examination, [which disclosed] * * * fresh rupture of the hymen and a condition of the genital parts indicating recent sexual intercourse, but not significant as to whether the same had been accomplished forcibly or otherwise. Her person nowhere showed any bruises or injuries, nor did her clothing, except for a rip about an inch long in her drawers. At this examination she stated to one of the physicians that she had not resisted or made any fight. * * * There were no marks upon his face, hands, or clothing of any struggle. * * *
>
> As the statement of facts discloses, the only * * * question was that of prosecutrix's physical resistance to the act of intercourse, and, as to this, [defense] counsel urges, with great force, that there was not evidence sufficient to satisfy any reasonable mind, beyond reasonable doubt, of such resistance as the law makes *sine qua non* to the crime of rape. * * * Not only must there be entire absence of mental consent or assent, but there must be the most vehement exercise of every physical means or faculty within the woman's power to resist the penetration of her person,

and this must be shown to persist until the offense is consummated. * * * Among the corroborating circumstances almost universally present in cases of actual rape are the signs and marks of the struggle upon the clothing and persons of the participants, and the complaint by the sufferer at the earliest opportunity. In the present case the former is absolutely wanting, for the one-inch rip in prosecutrix's underwear was not shown to be of a character or location significant of force or violence. Not a bruise or scratch on either was proved, and none existed on prosecutrix, for she was carefully examined by physicians. Her outer clothing not only presented no tearing, but no disarray, so far as the testimony goes. When one pauses to reflect upon the terrific resistance which the determined woman should make, such a situation is well-nigh incredible. * * * We are convinced that there was no evidence of the resistance which is essential to the crime of rape, and that the motion for new trial should have been granted on that ground.

See also Moss v. State, 208 Miss. 531, 45 So.2d 125 (1950) ("[A] mere tactical surrender in the face of the assumed superior physical force is not enough. Where the penalty for the defendant may be supreme, so must resistance be unto the uttermost.").

5. *Resistance (part 3)*. Should the law require a victim to resist her aggressor? Consider the following:

To some degree, [statutory] variations of the resistance inquiry share common faults. First, resistance may prove an invitation to danger of death or serious bodily harm. Second, it is wrong to excuse the male assailant on the ground that his victim failed to protect herself with the dedication and intensity that a court might expect of a reasonable person in her situation. As a practical matter, juries may require resistance to show that the male compelled her to submit, but there is little reason to encase this generalization in a rule of law. Where the proof establishes that the actor did compel submission to intercourse by force, the failure of a weak or fearful victim to display "utmost" or even "earnest" resistance should not be exculpatory.

American Law Institute, Model Penal Code and Commentaries, Comment to § 213.1 at 304–06 (1980).

Can you think of any good reason *for* the requirement?

6. Some critics of the resistance rule say that its abolition would bring "the law of rape into conformity with other crimes such as robbery, kidnapping, and assault, which require force, fear, and nonconsent to convict," but which do "not demand resistance as a * * * predicate to conviction." People v. Barnes, 42 Cal.3d 284, 228 Cal.Rptr. 228, 721 P.2d 110 (1986). Is there any *valid* reason, however, why fair-minded jurors would treat non-resistance by a supposed rape victim differently than non-resistance by a supposed robbery victim?

7. *Rethinking rape laws.* Why did traditional rape law, as set out in cases such as *Alston* and *Rusk*, develop as it did? Professor Anne Coughlin contends that rape laws historically were not intended to protect women's sexual autonomy, but neither were they meant as a means of enforcing male

domination of women. Instead, rape laws developed at a time when "sexuality was [decreed to be] a force so dangerous that it could not safely be left to self-regulation, but rather should be closely confined, by state law, within marital relationships." Anne M. Coughlin, *Sex and Guilt*, 84 Va. L. Rev. 1, 6 (1998). In other words, "the exercise of sexual autonomy"—by men *and* women— "[f]ar from being positively valued and protected * * * was something to be discouraged, even criminalized." Id. at 6–7. Coughlin argues that "[w]e inherited the rape crime from a culture in which rape was only one of two basic categories of heterosexual offenses. The other category of offenses consisted of consensual sexual intercourse outside marriage—fornication and adultery—in which the man and the woman were accomplices." Id. at 7. Coughlin suggests that traditional rape law doctrine makes sense if we examine rape law by "recaptur[ing] the ways of thinking about heterosexual intercourse underlying the fornication and adultery laws." Id. As Coughlin explains, id. at 30–38, in Victorian times, all <u>consensual sexual activities outside of marriage were immoral and criminal, and both parties to the act were guilty</u>:

> Viewed from this perspective, the traditional elements of rape begin to mimic perfectly the substantive arguments that we would expect a woman to make if she were trying to defend herself against an accusation of fornication or adultery. * * * To contradict the damaging inferences of their own sexual complicity to which their rape complaints inevitably gave rise, we would expect women to pursue the few well-worn defensive strategies available to those accused of criminal wrongdoing, and each of these strategies had the effect of attributing sole responsibility for the intercourse to the man. In short, like any other person who was implicated in criminal activity, a woman suspected of fornication or adultery could attack the elements of the prosecution's prima facie case, or, if that strategy failed, she could interpose an affirmative excuse to liability. * * *

> [One] * * * defensive strategy that a woman suspected of a sexual infraction might pursue would be to assert a failure of the actus reus element of the offense in question. * * *

> * * * [T]he woman suspected of fornication or adultery would not be responsible for the sexual offense if she established that the man actually had physically forced her to participate. If the woman's bodily movements were produced not by her "effort or determination," but by the man's exercise of superior physical strength, then she was merely an "inanimate thing" that the man had used to perpetrate an illicit objective that was entirely his own. * * *

> In the view of criminal law theorists, courts would and should be reluctant in such cases to conclude that the man literally had forced the woman to transgress unless she attempted to resist him. Thus, the commentators who discuss hypothetical potential failures of actus reus in other contexts remark that evidence of resistance by the accused adds substantial weight to her claim that she should not be punished because she committed no act at all. * * * As a component of the woman's failure of actus reus defense, the resistance requirement was not engrafted onto

rape doctrine merely to provide evidence of the woman's subjective opposition to the sexual penetration, as contemporary commentators suggest. Rather, its function was to support her claim that the intercourse had occurred without even that minimal connection between her mind and the illegal conduct in which her body participated that is the foundation of criminal responsibility.

[Another] defense that a woman might interpose to a fornication or adultery charge is that she had submitted to the unlawful intercourse under duress. * * *

When we compare the elements of the duress defense to the elements of rape, the connection between the woman's sexual excuse and the man's sexual crime is irresistible. In particular, the primary substantive elements of the duress excuse are indistinguishable from the force and resistance elements of rape. The duress defense is satisfied only in cases where the accused shows that she was subject to precisely the same kinds of threats of force uttered by a rapist; that is, she must show that an assailant threatened to kill or inflict serious bodily injury on her if she refused to commit the crime he proposed. * * * When we recall that judges formerly would view rape complainants not merely as crime victims, but also as potential accomplices in fornication or adultery, we must question the commentators' assertion that the law has imposed on rape victims legal burdens different from and greater than those faced by other crime victims. Rather, the criminal law merely was holding suspected female perpetrators of sexual crimes to the same demanding standard that any offender was required to satisfy in order to secure an excuse to liability.

In view of changed attitudes regarding the criminalization of fornication and adultery, Coughlin reasons that the rules relating to rape can and should be reformed.

8. *Blaming the victim.* Many sexual assaults go unreported to the police. One reason for this is that society, and rape victims themselves, often assign some blame for sexual assaults to the victim. "[S]ocial stigma * * *, unfortunately, still attaches to the rape victim—family, friends and acquaintances frequently shun the victim, somehow blaming her (consciously or unconsciously) for her rape." In re Pittsburgh Action Against Rape, 494 Pa. 15, 428 A.2d 126 (1981) (Larsen J., dissenting).

Why do people assign blame to apparently innocent victims for their injuries? One explanation—one that applies well beyond the crime of rape—is that we want to believe that the world is just, i.e., that innocent persons—like ourselves—will not be victimized. Therefore, we rationalize that victims are partially responsible for their own fate. Melvin J. Lerner, *The Desire for Justice and Reactions to Victims* in Altruism and Helping Behavior 205 (J. Macaulay & L. Berkowitz eds. 1970).

In the rape context, this blame-the-victim tendency is exacerbated by cultural attitudes about "proper" behavior by women. For example, in one attitudinal study, male and female college students received a fictional account of a forcible rape that occurred while the victim was walking home alone late at night through a college campus. The perceived respectability of the victim was manipulated: some students were told that she was a social worker living with her husband. Others learned that the victim was a divorced topless dancer, out on bail awaiting trial for possession of heroin with intent to distribute.

The experimenters found that female students, more than their male counterparts, focused on the role of chance (being in the wrong place at the wrong time) as an explanation for the rape. Nonetheless, both males and females attached some blame for the rape to the victim, but their reasons differed. On the whole, males focused on the victim's perceived character; females were more apt to emphasize the victim's behavior on the night of the crime (the fact that she chose to walk alone, late at night, through the campus). See generally James Luginbuhl & Courtney Mullin, *Rape and Responsibility: How and How Much Is the Victim Blamed?*, 7 Sex Roles 547 (1981); see also L.G. Calhoun et al., *The Effects of Victim Physical Attractiveness and Sex of Respondent on Social Reactions to Victims of Rape*, 17 Brit.J.Soc. & Clin.Psychol. 191 (1978).

Sex differences also emerged when the students were asked to assign a penalty (from 1 to 99 years) for the rape. For females, the victim's degree of respectability was irrelevant to the penalty (43.8 years for the rape of the "respectable" victim, 45.8 years for the "unrespectable"). Males, however assigned significantly fewer years' penalty for the rape of the topless dancer (17.6 years versus 53.7 years for the rape of the social worker).

9. *What is wrong with this statute?* Vermont defines sexual assault, in part, as follows:

No person shall engage in a sexual act with another person and compel the other person to participate in a sexual act: (1) without the consent of the other person; or (2) by threatening or coercing the other person; or (3) by placing the other person in fear that any person will suffer imminent bodily injury * * *. 13 V.S.A. § 3252 (2011).

Why do we need to have to consent?

Policy issues entirely aside, do you see something wrong with how the Vermont legislature drafted its sexual assault statute?

2. "NO" (OR THE ABSENCE OF "YES") AS "FORCE"?

"I told him to stop—maybe he didn't hear me. * * * I didn't hit him or anything. * * * And plus I started crying a little bit and he shouted, 'Shut up!' Right? * * * At first I didn't even know it was rape. * * * I just didn't want to hear it. * * * I don't know if I can ever think of myself as a [rape] survivor. * * * I guess because it was 'date rape.' It's like something will happen—the walls will crumble— if I say the word."[a]

---

a. Charlotte Pierce–Baker, Surviving the Silence: Black Women's Stories of Rape 98, 103–104 (1998) (describing the experience of a 15–year–old female).

SUSAN ESTRICH—RAPE

95 Yale Law Journal 1087 (1986), 1092–93

* * * At one end of the spectrum is the "real" rape, what I will call the traditional rape: A stranger puts a gun to the head of his victim, threatens to kill her or beats her, and then engages in intercourse. In that case, the law—judges, statutes, prosecutors and all—generally acknowledge that a serious crime has been committed. But most cases deviate in one or many respects from this clear picture, making interpretation far more complex. Where less force is used or no other physical injury is inflicted, where threats are inarticulate, where the two know each other, where the setting is not an alley but a bedroom, where the initial contact was not a kidnapping but a date, where the woman says no but does not fight, the understanding is different. In such cases, the law, as reflected in the opinions of the courts, the interpretation, if not the words, of the statutes, and the decisions of those within the criminal justice system, often tell us that no crime has taken place and that fault, if any is to be recognized, belongs with the woman. In concluding that such acts—what I call, for lack of a better title, "non-traditional" rapes—are not criminal, and worse, that the woman must bear any guilt, the law has reflected, legitimized, and enforced a view of sex and women which celebrates male aggressiveness and punishes female passivity. And that vision, while under attack in recent years, continues to be a dominant force in our society and in the law of rape. * * *

Some of those who have written about rape from a feminist perspective intimate that nothing short of political revolution can redress the failings of the traditional approach to rape, that most of what passes for "sex" in our capitalist society is coerced, and that no lines can or should be drawn between rape and what happens in tens of millions of bedrooms across America.

So understood, this particular feminist vision of rape shares one thing with the most traditional sexist vision: the view that non-traditional rape is not fundamentally different from what happens in tens of millions of bedrooms across America. According to the radical feminist, all of it is rape; according to the traditionalist, it is all permissible sex and seduction. In policy terms, neither is willing to draw lines between rape and permissible sex. As a result, the two visions, contradictory in every other respect, point to the same practical policy implications.

My own view is different from both of these. I recognize that both men and women in our society have long accepted norms of male aggressiveness and female passivity which lead to a restricted understanding of rape. And I do not propose, nor do I think it feasible, to punish all of the acts of sexual intercourse that could be termed coerced. But lines can be drawn between these two alternatives. The law should be understood to prohibit claims and threats to secure sex that would be prohibited by extortion law and fraud or false pretenses law as a means to secure money. The law should evaluate the conduct of "reasonable" men, not according to a *Playboy*-macho philosophy that says "no means yes," but by according respect to a woman's words. If * * * silence does not negate consent, at least crying and saying "no" should.

SUSAN AGER—THE INCIDENT

Detroit Free Press Magazine, Mar. 22, 1992, p. 17

We were alone beneath the stars, high in the mountains, miles from the nearest light, our sleeping bags unrolled on the ground, weary from a long drive and anticipating sleep.

Or so I thought.

We were not lovers, merely acquaintances. We worked together. We respected each other. He owned a few acres in the mountains, and I admired that back-to-the-land streak in anyone. So we agreed to make this weekend camping trip together to his patch of earth.

A few days earlier, oh so briefly, I thought about saying something. Issuing a "don't-get-any-ideas" warning. But I didn't. I thought he'd feel insulted.

He did not worry so much about my feelings.

For hours on that starlit night he pestered me. Stroked me. Whispered to me first, then argued, then whined: "Oh, come on. You'll love it. Why'd you come up here with me then? Just once. It's such a beautiful night. You'll enjoy it, really. Come on. Please?"

I didn't scream, because there was no one to hear. I didn't fight, because there was nowhere to run. It was his car, and he had the keys. Instead, I curled up. I buried my head against my chest while he touched me. I slapped blindly at his touches, as if I were batting away mosquitos.

Because this happened more than a decade ago, I can't remember with precision how long he continued. * * * I wore no watch that night.

All I know is that he went on forever. Unrelenting.

Finally, weary and weepy, I gave up. I remember the sting of my tears rolling down my cheeks and into my ears as I lay on my back and he moaned.

Then, I fell instantly into sleep, as if from the top of a mountain.

Our weekend ended early, because I was sullen and that made him angry. There was nothing to say on the long ride home.

I never called what happened that night "rape." I still don't.

But it wasn't bliss, either.

I wonder why it has no name. Because it happens all the time: Men push. We submit.

No violence, no shouting, no cries of "rape" afterwards. Just sadness and defeat.

How many of us women have watched this sort of thing happen to us, as if we were outside our bodies, in the 30 years since a confluence of factors made sexual interaction easier, at least practically speaking?

That night in the mountains I surrendered for one reason: I was tired and wanted to escape.

But we surrender for reasons besides fatigue.

• Duty: Some women may feel an obligation to reward men who've been particularly kind, or patient, or ardent. Other women may feel an obligation to be a good-and-ready wife.

• Ambiguity: Part of us wants sex, the other part is wary. And as the train is moving toward the station, so to speak, we're still not sure. We may surrender at the same moment that we conclude, "No, this is stupid."

Some men claim not to understand this. But most women know there is a vast geography of shifting sentiment between Yes and No.

• Hope: Sometimes we surrender because our disinterest might turn into delight. A friend calls this the "No-but-I-could-be-convinced" approach. Sometimes it works. Often it doesn't, and we wonder why we gave in.

We make these excuses for our surrenders, but that's no consolation for the vanquished.

Years after that night in the mountains, I'm surprised to find how angry I am about it. Angrier than I was then. At both him and me, and the games people play.

Now, wiser and less polite, I would not whimper but shout! Not for help, but for my own integrity—to let him know how I felt about his boorish presumptions.

I would surrender only if he held me down and forced me to. And then I could call it rape.

NOTES AND QUESTIONS

1. Do you agree with Susan Ager that what she experienced was not rape?

2. How *should* the law deal with conduct such as occurred in *The Incident*? Consider:

> The truth is that there are many fine[ ] distinctions which we need to recognize and to which we need to develop a sensitivity. We do this in other areas * * *. We know generally that there is a difference between actions which (*a*) infringe others' rights * * *, (*b*) don't infringe others' rights but are nonetheless wrong (like failing to give to someone in need), (*c*) are not wrong but which * * * evince bad character (giving to the needy * * * to feel your own superiority), and (*d*) are none of these yet may * * * be regrettable for their repercussions. What we need to

understand is that sex is at least as complex as other areas of human interaction and has just as many varieties of wrong as well as of good * * *.

Sarah Conly, *Seduction, Rape, and Coercion*, 115 Ethics 96, 120–121 (2004).

Should "The Incident" be considered boorish behavior but outside the scope of the criminal law? If it *should* be criminalized, how should the conduct be measured? In your view, is acquaintance rape a lesser offense than forcible rape? On the other hand, might it be argued that acquaintance rape is as bad as traditional rape—yes, violence is absent, but perhaps the violation of the trust of the victim is as serious as physical harm?

Consider these questions as we proceed.

COMMONWEALTH v. BERKOWITZ

Superior Court of Pennsylvania, 1992.
415 Pa.Super. 505, 609 A.2d 1338.

PER CURIAM: * * *

I. FACTS AND PROCEDURAL HISTORY

In the spring of 1988, appellant and the victim were both college sophomores at East Stroudsburg State University, ages twenty and nineteen years old, respectively. They had mutual friends and acquaintances. On April nineteenth of that year, the victim went to appellant's dormitory room. What transpired in that dorm room between appellant and the victim thereafter is the subject of the instant appeal.

During a one day jury trial held on September 14, 1988, the victim gave the following account during direct examination by the Commonwealth. At roughly 2:00 on the afternoon of April 19, 1988, after attending two morning classes, the victim returned to her dormitory room. There, she drank a martini to "loosen up a little bit" before going to meet her boyfriend, with whom she had argued the night before. Roughly ten minutes later she walked to her boyfriend's dormitory lounge to meet him. He had not yet arrived.

Having nothing else to do while she waited for her boyfriend, the victim walked up to appellant's room to look for Earl Hassel, appellant's roommate. She knocked on the door several times but received no answer. She therefore wrote a note to Mr. Hassel, which read, "Hi Earl, I'm drunk. That's not why I came to see you. I haven't seen you in a while. I'll talk to you later, [victim's name]." She did so, although she had not felt any intoxicating effects from the martini, "for a laugh."

After the victim had knocked again, she tried the knob on the appellant's door. Finding it open, she walked in. She saw someone lying on the bed with a pillow over his head, whom she thought to be Earl Hassel. After lifting the pillow from his head, she realized it was appellant. She asked appellant which dresser was his roommate's. He told her, and the victim left the note.

Before the victim could leave appellant's room, however, appellant asked her to stay and "hang out for a while." She complied because she "had time to kill" and because she didn't really know appellant and wanted to give him "a fair chance." Appellant asked her to give him a back rub but she declined, explaining that she did not "trust" him. Appellant then asked her to have a seat on his bed. Instead, she found a seat on the floor, and conversed for a while about a mutual friend.[1] No physical contact between the two had, to this point, taken place.

Thereafter, however, appellant moved off the bed and down on the floor, and "kind of pushed [the victim] back with his body. It wasn't a shove, it was just kind of a leaning-type of thing." Next appellant "straddled" and started kissing the victim. The victim responded by saying, "Look, I gotta go. I'm going to meet [my boyfriend]." Then appellant lifted up her shirt and bra and began fondling her. The victim then said "no."

After roughly thirty seconds of kissing and fondling, appellant "undid his pants and he kind of moved his body up a little bit." The victim was still saying "no" but "really couldn't move because [appellant] was shifting at [her] body so he was over [her]." Appellant then tried to put his penis in her mouth. The victim did not physically resist, but rather continued to verbally protest, saying "No, I gotta go, let me go," in a "scolding" manner.

Ten or fifteen more seconds passed before the two rose to their feet. Appellant disregarded the victim's continual complaints that she "had to go," and instead walked two feet away to the door and locked it so that no one from the outside could enter.[2]

Then, in the victim's words, "[appellant] put me down on the bed. It was kind of like—he didn't throw me on the bed. It's hard to explain. It was kind of like a push but no * * *." She did not bounce off the bed. "It wasn't slow like a romantic kind of thing, but it wasn't a fast shove either. It was kind of in the middle."

Once the victim was on the bed, appellant began "straddling" her again while he undid the knot in her sweatpants. He then removed her sweatpants and underwear from one of her legs. The victim did not physically resist in any way while on the bed because appellant was on top of her, and she "couldn't like go anywhere." She did not scream out at anytime because, "[i]t was like a dream was happening or something."

Appellant then used one of his hands to "guide" his penis into her vagina. At that point, after appellant was inside her, the victim began saying "no, no to him softly in a moaning kind of way * * * because it was just so scary." After about thirty seconds, appellant pulled out his penis and ejaculated onto the victim's stomach.

---

1. On cross-examination, the victim testified that during this conversation she had explained she was having problems with her boyfriend.

2. The victim testified that she realized at the time that the lock was not of a type that could lock people inside the room.

Immediately thereafter, appellant got off the victim and said, "Wow, I guess we just got carried away." To this the victim retorted, "No, we didn't get carried away, you got carried away." The victim then quickly dressed, grabbed her school books and raced downstairs to her boyfriend who was by then waiting for her in the lounge.

Once there, the victim began crying. Her boyfriend and she went up to his dorm room where, after watching the victim clean off appellant's semen from her stomach, he called the police.

Defense counsel's cross-examination elicited more details regarding the contact between appellant and the victim before the incident in question. The victim testified that roughly two weeks prior to the incident, she had attended a school seminar entitled, "Does 'no' sometimes means 'yes'?" Among other things, the lecturer at this seminar had discussed the average length and circumference of human penises. After the seminar, the victim and several of her friends had discussed the subject matter of the seminar over a speaker-telephone with appellant and his roommate Earl Hassel. The victim testified that during that telephone conversation, she had asked appellant the size of his penis. According to the victim, appellant responded by suggesting that the victim "come over and find out." She declined.

When questioned further regarding her communications with appellant prior to the April 19, 1988 incident, the victim testified that on two other occasions, she had stopped by appellant's room while intoxicated. During one of those times, she had laid down on his bed. When asked whether she had asked appellant again at that time what his penis size was, the victim testified that she did not remember.

Appellant took the stand in his own defense and offered an account of the incident and the events leading up to it which differed only as to the consent involved. According to appellant, the victim had begun communication with him after the school seminar by asking him of the size of his penis and of whether he would show it to her. Appellant had suspected that the victim wanted to pursue a sexual relationship with him because she had stopped by his room twice after the phone call while intoxicated, laying down on his bed with her legs spread and again asking to see his penis. He believed that his suspicions were confirmed when she initiated the April 19, 1988 encounter by stopping by his room (again after drinking), and waking him up.

Appellant testified that, on the day in question, he did initiate the first physical contact, but added that the victim warmly responded to his advances by passionately returning his kisses. He conceded that she was continually "whispering * * * no's," but claimed that she did so while "amorously * * * passionately" moaning. In effect, he took such protests to be thinly veiled acts of encouragement. When asked why he locked the door, he explained that "that's not something you want somebody to just walk in on you [doing.]"

According to appellant, the two then laid down on the bed, the victim helped him take her clothing off, and he entered her. He agreed that the victim continued to say "no" while on the bed, but carefully qualified his agreement, explaining that the statements were "moaned passionately." According to appellant, when he saw a "blank look on her face," he immediately withdrew and asked "is anything wrong, is something the matter, is anything wrong." He ejaculated on her stomach thereafter because he could no longer "control" himself. Appellant testified that after this, the victim "saw that it was over and then she made her move. She gets right off the bed * * * she just swings her legs over and then she puts her clothes back on." Then, in wholly corroborating an aspect of the victim's account, he testified that he remarked, "Well, I guess we got carried away," to which she rebuked, "No, we didn't get carried, you got carried away."

After hearing both accounts, the jury convicted appellant of rape and indecent assault. * * * Appellant was then sentenced to serve a term of imprisonment of one to four years for rape and a concurrent term of six to twelve months for indecent assault. * * *

II.   SUFFICIENCY OF THE EVIDENCE

Appellant's argument in this regard was well summarized by appellant's counsel in his brief. * * *

Mr. Berkowitz prays that this Court overturns his rape conviction. He asks that this Court define the parameters between what may have been unacceptable social conduct and the criminal conduct necessary to support the charge for forcible rape.

We contend that upon review, the facts show no more than what legal scholars refer to as "reluctant submission." The complainant herself admits that she was neither hurt nor threatened at any time during the encounter. She admits she never screamed or attempted to summon help. The incident occurred in a college dormitory in the middle of the afternoon. There has never been an affirmed conviction for forcible rape under similar circumstances. Not one factor which this Court has considered significant in prior cases, exists here. The uncontroverted evidence fails to establish forcible compulsion.

The Commonwealth counters:

Viewing the evidence and its inferences in the light most favorable to the Commonwealth, the jury's conclusion that the Defendant's forcible conduct overcame [the victim's] will is reasonable. The assault was rapid and the victim was physically overcome. Because she was acquainted with the Defendant, [the victim] had no reason to be fearful or suspicious of him and her resorting to verbal resistance only is understandable. More importantly, perhaps, it is only her lack of consent that is truly relevant. It is entirely reasonable to believe that the Defendant sat on her, pushed her on the bed and penetrated her before she had time to fully realize her plight and raise a hue and cry.

If the law required active resistance, rather the simple absence of consent, speedy penetration would immunize the most violent attacks and the goal-oriented rapist would reap an absurd reward. Certainly a victim must communicate her objections. But, contrary to the Defendant's arguments, Pennsylvania law says she can "just say no." [The victim] said "no." She said it repeatedly, clearly and sternly. She was rapidly, forcibly raped and deserves the protection of the law.

With the Commonwealth's position, the trial court agreed. We cannot.

In viewing the evidence, we remain mindful that credibility determinations were a matter solely for the fact finder below. On appeal, we must examine the evidence in the light most favorable to the Commonwealth drawing all reasonable inferences therefrom. If a jury could have reasonably determined from the evidence adduced that all of the necessary elements of the crime were established, then the evidence will be deemed sufficient to support the verdict.

In Pennsylvania, the crime of rape is defined by statute as follows:

A person commits a felony of the first degree when he engages in sexual intercourse with another person not his spouse:

>   (1) by forcible compulsion;

>   (2) by threat of forcible compulsion that would prevent resistance by a person of reasonable resolution;

>   (3) who is unconscious; or

>   (4) who is so mentally deranged or deficient that such person is incapable of consent.

18 Pa.C.S.A. § 3121. A statutory caveat to this rule may be found in section 3107 of title 18.

Resistance Not Required

The alleged victim need not resist the actor in prosecution under this chapter: Provided, however, that nothing in this section shall be construed to prohibit a defendant from introducing evidence that the alleged victim consented to the conduct in question.

The contours of Pennsylvania's rape statute, however, are not immediately apparent. As our Supreme Court explained in the landmark case, *Commonwealth v. Rhodes*, 510 Pa. 537, 510 A.2d 1217 (1986):

"[F]orcible compulsion" as used in section 3121(1) includes not only physical force or violence but also moral, psychological or intellectual force used to compel a person to engage in sexual intercourse against that person's will.

Closely related to section 3121(1) is section 3121(2) which applies to the situation where "forcible compulsion" is not actually used but is threatened. That section uses the phrase "by threat of forcible compulsion that would prevent resistance by a person of reasonable resolution." The Model Penal Code used the terminology "compels her to submit by any threat that would prevent resistance by a woman of ordinary resolution" and graded that offense as gross sexual imposition, a felony of the third degree. The Pennsylvania legislature rejected the concept that sexual intercourse compelled by "gross imposition" should be graded as a less serious offense and, therefore, enacted section 3121(2). By use of the phrase "person of reasonable resolution," the legislature introduced an objective standard regarding the use of *threats* of forcible compulsion to prevent resistance (as opposed to actual application of "forcible compulsion.")

The determination of whether there is sufficient evidence to demonstrate beyond a reasonable doubt that an accused engaged in sexual intercourse by forcible compulsion (which we have defined to include "not only physical force or violence, but also moral, psychological or intellectual force used to compel a person to engage in sexual intercourse against that person's will"), or by the threat of such forcible compulsion that would prevent resistance by a person of reasonable resolution *is, of course, a determination that will be made in each case based upon the totality of the circumstances that have been presented to the fact finder.* Significant factors to be weighed in that determination would include the respective ages of the victim and the accused, the respective mental and physical conditions of the victim and the accused, the atmosphere and physical setting in which the incident was alleged to have taken place, the extent to which the accused may have been in a position of authority, domination or custodial control over the victim, and whether the victim was under duress. This list of possible factors is by no means exclusive.

Before us is not a case of mental coercion. There existed no significant disparity between the ages of appellant and the victim. They were both college sophomores at the time of the incident. Appellant was age twenty; the victim was nineteen. The record is devoid of any evidence suggesting that the physical or mental condition of one party differed from the other in any material way. Moreover, the atmosphere and physical setting in which the incident took place was in no way coercive. The victim walked freely into appellant's dorm room in the middle of the afternoon on a school day and stayed to talk of her own volition. There was no evidence to suggest that appellant was in any position of authority, domination or custodial control over the victim. Finally, no record evidence indicates that the victim was under duress. Indeed, nothing in the record manifests any intent of appellant to impose "moral, psychological or intellectual" coercion upon the victim. *See and compare Commonwealth v. Rhodes, supra* (position of authority, isolated area of the incident and explicit commands sufficient to prove mental coercion); *Commonwealth v. Ables*, 404 Pa.Superior Ct. [169], 590 A.2d [334 (1991)] (position of trust and confidence coupled with emotional exploitation sufficient to establish moral coercion); *Commonwealth v. Ruppert*, 397 Pa.Super. 132, 579 A.2d 966 (1990) (father-daughter relationship coupled with showing of sexually explicit pictures sufficient to establish psychological coercion); *Commonwealth v.*

Frank, 395 Pa.Super. 412, 577 A.2d 609 (1990) (therapist-patient relationship coupled with threat sufficient for psychological coercion); *Commonwealth v. Dorman*, [377 Pa.Super. 419, 547 A.2d 757 (1988)] (appellant's position of authority and trust and remote location of the incident sufficient to establish psychological coercion).

Nor is this a case of a threat of forcible compulsion. When asked by defense counsel at trial whether appellant had at any point threatened her in any manner, the victim responded, "No, he didn't." Moreover, careful review of the record fails to reveal any express or even implied threat that could be viewed as one which, by the objective standard applicable herein, "would prevent resistance by a person of reasonable resolution." *Compare Commonwealth v. Poindexter*, 372 Pa.Super. 566, 539 A.2d 1341 (1988) (father's reproaches and threats sufficient to establish coercion toward daughters); *Commonwealth v. Williams*, 294 Pa.Super. 93, 439 A.2d 765 (1982) (threat that victim would be killed if she resisted sufficient to establish forcible compulsion).

Rather, the Commonwealth contends that the instant rape conviction is supported by the evidence of actual physical force used to complete the act of intercourse. Essentially, the Commonwealth maintains that, viewed in the light most favorable to it, the record establishes that the victim did not consent to engage in the intercourse, and thus, any force used to complete the act of intercourse thereafter constituted "forcible compulsion." * * *

What is comparatively uncertain * * * is the precise degree of actual physical force necessary to prove "forcible compulsion." As the *Rhodes* Court has made clear, no precise definition of the term "forcible compulsion" may be found. * * * Rather, the Court left that delineation to evolve "in the best tradition of the common law—by development of a body of case law. * * * [W]hether there is sufficient evidence to demonstrate * * * that an accused engaged in sexual intercourse by forcible compulsion * * * is, of course, a determination that will be made in each case based on the *totality of the circumstances*." * * *

Here, the victim testified that the physical aspects of the encounter began when appellant "kind of pushed me back with his body. It wasn't a shove, it was just kind of a leaning-type thing." She did not testify that appellant "pinned" her to the floor with his hands thereafter; she testified that he "started kissing me * * * [and] lift[ing] my shirt [and] bra * * * straddling me kind of * * * shifting at my body so that he was over me." When he attempted to have oral sex with her, appellant "knelt up straight * * * [and] tried to put his penis in my mouth * * * and after he obviously couldn't * * * he, we got up." Although appellant then locked the door, his act cannot be seen as an attempt to imprison the victim since she knew and testified that the type of lock on the door of appellant's dorm room simply prevented those on the outside from entering but could be opened from the inside without hindrance. Appellant did not push, shove or throw the victim to his bed; he "put" her on the bed, not in a "romantic" way, but not with a "fast shove either." Once on the bed, appellant did not try to restrain the victim with his hands in any fashion. Rather, while she was "just kind of laying there," he "straddled" her, "quick[ly] undid" the knot in her sweatpants, "took off" her sweatpants and underwear, placed the "weight of his body" on top of her and "guided" his penis inside her vagina.

Even in the light most favorable to the Commonwealth, the victim's testimony as to the physical aspects of the encounter cannot serve as a basis to prove "forcible compulsion." The cold record is utterly devoid of any evidence regarding the respective sizes of either appellant or the victim. As such, we are left only to speculate as to the coercive effect of such acts as "leaning" against the victim or placing the "weight of his body" on top of her. This we may not do. Moreover, even if the record indicated some disparity in the respective weights or strength of the parties, such acts are not themselves inconsistent with consensual relations. Except for the fact that appellant was on top of the victim before and during intercourse, there is no evidence that the victim, if she had wanted to do so, could not have removed herself from appellant's bed and walked out of the room without any risk of harm or danger to herself whatsoever. These circumstances simply cannot be bootstrapped into sexual intercourse by forcible compulsion.

Similarly inconclusive is the fact that the victim testified that the act occurred in a relatively brief period of time. The short time frame might, without more, indicate that the victim desired the sexual encounter as easily as it might that she didn't, given the fact that no threats or mental coercion were alleged. At most, therefore, the physical aspects of the encounter establishes that appellant's sexual advances may have been unusually rapid, persistent and virtually uninterrupted. However inappropriate, undesirable or unacceptable such conduct may be seen to be, it does not, standing alone, prove that the victim was "forced to engage in sexual intercourse against her will."

The only evidence which remains to be considered is the fact that both the victim and appellant testified that throughout the encounter, the victim repeatedly and continually said "no."[6] Unfortunately for the Commonwealth, under the existing statutes, this evidence alone cannot suffice to support a finding of "forcible compulsion."

Evidence of verbal resistance is unquestionably relevant in a determination of "forcible compulsion." At least twice previously this Court has given weight to the failure to heed the victim's oral admonitions. In each such case, however, evidence of verbal resistance was only found sufficient where coupled with a sufficient threat of forcible compulsion, mental

6. The accounts differed in this respect only as to the tone in which the word was spoken. Appellant claimed it was whispered "passionately." The victim testified that she voiced her objections *before* the intercourse in a "scolding" manner. At trial, it was peculiarly for the jury to determine the credibility of the parties. On appeal, we must view the record in the light most favorable to the Commonwealth. Viewed in this way, we must consider the victim's admonitions *before* the intercourse to be sincere protests. * * *

coercion, or actual physical force of a type inherently inconsistent with consensual sexual intercourse. Thus, although evidence of verbal protestations may be relevant to prove that the intercourse was against the victim's will, it is not dispositive or sufficient evidence of "forcible compulsion."

If the legislature had intended to define rape, a felony of the first degree, as non-consensual intercourse, it could have done so. It did not do this. It defined rape as sexual intercourse by "forcible compulsion." If the legislature means what it said, then where as here no evidence was adduced by the Commonwealth which established either that mental coercion, or a threat, or force inherently inconsistent with consensual intercourse was used to complete the act of intercourse, the evidence is insufficient to support a rape conviction.[7] Accordingly, we hold that the trial court erred in determining that the evidence adduced by the Commonwealth was sufficient to convict appellant of rape. * * *

For the foregoing reasons, we conclude that the evidence adduced by the Commonwealth was insufficient to convict appellant of rape, and that a new trial is warranted [on other grounds] on the indecent assault charge. * * * Accordingly, we *discharge* appellant as to the rape conviction and *reverse* and *remand* for a new trial in accordance with this opinion.

NOTES AND QUESTIONS

1. Do you feel Berkowitz was guilty, as charged? Do you think his conduct *should* be criminal? Did he deserve the original one-to-four year prison sentence? Less? More?

Here is what Deborah Zubow, of the Women's International League for Peace and Freedom, said about *Berkowitz*: "What is it about the word 'no' they don't understand? Obviously the court has a difficult time comprehending the most unambiguous word in the English language. How else could it have ruled that a woman who repeatedly * * * told a man she did not want to have sex with him had not been raped?" Editorial, *When "No" Means Nothing*, St. Louis Post–Dispatch, June 6, 1994, at 6B (quoting Zubow).

On the other hand here is what Professor Camille Paglia (University of the Arts) said: "Oh, please, she goes into the room of a man who's in bed and

---

7. It may be argued that our conclusion requires the victim, whose *verbal* resistance did not deter the sexual advances, to *physically* resist, in violation of the "no resistance requirement." In this regard, we note the following. Although the "no resistance requirement" does not, on its face, in any way restrict the situations to which it may apply, it appears that the statute must have limits. Section 3121(2) of title 18, which describes the threat element of rape, states that rape occurs when a person "engages in sexual intercourse with another * * * by threat of forcible compulsion *that would prevent resistance* by a person of reasonable resolution." If the "no resistance requirement" were applied in that setting, the description of the type of threat which is sufficient would be rendered wholly meaningless. To be consistent, therefore, the "no resistance requirement" must be applied only to prevent any *adverse inference* to be drawn against the person who, *while* being "forcibly compelled" to engage in intercourse, chooses not to physically resist. Since there is no evidence that the instant victim was at any time "forcibly compelled" to engage in sexual intercourse, our conclusion is not at odds with the "no resistance requirement."

sits on the floor with her breasts sticking up: What are we teaching our girls? * * * When you go into a man's room and stretch on the floor, you are sending a signal." Nancy E. Roman, *Scales of Justice Weigh Tiers of Sexual Assault; State May Reform Rape Law*, Washington Times, June 16, 1994, at A* (quoting Paglia).

2.   According to Professor Dan Kahan, when there are factual disputes or different reasonable inferences one can draw from those facts, "individuals naturally gravitate toward factual perceptions that reflect their group [cultural-value] commitments." Dan M. Kahan, *Culture, Cognition, and Consent: Who Perceives What, and Why, in Acquaintance–Rape Cases*, 158 U. Pa. L. Rev. 729, 732 (2010). Thus, in an experimental study of attitudes about the *Berkowitz* facts, Kahan found that those "who adhere to a largely traditional cultural style, one that prescribes highly differentiated gender roles and features a commitment to hierarchical forms of authority * * * are highly likely to believe that 'no' did not mean 'no' in *Berkowitz*" and, therefore, that no rape occurred. "In contrast, persons who subscribe to a more egalitarian cultural style that denies the legitimacy of hierarchical forms of social organization, including those founded on gender"—specifically, those who "judge[ ] the character of men and women by largely unitary measure and treat[ ] female sexuality as a legitimate expression of individual autonomy"— were far more likely to believe that the complainant did not consent and, thus, that Berkowitz was guilty of rape. *Id*. at 733, 757. The study found that, overall, women were no more likely to favor conviction than men. Gender only mattered in conjunction with cultural values. *Id*. at 733–734.

3.   *Aftermath*. The Supreme Court of Pennsylvania upheld the Superior Court's discharge of Berkowitz's rape conviction, but it reinstituted his conviction for indecent assault. 537 Pa. 143, 641 A.2d 1161 (1994). Berkowitz, who was free on bail during the appeal stage and had transferred to Rutgers University after the trial, began serving his six to twelve month sentence on August 1, 2004. As a result of the case, the Pennsylvania legislature enacted a new offense prohibiting nonforcible, nonconsensual sexual intercourse. (18 Pa.C.S.A. § 3124.1, see p. 397, supra.)

4.   Model Penal Code § 213.1(2) provides that a criminal offense occurs—"gross sexual imposition," a lesser offense than rape—if a male compels intercourse with a female "by any threat that would prevent resistance by a woman of ordinary resolution." Would this provision apply to Berkowitz's conduct?

5.   The defendant testified that the rape complainant kept saying "no" in a "passionate" manner. In contrast, the woman said that she uttered the words in a "scolding" manner. Footnote 6 characterizes the issue of the tone as one of credibility. Could it be, however, that she intended her "no's" to communicate her wish for Berkowitz to desist, but that he honestly heard them as passionate in nature? If so, what is the legal significance of this misunderstanding?

6.   Do you believe that any of the evidence introduced at trial should have been excluded? If so, what evidence, and why?

STATE OF NEW JERSEY IN THE INTEREST OF M.T.S.

Supreme Court of New Jersey, 1992.
129 N.J. 422, 609 A.2d 1266.

HANDLER, J. [in an unanimous opinion]

Under New Jersey law a person who commits an act of sexual penetration using physical force or coercion is guilty of second-degree sexual assault. The sexual assault statute does not define the words "physical force." The question posed by this appeal is whether the element of "physical force" is met simply by an act of non-consensual penetration involving no more force than necessary to accomplish that result.

That issue is presented in the context of what is often referred to as "acquaintance rape." The record in the case discloses that the juvenile, a seventeen-year-old boy, engaged in consensual kissing and heavy petting with a fifteen-year-old girl and thereafter engaged in actual sexual penetration of the girl to which she had not consented. There was no evidence or suggestion that the juvenile used any unusual or extra force or threats to accomplish the act of penetration.

The trial court determined that the juvenile was delinquent for committing a sexual assault. The Appellate Division reversed the disposition of delinquency, concluding that non-consensual penetration does not constitute sexual assault unless it is accompanied by some level of force more than that necessary to accomplish the penetration. We granted the State's petition for certification.

I

The issues in this case are perplexing and controversial. * * *

On Monday, May 21, 1990, fifteen-year-old C.G. was living with her mother, her three siblings, and several other people, including M.T.S. and his girlfriend. A total of ten people resided in the three-bedroom townhome at the time of the incident. M.T.S., then age seventeen, was temporarily residing at the home with the permission of the C.G.'s mother; he slept downstairs on a couch. C.G. had her own room on the second floor. At approximately 11:30 p.m. on May 21, C.G. went upstairs to sleep after having watched television with her mother, M.T.S., and his girlfriend. When C.G. went to bed, she was wearing underpants, a bra, shorts, and a shirt. At trial, C.G. and M.T.S. offered very different accounts concerning the nature of their relationship and the events that occurred after C.G. had gone upstairs. The trial court did not credit fully either teenager's testimony.

C.G. stated that earlier in the day, M.T.S. had told her three or four times that he "was going to make a surprise visit up in [her] bedroom." She said that she had not taken M.T.S. seriously and considered his comments a joke because he frequently teased her. She testified that

M.T.S. had attempted to kiss her on numerous other occasions and at least once had attempted to put his hands inside of her pants, but that she had rejected all of his previous advances.

C.G. testified that on May 22, at approximately 1:30 a.m., she awoke to use the bathroom. As she was getting out of bed, she said, she saw M.T.S., fully clothed, standing in her doorway. According to C.G., M.T.S. then said that "he was going to tease [her] a little bit." C.G. testified that she "didn't think anything of it"; she walked past him, used the bathroom, and then returned to bed, falling into a "heavy" sleep within fifteen minutes. The next event C.G. claimed to recall of that morning was waking up with M.T.S. on top of her, her underpants and shorts removed. She said "his penis was into [her] vagina." As soon as C.G. realized what had happened, she said, she immediately slapped M.T.S. once in the face, then "told him to get off [her], and get out." She did not scream or cry out. She testified that M.T.S. complied in less than one minute after being struck; according to C.G., "he jumped right off of [her]." She said she did not know how long M.T.S. had been inside of her before she awoke.

C.G. said that after M.T.S. left the room, she "fell asleep crying" because "[she] couldn't believe that he did what he did to [her]." She explained that she did not immediately tell her mother or anyone else in the house of the events of that morning because she was "scared and in shock." According to C.G., M.T.S. engaged in intercourse with her "without [her] wanting it or telling him to come up [to her bedroom]." By her own account, C.G. was not otherwise harmed by M.T.S. * * *

According to M.T.S., he and C.G. had been good friends for a long time, and their relationship "kept leading on to more and more." He had been living at C.G.'s home for about five days before the incident occurred; he testified that during the three days preceding the incident they had been "kissing and necking" and had discussed having sexual intercourse. The first time M.T.S. kissed C.G., he said, she "didn't want him to, but she did after that." He said C.G. repeatedly had encouraged him to "make a surprise visit up in her room."

M.T.S. testified that at exactly 1:15 a.m. on May 22, he entered C.G.'s bedroom as she was walking to the bathroom. He said C.G. soon returned from the bathroom, and the two began "kissing and all," eventually moving to the bed. Once they were in bed, he said, they undressed each other and continued to kiss and touch for about five minutes. M.T.S. and C.G. proceeded to engage in sexual intercourse. According to M.T.S., who was on top of C.G., he "stuck it in" and "did it [thrust] three times, and then the fourth time [he] stuck it in, that's when [she] pulled [him] off of her." M.T.S. said that as C.G. pushed him off, she said "stop, get off," and he "hopped off right away."

According to M.T.S., after about one minute, he asked C.G. what was wrong; she replied with a back-hand to his face. He recalled asking C.G. what was wrong a second time, and her replying, "how can you take advantage of me or something like that." * * *

On May 23, 1990, M.T.S. was charged with conduct that if engaged in by an adult would constitute second-degree sexual assault of the victim, contrary to *N.J.S.A.* 2C:14–2c(1). * * *

Following a two-day trial on the sexual assault charge, M.T.S. was adjudicated delinquent. After reviewing the testimony, the court concluded that the victim had consented to a session of kissing and heavy petting with M.T.S. The trial court did not find that C.G. had been sleeping at the time of penetration, but nevertheless found that she had not consented to the actual sexual act. Accordingly, the court concluded that the State had proven second-degree sexual assault beyond a reasonable doubt. On appeal, * * * the Appellate Division determined that the absence of force beyond that involved in the act of sexual penetration precluded a finding of second-degree sexual assault. It therefore reversed the juvenile's adjudication of delinquency for that offense.

II

The New Jersey Code of Criminal Justice, *N.J.S.A.* 2C:14–2c(1), defines "sexual assault" as the commission "of sexual penetration" "with another person" with the use of "physical force or coercion."[1] An unconstrained reading of the statutory language indicates that both the act of "sexual penetration" and the use of "physical force or coercion" are separate and distinct elements of the offense. Neither the definitions section of *N.J.S.A.* 2C:14–1 to B8, nor the remainder of the Code of Criminal Justice provides assistance in interpreting the words "physical force." The initial inquiry is, therefore, whether the statutory words are unambiguous on their face and can be understood and applied in accordance with their plain meaning. * * *

The parties offer two alternative understandings of the concept of "physical force" as it is used in the statute. The State would read "physical force" to entail any amount of sexual touching brought about involuntarily. A showing of sexual penetration coupled with a lack of consent would satisfy the elements of the statute. The Public Defender urges an interpretation of "physical force" to mean force "used to overcome lack of consent." That definition equates force with violence and leads to the conclusion that sexual assault requires the application of some amount of force in addition to the act of penetration.

Current judicial practice suggests an understanding of "physical force" to mean "any degree of physical power or strength used against the victim, even though it entails no injury and leaves no mark." Resort to common experience or understanding does not yield a conclusive meaning. The dictionary provides several definitions of "force," among which are

---

1. The sexual assault statute, *N.J.S.A.:* 2C:14–2c(1), reads as follows:

c. An actor is guilty of sexual assault if he commits an act of sexual penetration with another person under any one of the following circumstances:

(1) The actor *uses physical force or coercion,* but the victim does not sustain severe personal injury; * * *

[For the rest of § 2C:14–2, see p. 394 supra.]

the following: (1) "power, violence, compulsion, or constraint exerted upon or against a person or thing," (2) "a general term for exercise of strength or power, esp. physical, to overcome resistance," or (3) "strength or power of any degree that is exercised without justification or contrary to law upon a person or thing." *Webster's Third New International Dictionary* 887 (1961).

Thus, as evidenced by the disagreements among the lower courts and the parties, and the variety of possible usages, the statutory words "physical force" do not evoke a single meaning that is obvious and plain. * * * When a statute is open to conflicting interpretations, the court seeks the underlying intent of the legislature, relying on legislative history and the contemporary context of the statute. * * * We also remain mindful of the basic tenet of statutory construction that penal statutes are to be strictly construed in favor of the accused. Nevertheless, the construction must conform to the intent of the Legislature.

The provisions proscribing sexual offenses found in the Code of Criminal Justice, *N.J.S.A.* 2C:14–2c(1), became effective in 1979, and were written against almost two hundred years of rape law in New Jersey. The origin of the rape statute that the current statutory offense of sexual assault replaced can be traced to the English common law. Under the common law, rape was defined as "carnal knowledge of a woman against her will." American jurisdictions generally adopted the English view, but over time states added the requirement that the carnal knowledge have been forcible, apparently in order to prove that the act was against the victim's will. As of 1796, New Jersey statutory law defined rape as "carnal knowledge of a woman, forcibly and against her will." Those three elements of rape—carnal knowledge, forcibly, and against her will—remained the essential elements of the crime until 1979.

Under traditional rape law, in order to prove that a rape had occurred, the state had to show both that force had been used and that the penetration had been against the woman's will. Force was identified and determined not as an independent factor but in relation to the response of the victim, which in turn implicated the victim's own state of mind. "Thus, the perpetrator's use of force became criminal only if the victim's state of mind met the statutory requirement. The perpetrator could use all the force imaginable and no crime would be committed if the state could not prove additionally that the victim did not consent." Although the terms "non-consent" and "against her will" were often treated as equivalent, under the traditional definition of rape, both formulations squarely placed on the victim the burden of proof and of action. Effectively, a woman who was above the age of consent had actively and affirmatively to withdraw that consent for the intercourse to be against her will. * * *

The presence or absence of consent often turned on credibility. To demonstrate that the victim had not consented to the intercourse, and also that sufficient force had been used to accomplish the rape, the state had to prove that the victim had resisted. According to the oft-quoted Lord Hale, to be deemed a credible witness, a woman had to be of good fame, disclose the injury immediately, suffer signs of injury, and cry out for help. 1 Matthew Hale, *History of the Pleas of the Crown* 633 (1st ed. 1847). Courts and commentators historically distrusted the testimony of victims, "assuming that women lie about their lack of consent for various reasons: to blackmail men, to explain the discovery of a consensual affair, or because of psychological illness." Evidence of resistance was viewed as a solution to the credibility problem; it was the "outward manifestation of nonconsent, [a] device for determining whether a woman actually gave consent." * * *

The judicial interpretation of the pre-reform rape law in New Jersey, with its insistence on resistance by the victim, greatly minimized the importance of the forcible and assaultive aspect of the defendant's conduct. Rape prosecutions turned then not so much on the forcible or assaultive character of the defendant's actions as on the nature of the victim's response. * * *

The importance of resistance as an evidentiary requirement set the law of rape apart from other common-law crimes, particularly in the eyes of those who advocated reform of rape law in the 1970s. * * *

To refute the misguided belief that rape was not real unless the victim fought back, reformers emphasized empirical research indicating that women who resisted forcible intercourse often suffered far more serious injury as a result. That research discredited the assumption that resistance to the utmost or to the best of a woman's ability was the most reasonable or rational response to a rape.

The research also helped demonstrate the underlying point of the reformers that the crime of rape rested not in the overcoming of a woman's will or the insult to her chastity but in the forcible attack itself— the assault on her person. Reformers criticized the conception of rape as a distinctly sexual crime rather than a crime of violence. They emphasized that rape had its legal origins in laws designed to protect the property rights of men to their wives and daughters. Although the crime had evolved into an offense against women, reformers argued that vestiges of the old law remained, particularly in the understanding of rape as a crime against the purity or chastity of a woman. The burden of protecting that chastity fell on the woman, with the state offering its protection only after the woman demonstrated that she had resisted sufficiently. * * *

Critics of rape law agreed that the focus of the crime should be shifted from the victim's behavior to the defendant's conduct, and particularly to its forceful and assaultive, rather than sexual, character. Reformers also shared the goals of facilitating rape prosecutions and of sparing victims much of the degradation involved in bringing and trying a charge of rape. There were, however, differences over the best way to redefine the crime. * * * Nonetheless, all proponents of reform shared a central premise: that the burden of showing non-consent should not fall on the victim of the crime. In dealing with the problem of consent the reform goal was not so much to purge the entire concept of consent from the law as to eliminate the burden that had been placed on victims to prove they had not consented.

Similarly, with regard to force, rape law reform sought to give independent significance to the forceful or assaultive conduct of the defendant and to avoid a definition of force that depended on the reaction of the victim. In urging that the "resistance" requirement be abandoned, reformers sought to break the connection between force and resistance.

III

* * * The circumstances surrounding the actual passage of the current law reveal that it was conceived as a reform measure reconstituting the law to address a widely-sensed evil and to effectuate an important public policy. Those circumstances are highly relevant in understanding legislative intent and in determining the objectives of the current law.

In October 1971, the New Jersey Criminal Law Revision Commission promulgated a Final Report and Commentary on its proposed New Jersey Penal Code. The proposed Code substantially followed the American Law Institute's Model Penal Code (MPC) with respect to sexual offenses. See *M.P.C.* §§ 213.1 to 213.4. * * *

The Legislature did not endorse the Model Penal Code approach to rape. Rather, it passed a fundamentally different proposal in 1978 when it adopted the Code of Criminal Justice. The new statutory provisions covering rape were formulated by a coalition of feminist groups assisted by the National Organization of Women (NOW) National Task Force on Rape. * * * The NOW bill had been modeled after the 1976 Philadelphia Center for Rape Concern Model Sex Offense Statute. The Model Sex Offense Statute in turn had been based on selected provisions of the Michigan Criminal Sexual Conduct Statute * * *. The stated intent of the drafters of the * * * Model Statute had been to remove all features found to be contrary to the interests of rape victims. * * *

The reform statute defines sexual assault as penetration accomplished by the use of "physical force" or "coercion," but it does not define either "physical force" or "coercion" or enumerate examples of evidence that would establish those elements. * * * The task of defining "physical force" therefore was left to the courts. * * *

* * * [T]he New Jersey Code of Criminal Justice does not refer to force in relation to "overcoming the will" of the victim, or to the "physical overpowering" of the victim, or the "submission" of the victim. It does not require the demonstrated non-consent of the victim. * * *

The Legislature's concept of sexual assault and the role of force was significantly colored by its understanding of the law of assault and battery. As a general matter, criminal battery is defined as "the unlawful application of force to the person of another." The application of force is criminal when it results in either (a) a physical injury or (b) an offensive touching. * * * Thus, by eliminating all references to the victim's state of mind and conduct, and by broadening the definition of penetration to cover not only sexual intercourse between a man and a woman but a range of acts that invade another's body or compel intimate contact, the Legislature emphasized the affinity between sexual assault and other forms of assault and battery. * * *

* * * We are thus satisfied that an interpretation of the statutory crime of sexual assault to require physical force in addition to that entailed in an act of involuntary or unwanted sexual penetration would be fundamentally inconsistent with the legislative purpose to eliminate any consideration of whether the victim resisted or expressed non-consent. * * *

Because the statute eschews any reference to the victim's will or resistance, the standard defining the role of force in sexual penetration must prevent the possibility that the establishment of the crime will turn on the alleged victim's state of mind or responsive behavior. We conclude, therefore, that any act of sexual penetration engaged in by the defendant without the affirmative and freely-given permission of the victim to the specific act of penetration constitutes the offense of sexual assault. Therefore, physical force in excess of that inherent in the act of sexual penetration is not required for such penetration to be unlawful. The definition of "physical force" is satisfied under *N.J.S.A.* 2C:14–2c(1) if the defendant applies any amount of force against another person in the absence of what a reasonable person would believe to be affirmative and freely-given permission to the act of sexual penetration.

Under the reformed statute, permission to engage in sexual penetration must be affirmative and it must be given freely, but that permission may be inferred either from acts or statements reasonably viewed in light of the surrounding circumstances. Persons need not, of course, expressly announce their consent to engage in intercourse for there to be affirmative permission. Permission to engage in an act of sexual penetration can be and indeed often is indicated through physical actions rather than words. Permission is demonstrated when the evidence, in whatever form, is sufficient to demonstrate that a reasonable person would have believed that the alleged victim had affirmatively and freely given authorization to the act. * * *

Today the law of sexual assault is indispensable to the system of legal rules that assures each of us the right to decide who may touch our bodies, when, and under what circumstances. The decision to engage in sexual relations with another person is one of the most private and intimate decisions a person can make. Each person has the right not only to decide whether to engage in sexual contact with another, but also to control the circumstances and character of that contact. No one, neither a spouse, nor a friend, nor an acquaintance, nor a stranger, has the right or the privilege to force sexual contact. * * *

We emphasize as well that what is now referred to as "acquaintance rape" is not a new phenomenon. * * * Notwithstanding the stereotype of rape as a violent attack by a stranger, the vast majority of sexual assaults are perpetrated by someone known to the victim. One respected study indicates that more than half of all rapes are committed by male relatives, current or former husbands, boyfriends or lovers. Diana Russell, *The Prevalence and Incidence of Forcible Rape and Attempted Rape of Females,* 7 Victimology 81 (1982). Similarly, contrary to common myths, perpetrators generally do not use guns or knives and victims generally do not suffer external bruises or cuts. Although this more realistic and accurate view of rape only recently has achieved widespread public circulation, it was a central concern of the proponents of reform in the 1970s. * * *

IV * * *

In short, in order to convict under the sexual assault statute in cases such as these, the State must prove beyond a reasonable doubt that there was sexual penetration and that it was accomplished without the affirmative and freely-given permission of the alleged victim. * * * If there is evidence to suggest that the defendant reasonably believed that such permission had been given, the State must demonstrate either that defendant did not actually believe that affirmative permission had been freely-given or that such a belief was unreasonable under all of the circumstances. Thus, the State bears the burden of proof throughout the case. * * *

We acknowledge that cases such as this are inherently fact sensitive and depend on the reasoned judgment and common sense of judges and juries. The trial court concluded that the victim had not expressed consent to the act of intercourse, either through her words or actions. We conclude that the record provides reasonable support for the trial court's disposition.

Accordingly, we reverse the judgment of the Appellate Division and reinstate the disposition of juvenile delinquency for the commission of second-degree sexual assault.

NOTES AND QUESTIONS

1. Do you agree with *M.T.S.* as a matter of statutory interpretation? Consider:

> The net result [of *M.T.S.*] is that force is largely eliminated as a separate legal requirement. Nonconsent becomes the touchstone of criminal conduct. Somewhat ironically, the outcome brings the tactics of rape reform full circle. New Jersey * * * revised its statutes * * * to eliminate all references to victim consent and to focus instead on the forcible character of the defendant's conduct. The hope * * * was that an emphasis on force rather than consent would cut through the difficulties of proof and facilitate effective enforcement. With *M.T.S.*, the New Jersey Supreme Court rewrote its statute to take just the opposite approach * * *.

Stephen J. Schulhofer, Unwanted Sex: The Culture of Intimidation and the Failure of Law 96 (1998). Nonetheless, as a matter of public policy, Professor

Not defenseble on statutory interp. grounds

Schulhofer agrees with *M.T.S.* that "actual permission—nothing less than positive willingness, clearly communicated—should ever count as consent." Id. at 271. Do you agree?

2. Do you agree with Susan Estrich's observation that "if a thief stripped his victim, flattened that victim on the floor, lay down on top, and took the victim's wallet or jewelry, few would pause before concluding forcible robbery." Susan Estrich, Real Rape 59 (1987). If you agree, does that support the conclusion that the defendant used "force" in *M.T.S.*?

[handwritten margin note: force not inherent in any part of robbery]

3. What constitutes "freely given" permission under *M.T.S.*? What if a high school female acquiesces to having intercourse as the result of peer pressure? Or, what if a wealthy corporate executive and unemployed single mother begin dating and she eventually moves into his home in a sexual relationship. They live together happily, but after awhile, he tells her that he is no longer happy with their sexual relationship and, if she is not willing to have sexual relations more often in the future, he will kick her and her young children out of his house. As a result, she has intercourse with him more often. Is this "freely given" permission, or does the economic-power differential render this rape? See Stephen J. Schulhofer, *Taking Sexual Autonomy Seriously: Rape Law and Beyond*, 11 Law & Phil. 35, 88 (1992).

[handwritten margin note: Difference is whether threat is lawful or unlawful]

4. *No, yes, or negotiate?* Professor Michelle Anderson advocates a "Negotiation Model" to sexual relations, which requires

> consultation, reciprocal communication, and the exchange of views before a person initiates sexual penetration. It requires communication that is verbal unless partners have established a context between them in which they may accurately assess one's nonverbal behavior. The verbal communication must be such that it would indicate to a reasonable person that sexual penetration has been freely and explicitly agreed to.

Michelle J. Anderson, *Negotiating Sex*, 78 So. Cal. L. Rev. 1401, 1421 (2005).

According to Professor Anderson, this model is preferable to the "No Model" of sexual relations ("no means no," but in the absence of "no" an actor may proceed to sexual penetration) or "Yes Model" ("sexual penetration is illegal unless one's partner physically or verbally grants permission for it," id. at 1411).

Is this how *you* want sexual relations to occur? Why, or why not? *Should* violation of the Negotiation Model constitute a crime? If not, which of the remaining models do you think should determine criminal responsibility in sexual relations, or is there another model you would advocate?

5. *"No" means "no"?* In the past, male-dominant female-submissive "sexual courtship" was the social norm. One court observed, "[m]any men have been conditioned to believe that initial refusals [by women] are an essential part of the 'mating game' ritual which dictates that women must resist somewhat to make themselves more attractive to men * * *." Deborah S. v. Diorio, 153 Misc.2d 708, 583 N.Y.S.2d 872 (1992).

In one study of the behavior of 610 undergraduate women, 39% of the respondents admitted that they engaged in "token resistance," i.e., objecting and putting up mild resistance to the male's sexual overtures, even though they "had every intention to and [were] willing to engage in sexual intercourse.'' Among sexually experienced females, this behavior rose to 61 per-cent. Charlene L. Muehlenhard & Lisa C. Hollabaugh, *Do Women Sometimes Say No When They Mean Yes? The Prevalence and Correlates of Women's Token Resistance to Sex,* 54 J. of Personality & Soc. Psychol. 872 (1988). Among the reasons given by the undergraduate women for their behavior was fear of appearing promiscuous, self-consciousness or embarrassment, and game playing (e.g., ''I wanted him to beg,'' ''I wanted him to talk me into it,'' or ''I wanted him to be more physically aggressive'').

In view of these results, does the ''No Model'' (see Note 4) seem appropriate? *Should* the law treat ''no'' followed by sexual intercourse as rape in all circumstances, regardless of whether the ''no'' *really* meant ''no'' in the given situation? If your answer is yes to this question, how long does this ''no'' last? Must the male stop asking and wait for the female affirmatively to say yes? What about ''a woman who says no to her lover before dinner and then changes her mind after several hours of relaxation and intimate conver-sation''? Schulhofer, Note 3 supra, at 43. Suppose he nags her and she finally says yes?

For more on this subject, see Dan Subotnik, *''Hands Off'': Sex, Femi-nism, Affirmative Consent, and the Law of Foreplay,* 16 S. Cal. Rev. L. & Soc. Just. 249 (2007).

6. Is the ''sexual script'' described in Note 5 an historic relic? Perhaps, but if so, males may be slow to realize or accept it. Surveys of law students in the 1990s at Rutgers University at Newark found that

> community norms are moving in the direction of respecting a woman's sexual autonomy. * * * Nonetheless, remnants still persist of the old view that women want sex more than they acknowledge. The data strongly suggest that a woman who does not accompany ''no'' with force is not as likely to be believed. The data suggest that men, more than women, cling to the idea that ''no'' means maybe.

George C. Thomas III & David Edelman, *Consent to Have Sex: Empirical Evidence About ''No'',* 61 U. Pitt. L. Rev. 579, 616 (2000). If ''no'' *really* means ''no'' to a female, but ''no'' *really* means ''maybe'' to a male, what is the legal significance of this fact?

7. Is there any argument for *not* using the criminal law to deal with nonviolent acquaintance rapes? One commentator recommends mediation, rather than prosecution, in such circumstances:

> Rape is a frequent and serious occurrence in our society. Most rapes are simple rapes in which the victim and offender were acquainted prior to the rape and in which physical violence was absent. Simple rape causes serious emotional trauma for a victim, resulting in a need to regain self-esteem and control over her life. Shortcomings within the criminal justice system, however, discourage many victims of simple rape from reporting the crime. Even if a victim reports a simple rape, bias against victims of simple rape dramatically reduces the likelihood of a serious police investi-gation, trial, and conviction. When the criminal justice does deal with a simple rape case, the system fails to allow the parties control over their dispute. In addition, the criminal justice system deals ineffectively with

underlying causes for the rape, and thus, fails to educate the parties or reform the offender. Mediation, a process in which the victim and the offender meet with the aid of a neutral third party, avoids the bias of the criminal justice system against the rape victim. Mediation provides a victim with assistance in overcoming the feelings of powerlessness that resulted from the rape. Mediation also allows the victim and offender to confront each other and to deal with any miscommunication or misinterpretation of behavior that led to the rape. Ultimately, mediation allows an offender to face up to what he has done, while avoiding the stigma of a rape prosecution.

Deborah Gartzke Goolsby, Comment, *Using Mediation in Cases of Simple Rape*, 47 Wash. & Lee L.Rev. 1183, 1213–14 (1990). What do you think?

Another view is that a tort action may be a more effective remedy than a criminal prosecution in dealing with nonaggravated rapes. See Nora West, Note, *Rape in the Criminal Law and the Victim's Tort Alternative: A Feminist Analysis*, 50 U. Toronto Fac.L.Rev. 96 (1992). By suing, the rape victim is empowered vis-a-vis the attacker by personally "prosecuting" the offense. She retains greater control over the issues than would be possible in a criminal action, because in the latter circumstance the prosecutor determines what charges to bring and may participate in plea bargaining with the defense, against the victim's wishes. With the lesser standard of proof in a civil action, as well, the plaintiff is better positioned than a public prosecutor to obtain redress, and the civil remedy of money damages may be a more satisfactory outcome for the victim of acquaintance rape than imprisonment of the rapist.

8. *Marital immunity.* Forcible sexual intercourse between married couples did not constitute common law rape, although it could constitute a different and lesser offense, such as battery. According to Sir Matthew Hale, "the husband cannot be guilty of a rape committed by himself upon his lawful wife, for by their mutual matrimonial consent and contract the wife hath given up herself in this kind unto her husband, which she cannot retract." 1 Hale, History of the Pleas of the Crown *629 (1736). Other early justifications of the marital exemption rule included: the wife was the property of her husband and, thus, could not object to intercourse; by marriage, the woman retained no independent legal existence in the marital relationship; and a rape prosecution of a husband would violate marital privacy and undermine efforts at marital reconciliation.

The rule is eroding. The House of Lords unanimously abolished the marital exemption rule in England in R. v. R., [1991] 4 All Eng.Rep. 481. In the United States, by 2001, twenty-four states had abolished marital immunity for all sexual offenses. Michelle J. Anderson, *Marital Immunity, Intimate Relationships, and Improper Inferences: A New Law on Sexual Offenses by Intimates*, 54 Hastings L.J. 1465, 1468 (2003). Nonetheless, a "majority of states still retain some form of the common law regime: They criminalize a narrower range of offenses if committed within marriage, subject the marital rape they do recognize to less serious sanctions, and/or create special procedural hurdles for marital rape prosecutions." Jill Elaine Hasday, *Contest and Consent: A History of Marital Rape*, 88 Calif. L. Rev. 1373, 1375 (2000).

Is there justification for treating forcible rape by a husband less seriously than a similar rape outside of wedlock?

3. *MENS REA*

COMMONWEALTH v. SHERRY

Supreme Judicial Court of Massachusetts, 1982.
386 Mass. 682, 437 N.E.2d 224.

LIACOS, JUSTICE.

Each defendant was indicted on three charges of aggravated rape and one charge of kidnapping. A jury acquitted the defendants of kidnapping and convicted them of [three counts of] * * * the lesser included offense of rape without aggravation. Each defendant was sentenced on each conviction to be imprisoned * * * for a term of not more than five years nor less than three years. Six months of the sentence was to be served, with the balance of the sentence to be suspended. On completion of the sentence served, each defendant was to be placed on probation for the term of one year. * * *

There was evidence of the following facts. The victim, a registered nurse, and the defendants, all doctors, were employed at the same hospital in Boston. The defendant Sherry, whom the victim knew professionally, with another doctor was a host at a party in Boston for some of the hospital staff on the evening of September 5, 1980. The victim was not acquainted with the defendants Hussain and Lefkowitz prior to this evening.

According to the victim's testimony, she had a conversation with Hussain at the party, during which he made sexual advances toward her. Later in the evening, Hussain and Sherry pushed her and Lefkowitz into a bathroom together, shut the door, and turned off the light. They did not open the door until Lefkowitz asked them to leave her in peace. At various times, the victim had danced with both Hussain and Sherry.

Some time later, as the victim was walking from one room to the next, Hussain and Sherry grabbed her by the arms and pulled her out of the apartment as Lefkowitz said, "We're going to go up to Rockport." The victim verbally protested but did not physically resist the men because she said she thought that they were just "horsing around" and that they would eventually leave her alone.[3] She further testified that once outside, Hussain carried her over his shoulder to Sherry's car and held her in the front seat as the four drove to Rockport. En route, she engaged in superficial conversation with the defendants. She testified that she was not in fear at this time. When they arrived at Lefkowitz's home in Rockport, she asked to be taken home. Instead, Hussain carried her into the house.

---

3. The victim testified that she was not physically restrained as they rode down an elevator with an unknown fifth person, or as they walked through the lobby of the apartment building where other persons were present.

Once in the house, the victim and two of the men smoked some marihuana, and all of them toured the house. Lefkowitz invited them into a bedroom to view an antique bureau, and, once inside, the three men began to disrobe. The victim was frightened. She verbally protested, but the three men proceeded to undress her and maneuver her onto the bed. One of the defendants attempted to have the victim perform fellatio while another attempted intercourse. She told them to stop. At the suggestion of one of the defendants, two of the defendants left the room temporarily. Each defendant separately had intercourse with the victim in the bedroom. The victim testified, that she felt physically numbed and could not fight; she felt humiliated and disgusted. After this sequence of events, the victim claimed that she was further sexually harassed and forced to take a bath. * * *

The defendants testified to a similar sequence of events, although the details of the episode varied significantly. According to their testimony, Lefkowitz invited Sherry to accompany him from the party to a home that his parents owned in Rockport. The victim was present when this invitation was extended and inquired as to whether she could go along. As the three were leaving, Sherry extended an invitation to Hussain. At no time on the way out of the apartment, in the elevator, lobby, or parking lot did the victim indicate her unwillingness to accompany the defendants.

Upon arrival in Rockport, the victim wandered into the bedroom where she inquired about the antique bureau. She sat down on the bed and kicked off her shoes, whereupon Sherry entered the room, dressed only in his underwear. Sherry helped the victim get undressed, and she proceeded to have intercourse with all three men separately and in turn. Each defendant testified that the victim consented to the acts of intercourse. * * *

* * * The defendants * * * contend that because the judge failed to give two instructions exactly as requested, the judge's jury charge, considered as a whole, was inadequate and the cause of prejudicial error. The requested instructions in their entirety are set out in the margin.[8] * * *

The instructions given by the trial judge placed before the jury the essential elements of the crime required to be proved. The judge instructed the jury that intercourse must be accomplished with force "such [as] to overcome the woman's will; that it be sufficient to accomplish the man's purpose of having sexual intercourse against her will" or by threats of bodily harm, inferred or expressed, which engendered fear "reasonable in the circumstances * * * so that it was reasonable for her not to resist." * * *

These instructions correctly stated the elements of proof required for a rape conviction. * * *

---

8. "Unless you find beyond a reasonable doubt that [the victim] clearly expressed her lack of consent, or was so overcome by force or threats of bodily injury that she was incapable of consenting, and unless you find beyond a reasonable doubt that the accused had actual knowledge of [the victim's] lack of consent, then you must find them not guilty." * * *

[Handwritten margin note: "reasonable mistake of fact is defense"]

To the extent the defendants * * * appear to have been seeking to raise a defense of good faith mistake on the issue of consent, the defendants' requested instruction would have required the jury to "find beyond a reasonable doubt that the accused had *actual knowledge* of [the victim's] lack of consent" (emphasis added). The defendants, on appeal, argue that mistake of fact negating criminal intent is a defense to the crime of rape. The defense of mistake of fact, however, requires that the accused act in good faith and with reasonableness. Whether a reasonable good faith mistake of fact as to the fact of consent is a defense to the crime of rape has never, to our knowledge, been decided in this Commonwealth. We need not reach the issue whether a reasonable and honest mistake to the fact of consent would be a defense, for even if we assume it to be so, the defendants did not request a jury instruction based on a reasonable good faith mistake of fact. We are aware of no American court of last resort that recognizes mistake of fact, without consideration of its reasonableness as a defense; nor do the defendants cite such authority. There was no error. * * *

NOTES AND QUESTIONS

1. Notice that the *Sherry* court did not have to reach the issue of whether it approved of a general rule that a reasonable mistake of fact as to a victim's consent is a defense in a forcible rape prosecution, but it later answered this question in the negative in Commonwealth v. Lopez, 433 Mass. 722, 745 N.E.2d 961 (2001):

[Handwritten margin note: "no mistake of fact permitted (minority rule)"]

Any perception (reasonable, honest, or otherwise) of the defendant as to the victim's consent is * * * not relevant to a rape prosecution.

This is not to say, contrary to the defendant's suggestion, that the absence of any mens rea as to the consent element transforms rape into a strict liability crime. It does not. Rape, at common law and pursuant to [the Massachusetts rape statute] is a general intent crime, and proof that the defendant intended sexual intercourse by force coupled with proof that the victim did not in fact consent is sufficient to maintain a conviction. * * *

We * * * have concerns that the mistake of fact defense would tend to eviscerate the long-standing rule in this Commonwealth that victims need not use any force to resist an attack. A shift in focus from the victim's to the defendant's state of mind might require victims to use physical force in order to communicate an unqualified lack of consent to defeat any honest and reasonable belief as to consent. The mistake of fact defense is incompatible with the evolution of our jurisprudence with respect to the crime of rape.

We are cognizant that our interpretation is not shared by the majority of other jurisdictions.

Indeed, as the *Lopez* court recognized, the Massachusetts position is a minority one. The majority rule in the United States is that "[i]f a defendant entertains a reasonable * * * belief that a prosecutrix voluntarily consented

* * * to engage in sexual intercourse, * * * he does not possess the wrongful intent that is a prerequisite" to a rape conviction. People v. Mayberry, 15 Cal.3d 143, 125 Cal.Rptr. 745, 542 P.2d 1337 (1975); see Rosanna Cavallaro, *A Big Mistake: Eroding the Defense of Mistake of Fact About Consent in Rape*, 86 J. Crim. L. & Criminology 815 (1996).

Which is better: the general rule or the Massachusetts minority approach? Consider:

> Before rape law reform, the issue of *mens rea* rarely arose in rape trials. As a practical matter, the *actus reus* proved the *mens rea*. If a male used or threatened force to obtain intercourse, then it was evident that he purposely or knowingly had nonconsensual sexual relations. If his conduct was not forcible, the female had to resist, and this gave the male reasonable warning of her lack of consent: if he proceeded against her resistance, a jury could reasonably assume that he knew she did not want sexual relations. At a minimum, the resistance meant that the male acted recklessly or negligently in regard to her wishes. * * *

> With the abandonment or softening of the resistance requirement and the increased willingness of lawmakers to permit prosecutions for nonforcible forms of nonconsensual intercourse * * * the risk of conviction in the absence of *mens rea* is enhanced.

Joshua Dressler, *Where We Have Been, and Where We Might Be Going: Some Cautionary Reflections on Rape Law Reform*, 46 Clev. St. L. Rev. 409, 431–432 (1998).

On the other hand, is it fair to say that the "reasonable mistake defense" means that "a woman [was] raped but not by a rapist"? Catherine A. MacKinnon, *Feminism, Marxism, Method, and the State: Toward Feminist Jurisprudence*, 8 Signs 635, 654 (1983).

How does *Lopez* get around the argument that it has converted rape into a strict liability crime?

intent to have sex intercourse

2. Do you think there is any *real* possibility that the defendants in *Sherry* were genuinely mistaken regarding the victim's wishes? Is it not fair to suggest that either she consented (as they asserted at trial) or that she did not consent and they perfectly well knew it?

In People v. Williams, 4 Cal.4th 354, 14 Cal.Rptr.2d 441, 841 P.2d 961 (1992), the California Supreme Court held that, in a rape prosecution, a "reasonable mistake of fact" instruction regarding the complainant's consent should not be given unless there is "substantial evidence of equivocal conduct" on the part of the alleged victim. In *Williams*, the defendant testified that "Deborah" had "initiated sexual contact, fondled him to overcome his impotence, and inserted his penis inside herself." In stark contrast, she testified that he punched her in the eye, prevented her from escaping, ordered her to disrobe, and warned her that he "did not like to hurt people." According to the court, the defendant's testimony, if believed, established actual consent; her testimony, if established, "preclude[d] any reasonable belief of consent. These wholly divergent accounts create no middle ground from which Williams could argue he reasonably misinterpreted Deborah's conduct." Therefore, no mistake-of-fact instruction was appropriate.

Williams

Can you see why a concurring justice in *Williams* stated that the "equivocal conduct" rule means that a defendant has a better chance of getting a mistake instruction if his claim of *actual* consent is *weaker*?

3. *Mistake and "no" by the complainant.* Assume a female forthrightly says "no" to a male's sexual overtures. Is this a case in which you would deny the defendant a "reasonable mistake" jury instruction? Consider concurring Justice Brown's remarks in Commonwealth v. Lefkowitz, 20 Mass.App.Ct. 513, 481 N.E.2d 227 (1985):

> I am prepared to say that when a woman says "no" to someone any implication other than a manifestation of non-consent that might arise in that person's psyche is legally irrelevant, and thus no defense. Any further action is unwarranted and the person proceeds at his peril. In effect, he assumes the risk. * * * I find no social utility in establishing a rule defining non-consensual intercourse on the basis of the subjective (and quite likely wishful) view of the more aggressive player in the sexual encounter.

Is this "assumption of risk" approach fair? Consider:

> "No means no" is an excellent rule to teach men (and women) in our culture. And, it is an excellent starting point * * * in rape trials. But, bright-line rules such as this can only result, at best, in the correct outcome *most* of the time. Such rules do not assure justice to the individual whose case might not fit the bright-line assumptions. * * * If no does not always means no, there can surely be cases in which a reasonable person could *believe* that no does not mean no in the specific incident, *even when it does.* Such cases will be relatively few in number, but it is improper to convict a person on the basis of the law of averages. It is wrong to use the bludgeon of the criminal law to impose rules intended to change cultural attitudes when this means punishing an individual for rape who made a mistake that the community, represented by the jurors, would characterize as reasonable.

Dressler, Note 1 supra, at 433.

4. *Mistake and miscommunication between the sexes.* According to social scientists, women "commonly use[ ] nonverbal methods to give consent to sexual intercourse." E. Sandra Byers & Kim Lewis, *"Dating Couples" Disagreements Over the Desired Level of Sexual Intimacy*, 24 J. Sex Research 15, 26 (1988). Nonverbal cues of any sort, of course, are subject to misinterpretation, but the risk of mistake is heightened in social relationships, in part because of an "overlap in the cues used to convey friendliness and seduction." Antonia Abbey, *Misperception as an Antecedent of Acquaintance Rape: A Consequence of Ambiguity in Communication Between Men and Women* in Acquaintance Rape: The Hidden Crime 96 (Andrea Parrot & Laurie Bechhofer eds. 1991).

Males tend to interpret friendly behavior by females as motivated by sexual interest. Susan Haworth–Hoeppner, *What's Gender Got To Do With It: Perceptions of Sexual Coercion in a University Community*, 38 Sex Roles 757, 758 (1998). For example, one effect of a grocery store edict that its employees (primarily female) smile and make eye contact with their customers was that many male shoppers mistook this company-required friendliness for flirting, with the result that male customers propositioned the female clerks. Kim Curtis, *Clerks Frown on Service With a Smile*, Chicago Sun–Times, Sept. 3, 1998, at 26.

Is it possible, therefore, that a "woman may believe she has communicated her unwillingness to have sex and other women would agree, thus making it a 'reasonable' female expression. Her male partner might still believe she is willing and other men would agree with his interpretation, thus making it a 'reasonable' male interpretation." Robin D. Weiner, *Shifting the Communication Burden: A Meaningful Consent Standard in Rape*, 6 Harv. Women's L.J. 143, 147 (1983). If so, how should the criminal law deal with this communication problem?

5. *The "kinky wife" case.* One of the most controversial twentieth century rape cases arose in England in Regina v. Morgan, [1976] A.C. 182: Morgan invited three fellow members of the Royal Air Force to his home in order to have intercourse with his wife. According to the men, who were intoxicated, the husband (who was also their military superior) falsely told them that his wife was "kinky" and could not "be turned on" except by use of force. With his assistance, they each had forcible nonconsensual intercourse with the victim. At their trial, the defendants asserted that, based on Morgan's representations, they believed (albeit unreasonably) that his wife was feigning nonconsent when she unsuccessfully fought off their advances.

Morgan

The House of Lords, by a 3–2 vote, held that a defendant may *not* properly be convicted of rape if he honestly believed that the woman consented, even if such belief was *not* based on reasonable grounds.

At the time of the case, Section 1 of the Sexual Offenses Act of 1956 provided that it was an offense "for a man to rape a woman." The word "rape" was not defined by statute. Lord Hailsham of St. Marylebone explained his vote this way:

> Once one has accepted, what seems to me to be abundantly clear, that the prohibited act in rape is non-consensual sexual intercourse, and that the guilty state of mind is an intention to commit it, it seems to me to follow as a matter of inexorable logic that there is no room either for a "defence" of honest belief or mistake, or of a defence of honest and reasonable belief and mistake. Either the prosecution proves that the accused had the requisite intent, or it does not.

What is Lord Hailsham's getting at?

Morgan evoked outrage in the British public and legal community. In response to public reaction, the Parliament enacted the Sexual Offences (Amendment) Act of 1976, which now provides, in part:

> A man commits rape if (a) he has unlawful sexual intercourse with a woman who at the time of the intercourse does not consent to it; and (b) at that time he knows that she does not consent to the intercourse or he is reckless as to whether she consents to it.

How would the Model Penal Code resolve the *Morgan* controversy?

MPC ?

6. *Problem: culture and mistaken beliefs.* How should the law handle the following events, which occurred in a Laotian–American community in Fresno, California, as described by Michael Fisher, *The Human Rights Implications of a "Cultural Defense,"* 6 S.Cal. Interdisciplinary L.J. 663, 686 (1998):

> Moua engaged in sexual intercourse with [a woman] as the consummating part of the Hmong "marriage by capture" ritual. The custom requires that the woman, even if she is willing to marry the man, must protest in order to show her purity. The man, for his part, is required to force her to cooperate in order to prove his braveness and readiness to be a providing husband.

The victim was also from the Hmong culture, but she had rejected "aspects of her parents' culture," including the "marriage by capture" ritual. Her resistance was genuine. Doriane Lambelet Coleman, *Individualizing Justice Through Multiculturalism: The Liberals' Dilemma*, 96 Colum. L. Rev. 1093, 1150 (1996). Was Moua's mistake of fact reasonable? Should his mistake be evaluated by the standard of a reasonable person from his cultural background?

C. RAPE BY FRAUD OR NON-PHYSICAL THREATS

BORO v. SUPERIOR COURT

California Court of Appeal, First District, 1985.
163 Cal.App.3d 1224, 210 Cal.Rptr. 122.

NEWSOM, ASSOCIATE JUSTICE.

By timely petition filed with this court, petitioner Daniel Boro seeks a writ of prohibition to restrain further prosecution of Count II of the information on file against him * * * charging him with a violation of Penal Code section 261, subdivision (4), rape: "an act of sexual intercourse accomplished with a person not the spouse of the perpetrator, under any of the following circumstances: * * * (4) Where a person is at the time unconscious of the nature of the act, and this is known to the accused."

Petitioner contends that his motion to dismiss should have been granted * * * because the evidence at the preliminary hearing proved that the prosecutrix, Ms. R., was aware of the "nature of the act" within the meaning of section 261, subdivision (4). The Attorney General contends the opposite, arguing that the victim's agreement to intercourse was predicated on a belief—fraudulently induced by petitioner—that the sex act was necessary to save her life, and that she was hence unconscious of the *nature* of the act within the meaning of the statute.

In relevant part the factual background may be summarized as follows. Ms. R., the rape victim, * * * received a telephone call from a person who identified himself as "Dr. Stevens" and said that he worked at Peninsula Hospital.

"Dr. Stevens" told Ms. R. that he had the results of her blood test and that she had contracted a dangerous, highly infectious and perhaps fatal disease; that she could be sued as a result; that the disease came from using public toilets; and that she would have to tell him the identity of all her friends who would then have to be contacted in the interest of controlling the spread of the disease.

"Dr. Stevens" further explained that there were only two ways to treat the disease. The first was a painful surgical procedure—graphically described—costing $9,000, and requiring her uninsured hospitalization for six weeks. A second alternative, "Dr. Stevens" explained, was to have sexual intercourse with an anonymous donor who had been injected with a serum which would cure the disease. The latter, non-surgical procedure would only cost $4,500. When the victim replied that she lacked sufficient funds the "doctor" suggested that $1,000 would suffice as a down payment. The victim thereupon agreed to the non-surgical alternative and consented to intercourse with the mysterious donor, believing "it was the only choice I had."

After discussing her intentions with her work supervisor, the victim proceeded to the Hyatt Hotel in Burlingame as instructed, and contacted "Dr. Stevens" by telephone. The latter became furious when he learned Ms. R. had informed her employer of the plan, and threatened to terminate his treatment, finally instructing her to inform her employer she had decided not to go through with the treatment. Ms. R. did so, then went to her bank, withdrew $1,000 and, as instructed, checked into another hotel and called "Dr. Stevens" to give him her room number.

About a half hour later the defendant "donor" arrived at her room. When Ms. R. had undressed, the "donor," petitioner, * * * had sexual intercourse with her.

At the time of penetration, it was Ms. R.'s belief that she would die unless she consented to sexual intercourse with the defendant: as she testified, "My life felt threatened, and for that reason and that reason alone did I do it." * * *

Upon the basis of the evidence just recounted, petitioner was charged with five crimes, as follows: Count I: section 261, subdivision (2)—rape: accomplished against a person's will by means of force or fear of immediate and unlawful bodily injury on the person or another. Count II: section 261, subdivision (4)—rape "[w]here a person is at the time unconscious of the nature of the act, and this is known to the accused." Count III: section 266—procuring a female [for purposes of prostitution] to have illicit carnal connection with a man "by any false pretenses, false representation, or other fraudulent means* * *." Count IV: section 664/487—attempted grand theft. Count V: section 459—burglary (entry into the hotel room with intent to commit theft).

A * * * motion to set aside the information was granted as to counts I and III—the latter by concession of the district attorney. Petitioner's sole challenge is to denial of the motion to dismiss count II.

[handwritten: Counts I & III dismissed]

The People's position is stated concisely: "We contend, quite simply, that at the time of the intercourse Ms. R., the victim, was 'unconscious of the nature of the act': because of [petitioner's] misrepresentation she believed it was in the nature of a medical treatment and not a simple, ordinary act of sexual intercourse." Petitioner, on the other hand, stresses that the victim was plainly aware of the *nature* of the act in which she voluntarily engaged, so that her motivation in doing so (since it did not fall within the proscription of section 261, subdivision (2)) is irrelevant.

Our research discloses sparse California authority on the subject. * * * In *People v. Minkowski* (1962) 204 Cal.App.2d 832, 23 Cal.Rptr. 92, the defendant was a physician who "treated" several victims for menstrual cramps. Each victim testified that she was treated in a position with her back to the doctor, bent over a table, with feet apart, in a dressing gown. And in each case the "treatment" consisted of the defendant first inserting a metal instrument, then substituting an instrument which "felt different"—the victims not realizing that the second instrument was in fact the doctor's penis. The precise issue before us was never tendered in *People v. Minkowski* because the petitioner there *conceded* the sufficiency of evidence to support the element of consciousness.

The decision is useful to this analysis, however, because it exactly illustrates certain traditional rules in the area of our inquiry. Thus, as a leading authority has written, "if deception causes a misunderstanding as to the fact itself (fraud in the *factum*) there is no legally-recognized consent because what happened is not that for which consent was given; whereas consent induced by fraud is as effective as any other consent, so far as direct and immediate legal consequences are concerned, if the deception relates not to the thing done but merely to some collateral matter (fraud in the inducement)." (Perkins & Boyce, Criminal Law (3d ed. 1982) ch. 9, § 3, p. 1079.)

The victims in *Minkowski* consented, not to sexual intercourse, but to an act of an altogether different nature, penetration by medical instrument. The consent was to a pathological, and not a carnal, act, and the mistake was, therefore, in the *factum* and not merely in the inducement.

Another relatively common situation in the literature on this subject—discussed in detail by Perkins is the fraudulent obtaining of intercourse by impersonating a spouse. As Professor Perkins observes, the courts are not in accord as to whether the crime of rape is thereby committed. "[T]he disagreement is not in regard to the underlying principle but only as to its application. Some courts have taken the position that such a misdeed is fraud in the inducement on the theory that the woman consents to exactly what is done (sexual intercourse) and hence there is no rape; other courts, with better reason it would seem, hold such a misdeed to be rape on the theory that it involves fraud in the *factum* since the woman's consent is to an innocent act of marital intercourse while what is actually perpetrated upon her is an act of adultery. * * * "

In California, of course, we have by statute[3] adopted the majority view that such fraud is in the *factum,* not the inducement, and have thus held it to vitiate consent. It is otherwise, however, with respect to the conceptually much murkier statutory offense with which we here deal, and the language of which has remained essentially unchanged since its enactment.

The language itself could not be plainer. It defines rape to be "an act of sexual intercourse" with a non-spouse, accomplished where the victim is "at the time unconscious of the nature of the act * * *." Nor, as we have just seen, can we entertain the slightest doubt that the Legislature well understood how to draft a statute to encompass fraud in the *factum* (§ 261, subd. (5)) and how to specify fraud in the inducement as vitiating consent. Moreover, courts of this state have previously confronted the general rule that fraud in the inducement does not vitiate consent. * * *

If the Legislature * * * had desired to correct the [gap in the law by prohibiting fraud in the inducement,][5] it could certainly have done so. * * *

To so conclude is not to vitiate the heartless cruelty of petitioner's scheme, but to say that it comprised crimes of a different order than a violation of section 261, subdivision (4). * * *

NOTES AND QUESTIONS

1. *Follow-up.* As a response to this case, the California legislature enacted Penal Code § 266c (see p. 392), which makes it an offense to induce another person to consent to a sexual act by fraud or fear. Apparently, however, Daniel Boro didn't learn about the new law or didn't care: A year later he was arrested under the new provision after he induced a woman to have intercourse with him because, he told her, it was the fastest way to cure a fatal blood disease. (She paid him $750 for his medical services.) Ken Chavez, *Woman Says Ruse Tricked Her Into Sex*, Los Angeles Times, April 22, 1987, at pt. 2, p. 4.

2. Since Boro told the victim that she had contracted a "perhaps fatal" disease, and the victim testified that "my life felt threatened," why was Count I (forcible rape) dismissed?

No Threat to kill?

3. How would *Boro* be resolved under the Model Penal Code? Consider Article 13 of the Code.

4. In State v. Brooks, 46 Kan.App.2d 601, 265 P.3d 1175 (2011), the Kansas Court of Appeals considered the following issue: "If a woman has sex with a man to avoid his publicizing her acutely embarrassing past or present

---

3. Section 261, subdivision (5) reads as follows: "Where a person submits under the belief that the person committing the act is the victim's spouse, and this belief is induced by any artifice, pretense, or concealment practiced by the accused, with intent to induce the belief."

5. It is not difficult to conceive of reasons why the Legislature may have consciously wished to leave the matter where it lies. Thus, as a matter of degree, where consent to intercourse is obtained by promises of travel, fame, celebrity and the like—ought the liar and seducer to be chargeable as a rapist? Where is the line to be drawn?

conduct—and she makes clear to him that she would otherwise not do so—has he committed rape?'' What *should* the answer be? In essence, how *should* the law treat intercourse obtained by fraud or non-physical threats? Consider these two contrasting views:

> Lying to secure money is unlawful theft by deception or false pretenses, a lesser crime than robbery, but a crime nonetheless. Yet lying to secure sex is old-fashioned seduction—not first-degree rape, not even third-degree rape. A threat to expose sexual information has long been considered a classic case of extortion, if not robbery itself. But securing sex itself by means of a threat short of force has, in many jurisdictions, been considered no crime at all.
>
> To the argument that it is either impossible or unwise for the law to regulate sexual "bargains" short of physical force, the law of extortion stands as a sharp rebuke: It has long listed prohibited threats in fairly inclusive terms. While extortion may be a lesser offense than robbery, it is nonetheless prohibited.
>
> It is almost certainly impossible to expect that the law could address all of the techniques of power and coercion which men use against women in sexual relations. I am not suggesting that we try.[96] Rather, I am suggesting that we do something that is actually quite easy—prohibit fraud to secure sex to the same extent we prohibit fraud to secure money, and prohibit extortion to secure sex to the same extent we prohibit extortion to secure money.

Susan Estrich, *Rape*, 95 Yale L.J. 1–87, 1118–1120 (1986). Now consider this response to Estrich:

> Estrich [states that if a defendant seeks money, not sex, they may be] convicted of theft by deception or false pretenses since, among other things, victim foolishness would have afforded them no defense.
>
> That insight is true as far as it goes, but what bearing does it have on rape law? Does Estrich really mean to suggest that if * * * [a] defendant has misrepresented himself as a talent scout and told [a] * * * complainant, without any sort of intimidation, "Come to bed with me, and I'll make you a star," he should be convicted of *rape?* Fraud, perhaps; or mail fraud, if he wrote her a letter containing the lies—though I must confess to minimal sympathy for the idea that the law should protect, via criminal sanctions, the cheated expectations of women who sought to sleep their way to the top but discovered, too late, that they were dealing with swindlers. *A fortiori,* the notion that rape, one of the gravest possible infringements of human integrity, should be expanded to include situations where the woman attempts to sell her body and fails to receive the bargained-for price simply makes a mockery of women's long efforts to achieve autonomy, respect, and equality.

---

96. Nor am I arguing that these cases must of necessity be considered in the same category as first degree, armed and brutal rape. I am more than willing to treat them as a lesser degree of "rape" and to impose lighter punishment in the same way that the unarmed robber, or the blackmailer, is treated as a less serious offender than the one who uses a deadly weapon in a robbery.

What, finally, would be the limits of liability for rape by fraud? Many females presumably yield to male advances because the man insists: "I love you." If false, is this representation "material"? To a "reasonable" woman? Does it matter whether the woman is reasonable? Whether her exploiter knows that she isn't? What if the man represents that he is rich and famous whereas, in truth, he is poor and unknown? Or to take a more earnest tack, suppose that a woman makes love with a man in reliance on his falsehood that he is AIDS-free? In that case, the woman is surely a victim and the lying man, a despicable predator. But is he a rapist? The foregoing problems and many others would readily occur to thoughtful readers, not merely to nit-picking scholars. Estrich has failed to work them through. Thus, her approach to this tricky topic cannot, as it stands, be taken seriously. * * *

[Also,] * * * what sorts of threats should qualify as the equivalent of "force" in rape? Surely, not all. Again, her treatment of a major issue is extremely sketchy. * * *

If Estrich really intends to propose that *any* threat sufficient to trigger a charge of extortion should serve to support a conviction of rape, then the latter crime could comprise obtaining sex by the following threatened actions: firing, or failing to hire, a woman; taking her canary; exposing her secret love affair; telling a prospective mortgagee that she frequently fails to honor her debts. Plainly, at some point (sooner, I would hope, where one's body, as opposed to one's money, is involved), the law should encourage the imposed-on woman to complain to the authorities or file civil suit (on grounds of sexual harassment, for instance) rather than yield. I believe that this seemingly harsher approach, at least to my more trivial examples, would demonstrate greater respect for women than "empower[ing] them with the weapon of a rape charge" and thereby implying that one should not expect weak females to defend their own sexual autonomy against any form of unpleasantness or pressure. I also believe that some threats of middling severity like loss of employment, especially to a person who depends on the income, might properly be criminalized as "coercion." But to call the resulting intercourse "rape" to my mind fails "to make clear that loss of bodily integrity" due to the gravest threats "is a different and greater injury" than its loss on account of lesser menaces, "and thus merits greater punishment," including the stigma of the label "rapist."

Vivian Berger, *Not So Simple Rape*, 7 Crim. Just. Ethics (Winter/Spring 1988), at 69, 76–77.

By the way, returning to the *Brooks* case with which we started this Note, the court ruled, 2–1, that the defendant's conduct did *not* fall within the scope of the Kansas rape statute, but that he *was* guilty of the lesser offense of blackmail. The majority stated that it was "dismayed at the result * * *. The outcome leaves [the victim] without a full measure of justice for what Brooks did to her in this case." What result under the Model Penal Code?

5. Suppose that a college professor offers a student an "A" in his class if she sleeps with him. Should this constitute rape, if intercourse occurs? Does this constitute gross sexual imposition under Model Penal Code § 213.1,

subdivision (2)? What if he tells her he will give her an "F" if she does not sleep with him?

D. RAPE SHIELD LAWS

STATE v. HERNDON

Court of Appeals of Wisconsin, 1988.
145 Wis.2d 91, 426 N.W.2d 347.

MOSER, PRESIDING JUDGE. * * *

A DEFENDANT'S CONSTITUTIONAL RIGHT TO CONFRONT ADVERSE WITNESSES AND PRESENT WITNESSES IN HIS BEHALF

The sixth amendment to the United States Constitution guarantees a defendant a fair trial by providing him with the right to cross-examine all witnesses against him.[b] "The right of cross-examination is more than a desirable rule of trial procedure. It is implicit in the constitutional right of confrontation, and helps assure the 'accuracy of the truth-determining process'" by revealing any possible biases, prejudices or ulterior motives of the witness. * * *

The sixth amendment to the United States Constitution also guarantees a defendant the right to compulsory process of witnesses to testify in his behalf * * *. As the United States Supreme Court has stated, "[f]ew rights are more fundamental than that of an accused to present witnesses in his own defense." * * * A violation of this right may deprive the defendant of a fair trial.

The United States Supreme Court, when addressing a state statute that impinges on confrontation and compulsory process rights, has resorted to a balancing test [in which the state's interest in enacting a statute is weighed against the defendant's constitutional interests]. * * *

RAPE SHIELD LAWS AND DEFENDANTS' RIGHTS

Rape shield laws have been enacted by * * * every state. Generally speaking, these laws deny a defendant in a sexual assault case the opportunity to examine the complainant concerning her prior sexual conduct [with third parties] or reputation [for sexual conduct]. They also deny the defendant the opportunity to offer extrinsic evidence of the prior sexual conduct or reputation of the complainant. * * *

The policy underlying * * * rape shield law[s] * * * is four-fold. First, the law prevents the defendant from harassing and humiliating the complainant with evidence of either her reputation for chastity or of specific prior sexual acts. Second, this type of evidence generally has no bearing on whether the complainant consented to sexual conduct with the defendant at the time in question. Third, exclusion of the evidence keeps

b. The Sixth Amendment reads, in part: "In all criminal prosecutions, the accused shall enjoy the right * * * to be confronted with the witnesses against him [and] to have compulsory process for obtaining witnesses in his favor * * *."

the jury focused only on issues relevant to the case at hand. Finally, the law promotes effective law enforcement because a victim will more readily report and testify in sexual assault cases if she does not fear that her prior sexual conduct will be brought before the public. * * *

Since their creation, rape shield laws have generally passed constitutional muster despite challenges based upon the sixth amendment rights to confront adverse witnesses and present evidence in a defendant's behalf. Courts have almost always held that these rights are not absolute, and that evidence of the prior sexual conduct of the complainant is only marginally relevant. Because the probativeness of the evidence is so minuscule when weighed against the potential prejudice to the complaining witness that the receipt of such evidence may engender in the fact finders, the sixth amendment rights must bend to protect the innocent victims. On the other hand, the courts have also universally held that both cross-examination and witnesses brought on behalf of the defendant may show prior consensual sex if that evidence shows a complainant's unique pattern of conduct similar to the pattern of the case at hand or shows that the complainant may be biased or have a motive to fabricate the charges. In such cases, the issues of a witness' bias and credibility are not collateral, and the rape shield laws must give way to the defendant's sixth amendment rights. * * *

PEOPLE v. WILHELM

Michigan Court of Appeals, 1991.
190 Mich.App. 574, 476 N.W.2d 753.

PER CURIAM.

* * * Following a jury trial, defendant was convicted of third-degree criminal sexual conduct. Defendant was sentenced to from three years and nine months to ten years' imprisonment. Defendant appealed as of right. * * *

Defendant * * * claims that the trial court abused its discretion when it prohibited him from introducing certain testimony concerning alleged prior acts of the victim. Both the victim and defendant were in a bar. They were not together. Defendant claimed that he observed the victim lift her shirt and expose her breasts to two men who were sitting at her table. The victim also allegedly allowed one of the two men to "fondle" her breasts. Defendant claimed that another witness had also seen this activity.

During trial, the prosecutor learned that defendant intended to introduce this evidence. The prosecutor argued that the rape-shield statute[1]

___

1. M.C.L. § 750.520j; M.S.A. § 28.788(10) provides:

(1) Evidence of specific instances of the victim's sexual conduct, opinion evidence of the victim's sexual conduct, and reputation evidence of the victim's sexual conduct shall not be admitted * * * unless and only to the extent that the judge finds that the following proposed evidence is material to a fact at issue in the case and that its inflammatory or prejudicial nature does not outweigh its probative value:

(a) Evidence of the victim's past sexual conduct with the actor.

prohibited evidence of the victim's sexual conduct with another. Defendant moved to have this evidence admitted as relevant to the issue whether the victim had consented to intercourse with him later that same evening in his boat that was parked in his parents' driveway. * * *

Defendant argued that * * * another state's similar rape-shield statute had been held not to prohibit such evidence, citing *State v. Colbath,* 130 N.H. 316, 540 A.2d 1212 (1988). * * *

In *Colbath,* the defendant and the victim were in a tavern. The victim directed unspecified "sexually provocative attention" toward several men in the tavern, including the defendant. The defendant testified that he had felt the victim's breasts and bottom and that she had rubbed his crotch before they left the tavern and went to the defendant's trailer. There they had intercourse, which the defendant claimed was consensual and the victim claimed was not. While in the trailer, the defendant's live-in female companion came home, suspecting the defendant's infidelity. Upon discovering the pair, she violently assaulted the victim and dragged her outside by the hair. The trial court ruled that the evidence was inadmissible under New Hampshire's rape-shield law. Nonetheless, a state's witness testified that the victim had left the tavern in the company of various men several times during the afternoon and that the victim was "hanging all over everyone and making out with Richard Colbath and a few others." The trial court instructed the jury that the evidence was irrelevant. The New Hampshire Supreme Court declined the defendant's request to rule that its rape-shield law did not apply because the victim's right to privacy was not invaded by a discussion of acts that occurred in a bar open to the public. Instead, the court ruled that the defendant's right of confrontation required that the defendant be allowed to demonstrate that the probative value of statutorily inadmissible evidence in the context of his particular case outweighed its prejudicial effect on the victim. In doing so, the court noted:

> As soon as we address this process of assigning relative weight to prejudicial and probative force, it becomes apparent that the public character of the complainant's behavior is significant. On the one hand, describing a complainant's open, sexually suggestive conduct in the presence of patrons of a public bar obviously has far less potential for damaging the sensibilities than revealing what the same person may have done in the company of another behind a closed door. On the other hand, evidence of public displays of general interest in sexual activity can be taken to indicate a contemporaneous receptiveness to sexual advances that cannot be inferred from evidence of private behavior with chosen sex partners.

(b) Evidence of specific instances of sexual activity showing the source or origin of semen, pregnancy, or disease.

(2) If the defendant proposes to offer evidence described in subsection (1)(a) or (b), the defendant within 10 days after the arraignment on the information shall file a written motion and offer of proof. The court may order an in camera hearing to determine whether the proposed evidence is admissible under subsection (1). * * *

In this case, for example, the jury could have taken evidence of the complainant's openly sexually provocative behavior toward a group of men as evidence of her probable attitude toward an individual within that group. Evidence that the publicly inviting acts occurred closely in time to the alleged sexual assault by one such man could have been viewed as indicating the complainant's likely attitude at the time of the sexual activity in question. It would, in fact, understate the importance of such evidence in this case to speak of it merely as relevant. We should recall that the fact of intercourse was not denied, and that the evidence of assault was subject to the explanation that the defendant's jealous living [sic? live-in] companion had inflicted the visible injuries. The companion's furious behavior had further bearing on the case, as well, for the jury could have regarded her attack as a reason for the complainant to regret a voluntary liaison with the defendant, and as a motive for the complainant to allege rape as a way to explain her injuries and excuse her undignified predicament. * * *

* * * [D]efendant claims that the public nature of the victim's activities should remove them from the protection of the rape-shield statute. We disagree. The statute itself does not make this distinction. Defendant treats the statute's purpose of protecting the victim's privacy as though it extends only to private acts. * * * [O]ne of the purposes of the law is to encourage victims to report and testify without fear that the trial court's proceedings would veer from an impartial examination of the accused's conduct on the date in question and instead take on the aspects of an inquisition during which the victim would be required to acknowledge and justify her sexual past. Moreover, we fail to see how a woman's consensual sexual conduct with another in public indicates to third parties that the woman would engage in similar behavior with them. * * * [E]vidence of a rape victim's unchastity is ordinarily insufficiently probative of her consent to intercourse with a defendant. * * *

Finally, defendant claims that the * * * preclusion of the evidence under the rape-shield law deprived him of his right of confrontation. We disagree. Evidence of a victim's sexual conduct with a third party is irrelevant to the issue whether she consented to sexual intercourse with the defendant. Defendant further argues that the victim's acts with the third persons were probative of the issue of consent because they occurred in a public place and shortly before the period of time during which he claims that the victim consented to sexual relations with him. Defendant apparently attempts to analogize his case with *Colbath*. We believe that *Colbath* is distinguishable. As noted therein, the victim's behavior constituted a public display of general interest in sexual activity in which the defendant was directly involved. Moreover, the victim in *Colbath* had left the bar with various men several times during the afternoon, and the beating she had received from the defendant's live-in companion in that case may have provided a motive for fabrication. * * * If believed, the victim's alleged conduct [in the present case] occurred with third parties and, although observed by defendant, was not relevant to the issue whether she consented to sexual intercourse with him later on the same evening. Because the evidence was irrelevant, defendant was not denied his right of confrontation. * * *

NOTES AND QUESTIONS

1. Do you agree with the *Wilhelm* court's analysis? Do you think that *Colbath* was properly decided?

2. As a matter of sound public policy, in a sexual assault prosecution where consent is the critical issue, should a defendant be able to introduce evidence of the following: (a) in a case in which *L* was charged with nonconsensual anal sex with *V* (who testified that she was a lesbian and, therefore, did not have consensual sex with men), that *V* had previously engaged in consensual anal sex with other men, State v. Lessley, 257 Neb. 903, 601 N.W.2d 521 (1999); and (b) that *V* expressed rape fantasies to the defendant, People v. Garcia, 179 P.3d 250 (Colo. App. 2007)?

Should a *prosecutor*, in order to prove *non*consent, be permitted to introduce evidence that *V* has never consented to intercourse with a male because she is a lesbian?

3. *Problem.* In Lewis v. Wilkinson, 307 F.3d 413 (6th Cir. 2002), Nathaniel Lewis and Christina Heaslet were friends who met during their first year at the University of Akron. One evening, Heaslet invited Lewis, whom she knew was "a flirt who was interested in her sexually," to her dormitory room, where sexual intercourse ultimately ensued, consensually according to Lewis's testimony, nonconsensually according to Heaslet's description of the events in the dormitory room. Then:

Heaslet * * * went to see Alison Legitt, the Resident Coordinator for the dormitory, who called the police. Heaslet did not want to speak to the police initially. She was taken to the hospital, but did not want to see a rape counselor, and for the first several hours did not wish to file any charges. Heaslet eventually agreed to see a counselor * * * and was encouraged by her counselor to keep a diary. Lewis was arrested [for rape] in his dormitory room * * *. * * *

Several weeks prior to the scheduled trial date, Lewis received in the mail an envelope that had been sent anonymously to his home address. The envelope contained xeroxed excerpts of Heaslet's diary. Lewis gave the envelope to his trial counsel, who disclosed the contents to the assistant prosecutor and the trial judge. Lewis's counsel requested the production of the entire diary. The State acquired Heaslet's complete diary and provided it to the court for *in camera* review. The State moved * * * to exclude reference to the diary except for certain limited portions. * * * The portions anonymously sent to Lewis were marked Exhibits "A", "B", "C" and "D". Defense counsel argued for permission to cross-examine Heaslet on excerpts "A", "B", "C" and "D", arguing they were relevant to Heaslet's veracity and motive to lie and spoke directly to the issue of consent. Defense counsel was particularly interested in excerpt "B" contained in the entry dated April 20, 1997:

I can't believe the trial's only a week away. I feel guilty (sort of) for trying to get Nate locked up, but his lack of respect for women is terrible. I remember how disrespectful he always was to all of us girls in the courtyard * * * he thinks females are a bunch of sex objects! And he's such a player! He was trying to get with Holly and me, and all the while he had a girlfriend. I think I pounced on Nate because he was the last straw. That, and because I've always seemed to need some drama in my life. Otherwise I get bored. That definitely needs to change. I'm sick of men taking advantage of me * * * and I'm sick of myself for giving in to them. I'm not a nympho like all those guys think. I'm just not strong enough to say no to them. I'm tired of being a whore. This is where it ends.

Citing the [Ohio] rape shield law, the trial court prohibited the defense from introducing the following language from Exhibit "B":

* * * and I'm sick of myself for giving in to them. I'm not a nympho like all those guys think. I'm just not strong enough to say no to them. I'm tired of being a whore. This is where it ends.

As a matter of sound public policy, do you agree with the trial court's ruling? Why, or why not? Would you have admitted all of Exhibit "B"? None of it?

E. STATUTORY RAPE

GARNETT v. STATE

Court of Appeals of Maryland, 1993.
332 Md. 571, 632 A.2d 797.

[See p. 185 for the case.]

NOTES AND QUESTIONS

1. The FBI's National Incident–Based Reporting System has concluded that in the year 2000: there was one statutory rape for every three forcible rapes involving a juvenile victim reported to the police; 95% of statutory rape victims were female, and 99% of the offenders were male; 70% of male offenders were age 21 or over; and the median age difference between male offenders and female statutory rape victims was six years. U.S. Dept. of Justice, Office of Juvenile Programs, Statutory Rape Known to Law Enforcement (Aug. 2005).

2. According to Catherine L. Carpenter, *On Statutory Rape, Strict Liability, and the Public Welfare Offense Model*, 53 Am. U. L. Rev. 313 (2003), only three states treat statutory rape as a traditional, *mens rea*-required offense. Moreover, the consequence of conviction is far from trivial, as Professor Carpenter writes, at 374, 376:

Statutory rape laws carry a wide range of penalties, including serious consequences such as sentences of twenty years and beyond. * * *

Whether it carries significant prison time or minimal jail time, conviction of statutory rape in most jurisdictions bears the public equivalent of the "scarlet letter"—the requirement that sex offenders, after serving their sentences, must register with law enforcement officials. Further, in most states, * * * officials [must] notify members of the community of the offender's location.

3.   *Origins of statutory rape law.* Michelle Oberman, *Turning Girls Into Women: Re–Evaluating Modern Statutory Rape Law*, 85 J. Crim. L. & Criminology 15, 24–25 (1994):

> Statutory rape, which is "at least as ancient as the 4000–year–old Code of Hammurabi" was codified in English law in 1275. Essentially, statutory rape criminalizes acts which would not otherwise be classified as rape. Initially, the age of consent was twelve; in 1576, the age was lowered to ten.

> Statutory rape laws were absorbed into the American legal system via the English common law. Early American lawmakers set the age of consent at ten, but over the course of the nineteenth century, the states gradually raised the age, some to as high as eighteen or twenty-one. Some states provided increased penalties for adult men who had sex with pre-pubescent girls, and lesser penalties when the male was younger than the female.

> Statutory rape laws were gender-specific, criminalizing sexual relations with young females, but not with young males. Commentators note that the laws reflected the historical legal perception of women and girls as "special property in need of special protection." American courts in the 19th century originally adopted statutory rape as a strict liability offense, in accordance with English law. It did not matter whether the victim looked older than the age of consent, that she consented, or even that she initiated sexual contact.

4.   Why is intercourse with an underage female a crime? The California Supreme Court explained (and questioned the wisdom of) the offense this way in People v. Hernandez, 61 Cal.2d 529, 39 Cal.Rptr. 361, 393 P.2d 673 (1964):

> Consent of the female is often an unrealistic and unfortunate standard for branding sexual intercourse a crime as serious as forcible rape. Yet the consent standard has been deemed to be required by important policy goals. We are dealing here, of course, with statutory rape where, in one sense, the lack of consent of the female is not an element of the offense. In a broader sense, however, the lack of consent is deemed to remain an element but the law makes a conclusive presumption of the lack thereof because she is presumed too innocent and naive to understand the implications and nature of her act. * * *

> The assumption that age alone will bring an understanding of the sexual act to a young woman is of doubtful validity. Both learning from the cultural group to which she is a member and her actual sexual experiences will determine her level of comprehension. The sexually experienced 15–year old may be far more acutely aware of the implications of sexual intercourse than her sheltered cousin who is beyond the age of consent. A girl who belongs to a group whose members indulge in sexual intercourse at an early age is likely to rapidly acquire an insight

into the rewards and penalties of sexual indulgence. Nevertheless, even in circumstances where a girl's actual comprehension contradicts the law's presumption, the male is deemed criminally responsible for the act, although himself young and naive and responding to advances which may have been made to him.

In view of these observations, should feminists favor or oppose statutory rape legislation? Professor Oberman, Note 3 supra, at 27–29, 31–32, has described the feminists' involvement in statutory rape law reform:

By the mid–1800s, statutory rape laws were supported by Victorian feminists as well as "repressive moralists." Victorian feminist support grew out of concern over what some have labeled "social purity." While this cause may sound moralistic and repressive to modern ears, and while much of the rhetoric reflected an "obsessive concern with the social and sexual habits of the poor," the social purity movement pursued goals which easily fall within a modern feminist and progressive agenda. * * *

Victorian feminists saw youthful sexual activity as a tragic first step in the transformation of girls from chaste maidens to "fallen women," or, more immediately, child-prostitutes. Thus, Victorian feminists mobilized in an effort to strengthen statutory rape laws. One such mobilization took place in 1885, when approximately 250,000 people gathered in London's Hyde Park to demand passage of a bill raising the age of consent for girls from thirteen to sixteen. * * *

Feminist support for these reforms raised eyebrows among some of the supporters' progressive contemporaries. For example, when the coalition of feminists and "moralists" successfully secured the passage of the Criminal Law Amendment Act of 1885, raising the age of consent for girls, one observer commented, "It is * * * strange that many of the very women who have braved insult and calumny in demanding these rights were among the first and loudest supporters of the measure for their furthest restriction."

In the late twentieth century, feminists themselves became troubled by this apparent inconsistency, and many voiced concern that statutory rape laws amounted to state repression of female sexuality. This concern, among others, led feminists in the 1970s to oppose gender-based statutory rape laws, arguing that they perpetuated offensive gender stereotypes and restricted the sexual autonomy of young women.

This feminist "about-face" reflected the influence of the late 1960's and early 1970's sexual liberation movement, which coincided with the fledgling women's liberation movement, and gave the era's activists, including its feminists, a decidedly "pro-sex" character.

5. *Statutory rape law in a promiscuous society.* Professor Oberman reports that there has been a recent rekindling of interest in the enforcement of statutory rape laws, but for non-moralistic reasons. Michelle Oberman, *Regulating Consensual Sex with Minors: Defining a Role for Statutory Rape*, 48 Buffalo L. Rev. 703, 706 (2000).

Recent studies reveal that by age sixteen, half of U.S. teenagers have had sexual intercourse, which means that an enormous number of illicit acts of intercourse occur daily. Prosecution of every, or even many, of these violations of the law is impossible. However, Oberman points out, a recent study shows that "a startlingly high number of babies born to young teen mothers were fathered by adult men." Id. at 705. These mothers, disproportionately, do not complete high school and are more likely to need public assistance over the years. Selective enforcement of statutory rape laws is seen by some as a means to combat the teenage pregnancy problem. Oberman believes this focus may be appropriate if statutory rape laws are reformulated to "more closely approximate[ ] the goal of protecting a vulnerable population from sexual exploitation * * *." Id. at 707. For her suggested reforms, see id. at 775–784.

In light of this problem, the Supreme Court has upheld gender-specific statutory rape laws against constitutional attack on equal protection grounds. Michael M. v. Superior Court of Sonoma County, 450 U.S. 464, 101 S.Ct. 1200, 67 L.Ed.2d 437 (1981). The Court reasoned that a state might justifiably protect young females, but not young males, from underage sexuality in order to deter teenage pregnancy. It said that "virtually all of the significant harmful and inescapably identifiable consequences of teenage pregnancy fall on the young female."

Constitutional law issues, aside, the *wisdom* of gender-specific statutory rape laws has been questioned. Research demonstrates that "when an older woman takes advantage of a [young boy] sexually, significant negative after-shocks, such as substance abuse, suicidal thoughts, sexual disorders, and violent behavior, are quite common in the population of male victims." Kay L. Levine, *No Penis, No Problem*, 33 Fordham Urb. L.J. 357, 397 (2006).

6. *Problem.* A 12-year-old boy engaged in consensual sexual conduct with two other boys, one age 11, one age 12. He was prosecuted in juvenile court for statutory rape, defined as follows:

> No person shall engage in sexual conduct with another who is not the spouse of the offender * * *, when one of the following applies: * * * (b) The other person is less than 13 years of age, whether or not the offender knows the age of the other person.

The Ohio Supreme Court ruled that prosecution of the defendant under this statute was unconstitutional. In re D.B., 129 Ohio St.3d 104, 950 N.E.2d 528 (2011). Look at the statute carefully to see if you can figure out why the state high court ruled as it did.

All under age - violated due process & equal protection

CHAPTER 9

GENERAL DEFENSES TO CRIMES

■ ■ ■

A. CATEGORIES OF DEFENSES

PAUL H. ROBINSON—CRIMINAL LAW DEFENSES: A SYSTEMATIC ANALYSIS

82 Columbia Law Review 199 (1982), 200, 202–05, 208–11, 213–14, 221, 229–32

Unlike many aspects of the criminal law, defenses have not yet been the subject of comprehensive conceptual analysis. The general nature and scope of most defenses have been perpetuated for centuries with little or no question. Current debates commonly focus on whether a particular defense should apply in a particular circumstance, but rarely consider the larger perspective. How do circumstances covered by one defense compare with those of other defenses? Do defenses overlap? If so, will the outcome in identical situations vary with the defense asserted? Should it? Are there gaps between defenses, that is, circumstances in which our common sense of justice suggests that the defendant should be exculpated, yet where no defense applies? Do defenses based on theoretically analogous grounds of exculpation generate analogous results? The general inquiry, which seems never to have been undertaken, is: how does the collection of recognized defenses operate as a system? * * *

There are, no doubt, many people who believe that defenses defy such systemization. Defenses, it might be argued, are the embodiment of such complex human notions of fairness and morality, tempered by the demands of utility and efficiency, that they are too complex and perhaps too illogical to be reduced to an integrated, comprehensive, and internally consistent system of exculpation. * * *

This Article attempts to provide some measure of conceptual organization for criminal law defenses * * *.

I. A SYSTEM OF DEFENSES

The term "defense" is commonly used, at least in a casual sense, to mean any set of identifiable conditions or circumstances which may prevent a conviction for an offense. * * * Upon examining the functions of and the rationales supporting these rules and doctrines, five general categories become apparent. They may be termed: failure of proof defenses, offense modification defenses, justifications, excuses, and nonexculpatory public policy defenses. * * *

A.   Failure of Proof Defenses

Failure of proof defenses consist of instances in which, because of the conditions that are the basis for the "defense," all elements of the offense charged cannot be proven. They are in essence no more than the negation of an element required by the definition of the offense. * * *

mistake of fact & law

Mistake provides a clear example * * *. Assume, for example, that incest is defined as having intercourse with a person the actor knows to be an ancestor, descendant, or sibling. If the actor honestly believes that the person with whom he is having intercourse in not a relative, one might term his mistake a "defense." In reality, the actor's mistaken belief prevents a state from proving the required mental element of knowledge of the familial relationship. When this sort of mistake of fact is recognized as a "defense," it is considered not a general mistake excuse, but only a failure of proof defense. * * *

B.   Offense Modifications

Offense-modification defenses are real defenses in the sense that they do more than simply negate an element of an offense. They apply even where all elements of the offense are satisfied. They are distinguishable from general defenses (like self-defense or insanity), however, because they introduce criminalization decisions similar to those used in defining offenses, rather than giving effect to general principles of exculpation. They provide a more sophisticated account, when needed, of the harm or evil sought to be prohibited by the definition of the offense.

A parent, against the advice of police, pays a $10,000 ransom to the kidnapper of his child. A businessman pays monthly extortion payments to a racketeer. These persons may well satisfy the elements required for complicity in kidnapping and extortion, yet they will nonetheless have a defense to these charges. * * *

paying kidnapper not complicity

There is a single principle behind these modifications of the definition of an offense: while the actor has apparently satisfied all elements of the offense charged, he has not in fact caused the harm or evil sought to be prevented by the statute defining the offense. * * *

In many cases the defenses of this group are given no formal name, but exist only as accepted rules. For example, with regard to the kidnapping and extortion examples above, a common rule provides that the victim of a crime may not be held as an accomplice even though his conduct has in a significant sense aided the commission of the crime. * * *

Some offense modifications are considered defenses, rather than simply rules or doctrines, but they operate similarly to modify the definition of offenses. * * *

Offense modifications, like failure of proof defenses, commonly apply to only one specific offense. * * *

C. *Justifications*

Unlike failure of proof and offense modification defenses, justification defenses are not alterations of the statutory definition of the harm sought to be prevented or punished by an offense. The harm caused by the justified behavior remains a legally recognized harm which is to be avoided whenever possible. Under special justifying circumstances, however, that harm is outweighed by the need to avoid an even greater harm or to further a greater societal interest.

self-defense

A forest fire rages toward a town of 10,000 unsuspecting inhabitants. The actor burns a field of corn located between the fire and the town; the burned field then serves as a firebreak, saving 10,000 lives. The actor has satisfied all elements of the offense of arson by setting fire to the field with the purpose of destroying it. The immediate harm he has caused— the destruction of the field—is precisely the harm which the statute serves to prevent and punish. Yet the actor is likely to have a complete defense, because his conduct and its harmful consequences were justified. The conduct in this instance is tolerated, even encouraged, by society. * * *

D. *Excuses*

Excuses, like justifications, are usually general defenses applicable to all offenses even though the elements of the offense are satisfied. Excuses admit that the deed may be wrong, but excuse the actor because conditions suggest that the actor is not responsible for his deed. For instance, suppose that the actor knocks the mailman over the head with a baseball bat because she believes he is coming to surgically implant a radio receiver which will take control of her body. The defendant has satisfied all elements of the offense of aggravated assault—she struck the mailman with a deadly weapon with the purpose of causing him bodily injury. This is precisely the harm sought to be prevented by the statute, and it is not outweighed by any greater societal harm avoided or greater societal interest furthered. It is conduct that society would in fact condemn and seek to prevent. The defendant is exculpated only because her condition at the time of the offense—her paranoid delusion—suggests that she has not acted through a meaningful exercise of free will and therefore is not an appropriate subject for criminal liability. * * *

insanity

E. *Nonexculpatory Public Policy Defenses*

In 1971 the actor forcibly takes a wallet from an old man at gun point. The crime goes unsolved until 1978 when he is identified and arrested. Although he has committed the offense, caused the harm sought to be prevented by the statute, and has no claim that his conduct is justified or excused, the actor may nonetheless have a defense. The statute of limitations may bar his conviction for robbery despite his clear culpability because by foregoing that conviction society furthers other, more important, public interests.

Time limitations on criminal prosecutions are often supported as fostering a more stable and forward-looking society. * * * These rationales may justify current statutes of limitations, but it must be noted that they are not based on a lack of culpability of the defendant. They are purely public policy arguments. * * *

Other public policy-based bars to prosecution include diplomatic immunity, judicial, legislative, and executive immunities, * * * and incompetency. Each of the * * * forms of immunity furthers important societal interests * * *.

This balancing of countervailing public policy interests, both societal and personal, should be distinguished from the balancing which occurs in justification defenses. In the latter, the harm done by defendant's act is outweighed by the societal benefit that it creates, and, as a result, he is not blameworthy. In nonexculpatory defenses, the defendant's conduct is harmful, and creates no societal benefit; the defendant is blameworthy. The societal benefit underlying the defense arises not from his conduct, but from foregoing his conviction. The defendant escapes conviction in spite of his culpability.

JOSHUA DRESSLER—JUSTIFICATIONS AND EXCUSES: A BRIEF REVIEW OF THE CONCEPTS AND THE LITERATURE

33 Wayne Law Review 1155 (1987), 1155, 1157–59, 1161–63, 1167–69, 1171–73

I. INTRODUCTION * * *

An important feature of the new literature regarding criminal law defenses is the rebirth of interest in the concepts of "justification" and "excuse." In early English common law the legal profession paid considerable attention to the differences between these doctrines. A practical reason may have inspired the interest: justifiable homicide (e.g., killing to prevent the commission of an atrocious felony) resulted in acquittal of the actor; excusable homicide (e.g., killing by a person suffering from an insane delusion) resulted in the forfeiture of the actor's property and a need for a pardon to avoid the death penalty.

Today, a successful claim of excuse has the same direct effect as a justification: acquittal of the defendant. Probably because of this, the interest of nineteenth and twentieth century lawyers and most legal scholars in the inherent differences between the two classes of exculpatory claims waned. Indeed, until recently, the absence of interest in the subject was nearly complete. American casebooks ignored the distinctions; the topic received scant attention in American law journals; and treatise authors ignored the differences or, perhaps worse, suggested that the differences were of no concern to lawyers. In light of this, it is not surprising that courts often use the words "justification" and "excuse" interchangeably.

In recent years, the academic landscape has changed. * * *

* * * The field is now fairly rich in literature that defines the contours of justification and excuse defenses or that uses the concepts to determine whether particular conduct should be justified, excused, or punished. * * *

II. Justification and Excuse: The Basics

A person steeped in the justification-excuse debate or, indeed, any person who uses the English language with care is apt to wince upon hearing another say something like "the justification of self-defense *excuses* a person who injures an aggressor." The words "justification" and "excuse" are not interchangeable in the taxonomy of criminal law defenses or in proper English usage. A justification does not excuse conduct; an excuse does not justify conduct.

In its simplest form, and subject to substantial complexity and debate as to its precise contours, justified conduct is conduct that is "a good thing, or the right or sensible thing, or a permissible thing to do." A defendant who raises a justification defense in a criminal prosecution says, in essence, "I did nothing wrong for which I should be punished." To say that conduct is justified is to suggest that something which ordinarily would be considered wrong or undesirable—i.e., that would constitute "social harm,"—is, in light of the circumstances, socially acceptable or tolerable. A justification, in other words, negates the social harm of an offense. *justification*

An excuse is in the nature of a claim that although the actor has harmed society, she should not be blamed or punished for causing that harm. The criminal defendant who asserts an excusing defense says, in essence, "I admit, or you have proved beyond a reasonable doubt, that I did something I should not have done, but I should not be held criminally accountable for my actions." Whereas a justification negates the social harm of an offense, an excuse negates the moral blameworthiness of the *excuse* actor for causing the harm. Just as we do not punish people for committing harmless acts, we ordinarily do not punish them for blamelessly causing harm. The existence of excuses in the law is evidence of this fact. * * *

III. Why Should We Care About All of This?

A. *Generally*

Sir Henry Maine once observed that "nobody cares about criminal law except theorists and habitual criminals." Unfortunately, lawyers, judges, and lawmakers rarely are accused of being theorists, so it is difficult to convince the legal community that it should care about the justification-excuse distinction. The practical application of the distinction must be demonstrated.

Many of the scholars involved in the justification-excuse debate have sought, and I believe convincingly so, to demonstrate the importance of their work to the legal system. Some of their points suggest that, at least occasionally, a lawyer can take advantage of her knowledge of the justification-excuse dichotomy to win a criminal case. More significantly, the distinctions should prove valuable to those responsible for developing coherent and morally just rules of criminal responsibility. Some reasons why the subject should concern the legal community follow.

B. Sending Clear Messages

Austin has observed that "words are our tools, and, as a minimum we should use clean tools: we should know what we mean and what we do not, and we must forearm ourselves against the traps that language sets us."[50] These thoughts apply with special force to lawyers and judges. Words, after all, are their professional tools. As the words "justification" and "excuse" are not synonyms, the legal profession should not treat them as such. The importance of using clean tools is especially significant in the criminal law. Criminal statutes and rules of criminal responsibility express, or at least intend to express, the basic moral values of the community. Specifically, justification defenses reflect society's judgment that certain conduct is tolerable or desirable while excuse defenses recognize those circumstances in which society considers it morally unjust to punish and stigmatize wrongdoers. When the law fails to focus on the justification-excuse distinction it risks sending a false message. * * *

C. Providing Theoretical Consistency in the Criminal Law

Consideration of the justification-excuse distinction should be a valuable part of the process by which legislatures and courts coherently define criminal defenses. For example, * * * the heat-of-passion defense to murder suffers from a lack of sufficient consideration of the justification-excuse distinction by the courts that developed the doctrine.

Specifically, lawmakers failed to determine whether provoked killings are less serious offenses because the victim of the provocation is partially justified in killing the provoker—i.e., the victim's provocation results in partial moral forfeiture of her right to life—or whether she is partially excused for the homicide—i.e., the victim's life is fully valued but the actor's understandable passion reduces her moral blameworthiness. Unfortunately, some of the common law rules pertaining to the defense are based on a justification theory; other features fit the excuse mold. Only by alerting ourselves to the justification-excuse distinction can the elements of the defense be reconciled with the theory. * * *

D. Burden of Proof

A plausible argument can be made for the rule that legislatures ought to require the government to carry the burden of persuasion regarding

---

50. J.L. Austin, [*A Plea for Excuses*, in Freedom and Responsibility (H. Morris ed. 1961)], at 9.

justification defenses, but that the defendant should shoulder the burden with excuses.

The thesis is that the prosecutor is allocated the burden of proof regarding elements of a crime because no one should be punished if a reasonable doubt exists that she has committed an unlawful act. Justified conduct is lawful conduct. If the defendant is required to carry the burden of persuasion regarding a justification, she may be punished even though the factfinder is not satisfied beyond a reasonable doubt that she has acted wrongly. With excused conduct, however, all of the elements of the crime have been proved and the conduct was determined to be unjustifiable. In these circumstances, it is not unfair to require the defendant to persuade the jury that it should show compassion by excusing her for her unjustified, socially injurious conduct.

E.   Accomplice Liability

In some cases, the liability of an accomplice to a crime could be affected by the justification-excuse distinction. If *A* provides *D* with a gun in order to kill *V*, and *D* is acquitted on the ground of self-defense, it follows that *A* should also be acquitted of the offense since she has aided the primary party to commit a socially acceptable act. If *D* is acquitted on the ground of an excuse—let us assume, insanity—no reason of logic or policy requires the acquittal of *A*, assuming that she is not also insane or otherwise excused. After all, *D*'s insanity acquittal does not negate the fact that *A* provided a gun to an insane person who committed a socially harmful act.

Accomplice Liability

Notes and Questions

1.   Most scholars reason that claims of justification logically precede pleas of excuse. Can you see why?

B.   BURDEN OF PROOF

PATTERSON v. NEW YORK

Supreme Court of the United States, 1977.
432 U.S. 197, 97 S.Ct. 2319, 53 L.Ed.2d 281.

Mr. Justice White delivered the opinion of the Court.

The question here is the constitutionality under the Fourteenth Amendment's Due Process Clause of burdening the defendant in a New York State murder trial with proving the affirmative defense of extreme emotional disturbance as defined by New York law.

I

After a brief and unstable marriage, the appellant, Gordon Patterson, Jr., became estranged from his wife, Roberta. Roberta resumed an association with John Northrup, a neighbor to whom she had been engaged prior to her marriage to appellant. On December 27, 1970, Patterson borrowed a rifle from an acquaintance and went to the residence of his father-in-law. There, he observed his wife through a window in a state of semiundress in the presence of John Northrup. He entered the house and killed Northrup by shooting him twice in the head.

Patterson was charged with second-degree murder. In New York [see p. 243 for the statute—ed.] there are two elements of this crime: (1) "intent to cause the death of another person"; and (2) "caus[ing] the death of such person or of a third person." Malice aforethought is not an element of the crime. In addition, the State permits a person accused of murder to raise an affirmative defense that he "acted under the influence of extreme emotional disturbance for which there was a reasonable explanation or excuse."

New York also recognizes the crime of manslaughter. A person is guilty of manslaughter if he intentionally kills another person "under circumstances which do not constitute murder because he acts under the influence of extreme emotional disturbance." Appellant confessed before trial to killing Northrup, but at trial he raised the defense of extreme emotional disturbance.

The jury was instructed as to the elements of the crime of murder. Focusing on the element of intent, the trial court charged:

"Before you, considering all of the evidence, can convict this defendant or anyone of murder, you must believe and decide that the People have established beyond a reasonable doubt that he intended, in firing the gun, to kill either the victim himself or some other human being. * * *

"Always remember that you must not expect or require the defendant to prove to your satisfaction that his acts were done without the intent to kill. Whatever proof he may have attempted, however far he may have gone in an effort to convince you of his innocence or guiltlessness, he is not obliged, he is not obligated to prove anything. It is always the People's burden to prove his guilt, and to prove that he intended to kill in this instance beyond a reasonable doubt."

The jury was further instructed, consistently with New York law, that the defendant had the burden of proving his affirmative defense by a preponderance of the evidence. The jury was told that if it found beyond a reasonable doubt that appellant had intentionally killed Northrup but that appellant had demonstrated by a preponderance of the evidence that he had acted under the influence of extreme emotional disturbance, it had to find appellant guilty of manslaughter instead of murder.

The jury found appellant guilty of murder. * * * While appeal to the New York Court of Appeals was pending, this Court decided *Mullaney v. Wilbur,* 421 U.S. 684, 95 S.Ct. 1881, 44 L.Ed.2d 508 (1975), in which the Court declared Maine's murder statute unconstitutional. Under the Maine statute, a person accused of murder could rebut the statutory presumption that he committed the offense with "malice aforethought" by proving that he acted in the heat of passion on sudden provocation.[a] The Court held that this scheme improperly shifted the burden of persuasion from the prosecutor to the defendant and was therefore a violation of due process. In the Court of Appeals appellant urged that New York's murder statute is functionally equivalent to the one struck down in *Mullaney* and that therefore his conviction should be reversed.

The Court of Appeals rejected appellant's argument, holding that the New York murder statute is consistent with due process. The Court distinguished *Mullaney* on the ground that the New York statute involved no shifting of the burden to the defendant to disprove any fact essential to the offense charged since the New York affirmative defense of extreme emotional disturbance bears no direct relationship to any element of murder. * * *

II

It goes without saying that preventing and dealing with crime is much more the business of the States than it is of the Federal Government, and that we should not lightly construe the Constitution so as to intrude upon the administration of justice by the individual States. * * *

In determining whether New York's allocation to the defendant of proving the mitigating circumstances of severe emotional disturbance is consistent with due process, it is * * * relevant to note that this defense is a considerably expanded version of the common-law defense of heat of passion on sudden provocation and that at common law the burden of proving the latter, as well as other affirmative defenses—indeed, "all * * * circumstances of justification, excuse or alleviation"—rested on the defendant. * * *

In 1895 the common-law view was abandoned with respect to the insanity defense in federal prosecutions. *Davis v. United States,* 160 U.S. 469, 16 S.Ct. 353, 40 L.Ed. 499 (1895). This ruling had wide impact on the practice in the federal courts with respect to the burden of proving various affirmative defenses, and the prosecution in a majority of jurisdictions in this country sooner or later came to shoulder the burden of proving the sanity of the accused and of disproving the facts constituting other affirmative defenses, including provocation. *Davis* was not a constitutional ruling, however, as *Leland v. Oregon,* [343 U.S. 790, 72 S.Ct. 1002, 96 L.Ed. 1302 (1952)], made clear.

---

a. The Maine murder statute, Me.Rev.Stat.Ann., Tit. 17, § 2651 (1964), provided: "Whoever unlawfully kills a human being with malice aforethought, either express or implied, is guilty of murder and shall be punished by imprisonment for life."

The manslaughter statute, Me.Rev.Stat.Ann., Tit. 17, § 2251 (1964), read in pertinent part: "Whoever unlawfully kills a human being in the heat of passion, on sudden provocation, without express or implied malice aforethought * * * shall be punished by a fine of not more than $1,000 or by imprisonment for not more than 20 years."

At issue in *Leland v. Oregon* was the constitutionality under the Due Process Clause of the Oregon rule that the defense of insanity must be proved by the defendant beyond a reasonable doubt. [The Court in *Leland* upheld the Oregon rule, stating that *Davis* "obviously establish[ed] no constitutional doctrine."] * * *

In 1970, the Court declared that the Due Process Clause "protects the accused against conviction except upon proof beyond a reasonable doubt of every fact necessary to constitute the crime with which he is charged." *In re Winship*, 397 U.S. 358, 364, 90 S.Ct. 1068, 1073, 25 L.Ed.2d 368 (1970). Five years later, in *Mullaney v. Wilbur*, the Court further announced that under the Maine law of homicide, the burden could not constitutionally be placed on the defendant of proving by a preponderance of the evidence that the killing had occurred in the heat of passion on sudden provocation. The Chief Justice and Mr. Justice Rehnquist, concurring, expressed their understanding that the *Mullaney* decision did not call into question the ruling in *Leland v. Oregon, supra,* with respect to the proof of insanity.

Subsequently, the Court confirmed that it remained constitutional to burden the defendant with proving his insanity defense when it dismissed, as not raising a substantial federal question, a case in which the appellant specifically challenged the continuing validity of *Leland v. Oregon.* * * * *Rivera v. Delaware*, 429 U.S. 877, 97 S.Ct. 226, 50 L.Ed.2d 160 (1976) * * *.

III

We cannot conclude that Patterson's conviction under the New York law deprived him of due process of law. The crime of murder is defined by the statute, which represents a recent revision of the state criminal code, as causing the death of another person with intent to do so. The death, the intent to kill, and causation are the facts that the State is required to prove beyond a reasonable doubt if a person is to be convicted of murder. No further facts are either presumed or inferred in order to constitute the crime. The statute does provide an affirmative defense—that the defendant acted under the influence of extreme emotional disturbance for which there was a reasonable explanation—which, if proved by a preponderance of the evidence, would reduce the crime to manslaughter, an offense defined in a separate section of the statute. It is plain enough that if the intentional killing is shown, the State intends to deal with the defendant as a murderer unless he demonstrates the mitigating circumstances.

Here, the jury was instructed in accordance with the statute, and the guilty verdict confirms that the State successfully carried its burden of proving the facts of the crime beyond a reasonable doubt. * * * It seems to us that the State satisfied the mandate of *Winship* that it prove beyond a reasonable doubt "every fact necessary to constitute the crime with which [Patterson was] charged."

In convicting Patterson under its murder statute, New York did no more than *Leland* and *Rivera* permitted it to do without violating the Due Process Clause. Under those cases, once the facts constituting a crime are established beyond a reasonable doubt, based on all the evidence including the evidence of the defendant's mental state, the State may refuse to sustain the affirmative defense of insanity unless demonstrated by a preponderance of the evidence.

The New York law on extreme emotional disturbance follows this pattern. This affirmative defense * * * does not serve to negative any facts of the crime which the State is to prove in order to convict of murder. It constitutes a separate issue on which the defendant is required to carry the burden of persuasion; and unless we are to overturn *Leland* and *Rivera,* New York has not violated the Due Process Clause, and Patterson's conviction must be sustained.

We are unwilling to reconsider *Leland* and *Rivera.* But even if we were to hold that a State must prove sanity to convict once that fact is put in issue, it would not necessarily follow that a State must prove beyond a reasonable doubt every fact, the existence or nonexistence of which it is willing to recognize as an exculpatory or mitigating circumstance affecting the degree of culpability or the severity of the punishment. Here, in revising its criminal code, New York provided the affirmative defense of extreme emotional disturbance, a substantially expanded version of the older heat-of-passion concept; but it was willing to do so only if the facts making out the defense were established by the defendant with sufficient certainty. The State was itself unwilling to undertake to establish the absence of those facts beyond a reasonable doubt, perhaps fearing that proof would be too difficult and that too many persons deserving treatment as murderers would escape that punishment if the evidence need merely raise a reasonable doubt about the defendant's emotional state. It has been said that the new criminal code of New York contains some 25 affirmative defenses which exculpate or mitigate but which must be established by the defendant to be operative. The Due Process Clause, as we see it, does not put New York to the choice of abandoning those defenses or undertaking to disprove their existence in order to convict of a crime which otherwise is within its constitutional powers to sanction by substantial punishment.

The requirement of proof beyond a reasonable doubt in a criminal case is "bottomed on a fundamental value determination of our society that it is far worse to convict an innocent man than to let a guilty man go free." The social cost of placing the burden on the prosecution to prove guilt beyond a reasonable doubt is thus an increased risk that the guilty will go free. While it is clear that our society has willingly chosen to bear a substantial burden in order to protect the innocent, it is equally clear that the risk it must bear is not without limits; and Mr. Justice Harlan's aphorism provides little guidance for determining what those limits are. Due process does not require that every conceivable step be taken, at whatever cost, to eliminate the possibility of convicting an innocent person. Punishment of those found guilty by a jury, for example, is not forbidden merely because there is a remote possibility in some instances that an innocent person might go to jail.

* * * If the State * * * chooses to recognize a factor that mitigates the degree of criminality or punishment, we think the State may assure itself that the fact has been established with reasonably certainty. To recognize at all a mitigating circumstance does not require the State to prove its non-existence in each case in which the fact is put in issue, if in its judgment this would be too cumbersome, too expensive, and too inaccurate.

We thus decline to adopt as a constitutional imperative, operative countrywide, that a State must disprove beyond a reasonable doubt every fact constituting any and all affirmative defenses related to the culpability of an accused. * * * We * * * will not disturb the balance struck in previous cases holding that the Due Process Clause requires the prosecution to prove beyond a reasonable doubt all of the elements included in the definition of the offense of which the defendant is charged. Proof of the nonexistence of all affirmative defenses has never been constitutionally required; and we perceive no reason to fashion such a rule in this case and apply it to the statutory defense at issue here.

This view may seem to permit state legislatures to reallocate burdens of proof by labeling as affirmative defenses at least some elements of the crimes now defined in their statutes. But there are obviously constitutional limits beyond which the States may not go in this regard. "[I]t is not within the province of a legislature to declare an individual guilty or presumptively guilty of a crime." The legislature cannot "validly command that the finding of an indictment, or mere proof of the identity of the accused, should create a presumption of the existence of all the facts essential to guilt." * * * [T]he fact that a majority of the States have now assumed the burden of disproving affirmative defenses—for whatever reasons—[does not] mean that those States that strike a different balance are in violation of the Constitution.

IV

It is urged that *Mullaney v. Wilbur* necessarily invalidates Patterson's conviction. In *Mullaney* the charge was murder, which the Maine statute defined as the unlawful killing of a human being "with malice aforethought, either express or implied." * * * Malice as the statute indicated and as the court instructed, * * * was to be implied from "any deliberate, cruel act committed by one person against another suddenly * * * or without a considerable provocation," in which event an intentional killing was murder unless by a preponderance of the evidence it was shown that the act was committed "in the heat of passion, on sudden provocation." The instructions emphasized that " 'malice aforethought and heat of passion on sudden provocation are two inconsistent things'; thus, by proving the latter the defendant would negate the former." * * *

* * * This Court, accepting the Maine court's interpretation of the Maine law, unanimously agreed with the Court of Appeals that Wilbur's due process rights had been invaded by the presumption casting upon him the burden of proving by a preponderance of the evidence that he had acted in the heat of passion upon sudden provocation.

Mullaney's holding, it is argued, is that the State may not permit the blameworthiness of an act or the severity of punishment authorized for its commission to depend on the presence or absence of an identified fact without assuming the burden of proving the presence or absence of that fact, as the case may be, beyond a reasonable doubt.[15] In our view, the *Mullaney* holding should not be so broadly read. * * *

Mullaney surely held that a State must prove every ingredient of an offense beyond a reasonable doubt, and that it may not shift the burden of proof to the defendant by presuming that ingredient upon proof of the other elements of the offense. This is true even though the State's practice, as in Maine, had been traditionally to the contrary. Such shifting of the burden of persuasion with respect to a fact which the State deems so important that it must be either proved or presumed is impermissible under the Due Process Clause.

It was unnecessary to go further in *Mullaney*. The Maine Supreme Judicial Court made it clear that malice aforethought, * * * in the sense of the absence of provocation, was part of the definition of that crime. Yet malice, *i.e.*, lack of provocation, was presumed and could be rebutted by the defendant only by proving by a preponderance of the evidence that he acted with heat of passion upon sudden provocation. In *Mullaney* we held that however traditional this mode of proceeding might have been, it is contrary to the Due Process Clause as construed in *Winship*.

As we have explained, nothing was presumed or implied against Patterson; and his conviction is not invalid under any of our prior cases. The judgment of the New York Court of Appeals is [affirmed].

MR. JUSTICE POWELL, with whom MR. JUSTICE BRENNAN and MR. JUSTICE MARSHALL join, dissenting.

In the name of preserving legislative flexibility, the Court today drains *In re Winship* of much of its vitality. Legislatures do require broad discretion in the drafting of criminal laws, but the Court surrenders to the legislative branch a significant part of its responsibility to protect the presumption of innocence.

I * * *

Mullaney held invalid Maine's requirement that the defendant prove heat of passion. The Court today, without disavowing the unanimous

---

15. There is some language in *Mullaney* that has been understood as perhaps construing the Due Process Clause to require the prosecution to prove beyond a reasonable doubt any fact affecting "the degree of criminal culpability." It is said that such a rule would deprive legislatures of any discretion whatsoever in allocating the burden of proof, the practical effect of which might be to undermine legislative reform of our criminal justice system. * * * The Court did not intend *Mullaney* to have such far-reaching effect.

holding of *Mullaney,* approves New York's requirement that the defendant prove extreme emotional disturbance. The Court manages to run a constitutional boundary line through the barely visible space that separates Maine's law from New York's. It does so on the basis of distinctions in language that are formalistic rather than substantive.

This result is achieved by a narrowly literal parsing of the holding in *Winship:* "[T]he Due Process Clause protects the accused against conviction except upon proof beyond a reasonable doubt of every fact necessary to constitute the crime with which he is charged." The only "facts" necessary to constitute a crime are said to be those that appear on the face of the statute as a part of the definition of the crime. Maine's statute was invalid, the Court reasons, because it "defined [murder] as the unlawful killing of a human being 'with malice aforethought, either express or implied.' " "[M]alice," the Court reiterates, "in the sense of the absence of provocation, was part of the definition of that crime." *Winship* was violated only because this "fact"—malice—was "presumed" unless the defendant persuaded the jury otherwise by showing that he acted in the heat of passion. New York, in form presuming no affirmative "fact" against Patterson, and blessed with a statute drafted in the leaner language of the 20th century, escapes constitutional scrutiny unscathed even though the effect on the defendant of New York's placement of the burden of persuasion is exactly the same as Maine's.

This explanation of the *Mullaney* holding bears little resemblance to the basic rationale of that decision. But this is not the cause of greatest concern. The test the Court today establishes allows a legislature to shift, virtually at will, the burden of persuasion with respect to any factor in a criminal case, so long as it is careful not to mention the nonexistence of that factor in the statutory language that defines the crime. The sole requirement is that any references to the factor be confined to those sections that provide for an affirmative defense.

Perhaps the Court's interpretation of *Winship* is consistent with the letter of the holding in that case. But little of the spirit survives. Indeed, the Court scarcely could distinguish this case from *Mullaney* without closing its eyes to the constitutional values for which *Winship* stands. As Mr. Justice Harlan observed in *Winship,* "a standard of proof represents an attempt to instruct the factfinder concerning the degree of confidence our society thinks he should have in the correctness of factual conclusions for a particular type of adjudication." Explaining *Mullaney,* the Court says today, in effect, that society demands full confidence before a Maine factfinder determines that heat of passion is missing—a demand so insistent that this Court invoked the Constitution to enforce it over the contrary decision by the State. But we are told that society is willing to tolerate far less confidence in New York's factual determination of precisely the same functional issue. One must ask what possibly could explain this difference in societal demands. According to the Court, it is because Maine happened to attach a name—"malice aforethought"—to the absence of heat of passion, whereas New York refrained from giving a name to the absence of extreme emotional disturbance.

With all respect, this type of constitutional adjudication is indefensibly formalistic. * * * Nothing in the Court's opinion prevents a legislature from applying this new learning to many of the classical elements of the crimes it punishes.[8] * * *

* * * This decision simply leaves us without a conceptual framework for distinguishing abuses from legitimate legislative adjustments of the burden of persuasion in criminal cases.

II

It is unnecessary for the Court to retreat to a formalistic test for applying *Winship*. Careful attention to the *Mullaney* decision reveals the principles that should control in this and like cases. * * * In *Mullaney* we concluded that heat of passion was one of the "facts" described in *Winship*—that is, a factor as to which the prosecution must bear the burden of persuasion beyond a reasonable doubt. We reached that result only after making two careful inquiries. First, we noted that the presence or absence of heat of passion made a substantial difference in punishment of the offender and in the stigma associated with the conviction. Second, we reviewed the history, in England and this country, of the factor at issue. Central to the holding in *Mullaney* was our conclusion that heat of passion "has been, almost from the inception of the common law of homicide, the single most important factor in determining the degree of culpability attaching to an unlawful homicide."

Implicit in these two inquiries are the principles that should govern this case. The Due Process Clause requires that the prosecutor bear the burden of persuasion beyond a reasonable doubt only if the factor at issue makes a substantial difference in punishment and stigma. * * * But a substantial difference in punishment alone is not enough. It also must be shown that in the Anglo–American legal tradition the factor in question historically has held that level of importance. If either branch of the test is not met, then the legislature retains its traditional authority over matters of proof. * * *

I hardly need add that New York's provisions allocating the burden of persuasion as to "extreme emotional disturbance" are unconstitutional when judged by these standards. "Extreme emotional disturbance" is * * * the direct descendant of the "heat of passion" factor considered at

---

8. For example, a state statute could pass muster under the only solid standard that appears in the Court's opinion if it defined murder as mere physical contact between the defendant and the victim leading to the victim's death, but then set up an affirmative defense leaving it to the defendant to prove that he acted without culpable *mens rea*. The State, in other words, could be relieved altogether of responsibility for proving anything regarding the defendant's state of mind, provided only that the face of the statute meets the Court's drafting formulas.

To be sure, it is unlikely that legislatures will rewrite their criminal laws in this extreme form. * * * But it is completely foreign to this Court's responsibility for constitutional adjudication to limit the scope of judicial review because of the expectation—however reasonable—that legislative bodies will exercise appropriate restraint.

length in *Mullaney*. I recognize, of course, that the differences between Maine and New York law are not unimportant to the defendant; there is a somewhat broader opportunity for mitigation. But none of those distinctions is relevant here. The presence or absence of extreme emotional disturbance makes a critical difference in punishment and stigma, and throughout our history the resolution of this issue of fact, although expressed in somewhat different terms, has distinguished manslaughter from murder. * * *

NOTES AND QUESTIONS

1. *Burden of production.* Two burdens of proof arise in criminal trials. The first is the burden of production (or the "burden of going forward"). The party on whom this burden is placed has the initial obligation to introduce evidence in support of the matter at issue. The prosecutor has the burden of production regarding the elements of a crime; the defendant typically has the burden of production in regard to affirmative defenses. For example, in *Patterson*, the State of New York was required to produce evidence that Patterson caused the death, and that he did so intentionally. Patterson had the burden of producing evidence regarding the affirmative defense of extreme emotional disturbance.

How much evidence must a defendant present to require submission of a defense to the jury? Courts variously require a defendant to present "more than a scintilla" of evidence, "slight evidence," "some credible evidence" or "evidence sufficient to raise a reasonable doubt" in regard to the issue at stake. 1 Paul H. Robinson, Criminal Law Defenses 35–36 (1984).

If a defendant produces sufficient evidence of a defense to require submission of the defense to the jury, the next burden to consider is the burden of *persuasion*, i.e., the burden of convincing the factfinder of the truth of the claim in question. This was the issue in *Winship, Mullaney,* and *Patterson*.

2. *Elements versus defenses.* In Martin v. Ohio, 480 U.S. 228, 107 S.Ct. 1098, 94 L.Ed.2d 267 (1987), *M* killed *V*, her husband. *M* was charged with aggravated murder, defined in part under Ohio law as a killing "purposely, and with prior calculation and design." *M* claimed that she acted in self-defense. Under state law, self-defense contained three elements: (1) the defendant was not at fault in creating the difficulty; (2) the defendant did not violate any duty to avoid killing *V* by retreating; and, most pertinently here, (3), "the defendant had an honest belief that she was in imminent danger of death or great bodily harm."

The judge instructed the jury that the prosecutor had to prove the elements of aggravated murder beyond a reasonable doubt. He also instructed the jury, pursuant to statute, that *M* had to prove self-defense by a preponderance of the evidence. *M* argued that the latter instruction violated the *Winship* doctrine. Look carefully at the statutory definitions of aggravated murder and self-defense set out above. Can you articulate the specific basis of *M*'s due process claim, in light of *Patterson*?

Justice Byron White, speaking for a five-justice majority (and again over the dissent of Justice Powell), rejected the due process claim:

> The State did not * * * seek to shift to [*M*] the burden of proving any of [the] elements [of aggravated murder], and the jury's verdict [of guilt] reflects that none of her self-defense evidence raised a reasonable doubt about the State's proof that she purposefully killed with prior calculation and design. * * *
>
> It would be quite different if the jury had been instructed that self-defense evidence could not be considered in determining whether there was a reasonable doubt about the State's case, *i.e.*, that self-defense evidence must be put aside for all purposes unless it satisfied the preponderance standard. Such an instruction would relieve the State of its burden and plainly run afoul of *Winship*'s mandate. The instructions in this case could be clearer in this respect, but when read as a whole, we think they are adequate to convey to the jury that all of the evidence, including the evidence going to self-defense, must be considered in deciding whether there was a reasonable doubt about the sufficiency of the State's proof of the elements of the crime.

Let's test the Court's assumption that the instructions adequately explained the burden-of-proof issues to the jury. If *you* were a juror, would *you* understand who has the burden of persuasion—and quantum of proof—in regard to: (a) whether *M* killed *V*; (b) whether *M* killed *V* purposely; (c) whether *M* killed *V* with prior calculation and design; (d) whether *M* was at fault in the difficulty; (e) whether *M* should have retreated before killing *V*; and (f) whether *M* honestly believed that she was in imminent danger of death or great bodily harm?

3. Constitutional issues aside, who has the burdens of production and persuasion regarding defenses in Model Penal Code jurisdictions? Consider Sections 1.12 and 1.13(9).

4. *Elements versus sentencing factors.* Many states have devised sentencing systems in which "sentencing facts," if proven to a judge (not a jury) by preponderance of the evidence (not beyond a reasonable doubt) at a post-conviction hearing, may result in more severe punishment of the convicted defendant than would otherwise be permitted. For example, a jurisdiction might define Crime X as containing elements 1, 2, and 3, which if proven beyond a reasonable doubt, may result in a sentence of from 1 to 5 years in prison. But, if the prosecutor proves "sentencing fact" 4 by preponderance of the evidence, in a hearing before the judge after conviction, the defendant may receive a 10–year prison sentence.

Does such a sentencing system violate a defendant's constitutional right to trial by jury and/or her due process right to have "every *fact* necessary to constitute the crime charged" proven beyond a reasonable doubt? The Supreme Court answered both questions affirmatively in Apprendi v. New Jersey, 530 U.S. 466, 120 S.Ct. 2348, 147 L.Ed.2d 435 (2000). It ruled that a defendant has a constitutional right to have any fact (other than the fact of a prior conviction) that would expose her to a sentence beyond the maximum amount provided by the criminal statute in question—and, thus, would subject the defendant to a greater punishment than that authorized by the jury's guilty verdict (as with sentencing fact 4 in the example above)—determined by a jury, and not a judge, and that such fact be proven beyond a reasonable doubt.

C. PRINCIPLES OF JUSTIFICATION

1. STRUCTURE AND UNDERLYING THEORIES OF JUSTIFICATION DEFENSES

1 PAUL H. ROBINSON—CRIMINAL LAW DEFENSES
(1984) § 24(b), pp. 86–88**b**

All justification defenses have the same internal structure:

> *triggering conditions* permit a *necessary* and *proportional response*

Triggering conditions are the circumstances that must exist before an actor will be eligible to act under a justification. For example, in defensive force justifications the justification is triggered if an aggressor presents a threat of unjustified harm to a protected interest, as by attempting to burn the defendant's chicken coop. * * *

The triggering conditions of a justification defense do not give an actor the privilege to act without restriction. To be justified, the responsive conduct must satisfy two requirements:

(1) it must be *necessary* to protect or further the interest at stake, and

(2) it must cause only a harm that is *proportional* or reasonable in relation to the harm threatened or the interest to be furthered.

The *necessity requirement* demands that the defendant act only when and to the extent necessary to protect or further the interest at stake. Thus, where an aggressor announces his intention to assault the actor at noon the next day, the threat provides the triggering condition for self-defense. But, if indeed the actor is in no danger at the time, he is not justified in immediately using physical force against the aggressor. * * *

The *proportionality requirement* places a limit on the maximum harm that may be used in protection or furtherance of an interest. It bars justification when the harm caused by the actor may be necessary to protect or further the interest at stake, but is too severe in relation to the value of the interest. Where an actor has no other option but deadly force to prevent the stealing of apples from her orchard, a jurisdiction that prohibits deadly force to protect property essentially requires the actor to sacrifice her apples out of regard for the thieves' lives.

---

b. Reprinted from Criminal Law Defenses, Paul H. Robinson, copyright © 1984, with permission of the West Publishing Company.

JOSHUA DRESSLER—UNDERSTANDING CRIMINAL LAW

(5th Edition, 2009) 208–211

[A] Searching for an Explanatory Theory

* * * [J]ustified conduct is conduct that under ordinary circumstances is criminal, but which under the special circumstances encompassed by the justification defense is not wrongful and is even, perhaps, affirmatively desirable. A justified act is one that "the law does not condemn, or even welcomes."

* * * What makes ordinarily bad conduct justifiable? Why is it, for example, that *D* is justified in killing *V* to protect herself from *V*'s unlawful lethal assault or from *V*'s intrusion into her home, but that she is not justified in killing *V* to protect her dog or her television set from theft? * * * [I]s there a single moral theory that unifies the various justification defenses—some principle that explains why something bad (socially harmful) becomes good or, at least, tolerable?

It would be convenient if there were a single, unifying principle of justification, but there is none. * * * What follows is a brief summary of various justification principles. * * *

[B] "Public Benefit" Theory

At early common law, justification defenses had a strong public-benefit cast to them. Generally speaking, conduct was not justified unless it was performed in the public's interest, and in most cases was limited to the actions of public officers.

For example, Blackstone identified three sets of circumstances in which homicides were justifiable: (1) when a public officer was commanded to take a life (e.g., when the warden executed a convicted felon); (2) when a public officer, although not commanded to do so, took a life in order to advance the public welfare (e.g., when an officer killed a felon resisting arrest); and (3) when a private party took a life in order to prevent the commission of a forcible, atrocious felony.

A homicide in these circumstances is considered justifiable because society benefits from the actor's conduct. But, there is more to this justification principle: The benefit to society is not incidental to some self-interested goal of the actor; it is the underlying motivation for the actor's conduct. Although strands of the public-benefit concept remain today, it is no longer the dominant theory of justification.

[C] "Moral Forfeiture" Theory

* * * The moral-forfeiture principle of justification * * * is based on the view that people possess certain moral rights or interests that society recognizes through its criminal laws, e.g., the right to life, but which may be forfeited by the holder of the right.

The *forfeiture* of a right must be distinguished from its *waiver*. Some moral interests are not waivable. For example, a person may not legally consent to her own death. The right to life is inviolable in this sense. Nonetheless, even this nonwaivable right can be *forfeited*—nonconsensually lost—as the result of an actor's voluntary decision to violate the rights of another. In such circumstances, society may determine * * * that it will no longer recognize the wrongdoer's interest in her life.

The moral-forfeiture doctrine is frequently called upon to explain why an aggressor or fleeing felon may justifiably be killed: As a result of *V*'s freely-chosen decision to wrongfully threaten *D*'s life or to commit a dangerous felony, *V* forfeits her right to life; consequently, when *D* kills *V* in self-defense or in order to prevent *V*'s escape, no socially recognized harm has occurred. From the law's perspective, *V*'s life is worth no more than that of an insect or inanimate body. * * *

[D] "Moral Rights" Theory

Conduct may be justified on the ground that the actor has a right to protect a particular moral interest. This theory of justification differs significantly from the moral-forfeiture principle described in the preceding subsection. The forfeiture doctrine focuses on the wrongdoing of the "victim" (e.g., the aggressor) whereas the moral-rights theory focuses on the interests of the defendant. Whereas forfeiture works in a negative way to deny that there is a socially protected interest harmed when the wrongdoer is injured or killed, the moral-rights theory works in a positive sense to provide the actor with an affirmative right to protect her threatened moral interest.

For example, when *D* kills or seriously injures *V*, a lethal aggressor, her conduct may be justified because she was enforcing a natural right of autonomy that *V*'s conduct threatened. *D* is a right-holder protecting her interest against *V*, the outlaw who would violate her right. This principle of justification does not treat *V*'s death as socially irrelevant, as the forfeiture doctrine does; rather, it views *D*'s conduct as affirmatively proper. * * *

[E] "Superior Interest" (or "Lesser Harm") Theory

Another theory of justification authorizes conduct when the interests of the defendant outweigh those of the person she harms. Pursuant to this principle, the interests of the parties, and, more broadly, the values that they seek to enforce, are balanced. In each case there is a superior, or at least a non-inferior, interest. As long as such an interest is pursued the conduct is justified.

For example, if *D* trespasses by entering *V*'s house in order to avoid a tornado, her conduct is justified. Protection of human life is more important than property protection. Similarly, the use of nonlethal force upon a lethal aggressor is justifiable because preservation of life is more important than prevention of injury to another. As these examples suggest, the superior-interest theory of justification is consistent with the utilitarian goal of promoting individual conduct that reduces overall harm. It is also consistent with the non-utilitarian concept of weighing moral rights and identifying the superior one.

2. SELF-DEFENSE

a. General Principles

UNITED STATES v. PETERSON

United States Court of Appeals, District of Columbia Circuit, 1973.
483 F.2d 1222.

SPOTTSWOOD W. ROBINSON, III, CIRCUIT JUDGE:

Indicted for second-degree murder, and convicted by a jury of manslaughter as a lesser included offense, Bennie L. Peterson [appeals] * * *. * * * He complains * * * that the judge twice erred in the instructions given the jury in relation to his claim that the homicide was committed in self-defense. One error alleged was an instruction that the jury might consider whether Peterson was the aggressor in the altercation that immediately foreran the homicide. The other was an instruction that a failure by Peterson to retreat, if he could have done so without jeopardizing his safety, might be considered as a circumstance bearing on the question whether he was justified in using the amount of force which he did. * * * [W]e affirm Peterson's conviction.

alleged errors

(1)

(2)

I

The events immediately preceding the homicide are not seriously in dispute. * * * Charles Keitt, the deceased, and two friends drove in Keitt's car to the alley in the rear of Peterson's house to remove the windshield wipers from the latter's wrecked car. While Keitt was doing so, Peterson came out of the house into the back yard to protest. After a verbal exchange, Peterson went back into the house, obtained a pistol, and returned to the yard. In the meantime, Keitt had reseated himself in his car, and he and his companions were about to leave.

Upon his reappearance in the yard, Peterson paused briefly to load the pistol. "If you move," he shouted to Keitt, "I will shoot." He walked to a point in the yard slightly inside a gate in the rear fence and, pistol in hand, said, "If you come in here I will kill you." Keitt alighted from his car, took a few steps toward Peterson and exclaimed, "What the hell do you think you are going to do with that?" Keitt then made an about-face, walked back to his car and got a lug wrench. With the wrench in a raised position, Keitt advanced toward Peterson, who stood with the pistol pointed toward him. Peterson warned Keitt not to "take another step" and, when Keitt continued onward shot him in the face from a distance of about ten feet. Death was apparently instantaneous. * * *

III

More than two centuries ago, Blackstone, best known of the expositors of the English common law, taught that "all homicide is malicious, and of course, amounts to murder, unless * * * *justified* by the command or permission of the law; *excused* on the account of accident or self-preservation; or *alleviated* into manslaughter, by being either the involuntary consequence of some act not strictly lawful, or (if voluntary) occasioned by some sudden and sufficiently violent provocation.''

Tucked within this greatly capsulized schema of the common law of homicide is the branch of law we are called upon to administer today. No issue of justifiable homicide, within Blackstone's definition is involved.[35] But Peterson's consistent position is that as a matter of law his conviction * * * was wrong, and that his act was one of self-preservation—excused homicide. * * *

Self-defense, as a doctrine legally exonerating the taking of human life, is as viable now as it was in Blackstone's time, and in the case before us the doctrine is invoked in its purest form. But ''[t]he law of self-defense is a law of necessity;'' the right of self-defense arises only when the necessity begins, and equally ends with the necessity; and never must the necessity be greater than when the force employed defensively is deadly.[40] The ''necessity must bear all semblance of reality, and appear to admit of no other alternative, before taking life will be justifiable as excusable.'' Hinged on the exigencies of self-preservation, the doctrine of homicidal self-defense emerges from the body of the criminal law as a limited though important exception to legal outlawry of the arena of self-help in the settlement of potentially fatal personal conflicts.

So it is that necessity is the pervasive theme of the well defined conditions which the law imposes on the right to kill or maim in self-defense. There must have been a threat, actual or apparent, of the use of deadly force against the defender. The threat must have been unlawful and immediate. The defender must have believed that he was in imminent peril of death or serious bodily harm, and that his response was necessary to save himself therefrom. These beliefs must not only have been honestly entertained, but also objectively reasonable in light of the surrounding circumstances. It is clear that no less than a concurrence of these elements will suffice. * * *

IV * * *

* * * The first of Peterson's complaints centers upon an instruction that the right to use deadly force in self-defense is not ordinarily available to one who provokes a conflict or is the aggressor in it. Mere words, the judge explained, do not constitute provocation or aggression; and if Peter-

---

35. By the early common law, justification for homicide extended only to acts done in execution of the law, such as homicides in effecting arrests and preventing forcible felonies, and homicides committed in self-defense were only excusable. The distinction between justifiable and excusable homicide was important because in the latter case the slayer, considered to be not wholly free from blame, suffered a forfeiture of his goods. However, with the passage of 24 Henry VIII, ch. 5 (1532), the basis of justification was enlarged, and the distinction has largely disappeared. More usually the terms are used interchangeably, each denoting a legally non-punishable act, entitling the accused to an acquittal.

40. When we speak of deadly force, we refer to force capable of inflicting death or serious bodily harm.

son precipitated the altercation but thereafter withdrew from it in good faith and so informed Keitt by words or acts, he was justified in using deadly force to save himself from imminent danger or death or grave bodily harm. * * * Peterson contends that there was no evidence that he either caused or contributed to the conflict, and that the instructions on that topic could only [have] misled the jury.

It has long been accepted that one cannot support a claim of self-defense by a self-generated necessity to kill. The right of homicidal self-defense is granted only to those free from fault in the difficulty; it is denied to slayers who incite the fatal attack, encourage the fatal quarrel or otherwise promote the necessitous occasion for taking life. The fact that the deceased struck the first blow, fired the first shot or made the first menacing gesture does not legalize the self-defense claim if in fact the claimant was the actual provoker. In sum, one who is the aggressor in a conflict culminating in death cannot invoke the necessities of self-preservation. Only in the event that he communicates to his adversary his intent to withdraw and in good faith attempts to do so is he restored to his right of self-defense.

free from fault

aggressor

withdrawal

This body of doctrine traces its origin to the fundamental principle that a killing in self-defense is excusable only as a matter of genuine necessity. Quite obviously, a defensive killing is unnecessary if the occasion for it could have been averted, and the roots of that consideration run deep with us. * * *

In the case at bar, the trial judge's charge fully comported with these governing principles. The remaining question, then, is whether there was evidence to make them applicable to the case. A recapitulation of the proofs shows beyond peradventure that there was.

It was not until Peterson fetched his pistol and returned to his back yard that his confrontation with Keitt took on a deadly cast. Prior to his trip into the house for the gun, there was, by the Government's evidence, no threat, no display of weapons, no combat. There was an exchange of verbal aspersions and a misdemeanor[57] against Peterson's property[58] was in progress but, at this juncture, nothing more. * * *

The evidence is uncontradicted that when Peterson reappeared in the yard with his pistol, Keitt was about to depart the scene. * * * The uncontroverted fact that Keitt was leaving shows plainly that so far as he was concerned the confrontation was ended. It demonstrates just as plainly that even if he had previously been the aggressor, he no longer was.

Not so with Peterson, however, as the undisputed evidence made clear. Emerging from the house with the pistol, he paused in the yard to load it, and to command Keitt not to move. He then walked through the yard to the rear gate and, displaying his pistol, dared Keitt to come in, and

---

57. It is well settled that deadly force cannot be employed to arrest or prevent the escape of a misdemeanant.

58. The law never tolerates the use of deadly force in the protection of one's property.

no deadly force to protect property

threatened to kill him if he did. While there appears to be no fixed rule on the subject, the cases hold, and we agree, that an affirmative unlawful act reasonably calculated to produce an affray foreboding injurious or fatal consequences is an aggression which, unless renounced, nullifies the right of homicidal self-defense. We cannot escape the abiding conviction that the jury could readily find Peterson's challenge to be a transgression of that character.

aggression defined

The situation at bar is not unlike that presented in *Laney* [294 Fed. 412 (1923)]. There the accused, chased along the street by a mob threatening his life, managed to escape through an areaway between two houses. In the back yard of one of the houses, he checked a gun he was carrying and then returned to the areaway. The mob beset him again, and during an exchange of shots one of its members was killed by a bullet from the accused's gun. In affirming a conviction of manslaughter, the court reasoned:

position of comparative safety

> It is clearly apparent * * * that, when defendant escaped from the mob into the back yard * * * he was in a place of comparative safety, from which, if he desired to go home, he could have gone by the back way, as he subsequently did. The mob had turned its attention to a house on the opposite side of the street. According to Laney's testimony, there was shooting going on in the street. His appearance on the street at that juncture could mean nothing but trouble for him. Hence, when he adjusted his gun and stepped out into the areaway, he had every reason to believe that his presence there would provoke trouble. We think his conduct in adjusting his revolver and going into the areaway was such as to deprive him of any right to invoke the plea of self-defense.

Similarly, in Rowe v. United States [370 F.2d 240 (D.C.Cir.1966)], the accused was in the home of friends when an argument, to which the friends became participants, developed in the street in front. He left, went to his nearby apartment for a loaded pistol and returned. * * * [W]hen a group of five men began to move toward him, he began to shoot at them, killing two, and wounding a third. We observed that the accused "left an apparently safe haven to arm himself and return to the scene," and that "he inflamed the situation with his words to the men gathered there, even though he could have returned silently to the safety of the [friends'] porch." We held that

> [t]hese facts could have led the jury to conclude that [the accused] returned to the scene to stir up further trouble, if not actually to kill anyone, and that his actions instigated the men into rushing him. Self-defense may not be claimed by one who deliberately places himself in a position where he has reason to believe "his presence * * * would provoke trouble."

We noted the argument "that a defendant may claim self-defense if he arms himself in order to proceed upon his normal activities, even if he realizes that danger may await him"; we responded by pointing out "that the jury could have found that the course of action defendant here followed was for an unlawful purpose." We accordingly affirmed his conviction of manslaughter over his objection that an acquittal should have been directed.

We are brought much the readier to the same conclusion here. We think the evidence plainly presented an issue of fact as to whether Peterson's conduct was an invitation to and provocation of the encounter which ended in the fatal shot. We sustain the trial judge's action in remitting that issue for the jury's determination.

V

The second aspect of the trial judge's charge as to which Peterson asserts error concerned the undisputed fact that at no time did Peterson endeavor to retreat from Keitt's approach with the lug wrench. The judge instructed the jury that if Peterson * * * could have safely retreated but did not do so, that failure was a circumstance which the jury might consider, together with all others, in determining whether he went further in repelling the danger, real or apparent, than he was justified in going.

Peterson contends that this imputation of an obligation to retreat was error, even if he could safely have done so. He points out that at the time of the shooting he was standing in his own yard, and argues he was under no duty to move. We are persuaded to the conclusion that in the circumstances presented here, the trial judge did not err in giving the instruction challenged.

Within the common law of self-defense there developed the rule of "retreat to the wall," which ordinarily forbade the use of deadly force by one to whom an avenue for safe retreat was open. This doctrine was but an application of the requirement of strict necessity to excuse the taking of human life, and was designed to insure the existence of that necessity. Even the innocent victim of a vicious assault had to elect a safe retreat, if available, rather than resort to defensive force which might kill or seriously injure.

In a majority of American jurisdictions, contrarily to the common law rule, one may stand his ground and use deadly force whenever it seems reasonably necessary to save himself. While the law of the District of Columbia on this point is not entirely clear, it seems allied with the strong minority adhering to the common law. * * *

That is not to say that the retreat rule is without exceptions. Even at common law it was recognized that it was not completely suited to all situations. Today it is the more so that its precept must be adjusted to modern conditions nonexistent during the early development of the common law of self-defense.[86] One restriction on its operation comes to the

___

86. " * * * Time, place, and conditions may create a situation which would clearly justify a modification of the rule. For example, the common-law rule, which required the assailed to retreat to the wall, had its origin before the general introduction of firearms. If a person is threatened with death or great bodily harm by an assailant, armed with a modern rifle, in open

fore when the circumstances apparently foreclose a withdrawal with safety. The doctrine of retreat was never intended to enhance the risk to the innocent; its proper application has never required a faultless victim to increase his assailant's safety at the expense of his own. On the contrary, he could stand his ground and use deadly force otherwise appropriate if the alternative were perilous, or if to him it reasonably appeared to be. * * *

The trial judge's charge to the jury incorporated [this limit] on the retreat rule. Peterson, however, invokes another—the so-called "castle" doctrine. It is well settled that one who through no fault of his own is attacked in his home is under no duty to retreat therefrom. The oft-repeated expression that "a man's home is his castle" reflected the belief in olden days that there were few if any safer sanctuaries than the home. The "castle" exception, moreover, has been extended by some courts to encompass the occupant's presence within the curtilage outside his dwelling. Peterson reminds us that when he shot to halt Keitt's advance, he was standing in his yard and so, he argues, he had no duty to endeavor to retreat.

Despite the practically universal acceptance of the "castle" doctrine in American jurisdictions wherein the point has been raised, its status in the District of Columbia has never been squarely decided. But whatever the fate of the doctrine in the District law of the future, it is clear that in absolute form it was inapplicable here. The right of self-defense, we have said, cannot be claimed by the aggressor in an affray so long as he retains that unmitigated role. It logically follows that any rule of no-retreat which may protect an innocent victim of the affray would, like other incidents of a forfeited right of self-defense, be unavailable to the party who provokes or stimulates the conflict. Accordingly, the law is well settled that the "castle" doctrine can be invoked only by one who is without fault in bringing the conflict on. That, we think, is the critical consideration here.

We need not repeat our previous discussion of Peterson's contribution to the altercation which culminated in Keitt's death. It suffices to point out that by no interpretation of the evidence could it be said that Peterson was blameless in the affair. * * *

NOTES AND QUESTIONS

1. *Problems.*

A.   Dina ordinarily walks along a particular street in a residential area as part of her daily exercise regimen. One day Arthur, the resident bully, informs her that if she comes that way again he will kill her. Dina could just as conveniently walk along another street, but believing that "I have every right to walk where I choose," she decides the next day to arm herself with a licensed gun and walk along the now forbidden route with her weapon visible

---

space, away from safety, it would be ridiculous to require him to retreat. Indeed, to retreat would be to invite almost certain death." Laney v. United States, *supra.*

to onlookers. Arthur appears and comes toward her menacingly. Dina shoots and kills him. Does she have a valid self-defense claim under *Peterson?* How would Model Penal Code § 3.04 handle these facts?

B.   Defendant invited some friends over for a night of drinking. During the evening, one of his drunk guests passed out, only to awaken to find his wife in bed with the defendant. The guest, in a fit of rage, lunged at the defendant with a knife. The defendant grabbed a gun from beneath his bed and shot the guest dead. Self-defense under *Peterson?* What about under the M.P.C.? See Mark Curriden, *Small–Town Justice,* A.B.A. J., Nov. 1994, at 64.

2.   Suppose that Jim unlawfully throws a punch at Frank, but Frank escalates the affair by pulling a gun on Jim. Does Jim, the initial aggressor, *now* have the right to kill Frank? The Commentary to the Model Penal Code explains the M.P.C. and non-Code approach to this situation:

> The typical case to be imagined is this: *A* attacks *B* with his fists; *B* defends himself, and manages to subdue *A* to the extent of pinning him to the floor. *B* then starts to batter *A*'s head savagely against the floor. *A* manages to rise, and since *B* is still attacking him and *A* now fears that if he is thrown again to the floor he will be killed, *A* uses a knife. *B* is killed or seriously wounded.

> The solution to this situation under the provisions of [Section 3.04] is as follows: *B* is entitled to defend himself against *A*'s attack, but only to the extent of using moderate, nondeadly force. He is given this privilege by Subsection (1). *B* exceeds the bounds of "necessary" force under that provision, however, when, after reducing *A* to helplessness, he batters *A*'s head on the floor. Since this excessive force is, in its turn, unlawful, under Subsection (1) *A* is entitled to defend himself against it and, if he believes that he is then in danger of death or serious bodily harm without apparent opportunity for safe retreat, *A* is also entitled to use his knife in self-protection. *A* of course is criminally liable for his initial battery on *B,* but would have a justifying defense that he could raise against prosecution for the ultimate homicide or wounding. Subsection (2)(b)(i), depriving *A* of his justification on the ground of initial aggression, would not become operative unless *A* entered the encounter with the purpose of causing death or serious bodily harm.

> This conclusion—that an initial aggressor is accountable for his original unlawful use of force but not for his defense against a disproportionate return of force by his victim—is surely not unreasonable on its face. There is, however, * * * authority, both common law and statutory, demanding that a person claiming self-defense be free from fault in bringing on the difficulty. But the principle is not, on the whole, unqualified. The original aggressor is usually deemed to have a right of self-defense that is "imperfect"; before it may be exercised he must give notice of his wish to desist from the struggle and attempt in good faith to withdraw.

American Law Institute, Model Penal Code and Commentaries, Comment to § 3.04 at 49–51 (1985).

3. *The necessity requirement.* As *Peterson* teaches, self-defense has a necessity component. As explained in Stiers v. State, 229 S.W.3d 257 (Mo.App. W.D. 2007), "[t]o warrant the use of deadly force in self-defense, [there] must be present * * * an attempt by the defender to do all within his or her power consistent with his or her own personal safety to avoid the danger and need to take a life." In this regard, consider this case:

In State v. Dill, 461 So.2d 1130 (La.App.1984), the defendant (5'4", 145 lbs.) was in his car, preparing to leave a public parking lot, when the decedent (6'0", 200 lbs.) walked over and requested help to start his own vehicle. The defendant said he would only help if the decedent paid him five dollars. After a verbal exchange, the decedent lunged at the defendant with a knife through the defendant's open car window. The defendant emerged with a gun and immediately shot the decedent in the head. If you were on the jury, would you acquit the defendant on the ground of self-defense? Was the shooting necessary? Did the defendant have any reasonable alternatives?

4. *The imminency requirement.* As *Peterson* states, use of deadly force in unjustifiable at common law unless the actor is responding to actual or apparent "imminent peril of death or serious bodily harm." What is the justification for the imminency requirement?

In what way does the Model Penal Code differ from the common law on this subject? Consider the following scenario devised by Professor Robert Schopp: Two hikers (X and Y) agree to engage in a ten-day race across a desert that contains a single water hole half-way to the finish line. Each racer, therefore, maintains a five or six day supply of water in a canteen, which they intend to replenish at the water hole. During the first few days, Y attempts to sabotage X by changing trail makers and unsuccessfully attempting to steal X's canteen. Schopp's story proceeds:

As day five begins, both hikers are almost out of water * * *. As Y passes X on the trail * * *, Y holds up a box of rat poison and says to X, "I'll get you this time; I'll beat you to the water hole, get my water, and poison the rest * * *." Both hikers walk all day, but due to a sprained ankle X can barely keep up with Y. That evening, * * * Y says, "I'll walk all night and get to the water hole before morning." As Y begins to walk away, X, who is unable to continue that night, says, "wait," but Y walks in the direction of the water hole. X shoots Y, convinced * * * that this is the only way to prevent Y from poisoning the water hole the next morning.

Robert F. Schopp et al., *Battered Woman Syndrome, Expert Testimony, and the Distinction Between Justification and Excuse,* 1994 U. Ill. L. Rev. 45, 66–67.

Does X have a valid self-defense claim under the common law? Model Penal Code?

5. *Retreat.* What are the arguments for and against the retreat rule set out in *Peterson?* Weigh these judicial observations:

Self-defense is measured against necessity. From that premise one could readily say there was no necessity to kill in self-defense if the use of deadly force could have been avoided by retreat. The critics of the retreat rule do not quarrel with the theoretical validity of this conclusion, but rather condemn it as unrealistic. The law of course should not denounce conduct as criminal when it accords with the behavior of reasonable men. Upon this level, the advocates of no-retreat say the manly thing is to hold one's ground, and hence society should not demand what smacks of cowardice. Adherents of the retreat rule reply it is better that the assailed shall retreat than that the life of another be needlessly spent. They add that not only do right-thinking men agree, but further a rule so requiring may well induce others to adhere to that worthy standard of behavior. * * *

We believe the following principles are sound:

1. The issue of retreat arises only if the defendant resorted to a deadly force. It is deadly force which is not justifiable when an opportunity to retreat is at hand. Model Penal Code [§ 3.04(2)(b)(ii)]. As defined in [§ 3.11(2),] a deadly force means "force which the actor uses with the purpose of causing or which he knows to create a substantial risk of causing death or serious bodily harm." * * *

2. What constitutes an opportunity to retreat which will defeat the right of self-defense? As [§ 3.04(2)(b)(ii)] of the Model Penal Code states, deadly force is not justifiable "if the actor *knows* that he can avoid the necessity of using such force *with complete safety* by retreating * * *." We emphasize "knows" and "with complete safety." One who is wrongfully attacked need not risk injury by retreating, even though he could escape with something less than serious bodily injury. It would be unreal to require nice calculations as to the amount of hurt, or to ask him to endure any at all. And the issue is not whether in retrospect it can be found the defendant could have retreated unharmed. Rather the question is whether he knew the opportunity was there, and of course in that inquiry the total circumstances including the attendant excitement must be considered.

State v. Abbott, 36 N.J. 63, 174 A.2d 881 (1961).

6. *The "castle" exception. Peterson* notes that even when a duty to retreat otherwise exists, a person is not required to retreat from her home. But, if retreating makes sense outside the home—and, in any case, is not required if there is no known safe place to which to retreat (see Note 5)—why shouldn't the same principles apply *in* the home, i.e., a person should be required to retreat from her home if, but only if, she can do so safely and thereby prevent the unnecessary death of an aggressor? *[margin handwriting: Castle exception]*

How far should the castle exception extend? Should an innocent person be required to retreat from her home if the aggressor also lives there? Notice Model Code § 3.04(2)(b)(ii)(1) in this regard: an innocent person "is not obliged to retreat from his dwelling or place of work, unless he * * * is assailed in his place of work by another person whose place of work the actor knows it to be." Why do you think the drafters distinguished between *[margin handwriting: MPC]*

[bottom handwriting: wife not required to retreat]

workplaces and dwellings in regard to the scope of the exception? See American Law Institute, Model Penal Code and Commentaries, Comment to § 3.04 at 56 (1985).

7. *The proportionality requirement.* Deadly force may not be used to repel a *non*deadly attack, even if this is the only way to avoid injury. Assume that Joshua unlawfully threatens to strike Donald, and the only way Donald can avoid the blow is to push Joshua away. Donald may be justified in pushing Joshua because the shove is a nondeadly response to a nondeadly assault. However, if the shove would likely cause death or serious bodily injury to Joshua—for example, if Donald pushes him into oncoming traffic on a busy street—then the common law requires Donald to suffer the assault, rather than risk the death of the nondeadly aggressor. Should this be the rule?

[margin note: Proportionality]

8. *Expanding self-defense law.* As a result of public pressure and, in particular, successful lobbying by the National Rifle Association (sometimes over the objection of local prosecutors and police officials), approximately fifteen state legislatures have expanded their self-defense provisions (as well as other defenses relating to the use of deadly force). Adam Liptak, *15 States Expand Victims' Rights on Self Defense*, N.Y. Times, Aug. 7, 2006, at A1. Most of the states have modeled their so-called "Stand Your Ground" laws on one enacted in Florida:

[margin note: Stand your ground law in Florida]

(1) A person is presumed to have held a reasonable fear of imminent peril of death or great bodily harm to himself or herself or another when using [deadly] defensive force * * * if

(a) The person against whom the defensive force was used was in the process of unlawfully and forcefully entering, or had unlawfully and forcibly entered, a dwelling, residence, or occupied vehicle, or if that person had removed or was attempting to remove another against that person's will from the dwelling, residence, or occupied vehicle; * * *

(2) The presumption set forth in subsection (1) does not apply if: * * *

(c) The person who uses defensive force is engaged in an unlawful activity or is using the dwelling, residence, or occupied vehicle to further an unlawful activity * * *

(3) A person who is not engaged in an unlawful activity and who is attacked in any * * * place where he or she has a right to be has no duty to retreat and has the right to stand his or her ground and meet force with force, including deadly force if he or she reasonably believes it is necessary to do so to prevent death or great bodily harm to himself or herself or another or to prevent the commission of a forcible felony. Florida Stat. § 776.013 (2012).

Florida law also provides that, subject to a limited exception, a "person who uses force as permitted in § 776.013 * * * is * * * immune from criminal prosecution and civil action for the use of such force * * *." Florida Stat. § 776.032. This provision grants a defendant a statutory right to a pretrial hearing to assert immunity and avoid being subjected to a trial. Dennis v. State, 51 So.3d 456 (Fla. 2010).

Does this legislation entitle a person in a bar to stand his or her ground and meet force with force, even if she could in complete safety avoid use of deadly force by leaving the bar?

Do you believe the "Stand Your Ground" legislation will deter unlawful aggression, or will it result in unnecessary "shoot-first, ask-questions-later" deaths?

9. *Self-defense: rationale.* In Blackstone's time, killing in self-protection constituted *excusable* homicide, based on "the great universal principle of self-preservation, which prompts every man to save his own life preferably to that of another, where one of them must inevitably perish." 4 Blackstone, Commentaries on the Law of England *186 (1769).

Do you find the claim that a defensive killing is excusable—that the killing is wrong, but the killer should not be blamed for saving his own life—more persuasive than the modern view of the criminal law that the taking of the life of the aggressor is justifiable? If you think that such killings *are* justifiable (at least when they satisfy the requirements set out in *Peterson*), why, *precisely*, is this the case? In this context, consider pp. 479–481 supra.

10. *Self-defense and innocent aggressors: a thought experiment.* Bill, a police officer, is visiting his neighbor on a social visit. Eight-year-old neighbor Alice comes into the living room playing "cops and robbers." The only problem is that Alice has a *real* loaded gun in her possession. She giggles, "I am a robber," and she fires the gun once in the direction of "Cop Bill," missing him. She is about to fire the gun a second time. Bill, aware that he has no place he can safely retreat, and unable to convince Alice to put her gun down, fires his weapon at Alice, killing her. Would you characterize Bill's actions as justifiable? Excusable? Consider whether your answer to this thought experiment conforms with your answers to Note 9. See Laurence A. Alexander, *Justification and Innocent Aggressors,* 33 Wayne L.Rev. 1177 (1987); George P. Fletcher, *Proportionality and the Psychotic Aggressor: A Vignette in Comparative Criminal Theory,* 8 Israel L.Rev. 367 (1973); Mordechai Kremnitzer, *Proportionality and the Psychotic Aggressor: Another View,* 18 Israel L.Rev. 178 (1983).

11. Does it ultimately matter whether "self-defense" is considered a justification or an excuse? The *Peterson* court did not think so (see footnote 35, p. 482 supra). On the other hand, reconsider Part III of the Dressler excerpt (pp. 465–467). As you read the materials that follow, consider where you come out on this question.

b. "Reasonable Belief" Requirement

i. *In General*

The next case describes the facts regarding one of the most publicized and nationally debated criminal (or, at least, allegedly criminal) incidents in the United States in the 1980s. In the center of the controversy was Bernhard Hugo Goetz, better known after this case as Bernie Goetz or, to some, "the subway vigilante."

PEOPLE v. GOETZ

Court of Appeals of New York, 1986.
68 N.Y.2d 96, 506 N.Y.S.2d 18, 497 N.E.2d 41.

CHIEF JUDGE WACHTLER.

A Grand Jury has indicted defendant on attempted murder, assault, and other charges for having shot and wounded four youths on a New York City subway train after one or two of the youths approached him and asked for $5. The lower courts, concluding that the prosecutor's charge to the Grand Jury on the defense of justification was erroneous, have dismissed the attempted murder, assault and weapons possession charges. We now reverse and reinstate all counts of the indictment.

I.

The precise circumstances of the incident giving rise to the charges against defendant are disputed, and ultimately it will be for a trial jury to determine what occurred. We feel it necessary, however, to provide some factual background to properly frame the legal issues before us. Accordingly, we have summarized the facts as they appear from the evidence before the Grand Jury. * * *

Facts given to grand jury

On Saturday afternoon, December 22, 1984, Troy Canty, Darryl Cabey, James Ramseur, and Barry Allen boarded an IRT express subway train in The Bronx and headed south toward lower Manhattan. The four youths rode together in the rear portion of the seventh car of the train. Two of the four, Ramseur and Cabey, had screwdrivers inside their coats, which they said were to be used to break into the coin boxes of video machines.

Defendant Bernhard Goetz boarded this subway train * * * in Manhattan and sat down on a bench towards the rear section of the same car occupied by the four youths. Goetz was carrying an unlicensed .38 caliber pistol loaded with five rounds of ammunition in a waistband holster. * * *

* * * Canty approached Goetz, possibly with Allen beside him, and stated "give me five dollars." Neither Canty nor any of the other youths displayed a weapon. Goetz responded by standing up, pulling out his handgun and firing four shots in rapid succession. The first shot hit Canty in the chest; the second struck Allen in the back; the third went through Ramseur's arm and into his left side; the fourth was fired at Cabey, who apparently was then standing in the corner of the car, but missed, deflecting instead off of a wall of the conductor's cab. After Goetz briefly surveyed the scene around him, he fired another shot at Cabey, who then was sitting on the end bench of the car. The bullet entered the rear of Cabey's side and severed his spinal cord.

All but two of the other passengers fled the car when, or immediately after, the shots were fired. The conductor, who had been in the next car, heard the shots and instructed the motorman to radio for emergency assistance. The conductor then went into the car where the shooting occurred and saw Goetz sitting on a bench, the injured youths lying on the floor or slumped against a seat, and two women who had apparently taken cover, also lying on the floor. Goetz told the conductor that the four youths had tried to rob him.

While the conductor was aiding the youths, Goetz * * * jumped onto the tracks and fled. * * * Ramseur and Canty, initially listed in critical condition, have fully recovered. Cabey remains paralyzed, and has suffered some degree of brain damage.

On December 31, 1984, Goetz surrendered to police in Concord, New Hampshire * * *. Goetz admitted that he had been illegally carrying a handgun in New York City for three years. He stated that he had first purchased a gun in 1981 after he had been injured in a mugging. Goetz also revealed that twice between 1981 and 1984 he had successfully warded off assailants simply by displaying the pistol.

According to Goetz's statement, the first contact he had with the four youths came when Canty, sitting or lying on the bench across from him, asked "how are you," to which he replied "fine." Shortly thereafter, Canty, followed by one of the other youths, walked over to the defendant and stood to his left, while the other two youths remained to his right, in the corner of the subway car. Canty then said "give me five dollars." Goetz stated that he knew from the smile on Canty's face that they wanted to "play with me." Although he was certain that none of the youths had a gun, he had a fear, based on prior experiences, of being "maimed."

Goetz then established "a pattern of fire," deciding specifically to fire from left to right. His stated intention at that point was to "murder [the four youths], to hurt them, to make them suffer as much as possible." When Canty again requested money, Goetz stood up, drew his weapon, and began firing, aiming for the center of the body of each of the four. Goetz recalled that the first two he shot "tried to run through the crowd [but] they had nowhere to run." Goetz then turned to his right to "go after the other two." One of these two "tried to run through the wall of the train, but * * * he had nowhere to go." The other youth (Cabey) "tried pretending that he wasn't with [the others]" by standing still, holding on to one of the subway hand straps, and not looking at Goetz. Goetz nonetheless fired his fourth shot at him. He then ran back to the first two youths to make sure they had been "taken care of." Seeing that they had both been shot, he spun back to check on the latter two. Goetz noticed that the youth who had been standing still was now sitting on a bench and seemed unhurt. As Goetz told the police, "I said '[y]ou seem to be all right, here's another'," and he then fired the shot which severed Cabey's spinal cord. Goetz added that "if I was a little more under self-control * * * I would have put the barrel against his forehead and fired." He also admitted that "if I had had more [bullets], I would have shot them again, and again, and again."

II.   * * *

* * * [T]he * * * Grand Jury filed a 10–count indictment, containing four charges of attempted murder, four charges of assault in the first degree, one charge of reckless endangerment in the first degree, and one charge of criminal possession of a weapon in the second degree. * * *

* * * Goetz moved to dismiss the charges * * * alleging, among other things, * * * that the prosecutor's instructions to that Grand Jury on the defense of justification were erroneous * * *.

[The trial court] * * * granted Goetz's motion * * *. The court, after inspection of the Grand Jury minutes, * * * held * * * that the prosecutor, in * * * elaborating upon the justification defense, had erroneously introduced an objective element into this defense by instructing the grand jurors to consider whether Goetz's conduct was that of a "reasonable man in [Goetz's] situation". The court * * * concluded that the statutory test for whether the use of deadly force is justified to protect a person should be wholly subjective, focusing entirely on the defendant's state of mind when he used such force. It concluded that dismissal was required for this error because the justification issue was at the heart of the case. * * *

On appeal by the People, a divided Appellate Division affirmed [the] dismissal of the charges. * * *

III.

Penal Law article 35 recognizes the defense of justification, which "permits the use of force under certain circumstances." One such set of circumstances pertains to the use of force in defense of a person, encompassing both self-defense and defense of a third person. Penal Law § 35.15(1) sets forth the general principles governing all such uses of force: "[a] person may * * * use physical force upon another person when and to the extent he *reasonably believes* such to be necessary to defend himself or a third person from what he *reasonably believes* to be the use or imminent use of unlawful physical force by such other person" (emphasis added).

Section 35.15(2) sets forth further limitations on these general principles with respect to the use of "deadly physical force": "A person may not use deadly physical force upon another person under circumstances specified in subdivision one unless (a) He *reasonably believes* that such other person is using or about to use deadly physical force * * * or (b) He *reasonably believes* that such other person is committing or attempting to commit a kidnapping, forcible rape, forcible sodomy or robbery" (emphasis added).

Thus, consistent with most justification provisions, Penal Law § 35.15 permits the use of deadly physical force only where requirements as to triggering conditions and the necessity of a particular response are met. As to the triggering conditions, the statute requires that the actor "reasonably believes" that another person either is using or about to use deadly physical force or is committing or attempting to commit one of certain enumerated felonies, including robbery. As to the need for the use of deadly physical force as a response, the statute requires that the actor "reasonably believes" that such force is necessary to avert the perceived threat.

Because the evidence before the * * * Grand Jury included statements by Goetz that he acted to protect himself from being maimed or to avert a robbery, the prosecutor correctly chose to charge the justification defense in section 35.15 to the Grand Jury. * * *

When the prosecutor had completed his charge, one of the grand jurors asked for clarification of the term "reasonably believes." The prosecutor responded by instructing the grand jurors that they were to consider the circumstances of the incident and determine "whether the defendant's conduct was that of a reasonable man in the defendant's situation." It is this response by the prosecutor—and specifically his use of "a reasonable man"—which is the basis for the dismissal of the charges by the lower courts. As expressed repeatedly in the Appellate Division's plurality opinion, because section 35.15 uses the term "*he* reasonably believes," the appropriate test, according to that court, is whether a defendant's beliefs and reactions were "reasonable *to him.*" Under that reading of the statute, a jury which believed a defendant's testimony that he felt that his own actions were warranted and were reasonable would have to acquit him, regardless of what anyone else in defendant's situation might have concluded. Such an interpretation defies the ordinary meaning and significance of the term "reasonably" in a statute, and misconstrues the clear intent of the Legislature, in enacting section 35.15, to retain an objective element as part of any provision authorizing the use of deadly physical force.

Penal statutes in New York have long codified the right recognized at common law to use deadly physical force, under appropriate circumstances, in self-defense. These provisions have never required that an actor's belief as to the intention of another person to inflict serious injury be correct in order for the use of deadly force to be justified, but they have uniformly required that the belief comport with an objective notion of reasonableness. * * *

In 1961 the Legislature established a Commission to undertake a complete revision of the Penal Law and the Criminal Code. * * * The drafting of the general provisions of the new Penal Law, including the article on justification, was particularly influenced by the Model Penal Code. While using the Model Penal Code provisions on justification as general guidelines, however, the drafters of the new Penal Law did not simply adopt them verbatim.

The provisions of the Model Penal Code with respect to the use of deadly force in self-defense reflect the position of its drafters that any culpability which arises from a mistaken belief in the need to use such force should be no greater than the culpability such a mistake would give rise to if it were made with respect to an element of a crime. Accordingly, under Model Penal Code § 3.04(2)(b), a defendant charged with murder (or attempted murder) need only show that he *"believe[d]* that [the use of deadly force] was necessary to protect himself against death, serious bodily injury, kidnapping or [forcible] sexual intercourse" to prevail on a self-defense claim (emphasis added). If the defendant's belief was wrong, and was recklessly, or negligently formed, however, he may be convicted of the type of homicide charge requiring only a reckless or negligent, as the case may be, criminal intent (*see,* Model Penal Code § 3.09[2]).

The drafters of the Model Penal Code recognized that the wholly subjective test set forth in section 3.04 differed from the existing law in most States by its omission of any requirement of reasonableness. * * *

New York did not follow the Model Penal Code's equation * * * choosing instead to use a single statutory section which would provide either a complete defense or no defense at all to a defendant charged with any crime involving the use of deadly force. The drafters of the new Penal Law adopted in large part the structure and content of Model Penal Code § 3.04, but, crucially, inserted the word "reasonably" before "believes."

The plurality below agreed with defendant's argument that the change in the statutory language from "reasonable ground," used prior to 1965, to "he reasonably believes" in Penal Law § 35.15 evinced a legislative intent to conform to the subjective standard contained in Model Penal Code § 3.04. This argument, however, ignores the plain significance of the insertion of "reasonably." Had the drafters of section 35.15 wanted to adopt a subjective standard, they could have simply used the language of section 3.04. * * *

We cannot lightly impute to the Legislature an intent to fundamentally alter the principles of justification to allow the perpetrator of a serious crime to go free simply because that person believed his actions were reasonable and necessary to prevent some perceived harm. To completely exonerate such an individual, no matter how aberrational or bizarre his thought patterns, would allow citizens to set their own standards for the permissible use of force. It would also allow a legally competent defendant suffering from delusions to kill or perform acts of violence with impunity, contrary to fundamental principles of justice and criminal law.

We can only conclude that the Legislature retained a reasonableness requirement to avoid giving a license for such actions. * * *

Goetz also argues that the introduction of an objective element will preclude a jury from considering factors such as the prior experiences of a given actor and thus, require it to make a determination of "reasonableness" without regard to the actual circumstances of a particular incident. This argument, however, falsely presupposes that an objective standard means that the background and other relevant characteristics of a particular actor must be ignored. To the contrary, we have frequently noted that a determination of reasonableness must be based on the "circumstances" facing a defendant or his "situation." Such terms encompass more than the physical movements of the potential assailant. As just discussed, these terms include any relevant knowledge the defendant had about that person. They also necessarily bring in the physical attributes of all persons involved, including the defendant. Furthermore, the defendant's circumstances encompass any prior experiences he had which could provide a reasonable basis for a belief that another person's intentions were to injure or rob him or that the use of deadly force was necessary under the circumstances. * * *

Accordingly, the order of the Appellate Division should be reversed, and the dismissed counts of the indictment reinstated.

NOTES AND QUESTIONS

1. *Some background.* At the time of the incident, New York City was experiencing unprecedented rates of crime, well above the national average, and the City's subways were the source of considerable crime and fear of it. A New York Times poll found that half of the City's residents considered crime the "worst thing about living in the city, and also that many think it justifies taking matters into their own hands." Robert D. McFadden, *Poll Indicates Half of New Yorkers See Crime as City's Chief Problem*, New York Times, Jan. 14, 1985.

2. Why did the prosecutor, rather than a judge, instruct the grand jurors on the law of self-defense? The answer lies in the fact that judges are not present during grand jury proceedings. A prosecutor presides: she subpoenas the witnesses whom she believes will provide relevant testimony in the investigation; she questions them in the jurors' presence; and, at the conclusion of the investigation, she instructs the grand jurors on the relevant law. The jurors then determine if there is probable cause to issue an indictment against one or more persons for a crime.

3. *The aftermath.* Goetz was tried by a jury composed of eight men and four women, ten whites and two African–Americans. The jury acquitted Goetz of all charges in the indictment except for possession of a concealed weapon, for which he received a one-year jail sentence. At his sentencing, Goetz told the judge, "I do feel that this case is really more about deterioration in society than it is about me." Anthony M. DeStefano, *Goetz Resentenced, Starts 1–Year Jail Term At Rikers,* Newsday, Jan. 14, 1989, at 3. Goetz was released from jail after eight months. For a fascinating analysis of the case, see George P. Fletcher, A Crime of Self Defense (1988).

In 1996, in a new chapter of the story, a six-member civil jury of four African–Americans and two Hispanics ordered Goetz to pay Darrell Cabey, paralyzed in the shooting, $18 million in compensatory damages and $25 million in punitive damages. Adam Nossiter, *Bronx Jury Orders Goetz to Pay $43 Million to Shooting Victim*, New York Times, April 24, 1996, at A1. Goetz thereafter declared bankruptcy and, in 2004, claimed that he had not "paid a penny" of the judgment.

4. *Making sense of the verdict.* Why did the jury acquit Goetz of attempted murder of the four youths? What message did the jury implicitly send by its verdict? Professor Stephen Carter believes that Goetz's attorney,

and maybe the jurors, had one picture of Goetz, whereas the public that praised Goetz had another:

> As folk hero, * * * Bernhard Goetz is ultimately a disturbing figure. Even Mr. Goetz's defense painted him as something less than heroic. The defense was weakest on the issue of why he fired a second shot at a helpless Darrel Cabey * * *. [Goetz's] defense attorney offered a version of events in which, once the gun was drawn, Mr. Goetz's self-preserving instinct took command. Matters moved so quickly that his instinct would not let him stop * * *. In other words, his mind was not in control; he did not know what he was doing.

> The jury plainly accepted the rapid-fire theory as a reasonable explanation of Mr. Goetz's behavior. Mr. Goetz's public, however, the millions who apparently believe that they would have done precisely what he did and that the punks he shot got what they deserved, does not base its enthusiasm on the understanding he was out of control. On the contrary, the notion that he was *in* control is part of the appeal of the situation. To his public, Mr. Goetz was cool and calculating, showing the courage that millions of others would wish for themselves.

Stephen L. Carter, *When Victims Happen to be Black,* 97 Yale L.J. 420, 422–23 (1988).

Does the "rapid fire" theory fit within self-defense doctrine?

A juror in the case has offered his own explanation of why the jurors acquitted Goetz. He focused on self-defense law itself:

> According to the law, explained by [the judge], once the implied threat of deadly force is present a person can shoot to defend himself if he cannot retreat "with complete safety." When a person is confronted by two or more persons within the close confines of a moving subway car, a strong argument can be made that the person's safety is not ensured. I believe that a truly reasonable person with a proper respect for the sanctity of human life should do more than Goetz did to try to avoid shooting preemptively. Nothing more, however, is required by the law.

Mark Lesley & Charles Shuttleworth, Subway Gunman: A Juror's Account of the Bernhard Goetz Trial 315 (1988).

5. *Making sense of the verdict—again.* In their own study of a hypothetical case patterned on *Goetz* (the "beleaguered commuter"case), two scholars found that "persons of egalitarian and communitarian worldviews, and persons who describe[d] themselves as liberals or Democrats, [were] more likely to convict than persons of hierarchical and individualist views, and those who describe[d] themselves as conservatives or Republicans." Dan M. Kahan & Donald Braman, *The Self–Defensive Cognition of Self–Defense,* 45 Am. Crim. L. Rev. 1, 44–45 (2008). However, the reason for this dichotomy, they claim, is *not* that jurors and the public in general "willfully overid[e] their perception of doctrinally relevant facts to satisfy their partisan values."

Rather, consistent with the dynamic of self-defensive cognition, they are subconsciously relying on their values to determine what the facts are. Confronted with factual disputes, individuals are motivated to adopt (and to persist in) the beliefs that cohere best with their defining cultural and ideological commitments, both to avoid a form of dissonance and to protect their connection to others who share their values.

Id. at 62.

6. *What does the "reasonable person" think about in a New York subway?* According to the court—and in your opinion—are any of the following matters relevant in determining whether a reasonable person would have believed that the youths intended to seriously harm Goetz: (1) that two of the youths were armed with screwdrivers; (2) that Goetz had previously been mugged; (3) the clothing worn by the youths (for example, if they had been dressed in suits and ties or, on the other hand, in clothing identified with gangs in the area); (4) that one of the youths said, "give me five dollars"; (5) that the victims were young, African–American males; and (6) that Goetz was a middle-aged white male. Are there other matters that you, as a reasonable person, would have taken into consideration if you had been in Goetz's shoes?

7. *Race and the "reasonable person."* The Goetz incident provoked considerable discussion regarding the racial overtones of the case, the question of whether a reasonable person ever takes race into consideration in deciding whether to use force in an ambiguous situation, and even whether "reasonable racist" is an oxymoron. Consider the following three perspectives:

Richard Cohen, Closing the Door on Crime, Washington Post Magazine, Sept. 7, 1986, at W13 [written before the criminal trial began]: In order to be admitted to certain Washington jewelry stores, customers have to ring a bell. The ring-back that opens the door is almost perfunctory. According to the owner of one store, only one type of person does not get admitted: Young black males. The owner says they are the ones who stick him up.

Nearby is a men's clothing shop—upscale, but not really expensive. When young black males enter this store, the sales help are instructed to leave their customers and, in the manner of defensive backs in football, "collapse" on the blacks. Politely, but firmly, they are sort of shooed out of the store. The owner's explanation for this? Young blacks are his shoplifters.

Are these examples of racism? The shopkeepers either think so or think they can be accused of it. * * *

Interestingly, though, a black colleague of mine thinks otherwise. He, too, would turn away young blacks if he owned a jewelry store, although he said he would make his judgments on more than race, sex and youth. He would also take into account such factors as dress and even walk. * * * For the record, though, another black colleague called the policies "racist"—a label she applied to black store owners who follow similar practices.

As for me, I'm with the store owners, although I was not at first. It took Bernhard Goetz, of all people, to expose my sloppy thinking. * * *

It was reasonable for Goetz to assume that he was about to be mugged. The youths asked for money, which, in New York and elsewhere, is just a boilerplate precede to a mugging. It was then that Goetz reportedly pulled his gun and shot them all—one allegedly in the back as the youth lay on the subway floor. You would have a hard time making the case that the last alleged squeeze of the trigger was "reasonable."

But how about the rest of his actions? There were some who yelled at the time that Goetz was motivated by racism—that he would not have pulled either the gun or its trigger if his putative assailants had been white. Maybe. But * * * [e]specially in cities like Washington and New York, the menace comes from young black males. Both blacks and whites believe those young black males are the ones most likely to bop them over the head. In the Goetz case, it matters not at all that the four men he shot had extensive arrest records. Goetz had no way of knowing that. As far as he was concerned, the four youths wore their records on their faces.

The Goetz case has its own complications * * *, but the factors present are the same the Washington storekeepers take into account when they decide how to treat a customer. Like Goetz, they are reacting out of fear to a combination of race, youth and sex. * * *

Of course, all policies based on generalities have their injustices. A storekeeper might not know that the youths he has refused to admit are theology students—rich ones at that. But then insurance companies had no way of knowing I was not a typical teen-age driver. I paid through the nose anyway.

A nation with our history is entitled to be sensitive to race and racism—and we are all wary of behavior that would bring a charge of racism. But the mere recognition of race as a factor—especially if those of the same race recognized the same factor—is not in itself racism. * * * Let he who would open the door throw the first stone.

Rosemary L. Bray, It's Ten O'clock and I Worry About Where My Husband Is, Glamour, April 1990, at 302: He phoned more than an hour ago, to say he was on his way home. But I have yet to hear the scrape of the iron gate, the rattling keys, so I worry.

Most married women fret about a tardy husband; young black women like myself worry more. For most people in New York—truth be told—the urban bogeyman is a young black man in sneakers. But we live in Central Harlem, where every young man is black and wears sneakers, so we learn to look into the eyes of young males and discern the difference between youthful bravado and the true dangers of the streets. No, I have other fears. I fear white men in police uniforms; white teenagers driving by in a car with Jersey plates; thin panicky, middle-aged white men on the subway. Most of all, I fear that their path and my husband's path will cross one night as he makes his way home.

Bob is tall—5'10" or so, dark, with thick hair and wire-rimmed glasses. He carries a knapsack stuffed with work from the office, old crossword puzzles, Philip Glass tapes, *Ebony Man* and *People* magazines. When it rains, he carries his good shoes in the bag and wears his Reebok sneakers. He cracks his knuckles a lot, and wears a peculiar grimace when his mind is elsewhere. He looks dear and gentle to me—but then, I have looked into those eyes for a long time.

I worry that some white person will see that grim, focused look of concentration and see the intent to victimize. I fear that some white person will look at him and see only his or her nightmare—another black man in sneakers. In fact, my husband *is* another black man in sneakers. He's also a writer, an amateur cyclist, a lousy basketball player, his parents' son, my life's companion. When I put aside the book I'm reading to peek out the window, the visions in my head are those of blind white panic at my husband's black presence, visions of a flashing gun, a gleaming knife: I see myself a sudden, horrified widow at thirty-four.

Once upon a time, I was vaguely ashamed of my paranoia about his safety in the world outside our home. After all, he is a grown man. But he is a grown black man on the streets alone, a menace to white New Yorkers—even the nice, sympathetic, liberal ones who smile at us when we're together. And I am reminded, over and over, how dangerous white people still can be, how their fears are a hazard to our health. When white people are ruled by their fears of everything black, every black woman is an addict, a whore; every black man is a rapist—even a murderer. * * *

So when it's ten o'clock and he's not home yet, my thoughts can't help but wander to other black men—husbands, fathers, sons, brothers—who never do make it home, and to other black women whose fingers no longer rest at a curtain's edge. Even after I hear the scrape of our iron gate, the key in the lock, even after I hear that old knapsack hit the floor of the downstairs hallway and Bob's voice calling to me, my thoughts return to them.

Jody D. Armour, Race Ipsa Loquitur: Of Reasonable Racists, Intelligent Bayesians, and Involuntary Negrophobes, 46 Stan.L.Rev. 781, 787–90, 792–93, 795–96, 799–800, 802–803 (1994): The Reasonable Racist asserts that, even if his belief that blacks are "prone to violence" stems from pure prejudice, he should be excused for considering the victim's race before using force because most similarly situated Americans would have done so as well. For inasmuch as the criminal justice system operates on the assumption that "blame is reserved for the (statistically) deviant," an individual racist in a racist society cannot be condemned for an expression of human frailty as ubiquitous as racism.

With regard to his claim that average Americans share his fear of black violence, the Reasonable Racist can point to evidence such as a 1990 University of Chicago study which found that over 56 percent of Americans consciously believe that blacks tend to be "violence prone." Moreover, numerous recent news stories chronicle the widespread exclusion of blacks from shops and taxicabs by anxious storekeepers and cabdrivers, many of whom openly admit to making race-based assessments of the danger posed by prospective patrons. Few would want to agree with the Reasonable Racist's assertion that every white person in America harbors racial animus as he does; nonetheless, it is unrealistic to dispute the depressing conclusion that, for many Americans, crime has a black face.

The flaw in the Reasonable Racist's self-defense claim lies in his primary assumption that the sole objective of criminal law is to punish those who deviate from statistically defined norms. For even if the "typical" American believes that blacks' "propensity" toward violence justifies a quicker and more forceful response when a suspected assailant is black, this fact is legally significant only if the law defines *reasonable* beliefs as *typical* beliefs. The reasonableness inquiry, however, extends beyond typicality to consider the social interests implicated in a given situation. Hence not all "typical" beliefs are per se reasonable. * * *

* * * With respect to race, prevailing beliefs and attitudes may fall short of what we can fairly expect of people from the standpoint of * * * "social morality." If we accept that racial discrimination violates contemporary social morality, then an actor's failure to overcome his racism for the sake of another's health, safety, and personal dignity is blameworthy and thus unreasonable, independent of whether or not it is "typical." Although in most cases the beliefs and reactions of typical people reflect what may fairly be expected of a particular actor, this rule of thumb should not be transformed into or confused with a normative or legal principle. Nevertheless, this is precisely the error the "Reasonable Racist" makes in claiming that the moral norm implicit in the objective test of reasonableness extends no further than the proposition that "blame is reserved for the (statistically) deviant." * * *

A second argument which a defendant may advance to justify acting on race-based assumptions is that, given statistics demonstrating blacks' disproportionate involvement in crime, it is reasonable to perceive a greater threat from a black person than a white person. Walter Williams, a conservative black economist, refers to such an individual an "Intelligent Bayesian," named for Sir Thomas Bayes, the father of statistics. * * * While the Reasonable Racist explicitly admits his prejudice and bases his claim for exoneration on the prevalence of racial animus, the Intelligent Bayesian invokes the "objectivity" of numbers. * * *

Even if we accept the Bayesian's claim that his greater fear of blacks results wholly from his unbiased analysis of crime statistics, biases in the criminal justice system undermine the reliability of the statistics themselves. A *Harvard Law Review* survey of race and the criminal process, for example, found that "[a]n examination of empirical studies suggests * * * that racial discrimination by police officers in choosing whom to arrest most likely causes arrest statistics to exaggerate what differences might exist in crime patterns between blacks and whites, thus making any reliance on arrest patterns misplaced." Consequently, although the rate of robbery arrests among blacks is roughly twelve times that of nonblacks, it does not necessarily follow that a particular black person is twelve times more likely to be a robber than a nonblack.

Although biases in the criminal justice system exaggerate the differences in rates of violent crime by race, it may, tragically, still be true that blacks commit a disproportionate number of crimes. Given that the blight of institutional racism continues to disproportionately limit the life chances of African–Americans, and that desperate circumstances increase the likelihood that individuals caught in this web may turn to desperate undertakings, such a disparity, if it exists, should sadden but not surprise us. * * *

To the extent that socioeconomic status explains the overinvolvement of blacks in robbery and assault (assuming that there is, in fact, such overinvolvement), race serves merely as a proxy for socioeconomic status. But if race is a proxy for socioeconomic factors, then race loses its predictive value when one controls for those factors. Thus, if an individual is walking through an impoverished, "crime-prone neighborhood," * * * and if he has already weighed the character of the neighborhood in judging the dangerousness of his situation, then it is illogical for him to consider the racial identity of the person whose suspicious footsteps he hears. For he has already taken into account the socioeconomic factors for which race is a proxy, and considering the racial identity of the ambiguous person under such circumstances constitutes * * * "doublecounting." * * *

Ultimately, race-based evidence of reasonableness impairs the capacity of jurors to rationally and fairly strike a balance between the costs of waiting (increased risk for the person who perceives imminent attack) and the costs of not waiting (injury or death to the immediate victim, exclusion of blacks from core community activities, and, ultimately, reduction of individuals to predictable objects). * * *

* * * And surely a paragon of rational thinking like the Intelligent Bayesian would not press for the admission of evidence that subverts the rationality of the factfinding process. * * *

* * * In contrast to both the "Reasonable Racist" * * * and the "Intelligent Bayesian" * * *, [is] fear [that may] emerge[] after a violent personal assault [perpetrated by a person of color.] To what extent, then, should "involuntary negrophobia" be relevant to claims of self-defense?

Suppose [that a] patron [at an ATM machine, at night, shoots a] young black man [she observes in the shadows, who is dressed in a trench coat with an upturned collar and a hat pulled down even with his eyes, and who makes a movement to pull something out from his coat. Suppose further that the patron] had been mugged by black teenagers nine months before the * * * shooting. Suppose further that after the mugging she developed what her psychiatrist diagnosed as a post-traumatic stress disorder, triggered by contact with blacks, which induced her to overestimate the black victim's threat [at the ATM machine] on the night of the shooting. Under these circumstances, the defendant could claim that her admittedly paranoid fear of the young black victim was "reasonable" for someone mugged in the past by black assailants.

* * * The doctrinal foundation of the negrophobe's claim is the widely accepted "subjective" test of reasonableness, which takes into account both the defendant's past experiences and the psychological effects of those experiences. Under this standard of reasonableness, the factfinder compares the defendant's judgments not to those of a typical person drawn from the general population, but to those of a person *in the situation* of the defendant. The defendant's "situation" * * * includes not only the immediate circumstances of the fatal encounter, but also the psychological effects of experiences that she has undergone prior to the fatal encounter. Thus, as long as a "typical" person could develop the same misperceptions as did the defendant under exposure to the same external forces, the defendant's misperceptions will be found reasonable.* * *

* * * [We ought to be] concerned * * * were the courts to sanction the claim that race-based fear can be so involuntary as to provide a basis of exculpation. * * *

* * * Blacks, already concerned with a perceived dual standard operating in the court system, would justifiably perceive the courts' crediting of such claims as the advent of a new legal loophole potentially enabling racists to express their venomous prejudices without consequence. Furthermore, to the extent that the legal system signals to either reasonable or "pathological" racists that they may act without fear of serious consequences, it may ultimately inhibit blacks' full participation in society.

8.   Would it be desirable in a case such as *Goetz* to require juries *not* to ignore race, but rather to focus on it, but in a different way? Should a judge in her instructions to the jury require them to do "race-switching," i.e., to ask themselves whether, if the races of the defendant and the victim were switched, they would see the homicide in a different light? Consider:

> For example, if a White male defendant has killed a Black man and claims he acted in self-defense, there is a danger that the Black-as-Criminal stereotype will bias the jury in favor of the defendant. Encouraging jurors to think about whether they would feel the defendant acted reasonably in self-defense if he was Black and his victim White, all other facts the same, would help illuminate the role of race and racial stereotypes.

Cynthia Lee, Murder and the Reasonable Man: Passion and Fear in the Criminal Courtroom 224 (2003).

9.   *"Reasonable belief": justification or excuse?* Contemplate the following standard jury instruction regarding the "reasonable belief" rule:

> If the defendant had reasonable grounds to believe and actually did believe that he was in imminent danger of death or serious bodily harm and that deadly force was necessary to repel such danger, he would be justified in using deadly force in self-defense, even though it may afterwards have turned out that the appearances were false. If these requirements are met he could use deadly force even though there was in fact neither purpose on the part of the person to kill him or do him serious bodily harm, nor imminent danger that it would be done, nor actual necessity that deadly force be used in self-defense.

Fresno Rifle and Pistol Club, Inc. v. Van de Kamp, 746 F.Supp. 1415 (E.D.Cal.1990) (quoting E. Devitt and C. Blackmar, Federal Jury Instructions § 41.20 (3d ed. 1977)).

How can it ever be justifiable to kill an innocent person, i.e., an apparent aggressor who actually means no harm? Some scholars contend that conduct is unjustifiable unless it is objectively right, i.e., unless the person against whom self-defensive action is taken *in fact* represents an imminent, unlawful threat. When a person acts on the basis of false (albeit reasonable) appearances, these commentators would *excuse* the actor, rather than justify the conduct. See George P. Fletcher, Rethinking Criminal Law 762–69 (1978); Paul H. Robinson, *A Theory of Justification: Societal Harm as a Prerequisite for Criminal Liability,* 23 UCLA L.Rev. 266, 271–73, 283–84 (1975).

Are these commentators correct? Can you defend the common law and modern rule that killing in "self-defense" is justified based on reasonable (even, if incorrect) appearances? See Joshua Dressler, *New Thoughts About the Concept of Justification in the Criminal Law: A Critique of Fletcher's*

Thinking and Rethinking, 32 UCLA L.Rev. 61, 92–95 (1984); Kent Greenawalt, *Distinguishing Justifications From Excuses,* 49 Law & Contemp. Probs., Summer, 1986, at 89, 93–96, 101–03.

Does this dispute have practical implications? Suppose that Eunice reasonably, but incorrectly, believes that Violet is about to kill her. If Eunice pulls out a gun in order to kill Violet in "self-defense," may Violet kill *her* in self-defense? Why might Violet's right of self-defense depend on whether Eunice's claim is treated as a justification or an excuse?

[handwritten margin note: Eunice & Violet]

10. *Unreasonable belief: "imperfect" defense?* The negative implication of the reasonable-belief rule is that a person who acts on the basis of a genuine, but *unreasonable,* belief that deadly force is necessary for self-protection cannot successfully claim self-defense. Thus, an actor who mistakenly kills an innocent person or who uses more force than necessary to combat real aggression will be acquitted if her mistake was reasonable, but will be convicted of murder if her mistake was unreasonable. Is this a sensible solution?

[handwritten margin note: imperfect defense]

Many states now recognize "imperfect" or "incomplete" justification defenses. In these jurisdictions, a defendant is guilty of manslaughter, rather than murder, if she kills the decedent while harboring a genuine, but unreasonable, belief that the decedent constitutes an imminent threat to her life. E.g., In re Christian S., 7 Cal.4th 768, 30 Cal.Rptr.2d 33, 872 P.2d 574 (1994). How does the Model Penal Code handle this situation? See Sections 3.04 and 3.09.

Some states recognize an imperfect defense in other circumstances. For example, various jurisdictions allow a defendant to claim an imperfect defense if she uses deadly force in response to a nondeadly assault. E.g., State v. Clark, 69 Kan. 576, 77 P. 287 (1904). Other states allow the imperfect defense "where the homicide would fall within the perfect self defense doctrine but for the fault of the defendant in provoking or initiating the difficulty at the nondeadly force level." State v. Faulkner, 301 Md. 482, 489, 483 A.2d 759, 763 (1984); see also State v. McAvoy, 331 N.C. 583, 417 S.E.2d 489 (1992).

11. *Self-defense and innocent bystanders.* When Goetz shot the four youths, innocent subway passengers were sitting nearby. Suppose that an errant bullet from Goetz's gun had struck and killed one of the bystanders. Should Goetz's self-defense claim against the youths apply in a prosecution for the death of the bystander? How would the Model Penal Code answer this question? See Sections 3.04 and 3.09. *[handwritten: Reason for taking risk factored into analysis]*

[handwritten margin note: innocent bystanders]

[handwritten margin note: transferred intent]

12. *Self-defense and innocent shields.* In July, 2005, José Paul Pena engaged members of the Los Angeles Police Department in a street shootout. Pena fired forty shots at the officers, who fired ninety bullets at Pena even though he was holding his 19–month–old daughter, Susie Marie, as a shield. Police bullets struck and killed both Pena and his daughter. John M. Broder, *Man and Young Daughter Die in Shootout With Police,* N.Y. Times, July 12, 2005, at A20; John M. Broder, *Child in Shootout Was Killed by Police, Officials Say,* N.Y. Times, July 14, 2005, at A14. Focusing here only on the officer whose bullet killed Susie Marie Pena, would that officer have a valid self-defense claim if he were prosecuted for the infant's death? Apply the MPC.

[handwritten margin note: shield hypo]

ii. The "Reasonable Person": Objective, Subjective, or a Mixed Standard?

STATE v. WANROW

Supreme Court of Washington, 1977.
88 Wash.2d 221, 559 P.2d 548.

UTTER, ASSOCIATE JUSTICE.

Yvonne Wanrow was convicted by a jury of second-degree murder * * *. She appealed her conviction * * *.

Facts

On the afternoon of August 11, 1972, defendant's (respondent's) two children were staying at the home of Ms. Hooper, a friend of defendant. Defendant's son was playing in the neighborhood and came back to Ms. Hooper's house and told her that a man tried to pull him off his bicycle and drag him into a house. Some months earlier, Ms. Hooper's 7–year–old daughter had developed a rash on her body which was diagnosed as venereal disease. Ms. Hooper had been unable to persuade her daughter to tell her who had molested her. It was not until the night of the shooting that Ms. Hooper discovered it was William Wesler (decedent) who alleged- ly had violated her daughter. A few minutes after the defendant's son related his story to Ms. Hooper about the man who tried to detain him, Mr. Wesler appeared on the porch of the Hooper house and stated through the door, "I didn't touch the kid, I didn't touch the kid." At that moment, the Hooper girl, seeing Wesler at the door, indicated to her mother that Wesler was the man who had molested her. Joseph Fah, Ms. Hooper's landlord, saw Wesler as he was leaving and informed Shirley Hooper that Wesler had tried to molest a young boy who had earlier lived in the same house, and that Wesler had previously been committed to the Eastern State Hospital for the mentally ill. Immediately after this revelation from Mr. Fah, Ms. Hooper called the police who, upon their arrival at the Hooper residence, were informed of all the events which had transpired that day. Ms. Hooper requested that Wesler be arrested then and there, but the police stated, "We can't, until Monday morning." Ms. Hooper was urged by the police officer to go to the police station Monday morning and "swear out a warrant." Ms. Hooper's landlord, who was present during the conversation, suggested that Ms. Hooper get a baseball bat located at the corner of the house and "conk him over the head" should Wesler try to enter the house uninvited during the weekend. To this suggestion, the policeman replied, "Yes, but wait until he gets in the house." (A week before this incident Shirley Hooper had noticed someone prowling around her house at night. Two days before the shooting someone had attempted to get into Ms. Hooper's bedroom and had slashed the window screen. She suspected that such person was Wesler.)

That evening, Ms. Hooper called the defendant and asked her to spend the night with her in the Hooper house. At that time she related to Ms. Wanrow the facts we have previously set forth. The defendant arrived sometime after 6 p.m. with a pistol in her handbag. The two women ultimately determined that they were too afraid to stay alone and decided to ask some friends to come over for added protection. The two women then called the defendant's sister and brother-in-law, Angie and Chuck Michel. The four adults did not go to bed that evening, but remained awake talking and watching for any possible prowlers. There were eight young children in the house with them. At around 5 a.m., Chuck Michel, without the knowledge of the women in the house, went to Wesler's house, carrying a baseball bat. Upon arriving at the Wesler residence, Mr. Michel accused Wesler of molesting little children. Mr. Wesler then suggested that they go over to the Hooper residence and get the whole thing straightened out. Another man, one David Kelly, was also present, and together the three men went over to the Hooper house. Mr. Michel and Mr. Kelly remained outside while Wesler entered the residence.

The testimony as to what next took place is considerably less precise. It appears that Wesler, a large man who was visibly intoxicated, entered the home and when told to leave declined to do so. A good deal of shouting and confusion then arose, and a young child, asleep on the couch, awoke crying. The testimony indicates that Wesler than approached this child, stating, "My what a cute little boy," or words to that effect, and that the child's mother, Ms. Michel, stepped between Wesler and the child. By this time Hooper was screaming for Wesler to get out. Ms. Wanrow, a 5'4" woman who at the time had a broken leg and was using a crutch, testified that she then went to the front door to enlist the aid of Chuck Michel. She stated that she shouted for him and, upon turning around to reenter the living room, found Wesler standing directly behind her. She testified to being gravely startled by this situation and to having then shot Wesler in what amounted to a reflex action. * * *

Reversal of respondent's conviction is * * * required by a * * * serious error committed by the trial court. * * *

In the opening paragraph of instruction No. 10, the jury, in evaluating the gravity of the danger to the respondent, was directed to consider only those acts and circumstances occurring "at or immediately before the killing * * *."[7] This is not now, and never has been, the law of self-defense in Washington. On the contrary, the justification of self-defense is to be evaluated in light of *all* the facts and circumstances known to the defendant, including those known substantially before the killing.

In *State v. Ellis*, 30 Wash. 369, 70 P. 963 (1902), this court reversed a first-degree murder conviction obtained under self-defense instructions quite similar to that in the present case. The defendant sought to show that the deceased had a reputation and habit of carrying and using deadly weapons when engaged in quarrels. The trial court instructed that threats

---

7. [The first paragraph of instruction] No. 10 reads:

"To justify killing in self-defense, there need be no actual or real danger to the life or person of the party killing, but there must be, or reasonably appear to be, at or immediately before the killing, some overt act, or some circumstances which would reasonably indicate to the party killing that the person slain, is, at the time, endeavoring to kill him or inflict upon him great bodily harm.["]

were insufficient justification unless " 'at the time of the alleged killing the deceased was making or immediately preceding the killing had committed some overt act * * *' " This court found the instruction "defective and misleading", stating * * *[:]

> [I]t is apparent that a man who habitually carries and uses such weapons in quarrels must cause greater apprehension of danger than one who does not bear such reputation * * * The vital question is the reasonableness of the defendant's apprehension of danger * * * The jury are [sic] entitled to stand as nearly as practicable in the shoes of defendant, and from this point of view determine the character of the act.

Thus, circumstances predating the killing by weeks and months were deemed entirely proper, and in fact essential, to a proper disposition of the claim of self-defense. * * *

The second paragraph of instruction No. 10 contains an equally erroneous and prejudicial statement of the law. That portion of the instruction reads:

> However, when there is no reasonable ground for the person attacked to believe that *his* person is in imminent danger of death or great bodily harm, and it appears to *him* that only an ordinary battery is all that is intended, and all that *he* has reasonable grounds to fear from *his* assailant, *he* has a right to stand *his* ground and repel such threatened assault, yet *he* has no right to repel a threatened assault with naked hands, by the use of a deadly weapon in a deadly manner, unless *he* believes, *and has reasonable grounds* to believe, that *he* is in imminent danger of death or great bodily harm.

gendered instruction

(Italics ours.) In our society women suffer from a conspicuous lack of access to training in and the means of developing those skills necessary to effectively repel a male assailant without resorting to the use of deadly weapons. Instruction No. 12 does indicate that the "relative size and strength of the persons involved" may be considered; however, it does not make clear that the defendant's actions are to be judged against her own subjective impressions and not those which a detached jury might determine to be objectively reasonable. * * *

The second paragraph of instruction No. 10 not only establishes an objective standard, but through the persistent use of the masculine gender leaves the jury with the impression the objective standard to be applied is that applicable to an altercation between two men. The impression created—that a 5′4″ woman with a cast on her leg and using a crutch must, under the law, somehow repel an assault by a 6′2″ intoxicated man without employing weapons in her defense, unless the jury finds her determination of the degree of danger to be objectively reasonable—constitutes a separate and distinct misstatement of the law and, in the context of this case, violates the respondent's right to equal protection of the law. The respondent was entitled to have the jury consider her actions in the light of her own perceptions of the situation, including those perceptions which were the product of our nation's "long and unfortunate history of sex discrimination." *Frontiero v. Richardson*, 411 U.S. 677, 684, 93 S.Ct. 1764, 1769, 36 L.Ed.2d 583 (1973). Until such time as the effects of that history are eradicated, care must be taken to assure that our self-defense instructions afford women the right to have their conduct judged in light of the individual physical handicaps which are the product of sex discrimination. To fail to do so is to deny the right of the individual woman involved to trial by the same rules which are applicable to male defendants. The portion of the instruction above quoted misstates our law in creating an objective standard of "reasonableness." It then compounds that error by utilizing language suggesting that the respondent's conduct must be measured against that of a reasonable male individual finding himself in the same circumstances. * * *

We conclude that the instruction here in question contains an improper statement of the law on a vital issue in the case * * * and therefore is a proper basis for a finding of reversible error.

Finally, * * * the trial court cannot be said to have abused its discretion in this case in declining to allow defendant's counsel to call an expert witness to present opinion evidence on the effects of defendant's Indian culture upon her perception and actions. * * *

* * * [T]he conviction [is] reversed, and the case remanded for a new trial.

NOTES AND QUESTIONS

1. *Aftermath.* Upon remand, the Government sought to prosecute Wanrow again for second-degree murder, but this time on a felony-murder theory—the predicate felony being the assault upon Wesler. Prior to the second trial, Wanrow moved to have the felony-murder charge dismissed on the ground that the felony assault merged with the homicide and, therefore, could not serve as a basis for the prosecution. (See generally p. 326, supra.) The trial court denied the motion. The state supreme court ultimately affirmed the trial court's ruling, holding that Washington had no felony-murder merger rule. State v. Wanrow, 91 Wn. 301, 588 P.2d 1320 (1978). Wanrow subsequently pled guilty to manslaughter and was placed on five years' probation.

2. In view of the court's ruling about the relevance of Wanrow's gender, why was her Native American culture irrelevant?

3. *Explaining the outcome.* Susan Estrich, Getting Away With Murder 39 (1998):

So why did the jury convict? The sexism in the instruction * * * seems the least persuasive explanation. A mother protecting her young? What could be a more conventionally acceptable reason for deadly force, even in the old common law days? It goes back as far as the jealous-husband defense. You couldn't find a sexist man alive who doesn't think his wife should kill the SOB. And this woman is on crutches, to boot.

Estrich hypothesizes that the jury may have convicted Wanrow because of a 911 tape played to the jury in which Wanrow all-too-coolly reported the killing. Another scholar, as well, has raised the possibility that the events in *Wanrow* did not occur as the defense claimed:

> The facts of *Wanrow* are quite * * * bizarre. The victim had been invited into a house in which the defendant, Wanrow, was staying precisely because she was afraid of [Wesler]. The ostensible purpose of the invitation [to Wesler] was to straighten the victim out, but the two men who were to do this "straightening" were outside the house at the time, leaving Wanrow and her small children alone in the house with one other woman. * * * It somewhat staggers the imagination to believe that a putative child molester, called into a house at 5 a.m. * * *, which he knew was surrounded by several men with weapons, would act in any way which would [cast] even suspicion upon him.

Richard Singer, *The Resurgence of Mens Rea: II–Honest but Unreasonable Mistake of Fact in Self Defense,* 28 B.C.L.Rev. 459, 498 n. 214 (1987).

4. Did the court correctly characterize the opening paragraph of Instruction 10: Does it actually direct jurors to consider only those acts and circumstances occurring at or immediately prior to the killing? If this is not its import, what do you think the trial judge had in mind?

5. Under *Wanrow,* is a woman's reaction to apparent aggression measured by the standard of a "reasonable woman" or according to her own subjective impression of what is reasonable under the circumstances?

6. *Feminist commentary on Wanrow. Wanrow* is treated by some commentators as "a case central to feminist commentary on self-defense." Shirley Sagawa, Note, *A Hard Case for Feminists: People v. Goetz,* 10 Harv.Wom.L.J. 253, 268 (1987). But, is the case really feminist in its perspective: Does the court's discussion of the effects of sex discrimination on women improperly "play on the stereotype of victimized and mistreated women that has historically limited women's claims for equal treatment and suggest that the court's responsiveness to Yvonne Wanrow's claim was shaped by patriarchal solicitude"? Elizabeth M. Schneider, *Describing and Changing: Women's Self–Defense Work and the Problem of Expert Testimony on Battering,* 9 Women's Rts.L.Rep. 195, 214 (1986).

7. According to Professor Victoria Nourse, *After the Reasonable Man: Getting Over the Subjectivity/Objectivity Question,* 11 New Crim. L. Rev. 33, 49 (2008), the "reasonable woman" standard in *Wanrow* has costs,

> including a vast amount of backlash, and acceptance of a far weaker kind of equality than might have been achieved with a stronger frontal assault on the law's double standards.

> For men to judge women by the standards of men, given that gender identity is in part constructed by the use of violence, is to create a double standard. To the extent the "reasonable woman" standard fought that tendency, it must be considered a victory. But it is not a victory without cost. Long before the reasonable woman standard appeared on the scene, the law said that characteristics such as the defendant's height and weight and prior violent encounters between the parties were relevant to

self-defense claims. Why then did women need a special "subjective woman" standard? They needed it because * * * [without it] the jury was more likely to ask the wrong question (would a man, following male norms of use of violence, have felt the need to use violence in an intimate relationship?) than the right question (if men in the O.K. Corral could use violence at the movement of a finger, why shouldn't she be able to use violence?). Without some kind of corrective, there is every reason to believe that the jury will not see women as "legitimate" users of violence, and instead apply a rule that emphasizes their stereotypical role as pacifist caretakers.

8. Some feminist commentators believe that traditional self-defense rules are male-oriented and, therefore, unfair to women who kill men, especially abusive men:

> Although, as compared to men, women rarely kill, it is significant that when women do kill, they frequently kill men whom they knew well, often husbands or lovers. * * * It has been said that female homicide is so different from male homicide that women and men may be said to live in two difficult cultures, each with its own "subculture of violence." If this is true then it should come as no surprise that laws created to address male homicide * * * do not adequately address circumstances under which women kill. * * *

> * * * The traditional elements of self-defense are based on the paradigm of an encounter between two men of roughly equal physical size and ability. The traditional model anticipates a one-time attack/defense. The defendant is threatened with an attack that could potentially result in serious bodily harm or death and therefore is justified in protecting himself. This model presumes that the authorities will step in at the first possible opportunity; therefore, the defendant only need defend himself as far as is necessary, at that moment, to keep the aggressor at bay.

> This model * * * does not accommodate a scenario that includes repeated attacks over time (battering), nor does it need to because men are not, in significant numbers, subjected to repeated and vicious physical abuse during the course of their *everyday lives*. This definition of "necessity" does not contemplate having to live in an environment dominated by regular, vicious, physical abuse without the possibility of intervention or recourse to the law. Since necessity does not contemplate living with such physical abuse, the possibility of a fundamental right to a life *free from abuse* never enters into the equation that balances the rights of the attacker against the rights of a woman to preserve her physical integrity.

Deborah Kochan, *Beyond the Battered Woman Syndrome: An Argument for the Development of New Standards and the Incorporation of a Feminine Approach to Ethics*, 1 Hastings Women's L.J. 89, 95–98 (1989).

In light of these observations, should women who kill men be held to a different set of legal standards of self-defense than men who kill other men? Specifically, should a woman (but not a man) be permitted to use a deadly weapon to repel nondeadly force? Professor Susan Estrich reflected on this question in her review of a book by Cynthia Gillespie [Justifiable Homicide: Battered Women, Self–Defense and the Law (1989)]:

In Gillespie's view, in a point she repeats often, [self-defense] rules were designed to define "manly behavior." But that is not so, really. In many cases, the rules exist not so much to define manly behavior as to limit manly instincts—in order to preserve human life.

It might be "manly" to respond to a slight or an insult with deadly force, but the requirement that the threat be one of death or serious bodily harm does not permit it. Similarly, the imminence requirement is at least intended as a limit on vigilante revenge for attacks on one's family that occurred hours or days before. The retreat requirement is opposed by many precisely because it limits the manly instinct to stand one's ground and fight; it calls on men, and I think appropriately so, to sacrifice this aspect of manhood to the preservation of human life.

This is not to say that the automatic, unthinking application of these requirements to fights between men and women, or husbands and wives in particular, does not raise potential problems. The effect of the rule disallowing deadly response where nondeadly force is threatened may be particularly harsh for women, for their alternatives may be more limited. To expect or demand that women, who are likely to be smaller and less adept with their fists than most men, respond like schoolboys in the yard when attacked may be to leave them utterly without defenses.

A similar problem arises in rape law, where the requirement of force has been defined according to a woman's response, and where her failure to "fight back" in traditional, schoolboy terms—to use her hands or her fists to resist an unarmed man—leads some courts to conclude that there must have been no force in the first instance. But the answer, it seems to me, is a great deal easier in rape law: I have argued, as other have, that a woman should not be required to fight back with her hands and fists, that it should be enough if she *says* no, and that a man who proceeds in the face of such verbal resistance may fairly be held to have used force.

The hard question in self-defense cases, however, is not whether it will suffice for a woman to use *less* force than her male attacker; it is whether she is privileged to use more, to use deadly force when he may not. It is easy to characterize the current rule as one written by men and for men. But what should the rule for women be? Should a woman be privileged to respond to a fist with a gun? Cynthia Gillespie seems to say yes; indeed, she almost assumes it. But would she let a small, diminutive man do the same? Would she let a woman respond that way to the attack of her strong and aggressive sister? Should we? For me, at least, Gillespie's automatic response is not always so automatic; it requires careful consideration of the individual woman and the individual facts.

Susan Estrich, *Defending Women,* 88 Mich.L.Rev. 1430, 1431–32 (1990).

iii. *Battered Women, Battered Woman Syndrome and Beyond*

According to estimates from the National Crime Victimization survey, there were just fewer than 700,000 nonfatal violent cases of intimate partner violence in the year 2001. A disproportionate number of the victims were women. On average between 2001 and 2005, nonfatal intimate partner victimizations represented 22% of all nonfatal violent victimizations against females age 12 or older, and 4% against males age 12 or older. Bureau of Justice Statistics, Intimate Partner Violence in the U.S. (Dec. 2007, NCJ 210675).

STATE v. NORMAN

Court of Appeals of North Carolina, 1988.
89 N.C.App. 384, 366 S.E.2d 586.

PARKER, JUDGE.

* * * The primary issue presented on this appeal is whether the trial court erred in failing to instruct on self-defense. We answer in the affirmative and grant a new trial.

FACTS

At trial the State presented the testimony of a deputy sheriff * * * who testified that * * * he was dispatched to the Norman residence. There, in one of the bedrooms, he found decedent, John Thomas "J.T." Norman (herein decedent or Norman) dead, lying on his left side on a bed. The State presented an autopsy report, stipulated to by both parties, concluding that Norman had died from two gunshot wounds to the head. The deputy sheriff also testified that * * * defendant told the officer that decedent, her husband, had been beating her all day, that she went to her mother's house nearby and got a .25 automatic pistol, that she returned to her house and loaded the gun, and that she shot her husband [while he slept.] * * *

Defendant's evidence, presented through several different witnesses, disclosed a long history of verbal and physical abuse leveled by decedent against defendant. Defendant and Norman had been married twenty-five years at the time of Norman's death. Norman was an alcoholic. He had begun to drink and to beat defendant five years after they were married. The couple had five children, four of whom are still living. When defendant was pregnant with her youngest child, Norman beat her and kicked her down a flight of steps, causing the baby to be born prematurely the next day.[c]

Norman, himself, had worked one day a few months prior to his death; but aside from that one day, witnesses could not remember his ever working. Over the years and up to the time of his death, Norman forced defendant to prostitute herself every day in order to support him. If she begged him not to make her go, he slapped her. Norman required defendant to make a minimum of one hundred dollars per day; if she failed to make this minimum, he would beat her.

---

c. According to the state supreme court, "[t]he defendant said her husband's abuse occurred only when he was intoxicated, but that he would not give up drinking. She said she and her husband 'got along well when he was sober,' and that he was 'a good guy' when he was not drunk."

Norman commonly called defendant "Dogs," "Bitches," and "Whores," and referred to her as a dog. Norman beat defendant "most every day," especially when he was drunk and when other people were around, to "show off." He would beat defendant with whatever was handy—his fist, a fly swatter, a baseball bat, his shoe, or a bottle; he put out cigarettes on defendant's skin; he threw food and drink in her face and refused to let her eat for days at a time; and he threw glasses, ashtrays, and beer bottles at her and once smashed a glass in her face. Defendant exhibited to the jury scars on her face from these incidents. Norman would often make defendant bark like a dog, and if she refused, he would beat her. He often forced defendant to sleep on the concrete floor of their home and on several occasions forced her to eat dog or cat food out of the dog or cat bowl.

Norman often stated both to defendant and to others that he would kill defendant. He also threatened to cut her heart out.

Witnesses for the defense also testified to the events in the thirty-six hours prior to Norman's death. On or about the morning of 10 June 1985, Norman forced defendant to go to a truck stop or rest stop on Interstate 85 in order to prostitute to make some money. * * * Some time later that day, Norman went to the truck stop, apparently drunk, and began hitting defendant in the face with his fist and slamming the car door into her. He also threw hot coffee on defendant. On the way home, Norman's car was stopped by police, and he was arrested for driving under the influence.

When Norman was released from jail the next morning, on 11 June 1985, he was extremely angry and beat defendant. Defendant's mother said defendant acted nervous and scared. Defendant testified that during the entire day, when she was near him, her husband slapped her, and when she was away from him, he threw glasses, ashtrays, and beer bottles at her. Norman asked defendant to make him a sandwich; when defendant brought it to him, he threw it on the floor and told her to make him another. Defendant made him a second sandwich and brought it to him; Norman again threw it on the floor, telling her to put something on her hands because he did not want her to touch the bread. Defendant made a third sandwich using a paper towel to handle the bread. Norman took the third sandwich and smeared it in defendant's face.

On the evening of 11 June 1985, at about 8:00 or 8:30 p.m., a domestic quarrel was reported at the Norman residence. The officer responding to the call testified that defendant was bruised and crying and that she stated her husband had been beating her all day and she could not take it any longer. The officer advised defendant to take out a warrant on her husband, but defendant responded that if she did so, he would kill her. A short time later, the officer was again dispatched to the Norman residence. There he learned that defendant had taken an overdose of "nerve pills," and that Norman was interfering with emergency personnel who were trying to treat defendant. Norman was drunk and was making statements such as, " 'If you want to die, you deserve to die. I'll give you more pills,' " and " 'Let the bitch die * * *. She ain't nothing but a dog. She don't deserve to live.' " Norman also threatened to kill defendant, defendant's mother, and defendant's grandmother. * * * Defendant was taken to Rutherford Hospital.

The therapist on call at the hospital that night stated that defendant was angry and depressed and that she felt her situation was hopeless.[d] On the advice of the therapist, defendant did not return home that night, but spent the night at her grandmother's house.

The next day, 12 June 1985, the day of Norman's death, Norman was angrier and more violent with defendant than usual. According to witnesses, Norman beat defendant all day long. Sometime during the day, Lemuel Splawn, Norman's best friend, called Norman and asked Norman to drive with him to Spartanburg, where Splawn worked, to pick up Splawn's paycheck. Norman arrived at Splawn's house some time later. Defendant was driving. During the ride to Spartanburg, Norman slapped defendant for following a truck too closely and poured a beer on her head. Norman kicked defendant in the side of the head while she was driving and told her he would " 'cut her breast off and shove it up her rear end.' "

Later that day, one of the Normans' daughters, Loretta, reported to defendant's mother that her father was beating her mother again. Defendant's mother called the sheriff's department, but no help arrived at that time. Witnesses stated that back at the Norman residence, Norman threatened to cut defendant's throat, threatened to kill her, and threatened to cut off her breast. Norman also smashed a doughnut on defendant's face and put out a cigarette on her chest.

In the late afternoon, Norman wanted to take a nap. He lay down on the larger of the two beds in the bedroom. Defendant started to lie down on the smaller bed, but Norman said, " 'No bitch * * * Dogs don't sleep on beds, they sleep in [sic] the floor.' " Soon after, one of the Normans' daughters, Phyllis, came into the room and asked if defendant could look after her baby. Norman assented. When the baby began to cry, defendant took the child to her mother's house, fearful that the baby would disturb Norman. At her mother's house, defendant found a gun. She took it back to her home and shot Norman.

Defendant testified that things at home were so bad she could no longer stand it. She explained that she could not leave Norman because he would kill her. She stated that she had left him before on several occasions and that each time he found her, took her home, and beat her. She said that she was afraid to take out a warrant on her husband because he had said that if she ever had him locked up, he would kill her when he got out. She stated she did not have him committed because he told her he would see the authorities coming for him and before they got to him he would

---

d. According to the state supreme court, the therapist also testified "that the defendant threatened a number of times that night to kill her husband and that she said she should kill him because of the things he had done to her."

cut defendant's throat. Defendant also testified that when he threatened to kill her, she believed he would kill her if he had the chance.

The defense presented the testimony of two expert witnesses in the field of forensic psychology, Dr. William Tyson and Dr. Robert Rollins. Based on an examination of defendant and an investigation of the matter, Dr. Tyson concluded that defendant "fits and exceeds the profile, of an abused or battered spouse." Dr. Tyson explained that in defendant's case the situation had progressed beyond mere " 'Wife battering or family violence' " and had become "torture, degradation and reduction to an animal level of existence, where all behavior was marked purely by survival * * *." Dr. Tyson stated that defendant could not leave her husband because she had gotten to the point where she had no belief whatsoever in herself and believed in the total invulnerability of her husband. He stated, "Mrs. Norman didn't leave because she believed, fully believed that escape was totally impossible * * *. She fully believed that [Norman] was invulnerable to the law and to all social agencies that were available; that nobody could withstand his power. As a result, there was no such thing as escape." Dr. Tyson stated that the incidences of Norman forcing defendant to perform prostitution and to eat pet food from pet dishes were parts of the dehumanization process. Dr. Tyson analogized the process to practices in prisoner-of-war camps in the Second World War and the Korean War.

When asked if it appeared to defendant reasonably necessary to kill her husband, Dr. Tyson responded, "I think Judy Norman felt that she had no choice, both in the protection of herself and her family, but to engage, exhibit deadly force against Mr. Norman, and that in so doing, she was sacrificing herself, both for herself and for her family."

Dr. Rollins was defendant's attending physician at Dorothea Dix Hospital where she was sent for a psychiatric evaluation after her arrest. Based on an examination of defendant, laboratory studies, psychological tests, interviews, and background investigation, Dr. Rollins testified that defendant suffered from "abused spouse syndrome." Dr. Rollins defined the syndrome in the following way:

> The "abused spouse syndrome" refers to situations where one spouse has achieved almost complete control and submission of the other by both psychological and physical domination. It's, to start with, it's usually seen in the females who do not have a strong sense of their own adequacy who do not have a lot of personal or occupational resources; it's usually associated with physical abuse over a long period of time, and the particular characteristics that interest us are that the abused spouse comes to believe that the other person is in complete control; that they themselves are worthless and they cannot get away; that there's no rescue from the other person.

When asked, in his opinion, whether it appeared reasonably necessary that defendant take the life of J.T. Norman, Dr. Rollins responded, "In my opinion, that course of action did appear necessary to Mrs. Norman."

However, Dr. Rollins stated that he found no evidence of any psychotic disorder * * *.

LEGAL ANALYSIS * * *

The question * * * arising on the facts in this case is whether the victim's passiveness at the moment the [homicidal] act occurred precludes defendant from asserting * * * self-defense.

Applying the criteria of * * * self-defense to the facts of this case, we hold that the evidence was sufficient to submit an issue of * * * self-defense to the jury. An examination of the elements of * * * self-defense reveals that both subjective and objective standards are to be applied in making the crucial determinations. The first requirement that it appear to defendant and that defendant believe it necessary to kill the deceased in order to save herself from death or great bodily harm calls for a subjective evaluation. This evaluation inquires as to what the defendant herself perceived at the time of the shooting. The trial was replete with testimony of forced prostitution, beatings, and threats on defendant's life. The defendant testified that she believed the decedent would kill her, and the evidence showed that on the occasions when she had made an effort to get away from Norman, he had come after her and beat her. * * * Both experts testified that in their opinion, defendant believed killing the victim was necessary to avoid being killed. This evidence would permit a finding by a jury that defendant believed it necessary to kill the victim to save herself from death or serious bodily harm.

Unlike the first requirement, the second element of self-defense—that defendant's belief be reasonable * * *—is measured by the objective standard of the person of ordinary firmness under the same circumstances. Again, the record is replete with sufficient evidence to permit but not compel a juror, representing the person of ordinary firmness, to infer that defendant's belief was reasonable under the circumstances in which she found herself. Both expert witnesses testified that defendant exhibited severe symptoms of battered spouse syndrome, a condition that develops from repeated cycles of violence by the victim against the defendant. Through this repeated, sometimes constant, abuse, the battered spouse acquires what the psychologists denote as a state of "learned helplessness," defendant's state of mind as described by Drs. Tyson and Rollins. * * * The inability of a defendant to withdraw from the hostile situation and the vulnerability of a defendant to the victim are factors considered * * * in determining the reasonableness of a defendant's belief in the necessity to kill the victim. * * *

* * * Psychologists and sociologists report that battered spouse syndrome usually has three phases—the tension-building phase, the violent phase, and the quiet or loving phase. During the violent phase, the time when the traditional concept of self-defense would mandate that defendant protect herself, i.e., at the moment the abusing spouse attacks, the battered spouse is least able to counter because she is immobilized by fear, if not actually physically restrained.

Mindful that the law should never casually permit an otherwise unlawful killing of another human being to be justified or excused, this Court is of the opinion that with the battered spouse there can be, under certain circumstances, * * * killing of a passive victim that does not preclude the defense of * * * self-defense. Given the characteristics of battered spouse syndrome, we do not believe that a battered person must wait until a deadly attack occurs or that the victim must in all cases be actually attacking or threatening to attack at the very moment defendant commits the unlawful act for the battered person to act in self-defense. Such a standard, in our view, would ignore the realities of the condition. * * *

* * * Based on this evidence, a jury, in our view, could find that decedent's sleep was but a momentary hiatus in a continuous reign of terror by the decedent, that defendant merely took advantage of her first opportunity to protect herself, and that defendant's act was not without the provocation required for * * * self-defense.

Finally, the expert testimony considered with the other evidence would permit reasonable minds to infer that defendant did not use more force than reasonably appeared necessary to her under the circumstances to protect herself from death or great bodily harm. * * *

STATE v. NORMAN

Supreme Court of North Carolina, 1989.
324 N.C. 253, 378 S.E.2d 8.

MITCHELL, JUSTICE. * * *

The Court of Appeals granted a new trial, citing as error the trial court's refusal to submit a possible verdict of acquittal by reason of * * * self-defense. Notwithstanding the uncontroverted evidence that the defendant shot her husband three times in the back of the head as he lay sleeping in his bed, the Court of Appeals held that the defendant's evidence that she exhibited what has come to be called "the battered wife syndrome" entitled her to have the jury consider whether the homicide was an act of * * * self-defense and, thus, not a legal wrong.

We conclude that the evidence introduced in this case would not support a finding that the defendant killed her husband due to a reasonable fear of imminent death or great bodily harm, as is required before a defendant is entitled to jury instructions concerning * * * self-defense. Therefore, the trial court properly declined to instruct the jury on the law relating to self-defense. Accordingly, we reverse the Court of Appeals. * * *

The right to kill in self-defense is based on the necessity, real or reasonably apparent, of killing an unlawful aggressor to save oneself from *imminent* death or great bodily harm at his hands. Our law has recognized that self-preservation under such circumstances springs from a primal impulse and is an inherent right of natural law. * * *

The killing of another human being is the most extreme recourse to our inherent right of self-preservation and can be justified in law only by the utmost real or apparent necessity brought about by the decedent. For that reason, our law of self-defense has required that a defendant claiming that a homicide was justified * * * establish that she reasonably believed at the time of the killing she otherwise would have immediately suffered death or great bodily harm. Only if defendants are required to show that they killed due to a reasonable belief that death or great bodily harm was imminent can the justification for homicide remain clearly and firmly rooted in necessity. The imminence requirement ensures that deadly force will be used only where it is necessary as a last resort in the exercise of the inherent right of self-preservation. * * *

The term "imminent," as used to describe such perceived threats of death or great bodily harm as will justify a homicide by reason of * * * self-defense, has been defined as "immediate danger, such as must be instantly met, such as cannot be guarded against by calling for the assistance of others or the protection of the law." Black's Law Dictionary 676 (5th ed. 1979). * * *

The evidence in this case did not tend to show that the defendant reasonably believed that she was confronted by a threat of imminent death or great bodily harm. The evidence tended to show that no harm was "imminent" or about to happen to the defendant when she shot her husband. The uncontroverted evidence was that her husband had been asleep for some time when she walked to her mother's house, returned with the pistol, fixed the pistol after it jammed and then shot her husband three times in the back of the head. The defendant was not faced with an instantaneous choice between killing her husband or being killed or seriously injured. Instead, *all* of the evidence tended to show that the defendant had ample time and opportunity to resort to other means of preventing further abuse of her husband. * * *

Additionally, the lack of any belief by the defendant—reasonable or otherwise—that she faced a threat of imminent death or great bodily harm from the drunk and sleeping victim in the present case was illustrated by * * * her own expert witnesses when testifying about her subjective assessment of her situation at the time of the killing. * * *

Dr. Tyson * * * testified that the defendant "believed herself to be doomed * * * to a life of the worst kind of torture and abuse, degradation that she had experienced over the years in a progressive way; that it would only get worse, and that death was inevitable." Such evidence of the defendant's speculative beliefs concerning her remote and indefinite future, while indicating she had felt generally threatened, did not tend to show that she killed in the belief—reasonable or otherwise—that her husband presented a threat of *imminent* death or great bodily harm. * * *

We are not persuaded by the reasoning of our Court of Appeals in this case that when there is evidence of battered wife syndrome, neither an actual attack nor threat of attack by the husband at the moment the wife uses deadly force is required to justify the wife's killing of him in * * * self-defense. The Court of Appeals concluded that to impose such require-ments would ignore the "learned helplessness," meekness and other realities of battered wife syndrome and would effectively preclude such women from exercising their right of self-defense. Other jurisdictions which have addressed this question under similar facts are divided in their views, and we can discern no clear majority position on facts closely similar to those of this case. * * *

* * * [S]tretching the law of self-defense to fit the facts of this case would require changing the "imminent death or great bodily harm" requirement to something substantially more indefinite than previously required and would weaken our assurances that justification for the taking of human life remains firmly rooted in real or apparent necessity. That result in principle could not be limited to a few cases decided on evidence as poignant as this. The relaxed requirements * * * proposed by our Court of Appeals would tend to categorically legalize the opportune killing of abusive husbands by their wives solely on the basis of the wives' testimony concerning their subjective speculation as to the probability of future felonious assaults by their husbands. Homicidal self-help would then become a lawful solution, and perhaps the easiest and most effective solution, to this problem. * * *

Reversed.

MARTIN, JUSTICE, dissenting.

At the outset it is to be noted that the peril of fabricated evidence is not unique to the trials of battered wives who kill. The possibility of invented evidence arises in all cases in which a party is seeking the benefit of self-defense. Moreover, in this case there were a number of witnesses other than defendant who testified as to the actual presence of circum-stances supporting a claim of self-defense. This record contains no reason-able basis to attack the credibility of evidence for the defendant. * * *

* * * Defendant does not seek to expand or relax the requirements of self-defense and thereby "legalize the opportune killing of allegedly abu-sive husbands by their wives," as the majority overstates. * * * The proper issue for this Court is to determine whether the evidence, viewed in the light most favorable to the defendant, was sufficient to require the trial court to instruct on the law of self-defense. I conclude that it was. * * *

Evidence presented by defendant described a twenty-year history of beatings and other dehumanizing and degrading treatment by her hus-band. In his expert testimony a clinical psychologist * * * described the defendant as a woman incarcerated by abuse, by fear, and by her convic-tion that her husband was invincible and inescapable * * *.

* * * This, in fact, is a state of mind common to the battered spouse, and one that dramatically distinguishes Judy Norman's belief in the imminence of serious harm from that asserted by [defendants in other

cases]. * * * For the battered wife, if there is no escape, if there is no window of relief or momentary sense of safety, then the next attack, which could be the fatal one, is imminent. In the context of the doctrine of self-defense, "imminent" is a term the meaning of which must be grasped from the defendant's point of view. Properly stated, * * * the question is not whether the threat was *in fact* imminent, but whether defendant's belief in the impending nature of the threat, given the circumstances as she saw them, was reasonable in the mind of a person of ordinary firmness.

Defendant's intense fear * * * evident in the testimony of witnesses who recounted events of the last three days of the decedent's life * * * could have led a juror to conclude that defendant reasonably perceived a threat to her life as "imminent," even while her husband slept. * * *

In *State v. Wingler,* 184 N.C. 747, 115 S.E. 59 (1922), in which the defendant was found guilty for the murder of his wife, Justice * * * Stacy recognized the pain and oppression under which a woman suffers at the hands of an abusive husband: "The supreme tragedy of life is the immolation of woman. With a heavy hand, nature exacts from her a high tax of blood and tears." By his barbaric conduct over the course of twenty years, J.T. Norman reduced the quality of the defendant's life to such an abysmal state that, given the opportunity to do so, the jury might well have found that she was justified in acting in self-defense for the preservation of her tragic life. * * *

NOTES AND QUESTIONS

1. At trial, when asked why she killed her husband, Judy Norman testified:

> Because I was scared of him and I knowed when he woke up, it was going to be the same thing, and I was scared when he took me to the truck stop that night it was going to be worse than he had ever been. I just couldn't take it no more. There ain't no way [crying], even if it means going to prison. It's better than living in that. That's worse hell than anything [crying]. Transcript, File No. 85–CRS–3890, page 142.

2. Judy Norman was convicted of voluntary manslaughter and sentenced to prison for six years. On July 9, 1989, two months after she entered the North Carolina Correctional Institute for Women, her sentence was commuted by the Governor of North Carolina. Judy Norman's plight and the issues raised by her case are considered in detail in Richard A. Rosen, *On Self–Defense, Imminence, and Women Who Kill Their Batterers,* 71 N.C.L.Rev. 371 (1993).

3. In view of the fact that the jury was not instructed on self-defense, why do you think Norman was convicted of voluntary manslaughter, rather than murder?

4. Review Note 5, p. 498. The authors reported that in a vignette based on *Norman,* the position of respondents was the reverse of the outcome in the "beleaguered commuter" case (*Goetz*): persons with an egalitarian worldview,

as well as liberals and Democrats were more likely to acquit the battered woman than were individualists, conservatives, and Republicans. Was *your* response to *Goetz* and *Norman* in accord with their findings?

5. In 2008, Barbara Sheehan, after many years of alleged abuse by her police-officer husband, shot him five times with a .38 caliber revolver while he was shaving one morning. She then picked up his Glock and shot him six more times as he lay on the floor. She claimed self-defense. After a month-long trial, a New York jury of nine women and three men acquitted her of murder, although she was convicted of a gun possession charge. The latter offense carried a potential prison sentence of 3½ to 15 years. The judge sentenced her to a five-year prison term on the charge. For more details on the case, see New York Times, April 26, 2001; October 6, 2011; and November 10, 2011.

6. Battered woman cases may be roughly divided into three categories. First are confrontational homicides, i.e., cases in which the battered woman kills her abusive partner when he poses an immediate threat of death or serious injury to her. Such cases apparently represent about 75% of the reported cases. Holly Maguigan, *Battered Women and Self–Defense: Myths and Misconceptions in Current Reform Proposals,* 140 U.Pa.L.Rev. 379, 397 (1991). *Norman* represents a second category of cases, so-called "non-confrontational" homicides, in which the abuser is killed while asleep or during some other lull in the violence.

A very few cases fall into a third grouping, in which the woman hires a third party to kill the batterer, e.g., People v. Yaklich, 833 P.2d 758 (Colo.App. 1991), or plots with a relative for the latter to kill the man, e.g., People v. Erickson, 57 Cal.App.4th 1391, 67 Cal.Rptr.2d 740 (1997) (mother plotted with her son for the latter to kill her abusive boyfriend, which he did).

7. For a moment, ignore the testimony in *Norman* about "abused spouse syndrome" (or "battered woman syndrome," see Note 12). Knowing what you know about Judy and J.T. Norman, how he abused her (but, remember: ignore the syndrome testimony), and the facts relating to the homicide, do you believe that Judy was *justified* in killing J.T. while he slept? If so, what made this intentional killing "proper," "good" or, at least "non-wrongful," as the concept of "justification" implies? Can you provide a moral theory to justify his death?

If you don't believe Judy Norman was justified in killing her husband when she did, why not? If she was *not* justified, would you *excuse* her, i.e., would you say that the killing was wrongful but that society should hold her morally blameless for her actions? Why, or why not? (Remember again, right now ignore the syndrome testimony!)

If a battering victim is going to be acquitted of killing her abusive partner while he is asleep, does it matter whether her defense is labeled a justification or an excuse? Are there practical implications to the label attached? For example, suppose that J.T. Norman had awakened when his wife placed the gun at his temple. At that moment, would *he* have been justified in killing *her*? Do *his* rights in this situation depend on how we describe *her* defense claim?

8. *The imminency requirement and battered women.* Self-defense law contains a necessity element—deadly force against an aggressor may not be used unless it is necessary. So, is there any need for an imminency rule, as well? Consider the following observation by Professor Rosen, Note 2 supra, at 375–76:

> On one level the view of the majority of the North Carolina Supreme Court is unassailable—the threat of death or great bodily harm was not imminent when Ms. Norman shot her husband, not, at least, by any reasonable interpretation of the word imminent.[6] At the time she killed her husband, Ms. Norman had at least several hours of peace and safety before her, and even more if she chose to be absent when her husband awoke. Thus, to the extent the court was simply applying the settled law * * * its decision was surely correct. The attempt by the dissent to wrestle the facts of this case into the confines of the imminence requirement, while understandable and perhaps even laudable, was unpersuasive. * * *

> At a deeper level, however, the decision is disturbing. It is difficult to imagine that Ms. Norman had any choice but to act as she did in order to avoid a grave risk of death or serious harm at the hands of her husband. By relying on the imminence requirement, the North Carolina Supreme Court never answered the question whether it was *necessary* for Ms. Norman to kill her husband to avoid great bodily harm or death. And is not *this* the proper question that should be addressed in *Norman* and similar cases?

Similarly, consider these observations of Stephen J. Morse, *Neither Desert Nor Disease*, 5 Legal Theory 265, 305–07:

> It is * * * fair to infer that [Judy Norman's] community was not well-served by shelters or other institutions devoted to protecting victims of domestic violence. * * * Almost certainly, even if Judy had filed a [criminal] complaint * * *, it is highly unlikely that he would have served serious time or that jail would have reformed his drinking and violent tendencies, and it is correspondingly likely that he would have emerged from incarceration more disposed than ever to hurt Judy.

> Moreover, even if her husband was imprisoned for a time, * * * Judy lacked the resources and skills to move to another location, where she could live an economically and socially viable life with her children and where J.T. could not find her. Finally, Judy could have armed herself and waited for the next assault, but this would have been a dreadfully risky strategy that was likely to result in her death if she failed to kill J.T.

> In sum, while her husband was asleep in the bed, it was entirely reasonable for Judy Norman to conclude that it was completely predictable that he would abuse her brutally in the near future, and * * * it was

---

6. Black's Law Dictionary 750 (6th ed. 1990), defines "imminent" as "[s]omething which is threatening to happen at once"; "something to happen upon the instant"; "something * * * on the point of happening." Under the Webster's Third New International Dictionary 1130 (1976) definition, "imminent" connotes something "ready to take place; near at hand; impending." As these definitions indicate, and as courts have consistently found, imminence unquestionably includes a temporal requirement.

entirely reasonable for Judy Norman to believe that no one was really able to protect her and that there was nowhere to hide. * * *

To protect Judy, * * * the law might permit a broader, private preemptive response to danger, justified by the danger and by the lack of reasonable alternatives.

Are Professors Rosen and Morse on to something? Former President George Bush declared in 2002 that the United States "must be prepared to stop rogue states and their terrorist client *before they are able to threaten or use* weapons of mass destruction * * *." *The National Security Strategy of the United States*, http://www/nytimes/com/2002/09/20/politics/20STEXT_FULL. html. If "preemptive self-defense" is conducted at the international level, is there any reason to deny the right to a battered woman to kill her "rogue" or "terrorist" partner before he is able "to threaten or use" deadly force?

Professor Jane Moriarty, while rejecting the Bush Doctrine as extreme, defends so-called "anticipatory self-defense" (ASD). She writes that "[t]hose who favor ASD in international law do not restrict the doctrine to the moment when the missile is in the air." Thus, for example "[p]ursuant to international law, ASD may be legitimately invoked if a targeted country has been victimized by prior attacks and learns more attacks are planned. When a prior aggressor threatens to commit future violence, international law treats the threat as real. So should domestic criminal law." Jane Campbell Moriarty, *"While Dangers Gather": The Bush Preemption Doctrine, Battered Women, Imminence, and Anticipatory Self–Defense*, 30 N.Y.U. Rev. Law & Soc. Change 1, 15, 25 (2005).

Not all commentators agree with those who would abandon an imminency requirement. Some scholars fear that abandonment of a strict temporal requirement—"[a]dmittedly, * * * a tempting direction to go when we look at evil persons such as J.T. Norman and when we see the 'solution' of execution of the sleeping abuser as a way of relieving the victim's agony"—would "expand[] the lawful use of deadly force to a point dangerous to the community and debilitating to our belief in the general sanctity of human life." Joshua Dressler, *Battered Women and Sleeping Abusers: Some Reflections*, 3 Ohio St. J. Crim. L. 457, 468 (2006); see also United States v. Slocum, 486 F.Supp.2d 1104, 1109 (C.D. Cal. 2007) ("Civilized society does not recognize self-defense as a justification for [homicide] so that defendants may preemptively strike and kill their enemies, * * * no matter how potentially formidable these enemies may be."). And, there is more, say advocates of an imminency rule:

> [T]he imminence requirement is more than a proxy for necessity. Rather it is conceptually related to the concepts of aggression and defensive conduct. Without aggression, there is no self-defense, only self-preference. * * * [F]or self-defense, we cannot supplant imminence with necessity. * * * Self-defense is uniquely justified by the fact that the defender is responding to aggression. Imminence, far from simply establishing necessity, is conceptually tied to self-defense by staking out the type of threats that constitute aggression.

Kimberly Kessler Ferzan, *Defending Imminence: From Battered Women to Iraq*, 46 Ariz. L. Rev.213, 262 (2004).

Finally, some proponents of the imminency rule believe it is defensible as "a response to the fundamental political concern of regulating and controlling the use of violence in society." The imminency requirement

> ultimately rests on the venerable natural law principle * * * that no one should be a judge in his own case; the decision to use force against another person must be made by an objective and disinterested authority. * * * Thus, the state reserves the right to the use of retaliatory (punitive) force against past harm, as well as preemptive/preventive force against future threats. The single exception to this principle is where the immediacy of the threat rendered it impossible to resort to external protection, and thus licensed self-help. Even in such cases, notably, the state has always reserved the right to be the arbiter after the fact as to whether the defensive force used was justified from an impartial perspective.

Whitley R.P. Kaufman, *Self–Defense, Imminence, and the Battered Woman*, 10 New Crim. L. Rev. 342, 359–360 (2007).

How do you come out on this debate? If you *would* remove the imminency requirement—and only require proof that the deadly force was necessary—would you do it only in abuse cases, or do your reasons justify abandonment of the requirement in *all* self-defense cases?

9. In regard to the imminency issue, how would *Norman* be resolved in a jurisdiction applying Model Penal Code § 3.04? For help, see p. 488, Note 4.

10. *Other justifying theories (part 1)*. Rather than focus on the physical harm that Judy Norman was experiencing, should her acts be justified on the ground that she was defending herself against continued psychological degradation? Professor Charles Ewing has proposed that the law permit the use of deadly force to prevent serious psychological injury, defined by him as "gross and enduring impairment of one's psychological functioning that significantly limits the meaning and value of one's physical existence." Charles Patrick Ewing, *Psychological Self–Defense*, 14 Law & Hum.Behav. 579, 587 (1990). For a critique of the doctrine of psychological self-defense, see Stephen J. Morse, *The Misbegotten Marriage of Soft Psychology and Bad Law*, 14 Law & Hum.Behav. 595 (1990).

11. *Other justifying theories (part 2)*. To the extent that a kidnap victim may use deadly force to escape her situation (see, e.g., Model Penal Code § 3.04(2)(b)), it is appropriate to argue that Judy Norman was prevented over time from escaping J.T. or obtaining successful aid and, therefore, is justified in killing him on *that* ground?

12. *Battered woman syndrome (BWS)*. BWS (or now often called "battered *spouse* syndrome") is explained this way in State v. Smullen, 380 Md. 233, 844 A.2d 429 (2004):

> Dr. Lenore Walker, an academic and clinical psychologist, is usually credited with first describing the battered spouse syndrome, which she called the "battered woman syndrome." *See* Lenore E. Walker, THE BATTERED WOMAN (1979); *also* The Battered Woman Syndrome (1984) and *Battered Woman Syndrome and Self–Defense*, 6 Notre Dame J.L. Ethics & Pub. Pol'y 321 (1992). Dr. Walker identified a "battered woman" as one

who is repeatedly subjected to any forceful physical or psychological behavior by a man in order to coerce her to do something he wants her to do without any concern for her rights. She described three phases to the battering cycle, which, she said, may vary in both time and intensity. Phase I she referred to as the "tension-building" phase, in which minor incidents of physical, sexual, or emotional abuse occur. The woman is not severely abused, but the batterer begins to express hostility toward her. Phase II consists of an acute battering incident, in which the batterer "typically unleashes a barrage of verbal and physical aggression that can leave the woman severely shaken and injured." Phase III is a contrition stage, in which the batterer apologizes, seeks forgiveness, and promises to change. The apparent transformation of the abuser back into a loving partner, according to Walker, "provides the positive reinforcement for remaining in the relationship."

The essence of the syndrome is that this cycle repeats, and, indeed, Walker asserts that the syndrome does not exist unless it has repeated at least once. Worse, perhaps, than the mere repetition, is the fact that, over time, the cycle becomes more intense, more frequent, more violent, and often more lethal. One aspect of the syndrome is what had been described as "learned helplessness"—where, after repeated abuse, women come to believe that they cannot control the situation and thus become passive and submissive. The etiology of this aspect is described in Erin Masson, Admissibility of Expert or Opinion Evidence of Battered-Woman Syndrome on Issue of Self-Defense, 58 ALR 5th 749, 762–763 (1998):

"Through experience, the victim learns that when she attempts to defend herself—by reaching out to others or trying to leave—that she will be the victim of more severe violence. The batterer blames the abusive relationship on her inability to respond to his ever-increasing demands so that the most effective short-term method of reducing incidents of violence is to be more subservient."

This is a key aspect in the purported relevance of the syndrome in a self-defense context, as it offers an explanation of why the defendant, having been previously subjected to abuse, simply did not leave the home or take some other action against her abuser. * * *

Another aspect of the battered spouse syndrome directly relevant in a self-defense context, is that the victim becomes able to sense the escalation in the frequency and intensity of the violence and thus becomes more sensitive to the abuser's behavior. As described by Elizabeth Bochnak, Women's Self–Defense Cases: Theory and Practice (1981) * * *:

"The battered woman learns to recognize the small signs that precede periods of escalated violence. She learns to distinguish subtle changes in tone of voice, facial expressions, and levels of danger. She is in a position to know, perhaps with greater certainty than someone attacked by a stranger, that the batterer's threat is real and will be acted upon."

Walker's studies indicated that retaliation by the abused woman often occurred when the cycle lapsed back from Phase III to Phase I. * * * In describing the cases in which the woman had been tried for murder, Walker recounted that several factors were common to all of the cases:

> "First, each woman stated that she was convinced the batterer was going to kill her. Violent assaults had taken place previously in all of the these cases. In the final incident, however, something different was noted by these women which convinced them that the batterer really was going to kill them this time."

Dr. Walker has opined that the battered woman syndrome constitutes a subgroup of Post–Traumatic Stress Disorder, which is recognized by the American Psychiatric Association as a mental disorder. *See* Diagnostic and Statistical Manual of Mental Disorders, American Psychiatric Association, 4th ed. § 309.81(DSM–IV), although, as critics have pointed out, DSM–IV does not, itself, mention the battered woman syndrome. Other writers have compared the battered spouse syndrome to the Stockholm syndrome of traumatic bonding, which offers an explanation of why hostages sometimes come to identify with their captors.

Dr. Lenore Walker's research has been criticized as lacking empirical support and potentially demeaning to women. See, e.g., Robert F. Schopp, Barbara J. Sturgis, & Megan Sullivan, *Battered Woman Syndrome, Expert Testimony, and the Distinction Between Justification and Excuse*, 1994 U.Ill. L.Rev. 45, 63; David L. Faigman & Amy J. Wright, *The Battered Woman Syndrome in the Age of Science*, 39 Ariz.L.Rev. 67, 69 (1997); David L. Faigman, Note, *Battered Woman Syndrome and Self–Defense: A Legal and Empirical Dissent,* 72 Virg.L.Rev. 619 (1986).

Despite criticisms, most courts now admit BWS testimony in appropriate self-defense cases.[e] The clear trend is to permit syndrome evidence in cases of confrontational homicides, assuming that the defendant presents evidence of a history of abuse. Courts are divided on how to deal with nonconfrontational cases. Some courts, as in *Norman*, do *not* permit a self-defense instruction in such cases, so the syndrome evidence is not "relevant to the task at hand." Other jurisdictions, however, permit self-defense to be claimed in nonconfrontational cases if it is supported by syndrome evidence. See State v. Gallegos, 104 N.M. 247, 719 P.2d 1268 (Ct.App.1986); State v. Leidholm, 334 N.W.2d 811 (N.D.1983).

13. For what specific purposes may or should expert testimony regarding BWS be introduced in self-defense cases? Do you think such evidence is relevant: (1) to buttress the battered woman's claim that she was repeatedly beaten by her spouse; (2) in determining whether she *subjectively* believed that she was confronting an imminent deadly threat; and/or (3) in determining whether she satisfied the *objective* "reasonable belief" requirement of self-defense? The next excerpt speaks to these questions.

---

e. Some states provide by statute for the admissibility of battered woman syndrome expert testimony in specified circumstances. E.g., Cal. Evid. Code § 1107 (2011); Md.Cts. & Jud.Proc. Code Ann. § 10–916 (2011); Ohio Rev.Code § 2901.06 (2011).

STEPHEN J. MORSE—THE "NEW SYNDROME EXCUSE SYNDROME"

Criminal Justice Ethics, Vol. 14, No. 1, Winter/Spring 1995, at 3, 11–13

Syndrome evidence may be relevant in a number of ways to an objectively reasonable assessment of the need to use deadly force. First, the evidence may dispel myths or correct seemingly sensible but erroneous inferences that might affect the factfinder's assessment. For example, suppose a defendant claiming self-defense tries to buttress the honesty and reasonableness of her belief that she needed to use deadly force by providing a history of battering by the person she killed. Ordinary people might find the history unbelievable and the present claim less credible because they do not believe the defendant would have stayed in such a relationship. They might not believe that the defendant suffered repeated attacks because ordinary observers think that she would have left the relationship. Consequently, they might also infer that there probably was not much danger on the present occasion either. Syndrome evidence will support the honesty and reasonableness of the defendant's belief and the proportionality of her defensive force because it will explain why people subjected repeatedly to terrible physical abuse stay with the abuser.

Second, it is possible that battering syndrome sufferers may be especially acute observers of cues that presage imminent violence from the abuser. That is, although the situation may appear non-threatening to the ordinary person—say, the batterer has a funny look in his eyes or he just crushed a beer can in his hand in a particularly harsh manner—the battered syndrome suffering defendant may know quite reasonably that that look or that gesture is always or almost always followed by dreadful violence. If the sufferer has such skills of hypervigilance and if the batterer did exhibit the prodromal cues—both of which are factual questions—then the defendant's belief is once again reasonable by standard, objective standards.

In both examples, syndrome evidence was used to support an entirely traditional, unreformed, unsubjectivized self-defense justification. The law is simply taking advantage of fresh scientific/clinical evidence to apply old objective doctrine. This is nothing more than the exercise of rationality, for which the law prides itself mightily. Such limited uses of syndrome evidence in the realm of justification is entirely to be applauded when the factual evidence meets the usual evidentiary tests of reliability and validity.

[Some battered woman] sufferers want more, however. They wish to expand justifications in cases that lack the usual criteria of justification. For example, suppose a syndrome sufferer's belief about the need to use defensive force is objectively *un*reasonable. The primary expansionist move is to attempt to endow the objective, reasonable person standard with the syndrome of the accused. Thus, instead of asking what the reasonable person would have believed and done in these circumstances, advocates wish to ask what a "reasonable syndrome sufferer" would have believed and done. * * *

* * * Can the sufferer's honest but unreasonable belief in the need to use deadly force *justify* rather than excuse killing the batterer when there

is no immediate danger and there are alternatives available to safeguard her? * * *

Expansionists * * * argue that the battered victim syndrome affects the sufferer's cognitive and volitional functioning, making it difficult or impossible for the sufferer to recognize or to utilize the alternatives. For example, the syndrome might produce such a sense of helplessness, hopelessness, and unworthiness that the sufferer honestly but *erroneously* believes that there is "no other way out." Or, she may know that alternatives exist and that she ought to take advantage of them, but depression associated with the syndrome robs her of volition, rendering her incapable of making use of the alternatives. These in fact are precisely the types of claims made about battered victim syndrome sufferers by those who have studied domestic violence.

Now, if these assertions are true, and I believe that they often are, the defendant is really claiming an excuse based on impaired rationality or volition. If there were reasonable alternatives available, killing the batterer on the occasion was *not* the right thing to do, and it should not be justified. * * * If the syndrome suffering defendant is to have an affirmative defense in such cases, it must be an excuse.

NOTES AND QUESTIONS

1. According to Sue Osthoff & Holly Maguigan, *Explaining Without Pathologizing*: *Testimony on Battering and Its Effects,* in Current Controversies on Family Violence (Donileen R. Loseke et al. eds., 2005), at 229–231:

> Over the years, experiences in criminal courts persuaded advocates, lawyers, and researchers to move beyond the "battered woman syndrome" formulation to more comprehensive testimony. They came to understand that BWS fails to capture the full experience of battered women, and that its risks subjecting women who are battered to labels that deny their diversity and that portray them as helpless and incapacitated * * *.

> The "syndrome" label may encourage jurors to receive the defendant as pathological. Such a perception is at odds with a defense argument that the woman's actions were actually reasonable in light of the circumstances. * * *

> More recent work has made it clear that BWS is no longer the appropriate term to describe either the state of our knowledge or the content of expert testimony. The phrase, "testimony on battering and its effects" more accurately describes the expert evidence because it focuses on battered women's experiences, moves their social context to the foreground, emphasizes the diversity of their range of reactions, and highlights the utility of expert testimony to explain the psychological sequelae of living with violence.

2. *Subjectivization of the "reasonable belief" standard: how far should the law go?* If courts take into consideration BWS evidence in self-defense cases, what other characteristics of a defendant ought to be considered in

evaluating an actor's "reasonable beliefs"? What do you think of the following standard, announced in State v. Leidholm, 334 N.W.2d 811 (N.D.1983):

> [A]n accused's actions are to be viewed from the standpoint of a person whose mental and physical characteristics are like the accused's and who sees what the accused sees and knows what the accused knows. For example, if the accused is a timid, diminutive male, the factfinder must consider these characteristics in assessing the reasonableness of his belief. If, on the other hand, the accused is a strong, courageous, and capable female, the factfinder must consider these characteristics in judging the reasonableness of her belief. * * *

> Hence, a correct statement of the law of self-defense is one in which the court directs the jury to assume the physical and psychological properties peculiar to the accused, viz., to place itself as best it can in the shoes of the accused, and then decide whether or not the particular circumstances surrounding the accused at the time he used force were sufficient to create in his mind a sincere and reasonable belief that the use of force was necessary to protect himself from imminent and unlawful harm.

3. *The "reasonable person": beliefs and culture.* Consider People v. Romero, 69 Cal.App.4th 846, 81 Cal.Rptr.2d 823 (1999), in which defense counsel sought to introduce expert testimony "on the sociology of poverty, and the role of honor, paternalism, and street fighting in the Hispanic culture," on the ground that her Hispanic client's belief that he needed to use deadly force, and that he should not retreat from a street confrontation, should be considered by the jury from his cultural background? Should such testimony be permitted? Why, or why not?

3. DEFENSE OF OTHERS

PEOPLE v. KURR

Court of Appeals of Michigan, 2002.
253 Mich.App. 317, 654 N.W.2d 651.

METER, PRESIDING JUSTICE.

Defendant, who killed her boyfriend, Antonio Pena, with a knife, appeals * * * from her conviction by a jury of voluntary manslaughter. * * * Defendant argues on appeal that she should have been allowed a jury instruction regarding the defense of others because the jurors could have concluded that she killed Pena while defending her unborn children.[1] We agree that a defense of others jury instruction was appropriate here and therefore reverse defendant's conviction and remand this case for a new trial.

Defendant stabbed Pena on October 9, 1999. According to a Kalamazoo police officer, defendant told him that she and Pena had argued that day over Pena's cocaine use. Defendant told the officer that Pena subsequently punched her two times in the stomach and that she warned Pena

---

1.   * * * [Apparently,] she had been carrying quadruplets at the time of the stabbing.

not to hit her because she was carrying his babies. Defendant stated that when Pena came toward her again, she stabbed him in the chest. He died as a result of the stab wound.

Months before trial, defendant moved for permission to present testimony and to argue that she killed Pena in defense of her unborn children. The trial court concluded that a person could assert the defense of others theory * * *. * * *

At trial, defendant presented evidence of Pena's assaultive nature. * * * The parties also presented testimony regarding defendant's * * * pregnancy. * * *

At the conclusion of the trial, defendant requested a jury instruction on the defense of others. * * * Despite its earlier ruling, the trial court disallowed a defense of others instruction, noting that (1) the fetus or fetuses would have been only sixteen or seventeen weeks in gestation at the time of the stabbing and (2) according to a physician's trial testimony, a fetus under twenty-two weeks old is nonviable, i.e., it is not capable of surviving outside the mother's womb. The trial court concluded that in order for defendant to assert a defense of others theory, there had "to be a living human being existing independent of [defendant] * * *." It stated: "Even under the evidence in this case, under 22 weeks, there are no ['others']. And, that's my theory." The trial court did allow a self-defense jury instruction.

* * * In order to determine whether the court should indeed have given the defense of others instruction, we must initially decide the purely legal question whether a nonviable fetus constitutes an "other" in the context of this defense. With certain restrictions, we conclude that it does.

"In Michigan, the killing of another person in self-defense is justifiable homicide if the defendant honestly and reasonably believes that his life is in imminent danger or that there is a threat of serious bodily harm." * * * Case law in Michigan also allows a person to use deadly force in defense of another. Traditionally, the "defense of others" concept applied solely to those persons with whom the defendant had a special relationship, such as a wife or brother. * * * [T]he defense now makes no distinction between strangers and relatives with regard to its application.

We conclude that in this state, the defense should also extend to the protection of a fetus, viable or nonviable, from an assault against the mother, and we base this conclusion primarily on the fetal protection act adopted by the Legislature in 1998. This act punishes individuals who harm or kill fetuses or embryos under various circumstances. [This Act] set forth penalties for harming a fetus or embryo during an intentional assault against a pregnant woman[,] punishes an individual for causing a miscarriage or stillbirth with malicious intent toward the fetus or embryo or for causing a miscarriage or stillbirth while acting "in wanton or willful disregard of the likelihood that the natural tendency of [his] conduct is to cause a miscarriage or stillbirth or great bodily harm to the embryo or fetus." [The Act] punishes an individual for harming or killing a fetus or embryo during an intentional assault [or grossly negligent act] against a pregnant woman without regard to the individual's * * * state of mind concerning the fetus or embryo.

The plain language of these provisions shows the Legislature's conclusion that fetuses are worthy of protection as living entities as a matter of public policy. Indeed, we note that a violation of [one provision of the Act] is punishable by up to life imprisonment, nearly the harshest punishment available in our state. Moreover, in enacting the fetal protection act, the Legislature did not distinguish between fetuses that are viable, or capable of surviving outside the womb, and those that are nonviable. In fact, the Legislature used the term "embryo" as well as the term "fetus" in describing the prohibited conduct * * *. * * *

Because the act reflects a public policy to protect even an embryo from unlawful assaultive or negligent conduct, we conclude that the defense of others concept does extend to the protection of a nonviable fetus from an assault against the mother. We emphasize, however, that the defense is available *solely* in the context of an assault against the mother. Indeed, the Legislature has *not* extended the protection of the criminal laws to embryos existing outside a woman's body, i.e., frozen embryos stored for future use, and we therefore *do not* extend the applicability of the defense of others theory to situations involving these embryos.

We acknowledge that in *Ogas v. Texas*, 655 S.W.2d 322, 325 (Tex. App., 1983), the Texas Court of Appeals rejected the defendant's assertion that she was entitled to use deadly force to protect her unborn child. However, unlike Michigan, Texas has codified the defense of others theory in its criminal statutes. See Tex. Penal Code Ann. § 9.33. Section 9.33 provides that one may use deadly force against another to protect a third "person," and "person" is defined by the penal code as "an individual, corporation, or association." Moreover, and significantly, "individual" is defined as a "human being who has been born and is alive." * * *

Michigan has not similarly codified the defense of others theory in its criminal statutes, and we are therefore not bound by restrictive statutory definitions. Our Legislature, as noted earlier, has expressed its intent that fetuses and embryos be provided strong protection under the law from assaults against pregnant women, and we believe that our decision today effectuates that intent. * * *

A number of cases exist in which antiabortion activists on trial for criminal conduct have unsuccessfully raised the defense of others theory. For example, in *Louisiana v. Aguillard*, 567 So. 2d 674, 675 (La.App., 1990), the defendants were prosecuted for criminal trespass, obstructing public passage, and resisting an officer after they protested abortions at an abortion clinic. The Louisiana Court of Appeals held that they were not entitled to assert a defense of others theory because a woman's right to obtain an abortion is constitutionally protected. * * *

The distinction between the abortion cases and the instant case is straightforward. * * * The defense of others theory is available only if a person acts to prevent *unlawful* bodily harm against another. Because clinics that perform abortions are engaging in lawful activity, the defense of others theory does not apply. * * * Our holding today does not apply to what the United States Supreme Court has held to constitute lawful abortions. * * *

We conclude that the failure to give a defense of others jury instruction deprived defendant of her due process right to present a defense. The prosecutor argues that the instructions as given were sufficient because they included a self-defense theory, which the jury rejected, and because the court allowed defendant to present testimony concerning her pregnancy in order to justify her decision to defend herself. This argument is disingenuous. Indeed, in light of the punches to defendant's stomach, the jury could have rejected defendant's self-defense theory while at the same time finding that defendant killed Pena in defense of her unborn children. * * * Because the jury instructions essentially excluded consideration of defendant's viable defense of others theory, a new trial is warranted.

We emphasize that our decision today is a narrow one. We are obviously aware of the raging debate occurring in this country regarding the point at which a fetus becomes a person entitled to *all* the protections of the state and federal constitutions. This issue, however, is not raised by the parties, is not pertinent to the resolution of the instant case, and does not drive our ruling today. * * *

NOTES AND QUESTIONS

1. *Follow-up.* Jaclyn Kurr was retried in 2003, reconvicted of voluntary manslaughter, and sentenced to a term of imprisonment of from five to twenty years. Kurr was released on parole on March 11, 2009.

[handwritten margin note: arrested again]

2. In 2011, the House Judiciary Committee of South Dakota voted, 9–3, to amend the State's Penal Code, as follows (the proposed amendment is underlined):

> Homicide is justifiable if committed by any person in the lawful defense of such person, or of his or her husband, wife, parent, child, master, mistress, or servant, or the unborn child of any such enumerated person, if there is reasonable ground to apprehend a design to commit a felony, or to do some great personal injury, and imminent danger of such design being accomplished.

According to the February 16, 2011 issue of the New York Times, "[t]he phrasing caused concern and disbelief on both sides of the abortion debate, with activists in [both] movements calling the language poorly conceived at best * * *." Was the concern justified?

3. In general, a person is justified today in using force to protect a third party from unlawful use of force by an aggressor. The intervenor's right to use force in such circumstances parallels the third party's right of self-defense. Put differently, she may use force when, and to the extent that, the

third party would *apparently* be justified in using force to protect himself. (The significance of the word "apparently" is considered in Note 4 below.)

The Model Penal Code version of this defense is set out in Section 3.05 of the Code. How would *Kurr* be decided pursuant to the Code? (Hint: look beyond Section 3.05 for the answer.)

4. *A* observes *B* threatening to use force against *C*. From *A*'s perspective—and we will assume from the perspective of a reasonable person in *A*'s shoes—*C* is an innocent person about to become the victim of *B*'s unlawful aggression, so *A* comes to *C*'s aid by using force against *B*. Unfortunately, it turns out that *B* was not a aggressor, but an undercover police officer lawfully threatening to use force against wrongdoer *C*. Should *A*, who acted on the basis of reasonable appearances, be entitled to claim defense-of-others?

At one point, most jurisdictions applied the "alter ego rule": a person who comes to the aid of another is placed in the shoes of the individual for whom she was providing assistance. Put differently, the right to defend another is no greater than the right of the third person to defend himself. Since *C* had no right to defend himself in this example, *A* cannot validly assert defense-of-others in an "alter ego" jurisdiction.

This is no longer the majority rule. Most states now provide that if *A* acts on the basis of a reasonable belief, the defense applies to *A*, even if *C* has no right of self-defense. What do you think is the rationale for this rule? Which approach—the alter ego rule or the "reasonable belief" standard—is preferable?

4. DEFENSE OF HABITATION/PROPERTY AND LAW ENFORCEMENT DEFENSES

It was New Year's Eve, December 31, 2011. Sarah McKinley, an 18–year–old mother of a three-month-old son—her husband had died of cancer just a week earlier—called 911 to report that a man was at her door attempting to enter. She told the 911 dispatcher, "There's a guy at my door and I'm here by myself with my infant baby. Can I please get a dispatcher out here immediately?" In the conversation, she said, "I've got two guns in my hand. Is it OK to shoot him if he comes in my door?" (Los Angeles Times, Jan. 5, 2012.)

What would *you* have told her? Suppose that she had said (accurately), "I have barricaded the front door with my sofa. I have a 12–gauge shotgun. Would it be legal to shoot him through the door?" Remember, she doesn't know the would-be intruder's purpose or whether he is armed or unarmed. Consider, now, the following case.

STATE v. BOYETT

Supreme Court of New Mexico, 2008.
144 N.M. 184, 185 P.3d 355.

SERNA, JUSTICE.

Defendant Cecil Boyett appeals from his conviction for the first degree murder of Deborah Rhodes (Victim) * * *. He alleges that the trial court erred in refusing to instruct the jury on his theory of the case * * *. * * *

I. BACKGROUND

Defendant and Victim had a rancorous history. The enmity that each harbored for the other apparently had its roots in a romantic interest that both had in Renate Wilder (Wilder).

Wilder and Victim were childhood friends who eventually moved in together and started an intimate relationship. Although their romance ended, the two remained close friends, living and working together. Wilder later met Defendant, and the two became romantically involved. Wilder eventually supplanted Victim's presence in her life with that of Defendant. She fired Victim from her bar and gave Victim's former job to Defendant. She ousted Victim from her home with the help of a restraining order and invited Defendant to move in. At one point, Victim discovered the entwined couple near the hot tub behind Wilder's house. Enraged, Victim retrieved a gun from the house and used it to threaten the couple. Disdain developed between Defendant and Victim, and Victim only occasionally returned to Wilder's home after she was forced out.

Following a protracted courtship, Wilder and Defendant planned to marry on February 6, 2004. A few days prior to her wedding, Wilder absconded from the home that she shared with Defendant. She spent that time with Victim and did not tell Defendant where she was or what she was doing. Wondering as to her whereabouts, Defendant engaged in a variety of activities aimed at locating her but was unsuccessful in his attempts; he rightfully suspected that she was with Victim although he was unable, at that time, to confirm his suspicions.

On the afternoon of February 5, 2004, Wilder departed Victim's company to return to her own home but had a car accident along the way. The accident occurred near Victim's residence and, for a variety of reasons, Victim offered to claim responsibility for it. Wilder accepted and departed the scene on foot, walking back to the house that she shared with Defendant. Shortly after Wilder returned to the house, Victim arrived. Victim's visit concluded when Defendant shot her in the head with a .357 revolver from approximately four feet away, but the events leading to that end were disputed at trial.

[The prosecutor argued that Victim arrived at the house to return Wilder's car keys, that Defendant opened the front door, shouted at her to leave, and then immediately shot her.]

Defendant's version of events was quite different. He claimed that Victim came to the house that day intent on killing him to prevent his impending marriage to Wilder. Defendant testified that he heard a loud banging at the front door, grabbed the gun that he kept nearby, and opened the door only to find a furious Victim on the doorstep. Defendant said that he shouted at Victim, telling her to get off his property, but in the process of trying to run her off, he observed her draw the gun that he knew she routinely carried. In fear for his life, Defendant raised his revolver and shot Victim. Defendant asserted that if he had not shot her, she would have fired her gun and fatally wounded him.

Defendant * * * argued that he was not guilty because he acted lawfully in shooting Victim, either in self defense, defense of another, or defense of habitation. * * *

* * * The trial court concluded that the jury instruction related to defense of habitation * * * did not apply in this case because Defendant did not shoot Victim inside his home. * * *

II. DEFENDANT WAS NOT ENTITLED TO THE REQUESTED JURY INSTRUCTIONS * * *

The trial court denied the defense of habitation instruction based on its conclusion that the defense applies to only those situations in which an intruder is killed within the home. Picking up the torch lit by the trial court, the State now argues that the defense should be limited to situations in which a person forcibly enters a home and is killed while intruding therein. By that argument, the State seeks our endorsement of a bright line rule that would require an intruder to cross the threshold before an occupant's use of force to repel that entry could be justified by defense of habitation. Despite the State's contention, we are unwilling to draw such a bright line.

Defense of habitation has long been recognized in New Mexico. *See, e.g., State v. Bailey*, 27 N.M. 145, 162–63, 198 P. 529, 534 (1921). It gives a person the right to use lethal force against an intruder when such force is necessary to prevent the commission of a felony in his or her home. The defense is grounded in the theory that "[t]he home is one of the most important institutions of the state, and has ever been regarded as a place where a person has a right to stand his [or her] ground and repel, force by force, to the extent necessary for its protection." *State v. Couch*, 52 N.M. 127, 134, 193 P.2d 405, 409 (1946). Ultimately, in every purported defense of habitation, the use of deadly force is justified only if the defendant reasonably believed that the commission of a felony in his or her home was immediately at hand and that it was necessary to kill the intruder to prevent that occurrence.

This Court has refused to extend the defense to situations in which the victim was fleeing from the defendant, as well as situations in which the victim had lawfully entered the defendant's home. But our courts have never held that entry into the defendant's home is a prerequisite for the defense. On the contrary, the seminal New Mexico case on defense of habitation was clear that, in certain circumstances, it may justify an occupant's use of lethal force against an intruder who is outside the home. *Bailey*, 27 N.M. at 162, 198 P. at 534.

In addition to providing a defense for the killing of an intruder already inside the defendant's home, *Bailey* explained that defense of habitation justifies killing an intruder who is assaulting the defendant's home with the intent of reaching its occupants and committing a felony against them. Protecting a defendant's right to prevent forced entry necessitates that the defense apply when an intruder is outside the home but endeavoring to enter it. This interpretation of defense of habitation is supported by *Couch*, where the defendant fired a shotgun from within his home at an intruder who was outside, pelting the home with rocks. Prior to the night of the shooting, the defendant's home had repeatedly been broken into, which caused he and his wife to "suffer intensely from apprehension of violence at the hands of the unknown intruder." When the later assault on their home occurred, both the defendant and his wife believed that the attackers were the same people who had previously broken in. This Court concluded that, even though the victim was killed outside the home, the defendant was entitled to an instruction on defense of habitation because he could reasonably have believed that the person attacking it intended to enter and commit violence against the occupants.

The proposition that defense of habitation allows one to kill to prevent an intruder's forced entry is well supported by the law in other jurisdictions and treatises on the subject. *See, e.g., People v. Curtis*, 30 Cal. App. 4th 1337, 37 Cal.Rptr.2d 304, 318 (Ct. App. 1994) ("Defense of habitation applies where the defendant uses reasonable force to exclude someone he or she reasonably believes is trespassing in, *or about to trespass in*, his or her home." (emphasis added)); [citing and quoting other cases]; *see also* 40 C.J.S. *Homicide* § 164 (2006) ("People may defend their dwellings against those who *endeavor by violence to enter them* and who appear to intend violence to persons inside...." (emphasis added)); 2 Wharton's Criminal Law § 131 (15th ed. 1994) ("When a dwelling house is entered or *attempted to be entered by force* ... the occupant may use deadly force, if reasonably necessary, to prevent or terminate such entry." (emphasis added)).

Based on our precedent and the authorities cited above, we cannot accept the position that defense of habitation requires an intruder to cross the threshold of the defendant's home. Instead, we emphasize that a person has a right to defend his or her residence not only when an intruder is already inside the home, but also when an intruder is outside the home and attempting to enter to commit a violent felony.

We recognize that "[t]he term felony in former times carried a connotation of greater threat than" it does today. "In the common law, the rule developed that use of lethal force to prevent a felony was only justified if the felony was a forcible and atrocious crime." Felonies are no longer constrained to forcible and atrocious crimes, and were we not to update *Bailey*'s "felony" language, defense of habitation may apply to situations in which an intruder attempts to force entry into a home with the purpose of committing a non-violent felony, such as bribing a public official therein. Seeking to avoid such absurdity, we turn to our prior decisions to determine the meaning of "felony" as it is used in the defense of habitation context.

As noted above, the defendant in *Couch* was entitled to an instruction on defense of habitation because he could have reasonably believed that the people who were attacking his home intended violence against its occupants. Later, * * * this Court held that the defendant did not qualify for a defense of habitation instruction because, among other things, no evidence had been presented that the victim "enter[ed] the house in order to commit a felony involving violence." Those authorities show that the term "felony" in the defense of habitation context is properly limited to those felonies involving violence. In other words, the felony that the defendant acted to prevent must have been one that would have resulted in violence against the occupants were it not prevented; in the event of any other felony, a defense of habitation instruction would be unwarranted.

Because defense of habitation is not restricted to instances in which the victim is killed inside the defendant's home, the trial court in this case erred when it excluded the instruction on that ground. Defendant would have been entitled to an instruction on the defense if some evidence reasonably tended to show that he killed Victim to prevent her from forcing entry into his home and committing a violent felony once inside. Thus, the question we must now answer is whether, when viewed in the light most favorable to giving the instruction, the evidence supports that theory. We decide that it does not.

Defendant asserts that the following evidence is enough to support his theory that he had a reasonable belief that killing Victim was necessary to prevent a felony from occurring within his home: (1) Victim hated Defendant; (2) she knocked on the door to Defendant's home; (3) she had threatened him with a gun in the past; (4) she was furious that the couple was to be married the next day; and (5) she always carried a loaded gun. Absent from that evidence is any demonstration that Victim was "endeavor[ing] by violence to enter" his home or that she "intend[ed] violence to persons inside." Assuming that Defendant reasonably believed that Victim intended to commit a felony in his home, defense of habitation would have justified his actions only if he could show that Victim was attempting to force entry to his home. For example, if the evidence showed that Victim was trying to break through Defendant's front door at the time he killed her, defense of habitation would apply. However, under the facts of this case, there is no evidence reasonably tending to support the theory that Victim was attempting to force entry at the time Defendant killed her. After knocking on the door, Victim had retreated some four feet from it and was waiting for it to open. No evidence shows that, at the time she was killed, Victim was attempting to gain entry to Defendant's home with the intent to commit a violent felony therein.

Defendant's argument * * * justifies the instructions that Defendant received on self defense, and defense of another, it does not give rise to an instruction on defense of habitation because it does not allege any attempted forced entry on Victim's part.

Because there is no evidence to support the theory that Defendant killed Victim in defense of his habitation, refusing the instruction was not in error.

Notes and Questions

1. The former Attorney General of South Carolina stated in 2001 his policy regarding homes: "invade a home and invite a bullet." David Firestone, *South Carolina Killing Is Becoming Political*, New York Times, March 16, 2001, at A11. Should this be the rule—a person may shoot any intruder, regardless of any other circumstances? Is that what *Boyett* suggests?

2. Why does the law recognize a defense of habitation? Does it justify use of deadly force that is not already encompassed by the defenses of self-defense and defense-of-other?

When does the Model Penal Code justify use of deadly force against an intruder? Look at Section 3.06.

3. *Deadly force in defense of personal property.* Don't confuse the defense habitation with a defense of personal property. The general, although not universal, rule is that a person may *not* use deadly force solely to protect personal property.

Use of deadly force aside, should a person be permitted to *threaten* the use of deadly force to protect personal property? Suppose Bob attempts to steal Albert's laptop computer. Albert points an unloaded firearm at Bob and threatens to kill him unless Bob releases the laptop. If Albert is charged with brandishing a firearm, should he be able to defend himself on the basis of defense-of-property? See Commonwealth v. Alexander, 260 Va. 238, 531 S.E.2d 567 (2000).

Under what circumstances, if any, may a person use deadly force to protect personal property under the Model Penal Code? Reconsider MPC § 3.06.

4. Let's return to teen mother Sarah McKinley's situation described on p. 534. Under *Boyett*, was she justified in shooting to kill the intruder based on defense of habitation? What if the intruder was unarmed and intended only to take personal property? What if the intruder could not get in?

5. Now to the rest of Sarah McKinley's story. As it turns out, there were two men on the outside. They wanted to enter in order to look for painkilling drugs they suspected her late husband had used in the final stages of his illness. McKinley barricaded the door with her sofa. The intruders did not enter for approximately 21 minutes. During this time, she gave her baby a bottle so he would not cry. With no police officer yet in sight, one of the men finally pushed his way inside. McKinley shot him when he entered. The intruder died clutching a knife in his gloved left hand. His accomplice, Dustin Louis Stewart, fled, but later turned himself in to the police. McKinley was not prosecuted for any offense. For what offenses could Stewart be prosecuted?

6. Some defense-of-habitation cases involve a different scenario than the McKinley story. For example, in Dallas, Texas, a home owner was awakened

at 4 a.m. by someone banging and kicking at his back door. Fearing a burglar, he shot through the closed door, shooting his unarmed and harmless neighbor. Gretel C. Kovach, *Musician Is Killed For Banging on a Door*, New York Times, Sept. 5, 2007, at A23 (National Edition).

Another tragic scenario: Police officers seek to enter a home to execute a search warrant. Perhaps they have the right house for the search, perhaps they have made a mistake. In any case, the resident, unaware of the identity of the intruders, shoots and kills an officer. If she believed that the intruders were burglars, should she be permitted to claim defense-of-habitation, or should the law be that the defense only applies if "the entry * * * itself must have been *in fact* unlawful, regardless of what a defendant might have believed * * *." Fair v. State, 288 Ga. 244, 702 S.E.2d 420 (2010) (interpreting a state statute).

7. Hector Soto, 21, who had recently moved into an apartment complex, went out with friends to celebrate his upcoming graduation. Friends drove him back to the apartment building. Intoxicated and confused because the buildings in the complex looked the same, Soto attempted to enter the wrong apartment. When his key failed, he entered an open window and headed to the bathroom (you can imagine why). Tom Bradford, the resident of the apartment, encountered Soto and killed him. Lance Pugmire, *Man Made Fatal Error in Address*, Los Angeles Times, Jan. 10, 2006, at B9.

The defense of habitation usually is asserted when an occupant of a home uses deadly force to *prevent* intrusion into his "castle." Assume Bradford would have been justified in using deadly force as Soto entered the apartment through the window. Should he be permitted to use deadly force against Soto *after* the entry? What are the competing arguments? Compare State v. McCombs, 297 N.C. 151, 253 S.E.2d 906 (1979) (disallowing the defense) with People v. Stombaugh, 52 Ill.2d 130, 284 N.E.2d 640 (1972) (permitting the defense).

8. *And then there is this perhaps—but, only perhaps—apocryphal story. . . .* An elderly woman completed her shopping and returned to her car. She found four men inside. She dropped her shopping bags, drew a handgun, yelled at them at the top of her lungs that she would use the gun unless they got out of the car. The men "didn't wait around for a second invitation, but got out and ran like mad." Our elderly hero loaded her shopping bags into the car, and got into the driver's seat. Oops. Her key would not fit the ignition. No wonder. It was not her car. Her car was identical looking, but parked four spaces down. She embarrassedly loaded her bags (this time, into her own car) and drove to the police station. There, a police sergeant broke into laughter after she reported what had happened. He pointed to the other end of the room where four men, pale faced, were reporting a carjacking by a mad elderly woman. Lisa Denton, *Laugh Lines*, Chattanooga Times, Feb. 25, 2000, at 23.

9. *Crime prevention and arrest.* The defenses of habitation and property are, of course, generally raised by private persons. In contrast, when a law enforcement officer uses force, particularly deadly force, she will typically plead one of two law enforcement defenses: crime prevention (use of force to prevent a crime) or arrest (use of force in the effectuation of the arrest, often

when the arrestee seeks to escape). Ordinary citizens—alone or while assisting an officer—may also claim one of these defenses, although the facts will often trigger other defenses (e.g., self-defense or defense of habitation), as well.

Deadly force is never justified to prevent misdemeanors or to arrest a misdemeanant. At early common law, however, law enforcement officers could use deadly force, when necessary, to prevent the commission of *any* felony or to effectuate the arrest of *any* felon. In more recent years, many states by statute or case law have limited the use of deadly force in law enforcement, to forcible ("atrocious") felonies. Joshua Dressler, Understanding Criminal Law § 21.03 (5th ed. 2009).

There is also a constitutional law aspect to the law enforcement defenses. The Fourth Amendment to the United States Constitution prohibits "unreasonable searches and seizures." An arrest is a "seizure" of a person; therefore, it is unconstitutional for a law enforcement officer to seize a person in an unreasonable way. One such "unreasonable" way to seize a person is to use excessive force under the circumstances of the particular case. Thus, for example, the use of deadly force to effectuate the arrest of a fleeing unarmed youth, suspected of a nonviolent felony, constitutes an unreasonable seizure of the youth. Tennessee v. Garner, 471 U.S. 1, 105 S.Ct. 1694, 85 L.Ed.2d 1 (1985). However, the Supreme Court has held that the Fourth Amendment is *not* violated when a police officer rams a fleeing motorist's car from behind during a high-speed chase, in view of the danger inherent in the driver's conduct. Scott v. Harris, 550 U.S. 372, 127 S.Ct. 1769, 167 L.Ed.2d 686 (2007).

[handwritten margin note: 4th Amendment]

5. NECESSITY ("CHOICE OF EVILS")

a. General Principles

NELSON v. STATE

Supreme Court of Alaska, 1979.
597 P.2d 977.

MATTHEWS, JUSTICE.

Shortly after midnight on May 22, 1976, Dale Nelson drove his four-wheel drive truck onto a side road off the [highway] * * *. His truck became bogged down in a marshy area about 250 feet off the highway. Nelson testified that he was afraid the truck might tip over in the soft ground. He and his two companions, Lynnette Stinson and Carl Thompson, spent an hour unsuccessfully trying to free the vehicle. At about 1:00, Nelson began walking with Stinson down the highway. An acquaintance drove by and offered to help, but was unable to render much assistance. He then drove Nelson and Stinson to a Highway Department Yard where heavy equipment was parked. The yard was marked with "no-trespassing" signs. After waiting several hours for someone to come by, they decided to take a dump truck and use it to pull out Nelson's vehicle. The dump truck also became stuck.

At approximately 10:00 that morning a man identified only as "Curly" appeared. His vehicle was also stuck further down the highway. Curly offered to assist Nelson. They returned to the heavy equipment yard and took a front-end loader, which they used to free the dump truck. They then used the dump truck to free Curly's car. The dump truck was returned to the equipment yard, but when Nelson attempted to use the front-end loader to free his own truck the front-end loader also became bogged down.

Frustrated and tired after twelve hours of attempting to free his vehicle, Nelson and his companions quit and went to sleep. Two of them slept in a tent. One of them went to sleep in the truck. They were awakened by a Highway Department employee, who placed them under citizen's arrest.

Considerable damage was done to both the front-end loader and the dump truck as a result of Nelson's attempt to free his truck. * * * Nelson was convicted in district court of reckless destruction of personal property in violation of AS 11.20.515(b)[2] and joyriding in violation of AS 28.35.010.[3] This conviction was affirmed on appeal to the superior court.

The sole question presented is whether the jury was properly instructed on the defense of necessity. Nelson requested an instruction which read:

> You are instructed that the defendant is allowed to use a motor vehicle of another person without permission if the use is for an emergency in the case of immediate and dire need.

> You are further instructed that once the defendant has raised the issue of emergency or necessity, the state must prove the lack of emergency or necessity beyond a reasonable doubt.

Over Nelson's objection, the court gave an instruction on the necessity defense which read as follows:

> You are instructed that it is a defense to a crime such as joyriding or taking someone else's motor vehicle without his permission that the person acted out of necessity in a case of immediate and dire need. However, such a defense exists only when natural forces create a situation wherein it becomes necessary for a person to violate the law in order to avoid a greater evil to himself or his property. The harm

---

2. AS 11.20.515(b) provides:

A person who wilfully interferes with or tampers with property not his own, with the purpose to harm the property of another person, or with reckless disregard for the risk of harm to or loss of the property, is guilty of malicious mischief and, upon conviction, is punishable by imprisonment for not more than one year, or by a fine of not less than $100 nor more than $5,000 or by both.

3. AS 28.35.010(a) provides in part:

Driving a vehicle without owner's consent. (a) A person who drives, tows away, or takes a vehicle not his own without the consent of the owner, with intent temporarily to deprive the owner of possession of the vehicle, or a person who is a party or accessory to or an accomplice in the driving or unauthorized taking is guilty of a misdemeanor, and upon conviction is punishable by imprisonment for not less than 30 days nor more than one year, and by a fine of not less than $100 nor more than $1,000.

which is to be avoided must be the greater harm and it must be immediate and dire. Where a reasonable alternative other than violating the law is available in order to avoid the harm the defense of necessity is not applicable.

Nelson argues that the jury instruction was erroneous because it allowed the jury to apply what he calls an "objective, after-the-fact" test of need and emergency, rather than a "subjective, reasonable man" test. By this we assume Nelson means that he was entitled to have explained to the jury that they must view the question of necessity from the standpoint of a reasonable person knowing all that the defendant did at the time he acted.

We affirm the conviction. We note at the outset that the instruction proposed by Nelson is similarly lacking of any explicit language allowing the jury to find necessity if there was a reasonable belief that an emergency existed as opposed to an actual emergency. Thus, even if Nelson's proposed instruction had been given verbatim the alleged error would not have been corrected. * * *

The defense of necessity may be raised if the defendant's actions, although violative of the law, were necessary to prevent an even greater harm from occurring.

> The rationale of the necessity defense is not that a person, when faced with the pressure of circumstances of nature, lacks the mental element which the crime in question requires. Rather, it is this reason of public policy: the law ought to promote the achievement of higher values at the expense of lesser values, and sometimes the greater good for society will be accomplished by violating the literal language of the criminal law.

W. LaFave & A. Scott, *Criminal Law* § 50 at 382 (1972).

Commentators generally agree that there are three essential elements to the defense: 1) the act charged must have been done to prevent a significant evil; 2) there must have been no adequate alternative; 3) the harm caused must not have been disproportionate to the harm avoided.

The instruction given adequately describes these requirements for the jury. Nelson argues that he was entitled to wording which would explicitly allow the jury to find a necessity defense if a reasonable person at the time of acting would have believed that the necessary elements were present. Nelson is correct in stating that the necessity defense is available if a person acted in the reasonable belief that an emergency existed and there were no alternatives available even if that belief was mistaken. Moreover, the person's actions should be weighed against the harm reasonably foreseeable at the time, rather than the harm that actually occurs.[6]

---

6. * * * [T]he defendant must also have acted in the belief that the reasonably foreseeable harm resulting from the violation would be less than the harm resulting from compliance with the law. However, here the defendant's belief is not by itself sufficient. An objective determination must be made as to whether the defendant's value judgment was correct, given the facts as

Assuming that the instruction given was not worded adequately to convey these concepts to the jury, we would find the error harmless, for Nelson failed to make out a case for the necessity defense. The "emergency" situation claimed by Nelson to justify his appropriation of the construction equipment was the alleged danger that his truck, stuck in the mud, might tip over, perhaps damaging the truck top. However by the time Nelson decided to use the equipment the truck had already been stuck for several hours. The dire nature of the emergency may be judged by the fact that some twelve hours later, having unsuccessfully attempted to remove the vehicle from the mud, one of Nelson's companions fell asleep in the truck, which had still not tipped over.

Nor can it be said that Nelson had no lawful alternatives in his situation. The record shows that during the time Nelson was trying to free the vehicle people stopped on several different occasions and offered their services in the form of physical assistance, rides, or offers to telephone state troopers or a tow truck.

Finally, it cannot be said that the harm sought to be avoided in this case—potential damage to Nelson's truck—was greater than the harm caused by Nelson's illegal actions. Even disregarding the actual damage to the equipment caused by Nelson's use, the seriousness of the offenses committed by Nelson were disproportionate to the situation he faced. The legislature has made this clear by making reckless destruction of personal property a crime punishable by imprisonment for up to one year and a $5,000 fine, and joyriding punishable by imprisonment for up to one year and a $1,000 fine. The equipment taken by Nelson was marked with no trespassing signs. Nelson's fears about damage to his truck roof were no justification for his appropriation of sophisticated and expensive equipment.

AMERICAN LAW INSTITUTE, MODEL PENAL CODE AND COMMENTARIES, COMMENT TO § 3.02

(1985), 9–14

1. *Codification of a Principle of Necessity.* This section [§ 3.02 of the Code] accepts the view that a principle of necessity, properly conceived, affords a general justification for conduct that would otherwise constitute an offense. It reflects the judgment that such a qualification on criminal liability, like the general requirements of culpability, is essential to the rationality and justice of the criminal law, and is appropriately addressed in a penal code. Under this section, property may be destroyed to prevent the spread of a fire. A speed limit may be violated in pursuing a suspected criminal. An ambulance may pass a traffic light. Mountain climbers lost in a storm may take refuge in a house or may appropriate provisions. Cargo may be jettisoned or an embargo violated to preserve the vessel. An alien

---

he reasonably perceived them. The majority of jurisdictions appear to hold that this determination must be made, at least initially, by the court.

may violate a curfew in order to reach an air raid shelter. A druggist may dispense a drug without the requisite prescription to alleviate grave distress in an emergency. A developed legal system must have better ways of dealing with such problems than to refer only to the letter of particular prohibitions, framed without reference to cases of this kind.

Although the point has not been entirely free from controversy, necessity seems clearly to have standing as a common law defense; such issue as there was related to its definition and extent. Because judicial decisions were rare, and the problems had received scant legislative attention, it was difficult to say even in a particular jurisdiction what the standing and scope of the defense might be. It was, therefore, believed essential to address the question in the formulation of an integrated code.

2. *Limitations on Scope of Defense.* The Code's principle of necessity is subject to a number of limitations. First, the actor must actually believe that his conduct is necessary to avoid an evil. If a druggist who sells a drug without a prescription is unaware that the recipient requires it immediately to save his life, the actual necessity of the transaction will not exculpate the druggist. * * *

Second, the necessity must arise from an attempt by the actor to avoid an evil or harm that is greater than the evil or harm sought to be avoided by the law defining the offense charged. An equal or a lesser harm will not suffice. * * *

Third, the balancing of evils is not committed to the private judgment of the actor; it is an issue for determination at the trial. Thus, even if the defendant genuinely believes that the life of another is less valuable than his own financial security, his conduct would not be justified under Subsection (1)(a); for it requires that the harm or evil sought to be avoided be greater than that which would be caused by the commission of the offense, not that the defendant believe it to be so. * * * The Code does not resolve the question of how far the balancing of values should be determined by the court as a matter of law or submitted to the jury. There was disagreement in the Council of the Institute over the proper distribution of responsibility and it was decided that this question was best remitted to the law that generally governs the respective functions of the court and jury.

Fourth, under Subsections (1)(b) and (1)(c), the general choice of evils defense cannot succeed if the issue of competing values has been previously foreclosed by a deliberate legislative choice, as when some provision of the law deals explicitly with the specific situation that presents the choice of evils or a legislative purpose to exclude the claimed justification otherwise appears. * * * The legislature, so long as it acts within constitutional limits, is always free to make such a choice and have its choice prevail. * * *

The fifth limitation is dealt with in Subsection (2). * * *

When the actor has made a proper choice of values, his belief in the necessity of his conduct to serve the higher value will exculpate—unless the crime involved can be committed recklessly or negligently. When the latter is the case, recklessness or negligence in bringing about the situation requiring the choice of evils or in appraising the necessity for his conduct may be the basis for conviction. This treatment of the matter thus precludes conviction of a purposeful offense when the actor's culpability inheres in recklessness or negligence, while sanctioning conviction for a crime for which that level of culpability is otherwise sufficient to convict. What will constitute recklessness or negligence in the particular circumstances, of course, is an issue to be resolved under the definition of these terms in Section 2.02.

NOTES AND QUESTIONS

1. *Fault in creating the emergency.* Does Model Penal Code § 3.02(2) state a sensible limitation on the scope of the necessity defense? Suppose that Paul recklessly starts a fire in a heavily wooded area that immediately threatens to burn down a row of occupied houses. Paul correctly concludes that the only way to save the homes is for him to burn down Jennifer's unoccupied house as a firebreak, which he does, thereby saving the other houses and, perhaps, lives. If Paul is prosecuted for arson (defined, "purposely, knowingly, recklessly burning a dwelling house"), does he have a valid necessity claim? *Should* he be permitted the defense? See Paul H. Robinson, *Causing the Conditions of One's Own Defense: A Study in the Limits of Theory in Criminal Law Doctrine,* 71 Va.L.Rev. 1, 3–4, 8–13, 17–20 (1985).

2. How does Model Penal Code § 3.02 differ from the common law necessity defense, as explained in *Nelson?*

3. Michael H. Hoffheimer, *Codifying Necessity: Legislative Resistance to Enacting Choice-of-Evils Defenses to Criminal Liability,* 82 Tulane L. Rev. 191, 196 (2007):

> It is time for a reality check. * * * Only two states have enacted the Model Penal Code's version of the [necessity, or choice-of-evils] defense verbatim—a third has adopted it with modifications. Furthermore, those states that do codify some form of the necessity defense almost universally impose significant limits on the defense that parallel restrictions imposed by jurisdictions that recognize the defense by common law judicial decisions.

Courts generally apply the non-MPC version of the defense quite strictly. For example, consider People v. Fontes, 89 P.3d 484 (Colo.App. 2003):

> Defendant was arrested after he presented a false identification card to a convenience store clerk and attempted to cash a forged payroll check in the amount of $454.75. At trial, his wife testified * * * that defendant had intended to use the money from the check to buy food for the couple's children.

> As part of his offer of proof, defendant indicated that his three children, who ranged in age from sixteen months to eleven years, suffered

from severe health problems. On the date the crimes occurred, the children had not eaten for more than twenty-four hours, and three different food banks has turned down defendant's requests for food. Defendant feared that a lack of food would exacerbate his children's health problems, and lead to malnutrition and death. * * *

While we are not without sympathy for the downtrodden, the law is clear that economic necessity alone cannot support a choice of crime. Although economic necessity may be an important issue in sentencing, a choice of evils defense cannot be based upon economic necessity.

Why would the court bar *all* economic necessity claims?

4. The State of Louisiana prohibits "looting," punishable by imprisonment for not more than fifteen years. Looting is defined, in part, as

the intentional entry by a person without authorization into any * * * place of abode * * * or any structure belonging to another and used in whole or in part as a place of business, * * * in which normal security of property is not present by virtue of a hurricane, flood, fire, act of God, or * * * by virtue of a riot, mob, or other human agency, and the obtaining or exerting control over or damaging or removing property of the owner. La. R.S. § 14:62.5 (2008).

Now, consider victims of Hurricane Katrina, a number of whom broke into businesses to take children's clothing, food, water, and needed medications, for themselves or their family. If such a victim asserted a Model Penal Code choice-of-evils defense in a looting prosecution, how would you characterize the harm *she* has caused? Is it trivial compared to the harm she sought to prevent? Consider:

[T]he calculation of evils * * * caused[] [in looting cases] is actually more complicated than [a] simple account would suggest. Although the more direct harms caused by the offender's looting are those suffered by the person or entity whose premises are looted, less direct harms accrue to the community generally, including the loss of civil order and the sense of fear that such loss is likely to cause. We must also consider the possibility that looting tends to be contagious * * *. And such looting might also cause more remote, but still significant, harms: for example, the store whose goods were looted might have its insurance premiums increased; as a result, it might decide to raise its prices or even close for good; the premises might remain vacant and boarded up; the incident might mark the beginning of the community's slide into decline.

Stuart P. Green, *Looting, Law, and Lawlessness*, 81 Tulane L. Rev. 1129, 1152–53 (2007).

Do you find all of these "harms" a realistic concern in the context of Katrina? In view of the potential complexities in balancing harms in *any* necessity case, involving *any* crime, whom do you consider better qualified to conduct the process, a judge or jury? If *you*, as a juror, were balancing the harms in a Katrina looting case, what more (if anything) would you feel you need to know to decide whether the "looter" was justified in her conduct?

5. *Problem.* D engaged in heavy drinking in the early evening. Later, he awoke in his apartment and discovered that he was lying in a pool of blood

and that he was bleeding from a wound that required immediate medical attention. He had no telephone in the apartment and lived alone. He tried to drive himself to the hospital, but he was arrested for driving under the influence of alcohol on the way there. Butterfield v. State, 167 Tex.Crim. 64, 317 S.W.2d 943 (1958). Do the facts support a valid choice-of-evils defense under the Model Penal Code?

Suppose we change one fact: when *D* awakened from his heavy drinking, he discovered that his small child had ingested a life-threatening poison. Does *this* support a valid choice-of-evils defense to driving while intoxicated?

b. Civil Disobedience

UNITED STATES v. SCHOON

United States Court of Appeals, Ninth Circuit, 1991.
971 F.2d 193.

Bᴏᴏᴄʜᴇᴠᴇʀ, Cɪʀᴄᴜɪᴛ Jᴜᴅɢᴇ:

Gregory Schoon, Raymond Kennon, Jr., and Patricia Manning appeal their convictions for obstructing activities of the Internal Revenue Service Office in Tucson, Arizona, and failing to comply with an order of a federal police officer. Both charges stem from their activities in protest of United States involvement in El Salvador. They claim the district court improperly denied them a necessity defense. Because we hold the necessity defense inapplicable in cases like this, we affirm.

I.

On December 4, 1989, thirty people, including appellants, gained admittance to the IRS office in Tucson, where they chanted "keep America's tax dollars out of El Salvador," splashed simulated blood on the counters, walls, and carpeting, and generally obstructed the office's operation. After a federal police officer ordered the group, on several occasions, to disperse or face arrest, appellants were arrested.

At a bench trial, appellants proffered testimony about conditions in El Salvador as the motivation for their conduct. They attempted to assert a necessity defense, essentially contending that their acts in protest of American involvement in El Salvador were necessary to avoid further bloodshed in that country. While finding appellants motivated solely by humanitarian concerns, the court nonetheless precluded the defense as a matter of law * * *. The sole issue on appeal is the propriety of the court's exclusion of a necessity defense as a matter of law.

II.

* * * To invoke the necessity defense, * * * the defendants colorably must have shown that: (1) they were faced with a choice of evils and chose the lesser evil; (2) they acted to prevent imminent harm; (3) they reasonably anticipated a direct causal relationship between their conduct and the

harm to be averted; and (4) they had no legal alternatives to violating the law. * * *

The district court denied the necessity defense on the grounds that (1) the requisite immediacy was lacking; (2) the actions taken would not abate the evil; and (3) other legal alternatives existed. Because the threshold test for admissibility of a necessity defense is a conjunctive one, a court may preclude invocation of the defense if "proof is deficient with regard to any of the four elements."

While we could affirm substantially on those grounds relied upon by the district court, we find a deeper, systemic reason for the complete absence of federal case law recognizing a necessity defense in an indirect civil disobedience case. As used in this opinion, "civil disobedience" is the wilful violation of a law, undertaken for the purpose of social or political protest. * * * Indirect civil disobedience involves violating a law or interfering with a government policy that is not, itself, the object of protest. Direct civil disobedience, on the other hand, involves protesting the existence of a law by breaking that law or by preventing the execution of that law in a specific instance in which a particularized harm would otherwise follow. This case involves indirect civil disobedience because these protestors were not challenging the laws under which they were charged. In contrast, the civil rights lunch counter sit-ins, for example, constituted direct civil disobedience because the protestors were challenging the rule that prevented them from sitting at lunch counters. Similarly, if a city council passed an ordinance requiring immediate infusion of a suspected carcinogen into the drinking water, physically blocking the delivery of the substance would constitute direct civil disobedience: protestors would be preventing the execution of a law in a specific instance in which a particularized harm—contamination of the water supply—would otherwise follow.

* * * Today, we conclude, for the reasons stated below, that the necessity defense is inapplicable to cases involving indirect civil disobedience.

III.

Necessity is, essentially, a utilitarian defense. It therefore justifies criminal acts taken to avert a greater harm, maximizing social welfare by allowing a crime to be committed where the social benefits of the crime outweigh the social costs of failing to commit the crime. Pursuant to the defense, prisoners could escape a burning prison, a person lost in the woods could steal food from a cabin to survive, an embargo could be violated because adverse weather conditions necessitated sale of the cargo at a foreign port, a crew could mutiny where their ship was thought to be unseaworthy, and property could be destroyed to prevent the spread of fire.

What all the traditional necessity cases have in common is that the commission of the "crime" averted the occurrence of an even greater "harm." In some sense, the necessity defense allows us to act as individual legislatures, amending a particular criminal provision or crafting a one-time exception to it, subject to court review, when a real legislature would formally do the same under those circumstances. For example, by allowing prisoners who escape a burning jail to claim the justification of necessity, we assume the lawmaker, confronting this problem, would have allowed for an exception to the law proscribing prison escapes.

Because the necessity doctrine is utilitarian, however, strict requirements contain its exercise so as to prevent nonbeneficial criminal conduct. For example, " '[i]f the criminal act cannot abate the threatened harm, society receives no benefit from the criminal conduct.' " Similarly, to forgive a crime taken to avert a lesser harm would fail to maximize social utility. * * * Likewise, criminal acts cannot be condoned to thwart threats, yet to be imminent, or those for which there are legal alternatives to abate the harm.

Analysis of three of the necessity defense's four elements leads us to the conclusion that necessity can never be proved in a case of indirect civil disobedience. We do not rely upon the imminent harm prong of the defense because we believe there can be indirect civil disobedience cases in which the protested harm is imminent.

A.

1. Balance of Harms

It is axiomatic that, if the thing to be averted is not a harm at all, the balance of harms necessarily would disfavor any criminal action. Indirect civil disobedience seeks first and foremost to bring about the repeal of a law or a change of governmental policy, attempting to mobilize public opinion through typically symbolic action. * * * Thus, the most immediate "harm" this form of protest targets is the *existence* of the law or policy. However, the mere existence of a constitutional law or governmental policy cannot constitute a legally cognizable harm.

There may be, of course, general harms that result from the targeted law or policy. Such generalized "harm," however, is too insubstantial an injury to be legally cognizable. * * * The law could not function were people allowed to rely on their *subjective* beliefs and value judgments in determining which harms justified the taking of criminal action. *See United States v. Moylan,* 417 F.2d 1002, 1008–09 (4th Cir.1969) ("Exercise of a moral judgment based upon individual standards does not carry with it legal justification or immunity from punishment for breach of the law* * *. Toleration of such conduct would [be] inevitably anarchic.").

The protest in this case was in the form of indirect civil disobedience, aimed at reversal of the government's El Salvador policy. That policy does not violate the Constitution, and appellants have never suggested as much. There is no evidence that the procedure by which the policy was adopted was in any way improper; nor is there any evidence that appellants were prevented systematically from participating in the democratic processes through which the policy was chosen. The most immediate harm the appellants sought to avert was the existence of the government's El Salvador policy, which is not in itself a legally cognizable harm. Moreover, any harms resulting from the operation of this policy are insufficiently concrete to be legally cognizable as harms for purposes of the necessity defense.

Thus, as a matter of law, the mere existence of a policy or law validly enacted by Congress cannot constitute a cognizable harm. If there is no cognizable harm to prevent, the harm resulting from criminal action taken for the purpose of securing the repeal of the law or policy necessarily outweighs any benefit of the action.

2. Causal Relationship Between Criminal Conduct and Harm to Be Averted

This inquiry requires a court to judge the likelihood that an alleged harm will be abated by the taking of illegal action. * * * In the traditional cases, a prisoner flees a burning cell and averts death, or someone demolishes a home to create a firebreak and prevents the conflagration of an entire community. The nexus between the act undertaken and the result sought is a close one. Ordinarily it is the volitional illegal act alone which, once taken, abates the evil.

In political necessity cases involving indirect civil disobedience against congressional acts, however, the act alone is unlikely to abate the evil precisely because the action is indirect. Here, the IRS obstruction, or the refusal to comply with a federal officer's order, are unlikely to abate the killings in El Salvador, or immediately change Congress's policy; instead, it takes another *volitional* actor not controlled by the protestor to take a further step; Congress must change its mind.

3. Legal Alternatives

A final reason the necessity defense does not apply to these indirect civil disobedience cases is that legal alternatives will never be deemed exhausted when the harm can be mitigated by congressional action. * * *

B.   * * *

The real problem here is that litigants are trying to distort to their purposes an age-old common law doctrine meant for a very different set of circumstances. What these cases are really about is gaining notoriety for a cause—the defense allows protestors to get their political grievances discussed in a courtroom. It is precisely this political motive that has left some courts, like the district court in this case, uneasy. Because these attempts to invoke the necessity defense "force the courts to choose among causes they should make legitimate by extending the defense of necessity," and because the criminal acts, themselves, do not maximize social good, they should be subject to a *per se* rule of exclusion. * * *

FERNANDEZ, CIRCUIT JUDGE, concurring:

I agree with much of what the majority says regarding the application of the necessity defense to this type of case.

I do not mean to be captious in questioning whether the necessity defense is grounded on pure utilitarianism,[1] but fundamentally, I am not so sure that this defense of justification should be grounded on utilitarian theory alone rather than on a concept of what is right and proper conduct under the circumstances. * * *

NOTES AND QUESTIONS

1.   Even without a *per se* rule of exclusion, trial courts rarely instruct juries on the defense of necessity in indirect civil disobedience cases, a position approved by virtually all appellate courts. This does not mean, however, that the defense is never successfully used by protesters. Occasionally, a trial judge permits a defendant to raise the necessity claim, and the factfinder sends a "political message" by acquitting the defendant. Because a defendant may not constitutionally be retried after an acquittal, the prosecutor is barred from seeking a new trial on the ground that the judge erred in allowing the defense to be raised.

2.   As explained in Steven M. Bauer & Peter J. Eckerstrom, *The State Made Me Do It: The Applicability of the Necessity Defense to Civil Disobedience*, 39 Stanford L. Rev. 1173, 1184–1198 (1987), three arguments are frequently made in defense of political necessity claims. First, such a defense "empowers the individual primarily by presenting a forum in which stifled minority or unheeded majority viewpoints receive a public hearing and a governmental response." By allowing defendants to raise a political necessity claim, the law "conveys the symbolic message that our society highly values political input and gives special attention to apparent systemic failures in our form of democratic government."

Second, the political necessity defense "places the jury in a position to acquit the defendant, nullifying the effect of the law that has been broken." Such "empowerment" of the jury "conforms with a longstanding American willingness to use citizens as a buffer between the defendant and the harsh and sometimes arbitrary enforcement of the law."

Third, "[t]he airing of political necessity arguments generally improves the quality and quantity of public discussion." When courts treat a political defendant's claims with seriousness, this "stimulate[s] a higher quality of discussion outside the courtroom as the media reports on the trial's progress."

Opponents of a political necessity defense contend that those who civilly disobey the law should accept the legal consequences of their actions, rather than seek to avoid punishment by raising a defense. Anti-defense advocates contend:

> [A] civil disobedient must accept enforcement of laws with which he disagrees if he is to expect enforcement of his prospective social agenda. * * * [H]e must ritualize his respect for law in general, even as he uses

---

1. For example, without questioning the defense itself, one might question the utility of permitting a condemned mass murderer to escape from a prison conflagration.

the persuasive strategy of defying a particular law. * * * The civil disobedient must demonstrate his respect for law not only to demonstrate prospective philosophical consistency, but also to resolve the present philosophical dilemma of his own lawbreaking. In acting on conscience, the civil disobedient asserts a subjective moral vision. He cannot expect that vision to be binding on the rest of society unless it is endorsed through the democratic process. * * * By breaking the law while accepting its punishment, the civil disobedient can accommodate both his individual moral viewpoint and his ethical bond to accede to the mandate of the community.

Opponents of the defense also assert that advocacy of the defense violates the principle of majority rule. It permits a jury—or even one hold-out on a jury—to frustrate the public will, as demonstrated through the electoral process.

Finally, opponents of a political necessity defense contend that juries lack the expertise to make the policy judgments that civil disobedients call on them to make. Even if jurors were generally equipped, the courtroom—with its technical rules of evidence—is not as suitable a forum for policymaking as the legislative process. Moreover, "factors that have nothing to do with the policy issue often enter into a jury's consideration. Subjective notions about the parties, actions by the judge, and the lawyers' ability to inflame the jury may influence its decision."

3. Should civil disobedients be convicted, but not punished? Do you agree that "[c]ivil resisters, for the most part, are people of passion and principle who are driven to lead by example. * * * It is unrealistic not to recognize that these individuals differ from the common egotistic criminal"? Matthew Lippman, *Reflections on Non–Violent Resistance and the Necessity Defense,* 11 Hous.J.Int'l L. 277, 304 (1989). If you agree, is there any valid basis for punishing these people? Will punishment deter them or other similarly impassioned and principled opponents of government policies or laws? Is the justification for punishing a disobedient that the actor's behavior "identifies a form of arrogance [in believing that he knows better than the majority what is good for society,] which organized society cannot tolerate"? United States v. Cullen, 454 F.2d 386 (7th Cir.1971).

4. *Update.* Gregory Schoon is now a professional artist: <www.greg schoonfineart.com>.

c. Defense to Murder?

THE QUEEN v. DUDLEY AND STEPHENS

Queen's Bench Division, 1884.
14 Q.B.D. 273.

LORD COLERIDGE, C.J.

[The facts are set out at p. 49 supra.]

* * * From these facts, stated with the cold precision of a special verdict, it appears sufficiently that the prisoners were subject to terrible

temptation, to sufferings which might break down the bodily power of the strongest man, and try the conscience of the best. * * * But nevertheless this is clear, that the prisoners put to death a weak and unoffending boy upon the chance of preserving their own lives by feeding upon his flesh and blood after he was killed, and with the certainty of depriving *him* of any possible chance of survival. The verdict finds in terms that "if the men had not fed upon the body of the boy they would *probably* not have survived," and that "the boy being in a much weaker condition was *likely* to have died before them." They might possibly have been picked up next day by a passing ship; they might possibly not have been picked up at all; in either case it is obvious that the killing of the boy would have been an unnecessary and profitless act. It is found by the verdict that the boy was incapable of resistance, and, in fact, made none; and it is not even suggested that his death was due to any violence on his part attempted against, or even so much as feared by, those who killed him. Under these circumstances the jury say that they are ignorant whether those who killed him were guilty of murder, and have referred it to this Court to determine what is the legal consequence which follows from the facts which they have found. * * *

There remains to be considered the real question in the case— whether killing under the circumstances set forth in the verdict be or be not murder. The contention that it could be anything else was, to the minds of us all, both new and strange, and we stopped the Attorney General in his negative argument in order that we might hear what could be said in support of a proposition which appeared to us to be at once dangerous, immoral, and opposed to all legal principle and analogy. All, no doubt, that can be said has been urged before us, and we are now to consider and determine what it amounts to. First it is said that it follows from various definitions of murder in books of authority, which definitions imply, if they do not state, the doctrine, that in order to save your own life you may lawfully take away the life of another, when that other is neither attempting nor threatening yours, nor is guilty of any illegal act whatever towards you or any one else. But if these definitions be looked at they will not be found to sustain this contention. The earliest in point of date is the passage cited to us from Bracton, who lived in the reign of Henry III. * * * But in the very passage as to necessity, on which reliance has been placed, it is clear that Bracton is speaking of necessity in the ordinary sense—the repelling by violence, violence justified so far as it was neces- sary for the object, any illegal violence used towards oneself. * * *

It is, if possible, yet clearer that the doctrine contended for receives no support from the great authority of Lord Hale. * * * Lord Hale regarded the private necessity which justified, and alone justified, the taking the life of another for the safeguard of one's own to be what is commonly called "self-defence."

But if this could be even doubtful upon Lord Hale's words, Lord Hale himself has made it clear. For in the chapter in which he deals with the exemption created by compulsion or necessity he thus expresses himself:—

"If a man be desperately assaulted and in peril of death, and cannot otherwise escape unless, to satisfy his assailant's fury, he will kill an innocent person then present, the fear and actual force will not acquit him of the crime and punishment of murder, if he commit the fact, for he ought rather to die himself than kill an innocent * * *." * * *

Is there, then, any authority for the proposition which has been presented to us? Decided cases there are none. * * * The American case cited by my Brother Stephen in his Digest, from Wharton on Homicide, in which it was decided, correctly indeed, that sailors had no right to throw passengers overboard to save themselves, but on the somewhat strange ground that the proper mode of determining who was to be sacrificed was to vote upon the subject by ballot,[f] can hardly * * * be an authority satisfactory to a court in this country. * * *

The one real authority of former time is Lord Bacon, who, in his commentary * * * lays down the law as follows:—"Necessity carrieth a privilege in itself. * * * [I]f a man steal viands to satisfy his present hunger, this is no felony nor larceny. So if divers be in danger of drowning by the casting away of some boat or barge, and one of them get to some plank, or on the boat's side to keep himself above water, and another to save his life thrust him from it, whereby he is drowned, this is neither se defendendo or by misadventure, but justifiable." On this it is to be observed that Lord Bacon's proposition that stealing to satisfy hunger is no larceny is * * * expressly contradicted by Lord Hale * * *. And for the proposition as to the plank or boat, it is said to be derived from the canonists. At any rate he cites no authority for it, and it must stand upon his own. * * * There are many conceivable states of things in which it might possibly be true, but if Lord Bacon meant to lay down the broad proposition that a man may save his life by killing, if necessary, an innocent and unoffending neighbour, it certainly is not law at the present day. * * *

* * * Now it is admitted that the deliberate killing of this unoffending and unresisting boy was clearly murder, unless the killing can be justified by some well-recognised excuse admitted by the law. It is further admitted that there was in this case no such excuse, unless the killing was justified by what has been called "necessity." But the temptation to the act which existed here was not what the law has ever called necessity. Nor is this to be regretted. Though law and morality are not the same, and many things may be immoral which are not necessarily illegal, yet the

---

f. United States v. Holmes, 26 F.Cas. 360, 1 Wall.Jr.C.C. 1 (C.C.E.D. Pa. 1842). The trial judge instructed the jury that if "two persons who owe no duty to one another * * * should, by accident, not attributable to either, be placed in a situation where one cannot survive[,] [n]either is bound to save the other's life by sacrificing his own, nor would either commit a crime in saving his own life in a struggle for the only means of safety; but, if the source of danger, although obvious, is not imminent, the decision of who should be sacrificed among persons in equal relations to each other must be made by lot."

Holmes, a member of the crew who assisted in throwing passengers off an overcrowded boat following a shipwreck, was convicted of manslaughter and sentenced to six months' imprisonment and a fine of $20.

absolute divorce of law from morality would be of fatal consequence; and such divorce would follow if the temptation to murder in this case were to be held by law an absolute defence of it. It is not so. To preserve one's life is generally speaking a duty, but it may be the plainest and highest duty to sacrifice it. War is full of instances in which it is a man's duty not to live, but to die. The duty, in case of shipwreck, of a captain to his crew, of the crew to the passengers, of soldiers to women and children * * *; these duties impose on men the moral necessity, not of the preservation, but of the sacrifice of their lives for others, from which in no country, least of all, it is to be hoped, in England, will men ever shrink, as indeed, they have not shrunk. It is not correct, therefore, to say that there is any absolute or unqualified necessity to preserve one's life. * * * [I]t is enough in a Christian country to remind ourselves of the Great Example whom we profess to follow. It is not needful to point out the awful danger of admitting the principle which has been contended for. Who is to be the judge of this sort of necessity? By what measure is the comparative value of lives to be measured? Is it to be strength, or intellect, or what? It is plain that the principle leaves to him who is to profit by it to determine the necessity which will justify him in deliberately taking another's life to save his own. In this case the weakest, the youngest, the most unresisting, was chosen. Was it more necessary to kill him than one of the grown men? The answer must be "No"—

"So spake the Fiend, and with necessity,

The tyrant's plea, excused his devilish deeds."

It is not suggested that in this particular case the deeds were "devilish," but it is quite plain that such a principle once admitted might be made the legal cloak for unbridled passion and atrocious crime. * * *

It must not be supposed that in refusing to admit temptation to be an excuse for crime it is forgotten how terrible the temptation was; how awful the suffering; how hard in such trials to keep the judgment straight and the conduct pure. We are often compelled to set up standards we cannot reach ourselves, and to lay down rules which we could not ourselves satisfy. But a man has no right to declare temptation to be an excuse, though he might himself have yielded to it, nor allow compassion for the criminal to change or weaken in any manner the legal definition of the crime. It is therefore our duty to declare that the prisoners' act in this case was wilful murder, that the facts as stated in the verdict are no legal justification of the homicide; and to say that in our unanimous opinion the prisoners are upon this special verdict guilty of murder.[1]

The Court then proceeded to pass sentence of death upon the prisoners.[2]

---

1. My brother Grove has furnished me with the following suggestion, too late to be embodied in the judgment but well worth preserving: "If the two accused men were justified in killing Parker, then if not rescued in time, two of the three survivors would be justified in killing the third, and of the two who remained the stronger would be justified in killing the weaker, so the three men might be justifiably killed to give the fourth a chance of surviving."

2. This sentence was afterwards commuted by the Crown to six months' imprisonment.

NOTES AND QUESTIONS

1. Does *Dudley and Stephens* stand for the proposition that the killing of an innocent person, even to save the lives of a greater number of innocents, is *never* justifiable? If not, what *is* Lord Coleridge saying?

2. What *should* the law be in this regard? In your view, is it ever justifiable (and, if so, when) to intentionally kill an innocent person?

3. The Model Penal Code does not rule out the use of its choice-of-evils provision in homicide cases:

> The Model Code rejects any limitations on necessity cast in terms of particular evils to be avoided or particular evils to be justified * * *. * * * [T]his section reflects the view that the principle of necessity is one of general validity. It is widely accepted in the law of torts and there is even greater need for its acceptance in the law of crime. While there may be situations, such as rape, where it is hardly possible to claim that greater evil was avoided than that sought to be prevented by the law defining the offense, this is a matter that is safely left to the determination and elaboration of the courts.
>
> It would be particularly unfortunate to exclude homicidal conduct from the scope of the defense. For, recognizing that the sanctity of life has a supreme place in the hierarchy of values, it is nonetheless true that conduct that results in taking life may promote the very value sought to be protected by the law of homicide. Suppose, for example, that the actor makes a breach in a dike, knowing that it will inundate a farm, but taking the only course available to save a whole town. If he is charged with homicide of the inhabitants of the farm house, he can rightly point out that the object of the law of homicide is to save life, and that by his conduct he has effected a net saving of innocent lives. The life of every individual must be taken in such a case to be of equal value and the numerical preponderance in the lives saved compared to those sacrificed surely should establish legal justification for the act. * * * Although the view is not universally held that it is ethically preferable to take one innocent life than to have many lives lost,[15] most persons probably think a net saving of lives is ethically warranted if the choice among lives to be saved is not unfair. Certainly the law should permit such a choice.

---

15. Roman Catholic moralists have generally taken the position that one should not cause effects that are directly evil even if they are thought to be a necessary means to a greater good. Thus, it is considered wrong to terminate the life of a fetus even if that is the only way the mother can be saved and even if the fetus will die in any event. On the other hand, an ordinary operation designed directly to protect the mother's health is permissible, even if an inevitable effect is the death of the fetus, under the so-called principle of "double effect" that death is only permitted, not intended, and is not itself a means to saving the mother's life.

Many acts justifiable under this section would also be justifiable under the principle of "double effect." Diverting a flood to destroy a farmhouse instead of a town would be acceptable since the destruction of the farmhouse is not intended and is not a means of saving the town. Suppose, however, the citizens of a town receive a credible threat, say from a foreign invader, that everyone in the town will be killed unless the townspeople themselves kill their mayor, who is hiding. If the townspeople accede, they would have a substantial argument against criminal liability under this section but their act would be immoral under the double effect analysis, since they have intended to kill the mayor and it is his death that is the means to their safety.

American Law Institute, Model Penal Code and Commentaries, Comment to § 3.02 at 14–15 (1985).

Not all commentators agree with the Model Penal Code's approach:

> On a utilitarian theory of justice, the matter is open to debate. The particular act did reduce aggregate harm: By killing one, three survived who probably otherwise would not have. However, * * * it is not clear whether a legal system which institutionalizes the permissibility of such killings would, on balance, prevent more harm than it causes. This is where the mariners and the Crown diverged—with the mariners concerned with increasing chances of survival in shipwrecks, and the Crown and the courts concerned with long-run risks of diluting the deterrent force of the homicide prohibition. It is difficult to imagine how one could obtain evidence supporting either contention.
>
> Once one begins to doubt a purely utilitarian theory of justice, however, the answer begins to change. It becomes questionable whether such killings could ever be justified. The German courts * * * have historically been influenced by Kantian ethics, and would probably interpret the choice-of-evils provision in the German code as not permitting homicide to save others' lives.
>
> While Kantian ethics once were largely ignored in American legal philosophy, that has ceased to be true in recent years. Many leading writers on ethics and jurisprudence are now explicitly Kantian in their insistence on the preeminent value of individuals. Each person's life is as important as the lives of other persons. Hence, it is not just to sacrifice A's existence in order to promote the interests—or even, to save the lives—of B, C, and D. * * * If correct, it means that Dudley and Stephens's act of homicide cannot be justifiable. * * * Were one to accept this conclusion, it would require amending the Model Penal Code's choice-of-evils provision. The principle of preferring the lesser evil * * * should have applicability only when the act invades interests of the victim that are of less importance for him than the interests the actor stands to lose from compliance: for example, when I break into your house and steal your food in order to prevent myself from starving. The principle should not apply when I exact the ultimate sacrifice from you.

Andrew von Hirsch, *Lifeboat Law,* 4 Crim.Just.Ethics (Summer/Fall 1985), at 88, 90.

4. *A thought experiment.* It seems reasonable to conclude that suicide terrorists are not deterred by the threat of the death penalty. So, assume that the Central Intelligence Agency determines that the way to deter suicide terrorism is to develop a sanction worse than death. In this regard, consider Professor Paul Butler's thought experiment in his article, *Terrorism and Utilitarianism: Lessons From, and for, Criminal Law,* 93 J. Crim. L. & Criminology 1, 14 (2002):

> Imagine that the [CIA] let it be known that its agents will assassinate five members of the immediate family of any terrorist who dies in a suicide attack. * * * The CIA's objective is to prevent future terrorism. Thus, to send a message to potential terrorists, it plans to kill five family

members of each of the nineteen September 11 suicide terrorists. Should it? Does your answer depend upon how certain we are of the potential for future terrorism and the deterrent effect of the CIA's act? Suppose we knew that the CIA's act would deter at least one future attack, in which many more lives would be lost than the ninety-five that the CIA would take?

How would you answer Professor Butler's questions?

5. *A modern Dudley and Stephens dilemma?* Consider the English case of Re A (children) (conjoined twins: surgical separation), [2001] 2 WLR 480 (Court of Appeal, Civil Division):

> It truly is a unique case. In a nutshell the problem is this. Jodie and Mary are conjoined twins. They each have their own brain, heart and lungs and other vital organs and they each have arms and legs. They are joined at the lower abdomen. Whilst not underplaying the surgical complexities, they can be successfully separated. But the operation will kill the weaker twin, Mary. That is because her lungs and heart are too deficient to oxygenate and pump blood through her body. * * * She is alive only because a common artery enables her sister, who is stronger, to circulate life sustaining oxygenated blood for both of them. Separation would require the clamping and then the severing of that common artery. Within minutes of doing so Mary will die. Yet if the operation does not take place, both will die within three to six months, or perhaps a little longer, because Jodie's heart will eventually fail. The parents cannot bring themselves to consent to the operation. The twins are equal in their eyes and they cannot agree to kill one even to save the other. As devout Roman Catholics they sincerely believe that it is God's will that their children are afflicted as they are and they must be left in God's hands. The doctors are convinced they can carry out the operation so as to give Jodie a life which will be worthwhile.

The Court of Appeal authorized the surgical separation. There was no further appeal. The operation occurred at Saint Mary's Hospital, in Manchester, England. The surgery lasted twenty hours. The final separation took place in silence. Two pediatric surgeons, one a Catholic and the other an evangelical Christian, made the final cut, "as they felt it was inappropriate for one person to assume the entire responsibility as the cause of Mary's death." Charles I. Lugosi, *Playing God: Mary Must Die so Jodie May Live Longer*, 17 Issues in Law & Medicine 123, 136 (2001). As predicted, Mary died moments later.

First, as a purely legal matter, do you agree with the observation that "the laws of England appear to have changed. * * * [T]he Court of Appeal [has] now in effect adopted the defense's position in *Dudley and Stephens*." Id. at 139. Is there a principled way to distinguish the dilemma facing the parties in *Dudley and Stephens* from the case confronting the parents and doctors here? Is there any other justification defense—other than necessity—that might apply to the Conjoined Twins case?

Second, however you answer the preceding questions, do *you* believe the court acted properly?

6. Consider the following two hypotheticals that involve the taking of innocent life. Would you justify either of these homicides? How do these hypotheticals compare to *Dudley and Stephens* and/or the Conjoined Twins case (Note 5)—are they similar to them, or do they present an easier (or harder) case than those earlier decisions?

Hypothetical 1: F drives a trolley car. As the trolley rounds a bend, *F* sees five workers repairing the track. The only way to avoid striking and killing them is to stop the trolley, but the brakes unexpectedly fail. *F* sees a spur of track that would lead the trolley off to the right, but there is a single workman on the spur. *F* turns the trolley onto the spur, killing that workman, but saving the lives of the other five workers. Philippa Foot, *The Problem of Abortion and the Doctrine of Double Effect* in Virtues and Vices and Other Essays in Moral Philosophy 19 (1978).

Hypothetical 2: G is a surgeon with five desperately ill patients, two of whom need a lung transplant, two of whom require a kidney, and one of whom is waiting for a healthy heart. Each will die within 24 hours without the needed organ, but none are available. *H* comes to the hospital for a routine physical. *H* is in excellent health, with the appropriate blood-type and tissue matches to allow his organs to be transplanted into all of the dying patients. Without *H*'s consent, *G* harvests *H*'s heart, lungs, and kidneys. *H* dies, but *G*'s five patients survive and live long, healthy lives. Judith Jarvis Thomson, *The Trolley Problem*, 94 Yale L.J. 1395, 1396 (1985); see Robert Hallborg, Jr., *Comparing Harms: The Lesser–Evil Defense and the Trolley Problem*, 3 Legal Theory 291 (1997).

7. Assuming arguendo that Dudley and Stephens were not justified in killing the youth, should they have been *excused*? That is, do you believe that they should not morally and legally be blamed for their actions, even if those actions were wrong (unjustifiable)? You may want to think about this question as we turn to the principles of excuse.

D. PRINCIPLES OF EXCUSE

1. WHY DO WE EXCUSE WRONGDOERS?

SANFORD H. KADISH—EXCUSING CRIME

75 California Law Review 257 (1987), 263–65

Why we have excuses is less obvious than why we have other defenses. Let us start with Jeremy Bentham's explanation. He saw the point of excuses to be that they identified situations in which conduct is nondeterrable, so that punishment would be so much unnecessary evil. For since only the nondeterrable are excused, withholding punishment offers no comfort to those who are deterrable. The trouble is, as is now widely appreciated, that this does not follow, for punishing all, whether or not they happen to be deterrable, closes off any hope a deterrable offender might otherwise harbor that he could convince a jury that he was among the nondeterrable. Moreover, without excuses, prosecutions would be faster and cheaper, convictions more reliable, and the deterrent threat more credible. Indeed, we have in our law a class of offenses, strict liability offenses, that dispenses with mens rea requirements on just these grounds. Have we not given up something of value for the increased effectiveness that strict liability arguably provides, something that is not captured in Bentham's rationale?

Professor [H.L.A.] Hart [has] * * * offered a different account of excuses. He argued that by confining liability to cases in which persons have freely chosen, excuses serve to maximize the effect of a person's choices within the framework of coercive law, thereby furthering the satisfaction people derive in knowing that they can avoid the sanction of the law if they choose.

This rationale is an improvement over Bentham, inasmuch as Hart gives us a reason why we might want to put up with the loss of deterrence caused by excuses. But does this account capture the full force of a system of excuses? Suppose we preferred the risk of accidentally being victims of law enforcement to the increased risk of being victims of crime. That would be a plausible choice, particularly for a public obsessed with rising crime rates. Would we then feel there was nothing more problematic in giving up excuses than that we would be trading one kind of satisfaction for another? I think not. Something is missing in this account.

Hart's account focuses on the interests and satisfactions of the great majority of us who never become targets of law enforcement—our security in knowing we will not be punished if we do not choose to break the law. What is missing is an account of the concern for the innocent person who is the object of a criminal prosecution. Hart's essay does refer to the satisfaction of the lawbreaker in knowing the price he must pay to get what he wants by breaking the law. But it is doubtful that this is a satisfaction the law has any interest in furthering, for the point of the criminal law is surely to keep people from engaging in prohibited conduct, not to give them a choice between complying with the law or suffering punishment. The law's concern is for the person accused who has not made a culpable choice to break the law, not with furthering the interests of persons who would like to.

To blame a person is to express a moral criticism, and if the person's action does not deserve criticism, blaming him is a kind of falsehood and is, to the extent the person is injured by being blamed, unjust to him. It is this feature of our everyday moral practices that lies behind the law's excuses. Excuses, then, as Hart himself recognized * * *, represent no sentimental compromise with the demands of a moral code; they are, on the contrary, of the essence of a moral code. * * *

Of course, one might escape excuses altogether by withdrawing the element of blame from a finding of criminality. Indeed, there are some—though not so many as there were a generation ago—who would prefer that the criminal law reject all backward-looking judgments of punishment, blame, and responsibility, and concern itself exclusively with identifying and treating those who constitute a social danger. Whether it would be desirable to loosen punishment from its mooring in blame is a large and much discussed question. I will confine myself here to two observations. First, such a dissociation would not likely succeed. People would continue to see state coercion as punishment, notwithstanding official declarations that the state's only interest is the individual's welfare and social protection. Second, it is very doubtful that we should want it to succeed, since blame and punishment give expression to the concept of personal responsibility which is a central feature of our moral culture.

JOSHUA DRESSLER—UNDERSTANDING CRIMINAL LAW

(5th ed, 2009), 211–215

§ 17.03   Underlying Theories of "Excuse"

[A]   Searching for an Explanatory Theory

An excuse defense "is in the nature of a claim that although the actor has harmed society, she should not be blamed or punished for causing that harm." The question that must be answered here is: Is there a single principle that determines when the law will abstain from blaming a person who has caused social harm and, as a result, not hold her legally accountable in a criminal prosecution?

As with justifications, no single theory explains every excuse defense. * * * However, unlike justification defenses, which are often (but need not) be explained on utilitarian grounds, excuses in the criminal law are far more plausibly defended in non-utilitarian terms. As Professor Sanford Kadish has observed [in the excerpt above], "[s]omething is missing" in the utilitarian account of excuses * * *.

* * * [V]arious nonconsequentialist moral theories are surveyed [below]. * * *

[C]   Causation Theory

Perhaps the broadest excuse theory states that a person should not be blamed for her conduct if it was caused by factors outside her control.[26] For example, according to a causal theorist, D should be excused if she commits a crime because of a mental illness or a coercive deadly threat: Since she is not to blame for being ill or the victim of coercion—the cause of her actions—she is not to blame for the crime itself. * * *

It is * * * not evident that the causation principle conforms with our moral intuitions. A person who commits a crime due to self-induced intoxication, for example, may be able to show that her propensity to become intoxicated was caused by genetic or environmental factors over which she had no control; yet we do not consider such a wrongdoer morally blameless. Indeed, acceptance of the causal principle of excuses

---

26. For a full exposition of this theory, which the author ultimately rejects, see [Michael S. Moore, *Causation and the Excuses*, 73 Calif.L.Rev. 1091 (1985)].

could threaten to lead society down "the cul-de-sac of * * * determinism," in which *nobody* can be blamed or punished for her wrongful conduct.

[D] Character Theory

Various theorists treat a person's moral character as central to the concept of deserved punishment. According to one character theory, punishment should be proportional to a wrongdoer's moral desert, and that desert should be measured by the actor's character. Normally, we infer bad character from an actor's wrongful conduct; these character theorists argue that excuses should be recognized in the law in those circumstances in which bad character cannot be inferred from the offender's wrongful conduct.

For example, if *D* robs a bank, we would ordinarily infer that she is a greedy person who lacks concern for the rights of others, i.e., that she possesses a bad character. However, we would not infer bad character if we learned that she robbed the bank because terrorists threatened to kill her child if she did not cooperate. In such circumstances, we assume that even a person of good moral character would probably violate the law. Therefore, we excuse her actions. * * *

* * * [C]ritics raise various objections to * * * the character theory of excuses. First, if excuse law were genuinely based on character, a court would need to look at a person's entire life, and not solely at the circumstances surrounding the particular criminal act, in order to evaluate her moral desert. But, * * * "there are staggering obstacles in the way of our making [character] judgments about others." God, it may be argued, can judge our character, but mortals lack "the knowledge required to impute deep character depravity to others with any degree of reliability" * * *.

Second, the theory does not explain why we *do* punish people of *good* character who commit out-of-character offenses. * * *

Third, causal theorists argue that the character theory assumes that people are responsible for their character—and, thus, may be blamed for their bad character—but this may not be the case. They argue that one's character is shaped by powerful genetic and environmental factors beyond the individual's control. Defenders of the character theory argue, however, that a person *may* properly be held responsible for her character traits, even if she did not initially choose them, because she is responsible for *retaining* them.

[E] "Free Choice" (or Personhood) Theory

Advocates of the free-choice theory claim that a person may properly be blamed for her conduct "if, but only if, [s]he had the capacity and fair opportunity to function in a uniquely human way, *i.e.*, freely to choose whether to violate the moral/legal norms of society." According to this account, "free choice" exists if, at the time of the wrongful conduct, the actor has the substantial capacity and fair opportunity to: (1) understand the facts relating to her conduct; (2) appreciate that her conduct violates society's mores; and (3) conform her conduct to the dictates of the law. A person lacking the *substantial capacity* in any of these regards essentially suffers from some serious *internal disability* and, therefore, does not deserve to be punished because she lacks the basic attributes of person-hood that qualify her as a moral agent. Alternatively, a person who lacks "free choice" under the *no-fair-opportunity* prong does not deserve punishment because some *external* factor is acting upon her on this particular occasion such that it is unjust to blame her for her wrongful conduct.

Critics of the choice theory believe that it is too narrow. Causal theorists argue, for example, that because "free choice" is defined in terms of the actor's capacity and opportunity *at the moment of the criminal act* to obey the law, morally significant events arising earlier are excluded from the picture. For example, although a person may have had free choice regarding whether to rob a particular liquor store on a particular occasion, she may not have had a fair opportunity to avoid the conditions that hardened her character and made committing the crime seem inevitable.

NOTES AND QUESTIONS

1. As you consider the excuse defenses described in this chapter, ask yourself which one of the preceding moral theories (or the utilitarian rationale described in Kadish, supra) best explains the law of excuses that has developed, and which one, if any, approximates your own judgments about moral culpability.

2. DURESS

a. General Principles

UNITED STATES v. CONTENTO–PACHON

United States Court of Appeals, Ninth Circuit, 1984.
723 F.2d 691.

BOOCHEVER, CIRCUIT JUDGE.

This case presents an appeal from a conviction for unlawful possession with intent to distribute a narcotic controlled substance in violation of 21 U.S.C. § 841(a)(1) (1976). At trial, the defendant attempted to offer evidence of duress and necessity defenses. The district court excluded this evidence on the ground that it was insufficient to support the defenses. We reverse because there was sufficient evidence of duress to present a triable issue of fact.

I.   FACTS

The defendant-appellant, Juan Manuel Contento–Pachon, is a native of Bogota, Colombia and was employed there as a taxicab driver. He asserts that one of his passengers, Jorge, offered him a job as the driver of a privately-owned car. Contento–Pachon expressed an interest in the job and agreed to meet Jorge and the owner of the car the next day.

Instead of a driving job, Jorge proposed that Contento–Pachon swallow cocaine-filled balloons and transport them to the United States. Contento–Pachon agreed to consider the proposition. He was told not to mention the proposition to anyone, otherwise he would "get into serious trouble." Contento–Pachon testified that he did not contact the police because he believes that the Bogota police are corrupt and that they are paid off by drug traffickers.

Approximately one week later, Contento–Pachon told Jorge that he would not carry the cocaine. In response, Jorge mentioned facts about Contento–Pachon's personal life, including private details which Contento–Pachon had never mentioned to Jorge. Jorge told Contento–Pachon that his failure to cooperate would result in the death of his wife and three year-old child.

The following day the pair met again. Contento–Pachon's life and the lives of his family were again threatened. At this point, Contento–Pachon agreed to take the cocaine into the United States.

The pair met two more times. At the last meeting, Contento–Pachon swallowed 129 balloons of cocaine. He was informed that he would be watched at all times during the trip, and that if he failed to follow Jorge's instruction he and his family would be killed.

After leaving Bogota, Contento–Pachon's plane landed in Panama. Contento–Pachon asserts that he did not notify the authorities there because he felt that the Panamanian police were as corrupt as those in Bogota. Also, he felt that any such action on his part would place his family in jeopardy.

When he arrived at the customs inspection point in Los Angeles, Contento–Pachon consented to have his stomach x-rayed. The x-rays revealed a foreign substance which was later determined to be cocaine.

At Contento–Pachon's trial, the government moved to exclude the defenses of duress and necessity. The motion was granted. We reverse.

A. *Duress*

There are three elements of the duress defense: (1) an immediate threat of death or serious bodily injury, (2) a well-grounded fear that the threat will be carried out, and (3) no reasonable opportunity to escape the threatened harm. * * *

* * * We examine the elements of duress.

Immediacy: The element of immediacy requires that there be some evidence that the threat of injury was present, immediate, or impending. "[A] veiled threat of future unspecified harm" will not satisfy this requirement. The district court found that the initial threats were not immediate because "they were conditioned on defendant's failure to cooperate in the future and did not place defendant and his family in immediate danger."

Evidence presented on this issue indicated that the defendant was dealing with a man who was deeply involved in the exportation of illegal substances. Large sums of money were at stake and, consequently, Contento–Pachon had reason to believe that Jorge would carry out his threats. Jorge had gone to the trouble to discover that Contento–Pachon was married, that he had a child, the names of his wife and child, and the location of his residence. These were not vague threats of possible future harm. According to the defendant, if he had refused to cooperate, the consequences would have been immediate and harsh.

Contento–Pachon contends that he was being watched by one of Jorge's accomplices at all times during the airplane trip. As a consequence, the force of the threats continued to restrain him. Contento–Pachon's contention that he was operating under the threat of immediate harm was supported by sufficient evidence to present a triable issue of fact.

Escapability: The defendant must show that he had no reasonable opportunity to escape. The district court found that because Contento–Pachon was not physically restrained prior to the time he swallowed the balloons, he could have sought help from the police or fled. Contento–Pachon explained that he did not report the threats because he feared that the police were corrupt. The trier of fact should decide whether one in Contento–Pachon's position might believe that some of the Bogota police were paid informants for drug traffickers and that reporting the matter to the police did not represent a reasonable opportunity of escape.

If he chose not to go to the police, Contento–Pachon's alternative was to flee. We reiterate that the opportunity to escape must be reasonable. To flee, Contento–Pachon, along with his wife and three year-old child, would have been forced to pack his possessions, leave his job, and travel to a place beyond the reaches of the drug traffickers. A juror might find that this was not a reasonable avenue of escape. Thus, Contento–Pachon presented a triable issue on the element of escapability. * * *

B. *Necessity*

The defense of necessity is available when a person is faced with a choice of two evils and must then decide whether to commit a crime or an alternative act that constitutes a greater evil. Contento–Pachon has attempted to justify his violation of 21 U.S.C. § 841(a)(1) by showing that the alternative, the death of his family, was a greater evil.

Traditionally, in order for the necessity defense to apply, the coercion must have had its source in the physical forces of nature. The duress defense was applicable when the defendant's acts were coerced by a human force. This distinction served to separate the two similar defenses. But modern courts have tended to blur the distinction between duress and necessity.

It has been suggested that, "the major difference between duress and necessity is that the former negates the existence of the requisite mens rea for the crime in question, whereas under the latter theory there is no actus reus." *United States v. Micklus,* 581 F.2d 612, 615 (7th Cir.1978). The theory of necessity is that the defendant's free will was properly exercised to achieve the greater good and not that his free will was overcome by an outside force as with duress.

The defense of necessity is usually invoked when the defendant acted in the interest of the general welfare. * * *

Contento–Pachon's acts were allegedly coerced by human, not physical forces. In addition, he did not act to promote the general welfare. Therefore, the necessity defense was not available to him. Contento–Pachon mischaracterized evidence of duress as evidence of necessity. The district court correctly disallowed his use of the necessity defense.

II. CONCLUSION

Contento–Pachon presented credible evidence that he acted under an immediate and well-grounded threat of serious bodily injury, with no opportunity to escape. Because the trier of fact should have been allowed to consider the credibility of the proffered evidence, we reverse. * * *

COYLE, DISTRICT JUDGE (dissenting in part and concurring in part): * * *

In * * * excluding the defense of duress, the trial court specifically found Contento–Pachon had failed to present sufficient evidence to establish the necessary elements of immediacy and inescapability. In its Order the district court stated:

> The first threat made to defendant and his family about three weeks before the flight was not immediate; the threat was conditioned upon defendant's failure to cooperate in the future and did not place the defendant and his family in immediate danger or harm. Moreover, after the initial threat and until he went to the house where he ingested the balloons containing cocaine, defendant and his family were not physically restrained and could have sought help from the police or fled. No such efforts were attempted by defendant. Thus, defendant's own offer of proof negates two necessary elements of the defense of duress.

* * * This finding is adequately supported by the record. * * *

I agree with the majority, however, that the district court properly excluded Contento–Pachon's necessity defense.

NOTES AND QUESTIONS

1. Joshua Dressler, *Exegesis of the Law of Duress: Justifying the Excuse and Searching For Its Proper Limits,* 62 S.Cal.L.Rev. 1331, 1335 (1989):

> Reduced to a[n] * * * easily digested analytic form, * * * [a defendant] will be acquitted of an offense other than murder on the basis of duress if he pleads and proves that (1) [another person] unlawfully threatened

imminently to kill or grievously injure him or another person; and (2) he was not at fault in exposing himself to the threat.

2. If the defendant was entitled to an instruction on duress, as the appellate court ruled, why was he not also entitled to an instruction on necessity?

3. *Duress and mens rea.* Does a coerced person lack the requisite *mens rea* of an offense? Is that why a coerced person is acquitted of a crime? Consider these observations from Hibbert v. The Queen, 99 C.C.C.3d 193 (1995):

> That threats of death or serious bodily harm can have an effect on a person's state of mind is indisputable. However, it is also readily apparent that a person who carries out the *actus reus* of a criminal offence in response to such threats will not necessarily lack the *mens rea* for that offence. Whether he or she does or not will depend both on what the mental element of the offence in question happens to be, and on the facts of the particular case. As a practical matter, though, situations where duress will operate to "negate" *mens rea* will be exceptional, for the simple reason that the types of mental states that are capable of being "negated" by duress are not often found in the definitions of criminal offences.

> In general, a person who performs an action in response to a threat will *know* what he or she is doing, and will be aware of the probable consequences of his or her actions. Whether or not he or she *desires* the occurrence of these consequences will depend on the particular circumstances. For example, a person who is forced at gunpoint to drive a group of armed ruffians to a bank will usually know that the likely result of his or her actions will be that an attempt will be made to rob the bank, but he or she may not desire this result—indeed, he or she may strongly wish that the robbers' plans are ultimately foiled, if this could occur without risk to his or her own safety. In contrast, a person who is told that his or her child is being held hostage at another location and will be killed unless the robbery is successful will almost certainly have an active subjective desire that the robbery succeed. While the existence of threats clearly has a bearing on the *motive* underlying each actor's respective decision to assist in the robbery, only the first actor can be said not to *desire* that the robbery take place, and neither actor can be said not to have knowledge of the consequences of their actions. To determine whether *mens rea* is "negated" in a particular case, therefore, the first question that must be asked is whether the mental element of the offence in question is defined in such a way that either an actor's motives or his or her immediate desires have any direct relevance.

Did Contento–Pachon have the requisite *mens rea* to be convicted of *his* offense?

4. *"Duress" as a justification defense.* In his influential treatise, Professor Wayne LaFave once treated duress as a justification defense. See Wayne R. LaFave, Criminal Law § 5.3 (3d ed. 2000). Was he correct in doing so? Look at the elements of the defense set out in Note 1, and consider the crimes

for which the defense may be pleaded. Does duress appear to be a justification defense? Is duress a justification or excuse defense in the Model Penal Code?

If duress *is* a justification defense as LaFave claims, how does it differ from the defense of necessity?

Intuitively, is duress an excuse or a justification? For example, suppose that Agnes threatens to poke out an eye of Brian's infant daughter unless he rapes Cecilia, and Brian accedes to the threat. To the extent that a jury would be inclined to acquit Brian, is the reason that he did the right or permissible thing (justification) or is it that we do not believe it is just to hold him accountable for his actions under these extreme circumstances (excuse)?

For scholarly debate on this subject, see Peter Westen & James Mangiafico, *The Criminal Defense of Duress: A Justification, Not an Excuse—And Why It Matters*, 6 Buffalo Crim. L. Rev. 833 (2003); and Kyron Huigens, *Duress Is Not a Justification*, 2 Ohio St. J. Crim. L. 303 (2004).

5. *"Duress" as an excuse defense.* Assuming duress is an excuse, what is the rationale of the defense? According to the drafters of the Model Penal Code, condemnation of a coerced actor "is bound to be an ineffective threat; what is, however, more significant is that it is divorced from any moral base and is unjust." American Law Institute, Model Penal Code and Commentaries, Comment to § 2.09 at 375 (1985).

Jerome Hall disagrees with the deterrence argument. According to Hall, "it certainly has not been, and probably cannot be, established that the drive of self-preservation is irresistible, that conduct in such situations is inexorably fixed. * * * In many ordinary matters, it is a common experience to act against a very strong desire * * *." Jerome Hall, General Principles of Criminal Law 445–46 (2d ed. 1960). The wise course, he says, "is to proceed on the hypothesis that a substantial percentage of persons * * * will act against their instinctual desires * * *." Id., at 446–47. Do you agree?

Regarding the "more significant" argument raised in the Model Code Commentary, namely, that it is morally unjust to punish a coerced actor, consider the following observations:

A coerced wrongdoer is unlike the insane person. The coerced actor is a whole person, free of sickness. As such, he possess the capacity for free choice; he has practical reasoning skills. * * *

Furthermore, the coerced actor not only possesses the capacity to understand the attendant factual and legal circumstances, but he does *in fact* realize what it is he is doing. When *D* steals a watch under duress, he knows that he is taking a watch; when he commits perjury, he realizes that he is uttering a falsehood under oath; and when he succumbs to a kill-or-be-killed command, he knows perfectly well that he is taking a human life. * * *

Indeed, what most weakens the case for excuse is that the coerced actor *chooses* to violate the law. He chooses to commit the criminal offense rather than to accept the threatened consequences. He would not have chosen to commit the crime but for the threat, but it *is* still his choice, albeit a hard and excruciatingly difficult choice. His act may be unwilling, but it is not unwilled.

In no other circumstances does the law excuse a person for his rational and intentionally chosen harmful acts. Only duress cases excuse one who "self-consciously subordinates [the law] to the primacy of the person who is the subject of the desire."

Joshua Dressler, Note 1 supra, at 1359–60.

If the preceding statement accurately describes duress, what is the moral foundation for excusing coerced wrongdoers? The Commentary provides the following explanation:

[L]aw is ineffective in the deepest sense, indeed * * * it is hypocritical, if it imposes on the actor who has the misfortune to confront a dilemmatic choice, a standard that his judges are not prepared to affirm that they should and could comply with if their turn to face the problem should arise.

American Law Institute, Model Penal Code and Commentaries, Comment to § 2.09 at 374–75 (1985).

Is this a satisfactory explanation? What about Lord Coleridge's observation in *Dudley and Stephens* (p. 553 supra) that "[w]e are often compelled to set up standards we cannot reach ourselves, and to lay down rules which we could not ourselves satisfy"?

Consider the moral theories of excuse set out in the Dressler excerpt (p. 562–564 supra). Do you find one of them especially convincing in the context of duress?

6. *Model Penal Code.* How does the Code's definition of duress (§ 2.09) differ from the common law, as described in Note 1?

7. *The Model Penal Code and "threats" that were not threats.* What if a person incorrectly believes that a threat to use unlawful force has been made? Is such a person entitled to claim duress? The Commentary explains:

Although the language is not * * * explicit * * *, the intent [of Section 2.09] is to give effect to the defense when the actor mistakenly believes that a threat to use unlawful force has been made. One's culpability for an offense would be no greater than one's culpability in assessing the presence of a threat that, if genuine, would give rise to the defense of duress. Thus if one reasonably but mistakenly believed he had been threatened, he would be liable for no offense if a person of reasonable firmness would not have been able to resist such a threat. If one's mistaken belief was recklessly or negligently formed, he could be liable only for a crime of recklessness or negligence.

American Law Institute, Model Penal Code and Commentaries, Comment to § 2.09 at 380 (1985).

8. *"The person of reasonable firmness."* Model Penal Code § 2.09 measures the defendant's conduct against the standard of "a person of reasonable firmness." Since duress is an excuse, why is the test objective, rather than focusing on the subjective capacities of the coerced individual? For example, suppose that John wants to prove at trial that he is a timid individual and, therefore, had "no choice" but to commit a serious crime when a minor threat

was issued? Is it fair to hold him to a standard that he cannot meet? The Commentary explains the drafters' reasoning:

The case of concern here is that in which the actor makes a choice, but claims in his defense that he was so intimidated that he was unable to choose otherwise. Should such psychological incapacity be given the same exculpative force as the physical incapacity that may afford a defense under Section 2.01? * * *

In favor of allowing the defense, it may be argued that the legal sanction cannot be effective in the case supposed and that the actor may not properly be blamed for doing what he had to choose to do. It seems clear, however, that the argument in its full force must be rejected. The crucial reason is the same as that which elsewhere leads to an unwillingness to vary legal norms with the individual's capacity to meet the standards they prescribe, absent a disability that is both gross and verifiable, such as the mental disease or defect that may establish irresponsibility [under § 4.01]. * * * To make liability depend upon the fortitude of any given actor would be no less impractical or otherwise impolitic than to permit it to depend upon such other variables as intelligence or clarity of judgment, suggestibility or moral insight.

Moreover, the legal standard may gain in its effectiveness by being unconditional in this respect. * * * [L]egal norms and sanctions operate not only at the moment of the climactic choice, but also in the fashioning of values and of character.

Though, for the foregoing reasons, the submission that the actor lacked the fortitude to make the moral choice should not be entertained as a defense, a different situation is presented if the claimed excuse is based upon the incapacity of men in general to resist the coercive pressures to which the individual succumbed.

American Law Institute, Model Penal Code and Commentaries, Comment to § 2.09 at 373–74 (1985).

Although Section 2.09 generally states an objective standard, some subjectivization is invited, id. at 375:

The standard is not, however, wholly external in its reference; account is taken of the actor's "situation," a term that should here be given the same scope it is accorded in appraising recklessness and negligence. Stark, tangible factors that differentiate the actor from another, like his size, strength, age, or health, would be considered in making the exculpatory judgment. Matters of temperament would not.

In evaluating the actor's "situation," how broadly or narrowly should courts "time-frame"? That is, consider the following observation:

Part of the complexity of the issue [of] * * * the distinction between subjective and objective evidence * * * can be demonstrated by changing the "snapshot" of circumstances that is shown to a jury in any particular case. If the jury sees the defendant's circumstances immediately prior to commission of the crime and there is no gun held to her head or other markedly extreme duress, the jury may conclude that any fear of imminent death or violence was unreasonable. However, if the defendant is permitted to pull the camera back to provide the broader picture, so to speak, of her circumstances, the jury could learn of a pattern of violence, control, and coercion leading up to the criminal act.

United States v. Marenghi, 893 F.Supp. 85 (D.Me.1995).

Consider the time-framing issue as you consider the following Notes.

9. *Battered women "compelled" to commit crimes: How does (and should) the MPC handle it?* In State v. B.H., 183 N.J. 171, 870 A.2d 273 (2005), B.H. engaged in sexual intercourse with her stepson in a motel room while her husband, S.H., observed. The State of New Jersey charged B.H. with aggravated sexual assault and endangering the welfare of a child.

Under one version of the facts (B.H.'s statements to the police), B.H. committed the acts although S.H. did not threaten her in any manner on the day of the incident. Instead, B.H. testified at trial that she was victim of regular incidents of "physical, sexual, and emotional abuse" perpetrated by S.H., throughout their marriage, such as being "beaten about her breasts," "choked until she would almost pass out," "sexually violent practices that involved recurrent incidents of rape in various forms," and other humiliating acts not described by the court.

B.H. presented a duress defense based on Model Penal Code § 2.09. In support of this claim, the defense introduced expert testimony about battered woman syndrome (BWS). At the conclusion of the trial, the judge instructed the jury that "the sole purpose for which that evidence is offered to you is to explain why the defendant continued to live with her husband and why she hadn't left him." Why would the fact that B.H. did not leave her husband be relevant in a duress case? In what way is BWS evidence relevant in that regard?

The defense objected to this limitation on the BWS evidence. Based on what you know about BWS evidence (p. 525, Note 12), how else might BWS evidence arguably be relevant in a Model Penal Code duress case? Based on the Commentary to the MPC, as set out in Notes 7–8, supra, was the trial court correct in limiting the use of the expert's BWS testimony?

10. *Battered women and duress: Judy Norman redux.* Think back to Judy Norman (p. 513 supra), who killed her abusive husband as he slept. Would she have a basis for claiming duress under Model Penal Code § 2.09? As a public policy matter, do you think such a claim would be preferable to self-defense or to any other justification or excuse defense? Why, or why not? See Joshua Dressler, *Battered Women and Sleeping Abusers: Some Reflections,* 3 Ohio St. J. Crim. L. 457 (2006).

b. Necessity Versus Duress

PEOPLE v. UNGER
Supreme Court of Illinois, 1977.
66 Ill.2d 333, 5 Ill.Dec. 848, 362 N.E.2d 319.

RYAN, JUSTICE.

Defendant, Francis Unger, was charged with the crime of escape, and was convicted following a jury trial * * *. * * * The conviction was reversed upon appeal * * *. We * * * affirm the judgment of the appellate court.

At the time of the present offense, the defendant was confined at the Illinois State Penitentiary in Joliet, Illinois. Defendant was serving a one- to three-year term as a consequence of a conviction for auto theft in Ogle County. Defendant began serving this sentence in December of 1971. On February 23, 1972, the defendant was transferred to the prison's mini- mum security, honor farm. It is undisputed that on March 7, 1972, the defendant walked off the honor farm. Defendant was apprehended two days later in a motel room in St. Charles, Illinois.

At trial, defendant testified that prior to his transfer to the honor farm he had been threatened by a fellow inmate. This inmate allegedly brandished a six-inch knife in an attempt to force defendant to engage in homosexual activities. Defendant was 22 years old and weighed approxi- mately 155 pounds. He testified that he did not report the incident to the proper authorities due to fear of retaliation. Defendant also testified that he is not a particularly good fighter.

Defendant stated that after his transfer to the honor farm he was assaulted and sexually molested by three inmates, and he named the assailants at trial. The attack allegedly occurred on March 2, 1972, and from that date until his escape defendant received additional threats from inmates he did not know. On March 7, 1972, the date of the escape, defendant testified that he received a call on an institution telephone. Defendant testified that the caller, whose voice he did not recognize, threatened him with death because the caller had heard that defendant had reported the assault to prison authorities. Defendant said that he left the honor farm to save his life and that he planned to return once he found someone who could help him. None of these incidents were reported to the prison officials. * * *

Defendant's first trial for escape resulted in a hung jury. The jury in the second trial returned its verdict after a five-hour deliberation. The following instruction (People's Instruction No. 9) was given by the trial court over defendant's objection.

> "The reasons, if any, given for the alleged escape are immaterial and not to be considered by you as in any way justifying or excusing, if there were in fact such reasons."

The appellate court majority found that the giving of People's Instruction No. 9 was reversible error. Two instructions which were tendered by defendant but refused by the trial court are also germane to this appeal. Defendant's instructions Nos. 1 and 3 were predicated upon the affirma- tive defenses of compulsion and necessity. Defendant's instructions Nos. 1 and 3 read as follows:

> "It is a defense to the charge made against the Defendant that he left the Honor Farm of the Illinois State Penitentiary by reason of necessity if the accused was without blame in occasioning or develop-

ing the situation and reasonably believed such conduct was necessary to avoid a public or private injury greater than the injury which might reasonably result from his own conduct.''

"It is a defense to the charge made against the Defendant that he acted under the compulsion of threat or menace of the imminent infliction of death or great bodily harm, if he reasonably believed death or great bodily harm would be inflicted upon him if he did not perform the conduct with which he is charged.''

The principal issue in the present appeal is whether it was error for the court to instruct the jury that it must disregard the reasons given for defendant's escape and to conversely refuse to instruct the jury on the statutory defenses of compulsion and necessity. * * * The State contends that, under the facts and circumstances of this case, the defenses of compulsion and necessity are, as a matter of law, unavailable to defendant. * * *

Proper resolution of this appeal requires some preliminary remarks concerning the law of compulsion and necessity as applied to prison escape situations. Traditionally, the courts have been reluctant to permit the defenses of compulsion and necessity to be relied upon by escapees. This reluctance appears to have been primarily grounded upon considerations of public policy. Several recent decisions, however, have recognized the applicability of the compulsion and necessity defenses to prison escapes. In *People v. Harmon* (1974), 53 Mich.App. 482, 220 N.W.2d 212, the defense of duress was held to apply in a case where the defendant alleged that he escaped in order to avoid repeated homosexual attacks from fellow inmates. In *People v. Lovercamp* (1974), 43 Cal.App.3d 823, 118 Cal.Rptr. 110, a limited defense of necessity was held to be available to two defendants whose escapes were allegedly motivated by fear of homosexual attacks.

As illustrated by *Harmon* and *Lovercamp*, different courts have reached similar results in escape cases involving sexual abuse, though the question was analyzed under different defense theories. A certain degree of confusion has resulted from the recurring practice on the part of the courts to use the terms "compulsion" (duress) and "necessity" interchangeably, though the defenses are theoretically distinct. It has been suggested that the major distinction between the two defenses is that the source of the coercive power in cases of compulsion is from human beings, whereas in situations of necessity the pressure on the defendant arises from the forces of nature. Also, * * * the defense of compulsion generally requires an impending, imminent threat of great bodily harm together with a demand that the person perform the specific criminal act for which he is eventually charged. Additionally, where the defense of compulsion is successfully asserted the coercing party is guilty of the crime.

It is readily discernible that prison escapes induced by fear of homosexual assaults and accompanying physical reprisals do not conveniently fit within the traditional ambits of either the compulsion or the necessity defense. However, it has been suggested that such cases could best be analyzed in terms of necessity. One commentator has stated that the relevant consideration should be whether the defendant chose the lesser of two evils, in which case the defense of necessity would apply, or whether he was unable to exercise a free choice at all, in which event compulsion would be the appropriate defense.

In our view, the defense of necessity is the appropriate defense in the present case. In a very real sense, the defendant here was not deprived of his free will by the threat of imminent physical harm which * * * appears to be the intended interpretation of the defense of compulsion as set out in * * * the Criminal Code. * * * Rather, if defendant's testimony is believed, he was forced to choose between two admitted evils by the situation which arose from actual and threatened homosexual assaults and fears of reprisal. Though the defense of compulsion would be applicable in the unlikely event that a prisoner was coerced by the threat of imminent physical harm to perform the specific act of escape, no such situation is involved in the present appeal. We, therefore, turn to a consideration of whether the evidence presented by the defendant justified the giving of an instruction on the defense of necessity.

The defendant's testimony was clearly sufficient to raise the affirmative defense of necessity. * * * Defendant testified that he was subjected to threats of forced homosexual activity and that, on one occasion, the threatened abuse was carried out. He also testified that he was physically incapable of defending himself and that he feared greater harm would result from a report to the authorities. Defendant further testified that just prior to his escape he was told that he was going to be killed, and that he therefore fled the honor farm in order to save his life. * * * It is clear that defendant introduced some evidence to support the defense of necessity. * * * [T]hat is sufficient to justify the giving of an appropriate instruction.

The State, however, would have us apply a more stringent test to prison escape situations. The State refers to the *Lovercamp* decision, where only a limited necessity defense was recognized. In *Lovercamp,* it was held that the defense of necessity need be submitted to the jury only where five conditions had been met. Those conditions are:

"(1) The prisoner is faced with a specific threat of death, forcible sexual attack or substantial bodily injury in the immediate future;

(2) There is no time for a complaint to the authorities or there exists a history of futile complaints which make any result from such complaints illusory;

(3) There is no time or opportunity to resort to the courts;

(4) There is no evidence of force or violence used towards prison personnel or other 'innocent' persons in the escape; and

(5) The prisoner immediately reports to the proper authorities when he has attained a position of safety from the immediate threat."

The State correctly points out that the defendant never informed the authorities of his situation and failed to report immediately after securing a position of safety. Therefore, it is contended that, under the authority of *Lovercamp,* defendant is not entitled to a necessity instruction. We agree with the State and with the court in *Lovercamp* that the above conditions are relevant factors to be used in assessing claims of necessity. We cannot say, however, that the existence of each condition is, as a matter of law, necessary to establish a meritorious necessity defense.

The preconditions set forth in *Lovercamp* are, in our view, matters which go to the weight and credibility of the defendant's testimony. * * * The absence of one or more of the elements listed in *Lovercamp* would not necessarily mandate a finding that the defendant could not assert the defense of necessity.

By way of example, in the present case defendant did not report to the authorities immediately after securing his safety. * * * However, defendant testified that he intended to return to the prison upon obtaining legal advice from an attorney and claimed that he was attempting to get money from friends to pay for such counsel. Regardless of our opinion as to the believability of defendant's tale, this testimony, if accepted by the jury, would have negated any negative inference which would arise from defendant's failure to report to proper authorities after the escape. The absence of one of the *Lovercamp* preconditions does not alone disprove the claim of necessity and should not, therefore, automatically preclude an instruction on the defense. * * *

NOTES AND QUESTIONS

1. Since prison escape cases do not neatly fit within the ambit of either the necessity or duress defense, does it matter which label is attached? If you represented a prison escapee, which defense would you prefer to use? Consider the following Notes in this regard.

2. *Balancing the interests.* Does the choice-of-evils calculus involved in a necessity claim support or hurt an escapee's chances for acquittal? Does it matter whether the inmate was in prison, as in *Unger,* for car theft or e.g., for rape? What if the car thief/rapist claims duress, instead?

3. *Effect on third parties: the prison guard.* Suppose that a prison guard had discovered Unger as he was escaping. Would she have been justified in preventing Unger's escape, by force if necessary? Would Unger have been justified in using defensive force against *her*? Do the answers to these questions depend on whether Unger's escape is justified or merely excused?

According to Professor Fletcher, a "determination that the conduct [of a prisoner] is justified presupposes a judgment about the superior social interest in the conflict. If the superior social interest is represented by the party seeking to [escape] * * *, it is also in the social interest to suppress resistance [by the guard]." George P. Fletcher, Rethinking Criminal Law 761 (1978). In short, if a prisoner is justified in escaping, a guard is not justified in preventing the escape. In contrast, if the inmate is only excused for escaping,

Fletcher believes the guard is justified in resisting the escape. Professor David Dolinko disagrees:

> Whatever the validity of [Fletcher's] argument as applied to justified actions in general, it neglects the special features present in an escape situation. * * *
>
> * * * [E]ven if the lesser-evils principle is the basis for holding a prisoner's escape attempt justified, a prison guard can be justified by that same principle in foiling the escape. * * *
>
> Suppose that a prisoner is attempting to escape in circumstances that justify his actions as the lesser evil. His escape would inflict a certain amount of harm, because to some degree it would weaken prison discipline, encourage other escape attempts, and possibly raise the level of tension and violence in the prison. This harm is by hypothesis outweighed by the harm the prisoner would avoid if he escapes: assume that this harm consists of a threatened sexual assault. Now consider a prison guard who discovers the inmate attempting to escape and acts to prevent the escape. The harm inflicted by the guard's action is precisely that which would have been avoided by the escape: subjecting the prisoner to sexual assault. But the harm that the guard's action averts is *not* necessarily the same as the harm which the escape would have inflicted— it may well be greater. The prisoner's escape, in itself, would have undermined prison discipline to some degree; but for a guard to witness a prisoner escaping and take no action to stop him would represent a much greater blow to discipline. Hence it is at least possible that the harm the guard's intervention averts might outweigh the harm of sexual assault on the inmate, even though that harm in turn outweighs the harm the escape would have wrought. If so, both the prisoner's escape attempt and the guard's intervention would be justified as choices of the lesser evil. Consequently, it is false to claim that interference with an action justified by the choice of evils principle (that is, by the defense of necessity) must be wrongful.

David Dolinko, *Intolerable Conditions as a Defense to Prison Escapes,* 26 UCLA L. Rev. 1126, 1176, 1178, 1180–81 (1979).

Professor Fletcher replied:

> The purpose of the legal system is * * * to resolve these conflicts based on plausible but inconsistent assertions of right. If the parties assert conflicting rights, then respect for their definition of the dispute requires that we search for the superior claim of right. * * *
>
> * * * [W]e have to recognize that every decision about rights entails a judgment about whether other parties have a right to prevent the rightful conduct. We cannot affirm a right in the prisoner to escape and at the same time grant the guard a right to keep him in prison. Conversely, if the guard has a right to keep convicted felons in prison, the inmates cannot have a right to escape.

George P. Fletcher, *Should Intolerable Prison Conditions Generate a Justification or an Excuse for Escape?,* 26 UCLA L.Rev. 1355, 1364–65 (1979).

4. *Effect on third parties: accomplices.* Suppose that Unger had obtained help in escaping. Would his accomplice's liability depend on the nature of Unger's claim? (See p. 864 infra.)

5. *Model Penal Code.* How would *Unger* be decided under the Model Code? Could the defendant successfully raise either or both Sections 2.09 and 3.02?

Suppose that a guard had killed Unger because it was the only way to prevent the escape. In an ensuing murder prosecution, would the guard have a valid defense? See Section 3.07(3). Would it matter whether the guard knew why Unger was fleeing?

c. Defense to Murder?

PEOPLE v. ANDERSON

Supreme Court of California, 2002.
28 Cal.4th 767, 122 Cal.Rptr.2d 587, 50 P.3d 368.

CHIN, J.

Over two centuries ago, William Blackstone, the great commentator on the common law, said that duress is no excuse for killing an innocent person: "And, therefore, though a man be violently assaulted, and hath no other possible means of escaping death, but by killing an innocent person, this fear and force shall not acquit him of murder; for he ought rather to die himself than escape by the murder of an innocent."

We granted review to decide whether these words apply in California. We conclude that, as in Blackstone's England, so today in California: fear for one's own life does not justify killing an innocent person. Duress is not a defense to murder. We also conclude that duress cannot reduce murder to manslaughter. * * * [I]f a new form of manslaughter is to be created, the Legislature, not this court, should do it.

I. THE FACTS AND PROCEDURAL HISTORY

Defendant was charged with kidnapping and murdering Margaret Armstrong in a camp area near Eureka * * *. Defendant and others apparently suspected the victim of molesting two girls who resided in the camp. Ron Kiern, the father of one of the girls, pleaded guilty to Armstrong's second degree murder and testified at defendant's trial. [The defendant claimed he killed the victim because Kiern threatened to "beat the shit out of [him]" if he failed to do so.] * *

A jury convicted defendant of first degree murder and kidnapping. * * *

II. DISCUSSION

A. Whether Duress Is a Defense to Murder

At common law, the general rule was, and still is today, what Blackstone stated: duress is no defense to killing an innocent person.

"Stemming from antiquity, the nearly 'unbroken tradition' of Anglo–American common law is that duress never excuses murder, that the person threatened with his own demise 'ought rather to die himself, than escape by the murder of an innocent.' "

The basic rationale behind allowing the defense of duress for other crimes "is that, for reasons of social policy, it is better that the defendant, faced with a choice of evils, choose to do the lesser evil (violate the criminal law) in order to avoid the greater evil threatened by the other person." This rationale, however, "is strained when a defendant is confronted with taking the life of an innocent third person in the face of a threat on his own life. * * * When the defendant commits murder under duress, the resulting harm—i.e. the death of an innocent person—is at least as great as the threatened harm—i.e. the death of the defendant." We might add that, when confronted with an apparent kill-an-innocent-person-or-be-killed situation, a person can always choose to resist. As a practical matter, death will rarely, if ever, inevitably result from a choice not to kill. The law should require people to choose to resist rather than kill an innocent person.

A state may, of course, modify the common law rule by statute. * * * Defendant contends the California Legislature modified the rule in the 19th century and made duress a defense to some murders.

Since its adoption in 1872, Penal Code section 26 has provided: "All persons are capable of committing crimes except those belonging to the following classes: [¶] * * * Persons (unless the crime be punishable with death) who committed the act or made the omission charged under threats of menaces sufficient to show that they had reasonable cause to and did believe their lives would be endangered if they refused." Defendant contends the reference to a "crime * * * punishable with death" means that the crimes to which duress is not a defense include only those forms of murder that are punishable with death, and that these forms change with changes in death penalty law. In 1872, when the current Penal Code was adopted, all first degree murder was punishable with death. Today only first degree murder with special circumstances is so punishable. Accordingly, defendant contends that today, duress is a defense to all murder except first degree murder with special circumstances. In effect, he argues that a killing under duress is either first degree murder with special circumstances or no crime at all. Because the prosecution did not allege special circumstances in this case, he continues, duress provides a full defense. * * *

In 1850, all murder was punishable with death. Not until 1856 was murder divided into degrees, with death the punishment for first degree but not second degree murder. This means that in 1850, duress was no defense to any murder. Thus, like many of California's early penal statutes, section 26 effectively adopted the common law, although the Legislature used a problematic method in which to do so. The question before us is whether the exception for a crime punishable with death changes with every change in death penalty law, which would mean that by 1872, the exception included only first degree murder and today it includes only first degree murder with special circumstances. We think not, for several reasons.

We see no suggestion that the 1850, or any, Legislature intended the substantive law of duress to fluctuate with every change in death penalty law. * * *

Moreover, no reason appears for the Legislature to have silently abrogated the common law rule. The reasons for the rule applied as well to 19th-century California as to Blackstone's England. They apply, if anything, with greater force in California today. A person can always choose to resist rather than kill an innocent person. The law must encourage, even require, everyone to seek an alternative to killing. Crimes are often committed by more than one person; the criminal law must also, perhaps especially, deter those crimes. California today is tormented by gang violence. If duress is recognized as a defense to the killing of innocents, then a street or prison gang need only create an internal reign of terror and murder can be justified, at least by the actual killer. Persons who know they can claim duress will be more likely to follow a gang order to kill instead of resisting than would those who know they must face the consequences of their acts. Accepting the duress defense for any form of murder would thus encourage killing. Absent a stronger indication than the language of section 26, we do not believe the Legislature intended to remove the sanctions of the criminal law from the killing of an innocent even under duress. * * *

Accordingly, we conclude that duress is not a defense to any form of murder.

B.   Whether Duress Can Reduce Murder to a Lesser Crime

Defendant also argues that even if duress is not a complete defense to murder, at least it reduces the crime to manslaughter by negating malice. * * *

Some commentators do, indeed, argue that fear for one's own life, although not justifying the killing of an innocent, should at least mitigate murder to manslaughter. "The holding that a killing in such an extremity is necessarily murder has not been adequately considered. While moral considerations require the rejection of any claim of excuse, they do not require that the mitigation of the circumstances be overlooked. A killing in such an extremity is far removed from cold-blooded murder, and should be held to be manslaughter." * * *

* * * On the other hand, because duress can often arise in a criminal gang context, the Legislature might be reluctant to do anything to reduce the current law's deterrent effect on gang violence. These policy questions are for the Legislature, not a court, to decide. Accordingly, we reject defendant's argument that we should create a new form of voluntary manslaughter. His arguments are better directed to the Legislature.

Defendant also argues that, at least, duress can negate premeditation and deliberation, thus resulting in second degree and not first degree murder. We agree that a killing under duress, like any killing, may or may not be premeditated, depending on the circumstances. If a person obeys an order to kill without reflection, the jury might find no premeditation and thus convict of second degree murder. As with implied malice murder, this circumstance is not due to a special doctrine of duress but to the legal requirements of first degree murder. The trial court instructed the jury on the requirements for first degree murder. It specifically instructed that a killing "upon a sudden heat of passion or *other condition precluding the idea of deliberation*" would not be premeditated first degree murder. Here, the jury found premeditation. In some other case, it might not. It is for the jury to decide. But, unless and until the Legislature decides otherwise, a malicious, premeditated killing, even under duress, is first degree murder.

On a final point * * *. If one is not guilty of the underlying felony due to duress, one cannot be guilty of felony murder based on that felony. Here, for example, the court instructed the jury that duress could be a defense to the kidnapping charge. It also instructed on felony murder with kidnapping as the underlying felony. If the jury had found defendant not guilty of kidnapping due to duress (it did not), it could not have found that he killed during the commission of that kidnapping. Defendant could not have killed during the perpetration of a crime of which he was innocent. * * *

Concurring and Dissenting Opinion by KENNARD, J. * * *

Section 26, making duress a defense "unless the crime be punishable with death," implicitly incorporates by reference other statutory provisions defining crimes and prescribing their punishments. * * * By * * * referring generally to "a crime not punishable with death," the Legislature expressed an intention to incorporate the general body of law relating to capital punishment as it might change from time to time. * * *

The Legislature's decisions whether to allow a duress defense and whether to authorize the death penalty both reflect societal judgments about the seriousness of the offense in question. In the first instance, the societal judgment is whether an offense is so serious that an individual is expected to forfeit his or her life rather than commit it. In the second instance, the societal judgment is whether an offense is so serious that a person who has committed it should forfeit his or her life. The Legislature could reasonably have concluded that the same small category of highly serious offenses that warranted capital punishment could not be excused by a claim of duress. Also, if duress is not a defense to a noncapital crime, then the law has created a situation in which one is better off breaking the law than obeying it because by committing the crime one risks only a prison sentence, while by refusing to commit the crime one risks death or very serious injury from the person imposing the duress. The Legislature may well have concluded that a just system of laws does not place those who obey the law in a worse position than those who break it. * * *

The majority appears to argue that this court *must* construe section 26 as not permitting the defense of duress to any form of murder because sound considerations of public policy require that no amount of threats or menaces can justify the taking of innocent human life. * * * In general, this court may not substitute its public policy views for those of the Legislature under the guise of statutory construction. When the language of a statute is ambiguous, however, this court may prefer a resolution of the ambiguity that avoids absurd consequences or that no reasonable legislative body could have intended.

Here, a construction of section 26 that makes the defense of duress unavailable as to capital murder but available as to noncapital murder does not produce results that are absurd or that no reasonable legislative body could have intended. On the contrary, * * * the construction of section 26 that I have arrived at by applying well-established rules of statutory construction represents a moderate approach in line with mainstream legal thinking.

For example, the Model Penal Code allows the defense of duress to be asserted against *all* criminal charges, including murder. * * * In the official comment to this provision, the American Law Institute explains that "persons of reasonable firmness surely break at different points depending on the stakes that are involved"; it further observes "that even homicide may sometimes be the product of coercion that is truly irresistible, that danger to a loved one may have greater impact on a person of reasonable firmness than a danger to himself, and, finally, that long and wasting pressure may break down resistance more effectively than a threat of immediate destruction."

The states of Connecticut, New York, North Dakota, Tennessee, Texas, and Utah have adopted statutes similar to the Model Penal Code allowing duress as a defense to homicide. Also, the laws of most civil law countries—including Belgium, Greece, the Netherlands, Germany, Switzerland and Sweden—recognize duress as a defense to any crime, including murder.

As a leading commentator on the law of duress has stated, "duress always is a matter of line drawing about which reasonable minds can differ" Indeed, the weight of scholarly commentary favors the Model Penal Code's definition of duress and its abolition of the common law murder exception to the duress defense.

I do not here suggest that the Legislature should adopt the Model Penal Code approach * * *. I suggest only that a construction of section 26 under which duress is a defense to noncapital murder, but not to capital murder, represents a moderate, middle-of-the road approach that a legislative body plausibly could have adopted to resolve a difficult and complex issue on which reasonable minds may differ.* * *

* * * [U]nder the majority's construction, section 26 does not allow a duress defense even in situations of unintentional implied malice killings.

Imagine, for example, this scenario: Two armed robbers fleeing the scene of a store robbery force their way into a car that is leaving the parking lot. One robber holds a gun to the driver's head, while the other places a gun against the head of the driver's wife. They order the driver to take off at high speed and not to stop or slow down for stop signs or signal lights, threatening immediate death to the driver and his wife. If the driver complies, and an accident ensues resulting in the death of an innocent person, the driver could be prosecuted for second degree murder on an implied malice theory, and, under the majority's construction of section 26, the driver could not assert duress as a defense. I doubt that our Legislature intended to withhold the defense of duress under these or similar circumstances.[g]

The majority expresses concern that if defendants can assert a duress defense to noncapital murder, the defense may be used to excuse killings by gang members. But most if not all gang-motivated killings are capital murder because it is a special circumstance [under state law] that "the defendant intentionally killed the victim while the defendant was an active participant in a criminal street gang * * * and the murder was carried out to further the activities of the criminal street gang." Moreover, the defense of duress is not available to a defendant who recklessly or intentionally placed himself in a situation where coercion to commit criminal acts could reasonably be anticipated. Because persons who join criminal street gangs or terrorist organizations can anticipate pressure to commit crimes, the defense would usually be unavailable to those individuals. * * *

Here, defendant failed to present substantial evidence of duress. * * * Kiern did not threaten him with death, and there was no history of violence between the two men despite their long acquaintance. In addition, defendant voluntarily joined Kiern in the initial attack on the victim, thereby placing himself in the situation where he should have anticipated that Kiern would pressure him to commit further acts of violence. * * *

Because defendant presented insufficient evidence of duress to warrant a jury instruction on that defense, I agree with the majority that * * * defendant's conviction [should be affirmed].

---

g. The majority responded:

"The concurring and dissenting opinion * * * evokes the image of an innocent person who is forced at gunpoint by fleeing armed robbers to drive recklessly, and who is then charged with murder when a fatal accident ensues. In reality, the situation is not so grim. Although duress is not an affirmative defense to murder, the circumstances of duress would certainly be relevant to whether the evidence establishes the elements of implied malice murder. The reasons a person acted in a certain way, including threats of death, are highly relevant to whether the person acted with a conscious or wanton disregard for human life. This is not due to a special doctrine of duress but to the requirements of implied malice murder."

Notes and Questions

1. As a purely statutory matter, whose reading of the pertinent penal code section seems more plausible? As a matter of wise policy, do you believe duress should be a full defense to murder, reduce the offense to manslaughter, or neither? Why might some critics of the majority opinion say, "Even if duress should not be a defense, the majority's policy arguments are unpersuasive."

2. Under the Model Penal Code, if a jury determines that a person of reasonable firmness would *not* have killed in the actor's situation, of what crime *is* the defendant probably guilty?

3. *Necessity as an excuse.* As we saw earlier, necessitous circumstances can *justify* violation of a criminal law. Is there any reason why "necessity" should not also serve as an *excuse*? For example, assume that the law will excuse a particular crime committed as the result of a coercive human threat (duress). Does it logically follow that the law should also excuse the same offense if it arises from natural conditions of an equally coercive nature ("compulsion of circumstances")?

Look carefully at the Model Penal Code. Section 2.09 is limited to coercion arising from the use or threatened use of "unlawful" force, which means that coercive natural forces are not covered by the defense (since natural forces cannot be unlawful). Is there a principled way to distinguish coercive human threats from coercive natural conditions?

3. INTOXICATION

There are two legally relevant forms of intoxication in the criminal law: voluntary and involuntary. Almost all cases, including the following one, involve the former variety. Involuntary intoxication is considered in Note 7 following *Veach*.

UNITED STATES v. VEACH

United States Court of Appeals for the Sixth Circuit, 2006.
455 F.3d 628.

Martha Craig Daughtrey, Circuit Judge. The defendant, Darwin Veach, appeals from his conviction and sentence for resisting a federal law enforcement officer and threatening to assault and murder two federal law enforcement officers with intent to impede the performance of their official duties. * * *

I. Factual and Procedural Background

There is no dispute concerning the relevant facts underlying the defendant's convictions. The record establishes that Veach's automobile was involved in a collision with another vehicle in Cumberland Gap National Historic Park. When United States Park Rangers Greg Mullin and Karen Bradford arrived on the scene, they suspected that the defendant was intoxicated and performed various field sobriety tests and a portable breath test on Veach that confirmed their initial impressions.

While securing the defendant for transport, Ranger Mullin was forced to struggle with Veach, who "attempted to pull away from" Mullin. The defendant also pulled the officer "down to one knee, causing an abrasion on that knee." Furthermore, as Mullin drove the defendant to the police station for booking, Veach stated, "I'm going to mess with you; if I get a shot at you[,] God dammit I'll kill you, I will; and I'm going to cut your head off." Veach was later transported to a local hospital for treatment of a facial cut, and once there he again threatened to decapitate one of the rangers. On the way back to the detention center, Veach threatened Mullin and Bradford once more, saying, "I will put a fuckin' bullet straight in your fuckin' head. The sheriff won't always be in office and 15 years later I'll walk up on you * * *. I'm going to drive [you] all straight to hell."

Based on these facts, the jury convicted Veach of one count of resisting a federal law enforcement officer, 18 U.S.C. § 111(a)(1), and two counts of threatening to assault and murder a federal law enforcement officer with intent to impede such officer in the performance of official duties, 18 U.S.C. § 115(a)(1)(B).

II. DISCUSSION * * *

On appeal, Veach * * * maintains that the court erred in granting the government's motion *in limine* to exclude presentation of a defense of * * * voluntary intoxication. * * *

As we have held, "[i]t is well established that intoxication, whether voluntary or involuntary, may preclude the formation of specific-intent and thus serve to negate an essential element of certain crimes." It is, however, only "the mens rea of a specific-intent crime" that may be negated by a * * * voluntary intoxication defense; [this defense has] * * * no applicability to general intent crimes." To determine whether the district judge properly excluded the defendant's testimony relating to his level of intoxication at the time of the crimes charged, it is thus necessary to decide, first, whether 18 U.S.C. §§ 111(a)(1) and 115(a)(1)(B) are general or specific intent offenses. * * *

Pursuant to the provisions of 18 U.S.C. § 111(a)(1):

> Whoever forcibly assaults, resists, opposes, impedes, intimidates, or interferes with [any officer or employee of the United States or of any agency in any branch of the United States Government, or any person assisting such an officer or employee] while engaged in or on account of the performance of official duties * * * shall, where the acts * * * constitute only simple assault, be fined * * * or imprisoned not more than one year, or both * * *.

This statutory provision clearly indicates that any violator will be punished solely for the forcible assault on, resistance to, opposition to, impedance of, intimidation of, or interference with a designated individual. No other intent on the part of a defendant need be shown; the mere intentional performance of the prohibited act is sufficient to subject the perpetrator to federal criminal liability. The plain language of the statute thus supports the district judge's conclusion that voluntary intoxication * * * is not a viable defense to a charge of a violation of § 111. * * *

Unlike 18 U.S.C. § 111, however, § 115(a)(1)(B) does contain additional language not found in the former general intent statute. That latter statutory provision reads:

> Whoever threatens to assault, kidnap, or murder, a United States official, a United States judge, a Federal law enforcement officer, or an official whose killing would be a crime under [18 U.S.C. § 1114], *with intent to impede, intimidate, or interfere with such official, judge, or law enforcement officer while engaged in the performance of official duties, or with intent to retaliate against such official, judge, or law enforcement officer on account of the performance of official duties,* shall be punished as provided in subsection (b). (Emphasis added.)
>
> * * *

* * * [T]he additional, specific intent requirement in 18 U.S.C. § 115(a)(1)(B) differentiates that statute from 18 U.S.C. § 111(a)(1). Not only does § 115(a)(1)(B) require the government to prove beyond a reasonable doubt that the defendant threatened certain action against a government official but also that the defendant made such a threat for the specific purpose of interfering with the performance of official duties or of retaliating for the performance of such duties. * * *

Both the actual language of the statute itself and our allusions [in earlier cases] to the requirements for conviction under that provision lead to the inescapable conclusion that 18 U.S.C. § 115(a)(1)(B) contains a specific intent element that must be proven by the government beyond a reasonable doubt. Consequently, because a defendant must possess a particular *mens rea* in order to be guilty of the crimes described in that statute, in this case Veach should have been allowed to present evidence to the jury that he was too intoxicated at the time of his arrest to form the requisite specific intent. Instead, the district judge specifically forbade the defendant from "making intoxication * * * a defense" or from attempting to show "that he could not form an opinion."

That ruling was in error and prevented Veach from challenging effectively the government's assertion that it had proved all essential elements of a charge under 18 U.S.C. § 115(a)(1)(B) beyond a reasonable doubt. * * * [W]e must reverse Veach's § 115 convictions and remand this matter to the district court for retrial on those charges only. * * *

NOTES AND QUESTIONS

1. According to the court in the penultimate paragraph above, "the district judge specifically forbade the defendant from 'making intoxication * * * a defense'." Did the Sixth Circuit, by *its* holding regarding 18 U.S.C. § 115, render voluntary intoxication a "defense"? If so, is it an excuse defense? If not, what type defense is it?

2. How can it logically be the case that evidence of voluntary intoxication is admissible as to Section 115, but inadmissible regarding Section 111? If a person arguably is too intoxicated to "assault, kidnap, or murder, a United States official, * * * with intent intend to impede, intimidate, or interfere with such official * * * "—the language of Section 115—isn't he also too intoxicated to intentionally perform the prohibited act of Section 111, which is to "assault[], resist[], oppose[], impede[], intimidate[], or interfere[] with [any United States official]"? What is going on here?

Or consider this: Suppose voluntarily-intoxicated Bill is about to commit the act of nonconsensual intercourse with Violet when the police thankfully arrive and arrest him. He is charged with assault with intent to commit rape. Based on the principles described in *Veach*, is Bill entitled to introduce evidence of his voluntary intoxication in order to avoid conviction? What if he had completed his unlawful conduct before the police arrived and he had instead been charged with rape. Would he now be allowed to use his severely intoxicated condition as a defense? If he was too intoxicated to commit assault with intent to commit rape, isn't he also too intoxicated to commit rape? Put differently, shouldn't the two cases be treated alike—give Bill a defense in both or neither case? Why, or why not?

3. *Putting the "voluntary intoxication" issue in historical context.* In Montana v. Egelhoff, 518 U.S. 37, 116 S.Ct. 2013, 135 L.Ed.2d 361 (1996) (plurality opinion), Justice Scalia described the historical foundation of "voluntary intoxication" law this way:

By the [early] laws of England, * * * the intoxicated defendant "shall have no privilege by this voluntarily contracted madness, but shall have the same judgment as if he were in his right senses." 1 M. Hale, Pleas of the Crown *32–33. * * * Blackstone, citing Coke, explained that the law viewed intoxication "as an aggravation of the offence, rather than an excuse for any criminal misbehaviour." 4 W. Blackstone, Commentaries *25–26. This stern rejection of inebriation as a defense became a fixture of early American law as well. * * *

* * * Over the course of the 19th century, courts carved out an exception to the common law's traditional across-the-board condemnation of the drunken offender, allowing a jury to consider a defendant's intoxication when assessing whether he possessed the mental state needed to commit the crime charged, where the crime was one requiring a "specific intent." * * * Eventually, * * * the new view won out, and by the end of the 19th century, in most American jurisdictions, intoxication could be considered in determining whether a defendant was capable of forming the specific intent necessary to commit the crime charged.

A strong counter-trend is underway. Although some states retain the "specific intent"/"general intent" dichotomy, other states have narrowed or abolished the voluntary intoxication "defense." An example of the narrowing approach is 18 Pa. Cons. Stat. § 308 (2012), which provides:

Neither voluntary intoxication nor voluntary drugged condition is a defense to a criminal charge, nor may evidence of such conditions be introduced to negative the element of intent of the evidence, except that evidence of such intoxication or drugged condition of the defendant may be offered by the defendant whenever it is relevant to reduce murder from higher degree to a lower degree of murder.

An example of a statute that has abolished "voluntary intoxication" as a basis for acquittal is Mont. Code. Ann. § 45–2–203 (2012):

> A person who is in an intoxicated condition is criminally responsible for his conduct, and an intoxicated condition is not a defense to any offense and may not be taken into consideration in determining the existence of a mental state which is an element of the offense unless the defendant proves [that the intoxication was involuntary].

Is the latter penal provision constitutional? Consider that Montana defines the offense of "Deliberate Homicide" as "purposely or knowingly" causing the death of another human being. Mont. Code. Ann. § 45–5–102 (2008). What if Ally's mind is so clouded by alcohol that, when she kills the victim, she does not know that she has done so, and had no purpose for doing so. Does the conjunction of these two Montana penal provisions mean that she can be convicted of Deliberate Homicide although she lacked the requisite *mens rea* of the offense?

In *Egelhoff*, supra, the Supreme Court, by a 5–4 vote, upheld the Montana law against constitutional attack, although the majority was divided in its reasoning. Justice Scalia, for a four-justice plurality, rejected the defendant's argument that the statutory scheme violated the Due Process Clause:

> *In re Winship* [p. 9 supra] announced the proposition that the Due Process Clause requires proof beyond a reasonable doubt of every fact necessary to constitute the charged crime, and *Sandstrom v. Montana*, 442 U.S. 510, 524, 99 S.Ct. 2450, 2459, 61 L.Ed.2d 39 (1979), established a corollary, that a jury instruction which shifts to the defendant the burden of proof on a requisite element of mental state violates due process. These decisions simply are not implicated here because, * * * "[t]he burden is not shifted" under § 45–2–203. The trial judge instructed the jury that "[t]he State of Montana has the burden of proving the guilt of the Defendant beyond a reasonable doubt," and that "[a] person commits the offense of deliberate homicide if he purposely or knowingly causes the death of another human being." Thus, failure by the State to produce evidence of respondent's mental state would have resulted in an acquittal. That acquittal did not occur was presumably attributable to the fact * * * that the State introduced considerable evidence from which the jury might have concluded that respondent acted "purposely" or "knowingly." * * *
>
> Recognizing that *Sandstrom* is not directly on point, the Supreme Court of Montana [which declared the statute unconstitutional] described § 45–2–203 as a burden-*reducing*, rather than burden-shifting, statute. * * * What the court evidently meant is that, by excluding a significant line of evidence that might refute *mens rea*, the statute made it easier for the State to meet the requirement of proving *mens rea* beyond a reasonable doubt—reduced the burden in the sense of making the burden easier to bear. But *any* evidentiary rule can have that effect. "Reducing" the State's burden in this manner is not unconstitutional, unless the rule of

evidence itself violates a fundamental principle of fairness (which * * * this one does not). We have "reject[ed] the view that anything in the Due Process Clause bars States from making changes in their criminal law that have the effect of making it easier for the prosecution to obtain convictions." * * *

　　* * * The people of Montana have decided to resurrect the rule of an earlier era, disallowing consideration of voluntary intoxication when a defendant's state of mind is at issue. Nothing in the Due Process Clause prevents them from doing so * * *.

Justice Ginsburg provided the fifth vote upholding the Montana statute, but she reached the result by a very different path. She disagreed with the plurality's characterization of § 45–2–203 as a rule intended to keep out relevant exculpatory evidence (in this case, evidence of intoxication). Instead, she interpreted the provision as redefining "deliberate homicide" as follows:

> To obtain a conviction, the prosecution must prove only that (1) the defendant caused the death of another with actual knowledge or purpose, *or* (2) that the defendant killed "under circumstances that would otherwise establish knowledge or purpose 'but for' [the defendant's] voluntary intoxication." Accordingly, § 45–2–203 does not "lighte[n] the prosecution's burden to prove [the] mental-state element beyond a reasonable doubt," * * * for "[t]he applicability of the reasonable-doubt standard * * * has always been dependent on how a State defined the offense that is charged."

What does Justice Ginsburg mean by (2) above? Does she mean that a jury must assume a fact exists (that the actor was sober) that does not? How does the factfinder conduct the counter-factual exercise of determining what the drunk defendant's state of mind would have been if he had been sober?

　　4. *Model Penal Code.* Model Penal Code § 2.08(1) provides that intoxication is a defense if it "negatives an element of the offense." The common law "general intent"/"specific intent" distinction does not apply. Look with care, however, at § 2.08, subsection (2), which sets out a special definition of recklessness in the case of self-induced intoxication.

Is the effect of subsection (2) to treat a negligently intoxicated harmdoer as if she were reckless? If so, isn't it the case, as the Commentary to the Model Penal Code observes, that "the result of [the] special rule is bound to be a liability disproportionate to culpability"? The Commentary defends the special provision as follows:

> The [argument against the MPC rule] * * * is worthy of respect, but there are strong considerations on the other side. There is first the weight of the antecedent law which here, more clearly than in England, has tended toward a special rule for drunkenness in this context. Beyond this, there is the fundamental point that awareness of the potential consequences of excessive drinking on the capacity of human beings to gauge the risks incident to their conduct is by now so dispersed in our culture that it is not unfair to postulate a general equivalence between the risks created by the conduct of the drunken actor and the risks created by his conduct in becoming drunk. Becoming so drunk as to

destroy temporarily the actor's powers of perception and judgment is conduct that plainly has no affirmative social value to counterbalance the potential danger. The actor's moral culpability lies in engaging in such conduct. Added to this are the impressive difficulties posed in litigating the foresight of any particular actor at the time when he imbibes and the relative rarity of cases where intoxication really does engender unawareness as distinguished from imprudence. These considerations led to the conclusion, on balance, that the Model Code should declare that unawareness of risks, of which the actor would have been aware had he been sober, is immaterial. Most states with revised codes have taken a similar position.

American Law Institute, Model Penal Code and Commentaries, Comment to § 2.08 at 358–59 (1985).

5. *Intoxication and insanity.* The defense of insanity is considered in detail in the next section of the chapter. One essential condition for pleading insanity is that the defendant must suffer from a mental disease or defect. As currently understood, neither alcoholism nor drug addiction constitutes a mental disorder, so the insanity defense is not automatically available to persons suffering from either of these conditions.

Long-term and excessive use of alcohol or drugs, however, sometimes brings on an independent mental infirmity that persists even after the short-term effects of the intoxicating substance have worn off. Most jurisdictions that have considered the issue recognize a defense in such circumstances, even if the defendant possesses the requisite *mens rea* for the offense, but the defense is that of insanity—often termed "settled" or "fixed" insanity in this context—and not intoxication. E.g., Berry v. State, 950 N.E.2d 821 (Ind. Ct. App. 2011); People v. Chapman, 165 Mich.App. 215, 418 N.W.2d 658 (1987); Jones v. State, 648 P.2d 1251 (Okla.Crim.App.1982).

Should a person be excused if her "settled insanity" was induced by regular, voluntary ingestion of alcohol or narcotics? One court, State v. Sexton, 180 Vt. 34, 904 A.2d 1092 (2006), has answered the question this way:

The underlying rationale for the settled insanity doctrine is generally explained as an acknowledgment of "the futility of punishment, since the defective mental state is permanent," or, more commonly, as a compassionate concession that at some point a person's earlier voluntary decisions become so temporally and "morally remote" that the cause of the offense can reasonably be ascribed to the resulting insanity rather than the use of intoxicants.

The doctrine is not without its more contemporary critics. The author of one seminal article has opined that "the moral culpability of long term alcohol abuse and society's interest in preventing criminal behavior weigh heavily in favor of denying the settled insanity defense." Another commentator has noted the "injustice" and social costs of holding an intoxicated defendant responsible for his conduct while excusing another merely because he used enough drugs long enough to develop an underlying illness. At least one court has rejected the doctrine as based on an indefensible distinction between the person who drinks or takes drugs and is "momentarily 'mentally defective'" and the person who drinks or takes drugs and is " 'mentally defective' as an eventual, long-term result." Bieber v. People, 856 P.2d 811, 816 [(Colo. 1993)]. * * *

* * * To retain any moral or legal salience, the doctrine must—if it is ever justified—be limited to those cases where the initial choice to abuse alcohol or drugs has become so attenuated over time that it serves little or no purpose to hold the defendant accountable for that choice once a permanent mental illness has taken hold through years of chronic substance abuse.

6. *Involuntary intoxication.* On occasion a defendant will assert that she should be exculpated because of *involuntary* intoxication. Successful claims of this sort are rare. City of Minneapolis v. Altimus, 306 Minn. 462, 238 N.W.2d 851 (1976) summarizes the categories of involuntary intoxication:

> Four different kinds of involuntary intoxication have been recognized: Coerced intoxication, pathological intoxication, intoxication by innocent mistake, and unexpected intoxication resulting from the ingestion of a medically prescribed drug. Coerced intoxication is intoxication involuntarily induced by reason of duress or coercion. * * * Courts have strictly construed the requirement of coercion, however, so that acquittal by reason of coerced intoxication is an exceedingly rare result.
>
> Pathological intoxication has been defined as "intoxication grossly excessive in degree, given the amount of the intoxicant, to which the actor does not know he is susceptible." Model Penal Code, § 2.08(5)(c). Pathologically intoxicated offenders have been held not criminally responsible for their acts when they ingested the intoxicant not knowing of their special susceptibility to its effects. * * *
>
> Involuntary intoxication may also occur when intoxication results from an innocent mistake by the defendant about the character of the substance taken, as when another person has tricked him into taking the liquor or drugs. See, *People v. Penman,* 271 Ill. 82, 110 N.E. 894 (1915). In *Penman,* the defendant killed his victim after apparently taking cocaine tablets which, due to the deception of another, he believed to be breath purifiers. * * *
>
> The last kind of involuntary intoxication recognized in the case law arises when the defendant is unexpectedly intoxicated due to the ingestion of a medically prescribed drug

How does involuntary intoxication exculpate? First, an involuntarily intoxicated individual is entitled to acquittal if, as a result of the condition, he does not form the *mens rea* for the offense. That is, he will be exculpated if, as a result of involuntary intoxication, he lacks the specific intent, if any, of the offense. Also, "[a]lthough there is exceedingly little case law on the matter, it would seem that because the actor's intoxication was contracted in a nonculpable manner, he should also be acquitted of any general-intent offense." Joshua Dressler, Understanding Criminal Law 335 (5th ed. 2009).

Second, a person whose involuntary intoxication renders the individual "temporarily insane" is entitled to acquittal of any offense. That is, she is entitled to exculpation if, as a result of the intoxication (rather than a mental disease), the actor's condition satisfies that jurisdiction's definition of insanity. The defense, however, is involuntary intoxication, and not insanity. (Thus, the civil commitment procedures that often attach to an insanity acquittal do not apply here.)

4. INSANITY

a. Some Preliminaries

i. *Competency to Stand Trial*

A criminal trial may not proceed if the defendant is incompetent to stand trial. An individual can be incompetent for a variety of reasons, including that she is severely mentally ill or disabled, suffers from amnesia, or is unable to communicate with her attorney due to a physical handicap, such as an inability to speak. Generally speaking, a defendant is incompetent to stand trial unless she has sufficient present ability to consult with her lawyer "with a reasonable degree of rational understanding" and has "a rational as well as factual understanding of the proceedings" against her. Dusky v. United States, 362 U.S. 402, 80 S.Ct. 788, 4 L.Ed.2d 824 (1960) (internal quotation marks omitted).

The issue of competency, should it arise, ordinarily is considered at the defendant's initial appearance before a magistrate, but it may be raised at any time during the proceedings, even during the trial. Unless the parties agree that the defendant is incompetent, the judge ordinarily will appoint at least one mental health professional to examine the defendant, during which time the accused may be committed to a hospital or other suitable facility for the testing. E.g., Model Penal Code § 4.05.

A state may presume that a defendant is competent to stand trial and require her to prove her incompetency by a preponderance of evidence. Medina v. California, 505 U.S. 437, 112 S.Ct. 2572, 120 L.Ed.2d 353 (1992). However, it violates due process to impose a stricter burden on the defendant, such as "proof by clear and convincing evidence" of incompetency. Cooper v. Oklahoma, 517 U.S. 348, 116 S.Ct. 1373, 134 L.Ed.2d 498 (1996).

If a judge determines that the defendant is incompetent to stand trial, criminal proceedings are suspended, and the defendant is committed to a mental health facility, where she may be held until she regains competency, a period of time that may exceed the potential maximum sentence for the offense charged.

Constitutional issues arise when the defendant cannot be restored to competency. For example, in Jackson v. Indiana, 406 U.S. 715, 92 S.Ct. 1845, 32 L.Ed.2d 435 (1972), the defendant was described as a "mentally defective deaf mute with a mental level of a pre-school child," who could neither read, write, nor communicate to others except through very limited sign language. The examining doctors described the defendant's prognosis for competency as "rather dim." As defense counsel pointed out, the defendant's commitment under such circumstances amounted to a life sentence without a criminal trial.

The Supreme Court ruled that "[a]t the least, due process requires that the nature and duration of commitment bear some reasonable relation to the purpose for which the individual is committed." Therefore, the Court held:

> [A] person charged by the State with a criminal offense who is committed solely on account of his incapacity to proceed to trial cannot be held more than the reasonable period of time necessary to determine whether there is a substantial probability that he will attain the capacity in the foreseeable future. If it is determined that this is not the case, then the State must either institute the customary civil commitment proceeding that would be required to commit indefinitely any other citizen, or release the defendant.

Severely psychotic defendants sometimes can be restored to competency by the administration of antipsychotic drugs. May the government, therefore, require such a person to undergo administration of such medication in order to render her competent to stand trial? As a constitutional matter, "[t]he forcible injection of medication into a nonconsenting person's body represents a substantial interference with that person's liberty" interest under the due process clause. Washington v. Harper, 494 U.S. 210, 229, 110 S.Ct. 1028, 1041, 108 L.Ed.2d 178, 203 (1990). Therefore, the Supreme Court held in Sell v. United States, 539 U.S. 166, 123 S.Ct. 2174, 156 L.Ed.2d 197 (2003) that the

> Constitution permits the Government involuntarily to administer antipsychotic drugs to a mentally ill defendant facing serious criminal charges in order to render that defendant competent to stand trial, but *only if* the treatment is medically appropriate, is *substantially* unlikely to have side effects that may undermine the fairness of the trial, and, taking account of less intrusive alternatives, is *necessary significantly* to further important governmental trial-related interests. (Emphasis added.)

The Court opined that such conditions as would justify the use of antipsychotic drugs to restore competency will be rare.

ii. Pre–Trial Assertion of the Insanity Plea

Most states have instituted special procedures that must be followed if a defendant wishes to assert the insanity defense at trial. For example, a defendant who intends to claim insanity must often assert a special plea of "not guilty by reason of insanity" (NGRI), rather than (or in conjunction with) the general plea of "not guilty." Courts are divided on the question of whether a trial judge may interpose an insanity plea over the objections of a competent defendant. See David S. Cohn, *Offensive Use of the Insanity Defense: Imposing the Insanity Defense Over the Defendant's Objection,* 15 Hastings Const.L.Q. 295 (1988).

In many states and in the federal courts, a defendant who intends to introduce expert testimony relating to her mental condition at the time of the crime must notify the prosecutor of her plan within a specified period of time before trial, and submit to a psychiatric evaluation by a court appointed expert. If the defendant fails to comply with such rules, the judge may bar the party's expert testimony at trial. E.g., Fed.R.Crim.P. 12.2.

Some states now permit the factfinder to return a verdict of "guilty but mentally ill" (GBMI) in any case in which it could return a verdict of NGRI. E.g., Mich.Comp.Law Ann. § 768.36 (2012). A GBMI verdict is allowed if the prosecutor proves beyond a reasonable doubt all of the elements of the crime, no defenses (including insanity) are proven, and the defendant suffers from a mental illness.

Under the prototypical Michigan system, a GBMI-verdict defendant receives a sentence suitable for one who is found guilty of the offense for which she has been convicted. Upon sentencing, however, the defendant is evaluated to determine if psychiatric treatment is indicated. If it is, care may be provided in the prison or a mental health facility. If treatment is successfully completed before the defendant's sentence of imprisonment is completed, the inmate is returned to the prison's jurisdiction to serve the balance of the sentence.

Studies of jury verdicts in Michigan indicate that implementation of the GBMI law did not result in a reduction of NGRI verdicts in that state. E.g., Gare A. Smith & James A. Hall, *Evaluating Michigan's Guilty But Mentally Ill Verdict: An Empirical Study*, 16 U.Mich.J.L.Ref. 77 (1982). However, in Pennsylvania the number of successful insanity pleas dropped significantly after the GBMI verdict was instituted. R.D. Mackay & Jerry Kopelman, *The Operation of the "Guilty But Mentally Ill" Verdict in Pennsylvania*, 16 J. Psychiatry & Law 247 (Summer, 1988). Some mock jury studies also support the view that the GBMI option reduces markedly the number of likely NGRI verdicts. Caton F. Roberts et al., *Implicit Theories of Criminal Responsibility*, 11 Law & Hum. Behav. 207 (1987).

iii. Burden of Proof at Trial

Insanity is an affirmative defense. Therefore, the legislature may constitutionally require the defendant to persuade the factfinder that she was insane at the time of the crime. Leland v. Oregon, 343 U.S. 790, 72 S.Ct. 1002, 96 L.Ed. 1302 (1952). Nonetheless, until the 1980s, most states and the federal courts required the prosecutor to carry the burden of proof regarding the defendant's sanity. 2 Paul H. Robinson, Criminal Law Defenses § 173(a) at 284–85 (1984).

Public anger stemming from the insanity acquittal of John W. Hinckley, the attempted assassin of President Ronald Reagan, resulted in legislative action to make insanity acquittals harder to obtain. Today, a majority of states and Congress place the burden of persuasion regarding sanity on the defendant.

iv.   Post–Trial Disposition of Insanity Acquittees

A defendant found not guilty by reason of insanity (NGRI) rarely goes free immediately or even within a brief period of time following trial. In some jurisdictions, an insanity acquittee is automatically committed by the criminal court to a psychiatric facility for custody, care, and treatment of his mental illness. E.g., Model Penal Code § 4.08. In other states, commitment is not automatic, but local law commonly permits or requires the criminal court to order the acquittee detained temporarily in a mental health facility for observation and determination of whether he remains mentally ill and subject to civil commitment. E.g., Mich.Comp.Laws Ann. § 330.2050 (2009).

A person may not be civilly committed to a mental institution unless he is both presently mentally ill (or, at least, suffering from some mental abnormality) and dangerous to himself or others. Ordinarily, involuntary commitment is not permitted unless the State proves these two conditions—mental abnormality and dangerousness—by clear and convincing evidence. Addington v. Texas, 441 U.S. 418, 99 S.Ct. 1804, 60 L.Ed.2d 323 (1979). However, the Court held in Jones v. United States, 463 U.S. 354, 103 S.Ct. 3043, 77 L.Ed.2d 694 (1983), that when a person is acquitted of a crime (in *Jones*, shoplifting) on grounds of insanity, the acquittee may properly be institutionalized on the lesser standard of proof of preponderance of the evidence.

Why does the clear-and-convincing-evidence standard for proving mental illness and dangerousness not apply to an insanity acquittee? The Court explained:

> A verdict of not guilty by reason of insanity establishes two facts: (i) the defendant committed an act that constitutes a criminal offense, and (ii) he committed the act because of mental illness. * * *
>
> The fact that a person has been found, beyond a reasonable doubt, to have committed a criminal act certainly indicates dangerousness. * * * Indeed, this concrete evidence generally may be at least as persuasive as any predictions about dangerousness that might be made in a civil-commitment proceeding. We do not agree with petitioner's suggestion that the requisite dangerousness is not established by proof that a person committed a non-violent crime against property. This Court never has held that "violence" * * * is a prerequisite for a constitutional commitment.
>
> Nor can we say that it was unreasonable for Congress to determine that the insanity acquittal supports an inference of continuing mental illness. It comports with common sense to conclude that someone whose mental illness was sufficient to lead him to commit a criminal act is likely to remain ill and in need of treatment.

The *Jones* Court also held that a person found NGRI may be held in custody as long as he remains both mentally ill and dangerous, although this may, and often does, result in hospitalization for a period of time longer than the detainee could have been incarcerated if he had been convicted in criminal court.

v. Sexual Predator Laws: A New Strategy for Civil Commitment

In recent years many states have enacted "sexual predator laws," which provide a new way to institutionalize persons believed to be likely to commit acts of sexual violence in the future. For example, the State of Kansas enacted a law in 1994 establishing procedures for the "long-term care and treatment" of "sexually violent predators." Kan. Stat. Ann. § 59–29a01 *et seq* (1994). Under the law as originally drafted, a "sexually violent predator" is "any person who has been convicted of or charged with a sexually violent offense and who suffers from a mental abnormality or personality disorder which makes the person likely to engage in the predatory acts of sexual violence." A "mental abnormality" was defined as a "congenital or acquired condition, affecting the emotional or volitional capacity which predisposes the person to commit sexually violent offenses in a degree constituting such person a menace to the health and safety of others." In 2007, approximately 2,700 persons were under confinement pursuant to state predator laws. Monica Davey & Abby Goodnough, *Doubts Rise as States Hold Sex Offenders After Prison,* New York Times, Mar. 4, 2007, at A1.

Sexual predators usually are found fully responsible for their actions, i.e., they are not legally insane. Typically, therefore, predator laws are enforced against persons who have been convicted of sexual violence but who are due to be released from prison. Nonetheless, the laws potentially apply as well to persons charged with such crimes but declared incompetent to stand trial, to insanity acquittees, and even to persons found *not* guilty of sexual violence. Although procedures vary by jurisdiction, a prosecutor typically files a petition in a state court seeking the person's involuntary civil commitment. If a judge finds that there is probable cause to believe that the individual is a sexual predator, he is transferred to a mental facility for evaluation, after which a full hearing is held. Based on psychiatric evaluations, if a judge determines beyond a reasonable doubt that the individual is a sexually violent predator—that this individual is "likely to engage" in sexual violence in the future—the person is civilly committed until his condition "has so changed that [he] is safe to be at large." Because such persons are thought not to be "amenable to existing mental illness treatment modalities," Kan. Stat. Ann. § 59–29a01 (1994), the practical effect of such civil commitment may be life-long institutionalization based on a prediction of future behavior. Indeed, only approximately 250 persons nationally have ever been released unconditionally, and about half of these were released on technical grounds unrelated to treatment. Davey & Goodnaugh, supra. For example, Leroy Hendricks, whose case was the first to reach the United States Supreme Court, remained civilly committed, at age 72, although he was largely confined to a wheel chair as a result of complications from diabetes and a stroke. Id.

Sexual predator laws have withstood constitutional attack. Kansas v. Hendricks, 521 U.S. 346, 117 S.Ct. 2072, 138 L.Ed.2d 501 (1997), but the Supreme Court *has* warned that, in cases where the actor's lack of volitional control is at issue—typically the basis for commitment of sexual predators—due process requires that there "be proof of serious difficulty in controlling behavior * * * [that is] sufficient to distinguish the dangerous sexual offender whose serious mental illness, abnormality, or disorder subjects him to civil commitment from the dangerous but typical recidivist convicted in an ordinary criminal case." Kansas v. Crane, 534 U.S. 407, 122 S.Ct. 867, 151 L.Ed.2d 856 (2002).

b. Why Do We Excuse the Insane?: Some Initial Thoughts

UNITED STATES v. FREEMAN

United States Court of Appeals, Second Circuit, 1966.
357 F.2d 606.

KAUFMAN, CIRCUIT JUDGE: * * *

The criminal law * * * is an expression of the moral sense of the community. The fact that the law has, for centuries, regarded [insane] wrong-doers as improper subjects for punishment is a testament to the extent to which that moral sense has developed. Thus, society has recognized over the years that none of the three asserted purposes of the criminal law—rehabilitation, deterrence and retribution—is satisfied when the truly irresponsible * * * are punished.

What rehabilitative function is served when one who is mentally incompetent and found guilty is ordered to serve a sentence in prison? Is not any curative or restorative function better achieved in such a case in an institution designed and equipped to treat just such individuals? And how is deterrence achieved by punishing the incompetent? Those who are substantially unable to restrain their conduct are, by definition, undeterrable and their "punishment" is no example for others; those who are [insane] * * * can hardly be expected rationally to weigh the consequences of their conduct. Finally, what segment of society can feel its desire for retribution satisfied when it wreaks vengeance upon the incompetent? Although an understandable emotion, a need for retribution can never be permitted in a civilized society to degenerate into a sadistic form of revenge.

NOTES AND QUESTIONS

1. Is Judge Kaufman correct in asserting that punishment of the insane is incompatible with principles of rehabilitation, deterrence, and retribution? The following judicial comments are additional efforts to justify the defense.

2. State v. Singleton, 418 N.J.Super. 177, 12 A.3d 728 (N.J. Super. Ct. App. Div. 2011):

[T]he insanity defense comports with the fundamental purposes of our criminal law to ensure public safety. That is, criminal punishment serves to deter the defendant in choosing wrong over right, but "[i]f the defendant cannot understand the wrongfulness of his or her conduct, he or she will not understand the reason for the punishment, and that punishment will not serve as a deterrent to anyone."

3. Holloway v. United States, 148 F.2d 665 (D.C.Cir.1945):

To punish a man who lacks the power to reason is as undignified and unworthy as punishing an inanimate object or an animal. A man who cannot reason cannot be subject to blame. Our collective conscience does not allow punishment where it cannot impose blame.

4. United States v. Lyons, 739 F.2d 994 (5th Cir.1984) (Rubin, C.J., dissenting):

The insanity defense reflects the fundamental moral principles of our criminal law. An adjudication of guilt is more than a factual determination that the defendant pulled a trigger, took a bicycle, or sold heroin. It is a moral judgment that the individual is blameworthy. * * * Our concept of blameworthiness rests on assumptions that are older than the Republic: "man is naturally endowed with these two great faculties, understanding and liberty of will." "[H]istorically, our substantive criminal law is based on a theory of punishing the viscious [sic] will. It postulates a free agent confronted with a choice between doing right and wrong, and choosing freely to do wrong." Central, therefore, to a verdict of guilty is the concept of responsibility. * * * An acquittal by reason of insanity is a judgment that the defendant is not *guilty* because, as a result of his mental condition, he is unable to make an effective choice regarding his behavior.

5. State v. Johnson, 121 R.I. 254, 399 A.2d 469 (1979):

The law of criminal responsibility has its roots in the concept of free will. * * * Our law proceeds from this postulate and seeks to fashion a standard by which criminal offenders whose free will has been sufficiently impaired can be identified and treated in a manner that is both humane and beneficial to society at large. The problem has been aptly described as distinguishing between those cases for which a correctional-punitive disposition is appropriate and those in which a medical-custodial disposition is the only kind that is legally permissible.

6. *Evil versus sickness.* The dichotomy mentioned in Note 5 between correctional (criminal) and medical (civil) commitment suggests that the insanity defense is meant to distinguish between wickedness and sickness, to draw a line between the "bad and the mad." But, how do we draw such a line? Was Jeffrey Dahmer, who killed men, had sexual relations with the corpses, dismembered the bodies and, on occasion, cannibalized the victims, sick or evil? Was Hitler sick or evil? Are persons who kill for racist reasons mentally ill, as one highly respected clinical professor of psychiatry asserts? Alvin F. Poussaint, *They Hate. They Kill. Are They Insane?*, New York Times, Aug. 26, 1999, at A21.

As you read the materials that follow, ask yourself whether the law has devised a suitable way to distinguish sickness from evil. Or, is this a false dichotomy? Was paranoid schizophrenic Andrew Goldstein, who tossed Kendra Webdale to her death under a New York City subway train, correct when he told the court, "[i]f you kill somebody, you should be punished. * * * Jail or mental hospital, *it's all the same.*" Barbara Ross, *25 to Life for Subway Killer*, New York Daily News, May 5, 2000, at 30.

7. *Mental illness versus insanity.* Approximately 283,000 mentally ill offenders were incarcerated in 1998 in United States prisons and jails. U.S. Dept. of Justice, Mental Health and Treatment of Inmates and Probationers (July 1999, NCJ 174463). How can this be if we have an insanity defense? The answer—one that should be kept in mind throughout the materials that follow—is that *mental illness* is a medical concept, whereas *insanity* is a legal term. One can be mentally ill without being insane, but not vice-versa.

c. Struggling for a Definition: The Tests of Insanity

In light of competing social currents and developments in our understanding of human psychology, courts have struggled over the past two centuries to devise a suitable definition of insanity. The following case lays out four tests of insanity that American jurisdictions have adopted at one time or another. The court also summarizes some of the criticisms of each test. These criticisms, and other matters, are considered in greater detail in the Notes following the case.

STATE v. JOHNSON

Supreme Court of Rhode Island, 1979.
121 R.I. 254, 399 A.2d 469.

DORIS, JUSTICE.

The sole issue presented by this appeal is whether this court should abandon the *M'Naghten* test in favor of a new standard for determining the criminal responsibility of those who claim they are blameless by reason of mental illness. For the reasons stated herein, we have concluded that the time has arrived to modernize our rule governing this subject. [The court adopted a version of the Model Penal Code insanity defense discussed below.] * * *

Because language is inherently imprecise and there is a wide divergence of opinion within the medical profession, no exact definition of "insanity" is possible. * * * Any legal standard designed to assess criminal responsibility must satisfy several objectives. It must accurately reflect the underlying principles of substantive law and community values while comporting with the realities of scientific understanding. The standard must be phrased in order to make fully available to the jury such psychiatric information as medical science has to offer regarding the individual defendant, yet be comprehensible to the experts, lawyers, and jury alike. Finally, the definition must preserve to the trier of facts, be it judge or jury, its full authority to render a final decision. * * *

I.

The historical evolution of the law of criminal responsibility is a fascinating, complex story. For purposes of this opinion, however, an exhaustive historical discussion is unnecessary; a brief sketch will therefore suffice. The renowned "right-wrong" test had antecedents in England as early as 1582. In that year the *Eirenarcha*, written by William Lambard of the Office of the Justices of Peace, laid down as the test of criminal responsibility "knowledge of good or evil." During the 1700's the language of the test shifted its emphasis from "good or evil" to "know." During the eighteenth century, when these tests and their progeny were evolving, psychiatry was hardly a profession, let alone a science. Belief in demonology and witchcraft was widespread and became intertwined with the law of responsibility. So eminent a legal scholar as Blackstone adamantly insisted upon the existence of witches and wizards as late as the latter half of the eighteenth century. The psychological theories of phrenology and monomania thrived and influenced the development of the "right and wrong" test.[2] Both of these compartmentalized concepts have been soundly rejected by modern medical science which views the human personality as a fully integrated system. By historical accident, however, the celebrated case of Daniel M'Naghten froze these concepts into the common law just at the time when they were beginning to come into disrepute.

[THE *M'NAGHTEN* RULE][h]

Daniel M'Naghten attempted to assassinate Sir Robert Peel, Prime Minister of England, but mistakenly shot Peel's private secretary instead. This assassination had been preceded by several attempts on the lives of members of the English Royal House, including Queen Victoria herself. When M'Naghten was tried in 1843 the jury was charged with a test heavily influenced by the enlightened work of Dr. Isaac Ray who was severely critical of the "right and wrong" rule. After the jury acquitted M'Naghten the public indignation, spearheaded by the Queen, was so pronounced that the Judges of England were summoned before the House of Lords to justify their actions. In an extraordinary advisory opinion, issued in a pressure-charged atmosphere, Lord Chief Justice Tindal, speaking for all but one of the 15 judges, reversed the charge used at trial and articulated what has become known as the *M'Naghten* rules. The principal rule in *M'Naghten's Case*, 8 Eng.Rep. 718 (1843) states:

> "To establish a defense on the ground of insanity it must be clearly proved that, at the time of committing the act, the party accused was laboring under such a defect of reason, from disease of the mind, as not to know the nature and quality of the act he was doing, or if he did know it, that he did not know that what he was doing was wrong."

2. Phrenologists viewed the brain as divided into 35 distinct areas. Each area controlled a specific mental function. The sixth area, for example, was denominated "destructiveness." Monomania was a state of mind in which a single insane idea predominated while the rest of the thought processes remained normal.

h. The bracketed words, identifying the insanity tests, are not part of the original court opinion. They were added by the casebook editor for purposes of clarity.

This dual-pronged test, issued in response to the outrage of a frightened Queen, rapidly became the predominant rule in the United States. * * *

II.

The *M'Naghten* rule has been the subject of considerable criticism and controversy for over a century. The test's emphasis upon knowledge of right or wrong abstracts a single element of personality as the sole symptom or manifestation of mental illness. *M'Naghten* refuses to recognize volitional or emotional impairments, viewing the cognitive element as the singular cause of conduct. * * * One of the [other] most frequent criticisms of *M'Naghten* has been directed at its all-or-nothing approach, requiring total incapacity of cognition. We agree that:

> "Nothing makes the inquiry into responsibility more unreal for the psychiatrist than limitation of the issue to some ultimate extreme of total incapacity, when clinical experience reveals only a graded scale with marks along the way. * * *

> "The law must recognize that when there is no black and white it must content itself with different shades of gray." Model Penal Code, § 4.01, Comment at 158 (Tent.Draft No. 4, 1955).

By focusing upon total cognitive incapacity, the *M'Naghten* rule compels the psychiatrist to testify in terms of unrealistic concepts having no medical meaning. Instead of scientific opinions, the rule calls for a moral or ethical judgment from the expert which judgment contributes to usurpation of the jury's function as decision maker.

Probably the most common criticism of *M'Naghten* is that it severely restricts expert testimony, thereby depriving the jury of a true picture of the defendant's mental condition. * * *

III.

[The "Irresistible Impulse" or "Control" Test]

Responding to criticism of *M'Naghten* as a narrow and harsh rule, several courts supplemented it with the "irresistible impulse" test.[i] Under this combined approach, courts inquire into both the cognitive and volitional components of the defendant's behavior. Although a theoretical advance over the stringent right and wrong test, the irresistible impulse doctrine has also been the subject of widespread criticism. Similar to *M'Naghten*'s absolutist view of capacity to know, the irresistible impulse is considered in terms of a complete destruction of the governing power of the mind. A more fundamental objection is that the test produces the

---

i. E.g., Parsons v. State, 81 Ala. 577, 2 So. 854 (1887): " 'If * * * it shall be definitely established to be true that there is an unsound condition of the mind, that is, a diseased condition of the mind, in which, though a person abstractly knows that a given act is wrong, he is yet, by an *insane impulse*, * * * irresistibly driven to commit it, the law must * * * give to this condition * * * its exculpatory effect.' * * * We think it sufficient if the insane delusion—by which we mean the delusion proceeding from a *diseased mind*—* * * so subverts his will as to destroy his free agency by rending him powerless to resist by reason of *the duress of the disease*."

misleading notion that a crime impulsively committed must have been perpetrated in a sudden and explosive fit. Thus, the irresistible impulse test excludes those "far more numerous instances of crimes committed after excessive brooding and melancholy by one who is unable to resist sustained psychic compulsion or to make any real attempt to control his conduct."

[THE "PRODUCT" TEST]

The most significant break in the century-old stranglehold of *M'Naghten* came in 1954 when the Court of Appeals for the District of Columbia declared that, "an accused is not criminally responsible if his unlawful act was the product of mental disease or mental defect." *Durham v. United States*, 94 U.S.App.D.C. 228, 214 F.2d 862 (1954). The "product" test, first pioneered by the Supreme Court of New Hampshire in *State v. Pike*, 49 N.H. 399, 402 (1869), was designed to facilitate full and complete expert testimony and to permit the jury to consider all relevant information, rather than restrict its inquiry to data relating to a sole symptom or manifestation of mental illness. *Durham* generated voluminous commentary and made a major contribution in recasting the law of criminal responsibility. In application, however, the test was plagued by significant deficiencies. The elusive, undefined concept of productivity * * * gave the jury inadequate guidance. Most troublesome was the test's tendency to result in expert witnesses' usurpation of the jury function. As a result, in *Washington v. United States*, 129 U.S.App.D.C. 29, 390 F.2d 444 (1967), the court took the extreme step of proscribing experts from testifying concerning productivity altogether. Finally, in *United States v. Brawner*, 153 U.S.App.D.C. 1, 471 F.2d 969 (1972), the court abandoned *Durham*, decrying the "trial by label" that had resulted. The author of *Durham*, Chief Judge Bazelon, stated that testimony couched in terms of the legal conclusion that an act was or was not the product of mental disease invited the jury to abdicate its responsibility as ultimate decision maker, and acquiesce in the experts' conclusions. * * *

IV.

[MODEL PENAL CODE (AMERICAN LAW INSTITUTE) TEST]

Responding to the criticism of the *M'Naghten* and irresistible impulse rules, the American Law Institute incorporated a new test of criminal responsibility into its Model Penal Code. The Model Penal Code test [Section 4.01] has received widespread and evergrowing acceptance. * * * Although no definition can be accurately described as the perfect or ultimate pronouncement, we believe that the Model Penal Code standard represents a significant, positive improvement over our existing rule. Most importantly, it acknowledges that volitional as well as cognitive impairments must be considered by the jury in its resolution of the responsibility issue. * * * Additionally, the test employs vocabulary sufficiently in the common ken that its use at trial will permit a reasonable three-way dialogue between the law-trained judges and lawyers, the medical-trained experts, and the jury. * * *

AMERICAN LAW INSTITUTE, MODEL PENAL CODE AND COMMENTARIES COMMENT TO § 4.01

(1985), 168–72

The Model Code * * * standard relieves the defendant of responsibility under two circumstances: (1) when, as a result of mental disease or defect, the defendant lacked substantial capacity to appreciate the criminality [wrongfulness] of his conduct; (2) when, as a result of mental disease or defect, the defendant lacked substantial capacity to conform his conduct to the requirements of law.

The use of "appreciate" rather than "know" conveys a broader sense of understanding than simple cognition. The proposal as originally approved in 1955 was cast in terms of a person's lack of capacity to appreciate the "criminality" of his conduct, but the Institute accepted "wrongfulness" as an appropriate substitute for "criminality" in the Proposed Final Draft. Appreciating "wrongfulness" may be taken to mean appreciating that the community regards the behavior as wrongful. * * *

The part of the Model Code test relating to volition is cast in terms of capacity to conform one's conduct to the requirements of the law. Application of the principle calls for a distinction, inevitable for a standard addressed to impairment of volition, between incapacity and mere indisposition. In drawing this distinction, the Model Code formulation effects a substantial improvement over pre-existing standards.

In contrast to the M'Naghten and "irresistible impulse" criteria, the Model Code formulation reflects the judgment that no test is workable that calls for complete impairment of ability to know or to control. The extremity of these conceptions had posed the largest difficulty for the administration of the old standards. Disorientation, psychiatrists indicated, might be extreme and still might not be total; what clinical experience revealed was closer to a graded scale with marks along the way. Hence, an examiner confronting a person who had performed a seemingly purposive act might helpfully address himself to the extent of awareness, understanding and control. If, on the other hand, he had to speak to utter incapacity vel non under the M'Naghten test, his relevant testimony would be narrowly limited to the question of whether the defendant suffered from delusional psychosis, where the act would not be criminal if the facts were as the defendant deludedly supposed them to be. A test requiring an utter incapacity for self-control imposes a comparably unrealistic restriction on the scope of the relevant inquiry. To meet these difficulties, it was thought that the criterion should ask if the defendant, as a result of mental disease or defect, was deprived of "substantial capacity" to appreciate the criminality (or wrongfulness) of his conduct or to conform his conduct to the requirements of law, meaning by "substantial" a capacity of some appreciable magnitude when measured by the standard of humanity in general, as opposed to the reduction of capacity to the vagrant and trivial dimensions characteristic of the most severe afflictions of the mind.

The adoption of the standard of substantial capacity may well be the Code's most significant alteration of the prevailing tests. It was recognized, of course, that "substantial" is an open-ended concept, but its quantitative connotation was believed to be sufficiently precise for purposes of practical administration.

NOTES AND QUESTIONS

1. *The Constitution and the insanity defense. Johnson* sets out the four primary insanity definitions: (a) *M'Naghten*; (b) the control test; (c) the product rule; and (d) the Model Penal Code version. These tests are discussed in further detail in the materials that follow.

Would it be constitutional, however, for a state to narrow the *M'Naghten* test—to cut it in half? As *Johnson* explains, the *M'Naghten* rule provides that a person is insane and, therefore, not criminally responsible for his actions if, as a result of a mental disease or defect, he does not know "the nature and quality of the act he was doing" (sometimes characterized as the "cognitive incapacity" prong) *or* "did not know right from wrong" (the so-called "moral incapacity" prong). What if a state only recognized one of these prongs?

Consider the State of Arizona. After first defining insanity in full *M'Naghten* terms, it narrowed its insanity defense by deleting the cognitive incapacity prong—that is, the only basis for finding insanity in Arizona is whether a defendant, due to mental disease or defect, did not know right from wrong. In Clark v. Arizona, 548 U.S. 735, 126 S.Ct. 2709, 165 L.Ed.2d 842 (2006), the United Supreme Court considered the constitutionality—and the practical significance—of the Arizona approach:

[Defendant] Clark * * * insists that the [full] *M'Naghten* test represents the minimum that a government must provide in recognizing an alternative to criminal responsibility on grounds of mental illness or defect, and he argues that elimination of the *M'Naghten* reference to [cognitive incapacity violates the Due Process Clause because it] " 'offends [a] principle of justice so rooted in the traditions and conscience of our people as to be ranked as fundamental.' "

The claim entails no light burden, and Clark does not carry it. History shows no deference to *M'Naghten* that could elevate its formula to the level of fundamental principle, so as to limit the traditional recognition of a State's capacity to define crimes and defenses.

Even a cursory examination of the traditional Anglo–American approaches to insanity reveals significant differences among them, with four traditional strains variously combined to yield a diversity of American standards. [The Court summarized the four definitions of insanity set out in *Johnson*, supra.] Seventeen States and the Federal Government[j] have

---

j. The federal definition of insanity provides that "It is an affirmative defense to a prosecution under any Federal statute that, at the time of the commission of the acts constituting the offense,

adopted a recognizable version of the *M'Naghten* test with both its cognitive incapacity and moral incapacity components. One State has adopted only *M'Naghten*'s cognitive incapacity test, and 10 (including Arizona) have adopted the moral incapacity test alone. Fourteen jurisdictions, inspired by the Model Penal Code, have in place an amalgam of the volitional incapacity test and some variant of the moral incapacity test, satisfaction of either (generally by showing a defendant's substantial lack of capacity) being enough to excuse. Three States combine a full *M'Naghten* test with a volitional incapacity formula. And New Hampshire alone stands by the product-of-mental-illness test. * * * Finally, four States have no affirmative insanity defense[20] * * *. These four * * * allow consideration of evidence of mental illness directly on the element of *mens rea* defining the offense.

With this varied background, it is clear that no particular formulation has evolved into a baseline for due process, and that the insanity rule, like the conceptualization of criminal offenses, is substantially open to state choice. * * *

Nor does Arizona's abbreviation of the *M'Naghten* statement raise a proper claim that some constitutional minimum has been shortchanged. Clark's argument of course assumes that Arizona's former statement of the *M'Naghten* rule, with its express alternative of cognitive incapacity, was constitutionally adequate (as we agree). That being so, the abbreviated rule is no less so, for cognitive incapacity is relevant under that statement, just as it was under the more extended formulation, and evidence going to cognitive incapacity has the same significance under the short form as it had under the long.

Though Clark is correct that the application of the moral incapacity test (telling right from wrong) does not necessarily require evaluation of a defendant's cognitive capacity to appreciate the nature and quality of the acts charged against him, his argument fails to recognize that cognitive incapacity is itself enough to demonstrate moral incapacity. Cognitive incapacity, in other words, is a sufficient condition for establishing a defense of insanity, albeit not a necessary one. As a defendant can therefore make out moral incapacity by demonstrating cognitive incapacity, evidence bearing on whether the defendant knew the nature and quality of his actions is both relevant and admissible. In practical terms, if a defendant did not know what he was doing when he acted, he could not have known that he was performing the wrongful act charged as a crime.[23]

---

the defendant, as a result of a severe mental disease or defect, was unable to appreciate the nature and quality or the wrongfulness of his acts. Mental disease or defect does not otherwise constitute a defense." 18 U.S.C. § 17 (2006). In what ways does this test differ from the *M'Naghten* and Model Penal Code standards?

20. Idaho Code § 18–207 (2004); Kan. Stat. Ann. § 22–3220 (1995); Mont. Code Ann. §§ 46–14–102, 46–14–311 (2005); Utah Code Ann. § 76–2–305 (2003). We have never held that the Constitution mandates an insanity defense, nor have we held that the Constitution does not so require. This case does not call upon us to decide the matter.

23. He might, of course, have thought delusively he was doing something just as wrongful as the act charged against him, but this is not the test: he must have understood that he was committing the act charged and that it was wrongful.

Can you see why the Court believes that cognitive incapacity "is a sufficient condition for establishing insanity" in a jurisdiction that only recognizes the moral incapacity prong?

As footnote 20 demonstrates, it remains an open question whether a state violates the Constitution by abolishing the insanity defense, as four states have done. One state supreme court recently held that such abolition *does* violate due process. Finger v. State, 117 Nev. 548, 27 P.3d 66 (2001).

The *Clark* Court observed that the four states that have abolished the insanity defense *do* permit a defendant to introduce evidence of mental illness regarding the element of *mens rea*. That is, although the insanity defense has been abolished in those four states, a defendant may introduce mental-illness testimony to show, for example, that he was so far out of touch with reality that when he strangled the victim he believed he was squeezing an orange (and, therefore, did not have the requisite intent to kill).

As a matter of public policy, why might a state legislature allow mental illness evidence on the matter of *mens rea* but not to prove insanity? Finally, what if a state were to do the opposite—allow mental illness evidence on the issue of insanity, but *not* permit it to disprove *mens rea*? As to the latter situation, the *Clark* case had an answer. See p. 642.

2. *Why the change?* In *Johnson*, the court reported that the MPC definition of insanity "has received widespread and evergrowing acceptance." Indeed, at the time of *Johnson* a slim majority of states, and all but one of the federal circuits, endorsed the MPC standard. Yet, in *Clark* (Note 1) we see that in 2006 twenty-eight states applied all or part of the *M'Naghten* test, whereas only fourteen jurisdictions recognized the MPC test. What happened? The answer is simple: The insanity acquittal of John Hinckley for the attempted assassination of President Ronald Reagan galvanized public opposition to the insanity defense. A few legislatures responded to public outrage by abolishing the insanity defense; more typically, legislatures and courts returned to the *M'Naghten* standard. "When the dust cleared, the sun of the Model Penal Code test had set." Sanford H. Kadish, *Fifty Years of Criminal Law: An Opinionated Review*, 87 Calif. L. Rev. 943, 960 (1999).

3. *"Mental disease or defect."* All of the insanity tests require proof that the actor suffered from a "mental disease or defect" at the time of the crime, yet few courts define this crucial term. What seems clear, however, is that the definition of "mental disease or defect" "is, in the final analysis, a question of legal, moral, and policy—not of medical—judgment." United States v. Lyons, 731 F.2d 243 (5th Cir.1984).

The policy-driven approach to the issue is exemplified by decisions of courts and legislatures to exclude "sociopathy," now identified as "antisocial personality disorder," from the scope of the insanity defense. The essential characteristic of this condition is "a pervasive pattern of disregard for, and violation of, the rights of others that begins in childhood or early adolescence and continues into adulthood." American Psychiatric Association, Diagnostic and Statistical Manual of Mental Disorders 701 (4th ed. Text Revision 2004). The Model Penal Code, while not defining "mental disease or defect," expressly excludes this condition from coverage. M.P.C. § 4.01(2). The Commentary concedes that "[s]ome critics have regarded this [exclusion] as a presumptuous legal intervention in the realm of psychiatric theory," but the drafters concluded that the issue is one "of legal policy that cannot sensibly be resolved as a question of fact or medical terminology." American Law Institute, Model Penal Code and Commentaries, Comment to § 4.01 at 174 (1985).

4. *Cognition: M'Naghten's "know" versus M.P.C.'s "appreciate."* The *M'Naghten* test is often criticized because, by its language, it focuses on a defendant's *knowledge* of the nature and quality, and wrongfulness, of his conduct. In contrast, as the Commentary to the Model Penal Code points out, the Code standard uses the word "appreciate" rather than "know," in order to "convey[] a broader sense of understanding than simple cognition."

The difference here is subtle, but potentially important. A young child may "know" that she is pulling the trigger of a loaded gun, "know" that this causes a person "to die," and "know" that killing others is considered "bad." But, a young child does not "appreciate" the significance of her actions in a deeper sense: she does not truly understand what it means to die (she may even think that death is not permanent, that a dead person can come back to life much as a cartoon character does); she does not appreciate the emotional devastation her actions will have on others; and, as a result of all of this, she cannot fully understand the enormity of the wrongfulness of her conduct. In the same way, a mentally disturbed individual may lack this fundamental—deeper—appreciation of the significance of his conduct.

A primary purpose of the M.P.C. drafters' use of the term "appreciate," rather than *M'Naghten's* "know," is to more satisfactorily enable mental health experts to testify regarding this deeper sense of cognition.

5. *Should the law exculpate for volitional impairment?* The control and Model Penal Code tests provide that a person is not responsible for his actions if, due to mental disease or defect, he lacks the substantial capacity to control his conduct. Opposition to this prong, however, has grown in recent years, in part because of the views expressed by the American Psychiatric Association in its Statement on the Insanity Defense (1982). The A.P.A. stated that "[t]he line between an irresistible impulse and an impulse not resisted is probably no sharper than that between twilight and dusk." Therefore, it reported, "[m]any psychiatrists * * * believe that psychiatric testimony (particularly that of a conclusory nature) about volition is more likely to produce confusion for jurors" than expert testimony relating to cognition. One court, following up on the A.P.A. position, explained why it believed the volitional component of the insanity definition should be rejected:

> "[M]oral mistakes" in administering the insanity defense are greatest "when the experts and the jury are asked to speculate whether the defendant had the capacity to 'control' himself or whether he could have 'resisted' the criminal impulse." * * *
>
> One need not disbelieve in the existence of Angels in order to conclude that the present state of our knowledge regarding them is not such as to support confident conclusions about how many can dance on the head of a pin. In like vein, it may be that some day tools will be

discovered with which reliable conclusions about human volition can be fashioned. It appears to be all but a certainty, however, that despite earlier hopes they do not lie in our hands today. When and if they do, it will be time to consider again to what degree the law should adopt the sort of conclusions that they produce. But until then, we see no prudent course for the law to follow but to treat all criminal impulses—including those not resisted—as resistible. To do otherwise in the present state of medical knowledge would be to cast the insanity defense adrift upon a sea of unfounded scientific speculation, with the palm awarded case by case to the most convincing advocate of that which is presently unknown—and may remain so, because unknowable.

United States v. Lyons, 731 F.2d 243 (5th Cir.1984).

Do you agree with *Lyons*? Or, do you agree with Circuit Judge Alvin Rubin, who dissented in the case at 739 F.2d 994 (5th Cir.1984):

> The majority's fear that the [control] test invites "moral mistakes" is difficult to understand. The majority opinion concedes that some individuals cannot conform their conduct to the law's requirements. Other writers have concluded that a strictly cognitive insanity test will overlook some individuals who would be covered by a control test. Without citing any data that verdicts in insanity cases decided under a control test are frequently inaccurate, the majority embraces a rule certain to result in the conviction of at least some who are not morally responsible and the punishment of those for whom retributive, deterrent, and rehabilitative penal goals are inappropriate. A decision that virtually ensures undeserved, and therefore unjust, punishment in the name of avoiding moral mistakes rests on a peculiar notion of morality.

6. *The Durham "product" test. Durham v. United States*, explained briefly in *Johnson* at p. 602, was revolutionary in its purpose: to reject the idea that the human mind can be compartmentalized in terms of cognition and volition; and, relatedly, to permit psychiatrists to testify without limitation regarding a defendant's state of mind. Difficulties with the product test developed, however, as explained in United States v. Brawner, 471 F.2d 969 (D.C.Cir.1972):

> The rule was devised to facilitate the giving of testimony by medical experts in the context of a legal rule, with the jury called upon to reach a composite conclusion that had medical, legal and moral components. However the pristine statement of the *Durham* rule opened the door to "trial by label." * * * [T]he court failed to explicate what abnormality of mind was an essential ingredient of [the defense]. In the absence of a definition of "mental disease or defect," medical experts attached to them the meanings which would naturally occur to them—medical meanings— and gave testimony accordingly. The problem was dramatically highlighted by the weekend flip flop case, In re Rosenfield, 157 F.Supp. 18 (D.D.C.1957). The petitioner was described as a sociopath. A St. Elizabeths psychiatrist testified that a person with a sociopathic personality was not suffering from a mental disease. That was Friday afternoon. On

Monday morning, through a policy change at St. Elizabeths Hospital, it was determined as an administrative matter that the state of a psychopathic or sociopathic personality did constitute a mental disease.

The concern that medical terminology not control legal outcomes culminated in McDonald v. United States, 114 U.S.App.D.C. 120, 312 F.2d 847, 851 (en banc, 1962), where this court recognized that the term, mental disease or defect, has various meanings, depending upon how and why it is used, and by whom. Mental disease means one thing to a physician bent on treatment, but something different, if somewhat overlapping, to a court of law. We provided a legal definition of mental disease or defect, and held that it included "any abnormal condition of the mind which substantially affects mental or emotional processes and substantially impairs behavior controls." * * *

The *Durham* rule also required explication along other lines, notably the resolution of the ambiguity inherent in the formulation concerning actions that were the "product" of mental illness. * * * Carter v. United States, 102 U.S.App.D.C. 227 at 234, 235, 252 F.2d 608 at 615–616 (1957) * * * identified the "product" element of the rule with the "but for" variety of causation.

The pivotal "product" term continued to present problems, principally that it put expert testimony on a faulty footing. Assuming that a mental disease, in the legal sense, had been established, the fate of the defendant came to be determined by what came to be referred to by the legal jargon of "productivity." On the other hand, it was obviously sensible if not imperative that the experts having pertinent knowledge should speak to the crucial question whether the mental abnormality involved is one associated with aberrant behavior. But since "productivity" was so decisive a factor in the decisional equation, a ruling permitting experts to testify expressly in language of "product" raised in a different context the concern lest the ultimate issue be in fact turned over to the experts rather than retained for the jurors representing the community. * * *

It was in this context that the court came to the decision in Washington v. United States, 129 U.S.App.D.C. 29, 390 F.2d 444 (1967), which forbade experts from testifying as to productivity altogether.

Thus, a test intended to give psychiatrists a free rein was turned on its head. *Brawner* overruled *Durham*.

7. *Psychiatrists and lawyers: oil and water trying to mix?* Generally speaking, mental health professionals applauded *Durham.* Psychiatrists believed that they had won a significant battle in their "cold war" with lawyers regarding the proper role of psychiatry in the criminal justice system. One of the most influential combatants at the time was Dr. Karl Menninger, Chairman of the Board of Trustees of the Menninger Foundation in Topeka, Kansas. In a book on the subject, he described the deep divide between psychiatrists and lawyers:

Psychiatrists aspire to facts; they spend their lives trying to more accurately describe and understand misbehavior of all kinds. They believe in rules and laws related to their procedures with just as much conviction as the jurist believes in *his* laws. But these two sets of laws just do not jibe. * * *

Lawyers are concerned with placing or rebutting *blame* for specific acts of deviant, prohibited behavior; psychiatrists are interested in correcting total patterns of behavior. Instead of seeking for the *blame* or the exculpation of an accused, doctors seek the etiology, the explanation, the underlying motives, and contributing facts in the commission of certain undesirable acts. Lawyers and psychiatrists speak two different languages in regard to professional matters, and hence their common English tongue is of little help in meaningful communication with one another. * * *

For example, the word *justice,* which is so dear to lawyers, is one which the doctor *qua* scientist simply does not use or readily understand. No one thinks of justice as applying to the phenomena of physics. There is no "justice" in chemical reactions, in illness, or in behavior disorder.

Free will—to a lawyer—is not a philosophical theory or a religious concept or a scientific hypothesis. It is a "given," a *basic* assumption in legal theory and practice. To the psychiatrist, this position is preposterous; he seeks clear operational definitions of *free* and of *will.* On the other hand, the psychiatrist's assumption that motivation and mentation can go on *unconsciously* is preposterous to lawyers, constituting a veritable self-contradiction in terms.

Karl Menninger, The Crime of Punishment 91, 96–97 (1968). According to Menninger, "[t]he very word *justice* irritates scientists. No surgeon expects to be asked if an operation for cancer is just or not." Id. at 17.

If concepts like "justice" and "blame" bewilder or irritate scientists, many lawyers and courts are concerned lest the scientific view of crime become too embedded in the criminal law. Consider the following remarks by a federal district court judge:

Psychiatry and law approach the problem of human behavior from different philosophical perspectives. Psychiatry purports to be scientific and takes a deterministic position with regard to behavior. "Its view of human nature is expressed in terms of drives and dispositions which, like mechanical forces, operate in accordance with universal laws of causation." For psychiatry, what we do is determined by what we are, and there is little or no room for moral or ethical judgments. In a sense, all criminal behavior, whether it be the acts of the rapist, the forger, the embezzler, the sender of licentious literature through the mails or tax evasion by a reputable businessman, is evidence of mental disease. But the uncritical adoption of this point of view would completely do away with the concept of criminal responsibility.

United States v. Pollard, 171 F.Supp. 474 (E.D. Mich. 1959) (Levin, D.J.), reversed, 282 F.2d 450 (6th Cir.1960).

In view of these observations, imagine how a criminal justice system—and the criminal law you are studying—might look if the psychiatric community could reshape it. Would it be a worse or better one than the status quo?

8. *A different definition of insanity?* In view of the criticisms directed at the various insanity tests, which standard do you find most appealing? Or, should the defense be formulated in still another way? In *United States v. Brawner*, 471 F.2d 969 (D.C.Cir.1972), Judge Bazelon, concurring in part and dissenting in part, suggested an alternative standard:

> Our instruction to the jury should provide that a defendant is not responsible *if at the time of his unlawful conduct his mental or emotional processes or behavior controls were impaired to such an extent that he cannot justly be held responsible for his act.* This test would ask the psychiatrist a single question: what is the nature of the impairment of the defendant's mental and emotional processes and behavior controls? It would leave for the jury the question whether that impairment is sufficient to relieve the defendant of responsibility for the particular act charged.

> The purpose of this proposed instruction is to focus the jury's attention on the legal and moral aspects of criminal responsibility, and to make clear why the determination of responsibility is entrusted to the jury and not the expert witnesses.

Do you like this test?

9. *Much ado about nothing?* Does any of the debate regarding insanity tests really matter? One study of jury behavior in mock trials found that jurors poorly comprehended legal instructions regarding the insanity defense. More significantly, regardless of the legal standard used, jurors generally focused on the same factors, including the defendant's history of mental illness, ability to recall events from the offense, degree of remorse, and cognitive and volitional capacities. James R.P. Ogloff, *A Comparison of Insanity Defense Standards on Juror Decision Making,* 15 Law & Hum.Behav. 509 (1991); see also Norman J. Finkel, *Insanity Defenses: From the Jurors' Perspective*, 9 Law & Psych. Rev. 77 (1985) (finding that jurors reach the same results regardless of the insanity test).

In view of these findings, researcher Ogloff observed that "the 'justly responsible' test [see Note 8] is one formulation * * * that is surprisingly consistent with the conclusion that jurors apply their own sense of justice when determining whether to find a defendant [not guilty by reason of insanity]." Ogloff, supra, at 527. There is also evidence suggesting that juries reach the same verdict, regardless of whether they are instructed pursuant to one of the usual insanity tests or are told, simply, to use their own best judgment in deciding the case. Norman J. Finkel & Sharon F. Handel, *Jurors and Insanity: Do Test Instructions Instruct?*, 1 Forensic Rep. 65 (1988); Norman J. Finkel & Sharon F. Handel, *How Jurors Construe "Insanity"*, 13 Law & Hum.Behav. 41 (1989).

d. M'Naghten and the Model Penal Code in Greater Detail

i. Knowing/Appreciating the "Wrongfulness" of One's Actions

STATE v. WILSON

Supreme Court of Connecticut, 1997.
242 Conn. 605, 700 A.2d 633.

PALMER, ASSOCIATE JUSTICE.

This appeal requires us to define the term "wrongfulness" for purposes of the affirmative defense of insanity under General Statutes § 53a–13 (a).[2] * * *

The following facts are undisputed. The defendant and the victim, Jack Peters, were acquainted through the victim's son, Dirk Peters, with whom the defendant had attended high school. In early 1993, the defendant began to exhibit symptoms of a mental disorder manifested by a delusional belief that Dirk, assisted by the victim, systematically was destroying the defendant's life. Specifically, the defendant believed that, in 1981, Dirk had poisoned him with methamphetamine and had hypnotized him in order to obtain control of his thoughts. The defendant believed that Dirk had been acting with the approval of the victim, who, the defendant also believed, was the mastermind of a large organization bent on controlling the minds of others. The defendant further believed that Dirk and the victim were responsible for the defendant's loss of employment, sexual inadequacy, physical weakness and other incapacities, as well as the deaths of the defendant's mother and several family dogs. In addition, the defendant blamed the victim and Dirk for the breakup of the defendant's relationship with a former girlfriend.

Beginning in approximately February, 1993, the defendant began contacting law enforcement authorities to inform them of the conspiracy by the victim and Dirk to destroy his life and the lives of others. He informed the police that Dirk was continuing to drug and brainwash people, and that Dirk should be stopped. He blamed the victim and Dirk for his own drug involvement and claimed that they were ruining other people's lives as well.[7] In May and June, 1993, the defendant repeatedly called the police, requesting their assistance in combatting the mind control conspiracy by the victim and Dirk. The police informed him that it was impossible to investigate his allegations.

---

2. General Statutes § 53a–13 provides: "Lack of capacity due to mental disease or defect as affirmative defense. (a) In any prosecution for an offense, it shall be an affirmative defense that the defendant, at the time he committed the proscribed act or acts, lacked substantial capacity, as a result of mental disease or defect, either to appreciate the wrongfulness of his conduct or to control his conduct within the requirements of the law. * * * "

7. For example, the defendant sent audiotapes to the police, one of which was accompanied by a letter stating, "Hopefully, the decent people of the world can somehow be protected from [the] wrath of methamphetamine * * *. Maybe before dozens more people are similarly poisoned with this toxin at the hands of [Dirk] Peters * * *."

On August 5, 1993, the defendant went to see the victim at his home in the city of Greenwich. He quarreled with the victim and then shot him numerous times with a semiautomatic revolver that he had purchased two days earlier from a gun dealer in the city of New Haven.

Later that day, the defendant entered the Greenwich police headquarters and stated that he had shot the victim because he "had to do it." The defendant thereafter gave a sworn statement to the police in which he indicated, among other things, that: (1) his life had been ruined by Dirk, who had drugged, hypnotized and brainwashed him; (2) the victim had assisted Dirk in these activities; (3) Dirk and the victim were responsible for the defendant's schizophrenia; (4) the conduct of Dirk and the victim required "drastic action" and "drastic retribution"; and (5) the defendant had shot the victim repeatedly at the victim's home earlier that day.

At trial, the defendant raised his mental illness as an affirmative defense under § 53a–13. The jury, however, rejected the defendant's claim of insanity and convicted him of murder. The trial court rendered judgment sentencing the defendant to sixty years imprisonment. * * *

* * * In this case, the defendant requested that the trial court instruct the jury that wrongfulness is comprised of a moral element, so that "an accused is not criminally responsible for his offending act if, because of mental disease or defect, he believes that he is morally justified in his conduct—even though he may appreciate that his act is criminal." The trial court, however, refused to [so] instruct the jury * * *.[10] The defendant argues that the court's failure to charge the jury on this moral component of the insanity defense requires reversal. * * *

Our resolution of the defendant's claim requires us to answer [two] subordinate questions: (1) How should a trial court define the term "wrongfulness" as it is used in § 53a–13 (a) when a definitional instruction of that term is requested? [and] (2) Was such an instruction necessary in this case in view of the evidence presented at trial and the defendant's request to charge? * * *

I * * *

For purposes of this appeal, three features of the Model Penal Code test are noteworthy. First, like our prior common law standard, this test encompasses, albeit in a different form, both a cognitive and a volitional prong. * * *

---

10. The trial court instead instructed the jury in relevant part: "The first of the two alternative parts of this [insanity defense] is that the defendant lacked substantial capacity to appreciate the wrongfulness of his conduct. This means that he lacked substantial capacity to understand both intellectually and emotionally, that his actions were wrong. This does not include * * * a person whose faculties were impaired in some measure but were still sound enough for him to understand that his conduct was wrong. Not every mental deficiency or abnormality leaves a person without substantial capacity to appreciate the wrongfulness of his conduct. It is only when he lacks substantial capacity to appreciate that a particular act or course of conduct was wrong that this part of the affirmative defense excuses him from criminal liability."

Second, the Model Penal Code test focuses on the defendant's actual *appreciation of*, rather than merely his *knowledge of*, the wrongfulness of his conduct. The drafters of the Model Penal Code purposefully adopted the term "appreciate" in order to account for the defendant whose "detached or abstract awareness" of the wrongfulness of his conduct "does not penetrate to the affective level." As Herbert Wechsler, chief reporter for the Model Penal Code, stated in his model jury charge: "To appreciate the wrongfulness of conduct is, in short, to realize that it is wrong; to understand the idea as a matter of importance and reality; to grasp it in a way that makes it meaningful in the life of the individual, not as a bare abstraction put in words."

The third important feature of the Model Penal Code test, and the most relevant for purposes of this appeal, is its alternative phrasing of the cognitive prong. By bracketing the term "wrongfulness" and juxtaposing that term with "criminality," the drafters purposefully left it to the individual state legislatures to decide which of these two standards to adopt to describe the nature of the conduct that a defendant must be unable to appreciate in order to qualify as legally insane. The history of the Model Penal Code indicates that "wrongfulness" was offered as a choice so that any legislature, if it wishes, could introduce a "moral issue" into the test for insanity.

There is little dispute in this case that, by choosing the term "wrongfulness" instead of "criminality," the legislature intended to import this moral element into Connecticut's insanity statute. * * *

The more difficult question * * * is how properly to define the moral element inherent in the term "wrongfulness" under § 53a–13 (a). The defendant contends that morality must be defined in purely personal terms, such that a defendant is not responsible for his criminal acts as long as his mental disease or defect causes him *personally* to believe that those acts are morally justified, even though he may appreciate that his conduct is wrong in the sense that it is both illegal and contrary to societal standards of morality. The state, on the other hand, contends that morality must be defined by societal standards, such that a defendant is not responsible for his criminal acts *unless*, because of mental disease or defect, he lacks substantial capacity to appreciate that his actions were wrong under *society's* moral standards. Although we agree with the state that the proper test must incorporate principles of societal morality, we conclude that the state's interpretation of the cognitive prong of § 53a–13 (a) does not sufficiently account for a delusional defendant's own distorted perception of society's moral standards. Accordingly, we conclude that a defendant may establish that he lacked substantial capacity to appreciate the "wrongfulness" of his conduct if he can prove that, at the time of his criminal act, as a result of mental disease or defect, he substantially misperceived reality and harbored a delusional belief that society, *under the circumstances as the defendant honestly but mistakenly understood them*, would not have morally condemned his actions.

Before addressing the legislative and jurisprudential principles that undergird our interpretation of § 53a–13 (a), however, we first must consider the contrary view advanced by the defendant. We conclude that the defendant's efforts to define morality in purely personal terms are inconsistent with the Model Penal Code, judicial precedent, and the assumptions underlying our criminal law.

The text accompanying § 4.01 of the Model Penal Code, upon which § 53a–13 is modeled, suggests that its drafters intended that the moral element of "wrongfulness" be measured by a defendant's capacity to understand society's moral standards. In his model jury charge, for example, Professor Wechsler suggests the following language: "[A] person may have knowledge of the facts about his conduct and of the immediate surrounding circumstances and still be rendered quite incapable of grasping the idea that it is wrong, in the sense that it is condemned by the law and *commonly accepted moral standards.*" (Emphasis added.) * * * Although the rejection under the Model Penal Code of the personal standard is not beyond debate, we conclude that the drafters of § 4.01 did not intend that a defendant who appreciates *both* the illegality and the societal immorality of his actions be relieved of criminal responsibility due to his purely personal, albeit delusional, moral code.

Moreover, the large majority of other jurisdictions that have considered the cognitive prong of the insanity defense has chosen a societal, rather than a personal, standard. Although these courts generally have made this determination in the context of the *M'Naghten* test, to the extent that the use of the term "wrongfulness" in the Model Penal Code can be traced back to *M'Naghten*, the evolution of the *M'Naghten* test and the reasoning employed by courts interpreting that test inform an interpretation of our own insanity defense.

Finally, with respect to the fundamental policies that undergird our criminal law, defining the moral element of wrongfulness according to a purely personal standard tends to undermine the "moral culture on which our societal norms of behavior are based." There may well be cases in which a defendant's delusional ideation causes him to harbor personal beliefs that so cloud his cognition as to render him incapable of recognizing the broader moral implications of his actions. In such cases, the defendant would be entitled to be acquitted under the cognitive prong of the defense.

Those cases involving the so-called "deific command," in our view, fall into this category. Contrary to the defendant's position at oral argument, we are hard pressed to envision an individual who, because of mental disease or defect, truly believes that a divine power has authorized his actions, but, at the same time, also truly believes that such actions are immoral. An individual laboring under a delusion that causes him to believe in the divine approbation of his conduct is an individual who, in all practicality, is unlikely to be able fully to appreciate the wrongfulness of that conduct.

A defendant should not be relieved of criminal liability, however, if his mental illness does not deprive him of substantial capacity to appreciate the boundaries of societal morality and if he elects to transgress those boundaries in pursuit of a delusional personal belief system that he appreciates society would not itself accept. To permit otherwise "would seriously undermine the criminal law [by allowing] one who violated the law to be excused from criminal responsibility solely because, in his own conscience, his act was not morally wrong." * * *

* * * Although we agree with the state that the defendant's appreciation of morality must be defined in terms of his appreciation of society's moral standards, the state's test is insufficient in one important respect. Consider, for example, a defendant who, because of a mental delusion, misperceives reality and, on the basis of that misperception, engages in criminal conduct that he believes is necessary to advance a greater social good, but who, at the same time, also appreciates that society is unaware of the need to bring about this social good and, because of this ignorance, would not condone his actions.[20] Under the state's test, such an individual would probably not be considered legally insane because he retains substantial capacity to appreciate that, *objectively speaking*, society does not approve of his actions.

In our view, such an approach represents an overly restrictive interpretation of what the legislature intended by choosing the term "wrongfulness" instead of the term "criminality." * * * Under the state's test, * * * moral wrongfulness would be measured strictly in terms of society's objective disapproval; to the extent that this objective disapproval is embodied in the criminal code, the state's test renders morality and criminality virtually synonymous.[21] We are unwilling to negate the legislature's choice of the term "wrongfulness" by treating these otherwise distinct terms as virtually identical.

We conclude, rather, that a defendant does not truly "appreciate the wrongfulness of his conduct" as stated in § 53a–13 (a) if a mental disease or defect causes him both to harbor a distorted perception of reality and to believe that, *under the circumstances as he honestly perceives them*, his actions do not offend societal morality, even though he may also be aware that society, *on the basis of the criminal code*, does not condone his actions. Thus, a defendant would be entitled to prevail under § 53a–13 (a)

20. For example, a defendant might, because of a mental delusion, believe that his infant child suffers from a rare condition that will cause her to die unless she ingests certain medication that he can obtain only through theft. This hypothetical defendant might appreciate that society, objectively speaking, would disapprove of him stealing the medication but, nevertheless, may believe that, if society knew of his child's condition, it would no longer view his theft of the medication as immoral.

21. Although the drafters of the Model Penal Code recognized that few cases would arise in which the distinction between wrongfulness and criminality would be determinative, we do not infer from this recognition that the drafters intended these terms to have identical meanings. Rather, the drafters were simply observing that, in the typical case, the trier of fact may infer that a defendant who has the capacity to appreciate the illegality of his conduct also has the capacity to appreciate its immorality. That such an inference is possible, however, does not mean that it is compelled.

if, as a result of his mental disease or defect, he sincerely believes that society *would* approve of his conduct *if* it shared his understanding of the circumstances underlying his actions. This formulation appropriately balances the concepts of societal morality that underlie our criminal law with the concepts of moral justification that motivated the legislature's adoption of the term "wrongfulness" in our insanity statute. * * *

II * * *

The state contends that the defendant was not entitled to an instruction defining the term "wrongfulness" under § 53a–13 (a) because he failed to adduce sufficient evidence to support such an instruction. * * * Although the state does not seriously dispute that the defendant suffered from a mental disease that caused him to misperceive reality, the state claims that the evidence merely tended to show, in accordance with the purely personal standard we have rejected, that the defendant had followed his own subjective moral calculus in seeking revenge for the perceived actions of the victim and Dirk. * * *

At trial, the defense called several expert witnesses to testify regarding their examinations of the defendant and the conclusions drawn therefrom. Jay Berkowitz, a psychiatrist employed by the department of correction and working at the Bridgeport correctional center (center), testified that he had conducted a ninety minute interview and psychiatric evaluation of the defendant after the defendant's arrival at the center. Berkowitz testified that the defendant had expressed remorse for killing the victim but felt that it was something that he had to do in order to save other people. Sue Anne O'Brien, a psychiatric nurse who also worked at the center, testified that she had spoken with the defendant for approximately ninety minutes. O'Brien testified that the defendant believed that he had "saved all of us from this evil thing [that] was occurring," and she quoted the defendant as stating, " 'I saved you. I saved everyone here. I've saved the world.' "

Another expert witness, Leslie Kurt, a forensic psychiatrist, testified extensively with respect to her examination and diagnosis of the defendant, with whom she had met in a series of six interviews for a total of nearly twelve hours. Kurt stated that the defendant believed that the victim had used methamphetamine and hypnosis to gain control over people and had done nothing to prevent the intensely evil crimes of Dirk. According to Kurt, the defendant likened the victim to Sirhan Sirhan, Jim Jones and Charles Manson, and expressed a belief that he had a higher moral duty to stop the victim and Dirk. Kurt described the defendant's belief in a higher moral duty as something akin to a person believing, during World War II, that he or she had a moral obligation to assassinate Adolf Hitler even though that person understood that this killing would be illegal.

On the basis of this testimony, we conclude that the defendant presented sufficient evidence from which a jury reasonably could have found, by a preponderance of the evidence, that, due to a mental disease or defect, the defendant misperceived reality and, in acting on the basis of that misperception, did not substantially appreciate that his actions were contrary to societal morality. It is true, as the state maintains, that the defendant tried repeatedly, albeit unsuccessfully, to convince the police that the activities conducted by the victim and Dirk were dangerous and unlawful. Thus, it reasonably could be said that the defendant understood that society, unpersuaded of the danger posed by the victim, did not condone his actions. The test that we have adopted, however, requires a fact finder to look beyond the defendant's appreciation of society's objective disapproval of his actions and to inquire whether the defendant, as a result of mental disease or defect, truly believed that society, if it were aware of the circumstances as he honestly perceived them, would have condoned his actions.

* * * Accordingly, we conclude that the evidence presented at trial warranted an instruction defining the term "wrongfulness" in terms of societal morality consistent with our explication of that definition in part I of this opinion. * * *

The judgment is reversed and the case is remanded for a new trial. * * *

KATZ, ASSOCIATE JUSTICE, concurring. * * *

I concur in the result reached by the majority, and applaud what is obviously a carefully considered and thoughtfully drafted exegesis of the standard set forth in the American Law Institute's Model Penal Code as incorporated by General Statutes § 53a–13. I am concerned, nonetheless, that the test as interpreted by the majority may exclude certain defendants who are obviously impaired and for whom the interests of justice would not be served by a criminal conviction; specifically, those defendants who, *because of their mental illness*, adhere to a personal code of morality. * * *

I * * *

The majority has determined that under the Model Penal Code, a defendant who "appreciates" that society would not approve of his or her actions cannot invoke the insanity defense, even though that defendant is mentally ill and has acted under a delusional adherence to a personal moral code. I fail to understand the majority's reasoning, however, in light of statements by Herbert Wechsler, the chief reporter for the Model Penal Code, in which he clarifies what it means to "appreciate" the wrongfulness of one's actions. The majority cites to Wechsler's model jury instructions, which provide: "To appreciate the wrongfulness of conduct is, in short, to realize that it is wrong; to understand the idea as a matter of importance and reality; *to grasp it in a way that makes it meaningful to the life of the individual,* not as a bare abstraction put in words." Although recognizing that a defendant's personal moral code may be delusional, the majority underestimates the pivotal role of that defendant's mental illness. In other words, if the defendant's personal code is the *direct result* of the mental illness, then I am hard-pressed to understand how that defendant's knowledge of society's disapproval could be "a matter of importance and reality * * * meaningful in the life of the [defendant] * * *." I believe that such a defendant is unable to truly appreciate, as defined by Wechsler, the "wrongfulness" of his or her action. Nor am I alone in that belief—I need go no further than the aforementioned model jury instructions.

The majority cites to the model jury instructions in the Model Penal Code in support of its conclusion that "wrongfulness" incorporates societal standards. Reading one sentence further, however, I note that Wechsler provides the jury with an example of a defendant who cannot appreciate the wrongfulness of his actions: "If, for example, one has such a diseased conception of his own relationship to other people that he thinks himself to be an Oriental monarch, with absolute dominion over those about him, including the privilege to deal with or to terminate their lives as he sees fit, it hardly could be thought that such a person has substantial power to appreciate that conduct of that kind is contrary to both the law and moral standards that obtain in our community." This, I would argue, is *precisely* the person to whom the majority refers when it describes that individual who adheres to a "personal, albeit delusional, moral code." * * *

McDONALD, ASSOCIATE JUSTICE, dissenting. * * *

The majority now approves a jury instruction that provides a definition of wrong as something against societal morality, but not objectively speaking. * * * Under [the majority's] formula, a person who knows murder is wrong in the eyes of society and knows society does not share his perception that his victim needs to be killed may be excused if he believes, because of mental illness, that society would condone the killing if it, too, saw that need. This should not be written into our law. If the defendant recognizes his conduct is both criminal and wrong in the eyes of society, as murder clearly is, public safety demands that he be held responsible for his actions. I do not agree that it should be a defense that the defendant believes society did not approve of his conduct only because society failed to appreciate a needed "greater social good" which would come from those same actions.

It is hoped that we can still rely on the common sense of jurors, coping with these enigmatic instructions, to safeguard us. * * *

NOTES AND QUESTIONS

1. *Aftermath.* In October, 1999, before Andrew Wilson was scheduled to be retried for the 1993 homicide, he entered a plea of guilty and was sentenced to thirty years in prison. But, as they say, there is more to the story.

In 2009, convicted murderer Michael Skakel—despite asserting his innocence, he was convicted in 2002 for beating to death Martha Moxley with a golf club in 1975, when Skakel was fifteen years old—filed a motion in federal court claiming that state prosecutors concealed exculpatory evidence. What was the evidence? It was that, in 1993, Andrew Wilson's sister reported to police her fear that her brother was seriously mentally ill, dangerous, and that he claimed to know the identity of Moxley's murderer. And—here's the zinger—two months later Wilson was charged with shooting to death Jack Peters, *the father of the man Wilson told his sister was Moxley's killer.* Skakel's lawyer argued that either Wilson was telling the truth or that Wilson himself killed Martha Moxley. *Skakel Lawyers Cite Secret Evidence,* Connecticut Post, Jan. 9, 2009. (Later, Skakel's defense attorneys turned in another direction and sought a new trial based on a videotaped statement by Gitano Bryant, cousin of basketball star Kobe Bryant, that two of his friends had bragged about killing Moxley "caveman style." But, the Connecticut Supreme Court found no credibility in Bryant's account and, therefore, denied Skakel's motion for a new trial. Skakel v. Connecticut, 295 Conn. 447, 991 A.2d 414 (2010).)

2. *"Legal" versus "moral" wrong.* American Courts are sharply divided on whether the right-or-wrong prong of *M'Naghten* pertains to "moral wrong" or "legal wrong," just as jurisdictions that have adopted the Model Penal Code test are split on the "criminality"/"wrongfulness" option that the Code drafters provided to the legislatures. No jurisdiction currently applies the "personal morality" concept of wrongfulness that Justice Katz would have adopted.

Consider now two individuals. Mr. Moral knows what he is doing is illegal, but he believes (due to mental illness) that society would morally condone his actions. Ms. Legal believes that society would morally condemn her actions, but believes (due to mental illness) that her conduct is legal. In a "moral wrong" jurisdiction, Mr. Moral will be found insane, but Ms. Legal will be held responsible for her actions. In a "legal wrong" jurisdiction, the results will be reversed. Which set of outcomes do you find more sensible? Do you believe that Moral is more (or less) culpable than Legal? Is one of them more susceptible to deterrence?

[margin handwritten note: moral slightly more deterrable?]

3. *Deific decrees.* Consider these horrible facts:

- A Tyler, Texas woman, Deanna Laney, killed her two sons, six-year-old Luke and eight-year-old Joshua, in her front yard by bashing their heads in with rocks. According to five mental health experts, Laney suffered from psychotic delusions that God ordered her to kill her sons as a test of faith and then serve as a witness after the world ended. Lee Hancock, *Laney Said Dead Sons Would Return Alive,* Dallas News, April 2, 2004, at 3A. She was later declared insane.

- In another Texas case, a mother cut off her ten-month-old daughter's arms with a kitchen knife because God told her to do so. She, too, was found not guilty by reason of insanity. Wendy Hundley, *Dena Schlosser, Plano Mom Who Cut Off Baby's Arms, Moving to Outpatient Care,* Dallas Morning News, Nov. 8, 2008.

- An Oakland, California mother undressed her three sons and threw them into the San Francisco Bay. God told her to do so, she explained. "[S]he believed she was sending her children to heaven, a happy place

[margin handwritten note: Not likely to be deterred]

with cars and houses where they could receive mail." She was found not guilty by reason of insanity by a trial judge. Cecily Burt, *Mom Who Drowned Sons Ruled Insane*, San Jose Mercury News, Jan. 18, 2007, at B6.

These are examples of "deific decree" cases—cases in which a mentally disordered person believes that God has instructed or commanded her (or him) to do what she (or he) is now on trial for committing. Here is some background on the "deific decree" principle as explained in Lundgren v. Mitchell, 440 F.3d 754 (6th Cir. 2006):

> For over two hundred years, trial counsel have presented the insanity defense in "deific decree" cases in many states * * * and in England. *See State v. Lafferty*, 2001 UT 19, 20 P.3d 342, 363 (Utah 2001) (Mormon fundamentalist, who killed his sister-in-law and her infant child pursuant to God's "removal revelation," presented insanity defense to jury); *People v. Coddington*, 23 Cal.4th 529, 97 Cal.Rptr.2d 528, 2 P.3d 1081, 1103, 1110–14 (Cal. 2000) (defendant presented insanity defense to jury after strangling chaperones of two girls he sexually abused professedly because God commanded the actions); *State v. Blair*, 143 N.H. 669, 732 A.2d 448, 449–50 (N.H. 1999) (counsel presented insanity defense to jury in case in which husband bludgeoned his wife and son with a hammer after experiencing a "trance" in which God revealed that he would be cast into the lake of fire if he refused to do so); *People v. Serravo*, 823 P.2d 128, 130 (Colo. 1992) (en banc) (jury found defendant not guilty by reason of insanity for stabbing his wife "in order to sever the marriage bond" in accordance with God's purported instructions); *State v. Ryan*, 233 Neb. 74, 444 N.W.2d 610, 632 (Neb. 1989) (cult leader entered plea of not guilty by reason of insanity after following Yahweh's "command" to torture and kill an "unfaithful" cult member); *Laney v. State*, 486 So.2d 1242, 1245–46 (Miss. 1986) (defendant shot police officers because God purportedly commanded the act and presented insanity defense to jury); [many other cited cases are omitted]. * * *

> As early as 1800, the defense of not guilty by reason of insanity was successful in a deific decree case in England. *See generally Hadfield's Case*, 27 How. St. Tr. 1281 (K.B. 1800). James Hadfield, a former British soldier, fired a horse pistol at King George III in Drury Lane Theatre but missed the King's head by less than a foot-and-a-half. Hadfield believed that God had told him to sacrifice himself to save the world and chose assassinating the King as the surest way of assuring his own death. Renowned barrister Thomas Erskine defended Hadfield and entered an insanity plea, and the jury returned a verdict of not guilty by reason of insanity. * * *

In 1882, Charles Guiteau was tried for assassinating President James Garfield and relied upon the insanity defense, claiming that God told him to kill the President. The judge instructed the jury with citation to the above example of insanity * * *. *United States v. Guiteau*, 10 F. 161, 172 (D.D.C. 1882). In applying the *M'Naghten* rule, the judge specifically informed the jury that "if [Guiteau] was under an insane delusion that the Almighty had commanded him to do the act, and in consequence of

[handwritten margin note: Hadfield told to sacrifice himself— suicide by cop?]

that he was incapable of seeing that it was a wrong thing to do,—then he was not in a responsible condition of mind, and was an object of compassion, and not of justice, and ought to be now acquitted."

> Thirty years later, Justice Benjamin Cardozo * * * provided another [example]:
>
> A mother kills her infant child to whom she has been devotedly attached. She knows the nature and quality of the act; she knows that the law condemns it; but she is inspired by an insane delusion that God has appeared to her and ordained the sacrifice. It seems a mockery to say that, within the meaning of the statute, she knows that the act is wrong.

People v. Schmidt, 216 N.Y. 324, 110 N.E. 945, 949 (N.Y. 1915). According to Justice Cardozo, holding such a defendant criminally responsible would be "abhorrent," and a jury would likely disregard a jury instruction directing otherwise.

Look at Hadfield's delusion set out above. Now look at how the "deific decree" principle as explained in *Guiteau*. As the latter court explains the doctrine, was Hadfield acting as a result of a deific decree?

Reconsider the three mothers who killed their children. Accepting as true that they believed they had heard the voice of God tell them what to do, should they be relieved of legal responsibility for their actions?

If a court accepts a "deific decree" insanity defense, do you agree with two judges who asserted that it should make "no difference whether the mentally ill defendant claims he was commanded to kill by God, the President, the Pope, or a rock star." *State v. Winder*, 200 N.J. 231, 979 A.2d 312 (2009) (concurring opinion).

ii. Convincing the Jury: The Role of Experts

PEREZ v. CAIN

United States Court of Appeals, Fifth Circuit, 2008.
529 F.3d 588.

REAVLEY, CIRCUIT JUDGE:

[Salvador] Perez was convicted of first-degree murder of a police officer and sentenced to life in prison for shooting New Orleans Police Officer Chris McCormick. Perez asserted at trial that he was not guilty by reason of insanity. * * *

I. FACTUAL AND PROCEDURAL BACKGROUND

* * * Perez is currently a 61–year old Mexican citizen who formerly resided legally with his wife, Rosa, and five children on a small farm in Seguin, Texas. On the morning of July 15, 1996, Perez told his wife that he was going out to feed the cows. Instead, he left home with his 12–year old son, Salvatore Perez, Jr., and began a drive that ended with the tragic death of a police officer in New Orleans. Believing that he was being

pursued by people who wanted to kill him, Perez proceeded from Seguin toward Florida, where he had once lived. He constantly checked his mirrors for his pursuers and increased his speed to lose the other vehicles that he believed were chasing him.

Salvatore Perez, Jr. testified that his father drove on back roads and that he was preoccupied with other vehicles. When they stopped at a convenience store at one point, Perez suddenly became scared and began sounding the horn for his son to return to the vehicle so they could quickly leave. Salvatore Jr. described his father's hands as shaking and also reported that Perez would frequently push buttons on the roof of the vehicle, believing this action would throw off the pursuers. Perez also called his wife Rosa and reported that someone was trying to kill him and that a black car was following him. He also believed that Rosa was being held hostage.

Salvatore Jr. later told police that he and his father slept in a park on the first night. At about 4:00 a.m. or 5:00 a.m., Perez awoke and saw a brown Chevrolet truck in the park that he thought was looking for him. Perez next believed that a reddish car at a gas station was following him. Upon reaching New Orleans, Perez and his son ended up at the Fair Grounds. Salvatore Jr. told police that Perez saw the same black car at the Fair Grounds that had been following them from Texas, and Perez thought that gangsters who were chasing him were resting in the race-track barns.

On the morning of July 17, 1996, a Fair Grounds security guard encountered Perez and his son while investigating a report of a suspicious man near the barns. Perez held a small black handgun at his side. He pulled his son close to him and told the guard to leave him alone and not to take his kid. The guard retreated to call the police, but when police arrived Perez was not found. Later that evening, the Fair Grounds security discovered Salvatore Jr. alone and took him into custody. A police officer testified that Salvatore Jr. said he and his father had come to New Orleans in a van, that they were being pursued by gangs from Texas, and that his mother knew about Perez's behavior. The officer testified that Salvatore Jr. also said that his father had ripped off drug dealers. The officer located Perez's vehicle parked behind the Fair Grounds and had it impounded, but no drugs were ever found.

At approximately 10:30 p.m., a woman living adjacent to the Fair Grounds observed a man, possibly holding a gun, in her backyard shed where the hot water heater was located. Police were called, and Officer McCormick and his partner Officer Artie Jackson responded. Officer McCormick proceeded quickly down the back stairs of the apartment. Upon reaching the bottom step, a single shot rang out, striking McCormick in the chest. Officer Jackson immediately called for assistance and numerous officers responded. A canine unit discovered Perez hiding under the house next door. During the apprehension, Perez shot the police dog and was himself shot twice by police.

The state trial court appointed doctors to examine Perez and conducted several lunacy hearings to determine Perez's competency. Dr. Raphael Salcedo and Dr. Sarah Deland initially deemed Perez competent to stand trial, but in August 1997 Perez was determined to be a danger to himself or others and was transferred to the Feliciana Forensic Facility (FFF). Dr. David Carrington was Perez's treating psychiatrist at FFF. Dr. Carrington testified that Perez was not competent at the time of his admission to FFF. In Dr. Carrington's opinion, Perez had a disorganized thought process and a difficulty communicating that was not uncommon with someone who has a significant degree of mental illness. Dr. Carrington testified that Perez had auditory hallucinations of music and the sound of machinery. He also had delusions, such as the belief that he could communicate with his wife telepathically. Dr. Carrington testified on cross-examination that it was possible Perez's confinement prior to his transfer to FFF could have contributed to his condition at the time of the initial examination. Dr. Carrington gave Perez the anti-psychotic medication Haldol and examined him on a weekly basis for the first two months of his stay at FFF. Perez's condition improved somewhat after three weeks of taking Haldol, but he still had disorganized thought processes. Dr. Carrington increased the medication dosage, and Perez was eventually restored to competency. He was transferred back to Orleans Parish for trial in December 1997.

Perez conceded that he shot Officer McCormick but defended on the ground of insanity. Perez's defense included lay testimony from his wife and his son, Salvatore Jr. It also consisted of expert testimony from seven psychiatric experts about his delusions, including Dr. Salcedo and Dr. Deland. All seven experts agreed that Perez suffered from severe mental illness and delusions of paranoia and persecution. All seven experts also agreed that Perez was not malingering or feigning his mental condition. Six of the experts testified that Perez's mental illness prevented him from knowing right from wrong on the night of the shooting. The seventh expert, Dr. Carrington, was not asked about Perez's sanity at the time of the offense. Five of the experts were either court appointed or otherwise employed by the state.

Rosa Perez testified that approximately two weeks before her husband left home, he became very quiet and edgy in his behavior. She testified that Perez would often look out the window and whisper as if someone were watching or listening to him. She also implied that the night before he left, Perez had been afraid to go outside. On cross-examination, the state confronted Rosa with a statement she had given to Detective Joseph Catalanotto after the shooting. When the police had asked her whether Perez had any history of psychological problems, Rosa had responded, "No. Not that I know of." The statement also showed, however, that Rosa said Perez had been acting strangely for several days. The state also asked Rosa about a report from psychologist Dr. Carlos Kronberger, wherein Rosa reported that she did not remember Perez acting strangely the day he had left home.

Salvatore Jr. also testified that in the weeks before his father drove to New Orleans, Perez had grown quieter and more suspicious. He further described, as noted above, Perez's odd behavior in trying to evade pursuers. On redirect-examination, he admitted telling Detective Catalanotto that he thought a friend of his step-grandfather's had asked Perez to become involved in drug activities but Perez had declined. He also admitted stating that his father thought he had done something to make the drug buyers angry, but that he had also insisted his father was not involved with drugs.

The state did not call any expert witnesses or present any expert medical opinions concerning Perez's mental state. It also did not offer any lay testimony on the issue. Instead, it relied on its cross-examination of Perez's witnesses, and it called Detective Catalanotto as a rebuttal witness to testify about the statements from Rosa and Salvatore Jr. The state's theory throughout the trial was that Perez and his family fooled the medical experts by making up the story that Perez feared someone was trying to kill him.

The jury found Perez guilty and recommended life imprisonment. The trial court sentenced Perez to life imprisonment at hard labor, without the benefit of parole, probation, or suspension of sentence. [Perez appealed his conviction, in part on the ground that there was insufficient evidence introduced at trial to convict him. The Louisiana courts rejected his claim. He then filed a petition for writ of habeas corpus in the federal district court, claiming that his continued incarceration violated his contitutional right to liberty.] * * *

III.   DISCUSSION

The state challenges the district court's conclusion that the evidence was insufficient for the jury to find that Perez failed to show he was insane. In a federal habeas corpus proceeding, the Supreme Court's decision in *Jackson v. Virginia* [, 443 U.S. 307, 99 S.Ct. 2781, 61 L.Ed.2d 560 (1979),] provides the standard for testing the sufficiency of the evidence. The question is whether, after viewing the evidence in the light most favorable to the prosecution, *any* rational trier of fact could have found the essential elements of the crime beyond a reasonable doubt. * * *

In Louisiana, a criminal defendant is presumed to be sane and responsible for his actions. The defendant may rebut this presumption based on a preponderance of the evidence. Legal insanity is proved if the circumstances indicate that a mental disease or mental defect rendered the offender incapable of distinguishing between right and wrong with reference to the conduct in question. In light of Louisiana law on the issue of insanity, the question under the *Jackson* sufficiency standard is whether, viewing the evidence in the light most favorable to the state, any rational trier of fact could have found beyond a reasonable doubt that Perez did not prove by a preponderance of the evidence that he was insane at the time of the offense. * * *

The state was not required to present expert evidence to contradict Perez and establish that he was sane. Lay testimony alone may be used to successfully rebut an expert's opinion. We have recognized with respect to insanity, however, that the opinions of experts may not be arbitrarily ignored and that some reason must be objectively present for ignoring expert opinion testimony. Expert evidence may be rebutted by showing the incorrectness or inadequacy of the factual assumptions on which the opinion is based, the reasoning by which he progresses from his material to his conclusion, the interest or bias of the expert, inconsistencies or contradictions in his testimony as to material matters, material variations between the experts themselves, and defendant's lack of co-operation with the expert.

Even though the state did not present any direct evidence of Perez's mental condition, the state appellate court concluded that the evidence was sufficient for the jury to find Perez did not show he was insane for essentially three reasons: first, that there was a substantial delay, ranging from nine to seventeen months, between the shooting and the experts' examinations of Perez; second, that the experts based their opinions on information provided by Rosa Perez and Salvatore Perez, Jr., whose information about Perez's history was inconsistent with pretrial statements and therefore unreliable; and third, that all of Perez's behavior was consistent with and could be explained by his fear of rebuffed drug dealers. * * *

At the outset, we note that all of the experts who testified at trial that Perez was insane at the time of the offense were consistent in their opinions that Perez suffered from a severe mental illness. All of the experts were well-qualified, as the state stipulated at trial. Most of the experts were also disinterested due to their capacities as court appointees or employees of the state. * * *

With respect to the delay in the experts' examinations of Perez, the state appellate court found that the experts' opinions about Perez's status at the time of the offense were undermined for essentially two reasons. First, the court noted that a Charity Hospital record from the night of the shooting reported that when Perez was brought to the hospital he was oriented, responsive, and obeying commands. Second, Dr. Carrington admitted that Perez's condition at the time he first examined him at the FFF in August 1997 could have been attributed in some part to his thirteen months of incarceration in Orleans Parish prison. The state court apparently reasoned that a rational jury could have found that these facts together gave a more accurate picture of Perez's mental state at the time of the offense than the experts' subsequent examinations. We disagree.

The Charity Hospital notation cannot be considered in a vacuum. Dr. Carrington, the only expert who was asked about the record, explained that "oriented" meant that Perez knew who he was, where he was, and generally what time it was. He testified that "responsive" meant that Perez was "essentially * * * not unconscious." * * *

Dr. Carrington did testify that it was possible Perez's pretrial incarceration could have contributed to the condition in which he found Perez in August 1997. However, Dr. Carrington was not asked whether the incarceration was the sole cause of Perez's condition or even the degree to which Perez may have been affected, and he was not asked whether Perez was sane at the time of the offense. The jury was given nothing from which it could draw an inference about Perez's mental state on the night of the offense from Perez's pretrial incarceration possibly contributing to his state in August 1997. There was simply no rational basis for a jury to infer that Perez was sane at the time of the shooting and became insane due only to his living conditions after apprehension. * * *

We further agree with the district court's conclusion that impugning the veracity of Perez's wife and son was insufficient to permit the jury to ignore the experts' opinion and conclude that Perez was sane. Although the doctors did receive important information from Rosa Perez and Salvatore Jr., they did not rely solely on that information when formulating their opinions. They also considered information from personal examinations of Perez, test results, arrest reports, and witness testimony. * * *

We disagree that the record shows Perez may have been justified in his fears [of drug dealers]. As the district court held, there was no evidence that there actually were drug dealers in pursuit of Perez. Salvatore Jr. testified that he told police they were being followed by gangs from Texas because his father told him that. He did admit telling police his father thought his step-grandfather's friends sold drugs, but he also told police that his father was not involved with narcotics. Detective Catalanotto confirmed this statement. The record simply provides no basis for a rational jury to conclude that Perez was being chased by drug dealers from Texas, and Perez's behavior may not be so neatly explained away.

Furthermore, we agree with the district court that the medical experts personally observed psychotic behavior in Perez independently of whether anyone was pursuing him. For example, Dr. Carrington found that Perez had disorganized thought processes, characterized by difficulty communicating in a coherent manner, and had experienced hallucinations of music and the sound of machinery. Dr. Ritter testified that Perez's action when confronted by the Fair Grounds security guard, who could hardly be mistaken for a drug dealer while clad in uniform, was consistent with the delusions of persecution. Dr. Deland described Perez as presenting a very classic case of someone with a delusional belief of being persecuted and threatened. She specifically observed Perez's demeanor during her assessment and noted that people cannot generally manufacture such symptoms while under 24–hour observation, as Perez was at FFF.

* * * It is objectively unreasonable to conclude that a rational family man with no violent criminal history would suddenly flee with one son, leave his remaining family behind, drive to an unfamiliar city in an

unfamiliar state, hide in someone's backyard shed, and then shoot a police officer. * * *

The evidence that Perez produced as to his insanity was overwhelming. * * * The state produced insufficient evidence solely through cross-examination and argument to controvert Perez's claim. We therefore conclude that Perez established by a preponderance of the evidence that he was insane and that the state appellate court's conclusion that a rational jury could have found otherwise was an objectively unreasonable application of federal law.

NOTES AND QUESTIONS

1. *A matter of time.* On what date did the murder occur? In what year was Perez's conviction overturned?

2. In view of the fact the prosecutor had no experts willing to testify that Perez was sane, why do you think he went ahead anyway to prosecute Perez for murder and fight the insanity claim? For that matter, why do you think the jury rejected the insanity defense—after all, this court says that "no rational jury could have found otherwise" than that Perez was insane? Or, were the federal courts here wrong in overturning the jury's verdict?

3. The court here observed that "[m]ost of the experts were * * * disinterested due to their capacities as court appointees or employees of the state." Why does the fact they were appointed by the court or are employees of the state make them "disinterested"?

One difficulty often confronting juries in criminal trials, especially when insanity is pled, is that the prosecutor and the defense hire experts who testify in "polar opposite" manner. For example, in one case in which the competency of a defendant to stand trial was at issue, an expert testifying for the defendant—one who has been testifying for defendants for twenty years—told the court that the accused had an I.Q. of 58 and could not understand the proceedings. Meanwhile, a prosecution expert, who has testified for the state more than two hundred times, testified the defendant has an I.Q. of 88, well above the retardation level. Adam Liptak, *Experts Hired to Shed Light Can Leave U.S. Courts in Dark*, New York Times, Aug. 12, 2008, at A1. Would it be better if, as is the case in many parts of the world, expert witnesses are selected by the judge and paid from court funds rather than by one of the parties to the trial?

4. The proper role of mental health experts in criminal trials is a major source of controversy. State v. Johnson, 121 R.I. 254, 399 A.2d 469 (1979), articulated their role this way:

> Without question the essential dilemma in formulating any standard of criminal responsibility is encouraging a maximum informational input from the expert witnesses while preserving to the jury its role as trier of fact and ultimate decision maker. As one court has aptly observed:
>
> > "Ideally, psychiatrists—much like experts in other fields—should provide grist for the legal mill, should furnish the raw data upon which the legal judgment is based. It is the psychiatrist who informs

as to the mental state of the accused—his characteristics, his potentialities, his capabilities. But once this information is disclosed, it is
society as a whole, represented by judge or jury, which decides
whether a [person] with the characteristics described should or
should not be held accountable for his acts."

Do psychiatrists play too great or too little a role in criminal trials? Do
you agree with the observation that

[m]ental health experts are neither moral experts nor social value experts
* * *.

The best measuring instrument for determining if a person is crazy is
to find out as much as possible about the actor from those persons who
have had an opportunity to observe him directly in a wide variety of
circumstances. When much is learned about how the actor has behaved at
many different times and in particular circumstances, or at a particular
time and in particular circumstances, then all members of society will be
competent to judge if the person is crazy in general or if he was crazy at
the particular time in question. The current deference the law accords
mental health experts is misplaced. For legal purposes, the question of
who is crazy must be recognized as a social and moral judgment that
must be decided as such.

Stephen J. Morse, *Crazy Behavior, Morals, and Science: An Analysis of Mental
Health Law*, 51 So. Cal. L. Rev. 527, 560 (1978); but see Stephen J. Morse,
Excusing the Crazy: The Insanity Defense Reconsidered, 58 So. Cal. L. Rev.
777, 823 (1985) (offering the slightly revised view that experts should be
permitted to offer at trial "full, rich, clinical descriptions of [the defendant's]
thoughts, feelings and actions and relevant data based on sound scientific
studies," but still concluding that "[t]o remedy the 'circus atmosphere' of
insanity trials, experts should be prohibited from offering diagnoses, unvali-
dated explanations, and ultimate legal conclusions.").

A THOUGHT EXPERIMENT

You are a juror in a criminal trial. The defendant pleads not guilty by
reason of insanity. The judge informs you that this defense is not defined.
She explains that you have a free rein to decide whether the defendant
should be found guilty or not guilty by reason of insanity. (She does
inform you, however, that the burden of proof is on the defendant, by
preponderance of the evidence, to prove insanity.) The judge informs you
that when you provide your verdict, you must explain your reasons for it.

Here are the facts, as they were presented to you at trial. [State v.
Armstrong, 671 So.2d 307 (La.1996).]

On January 24, 1992, defendant [Armstrong] went to Loche's
Mortuary to obtain a copy of his father's death certificate, but left
while Mrs. Loche searched for the copy. About forty-five minutes
later, defendant returned to the mortuary's business office with a
briefcase. When Mrs. Loche, who was in the office with Rev. Fred
Neal, asked defendant if he still wanted the certificate, defendant
answered "no." Without saying anything to Rev. Neal, defendant

opened the briefcase and revealed a large butcher knife. Mrs. Loche ran for help, leaving Rev. Neal alone in the office with defendant.

Shortly thereafter, Officer Billy Womack arrived at the mortuary and found Rev. Neal on the floor of the office, while defendant stood over him with a bloody knife. Officer Womack asked defendant what was wrong, but defendant just stared at him. As Officer Womack checked Rev. Neal for vital signs, Mr. Loche yelled that defendant was "the one having the seizure." Officer Womack then drew his weapon and ordered defendant to drop the knife. Ignoring the officer, defendant walked up the nearby stairway as additional officers arrived. After pausing for a while, defendant turned and descended the stairs, while the officers tried to communicate with him. With Womack and other officers watching, defendant severed Rev. Neal's head from his body. Grinning, defendant picked up the head by the ears and held it up for the officers to see. According to Officer Womack's description, defendant "appeared to be a person possessed." He then put the head down, picked up Rev. Neal's headless body and placed it in a chair, picked up the head, and walked upstairs and dropped it in the toilet. Returning downstairs, defendant put the knife in the briefcase, put on his cap and walked toward the entrance door as if nothing had happened. The officers thereupon arrested him for murder. Officer Womack stated that he continually attempted to communicate with defendant, who did not respond, and that the officers never felt threatened by him.

Alright, that is the testimony. Do you feel you need expert testimony before deciding whether Armstrong should be held legally responsible for his actions? (Remember, you have a free rein on the insanity issue.) If so, what information would you want? How would that information assist you in reaching a verdict? If no further evidence is presented, what would your "insanity" verdict be, and why?

e. Should the Defense Be Abolished?

AMERICAN LAW INSTITUTE, MODEL PENAL CODE AND COMMENTARIES COMMENT TO § 4.01

(1985), 182–83

A variety of reasons for abolition have been advanced from quite different ideological perspectives. Though it oversimplifies matters somewhat, it clarifies understanding to distinguish two basic positions in favor of abolition. The first position is perhaps epitomized by President Nixon's support of abolition, which he said was * * * to curb "unconscionable abuse" of the insanity defense which had taken place under prior standards. This position does not challenge the traditional assumption that an important function of the system of criminal justice is to label serious wrongdoers as blameworthy; it asserts that the insanity defense is a device by which too many wrongdoers are escaping punishment. * * *

The other attack on the insanity defense is more complex and it goes to the roots of the criminal law. It shares with the first position a skepticism that distinctions can sensibly be made between those who are responsible and those who are not. Critics taking this view cite the rarity of the employment of the defense as evidence that most mentally ill defendants are being convicted despite the availability of the defense. They doubt that the stigma of those convicted and subsequently treated as mentally disturbed is any worse than the stigma of those who commit criminal acts and are committed to high security institutions for the mentally ill without undergoing trial or after being acquitted on grounds of insanity. They argue that there is little basis for withholding condemnation of those whose mental illness causes them to act criminally when those whose deprived economic and social background causes them to act criminally are condemned. They regard the adversarial debate over the responsibility of particular defendants as wasteful, confusing for the jury, and possibly harmful for those defendants who are mentally disturbed. They think psychiatric diagnosis should be employed primarily after conviction to determine what sort of correctional treatment is appropriate instead of prior to conviction to determine criminal responsibility. Ideally, in the view of some of these critics, criminal convictions generally should not be regarded as stigmatizing, but as determinants of dangerousness to which the community must respond.

NOTES AND QUESTIONS

1. Circuit Court Judge Alvin Rubin in United States v. Lyons, 739 F.2d 994 (5th Cir.1984), articulated the "unconscionable abuse" argument this way:

> Public opposition to any insanity-grounded defense is often based, either explicitly or implicitly, on the view that the plea is frequently invoked by violent criminals who fraudulently use it to evade just punishment. Some critics perceive the insanity defense as an opportunity for criminals to use psychiatric testimony to mislead juries. This perception depicts an insanity trial as a "circus" of conflicting expert testimony that confuses a naive and sympathetic jury. And it fears insanity acquittees as offenders who, after manipulating the criminal justice system, are soon set free to prey once again on the community.

However, Judge Rubin rejected the argument:

> Despite the prodigious volume of writing devoted to the plea, the empirical data that are available provide little or no support for these fearsome perceptions and in many respects directly refute them. Both the frequency and the success rate of insanity pleas are grossly overestimated by professionals and lay persons alike; the plea is rarely made, and even more rarely successful.[8] * * *

---

8. For example, one extensive study examined the opinions held by college students, the general public, state legislators, law enforcement officers, and mental health personnel in Wyoming. Estimates of the frequency with which criminal defendants entered the plea ranged from 13% to 57%. During the time period considered, however, the actual frequency was only

The perception that the defendant who successfully pleads insanity is quickly released from custody is also based only on assumption. Although an acquittal by reason of insanity ends the criminal jurisdiction of * * * the courts of a few states, the acquittee is not simply set free. "The truth is that in almost every case, the acquittee is immediately hospitalized and evaluated for dangerousness. Usually, the acquittee remains hospitalized for an extended time."

In sum, the available evidence belies many of the assumptions upon which much popular criticism of the insanity defense are based. The plea is rarely invoked, usually fails, and, when it is successful, the acquittees rarely go free.

The statistics Judge Rubin provided in the footnote are old and hardly comprehensive. In fact, regarding the frequency-of-use and success-rate figures for the insanity defense, "[w]hat is as startling as any other fact unearthed by empiricists is the realization that * * * officials in twenty states could provide no information whatsoever about the use of the plea." Michael L. Perlin, *Unpacking the Myths: The Symbolism Mythology of Insanity Defense Jurisprudence,* 40 Case W.Res.L.Rev. 599, 649 (1990). In one four-state study over a ten-year period, however, the insanity defense was raised in only 5,302 of 586,063 felony prosecutions, a rate of 0.9 percent. The defense was successful in 1,204 of these cases—22.7 percent of the insanity pleas, or 0.2 percent of all felony indictments. Henry J. Steadman, et al., Before and After Hinckley: Evaluating Insanity Defense Reform 150 (1993).

2. In the debate regarding the insanity defense, an influential critic of the insanity defense was the late Norval Morris, "a man of the liberal center, a former law school dean, a world-renowned scholar, and an influential pragmatic reformer." Phillip E. Johnson, *Book Review,* 50 U.Chi.L.Rev. 1534, 1536 (1983). Morris once wrote that "the defense of insanity is a tribute * * * to our hypocrisy rather than to our morality." Norval Morris, Madness and the Criminal Law 64 (1982). According to Morris, at id., the defense produces

> a morally unsatisfactory classification on the continuum between guilt and innocence. It applies in practice to only a few mentally ill criminals, thus omitting many others with guilt-reducing relationships between their mental illness and their crime; it excludes other powerful pressures on human behavior, thus giving excessive weight to the psychological over the social.

0.47%: one case in 200. Similarly, although estimates of its success rate varied from 19% to 44%, during the relevant period only one of the 102 defendants who entered the plea was acquitted by reason of insanity. One compendious British study, encompassing selected periods from 1740 to 1930, found the frequency of the plea to range between .29% to 1.30% with a success rate varying between 28.5% and 69.6%. 1 N. Walker, *Crime and Insanity in England* 67 (1968); 2 N. Walker and S. McCabe, Crime and Insanity in England (1973).

A somewhat dated survey of major metropolitan areas in the United States reported similar conclusions, finding that insanity pleas were rarely entered. The highest figures were obtained in California and the District of Columbia, where the data showed the plea was invoked in 1.3% and 5.1% of all felony dispositions respectively. A. Matthews, *Mental Disability and the Law* 26–30 (1970).

One source estimates fewer than 100 successful insanity pleas out of 50,000 federal criminal cases brought annually. Dershowitz, *Abolishing the Insanity Defense: The Most Significant Feature of the Administration's Proposed Criminal Code—An Essay,* 9 Crim.L.Bull. 434, 436 (1973).

According to Professor Morris, social disadvantage is more criminogenic than mental illness, yet the former condition—properly, he believes—is not an excuse for criminal conduct. He reasons that the defendant's mental condition, as well as social adversities, should be taken into account, but only at the sentencing stage.

How might a proponent of the insanity plea defend the insanity defense against Professor Morris's attack? Is there a suitable justification for recognizing a mental illness, but not a social deprivation, defense? (The issue of whether social deprivation should excuse criminal conduct is considered at p. 695.)

f. One Final Problem

You are a juror in a murder trial. The defendant pleads not guilty by reason of insanity. The jurisdiction applies the *M'Naghten* rule. The defendant testifies in his own defense. Here is his testimony.

EDGAR ALLAN POE—THE TELL–TALE HEART

(1843)**k**

TRUE! nervous, very, very dreadfully nervous I had been and am; but why will you say that I am mad? The disease had sharpened my senses, not destroyed, not dulled them. Above all was the sense of hearing acute. I heard all things in the heaven and in the earth. I heard many things in hell. How, then, am I mad? Hearken! and observe how healthily—how calmly I can tell you the whole story.

It is impossible to say how first the idea entered my brain; but once conceived, it haunted me day and night. Object there was none. Passion there was none. I loved the old man. He had never wronged me. He had never given me insult. For his gold I had no desire. I think it was his eye! yes, it was this! One of his eyes resembled that of a vulture, a pale blue eye, with a film over it. Whenever it fell upon me, my blood ran cold; and so by degrees, very gradually, I made up my mind to take the life of the old man, and thus rid myself of the eye forever.

Now this is the point. You fancy me mad. Madmen know nothing. But you should have seen me. You should have seen how wisely I proceeded; with what caution, with what foresight, with what dissimulation I went to work! I was never kinder to the old man than during the whole week before I killed him. And every night, about midnight, I turned the latch of his door and opened it—oh so gently! And then, when I had made an opening sufficient for my head, I put in a dark lantern, all closed, closed, that no light shone out, and then I thrust in my head. Oh, you would have laughed to see how cunningly I thrust it in! I moved it slowly—very, very slowly, so that I might not disturb the old man's sleep. It took me an hour to place my whole head within the opening so far that I could see him as he lay upon his bed. Ha! would a madman have been so wise as this? And

---

k. First published in *The Pioneer* in January, 1843.

then, when my head was well in the room, I undid the lantern cautiously—oh, so cautiously, cautiously (for the hinges creaked); I undid it just so
much that a single thin ray fell upon the vulture eye. And this I did for
seven long nights, every night just at midnight, but I found the eye always
closed; and so it was impossible to do the work; for it was not the old man
who vexed me, but his evil eye. And every morning, when the day broke, I
went boldly into the chamber, and spoke courageously to him, calling him
by name in a hearty tone, and inquiring how he has passed the night. So
you see he would have been a very profound old man, indeed, to suspect
that every night, just at twelve, I looked in upon him while he slept.

Upon the eighth night I was more than usually cautious in opening
the door. A watch's minute-hand moves more quickly than did mine.
Never before that night had I felt the extent of my own powers—of my
sagacity. I could scarcely contain my feelings of triumph. To think that
there I was, opening the door, little by little, and he not even to dream of
my secret deeds or thoughts. I fairly chuckled at the idea; and perhaps he
heard me; for he moved on the bed suddenly, as if startled. Now you may
think that I drew back, but no. His room was as black as pitch with the
thick darkness (for the shutters were close fastened, through fear of
robbers), and so I knew that he could not see the opening of the door, and
I kept pushing it on steadily, steadily.

I had my head in, and was about to open the lantern, when my thumb
slipped upon the tin fastening, and the old man sprang up in bed, crying
out, "Who's there?"

I kept quite still and said nothing. For a whole hour I did not move a
muscle, and in the meantime I did not hear him lie down. He was still
sitting up in the bed, listening: just as I have done, night after night,
hearkening to the death-watches in the wall.

Presently I heard a slight groan, and I knew it was the groan of
mortal terror. It was not a groan of pain or of grief; oh, no! it was the low
stifled sound that arises from the bottom of the soul when overcharged
with awe. I knew the sound well. Many a night, just at midnight, when all
the world slept, it has welled up from my own bosom, deepening, with its
dreadful echo, the terrors that distracted me. I say I knew it well. I knew
what the old man felt, and pitied him, although I chuckled at heart. I
knew that he had been lying awake ever since the first slight noise when
he had turned in the bed. His fears had been ever since growing upon him.
He had been trying to fancy them causeless, but could not. He had been
saying to himself: "It is nothing but the wind in the chimney, it is only a
mouse crossing the floor," or "It is merely a cricket which has made a
single chirp." Yes, he had been trying to comfort himself with these
suppositions; but he had found all in vain. All in vain; because Death, in
approaching him had stalked with his black shadow before him, and
enveloped the victim. And it was the mournful influence of the unper-
ceived shadow that caused him to feel, although he neither saw nor heard,
to feel the presence of my head within the room.

When I had waited a long time, very patiently, without hearing him lie down, I resolved to open a little, a very, very little crevice in the lantern. So I opened it—you cannot imagine how stealthily, stealthily—until, at length a simple dim ray, like the thread of the spider, shot from out the crevice and fell full upon the vulture eye.

It was open, wide, wide open, and I grew furious as I gazed upon it. I saw it with perfect distinctness, all a dull blue, with a hideous veil over it that chilled the very marrow in my bones; but I could see nothing else of the old man's face or person: for I had directed the ray as if by instinct precisely upon the damned spot.

And now have I not told you that what you mistake for madness is but overacuteness of the sense? now, I say, there came to my ears a low, dull, quick sound, such as a watch makes when enveloped in cotton. I knew that sound well, too. It was the beating of the old man's heart. It increased my fury, as the beating of a drum stimulates the soldier into courage.

But even yet I refrained and kept still. I scarcely breathed. I held the lantern motionless. I tried how steadily I could maintain the ray upon the eye. Meantime the hellish tattoo of the heart increased. It grew quicker and quicker, and louder and louder every instant. The old man's terror must have been extreme! It grew louder, I say, louder every moment! do you mark me well? I have told you that I am nervous: so I am. And now at the dead hour of the night, amid the dreadful silence of that old house, so strange a noise as this excited me to uncontrollable terror. Yet, for some minutes longer I refrained and stood still. But the beating grew louder, louder! I thought the heart must burst. And now a new anxiety seized me, the sound would be heard by a neighbor! The old man's hour had come! With a loud yell, I threw open the lantern and leaped into the room. He shrieked once—once only. In an instant I dragged him to the floor, and pulled the heavy bed over him. I then smiled gaily, to find the deed so far done. But, for many minutes, the heart beat on with a muffled sound. This, however, did not vex me; it would not be heard through the wall. At length it ceased. The old man was dead. I removed the bed and examined the corpse. Yes, he was stone, stone dead. I placed my hand upon the heart and held it there many minutes. There was no pulsation. He was stone dead. His eve would trouble me no more.

If still you think me mad, you will think so no longer when I describe the wise precautions I took for the concealment of the body. The night waned, and I worked hastily, but in silence. First of all I dismembered the corpse. I cut off the head and the arms and the legs.

I then took up three planks from the flooring of the chamber, and deposited all between the scantlings. I then replaced the boards so cleverly, so cunningly, that no human eye, not even his, could have detected anything wrong. There was nothing to wash out, no stain of any kind; no blood-spot whatever. I had been too wary for that. A tub had caught all; ha! ha!

When I had made an end of these labors, it was four o'clock; still dark as midnight. As the bell sounded the hour, there came a knocking at the street door. I went down to open it with a light heart; for what had I now to fear? There entered three men, who introduced themselves, with perfect suavity, as officers of the police. A shriek had been heard by a neighbor during the night; suspicion of foul play had been aroused; information had been lodged at the police office, and they (the officers) had been deputed to search the premises.

I smiled, for what had I to fear? I bade the gentlemen welcome. The shriek, I said, was my own in a dream. The old man, I mentioned, was absent in the country. I took my visitors all over the house. I bade them search—search well. I led them, at length, to his chamber. I showed them his treasures, secure, undisturbed. In the enthusiasm of my confidence, I brought chairs into the room, and desired them here to rest from their fatigues, while I myself, in the wild audacity of my perfect triumph, placed my own seat upon the very spot beneath which reposed the corpse of the victim.

The officers were satisfied. My manner had convinced them. I was singularly at ease. They sat, and while I answered cheerily, they chatted of familiar things. But, ere long, I felt myself getting pale and wished them gone. My head ached, and I fancied a ringing in my ears: but still they sat and still chatted. The ringing became more distinct: it continued and became more distinct: I talked more freely to get rid of the feeling; but it continued and gained definiteness, until, at length, I found that the noise was not within my ears.

No doubt I now grew very pale; but I talked more fluently, and with a heightened voice. Yet the sound increased, and what could I do? It was a low, dull, quick sound; much such a sound as a watch makes when enveloped in cotton. I gasped for breath; and yet the officers heard it not. I talked more quickly, more vehemently; but the noise steadily increased. I arose and argued about trifles, in a high key and with violent gesticulations, but the noise steadily increased. Why would they not be gone? I paced the floor to and fro with heavy strides, as if excited to fury by the observations of the men; but the noise steadily increased. Oh God! what could I do? I foamed, I raved, I swore! I swung the chair upon which I had been sitting, and grated it upon the boards, but the noise arose over all and continually increased. It grew louder, louder, louder! And still the men chatted pleasantly, and smiled. Was it possible they heard not? Almighty God! no, no! They heard! they suspected! they knew! they were making a mockery of my horror! this I thought, and this I think. But anything was better than this agony! Anything was more tolerable than this derision! I could bear those hypocritical smiles no longer! I felt that I must scream or die! and now—again! hark! louder! louder! louder! louder! —

"Villains!" I shrieked, "dissemble no more! I admit the deed! Tear up the planks! here, here! It is the beating of his hideous heart!"

Notes and Questions

1. What is your verdict? Why do you believe he is (in)sane?

5. DIMINISHED CAPACITY

STEPHEN J. MORSE—UNDIMINISHED CONFUSION IN DIMINISHED CAPACITY

75 Journal of Criminal Law & Criminology 1 (1984), 1, 5–7, 20–21

The diminished capacity doctrine allows a criminal defendant to introduce evidence of mental abnormality at trial either to negate a mental element of the crime charged, thereby exonerating the defendant of that charge, or to reduce the degree of crime for which the defendant may be convicted, even if the defendant's conduct satisfied all the formal elements of a higher offense. The first variant of diminished capacity, which I shall refer to as the "mens rea" variant, is the dominant approach in the United States. The second, * * * I shall refer to as the "partial responsibility" variant. * * *

A. The Mens Rea Variant

The prosecution always bears the burden of proving beyond a reasonable doubt its prima facie case, the definitional elements necessary to find the defendant guilty of the crime charged or lesser included offenses. Cases of strict liability aside, all crimes include a mental element, a mens rea, that the prosecution must prove. If the prosecution fails to carry its persuasion burden on a requisite mental element, the defendant must be acquitted of any crime that includes such an element in its definition. * * *

In light of these elementary principles of criminal law, it is clear that the mens rea variant of diminished capacity is not a separate defense that deserves to be called "diminished capacity" or any other name connoting that it is some sort of special, affirmative defense. The defendant is simply introducing evidence, in this case evidence of mental abnormality, to make the following claim: "I did not commit the crime charged because I did not possess the requisite mens rea." * * * Further, a defendant claiming no mens rea because of mental disorder is not asserting some lesser form of legal insanity, that is, he is not claiming that he is partially or less responsible for the crime charged. Rather, the defendant is straightforwardly denying the prosecution's prima facie case by attempting to cast doubt on the prosecution's claim that a requisite mental element was present at the time of the offense. He is claiming that he is not guilty of that crime at all, although he may be guilty of a lesser crime if all the elements of the latter are proven. It is as if, for example, a defendant charged with murder on an intent-to-kill theory pleads not guilty on the ground that he thought he was shooting at a tree and therefore lacked the requisite intent to kill.

The moral logic of the mens rea variant is as compelling and straightforward as the technical logic. In our system of criminal justice, culpability is dependent upon a finding of both an act *and* a requisite mental state. Moreover, culpability for the same act varies according to the accompanying mental state. * * * A defendant who lacks a required element is not blameworthy for an offense that includes that element, and it would be unjust as well as unconstitutional to punish him for it.

Many courts and legislatures have been convinced of the fundamental fairness and consequent necessity of allowing defendants to attempt to cast doubt on the prosecution's case using evidence of mental abnormality,[17] but they have usually placed illogical limitations on the defendant's ability to do so. A smaller number of courts and legislatures have refused to permit the admission of any evidence of mental abnormality, except on the issue of legal insanity.[19] * * *

B.   THE PARTIAL RESPONSIBILITY VARIANT

Partial responsibility is a form of lesser legal insanity: The defendant is claiming that, as a result of mental abnormality, he is not fully responsible for the crime proven against him. Even if the technical elements of an offense are satisfied, the defendant is less culpable and should be convicted of a lesser crime, or, at least, should be punished less severely. * * *

The rationales for holding a defendant partially responsible and for excusing him by reason of insanity differ only in degree. The preconditions for moral and legal responsibility are, *inter alia,* that the actor is reasonably rational and in control of his actions. Actors, such as small children, who lack reasonable cognitive or volitional capacity through no fault of their own may be dangerous, but are not considered fully responsible as moral agents. This basic intuition about the way cognitive and volitional capacity relate to responsibility is tracked by the insanity defense tests * * *.

Although the law draws a bright line for legal responsibility, human cognitive and volitional capacities and behaviors are clearly distributed along a very lengthy continuum of competence. All legally sane defendants will not be equally rational or equally in possession of self-control at the time of the prohibited act. When a legally sane defendant has impaired rationality or self-control because of mental abnormality—a cause he is allegedly unable to control—an argument for some form of lessened responsibility arises.

NOTES AND QUESTIONS

1.   People v. Wetmore, 22 Cal.3d 318, 583 P.2d 1308, 149 Cal.Rptr. 265 (1978):

---

17. The Model Penal Code was an early proponent of this view. Model Penal Code § 4.02.

19. * * * Unfortunately, courts constantly confuse partial responsibility with the mens rea variant and then reject the mens rea variant on the ground that the insanity defense is the only doctrine that considers nonresponsibility caused by mental abnormality.

The only evidence submitted to the trial court in this case was the testimony of Joseph Cacciatore, the victim of the burglary * * * and three psychiatric reports. Cacciatore testified that he left his apartment on March 7, 1975. When he returned three days later, he discovered defendant in his apartment. Defendant was wearing Cacciatore's clothes and cooking his food. The lock on the front door had been broken; the apartment lay in a shambles. Cacciatore called the police, who arrested defendant for burglary. Later Cacciatore discovered that a ring, a watch, a credit card, and items of clothing were missing.

The psychiatric reports submitted to the court explain defendant's long history of psychotic illness, including at least 10 occasions of hospital confinement for treatment. According to the reports, defendant, shortly after his last release from Brentwood Veteran's Hospital, found himself with no place to go. He began to believe that he "owned" property, and was "directed" to Cacciatore's apartment. When he found the door unlocked he was sure he owned the apartment. He entered, rearranged the apartment, destroyed some advertising he felt was inappropriate, and put on Cacciatore's clothes. When the police arrived, defendant was shocked and embarrassed, and only then understood that he did not own the apartment.

Based on the preceding facts, defendant Wetmore was charged with burglary. Using Professor Morse's dichotomy, which variant of diminished capacity is potentially implicated? If Wetmore is permitted to claim diminished capacity, and if the jury is persuaded by his factual claim, what is the practical outcome?

2. *The "partial responsibility" model of diminished capacity: common law and Model Penal Code.* California was the leading state to adopt a partial responsibility form of diminished capacity, although it did so as if it were applying the *"mens rea"* model described by Professor Morse in the preceding excerpt. Thus, the California Supreme Court held in an extended line of cases that evidence of mental illness short of insanity could be introduced to negate the element of premeditation or deliberation, so as to reduce a murder from first-degree to second-degree, or even to negate the element of malice aforethought, so as to lower the offense to manslaughter. Public outcry against the state court's rulings in controversial cases culminated in legislative abolition of this defense.

Today, the partial responsibility model of diminished capacity is usually recognized, if at all, in states that have adopted the Model Penal Code "extreme mental or emotional disturbance" manslaughter provision, that is, § 210.3(1)(b). This Code provision was considered earlier in the casebook (p. 284) in relation to the provocation doctrine. Is it sensible, however, to use the same statutory provision to deal with both heat-of-passion and diminished capacity? In this regard, consider the following observation:

> Diminished capacity involves a mental disturbance which peculiarly involves the killer. Heat of passion is a concession to human weakness, to a universal human condition. Diminished capacity is an effort to reduce punishment because the actor is not like all humans, whereas heat of

passion reduces punishment because the actor is, unfortunately, like most humans.

Joshua Dressler, *Rethinking Heat of Passion: A Defense in Search of a Rationale*, 73 J.Crim.L. & Criminology 421, 459–60 (1982).

Sometimes a defendant in a Model Penal Code jurisdiction will raise a claim that merges the disparate concepts of provocation and diminished capacity. For example, in State v. Dumlao, 6 Haw.App. 173, 715 P.2d 822 (1986), the defendant suffered from a "paranoid personality disorder" that caused him to become pathologically and irrationally jealous, and to believe that other persons, including his wife's relatives, were sexually intimate with her. As a result of these delusions, the defendant killed one of his wife's relatives in a rage.

Essentially, the court characterized Dumlao's "extreme mental or emotional disturbance" as his jealous rage rather than his paranoia. Then, pursuant to the Code's language, it held that the reasonableness of his rage should be "determined from the viewpoint of a person in the actor's situation under the circumstances as he believes them to be." Thus, the factfinder was called upon to consider the reasonableness of Dumlao's rage based on his irrational belief that his in-laws were having sexual relations with his wife!

3. *Abolish the "partial responsibility" defense?* Assume that there are two sane killers, Alice and Bob, each one of whom intentionally and unjustifiably takes the life of another person. Alice possesses normal mental capacities, whereas Bob suffers from some mental abnormality, e.g., moderate mental illness or retardation. In light of Bob's mental condition, should the criminal law treat his crime as a lesser homicide offense than that committed by Alice? Professor Morse once argued that the law should treat the two killers the same:

> How hard is it not to offend the law? How hard is it not to kill, burgle, rob, rape, and steal? The ability to resist the temptation to violate the law is not akin to the ability required to be a fine athlete, artist, plumber, or doctor. The person is not being asked to exercise a difficult skill; rather, he or she is being asked simply to refrain from engaging in antisocial conduct. Think * * * of all the factors mitigating against such behavior: parental, religious, and school training; peer pressures and cultural expectations; internalized standards ("superego"); fear of capture and punishment; fear of shame; and a host of others. Not all such factors operate on all actors or with great strength: there will be wide individual differences based on life experiences and, perhaps, biological factors. Nonetheless, for all persons there are enormous forces arrayed against lawbreaking. It is one thing to yield to a desire to engage in undesirable conduct such as to gossip, brag, or treat one's fellows unfairly; it is another to give in to a desire to engage in qualitatively more harmful conduct such as to kill, rape, burgle, rob, or burn.
>
> The substantive criminal law sets minimal ethical and legal standards that ask very little of us and are easy to meet. Even if an actor has rationality or self-control problems, it is not hard for a legally responsible person to avoid offending. * * *

As long as the function of conviction and sentencing is to punish the actor for what he has done, rather than for who he is, there is no injustice in treating alike actors whose behavior satisfies the elements of the same crime and meets the low threshold standard for legal responsibility.

Morse, *supra*, at 30–32. But, consider this response to Professor Morse:

> We should not punish persons for possessing bad character, nor should we mitigate or exculpate because of good character. But we ought to consider explanations for behavior that indicate that the actors' personal blameworthiness for the events—their moral accountability for the harm—is less than we ordinarily would expect.

> The difference between insanity and diminished capacity is one of degree. Just as we differentially punish people because of gradations in mens rea, no principled basis exists for ignoring gradations here. The [proffered] evidence is no less reliable in the case of diminished capacity than with insanity. As long as the jury, not the "expert," resolves the moral issues of accountability, there is no good reason for closing our eyes to partial responsibility claims.

> * * * [Consider] this * * * case[50][:] the defendant, Fisher, intentionally strangled a librarian. Fisher was not insane. Under Professor Morse's all-or-nothing approach, he was properly convicted of murder. * * * Yet, Fisher was mentally subnormal. * * * [H]e suffered from an aggressive psychopathic condition that affected his behavior. He killed suddenly, but intentionally; yet, he acted only after the victim called him a "black nigger." Are these factors individually or collectively irrelevant to his moral guilt and deserved punishment? Is it wrong for the jury to be permitted to evaluate their moral relevance? The Court said yes. Morse would say yes. I would say no. I agree with the observations of Justice Frankfurter:

>> A shocking crime puts law to its severest test. * * * Fisher is not the name of a theoretical problem. We are not hear [sic] dealing with an abstract man. * * * Murder cases are apt to be peculiarly individualized. * * * The bite of law is in its enforcement. This is especially true when careful or indifferent judicial administration has consequences so profound as * * * life and death.

> Fisher's impairment, and the victim's racial epithet, may not have been the legal causes of his conduct. His free will acts were the cause. Because he had free will, and chose to kill, he should be punished. But my intuition tells me that the information [proffered] by the defense would have been highly relevant to morally sensitive jurors in their decision regarding Fisher's degree of moral guilt. Jurors might conclude that it was harder for Fisher than for the juror *not* to kill.

Joshua Dressler, *Reaffirming the Moral Legitimacy of the Doctrine of Diminished Capacity: A Brief Reply to Professor Morse,* 75 J.Crim.L. & Criminology 953, 960–61 (1984).

---

50. Fisher v. United States, 328 U.S. 463, 66 S.Ct. 1318, 90 L.Ed. 1382 (1946).

In 1998, Professor Morse wrote that "I now believe, on further reflection, that the moral claim [for a partial responsibility defense] is sufficiently weighty to justify bearing the potential practical costs." Stephen J. Morse, *Excusing and the New Excuse Defenses: A Legal and Conceptual Review* in 23 Crime and Justice: A Review of Research 329, 397 (1998). Indeed, Morse would now recognize a "guilty but partially responsible" verdict for all offenses, resulting in lesser punishment than a guilty verdict, if the jury finds that, at the time of the offense, the "defendant suffered from substantially diminished rationality for which the defendant was not responsible and which substantially affected the defendant's criminal conduct." Stephen J. Morse, *Diminished Rationality, Diminished Responsibility*, 1 Ohio St. J. Crim. L. 289, 300 (2003).

4. *The "mens rea" model of diminished capacity: common law and Model Penal Code.* Professor Morse characterized the *"mens rea"* version of diminished capacity as the "dominant approach in the United States." As he observed, however, although Model Penal Code Section 4.02 permits introduction of evidence of mental abnormality "whenever it is relevant to prove that the defendant did or did not have a state of mind which is an element of the offense," many states limit use of such evidence to specific intent crimes.

As Professor Morse recognized in the preceding excerpt, however, some states have prohibited the admission of mental abnormality evidence *for all crimes* except on the issue of legal insanity. But, how can this be? If an offense contains a *mens rea* element and, therefore, the government has the constitutional burden to prove the requisite intent, how can a state deny a defendant the opportunity to put on evidence that might negate that element? Consider the next case, which speaks to this question.

CLARK v. ARIZONA

Supreme Court of the United States, 2006.
548 U.S. 735, 126 S.Ct. 2709, 165 L.Ed.2d 842.

JUSTICE SOUTER delivered the opinion of the Court. * * *

I

In the early hours of June 21, 2000, Officer Jeffrey Moritz of the Flagstaff Police responded in uniform to complaints that a pickup truck with loud music blaring was circling a residential block. When he located the truck, the officer turned on the emergency lights and siren of his marked patrol car, which prompted petitioner Eric Clark, the truck's driver (then 17), to pull over. Officer Moritz got out of the patrol car and told Clark to stay where he was. Less than a minute later, Clark shot the officer, who died soon after * * *. Clark ran away on foot but was arrested later that day * * *.

Clark was charged with first-degree murder under Ariz. Rev. Stat. Ann. § 13–1105(A)(3) for intentionally or knowingly killing a law enforcement officer in the line of duty.[1] In March 2001, Clark was found

---

1. Section 13–1105(A)(3) provides that "[a] person commits first degree murder if * * * intending or knowing that the person's conduct will cause death to a law enforcement officer, the person causes the death of a law enforcement officer who is in the line of duty."

incompetent to stand trial and was committed to a state hospital for treatment, but two years later the same trial court found his competence restored and ordered him to be tried. Clark waived his right to a jury, and the case was heard by the court.

At trial, Clark did not contest the shooting and death, but relied on his undisputed paranoid schizophrenia at the time of the incident in denying that he had the specific intent to shoot a law enforcement officer or knowledge that he was doing so, as required by the statute. Accordingly, the prosecutor offered circumstantial evidence that Clark knew Officer Moritz was a law enforcement officer. The evidence showed that the officer was in uniform at the time, that he caught up with Clark in a marked police car with emergency lights and siren going, and that Clark acknowledged the symbols of police authority and stopped. The testimony for the prosecution indicated that Clark had intentionally lured an officer to the scene to kill him, having told some people a few weeks before the incident that he wanted to shoot police officers. At the close of the State's evidence, the trial court denied Clark's motion for judgment of acquittal for failure to prove intent to kill a law enforcement officer or knowledge that Officer Moritz was a law enforcement officer.

In presenting the defense case, Clark claimed mental illness * * *. * * * [H]e aimed to rebut the prosecution's evidence of the requisite *mens rea*, that he had acted intentionally or knowingly to kill a law enforcement officer.

The trial court ruled that Clark could not rely on evidence bearing on insanity to dispute the *mens rea*. The court cited *State* v. *Mott*, 187 Ariz. 536, 931 P.2d 1046 (en banc), which "refused to allow psychiatric testimony to negate specific intent," and held that "Arizona does not allow evidence of a defendant's mental disorder short of insanity * * * to negate the *mens rea* element of a crime." * * *

At the close of the defense case * * *, the trial court denied Clark's renewed motion for a directed verdict grounded on failure of the prosecution to show that Clark knew the victim was a police officer. The judge then issued a * * * verdict of first-degree murder * * *. * * * The sentence was life imprisonment without the possibility of release for 25 years.

Clark moved to vacate the judgment and sentence, arguing, among other things, that Arizona's * * * *Mott* rule * * * violate[s] due process. * * * The court denied the motion. * * *

III * * *

A

Understanding Clark's claim requires attention to the categories of evidence with a potential bearing on *mens rea*. First, there is "observation evidence" in the everyday sense, testimony from those who observed what Clark did and heard what he said; this category would also include testimony that an expert witness might give about Clark's tendency to think in a certain way and his behavioral characteristics. This evidence may support a professional diagnosis of mental disease and in any event is the kind of evidence that can be relevant to show what in fact was on Clark's mind when he fired the gun. Observation evidence in the record covers Clark's behavior at home and with friends, his expressions of belief around the time of the killing that "aliens" were inhabiting the bodies of local people (including government agents),[27] his driving around the neighborhood before the police arrived, and so on. Contrary to the dissent's characterization, observation evidence can be presented by either lay or expert witnesses.

Second, there is "mental-disease evidence" in the form of opinion testimony that Clark suffered from a mental disease with features described by the witness. As was true here, this evidence characteristically but not always comes from professional psychologists or psychiatrists who testify as expert witnesses and base their opinions in part on examination of a defendant, usually conducted after the events in question. The thrust of this evidence was that, based on factual reports, professional observations, and tests, Clark was psychotic at the time in question, with a condition that fell within the category of schizophrenia.

Third, there is evidence we will refer to as "capacity evidence" about a defendant's capacity for cognition and moral judgment (and ultimately also his capacity to form *mens rea*). This, too, is opinion evidence. Here, as it usually does, this testimony came from the same experts and concentrated on those specific details of the mental condition that make the difference between sanity and insanity under the Arizona definition. * * *

B

It is clear that *Mott* itself imposed no restriction on considering evidence of the first sort, the observation evidence. We read the *Mott* restriction to apply, rather, to evidence addressing the two issues in testimony that characteristically comes only from psychologists or psychiatrists qualified to give opinions as expert witnesses: mental-disease evidence (whether at the time of the crime a defendant suffered from a mental disease or defect, such as schizophrenia) and capacity evidence (whether the disease or defect left him incapable of performing or experiencing a mental process defined as necessary for sanity such as appreciating the nature and quality of his act and knowing that it was wrong). * * *

27. Clark's parents testified that, in the months before the shooting and even days beforehand, Clark called them "aliens" and thought that "aliens" were out to get him. One night before the shooting, according to Clark's mother, Clark repeatedly viewed a popular film characterized by her as telling a story about "aliens" masquerading as government agents, a story Clark insisted was real despite his mother's protestations to the contrary. And two months after the shooting, Clark purportedly told his parents that his hometown, Flagstaff, was inhabited principally by "aliens," who had to be stopped, and that the only way to stop them was with bullets.

D * * *

Clark's argument is [that the *Mott* restrictions violate] a defendant's right as a matter of simple due process to present evidence favorable to himself on an element that must be proven to convict him. * * *

As Clark recognizes, however, the right to introduce relevant evidence can be curtailed if there is a good reason for doing that. "While the Constitution * * * prohibits the exclusion of defense evidence under rules that serve no legitimate purpose or that are disproportionate to the ends that they are asserted to promote, well-established rules of evidence permit trial judges to exclude evidence if its probative value is outweighed by certain other factors such as unfair prejudice, confusion of the issues, or potential to mislead the jury." And if evidence may be kept out entirely, its consideration may be subject to limitation, which Arizona claims the power to impose here. State law says that evidence of mental disease and incapacity may be introduced and considered, and if sufficiently forceful to satisfy the defendant's burden of proof under the insanity rule it will displace the presumption of sanity and excuse from criminal responsibility. But mental-disease and capacity evidence may be considered only for its bearing on the insanity defense, and it will avail a defendant only if it is persuasive enough to satisfy the defendant's burden as defined by the terms of that defense. The mental-disease and capacity evidence is thus being channeled or restricted to one issue and given effect only if the defendant carries the burden to convince the factfinder of insanity; the evidence is not being excluded entirely, and the question is whether reasons for requiring it to be channeled and restricted are good enough to satisfy the standard of fundamental fairness that due process requires. We think they are.

E * * *

Are there * * * characteristics of mental-disease and capacity evidence giving rise to risks that may reasonably be hedged by channeling the consideration of such evidence to the insanity issue on which, in States like Arizona, a defendant has the burden of persuasion? We think there are: in the controversial character of some categories of mental disease, in the potential of mental-disease evidence to mislead, and in the danger of according greater certainty to capacity evidence than experts claim for it.

To begin with, the diagnosis may mask vigorous debate within the profession about the very contours of the mental disease itself. Though we certainly do not "condem[n mental-disease evidence] wholesale," the consequence of this professional ferment is a general caution in treating psychological classifications as predicates for excusing otherwise criminal conduct.

Next, there is the potential of mental-disease evidence to mislead jurors (when they are the factfinders) through the power of this kind of evidence to suggest that a defendant suffering from a recognized mental disease lacks cognitive, moral, volitional, or other capacity, when that may not be a sound conclusion at all. Even when a category of mental disease is broadly accepted and the assignment of a defendant's behavior to that category is uncontroversial, the classification may suggest something very significant about a defendant's capacity, when in fact the classification tells us little or nothing about the ability of the defendant to form *mens rea* * * *. The limits of the utility of a professional disease diagnosis are evident in the dispute between the two testifying experts in this case; they agree that Clark was schizophrenic, but they come to opposite conclusions on whether the mental disease in his particular case left him bereft of cognitive or moral capacity [for purposes of the insanity defense]. Evidence of mental disease, then, can easily mislead; it is very easy to slide from evidence that an individual with a professionally recognized mental disease is very different, into doubting that he has the capacity to form *mens rea*, whereas that doubt may not be justified. * * * Because allowing mental-disease evidence on *mens rea* can thus easily mislead, it is not unreasonable to address that tendency by confining consideration of this kind of evidence to insanity, on which a defendant may be assigned the burden of persuasion.

There are, finally, particular risks inherent in the opinions of the experts who supplement the mental-disease classifications with opinions on incapacity: on whether the mental disease rendered a particular defendant incapable of the cognition necessary for moral judgment or *mens rea* or otherwise incapable of understanding the wrongfulness of the conduct charged. Unlike observational evidence bearing on *mens rea*, capacity evidence consists of judgment, and judgment fraught with multiple perils: a defendant's state of mind at the crucial moment can be elusive no matter how conscientious the enquiry, and the law's categories that set the terms of the capacity judgment are not the categories of psychology that govern the expert's professional thinking. Although such capacity judgments may be given in the utmost good faith, their potentially tenuous character is indicated by the candor of the defense expert in this very case. Contrary to the State's expert, he testified that * * * "no one knows exactly what was on [his] mind" at the time of the shooting. And even when an expert is confident that his understanding of the mind is reliable, judgment addressing the basic categories of capacity requires a leap from the concepts of psychology, which are devised for thinking about treatment, to the concepts of legal sanity, which are devised for thinking about criminal responsibility. In sum, these empirical and conceptual problems add up to a real risk that an expert's judgment in giving capacity evidence will come with an apparent authority that psychologists and psychiatrists do not claim to have. We think that this risk, like the difficulty in assessing the significance of mental-disease evidence, supports the State's decision to channel such expert testimony to consideration on the insanity defense, on which the party seeking the benefit of this evidence has the burden of persuasion.

It bears repeating that not every State will find it worthwhile to make the judgment Arizona has made * * *. The point here simply is that

Arizona has sensible reasons to assign the risks as it has done by channeling the evidence.[45] * * *

The judgment of the Court of Appeals of Arizona [that affirmed the conviction] is, accordingly, affirmed.

JUSTICE KENNEDY, with whom JUSTICE STEVENS and JUSTICE GINSBURG join, dissenting.

In my submission the Court is incorrect in holding that Arizona may convict petitioner Eric Clark of first-degree murder for the intentional or knowing killing of a police officer when Clark was not permitted to introduce critical and reliable evidence showing he did not have that intent or knowledge. * * *

I * * *

The Court[] * * * adopts an evidentiary framework that, in my view, will be unworkable in many cases. * * * These categories break down quickly when it is understood how the testimony would apply to the question of intent and knowledge at issue here. The most common type of schizophrenia, and the one Clark suffered from, is paranoid schizophrenia. The existence of this functional psychosis is beyond dispute, but that does not mean the lay witness understands it or that a disputed issue of fact concerning its effect in a particular instance is not something for the expert to address. Common symptoms of the condition are delusions accompanied by hallucinations, often of the auditory type, which can cause disturbances of perception. Clark's expert testified that people with schizophrenia often play radios loudly to drown out the voices in their heads. Clark's attorney argued to the trial court that this, rather than a desire to lure a policeman to the scene, explained Clark's behavior just before the killing. The observation that schizophrenics play radios loudly is a fact regarding behavior, but it is only a relevant fact if Clark has schizophrenia.

Even if this evidence were, to use the Court's term, mental-disease evidence, because it relies on an expert opinion, what would happen if the expert simply were to testify, without mentioning schizophrenia, that people with Clark's symptoms often play the radio loudly? This seems to be factual evidence, as the term is defined by the Court, yet it differs from mental-disease evidence only in forcing the witness to pretend that no one has yet come up with a way to classify the set of symptoms being described. More generally, the opinion that Clark had paranoid schizo-

---

45. Arizona's rule is supported by a further practical reason, though not as weighty as those just considered. As mentioned before, if substantial mental-disease and capacity evidence is accepted as rebutting *mens rea* in a given case, the affirmative defense of insanity will probably not be reached or ruled upon; the defendant will simply be acquitted (or perhaps convicted of a lesser included offense). If an acquitted defendant suffers from a mental disease or defect that makes him dangerous, he will neither be confined nor treated psychiatrically unless a judge so orders after some independent commitment proceeding. But if a defendant succeeds in showing himself insane, Arizona law (and presumably that of every other State with an insanity rule) will require commitment and treatment as a consequence of that finding without more. It makes sense, then, to channel capacity evidence to the issue structured to deal with mental incapacity when such a claim is raised successfully.

phrenia—an opinion shared by experts for both the prosecution and defense—bears on efforts to determine, as a factual matter, whether he knew he was killing a police officer. The psychiatrist's explanation of Clark's condition was essential to understanding how he processes sensory data and therefore to deciding what information was in his mind at the time of the shooting. Simply put, knowledge relies on cognition, and cognition can be affected by schizophrenia. The mental-disease evidence at trial was also intertwined with the observation evidence because it lent needed credibility. Clark's parents and friends testified Clark thought the people in his town were aliens trying to kill him. These claims might not be believable without a psychiatrist confirming the story based on his experience with people who have exhibited similar behaviors. It makes little sense to divorce the observation evidence from the explanation that makes it comprehensible. * * *

Clark seeks resolution of issues that can be complex and somewhat overlapping. In the end, however, we must decide whether he had the right to introduce evidence showing he lacked the intent or knowledge the statute itself sets forth in describing a basic element of the crime. * * *

II * * *

The central theory of Clark's defense was that his schizophrenia made him delusional. He lived in a universe where the delusions were so dominant, the theory was, that he had no intent to shoot a police officer or knowledge he was doing so. It is one thing to say he acted with intent or knowledge to pull the trigger. It is quite another to say he pulled the trigger to kill someone he knew to be a human being and a police officer. If the trier of fact were to find Clark's evidence sufficient to discount the case made by the State, which has the burden to prove knowledge or intent as an element of the offense, Clark would not be guilty of first-degree murder under Arizona law.

The Court * * * fails to recognize * * * the meaning of the offense element in question here. The *mens rea* element of intent or knowledge may, at some level, comprise certain moral choices, but it rests in the first instance on a factual determination. That is the fact Clark sought to put in issue. Either Clark knew he was killing a police officer or he did not.

The issue is not, as the Court insists, whether Clark's mental illness acts as an "excuse from customary criminal responsibility," but whether his mental illness, as a factual matter, made him unaware that he was shooting a police officer. If it did, Clark needs no excuse, as then he did not commit the crime as Arizona defines it. For the elements of first-degree murder, where the question is knowledge of particular facts—that one is killing a police officer—the determination depends not on moral responsibility but on empirical fact. Clark's evidence of mental illness had a direct and substantial bearing upon what he knew, or thought he knew, to be the facts when he pulled the trigger; this lay at the heart of the matter. * * *

This is not to suggest all general rules on the exclusion of certain types of evidence are invalid. If the rule does not substantially burden the defense, then it is likely permissible. Where, however, the burden is substantial, the State must present a valid reason for its *per se* evidentiary rule.

In the instant case Arizona's proposed reasons are insufficient to support its categorical exclusion. While the State contends that testimony regarding mental illness may be too incredible or speculative for the jury to consider, this does not explain why the exclusion applies in all cases to all evidence of mental illness. "A State's legitimate interest in barring unreliable evidence does not extend to *per se* exclusions that may be reliable in an individual case." * * *

The risk of jury confusion also fails to justify the rule. The State defends its rule as a means to avoid the complexities of determining how and to what degree a mental illness affects a person's mental state. The difficulty of resolving a factual issue, though, does not present a sufficient reason to take evidence away from the jury even when it is crucial for the defense. "We have always trusted juries to sort through complex facts in various areas of law." * * *

The Court undertakes little analysis of the interests particular to this case. By proceeding in this way it devalues Clark's constitutional rights. * * * The Court is correct that many mental diseases are difficult to define and the subject of great debate. Schizophrenia, however, is a well-documented mental illness, and no one seriously disputes either its definition or its most prominent clinical manifestations. The State's own expert conceded that Clark had paranoid schizophrenia and was actively psychotic at the time of the killing. The jury-confusion rationale, if it is at all applicable here, is the result of the Court's own insistence on conflating the insanity defense and the question of intent. Considered on its own terms, the issue of intent and knowledge is a straightforward factual question. A trier of fact is quite capable of weighing defense testimony and then determining whether the accused did or did not intend to kill or knowingly kill a human being who was a police officer. True, the issue can be difficult to decide in particular instances, but no more so than many matters juries must confront.

The Court says mental-illness evidence "can easily mislead," and may "tell us little or nothing about the ability of the defendant to form *mens rea*." These generalities do not, however, show how relevant or misleading the evidence in this case would be * * *. As explained above, the evidence of Clark's mental illness bears directly on *mens rea*, for it suggests Clark may not have known he was killing a human being. It is striking that while the Court discusses at length the likelihood of misjudgment from placing too much emphasis on evidence of mental illness, it ignores the risk of misjudging an innocent man guilty from refusing to consider this highly relevant evidence at all. Clark's expert, it is true, said no one could know exactly what was on Clark's mind at the time of the shooting. The expert testified extensively, however, about the effect of Clark's delusions on his perceptions of the world around him, and about whether Clark's behavior around the time of the shooting was consistent with delusional thinking. This testimony was relevant to determining whether Clark knew he was killing a human being. It also bolstered the testimony of lay witnesses, none of which was deemed unreliable or misleading by the state courts. * * *

Contrary to the Court's suggestion, the fact that the state and defense experts drew different conclusions about the effect of Clark's mental illness on his mental state only made Clark's evidence contested; it did not make the evidence irrelevant or misleading. The trial court was capable of evaluating the competing conclusions, as factfinders do in countless cases where there is a dispute among witnesses. In fact, the potential to mislead will be far greater under the Court's new evidentiary system, where jurors will receive observation evidence without the necessary explanation from experts.

The fact that mental-illness evidence may be considered in deciding criminal responsibility does not compensate for its exclusion from consideration on the *mens rea* elements of the crime. The evidence addresses different issues in the two instances. Criminal responsibility involves an inquiry into whether the defendant knew right from wrong, not whether he had the *mens rea* elements of the offense. * * *

Even if the analyses were equivalent, there is a different burden of proof for insanity than there is for *mens rea*. Arizona requires the defendant to prove his insanity by clear and convincing evidence. The prosecution, however, must prove all elements of the offense beyond a reasonable doubt. The shift in the burden on the criminal responsibility issue, while permissible under our precedent, cannot be applied to the question of intent or knowledge without relieving the State of its responsibility to establish this element of the offense. * * *

Future dangerousness is not, as the Court appears to conclude [in footnote 45], a rational basis for convicting mentally ill individuals of crimes they did not commit. Civil commitment proceedings can ensure that individuals who present a danger to themselves or others receive proper treatment without unfairly treating them as criminals. The State presents no evidence to the contrary, and the Court ought not to imply otherwise. * * *

* * * It is unclear * * * what would have happened in this case had the defendant wanted to testify that he thought Officer Moritz was an alien. If disallowed, it would be tantamount to barring Clark from testifying on his behalf to explain his own actions. If allowed, then Arizona's rule would simply prohibit the corroboration necessary to make sense of Clark's explanation. In sum, the rule forces the jury to decide guilt in a fictional world with undefined and unexplained behaviors but without mental illness. This rule has no rational justification and imposes a

significant burden upon a straightforward defense: He did not commit the crime with which he was charged.

NOTES AND QUESTIONS

1. Whose opinion—Justice Souter's or Justice Kennedy's—persuades you? For different perspectives on the case, see Ronald J. Allen, *Clark v. Arizona: Much (Confused) Ado About Nothing*, 4 Ohio St. J. Crim. L. 135 (2006); Peter Westen, *The Supreme Court's Bout with Insanity: Clark v. Arziona*, 4 Ohio St. J. Crim. L. 143 (2006).

2. Many years ago, Peter Arenella wrote the following about expert testimony in regard to the *mens rea* model of diminished capacity:

> The only difficulty with the *mens rea* model is its assumption that psychiatric analysis is directly relevant to the criminal law's state of mind elements. This premise is usually erroneous because most expert testimony does not speak to the criminal law's conception of intent.
>
> Consider the following hypothetical. Assume Mr. Fanatic believes that God has ordered him to kill his neighbor because the neighbor is an agent of the devil. Mr. Fanatic buys a gun and ammunition, invites his neighbor over for tea, and calmly blows his brains out, killing him instantly. Psychiatrists testify that Mr. Fanatic was suffering from paranoid schizophrenia as evidenced by his delusion that God had ordered the killing. * * * Mr. Fanatic would be exculpated under the insanity rule of the Model Penal Code. Yet the same evidence of mental abnormality would not refute the existence of either the specific intent to kill or premeditation and deliberation. Mr. Fanatic certainly intended to kill and his objective acts clearly evidenced a preconceived design to effectuate that intent in a calm, deliberate manner.
>
> Is this an illogical result? How can the defendant be insane, and therefore entitled to a complete defense, and yet not qualify for what is considered a "partial" defense? The simple answer is that there is no necessary connection between a judgment about the defendant's criminal responsibility and his mental capacity to entertain the state of mind required by the crime. As long as the *mens rea* element is defined in terms of the conscious mind's cognitive and affective functions, it is perfectly plausible that the defendant entertained the specific mental state but was still insane. In fact, most mentally abnormal offenders are fully capable of thinking about their criminal act before they do it, turning it over in their minds, planning the act, and then performing it in accordance with their preconceived plan. Evidence of how Fanatic's mental abnormality impaired his behavior controls or made it difficult for him to appreciate the act's gravity does not negate the existence of the required mental states; it merely explains them. Therefore, a psychiatric explanation of how a defendant's personality development led to his deviant behavior which does not dispute the presence of this conscious intent should not be admissible evidence under the strict *mens rea* model.
>
> Admittedly, there will be occasional cases in which the expert testimony establishes that the defendant was incapable of entertaining the

requisite intent. But given the criminal law's minimal definition of *mens rea,* the only type of mental abnormality that could establish such incapacity would be a severe mental disability that substantially interfered with the defendants reality-testing functions. However, evidence that the defendant's reality-testing functions were so impaired by mental illness that he did not realize what he was doing would also establish his insanity under either the *M'Naughton* or Model Penal Code tests. Thus, our analysis suggests that if courts administer the *mens rea* model honestly and only admit evidence that establishes that the defendant did not entertain the requisite mental state, the strict *mens rea* variant will rarely serve any purpose not satisfied by the insanity defense.

Peter Arenella, *The Diminished Capacity and Diminished Responsibility Defenses: Two Children of a Doomed Marriage,* 77 Colum.L.Rev. 827, 833–35 (1977).

In light of *Clark*, does Professor Arenella seem correct?

6. INFANCY

IN RE DEVON T.

Court of Special Appeals of Maryland, 1991.
85 Md.App. 674, 584 A.2d 1287.

MOYLAN, JUDGE.

In a world dizzy with change, it is reassuring to find Daniel M'Naghten alive and well in juvenile court. It was, of course, M'Naghten's bungled attempt to assassinate Prime Minister Sir Robert Peel, killing by mistake Sir Robert's private secretary Edward Drummond, that led to his prosecution for murder and the assertion of his now eponymic insanity defense. When the House of Lords placed its imprimatur upon the jury's acquittal by reason of insanity, "the M'Naghten test" was impressed indelibly upon the Common Law of Anglo–America.

The M'Naghten test, by name, crossed to New England within the year. It was adopted by the Court of Appeals in 1888 as the controlling standard in Maryland, * * * and remained the exclusive criterion of criminal insanity in this state until supplanted by the Acts of 1967, ch. 709.[1] * * *

What has not been adequately noted in the case law is that this cognitive capacity to distinguish right from wrong in the language of M'Naghten was not a characteristic of the insanity defense exclusively. It has traditionally been the common denominator criterion for a whole family of defenses based upon mental incapacity—insanity, infancy, mental retardation, intoxication (at least of the involuntary variety). The cause of the mental incapacity might vary from one such defense to the next but the ultimate nature of the resulting incapacity was a constant. In any of

---

1. The 1967 legislation, then codified as Md.Ann.Code art. 59, § 9(a), adopted the test for criminal insanity recommended by the American Law Institute and contained in § 4.01 of the Model Penal Code. * * *

its manifestations, criminal responsibility traditionally turned and largely still turns upon the difference between a mind doli capax (capable of malice or criminal intent) and a mind doli incapax (incapable of malice or criminal intent). Capability or capacity might be eroded in various ways but the ultimate quality of the required mental capacity itself was unchanging. * * *

Hence, we tentatively advance the traditional M'Naghten test as pertinent to our present review of an adjudication of juvenile delinquency in the Circuit Court for Baltimore City. For the moment, however, let Daniel M'Naghten retire to the wings as we bring onto the stage the contemporary players.

THE PRESENT CASE

The juvenile appellant, Devon T., was charged with committing an act which, if committed by an adult, would have constituted the crime of possession of heroin with intent to distribute. In the Circuit Court for Baltimore City, Judge Roger W. Brown found that Devon was delinquent. The heart of the case against Devon was that when on May 25, 1989, Devon was directed to empty his pockets by the security guard at the Booker T. Washington Middle School, under the watchful eye of the Assistant Principal, the search produced a brown bag containing twenty zip-lock pink plastic bags which, in turn, contained heroin. * * *

THE INFANCY DEFENSE GENERALLY

At the time of the offense, Devon was 13 years, 10 months, and 2 weeks of age. He timely raised the infancy defense. * * *

The case law and the academic literature alike conceptualize the infancy defense as but an instance of the broader phenomenon of a defense based upon lack of moral responsibility or capacity. The criminal law generally will only impose its retributive or deterrent sanctions upon those who are morally blameworthy—those who know they are doing wrong but nonetheless persist in their wrongdoing.

After several centuries of pondering the criminal capacity of children and experimenting with various cut-off ages, the Common Law settled upon its current resolution of the problem by late Tudor and early Stuart times. As explained by LaFave & Scott, *Criminal Law*, (2d ed. 1986), at 398, the resolution was fairly simple:

> "At common law, children under the age of seven are conclusively presumed to be without criminal capacity, those who have reached the age of fourteen are treated as fully responsible, while as to those between the ages of seven and fourteen there is a rebuttable presumption of criminal incapacity."

The authors make clear that infancy was an instance of criminal capacity generally:

> "The early common law infancy defense was based upon an unwillingness to punish those thought to be incapable of forming

criminal intent and not of an age where the threat of punishment could serve as a deterrent." * * *

Clark & Marshall, *A Treatise on the Law of Crimes,* (6th Wing. ed. 1958), emphasizes that the mental quality that is the *sine qua non* of criminal responsibility is the capacity to distinguish right from wrong. * * *

The reasoning behind the rule is made very clear, at 391:

> "A child is not criminally responsible unless he is old enough, and intelligent enough, to be capable of entertaining a criminal intent; and to be capable of entertaining a criminal intent he must be capable of distinguishing between right and wrong as to the particular act."

Walkover, *The Infancy Defense in the New Juvenile Court,* 31 UCLA L.Rev. 503, 507 (1984), distills the rationale to a single sentence:

> "The infancy defense was an essential component of the common law limitation of punishment to the blameworthy." * * *

THE INFANCY DEFENSE IN JUVENILE COURT

With the creation shortly after the turn of the present century of juvenile courts in America, diverting many youthful offenders from criminal courts into equity and other civil courts, the question arose as to whether the infancy defense had any pertinence to a juvenile delinquency adjudication. Under the initially prevailing philosophy that the State was acting in delinquency cases as *parens patriae* (sovereign parent of the country), the State was perceived to be not the retributive punisher of the child for its misdeeds but the paternalistic guardian of the child for its own best interests. Under such a regime, the moral responsibility or blameworthiness of the child was of no consequence. Morally responsible or not, the child was in apparent need of the State's rehabilitative intervention and the delinquency adjudication was but the avenue for such intervention.

This was the philosophy that persuaded this Court * * * to forbear from extending the defense of infancy to juvenile court proceedings as an inapposite criterion. * * *

Over the course of the century, however, buffeted by unanticipated urban deterioration and staggering case loads, the reforming vision of * * * the * * * founders of the movement faded. Although continuing to stress rehabilitation over retribution more heavily than did the adult criminal courts, delinquency adjudications nonetheless took on, in practice if not in theory, many of the attributes of junior varsity criminal trials. The Supreme Court, in * * * acknowledged this slow but inexorable transformation of the juvenile court apparatus into one with increasingly penal overtones. It ultimately guaranteed, therefore, a juvenile charged with delinquency most of the due process protections afforded an adult charged with crime. * * *

In terms of the applicability of the infancy defense to delinquency proceedings, the implications of the new dispensation are clear. A finding of delinquency, unlike other proceedings in a juvenile court, unmistakably connotes some degree of blameworthiness and unmistakably exposes the delinquent to, whatever the gloss, the possibility of unpleasant sanctions. Clearly, the juvenile would have as an available defense to the delinquency charge 1) the fact that he was too criminally insane to have known that what he did was wrong, 2) that he was too mentally retarded to have known that what he did was wrong, or 3) that he was too involuntarily intoxicated through no fault of his own to have known that what he did was wrong. It would be inconceivable that he could be found blameworthy and suffer sanctions, notwithstanding precisely the same lack of understanding and absence of moral accountability, simply because the cognitive defect was caused by infancy rather than by one of the other incapacitating mechanisms. * * *

In a juvenile delinquency adjudication, * * * the defense of infancy is now indisputably available in precisely the same manner as it is available in a criminal trial. * * *

What Is Criminal Capacity in an Infant?

Before the juvenile master, the appellant timely raised the infancy defense. One party or the other (it matters not which) introduced the undisputed fact * * * that at the time of the allegedly delinquent act, Devon was 13 years, 10 months, and 2 weeks of age. Thus, the issue of mental incapacity due to infancy was properly generated and before the court.

On that issue, Devon initially had the benefit of presumptive incapacity. The presumption having been generated, the State had the burdens (of both production and persuasion) of rebutting that presumption. * * *

To overcome the presumption of incapacity, then, what precisely was that quality of Devon's mind as to which the State was required to produce legally sufficient evidence? It was required to produce evidence permitting the reasonable inference that Devon—the Ghost of M'Naghten speaks:—"at the time of doing the act knew the difference between right and wrong." * * *

The analogy between incapacity due to infancy and incapacity due to insanity, mental retardation, or involuntary intoxication has lost some of its original symmetry to the extent that those latter incapacities have been broadened (directly or indirectly) to include a volitional as well as a cognitive component. The infancy defense retains its exclusive concern with the cognitive element. * * *

In short, when Devon walked around the Booker T. Washington Middle School with twenty zip-lock bags of heroin, apparently for sale or other distribution, could Devon pass the M'Naghten test? Was there legally sufficient data before him to permit Judge Brown to infer that

Devon knew the difference between right and wrong and knew, moreover, that what he was doing was wrong?

THE LEGAL SUFFICIENCY OF THE EVIDENCE TO PROVE DEVON'S KNOWLEDGE OF RIGHT AND WRONG

As we turn to the legal sufficiency of the evidence, it is important to know that the only mental quality we are probing is the cognitive capacity to distinguish right from wrong. Other aspects of Devon's mental and psychological make-up, such as his scholastic attainments, his I.Q., his social maturity, his societal adjustment, his basic personality, etc., might well require evidentiary input from psychologists, from parents, from teachers or other school authorities, etc. On knowledge of the difference between right and wrong, however, the general case law, as well as the inherent logic of the situation, has established that that particular psychic phenomenon may sometimes permissibly be inferred from the very circumstances of the criminal or delinquent act itself. * * *

On the issue of Devon's knowledge of the difference between right and wrong, if all we knew in this case were that Devon's age was at some indeterminate point between his seventh birthday and his fourteenth birthday, the State's case would be substantially weaker than it is now. The evidence before Judge Brown that Devon, at the time of the allegedly delinquent act, was 13 years, 10 months, and 2 weeks of age was substantial, although not quite sufficient, proof of his cognitive capacity.

The applicable common law on doli incapax with relation to the infancy defense establishes that on the day before their seventh birthday, no persons possess cognitive capacity. (0 per cent). It also establishes that on the day of their fourteenth birthday, all persons (at least as far as age is concerned) possess cognitive capacity. (100 per cent). On the time scale between the day of the seventh birthday and the day before the fourteenth birthday, the percentage of persons possessing such capacity steadily increases. The statistical probability is that on the day of the seventh birthday, at most a tiny fraction of one per cent will possess cognitive capacity. Conversely, on the day before the fourteenth birthday, only a tiny fraction of one per cent will lack such cognitive capacity. Assuming a steady rate of climb,[6] the midpoint where fifty per cent of persons will lack

---

6. The climb in cognitive capacity from the seventh birthday through the fourteenth birthday, of course, has not been charted with actuarial precision by the social sciences. The rise in maturity of the group as a whole may be a linear progression at a regular rate of climb. There may, however, be plateaus interrupting the upward progression. There might even be a parabolic curve, concentrating much of the statistical advance of the group as a whole into the last year or two rather than having it spread evenly across the course of the seven years.

Whatever the configuration of the maturity chart, however, Devon had moved 98.2 per cent of the way, on the timeline of his life, from his seventh birthday to his fourteenth birthday. Assuming a regular linear progression, simply for illustrative purposes, that would mean that of all persons in Devon's particular age group, 98.2 per cent would be expected to possess cognitive capacity and 1.8 per cent would be expected to lack it. The State's burden, therefore, would not be to prove that Devon was precociously above average but only to satisfy the court that Devon fell within the upper 98.2 per cent of his age group and not within the subnormal 1.8 per cent of it.

In any event, whatever the statistical rate of progress or the maturity curve might be, Devon had moved 98.2 per cent of the way from its beginning point to its terminus.

cognitive capacity and fifty per cent will possess it would be at 10 years and 6 months of age. That is the scale on which we must place Devon.

We stress that the burden in that regard, notwithstanding the probabilities, was nonetheless on the State. * * * The fact that the quantum of proof necessary to overcome presumptive incapacity diminishes in substantially the same ratio as the infant's age increases only serves to lessen the State's burden, not to eliminate it. * * *

We hold that the State successfully carried that burden. A minor factor, albeit of some weight, was that Devon was essentially at or near grade level in school. The report of the master, received and reviewed by Judge Brown, established that at the time of the offense, Devon was in middle school, embracing grades 6, 7, and 8. The report of the master, indeed, revealed that Devon had flunked the sixth grade twice, with truancy and lack of motivation as apparent causes. That fact nonetheless revealed that Devon had initially reached the sixth grade while still eleven years of age. That would tend to support his probable inclusion in the large majority of his age group rather than in a small and subnormal minority of it.

We note that the transcript of the hearing before the juvenile master shows that the master was in a position to observe first-hand Devon's receiving of legal advice from his lawyer, his acknowledgment of his understanding of it, and his acting upon it. His lawyer explained that he had a right to remain silent and that the master would not infer guilt from his exercise of that right. He acknowledged understanding that right. His lawyer also advised him of his right to testify but informed him that both the assistant state's attorney and the judge might question him about the delinquent act. Devon indicated that he wished to remain silent and say nothing. Although reduced to relatively simple language, the exchange with respect to the risk of self-incrimination and the privilege against self-incrimination forms a predicate from which an observer might infer some knowledge on Devon's part of the significance of incrimination. * * *

The transcript that was received and reviewed by Judge Brown revealed yet a further exchange between the juvenile master and Devon, also not without some significance. After Devon and his companion Edward had already been adjudicated delinquent and when no further risk of incrimination inhered, the master, prior to disposition, asked each of the two what, if anything, he would like to say and was met by "stonewalling" * * *. This inferable allegiance to the Underworld's "Code of Silence" suggests that Devon and Edward were no mere babies caught up in a web they did not comprehend. The permitted inference, rather, was that they were fully conscious of the ongoing war between lawful authority and those who flout it and had deliberately chosen to adhere to the latter camp.

We turn, most significantly, to the circumstances of the criminal act itself. * * *

* * * The case broke when a grandmother, concerned enough to have had her own live-in grandson institutionalized, complained to the authorities at Booker T. Washington Middle School that several of her grandson's classmates were being truant on a regular basis and were using her home, while she was out working, as the "hide out" from which to sell drugs. * * * Children who are unaware that what they are doing is wrong have no need to hide out or to conceal their activities. *

The most significant circumstance was the very nature of the criminal activity in which Devon engaged. It was not mere possession of heroin. It was possession of twenty packets of heroin with the intent to distribute. This was the finding of the court and it was supported by the evidence. There were no needle marks or other indications of personal use on Devon's body. * * *

We hold that the surrounding circumstances here were legally sufficient to overcome the slight residual weight of the presumption of incapacity due to infancy. * * *

NOTES AND QUESTIONS

1. To what extent should a youth be tried in an adult court, rather than a juvenile court, and, if convicted, be incarcerated in a prison, rather then held in a juvenile facility where rehabilitation can be undertaken? An increasing number of states—now more than thirty—permit prosecution of juveniles (even those presumptively incapable of committing an offense at common law) in adult courts, thus making them potentially subject to incarceration in adult prisons. Richard E. Redding, *Juvenile Transfer Laws: An Effective Deterrent to Delinquency?*, Juvenile Justice Bulletin, August 2008 (U.S. Dep't. of Justice, Office of Justice Programs). As a result, the United States Supreme Court has been called upon to determine whether incarcerative sentences of juveniles, although permissible if imposed on an adult, violate the Eighth Amendment bar on cruel and unusual punishment. The Court has held that, just as current standards of decency bar the execution of murderers who were under the age of eighteen at the time of the homicide (see p. 378), the Constitution prohibits a sentence of life imprisonment without possibility of parole for a nonhomicide crime committed by a youth under the age of eighteen. Graham v. Florida, 560 U.S. ___, 130 S.Ct. 2011, 176 L.Ed.2d 825 (2010).

2. Staci A. Gruber & Deborah A. Yurgelun–Todd, *Neurobiology and the Law: A Role in Juvenile Justice?*, 3 Ohio St. J. Crim. L. 321, 331 (2006):

> Based on neurobiological data alone, it is clear that children and adolescents are different both structurally and functionally from adults. In addition to documentable alterations which change during the trajectory of normal development, data from recent investigations provide evidence that brain maturation continues well past adolescence. Accordingly, the developmental factors which influence decision-making in adolescents may result in choices which are suggestive of cortical immaturity, poor judgment and impulsivity.

3. Elizabeth S. Scott & Laurence Steinberg, *Blaming Youth*, 81 Texas L. Rev. 799, 822–823, 825 (2003):

> Choice theorists adopt a model of culpability based on rationality and volition, positing the responsible moral agent as one who has the capacity to make a rational choice and a "fair opportunity" to choose the law-abiding course. * * *

> Character theory holds that criminal blameworthiness is premised on an implicit but powerful inference that the wrongful act is the product of the actor's bad character. * * * [T]he most defensible version of character theory * * * holds that the culpability of the criminal act varies depending not simply on the quality of his choice, but on its meaning as an expression of the actor's moral character. * * *

> * * * [A]nalysis of adolescent culpability within either of these theoretical frameworks points to the conclusion that young actors are less culpable than are typical adults. * * * [Y]oung law violators are poor decisionmakers with more restricted opportunities to avoid criminal choices than are adults. [Similarly,] * * * ordinary adolescents, whose identity is in flux and character unformed, are less culpable than typical adult criminals.

E. NEW DEFENSES?

1. EUTHANASIA

INTRODUCTION

- "A 63–year–old mother has been charged with shooting two of her [adult] sons as they lay side-by-side in a nursing home, their brains so wracked with the same hereditary disease that had killed their father that they were reduced to incoherent mumbling. Investigators said that after the shootings, * * * the woman, Carol Carr, calmly sat on a couch in the lobby and waited to be arrested." *Mother Apologizes For Killing Ill Sons*, New York Times, June 11, 2002, at A16 (Associated Press). Carr was indicted on two counts of murder. As part of a plea bargain, she pleaded guilty to assisted suicide, was sentenced to five years imprisonment, but was released after 21 months.

- An 86–year–old "devoted husband" smothered to death his Alzheimer-suffering, stroke-deteriorated wife of fifty-seven years in a London hospital, where she was receiving care for severe stomach pains. Originally charged with murder, he plead guilty to manslaughter. The judge, characterizing the man as "thoughtful, kind, and honest," imposed a nine-month suspended sentence. *Mercy for Husband, 86, Who Killed His Sick Wife*, Daily Mail, Oct. 11, 2008, at p. 40.

- "A doctor and two nurses were arrested Tuesday after the Louisiana attorney general accused them of using lethal injection to kill four elderly patients in a New Orleans hospital * * * in the aftermath of Hurricane Katrina." Adam Nossiter and Shaila De-wan, *Patient Deaths In New Orleans Bring Arrests*, New York Times, July 19, 2006, at A1. According to other news accounts, overheated elderly patients were dying around the doctors, medicine was running low, there was no electricity, chaos reigned, and nobody was coming to save the patients. A grand jury refused to indict the doctor and nurses. For more on the story, see Sheri Fink, *The Deadly Choices at Memorial*, N.Y. Times Magazine, Aug. 30, 2009, at 28.

● "The long, sorrowful struggle over Terri Schiavo's life ended Thursday morning when she died in her hospice bed almost two weeks after the removal of her feeding tubes, her parents and siblings absent, the husband they reviled at her side." Abby Goodnough, *Schiavo Dies, Ending Bitter Case Over Feeding Tube*, New York Times, April 1, 2005, at A1.

● Setting off a worldwide debate, the Netherlands legalized euthanasia for terminally ill people by physicians who obey strict rules. *Dutch Legalize Euthanasia, The First Such National Law*, New York Times, April 1, 2002, at A9.

● In 1994, Oregon voters enacted by ballot initiative the "Death With Dignity Act," which legalizes physician-assisted suicide for competent, terminally-ill patients. Through early 2009, 401 persons had used the law to hasten their death. In 2008, Washington voters passed a similar initiative. In 2009, at least 36 terminally ill persons took lethal injections prescribed by doctors pursuant to the new law. William Yardley, *At Least 36 Died in Washington State in 2009 Under New Assisted Suicide Law*, N.Y. Times, Mar. 5, 2010, at A10. And, in Montana, applying state homicide laws but avoiding a constitutional ruling, the state supreme court held that physicians may not be held liable under the state's homicide laws for providing aid in dying to a mentally competent, terminally ill patient. Baxter v. State, 354 Mont. 234, 224 P.3d 1211 (2009).

● According to an Associated Press–Ipsos poll in June 2007, 68% of Americans believe there are circumstances in which a patient should be allowed to die; 48% believe it should be legal for doctors to give terminally ill patients fatal drugs, while 44% say that such action should remain illegal. Cary McMullen, *When Life Ebbs Away*, The Ledger, July 8, 2007, at A1.

Euthanasia is not a formal defense in the United States. You may remember, however, that we have already seen cases this semester that seem to implicate euthanasia. In one case, doctors ended life support on a patient in a chronic vegetative state, much as occurred more recently with Terri Schiavo. The court in that earlier case (p. 142) characterized the events as an omission (failure to provide medical treatment), and ruled that the physicians owed no duty to provide life-extending hydration and nourishment to their patient. Perhaps the court reached this outcome because it felt that euthanasia should be a defense. In another case (p. 261), a loving son shot to death his seriously ill father in a hospital; his conviction of first-degree murder was affirmed. What are we to make of all of this? Should euthanasia be a defense, as it is in the Netherlands? If so, is *justifiable* or *excusable* homicide?

Then, consider the well publicized actions of Dr. Jack Kevorkian who assisted more than 130 persons commit suicide in Michigan. At early English common law, suicide was a crime. Those who committed the act suffered an ignominious burial and forfeiture of their property. And, although suicide is no longer an offense, many states prohibit suicide *assistance*. Should this be?

The following materials focus on the legal and moral issues relating to euthanasia and suicide assistance. The Canadian case with which we begin deals with euthanasia in tragic circumstances. As euthanasia is not a defense in Canada, the defense sought to bring the homicide within the recognized defense of necessity.

LATIMER v. THE QUEEN

Supreme Court of Canada, 2001.
1 S.C.R. 3, 193 D.L.R. (4th) 577.

BY THE COURT:

This appeal arises from the death of Tracy Latimer, a 12–year–old girl who had a severe form of cerebral palsy. Her father, Robert Latimer, took her life some seven years ago. He was found guilty of second degree murder. * * * [Latimer was sentenced to life in prison, with a mandatory minimum term of imprisonment of ten years.]

The law has a long history of difficult cases. We recognize the questions that arise in Mr. Latimer's case are the sort that have divided Canadians and sparked a national discourse. This judgment will not end that discourse.

Mr. Latimer perceived his daughter and family to be in a difficult and trying situation. It is apparent from the evidence in this case that he faced challenges of the sort most Canadians can only imagine. His care of his daughter for many years was admirable. His decision to end his daughter's life was an error in judgment. The taking of another life represents the most serious crime in our criminal law.

I. FACTS

The appellant, Robert Latimer, farmed in Wilkie, Saskatchewan. His 12–year–old daughter, Tracy, suffered a severe form of cerebral palsy. She was quadriplegic and her physical condition rendered her immobile. She was bedridden for much of the time. Her condition was a permanent one, caused by neurological damage at the time of her birth. Tracy was said to have the mental capacity of a four-month-old baby, and she could communicate only by means of facial expressions, laughter and crying. She was completely dependent on others for her care. Tracy suffered seizures despite the medication she took. It was thought she experienced a great deal of pain, and the pain could not be reduced by medication since the pain medication conflicted with her anti-epileptic medication and her difficulty in swallowing. Tracy experienced five to six seizures daily. She had to be spoon-fed, and her lack of nutrients caused weight loss.

There was evidence that Tracy could have been fed with a feeding tube into her stomach, an option that would have improved her nutrition and health, and that might also have allowed for more effective pain medication to be administered. The Latimers rejected the feeding-tube option as being intrusive and as representing the first step on a path to preserving Tracy's life artificially.

Tracy had a serious disability, but she was not terminally ill. Her doctors anticipated that she would have to undergo repeated surgeries, her breathing difficulties had increased, but her life was not in its final stages.

Tracy enjoyed music, bonfires, being with her family and the circus. She liked to play music on a radio, which she could use with a special button. Tracy could apparently recognize family members and she would express joy at seeing them. Tracy also loved being rocked gently by her parents.

Tracy underwent numerous surgeries in her short lifetime. In 1990, surgery tried to balance the muscles around her pelvis. In 1992, it was used to reduce the abnormal curvature in her back.

Like the majority of totally involved, quadriparetic children with cerebral palsy, Tracy had developed scoliosis, an abnormal curvature and rotation in the back, necessitating surgery to implant metal rods to support her spine. While it was a successful procedure, further problems developed in Tracy's right hip: it became dislocated and caused her considerable pain.

Tracy was scheduled to undergo further surgery on November 19, 1993. This was to deal with her dislocated hip and, it was hoped, to lessen her constant pain. The procedure involved removing her upper thigh bone, which would leave her lower leg loose without any connecting bone; it would be held in place only by muscle and tissue. The anticipated recovery period for this surgery was one year.

The Latimers were told that this procedure would cause pain, and the doctors involved suggested that further surgery would be required in the future to relieve the pain emanating from various joints in Tracy's body. According to the appellant's wife, Laura Latimer, further surgery was perceived as mutilation. As a result, Robert Latimer formed the view that his daughter's life was not worth living.

In the weeks leading up to Tracy's death, the Latimers looked into the option of placing Tracy in a group home in North Battleford. She had lived there between July and October 1993, just prior to her death, while her mother was pregnant. The Latimers applied to place Tracy in the home in

October, but later concluded they were not interested in permanently placing her in that home at that time.

On October 12, 1993, after learning that the doctors wished to perform this additional surgery, the appellant decided to take his daughter's life. On Sunday, October 24, 1993, while his wife and Tracy's siblings were at church, Robert Latimer carried Tracy to his pickup truck, seated her in the cab, and inserted a hose from the truck's exhaust pipe into the cab. She died from the carbon monoxide.[1] * * *

Mr. Latimer has been convicted of murder twice in this case. He was initially charged with first degree murder and convicted by a jury of second degree murder. * * * It turned out that the prosecutor had interfered with the jury selection process. The Crown conceded that a new trial could not be avoided. In the second trial, Mr. Latimer was again convicted of second degree murder, and it is from that conviction that this appeal arises. * * *

IV. Issues * * *

1. Should the jury have been entitled to consider the defence of necessity? * * *

V. Analysis * * *

(1) *The Availability of the Defence of Necessity*

(a) *The Three Requirements for the Defence of Necessity*

* * * The leading case on the defence of necessity is *Perka v. The Queen*, [1984] 2 S.C.R. 232, 28 B.C.L.R. (2d) 205. [Justice] Dickson * * * outlined the rationale for the defence:

> It rests on a realistic assessment of human weakness, recognizing that a liberal and humane criminal law cannot hold people to the strict obedience of laws in emergency situations where normal human instincts, whether of self-preservation or of altruism, overwhelmingly impel disobedience. The objectivity of the criminal law is preserved; such acts are still wrongful, but in the circumstances they are excusable. Praise is indeed not bestowed, but pardon is.

[Justice] Dickson insisted that the defence of necessity be restricted to those rare cases in which true involuntariness is present. * * * Were the criteria for the defence loosened * * *, some fear * * * that necessity would very easily become simply a mask for anarchy.

Perka outlined three elements that must be present for the defence of necessity. * * *

---

1. Some additional facts: Tracy was born "clinically dead" and was resuscitated. During her life she was incontinent and often vomited after feeding; consequently, the family kept a bucket near her while she was being fed. Robert actively participated in Tracy's care and nurturing. Laura and Robert cried together in bed shortly before the fatal act; Laura said that she wished she "could call a Dr. Kevorkian" [to assist in Tracy's death]. Nonetheless, the plan to kill Tracy was entirely Robert's; he never told Laura of his plan. Veronica Henderson, *The School Bus to Wilkie and the Walk to Colonus: Latimer, Antigone and the Role for Mercy in Sentencing*, 14 Windsor Rev. Legal & Social Issues 53 (2002).

To begin, there must be an urgent situation of clear and imminent peril. * * * It is not enough that the peril is foreseeable or likely; it must be on the verge of transpiring and virtually certain to occur. * * *

The second requirement for necessity is that there must be no reasonable legal alternative to disobeying the law. *Perka* proposed these questions: "Given that the accused had to act, could he nevertheless realistically have acted to avoid the peril or prevent the harm, without breaking the law? *Was there a legal way out?*" If there was a reasonable legal alternative to breaking the law, there is no necessity. * * *

The third requirement is that there be proportionality between the harm inflicted and the harm avoided. The harm inflicted must not be disproportionate to the harm the accused sought to avoid. * * *

Evaluating proportionality can be difficult. It may be easy to conclude that there is no proportionality in some cases, like the example given in *Perka* of the person who blows up a city to avoid breaking a finger. Where proportionality can quickly be dismissed, it makes sense for a trial judge to do so and rule out the defence of necessity before considering the other requirements for necessity. But most situations fall into a grey area that requires a difficult balancing of harms. * * *

(b) The Application of the Requirements for Necessity in This Case

The inquiry here is not whether the defence of necessity should in fact *excuse* Mr. Latimer's actions, but whether the jury should have been left to consider this defence. The correct test on that point is whether there is an air of reality to the defence. * * *

For the necessity defence, the trial judge must be satisfied that there is evidence sufficient to give an air of reality to each of the three requirements. If the trial judge concludes that there is no air of reality to any one of the three requirements, the defence of necessity should not be left to the jury.

In this case, there was no air of reality to the three requirements of necessity.

The first requirement is imminent peril. It is not met in this case. * * * [W]e are dealing not with an emergency but with an obstinate and long-standing state of affairs. Tracy's proposed surgery did not pose an imminent threat to her life, nor did her medical condition. In fact, Tracy's health might have improved had the Latimers not rejected the option of relying on a feeding tube. * * *

The second requirement for the necessity defence is that the accused had no reasonable legal alternative to breaking the law. In this case, there is no air of reality to the proposition that the appellant had no reasonable legal alternative to killing his daughter. He had at least one reasonable legal alternative: he could have struggled on, with what was unquestionably a difficult situation, by helping Tracy to live and by minimizing her pain as much as possible. The appellant might have done so by using a feeding tube to improve her health and allow her to take more effective pain medication, or he might have relied on the group home that Tracy stayed at just before her death. The appellant may well have thought the prospect of struggling on unbearably sad and demanding. It was a human response that this alternative was unappealing. But it was a reasonable legal alternative that the law requires a person to pursue before he can claim the defence of necessity. * * *

The third requirement for the necessity defence is proportionality; it requires the trial judge to consider, as a question of law rather than fact, whether the harm avoided was proportionate to the harm inflicted. It is difficult, at the conceptual level, to imagine a circumstance in which the proportionality requirement could be met for a homicide. We leave open, if and until it arises, the question of whether the proportionality requirement could be met in a homicide situation. * * * The famous case of *R. v. Dudley and Stephens* [pp. 49 and 553, supra] involving cannibalism on the high seas, is often cited as establishing the unavailability of the defence of necessity for homicide, although the case is not conclusive * * *. American jurisdictions are divided on this question, with a number of them denying the necessity defence for murder. The American Model Penal Code proposes that the defence of necessity would be available for homicide.

Assuming for the sake of analysis only that necessity could provide a defence to homicide, * * * [t]he harm avoided in the appellant's situation was, compared to death, completely disproportionate. The harm inflicted in this case was ending a life; that harm was immeasurably more serious than the pain resulting from Tracy's operation which Mr. Latimer sought to avoid. Killing a person—in order to relieve the suffering produced by a medically manageable physical or mental condition—is not a proportionate response to the harm represented by the non-life-threatening suffering resulting from that condition.

We conclude that there was no air of reality to any of the three requirements for necessity. * * *

Appeal dismissed.

NOTES AND QUESTIONS

1. *Follow-up.* Robert Latimer was released from prison on supervised parole in March 2008. One condition of his parole is that he may not "have responsibility for, or make decisions for, seriously disabled persons." *Latimer's Parole Extended*, Calgary Sun, Mar. 20, 2009, at p. 26. Latimer has a website, <http://www.robertlatimer.net>.

2. Did *Perka*—and, here, *Latimer*—view necessity as a justification or excuse defense? In determining what the elements of the defense should be, should it matter whether "necessity" is a justification or excuse?

3. What result in *Latimer* in a Model Penal Code jurisdiction? Consider Sections 3.02 and 2.09.

4. In thinking about euthanasia—the underlying and unstated issue in *Latimer*—it is helpful to distinguish between various forms of so-called

"mercy killing." Euthanasia can be passive (purposely omitting conduct that would save a life) or active (performing a killing act). In turn, either form of euthanasia can be voluntary (the person who died requested the omission or act) or involuntary (without consent). *Latimer* involved involuntary active euthanasia, the most controversial form. In your view, are *any* of these forms of euthanasia morally appropriate? If so, should the law recognize an explicit defense for euthanasia, and how would it be defined? Consider the following Notes as you think about these questions.

5. *Euthanasia versus suicide assistance.* However you ultimately answer the questions raised in the last Note, would your answer be the same for suicide assistance? Is there any moral difference to be drawn between, for example, active voluntary euthanasia and "merely" furnishing a person the means by which she takes her own life? For example, Dr. Jack Kevorkian devised a suicide-assistance machine: He would insert an intravenous tube into the patient's vein; the patient would then push a button, which injected lethal poison through the tubing into the vein. What difference does it make—legally or morally—if the "patient" pushes the button of the Kevorkian machine or Kevorkian pushes it himself because the "patient" is too weak to do it?

In one case, the patient pushed the button, but the poison did not enter her vein because of a problem with the tubing, so Kevorkian exerted pressure on the intravenous tubing to force the poison through the tubing into the individual's vein. As a matter of law, is that suicide assistance or murder?

Query: If you believe suicide assistance should be illegal, should it also be illegal for a person to attempt to commit suicide? If not, why not?

6. *Euthanasia, suicide assistance, and the Constitution.* Whatever you might personally believe about the morality of euthanasia or suicide assistance, is there a constitutional basis for permitting it in some circumstances? Does a person who is in great pain or terminally ill have a constitutional right to die? If so, might the person who helps her die have a constitutional right to assist in that goal either by furnishing the means for the death (suicide assistance) or by killing her if she cannot do it herself?

In People v. Kevorkian, 248 Mich.App. 373, 639 N.W.2d 291 (2001), Kevorkian administered a lethal drug to Thomas Youk. Youk, 52–years–old, was suffering in the final stages of amyotrophic lateral sclerosis (ALS), so-called Lou Gehrig's disease. He was physically unable to commit suicide, so he signed a consent form affirming his wish for Kevorkian to take his life. Kevorkian videotaped the procedure of injecting lethal potassium chloride into Youk's vein, and later discussed his actions with Mike Wallace on *60 Minutes.* Kevorkian was later convicted of second-degree murder. He sought to overturn the conviction on constitutional grounds. Here is what the court said on this matter:

> At the outset it is important to understand the nature of defendant's constitutional claims. The best way to do this is to state clearly the constitutional arguments that defendant does *not* raise.

> First, defendant does *not* ask us to hold that he acted properly in furtherance of [Youk]s] * * * right to refuse life-sustaining medical

treatment. In *Cruzan v. Director, Missouri Dep't of Health*, [497 U.S. 261 (1990)], the United States Supreme Court "assumed that the United States Constitution would grant a competent person a constitutionally protected right to refuse lifesaving hydration and nutrition," likely under a Fourteenth Amendment due process liberty interest analysis. More recently, in [*Washington v.*] *Glucksberg*, [521 U.S. 702 (1997)], the Court strengthened the constitutional basis for the *Cruzan* decision, interpreting *Cruzan* as holding that "the right to refuse unwanted medical treatment was so rooted in our history, tradition, and practice as to require special protection under the Fourteenth Amendment." Here, defendant does not, and could not, rely on *Cruzan*; factually, this case does not involve removing life support. * * *

Here, defendant [also] makes no attempt to assert that he was engaged in assisted suicide when he injected Youk with potassium chloride, causing his death. Rather, he asserts that * * * the right to be free from unbearable pain and suffering caused by a medical condition is inherently part of the liberty interests secured by the Fourteenth Amendment [Due Process Clause] * * *. Defendant then contends that he cannot be prosecuted for "aiding in Thomas Youk's assertion of his constitutional right to be free from intolerable pain and suffering." Although defendant's appellate counsel has carefully avoided using the words, * * * the record indicates that defendant was quite specific when describing his actions; he said he was engaged in "active euthanasia" and the consent form that Youk signed directly refers to such active euthanasia.

* * * In a nutshell, and using his own terminology, defendant asks us to legalize euthanasia. * * *

Defendant starts with the proposition that there is a right to privacy that is part of the liberty interest protected by the Fourteenth Amendment * * *. He then asserts that the "intensely personal and private right of a patient to be free from intolerable and irremediable suffering" is either part of or similar to this privacy right. * * *

It is one thing to assert, as defendant does, that there is a large body of case law suggesting that due process sometimes relies on the right to privacy to protect fundamental liberty interests. It is quite another thing, however, to conclude that the right to privacy encompasses euthanasia. As Justice Jackson once pointedly noted, the enduring nature of precedent gives judicial opinions a force all their own. [Justice Jackson wrote:]

> The principle then lies about like a loaded weapon. * * * Every repetition imbeds that principle more deeply in our law and thinking and expands it to new purposes. All who observe the work of courts are familiar with what Judge Cardozo described as "the tendency of a principle to expand itself to the limit of its logic."

Defendant urges us to pick up the loaded weapon of the right to privacy cases. * * *

We decline, however, to pick up this loaded weapon for three basic reasons. First, we can find no meaningful precedent for expanding the right to privacy to include a right to commit euthanasia so that an individual can be free from intolerable and irremediable suffering. * * *

Here, expanding the right to privacy would begin, as the steps in the progression of defendant's argument supporting voluntary euthanasia clearly indicate, the slide down the slippery slope toward [involuntary] euthanasia. * * *

Second, we conclude that by expanding the right to privacy as defendant suggests, we would, to a great extent, place the matter outside the arenas of public debate and legislative action. * * * If society is to recognize a right to be free from intolerable and irremediable suffering, it should do so through the action of the majority of the legislature, whose role it is to set social policy, or by action of the people through ballot initiative. * * *

Third, we observe that by expanding the right of privacy to include a right to commit euthanasia in order to end intolerable and irremediable suffering we would inevitably involve the judiciary in deciding questions that are simply beyond its capacity. There is no court that can answer the question of how *much* pain, or perception of pain by a third party, is necessary before the suffering becomes intolerable and irremediable. The role of the courts is to serve neither as physicians nor as theologians.

7. *Voluntary euthanasia: sanctity and quality of life arguments.* Most of the arguments relating to voluntary active euthanasia are similar to the arguments made in regard to suicide assistance. Opponents of euthanasia make "sanctity of life" arguments; defenders of euthanasia focus on "quality of life" considerations. Professor Philip Peters has articulated (although he does not endorse) the basic claim of those who assert that a state has an overriding interest in protecting the sanctity of life:

> For some people, especially those with a deep faith in God, life itself may have an intrinsic value that makes intentionally ending it morally wrong, at least in the absence of an equally compelling moral excuse. This view may reflect a belief that all humans, like Job, have a responsibility to live out their lives and that they lack the authority or the capacity to judge either the value of their own lives or the value of the lives of their wards. * * *

> Most importantly, this moral mandate partly explains the past criminality of suicide. At common law, suicide was *malum in se,* like murder, an offense against God and nature. Self-destruction was unnatural because it was contrary to the instinct for self-preservation. Suicide offended God because it breached God's proscription "Thou shalt not kill." It usurped God's right to end life. Suicide also cheapened life by treating it as alienable.

Disentangling the state's interest in the sanctity or intrinsic value of life from other policies served by the state's interest in the preservation of life is difficult, and, perhaps, a little unfair. The phrase "sanctity of life" itself has many possible meanings. At its core lies the idea that all life is equally valuable and worthy of respect regardless of age, handicap, race, or other attribute. In this respect, it constitutes a widely shared

liberal ideal, demanding protection of the vulnerable against error and
abuse. * * * But sanctity of life objections often run deeper than fears of
error or extension. * * * Under this view, a preference for death is itself
morally wrong and the state may legitimately refuse to condone it. Even
though this viewpoint may be interwoven with concerns about abuse and
extension, it seems appropriate to consider the moral objection in isolation from its related concerns.

Philip G. Peters, Jr., *The State's Interest in the Preservation of Life: From
Quinlan to Cruzan,* 50 Ohio St.L.J. 891, 951–52 (1989).

The quality-of-life argument for euthanasia often runs as follows:

> For the severely, irreversibly ill, a rational choice for euthanasia
> promotes control over the end of life. At stake * * * is a "matter of vital,
> exclusive importance: the timing, manner and circumstance of one's
> death." The choice has practical, philosophical and spiritual ingredients.

> Opponents of euthanasia often emphasize the spiritual nature of
> their views, rooting their opposition in the idea that life is a gift of God.
> The cliche about "playing God" when making life and death decisions is
> meant to restrain decisions favoring death. But it is wrong to leave the
> spiritual ground to euthanasia opponents. Decisions about death are
> inherently philosophical and, for believers in God, religious. Believers
> who contemplate euthanasia must necessarily resolve for themselves
> spiritual questions as to life's meaning and the proper realms of God and
> man. * * *

> Disease and its treatment rob the individual of a great deal. Some
> conditions cause a host of extreme physical effects: bones so brittle they
> easily break, severely impaired breathing, constant exhaustion, emacia-
> tion, paralysis, blindness, recurrent nausea and vomiting, persistent fever
> and inability to eat or sleep. Physical problems often come in multiples,
> with increasing bodily degradation and pain. Mental deterioration adds a
> different cluster of problems, from loss of memory and ability to perform
> everyday tasks to the inability to communicate with or even recognize
> others. Treatments for serious diseases often have their own toxic side
> effects, intensifying physical and mental suffering.

> The magnitude of psychological suffering that accompanies dire med-
> ical conditions is easily underestimated. The varied sources of psychic
> pain that grip the victim of catastrophic illness include losses of privacy,
> lifestyle and established routines; the destruction of one's sense of securi-
> ty and sense of normalcy; the painful awareness of one's former physical
> powers and present incapacities; the dreaded anticipation of future men-
> tal and physical deterioration; the loss of control over one's life and life
> plans; the unwanted dependence on machines and doctors; the loss of
> home and of social roles in the outside world brought about by hospital-
> ization; and the loss of hope, of optimism about the future, and of
> pleasure in life. For some there is the pain of knowing that one is
> destined * * * "to witness and endure a final stage not as an effective
> agent, but merely a deteriorating object." * * *

Finally, people have an interest in how they will be remembered. The manner of one's death may overshadow other facets of one's life, to the point of haunting loved ones who witness an intolerable death.

Stephen A. Newman, *Euthanasia: Orchestrating "The Last Syllable of ... Time,"* 53 U.Pitt.L.Rev. 153, 179–82 (1991).

8. *Euthanasia: slippery slopes?* Another feature of the euthanasia debate, seen also in *Kevorkian* (Note 6), concerns the "slippery slope" or "wedge principle." The concern is that even if passive euthanasia (e.g., omitting life-saving medical treatment so that a person may die) is morally permissible, its toleration will lead to acceptance of active voluntary euthanasia and, ultimately, to active *involuntary* euthanasia, as in *Latimer.* One of the richest debates in this regard took place in the 1950s with the publication of English scholar Glanville Williams's book, *The Sanctity of Life and the Criminal Law* (1957), in which he advocated legalization of voluntary euthanasia. Professor Yale Kamisar responded to Williams:

> Look, when the messenger cometh, shut the door, and hold him fast at the door; is not the sound of his master's feet behind him?[210]

> This is the "wedge principle," the "parade of horrors" objection, if you will, to voluntary euthanasia. * * * I agree with Williams that if a first step is "moral" it is moral wherever a second step may take us. The real point, however, the point that Williams sloughs, is that whether or not the first step is precarious, is perilous, is worth taking, rests in part on what the second step is likely to be.

> It is true that the "wedge" objection can always be advanced, the horrors can always be paraded. But it is no less true that on some occasions the objection is much more valid than it is on others. One reason why the "parade of horrors" cannot be too lightly dismissed in this particular instance is that Miss Voluntary Euthanasia is not likely to be going it alone for very long. Many of her admirers * * * would be neither surprised nor distressed to see her joined by Miss Euthanatize the Congenital Idiots and Miss Euthanatize the Permanently Insane and Miss Euthanatize the Senile Dementia. * * *

> Another reason why the "parade of horrors" argument cannot be too easily dismissed in this particular instance, it seems to me, is that the parade *has* taken place in our time and the order of procession has been headed by the killing of "incurables" and the "useless":

>> Even before the Nazis took open charge in Germany, a propaganda barrage was directed against the traditional compassionate nine-teenth-century attitudes toward the chronically ill, and for the adoption of a utilitarian, Hegelian point of view. * * * The beginnings at first were merely a subtle shift in emphasis in the basic attitude of the physicians. *It started with the acceptance of the attitude, basic in the euthanasia movement, that there is such a thing as life not worthy to be lived.* This attitude in its early stages concerned itself merely with the severely and chronically sick. Gradually the sphere of those

---

210. II *Kings,* VI, 32, quoted and applied in Sperry, *The Case Against Mercy Killing,* 70 Am.Mercury 271, 276 (1950).

to be included in this category was enlarged to encompass the socially unproductive, the ideologically unwanted, the racially unwanted and finally all non-Germans. * * *[213]

It can't happen here. Well, maybe it cannot, but no small part of our Constitution and no small number of our Supreme Court opinions stem from the fear that *it can happen here unless we darn well make sure that it does not* by adamantly holding the line, by swiftly snuffing out what are or might be small beginnings of what we do not want to happen here.

Yale Kamisar, *Some Non–Religious Views Against Proposed "Mercy–Killing" Legislation,* 42 Minn.L.Rev. 969, 1030–32, 1038 (1958).

Professor Williams replied to Kamisar:

Kamisar's particular bogey, the racial laws of Nazi Germany, is an effective one in the democratic countries. Any reference to the Nazis is a powerful weapon to prevent change in the traditional taboo on * * * euthanasia. * * *

But it is insufficient to answer the "wedge" objection in general terms; we must consider the particular fears to which it gives rise. Kamisar professes to fear certain other measures that the Euthanasia societies may bring up if their present measure is conceded to them. Surely, these other measures, if any, will be debated on their merits? Does he seriously fear that anyone in the United States is going to propose the extermination of people of a minority race or religion? Let us put aside such ridiculous fancies and discuss practical politics.

The author is quite right in thinking that a body of opinion would favour the legalization of the involuntary euthanasia of hopelessly defective infants, and some day a proposal of this kind may be put forward. The proposal would have distinct limits, just as the proposal for voluntary euthanasia of incurable sufferers has limits. I do not think that any responsible body of opinion would now propose the euthanasia of insane adults, for the perfectly clear reason that any such practice would greatly increase the sense of insecurity felt by the borderline insane and by the large number of insane persons who have sufficient understanding on this particular matter.

Kamisar expresses distress at a concluding remark in my book in which I advert to the possibility of old people becoming an overwhelming burden on mankind. I share his feeling that there are profoundly disturbing possibilities here; and if I had been merely a propagandist, intent upon securing agreement for a specific measure of law reform, I should have done wisely to have omitted all reference to this subject. Since, however, I am merely an academic writer, trying to bring such intelligence as I have to bear on moral and social issues, I deemed the topic too important and threatening to leave without a word. I think I have made it clear * * * that I am not for one moment proposing any euthanasia of the aged in the present society; such an idea would shock me as much as it shocks Kamisar and would shock everybody else. Still, the fact that we

---

213. Alexander, *Medical Science Under Dictatorship,* 241 New England Journal of Medicine 39, 44, 50 (1949) (emphasis added). * * *

may one day have to face is that medical science is more successful in preserving the body than in preserving the mind. It is not impossible that, in the foreseeable future, medical men will be able to preserve the mindless body until the age, say, of 1000, while the mind itself will have lasted only a tenth of that time. What will mankind do then? It is hardly possible to imagine that we shall establish huge hospital-mausolea where the aged are kept in a kind of living death. Even if it is desired to do this, the cost of the undertaking may make it impossible.

This is not an immediately practical problem, and we need not yet face it. The problem of maintaining persons afflicted with senile dementia is well within our economic resources as the matter stands at present. Perhaps some barrier will be found to medical advance which will prevent the problem from becoming more acute.

Glanville Williams, *"Mercy–Killing" Legislation—A Rejoinder,* 43 Minn. L.Rev. 1, 10–12 (1958).

9.   The euthanasia and suicide-assistance debate has raged for decades, although with greater intensity in recent years. Professor Yale Kamisar (Note 8) has been a part of that debate for more than 50 years. Relatively recently, he wrote about how difficult—"agonizingly subtle and complex"—the issues in this area have proven to be. The following is an excerpt of his remarks.

YALE KAMISAR—PHYSICIAN ASSISTED SUICIDE: THE PROBLEMS PRESENTED BY THE COMPELLING, HEARTWRENCHING CASE

88 Journal of Criminal Law and Criminology 1121 (1998), 1121–29, 1142–46

Now that the U.S. Supreme Court has upheld * * * state laws prohibiting the aiding of another to commit suicide, the spotlight will shift to the state courts, the state legislatures and state referenda. And once again proponents of physician-assisted suicide (PAS) will point to a heartwrenching case, perhaps the relatively rare case where a dying person is experiencing unavoidable pain (i.e., pain that not even the most skilled palliative care experts are able to mitigate), and ask: What would you want done to you if you were in this person's shoes?

That is a hard question for opponents of PAS to answer, but * * * I think it is the wrong question to ask. To put it another way, I think it is a very different question than one which asks: Should we enact a law allowing PAS under certain circumstances?

Different people oppose the legalization of PAS (or physician administered active voluntary euthanasia) for different reasons. I believe that what John Arras said of the twenty-four persons who made up the New York State Task Force on Life and the Law (New York Task Force)—all of whom wound up opposing the legalization of PAS/euthanasia—applies to opponents of PAS/euthanasia generally. As Professor Arras pointed out, the opponents fall into three major camps:

First, those who believe the practices are "inherently immoral." Second, those who are greatly disturbed by the fact that "physicians are being called upon to do the killing," a development they view as "fatally compromis[ing] the physician-patient relationship." Third, those who recognize that in certain rare instances PAS/euthanasia might constitute "a positive good," but nevertheless "shrink from endorsing" these practices because they fear the "social consequences" of legalization.

Professor Arras has disclosed that during his tenure with the New York Task Force he belonged to the third faction. So do I.

For those of us whose opposition to the legalization of PAS/euthanasia is based on grounds that put us in the third camp, the heartwrenching case, e.g., a person enduring the last stages of ALS (Lou Gehrig's disease) who, barely able to speak, begs for immediate death, is especially troublesome. Indeed, the heartwrenching case is a principal reason why there is so much support for PAS/euthanasia in this country. * * *

What should be done about the compelling cases, those that seem to cry out for PAS/euthanasia? A close look at the writings of some of the most forceful and persuasive opponents of any legalization of PAS/euthanasia discloses that they are not really opposed to the practice in *every* case as much as they are to its legalization. Thus Ezekiel Emanuel readily concedes that in some cases, such as those where a patient must suffer despite all available palliative care, "physician-assisted suicide or euthanasia can offer obvious benefits—can end a life that is worse than death."[13] * * *

John Arras is still another commentator opposed to the legalization of PAS/euthanasia who is not unhappy about physicians engaging in these practices in exceptional cases. (Indeed, * * * it seems that Professor Arras would be more unhappy if physicians did *not* perform PAS/euthanasia in compelling cases.) Thus Arras concluded a recent article with "a plea to maintain the legal status quo."[18] And what did he mean by the "legal status quo" ? To quote Arras, it is "a regime that does not legally sanction PAS and euthanasia, but nevertheless *covertly permits some particularly compassionate and courageous physicians to violate the law in fear and trembling*."

I think it fair to say that Arras and other prominent opponents of PAS * * * are defending the flat prohibition against PAS partly on the ground that it is *not really* a flat ban—partly on the ground that "the availability of informal practice and informally agreed-upon 'rights,' " especially in the most compelling cases, *reduces* the *pressure* to legalize these practices formally. Four decades ago I took essentially the same position. Now I am a good deal less sure which way the "availability of informal practice" cuts. * * *

Perhaps Arras (and Emanuel * * * and others who balk at the legalization of PAS/euthanasia but find it acceptable in certain individual cases) should be commended for forthrightly admitting that should *they*

---

13. Ezekiel Emanuel, *Whose Right to Die?*, ATLANTIC MONTHLY, Mar. 1997, at 73–78.

18. John D. Arras, *Physician–Assisted Suicide: A Tragic View*, 13 J. Contemp. Health L. & Pol'y 361, 365 (1997).

ever suffer such a "terrible fate" themselves (i.e., an unavoidably painful or degrading existence at the end of life), *they* "would hope to find a thoughtful, compassionate, and courageous physician to release them from their misery." Nevertheless, this concession is quite troubling.

In *Regina v. Dudley & Stephens* [pp. 49, 553], the famous British "necessity" case, the court recognized that the defendants had been "subject to terrible temptation" and to "sufferings which might break down the bodily power of the strongest man and try the conscience of the best," yet emphatically rejected "necessity" as a defense to criminal homicide. The court took comfort in the notion that "[w]e are often compelled to set up standards we cannot reach ourselves, and to lay down rules which we could not ourselves satisfy." (*Why?* one might ask.) I have taught *Dudley & Stephens* many times—but never without voicing great uneasiness about establishing or preserving criminal laws that "we could not ourselves satisfy."

Yet Professor Arras and others opposed to the legalization of PAS/euthanasia seem to be saying just that. * * *

The sympathy many opponents of PAS/euthanasia express for what they would say are the relatively few people who suffer an unavoidably agonizing death, and the ambivalence with which they view these hard cases while stoutly resisting any legalization of PAS/euthanasia, has not escaped the attention—or the displeasure—of their adversaries. A good example is Professor Sylvia Law's sharp response to some of the comments John Pickering made in expressing his opposition to PAS/euthanasia.

At the time he chaired the American Bar Association's Commission on Legal Problems of the Elderly, Pickering incurred strong criticism when, along the same lines as Arras and others, he distinguished between PAS/euthanasia as public policy and PAS/euthanasia as a response to the circumstances of an individual case. In leading the successful opposition to an attempt to have the ABA endorse proposals to legalize PAS, Pickering expressed agreement with the New York Task Force Report that PAS/euthanasia is "unwise public policy" and that "it poses great danger to the most vulnerable segments of our society—the elderly, the poor and the persons with disabilities."[30] But then he added: "At the same time I selfishly reserve my right to do in private what my family, my doctor and pastor and I, in loving consultation, voluntarily agree is best." Sylvia Law, a strong proponent of PAS, responded: "While [Mr. Pickering's] candor is refreshing, it may be wise to enact legal principles that are applicable to all. Formal rules, justified to protect the vulnerable and then ignored by the powerful, are apt to be unfair to all, and most especially to those they purport to protect."[32]

---

30. John H. Pickering, *The Continuing Debate over Active Euthanasia*, A.B.A. Bioethics Bull., Summer 1994, at 1, 15.

32. Sylvia Law, *Physician–Assisted Death: An Essay on Constitutional Rights and Remedies*, 55 Md. L. Rev. 292, 314 (1996).

Professor Law's criticism deserves a response * * *. * * *

As we have seen, some opponents of PAS/euthanasia defend the present regime partly on the ground that it *covertly permits* these practices to take place in the relatively few cases where such action is appropriate. But it is not at all clear which way this cuts. It may be contended that the availability of what might be called the underground practice of PAS/euthanasia reduces the pressure to legalize these acts, but it may also be argued that the current state of affairs results in "the worst of all worlds: unpopular laws stay on the books and are sporadically enforced against unwary defendants, but because of the prosecutor's need to avoid a jury, the crimes are not punished to the extent the legislature might think appropriate."

The American Law Institute's Model Penal Code has deservedly been called "the point of departure for criminal law scholarship." So I turned to the Code for help. But when I did so, different code provisions and commentaries seemed to point in different directions.

In rejecting the position taken by the *Dudley & Stevens* court and other courts which have refused to recognize as defenses to criminal homicide "necessity" (sometimes called "choice of evils") or "duress" (sometimes called "coercion"), the Reporters for the Model Penal Code explained:

[L]aw is ineffective in the deepest sense, indeed * * * it is hypocritical, if it imposes on the actor who has the misfortune to confront a dilemmatic choice, a standard that his judges are not prepared to affirm that they should and could comply with if their turn to face the problem should arise. Condemnation in such a case is bound to be an ineffective threat; what is, however, more significant is that it is divorced from any moral base and is unjust.

These are strong words and they seem to provide strong support for legalizing PAS/euthanasia—at least in those compelling individual cases where even some opposed to the legalization of PAS/euthanasia deem the acts appropriate. Yet, without carving out any exceptions for compelling cases, the Code elsewhere, to use its own description, "creates a separate offense of aiding or soliciting suicide," explaining:

The fact that penal sanctions will prove ineffective to deter [a suicidal individual from committing the act himself] does not mean that the criminal law is equally powerless to influence the behavior of those who would aid or induce another to take his own life. Moreover, in principle it would seem that the interests in the sanctity of life that are represented by the criminal homicide laws are threatened by one who expresses a willingness to participate in taking the life of another, even though the act may be accomplished with the consent, or at the request, of the suicide victim.

The only concession the Model Penal Code is willing to make for heartwrenching cases is "to rely upon mitigation of sentence when the ground therefor appears." But this concession fails to mitigate the ordeal of a criminal prosecution or the stigma of a conviction. It is almost as if those who drafted the assisted suicide section and wrote the accompanying commentary were unaware of the sections dealing with "necessity" and "duress" and the commentary accompanying those provisions.

I do not deny it is hard to defend an absolute prohibition when you not only expect the prohibition to be violated in certain situations, but you can visualize circumstances where you would understand and forgive the person who did so. The best analogy I can think of is the absolute prohibition against torture. There, too, if we thought about it for a while, we could envisage some dramatic individual cases where there would be tremendous pressure to violate the prohibition, e.g., the "ticking bomb" case.

According to the press, a series of killings by terrorists has led the Israeli government to authorize harsh interrogation of suspected militants. The Israeli government has defended its decision by making what some have called the "ticking bomb" argument—underscoring the need to resort to torture to obtain information that could prevent imminent killings. But various human-rights groups in Israel remain unconvinced that a very few dramatic cases justify an exception to the absolute ban against torture. They fear that once a crack appears in the absolute prohibition, the crack will eventually widen—and that torture will start taking place under circumstances far removed from the "ticking bomb" case.

This may shock some people, but I believe that if a "ticking bomb" case actually arose in this country—i.e., the authorities had good cause to believe that a powerful bomb had been hidden in a huge office or government building and would explode in the next twenty-four hours and also had reason to believe that a person in their custody knew how, when and where this was to occur—the authorities would not shrink from using torture. I also doubt (especially if the use of torture succeeded in preventing an imminent disaster) that most people would *want* the authorities to shrink from doing so.

For purposes of the present discussion, I need not answer the hard question of whether it should *ever* be permissible for law enforcement officials to resort to torture, e.g., to elicit information that would prevent a large explosion or some other calamity. I need only maintain that it is a very different question than whether we should *enact a law* formally sanctioning the use of torture in certain situations. It is much easier for the government to resort to torture in less-than-compelling situations when such methods are already formally permitted in some circumstances. On the other hand, by refusing to make any formal or official exceptions to the prohibition against torture, or by refusing to acknowledge that we should balance the costs and benefits of torture as a general matter, we strengthen the presumption against torture and maximize the likelihood that it will only be resorted to in the rarest and most compelling circumstances.

Here, as elsewhere, it is very hard to maintain absolute prohibitions. But here, as elsewhere, problems arise when one starts carving out exceptions. I venture to say that, however great the care with which one formulates the exceptions, "hard" cases are bound to emerge *on the other side* of the line and with it the pressure to extend the outer boundaries of the exceptions to embrace these new "hard" cases. * * *

* * * Sometimes, I am afraid, what appear to be agonizingly subtle and complex problems turn out to be just that.

NOTES AND QUESTIONS

1. For replies to Professor Kamisar's reflections, see Cristina L.H. Traina, *Religious Perspectives on Assisted Suicide*, 88 J.Crim.L. & Criminology 1147 (1998) and John Deigh, *Physician Assisted Suicide and Voluntary Euthanasia: Some Relevant Differences*, 88 J.Crim.L. & Criminology 1155 (1998).

2. ADDICTION/ALCOHOLISM CONSTITUTIONAL DEFENSE

ROBINSON v. CALIFORNIA

Supreme Court of the United States, 1962.
370 U.S. 660, 82 S.Ct. 1417, 8 L.Ed.2d 758.

MR. JUSTICE STEWART delivered the opinion of the Court.

A California statute makes it a criminal offense for a person to "be addicted to the use of narcotics."[1] This appeal draws into question the constitutionality of that provision of the state law, as construed by the California courts in the present case.

The appellant was convicted after a jury trial in the Municipal Court of Los Angeles. * * * Officer Brown testified that he had had occasion to examine the appellant's arms one evening on a street in Los Angeles some four months before the trial. The officer testified that at that time he had observed "scar tissue and discoloration on the inside" of the appellant's right arm, and "what appeared to be numerous needle marks and a scab which was approximately three inches below the crook of the elbow" on the appellant's left arm. The officer also testified that the appellant under questioning had admitted to the occasional use of narcotics. * * *

---

1. The statute is § 11721 of the California Health and Safety Code. It provides: "No person shall use, or be under the influence of, or be addicted to the use of narcotics, excepting when administered by or under the direction of a person licensed by the State to prescribe and administer narcotics. * * * Any person convicted of violating any provision of this section is guilty of a misdemeanor and shall be sentenced to serve a term of not less than 90 days nor more than one year in the county jail. * * * In no event does the court have the power to absolve a person who violates this section from the obligation of spending at least 90 days in confinement in the county jail."

The judge * * * instructed the jury that the appellant could be convicted under a general verdict if the jury agreed *either* that he was of the "status" *or* had committed the "act" denounced by the statute. "All that the People must show is either that the defendant did use a narcotic in Los Angeles County, or that while in the City of Los Angeles he was addicted to the use of narcotics * * *."

Under these instructions the jury returned a verdict finding the appellant "guilty of the offense charged." * * * We noted probable jurisdiction of this appeal because it squarely presents the issue whether the statute as construed by the California courts in this case is repugnant to the Fourteenth Amendment of the Constitution.

The broad power of a State to regulate the narcotic drugs traffic within its borders is not here in issue. * * *

Such regulation, it can be assumed, could take a variety of valid forms. A State might impose criminal sanctions, for example, against the unauthorized manufacture, prescription, sale, purchase, or possession of narcotics within its borders. In the interest of discouraging the violation of such laws, or in the interest of the general health or welfare of its inhabitants, a State might establish a program of compulsory treatment for those addicted to narcotics. Such a program of treatment might require periods of involuntary confinement. And penal sanctions might be imposed for failure to comply with established compulsory treatment procedures. Or a State might choose to attack the evils of narcotics traffic on broader fronts also—through public health education, for example, or by efforts to ameliorate the economic and social conditions under which those evils might be thought to flourish. In short, the range of valid choice which a State might make in this area is undoubtedly a wide one, and the wisdom of any particular choice within the allowable spectrum is not for us to decide. Upon that premise we turn to the California law in issue here.

It would be possible to construe the statute under which the appellant was convicted as one which is operative only upon proof of the actual use of narcotics within the State's jurisdiction. But the California courts have not so construed this law. Although there was evidence in the present case that the appellant had used narcotics in Los Angeles, the jury were instructed that they could convict him even if they disbelieved that evidence. The appellant could be convicted, they were told, if they found simply that the appellant's "status" or "chronic condition" was that of being "addicted to the use of narcotics." And it is impossible to know from the jury's verdict that the defendant was not convicted upon precisely such a finding. * * *

This statute, therefore, is not one which punishes a person for the use of narcotics, for their purchase, sale or possession, or for antisocial or disorderly behavior resulting from their administration. It is not a law which even purports to provide or require medical treatment. Rather, we deal with a statute which makes the "status" of narcotic addiction a criminal offense, for which the offender may be prosecuted "at any time before he reforms." California has said that a person can be continuously guilty of this offense, whether or not he has ever used or possessed any narcotics within the State, and whether or not he has been guilty of any antisocial behavior there.

It is unlikely that any State at this moment in history would attempt to make it a criminal offense for a person to be mentally ill, or a leper, or to be afflicted with a venereal disease. A State might determine that the general health and welfare require that the victims of these and other human afflictions be dealt with by compulsory treatment, involving quarantine, confinement, or sequestration. But, in the light of contemporary human knowledge, a law which made a criminal offense of such a disease would doubtless be universally thought to be an infliction of cruel and unusual punishment in violation of the Eighth and Fourteenth Amendments.

We cannot but consider the statute before us as of the same category. In this Court counsel for the State recognized that narcotic addiction is an illness.[8] Indeed, it is apparently an illness which may be contracted innocently or involuntarily.[9] We hold that a state law which imprisons a person thus afflicted as a criminal, even though he has never touched any narcotic drug within the State or been guilty of any irregular behavior there, inflicts a cruel and unusual punishment in violation of the Fourteenth Amendment. * * * Even one day in prison would be a cruel and unusual punishment for the "crime" of having a common cold. * * *

Reversed.

MR. JUSTICE DOUGLAS, concurring.

While I join the Court's opinion, I wish to make more explicit the reasons why I think it is "cruel and unusual" punishment in the sense of the Eighth Amendment to treat as a criminal a person who is a drug addict. * * *

As stated by Dr. Isaac Ray many years ago:

"Nothing can more strongly illustrate the popular ignorance respecting insanity than the proposition, equally objectionable in its humanity and its logic, that the insane should be punished for criminal acts, in order to deter other insane persons from doing the same thing." Treatise on the Medical Jurisprudence of Insanity (5th ed. 1871), p. 56.

Today we have our differences over the legal definition of insanity. But however insanity is defined, it is in end effect treated as a disease.

---

8. In its brief the appellee stated: "Of course it is generally conceded that a narcotic addict, particularly one addicted to the use of heroin, is in a state of mental and physical illness. So is an alcoholic." * * *

9. Not only may addiction innocently result from the use of medically prescribed narcotics, but a person may even be a narcotics addict from the moment of his birth.

While afflicted people may be confined either for treatment or for the protection of society, they are not branded as criminals.

Yet terror and punishment linger on as means of dealing with some diseases. As recently stated:

> " * * * the idea of basing treatment for disease on purgatorial acts and ordeals is an ancient one in medicine. It may trace back to the Old Testament belief that disease of any kind, whether mental or physical, represented punishment for sin; and thus relief could take the form of a final heroic act of atonement. This superstition appears to have given support to fallacious medical rationales for such procedures as purging, bleeding, induced vomiting, and blistering, as well as an entire chamber of horrors constituting the early treatment of mental illness. The latter included a wide assortment of shock techniques, such as the 'water cures' (dousing, ducking, and near-drowning), spinning in a chair, centrifugal swinging, and an early form of electric shock. All, it would appear, were planned as means of driving from the body some evil spirit or toxic vapor." Action for Mental Health (1961), pp. 27–28.

That approach continues as respects drug addicts. Drug addiction is more prevalent in this country than in any other nation of the western world. It is sometimes referred to as "a contagious disease." But those living in a world of black and white put the addict in the category of those who could, if they would, forsake their evil ways.

The first step toward addiction may be as innocent as a boy's puff on a cigarette in an alleyway. It may come from medical prescriptions. Addiction may even be present at birth. * * *

The impact that an addict has on a community causes alarm and often leads to punitive measures. Those measures are justified when they relate to acts of transgression. But I do not see how under our system *being an addict* can be punished as a crime. If addicts can be punished for their addiction, then the insane can also be punished for their insanity. Each has a disease and each must be treated as a sick person. * * *

The Eighth Amendment expresses the revulsion of civilized man against barbarous acts—the "cry of horror" against man's inhumanity to his fellow man.

By the time of Coke, enlightenment was coming as respects the insane. Coke said that the execution of a madman "should be a miserable spectacle, both against law, and of extreme inhumanity and cruelty, and can be no example to others." 6 Coke's Third Inst. (4th ed. 1797), p. 6. Blackstone endorsed this view of Coke.

We should show the same discernment respecting drug addiction. The addict is a sick person. He may, of course, be confined for treatment or for the protection of society. Cruel and unusual punishment results not from confinement, but from convicting the addict of a crime. * * * A prosecution for addiction, with its resulting stigma and irreparable damage to the good name of the accused, cannot be justified as a means of protecting society, where a civil commitment would do as well. * * * We would forget the teachings of the Eighth Amendment if we allowed sickness to be made a crime and permitted sick people to be punished for being sick. This age of enlightenment cannot tolerate such barbarous action.

MR. JUSTICE HARLAN, concurring.

I am not prepared to hold that on the present state of medical knowledge it is completely irrational and hence unconstitutional for a State to conclude that narcotics addiction is something other than an illness nor that it amounts to cruel and unusual punishment for the State to subject narcotics addicts to its criminal law. Insofar as addiction may be identified with the use or possession of narcotics within the State (or, I would suppose, without the State), in violation of local statutes prohibiting such acts, it may surely be reached by the State's criminal law. But in this case the trial court's instructions permitted the jury to find the appellant guilty on no more proof than that he was present in California while he was addicted to narcotics. Since addiction alone cannot reasonably be thought to amount to more than a compelling propensity to use narcotics, the effect of this instruction was to authorize criminal punishment for a bare desire to commit a criminal act.

* * * Accordingly, I agree that the application of the California statute was unconstitutional in this case and join the judgment of reversal.

[The dissenting opinion of MR. JUSTICE CLARK is deleted.]

MR. JUSTICE WHITE, dissenting.

If appellant's conviction rested upon sheer status, condition or illness or if he was convicted for being an addict who had lost his power of self-control, I would have other thoughts about this case. But this record presents neither situation. * * *

I am not at all ready to place the use of narcotics beyond the reach of the States' criminal laws. I do not consider appellant's conviction to be a punishment for having an illness or for simply being in some status or condition, but rather a conviction for the regular, repeated or habitual use of narcotics immediately prior to his arrest and in violation of the California law.[3] * * *

* * * The Fourteenth Amendment is today held to bar any prosecution for addiction regardless of the degree or frequency of use, and the Court's opinion bristles with indications of further consequences. If it is "cruel and unusual punishment" to convict appellant for addiction, it is difficult to understand why it would be any less offensive to the Four-

---

3. This is not a case where a defendant is convicted "even though he has never touched any narcotic drug within the State or been guilty of any irregular behavior there." The evidence was that appellant lived and worked in Los Angeles. He admitted before trial that he had used narcotics for three or four months, three or four times a week, usually at his place with his friends. He stated to the police that he had last used narcotics * * * in the City of Los Angeles on January 27, 8 days before his arrest. * * *

teenth Amendment to convict him for use on the same evidence of use which proved he was an addict. It is significant that in purporting to reaffirm the power of the States to deal with the narcotics traffic, the Court does not include among the obvious powers of the State the power to punish for the use of narcotics. I cannot think that the omission was inadvertent. * * *

NOTES AND QUESTIONS

1. The constitutional significance of *Robinson* cannot be fully understood without considering the next case, *Powell v. Texas.* However, standing alone, what is the apparent holding of *Robinson?* Why is it constitutionally impermissible for the State of California to punish Robinson? And what do you view as the underlying principle or principles animating the Court's holding?

2. *Implications of Robinson.* Based on *Robinson,* could California constitutionally punish a person for "being HIV-positive"? For "being a prostitute"? For being homeless? What about punishing a homeless person for "sitting, lying, or sleeping" on a public street or sidewalk? Based on *Robinson,* are any common law elements of criminal responsibility constitutionally mandated? Are any defenses mandated? For example, would it be constitutional for a state to abolish the insanity defense?

POWELL v. TEXAS

Supreme Court of the United States, 1968.
392 U.S. 514, 88 S.Ct. 2145, 20 L.Ed.2d 1254.

MR. JUSTICE MARSHALL announced the judgment of the Court and delivered an opinion in which THE CHIEF JUSTICE, MR. JUSTICE BLACK, and MR. JUSTICE HARLAN join.

In late December 1966, appellant was arrested and charged with being found in a state of intoxication in a public place, in violation of Vernon's Ann.Texas Penal Code, Art. 477 (1952), which reads as follows:

"Whoever shall get drunk or be found in a state of intoxication in any public place, or at any private house except his own, shall be fined not exceeding one hundred dollars."

* * * His counsel urged that appellant was "afflicted with the disease of chronic alcoholism," that "his appearance in public [while drunk was] * * * not of his own volition," and therefore that to punish him criminally for that conduct would be cruel and unusual, in violation of the Eighth and Fourteenth Amendments to the United States Constitution.

The trial judge * * * sitting without a jury * * * ruled as a matter of law that chronic alcoholism was not a defense to the charge. He found appellant guilty, and fined him $50. * * *

I.

The principal testimony was that of Dr. David Wade, a Fellow of the American Medical Association, duly certificated in psychiatry. * * * Dr.

Wade sketched the outlines of the "disease" concept of alcoholism; noted that there is no generally accepted definition of "alcoholism"; alluded to the ongoing debate within the medical profession over whether alcohol is actually physically "addicting" or merely psychologically "habituating"; and concluded that in either case a "chronic alcoholic" is an "involuntary drinker," who is "powerless not to drink," and who "loses his self-control over his drinking." He testified that he had examined appellant, and that appellant is a "chronic alcoholic," who "by the time he has reached [the state of intoxication] * * * is not able to control his behavior, and [who] * * * has reached this point because he has an uncontrollable compulsion to drink." Dr. Wade also responded in the negative to the question whether appellant has "the willpower to resist the constant excessive consumption of alcohol." He added that in his opinion jailing appellant without medical attention would operate neither to rehabilitate him nor to lessen his desire for alcohol.

On cross-examination, Dr. Wade admitted that when appellant was sober he knew the difference between right and wrong, and he responded affirmatively to the question whether appellant's act in taking the first drink in any given instance when he was sober was a "voluntary exercise of his will." Qualifying his answer, Dr. Wade stated that "these individuals have a compulsion, and this compulsion, while not completely overpowering, is a very strong influence, an exceedingly strong influence, and this compulsion coupled with the firm belief in their mind that they are going to be able to handle it from now on causes their judgment to be somewhat clouded."

Appellant testified concerning the history of his drinking problem. He reviewed his many arrests for drunkenness; testified that he was unable to stop drinking; stated that when he was intoxicated he had no control over his actions and could not remember them later, but that he did not become violent; and admitted that he did not remember his arrest on the occasion for which he was being tried. On cross-examination, appellant admitted that he had had one drink on the morning of the trial and had been able to discontinue drinking. * * *

* * * The State made no effort to obtain expert psychiatric testimony of its own, or even to explore with appellant's witness the question of appellant's power to control the frequency, timing, and location of his drinking bouts, or the substantial disagreement within the medical profession concerning the nature of the disease, the efficacy of treatment and the prerequisites for effective treatment. It did nothing to examine or illuminate what Dr. Wade might have meant by his reference to a "compulsion" which was "not completely overpowering," but which was "an exceedingly strong influence," or to inquire into the question of the proper role of such a "compulsion" in constitutional adjudication. * * *

Following this abbreviated exposition of the problem before it, the trial court indicated its intention to disallow appellant's claimed defense of "chronic alcoholism." Thereupon defense counsel submitted, and the trial court entered, the following "findings of fact":

> "(1) That chronic alcoholism is a disease which destroys the afflicted person's will power to resist the constant, excessive consumption of alcohol.

> "(2) That a chronic alcoholic does not appear in public by his own volition but under a compulsion symptomatic of the disease of chronic alcoholism.

> "(3) That Leroy Powell, defendant herein, is a chronic alcoholic who is afflicted with the disease of chronic alcoholism."

Whatever else may be said of them, those are not "findings of fact" in any recognizable, traditional sense in which that term has been used in a court of law; they are the premises of a syllogism transparently designed to bring this case within the scope of this Court's opinion in Robinson v. State of California. Nonetheless, the dissent would have us adopt these "findings" without critical examination; it would use them as the basis for a constitutional holding that "a person may not be punished if the condition essential to constitute the defined crime is part of the pattern of his disease and is occasioned by a compulsion symptomatic of the disease."

The difficulty with that position, as we shall show, is that it goes much too far on the basis of too little knowledge. In the first place, the record in this case is utterly inadequate to permit the sort of informed and responsible adjudication which alone can support the announcement of an important and wide-ranging new constitutional principle. We know very little about the circumstances surrounding the drinking bout which resulted in this conviction, or about Leroy Powell's drinking problem, or indeed about alcoholism itself. * * *

Furthermore, the inescapable fact is that there is no agreement among members of the medical profession about what it means to say that "alcoholism" is a "disease." One of the principal works in this field states that * * * *"*a disease is what the medical profession recognizes as such.*" In other words, there is widespread agreement today that "alcoholism" is a "disease," for the simple reason that the medical profession has concluded that it should attempt to treat those who have drinking problems. There the agreement stops. * * *

Nor is there any substantial consensus as to the "manifestations of alcoholism." E.M. Jellinek, one of the outstanding authorities on the subject, identifies five different types of alcoholics which predominate in the United States, and these types display a broad range of different and occasionally inconsistent symptoms. Moreover, wholly distinct types, relatively rare in this country, predominate in nations with different cultural attitudes regarding the consumption of alcohol. Even if we limit our consideration to the range of alcoholic symptoms more typically found in this country, there is substantial disagreement as to the manifestations of the "disease" called "alcoholism." * * *

The trial court's "finding" that Powell "is afflicted with the disease of chronic alcoholism," which "destroys the afflicted person's will power to resist the constant, excessive consumption of alcohol" covers a multitude of sins. Dr. Wade's testimony that appellant suffered from a compulsion which was an "exceedingly strong influence," but which was "not completely overpowering" is at least more carefully stated, if no less mystifying. * * * [C]onceptual clarity can only be achieved by distinguishing carefully between "loss of control" once an individual has commenced to drink and "inability to abstain" from drinking in the first place. Presumably a person would have to display both characteristics in order to make out a constitutional defense, should one be recognized. Yet the "findings" of the trial court utterly fail to make this crucial distinction, and there is serious question whether the record can be read to support a finding of either loss of control or inability to abstain. * * *

It is one thing to say that if a man is deprived of alcohol his hands will begin to shake, he will suffer agonizing pains and ultimately he will have hallucinations; it is quite another to say that a man has a "compulsion" to take a drink, but that he also retains a certain amount of "free will" with which to resist. It is simply impossible, in the present state of our knowledge, to ascribe a useful meaning to the latter statement. This definitional confusion reflects, of course, not merely the undeveloped state of the psychiatric art but also the conceptual difficulties inevitably attendant upon the importation of scientific and medical models into a legal system generally predicated upon a different set of assumptions.

II.

Despite the comparatively primitive state of our knowledge on the subject, it cannot be denied that the destructive use of alcoholic beverages is one of our principal social and public health problems. * * *

There is as yet no known generally effective method for treating the vast number of alcoholics in our society. * * * Thus it is entirely possible that, even were the manpower and facilities available for a full-scale attack upon chronic alcoholism, we would find ourselves unable to help the vast bulk of our "visible"—let alone our "invisible"—alcoholic population.

However, facilities for the attempted treatment of indigent alcoholics are woefully lacking throughout the country. It would be tragic to return large numbers of helpless, sometimes dangerous and frequently unsanitary inebriates to the streets of our cities without even the opportunity to sober up adequately which a brief jail term provides. * * *

One virtue of the criminal process is, at least, that the duration of penal incarceration typically has some outside statutory limit; this is universally true in the case of petty offenses, such as public drunkenness, where jail terms are quite short on the whole. "Therapeutic civil commitment" lacks this feature; one is typically committed until one is "cured." Thus, to do otherwise than affirm might subject indigent alcoholics to the risk that they may be locked up for an indefinite period of time under the same conditions as before, with no more hope than before of receiving effective treatment and no prospect of periodic "freedom."

Faced with this unpleasant reality, we are unable to assert that the use of the criminal process as a means of dealing with the public aspects of problem drinking can never be defended as rational. The picture of the penniless drunk propelled aimlessly and endlessly through the law's "revolving door" of arrest, incarceration, release and re-arrest is not a pretty one. But before we condemn the present practice across-the-board, perhaps we ought to be able to point to some clear promise of a better world for these unfortunate people. Unfortunately, no such promise has yet been forthcoming. If, in addition to the absence of a coherent approach to the problem of treatment, we consider the almost complete absence of facilities and manpower for the implementation of a rehabilitation program, it is difficult to say in the present context that the criminal process is utterly lacking in social value. * * *

III.   * * *

Appellant * * * seeks to come within the application of the Cruel and Unusual Punishment Clause announced in Robinson v. State of California * * *.

On its face the present case does not fall within that holding, since appellant was convicted, not for being a chronic alcoholic, but for being in public while drunk on a particular occasion. The State of Texas thus has not sought to punish a mere status, as California did in *Robinson;* nor has it attempted to regulate appellant's behavior in the privacy of his own home. Rather, it has imposed upon appellant a criminal sanction for public behavior which may create substantial health and safety hazards, both for appellant and for members of the general public, and which offends the moral and esthetic sensibilities of a large segment of the community. This seems a far cry from convicting one for being an addict, being a chronic alcoholic, being "mentally ill, or a leper * * *."

Robinson so viewed brings this Court but a very small way into the substantive criminal law. And unless *Robinson* is so viewed it is difficult to see any limiting principle that would serve to prevent this Court from becoming, under the aegis of the Cruel and Unusual Punishment Clause, the ultimate arbiter of the standards of criminal responsibility, in diverse areas of the criminal law, throughout the country.

It is suggested in dissent that *Robinson* stands for the "simple" but "subtle" principle that "[c]riminal penalties may not be inflicted upon a person for being in a condition he is powerless to change." In that view, appellant's "condition" of public intoxication was "occasioned by a compulsion symptomatic of the disease" of chronic alcoholism, and thus, apparently, his behavior lacked the critical element of *mens rea*. Whatever may be the merits of such a doctrine of criminal responsibility, it surely cannot be said to follow from *Robinson*. The entire thrust of *Robinson*'s interpretation of the Cruel and Unusual Punishment Clause is that criminal penalties may be inflicted only if the accused has committed some act, has engaged in some behavior, which society has an interest in preventing, or perhaps in historical common law terms, has committed some *actus reus*. It thus does not deal with the question of whether certain conduct cannot constitutionally be punished because it is, in some sense, "involuntary" or "occasioned by a compulsion." * * *

Ultimately, then, the most troubling aspects of this case, were *Robinson* to be extended to meet it, would be the scope and content of what could only be a constitutional doctrine of criminal responsibility. In dissent it is urged that the decision could be limited to conduct which is "a characteristic and involuntary part of the pattern of the disease as it afflicts" the particular individual, and that "[i]t is not foreseeable" that it would be applied "in the case of offenses such as driving a car while intoxicated, assault, theft, or robbery." That is limitation by fiat. In the first place, nothing in the logic of the dissent would limit its application to chronic alcoholics. If Leroy Powell cannot be convicted of public intoxication, it is difficult to see how a State can convict an individual for murder, if that individual, while exhibiting normal behavior in all other respects, suffers from a "compulsion" to kill, which is an "exceedingly strong influence," but "not completely overpowering." * * *

Traditional common-law concepts of personal accountability and essential considerations of federalism lead us to disagree with appellant. We are unable to conclude, on the state of this record or on the current state of medical knowledge, that chronic alcoholics in general, and Leroy Powell in particular, suffer from such an irresistible compulsion to drink and to get drunk in public that they are utterly unable to control their performance of either or both of these acts and thus cannot be deterred at all from public intoxication. And in any event this Court has never articulated a general constitutional doctrine of *mens rea*.

We cannot cast aside the centuries-long evolution of the collection of interlocking and overlapping concepts which the common law has utilized to assess the moral accountability of an individual for his antisocial deeds. The doctrines of *actus reus, mens rea,* insanity, mistake, justification, and duress have historically provided the tools for a constantly shifting adjustment of the tension between the evolving aims of the criminal law and changing religious, moral, philosophical, and medical views of the nature of man. This process of adjustment has always been thought to be the province of the States.

Nothing could be less fruitful than for this Court to be impelled into defining some sort of insanity test in constitutional terms. Yet, that task would seem to follow inexorably from an extension of *Robinson* to this case. If a person in the "condition" of being a chronic alcoholic cannot be criminally punished as a constitutional matter for being drunk in public, it would seem to follow that a person who contends that, in terms of one test, "his unlawful act was the product of mental disease or mental defect," Durham v. United States, 94 U.S.App.D.C. 228, 241, 214 F.2d 862, 875, 45 A.L.R.2d 1430 (1954), would state an issue of constitutional dimension with regard to his criminal responsibility had he been tried under some different and perhaps lesser standard, e.g., the right-wrong test of *M'Naghten's Case.* * * * But formulating a constitutional rule would reduce, if not eliminate, that fruitful experimentation, and freeze the developing productive dialogue between law and psychiatry into a rigid constitutional mold. It is simply not yet the time to write the Constitutional formulas cast in terms whose meaning, let alone relevance, is not yet clear either to doctors or to lawyers.

Affirmed.

MR. JUSTICE BLACK, whom MR. JUSTICE HARLAN joins, concurring. * * *

Those who favor the change now urged upon us rely on their own notions of the wisdom of this Texas law to erect a constitutional barrier, the desirability of which is far from clear. To adopt this position would significantly limit the States in their efforts to deal with a widespread and important social problem and would do so by announcing a revolutionary doctrine of constitutional law that would also tightly restrict state power to deal with a wide variety of other harmful conduct.

I. * * *

Jailing of chronic alcoholics is definitely defended as therapeutic, and the claims of therapeutic value are not insubstantial. As appellee notes, the alcoholics are removed from the streets, where in their intoxicated state they may be in physical danger, and are given food, clothing, and shelter until they "sober up" and thus at least regain their ability to keep from being run over by automobiles in the street. * * *

Apart from the value of jail as a form of treatment, jail serves other traditional functions of the criminal law. For one thing, it gets the alcoholics off the street, where they may cause harm in a number of ways to a number of people, and isolation of the dangerous has always been considered an important function of the criminal law. In addition, punishment of chronic alcoholics can serve several deterrent functions—it can give potential alcoholics an additional incentive to control their drinking, and it may, even in the case of the chronic alcoholic, strengthen his incentive to control the frequency and location of his drinking experiences.

These values served by criminal punishment assume even greater significance in light of the available alternatives for dealing with the problem of alcoholism. Civil commitment facilities may not be any better than the jails they would replace. * * *

* * * From what I have been able to learn about the subject, it seems to me that the present use of criminal sanctions might possibly be unwise, but I am by no means convinced that *any* use of criminal sanctions would inevitably be unwise or, above all, that I am qualified in this area to know what is legislatively wise and what is legislatively unwise.

II.

I agree with Mr. Justice Marshall that the findings of fact in this case are inadequate to justify the sweeping constitutional rule urged upon us. I could not, however, consider any findings that could be made with respect to "voluntariness" or "compulsion" controlling on the question whether a specific instance of human behavior should be immune from punishment as a constitutional matter. When we say that appellant's appearance in public is caused not by "his own" volition but rather by some other force, we are clearly thinking of a force that is nevertheless "his" except in some special sense.[1] The accused undoubtedly commits the proscribed act and the only question is whether the act can be attributed to a part of "his" personality that should not be regarded as criminally responsible. Almost all of the traditional purposes of the criminal law can be significantly served by punishing the person who in fact committed the proscribed act, without regard to whether his action was "compelled" by some elusive "irresponsible" aspect of his personality. As I have already indicated, punishment of such a defendant can clearly be justified in terms of deterrence, isolation, and treatment. * * * For these reasons, much as I think that criminal sanctions should in many situations be applied only to those whose conduct is morally blameworthy, I cannot think the States should be held constitutionally required to make the inquiry as to what part of a defendant's personality is responsible for his actions and to excuse anyone whose action was, in some complex, psychological sense, the result of a "compulsion."

III.

The rule of constitutional law urged by appellant is not required by Robinson v. State of California. In that case we held that a person could not be punished for the mere status of being a narcotics addict. * * *

Punishment for a status is particularly obnoxious, and in many instances can reasonably be called cruel and unusual, because it involves punishment for a mere propensity, a desire to commit an offense; the mental element is not simply one part of the crime but may constitute all of it. This is a situation universally sought to be avoided in our criminal law; the fundamental requirement that some action be proved is solidly established even for offenses most heavily based on propensity, such as attempt, conspiracy, and recidivist crimes. * * *

The reasons for this refusal to permit conviction without proof of an act are difficult to spell out, but they are nonetheless perceived and universally expressed in our criminal law. Evidence of propensity can be considered relatively unreliable and more difficult for a defendant to rebut; the requirement of a specific act thus provides some protection against false charges. Perhaps more fundamental is the difficulty of distinguishing, in the absence of any conduct, between desires of the day-

---

1. If an intoxicated person is actually carried into the street by someone else, "he" does not do the act at all, and of course he is entitled to acquittal. E.g., Martin v. State, 31 Ala.App. 334, 17 So.2d 427 (1944).

dream variety and fixed intentions that may pose a real threat to society; extending the criminal law to cover both types of desire would be unthinkable, since "[t]here can hardly be anyone who has never thought evil. When a desire is inhibited it may find, expression in fantasy; but it would be absurd to condemn this natural psychological mechanism as illegal."

In contrast, crimes that require the State to prove that the defendant actually committed some proscribed act involve none of these special problems. In addition, the question whether an act is "involuntary" is, as I have already indicated, an inherently elusive question, and one which the State may, for good reasons, wish to regard as irrelevant. In light of all these considerations, our limitation of our *Robinson* holding to pure status crimes seems to me entirely proper.

IV.

The rule of constitutional law urged upon us by appellant would have a revolutionary impact on the criminal law, and any possible limits proposed for the rule would be wholly illusory. If the original boundaries of *Robinson* are to be discarded, any new limits too would soon fall by the wayside and the Court would be forced to hold the States powerless to punish any conduct that could be shown to result from a "compulsion," in the complex, psychological meaning of that term. * * *

The real reach of any such decision, however, would be broader still, for the basic premise underlying the argument is that it is cruel and unusual to punish a person who is not morally blameworthy. I state the proposition in this sympathetic way because I feel there is much to be said for avoiding the use of criminal sanctions in many such situations. But the question here is one of constitutional law. The legislatures have always been allowed wide freedom to determine the extent to which moral culpability should be a prerequisite to conviction of a crime. The criminal law is a social tool that is employed in seeking a wide variety of goals, and I cannot say the Eighth Amendment's limits on the use of criminal sanctions extend as far as this viewpoint would inevitably carry them. * * *

MR. JUSTICE WHITE, concurring in the result.

If it cannot be a crime to have an irresistible compulsion to use narcotics, Robinson v. State of California, I do not see how it can constitutionally be a crime to yield to such a compulsion. Punishing an addict for using drugs convicts for addiction under a different name. Distinguishing between the two crimes is like forbidding criminal conviction for being sick with flu or epilepsy but permitting punishment for running a fever or having a convulsion. Unless *Robinson* is to be abandoned, the use of narcotics by an addict must be beyond the reach of the criminal law. Similarly, the chronic alcoholic with an irresistible urge to consume alcohol should not be punishable for drinking or for being drunk.

Powell's conviction was for the different crime of being drunk in a public place. * * *

The trial court said that Powell was a chronic alcoholic with a compulsion not only to drink to excess but also to frequent public places when intoxicated. Nothing in the record before the trial court supports the latter conclusion, which is contrary to common sense and to common knowledge. The sober chronic alcoholic has no compulsion to be on the public streets; many chronic alcoholics drink at home and are never seen drunk in public. Before and after taking the first drink, and until he becomes so drunk that he loses the power to know where he is or to direct his movements, the chronic alcoholic with a home or financial resources is as capable as the non-chronic drinker of doing his drinking in private, of removing himself from public places and, since he knows or ought to know that he will become intoxicated, of making plans to avoid his being found drunk in public. For these reasons, I cannot say that the chronic alcoholic who proves his disease and a compulsion to drink is shielded from conviction when he has knowingly failed to take feasible precautions against committing a criminal act, here the act of going to or remaining in a public place. On such facts the alcoholic is like a person with smallpox, who could be convicted for being on the street but not for being ill, or, like the epileptic, who would be punished for driving a car but not for his disease.

The fact remains that some chronic alcoholics must drink and hence must drink *somewhere*. Although many chronics have homes, many others do not. * * * For some of these alcoholics I would think a showing could be made that resisting drunkenness is impossible and that avoiding public places when intoxicated is also impossible. As applied to them this statute is in effect a law which bans a single act for which they may not be convicted under the Eighth Amendment—the act of getting drunk.

It is also possible that the chronic alcoholic who begins drinking in private at some point becomes so drunk that he loses the power to control his movements and for that reason appears in public. The Eighth Amendment might also forbid conviction in such circumstances, but only on a record satisfactorily showing that it was not feasible for him to have made arrangements to prevent his being in public when drunk and that his extreme drunkenness sufficiently deprived him of his faculties on the occasion in issue. * * *

MR. JUSTICE FORTAS, with whom MR. JUSTICE DOUGLAS, MR. JUSTICE BRENNAN, and MR. JUSTICE STEWART join, dissenting. * * *

The issue posed in this case is a narrow one. There is no challenge here to the validity of public intoxication statutes in general or to the Texas public intoxication statute in particular. * * *

The sole question presented is whether a criminal penalty may be imposed upon a person suffering the disease of "chronic alcoholism" for a condition—being "in a state of intoxication" in public—which is a characteristic part of the pattern of his disease and which, the trial court found, was not the consequence of appellant's volition but of "a compulsion symptomatic of the disease of chronic alcoholism." * * *

Robinson stands upon a principle which, despite its subtlety, must be simply stated and respectfully applied because it is the foundation of individual liberty and the cornerstone of the relations between a civilized state and its citizens: Criminal penalties may not be inflicted upon a person for being in a condition he is powerless to change. In all probability, Robinson at some time before his conviction elected to take narcotics. But the crime as defined did not punish this conduct.[29] The statute imposed a penalty for the offense of "addiction"—a condition which Robinson could not control. Once Robinson had become an addict, he was utterly powerless to avoid criminal guilt. He was powerless to choose not to violate the law.

In the present case, appellant is charged with a crime composed of two elements—being intoxicated and being found in a public place while in that condition. The crime, so defined, differs from that in *Robinson*. The statute covers more than a mere status. But the essential constitutional defect here is the same as in *Robinson*, for in both cases the particular defendant was accused of being in a condition which he had no capacity to change or avoid. * * *

* * * [H]ere the findings of the trial judge call into play the principle that a person may not be punished if the condition essential to constitute the defined crime is part of the pattern of his disease and is occasioned by a compulsion symptomatic of the disease. This principle, narrow in scope and applicability, is implemented by the Eighth Amendment's prohibition of "cruel and unusual punishment," as we construed that command in *Robinson*. * * *

NOTES AND QUESTIONS

1. Is *Powell* consistent with the holding of *Robinson*? Is *Powell* consistent with the underlying reasoning of *Robinson*? If not, why do you think the Supreme Court changed directions?

2. In Jones v. City of Los Angeles, 444 F.3d 1118 (9th Cir. 2006), six homeless persons, unable to find shelter, filed an Eighth Amendment challenge to the enforcement of a Los Angeles City ordinance that criminalized "sitting, lying or sleeping on public streets and sidewalks" at all hours. The Ninth Circuit, 2–1, held that the ordinance violated the Eighth Amendment when enforced against persons guilty only of "involuntary sitting, lying, or sleeping on public sidewalks that is an unavoidable consequence of being human and homeless without shelter in the City of Los Angeles."[m] (Subsequently, the City of Los Angeles agreed not to enforce the ordinance, and the

---

29. The Court noted in *Robinson* that narcotic addiction "is apparently an illness which may be contracted innocently or involuntarily." In the case of alcoholism it is even more likely that the disease may be innocently contracted, since the drinking of alcoholic beverages is a common activity, generally accepted in our society, while the purchasing and taking of drugs are crimes. * * *

m. See also State v. Adams, 91 So.3d 724 (Ala.Crim.App.2010) (holding, under *Robinson–Powell*, that the Eighth Amendment bars punishment of indigent homeless sex offenders for failing to provide the actual address where they reside, as required under state law).

parties filed a joint motion seeking dismissal of the appeal and requesting that the appellate court's opinion be vacated, which it was. 505 F.3d 1006 (9th Cir. 2007).)

Is *Jones* consistent with *Robinson–Powell*? Precedent aside, do you agree with the result as a constitutional matter?

Consider the comments of one critic of *Jones* who asked:

[W]hy in principle would *Jones* be limited to the homeless? Why would homeless people be protected from punishment * * * without similar protection afforded to alcoholics and drug addicts who commit criminal acts linked to their "disease status"? Surely pedophiles will soon make compelling arguments under *Jones* that their sexual acts are compulsive, irresistible actions inherent in their "disease" and are thus unpunishable under the Eighth Amendment.

Martin R. Gardner, *Rethinking Robinson v. California in the Wake of Jones v. Los Angeles: Avoiding the "Demise of the Criminal Law" by Attending to "Punishment,"* 98 J. Crim. L. & Criminology 429, 459 (2008).

Are Professor Gardner's concerns legitimate? Would it be bad if there was a constitutional-based defense that prohibited the punishment of alcoholics, addicts, and pedophiles for criminal acts "linked" to their conditions? Is there a principled way to draw a line between the homeless and these persons?

The next two Notes consider whether a constitutional defense can be justified on retributive or utilitarian grounds.

3. *Retributivism.* In assessing an individual's blameworthiness for a crime, is the pertinent issue whether the actor is to blame for becoming an alcoholic or addict? Or, is the appropriate question whether—however one's alcoholism or addiction arose—the actor had sufficient free will to avoid committing the offense at the time of the crime?

Suppose that a person *is* to blame for becoming an addict. Does it follow from this that she deserves to be punished for her later, arguably morally involuntary, addiction-related conduct? Yes, according to the following anti-drug message to adolescents:

Here * * * is the truth about crack, and many other drugs. If you do it once, you are significantly more likely to mess up your life than you otherwise would have been. If you do it a second time, the chances rise again. And so on. At some point * * * continued use entails some degree of ongoing damage to your life and the chances of something truly catastrophic happening becomes high. * * * At a certain point it may in some sense be beyond your power to step back from the brink. *Still, when catastrophe strikes, it's all your fault, for * * * you knew, or should have known, the odds when you went into the game * * *.*

"The Barry Bust," *The New Republic,* Vol. 202, No. 7, Feb. 12, 1990, at 8, 9 (emphasis added).

Do you agree with the italicized conclusion? Or, do you find Circuit Judge Wright's observation in United States v. Moore, 486 F.2d 1139 (D.C.Cir.1973) (dissenting opinion), more persuasive:

It is of course true that there may have been a time in the past before the addict lost control when he made a conscious decision to use drugs. But imposition of punishment on this basis would violate the long-standing rule that "[t]he law looks to the immediate, and not to the remote cause; to the actual state of the party, and not to the causes, which remotely produced it." * * * "A sick person is a sick person though he exposed himself to contagion." I would adhere to that view today, for no matter how the addict came to be addicted, once he has reached that stage he clearly is sick, and a bare desire for vengeance cannot justify his treatment as a criminal.

Reconsider the theories of excuse described earlier in the casebook (beginning at p. 562). Is exculpation defensible according to one or more of these theories?

4. *Utilitarianism.* Does conviction and punishment of drug addicts and alcoholics for their offenses have utilitarian value? Are such persons deterrable? Would their punishment deter others? Consider Steven S. Nemerson, *Alcoholism, Intoxication, and the Criminal Law,* 10 Cardozo L.Rev. 393, 439–42 (1988), relating to alcoholism:

> Punishing individuals who are actually blameless as a result of alcoholism-induced intoxication may * * * serve to maximize utility by its effects on pre-crime drinking by some alcoholics.

> * * * [P]sychological denial of their inability to control the amount and results of their drinking "immunizes" [alcoholics] from the deterrent force of the threat or imposition of punishment. But punishment for crime by intoxicated alcoholics is not necessarily inefficacious as to all those in this class. Some do entertain limited doubts about their control over their own drinking and subsequent conduct. Some at least realize that in the past their drinking has led to unpredicted, undesired, and perhaps even criminal, consequences. To the extent that such doubts exist—to the extent that they acknowledge their own "problem drinking"—such individuals may be amenable to the deterrent force of punishment. * * *

> While an alcoholic not undergoing treatment has little or no control over whether he will drink, he does retain some control over when he will begin to drink. To the extent that drinking under certain conditions or in certain settings is more likely to result in criminal behavior, punishment of alcoholics for their crimes may serve to channel alcoholics's drinking into less potentially dangerous environments. * * *

> The fact that the alcoholic may not be morally blameworthy for his criminal acts does not negate the practical effect of imposing punishment for those acts. Treating the offender *as if he were morally responsible* serves to promote rehabilitation.

Are you persuaded? Do these arguments apply with equal force to persons addicted to narcotics?

5. For the perspectives of a participant in the *Powell* case from the State's perspective, three decades later, see David Robinson, Jr., *Powell v.*

Texas: The Case of the Intoxicated Shoeshine Man Some Reflections a Generation Later by a Participant, 26 Am. J. Crim. L. 401 (1999).

3. "SEVERE ENVIRONMENTAL DEPRIVATION" DEFENSE

In United States v. Alexander, 471 F.2d 923 (D.C.Cir.1972), the defendants, who were African–American, got into a verbal dispute in a hamburger shop with the victim, a white soldier in the Marines. When the soldier either said "What you God-damn niggers want?" or "What do you want, dirty nigger bastard?," one of the defendants shot to death the Marine. The defense introduced expert testimony that the defendant acted as the result of an irresistible impulse to shoot, and that the impulse was the result of the defendant's socially and economically deprived childhood in Watts, California, in which his father abandoned the family, he lived in economically dire straits, received little love and attention from his mother, and was the victim of racist treatment. According to the psychiatrist, the defendant experienced impaired behavior controls as the result of his "rotten social background."

The trial judge instructed the jury to disregard the testimony regarding the defendant's socially deprived background and to consider only the defendant's insanity plea. The Court of Appeal affirmed, but Judge Bazelon dissented. He would have required the trial judge to instruct the jury to consider the testimony (Bazelon described it as "rotten social background" testimony) and to acquit him if it found that, as a result of the condition, his behavioral controls were seriously undermined.

A few years later, Judge Bazelon formulated the following general proposition:

> Those who see the law as a moral force insist that the law should not convict unless it can condemn. According to this view, a decision for conviction requires the following three determinations: (1) a condemnable act was committed by the actor-defendant; (2) the actor can be condemned—that is, he could reasonable have been expected to have conformed his behavior to the demands of the law; and (3) society's own conduct in relation to the actor entitles it to sit in condemnation of him with respect to the condemnable act.

David L. Bazelon, *The Morality of the Criminal Law*, 49 S.Cal.L.Rev. 385, 388 (1976).

In *your* view, should a person who commits a crime because of social deprivation be acquitted on the ground that he does not deserve to be condemned (Bazelon's second element) or that society lacks standing to judge the actor (the third element). In thinking about this, consider the following materials.

RICHARD DELGADO—"ROTTEN SOCIAL BACKGROUND": SHOULD THE CRIMINAL LAW RECOGNIZE A DEFENSE OF SEVERE ENVIRONMENTAL DEPRIVATION?

3 Law & Inequality 9 (1985), 9–10, 54–55, 68–72

There is * * * a strong relationship between environmental adversity and criminal behavior. Of course, not all poor persons violate the law and not all those from privileged backgrounds are law-abiding; it remains, however, that of more than one million offenders entangled in the correctional system, the vast majority are members of the poorest class. Unless we are prepared to argue that offenders are poor because they are criminal, we should be open to the possibility that many turn to crime because of poverty—that poverty is, for many, a determinant of criminal behavior. * * *

An environment of extreme poverty and deprivation creates in individuals a propensity to commit crimes. In some cases, a defendant's impoverished background so greatly determines his or her criminal behavior that we feel it unfair to punish the individual. This sense of unfairness arises from the morality of the criminal law itself, in that "our collective conscience does not allow punishment where it cannot impose blame." And blame is inappropriate when a defendant's criminal behavior is caused by extrinsic factors beyond his or her control. * * *

According to most retributive theories, punishment is inflicted simply because justice requires (or permits) it * * *. From society's perspective, the wrongdoer has taken unfair advantage of the agreed-upon sharing of benefits and burdens, and therefore the wrongdoer owes something to society as a result of renouncing the burden of self-restraint which others have assumed. Punishment exacts the debt and restores moral equilibrium. * * *

How does this theory of punishment apply to an RSB defendant? The view that the criminal needs punishment "to heal the laceration of the bonds that joined him to society" assumes the actual existence of a community to which each individual is bonded in a meaningful way. This assumption has been challenged. * * * [A]ny * * * sense of community is destroyed by the unequal distribution of wealth, which consigns some to poverty, and by unequal laws. * * *

If the community excludes certain persons, is it entitled to punish those individuals on the basis of a debt they owe the community? * * * Like others, Professor [Jeffrie] Murphy draws [the conclusion that punishment is morally unjustifiable] by showing that there is little basis for community in the reality of rotten social background:

> [T]o think that [the notion of community] applies to the typical criminal from the poorer classes is to live in a world of social and political fantasy. Criminals typically are not members of a shared

community of values with their jailers; they suffer from what Marx calls alienation. And they certainly would be hard pressed to name the benefits for which they are supposed to owe obedience.

Thus, even if an RSB defendant is responsible for his or her acts, retribution theory provides little moral basis to punish him or her for those acts. * * *

Deterrence theory argues that punishment prevents crime by making an example of the criminal; punishment functions as a threat and warning. * * *

Both functions are at best weakly served by inflicting punishment on an RSB defendant. Although some who live in poverty do heed the law's sanction, many will not be deterred. These include the RSB person who commits crime out of rage or on the basis of political principle. Moreover, the threat of punishment is unlikely to deter the desperately poor, who commit crimes out of economic necessity. * * * For a deterrent to work, it must threaten the individual with loss of things he or she considers valuable. When an individual lives a miserable, impoverished life, he or she has little, if anything, to fear from a deterrent, sometimes not even the loss of his or her freedom. * * *

NOTES AND QUESTIONS

1. Are you persuaded by Delgado's arguments? Can you defend your proposition—either for or against the defense—on utilitarian or retributive grounds?

2. Sanford H. Kadish, *Excusing Crime,* 75 Calif.L.Rev. 257, 284 (1987):

> Social deprivation may well establish a credible explanation of how the defendant has come to have the character he has. But it [does not] establish a moral excuse any more than a legal one, for there is a difference between explaining a person's wrongful behavior and explaining it away. Explanations are not excuses if they merely explain how the defendant came to have the character of someone who could do such a thing. Otherwise, there would be no basis for moral responsibility in any case where we knew enough about the person to understand him.

3. R. A. Duff, *Law, Language and Community: Some Preconditions of Criminal Liability*, 18 Oxford J. Legal Studies 189, 204–205 (1998):

> Claims about what people "could" do sometimes amount to claims, not about what is in some strict sense * * * psychologically possible for them, but rather about what could reasonably be expected of them. Thus to say that someone "could not" resist a threat * * * might be to say, not that it was impossible for him to resist it, but rather that we could not reasonably expect or demand that he resist it * * *. * * * I have said[] that it is a precondition of criminal liability that the language of the law be one which the defendant * * * could reasonably be expected to speak in her own voice * * *. * * * Can we honestly insist that it is reasonable to expect those who are seriously and unjustly disadvantaged by the

political and economic structures which the law protects to accept the language of the law * * * as a language which they can speak in their own voices?

4. For recent debate on this topic, see a symposium, *"Rotten Social Background" 25 Years Later*, starting at 2 Ala. C.R. & C.L. L. Rev. 1 (2012).

4. CULTURAL DEFENSE

Under what circumstances, if any, should a person's good-faith belief in the propriety of specific conduct, which belief is based on one's cultural upbringing, negate or mitigate the actor's criminal responsibility? The materials that follow invite consideration of this question.

STATE v. KARGAR

Supreme Judicial Court of Maine, 1996.
679 A.2d 81.

DANA, JUSTICE.

Mohammad Kargar, an Afghani refugee, appeals from the judgments entered in the Superior Court * * * convicting him of two counts of gross sexual assault in violation of 17–A M.R.S.A. § 253(1)(B) (Supp.1995) (Class A).[1] Kargar contends on appeal that the court erred in denying his motion to dismiss pursuant to the *de minimis* statute, 17–A M.R.S.A. § 12 (1983). * * *

On June 25, 1993, Kargar and his family, refugees since approximately 1990, were babysitting a young neighbor. While the neighbor was there, she witnessed Kargar kissing his eighteen-month-old son's penis. When she was picked up by her mother, the girl told her mother what she had seen. The mother had previously seen a picture of Kargar kissing his son's penis in the Kargar family photo album. After her daughter told her what she had seen, the mother notified the police.

Peter Wentworth, a sergeant with the Portland Police Department, went to Kargar's apartment to execute a search warrant. * * * The picture of Kargar kissing his son's penis was found in the photograph album. Kargar admitted that it was him in the photograph and that he was kissing his son's penis. Kargar told Wentworth that kissing a young son's penis is accepted as common practice in his culture. Kargar also said it was very possible that his neighbor had seen him kissing his son's penis. Kargar was arrested and taken to the police station.

Prior to the jury-waived trial Kargar moved for a dismissal of the case pursuant to the *de minimis* statute. With the consent of the parties, the court held the trial phase of the proceedings first, followed by a hearing on

---

1. 17–A M.R.S.A. § 253(1)(B) (Supp.1995) provides, in pertinent part:

1. A person is guilty of gross sexual assault if that person engages in a sexual act with another person and: * * *

B. The other person, not the actor's spouse, has not in fact attained the age of 14 years.

the *de minimis* motion. The *de minimis* hearing consisted of testimony from many Afghani people who were familiar with the Afghani practice and custom of kissing a young son on all parts of his body.[2] Kargar's witnesses, all relatively recent emigrants from Afghanistan, testified that kissing a son's penis is common in Afghanistan, that it is done to show love for the child, and that it is the same whether the penis is kissed or entirely put into the mouth because there are no sexual feelings involved.[3] The witnesses also testified that pursuant to Islamic law any sexual activity between an adult and a child results in the death penalty for the adult. Kargar also submitted statements from Professor Ludwig Adamec of the University of Arizona's Center for Near Eastern Studies and Saifur Halimi, a religious teacher and Director of the Afghan Mujahideen Information Bureau in New York. Both statements support the testimony of the live witnesses. The State did not present any witnesses during the *de minimis* hearing. Following the presentation of witnesses the court denied Kargar's motion and found him guilty of two counts of gross sexual assault.

I.

Maine's *de minimis* statute provides, in pertinent part:

1. The court may dismiss a prosecution if, ... having regard to the nature of the conduct alleged and the nature of the attendant circumstances, it finds the defendant's conduct:

> **A.** Was within a customary license or tolerance, which was not expressly refused by the person whose interest was infringed and which is not inconsistent with the purpose of the law defining the crime; or

> **B.** Did not actually cause or threaten the harm sought to be prevented by the law defining the crime or did so only to an extent too trivial to warrant the condemnation of conviction; or

> **C.** Presents such other extenuations that it cannot reasonably be regarded as envisaged by the Legislature in defining the crime.

* * * Kargar asserts that the court erred *as a matter of law* because it found culture, lack of harm, and his innocent state of mind irrelevant to its *de minimis* analysis. We agree.

II.

Maine's *de minimis* statute is based on the Model Penal Code [Section 2.12] and the Hawaii Penal Code, and its purpose is to "introduce[ ] a desirable degree of flexibility in the administration of the law." The

---

2. Kargar testified during the *de minimis* hearing that the practice was acceptable until the child was three, four, or five years old.

3. Kargar testified during the *de minimis* hearing that his culture views the penis of a child as not the holiest or cleanest part of the body because it is from where the child urinates. Kargar testified that kissing his son there shows how much he loves his child precisely because it is not the holiest or cleanest part of the body.

language of the statute expressly requires that courts view the defendant's conduct "having regard to the nature of the conduct alleged and the nature of the attendant circumstances." Each *de minimis* analysis will therefore always be case-specific. The Model Penal Code traces the history of *de minimis* statutes to section 13 of England's Stephen's Draft Code of 1879. As justification for the proposed section 13 it was suggested that courts should have the "power to discharge without conviction, persons who have committed acts which, though amounting in law to crimes, do not under the circumstances involve any moral turpitude."

When making a determination under the *de minimis* statute, an objective consideration of surrounding circumstances is authorized. Although we have not had occasion to articulate circumstances worthy of cognizance, we agree with the courts of New Jersey and Hawaii that the following factors are appropriate for *de minimis* analysis:

> the background, experience and character of the defendant which may indicate whether he knew or ought to have known of the illegality; the knowledge of the defendant of the consequences to be incurred upon violation of the statute; the circumstances concerning the offense; the resulting harm or evil, if any, caused or threatened by the infraction; the probable impact of the violation upon the community; the seriousness of the infraction in terms of punishment, bearing in mind that punishment can be suspended; mitigating circumstances as to the offender; possible improper motives of the complainant or prosecutor; and any other data which may reveal the nature and degree of the culpability in the offense committed by the defendant.
> * * *

III.

Our review of the record in the instant case reveals that the court, in its analysis of section 12(1)(C), denied Kargar's motion without considering the full range of relevant factors. The court's interpretation of the subsection, which focused on whether the conduct met the definition of the gross sexual assault statute, operated to nullify the effect of the *de minimis* analysis called for by the statute. The focus is not on whether the conduct falls within the reach of the statute criminalizing it. If it did not, there would be no need to perform a *de minimis* analysis. The focus is on whether the admittedly criminal conduct was envisioned by the Legislature when it defined the crime. If the Legislature did not intend that there be an individual, case-specific analysis then there would be no point to the *de minimis* statute. Subsection 1(C) provides a safety valve for circumstances that could not have been envisioned by the Legislature. * * * Because the Legislature did in fact allow for unanticipated "extenuations," the trial court was required to consider the possibility that the result of a Class A conviction *in this case* could not have been anticipated by the Legislature when it defined the crime of gross sexual assault.

IV.

In order to determine whether this defendant's conduct was anticipated by the Legislature when it defined the crime of gross sexual assault it is instructive to review the not-so-distant history of that crime. 17–A M.R.S.A. § 253(1)(B) makes criminal any sexual act with a minor (nonspouse) under the age of fourteen. A sexual act is defined as, among other things, "direct physical contact between the genitals of one and the mouth * * * of the other." Prior to 1985 the definition of this type of sexual act included a sexual gratification element. The Legislature removed the sexual gratification element because, "given the physical contacts described, no concern exists for excluding 'innocent' contacts." Thus, the 1985 amendment to section 251(1)(C) illuminates the fact that an "innocent" touching such as occurred in this case has not forever been recognized as inherently criminal by our own law. The Legislature's inability to comprehend "innocent" genital-mouth contact is highlighted by reference to another type of "sexual act," namely, "[a]ny act involving direct physical contact between the genitals * * * of one and an instrument or device manipulated by another." The Legislature maintained the requirement that for this type of act to be criminal it must be done for the purpose of either sexual gratification or to cause bodily injury or offensive physical contact. Its stated reason for doing so was that "a legitimate concern exists for excluding 'innocent' contacts, such as for proper medical purposes or other valid reasons."

All of the evidence presented at the *de minimis* hearing supports the conclusion that there was nothing "sexual" about Kargar's conduct. There is no real dispute that what Kargar did is accepted practice in his culture. * * *

* * * Although the court responded to [a] call for leniency by imposing an entirely suspended sentence, the two convictions expose Kargar to severe consequences independent of any period of incarceration, including his required registration as a sex offender pursuant to 34–A M.R.S.A. § 11003 (Supp.1995), and the possibility of deportation pursuant to 8 U.S.C.A. § 1251(a)(2)(A)(i)(I) (West Supp.1996). These additional consequences emphasize why the factors recognized by the court during the sentencing hearing were also relevant to *the de minimis* analysis.

Although it may be difficult for us as a society to separate Kargar's conduct from our notions of sexual abuse, that difficulty should not result in a felony conviction in this case. The State concedes that dismissing this case pursuant to the *de minimis* statute would pose little harm to the community. The State is concerned, however, with the potential harm caused by courts using the factors of this case to allow for even more exceptions to the criminal statutes. It argues that exceptions should be made by the Legislature, which can gather data, debate social costs and benefits, and clearly define what conduct constitutes criminal activity. The flaw in the State's position is that the Legislature has already clearly defined what conduct constitutes gross sexual assault. It has also allowed for the adjustment of the criminal statutes by courts in extraordinary cases where, for instance, the conduct cannot reasonably be regarded as envisaged by the Legislature in defining the crime.

* * * Precisely because the Legislature did not envision the extenuating circumstances present in this case, to avoid an injustice the *de minimis* analysis set forth in section 12(1)(C) requires that Kargar's convictions be vacated.

NOTES AND QUESTIONS

1.   Most jurisdictions do not have a *de minimis* statute. Therefore, a person in Kargar's situation would have to hope that a prosecutor would not bring charges, that a jury would nullify the law and acquit, or that the judge would be lenient in sentencing after conviction. Do you consider one of these alternatives preferable to the use of a *de minimis* statute? On the other hand, do you believe that a person's cultural beliefs should be irrelevant in determining guilt or innocence and in sentencing?

2.   Should a legislature enact a stand-alone "cultural defense"? If so, under what circumstances should individuals be acquitted for acting in conformity with their cultural beliefs? The following materials consider the propriety of such a defense.

THE CULTURAL DEFENSE IN THE CRIMINAL LAW

99 Harvard Law Review 1293 (1986), 1296, 1298–1304, 1308–1311

II.   THE RATIONALE FOR THE CULTURAL DEFENSE * * *

The American criminal justice system is committed to securing justice for the individual defendant. In the context of the criminal law, the ultimate aim of this principle of individualized justice is to tailor punishment to fit the degree of the defendant's personal culpability. The American legal system recognizes that, because of mitigating circumstances, it may be unjust to punish a particular defendant to the limits of the law. Consistent with the principle of individualized justice, courts have recently recognized new criminal defenses. The battered spouse defense, for example, was created in response to situations in which convicting the defendant would be unfair, but traditional defenses of self-defense and insanity would not be entirely appropriate.

Similarly, the principle of individualized justice militates in favor of the cultural defense. There are two situations in which strict application of the law might be unfair to a person raised in a foreign culture. First, such a person may have committed a criminal act solely because she was ignorant of the applicable law. Although ignorance of the law is generally no excuse in a criminal prosecution, fairness to the individual defendant suggests that ignorance of the law ought to be a defense for persons who were raised in a foreign culture. Treating persons raised in a foreign culture differently should not be viewed as an exercise in favoritism, but rather as a vindication of the principles of fairness and equality that underlie a system of individualized justice. It may be fair to impute knowledge of American law to persons raised in this country: various socializing institutions such as the family, school, and place of worship can reasonably be expected to have instructed these persons about the norms upon which society's laws are based. A new immigrant, however, has not been given the same opportunity to absorb—through exposure to important socializing institutions—the norms underlying this nation's criminal laws. The principle of individualized justice demands that the law take this factor into account.

Second, an ordinarily law-abiding person raised in a foreign culture may have committed a criminal act solely because the values of her native culture compelled her to do so. Mere awareness that her act is contrary to the law may not be enough to override her adherence to fundamental cultural values. Laws are more effective in commanding obedience when individuals internalize the underlying norms to the point where they believe that the law embodies morally correct values. A society's socializing institutions not only make its members aware of its norms, but also instill in its people a sense that they are morally obligated to abide by their culture's norms. Thus, persons raised in other cultures, who are subject to influences that inculcated in them a different set of norms, will likely feel morally obligated to follow those norms. Once norms have acquired this moral dimension, conformity with conflicting laws becomes more difficult. For this reason, a person's cultural background represents a relevant individual factor that a just legal system should take into account.

Through its commitment to individualized justice, the legal system advances a second principle that favors the recognition of a cultural defense: cultural pluralism. By judging each person according to the standards of her native culture, the principle of individualized justice preserves the values of that culture, and thus maintains a culturally diverse society. * * * [C]ultural pluralism emanates from the principle of equality underlying the American system of justice. Equality among different ethnic groups ultimately requires that each group respect other groups' right to be different and that the majority not penalize a minority group simply because it is different.

A third justification for encouraging cultural pluralism is that the amount of diversity in the United States measures, in part, the value that the majority places on liberty. Cultural pluralism is an inevitable product of this nation's commitment to liberty. In a nation with members drawn from diverse backgrounds, allowing people the freedom to live by their values will lead to a culturally pluralistic society. By quashing cultural values that diverge from mainstream norms, the majority foists upon all others a single orthodoxy—a result repugnant to the American political paragon. * * *

Individualized justice and cultural pluralism, however, are not the only ideals that are fundamental to society. Any commitment to these ideals must be constrained by a conflicting objective in the law: the desire to lay down a set of common values that society considers important for everyone to share. Perhaps the principal reason for imposing a set of common values is to maintain social order. Societies usually regard the preservation of social order—societal self-protection—as a primary aim. To maintain this order, it has been argued, societies must lay down a body of positive law that compels the obedience of all regardless of individual notions of morality: if each person were required to adhere to the law only to the extent that it was consistent with her own values, societies would tend toward anarchy. Legal systems attempt to compel this obedience by imposing punitive sanctions in order to deter people from breaking the law.

* * * Courts may oppose the cultural defense because they feel that it would undermine the specific deterrent effects of the law. A person punished for breaking a law would normally be less likely to misbehave again than one who received no punishment. Courts may also resist a cultural defense because they suspect that the defense would detract from the law's general deterrent effects. According to some observers, general deterrence is most effective when punishment for committing a proscribed act is certain. Thus, members of immigrant groups might be less deterred by the law if their transgressions could be excused by their cultural values.

In many cases, however, it is questionable whether recognition of the cultural defense would significantly impair the deterrent capacity of the law. Specific deterrence will often be needless in cases of culturally motivated crimes. In situations in which the defendant's conduct was triggered by extraordinary circumstances that are unlikely to recur, specific deterrence is unnecessary. More important, because these criminal acts often stem solely from ignorance of the existing laws—and not from any malevolent motive—punishment is unnecessary to deter similar conduct in the future: the mere invocation of the criminal process is likely to have a normative effect on the accused such that she will not commit similar violations in the future. Particularly if the defendant is informed that her ignorance will excuse her only once, then much of the specific deterrent effect of the law will be preserved. The defendant will know that she faces the regular punishment should she repeat her actions.

Punishing the defendant in cultural defense cases will serve as an effective *general* deterrent in only one of the two categories of culturally related crimes. In the first category—in which members of an ethnic culture commit crimes out of ignorance of the law—punishing the defendant may serve to instruct other members of her culture of the law, and thus may advance the goal of general deterrence. In such cases, however, punishment may not be necessary to accomplish this educational function. Efforts of local government agencies targeted at informing recent immigrant communities of the laws and other social norms would be a more far-reaching method of deterrence than punishing those few individuals who come in contact with the law. * * *

In the other category of culturally related crimes—those motivated by a sense of moral and social compulsion—punishing the defendant may only marginally deter others in her culture whose actions are similarly motivated. Further, to the extent that extreme acts induced by adherence to cultural mores * * * are relatively rare, the threat to social order, and thus the need for deterrence, becomes less pressing. * * *

III.   DEFINING THE SCOPE OF THE CULTURAL DEFENSE

Judicial rejection of a cultural defense may rest on the concern that once the defense is introduced, it will be impossible to define its proper scope. Thus, before courts recognize the defense, they must first identify factors that delineate its boundaries. These factors must determine in a principled way under what circumstances and to what extent a cultural defense should apply. Some of these factors can be derived from the principles of individualized justice and cultural pluralism. Other factors follow readily from the interests, such as societal self-protection and sense of community, that are promoted by common values. The crucial objective in defining the scope of the defense is to advance the goals of individualized justice and cultural pluralism while recognizing the concerns reflected in the desire for common values. The factors proposed below are each intimately tied to one or more of these three principles. The task of the courts would be to balance these factors in each case in order to arrive at the appropriate scope of the cultural defense.

The interest in societal self-protection directs courts to evaluate factors such as the probability of recurrence and severity of the crime in determining whether and to what extent to recognize a cultural defense in a particular case. Judicial receptiveness to a cultural defense should vary inversely with both the likelihood of recurrence and the severity of the crime. * * * With respect to the question of severity, at least three variables are relevant. First, courts should consider whether the crime is victimless. * * * Second, if there is a victim, courts should inquire whether the crime is confined to voluntary participants within the defendant's culture. A cultural defense should more readily be admitted when the crime is limited to persons capable of meaningful consent who belong to that culture and subscribe to its tenets. Third, when there is a victim, courts should ask whether serious bodily or emotional harm was inflicted.

The desire for social order further demands that courts consider factors such as the identifiability, degree of self-containment, and size of the defendant's cultural group. Identifiability is important because membership in the exempted group would otherwise be difficult to ascertain, thus complicating the task of applying the defense. Self-containment is important because it tends both to insulate the rest of society from harm and to minimize the loss of general deterrence that may accompany a judicial decision excusing a particular forbidden act. Finally, the size of the exempted group is significant because exempting a large percentage of the population from a law would itself impose significant costs and would also send a conspicuous signal to the remaining population that the proscribed conduct is acceptable. When recognizing the cultural defense is likely to create any of these dangers, courts will understandably be loath to do so.

Consistent with the goals of individualizing justice and fostering cultural pluralism are factors that direct an inquiry into the influence of the defendant's culture on her behavior. Courts might, for example, measure the degree of the defendant's assimilation into the mainstream culture. The less assimilated the accused, the more compelling are justice-based arguments that it is unfair to punish her for not complying with the law. Moreover, the less assimilated the accused, the more a cultural defense will encourage pluralism by maintaining a spectrum of widely divergent values.

A desire to maintain pluralism should further lead courts to assess the importance of the cultural value that impelled the prohibited act. Because a cultural defense confers a partial "exemption" from an otherwise legitimate law, only values of sufficient importance to the defendant's culture should be protected. Honor, for example, is considered a fundamental principle in the Japanese and Lebanese Muslim cultures. Thus, individuals in these cultures who are motivated by honor to commit prohibited acts may well be entitled to a cultural defense—subject, of course, to appropriate regard for social order and the desire to build a sense of community among all members of society.

By considering these factors, courts will be able to determine when and to what extent a cultural defense should apply. The precise way in which courts will balance these factors will, of course, vary from case to case. But as long as the evolutionary process of identifying and refining relevant factors is based on an accommodation of society's several interests in establishing a set of common values with the ideals of individualizing justice and maintaining cultural pluralism, courts can minimize interference with society's diverse cultures while preserving the stability of community life.

NOTES AND QUESTIONS

1. Is the cultural defense that the preceding article advocates better understood as a justification or excuse defense? Professor Elaine M. Chiu, in *Culture as Justification, Not Excuse*, 43 Am. Crim. L. Rev. 1317, 1373–74 (2006), writes:

> * * * The distinction between justification and excuse is not minor. Indeed, it is quite meaningful and warrants the attention of scholars as well as jurists and legislators as they struggle with finding a place for culture in the criminal law. * * *

> [My] proposal * * * is to shift the current orientation of thinking about culturally motivated defendants * * * from excuse to justification. Instead of entrusting their fate to the discretion of individual law enforcement officers or straining the truth into ill-fitting excuse defenses, such

defendants should be able to advocate that their acts were justified acts. They should be able to contend that given their cultural background, their community, their beliefs and values, they committed an act of lesser harm to avoid even greater harm.

2. Women or children are quite often the victims in criminal cases in which a cultural defense would be implicated. For example, a Taiwanese man in the United States was charged with attempted murder of his 10–month–old daughter after he slammed her into a door jam. He suggested that in his culture "the father reigns supreme and the life of a female child may be expendable." *Cultural Belief Complicates Beating Case*, San Antonio Express–News, Feb. 14, 1996. According to one report, newborn twins in one Native American tribe were customarily abandoned in the forest or tossed into rivers, because they were believed to bring bad luck. Jared Kotler, *Twins Born Into Two Worlds*, San Francisco Chronicle, August 19, 1999, at A14. Also, reconsider the case considered earlier in this casebook: a rape case in which a male believed a female consented to the "marriage-by-capture" tradition of his culture (p. 446, Note 6).

Doriane Lambelet Coleman, *Individualizing Justice Through Multiculturalism: The Liberals' Dilemma*, 96 Colum. L. Rev. 1093, 1094–1095, 1166–1167 (1996) considers the gender aspect of the cultural defense:

> Allowing sensitivity to a defendant's culture to inform the application of laws to that individual is good multiculturalism. It also is good progressive criminal defense philosophy, which has as a central tenet the idea that the defendant should get as much individualized (subjective) justice as possible. * * *

> For legal scholars and practitioners who believe in a progressive civil and human rights agenda, [discussion of the defense] also raise[s] an important question: What happens to the victims—almost always minority women and children—when multiculturalism and individualized justice are advanced by dispositive cultural evidence? The answer, both in theory and in practice, is stark: They are denied the protection of the criminal laws * * *. * * *

> * * * Respect for * * * newcomers requires that we view multiculturalism as a positive and even necessary factor in the debate about how to resolve these conflicts. * * *

> Nevertheless, multiculturalism should not be permitted either intentionally or incidentally to erode the progress we have made as a culture in protecting the rights of minorities, women, and children * * *. The antidiscrimination principle responsible for this progress is at the core of the broader American culture, a culture which logically also should enjoy multiculturalism's embrace.

> The cultural defense is irreconcilable with this core because it permits customary practices such as female genital mutilation, mother-child suicide, marriage-by-capture, and other gender-motivated violence to escape the full sanction of the criminal law. For that reason, it must yield.

CHAPTER 10

INCHOATE OFFENSES

■ ■ ■

A. OVERVIEW

AMERICAN LAW INSTITUTE—MODEL PENAL CODE AND COMMENTARIES, COMMENT TO ARTICLE 5

(1985), 293–294

Article 5 [of the Model Penal Code] undertakes to deal systematically with [the crimes of] attempt, solicitation and conspiracy. These offenses have in common the fact that they deal with conduct that is designed to culminate in the commission of a substantive offense, but has failed in the discrete case to do so or has not yet achieved its culmination because there is something that the actor or another still must do. The offenses are inchoate in this sense.

These, to be sure, are not the only crimes so defined that their commission does not rest on proof of the occurrence of the evil that it is the object of the law to prevent; many specific, substantive offenses also have a large inchoate aspect. This is true not only with respect to crimes of risk creation, such as reckless driving, or specific crimes of preparation, such as possession with unlawful purpose. It is also true, at least in part, of crimes like larceny, forgery, kidnapping and even arson, not to speak of burglary, where a purpose to cause greater harm than that which is implicit in the actor's conduct is an element of the offense. This reservation notwithstanding, attempt, solicitation and conspiracy have such generality of definition and of application as inchoate crimes that it is useful * * * to confront the common problems they present.

Burglary

* * * General deterrence is at most a minor function to be served in fashioning provisions of the penal law addressed to these inchoate crimes; that burden is discharged upon the whole by the law dealing with the substantive offenses.

Other and major functions of the penal law remain, however, to be served. They may be summarized as follows:

708

First: When a person is seriously dedicated to commission of a crime, a firm legal basis is needed for the intervention of the agencies of law enforcement to prevent its consummation. In determining that basis, there must be attention to the danger of abuse; equivocal behavior may be misconstrued by an unfriendly eye as preparation to commit a crime. It is no less important, on the other side, that lines should not be drawn so rigidly that the police confront insoluble dilemmas in deciding when to intervene, facing the risk that if they wait the crime may be committed while if they act they may not yet have any valid charge.

Second: Conduct designed to cause or culminate in the commission of a crime obviously yields an indication that the actor is disposed towards such activity, not alone on this occasion but on others. There is a need, therefore, subject again to proper safeguards, for a legal basis upon which the special danger that such individuals present may be assessed and dealt with. They must be made amenable to the corrective process that the law provides.

Third: Finally, and quite apart from these considerations of prevention, when the actor's failure to commit the substantive offense is due to a fortuity, as when the bullet misses in attempted murder or when the expected response to solicitation is withheld, his exculpation on that ground would involve inequality of treatment that would shock the common sense of justice. Such a situation is unthinkable in any mature system designed to serve the proper goals of penal law.

NOTES AND QUESTIONS

1. Ira P. Robbins, *Double Inchoate Crimes,* 26 Harv. J. on Legis. 1, 3–4 (1989):

> The inchoate crimes of attempt, conspiracy, and solicitation are well established in the American legal system. "Inchoate" offenses allow punishment of an actor even though he has not consummated the crime that is the object of his efforts. * * *
>
> Most American jurisdictions treat inchoate offenses as substantive crimes, distinct and divorced from the completed crimes toward which they tend. Accordingly, attempt, conspiracy, and solicitation are defined broadly to encompass acts leading to the commission of any completed crime. Rather than try to enumerate every act to which inchoate liability attaches, however, legislatures have enacted relatively short statutes containing abstract conceptual terms with universal application. The Model Penal Code's provision for attempt liability, for example, represents a middle-ground approach to this problem. It prohibits an act that constitutes a "substantial step" toward the completed offense. The Code then fleshes out the abstract term "substantial step" by listing several nonexclusive examples that have application to numerous completed crimes. It has fallen to the courts to elaborate on the scope of inchoate offenses and decide when to administer them.

Thus, the concept of substantive inchoate crimes, by requiring a high degree of judicial interpretation, has vested great discretion in the judiciary. This discretion is similar to that of earlier courts in creating common-law offenses. In both circumstances, the court analyzes the policies underlying the criminal law and decides whether those policies require courts to punish certain acts.

2.   Professor Robbins points out (Note 1) that because inchoate offenses are typically defined broadly and abstractly, the judiciary is vested with tremendous interpretative discretion. For the same reason, police officers who come upon activities they regard as suspicious have considerable enforcement discretion. For example, consider the incident described in McQuirter v. State, 36 Ala.App. 707, 63 So.2d 388 (1953):

One summer evening, a woman walked with her two children and a neighbor's child past a parked truck in which a man, McQuirter, "said something unintelligible, opened the truck door, and placed his foot on the running board." McQuirter followed the woman and children, approaching within two or three feet of them. Fearful, the woman stopped at a friend's house. After ten minutes, she proceeded on her way, but McQuirter was still there and "came toward her from behind a telephone pole." The woman instructed the children to run to an acquaintance's house, which they did. When the resident of the house came out and investigated, McQuirter turned and walked away.

Suppose that a police officer had observed the preceding events. Should she have arrested McQuirter? If so, for what crime? Alternatively, should the officer have detained McQuirter to inquire as to his intentions? The difficulty with the latter option is that an officer may not constitutionally detain someone against his will unless she has reason to suspect that crime is afoot. Terry v. Ohio, 392 U.S. 1, 88 S.Ct. 1868, 20 L.Ed.2d 889 (1968). Do the facts here support a reasonable inference that McQuirter intended to commit a crime? What crime?

In actuality, no police officer was present, the woman arrived home safely, and McQuirter went to his home. Nonetheless, he was later arrested, prosecuted and convicted of the inchoate offense of "attempt to commit an assault with intent to rape." Is this a good outcome,[a] or do you believe that McQuirter was punished for innocent conduct "misconstrued by an unfriendly eye"? Does your view of the case change when you learn that McQuirter was an African–American and the woman, described by the Alabama court as "Mrs. Ted Allen," was white?[b]

What does this case suggest about inchoate offenses in general? For example, is there too great a risk that innocent persons will be arrested, tried, convicted, and punished for nothing more than suspicious-appearing behavior? Innocence aside, do some inchoate offenses come unacceptably close to

***

a.   Does your outlook on the case change when you learn that the Chief of Police testified at McQuirter's trial that the defendant confessed that he intended to rape the woman? McQuirter, however, denied making these statements.

b.   The appellate court believed that these facts were relevant: "In determining the question of intention the jury may consider social conditions and customs founded upon racial differences, such as that the prosecutrix was a white woman and defendant was a Negro man."

punishing persons for criminal thoughts alone? On the other hand, can a society adequately protect itself without punishing inchoate conduct? At what point should the Government be permitted to intervene, arrest, and punish persons for acting on their criminal thoughts?

Keep these questions in the forefront of your mind as you consider the materials in this chapter.

B. ATTEMPT

1. GENERAL PRINCIPLES

IRA P. ROBBINS—DOUBLE INCHOATE CRIMES

26 Harvard Journal on Legislation 1 (1989), 9–12

Although the law of attempt has roots in the early English law, its formulation as a general substantive offense is a relatively recent development.[22] * * * Many American jurisdictions now make specific provisions for the punishment of attempts to commit certain offenses, and almost all cover the rest of the field with a general attempt statute. With a few exceptions, these general statutes cover attempts to commit any felony or misdemeanor.

Among modern American jurisdictions, * * * the rule of merger operates * * * to the extent that a defendant cannot be convicted of both a completed offense and an attempt to commit it. All jurisdictions treat attempt as a lesser included offense of the completed crime. Moreover, many jurisdictions have held that a defendant may be convicted of the attempt if the state proves the completed crime, and several states so provide by statute.

* * * The principal purpose behind punishing an attempt * * * is not deterrence. The threat posed by the sanction for an attempt is unlikely to deter a person willing to risk the penalty for the object crime. Instead, the primary function of the crime of attempt is to provide a basis for law-enforcement officers to intervene before an individual can commit a completed offense.

NOTES AND QUESTIONS

1. Criminal attempts are of two varieties—incomplete and complete. In the former case, the actor does some of the acts that she set out to do, but then desists or is prevented from continuing by an extraneous factor, e.g., the intervention of a police officer. In contrast, with a completed attempt, the

---

22. The modern doctrine of attempt has its origin in the case of Rex v. Scofield, Cald.Mag.Rep. 397 (1784). * * * Prior to *Scofield,* * * * the courts imposed attempt liability only for two categories of offenses: attempted treason and attempts to subvert justice, such as subornation of perjury and attempted bribery of the King's officials.

The court in *Scofield* established the premises that a criminal intent may make criminal an act that was otherwise innocent in itself, and, conversely, that the completion of an act, criminal in itself, was not necessary to constitute a crime. * * *

actor does every act planned, but is unsuccessful in producing the intended result, e.g., she shoots and misses the intended victim.

Professor Robbins states that the primary purpose of attempt laws is to provide a basis for police intervention before an offense is completed. This rationale might explain incomplete attempts, but what is the basis for punishing a completed attempt?

2. *The role of "harm" in criminal attempts.* Is there any social harm in a criminal attempt? For example, if Oscar lies in wait to kill Paul, but is arrested before he can pull the trigger—perhaps before Paul even arrives on the scene—what harm has Oscar caused? Or, suppose that Tammy fires a gun at Ursula who is asleep, but the gun misfires. Tammy, disgusted, abandons her efforts to kill Ursula. Ursula goes about her life unaware of the events. Where is the harm in Tammy's actions? If there is no harm, are we punishing harmless conduct merely because of the actor's illicit thoughts?

Some commentators believe that punishment in the absence of harm is unjustifiable. Professor Paul Robinson writes:

> If one views deterrence as the proper function of the criminal law, a harm requirement is appropriate. To the extent that the criminal law punishes nonharmful conduct, it weakens the stigma and deterrent effect of criminal conviction for harmful conduct. If a defendant who has caused no harm feels that he is punished unjustifiably, rehabilitative efforts will be hampered. Indeed, one may ask: If no harm has been caused, what harm will be deterred by punishment, and what harm-causing characteristic will be rehabilitated? If one believes that the role of the criminal law is to provide retribution, a harm requirement is also proper; in the absence of harm there is nothing for which to seek retribution. * * * The consistency of a requirement of harm with these fundamental purposes of the criminal law is reflected in the fact that harm has, from the earliest of civilized times, been treated as a de facto requirement.

Paul H. Robinson, *A Theory of Justification: Societal Harm as a Prerequisite for Criminal Liability,* 23 UCLA L. Rev. 266, 266–267 (1975).

If social harm *is* a de facto requirement of the criminal law, does this mean that laws punishing attempts are unjustifiable, or do attempts cause "social harm"? If it is the latter, what *is* the social harm of a criminal attempt? Or, is Robinson simply wrong, and punishment of criminal attempts is justifiable even in the absence of harm? The following article excerpt considers these questions further.

ANDREW ASHWORTH—CRIMINAL ATTEMPTS AND THE ROLE OF RESULTING HARM UNDER THE CODE, AND IN THE COMMON LAW

19 Rutgers Law Journal 725 (1988), 734–738

What is the justification for criminalising incomplete attempts? Prevention is surely the main reason for penalising preliminary steps on the way to inflicting a prohibited harm. The law should authorise agents of law enforcement to intervene before the major harm is done. This is one of the few ways in which criminal law can realistically provide protection of rights. But to justify intervention (by arrest and perhaps overnight detention) is not to justify punishment. What has the incomplete attempter done that is wrong?

The answer depends on the chosen rationale for criminal punishment. Modern retributivist theories purport to justify punishment if and insofar as it tends to "restore an order of fairness which was disrupted by the criminal's criminal act." A crime disturbs the order of things ordained by law. The offender deserves punishment because he has chosen to disturb this order in a prohibited way. The punishment is necessary so as to restore, at least symbolically, that order.

This general theory of "just deserts," however, is not sufficiently specific to be applied to the incomplete attempter. It can be developed in either of two ways. A "harm-based" form of retributivism would link the justification for punishment to the culpable causing of harm: both the justification for and the measure of punishment derive from the culpable causing of a prohibited harm. This would seem to indicate impunity for incomplete attempters on the ground that, whatever their culpability, they have not yet caused the prohibited harm. The only way to circumvent this would be to argue for an extended definition of harm, * * * whereby a preliminary act manifesting an intent to commit a substantive crime is presumed to cause apprehension or fear in others. Some systems of criminal law do contain offences of this kind, but the actual or possible causation of apprehension in other persons does not generally form part of the definition of attempts. Thus, the harm-based version of retributivism * * * does not readily yield a justification for punishing incomplete attempts.

An intent-based form of retributivism would start with the proposition that the technique of the criminal law is to impose on individuals in society various duties of self-restraint, in order to provide a basic security of person, property, amenity, and so on. A person who voluntarily casts off this burden of self-restraint deserves punishment, in that he or she has used unfair means to gain an advantage over law-abiding citizens. The purpose of criminal punishment then is to counter-balance, at least symbolically, a voluntary breaking of the rules. Since fairness is an integral element in this "just deserts" approach, it would be wrong to allow random or chance factors to determine the threshold of criminal liability or the quantum of punishment. In criminal endeavours, as in other spheres of life, things do not always turn out as one expects. The emphasis in criminal liability should be upon what D was trying to do, intended to do and believed he was doing, rather than upon the actual consequences of his conduct. The point may be restated in terms of the "intent principle" and the "belief principle": the intent principle is that individuals should be held criminally liable for what they intended to do, and not according to what actually did or did not occur; the belief principle is that individuals should be judged on the basis of what they believed they were doing, not on the basis of actual facts and circumstances which were not known to them at the time.

Applying the intent principle, one must ask whether a person who takes substantial steps towards the commission of the substantive offence, with intent to commit that offence, has already manifested sufficient non-self-restraint so as to deserve punishment (subject to debate about the stage required as the actus reus of an attempt). Whether the endeavour is successful, in terms of committing the substantive offence, may well depend on matters which to D are pure chance—whether the police learn about the plan and intervene before D does all that was planned; whether something fails to work in the way D envisaged; whether the victim behaves unexpectedly, and so on. The fact that D appears in court for the substantive offence and E (who set out to commit the same crime) is charged only with an attempt may have been determined simply by twists of fate, unrelated to the efforts they made or to their relative culpability. The actual outcomes of their efforts should not make the difference between criminal liability and no liability at all * * *. For the intent-based retributivist, * * * once D has reached a sufficient stage in acting with the settled purpose of committing a substantive offence, criminal liability is individually deserved and socially fair.

How do the two versions of retributive theory apply to complete attempts, in which D has done all the acts intended without producing the prohibited outcome? Harm-based retributivism might be thought to tell more strongly here than for incomplete attempts, since a complete attempt may sometimes create more apprehension and alarm. Yet the absence of apprehension from the definition of attempts, together with the fact that many * * * attempts may be completed without causing alarm to anyone, weakens this argument. Intent-based retributivism, on the other hand, has its clearest application here. In a complete attempt D has done everything planned, and the non-occurrence of the consequence is unexpected and often outside his control. It can therefore be maintained that there is no relevant moral difference, for the purposes of punishment as distinct from compensation, between D's culpability and that of the substantive offender whose attempt succeeded. They equally deserve to be convicted of a crime, even if their offences are labelled differently.

Turning to consequentialist justifications, there is little difficulty in supporting the conviction of the incomplete attempter. Assuming that D has done a sufficient preliminary act and that it can be established that he intended to commit the substantive offence, this may be accepted as sufficient evidence of a dangerous disposition, and it supplies a good reason for intervening so as to prevent the consummation of the attempt. For the consequentialist, it is not a sufficient justification for punishment that it is said to be deserved. Since punishment involves the infliction of unpleasant consequences, it must be clear that any penalty will have a preventive (or other beneficial) effect which is not outweighed by any negative consequences it may have. As one measure of social defence, punishment must be aimed at those who have shown a disposition to cause prohibited harms. The complete attempter has unambiguously shown his willingness to try to bring about a proscribed consequence. The fact that chance interposed itself on this occasion and the result failed to follow does not reduce the dangerousness of this individual to any significant extent.

* * * Thus, both incomplete and complete attempts may support, although to a different extent, similar predictions about the defendant's propensities to do harm as may the substantive offence.

NOTES AND QUESTIONS

1. *"Objectivism" and "subjectivism."* In his influential book, Rethinking Criminal Law (1978), Professor George Fletcher describes two "patterns of criminality" that are important to understanding the development of criminal law doctrine.

The critical feature of one pattern—he calls it "the pattern of manifest criminality"—is that the offense "be objectively discernible at the time that it occurs. The assumption is that a neutral third-party observer could recognize the activity as criminal even if he had no special knowledge about the offender's intention." Id. at 115–116. Following this pattern, the actor's mental state does not arise as a legal issue unless and until the wrongfulness of her conduct is demonstrated by her actions. Only then does her action "generate apprehension" in the mind of the neutral third-party observer. Id. at 142. In the context of criminal attempts, Fletcher call this the "objectivist" theory of attempts, because it focuses on the actor's conduct, and "does not presuppose a prior determination of the actor's intent." Id. at 138. *[handwritten: objectivist]*

The competing pattern, "subjective criminality," focuses on the actor's intentions, rather than on externalities. In the realm of attempts, the subjectivist theory suggests that "the act of execution is important so far as it verifies the firmness of the intent," but has no independent significance. Id. Any act that verifies the person's commitment to carry out her criminal plan is sufficient to justify the criminal sanction. *[handwritten: subjectivist]*

In considering the materials on inchoate offenses that follow in this chapter, reflect on whether objectivist or subjectivist patterns of criminality have predominated.

2. The Ashworth excerpt you just read seeks to provide potential justifications for punishing incomplete and complete attempts. The remaining question—which Ashworth touches upon, at least by implication—is whether a criminal attempt, e.g., an attempted robbery or attempted murder, should be treated as a lesser offense than a successfully completed crime, e.g., robbery or murder, respectively. We turn to that question now, but keep Ashworth's ideas in mind as you proceed.

2. GRADING CRIMINAL ATTEMPTS

AMERICAN LAW INSTITUTE, MODEL PENAL CODE AND COMMENTARIES, COMMENT TO § 5.05

(1985), 485–486, 489–490

1. *Background.* Earlier law reflected no general or coherent theory for determining the sanctions that should be authorized upon conviction of attempt, solicitation or conspiracy. The maxima for these crimes were frequently fixed lower than for the substantive offense that was the actor's object * * *. * * *

The former statutes fitted into a number of identifiable patterns, some of which have been carried over in recent revisions. One common provision set specific maximum penalties, ranging from 10 to 50 years, for attempts to commit crimes punishable by death or life imprisonment, and fixed the penalty for all other attempts at one half of the maximum for the completed crime. * * *

2. *Grading.* Subsection (1) of 5.05 departs from the law that preceded promulgation of the Model Code by treating attempt, solicitation and conspiracy on a parity for purposes of sentence and by determining the grade or degree of the inchoate crime by the gravity of the most serious offense that is its object. Only when the object is a capital crime or a felony of the first degree does the Code deviate from this solution, grading the inchoate offense in that case as a felony of the second degree.

The theory of this grading system may be stated simply. To the extent that sentencing depends upon the antisocial disposition of the actor and the demonstrated need for a corrective sanction, there is likely to be little difference in the gravity of the required measures depending on the consummation or the failure of the plan. It is only when and insofar as the severity of sentence is designed for general deterrent purposes that a distinction on this ground is likely to have reasonable force. It is doubtful, however, that the threat of punishment for the inchoate crime can add significantly to the net deterrent efficacy of the sanction threatened for the substantive offense that is the actor's object, which he, by hypothesis, ignores. Hence, there is a basis for economizing in use of the heaviest and most afflictive sanctions by removing them from the inchoate crimes. The sentencing provisions for second degree felonies, including the provision for extended terms, should certainly suffice to meet whatever danger is presented by the actor.

NOTES AND QUESTIONS

1. *The role of luck in the criminal law.* Consider two persons, Alice and Bob. Both form the intent to kill someone. Both purchase a gun, both load their gun, both point their gun at their intended victim's head. Both pull the trigger. Alice kills her victim, but Bob fails because the gun misfires. Alice is guilty of murder; Bob is guilty of attempted murder. As the Model Penal Code

[handwritten margin note: traditional rule — attempts punished less severely]

excerpt suggests, the traditional rule—one that the drafters of the Code hoped to supplant except for the most serious offenses (such as murder)—is that criminal attempts are graded and punished less severely than completed offenses. So Bob will be punished less severely than Alice because of good (or, from his perspective, bad) luck, i.e., a factor entirely beyond his control. As one scholar has put it, "the reward for failing, no matter how hard you try to succeed or how close you come, is a lesser punishment." Sanford H. Kadish, *The Criminal Law and the Luck of the Draw*, 84 J. Crim. L. & Criminology 679, 682 (1994).

Or, consider this: Since 1960, the aggravated assault rate has risen by several hundred percent, whereas the murder rate during the same period has remained relatively flat overall. Why would this be? Professor Anthony Harris, director of the Criminal Justice Program at the University of Massachusetts, has come up with an explanation: as a result of improvements in emergency medical care, more assault victims' lives are being saved today than four decades ago. Anthony R. Harris, *Murder and Medicine: The Lethality of Criminal Assault 1960–1999*, 6 Homicide Stud. 128 (2002). Thus, many murderers of the 1960s are, today, "only" attempted murderers. It follows from this that the "lethality rate" is higher if a shooting or stabbing occurs in a community with poor emergency services than if a similar attack occurs near a high-tech trauma center. Should the fortuity of where the violence occurred, or perhaps the economic status of the victim, affect the overall punishment of the wrongdoer?

Should an attempt—attempted murder, attempted battery, attempted larceny—be treated as a less serious offense than the target crime, or as one of equal seriousness? How would a utilitarian answer this question? A retributivist? How would subjectivists and objectivists (p. 715, Note 1) answer these questions? How do *you* answer this question? Why do you think criminal attempts, in the past, have nearly always been punished more leniently than completed, successful crimes?

3. MENS REA

PEOPLE v. GENTRY

Appellate Court of Illinois, First District, 1987.
157 Ill.App.3d 899, 109 Ill.Dec. 895, 510 N.E.2d 963.

Justice Linn delivered the opinion of the court:

Following a jury trial, defendant, Stanley Gentry, was convicted of attempt murder (Ill.Rev.Stat.1983, ch. 38, par. 8–4(a)).[c] * * *

On appeal, Gentry asserts that his conviction should be reversed because * * * the trial court's instruction regarding the intent necessary for attempt murder was prejudicially erroneous * * *.

The record indicates that on December 13, 1983, Gentry and Ruby Hill, Gentry's girlfriend, were in the apartment they shared * * *. At

---

c. Paragraph 8–4(a) read: "A person commits an attempt when, with the intent to commit a specific offense, he does any act which constitutes a substantial step toward the commission of that offense."

approximately 9:00 p.m. the couple began to argue. During the argument, Gentry spilled gasoline on Hill, and the gasoline on Hill's body ignited. Gentry was able to smother the flames with a coat, but only after Hill had been severely burned. Gentry and Hill were the only eyewitnesses to the incident. * * *

The victim, Ruby Hill, * * * testified at trial. Hill stated that she and Gentry had been drinking all afternoon and that both of them were "pretty high." She further testified that Gentry had poured gasoline on her and that the gasoline ignited only after she had gone near the stove in the kitchen. Hill also related how Gentry tried to snuff the fire out by placing a coat over the flames. * * *

At the close of the presentation of evidence in this case, the following instructions were given. First, the trial court defined "attempt" as it relates to the underlying felony of murder:

> "A person commits the offense of [attempt] murder when he, *with intent to commit the offense of murder* does any act which constitutes a substantial step toward the commission of the offense of murder. The offense attempted need not have been completed."

Second, * * * the trial court defined the crime of murder, including all four culpable mental states:

> "A person commits the crime of [attempt] murder where he kills an individual if, in performing the acts which cause the death, he intends to kill *or* do great bodily harm to that individual, *or* he knows that such acts will cause death to that individual; *or* he knows that such acts create a strong probability of death or great bodily harm to that individual."

Gentry contends that the inclusion of all the alternative states of mind in the definitional murder instruction was erroneous because the crime of attempt murder requires a showing of specific intent to kill. Gentry posits that inclusion of all four alternative states of mind permitted the jury to convict him of attempt * * * upon a finding that he intended to harm Hill, or acted with the knowledge that his conduct created a strong probability of death or great bodily harm to Hill, even if the jury believed that Gentry did not act with specific intent to kill. We agree with Gentry's position that the jury was misinstructed in this case.

Our supreme court has repeatedly held that a finding of specific intent to kill is a necessary element of the crime of attempt murder. Indeed, a trial court instructing a jury on the crime * * * must make it clear that specific intent to kill is the pivotal element of that offense, and that intent to do bodily harm, or knowledge that the consequences of defendant's act may result in death or great bodily harm, is not enough. * * *

* * * The State labels as illogical those cases which distinguish between the specific intent to kill and the three other alternative states of mind also found in the definitional murder instruction.

The State would read the attempt * * * instruction as requiring a showing of any of the alternative mental states sufficient for a conviction of murder. In other words, the State makes no distinction between the mental state required to prove murder and the mental state required to prove attempt murder. We find the State's analysis and conclusion to be erroneous and lacking in legal substance since it fails to contain the judicial reasoning which recognizes the distinction between the intent elements of murder and attempt murder.

Specifically, we cite the *Kraft* case, where defendant's attempt murder conviction was reversed where the jury instructions would have permitted a conviction without a finding of specific intent to kill. (133 Ill.App.3d 294, 88 Ill.Dec. 546, 478 N.E.2d 1154.) In reversing the defendant's attempt murder conviction in that case, the *Kraft* court analyzed the distinction between the culpable mental states required for murder and attempt * * * noting as follows:

> "Our criminal code contains separate statutory definitions for the four culpable mental states of intent, knowledge, recklessness, and negligence, with knowledge encompassing a distinct and less purposeful state of mind than intent * * *. [O]ur state legislature manifested a desire to treat intent and knowledge as distinct mental states when imposing criminal liability for conduct * * *. Knowledge is not intent as defined by our statutes and the jury instructions should reflect this distinction. Accordingly, in a prosecution for attempted murder, where alternative culpable mental states will satisfy the target crime of murder, but only one is compatible with the mental state imposed by our attempt statute, the incompatible elements must be omitted from the jury instructions."

Consequently, it is sufficient only for us to say that we recognize the distinction between the alternative states of mind delineated in the definitional murder instruction, as well as the fact that only the specific intent to kill satisfies the intent element of the crime of attempt murder. * * *

* * * [W]e reverse defendant's conviction and sentence, and remand this cause for a new trial in front of a properly instructed jury.

NOTES AND QUESTIONS

1. Criminal attempts involve two "intents" (in common law parlance). First, the actor's conduct—the conduct that constitutes the attempt (as examined in the next chapter subsection)—must be intentional. For example, suppose that Donald aims and fires a loaded gun at George, wounding but not killing George. On these facts, Donald could realistically be charged with attempted murder. First, the act of firing the loaded gun at George was intentionally performed. Second, Donald quite arguably committed that act with the specific intention of committing the completed offense (killing George).

The two intentions often merge. Thus, if Donald accidentally pulled the trigger of the gun (i.e., the first intent is missing), it would likely follow that he did not intend to kill George (the second intent). Similarly, if Donald *did* intend to aim and pull the trigger of the gun, the prosecutor's claim that Donald intended to kill George becomes much stronger. Nonetheless, *the latter intent must also be proven beyond a reasonable doubt*. It is possible, for example, that Donald intentionally pulled the trigger of the gun with the intention of missing George (scaring him) or merely wounding him, in which case an attempted murder conviction would be inappropriate—the first intention, but not the second one, has been proven. Typically, therefore, it is the second intention—the intent to cause the completed offense—that becomes the key *mens rea* issue.

2. What was really going on in *Gentry*? Do you believe that the events occurred as Hill testified?

3. The court's application of the Illinois attempt statute tracks the common law. In view of the fact that an attempt is usually punished less severely, and never more severely, than the target offense, why does the common law require a *more* culpable state of mind for an attempted murder than for the completed crime?

Is the intent requirement appropriate in view of the purposes of attempt laws? Do you agree with the following observation by Holmes?

> Acts should be judged by their tendency under the known circumstances, not by the actual intent which accompanies them. ¶ It may be true that in the region of attempts, as elsewhere, the law began with cases of actual intent, as those cases are the most obvious ones. But it cannot stop with them, unless it attaches more importance to the etymological meaning of the word *attempt* than to the general principles of punishment.

Oliver Wendell Holmes, The Common Law 66 (1881).

4. *Model Penal Code: a quick primer*. Model Penal Code Section 5.01 is not artfully drafted. To help:

> To analyze an attempt issue under subsection (1), it is necessary to ask and answer one or two questions. First, does the case involve a complete or incomplete attempt? Second, if the case involves a complete attempt, is the target offense a "result" crime (e.g., murder) or a "conduct" crime (e.g., driving an automobile under the influence of alcohol)?
>
> Subsections (1)(a) and (1)(b) pertain to *completed* attempts. Specifically, subsection (1)(a) should be considered when the target offense of the completed attempt involves conduct; subsection (1)(b) applies to results. If the prosecution involves an *incomplete* attempt, subsection (1)(c) is used. However, this subsection must be read in conjunction with subsection (2), which elaborates on the meaning of "substantial step."

Joshua Dressler, Understanding Criminal Law § 27.09[B][2], at 413–414 (5th ed. 2009).

5. Assume that the prosecutor introduced evidence at Gentry's trial that he purposely doused Hill with gasoline, lit a match, and tossed it at her, but

that the match fell harmlessly into a bucket of water. Based on this version of the facts, if the prosecution had arisen in a Model Penal Code jurisdiction, would Gentry be guilty of attempted murder if he performed these actions: (a) in order to kill her; (b) in order to scare her, although he knew that his conduct might result in her death; or (c) as a practical joke—he meant no harm—and failed to realize how frightening and dangerous his actions were. If Gentry would *not* be guilty of attempted murder, is he guilty of any other MPC offense on these facts? Look at Article 211 for possibilities.

6. Bob wants to demolish a building. He realizes that people are in the structure and believes that they will be killed in the demolition, although he does not want them to die. He detonates a bomb to demolish the building, but the bomb proves defective. At common law, is Bob guilty of attempted murder? What would be the outcome under the Model Penal Code? See American Law Institute, Model Penal Code and Commentaries, Comment to § 5.01 at 304–305 (1985).

7. *Problem.* S was informed that he tested positive for the presence of the Human Immunodeficiency Virus (HIV), the virus that causes Acquired Immune Deficiency Syndrome (AIDS). Health professionals warned S that he should not have sexual relations without informing his partners of his "HIV positive" status, and that he should practice "safe sex" (including the use of condoms) in order to avoid transmitting the disease to his sexual partners. A month later, S raped a woman. The sexual act occurred without condoms. S was charged with attempted murder. Is he guilty? Smallwood v. State, 106 Md.App. 1, 661 A.2d 747 (1995), *rev'd,* 343 Md. 97, 680 A.2d 512 (1996); see also State v. Hinkhouse, 139 Or.App. 446, 912 P.2d 921 (1996).

BRUCE v. STATE

Court of Appeals of Maryland, 1989.
317 Md. 642, 566 A.2d 103.

Murphy, Chief Judge.

The question presented is whether "attempted felony murder" is a crime in this State.

On December 2, 1986, three men entered Barry Tensor's shoe store. One man, later identified as Leon Bruce, was masked and armed with a handgun. He ordered Tensor to open the cash register. * * * Upon finding it empty, Bruce demanded to know where the money could be found. Tensor testified:

> "I said it's empty, that is all there is and then he took the gun and aimed it right at my face, at my head. And he said I'm going to kill you in a very serious voice, and the gun was continuously held right at my face.

> "At that point, I was incredibly afraid and I just tucked my head down and kind of tried to get out of the way and ducked down and moved forward. And at that point, I guess I banged into him or something and he shot me."

Tensor was hospitalized for five weeks from a gunshot wound to his stomach.

* * * A jury * * * found [Bruce] * * * guilty of attempted first degree felony murder, guilty of robbery with a deadly weapon, and guilty of * * * two handgun charges. * * *

On appeal * * *, Bruce argued that attempted felony murder was not a crime in Maryland. We granted certiorari * * * to consider the significant issue raised in the case.

Maryland Code Article 27, § 407 provides that murder "perpetrated by means of poison, or lying in wait, or by any kind of wilful, deliberate and premeditated killing shall be murder in the first degree." Section 410—the so-called felony murder statute—provides that all murder committed in the perpetration of, or attempt to perpetrate, certain designated felonies, of which robbery is one, is also murder in the first degree. These statutes do not create new statutory crimes but rather divide the common law crime of murder into degrees for purposes of punishment.

* * * To secure a conviction for first degree murder under the felony murder doctrine, the State is required to prove a specific intent to commit the underlying felony and that death occurred in the perpetration or attempt to perpetrate the felony; it is not necessary to prove a specific intent to kill or to demonstrate the existence of wilfulness, deliberation, or premeditation. * * *

In determining whether attempted felony murder is a crime in Maryland, we note that criminal attempts are * * * applicable to any existing crime, whether statutory or common law. *Cox v. State,* 311 Md. 326, 329–30, 534 A.2d 1333 (1988). Under Maryland law, a criminal attempt consists of a specific intent to commit the offense coupled with some overt act in furtherance of the intent which goes beyond mere preparation.

In *Cox,* the question presented was whether an individual could be convicted of attempted voluntary manslaughter. Recognizing that criminal attempt is a specific intent crime, we held that an individual may be convicted of the crime of attempted voluntary manslaughter since the substantive offense is "an *intentional* homicide, done in a sudden heat of passion, caused by adequate provocation." On the other hand, we noted that involuntary manslaughter is an *"unintentional* killing done without malice, by doing some unlawful act endangering life, or in negligently doing some act lawful in itself"; accordingly, we held that it may not form the basis of a criminal conviction for attempt.

* * * Because a conviction for felony murder requires no specific intent to kill, it follows that because a criminal attempt is a specific intent crime, attempted felony murder is not a crime in Maryland. * * *

NOTES AND QUESTIONS

1. *Yes, but . . .* Nearly all states agree with the analysis in *Bruce,* but Florida does not. Florida Stat. § 782.051 (2006) provides that "[a]ny person

[handwritten margin note: Contra Florida]

who perpetrates or attempts to perpetrate any [enumerated] felony * * * and who commits, aids, or abets an intentional act that is not an essential element of the felony and that could, but does not, cause the death of another," is guilty of attempted felony-murder, an offense punishable by imprisonment for a term not exceeding life.

Based on this statute, former National Football League star Barret Robbins was charged with attempted felony-murder when, while allegedly committing a burglary, he struck an arriving police officer several times with his fist. Frank Blinebury, *The Last Fall of a Football Star*, Houston Chron. Jan. 26, 2005, at p. 1. (Subsequently, the prosecutor reduced the charges to felony battery and resisting arrest, to which Robbins pled guilty.)

2. *A different type of mens rea issue.* Suppose that Robert attempts to have sexual intercourse with an underage female, mistakenly believing that she is old enough to consent, but he is arrested before the intercourse occurs. He is charged with attempted statutory rape. In what way does the *mens rea* issue here differ from that in *Bruce*?

[handwritten margin note: att. stat. rape under MPC]

As a matter of policy, should Robert be convicted of the attempt? Here is how the Model Penal Code would handle this case:

> The requirement of purpose extends to the conduct of the actor and to the results that his conduct causes, but his purpose need not encompass all of the circumstances included in the formal definition of the substantive offense.[9] As to them, it is sufficient that he acts with the culpability that is required for commission of the completed crime.
>
> * * * Assume, for example, a statute that provides that sexual intercourse with a female under a prescribed age is an offense, and that a mistake as to age will not afford a defense no matter how reasonable its foundation. The policy of the substantive offense as to age, therefore, is one of strict liability, and if the actor has sexual intercourse with a female, he is guilty or not, depending upon her age and irrespective of his views as to her age. Suppose, however, that he is arrested before he engages in the proscribed conduct, and that the charge is an attempt to commit the offense. Should he then be entitled to rely on a mistake as to age as a defense? Or should the policy of the substantive crime on this issue carry over to the attempt as well? * * *
>
> Under the formulation in Subsection (1)(c),[11] the proffered defense would not succeed * * *. In the statutory rape example, the actor must have a purpose to engage in sexual intercourse with a female[12] in order to

---

9. The "circumstances" of the offense refer to the objective situation that the law requires to exist, in addition to the defendant's act or any results that the act may cause. The elements of "nighttime" in burglary, "property of another" in theft, "female not his wife" in rape, and "dwelling" in arson are illustrations. "Conduct" refers to "breaking and entering" in burglary, "taking" in theft, "sexual intercourse" in rape and "burning" in arson. Results, of course, include "death" in homicide. While these terms are not airtight categories, they have served as a helpful analytical device in the development of the Code.

11. Subsection (1)(a) would not apply * * * because * * * the defendant would have committed the substantive offense if he had successfully completed his conduct. [Since] he did not complete his planned course of conduct, Subsection (1)(c) would apply. * * *

12. It is assumed that the culpability standard for the "female" element of the offense is knowledge, and thus it would be the same for the attempt.

be charged with the attempt, and must engage in a substantial step in a course of conduct planned to culminate in his commission of that act. With respect to the age of the victim, however, it is sufficient if he acts "with the kind of culpability otherwise required for the commission of the crime," which in the case supposed is none at all. Since, therefore, mistake as to age is irrelevant with respect to the substantive offense, it is likewise irrelevant with respect to the attempt. * * *[13]

The judgment is thus that if the defendant manifests a purpose to engage in the type of conduct or to cause the type of result that is forbidden by the criminal law, he has sufficiently exhibited his dangerousness to justify the imposition of criminal sanctions, so long as he otherwise acts with the kind of culpability that is sufficient for the completed offense. The objective is to select out those elements of the completed crime that, if the defendant desires to bring them about, indicate with clarity that he poses the type of danger to society that the substantive offense is designed to prevent. This objective is well served by the Code's approach, followed in a number of recently enacted and proposed revisions, of allowing the policy of the substantive offense to control with respect to circumstance elements.

American Law Institute, Model Penal Code and Commentaries, Comment to § 5.01 at 301–303 (1985).

4. ACTUS REUS

a. General Principles

Both as fascinating and as fruitless as the alchemists' quest for the philosopher's stone has been the search, by judges and writers, for a valid, single statement of doctrine to express when, under the law of guilt, preparations to commit a crime becomes a criminal attempt thereat. John S. Strahorn, Jr., *Preparation for Crime as a Criminal Attempt*, 1 Wash & Lee L. Rev. 1, 1 (1939).

UNITED STATES v. MANDUJANO

United States Court of Appeals, Fifth Circuit, 1974.
499 F.2d 370.

RIVES, CIRCUIT JUDGE. * * *

Section 846 of Title 21, entitled "Attempt and conspiracy," provides that,

---

It should also be noted that the language "under the circumstances as he believes them to be," as well as its counterpart language in Subsections (1)(a) and (1)(b), does not affect the analysis of cases like the one[ ] posed. This language is designed to deal with the so-called "impossibility" cases [see p. 745 infra], where the actor believes an element of the offense to exist but where in fact it does not. In that situation, the actor is measured by "the circumstances as he believes them to be." In cases like [the statutory rape illustration], the actor's mistaken belief as to the particular circumstances is made irrelevant by law.

13. It should be noted that while offenses involving strict liability were chosen for clarity of illustration, the analysis would be the same for circumstance elements where the culpability level is set at recklessness or negligence. For example, if negligence as to age * * * were required and sufficient for the substantive offense, the same would hold true for the attempt.

"Any person who attempts or conspires to commit any offense defined in this subchapter is punishable by imprisonment or fine or both which may not exceed the maximum punishment prescribed for the offense, the commission of which was the object of the attempt or conspiracy." * * *

Apparently there is no legislative history indicating exactly what Congress meant when it used the word "attempt" in section 846. * * * In United States v. Noreikis, 7 Cir.1973, 481 F.2d 1177, * * * the court commented that,

"While it seems to be well settled that mere preparation is not sufficient to constitute an attempt to commit a crime, it seems equally clear that the semantical distinction between preparation and attempt is one incapable of being formulated in a hard and fast rule. The procuring of the instrument of the crime might be preparation in one factual situation and not in another. * * * " * * *

The courts in many jurisdictions have tried to elaborate on the distinction between mere preparation and attempt. See the Comment at 39–48 of Tent. Draft No. 10, 1960 of the Model Penal Code.[5] In cases involving statutes other than section 846, the federal courts have confronted this issue on a number of occasions. * * *

In United States v. Coplon, 2 Cir.1950, 185 F.2d 629, * * * Judge Learned Hand surveyed the law and addressed the issue of what would constitute an attempt:

"Because the arrest in this way interrupted the consummation of the crime one point upon the appeal is that her conduct still remained in the zone of 'preparation,' and that the evidence did not prove an 'attempt.' This argument it will be most convenient to answer at the outset. A neat doctrine by which to test when a person, intending to commit a crime which he fails to carry out, has 'attempted' to commit it, would be that he has done all that it is within his power to do, but has been prevented by intervention from outside; in short, that he has passed beyond any *locus pœnitentiae*. Apparently that was the original notion, and may still be law in England; but it is certainly not now

---

5. This comment to the Model Penal Code catalogues a number of formulations which have been adopted or suggested, including the following:

(a) The physical proximity doctrine—the overt act required for an attempt must be proximate to the completed crime, or directly tending toward the completion of the crime, or must amount to the commencement of the consummation.

(b) The dangerous proximity doctrine—a test given impetus by Mr. Justice Holmes whereby the greater the gravity and probability of the offense, and the nearer the act to the crime, the stronger is the case for calling the act an attempt.

(c) The indispensable element test—a variation of the proximity tests which emphasizes any indispensable aspect of the criminal endeavor over which the actor has not yet acquired control.

(d) The probable desistance test—the conduct constitutes an attempt if, in the ordinary and natural course of events, without interruption from an outside source, it will result in the crime intended. * * *

([e]) The res ipsa loquitur or unequivocality test—an attempt is committed when the actor's conduct manifests an intent to commit a crime.

generally the law in the United States, for there are many decisions which hold that the accused has passed beyond 'preparation,' although he has been interrupted before he has taken the last of his intended steps. * * * "

In Mims v. United States, 5 Cir.1967, 375 F.2d 135, 148, we noted that, "Much ink has been spilt in an attempt to arrive at a satisfactory standard for telling where preparations ends [sic] and attempt begins," and that the question had not been decided by this Court. The Court in *Mims,* did note that the following test from People v. Buffum, 40 Cal.2d 709, 256 P.2d 317, 321, has been "frequently approved":

> " 'Preparation alone is not enough, there must be some *appreciable fragment* of the crime committed, it must be in such progress that it will be consummated unless interrupted by circumstances independent of the will of the attempter, and the act must not be equivocal in nature. * * * ' "

NOTES AND QUESTIONS

1. Depending on whether a court takes a more subjectivist or objectivist approach (p. 715, Note 1 supra) to attempt law, the line between preparation and perpetration—thus, the line of demarcation for the crime of attempt—may be drawn relatively early or late in the process. The "tests" set out in *Mandujano* are nothing more than alternative potential standards (and, loose ones at that) for line drawing. Here are some other not entirely consistent observations about the demarcation line:

A. United States v. Oviedo, 525 F.2d 881 (5th Cir.1976):

> When the question before the court is whether certain conduct constitutes mere preparation * * * or an attempt * * *, the possibility of error is mitigated by the requirement that the objective acts of the defendant evidence commitment to the criminal venture and corroborate the *mens rea.* To the extent that this requirement is preserved it prevents the conviction of persons engaged in innocent acts on the basis of a *mens rea* proved through speculative inferences, unreliable forms of testimony, and past criminal conduct.

> Courts could have approached the preparation-attempt determination in another fashion, eliminating any notion of particular objective facts, and simply could have asked whether the evidence at hand was sufficient to prove the necessary intent. But this approach has been rejected for precisely the reasons set out above, for conviction upon proof of mere intent provides too great a possibility of speculation and abuse. * * *

> Thus, we demand that in order for a defendant to be guilty of a criminal attempt, the objective acts performed, without any reliance on the accompanying *mens rea,* mark the defendant's conduct as criminal in nature. The acts should be unique rather than so commonplace that they are engaged in by persons not in violation of the law.

B. Stokes v. State, 92 Miss. 415, 46 So. 627 (1908):

At last, it is the safety of the public and their protection which is to be guarded. * * * ¶ When the intent to commit crime, or, to put it more accurately, when the only proof is that it is the declared intention of a person to commit a crime merely, with no act done in furtherance of the intent, however clearly may be proved this intention, it does not amount to an attempt, and it cannot be punished as such. But, whenever the design of a person to commit crime is clearly shown, slight acts done in furtherance of this design will constitute an attempt, and this court will not destroy the practical and commonsense administration of the law with subtleties as to what constitutes preparation and what an act done toward the commission of a crime. * * * Too many loopholes have been made whereby parties are enabled to escape punishment for that which is known to be criminal in its worse sense.

C. People v. Luna, 170 Cal.App.4th 535, 87 Cal.Rptr.3d 781 (2009): "[W]here the intent to commit crime is clearly shown, an act done toward the commission of the crime may be sufficient for an attempt even though that same act would be insufficient if the intent is not clearly as shown."

D. Francis B. Sayre, *Criminal Attempts*, 41 Harv. L. Rev. 821, 846 (1928):

The more serious the crime attempted or the greater the menace to the social security from similar efforts on the part of the defendant * * *, the further back in the series of acts leading up to the consummated crime should the criminal law reach in holding the defendant guilty for attempt.

E. Arnold N. Enker, *Impossibility in Criminal Attempts—Legality and the Legal Process,* 53 Minn. L. Rev. 665, 674 (1969):

Cases arising along the preparation-attempt spectrum are handled in terms of their similarities to and differences from the substantive crime attempted, and in terms of analogy to previously decided or hypothetical attempt cases. In deciding, the court weighs several factors, principally: whether the act at issue is sufficiently close to the substantive crime or close enough to potential irreparable harm so as to preclude any further postponement of official intervention; whether the defendant's conduct has progressed to the point that one may be reasonably certain that he is firmly committed to a specific illegal venture rather than merely contemplating the possible future commission of a crime; and whether the act is sufficiently unambiguous to demonstrate the actor's illegal intent.

F. United States v. Williamson, 42 M.J. 613 (N–M.Ct.Crim.App.1995): "The facts may reveal that the line of demarkation [sic] [between preparation and perpetration] is not a line at all but a murky 'twilight zone.'"

AN INITIAL EFFORT AT DRAWING THE PREPARATION– PERPETRATION LINE

1. At 3:00 p.m., Anne places ammunition in her gun.

2. At 3:30 p.m., Anne places the loaded gun in the glove compartment of her car and begins to drive her automobile.

3. At 3:55 p.m., Anne reaches a destination, parks her car on the street in front of Bob's house.

4. At 3:56 p.m., Anne gets out of her car, and surveys the area.

5. At 4:00 p.m., Anne returns to her parked car and reads a newspaper.

6. At 5:15 p.m., Anne pulls the weapon out of the glove compartment and stations herself behind a bush, gun in hand.

7. At 5:20 p.m., Bob drives his car into the driveway. Anne aims the gun in Bob's direction.

8. Seconds later, Bob gets out of his car.

9. Seconds later, as Anne puts her finger on the gun trigger, Bob's young daughter runs out of the house and hugs him in the driveway.

10. Anne tearfully puts her gun down, re-enters her car, and drives away. *— changed mind - abandonment · or too late?*

NOTES AND QUESTIONS

1. Is Anne guilty of attempted murder? If so, at precisely what point did the attempt occur? What is your justification for drawing the line where you did? Keep in mind that the only evidence you have as to what Anne intended at any moment in time is what she is described as having done up to and including that moment.

2. Suppose at Step 7, Bob does *not* come home. He is out of town and will not be back in town for a week. Would this affect your analysis? Why, or why not?

3. Suppose at Step 7, Bob was already inside his house, dead from a heart attack suffered the night before. Would this affect your analysis? Why, or why not? *Impossibility*

4. What if you knew before Step 1 that Anne intended to kill Bob. Maybe she even called the police and said, "Bob is a terrible man. He needs to die. I am going to make sure that it happens today." Now, with that knowledge, would you find an attempt at an earlier step than before? If so, at what step would you say that Anne attempted to murder Bob? *Still need actus reus*

5. Anne, of course, never fired the gun. Should the rule of criminal attempts be that a person is not guilty until she performs the last act? Consider:

> When an actor forms an intention and engages in * * * preparatory behavior, she may know that what she intends to do is forbidden by the criminal law, but she also knows that she retains complete control over whether she will actually so act. * * * She has the ability to choose not to risk harm to her victim.

> It is only when the actor does something that * * * increases the risk of harm to the victim in a way that she no longer can control that she has engaged in a culpable act. This is the point where "what she does" ceases to be guided by her reason and will. * * * It is at this moment that the law calls upon the actor to refrain from acting, and she acts culpably when she ignores the law's commands.

Larry Alexander & Kimberly Kessler Ferzan (with Stephen Morse), Crime and Culpability: A Theory of Criminal Law 216 (2009) (proposing that, subject to two qualifications, "last acts" alone are the appropriate targets of criminal liability).

b. Distinguishing Preparation From Perpetration: The Tests at Work

COMMONWEALTH v. PEASLEE

Supreme Judicial Court of Massachusetts, 1901.
177 Mass. 267, 59 N.E. 55.

HOLMES, C.J. This is an indictment for an attempt to burn a building and certain goods therein, with intent to injure the insurers of the same. * * * The defense is that the overt acts alleged and proved do not amount to an offense. It was raised by a motion to quash, and also by a request to the judge to direct a verdict for the defendant. We will consider the case in the first place upon the evidence, apart from any question of pleading, and afterwards will take it up in connection with the indictment as actually drawn.

The evidence was that the defendant had constructed and arranged combustibles in the building in such a way that they were ready to be lighted, and if lighted would have set fire to the building and its contents. To be exact, the plan would have required a candle which was standing on a shelf six feet away to be placed on a piece of wood in a pan of turpentine and lighted. The defendant offered to pay a younger man in his employment if he would go to the building, seemingly some miles from the place of the dialogue, and carry out the plan. This was refused. Later the defendant and the young man drove towards the building, but when within a quarter of a mile the defendant said that he had changed his mind, and drove away. This is as near as he ever came to accomplishing what he had in contemplation.

The question on the evidence, more precisely stated, is whether the defendant's acts come near enough to the accomplishment of the substantive offense to be punishable. * * * The most common types of an attempt are either an act which is intended to bring about the substantive crime, and which sets in motion natural forces that would bring it about in the expected course of events, but for the unforeseen interruption, as, in this case, if the candle had been set in its place and lighted, but had been put out by the police, or an act which is intended to bring about the substantive crime, and would bring it about but for a mistake of judgment in a matter of nice estimate or experiment, as when a pistol is fired at a man, but misses him, or when one tries to pick a pocket which turns out to be empty. In either case the would-be criminal has done his last act.

Obviously new considerations come in when further acts on the part of the person who has taken the first steps are necessary before the substantive crime can come to pass. In this class of cases there is still a chance that the would-be criminal may change his mind. In strictness, such first steps cannot be described as an attempt, because that word suggests an act seemingly sufficient to accomplish the end, and has been supposed to have no other meaning. That an overt act, although coupled with an intent to commit the crime, commonly is not punishable if further acts are contemplated as needful, is expressed in the familiar rule that preparation is not an attempt. But some preparations may amount to an attempt. It is a question of degree. If the preparation comes very near to the accomplishment of the act, the intent to complete it renders the crime so probable that the act will be a misdemeanor, although there is still a locus poenitentiae, in the need of a further exertion of the will to complete the crime. As was observed in a recent case, the degree of proximity held sufficient may vary with circumstances, including, among other things, the apprehension which the particular crime is calculated to excite. Com. v. Kennedy, 170 Mass. 18, 22, 48 N.E. 770. See also, Com. v. Willard, 22 Pick. 476. * * *

Under the cases last cited, we assume that there was evidence of a crime, and perhaps of an attempt. The latter question we do not decide. Nevertheless on the pleadings [which failed to allege the solicitation of the employee to set the fire] a majority of the court is of opinion that the exceptions must be sustained. A mere collection and preparation of materials in a room for the purpose of setting fire to them, unaccompanied by any present intent to set the fire, would be too remote. If the accused intended to rely upon his own hands to the end, he must be shown to have had a present intent to accomplish the crime without much delay, and to have had this intent at a time and place where he was able to carry it out. We are not aware of any carefully considered case that has gone further than this. We assume, without deciding, that that is the meaning of the indictment; and it would have been proved if, for instance, the evidence had been that the defendant had been frightened by the police as he was about to light the candle. On the other hand, if the offense is to be made out by showing a preparation of the room, and a solicitation of some one else to set the fire, which solicitation, if successful, would have been the defendant's last act, the solicitation must be alleged as one of the overt acts. * * * If the indictment had been properly drawn, we have no question that the defendant might have been convicted.

Exceptions sustained.

Notes and Questions

1. Can solicitation to commit an offense, without more, constitute an attempt to commit that offense? What does Holmes *seem* to suggest in *Peaslee*? For more on this topic, see p. 775, Note 5.

2. Suppose that the employee had agreed to set the fire by himself, and that it was he, not Peaslee, who turned back a quarter of a mile from the building. Should that affect *Peaslee's* guilt for attempt?

3. Based on the evidence introduced at his trial, was Peaslee guilty of attempt under the "probable desistance" test of attempt, as that standard is summarized in footnote 5 of *Mandujano*, p. 725 supra?

The drafters of the Model Penal Code were critical of this test:

> *Probable Desistance Test.* Oriented largely toward the dangerousness of the actor's conduct * * * [t]his test seemed to require a judgment in each case that the actor had reached a point where it was unlikely that he would have voluntarily desisted from his efforts to commit the crime. But in cases applying this test no inquiry was made into the personality of the particular offender before the court. Rather, the question was whether *anyone* who went so far would stop short of the final step.[d] * * *

> Accepting for the time being the underlying assumption that probability of desistance, or actual abandonment of the criminal endeavor, negatives dangerousness sufficiently to warrant immunity from attempt liability, this test still does not appear to provide a workable standard. Is there an adequate empirical basis for predicting whether desistance is probable at various points in various type of cases? * * * [I]n actual operation the probable desistance test is linked entirely to the nearness of the actor's conduct to completion, this being the sole basis of unsubstantiated judicial appraisals of the probabilities of desistance. The test as applied appears to be little more than the physical proximity approach.

American Law Institute, Model Penal Code and Commentaries, Comment to § 5.01 at 324–325 (1985).

4. *Problem.* H's physician wrote a prescription for H for 30 pills containing codeine, a controlled substance. In a space on the prescription form to indicate refills, the doctor wrote "1." Later, H placed another "1" after the number, so that it appeared the doctor authorized 11 refills. H took the prescription to a pharmacy to have it filled for the first time. The pharmacist, aware that drugs containing codeine could legally be refilled no more than five times in a six-month period, contacted the doctor and learned that he had only authorized the one refill. The pharmacist filled H's initial order, and then called the police. H was prosecuted for attempted fraudulent acquisition of a controlled substance. State v. Henthorn, 218 Wis.2d 526, 581 N.W.2d 544 (Ct.App.1998). In your view, *should* W be convicted of attempt? What result if you apply the "probable desistance" test?

5. *Dangerous proximity test. Peaslee* is sometimes cited as an application of Holmes' "dangerous proximity" test (see footnote 5 of *Mandujano*). Holmes originally explained the doctrine in The Common Law 67–69 (1881):

> [L]ighting a match with intent to set fire to a haystack has been held to amount to a criminal attempt to burn it, although the defendant blew out the match on seeing that he was watched. * * *

> * * * If a man starts from Boston to Cambridge for the purpose of committing a murder when he gets there, but is stopped by the draw [bridge] and goes home, he is no more punishable than if he had sat in his

---

d. "The defendant's conduct must pass that point where most men, holding such an intention as the defendant holds, would think better of their conduct and desist." Berry v. State, 90 Wis.2d 316, 280 N.W.2d 204 (1979).

chair and resolved to shoot somebody, but on second thoughts had given up the notion. * * *

Eminent judges have been puzzled where to draw the line, or even to state the principle on which it should be drawn, between the two sets of cases. But the principle is believed to be similar to that on which all other lines are drawn by the law. Public policy, that is to say, legislative considerations, are at the bottom of the matter; the considerations being, in this case, the nearness of the danger, the greatness of the harm, and the degree of apprehension felt.

The following case has also been cited as one applying the dangerous proximity test.

PEOPLE v. RIZZO

Court of Appeals of New York, 1927.
246 N.Y. 334, 158 N.E. 888.

CRANE, J. The police of the city of New York did excellent work in this case by preventing the commission of a serious crime. It is a great satisfaction to realize that we have such wide-awake guardians of our peace. Whether or not the steps which the defendant had taken up to the time of his arrest amounted to the commission of a crime, as defined by our law, is, however, another matter. He has been convicted of an attempt to commit the crime of robbery in the first degree and sentenced to State's prison. There is no doubt that he had the intention to commit robbery if he got the chance. An examination, however, of the facts is necessary to determine whether his acts were in preparation to commit the crime if the opportunity offered, or constituted a crime in itself, known to our law as an attempt to commit robbery in the first degree. Charles Rizzo, the defendant, appellant, with three others, * * * planned to rob one Charles Rao of a payroll valued at about $1,200 which he was to carry from the bank for the United Lathing Company. These defendants, two of whom had firearms, started out in an automobile, looking for Rao or the man who had the payroll on that day. Rizzo claimed to be able to identify the man and was to point him out to the others who were to do the actual holding up. The four rode about in their car looking for Rao. They went to the bank from which he was supposed to get the money and to various buildings being constructed by the United Lathing Company. At last they came to One Hundred and Eightieth street and Morris Park avenue. By this time they were watched and followed by two police officers. As Rizzo jumped out of the car and ran into the building all four were arrested. The defendant was taken out from the building in which he was hiding. Neither Rao nor a man named Previti, who was also supposed to carry a payroll, were at the place at the time of the arrest. The defendants had not found or seen the man they intended to rob; no person with a payroll was at any of the places where they had stopped and no one had been pointed out or identified by Rizzo. * * *

Does this constitute the crime of an attempt to commit robbery in the first degree? * * *

In Hyde v. U.S., 225 U.S. 347, 32 S.Ct. 793, 56 L.Ed. 1114, it was stated that the act amounts to an attempt when it is so near to the result that the danger of success is very great. "There must be dangerous proximity to success." * * *

Commonwealth v. Peaslee, 177 Mass. 267, 59 N.E. 55, refers to the acts constituting an attempt as coming *very near* to the accomplishment of the crime.

How shall we apply this rule of immediate nearness to this case? * * * To constitute the crime of robbery the money must have been taken from Rao by means of force or violence, or through fear. The crime of attempt to commit robbery was committed if these defendants did an act tending to the commission of this robbery. Did the acts above described come dangerously near to the taking of Rao's property? Did the acts come so near the commission of robbery that there was reasonable likelihood of its accomplishment but for the interference? Rao was not found; the defendants were still looking for him; no attempt to rob him could be made, at least until he came in sight * * *. In a word, these defendants had planned to commit a crime and were looking around the city for an opportunity to commit it, but the opportunity fortunately never came. * * *

For these reasons, the judgment of conviction of this defendant, appellant, must be reversed and a new trial granted. * * *

NOTES AND QUESTIONS

1. Based on the dangerous proximity test, should *D* be convicted of attempt in the following cases?

A. *D* conversed in a Yahoo chat room with an undercover police officer who, using the screen name "Skatergurl," described himself as a fourteen-year old girl. *D* wanted to have intercourse with Skatergurl and the two arranged to meet at a local middle school between 2:00 and 2:15 a.m. that night. Before signing off, *D* asked, "you wanna have sex, honestly?" Skatergurl responded, "I can try." *D* told Skatergurl he would arrive in a black or red car and confirmed what he would be wearing. *D* was arrested when he pulled into the school parking lot in a red Toyota Celica at 2:30 a.m. *D* was charged with attempted sexual conduct with a minor. State v. Reid, 383 S.C. 285, 679 S.E.2d 194 (Ct.App. 2009).

B. After extensive negotiations, *D* hired burglars to stage a fake theft of various antiquities he owned, in order that he could fraudulently recover $18 million in insurance proceeds from Lloyd's of London. *D* provided the burglars with a diagram of the warehouse where the valuables were stored. Two days later, the burglars broke into the warehouse, but they were arrested before the antiquities could be removed. *D* was charged, along with others, with attempted grand larceny. People v. Mahboubian, 74 N.Y.2d 174, 544 N.Y.S.2d 769, 543 N.E.2d 34 (1989).

2. How should *Mahboubian* (Note 1B.) be resolved under the indispensable element test (footnote 5 of *Mandujano*)? That standard is explained by the American Law Institute:

Objectwest indispensable element test (proximity)

Some decisions seem to stand for the proposition that if the successful completion of a crime requires the assent or action of some third person, that assent or action must be forthcoming before the actor can be guilty of an attempt. Thus, if A and B plan to defraud a life insurance company by pretending that A, the insured, is dead, and if C, the beneficiary, must file a formal claim before any proceeds can be paid, it has been held that the acts of A and B cannot amount to an attempt to defraud the insurance company until C files a claim or agrees to file a claim. * * *

An analogous group of cases supports the view that a person cannot be guilty of an attempt if he lacks a means essential to completion of the offense. Thus, it has been held that one cannot be guilty of an attempt * * * to vote illegally until he obtains a ballot.

American Law Institute, Model Penal Code and Commentaries, Comment to § 5.01 at 323–324 (1985).

PEOPLE v. MILLER

Supreme Court of California, 1935.
2 Cal.2d 527, 42 P.2d 308.

SHENK, JUSTICE.

The defendant was charged by * * * amended information * * * with "attempt to commit murder, in that on or about the 17th day of March, 1934, * * * he did, then and there, wilfully, unlawfully and feloniously, attempt to murder one Albert Jeans." The jury found the defendant guilty as charged in the amended information. * * *

The evidence is practically without conflict. On the day in question, the defendant, somewhat under the influence of liquor and in the presence of others at the post office in the town of Booneville, threatened to kill Albert Jeans * * *. On that day Jeans was employed on the hop ranch of Ginochio, who was the constable of Booneville. About 4 o'clock that afternoon, while Constable Ginochio, Jeans, and others were planting hops, the defendant entered the hop field of Ginochio carrying a .22-caliber rifle. Ginochio was about 250 or 300 yards away and Jeans about 30 yards beyond him. The defendant walked in a direct line toward Ginochio. When the defendant had gone about 100 yards, he stopped and appeared to be loading his rifle. At no time did he lift his rifle as though to take aim. Jeans, as soon as he perceived the defendant, fled on a line at about right angles to Miller's line of approach, but whether before or after the stopping motion made by the defendant is not clear. The defendant continued toward Ginochio, who took the gun into his own possession; the defendant offering no resistance. The gun was found to be loaded with a .22-caliber long, or high-speed, cartridge. The foregoing are the salient facts stated without the color afforded by the epithets and language used by the defendant in making his threats. * * *

We are mindful of the fact that language appearing in Stokes v. State, 92 Miss. 415, 46 So. 627, 629, that, "whenever the design of a person to commit crime is clearly shown, slight acts done in furtherance of this

Objectivist Unequivocality test [handwritten margin note]

design will constitute an attempt," has received approval. The statement, however, * * * is not in conflict with the usual statements of the tests applied to aid in drawing the line at the point where preparation leaves off and execution has commenced. It still presupposes some direct act or movement in execution of the design, as distinguished from mere preparation, which leaves the intended assailant only in the condition to commence the first direct act toward consummation of his design. The reason for requiring evidence of a direct act, however slight, toward consummation of the intended crime, is * * * that in the majority of cases up to that time the conduct of the defendant, consisting merely of acts of preparation, has never ceased to be equivocal; and this is necessarily so, irrespective of his declared intent. It is that quality of being equivocal that must be lacking before the act becomes one which may be said to be a commencement of the commission of the crime, or an overt act, or before any fragment of the crime itself has been committed, and this is so for the reason that, so long as the equivocal quality remains, no one can say with certainty what the intent of the defendant is. * * *

* * * In the present case, up to the moment the gun was taken from the defendant, no one could say with certainty whether the defendant had come into the field to carry out his threat to kill Jeans or merely to demand his arrest by the constable. Under the authorities, therefore, the acts of the defendant do not constitute an attempt to commit murder. * * *

NOTES AND QUESTIONS

1. According to one California court, "[o]ther jurisdictions have not stood in line for a chance to follow *Miller*'s logic. * * * It could be argued that in this jurisdiction, *Miller*'s command is treated as a request to create grounds to ignore it." People v. Jiminez, 279 Cal.Rptr. 157 (App.1991), *review granted and opinion superseded*, 282 Cal.Rptr. 125, 811 P.2d 11 (1991).

2. According to one commentator, the point of the unequivocality test is to "judge whether the defendant has outwardly embodied or publicly manifested his intent in actions that, in their context, would thus signify to the reasonable observer a culpable choice." Alan Brudner, Punishment and Freedom: A Liberal Theory of Penal Justice 122 (2009). This judgment is to be made without considering any statement the defendant may have made before, during, or after the incident regarding her state of mind. As the test has been explained:

> [I]t is as though a cinematograph film, which has so far depicted merely the accused person's acts without stating what was his intention, had been suddenly stopped, and the audience were asked to say to what end those acts were directed. If there is only one reasonable answer to this question then the accused has done what amounts to an "attempt" to attain that end. If there is more than one reasonably possible answer, then the accused had not yet done enough.

J.W.C. Turner, *Attempts to Commit Crimes*, 5 Cambridge L.J. 230, 237–38 (1934).

Is this a sensible test? Although ultimately critical of this version of the doctrine, the American Law Institute offers these justifications for the standard:

> [T]he res ipsa loquitur rule * * * may be viewed entirely as a matter of procedure, as a device to prevent liability based solely on confessions and other representations of purpose[119] because of the risks they raise when considered with the other probative weaknesses[120] incident to attempt liability. Whether the requirement of unequivocality is considered part of the substantive definition of attempt or as a separate rule of evidence, it can be realistically administered only by means of a procedural mechanism—by excluding from the jury, in whole or in part, the actor's incriminating representations of purpose. If problems of proof are the basis of the preparation-attempt distinction, then the res ipsa loquitur approach has some merit. * * *
>
> A second point of departure in considering the * * * test is its relation to the manifested dangerousness of the actor. * * * The assumption underlying [the test] * * * is that there is some relationship between the actor's state of mind and the external appearance of his acts. While the actor's behavior is externally equivocal the criminal purpose in his mind is likely to be unfixed—a subjective equivocality. But once the actor must desist or perform acts that he realizes would incriminate him if all external facts were known, in all probability a firmer state of mind exists.

American Law Institute, Model Penal Code and Commentaries, Comment to § 5.01 at 326–29 (1985).

Does the unequivocality doctrine work as it should? What if a person enters a neighbor's barn, walks up to a haystack, and pulls out a match. Does this unequivocally demonstrate the actor's intention to set a fire, or must she light the match first? If she lights the match, is it now unequivocal? Suppose that she then pulls out a cigar, lights it, and sits down on the floor of the barn and reads a newspaper. See Glanville Williams, Criminal Law: The General Part 630 (2d ed. 1961).

3. In United States v. Buffington, 815 F.2d 1292 (9th Cir.1987), the police learned from an informant that *D1, D2,* and *D3* intended to rob a specific bank, and that *D3,* a male, would be dressed as a female. The police put the area under surveillance, during which time they observed three persons, including a male dressed as a female, drive slowly past the bank, look in, drive to an adjacent street, turn around, and again peer into the bank.

As the police continued to watch, the driver parked the car 150 feet from a drug store, and about 50 feet from the bank. *D1* entered the drug store and

---

119. Statements made by the actor before or during the act are not reliable because the actor may have been bluffing or he may have entertained an idea or inclination without really acting on it, the act in question being motivated by a noncriminal purpose.

120. There are a number of differences between the conduct questioned in an attempt case and the conduct questioned in a case involving the completed crime. In an attempt case the conduct involved is noncausal, so at the outset there is the opportunity to charge a crime where nothing is amiss. There is no corpus delicti to verify the fact that somebody has caused some sort of trouble. Moreover, in a case of a completed crime the last proximate act must be proved. * * * Thus, as to any substantive crime, the chances are that more steps will have to be proved if the completed crime is involved than if the attempt is charged.

walked to a window overlooking the bank. He did not inspect or purchase goods there, but after three minutes stood in a cashier's line at the store.

Simultaneously, *D2* got out of the parked car, wearing a large coat, hat, and long scarf. (The weather that day was inclement.) *D3*, the male in female clothing, then exited and stood by the car door. Both faced the drug store. By coincidence, a major power outage occurred in the area at that moment, causing bank employees to lock their doors. The three men re-entered the car and left. The police stopped the vehicle and arrested the occupants. Inside the car, the police discovered two weapons, and found that *D2* was wearing five layers of coats or jackets.

You are on the jury hearing the case. The informant's statements to the police were ruled inadmissible at the trial on unrelated grounds. Therefore, all you have to work with are the events observed by the police during their surveillance and the post-arrest search of the car. Attempted bank robbery?

[handwritten margin note: Why bank robbery? Why not something else?]

STATE v. REEVES

Supreme Court of Tennessee, 1996.
916 S.W.2d 909.

[handwritten margin note: subjectivist substantial step test (MPC)]

DROWOTA, JUDGE. * * *

On the evening of January 5, 1993, Tracie Reeves and Molly Coffman, both twelve years of age and students at West Carroll Middle School, spoke on the telephone and decided to kill their homeroom teacher, Janice Geiger. The girls agreed that Coffman would bring rat poison to school the following day so that it could be placed in Geiger's drink. The girls also agreed that they would thereafter steal Geiger's car and drive to the Smoky Mountains. Reeves then contacted Dean Foutch, a local high school student, informed him of the plan, and asked him to drive Geiger's car. Foutch refused this request.

On the morning of January 6, Coffman placed a packet of rat poison in her purse and boarded the school bus. During the bus ride Coffman told another student, Christy Hernandez, of the plan; Coffman also showed Hernandez the packet of rat poison. Upon their arrival at school Hernandez informed her homeroom teacher, Sherry Cockrill, of the plan. Cockrill then relayed this information to the principal of the school, Claudia Argo.

When Geiger entered her classroom that morning she observed Reeves and Coffman leaning over her desk; and when the girls noticed her, they giggled and ran back to their seats. At that time Geiger saw a purse lying next to her coffee cup on top of the desk. Shortly thereafter Argo called Coffman to the principal's office. Rat poison was found in Coffman's purse and it was turned over to a Sheriff's Department investigator. * * *

Reeves and Coffman were found to be delinquent by the Carroll County Juvenile Court, and both appealed from that ruling to the Carroll County Circuit Court. After a jury found that the girls attempted to commit second degree murder * * *, * * * the trial court affirmed the juvenile court's order and sentenced the girls to the Department of Youth

Development for an indefinite period. * * * Because we have not addressed the law of criminal attempt since the comprehensive reform of our criminal law undertaken by the legislature in 1989, we granted that application. * * *

Before the passage of the reform legislation in 1989, the law of criminal attempt * * * was judicially defined. In order to submit an issue of criminal attempt to the jury, the State was required to present legally sufficient evidence of: (1) an intent to commit a specific crime; (2) an overt act toward the commission of that crime; and (3) a failure to consummate the crime. *Dupuy v. State*, 204 Tenn. 624, 325 S.W.2d 238, 240 (1959).

Of the elements of criminal attempt, the second, the "overt act" requirement, was by far the most problematic. By attempting to draw a sharp distinction between "mere preparation" to commit a criminal act, which did not constitute the required overt act, and a "direct movement toward the commission after the preparations had been made," which did, Tennessee courts construed the term "overt act" very narrowly. The best example of this extremely narrow construction occurred in *Dupuy*. In that case, the Memphis police sought to lay a trap for a pharmacist suspected of performing illegal abortions by sending a young woman to request these services from him. After the woman had made several attempts to secure his services, he finally agreed to perform the abortion. The pharmacist transported the young woman to a hotel room, laid out his instruments in preparation for the procedure, and asked the woman to remove her clothes. At that point the police came into the room and arrested the pharmacist, who then admitted that he had performed abortions in the past. The defendant was convicted under a statute that made it illegal to procure a miscarriage, and he appealed to this Court.

A majority of this Court reversed the conviction. After admitting that the defendant's "reprehensible" course of conduct would doubtlessly have resulted in the commission of the crime "had he not been thwarted in his efforts by the arrival of the police," the majority concluded that:

> While the defendant had completed his plan to do this crime the element of attempt [overt act] does not appear in this record. The proof shows that he did not use any of the instruments and did not touch the body of the girl in question. Under such facts we do not think that the defendant is guilty under the statute. * * *

As indicated above, the sharp differentiation in *Dupuy* between "mere preparation" and "overt act," or the "act itself," was characteristic of the pre–1989 attempt law. In 1989, however, the legislature enacted a general criminal attempt statute, Tenn. Code Ann. § 39–12–101, as part of its comprehensive overhaul of Tennessee's criminal law. * * * Section 39–12–101 provides, in pertinent part, as follows:

> (a) A person commits criminal attempt who, acting with the kind of culpability otherwise required for the offense:

(1) Intentionally engages in action or causes a result that would constitute an offense if the circumstances surrounding the conduct were as the person believes them to be;

(2) Acts with intent to cause a result that is an element of the offense, and believes the conduct will cause the result without further conduct on the person's part; or

(3) Acts with intent to complete a course of action or cause a result that would constitute the offense, under the circumstances surrounding the conduct as the person believe them to be, *and the conduct constitutes a substantial step toward the commission of the offense.*

(b) Conduct does not constitute a *substantial step* under subdivision (a)(3) unless the person's entire course of action is corroborative of the intent to commit the offense. * * *

* * * [O]ur task is to determine whether the defendant's actions in this case constitute a "substantial step" toward the commission of second degree murder under the new statute. * * * [T]he question is made more difficult by the fact that the legislature declined to set forth any definition of the term, preferring instead to "leave the issue of what constitutes a substantial step [to the courts] for determination in each particular case."

In addressing this issue, we first note that the legislature, in enacting § 39–12–101, clearly looked to the criminal attempt section set forth in the Model Penal Code. That section provides, in pertinent part, as follows:

(1) Definition of attempt. A person is guilty of an attempt to commit a crime if, acting with the kind of culpability otherwise required for commission of the crime, he:

mPC

(a) purposely engages in conduct which would constitute the crime if the attendant circumstances were as he believes them to be; or

(b) when causing a particular result is an element of the crime, does or omits to do anything with the purpose of causing or with the belief that it will cause such result without further conduct on his part; or

(c) purposely does or omits to do anything which, under the circumstances as he believes them to be, *is a substantial step in a course of conduct planned to culminate in his commission of the crime*[.]

Model Penal Code, Section 5.01 (emphasis added.)

The State argues that the striking similarity of Tenn. Code Ann. § 39–12–101 and the Model Penal Code evidences the legislature's intention to abandon the old law of criminal attempt and instead adopt the Model Penal Code approach. The State then avers that the model code contains examples of conduct which, if proven, would entitle, but not require, the jury to find that the defendant had taken a "substantial step;'' and that two of these examples are applicable to this case. The section of the model code relied upon by the State, § 5.01(2), provides, in pertinent part, as follows:

(2) Conduct which may be held substantial step under paragraph (1)(c). Conduct shall not be held to constitute a substantial step under paragraph (1)(c) of this Section unless it is strongly corroborative of the actor's criminal purpose. Without negativing the sufficiency of other conduct, the following, if strongly corroborative of the actor's criminal purpose, shall not be held insufficient as a matter of law: * * *

(e) *possession of materials to be employed in the commission of the crime, which are specially designed for such unlawful use or which can serve no lawful purpose of the actor under the circumstances;*

(f) *possession, collection or fabrication of materials to be employed in the commission of the crime, at or near the place contemplated for its commission, where such possession, collection or fabrication serves no lawful purpose of the actor under the circumstances;* * * *

The State concludes that because the issue of whether the defendant's conduct constitutes a substantial step may be a jury question under the model code, the jury was justified in finding her guilty of attempting to commit second degree murder.

The defendant counters by arguing that despite the similarity of Tenn. Code Ann. § 39–12–101 and the Model Penal Code's attempt provision, the legislature intended to retain the sharp distinction between "mere preparation" and the "act itself" characteristic of such decisions as *Dupuy.* She supports this assertion by pointing out that although the legislature could have easily included the examples set forth in § 5.01(2) of the model code, the Tennessee statute does not include the examples. The defendant concludes that the new statute did not substantially change Tennessee attempt law, and that her conviction must be reversed because her actions constitute "mere preparation" under *Dupuy.*

Initially, we cannot accept the argument that the legislature intended to explicitly adopt the Model Penal Code approach, including the examples set forth in § 5.01(2). Although § 39–12–101 is obviously based on the model code, we agree with the defendant that the legislature could have, if it had so desired, simply included the specific examples in the Tennessee statute. That it did not do so prohibits us from concluding that the legislature explicitly intended to adopt the model code approach in all its particulars.

This conclusion does not mean, however, that the legislature intended to retain the distinction between "mere preparation" and the "act itself." Moreover, while we concede that a strong argument can be made that the conviction conflicts with *Dupuy* because the defendant did not place the poison in the cup, but simply brought it to the crime scene, we also are well aware that the *Dupuy* approach to attempt law has been consistently and effectively criticized. * * * [D]istinguishing between "mere preparation" and the "act itself" in a principled manner is a difficult, if not impossible, task. The other principal ground of criticism of the *Dupuy* approach bears directly on the primary objective of the law—that of preventing inchoate crimes from becoming full-blown ones. Many courts and commentators have argued that failing to attach criminal responsibility to the actor—and therefore prohibiting law enforcement officers from taking action—until the actor is on the brink of consummating the crime endangers the public and undermines the preventative goal of attempt law.

The shortcomings of the *Dupuy* rule with respect to the goal of prevention are particularly evident in this case. As stated above, it is likely that under *Dupuy* no criminal responsibility would have attached unless the poison had actually been placed in the teacher's cup. This rigid requirement, however, severely undercuts the objective of prevention because of the surreptitious nature of the act of poisoning. Once a person secretly places a toxic substance into a container from which another person is likely to eat or drink, the damage is done. Here, if it had not been for the intervention of the teacher, she could have been rendered powerless to protect herself from harm.

After carefully weighing considerations of *stare decisis* against the persuasive criticisms of the *Dupuy* rule, we conclude that this artificial and potentially harmful rule must be abandoned. We hold that when an actor possesses materials to be used in the commission of a crime, at or near the scene of the crime, and where the possession of those materials can serve no lawful purpose of the actor under the circumstances, the jury is entitled, but not required, to find that the actor has taken a "substantial step" toward the commission of the crime if such action is strongly corroborative of the actor's overall criminal purpose. For the foregoing reasons, the [conviction] * * * is affirmed.

BIRCH, JUSTICE, concurring and dissenting. * * *

* * * Based upon this record, I would find that the "*entire* course of action" [as required under § 39–12–101(b)] of these two twelve-year-old girls was not "strongly corroborative" of intent to commit second-degree murder and that the evidence was insufficient as a matter of law. In looking at the "entire course of action," we should remember that these were twelve-year-old girls, not explosive-toting terrorists.

Accordingly, while I concur in the majority's abandonment of the rule stated in *Dupuy v. State,* I dissent from the conclusion of the majority in this case.

NOTES AND QUESTIONS

Jackson

1. United States v. Jackson, 560 F.2d 112 (2d Cir.1977):

The draftsmen of the Model Penal Code recognized the difficulty of arriving at a general standard for distinguishing acts of preparation from acts constituting an attempt. * * * The problem then was to devise a standard more inclusive than one requiring the last proximate act before attempt liability would attach, but less inclusive than one which would make every act done with the intent to commit a crime criminal. * * *

The formulation upon which the draftsmen ultimately agreed required, in addition to criminal purpose, that an act be a substantial step in a course of conduct designed to accomplish a criminal result, and that it be strongly corroborative of criminal purpose in order for it to constitute such a substantial step. The following differences between this test and previous approaches to the preparation-attempt problem were noted:

#1

First, this formulation shifts the emphasis from what remains to be done—the chief concern of the proximity tests—to what the actor *has already done.* The fact that further major steps must be taken before the crime can be completed does not preclude a finding that the steps already undertaken are substantial. It is expected, in the normal case, that this approach will broaden the scope of attempt liability.

MPC

#2

Second, although it is intended that the requirement of a substantial step will result in the imposition of attempt liability only in those instances in which some firmness of criminal purpose is shown, no finding is required as to whether the actor would probably have desisted prior to completing the crime. * * *

#3

Finally, the requirement of proving a substantial step generally will prove less of a hurdle for the prosecution than the *res ipsa loquitur* approach, which requires that the actor's conduct must itself manifest the criminal purpose. The difference will be illustrated in connection with the present section's requirement of corroboration. Here it should be noted that, in the present formulation, the two purposes to be served by the *res ipsa loquitur* test are, to a large extent, treated separately. Firmness of criminal purpose is intended to be shown by requiring a substantial step, while problems of proof are dealt with by the requirement of corroboration (although, under the reasoning previously expressed, the latter will also tend to establish firmness of purpose).

Model Penal Code § 5.01, Comment at 47 (Tent. Draft No. 10, 1960).

The draftsmen concluded that, in addition to assuring firmness of criminal design, the requirement of a substantial step would preclude attempt liability, with its accompanying harsh penalties, for relatively remote preparatory acts. At the same time, however, by not requiring a "last proximate act" or one of its various analogues it would permit the apprehension of dangerous persons at an earlier stage than the other approaches without immunizing them from attempt liability.

2. People v. Lehnert, 163 P.3d 1111 (Colo. 2007):

> The question [for the jury] whether particular conduct constitutes a substantial step, of course, remains a matter of degree and can no more be resolved by a mechanical rule, or litmus test, than could the question whether the actor's conduct was too remote or failed to progress beyond mere preparation. The requirement that the defendant's conduct amount to a "substantial step" * * *, however, provides the fact-finder with a much more specific and predictable basis for determining liability.

Do you agree?

3. Model Penal Code § 5.01(2) is intended to "give some definite content to the 'substantial step' requirement" of subsection (1)(c), which applies in cases of incomplete attempts. American Law Institute, Model Penal Code and Commentaries, Comment to § 5.01 at 332 (1985). If the prosecutor establishes that any one of the situations enumerated in subsection (2) has occurred, the trial judge is required to instruct the jury pursuant to subsection (1)(c), and must accept a verdict of guilty unless she determines that, as a matter of law, the conduct is not "strongly corroborative of the actor's criminal purpose." A small number of states and some federal courts have adopted the substantial step formula of subsection (1)(c), but (as in Tennessee) subsection (2) has not been widely followed. Id. at 331, 332.

4. How is the Model Penal Code's "substantial step" test similar to the unequivocality or res ipsa loquitur test? How is it different?

5. C was upset that his wife wanted a divorce. He spoke of killing his wife and then committing suicide. One evening, after heavy drinking with a friend, he announced, "Tonight's the night. I'm going to stab her in her throat, I'm going to stab her in her heart." C prayed with his friend, said good-bye, and asked his friend to take custody of his cats and dogs. C, with an ice pick, a box cutter, and a pair of binoculars, drove to the hospital where his wife worked at night. He backed up his car into the last row of the parking lot across the street from the emergency room where his wife worked. Meanwhile C's friend reported the threat to the police. When the police arrived, they found C in his vehicle, the vehicle lights off, and C asleep or passed out. Attempted murder? Collier v. State, 846 N.E.2d 340 (Ind. App. 2006). Apply the Model Penal Code.

6. S is a United States citizen and licensed physician specializing in emergency medicine. S worked at a military hospital in Riyadh, Saudi Arabia and periodically returned to the United States. While in the United States, S met with and provided F, an undercover FBI agent posing as a recruiter for al Qaeda, with his personal and work telephone number. He did so in order to permit *mujahideen* needing medical assistance to contact him in Riyadh. S and a friend then participated in *bayat*, "a ritual in which each swore an oath of allegiance to al Qaeda, promising to serve as a 'soldier of Islam' and to protect 'the path of al Qaeda.' * * * The men further swore obedience to 'the guardians of the pledge,' *i.e.*, Osama bin Laden, and his second in command * * *" United States v. Farhane, 634 F.3d 127, 133 (2d Cir. 2011). Assume

that *S* would be guilty of knowingly providing material support to a terrorist organization if he had actually provided medical assistance to *mujahideen* needing such assistance. Is he guilty here of attempted knowing provision of material support to a terrorist organization? Apply the Model Penal Code.

7. Reconsider the *Gentry* case (p. 717, supra). Imagine that Hill's father enters the apartment after her clothing catches fire but before Gentry does anything to smother the flames. Hoping that she will die, Hill's father does nothing to help her. He just watches as Gentry eventually puts out the flames. Is Hill's father guilty of attempted murder? Apply the Model Penal Code.

ONE FINAL PROBLEM

Okay, take everything you have learned so far, and consider United States v. Duran, 96 F.3d 1495 (D.C. Cir. 1996):

> In mid-September of 1994 Francisco Martin Duran, a 26–year–old upholsterer from a suburb of Colorado Springs, Colorado, began to purchase a number of assault weapons. Evidence presented at trial established that on September 13, Duran bought an assault rifle and about 100 rounds of ammunition. Two days later, he bought a thirty-round clip and had the rifle equipped with a folding stock. Thirteen days after that, Duran bought a shotgun, and the following day still more ammunition. On September 30, Duran left work and, without contacting his family or employer, began his journey to Washington, D.C. He purchased another thirty-round clip in Charlottesville, Virginia on October 10, and the next day bought a large overcoat in Richmond, Virginia. Later that day Duran arrived in Washington, D.C., and checked into a hotel. He stayed at various hotels in the Washington area between the tenth and the twenty-ninth of October.

> Shortly before 6:00 on the morning of October 29, Duran checked out of the Embassy Suites Hotel in Tysons Corner, drove to downtown Washington, and parked his truck on 17th Street, between D and E Streets. By early afternoon, he was standing in front of the north side of the White House, wearing the overcoat he had purchased earlier on his trip. As Duran stood by the White House fence, two eighth-grade students on a field trip, Robert DeCamp and Brent Owens, ran to a point along the fence thirteen feet away. DeCamp pointed toward a small group of men in dark suits standing near the White House. One of these men, civilian Dennis Basso, bore a strong resemblance to President Clinton. DeCamp remarked that the man "looked like Bill Clinton," and Owens said "Yeah, it does." Almost immediately after this exchange, Duran began firing the rifle at Basso.

Duran was indicted for violation of 18 U.S.C. § 1751(c), which prohibits the attempted assassination of the President of the United States. Is Duran guilty of this offense? In answering this question, consider: (a) does he have the requisite *mens rea*; and (b) did his acts proceed far enough to convict him of the offense? On (b), at what precise point would you say that he crossed the line of attempt? Apply the Model Penal Code and common law.

5. SPECIAL DEFENSES

a. Impossibility

PEOPLE v. THOUSAND

Supreme Court of Michigan, 2001.
465 Mich. 149, 631 N.W.2d 694.

YOUNG, J.

We granted leave in this case to consider whether the doctrine of "impossibility" provides a defense to a charge of attempt to commit an offense prohibited by law under M.C.L. § 750.92 * * *. The circuit court granted defendant's motion to quash and dismissed [the charge] * * * against him on the basis that it was legally impossible for him to have committed * * * the charged crime[]. * * *

I. FACTUAL AND PROCEDURAL BACKGROUND

Deputy William Liczbinski was assigned by the Wayne County Sheriff's Department to conduct an undercover investigation for the department's Internet Crimes Bureau. Liczbinski was instructed to pose as a minor and log onto "chat rooms" on the Internet for the purpose of identifying persons using the Internet as a means for engaging in criminal activity.

On December 8, 1998, while using the screen name "Bekka," Liczbinski was approached by defendant, who was using the screen name "Mr. Auto–Mag," in an Internet chat room. Defendant described himself as a twenty-three-year-old male from Warren, and Bekka described herself as a fourteen-year-old female from Detroit. Bekka indicated that her name was Becky Fellins, and defendant revealed that his name was Chris Thousand. During this initial conversation, defendant sent Bekka, via the Internet, a photograph of his face.

From December 9 through 16, 1998, Liczbinski, still using the screen name "Bekka," engaged in chat room conversation with defendant. During these exchanges, the conversation became sexually explicit. Defendant made repeated lewd invitations to Bekka to engage in various sexual acts, despite various indications of her young age.

During one of his online conversations with Bekka, after asking her whether anyone was "around there," watching her, defendant indicated that he was sending her a picture of himself. Within seconds, Liczbinski received over the Internet a photograph of male genitalia. Defendant asked Bekka whether she liked and wanted it and whether she was getting "hot" yet, and described in a graphic manner the type of sexual acts he wished to perform with her. Defendant invited Bekka to come see him at his house for the purpose of engaging in sexual activity. Bekka replied that she wanted to do so, and defendant cautioned her that they had to be careful, because he could "go to jail." Defendant asked whether Bekka looked "over sixteen," so that if his roommates were home he could lie.

The two then planned to meet at an area McDonald's restaurant at 5:00 p.m. on the following Thursday. Defendant indicated that they could go to his house, and that he would tell his brother that Bekka was seventeen. Defendant instructed Bekka to wear a "nice sexy skirt," something that he could "get [his] head into." Defendant indicated that he would be dressed in black pants and shirt and a brown suede coat, and that he would be driving a green Duster. Bekka asked defendant to bring her a present, and indicated that she liked white teddy bears.

On Thursday, December 17, 1998, Liczbinski and other deputy sheriffs were present at the specified McDonald's restaurant when they saw defendant inside a vehicle matching the description given to Bekka by defendant. * * * Liczbinski recognized defendant's face from the photograph that had been sent to Bekka. Defendant looked around for approximately thirty seconds before leaving the restaurant. Defendant was then taken into custody. * * *

Following a preliminary examination, defendant was bound over for trial on charges of * * * attempted distribution of obscene material to a minor [and related offenses against underage females].

Defendant brought a motion to quash the information, arguing that, because the existence of a child victim was an element of each of the charged offenses, the evidence was legally insufficient to support the charges. The circuit court agreed and dismissed the case, holding that it was legally impossible for defendant to have committed the charged offenses. The Court of Appeals affirmed the dismissal of the charges * * *. * * *

III. ANALYSIS

A. The "Impossibility" Doctrine

The doctrine of "impossibility" as it has been discussed in the context of inchoate crimes represents the conceptual dilemma that arises when, because of the defendant's mistake of fact or law, his actions could not possibly have resulted in the commission of the substantive crime underlying an attempt charge. Classic illustrations of the concept of impossibility include: (1) the defendant is prosecuted for attempted larceny after he tries to "pick" the victim's empty pocket; (2) the defendant is prosecuted for attempted rape after he tries to have nonconsensual intercourse, but is unsuccessful because he is impotent; (3) the defendant is prosecuted for attempting to receive stolen property where the property he received was not, in fact, stolen;[8] and (4) the defendant is prosecuted for attempting to hunt deer out of season after he shoots at a stuffed decoy deer. In each of

---

8. *People v. Jaffe*, 185 N.Y. 497, 78 N.E. 169 (1906).

these examples, despite evidence of the defendant's criminal intent, he cannot be prosecuted for the *completed* offense of larceny, rape, receiving stolen property, or hunting deer out of season, because proof of at least one element of each offense cannot be derived from his objective actions. The question, then, becomes whether the defendant can be prosecuted for the *attempted* offense, and the answer is dependent upon whether he may raise the defense of "impossibility."

Courts and legal scholars have drawn a distinction between two categories of impossibility: "factual impossibility" and "legal impossibility." It has been said that, at common law, legal impossibility is a defense to a charge of attempt, but factual impossibility is not. See American Law Institute, Model Penal Code and Commentaries (1985), comment to § 5.01, pp. 307–317; Perkins & Boyce, Criminal Law (3d ed.), p. 632; Dressler, Understanding Criminal Law (1st ed.), § 27.07[B], p. 349. However, courts and scholars alike have struggled unsuccessfully over the years to articulate an accurate rule for distinguishing between the categories of "impossibility."

"Factual impossibility," which has apparently never been recognized in any American jurisdiction as a defense to a charge of attempt, "exists when [the defendant's] intended end constitutes a crime but she fails to consummate it because of a factual circumstance unknown to her or beyond her control." An example of a "factual impossibility" scenario is where the defendant is prosecuted for attempted murder after pointing an unloaded gun at someone and pulling the trigger, where the defendant believed the gun was loaded.

The category of "legal impossibility" is further divided into two subcategories: "pure" legal impossibility and "hybrid" legal impossibility. Although it is generally undisputed that "pure" legal impossibility will bar an attempt conviction, the concept of "hybrid legal impossibility" has proven problematic. As Professor Dressler points out, the failure of courts to distinguish between "pure" and "hybrid" legal impossibility has created confusion in this area of the law.

"Pure legal impossibility exists if the criminal law does not prohibit *D*'s conduct or the result that she has sought to achieve."[e] In other words, the concept of pure legal impossibility applies when an actor engages in conduct that he believes is criminal, but is not actually prohibited by law: "There can be no conviction of criminal attempt based upon *D*'s erroneous notion that he was committing a crime." Perkins & Boyce, *supra.* As an example, consider the case of a man who believes that the legal age of consent is sixteen years old, and who [accurately] believes that a girl with whom he had consensual sexual intercourse is fifteen years old. If the law actually fixed the age of consent at fifteen, this man would not be guilty of

---

e. Ira P. Robbins, *Attempting the Impossible: The Emerging Consensus*, 23 Harv. J. on Legis. 377, 389 (1986): Pure legal impossibility arises "when the law does not proscribe the goal that the defendant sought to achieve."

attempted statutory rape, despite his mistaken belief that the law prohibited his conduct.

When courts speak of "legal impossibility," they are generally referring to what is more accurately described as "hybrid" legal impossibility.

Most claims of legal impossibility are of the hybrid variety. *Hybrid legal impossibility* exists if *D*'s goal was illegal, but commission of the offense was impossible due to a factual mistake by her regarding the legal status of some factor relevant to her conduct.[f] This version of impossibility is a "hybrid" because, as the definition implies and as is clarified immediately below, D's impossibility claim includes both a legal and a factual aspect to it.

Courts have recognized a defense of legal impossibility or have stated that it would exist if D receives unstolen property believing it was stolen; tries to pick the pocket of a stone image of a human; offers a bribe to a "juror" who is not a juror; tries to hunt deer out of season by shooting a stuffed animal; shoots a corpse believing that it is alive; or shoots at a tree stump believing that it is a human.

Notice that each of the mistakes in these cases affected the legal status of some aspect of the defendant's conduct. The status of property as "stolen" is necessary to commit the crime of "receiving stolen property with knowledge it is stolen"—i.e., a person legally is incapable of committing this offense if the property is not stolen. The status of a person as a "juror" is legally necessary to commit the offense of bribing a juror. The status of a victim as a "human being" (rather than as a corpse, tree stump, or statue) legally is necessary to commit the crime of murder or to "take and carry away the personal property *of another.*" Finally, putting a bullet into a stuffed deer can never constitute the crime of hunting out of season.

On the other hand, in each example of hybrid legal impossibility D was mistaken about a fact: whether property was stolen, whether a person was a juror, whether the victims were human or whether the victim was an animal subject to being hunted out of season. [Dressler, *supra.*]

As the Court of Appeals panel in this case accurately noted, it is possible to view virtually any example of "hybrid legal impossibility" as an example of "factual impossibility":

> "*Ultimately any case of hybrid legal impossibility may reasonably be characterized as factual impossibility.* * * * [B]y skillful characterization, one can describe virtually any case of hybrid legal impossibility, which is a common law defense, as an example of factual impossibility, which is *not* a defense."

---

f. The fifth edition of Dressler's Understanding Criminal Law, at p. 408, perhaps more precisely states that hybrid legal impossibility exists "if the actor's goal is illegal, but commission of the offense is impossible due to a *factual* mistake * * * regarding the *legal* status of some attendant circumstance that constitutes an element of the charged offense."

See also * * * *United States v. Thomas,* 13 USCMA 278, 283, 32
C.M.R. 278, 283, 1962 WL 4490 (1962) ("[w]hat is abundantly clear * * *
is that it is most difficult to classify any particular state of facts as
positively coming within one of these categories to the exclusion of the
other");[g] *State v. Moretti,* 52 N.J. 182, 189, 244 A.2d 499 (1968) ("[o]ur
examination of [authorities discussing the doctrine of impossibility] con-
vinces us that the application of the defense of impossibility is so fraught
with intricacies and artificial distinctions that the defense has little value
as an analytical method for reaching substantial justice").

It is notable that "the great majority of jurisdictions have now
recognized that legal and factual impossibility are 'logically indistinguishable' * * * and have abolished impossibility as a defense."[12] For example,
several states have adopted statutory provisions similar to Model Penal
Code § 5.01(1), [which abolishes the defense of legal impossibility—but
see Note 10 infra.—Ed.] * * *

In other jurisdictions, courts have considered the "impossibility"
defense under attempt statutes that did not include language explicitly
abolishing the defense. Several of these courts have simply declined to
participate in the sterile academic exercise of categorizing a particular set
of facts as representing "factual" or "legal" impossibility, and have
instead examined solely the words of the applicable attempt statute.

B. Attempted Distribution of Obscene Material to a Minor

The Court of Appeals panel in this case, after examining Professor
Dressler's exposition of the doctrine of impossibility, concluded that it was
legally impossible for defendant to have committed the charged offense of
attempted distribution of obscene material to a minor. The panel held
that, because "Bekka" was, in fact, an adult, an essential requirement of
the underlying substantive offense was not met (dissemination to a
minor), and therefore it was legally impossible for defendant to have
committed the crime.

We begin by noting that the concept of "impossibility," in either its
"factual" or "legal" variant, has never been recognized by this Court as a
valid defense to a charge of attempt. * * *

Finding no recognition of impossibility in our common law, we turn
now to the terms of the statute. MCL 750.92 provides, in relevant part:

> Any person who shall attempt to commit an offense prohibited by
> law, and in such attempt shall do any act towards the commission of
> such offense, but shall fail in the perpetration, or shall be intercepted

g. In *Thomas,* soldiers had sexual intercourse with a woman they believed had fallen
unconscious from intoxication. In fact, she had died. They were charged with attempted rape.
They asserted a claim of legal impossibility.

12. Apart from judicial abrogation of this doctrine, many states have done so by legislative
enactment. In a 1995 law review article, California Deputy Attorney General Kyle Brodie listed
twenty states that had specifically abolished the defense of impossibility by legislative enactment.
Brodie, *The obviously impossible attempt: A proposed revision to the Model Penal Code,* 15 N Ill U
L R 237, n. 39 (1995).

or prevented in the execution of the same, when no express provision is made by law for the punishment of such attempt, shall be punished as follows: * * *

3. If the offense so attempted to be committed is punishable by imprisonment in the state prison for a term less than 5 years, or imprisonment in the county jail or by fine, the offender convicted of such attempt shall be guilty of a misdemeanor * * *.

Under our statute, then, an "attempt" consists of (1) an attempt to commit an offense prohibited by law, and (2) any act towards the commission of the intended offense. We have further explained the elements of attempt under our statute as including "an intent to do an act or to bring about certain consequences which would in law amount to a crime; and * * * an act in furtherance of that intent which, as it is most commonly put, goes beyond mere preparation."

In determining whether "impossibility," were we to recognize the doctrine, is a viable defense to a charge of attempt under M.C.L. § 750.92, our obligation is to examine the statute in an effort to discern and give effect to the legislative intent that may reasonably be inferred from the text of the statute itself. * * *

We are unable to discern from the words of the attempt statute any legislative intent that the concept of "impossibility" provide any impediment to charging a defendant with, or convicting him of, an attempted crime, notwithstanding any factual mistake—regarding either the attendant circumstances or the legal status of some factor relevant thereto—that he may harbor. The attempt statute carves out no exception for those who, possessing the requisite criminal intent to commit an offense prohibited by law and taking action toward the commission of that offense, have acted under an extrinsic misconception.

Defendant in this case is not charged with the substantive crime of distributing obscene material to a minor in violation of M.C.L. § 722.675.[16] It is unquestioned that defendant could not be convicted of that crime, because defendant allegedly distributed obscene material not to "a minor," but to an adult man. Instead, defendant is charged with the distinct offense of attempt, which requires only that the prosecution prove

---

16. At the time of the alleged offense, M.C.L. § 722.675 provided, in relevant part:

(1) A person is guilty of distributing obscene matter to a minor if that person does either of the following:

(a) Knowingly disseminates to a minor sexually explicit visual or verbal material that is harmful to minors. * * *

(2) A person knowingly disseminates sexually explicit matter to a minor when the person knows both the nature of the matter and the status of the minor to whom the matter is disseminated.

(3) A person knows the nature of matter if the person either is aware of the character and content of the matter or recklessly disregards circumstances suggesting the character and content of the matter.

(4) A person knows the status of a minor if the person either is aware that the person to whom the dissemination is made is under 18 years of age or recklessly disregards a substantial risk that the person to whom the dissemination is made is under 18 years of age.

SEC. B   ATTEMPT   751

intention to commit an offense prohibited by law, coupled with conduct toward the commission of that offense. The notion that it would be "impossible" for the defendant to have committed the *completed* offense is simply irrelevant to the analysis. Rather, in deciding guilt on a charge of attempt, the trier of fact must examine the unique circumstances of the particular case and determine whether the prosecution has proven that the defendant possessed the requisite specific intent and that he engaged in some act "towards the commission" of the intended offense.

Because the nonexistence of a minor victim does not give rise to a viable defense to the attempt charge in this case, the circuit court erred in dismissing this charge on the basis of "legal impossibility." * * *

MARILYN J. KELLY, J. (* * * dissenting * * *).

I respectfully disagree with the majority's conclusion that the doctrine of "legal impossibility" has never been adopted in Michigan. There is ample evidence to the contrary in the case law of the state. Because "legal impossibility" is a viable defense, I would affirm the Court of Appeals decision affirming the circuit court's dismissal of attempted distribution of obscene material to a minor. * * *

Even if "legal impossibility" were not part of Michigan's common law, I would disagree with the majority's interpretation of the attempt statute. It does not follow from the fact that the statute does not expressly incorporate the concept of impossibility that the defense is inapplicable.

Examination of the language of the attempt statute leads to a reasonable inference that the Legislature did not intend to punish conduct that a mistake of legal fact renders unprohibited. The attempt statute makes illegal an " * * * attempt to *commit an offense prohibited by law* * * *." It does not make illegal an action not prohibited by law. Hence, one may conclude, the impossibility of completing the underlying crime can provide a defense to attempt.

This reasoning is supported by the fact that the attempt statute codified the common-law rule regarding the elements of attempt. At common law, "legal impossibility" is a defense to attempt. Absent a statute expressly abrogating "legal impossibility," this common-law rule continues to provide a viable defense.

This state's attempt statute, unlike the Model Penal Code and various state statutes that follow it, does not contain language allowing for consideration of a defendant's beliefs regarding "attendant circumstances." Rather, it takes an "objective" view of criminality, focusing on whether the defendant actually came close to completing the prohibited act. The impossibility of completing the offense is relevant to this objective approach because impossibility obviates the state's "concern that the actor may cause or come close to causing the harm or evil that the offense seeks to prevent."

The majority's conclusion, that it is irrelevant whether it would be impossible to have committed the completed offense, contradicts the language used in the attempt statute. If an element of the offense cannot be established, an accused cannot be found guilty of the prohibited act. The underlying offense in this case, disseminating or exhibiting sexual material to a minor, requires a minor recipient. Because the dissemination was not to a minor, it is legally impossible for defendant to have committed the prohibited act.

This Court should affirm the Court of Appeals decision, determining that it was legally impossible for defendant to have committed the charged offense of attempted distribution of obscene material to a minor. * * *

As judges, we often decide cases involving disturbing facts. However repugnant we personally find the criminal conduct charged, we must decide the issues on the basis of the law. I certainly do not wish to have child predators loose in society. However, I believe that neither the law nor society is served by allowing the end of removing them from society to excuse unjust means to accomplish it. In this case, defendant raised a legal impossibility argument that is supported by Michigan case law. The majority, in determining that legal impossibility is not a viable defense in this state, ignores that law. * * *

NOTES AND QUESTIONS

1. As a matter of statutory analysis, who has the better argument, the majority or the dissent?

2. Although *Thousand* and various scholars have drawn a distinction between "pure" and "hybrid" legal impossibility (although different terms are sometimes used), most courts speak simply of "factual" and "legal" impossibility. United States v. Oviedo, 525 F.2d 881, 883 (5th Cir.1976) provides definitions of these terms:

> Legal impossibility occurs when the actions which the defendant performs or sets in motion, even if fully carried out as he desires, would not constitute a crime. Factual impossibility occurs when the objective of the defendant is proscribed by the criminal law but a circumstance unknown to the actor prevents him from bringing about that objective.

3. *Factual versus legal impossibility: making sense of it.* Although many states have abolished the factual/legal impossibility distinction, not all jurisdictions have done so. Later Notes consider the wisdom of the abolitionist trend. But, for now, attempt (no pun intended) to understand the distinction.

Case law suggests that shooting at an empty bed, thinking there is someone in it, is a case of "factual impossibility" in an attempted murder prosecution; but it is "legal impossibility" to shoot a stuffed deer dummy in a prosecution for attempted shooting deer out of season. Assuming these cases are rightly decided, what is the relevant distinction? In light of these two cases, what if a would-be victim, aware of an impending bedroom assault, puts a mannequin in his bed: if the defendant shoots at what now is *not* an empty bed, but a bed with a dummy in it, is she no longer guilty of attempted murder? Suppose that the shooter, acting in the dark, had not seen the mannequin when she fired her gun?

4. *Jaffe and non-stolen goods. Thousand* cites (footnote 8) *Jaffe,* which is a leading case for the proposition that if a person receives non-stolen property, believing it is stolen, this is a case of legal impossibility, which bars conviction for the crime of attempted receipt of stolen property ("receipt of stolen property, knowing it is stolen"). This is to be distinguished from cases in which a would-be thief puts his hand in the empty pocket of a victim. *Jaffe* explained:

> "The crucial distinction between the case before us and the pickpocket cases, and others involving the same principle, lies not in the possibility or impossibility * * * of the commission of the crime, but in the fact that, in the present case, *the act, which it was doubtless the intent of the defendant to commit, would not have been a crime if it had been consummated.*" (Emphasis added)

Is the *Jaffe* court's reasoning persuasive? According to one scholar, it is not:

> The critics of *Jaffe* have not found much difficulty in demolishing the analysis contained in this passage. It has been pointed out that the *Jaffe* court's statement that "the act, which it was doubtless the intent of the defendant to commit would not have been a crime if it had been consummated" is very questionable and turns upon a choice of what is relevant in establishing what his intention was. It certainly seems no defiance of ordinary language to say that Jaffe intended to receive stolen goods, for, in speaking of a person's intention, we frequently incorporate his mistaken view of a situation, since belief and intent cannot be neatly separated. So, if I am sitting in a plane flying from New York to Los Angeles, which I mistakenly think is flying to London—my desired destination—it would be a perfectly reasonable statement to say that, at least until the mistake is pointed out to me, it was my intention to reach London on that plane. The rejection of *Jaffe* * * * is not only supported by such a view of intent but also by the policy underlying the law of attempts. Jaffe, in this way of looking at the facts, intended to commit an offense known to the law, so this is not a case of legal impossibility. Where the prosecution can discharge its burden of proof by showing beyond a reasonable doubt that an accused had such an intent, expressed in a sufficient overt act, then in terms of the prohibitions of the criminal law such a person is socially dangerous and deserves punishment.[h]

5. *The saga of Lady Eldon.* Consider the following famous story:

> Lady Eldon, when traveling with her husband on the Continent, bought what she supposed to be a quantity of French lace, which she hid, concealing it from Lord Eldon in one of the pockets of the coach. The package was brought to light by a custom officer at Dover. The lace turned out to be an English manufactured article of little value and, of course, not subject to duty. Lady Eldon had bought it at a price vastly above its value, believing it to be genuine, intending to smuggle it into England.

---

h. Graham Hughes, *One Further Footnote on Attempting the Impossible,* 42 N.Y.U. L. Rev. 1005, 1009 (1967). Copyright © 1967, New York University. Reprinted by permission.

1 Wharton, Criminal Law § 225, at 304 n.9 (12th ed. 1932).

Assume that despite her elevated social position in England, Lady Eldon was charged with the offense of attempting to smuggle a dutiable item into the country. Using the definitions found in Note 2, is this a case of factual or legal impossibility?

6.   Can you identify any underlying principle to explain why common-law courts tried to formulate rules for distinguishing between factual impossibility and hybrid legal impossibility, and thus between those cases in which impossibility was not a defense and those in which was? George Fletcher says: "[I]mpossible attempts are punishable if the behavior itself produces apprehension * * * in the mind of the ideal observer." George P. Fletcher, Basic Concepts of Criminal Law 177 (1998). Alan Brudner similarly says: "[W]hile impossibility of completion should not necessarily preclude culpability for attempt, liability should be excluded where * * * a reasonable observer could interpret the defendant's action as innocent." Alan Brudner, Punishment and Freedom: A Liberal Theory of Penal Justice 128 (2009). Helpful, nor not?

7.   *Model Penal Code.* The Code sweeps aside the defense of impossibility. Take a look at Section 5.01(1): can you see why "legal impossibility"—or, more accurately, the hybrid version—will not exculpate an actor? Apply Section 5.01 to the facts in *Thousand.*

8.   *Abolition of the legal impossibility defense.* Is abolition of the defense in so-called hybrid legal impossibility cases a good idea? Before turning to that question in the Notes that follow, think back to the debate between objectivism and subjectivism (p. 715, Note 1). Would objectivists have more reason to defend the retention of the defense than subjectivists? Consider this question as you read on.

9.   *The argument for abolition.* The reporters of the Model Penal Code have explained the drafters' rationale for abolishing the (hybrid) legal impossibility defense:

> Insofar as it has not rested on conceptual tangles that have been largely independent of policy considerations, the defense of impossibility seems to have been employed to serve a number of functions. First, it has been used to verify criminal purpose; if the means selected were absurd, there is good ground for doubting that the actor really planned to commit a crime. Similarly, if the defendant's conduct, objectively viewed, is ambiguous, there may be ground for doubting the firmness of his purpose to commit a criminal offense. A general defense of impossibility is, however, an inappropriate way of assuring that the actor has a true criminal purpose. * * *

> [Another] consideration that has been advanced in support of an impossibility defense is the view that the criminal law need not take notice of conduct that is innocuous, the element of impossibility preventing any dangerous proximity to the completed crime. The law of attempts, however, should be concerned with manifestations of dangerous character as well as with preventive arrests; the fact that particular conduct may not create an actual risk of harmful consequences, though it would if the circumstances were as the defendant believed them to be, should not

therefore be conclusive. The innocuous character of the particular conduct becomes relevant only if the futile endeavor itself indicates a
harmless personality, so that immunizing the conduct from liability
would not result in exposing society to a dangerous person.

American Law Institute, Model Penal Code and Commentaries, Comment to
§ 5.01 at 315–316 (1985).

10. *Rethinking the objections.* The drafters of the Code claim (id. at 309)
that "[i]n all of these cases [that recognize the impossibility defense] the
actor's criminal purpose has been clearly demonstrated; he went as far as he
could in implementing that purpose; and, as a result, his 'dangerousness' is
plainly manifested." Are the drafters correct? Reconsider Lady Eldon's lace
(Note 5 supra) and *Jaffe* (Note 4) in light of the following observations:

> The argument that Lady Eldon should be convicted of attempted
> smuggling is that having gone beyond preparatory acts to the point where
> she has committed the very act defined by the crime—importing the
> lace—it is clear that she is fully committed to her illegal escapade. Only
> the accidental absence of an external circumstance required by the
> statute—that the imported goods be dutiable—precludes liability for the
> substantive crime. Since she thought the goods were dutiable, intended to
> avoid paying the duty, and did all the acts that would have supported
> substantive liability had the facts been as she thought, she should be
> guilty of an attempt.
>
> But, we are entitled to ask, if Lady Eldon's handkerchief really is
> cheap linen, how do we know that she thought it was expensive dutiable
> lace? The facts state that she "hid" the lace, "concealing" it in a pocket,
> but those are loaded words that assume the very thing at issue, namely
> that she sought to avoid a duty she mistakenly believed due. Where there
> are present two objective factors—lace subject to import duty and an act
> of concealment—the coincidence of an objective motive to smuggle and
> conduct consistent with that motive and supportive of that goal is fair
> ground for the conclusion that Lady Eldon in fact intended to avoid
> paying the duty. If we remove the objective existence of the motive, the
> evidentiary basis for the conclusion that she intended to evade a duty
> believed due is correspondingly weakened. * * *
>
> Let us apply a similar analysis to another famous legal impossibility
> case, *People v. Jaffe.* * * *
>
> Those who would eliminate the defense of legal impossibility from
> the legal lexicon and would convict Jaffe of attempted possession of stolen
> goods because he thought they were stolen presumably would convict any
> other defendant of the same crime with respect to goods that had never
> been stolen if it could be proved that the defendant thought they were
> stolen. Having dispensed with the need for establishing the circumstance
> that the goods are stolen, they must permit this result if there is evidence
> of guilty belief. Assume two cases in which the sole direct evidence of the
> defendant's alleged belief that the goods are stolen is a confession or a
> testimony of an informer or an accomplice. In one case the goods
> possessed are in fact stolen; in the other they are not. It is reasonably
> clear that most of us would rest easier with a conviction in the first case

than in the second although we might have a difficult time articulating reasons for this distinction. * * * [I]t may * * * be that possession of stolen goods furnishes some evidence of belief that they are stolen while, clearly, possession of goods not in fact stolen furnishes no reason to believe that the defendant thought they were stolen.

The draftsmen of the Model Penal Code have argued that while eliminating legal impossibility as a defense, the Code adequately takes care of these problems by its separate provision requiring that the defendant's act corroborate his mens rea. But the Model Penal Code's requirement that the act corroborate the mens rea [Section 5.01(1)(c)— ed.] applies only to cases in the preparation-attempt continuum. Cases such as *Jaffe* and Lady Eldon are covered by separate provision [Section 5.01(1)(a)—ed.] which provides that where the defendant does any act which would constitute a crime under the circumstances as he thought them to be, he is guilty of an attempt. The corroboration requirement of section 5.01(2) does not apply to this section. Perhaps the draftsmen assumed that doing the act defined in the substantive crime will always supply at least as much corroboration of mens rea as is present in the substantive crime itself. If so, what they have failed to see is that the act in its narrow sense of the defendant's physical movements can be perfectly innocent in itself—possession of goods, bringing goods into the country—and that what gives the act character as corroborative of mens rea is often the objective element or the attendant circumstances that the goods possessed are in fact stolen, or that the goods brought into the country are in fact dutiable, or that the goods possessed are in fact narcotics.

Arnold N. Enker, *Impossibility in Criminal Attempts—Legality and the Legal Process*, 53 Minn. L. Rev. 665, 677, 679–680, 682–683 (1969).

The reporters of the Code responded in part to Professor Enker's criticism this way:

> [I]t should * * * be noted how unlikely it is that persons will be prosecuted on the basis of admissions alone; the person who has behaved in a wholly innocuous way is not a probable subject of criminal proceedings. So the issue posed over Subsections (1)(a) and (1)(b) is more theoretical than practical.

American Law Institute, Model Penal Code and Commentaries, Comment to § 5.01 at 319–320 (1985).

Is this a satisfactory response? For example, consider Anderton v. Ryan, [1985] 1 App.Cas. 560, 2 All Eng.Rep. 355, overruled by Regina v. Shivpuri, [1986] 1 App.Cas. 1, 2 All Eng.Rep. 334, in which *R* reported to the police a theft of her video cassette recorder. Later, she told the investigating officer, "I may as well be honest, it was a stolen one I bought, I should not have phoned you." *R* was prosecuted for "dishonestly handling stolen property knowing or believing it is stolen." Because the video recorder was never recovered, the prosecutor could not prove that it had been stolen before *R* bought it—as far as the Government knew it was *not* stolen. The issue facing the House of Lords, therefore, was whether *R* could be convicted of an attempted violation of the statute. Under the Model Code, she could be. As a policy matter, *should* she be? Consider:

> [T]he lack of an objective condition for liability poses a significant risk of enforcement error or abuse. Almost all of us jump at the chance to purchase an item we want at a bargain price, often from non-retail sources. How secure can those of us with * * * associations or characteristics that reduce our credibility with a jury be if a prosecutor can obtain a conviction for receiving stolen property merely by convincing a jury that we believed the property to be stolen? * * * Most prosecutors are entirely honest. But the incentives within the criminal justice system reward those who obtain convictions and "get the bad guys off the streets." * * * Furthermore, even in the absence of abuse, a subjectivist definition of attempt creates strong incentives for informers and those facing charges themselves to accuse others of possessing what they believed to be controlled substances, whether they do or not, in return for monetary payments or leniency in sentencing. To the extent that police and prosecutors rely on such evidence, the risk of enforcement error is greatly increased. * * *
>
> The subjectivists are entirely correct to point out that requiring an objective condition for attempt liability makes obtaining a conviction in non-abusive cases more difficult and will result in some who deserve punishment escaping liability. * * * [T]his is the price we pay for living in a liberal society; "the price of the choice made long ago in favour of guaranteeing that the innocent be protected * * *."

John Hasnas, *Once More unto the Breach: The Inherent Liberalism of the Criminal Law and Liability for Attempting the Impossible*, 54 Hastings L.J. 1, 60–61 (2002).

11. *"Pure legal impossibility" and illusory crimes.* The Model Penal Code drafters intended to abolish the "legal impossibility" defense, but they meant only to do so as to the hybrid variety. An actor is not guilty of an attempt in "pure legal impossibility" cases. The Commentary to Model Penal Code Section 5.01 states, at page 318:

> [I]t is, of course necessary that the result desired or intended by the actor constitute a crime. If, according to his beliefs as to relevant facts and legal relationships, the result desired or intended is not a crime, the actor will not be guilty of an attempt even though he firmly believes that his goal is criminal.

In this regard, consider the following observations:

> [Pure] [l]egal impossibility describes a situation in which the objective of the accused * * * does not constitute an offense known to the law, even though the accused may mistakenly believe the law to be other than it is. Mistake of law may not generally excuse, but neither can it in itself be a sufficient ground for indictment. So an American on a visit to England might quite reasonably have the mistaken belief that fornication is a crime in England since it is one in the American jurisdiction in which he resides. Such a mistaken belief clearly cannot subject him to prosecution for a nonexistent crime of committing the sexual act, and it would be

a strange notion to talk of a prosecution for attempting to commit a crime which is not on the statute book. How after all could the indictment be drafted, unless we recognized the existence of a general offense of doing what one mistakenly believed to be a crime? It will be noticed that the argument here does not essentially depend on the concept of attempt in the usual sense of that word, for it is not necessarily a case of trying and failing. The inappropriateness of convicting such a person remains whether he has committed sexual intercourse or only attempted it. The reason for not convicting him has nothing to do with the failure of the enterprise, but rather with the absence of any prohibition of the conduct whether completed or not.[i]

Can pure legal impossibility cases be explained and defended on grounds independent of attempt doctrine?

12. *Problems.* Are the following examples of factual impossibility, hybrid legal impossibility, or pure legal impossibility?

A. Albert puts his hand on Betty's shoulder without her consent, incorrectly believing that this constitutes the offense of rape. He is charged with attempted rape.

B. Oscar Ramiro Ortego–Hernandez stopped his black Honda Accord on Constitution Avenue in front of the Ellipse, the large field of grass between the White House and the Washington Monument. He fired nine shots from a semi-automatic rifle, mounted with a large scope, at the White House, several of which hit on or above the second floor, where the first family's residential quarters are located. President Obama and his wife were out of town at the time. Is Ortego–Hernandez guilty of attempted assassination of the President?

C. *United States v. Thomas,* as set out on p. 749, footnote g.

D. Carla tampers with a payroll check made out to her by altering the numbers on it, so that the check for "$500.00" reads "$1500.00." She attempts to cash it, but the bank teller, noticing the discrepancy (since the *words* on the check continued to read "five hundred dollars"), refuses to give her the extra money. Initially Carla is prosecuted for forgery, but this charge is unsustainable because the statute prohibits only "material" alterations of instruments, and prior state law provides that alterations of numbers and figures on a check are not material. Is Carla guilty of *attempted* forgery? See Wilson v. State, 85 Miss. 687, 38 So. 46 (1905).

13. *"Inherent" impossibility.* Leroy Ivy, a prison inmate, obtained a photograph of the judge who sentenced him to prison. Ivy intended to obtain a lock of the judge's hair from a person working in the judge's home, and then send it and the picture to a voodoo priest who would cast a death curse on the judge. Ivy was arrested before he could secure the lock of hair. Mark Curriden, *Voodoo Attempt?,* 75 A.B.A. J., Sept. 1989, at 48. Suppose that Ivy had obtained the lock of hair and successfully mailed it to the priest, who cast the curse, but the judge did not die. Would the priest (and Ivy, under concepts of complicity considered in Chapter 11) be guilty of attempted murder?

---

i. Graham Hughes, *One Further Footnote on Attempting the Impossible,* 42 N.Y.U. L. Rev. 1005, 1006 (1967). Copyright © 1967, New York University. Reprinted by permission.

Or, consider the case of Avigdor Eskin, who put a death curse on Israeli Prime Minister Yitzhak Rabin, and was prosecuted in that country for violating the Prevention of Terrorism Act. *Eskin Convicted of Incitement*, Jerusalem Post, May 29, 1997, at 3. Should the curse also constitute attempted murder?

Most commentators believe that an attempt prosecution should not lie in such circumstances:

> As Justice Holmes aptly said in Com. v. Kennedy, 170 Mass. 18, 48 N.E. 770: "As the aim of the law is not to punish sins, but is to prevent certain external results, the act done must come pretty near to accomplishing that result before the law will notice it." * * *
>
> * * * [Cases like this] belong[ ] to the category of "trifles," with which "the law is not concerned." Even though a "voodoo doctor" * * * actually believed that his malediction would surely bring death to the person on whom he was invoking it, [in light of the lack of proximity to the result] I cannot conceive of an American court upholding a conviction of such a maledicting "doctor" for attempted murder or even attempted assault and battery.

Commonwealth v. Johnson, 312 Pa. 140, 167 A. 344 (1933) (Maxes, J., dissenting).

Is this reasoning faulty? Is the use of a curse any less proximate to the result than firing an unloaded gun? Would Ivy or Eskin be guilty of attempted murder under the Model Penal Code? See Sections 5.05 and 6.12.

b. Abandonment

COMMONWEALTH v. McCLOSKEY

Superior Court of Pennsylvania, 1975.
234 Pa.Super. 577, 341 A.2d 500.

HOFFMAN, JUDGE:

Appellant contends that the Commonwealth's evidence at trial was insufficient to sustain his conviction for an attempted prison breach.

At the time of the alleged offense, appellant was serving a one-to three-year sentence for larceny in the Luzerne County Prison. At about 12:15 a.m., on December 26, 1972, James Larson, a Guard Supervisor at the prison, heard an alarm go off that indicated that someone was attempting an escape in the recreation area of the prison. The alarm was designed so that it could be heard in the prison office, but not in the courtyard. Larson immediately contacted Guards Szmulo and Banik. Initially, the guards checked the prison population, but found no one missing. The three men then conducted a search of the area where the alarm had been "tripped." Near the recreation yard between two wings of the prison, they found one piece of barbed wire that had been cut. In addition, Guard Szmulo found a laundry bag filled with civilian clothing. The bags are issued by the prison and are marked with a different number for each prisoner. A check revealed that the bag belonged to appellant.

At approximately 5:15 a.m., on December 26, the appellant voluntarily approached Larson. Appellant had spent that night on the nine p.m. to five a.m. shift at work in the boiler room, situated near the point where the alarm had been triggered. Appellant explained to Larson "I was gonna make a break last night, but I changed my mind because I thought of my family, and I got scared of the consequences." Appellant testified at trial that he had become depressed prior to his decision to escape because he had been denied a Christmas furlough on December 24, 1972. His testimony at trial was consistent with Larson's version of the episode: "* * * in the yard, I realized that I had shamed my family enough, and I did not want to shame them any more. * * * So I went back to the boiler room and continued working."

On April 18, 1973, the grand jury returned an indictment charging the appellant with prison breach. Appellant went to trial * * * before a judge sitting without a jury and was found guilty of attempted prison breach. * * * This appeal followed. * * *

In the instant case, the evidence on the record indicates that appellant scaled a fence within the prison walls that led to the recreation yard and then to the prison wall. * * * The Commonwealth's evidence supports the appellant's claim that he went only as far as the yard before giving up his plan to escape. * * * Thus appellant was still within the prison, still only contemplating a prison breach, and not yet attempting the act. He was thus in a position to abandon the criminal offense of attempted prison breach voluntarily, thereby exonerating himself from criminal responsibility.

Judgment of sentence is vacated and appellant ordered discharged on the conviction of attempted prison breach. * * *

CERCONE, JUDGE (concurring):

I agree with the majority that appellant's conviction for attempted prison breach should not be permitted to stand. However, I disagree with the basis for the majority's conclusion, that the acts done by appellant prior to his decision to abandon his escape were insufficient to constitute an attempt. I would have found little difficulty, for instance, in affirming appellant's conviction had he been apprehended by the guards immediately after he had snipped the barbed wire and crossed the inner fence. To hold otherwise is to require that prisoners must literally be plucked from the prison wall before their conduct may be characterized as attempted prison breach.

I respectfully suggest that the majority has fallen into a trap peculiarly common to the law of attempts. As Professor Perkins has stated in discussing when conduct ceases to be merely preparatory and becomes perpetration:

"The preparatory-perpetrating dichotomy is useful in discussing situations of a rather general nature, but the actual dividing line between the two is shadowy in the extreme. There is reason to believe that *in close cases the decision is based upon other considerations* and that the label attached is that appropriate to the conclusion reached—after it is reached." R. Perkins, Criminal Law 561 (2d ed. 1969). [Emphasis added.]

The "other consideration" which has influenced the majority herein is appellant's voluntary abandonment of his escape plan. In my opinion, appellant's abandonment of his plan is a sufficient defense to the crime of attempted prison breach and should be recognized as such.

As a practical matter, it has long been recognized that plans voluntarily abandoned are less likely to be found to be attempts than are plans carried to the same point, but interrupted by the apprehension of the perpetrators. Unfortunately, in jurisdictions where voluntary abandonment or renunciation of a criminal purpose has not been recognized as an affirmative defense, the courts have sought to give effect to the defendant's abandonment, *sub silentio,* by characterizing his conduct as "preparatory." That is precisely the error which the majority has made in the instant case. The difficulty with this position is that, with regard to the preparation-perpetration dichotomy, it breeds results superficially inconsistent. If voluntary abandonment is to be given effect in attempt cases, it should not be done covertly.

For some time the trend in the law has been to recognize voluntary abandonment as an affirmative and complete defense to a charge of attempt, despite the exhortations to the contrary by some commentators. And, in following this trend our legislature substantially adopted section 5.01 of the Model Penal Code in drafting the attempt provisions in our recently enacted Crimes Code. Our Code now recognizes that abandonment under circumstances indicating voluntariness, is a complete defense to a charge of attempt. Appellant, however, was charged under our old Penal Code which did not speak to whether voluntary abandonment was a defense to a charge of attempt. * * *

It is clear that this court long ago perceived voluntary abandonment to be an affirmative defense to the crime of attempt * * *.

Sound policy reasons also underlie the recognition of voluntary abandonment as an affirmative defense. As the drafters of the Model Penal Code have pointed out, the defense of complete and permanent abandonment should be allowed because voluntary abandonment negates the conclusion that the accused continues to be dangerous; and, the knowledge that voluntary abandonment exonerates one from criminal liability provides a motive to desist prior to completion of the crime.

Thus, I have concluded that the law in Pennsylvania recognized voluntary abandonment as an affirmative defense even prior to the adoption of the Crimes Code. In any event, the trend in the United States is so profoundly in favor of such a defense that we should have recognized its existence in the instant case even had the Crimes Code not been enacted. * * *

NOTES AND QUESTIONS

1. How do you respond to the following argument against the abandonment defense?

[T]he traditional view [is] that voluntary abandonment is not a defense where the elements of an attempt are already established, although it may be relevant to the issue of whether defendant possessed the requisite intent in the first place. Under this view, once a defendant has gone so far as to have committed a punishable attempt, the crime is "complete" and he or she cannot then abandon the crime and avoid liability anymore than a thief can abandon a larceny by returning the stolen goods.

People v. Kimball, 109 Mich.App. 273, 311 N.W.2d 343 (1981).

2. In a jurisdiction in which abandonment is a defense to an attempt, should the defense ever apply to a *completed* offense? For example, should a thief who voluntarily returns the goods she stole be permitted a defense? What about a burglar who, after breaking into a dwelling, voluntarily leaves without committing a felony therein? Are such cases distinguishable from attempts? See Paul R. Hoeber, *The Abandonment Defense to Criminal Attempt and Other Problems of Temporal Individuation,* 74 Cal. L. Rev. 377, 418–426 (1986); Evan Tsen Lee, *Cancelling Crime,* 30 Conn. L. Rev. 117 (1997); Daniel G. Moriarty, *Extending the Defense of Renunciation,* 62 Temple L. Rev. 1, 38–58 (1989).

3. *Problem.* Arin Ahmed, a 20–year–old Palestinian woman, decided to commit a suicide bombing in Israel. She explained what happened:

I got out of the car. * * * I saw a lot of people, mothers with children, teenage boys and girls. I remembered an Israeli girl my age whom I used to be in touch with. I suddenly understood what I was about to do and I said to myself: How can I do such a thing? I changed my mind. [I went home.] I stayed at home until [members of the Israeli Defense Forces (IDF)] came and arrested me.

Vered Levy–Barzilai, *Prisoners' Dilemmas,* Harper's Magazine, Sept. 2002, at 17, 21.

Do you believe Ahmed should be convicted of attempted murder? Is it relevant to you that, when interrogated by the IDF and asked what she would do if she were released, she said she would "leave this place immediately * * * [and] go to live in Jordan with my mother. I would draw a line across the past and never come back here." She explained, "I faltered. But it was a momentary stumble." If released, she would continue her college studies in Jordan, and "I'd never go near anything like this again. I'd continue my life normally."

How would her case be resolved if Israel had a law similar to Model Penal Code § 5.01(4)?

4. Under M.P.C. § 5.01(4), should the abandonment defense apply if a would-be rapist desists from having intercourse because: (a) the victim tearfully told him that her young daughter would be home from school "any time," and that "I am all she has because her daddy is dead," see Ross v.

State, 601 So.2d 872 (Miss.1992); (b) the victim convinced him that "you could be my boyfriend, and you do not have to have it this way"? People v. Taylor, 80 N.Y.2d 1, 586 N.Y.S.2d 545, 598 N.E.2d 693 (1992); or (c) the victim was pregnant, see Le Barron v. State, 32 Wis.2d 294, 145 N.W.2d 79 (1966).

5. When is it too late to abandon an attempt? Suppose that D, with the intent to kill, stabs V, feels immediate remorse, and rushes V to a hospital, where timely life-saving medical care is provided. See State v. Mahoney, 264 Mont. 89, 870 P.2d 65 (1994); State v. Smith, 409 N.E.2d 1199 (Ind.App. 1980). In an attempted murder prosecution, should D be able to claim the defense of abandonment? See American Law Institute, Model Penal Code and Commentaries, Comment to § 5.01 at 360 (1985).

6. ASSAULT

AMERICAN LAW INSTITUTE, MODEL PENAL CODE AND COMMENTARIES, COMMENT TO § 211.1

(1980), 175–178, 183–184

Mayhem and Battery. The common law punished actual injury to another as mayhem or battery, depending upon the kind of harm caused. Mayhem, a common-law felony, originally consisted of injury permanently impairing the victim's ability to defend himself or to annoy his adversary. * * *

Battery was a common-law misdemeanor of far broader scope. It covered any unlawful application of force to the person of another wilfully or in anger. The requirement of force could be satisfied directly, as by a blow of the fist or indirectly, as by the use of a mechanical agent. Moreover, the notion of force was not limited to actual violence but included any kind of offensive and unlawful contact. Offensive contact was rendered unlawful chiefly by lack of consent. Thus, common-law battery covered unwanted sexual advance as well as physical attack. * * * [I]t was not uncommon * * * for American statutes to consolidate battery with the offense of assault.

Assault. Originally, common-law assault was simply an attempt to commit a battery. * * * Typical legislation described the offense as "an unlawful attempt, coupled with a present ability, to commit a violent injury on the person of another." Under such an approach, no assault would be committed if the alleged assailant had no intent to injure or if his gun were unloaded. The requirement of "present ability," moreover, imported into the offense an even stricter notion of proximity to the completed act than characterized the law of criminal attempt. Thus, some actions that went far enough to have constituted an attempt would nevertheless fail to satisfy the more stringent proximity required of an assault.

It was recognized early in the development of the private law of damages that an action could be maintained against one who intentionally placed another in fear of bodily injury, even if he acted without any purpose to carry out the threat. The majority of jurisdictions at the time the Model Code was drafted had assimilated this civil notion of assault into the criminal law. In these jurisdictions, assault thus consisted either of an actual attempt to commit a battery or of an intentional subjection of another to reasonable apprehension of receiving a battery. The assault offense was thus expanded to include menacing as well as actual attempts to do physical harm to another. It also generally included so-called conditional assaults, *i.e.*, situations where the actor threatened violence without justification or excuse if the victim did not engage in conduct demanded by the actor. * * *

The Model Code Approach. Section 211.1 of the Model Code undertakes a substantial restructuring of prior law. It eliminates the common-law categories and many of the antecedent statutory variations in favor of a single integrated provision. * * *

Subsections (1)(a), (1)(c), and (2) include attempts as well as completed offenses, thus achieving a consolidation of what former law treated as the separate crimes of assault and battery, as well as their more serious counterparts. The special feature of the former law of assault requiring greater proximity to success than for a normal attempt is discarded, however, in favor of the normal application of attempt principles. References in Section 211.1 to "attempts" are meant to incorporate the terms of Section 5.01, which defines attempt generally.

NOTES AND QUESTIONS

1.   State v. Boutin, 133 Vt. 531, 346 A.2d 531 (1975):

The facts disclose that on the evening of August 29, 1973, the defendant [Boutin] and Gary Moore were involved in a scuffle in front of Al's Pizza in Island Pond, Vermont. Following the scuffle, the defendant picked up a bottle from a trash can nearby, while Moore grabbed a rock from the street. Two town constables heard the disturbance and, on investigating, found the defendant and Moore ten feet apart, with the defendant walking towards Moore with the bottle raised over his head and Moore backing away across the street. The constables requested the defendant to put down the bottle, and then the defendant turned on the officers. At no time did the defendant attempt to strike Moore or to throw the bottle or lunge towards Moore, nor did he ever get in closer proximity than ten feet.

Did Boutin commit a common law assault? Did he commit an assault pursuant to the "typical legislation" mentioned in the Model Penal Code Commentary (p. 763 supra)? Did he commit a simple assault according to Model Penal Code § 211.1?

2.   Practical joker Roberto blindfolds himself, stands outside a crowded room, aims his gun inside the room, and fires three times, at five second intervals, hitting nobody, as was his wish. Under the Model Penal Code, is Roberto guilty of assault or of reckless endangerment (Section 211.2)?

3. Is there a crime of "attempted assault"? No, according to Wilson v. State, 53 Ga. 205 (1874):

> Is there any such crime? * * * As an assault is itself an attempt to commit a crime, an attempt to make an assault can only be an attempt to attempt to do it, or to state the matter still more definitely, it is to do any act towards doing an act towards the commission of the offense. This is simply absurd. As soon as any act is done towards committing a violent injury on the person of another, the party doing the act is guilty of an assault, and he is not guilty until he has done the act. Yet it is claimed that he may be guilty of an attempt to make an assault, when, under the law, he must do an act before the attempt is complete. The refinement and metaphysical acumen that can see a tangible idea in the words an attempt to act is too great for practical use. It is like conceiving of the beginning of eternity or the starting place of infinity.

Professor Perkins disagrees:

> [I]t is apparent that reference may be made to an "attempt to assault" without logical absurdity. There is nothing absurd in referring to an attempt to frighten, which would constitute, if successful, a criminal assault in most jurisdictions. Where an attempt to commit a battery with present ability is the only basis on which a criminal assault may be established, an "attempt to assault" would mean in substance an attempt to commit a battery without present ability. Even where a criminal assault still has its original meaning as an attempt to commit a battery, reference to an attempt to assault is not necessarily absurd. Because of the recognized difference between the requirement of proximity for an assault and for a general criminal attempt, an attempt to assault would indicate an effort to accomplish a battery that had proceeded beyond the stage of preparation, but had not come close enough to completion to constitute an assault. It is not surprising, therefore, that there is a tendency to break away from the ancient view that there is no such offense known to the law as an attempt to commit an assault.

Rollin M. Perkins, *An Analysis of Assault and Attempts to Assault*, 47 Minn. L. Rev. 71, 81–82 (1962).

People v. O'Connell, 14 N.Y.S. 485 (1891), is an example of an attempted assault of the "attempted battery" variety. In O'Connell, O threatened V with an ax. The court reasoned that to be guilty of an assault, O had to be within reaching distance of V, but that such proximity was not needed for an attempted assault.

7. PUNISHING PRE–ATTEMPT CONDUCT

The inchoate offenses of solicitation and conspiracy (Sections C. and D. infra) punish specific types of preparatory conduct (conduct that has not yet reached the "attempt" stage). Legislatures have also sought to criminalize a broader range of threatening, but pre-attempt, conduct. Abuses associated with newer and more widely used technologies—e-mail, texting, Twitter, and so forth—have prompted new criminal prohibitions. Consider the following.

UNITED STATES V. ALKHABAZ

United States Court of Appeals, Sixth Circuit, 1997.
104 F.3d 1492.

BOYCE F. MARTIN, JR., CHIEF JUDGE. * * *

From November 1994 until approximately January 1995, [Abraham Jacob Alkhabaz, a.k.a. Jake] Baker and [Arthur] Gonda exchanged e-mail messages over the Internet, the content of which expressed a sexual interest in violence against women and girls. Baker sent and received messages through a computer in Ann Arbor, Michigan, while Gonda—whose true identity and whereabouts are still unknown—used a computer in Ontario, Canada.

Prior to this time, Baker had posted a number of fictional stories to "alt.sex.stories," a popular interactive Usenet news group. * * * Baker's fictional stories generally involved the abduction, rape, torture, mutilation, and murder of women and young girls. On January 9, Baker posted a story describing the torture, rape, and murder of a young woman who shared the name of one of Baker's classmates at the University of Michigan.

On February 9, Baker was arrested and appeared before a United States Magistrate Judge on a criminal complaint alleging violations of 18 U.S.C. § 875(c), which prohibits interstate communications containing threats to kidnap or injure another person. * * *

* * * On March 15, citing several e-mail messages between Gonda and Baker, a federal grand jury returned a superceding indictment, charging Baker and Gonda with five counts of violating * * * § 875(c). The e-mail messages supporting the superceding indictment were not available in any publicly accessible portion of the Internet.[1] * * *

Title 18, United States Code, Section 875(c) states:

> Whoever transmits in interstate or foreign commerce any communication containing any threat to kidnap any person or any threat to injure the person of another, shall be fined under this title or imprisoned not more than five years, or both.

The government must allege and prove three elements to support a conviction under Section 875(c): "(1) a transmission in interstate [or foreign] commerce; (2) a communication containing a threat; and (3) the threat must be a threat to injure [or kidnap] the person of another." In this case, the first and third elements cannot be seriously challenged by the defendant. However, the second element raises several issues that this Court must address. As this Court has recognized, "[i]t is one of the most fundamental postulates of our criminal justice system that conviction can

---

1. As the district court noted, "the government * * * abandoned the story [posted on January 9] as a basis of prosecution because it did not constitute a threat." United States v. Baker, 890 F.Supp. 1375, 1380 n.6 (E.D. Mich. 1995). The prosecution was thus based on the e-mail messages alone.

result only from a violation of clearly defined standards of conduct." Indeed, "[o]ur law does not punish bad purpose standing alone, however; instead we require that mens rea accompany the actus reus specifically proscribed by statute." * * * William Shakespeare's lines here illustrate sound legal doctrine.

His acts did not o'ertake his bad intent;

And must be buried but as an intent

That perish'd by the way: thoughts are no subjects,

Intents but merely thoughts. * * *

* * * Section 875(c) does not clearly define an actus reus. * * *

To determine what type of action Congress intended to prohibit, it is necessary to consider the nature of a threat. At their core, threats are tools that are employed when one wishes to have some effect, or achieve some goal, through intimidation. This is true regardless of whether the goal is highly reprehensible or seemingly innocuous. * * *

For example, the goal may be extortionate or coercive. In *United States v. Cox*, 957 F.2d 264 (6th Cir.1992), a bank repossessed the defendant's vehicle, including several personal items. The defendant then telephoned the bank and threatened to "hurt people" at the bank, unless the bank returned his property. * * *

Additionally, the goal, although not rising to the level of extortion, may be the furtherance of a political objective. For example, in *United States v. Kelner*, 534 F.2d 1020 (2d Cir.1976), the defendant threatened to assassinate Yasser Arafat, leader of the Palestine Liberation Organization (PLO), during a news conference. Kelner claimed that his sole purpose in issuing the threat was to inform the PLO that "we (as Jews) would defend ourselves and protect ourselves." Although Kelner's threat was not extortionate, he apparently sought to further the political objectives of his organization by intimidating the PLO with warnings of violence.

Finally, a threat may be communicated for a seemingly innocuous purpose. For example, one may communicate a bomb threat, even if the bomb does not exist, for the sole purpose of creating a prank. However, such a communication would still constitute a threat because the threatening party is attempting to create levity (at least in his or her own mind) through the use of intimidation.

The above examples illustrate threats because they demonstrate a combination of the mens rea with the actus reus. Although it may offend our sensibilities, a communication objectively indicating a serious expression of an intention to inflict bodily harm cannot constitute a threat unless the communication also is conveyed for the purpose of furthering some goal through the use of intimidation.

Accordingly, to achieve the intent of Congress, we hold that, to constitute "a communication containing a threat" under Section 875(c), a communication must be such that a reasonable person (1) would take the statement as a serious expression of an intention to inflict bodily harm (the mens rea), and (2) would perceive such expression as being communicated to effect some change or achieve some goal through intimidation (the actus reus).

The dissent argues that Congress did not intend to include as an element of the crime the furthering of some goal through the use of intimidation. Emphasizing the term "any" in the language of the statute, the dissent maintains that Congress did not limit the scope of communications that constitutes criminal threats. While we agree that Congress chose inclusive language to identify the types of threats that it intended to prohibit, we cannot ignore the fact that Congress intended to forbid only those communications that in fact constitute a "threat." The conclusion that we reach here is one that the term "threat" necessarily implies. * * *

Applying our interpretation of the statute to the facts before us, we conclude that the communications between Baker and Gonda do not constitute "communication[s] containing a threat" under Section 875(c). Even if a reasonable person would take the communications between Baker and Gonda as serious expressions of an intention to inflict bodily harm, no reasonable person would perceive such communications as being conveyed to effect some change or achieve some goal through intimidation. Quite the opposite, Baker and Gonda apparently sent e-mail messages to each other in an attempt to foster a friendship based on shared sexual fantasies. * * *

For the foregoing reasons, the judgment of the district court [quashing the indictment] is affirmed.

KRUPANSKY, CIRCUIT JUDGE, dissenting. * * *

Jake Baker * * *, an undergraduate student attending the University of Michigan in Ann Arbor, for some time prior to November 1994 and continuing until February 1995 was a regular contributor of sadistic fictional "short stories" intended for public dissemination and comment via a Usenet electronic bulletin board. The appellate record contains a substantial anthology of Baker's efforts. Overall, these misogynistic articles evince an extreme and morbid fascination with the concept of the physical and psychological abuse and torment of women and young girls, described in lurid detail, and often culminating in murder.

By November 1994, Baker's sadistic stories attracted the attention of an individual who called himself "Arthur Gonda," a Usenet service subscriber residing in Ontario, Canada, who apparently shared similarly misdirected proclivities. Baker and Gonda subsequently exchanged at least 41 private computerized electronic mail ("e-mail") communications between November 29, 1994 and January 25, 1995. Concurrently, Baker continued to distribute violent sordid tales on the electronic bulletin board. On January 9, 1995, Baker brazenly disseminated publicly, via the electronic bulletin board, a depraved torture-and-snuff [murder] story in which the victim shared the name of a female classmate of Baker's referred to below as "Jane Doe"[3] This imprudent act triggered notification of the University of Michigan authorities by an alarmed citizen on January 18, 1995. On the following day, Baker admitted to a University of Michigan investigator that he had authored the story and published it on the Internet. * * *

Later that month, pursuant to Baker's written consent, university security personnel searched the defendant's dormitory room, personal papers, and computer files including his unique e-mail compartment. This investigation surfaced a second violent and reprehensible tale featuring Jane Doe's actual name, as well as her accurate residential address. The search of Baker's electronic mailbox disclosed a chilling correspondence between the defendant and Gonda chronicling the two men's plans of abduction, bondage, torture, humiliation, mutilation, rape, sodomy, murder, and necrophilia. Most ominously, these messages cumulated in a conspiracy between the two men to realize their aberrant e-mail discussions and exchanges by implementing an actual abduction, rape, and murder of a female person. * * *

The words in section 875(c) are simple, clear, concise, and unambiguous. The plain, expressed statutory language commands only that the alleged communication must contain *any threat* to kidnap or physically injure *any person*, made for *any reason* or no reason. Section 875(c) by its terms does *not* confine the scope of criminalized communications to those directed to identified individuals and intended to effect some particular change or goal. * * *

By contrast to section 875(c), a companion statutory provision, 18 U.S.C. § 875(b), *criminalizes similar communications made with the intent to extort money or other value,* coupled with more severe penalties than those appertaining to a threat illegalized by section 875(c) * * *.

Patently, Congress sought to punish all interstate or international communications containing a threat to kidnap or injure any person; such communications accompanied by an intent to extort value (section 875(b)) could be punished more severely than those which are not coupled with the intent to extort (section 875(c)). * * *

The panel majority attempts to justify its improper fusion of an extra-legislative element re the "intent to intimidate some change or goal" upon section 875(c) by embracing an artificially narrow legal definition of the term "threat." * * * Undeniably, a simple, credible declaration of an intention to cause injury to some person, made for any reason, or for no reason whatsoever, may *also* constitute a "threat." For instance, Black's Law Dictionary 1480–81 (6th ed. 1990) adopts, among other definitions, the following:

3. Although the true name of "Jane Doe" was known to the district court and to this appellate forum, her identity has been concealed to spare this young woman any additional and unnecessary fear, emotional trauma, or embarrassment. The record reflected that during an interview concerning Baker's Jane Doe publication conducted by a University of Michigan investigator, Jane Doe "appeared to be controlling herself with great difficulty[,]" resulting in a recommendation for psychological counseling by University of Michigan personnel.

Threat. *A communicated intent to inflict physical or other harm on any person or on property. A declaration of an intention to injure another or his property by some unlawful act. A declaration of intention or determination to inflict punishment, loss, or pain on another, or to injure another or his property by the commission of some unlawful act. . . .*

The term, "threat" [sic] means an avowed present determination or intent to injure presently or in the future. * * *

* * * [A] "threat" is a category of expression which warrants no First Amendment protection. However, only communications which convey "true threats" (as opposed to, for example, inadvertent statements, mistakes, jests, hyperbole, innocuous talk, or political commentary not objectively intended to express a real threat) are "threats" outside the embrace of the First Amendment's guarantees.

Accordingly, in order to prove a "true threat" proscribed by 18 U.S.C. § 875(c) * * *, the prosecution must evidence to a rational jury's satisfaction *only* the following: (1) that the defendant transmitted the subject communication in interstate or foreign commerce, (2) that the communication contained a threat, (3) that the threat was one against the physical safety or freedom of some individual or class of persons (irrespective of the identity of the person or group threatened, the originator's motivation for issuing the threat, or the existence or nonexistence of any goal pursued by the threat), and (4) that the subject communication in its factual context would lead a reasonable, objective recipient to believe that the publisher of the communication was serious about his threat (regardless of the subjective intent of the speaker to make an actual threat or whether anyone actually felt frightened, intimidated, or coerced by the threat). * * *

Accordingly, I would reverse the district court's judgment which dismissed the superseding indictment as purportedly not alleging "true threats," and remand the cause to the lower court.

NOTES AND QUESTIONS

1. *Cyberstalking.* William Lawrence Cassidy was a self-proclaimed Buddhist American tulku (reincarnate master) living in California. Alyce Zeoli was a 61 year-old Buddhist leader in Maryland believed by her followers to be the only American-born female tulku. In 2007 Cassidy joined the center where Zeoli taught. Cassidy signed up under a false name and claimed to have lung cancer. Believing he was near death, members of Zeoli's center cared for Cassidy (spending about $10,000 in doing so). They eventually came to doubt Cassidy's claim to be a tulku and discovered that he did not in fact suffer from cancer. Cassidy left the center and started to post Twitter messages (tweets) about Zeoli, including the following:

"ya like haiku? Here's one for ya: 'Long limb, Sharp Saw, Hard Drop' "

"Zeoli is a demonic force who tries to destroy Buddhism"

"want it to all be over soon sweetie?"

"Zeoli you are a liar & a fraud & you corrupt Buddhism by your very presence: go kill yourself"

"Zeoli is no dakini: shes [sic] a grossly overweight 61 yr old burnt out freak with bad bowels & a lousy outlook: her crown is a joke"

"I have just one thing to say to Zeoli, and its [sic] form [sic] the heart: do the world a favor and go kill yourself. P.S. Have a nice day"

Over the course of two years Cassidy posted some 8,000 such tweets. Somini Sengupta, *Case of 8,000 Menacing Posts Test Limits of Twitter Speech*, N.Y. Times, Aug. 27, 2011, at A1; Complaint, United States v. Cassidy, No. 11–501 CBD (D. Md. Feb. 2, 2011). He was indicted for violating 18 U.S.C. § 2261A(2)(A), which provides in pertinent part:

> Whoever with the intent to kill, injure, harass, or place under surveillance with the intent to kill, injure, harass, or intimidate, or cause substantial emotional distress to a person in another State * * * uses the mail, any interactive computer service, or any facility of interstate * * * commerce to engage in a course of conduct that causes substantial emotional distress to that person * * * shall be punished * * *

Is Cassidy guilty? *Should* his conduct be criminal?

2. How should the law deal with people who are dangerous inasmuch as they have formed an intention to cause harm to others, but who have not yet committed a crime, not even an attempt? One answer, of course, is nothing. Another is to create new crimes that are really meant to punish little more than the "mental act" of forming an intent to cause harm.

For example, should it be a crime simply to *say* that one intends to cause harm to another, even before one has done anything in furtherance of that intention, and even if the intended victim never learns that he is the intended victim? What if the intended harm is a terrorist act that aims to cause death and destruction on a wide scale? As one commentator sees it:

> Forming the intention to commit a criminal act is the essence of inchoate crimes. And while the crime of stating the intention to commit unlawful, violent acts pushes the outer limits of the idea of an inchoate crime, it does not surpass those limits. As long as the crime itself is sufficiently serious, and the prospects for deterrence sufficiently low, there is reason to have such a crime. Further, those conditions are met when dealing with politically or religiously motivated terrorist crime.

Alec Walen, *Criminalizing Statements of Terrorist Intent: How to Understand the Law Governing Terrorist Threats, and Why It Should Be Used Over Long–Term Preventive Detention*, 101 J. Crim. L. & Criminology 803, 853 (2011).

Others argue that an actor who says he intends to commit a terrorist act should not be guilty of any crime, because he can always change his mind. Nonetheless, forming an intent to commit a terrorist act, together with "any act" in furtherance of that intention, should render him liable to preventive detention. Kimberly Kessler Ferzan, *Beyond Crime and Commitment: Justifying Liberty Deprivations of the Dangerous and Responsible*, 96 Minn. L. Rev. 141 (2011). What do you think?

C. SOLICITATION

STATE v. MANN

Supreme Court of North Carolina, 1986.
317 N.C. 164, 345 S.E.2d 365.

MARTIN, JUSTICE. * * *

Solicitation involves the asking, enticing, inducing, or counselling of another to commit a crime. The solicitor conceives the criminal idea and furthers its commission via another person by suggesting to, inducing, or manipulating that person. As noted by Weschler, Jones, and Korn in *The Treatment of Inchoate Crimes in the Model Penal Code of the American Law Institute: Attempt, Solicitation and Conspiracy,* 61 Colum.L.Rev. 571, 621–22 (1961), "the solicitor, working his will through one or more agents, manifests an approach to crime more intelligent and masterful than the efforts of his hireling," and a solicitation, "an attempt to conspire," may well be more dangerous than an attempt. Indeed, a solicitor may be more dangerous than a conspirator; a conspirator may merely passively agree to a criminal scheme, while the solicitor plans, schemes, suggests, encourages, and incites the solicitation. Further, the solicitor is morally more culpable than a conspirator; he keeps himself from being at risk, hiding behind the actor. * * *

NOTES AND QUESTIONS

1. At common law, a solicitation to commit any felony or a misdemeanor involving a breach of the peace or obstruction of justice, was indictable as a misdemeanor. Until the Model Penal Code was drafted, however, few state penal codes included a general criminal solicitation statute, although many states prohibited specific forms of solicitation, e.g., solicitation to commit murder or solicitation to commit prostitution. Consequently, in states that abolished common law offenses, most solicitations went unpunished. Nearly all states today include a general prohibition on criminal solicitations. American Law Institute, Model Penal Code and Commentaries, Comment to § 5.02 at 366–370 (1985).

Solicitation is a controversial crime because the offense is complete as soon as the solicitor asks, entices, or encourages another to commit the target offense. As observed in *Mann,* a solicitation may consist of nothing more than an attempt to conspire with another to commit an offense, which essentially makes solicitation a double inchoate offense.

2. *Merger.* The offense of solicitation merges into the crime solicited if the latter offense is committed or attempted by the solicited party. For example, if Agnes solicits Ben to murder Camille, and Ben refuses, Agnes is guilty of solicitation; if Ben agrees and kills or attempts to murder Camille, Agnes is guilty of murder or attempted murder, respectively, under complicity principles (see Chapter 11 infra), rather than of the offense of solicitation. If Ben agrees, but is arrested before the attempt, Agnes and Ben may be

prosecuted for conspiracy to commit murder (see subsection E. infra). Agnes's solicitation would merge into the conspiracy.

STATE v. COTTON

Court of Appeals of New Mexico, 1990.
109 N.M. 769, 790 P.2d 1050.

DONNELLY, JUDGE.

Defendant appeals his convictions of two counts of criminal solicitation. * * * [He was convicted of soliciting the felony offense of "Bribery or Intimidation of a Witness" (Count 1) and soliciting the felony of Custodial Interference (Count 2).]

In 1986, defendant, together with his wife Gail, five children, and a stepdaughter, moved to New Mexico. A few months later, defendant's wife and children returned to Indiana. Shortly thereafter, defendant's fourteen-year-old stepdaughter moved back to New Mexico to reside with him. In 1987, the Department of Human Services investigated allegations of misconduct involving defendant and his stepdaughter. * * *

In May 1987, defendant was arrested and charged with multiple counts of criminal sexual penetration of a minor and criminal sexual contact of a minor. While in the Eddy County Jail awaiting trial on those charges defendant discussed with his cell-mate James Dobbs * * * his desire to persuade his stepdaughter not to testify against him. During his incarceration defendant wrote numerous letters to his wife; in several of his letters he discussed his strategy for defending against the pending criminal charges.

On September 23, 1987, defendant addressed a letter * * * to his wife. In that letter he requested that she assist him in defending against the pending criminal charges by persuading his stepdaughter not to testify at his trial. The letter also urged his wife to contact the stepdaughter and influence her to return to Indiana or that she give her money to leave the state so that she would be unavailable to testify. After writing this letter defendant gave it to Dobbs and asked him to obtain a stamp for it so that it could be mailed later. Unknown to defendant, Dobbs removed the letter from the envelope, replaced it with a blank sheet of paper, and returned the sealed stamped envelope to him. Dobbs gave the original letter written by defendant to law enforcement authorities, and it is undisputed that defendant's original letter * * * was never in fact mailed nor received by defendant's wife.

On September 24 and 26, 1987, defendant composed another letter * * * to his wife. * * * The letter stated that * * * his wife should try to arrange for his stepdaughter to visit her in Indiana for Christmas; and that his wife should try to talk the stepdaughter out of testifying or to talk her into testifying favorably for defendant. Defendant also said in the letter that his wife should "warn" his stepdaughter that if she did testify for the state "it won't be nice * * * and she'll make [New Mexico] news," and that, if the stepdaughter was not available to testify, the prosecutor would have to drop the charges against defendant.

* * * It is * * * undisputed that the second letter * * * was never mailed to defendant's wife. * * *

The offense of criminal solicitation as provided in NMSA Section 30–28–3 (Repl.Pamp.1984), is defined in applicable part as follows:

> A.   Except as to bona fide acts of persons authorized by law to investigate and detect the commission of offenses by others, a person is guilty of criminal solicitation if, with the intent that another person engage in conduct constituting a felony, he solicits, commands, requests, induces, employs or otherwise attempts to promote or facilitate another person to engage in conduct constituting a felony within or without the state.

Defendant contends that the record fails to contain the requisite evidence to support the charges of criminal solicitation against him because defendant's wife, the intended solicitee, never received the two letters. * * *

* * * The state reasons that even in the absence of evidence indicating that the solicitations were actually communicated to or received by the solicitee, under our statute, proof of defendant's acts of writing the letters, attempts to mail or forward them, together with proof of his specific intent to solicit the commission of a felony constitutes sufficient proof to sustain a charge of criminal solicitation. We disagree.

The offense of criminal solicitation, as defined in Section 30–28–3 by our legislature, adopts in part, language defining the crime of solicitation as set out in the Model Penal Code promulgated by the American Law Institute. * * * As enacted by our legislature, however, Section 30–28–3 significantly omits one section of the Model Penal Code, Section 5.02(2), which pertains to the effect of an uncommunicated criminal solicitation.

The commentary to the American Law Institute Model Penal Code explains that "[g]eneral statutory provisions punishing solicitations were not common before the Model Penal Code."[1] Model Penal Code § 5.02, commentary 2, § 5.02, at 367 (1985). The Commentary further notes in Section 5.02 of its proposed draft of criminal solicitation that:

> Under Subsection (2) [of proposed Section 5.02 of the Model Penal Code], conduct "designed to effect" communication of the culpable message is sufficient to constitute criminal solicitation and there is therefore no need for a crime of attempted solicitation. * * *

However, as enacted by our legislature, Section 30–28–3 sets out the offense of criminal solicitation in a manner which differs in several

---

1.   As observed by the drafters of the Model Penal Code in their commentary to Section 5.02, prior to the promulgation of the American Law Institute proposed Criminal Solicitation statute, uncommunicated messages by a defendant could under some circumstances constitute attempted solicitation, but "it [is] considered doubtful whether an uncommunicated message could constitute a solicitation."

material respects from the proposed draft of the Model Penal Code. Among other things, * * * Section 30–28–3 specifically omits that portion of the Model Penal Code subsection declaring that an uncommunicated solicitation to commit a crime may constitute the offense of criminal solicitation.[2] The latter omission, we conclude, indicates an implicit legislative intent that the offense of solicitation requires some form of actual communication from the defendant to either an intermediary or the person intended to be solicited, indicating the subject matter of the solicitation. * * *

The question posed in the instant case is also discussed by the authors, W. LaFave and A. Scott. "What if the solicitor's message never reaches the person intended to be solicited, as where the intermediary fails to pass on the communication or the solicitee's letter is intercepted before it reaches the addressee? The act is nonetheless criminal, *although it may be that the solicitor must be prosecuted for an attempt to solicit on such facts.*" We apply a similar result in the present case. * * *

* * * Defendant's convictions for solicitation are reversed and the cause is remanded with instructions to set aside the convictions * * *.

NOTES AND QUESTIONS

1. Did the court correctly interpret and apply Section 30–28–3?

2. Alice and Beverly are cellmates. Alice, thinking aloud, says, "I ought to kill Corina" (another prisoner). Beverly reflects on Alice's comments, and realizes that she, too, would like Corina dead. Beverly tells Alice, "I agree. I will kill Corina." Is Alice guilty of solicitation to commit murder under Section 30–28–3? See Monoker v. State, 321 Md. 214, 582 A.2d 525 (1990).

3. *Problem.* H, the head of a white supremacist group, sent an e-mail to X, his chief of security but also an FBI informant, instructing him to get the home address of a federal judge. Later, H and X had conversations taped by the FBI, in which H asked about the address. X: "I'm working on it. When we get it, we can exterminate the rat." H: "Good. Well, whatever you want to do, basically. You know my position has always been that I'm going to fight within the law, but if you wish to do anything yourself, you can." Associated Press, *Bond Denied in Reported Plot to Kill Judge*, N.Y. Times, Jan. 24, 2003, at A19. Solicitation to commit murder under Model Penal Code § 5.02(1)?

4. Francisco asks Georgia to furnish him with tools so that he may burglarize Harold's house. Georgia refuses. Is Francisco guilty of solicitation under Section 30–28–3? Is he guilty of solicitation under the Model Penal Code? See Sections 5.02(1) and 2.06(3).

5. *Can a solicitation constitute an attempt?* In Mettler v. State, 697 N.E.2d 502 (Ind.App.1998), M left a letter in an envelope on his 18–year–old daughter's bed. Also inside the envelope was a five dollar bill and half of a

---

2. The American Law Institute, Model Criminal Code, Section 5.02(2) provides: "It is immaterial under Subsection (1) of this Section that the actor fails to communicate with the person he solicits to commit a crime if his conduct was designed to effect such communication." * * *

hundred dollar bill. The letter solicited his daughter to "come in the front door some night, without your panties on" and submit to fondling and other sexual acts. He promised her the other half of the hundred dollar bill if she complied. His daughter became frightened by the letter and left the house. At no time did *M* speak to his daughter concerning his sexual desires.

These acts constituted *solicitation* by *M* to have his daughter commit incest ("a person 18 years of age or older who engages in sexual intercourse * * * with another person, when the person knows that the other person is related to the person biologically as a parent [or] child, * * * commits incest"). But, do these same acts constitute *attempted* incest on his part? In most jurisdictions, in which solicitation is a less serious offense than an attempt, the distinction is important.

The Commentaries to the Model Penal Code provide this insight into the law:

> Whether the solicitation to commit a crime constitutes an attempt by the solicitor is a question that has been answered in several ways. One approach to the problem treats every solicitation as a specific type of attempt to be governed by ordinary attempt principles, the solicitation being an overt act that alone or together with other overt acts may surpass preparation and result in liability. A second position is that a naked solicitation is not an attempt, but a solicitation accompanied by other overt acts, for example, the offer of a reward or the furnishing of materials, does constitute an attempt. The third view is similar to the second except that in order to find the solicitor guilty of an attempt the other overt acts must proceed beyond what would be called preparation if the solicitor planned to commit the crime himself. Finally, there is the view that no matter what acts the solicitor commits, he cannot be guilty of an attempt because it is not his purpose to commit the offense personally. Although there has been considerable conflict, even among the decisions of the same jurisdiction, the trend has seemed to be toward the last two solutions * * *.

American Law Institute, Model Penal Code and Commentaries, Comment to § 5.02 at 368–369 (1985).

Did *M*'s conduct with his daughter constitute an attempt under any of the approaches described above?

6. *Problem.* People v. Decker, 21 Cal.Rptr.3d 126 (App. 2004), *aff'd*, 41 Cal.4th 1, 58 Cal.Rptr.3d 421, 157 P.3d 1017 (2007):

> A man wants his sister killed. With the specific intent of causing her death, he engages another person to murder her. He furnishes that person with specific information describing his sister, the means for gaining access to her residence, her work habits and the times she is likely to be at home. They agree on the means to commit the murder, other details, and price. The hired assassin warns that once he receives the down payment there will be no way to prevent the murder from occurring. The man reiterates his demand that there be no witnesses, and that if his sister is with her friend when the killing occurs, the friend also is to be killed. The man then hands the hired assassin the down payment.

It turns out that the person engaged to kill his sister is a detective posing as a killer and that he had no intention of actually killing the sister.

This scenario is no television script or law professor hypothetical. It is a real case. Should these facts constitute solicitation to commit murder (punishable in California of from three to nine years in prison) or attempted murder (fifteen years to life)? If the down payment had not been made (but everything else remained the same), would your answer change? What if he simply got the "other person" (the undercover officer) to agree to murder the sister, but none of the details or money arrangements had been made?

D. CONSPIRACY

1. GENERAL PRINCIPLES

PEOPLE v. CARTER

Supreme Court of Michigan, 1982.
415 Mich. 558, 330 N.W.2d 314.

* * * JUSTICE BLAIR MOODY, JR. * * *

Criminal conspiracy occupies a unique place in our criminal justice system. It is defined as "a partnership in criminal purposes," a mutual agreement or understanding, express or implied, between two or more persons to commit a criminal act or to accomplish a legal act by unlawful means. While the offense has its origins in the common law, it is now specifically proscribed by statute, which sets forth the penalties for its commission.

"The gist of the offense of conspiracy lies in the unlawful agreement." The crime is complete upon formation of the agreement; * * * it is not necessary to establish any overt act in furtherance of the conspiracy as a component of the crime.[3] However, a twofold specific intent is required for conviction: intent to combine with others, and intent to accomplish the illegal objective. * * *

It is a settled principle of black-letter law that conspiracy is a crime that is separate and distinct from the substantive crime that is its object. The guilt or innocence of a conspirator does not depend upon the accomplishment of the goals of the conspiracy. More importantly * * *, a conviction of conspiracy does not merge with a conviction of the completed offense. Thus, a defendant may be convicted and punished for both the conspiracy and the substantive crime. * * *

NOTES AND QUESTIONS

1. *Rationale of the crime.* Peter Buscemi, Note, *Conspiracy: Statutory Reform Since the Model Penal Code,* 75 Colum. L. Rev. 1122, 1122 n.5 (1975):

---

3. Many * * * states do require, as an element of proof of the crime, that an overt act in pursuance of the conspiratorial end be taken. The overt-act requirement tends to be relatively easy to meet; virtually any act, no matter how insignificant, may suffice.

Typically, conspiracy is said to perform a dual function. [First,] [i]n its aspect as an inchoate * * * crime, conspiracy has been employed to fill the gap created by a law of attempt too narrowly conceived. Where, in order to constitute attempt, preparation has had to proceed so far toward actual commission of a crime as to itself create an intolerable danger to society, conspiracy has entered the breach and provided an opportunity for earlier official intervention. [Second,] [i]n its role as weapon against group criminal activity, conspiracy has been used to combat the extraordinary dangers allegedly presented by multi-member criminal undertakings. In this guise, the offense has been characterized by vague definition and loose procedural standards. The usual response to criticism has been that such features are necessary to cope with the special threats posed by organized criminal conduct.

Of these two stated justifications, "the heart of the rationale lies in the fact—or at least the assumption—that collective action toward an antisocial end involves a greater risk to society than individual action toward the same end." *Developments in the Law—Criminal Conspiracy,* 72 Harv. L. Rev. 920, 923–924 (1959). The Supreme Court has presented the classic defense of this rationale:

> The distinctiveness between a substantive offense and a conspiracy to commit [it] is a postulate of our law. "It has long been recognized by the Court that the commission of the substantive offense and a conspiracy to commit it are separate and distinct offenses." * * *

> This settled principle derives from the reason of things in dealing with socially reprehensible conduct: collective criminal agreement—partnership in crime—presents a greater potential threat to the public than individual delicts. Concerted action both increases the likelihood that the criminal object will be successfully attained and decreases the probability that the individuals involved will depart from their path of criminality. Group association for criminal purposes often, if not normally, makes possible the attainment of ends more complex than those which one criminal could accomplish. Nor is the danger of a conspiratorial group limited to the particular end toward which it has embarked. Combination in crime makes more likely the commission of crimes unrelated to the original purpose for which the group was formed. In sum, the danger which a conspiracy generates is not confined to the substantive offense which is the immediate aim of the enterprise.

Callanan v. United States, 364 U.S. 587, 81 S.Ct. 321, 5 L.Ed.2d 312 (1961).

Is this argument entirely convincing? Consider the dialogue in Double Indemnity, the 1944 Billy Wilder *film noir* masterpiece, in which insurance agent Walter Neff (Fred MacMurray) assists Phyllis Dietrichson (Barbara Stanwyck) kill her husband. Barton Keyes (Edward G. Robinson), still unaware of Neff's involvement, says to Neff, "Murder is never perfect. It always come apart sooner or later. When two people are involved, it's usually sooner. * * * They may think it's twice as safe because there are two of them. But, it isn't twice as safe. It's ten times twice as dangerous." Why might this be? Consider the following observations about the supposed greater harm arising from conspiratorial relationships:

Though these assumed dangers from conspiracy have a romantically individualistic ring, they have never been verified empirically. It is hardly likely that a search for such verification would end in support of [the] suggestion that combination alone is *inherently* dangerous. This view is immediately refuted by reference to our own society, which is grounded in organization and agreement. More likely, empirical investigation would disclose that there is as much reason to believe that a large number of participants will increase the prospect that the plan will be leaked as that it will be kept secret; or that the persons involved will share their uncertainties and dissuade each other as that each will stiffen the others' determination. Most probably, however, the factors ordinarily mentioned as warranting the crime of conspiracy would be found to add to the danger to be expected from a group in certain situations and not in others; the goals of the group and the personalities of its members would make any generalization unsafe and hence require some other explanation for treating conspiracy as a separate crime in all cases.

Abraham S. Goldstein, *Conspiracy to Defraud the United States,* 68 Yale L.J. 405, 414 (1959).

Professor Neal Katyal disagrees with Professor Goldstein:

A wide body of psychological research over the last century reveals that people tend to act differently in groups than they do as individuals. Some of the work is tentative, thereby precluding robust results. Nevertheless, it is generally accepted that groups are more likely to polarize toward extremes, to take courses of action that advance the interests of the group even in the face of personal doubts, and to act with greater loyalty to each other. Much of the most influential research focuses on how group membership changes an individual's personal identity to produce a new *social identity.*

Neal Kumar Katyal, *Conspiracy Theory,* 112 Yale L.J. 1307, 1316 (2003).

2. As Justice Moody noted in *Carter,* a criminal conspiracy at common law involves an agreement to commit a crime or *to commit a lawful act in an unlawful manner.* The italicized language means that "it will be enough if the acts contemplated are corrupt, dishonest, fraudulent, or immoral * * *." State v. Kemp, 126 Conn. 60, 78, 9 A.2d 63, 72 (1939). For example, two persons who merely agree to perform an immoral (but not criminal) act, may be punished for common law conspiracy, although one person, acting by herself, would be guilty of no criminal offense if she committed the immoral act.

3. *Merger.* Suppose that April and Bill conspire to rob First State Bank, and subsequently rob it. According to *Carter,* are April and Bill guilty of both conspiracy to rob the bank and of robbery, or only of robbery? What would be the result under the Model Penal Code? See Section 1.07(1).

In a Model Code jurisdiction, does the conspiracy merge into the completed offense if Alice and Bill conspire to rob banks—not simply to rob a specific bank—and they are arrested after robbing First State Bank, but before they commit any further robberies? See American Law Institute, Model Penal Code and Commentaries, Comment to § 1.07 at 109 (1985).

4. *The relationship of conspiracy to the other inchoate offenses.* United States v. Anzalone, 40 M.J. 658, 663–664 (N–M.C.M.R. 1994), *rev'd in part on other grounds*, 43 M.J. 322 (A.F.C.M.A. 1995):

Th[e] spectrum of criminal conduct ranges from solicitation through the actual commission of the offense * * *. The spectrum might be viewed as follows:

Solicitation≫Conspiracy≫Attempt≫Substantive Crime

Solicitation occurs at the very outset of a criminal venture and consists of requesting seriously another person to commit an offense. However, soliciting another to commit an offense does not constitute an attempt. [This is not always so, see p. 775, Note 5.] The offense of solicitation is complete when the solicitation is made or advice is given with the specific wrongful intent to influence another or others to commit the offense. "It is not necessary that the person or persons solicited or advised agree to or act upon the solicitation or advice."

In our hierarchical analysis, conspiracy may be said to occur next. When the person solicited agrees to participate in a concerted action with the person soliciting to commit a crime, then a conspiracy is formed. When an overt act is committed by any of the persons involved, the crime of conspiracy is complete. Any overt act is enough, no matter how preliminary or preparatory in nature, as long as it is a manifestation that the agreement is being carried out.

An attempt, itself, occurs on the very threshold of completion of the substantive crime. Attempt requires an overt act done with the specific intent to commit the offense. Unlike conspiracy, "[t]he overt act required goes beyond preparatory steps and is a direct movement toward the commission of the offense." The final step in this hierarchical analysis is the actual commission of the offense.

5. *Attempted conspiracy?* Is "attempted conspiracy" a cognizable offense, or is that simply another way of describing the crime of solicitation? Can you suggest a scenario in which a person who attempts to conspire (as "conspiracy" is defined in *Carter*) is *not* guilty of the offense of common law solicitation?

6. Conspiracy is an inchoate offense. However, in most jurisdictions the existence of a conspiracy also constitutes the basis for holding a person accountable for the *completed* crimes of co-conspirators. The next case considers this subject.

[margin handwriting: Not every att. conspiracy a solicitation.]

PINKERTON v. UNITED STATES

Supreme Court of the United States, 1946.
328 U.S. 640, 66 S.Ct. 1180, 90 L.Ed. 1489.

MR. JUSTICE DOUGLAS delivered the opinion of the Court.

Walter and Daniel Pinkerton are brothers who live a short distance from each other on Daniel's farm. They were indicted for violations of the Internal Revenue Code. The indictment contained ten substantive counts and one conspiracy count. The jury found Walter guilty on nine of the substantive counts and on the conspiracy count. It found Daniel guilty on six of the substantive counts and on the conspiracy count. * * *

A single conspiracy was charged and proved. * * * Each of the substantive offenses found was committed pursuant to the conspiracy. * * *

It is contended that there was insufficient evidence to implicate Daniel in the conspiracy. But we think there was enough evidence for submission of the issue to the jury.

There is, however, no evidence to show that Daniel participated directly in the commission of the substantive offenses on which his conviction has been sustained, although there was evidence to show that these substantive offenses were in fact committed by Walter in furtherance of the unlawful agreement or conspiracy existing between the brothers. The question was submitted to the jury on the theory that each petitioner could be found guilty of the substantive offenses, if it was found at the time those offenses were committed petitioners were parties to an unlawful conspiracy and the substantive offenses charged were in fact committed in furtherance of it.[6]

Daniel relies on United States v. Sall [116 F.2d 745 (3d Cir.1940)]. That case held that participation in the conspiracy was not itself enough to sustain a conviction for the substantive offense even though it was committed in furtherance of the conspiracy. The court held that, in addition to evidence that the offense was in fact committed in furtherance of the conspiracy, evidence of direct participation in the commission of the substantive offense or other evidence from which participation might fairly be inferred was necessary.

We take a different view. We have here a continuous conspiracy. There is here no evidence of the affirmative action on the part of Daniel which is necessary to establish his withdrawal from it. * * * And so long as the partnership in crime continues, the partners act for each other in carrying it forward. It is settled that "an overt act of one partner may be the act of all without any new agreement specifically directed to that act." * * *

A different case would arise if the substantive offense committed by one of the conspirators was not in fact done in furtherance of the conspiracy, did not fall within the scope of the unlawful project, or was merely a part of the ramifications of the plan which could not be reasonably foreseen as a necessary or natural consequence of the unlawful agreement. But as we read this record, that is not this case.

Affirmed.

Mr. Justice Rutledge, dissenting in part.

---

6. * * * Daniel was not indicted as an aider or abettor, nor was his case submitted to the jury on that theory.

The judgment concerning Daniel Pinkerton should be reversed. In my opinion it is without precedent here and is a dangerous precedent to establish.

* * * The proof showed that Walter alone committed the substantive crimes. There was none to establish that Daniel participated in them, aided and abetted Walter in committing them, or knew that he had done so. Daniel in fact was in the penitentiary, under sentence for other crimes, when some of Walter's crimes were done. * * *

The court's theory seems to be that Daniel and Walter became general partners in crime by virtue of their agreement and because of that agreement without more on his part Daniel became criminally responsible as a principal for everything Walter did thereafter in the nature of a criminal offense of the general sort the agreement contemplated, so long as there was not clear evidence that Daniel had withdrawn from or revoked the agreement. Whether or not his commitment to the penitentiary had that effect, the result is a vicarious criminal responsibility as broad as, or broader than, the vicarious civil liability of a partner for acts done by a co-partner in the course of the firm's business.

Such analogies from private commercial law and the law of torts are dangerous, in my judgment, for transfer to the criminal field. Guilt there * * * remains personal, not vicarious, for the more serious offenses. It should be kept so. * * *

NOTES AND QUESTIONS

1. In *Pinkerton,* Daniel conspired with Walter, but apparently he did not aid and abet in the commission of the substantive offenses (footnote 6 supra). As will become clear in the next chapter, aiders-and-abettors (accomplices) are usually co-conspirators, and vice-versa, but (as here) this is not always the case. And, as will be seen, *accomplice* liability is often less expansive than *conspiracy* liability under the *Pinkerton* doctrine. It is critical, therefore, to keep these two forms of complicity doctrine—accomplice and conspiracy liability—separate.

2. *Problem. Developments in the Law—Criminal Conspiracy,* 72 Harv. L. Rev. 920, 996 (1959):

> *A* is the organizer and ringleader of a conspiracy to rob banks. He hires *B* and *C* to rob banks *1* and *2* respectively. Although *B* and *C* do not meet face-to-face, both know that they are members of a large conspiracy and each knows of the other's assignment. At *A*'s instigation, *D*, knowing of the conspiracy, steals a car for use in the robberies. *B* and *C* perform their robberies, the former using *D*'s car.

For purposes of the preceding hypothetical, you may assume that *A, B, C* and *D* are parties to a single conspiracy to rob banks. What completed offenses did each party *personally* commit? Of what offenses is each party guilty, as a co-conspirator, pursuant to the *Pinkerton* doctrine?

3. One effect of the *Pinkerton* rule is that it potentially makes relatively minor parties in a large conspiracy criminally responsible for many completed

offenses over which they had little or no control. For example, in Anderson v. Superior Court, 78 Cal.App.2d 22, 177 P.2d 315 (1947), abortionist (Stern) performed illegal abortions on pregnant women sent to him by Anderson and sixteen other conspirators, who received fees for their referrals. Stern, Anderson, and the sixteen other contacts were charged with one count of conspiracy to perform abortions and with 26 separate counts of abortion. That is, Anderson was prosecuted not only for the abortions performed on the women she directed to Stern, but also for those abortions performed on women sent to Stern by others. Thus, the prosecutor sought to have the relatively minor functionaries in the conspiracy held responsible for as many substantive crimes as the primary actor, Stern, was guilty.

The drafters of the Code, which rejects the *Pinkerton* doctrine, believed that the "law would lose all sense of just proportion if simply because of the conspiracy itself each [conspirator] were held accountable for thousands of additional offenses of which he was completely unaware and which he did not influence at all." American Law Institute, Model Penal Code and Commentaries, Comment to § 2.06 at 307 (1985). Do you agree with this criticism? Or do you concur in the statement that "[a]lthough it may appear to some that this rule is unduly harsh, such harshness may be considered as an occupational hazard confronting those who might be tempted to engage in a criminal conspiracy"? State v. Barton, 424 A.2d 1033 (R.I.1981)?

4. *Pinkerton and September 11.* Consider the following allegations in a federal indictment, dated December 11, 2001, of Zacarias Moussaoui, the alleged "20th hijacker," who was in jail on unrelated charges on September 11, 2001 when the attack on the United States occurred:

1. At all relevant times from in or about 1989 until the date of the filing of this Indictment, an international terrorist group existed which was dedicated to opposing non-Islamic governments with force and violence. This organization grew out of the "mekhtab al khidemat" (the "Services Office") organization which had maintained offices in various parts of the world, including Afghanistan, Pakistan * * *, and the United States. The group was founded by Usama Bin Laden and Muhammed Atef, a/k/a/ "Abu Hafs al Masry," together with "Abu Ubaidah al Banshiri," and others. From 1989 until in or about 1991, the group (hereafter referred to as "al Qaeda") was headquartered in Afghanistan and * * * Pakistan. * * *

16. From in or about 1989 until the date of the filing of this Indictment, * * * the defendant Zacarias Moussaoui * * * with other members and associates of al Qaeda and others known and unknown to the Grand Jury unlawfully, wilfully and knowingly combined, conspired, confederated and agreed to kill and maim persons within the United State, and to create a substantial risk of serious bodily injury to other persons by destroying and damaging structures, conveyances, and other real and personal property within the United States, in violation of the laws of States and the United States * * *, resulting in the deaths of thousands of persons on September 11, 2001.

[handwritten margin notes: "Would be guilty of every crime committed on 9/11 as well as the other crimes committed but nuge conspiracy if conspiracy is alleged all of these"]

Assuming the accuracy of these allegations, of what substantive offenses is Moussaoui guilty? Does *Pinkerton* permit prosecution of every single member of al Qaeda for every offense committed by each member?

5. *Some procedural features of conspiracy law.* Although this chapter focuses on the *substantive* crime of conspiracy, it is useful to be aware of at least a few of the procedural rules—many of which are controversial—that come into play in prosecutions of alleged conspiracies.

First, state and federal rules of evidence generally bar introduction of hearsay evidence at trial. "Hearsay" is a statement, made other than by a witness while testifying at trial, that is introduced to prove the truth of the matter stated. For example, in a criminal prosecution of Alice for murder, it would constitute hearsay to allow Bob to testify at trial that Carla said, "I saw Alice murder the victim," if the latter statement is introduced for its truth (that Alice murdered the victim). Such evidence is generally prohibited because it is both unreliable and unfair to Alice to use Carla's statement against her when Carla is not under oath and is not available for cross-examination.

[handwritten margin note: "#1 co-conspirators statements"]

One exception to the hearsay rule, however, is that an out-of-court statement made by a conspirator, while participating in the conspiracy, may be introduced in evidence against all of her co-conspirators. Thus, if Carla was Alice's co-conspirator in the murder, her statement *would* be admissible against Alice. In a perfect world, the prosecutor would be required to prove the existence of the conspiracy before allowing Carla's hearsay statement in evidence against Alice, but this does not always—or even typically—occur. As Justice Jackson explained in Krulewitch v. United States, 336 U.S. 440, 69 S.Ct. 716, 93 L.Ed. 790 (1949):

> Strictly, the prosecution should first establish *prima facie* the conspiracy and identify the conspirators, after which evidence of acts and declarations of each in the course of its execution are admissible against all. But the order of proof of so sprawling a charge is difficult for a judge to control. As a practical matter, the accused often is confronted with a hodgepodge of acts and statements by others which he may never have authorized or intended or even known about, but which help to persuade the jury of existence of the conspiracy itself. In other words, a conspiracy often is proved by evidence that is admissible only upon assumption that conspiracy existed.

Moreover, the existence of the conspiracy, and a particular defendant's participation in it, need only be proven by preponderance of the evidence in order for hearsay statements of co-conspirators to be introduced. Bourjaily v. United States, 483 U.S. 171, 107 S.Ct. 2775, 97 L.Ed.2d 144 (1987).

[handwritten margin note: "#2 Joint trials"]

Second, persons charged in a conspiracy are typically tried together rather than separately. Much of the evidence—and same witnesses—would need to be introduced at each alleged conspirator's trial, so one trial of all of the defendants is simpler for the witnesses and the prosecutor, as well as a more efficient way to expend finite judicial resources. But, is this approach fair to the defendants? Justice Jackson in *Krulewitch* has written:

A co-defendant in a conspiracy trial occupies an uneasy seat. There generally will be evidence of wrongdoing by somebody. It is difficult for the individual to make his own case stand on its own merits in the minds of jurors who are ready to believe that birds of a feather are flocked together. If he is silent, he is taken to admit it and if, as often happens, co-defendants can be prodded into accusing or contradicting each other, they convict each other.

Third, most states and federal law permit the government to bring a conspiracy prosecution in the jurisdiction in which *either* the alleged conspiracy itself was formed or *any* act in furtherance of that conspiracy allegedly occurred. Again, Justice Jackson has pointed out the concern:

> An accused, under the Sixth Amendment, has the right to trial "by an impartial jury of the State and district wherein the crime shall have been committed." The leverage of a conspiracy charge lifts this limitation from the prosecution and reduces its protection to a phantom, for the crime is considered so vagrant as to have been committed in any district where any one of the conspirators did any one of the acts, however innocent, intended to accomplish its object. The Government may, and often does, compel one to defend at a great distance from any place he ever did any act because some accused confederate did some trivial and by itself innocent act in the chosen district.

Fourth, the Supreme Court has held that, under federal law, a conspiracy does not automatically terminate simply because law enforcement officers have defeated the object of the conspiracy. United States v. Recio, 537 U.S. 270, 123 S.Ct. 819, 154 L.Ed.2d 744 (2003). For example, a conspiracy to distribute specific drugs does not end, even though the drugs in question have been seized by the police, if some of the conspirators do not realize that the conspiratorial objective has been frustrated. In such circumstances, the Court reasoned, the special conspiracy-related dangers of conspiratorial agreements remain in effect. Consequently, the special conspiracy rules that apply to conspiracies—e.g., the *Pinkerton* doctrine and admissibility of co-conspirator hearsay—can continue to apply although the conspiratorial objective has long since failed.

2. MENS REA

PEOPLE v. SWAIN

Supreme Court of California, 1996.
12 Cal.4th 593, 49 Cal.Rptr.2d 390, 909 P.2d 994.

BAXTER, ASSOCIATE JUSTICE.

Defendants Jamal K. Swain and David Chatman were each convicted of conspiracy to commit murder and other crimes, stemming from the drive-by shooting death of a 15–year–old boy. * * *

FACTS AND PROCEDURAL BACKGROUND

The question before us is one of law; the facts found by the Court of Appeal, summarized below, are not disputed.

Prosecution evidence established that a brown van passed through the Hunter's Point neighborhood of San Francisco about 2:00 a.m. on January 13, 1991. It slowed down near the spot where the young victim * * * and his friends were listening to music on the street.

A young * * * male who appeared to have no hair was driving the van. Suddenly several shots were fired from the front of the van. Defendant Chatman and another young man also fired guns from the rear of the van. One of the intended victims had yelled out "drive-by" as a warning of the impending shooting, so most of the people on the street ducked down. The 15–year–old victim, Hagbom Saileele, who was holding the radio from which music was playing, was shot twice from behind. He later died in surgery.

Afterward, defendant Swain was in jail and boasted to jailmates about what good aim he had with a gun: "He was talking about what a good shot he was. [¶] * * * [¶] He was saying he had shot that Samoan kid when they were in the van going about 30 miles an hour up a hill." * * * [At trial, Swain testified that he was in the van earlier in the evening, but had left prior to the incident because "the smell of marijuana bothered him."]

At trial, Chatman admitted he had been in the van, which was driven to Hunter's Point to retaliate for a car theft attributed to a neighborhood youth who was not the victim of the shooting. The original plan was allegedly to steal the car of the thief. Chatman admitted he had fired shots, but claimed he fired wildly and only in self-defense. In support of this self-defense theory, he testified he heard an initial shot and thought it was fired by someone outside the van shooting at him, so he returned the fire. * * *

The jury first returned a verdict finding defendant Chatman guilty of second degree murder and conspiracy. As instructed, the jury also made a finding that the target offense of the conspiracy was murder in the second degree. Several days later, the jury returned verdicts against defendant Swain, finding him not guilty of murder or its lesser included offenses, but guilty of conspiracy * * *. Once again, the jury made a finding under the conspiracy count that the target offense of the conspiracy was murder in the second degree. * * *

Both defendants appealed on several grounds, including the question of whether intent to kill is a required element of the crime of conspiracy to commit murder. More particularly, where, as here, the target offense is determined to be murder *in the second degree*, does conviction of conspiracy to commit murder necessarily require proof of express malice—the functional equivalent of intent to kill—or can one conspire to commit implied malice murder[, i.e., murder lacking an intent to kill]? * * *

DISCUSSION * * *

Defendants contend the jury should have been instructed that proof of intent to kill is required to support a conviction of conspiracy to commit murder, whether the target offense of the conspiracy—murder—is determined to be in the first or second degree. More particularly, defendants assert it was error to instruct the jury on the principles of *implied malice* second degree murder in connection with the determination of whether they could be found guilty of conspiracy to commit murder, since *implied malice* does not require a finding of intent to kill. As we shall explain, we agree. * * *

The crime of conspiracy is defined in the Penal Code as "two or more persons conspir[ing]" "[t]o commit any crime," together with proof of the commission of an overt act "by one or more of the parties to such agreement" in furtherance thereof. "Conspiracy is a 'specific intent' crime. * * * The specific intent required divides logically into two elements: (a) the intent to agree, or conspire, and (b) the intent to commit the offense which is the object of the conspiracy * * *. To sustain a conviction for conspiracy to commit a particular offense, the prosecution must show not only that the conspirators intended to agree *but also that they intended to commit the elements of that offense.*" * * *

Turning next to the elements of the target offense of the conspiracy here in issue, Penal Code section 187 defines the crime of murder as the "unlawful killing of a human being * * * with malice aforethought." Malice aforethought "may be express or implied." (Pen.Code, § 188.) "It is express when there is manifested a deliberate intention unlawfully to take away the life of a fellow creature. It is implied, when no considerable provocation appears, or when the circumstances attending the killing show an abandoned and malignant heart."

This court has observed that proof of unlawful "intent to kill" is the functional equivalent of express malice.

Penal Code section 189 distinguishes between murders in the first degree and murders in the second degree. "All murder which is perpetrated by means of a destructive device or explosive * * *, poison, lying in wait, torture, *or by any other kind of willful, deliberate, and premeditated killing,* or which is committed in the perpetration of, or attempt to perpetrate, [certain enumerated felonies], or any murder which is perpetrated by means of discharging a firearm from a motor vehicle, intentionally at another person outside of the vehicle with the intent to inflict death, is *murder of the first degree.* All other kinds of murders are of the second degree."

California law, in turn, recognizes three theories of *second degree murder.*

The first is unpremeditated murder with express malice [intent to kill].

The second, of particular concern here, is implied malice murder [based on a killing perpetrated with an abandoned and malignant heart].

The third theory is second degree felony murder.

* * * [T]he jury in this case was instructed on the elements of murder, including principles of *implied malice* second degree murder.

Under the instructions given, the jury could have based its verdicts finding defendants guilty of conspiracy to commit murder in the second degree on a theory of implied malice murder. * * *

We have noted that conspiracy is a specific intent crime requiring an intent to agree or conspire, and a further intent to commit the target crime, here murder, the object of the conspiracy. Since murder committed with intent to kill is the functional equivalent of *express malice* murder, conceptually speaking, no conflict arises between the specific intent element of conspiracy and the specific intent requirement for such category of murders. Simply put, where the conspirators agree or conspire with specific intent to kill and commit an overt act in furtherance of such agreement, they are guilty of conspiracy to commit express malice murder. The conceptual difficulty arises when the target offense of murder is founded on a theory of implied malice, which requires no intent to kill.

Implied malice murder, in contrast to express malice, requires instead an intent to do some act, the natural consequences of which are dangerous to human life. "*When the killing is the direct result of such an act,*" the requisite mental state for murder—malice aforethought—is implied. In such circumstances, " * * * * it is not necessary to establish that the defendant intended that his act would result in the death of a human being." * * *

* * * It is precisely due to this nature of *implied malice* murder that it would be *illogical* to conclude one can be found guilty of conspiring to commit murder where the requisite element of malice is implied. Such a construction would be at odds with the very nature of the crime of conspiracy * * *. * * *

We conclude that a conviction of conspiracy to commit murder requires a finding of intent to kill, and cannot be based on a theory of implied malice. * * *

Notes and Questions

1. Why was Swain not convicted of murder if he conspired with Chatman to kill the victim, as the jury found?

2. The defendants in *Swain* were convicted of conspiracy to commit *second degree* murder. The California Supreme Court has since held that "all conspiracy to commit murder is necessarily conspiracy to commit murder of the first degree * * *." People v. Cortez, 18 Cal.4th 1223, 77 Cal.Rptr.2d 733, 960 P.2d 537 (1998). Why would this be?

3. *Problem.* In People v. Barajas, 198 Mich.App. 551, 499 N.W.2d 396 (1993), *B* agreed to purchase one kilogram of cocaine from *X*. The parties, arrested before the delivery occurred, were prosecuted for conspiracy to possess over 650 grams of cocaine, in violation of state law. (Possession of 650 or fewer grams of cocaine constituted a lesser offense.) As it turned out, *X* intended to defraud *B*: the box that he intended to deliver contained only 26 grams of cocaine, mixed with baking soda. Are the parties guilty as charged? Does the answer depend on *when X* decided to defraud *B*?

[handwritten margin notes: "It is premeditated this murder 1°"] [handwritten bottom note: "plurality of mens rea issues"]

4. *Problem.* *A* and *B*, husband and wife, learn that their daughter *C* was raped by *D*. In heat of passion they agree to kill *D*. Three days later, *A* calmly kills *D*. Regarding the conspiracy: is this conspiracy to commit murder or conspiracy to commit voluntary manslaughter?

5. Jacob and Ken agree to detonate a bomb in a building they both know is occupied, in order to destroy it. Although they do not want anyone to die, they believe that people inside will be killed as a result of their actions. If the bomb explodes and occupants die, of what form of criminal homicide are they guilty? If the bomb does not go off, are they guilty of attempted murder? In either case, are they guilty of conspiracy to commit murder? Answer according to the Model Penal Code. See American Law Institute, Model Penal Code and Commentaries, Comment to § 5.03 at 407–408 (1985).

PEOPLE v. LAURIA

California Court of Appeal, Second District, 1967.
251 Cal.App.2d 471, 59 Cal.Rptr. 628.

FLEMING, ASSOCIATE JUSTICE.

In an investigation of call-girl activity the police focused their attention on three prostitutes actively plying their trade on call, each of whom was using Lauria's telephone answering service, presumably for business purposes.

On January 8, 1965, Stella Weeks, a policewoman, signed up for telephone service with Lauria's answering service. Mrs. Weeks, in the course of her conversation with Lauria's office manager, hinted broadly that she was a prostitute concerned with the secrecy of her activities and their concealment from the police. She was assured that the operation of the service was discreet and "about as safe as you can get." It was arranged that Mrs. Weeks need not leave her address with the answering service, but could pick up her calls and pay her bills in person.

On February 11, Mrs. Weeks talked to Lauria on the telephone and told him her business was modelling and she had been referred to the answering service by Terry, one of the three prostitutes under investigation. She complained that because of the operation of the service she had lost two valuable customers, referred to as tricks. Lauria defended his service and said that her friends had probably lied to her about having left calls for her. * * * In the course of his talk he said "his business was taking messages." * * *

On April 1 Lauria and the three prostitutes were arrested. Lauria complained to the police that this attention was undeserved, stating that * * * he kept separate records for known or suspected prostitutes for the convenience of himself and the police. * * * However, his service didn't "arbitrarily tell the police about prostitutes on our board. As long as they pay their bills we tolerate them." In a subsequent voluntary appearance before the Grand Jury Lauria * * * admitted he knew some of his customers were prostitutes, and he knew Terry was a prostitute because he had personally used her services, and he knew she was paying for 500 calls a month.

Lauria and the three prostitutes were [indicted] for conspiracy to commit prostitution, and nine overt acts were specified. Subsequently the trial court set aside the indictment as having been brought without reasonable or probable cause. The People have appealed, claiming that a sufficient showing of an unlawful agreement to further prostitution was made.

To establish agreement, the People need show no more than a tacit, mutual understanding between coconspirators to accomplish an unlawful act. Here the People attempted to establish a conspiracy by showing that Lauria, well aware that his codefendants were prostitutes who received business calls from customers through his telephone answering service, continued to furnish them with such service. This approach attempts to equate knowledge of another's criminal activity with conspiracy to further such criminal activity, and poses the question of the criminal responsibility of a furnisher of goods or services who knows his product is being used to assist the operation of an illegal business. Under what circumstances does a supplier become a part of a conspiracy to further an illegal enterprise by furnishing goods or services which he knows are to be used by the buyer for criminal purposes?

The two leading cases on this point face in opposite directions. In United States v. Falcone, 311 U.S. 205, 61 S.Ct. 204, 85 L.Ed. 128, the sellers of large quantities of sugar, yeast, and cans were absolved from participation in a moonshining conspiracy among distillers who bought from them, while in Direct Sales Co. v. United States, 319 U.S. 703, 63 S.Ct. 1265, 87 L.Ed. 1674, a wholesaler of drugs was convicted of conspiracy to violate the federal narcotic laws by selling drugs in quantity to a codefendant physician who was supplying them to addicts. The distinction between these two cases appears primarily based on the proposition that distributors of such dangerous products as drugs are required to exercise greater discrimination in the conduct of their business than are distributors of innocuous substances like sugar and yeast.

In the earlier case, *Falcone,* the sellers' knowledge of the illegal use of the goods was insufficient by itself to make the sellers participants in a conspiracy with the distillers who bought from them. Such knowledge fell short of proof of a conspiracy, and evidence on the volume of sales was too vague to support a jury finding that respondents knew of the conspiracy from the size of the sales alone.

In the later case of *Direct Sales,* the conviction of a drug wholesaler for conspiracy to violate federal narcotic laws was affirmed on a showing that it had actively promoted the sale of morphine sulphate in quantity and had sold codefendant physician, who practiced in a small town in South Carolina, more than 300 times his normal requirements of the drug, even though it had been repeatedly warned of the dangers of unrestricted sales of the drug. The court contrasted the restricted goods involved in

Direct Sales with the articles of free commerce involved in *Falcone:* "All articles of commerce may be put to illegal ends," said the court. "But all do not have inherently the same susceptibility to harmful and illegal use. * * * This difference is important for two purposes. One is for making certain that the seller knows the buyer's intended illegal use. The other is to show that by the sale he intends to further, promote and cooperate in it. This intent, when given effect by overt act, is the gist of conspiracy. While it is not identical with mere knowledge that another purposes unlawful action, it is not unrelated to such knowledge. * * * The step from knowledge to intent and agreement may be taken. There is more than suspicion, more than knowledge, acquiescence, carelessness, indifference, lack of concern. There is informed and interested cooperation, stimulation, instigation. And there is also a 'stake in the venture' which, even if it may not be essential, is not irrelevant to the question of conspiracy."

While *Falcone* and *Direct Sales* may not be entirely consistent with each other in their full implications, they do provide us with a framework for the criminal liability of a supplier of lawful goods or services put to unlawful use. Both the element of *knowledge* of the illegal use of the goods or services and the element of *intent* to further that use must be present in order to make the supplier a participant in a criminal conspiracy.

Proof of *knowledge* is ordinarily a question of fact and requires no extended discussion in the present case. The knowledge of the supplier was sufficiently established when Lauria admitted he knew some of his customers were prostitutes and admitted he knew that Terry, an active subscriber to his service, was a prostitute. * * * Because Lauria knew in fact that some of his customers were prostitutes, it is a legitimate inference he knew they were subscribing to his answering service for illegal business purposes and were using his service to make assignations for prostitution. On this record we think the prosecution is entitled to claim positive knowledge by Lauria of the use of his service to facilitate the business of prostitution.

The more perplexing issue in the case is the sufficiency of proof of *intent* to further the criminal enterprise. The element of intent may be proved either by direct evidence, or by evidence of circumstances from which an intent to further a criminal enterprise by supplying lawful goods or services may be inferred. Direct evidence of participation, such as advice from the supplier of legal goods or services to the user of those goods or services on their use for illegal purposes, * * * provides the simplest case. * * * But in cases where direct proof of complicity is lacking, intent to further the conspiracy must be derived from the sale itself and its surrounding circumstances in order to establish the supplier's express or tacit agreement to join the conspiracy. * * *

In examining precedents in this field we find that sometimes, but not always, the criminal intent of the supplier may be inferred from his knowledge of the unlawful use made of the product he supplies. Some consideration of characteristic patterns may be helpful.

1. Intent may be inferred from knowledge, when the purveyor of legal goods for illegal use has acquired a stake in the venture. For example, in Regina v. Thomas, (1957), 2 All.E.R. 181, 342, * * * when the accused rented a room at a grossly inflated rent to a prostitute for the purpose of carrying on her trade, a jury could find he was living on the earnings of prostitution. * * *

2. Intent may be inferred from knowledge, when no legitimate use for the goods or services exists. The leading California case is People v. McLaughlin, 111 Cal.App.2d 781, 245 P.2d 1076, in which the court upheld a conviction of the suppliers of horse-racing information by wire for conspiracy to promote bookmaking, when it had been established that wire-service information had no other use than to supply information needed by bookmakers to conduct illegal gambling operations. * * *

In such cases the supplier must necessarily have an intent to further the illegal enterprise since there is no known honest use for his goods. * * *

3. Intent may be inferred from knowledge, when the volume of business with the buyer is grossly disproportionate to any legitimate demand, or when sales for illegal use amount to a high proportion of the seller's total business. In such cases an intent to participate in the illegal enterprise may be inferred from the quantity of the business done. For example, in *Direct Sales,* supra, the sale of narcotics to a rural physician in quantities 300 times greater than he would have normal use for provided potent evidence of an intent to further the illegal activity. * * *

Yet there are cases in which it cannot reasonably be said that the supplier has a stake in the venture or has acquired a special interest in the enterprise, but in which he has been held liable as a participant on the basis of knowledge alone. * * * It seems apparent from these cases that a supplier who furnishes equipment which he *knows* will be used to commit a serious crime may be deemed from that knowledge alone to have intended to produce the result. Such proof may justify an inference that the furnisher intended to aid the execution of the crime and that he thereby became a participant. For instance, we think the operator of a telephone answering service with positive knowledge that his service was being used to facilitate the extortion of ransom, the distribution of heroin, or the passing of counterfeit money who continued to furnish the service with knowledge of its use, might be chargeable on knowledge alone with participation in a scheme to extort money, to distribute narcotics, or to pass counterfeit money. * * *

Logically, the same reasoning could be extended to crimes of every description. Yet we do not believe an inference of intent drawn from knowledge of criminal use properly applies to the less serious crimes classified as misdemeanors. The duty to take positive action to dissociate oneself from activities helpful to violations of the criminal law as far stronger and more compelling for felonies than it is for misdemeanors or petty offenses. In this respect, as in others, the distinction between felonies and misdemeanors, between more serious and less serious crime, retains continuing vitality. * * *

From this analysis of precedent we deduce the following rule: the intent of a supplier who knows of the criminal use to which his supplies are put to participate in the criminal activity connected with the use of his supplies may be established by (1) direct evidence that he intends to participate, or (2) through an inference that he intends to participate based on, (a) his special interest in the activity, or (b) the aggravated nature of the crime itself.

Rule

When we review Lauria's activities in the light of this analysis, we find no proof that Lauria took any direct action to further, encourage, or direct the call-girl activities of his codefendants and we find an absence of circumstances from which his special interest in their activities could be inferred. Neither excessive charges for standardized services, nor the furnishing of services without a legitimate use, nor an unusual quantity of business with call girls, are present. The offense which he is charged with furthering is a misdemeanor, a category of crime which has never been made a required subject of positive disclosure to public authority. Under these circumstances, although proof of Lauria's knowledge of the criminal activities of his patrons was sufficient to charge him with that fact, there was insufficient evidence that he intended to further their criminal activities, and hence insufficient proof of his participation in a criminal conspiracy with his codefendants to further prostitution. * * *

NOTES AND QUESTIONS

1. *Problem.* In just 62 working days, undercover Chicago police officers posing as "gang members, motorcycle toughs and camouflage-wearing soldiers of fortune" purchased 171 guns, many of which were illegal to possess in Chicago, in gun shops immediately outside Chicago city limits. Fran Spielman, *Chicago Sues Gun Dealers*, Chi. Sun–Times, Nov. 13, 1998, at 3. One of the shops was the source of a gun used to kill a Chicago police officer.

Assume that one of the gun dealers sold a gun to a *real* Chicago gang member (not an unlikely assumption). In which of the following cases, if any, would the dealer be guilty of conspiracy with the customer to commit murder under *Lauria*? Under M.P.C. § 5.03? As a matter of good public policy, where would *you* draw the conspiracy line?

A. The dealer knew that the purchaser was a member of a Chicago gang.

B. Same as (A), except that he also knew that a shooting war among rival gangs was underway.

C. Same as (B), and the customer told the gun dealer, "I need a gun to use in drive-by shootings of [members of the opposing gang]."

Affects liability under Pinkerton

D. Same as (B), and the customer told the dealer, "I need the gun for self-defense, in case [members of the opposing gang] try to kill me," but the purchaser uses the gun in an unprovoked gang shooting.

Red herring

2. *Problem.* Consider Jonathan Welsh, *New Radar Detectors Give Speed Freaks a Rush*, Wall St. J., Jan. 10, 2008, at D1:

> Radar detectors, one thought of as relics, are back on the radar.
>
> As people endure longer commutes * * *, they are increasingly tempted to hit the gas pedal harder. Police are fighting back with a web of electronic surveillance, from laser and radar speed traps to automatic cameras that spot speeders and issue tickets by mail.
>
> To improve their odds, committed speed demons (and scofflaws) are resorting to a new generation of high-end radar-detection devices. These gadgets, which include the $399 Valentine One * * *, promise to help drivers spot and avoid radar and laser speed traps. The new models * * * are touted as having better range and more sensitivity than their predecessors while generating fewer false alarms.

Scofflaw purchases a Valentine One from Merchant. Query: Based on what you have learned so far, do these facts state a conspiracy by Scofflaw, Merchant, and Valentine One Company to violate local traffic laws relating to speeding? (Put aside any special issues relating to holding corporations, as distinguished from individuals, liable for crimes.) What additional information, if any, do you need to answer the question?

3. *Mens rea and attendant circumstances.* Arnold to Babbit, "You ought to have intercourse with Christine. She likes you and I bet she wants to do it with you."

Babbit to Arnold, "Yeah, you are right. I am going to do it."

From these facts we may conclude that Arnold and Babbit have agreed for Babbit to have sexual intercourse with Christine (or, at least, to ask her for intercourse). But, is this agreement a conspiracy to commit a crime? Perhaps so if, for example, Christine is underage, and thus intercourse by Babbit with her would constitute statutory rape.

Let's assume that Christine is, indeed, underage, but that neither Arnold nor Babbit knew this fact. Further assume that in the jurisdiction in which these events occurred, statutory rape is a strict liability offense. Therefore, we can assume that if Babbit were to go through with the plan and have intercourse with Christine, he would be guilty of statutory rape, even if he reasonably thought Christine was of age to consent. However, even accepting these assumptions, can we say that Arnold and Babbit are guilty of "*conspiracy* to commit statutory rape"? Can't they plausibly argue that a person cannot be guilty of conspiracy unless they *knew* that Christine was underage? Put differently, although no culpability is required as to the female's age to be guilty of statutory rape, must there be proof of actual knowledge of the attendant circumstance to be guilty of *conspiracy* to commit statutory rape?

This issue does not arise often, but it does happen enough to be a serious issue. For another example, suppose that George and Karla agree to beat up Victor. They have conspired to commit a battery. What if, however, unbeknownst to George and Karla, Victor is an undercover police officer. May they now be convicted of the more serious offense of conspiracy to commit "battery upon a law enforcement officer"? If knowledge of the victim's status is not required for the underlying offense (a matter of legislative intent, to be determined), do we still require knowledge of the attendant circumstance (that Victor is a law enforcement officer) to be guilty of *conspiracy* to commit battery upon a law enforcement officer?

Case law is split in this regard. Some courts hold that conspiracy cannot be proven unless the parties have knowledge of the attendant circumstance, even if such knowledge is not required for the underlying crime. In short, a higher *mens rea* (as to an attendant circumstance) must be proven in a conspiracy case than for some target offenses. Other courts believe that the policies relating to the underlying offense should apply to the conspiracy charge: if the underlying offense is strict liability as to the attendant circumstance, the same rule should apply to conspiracy to commit that offense. Thus, in such a jurisdiction, as statutory rape is strict liability in nature, Arnold and Babbit would be guilty of conspiracy to commit statutory rape, although they did not know—and perhaps had no reason to know—that Christine was underage.

As for the Model Penal Code approach:

> The conspiracy provision in the Code does not attempt to solve the problem by explicit formulation * * *. * * * [I]t was believed that the matter is best left to judicial resolution as cases that present the question may arise, and that the formulations proposed afford sufficient flexibility for satisfactory decision. Under Subsection (1) of Section 5.03 it is enough that the object of the agreement is "conduct that constitutes the crime," which can be held to import no more than the mental state required for the substantive offense into the agreement to commit it. Although the agreement must be made "with the purpose of promoting or facilitating the commission of the crime," it is arguable, though by no means certain, that such a purpose may be proved although the actor did not know of the existence of a circumstance, which did exist in fact, when knowledge of the circumstance is not required for the substantive offense. Rather than press the matter further in this section, the Institute deliberately left the matter to interpretation in the context in which the issue is presented.

American Law Institute, Model Penal Code and Commentaries, Comment to § 5.03 at 413–414 (1985).

4. *The corrupt motive doctrine.* The last Note dealt with cases in which the actors did not know a critical *fact* that rendered their conduct unlawful (Christine's age, and Victor's identity as a police officer). What if the parties know all of the relevant facts but do not know that their agreed-upon goal is a crime. For example, suppose that A and B agree that B will drive his car 65 miles an hour, unaware that the speed limit on that highway is 55 miles-per-hour. Or, suppose political candidate C agrees to accept a contribution of $50 from D, although neither is aware than under new and complicated campaign reform legislation, this $50 contribution would be unlawful. Are they guilty of conspiracy to violate the election law?

A few courts apply what has come to be known as the "corrupt motive doctrine." This doctrine provides that, beyond the usual *mens rea* requirements, parties to an alleged conspiracy are not guilty unless they had a corrupt or wrongful motive for their planned actions. In the hypothetical cases here, there was no corrupt motive, so there would be no guilt.

Guidance is no excuse because exception

Is this doctrine inconsistent with any legal rules you have learned outside the conspiracy area? Do you find the rule appealing? Why, or why not?

3. ACTUS REUS

ABRAHAM S. GOLDSTEIN—CONSPIRACY TO DEFRAUD THE UNITED STATES

68 Yale Law Journal 405 (1959), 409–412

The agreement represents the actualization of the intent contemplated by the act-intent maxim. It is the "act" which expresses in concrete form the threat to society of an intent shared by two or more persons. Vicarious liability is imputed and hearsay admitted, statute of limitations tolled and venue attained—all by virtue of the terms of that agreement.

Yet "agreement" is almost as much a theoretical construct as the "intent" it is supposed to carry over the threshold from fancy to fact. Indeed, in most cases, it is proved by the very same evidence from which intent will be inferred. Thus, instead of anchoring intangible intent to a tangible act, the law of conspiracy makes intent an appendage of the equally intangible agreement. By pouring the same proof into the mold of "agreement" and by calling that "agreement" an "act"—passive though it may be—courts foster the already elaborate illusion that conspiracy reaches actual, not potential, harm.

The illusory quality of agreement is increased by the fact that it, like intent, must inevitably be based upon assumptions about what people acting in certain ways must have had in mind. It is ordinarily fashioned by a jury out of bits and pieces of circumstantial evidence, usually styled "overt acts," offered to prove that two or more persons are (or were) pursuing a given unlawful purpose. The sensation that the proof consists of little more than "bits and pieces" is, of course, intensified by the fact that acts and statements of each of several defendants are being offered into evidence as imputable to each of the other defendants. And overshadowing the entire proceeding is the uneasy feeling that the evidence may be taking the form cast for it in the indictment quite as much because the parties are seated together in the courtroom as defendants in a common trial as because they did, in fact, agree. This is not to say that words of caution are not uttered by judge to jury. Indeed, conspiracy cases are among the rare instances in which trial judges ask juries to be mindful of the vagaries of the process in which they are participating.

More important, however, jurors are also told that the existence of a conspiracy may be inferred from the unfolding of events over an extended period of time and that, though evidence like unexplained meetings of defendants is insufficient in and of itself, such evidence must be used if the crime is ever to be discovered. Judicial folklore is also shared. Conspirators, juries are advised, do not shout their plans from the rooftops. Nor do they cast them in written form or announce them in the presence of witnesses. The net effect of such commentary is to free juries from the automatic compliance with "law" which instructions ordinarily demand and to invite a "guilty" verdict on less evidence than might otherwise be required.

NOTES AND QUESTIONS

1. *Developments in the Law—Criminal Conspiracy*, 72 Harv. L. Rev. 920, 933 (1959):

The basic principle that a conspiracy is not established without proof of an agreement has been weakened, or at least obscured, by * * * the courts' unfortunate tendency to overemphasize a rule of evidence at the expense of a rule of law. Conspiracy is by nature a clandestine offense. It is improbable that the parties will enter into their illegal agreement openly; it is not necessary, in fact, that all the parties ever have direct contact with one another, or know one another's identity, or even communicate verbally their intention to agree. It is therefore unlikely that the prosecution will be able to prove the formation of the agreement by direct evidence, and the jury must usually infer its existence from the clear co-operation among the parties. But in their zeal to emphasize that the agreement need not be proved directly, the courts sometimes neglect to say that it need be proved at all.

COMMONWEALTH v. AZIM

Superior Court of Pennsylvania, 1983.
313 Pa.Super. 310, 459 A.2d 1244.

PER CURIAM:

Appellant Charles Azim * * * seeks dismissal of all the charges brought against him. * * *

Appellant was arrested, along with Mylice James and Thomas Robinson * * * for simple assault, robbery, and conspiracy. The victim of the robbery was Jerry Tennenbaum, a Temple University student. Appellant drove a car in which the other two men were passengers. Appellant stopped the car, Robinson called Tennenbaum over to the curb, the two passengers got out of the car, inflicted bodily injury on Tennenbaum, took his wallet which had fallen to the ground, and immediately left the scene in the same car driven by appellant. Robinson and appellant were tried to a jury and convicted as co-defendants * * *. * * *

In this appeal, appellant * * * argues that because his conspiracy conviction was not supported by sufficient evidence against him, the charges of assault and robbery must also fail.

* * * In *Commonwealth v. Volk*, 298 Pa.Super. 294, 444 A.2d 1182 (1982) * * * our Court maintained that * * *:

* * * "The essence of criminal conspiracy is a common understanding, no matter how it came into being, that a particular criminal objective be accomplished." By its very nature, the crime of conspiracy is frequently not susceptible of proof except by circumstantial

evidence. And although a conspiracy cannot be based upon mere suspicion or conjecture, a conspiracy "may be inferentially established by showing the relationship, conduct or circumstances of the parties, and the overt acts on the part of the co-conspirators have uniformly been held competent to prove that a corrupt confederation has in fact been formed."

At trial, the prosecution presented evidence that established that appellant was the driver of the car in which James and Robinson (the men who demanded money from Tennenbaum and beat and choked him) rode. Robinson was seated on the front seat, next to appellant. Robinson rolled down the car window, twice beckoned to the victim to come close to the car, and when Tennenbaum refused, the two passengers got out, assaulted Tennenbaum, and took his wallet. Appellant sat at the wheel, with the engine running and lights on, and the car doors open, while the acts were committed in the vicinity of the car. He then drove James and Robinson from the scene.

Among those circumstances relevant to proving conspiracy are association with alleged conspirators, knowledge of the commission of the crime, presence at the scene of the crime, and, at times, participation in the object of the conspiracy. Conspiracy to commit burglary has been found where the defendant drove codefendants to the scene of a crime and then later picked them up. * * * We find no merit in appellant's claim that he was merely a hired driver, with no knowledge of his passengers' criminal activity.

We hold that a rational factfinder could find, beyond a reasonable doubt, that appellant conspired with James and Robinson to commit assault and robbery. * * *

Once conspiracy is established and upheld, a member of the conspiracy is also guilty of the criminal acts of his co-conspirators * * *. * * *

NOTES AND QUESTIONS

1. *Conspiracy by choreography.* Reconsider (p. 783, Note 4) the indictment of Zacarias Moussaoui. Moussaoui was indicted on multiple conspiracy charges, including conspiracy to commit acts of terrorism transcending national boundaries (in violation of specified federal statutes) and various conspiracies relating to the September 11 attack on the United States. The lengthy indictment resulted in the following journalistic summary:

> At the heart of the government's charges against Mr. Moussaoui are accusations that he engaged in a narrow pattern of activities identical to ones conducted by the 19 hijackers—buying knives, purchasing flight training materials, receiving wire transfers from abroad—at about the same time as the others, even though he lived in another part of the country and had no apparent contact with them.
>
> Also, like Mohamed Atta, the man who authorities believe led the plot, the indictment said that Mr. Moussaoui made inquiries at a crop-

dusting company and possessed a computer disk with information about the aerial application of pesticides.

David Johnson & Philip Shenon, *Man Held Since August Is Accused of Helping in Sept. 11 Terror Plot*, N.Y. Times, Dec. 12, 2001, at A1, B7.

Assuming that Moussaoui did all of the acts alleged in the indictment, do you believe that this information, standing alone, proves that he conspired with the 19 hijackers to commit the terrorist acts of September 11? Why, or why not?

COMMONWEALTH v. COOK

Appeals Court of Massachusetts, 1980.
10 Mass.App.Ct. 668, 411 N.E.2d 1326.

GREANEY, JUSTICE.

The defendant [Dennis Cook] was tried before a jury * * * on an indictment charging conspiracy to commit rape. His motion for a required finding of not guilty was filed and denied at the conclusion of the Commonwealth's case, and he was subsequently convicted and sentenced on the indictment. On appeal he claims error in the denial of the motion. We hold that the evidence introduced up to the time the Commonwealth rested was insufficient to warrant his conviction of conspiracy and that, as a result, the judgment must be reversed. A summary of the Commonwealth's evidence follows.

At approximately 8:00 P.M. on the evening of July 16, 1977, the victim, age seventeen, went to Chicopee to visit some friends and to see her boyfriend. Upon discovering that her friends were not at home, she proceeded to the housing project where her boyfriend resided. As she passed the area of the project office, the defendant and his brother Maurice Cook attempted to engage her in conversation. Not knowing the Cooks, she spurned an invitation to join them and instead walked to her boyfriend's residence. After ascertaining that he was not at home, she reversed her route, intending to stay at her friends' home to await their return. As she passed the office area for the second time, she accepted the Cooks' renewed invitation to socialize, and she sat with the two brothers on a platform talking for approximately forty-five minutes. The area apparently was used as a common meeting point for informal socializing, and while the victim was there several other people were in the vicinity, one of whom recognized the victim and called her by name. There was evidence that the Cooks smoked marihuana and drank beer but that the victim declined to smoke marihuana because her boyfriend disliked her "flying high." She did take a drink of beer. The defendant told her that he and his brother were caring for a nearby home whose occupants were away on vacation. Because the victim was having difficulty remembering their names, the defendant told her that he worked at Smith and Wesson. He also showed her his plant identification card with his picture on it, and his brother informed her of his employer and his address and displayed his driver's license.

About 9:00 P.M. Maurice Cook indicated that he was out of cigarettes and suggested that the three walk to a convenience store located about a minute and a half away. The victim agreed. To reach the store, the trio proceeded along the street to a narrow path or trail located behind the project office. This path led down a hill through a wooded area to the rear of a well-lit service station adjacent to the convenience store. As they "walk[ed] towards the path" single file (with Maurice in front, the victim in the middle and the defendant in the rear), the victim "slipped * * * fell or something." She sat on the ground for a few seconds laughing when "Maurice turned around and jumped on me * * * and told me I was going to love it." After she screamed, Maurice covered her mouth with his hand, took off his belt and gave it to the defendant seated nearby. Maurice then scratched her with a stick or blunt object and said, "No blood, no blood." The defendant was overheard laughing and saying, "The bitch doesn't want to bleed, we'll make her bleed." Maurice then forcibly raped her. During the assault the victim lost consciousness. She awoke about 11:00 P.M. and went directly to her friends' home. The incident was subsequently reported to the police, and the Cooks were arrested. Maurice was indicted for rape and the defendant, in addition to the conspiracy indictment, was charged as an accessory to the rape.

1. A combination of two or more persons who seek by some concerted action to accomplish a criminal act may be punished as a conspiracy. It is essential to a conviction that the Commonwealth prove the existence of an agreement, because "[t]he gravamen of * * * conspiracy * * * is the unlawful agreement." * * * "It must [also] be shown that the defendant was aware of the objective of the conspiracy which was alleged." Proof of a conspiracy may rest entirely or mainly on circumstantial evidence, but "some record evidence" is not enough, and an acquittal must be ordered if any essential element of the crime is left to surmise, conjecture or guesswork.

We are of the opinion that the evidence, tested against the foregoing principles, was insufficient to establish a conspiracy. The circumstances under which the victim and the Cooks met and socialized were not indicative of a preconceived plan between the defendant and his brother to commit a sexual assault. Rather, the meeting and subsequent engagement were consistent with a chance social encounter common between young persons. The area where the group stayed prior to setting out for the store was used frequently as a gathering spot, and there was no evidence either that the Cooks attempted to conceal from others the fact that they were with the victim or that they consciously attempted to mislead her as to their identities. The evidence cuts directly against any such inference because of the special efforts made by the defendant and his brother to identify themselves by disclosing their names and places of employment, and by showing the victim their photographs. We do not think it plausible to infer that this conduct was an attempt by the Cooks to lull the victim into a false sense of security. Moreover, since all the conversation at the platform occurred in the victim's presence, the jury could not have properly inferred that a clandestine plan to commit an assault had been formulated during that period. While openness will not automatically sanitize a conspiracy, highly visible conduct has to be considered inconsistent with the shadowy environment which usually shrouds the crime. The purpose for leaving the area was on its face innocuous and was suggested by Maurice, not the defendant. While the route chosen was arguably suspicious, the evidence established that it also was selected by Maurice, not the defendant. There was evidence that the path provided a short, reasonably direct route to a gasoline station which was nearby, well-lighted, and visible from the crest of the hill. We do not think that the events up to the time the victim fell were sufficient to establish a criminal agreement or to warrant the jury in inferring the state of facts that the Commonwealth claims to have existed.

Nor was the prosecution's case strengthened by the circumstances surrounding the assault itself. There was no evidence that the defendant (or his brother for that matter) had anything to do with the victim's falling to the ground. The fact that Maurice's attack began immediately after the victim found herself in a compromising situation suggests spontaneity of action on his part rather than the purposeful execution of a predetermined plan. From that point on, the defendant's conduct fits the classic paradigm of an accomplice adding encouragement to a crime in progress. The fact that the defendant may have aided and abetted the crime does not * * * establish a conspiracy, particularly where the evidence shows that prior planning is not an inherent facet of the crime. "[N]either association with [a criminal] nor knowledge of illegal activity constitute proof of participation in a conspiracy."

In reaching our conclusion, we are mindful of the principle that proof of a tacit agreement to commit a crime may be enough to establish a conspiracy. But in this case it is just as reasonable to conclude that the defendant became implicated in the crime as an accomplice after it had commenced without any advance knowledge that it was to occur, as it is to infer that the minds of the parties had met in advance "understandingly, so as to bring about an intelligent and deliberate agreement to * * * commit the offense charged." "[W]hen the evidence tends to sustain either of two inconsistent propositions, neither * * * can be said to have been established by legitimate proof."

2. The remaining question raised by the Commonwealth's argument is whether the defendant can be convicted of conspiracy *solely* on the evidence tending to show his complicity as an accomplice in the commission of the substantive crime. We think on the evidence in this case such a conclusion would be unjustified.

Accomplice and conspiratorial liability are not synonymous, and one can be an accomplice aiding in the commission of a substantive offense without necessarily conspiring to commit it. The holdings which conceptually and practically separate the two types of criminal activity do so because of fundamental distinctions between them. As has already been discussed, the gist of conspiracy rests in the "agree[ment] [between the conspirators] to work in concert for the criminal or corrupt or unlawful purpose," and it is that agreement which constitutes the criminal act and which generally serves to manifest the requisite criminal intent. * * * Absent from the formulation of accomplice liability is the necessity of establishing an agreement or consensus in the same sense as those terms are used in describing the agreement or combination which hallmarks a conspiracy.[3] When a defendant is convicted of conspiring with others to commit a crime, the conviction stems from, and is designed to punish, the unlawful agreement which preexists commission of the substantive offense. This is why proof of the conspiracy typically involves circumstantial evidence aimed at establishing a consensus prior to the commission of the target offense. Execution of the crime thus represents performance of the agreement. But because the conspiracy for practical purposes is at least one step removed from the substantive offense, the offense does not substitute for the agreement and the factfinder's analysis of the conspiracy evidence is logically directed at ascertaining whether an underlying agreement exists. As the [Eighth] Circuit stated, in a different factual context: "To warrant a conviction for conspiracy * * * the evidence must disclose something further than participating in the offense which is the object of the conspiracy; there must be proof of the unlawful agreement, either express or implied, and participation with knowledge of the agreement." *Dickerson v. United States,* 18 F.2d 887, 893 (8th Cir.1927). * * * Implicit support for our conclusion is also contained in the following statement from *Commonwealth v. Stasiun,* 349 Mass. 38, 48, 206 N.E.2d 672 (1965): "[P]unishment [for conspiracy] is imposed for entering into the combination. This is not the same thing as participating in the substantive offense which was the object of the conspiracy." A contrary holding on the facts we are considering would confuse certain settled aspects of the law of conspiracy and would tend unnecessarily to expand its already elastic and pervasive definition by "blur[ring] the demarcation line between a conspiracy to commit an offense and the substantive offense which is the object of the conspiracy." * * * "[A]cts of aiding and abetting clearly make each actor a principal in the substantive offense * * * but cannot, without [more],[8] also make each other actor a principal

3. The Commonwealth's argument meshing the two concepts perhaps derives from misplaced reliance on Mr. Justice Holmes' famous epigram that a conspiracy is "a partnership in criminal purposes." *United States v. Kissel,* 218 U.S. 601, 608, 31 S.Ct. 124, 126, 54 L.Ed. 1168 (1910). Styling every joint venture crime as a type of partnership would automatically make each actor at the scene a member of a conspiracy. But a partnership contemplates the partners' arriving at an agreement before the partnership engages in its business. To avoid reasoning along such lines, the Model Penal Code rejected inclusion of "the analogy of partnership * * * in the formal definition [of conspiracy]" and instead rested "the core of the conspiracy idea * * * on the primordial conception of agreement." Model Penal Code, comments to § 5.03, at 116–117 (Proposed Official Draft 1962). * * *

8. Of course, a factfinder can consider and permissibly infer the existence of a conspiracy from the circumstances surrounding the commission of the crime. For example, the sophistication surrounding the execution of the Brinks' robbery (*Commonwealth v. Geagan,* 339 Mass. 487, 159 N.E.2d 870 [1959]), would warrant a conclusion that its perpetrators had conspired and prepared in advance to commit it. But there the facts establishing the "more" necessary to convict the accomplices of conspiracy consisted of the numerous incidental circumstances manifested at the

in the crime of conspiracy to commit such offense * * *." We conclude that in this case the evidence of the confederation at the scene was insufficient to warrant the defendant's conviction of conspiracy. * * *

NOTES AND QUESTIONS

1. Is *Cook* consistent with *Azim*?

2. In *Cook*, the court suggested that Dennis was an accomplice in the rape, but was not guilty of conspiracy to commit rape. In contrast, in *Pinkerton* (p. 780 supra), Daniel Pinkerton conspired with his brother, but was not an accomplice in the commission of the substantive tax offenses. We are reminded again, therefore, of the importance of not treating accomplice and conspiracy liability interchangeably.

As discussed in the next chapter, if *D1* commits crime X, and *D2* is determined to be an accomplice of *D1* in the commission of that crime, *D2* may be convicted of crime X as an accomplice, although crime X was committed by *D1*, rather than by *D2*. Therefore, consider this: Is there a way to convict a person for the crime of conspiracy by showing that, although she was not a co-conspirator, she was an accomplice in the crime of conspiracy? The answer is yes, but you need to be very careful in the analysis. Consider *Developments in the Law—Criminal Conspiracy*, 72 Harv. L. Rev. 920, 934–935 (1959):

> [A] verbal ambiguity * * * leads courts to deal with the crime of conspiracy as though it were a group rather than an act. If a "conspiracy" consists of the people who are working toward a proscribed object, and if one who aids and abets a substantive offense becomes liable as a principal thereto, then it follows that one who aids and abets these men in the attainment of their object becomes liable as a conspirator. * * * [T]his reasoning from a faulty premise * * * [is] difficult to discover since it is assumed rather than articulated * * *. But to aid and abet a crime it is necessary not merely to help the criminal, but to help him in the commission of the particular criminal offense. A person does not aid and abet a conspiracy by helping the "conspiracy" to commit a substantive offense, for the crime of conspiracy is separate from the offense which is its object. It is necessary to help the "conspiracy" in the commission of the crime of conspiracy, that is, in the commission of the act of agreement. Only then is it justifiable to dispense with the necessity of proving commission of the act of agreement by the defendant himself.

Can you suggest a set of facts in which *A* could be said to have aided in the commission of the crime of conspiracy by *B* and *C* to commit a bank robbery?

3. *Problem. D* owned a trucking business in Texas. *I*, a paid government informant, testified that *D* offered him $10,000 to commingle marijuana with a load of broccoli to be delivered to a buyer in North Carolina. *I* told Customs and Immigration Enforcement officers that the truck containing the marijua-

---

scene of the crime and elsewhere which demonstrated planning and pursuit of a prearranged systematic course of action. * * *

na would be located on *V*'s property on September 11, 2006. A search on that date, a search to which *D* consented, revealed 230 kilograms of marijuana hidden in the truck's sleeper compartment. *D* was prosecuted for conspiracy to possess marijuana with the intent to distribute. Other than the marijuana, the evidence against *D* was based on the testimony of *I*, who received $7,500 for his information prior to trial. Should *D* be convicted? United States v. Delgado, 672 F.3d 320 (5th Cir.2012) (en banc).

4. CONSPIRACY: BILATERAL OR UNILATERAL?

PEOPLE v. FOSTER

Supreme Court of Illinois, 1983.
99 Ill.2d 48, 75 Ill.Dec. 411, 457 N.E.2d 405.

UNDERWOOD, JUSTICE:

Following a jury trial * * * the defendant, James Foster, was convicted of conspiracy to commit robbery, and sentenced to an extended term of six years' imprisonment. * * *

On September 28, 1981, defendant initiated his plan to commit a robbery when he approached John Ragsdale in a Rantoul bar and asked Ragsdale if he was "interested in making some money." Defendant told Ragsdale of an elderly man, A.O. Hedrick, who kept many valuables in his possession. Although Ragsdale stated that he was interested in making money he did not believe defendant was serious until defendant returned to the bar the next day and discussed in detail his plan to rob Hedrick. In an effort to gather additional information, Ragsdale decided to feign agreement to defendant's plan but did not contact the police.

On October 1, defendant went to Ragsdale's residence to find out if Ragsdale was "ready to go." Since Ragsdale had not yet contacted the police he told defendant that he would not be ready until he found someone else to help them. Ragsdale informed the police of the planned robbery on October 3. Defendant and Ragsdale were met at Hedrick's residence the following day and arrested.

The appellate court determined that the conspiracy statute (Ill.Rev. Stat.1981, ch. 38, par. 8–2) required actual agreement between at least two persons to support a conspiracy conviction. Reasoning that Ragsdale never intended to agree to defendant's plan but merely feigned agreement, the court reversed defendant's conviction.

On appeal to this court the State argues that under the conspiracy statute it suffices if only one of the participants to the alleged conspiracy actually intends to agree to commit an offense. * * *

The question is whether the Illinois legislature, in amending the conspiracy statute in 1961, intended to adopt the unilateral theory of conspiracy. To support a conspiracy conviction under the unilateral theory only one of the alleged conspirators need intend to agree to the commission of an offense. Prior to the 1961 amendment the statute clearly encompassed the traditional, bilateral theory, requiring the actual agreement of at least two participants. The relevant portion of the former statute is as follows:

> "If any *two or more persons* conspire or *agree together* * * * to do any illegal act * * * they shall be deemed guilty of a conspiracy." (Emphasis added.)

The amended version of the statute provides:

> "*A person* commits conspiracy when, with intent that an offense be committed, *he agrees* with another to the commission of that offense." (Emphasis added.)

Since the statute is presently worded in terms of "a person" rather than "two or more persons" it is urged by the State that only one person need intend to agree to the commission of an offense. In support of its position the State compares the Illinois statute with the Model Penal Code conspiracy provision and the commentary thereto. The Model Penal Code provision is similar to section 8–2(a) in that it is also worded in terms of "a person":

> "*A person* is guilty of conspiracy with another person or persons to commit a crime if with the purpose of promoting or facilitating its commission *he*:
>
> (a) *agrees* with such other person or persons that they or one or more of them will engage in conduct which constitutes such crime or an attempt or solicitation to commit such crime * * *." (Emphasis added.) Model Penal Code sec. 5.03.

The commentary following section 5.03 expressly indicates the drafters' intent to adopt the unilateral theory of conspiracy. * * *

There is no question that the drafters of section 8–2(a) were aware of this provision since several references were made to the Model Penal Code in the committee comments to section 8–2. Consequently, the State reasons that the drafters would not have deleted the words "two or more persons" if they had intended to retain the bilateral theory. Similar reasoning was employed in *State v. Marian* (1980), 62 Ohio St.2d 250, 405 N.E.2d 267, and *State v. St. Christopher* (1975), 305 Minn. 226, 232 N.W.2d 798, where the courts were asked to interpret statutory provisions analogous to section 8–2(a). In each of those decisions it was determined that deletion of the words "two or more persons" from the State's conspiracy statute reflected a legislative intent to abandon the bilateral theory. The Ohio court, however, also relied to a considerable degree upon the absence from Ohio criminal law of a statute making solicitation to commit a crime an offense. Illinois does have such a statute.

While impressed with the logic of the State's interpretation of section 8–2(a), we are troubled by the committee's failure to explain the reason for deleting the words "two or more persons" from the statute. The committee comments to section 8–2 detail the several changes in the law of conspiracy that were intended by the 1961 amendment. The comments simply do not address the unilateral/bilateral issue. The State suggests that the new language was so clear on its face that it did not warrant additional discussion. We doubt, however, that the drafters could have intended what represents a rather profound change in the law of conspiracy without mentioning it in the comments to section 8–2. * * *

As earlier noted, Illinois does have a solicitation statute which embraces virtually every situation in which one could be convicted of conspiracy under the unilateral theory. Moreover, the penalties for solicitation and conspiracy are substantially similar. There would appear to have been little need for the legislature to adopt the unilateral theory of conspiracy in light of the existence of the solicitation statute. Even though the Model Penal Code also contains a separate solicitation offense and still provides for the unilateral theory, its commentary makes explicit its intent to do so. The absence of similar comments upon our statute seems difficult to explain if the intent was the same.

We cannot agree with the State's argument that section 8–2(b) of the statute supports a unilateral interpretation of section 8–2(a). Section 8–2(b) provides:

> "It shall not be a defense to conspiracy that the person or persons with whom the accused is alleged to have conspired: * * *

> (4) Has been acquitted, or

> (5) Lacked the capacity to commit an offense."

The State argues that subsections (4) and (5) focus on the culpability of only one of the conspirators and are therefore consistent with a legislative intent to adopt the unilateral theory. However, the committee comments clearly indicate that the limited purpose of those subsections is to avoid the recurrent problems inherent in conducting separate trials:

> "Previously, acquittal of all other conspirators absolved the remaining one, since, theoretically, there must be at least two guilty parties to a conspiracy. [Citation.] However, this rationale was rejected as being too technical and overlooking the realities of trials which involve differences in juries, contingent availability of witnesses, the varying ability of different prosecutors and defense attorneys, etc."

Additionally, if the drafters had intended to adopt the unilateral theory in section 8–2(a), it would have been unnecessary to include section 8–2(b) in the statute, since the provisions of section 8–2(b) are encompassed by the unilateral theory.

* * * We are also mindful of the rule of construction * * * which requires us to resolve statutory ambiguities in favor of criminal defendants.

For the above reasons we conclude that section 8–2(a) encompasses the bilateral theory of conspiracy. * * *

NOTES AND QUESTIONS

1. Many states approve of the Model Penal Code's unilateral definition of conspiracy. For example, in Miller v. State, 955 P.2d 892 (Wyo.1998), Miller was convicted of conspiracy to kidnap his victim, although the "co-conspirator," a man named Powell, served as a police informant at the time of the "agreement." The state supreme court explained why it believed that the unilateral version of conspiracy constituted "sound public policy":

> A person who believes he is conspiring with another to commit a crime is a danger to the public regardless of whether the other person in fact has agreed to commit the crime. As one text writer has expressed the proposition, "such an approach is justified in that a man who believes that he is conspiring and wishes to conspire to commit a crime has a guilty mind and has done all in his power to plot the commission of an unlawful purpose." Miller's case furnishes a textbook example of the justification for the unilateral approach. Miller's guilty mind was not diminished by the fact that Powell had made an agreement to serve as a law enforcement informant. It is true that Miller's chance of succeeding in kidnaping * * * under the circumstances was minimal, but Miller has "nonetheless engaged in conduct which provides unequivocal evidence of his firm purpose to commit a crime."

Some courts disapprove of the unilateral theory or, at least, see no need for it. United States v. Valigura, 50 M.J. 844 (A.Ct.Crim.App.1999):

> Two reasons have been given for making conspiratorial agreements illegal. One is to punish the special dangers inherent in group criminal activity. The second is to permit preventive steps against those who show a disposition to commit crime. The unilateral theory of conspiracy does not further the first purpose because when there is only a solo conspirator, there is perforce no "group" criminal activity. The increased danger is particularly nonexistent in a feigned conspiracy with a government agent who pretends agreement. There is no increased chance the criminal enterprise will succeed, no continuing criminal enterprise, and no greater difficulty of detection.
>
> The unilateral theory also does not further the second purpose beyond that which already exists in other multiple actor inchoate offenses, i.e., solicitation and attempted conspiracy. The punishable conduct in a unilateral conspiracy will almost always satisfy the elements of either solicitation or attempt[ed conspiracy]. The government will still be able to thwart the activity and punish the individual who attempts agreement with an undercover police officer. Thus, it is in the instant case. Although appellant dodges the conspiracy bullet, attempted conspiracy still finds its mark.

Who seems right?

2. *Foster* alludes to the "recurrent problems" that arise in bilateral conspiracy jurisdictions when separate trials of alleged conspirators are held. For example, in Commonwealth v. Byrd, 490 Pa. 544, 550–553, 417 A.2d 173, 176–177 (1980), Byrd and Smith, charged with conspiracy, were tried sepa-

rately. Byrd was convicted. Smith was later acquitted. Byrd then sought to overturn his conviction as a result of Smith's acquittal. In essence, his argument was that he cannot be guilty of conspiracy—an agreement by two or more persons—if the other person alleged to have participated in the conspiracy was found not guilty of the crime. The Pennsylvania Supreme Court rejected the claim:

> There is no doubt that the crime of conspiracy requires proof of more than a single participant. As Justice Cardozo once noted: "It is impossible in the nature of things for a man to conspire with himself." *Morrison v. California,* 291 U.S. 82, 92, 54 S.Ct. 281, 285, 78 L.Ed. 664 (1934). Nevertheless, such generalizations do not require that a valid conviction for conspiracy against one defendant must be held in limbo pending the outcome of the separate trial or trials of all alleged co-conspirators. Nor do they require that a valid conspiracy conviction must subsequently be nullified by the acquittal of the other or others charged.

> At the outset it is important to emphasize certain already well-established principles in this area. There is no doubt, for example, that one convicted of conspiracy is not entitled to relief simply because others charged have not yet been tried. That the prosecution has *nolle prossed* charges against one or all of the others indicted is equally insufficient to afford a single convicted conspirator any relief. So too, that the only other co-conspirators have been granted immunity and so cannot be tried does not bar conviction of the remaining defendant. And, indeed, it is established that where the other alleged co-conspirators are unapprehended, unindicted, dead, or even, in some instances, unknown, there is no basis to disturb a valid conviction for conspiracy. The only question still apparently open to any debate is whether an acquittal of all alleged co-conspirators should produce a different result. At least in the case, such as this, of a subsequent acquittal, we do not believe that it should.

> Admittedly, some authority * * * does assert that the acquittal of all but one conspirator requires the discharge of the remaining defendant. This rule, however, had its origins at a time when co-conspirators were jointly tried. In that circumstance a single jury would hear the evidence of conspiracy and, rightly, would not be permitted to find the evidence sufficient to prove a conspiracy involving only one of those charged. The acquittal rule that developed was thus clearly a rule of verdict consistency. * * * In the case of separate trials, however, this consistency rule loses much if not all of its force.

> An acquittal at any trial is never a guarantee that no crime has been committed. Rather it signifies only that the Commonwealth has not proved its case to the satisfaction of the jury. Thus in the present case, different verdicts may well have been due solely to the different composition of the two juries. Alternatively, the difference may have been due to a variety of other circumstances, including a difference in the proof offered at trial. * * * It is error to assume that the failure of a jury to convict one conspirator necessarily invalidates the Commonwealth's verdict, won from a different jury, at a separate trial.

As alluded to in *Byrd*, the general rule in bilateral conspiracy jurisdictions has been that a conviction of a single conspirator cannot stand if the alleged co-conspirators are acquitted *at the same trial*. Even this rule is breaking down. For example, in People v. Palmer, 24 Cal.4th 856, 15 P.3d 234, 103 Cal.Rptr.2d 13 (2001), in a two-person conspiracy trial, *X*, a 15–year old youth, was acquitted, while *Y*, a 29–year–old man, was convicted of conspiracy to murder. Although the court conceded that the acquittal rule "has deep common law roots," it declared it "a vestige of the past with no continuing vitality." It explained:

> Our criminal justice system, which permits a conviction only if the jury unanimously finds beyond a reasonable doubt that a defendant is guilty of the particular charge, gives the defendant the benefit of the doubt. Moreover, a jury clearly has the unreviewable *power,* if not the right, to acquit whatever the evidence. An inevitable result of this system, and one that society accepts in its quest to avoid convicting the innocent, is that some criminal defendants who are guilty will be found not guilty. This circumstance does not, however, mean that if one person receives lenient treatment from the system, all must. "[I]t is always possible for a jury to exercise lenity and acquit some of the defendants while convicting others who are in fact no more guilty, and when this happens the convicted defendants have no remedy. Such incongruities are built into the American system of criminal justice and can have no weight in our decision whether to reverse the denial of a new trial to the present defendants." Here, for example, [*X*]'s jury may have shown sympathy or lenience because he was 15 years old at the time of the crimes. The * * * jury may have felt no such sympathy for the 29 year old [*Y*]. [*Y*]'s verdict must stand or fall on its own merit, not in comparison to [*X*]'s.

5. SCOPE OF AN AGREEMENT: PARTY AND OBJECT DIMENSIONS

AMERICAN LAW INSTITUTE, MODEL PENAL CODE AND COMMENTARIES, COMMENT TO § 5.03

(1985), 422–424

* * * Much of the most perplexing litigation in conspiracy has been concerned less with the essential elements of the offense than with the scope to be accorded to a combination, i.e., the singleness or multiplicity of the conspiratorial relationships in a large, complex, and sprawling network of crime. The question here differs from that discussed above in that in most of these cases it is clear that each defendant has committed or conspired to commit one or more crimes; the question now is, to what extent is he a conspirator with each of the persons involved in the larger criminal network to commit the crimes that are their objects.

A narcotics operation may involve smugglers, distributors, and many retail sellers and may result in numerous instances of the commission of different types of crimes, as, for example, importing, possessing, and selling the narcotics. A vice ring may involve an overlord, lesser officers, and numerous runners and prostitutes; it may comprehend countless instances of the commission of such crimes as prostitution, placing a female in a house of prostitution, and receiving money from her earnings. Has a retailer conspired with the smugglers to import the narcotics? Has a prostitute conspired with the leaders of the vice ring to commit the acts of prostitution of each other prostitute who is controlled by the ring?

The inquiry may be crucial for a number of purposes. These include not only defining each defendant's liability, but also the propriety of joint prosecution, admissibility against a defendant of the hearsay acts and declarations of others, questions of multiple prosecution or conviction and double jeopardy, satisfaction of the overt act requirement or statutes of limitation, or rules of jurisdiction and venue, and possibly liability for substantive crimes executed pursuant to the conspiracy. The scope problem is thus central to the concern of courts and commentators about the use of conspiracy, a concern based on the conflict between the need for effective means of prosecuting large criminal organizations, and the dangers of prejudice to individual defendants.

KILGORE v. STATE

Supreme Court of Georgia, 1983.
251 Ga. 291, 305 S.E.2d 82.

BELL, JUSTICE.

Kilgore was convicted * * * for the murder of Roger Norman and was given a life sentence. He appeals.

In the early morning hours of July 8, 1981, the victim, Roger Norman, was traveling south on Interstate 59 (I–59) * * * to his home in Alabama. While driving, he was shot in the head and killed. * * *

At trial, the state introduced evidence of a conspiracy to kill Roger Norman. In particular, it introduced evidence of three previous attempts on Norman's life. As to the first attempt, David Oldaker testified that on February 6, 1981 Greg Benton, his cousin, asked him to go with him to Menton, Alabama, Norman's home. He testified that the purpose of the trip was to kill Norman and that Benton told him a crippled man named Tom who sold pharmaceuticals and lived in Soddy–Daisy, Tennessee, was the man who wanted Norman killed. This testimony was admitted over the hearsay objection of defense counsel. Tom Carden, who died on July 16, 1981, was Norman's brother in law and lived in Soddy–Daisy. He was a paraplegic. Oldaker and Benton went to Norman's home, where they unsuccessfully attempted to kill him. Kilgore was in no way implicated in this attempt.

Evidence did specifically connect Kilgore with the second attempt. Ed Williams, an employee of a truck stop located just off the interstate near Trenton, Georgia, testified that on the evening of June 8, 1981 he saw two cars traveling close to each other while crossing a bridge over I–59; that he heard sounds like a car backfiring; and that Norman's car pulled into the truck stop while the other car turned north on I–59. Norman, who had been on his way home from work, had been shot in the upper back. Sheriff Steele of Dade County testified that based on what Norman told him, he posted a lookout for a 1962 or 1963 Rambler with a dark bottom, white top, and Tennessee tags.

Constance Chambers, Kilgore's ex-girlfriend who lived with him from April through September of 1981, testified that on June 8, 1981, Kilgore and his cousin, Lee Berry, borrowed her 1964 Rambler. It had a dark green body, white top, and Tennessee tags. She testified that Kilgore returned to her apartment around 4:00 a.m. the next morning and told her they had killed a man near Trenton, Georgia. Later that day, Chambers testified that Kilgore received a phone call from Tom Carden, during which she heard Kilgore say "apparently we didn't get him" * * *. * * *

Concerning the circumstances leading up to Norman's death on July 8, 1981, Chambers' testimony shows the continuation of a conspiracy to kill Norman. She testified that on June 15, 1981 Kilgore received a phone call from Carden, during which she heard Kilgore tell Carden he needed more money to obtain a faster car and another man to help him. Shortly thereafter, Kilgore went to Carden's and picked up fifteen hundred dollars. Chambers also testified that on July 5, 1981 Kilgore received another call from Carden, after which she and Kilgore drove to Carden's trailer where Kilgore took fifteen thousand dollars from the mailbox. According to her testimony, they left Carden's and drove to a V.F.W. post where they met a friend of Kilgore's, Bob Price. She testified that Kilgore took a rifle out of his car, put it in Price's van, and left with him, while she drove home alone. * * *

Chambers testified that on July 7, 1981, the day preceding the murder, Kilgore and Price left her apartment about 6:00 p.m., each in a separate vehicle but driving in the same direction. She did not see Kilgore until noon the next day, July 8, when, she testified, he returned driving a blue Lincoln. * * *

Kilgore and Chambers spent several days in Florida, and Chambers testified that on the way home Kilgore told her that "all mighty hell is going to break loose. * * * we killed a man"; that they [he and Price] had killed him on I–59 * * *. * * *

Kilgore appeals and enumerates fifty-one errors. * * *

Kilgore apparently contends that the state did not prove he actually committed the murder, and that consequently, it must have been proceeding on the theory that his guilt was based upon a conspiracy; yet, he argues, the state did not prove a conspiracy because it did not prove an overt act occurred in Georgia. * * * However, * * * the conspiracy was merely an evidentiary tool used by the state to help prove Kilgore guilty of the murder of Norman. In fact, Kilgore could not have been tried for conspiracy since the object of the conspiracy was completed.[j] * * *

j. Under Georgia law, the crime of conspiracy merged into the completed offense.

He next argues that the trial court erred in admitting over objection the hearsay testimony of David Oldaker that Benton told him that the man who wanted Norman killed was a crippled man named Tom who sold pharmaceuticals and lived in a trailer in Soddy–Daisy, Tennessee. This testimony was the only evidence connecting Tom Carden to the February 1981 attempt. For the reasons which follow, we find that this hearsay testimony was inadmissible.

The testimony could only be admissible under the exception to the hearsay rule which provides that the out-of-court statements of one conspirator are admissible against all conspirators. Therefore, this testimony was only admissible if Oldaker, Benton, and Kilgore were co-conspirators.

To have a conspiracy, there must be an agreement between two or more persons to commit a crime. Here, there is no question that the evidence shows that Oldaker and Benton and Carden were co-conspirators in their attempt to kill Norman, and that Kilgore and Price and Carden were co-conspirators in the murder of Norman, but the question is whether Kilgore, who did not know of or communicate with Oldaker and Benton, and Oldaker and Benton, who likewise did not know of or communicate with Kilgore, can be considered to have agreed to and become co-conspirators in the murder of Norman. We find that they cannot.

The type of agreement necessary to form a conspiracy is not the "meeting of the minds" necessary to form a contract and may be a "mere tacit understanding between two or more people that they will pursue a particular criminal objective." Also, "there need not be any written statement or even a speaking of words which expressly communicates agreement. It is possible for various persons to be parties to a single agreement (and thus one conspiracy) even though they do not know the identity of one another, and even though they are not all aware of the details of the plan of operation."

However, limitations have been imposed upon the concept that persons who do not know each other can "agree" to commit a crime. An agreement, and thus one conspiracy, is more likely to be inferred in what have been termed "chain" conspiracies, "usually involving the distribution of narcotics or other contraband, in which there is successive communication or cooperation...." Because the parties should know by the large, ongoing nature of the conspiracy that the other members exist, and because the various "links" have a community of interest in that the success of one member's part is dependent upon the success of the whole enterprise, courts have treated links as co-conspirators despite a lack of communication or contact with one another. *United States v. Bruno*, 105 F.2d 921, 922 (2d Cir.1939), rev'd on other grounds, 308 U.S. 287, 60 S.Ct. 198, 84 L.Ed. 257 (1939). In *Bruno*, because of these considerations the court found but one conspiracy among many smugglers, middlemen, and retailers in a drug smuggling operation.

The "chain" conspiracy contrasts with the "wheel" conspiracy in which there is usually a "hub," or common source of the conspiracy, who deals individually with different persons, "spokes," who do not know each other. It is more difficult to infer an agreement among these spokes than among the links of a "chain" conspiracy because they are less likely to have a community of interest or reason to know of each other's existence since one spoke's success is usually not dependent on the other spokes' success, but instead on his dealings with the hub. This is the type of conspiracy, if any, with which we deal in this case. *Kotteakos v. United States,* [328 U.S. 750, 66 S.Ct. 1239, 90 L.Ed. 1557 (1946),] is the classic case of a "wheel" conspiracy. There, Brown, the hub, agreed with various persons, the spokes, on an individual basis to fraudulently procure loans for them for a 5% commission. Because most of the spokes had no connection with and had not aided each other, the court found that there was no common purpose or interest among the spokes and, thus, that they were not co-conspirators. * * *

In the instant case, we conclude that Kilgore was not a co-conspirator of Benton and Oldaker. Here, there was no community of interests between Benton and Oldaker on the one hand and Kilgore on the other. The success of Benton's and Oldaker's attempt to kill Norman was not dependent in any way on Kilgore. Likewise, the success of Kilgore's attempt to kill Norman was not aided by Oldaker and Benton, especially considering that they did not assist in further efforts to kill Norman.

In addition, Benton and Oldaker, as one spoke, and Kilgore, as another or replacement spoke, had no knowledge of and no reason to know of each other such that an agreement can be inferred between them. There was no reason for Kilgore to know of the previous attempt on Norman's life, as his success was not dependent on it. Likewise, Oldaker and Benton had no reason to know of another spoke. It could be argued that Oldaker and Benton should have known that if they failed Carden would find another spoke, and that, therefore, they can be deemed to have "agreed" with this spoke. However, we find this reasoning to be too speculative a ground on which to infer such an agreement.

For the above reasons, we find that Kilgore and Oldaker and Benton were not co-conspirators. Consequently, it was error to admit the hearsay testimony of Oldaker. * * *

Notes and Questions

1. People v. Macklowitz, 135 Misc.2d 232, 514 N.Y.S.2d 883 (1987):

    Numerous labels have been used in an effort to categorize different types of conspiracies. Chains, links, wheels, hubs and spokes are just a few of the terms utilized where there are several layers of actors involved with various, albeit related, roles and objectives. The most common distinction made is between wheel conspiracies and chain conspiracies. A wheel conspiracy involves an individual (or small group)—the hub, who transacts illegal dealings with the various other individuals—the spokes. The most common evidentiary issue in a wheel conspiracy is whether the separate transactions between the hub and individual spokes can be merged to form a single conspiracy.

In contrast, the chain conspiracy usually involves several layers of personnel dealing with a single subject matter, as opposed to a specific person. Drug trafficking is often cited as a classic example of a chain conspiracy inasmuch as it is characterized by manufacturing links, wholesaling links and retailing links. A single conspiracy can be proven if each link knew or must have known of the other links in the chain, and if each defendant intended to join and aid the larger enterprise. * * *

This structural analysis is not without confusion, as some conspiracies may be classified as chain/spoke combinations. For example, in narcotics trafficking, the links at either end might be comprised of a number of persons " * * * who may have no reason to know that others are performing a role similar to theirs—in other words the extreme links of a chain conspiracy may have elements of the spoke conspiracy."

Perhaps a more accurate way to visualize a complex conspiracy case would be to view it as a three-dimensional organic chemistry molecule with each part interacting continuously with another thereby forming and adhering to the whole, for a common purpose.

2. In *Kilgore,* according to the prosecutor's theory of the case, who were the parties to the conspiracy to kill Norman? Structurally, what would the conspiracy look like? What does the conspiracy look like under the court's interpretation of the facts?

3. In United States v. Bruno, 105 F.2d 921 (2d Cir.1939) (cited in *Kilgore*), Bruno was indicted with 87 others for conspiracy to import, sell and possess narcotics. The government proved that various members of the conspiracy smuggled narcotics into the port of New York, that these smugglers received compensation for the narcotics from middlemen, who in turn sold the drugs to retailers in New York and to a retail group working the Texas–Louisiana region. In turn, the retailers dispensed the drugs on the street or distributed them to smaller-level peddlers. The evidence did not disclose any cooperation or communication between the smugglers and the retailers; however, the smugglers were aware that the middlemen with whom they dealt sold to retailers, and the retailers knew that the middlemen were buying the drugs from importers. Is this a single wheel conspiracy, a single chain conspiracy, or something else?

4. In Kotteakos v. United States, 328 U.S. 750, 66 S.Ct. 1239, 90 L.Ed. 1557 (1946), also cited in *Kilgore,* the indictment charged a single 32–person conspiracy, in which it was alleged that Brown, the key figure in the scheme, obtained federal loans for at least eight sets of persons by assisting them in making false representations in their loan applications. Apparently, none of Brown's customers were aware of his arrangements with the others.

As the Supreme Court looked at the evidence, the Government proved the existence of a hub with spokes: Brown was at the hub, with eight spokes emanating outward. As there was no rim connecting the spokes, there was no wheel conspiracy. Under this interpretation, Brown should have been charged with at least eight counts of conspiracy, based on each fraudulent loan application.

Why do you think the prosecutor sought to treat the events as a single conspiracy, rather than as eight separate agreements? What additional facts, if proven, would have established a single wheel conspiracy?

5. United States v. McDermott, 245 F.3d 133 (2d Cir.2001):

The present prosecution arose out of a triangulated love affair involving the president of a prominent investment bank, a pornographic film star and a New Jersey businessman.

Until May 1999, McDermott was the president, CEO and Chairman of Keefe Bruyette & Woods, an investment bank headquartered in New York City that specializes in mergers and acquisitions in the banking industry. Around 1996, McDermott began having an extramarital affair with Kathryn Gannon. Gannon was an adult film star and an alleged prostitute who performed using the stage name "Marylin Star." During the course of their affair, McDermott made numerous stock recommendations to Gannon. Unbeknownst to McDermott, Gannon was simultaneously having an affair with Anthony Pomponio and passing these recommendations to him. Although neither Gannon nor Pomponio had extensive training or expertise in securities trading, together they earned around $170,000 in profits during the period relevant to this case.

The government indicted McDermott, Gannon and Pomponio for conspiracy to commit insider trading and for insider trading on the theory that McDermott's recommendations to Gannon were based on non-public, material information.

Based on the preceding information, should this three-person single conspiracy charge hold up? If not, what should the prosecutor have charged in regard to conspiracy?

6. Look again at the facts in *Anderson v. Superior Court*, as set out on p. 782, Note 3. How would you characterize the shape of the conspiracy according to the prosecutor's theory of the case? Based on the materials you have read, what do you believe is the correct way to characterize the situation: who conspired with whom to do what?

BRAVERMAN v. UNITED STATES

Supreme Court of the United States, 1942.
317 U.S. 49, 63 S.Ct. 99, 87 L.Ed. 23.

Mr. CHIEF JUSTICE STONE delivered the opinion of the Court. * * *

Petitioners were indicted, with others, on seven counts, each charging a conspiracy to violate a separate and distinct internal revenue law of the United States.[1] On the trial there was evidence from which the jury could

---

1. The seven counts respectively charged them with conspiracy, in violation of § 37 of the Criminal Code, unlawfully (1) to carry on the business of wholesale and retail liquor dealers without having the special occupational tax stamps required by statute, 26 U.S.C.A. Int.Rev.Code § 3253; (2) to possess distilled spirits, the immediate containers of which did not have stamps

have found that for a considerable period of time petitioners, with others, collaborated in the illicit manufacture, transportation, and distribution of distilled spirits involving the violations of statutes mentioned in the several counts of the indictment. At the close of the trial petitioners renewed a motion which they had made at the beginning to require the Government to elect one of the seven counts of the indictment upon which to proceed, contending that the proof could not and did not establish more than one agreement. In response the Government's attorney took the position that the seven counts of the indictment charged as distinct offenses the several illegal objects of one continuing conspiracy, that if the jury found such a conspiracy it might find the defendants guilty of as many offenses as it had illegal objects, and that each such offense the two-year statutory penalty could be imposed.

The trial judge submitted the case to the jury on that theory. The jury returned a general verdict finding petitioners "guilty as charged," and the court sentenced each to eight years' imprisonment. On appeal the Court of Appeals for the Sixth Circuit affirmed * * *. It found that "From the evidence may be readily deduced a common design of appellant and others, followed by concerted action" to commit the several unlawful acts specified in the several counts of the indictment. It concluded that the fact that the conspiracy was "a general one to violate all laws repressive of its consummation does not gainsay the separate identity of each of the seven conspiracies." * * *

Both courts below recognized that a single agreement to commit an offense does not become several conspiracies because it continues over a period of time, and that there may be such a single continuing agreement to commit several offenses. But they thought that in the latter case each contemplated offense renders the agreement punishable as a separate conspiracy.

The question whether a single agreement to commit acts in violation of several penal statutes is to be punished as one or several conspiracies is raised on the present record, not by the construction of the indictment, but by the Government's concession at the trial and here, reflected in the charge to the jury, that only a single agreement to commit the offenses alleged was proven. Where each of the counts of an indictment alleges a conspiracy to violate a different penal statute it may be proper to conclude, in the absence of a bill of exceptions bringing up the evidence, that several conspiracies are charged rather than one, and that the conviction is for each. But it is a different matter to hold, as the court below appears

affixed denoting the quantity of the distilled spirits which they contained and evidencing payment of all Internal Revenue taxes imposed on such spirits, 26 U.S.C.A. Int.Rev.Code § 2803; (3) to transport quantities of distilled spirits, the immediate containers of which did not have affixed the required stamps, 26 U.S.C.A. Int.Rev.Code § 2803; (4) to carry on the business of distillers without having given bonds as required by law, 26 U.S.C.A. Int.Rev.Code § 2833; (5) to remove, deposit and conceal distilled spirits in respect whereof a tax is imposed by law, with intent to defraud the United States of such tax, 26 U.S.C.A. Int.Rev.Code § 3321; (6) to possess unregistered stills and distilling apparatus, 26 U.S.C.A. Int.Rev.Code § 2810; and (7) to make and ferment mash, fit for distillation, on unauthorized premises, 26 U.S.C.A. Int.Rev.Code § 2834.

to have done in this case, that even though a single agreement is entered into, the conspirators are guilty of as many offenses as the agreement has criminal objects.

The gist of the crime of conspiracy as defined by the statute is the agreement or confederation of the conspirators to commit one or more unlawful acts * * *.

For when a single agreement to commit one or more substantive crimes is evidenced by an overt act, as the statute requires, the precise nature and extent of the conspiracy must be determined by reference to the agreement which embraces and defines its objects. Whether the object of a single agreement is to commit one or many crimes, it is in either case that agreement which constitutes the conspiracy which the statute punishes. The one agreement cannot be taken to be several agreements and hence several conspiracies because it envisages the violation of several statutes rather than one. * * *

NOTES AND QUESTIONS

1. In Albernaz v. United States, 450 U.S. 333, 101 S.Ct. 1137, 67 L.Ed.2d 275 (1981), the defendants were convicted of violations of two drug conspiracy statutes, 21 U.S.C. § 963 (1988) (conspiracy to import illegal narcotics), and 21 U.S.C. § 846 (1988) (conspiracy to distribute illegal narcotics). The judge imposed consecutive sentences on each count.

The Supreme Court held that the defendants could be convicted and punished under both statutes, even though the Government did not prove the existence of separate conspiratorial agreements to import and to distribute the drugs. The Court reasoned that, in light of the separate conspiracy statutes, Congress intended to permit imposition of separate penalties for violations of the two offenses. The Court distinguished *Braverman* on the ground that the defendants in that case were charged under a general conspiracy statute.

2. *Problem.* Terry and Luis murder Carol on January 1, murder Daniel on January 2, and rob and murder Elaine on January 3. Assuming that they acted conspiratorially, of how many counts of conspiracy are they guilty under *Braverman*?

3. *Model Penal Code.* The Code's method of determining the parties to, and objects of, a conspiracy does not track the common law, in part because of its unilateral view of conspiracy. As the Commentary explains:

The combined operation of Subsections (1), (2), and (3) is relied upon to delineate the identity and scope of a conspiracy. All three provisions focus on the culpability of the individual actor. Subsections (1) and (2) limit the scope of his conspiracy both in terms of its criminal objectives, to those crimes that he had the purpose of promoting or facilitating, and in terms of parties, to those with whom he agreed, except when the same crime that he conspired to commit is, to his knowledge, also the object of a conspiracy between one of his co-conspirators and another person or persons. Subsection (3) provides that his conspiracy is a single one despite a multiplicity of criminal objectives, as long as such crimes are the object of the same agreement or continuous conspiratorial relationship.

American Law Institute, Model Penal Code and Commentaries, Comment to § 5.03 at 425 (1985).

According to the Model Penal Code, of how many counts of conspiracy are Terry and Luis (Note 2) guilty?

6. DEFENSES

IANNELLI v. UNITED STATES

Supreme Court of the United States, 1975.
420 U.S. 770, 95 S.Ct. 1284, 43 L.Ed.2d 616.

MR. JUSTICE POWELL delivered the opinion of the Court.

This case requires the Court to consider Wharton's Rule, a doctrine of criminal law enunciating an exception to the general principle that a conspiracy and the substantive offense that is its immediate end are discrete crimes for which separate sanctions may be imposed.

I

Petitioners were tried under a six-count indictment alleging a variety of federal gambling offenses. Each of the eight petitioners, along with seven unindicted coconspirators and six codefendants, was charged, *inter alia,* with conspiring to violate and violating 18 U.S.C. § 1955, a federal gambling statute making it a crime for five or more persons to conduct, finance, manage, supervise, direct, or own a gambling business prohibited by state law. Each petitioner was convicted of both offenses, and each was sentenced under both the substantive and conspiracy counts. The Court of Appeals for the Third Circuit affirmed, finding that a recognized exception to Wharton's Rule permitted prosecution and punishment for both offenses. * * * For the reasons now to be stated, we affirm.

II

Wharton's Rule owes its name to Francis Wharton, whose treatise on criminal law identified the doctrine and its fundamental rationale:

"When to the idea of an offense plurality of agents is logically necessary, conspiracy, which assumes the voluntary accession of a person to a crime of such a character that it is aggravated by a plurality of agents, cannot be maintained. * * * In other words, when the law says, 'a combination between two persons to effect a particular end shall be called, if the end be effected, by a certain name,' it is not lawful for the prosecution to call it by some other name; and when the law says, such an offense—*e.g.,* adultery—shall have a certain punishment, it is not lawful for the prosecution to evade this limitation by indicting the offense as conspiracy." 2 F. Wharton,

Criminal Law § 1604, p. 1862 (12th ed. 1932).[5]

The Rule has been applied by numerous courts, state and federal alike. It also has been recognized by this Court, although we have had no previous occasion carefully to analyze its justification and proper role in federal law.

The classic formulation of Wharton's Rule requires that the conspiracy indictment be dismissed before trial. * * * Federal courts earlier adhered to this literal interpretation and thus sustained demurrers to conspiracy indictments. More recently, however, some federal courts have differed over whether Wharton's Rule requires initial dismissal of the conspiracy indictment. * * * In this case, and in United States v. Kohne, 347 F.Supp. 1178, 1186 (W.D.Pa.1972), * * * the courts held that the Rule's purposes can be served equally effectively by permitting the prosecution to charge both offenses and instructing the jury that a conviction for the substantive offense necessarily precludes conviction for the conspiracy.

Federal courts likewise have disagreed as to the proper application of the recognized "third-party exception," which renders Wharton's Rule inapplicable when the conspiracy involves the cooperation of a greater number of persons than is required for commission of the substantive offense. In the present case, the Third Circuit concluded that the third-party exception permitted prosecution because the conspiracy involved more than the five persons required to commit the substantive offense * * *. The Seventh Circuit reached the opposite result, however, reasoning that since § 1955 also covers gambling activities involving more than five persons, the third-party exception is inapplicable.

The Courts of Appeals are at odds even over the fundamental question whether Wharton's Rule ever applies to a charge for conspiracy to violate § 1955. * * *

As this brief description indicates, the history of the application of Wharton's Rule to charges for conspiracy to violate § 1955 fully supports the Fourth Circuit's observation that "rather than being a rule, [it] is a concept, the confines of which have been delineated in widely diverse fashion by the courts." With this diversity of views in mind, we turn to an examination of the history and purposes of the Rule.

III

A

Traditionally the law has considered conspiracy and the completed substantive offense to be separate crimes. Conspiracy is an inchoate offense, the essence of which is an agreement to commit an unlawful act.

---

5. The current edition of Wharton's treatise states the Rule more simply:

"An agreement by two persons to commit a particular crime cannot be prosecuted as a conspiracy when the crime is of such a nature as to necessarily require the participation of two persons for its commission." 1 R. Anderson, Wharton's Criminal Law and Procedure § 89, p. 191 (1957).

Unlike some crimes * * * the conspiracy to commit an offense and the subsequent commission of that crime normally do not merge into a single punishable act. Thus, it is well recognized that in most cases separate sentences can be imposed for the conspiracy to do an act and for the subsequent accomplishment of that end. Indeed, the Court has even held that the conspiracy can be punished more harshly than the accomplishment of its purpose.

The consistent rationale of this long line of decisions rests on the very nature of the crime of conspiracy. This Court repeatedly has recognized that a conspiracy poses distinct dangers quite apart from those of the substantive offense.

"This settled principle derives from the reason of things in dealing with socially reprehensible conduct: collective criminal agreement—partnership in crime—presents a greater potential threat to the public than individual delicts. * * * "

As Mr. Justice Jackson, no friend of the law of conspiracy, see Krulewitch v. United States, 336 U.S. 440, 445, 69 S.Ct. 716, 719, 93 L.Ed. 790 (1949), observed: "The basic rationale of the law of conspiracy is that a conspiracy may be an evil in itself, independently of any other evil it seeks to accomplish."

B

The historical difference between the conspiracy and its end has led this Court consistently to attribute to Congress "a tacit purpose—in the absence of any inconsistent expression—to maintain a long-established distinction between offenses essentially different,—a distinction whose practical importance in the criminal law is not easily overestimated." Wharton's Rule announces an exception to this general principle. * * *

Wharton's Rule first emerged at a time when the contours of the law of conspiracy were in the process of active formulation. The general question whether the conspiracy merged into the completed felony offense remained for some time a matter of uncertain resolution. That issue is now settled, however, and the Rule currently stands as an exception to the general principle that a conspiracy and the substantive offense that is its immediate end do not merge upon proof of the latter. If the Rule is to serve a rational purpose in the context of the modern law of conspiracy, its role must be more precisely identified.

C

This Court's prior decisions indicate that the broadly formulated Wharton's Rule * * * has current vitality only as a judicial presumption, to be applied in the absence of legislative intent to the contrary. The classic Wharton's Rule offenses—adultery, incest, bigamy, duelling—are crimes that are characterized by the general congruence of the agreement and the completed substantive offense. The parties to the agreement are the only persons who participate in commission of the substantive offense,[15] and the immediate consequences of the crime rest on the parties themselves rather than on society at large. Finally, the agreement that attends the substantive offense does not appear likely to pose the distinct kinds of threats to society that the law of conspiracy seeks to avert. It cannot, for example, readily be assumed that an agreement to commit an offense of this nature will produce agreements to engage in a more general pattern of criminal conduct.

The conduct proscribed by § 1955 is significantly different from the offenses to which the Rule traditionally has been applied. Unlike the consequences of the classic Wharton's Rule offenses, the harm attendant upon the commission of the substantive offense is not restricted to the parties to the agreement. Large-scale gambling activities seek to elicit the participation of additional persons—the bettors—who are parties neither to the conspiracy nor to the substantive offense that results from it. Moreover, the parties prosecuted for the conspiracy need not be the same persons who are prosecuted for commission of the substantive offense. An endeavor as complex as a large-scale gambling enterprise might involve persons who have played appreciably different roles, and whose level of culpability varies significantly. It might, therefore, be appropriate to prosecute the owners and organizers of large-scale gambling operations both for the conspiracy and for the substantive offense but to prosecute the lesser participants only for the substantive offense. Nor can it fairly be maintained that agreements to enter into large-scale gambling activities are not likely to generate additional agreements to engage in other criminal endeavors. * * * [T]he legislative history of § 1955 provides documented testimony to the contrary.

Wharton's Rule applies only to offenses that *require* concerted criminal activity, a plurality of criminal agents. In such cases, a closer relationship exists between the conspiracy and the substantive offense because *both* require collective criminal activity. The substantive offense therefore presents some of the same threats that the law of conspiracy normally is thought to guard against, and it cannot automatically be assumed that the Legislature intended the conspiracy and the substantive offense to remain as discrete crimes upon consummation of the latter. Thus, absent legislative intent to the contrary, the Rule supports a presumption that the two merge when the substantive offense is proved.

---

15. An exception to the Rule generally is thought to apply in the case in which the conspiracy involves more persons than are required for commission of the substantive offense. For example, while the two persons who commit adultery cannot normally be prosecuted both for that offense and for conspiracy to commit it, the third-party exception would permit the conspiracy charge where a "matchmaker"—the third party—had conspired with the principals to encourage commission of the substantive offense. The rationale supporting this exception appears to be that the addition of a third party enhances the dangers presented by the crime. Thus, it is thought that the legislature would not have intended to preclude punishment for a combination of greater dimension than that required to commit the substantive offense.

Our determination that Congress authorized prosecution and conviction for both offenses in all cases, see Part IV, *infra,* makes it unnecessary to decide whether the exception to Wharton's Rule could properly be applied to conspiracies to violate § 1955 involving more than five persons. * * *

3d party exception

But a legal principle commands less respect when extended beyond the logic that supports it. In this case, the significant differences in characteristics and consequences of the kinds of offenses that gave rise to Wharton's Rule and the activities proscribed by § 1955 counsel against attributing significant weight to the presumption the Rule erects. More important, * * * the Rule * * * must defer to a discernible legislative judgment. We turn now to that inquiry.

IV

The basic purpose of the Organized Crime Control Act of 1970 was "to seek the eradication of organized crime in the United States by strengthening the legal tools in the evidence-gathering process, by establishing new penal prohibitions, and by providing enhanced sanctions and new remedies to deal with the unlawful activities of those engaged in organized crime." The content of the Act reflects the dedication with which the Legislature pursued this purpose. * * *

Major gambling activities were a principal focus of congressional concern. Large-scale gambling activities were seen to be both a substantive evil and a source of funds for other criminal conduct. * * *

* * * We conclude, therefore, that the history and structure of the Organized Crime Control Act of 1970 manifest a clear and mistakable legislative judgment that more than outweighs any presumption of merger between the conspiracy to violate § 1955 and the consummation of that substantive offense. * * *

NOTES AND QUESTIONS

1. In jurisdictions that still apply Wharton's Rule, it is typically only invoked in cases in which the target offense of the conspiracy has been committed or attempted; thus, the rule only serves to require merger of the conspiracy into the completed or attempted offense. However, the rule as originally announced by Wharton also barred prosecution of conspiracies in which the target offense was neither committed nor attempted. Is either version of Wharton's Rule sensible?

2. Does Wharton's Rule apply in the following cases? (Assume that the criminal object of the conspiracy was committed by the parties.)

A. Conspiracy by D1 to "barter, exchange, or offer" an illegal narcotic to D2. State v. Cavanaugh, 23 Conn.App. 667, 583 A.2d 1311 (1990). What about conspiracy by D3 to sell an illegal drug to D4? Or, conspiracy to "possess a controlled substance with intent to deliver"? Johnson v. State, 587 A.2d 444 (Del.1991).

B. D5 is on trial for several federal offenses. He persuades D6 (his girlfriend) to testify falsely on his behalf under oath, which she does. Thereafter, D5 is charged with conspiracy to suborn perjury and subornation of perjury. "Whoever procures another to commit any perjury is guilty of subornation of perjury" under 18 U.S.C. § 1622. A conviction under § 1622 requires that the person suborned actually commit perjury. Is D5's conviction for conspiracy to suborn perjury barred under Wharton's rule? See United 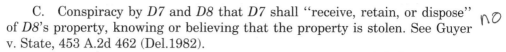 States v. Ruhbayan, 406 F.3d 292 (4th Cir. 2005).

C. Conspiracy by *D7* and *D8* that *D7* shall "receive, retain, or dispose" *no* of *D8*'s property, knowing or believing that the property is stolen. See Guyer v. State, 453 A.2d 462 (Del.1982).

D. Conspiracy by *D9*, a public official, and *D10*, a private party, to *yes* commit bribery, which is defined as the "giving and receiving of money or property to a public official in order to influence the official's vote or judgment on a public matter." See People v. Wettengel, 98 Colo. 193, 58 P.2d 279 (1935). What if the statute prohibits an "offer to give or receive" a bribe? *no* See People v. Incerto, 180 Colo. 366, 505 P.2d 1309 (1973).

GEBARDI v. UNITED STATES

Supreme Court of the United States, 1932.
287 U.S. 112, 53 S.Ct. 35, 77 L.Ed. 206.

legislative exemption

MR. JUSTICE STONE delivered the opinion of the Court.

This case is here on certiorari, to review a judgment of conviction for conspiracy to violate the Mann Act ([18 USCA § 397 et seq.]). Petitioners, a man and a woman, not then husband and wife, were indicted for conspiring together * * * to transport the woman from one state to another for the purpose of engaging in sexual intercourse with the man. At the trial * * * there was evidence from which the court could have found that the petitioners had engaged in illicit sexual relations in the course of each of the journeys alleged; that the man purchased the railway tickets for both petitioners for at least one journey; and that in each instance the woman, in advance of the purchase of the tickets, consented to go on the journey and did go on it voluntarily for the specified immoral purpose. There was no evidence supporting the allegation that any other person had conspired. The trial court * * * gave judgment of conviction * * *.

The only question which we need consider here is whether * * * the evidence was sufficient to support the conviction. * * *

Section 2 of the Mann Act, violation of which is charged by the indictment here as the object of the conspiracy, imposes the penalty upon "any person who shall knowingly transport or cause to be transported, or aid or assist in obtaining transportation for, or in transporting, in interstate or foreign commerce * * * any woman or girl for the purpose of prostitution or debauchery, or for any other immoral purpose. * * * " Transportation of a woman or girl whether with or without her consent, or causing or aiding it, or furthering it in any of the specified ways, are the acts punished, when done with a purpose which is immoral within the meaning of the law.

The act does not punish the woman for transporting herself; it contemplates two persons—one to transport and the woman or girl to be transported. For the woman to fall within the ban of the statute she must, at the least, "aid or assist" some one else in transporting or in procuring transportation for herself. But such aid and assistance must * * * be more active than mere agreement on her part to the transportation and its immoral purpose. For the statute is drawn to include those cases in which the woman consents to her own transportation. Yet it does not specifically impose any penalty upon her, although it deals in detail with the person by whom she is transported. In applying this criminal statute we cannot infer that the mere acquiescence of the woman transported was intended to be condemned by the general language punishing those who aid and assist the transporter, any more than it has been inferred that the purchaser of liquor was to be regarded as an abettor of the illegal sale. The penalties of the statute are too clearly directed against the acts of the transporter as distinguished from the consent of the subject of the transportation. * * *

* * * We come thus to the main question in the case, whether, admitting that the woman by consenting, has not violated the Mann Act, she may be convicted of a conspiracy with the man to violate it. * * *

* * * [W]e perceive in the failure of the Mann Act to condemn the woman's participation in those transportations which are effected with her mere consent, evidence of an affirmative legislative policy to leave her acquiescence unpunished. We think it a necessary implication of that policy that when the Mann Act and the conspiracy statute came to be construed together, as they necessarily would be, the same participation which the former contemplates as an inseparable incident of all cases in which the woman is a voluntary agent at all, but does not punish, was not automatically to be made punishable under the latter. It would contravene that policy to hold that the very passage of the Mann Act effected a withdrawal by the conspiracy statute of that immunity which the Mann Act itself confers.

It is not to be supposed that the consent of an unmarried person to adultery with a married person, where the latter alone is guilty of the substantive offense, would render the former an abettor or a conspirator, or that the acquiescence of a woman under the age of consent would make her a co-conspirator with the man to commit statutory rape upon herself. The principle, determinative of this case, is the same.

On the evidence before us the woman petitioner has not violated the Mann Act and, we hold, is not guilty of a conspiracy to do so. As there is no proof that the man conspired with anyone else to bring about the transportation, the convictions of both petitioners must be reversed.

NOTES AND QUESTIONS

1. What would be the result under Model Penal Code § 5.04?

PEOPLE v. SCONCE

California Court of Appeal, Second District, 1991.
228 Cal.App.3d 693, 279 Cal.Rptr. 59.

KLEIN, PRESIDING JUSTICE.

The People filed an information charging * * * David Wayne Sconce (Sconce) with conspiracy to commit murder. The trial court set the information aside [prior to trial] because it found Sconce effectively had withdrawn from the conspiracy. The People appeal. * * *

FACTUAL * * * BACKGROUND

This case involves Sconce's alleged formation of a conspiracy [with Bob Garcia] to kill Elie Estephan (Estephan). * * *

[Sconce offered Bob Garcia $10,000 to kill Estephan, the estranged husband of Cindy Strunk Estephan. Sconce told Garcia that he, Cindy, and a man named Sallard were plotting the murder. Garcia agreed to find someone to kill Estephan or to do it himself. Pursuant to the agreement, Garcia contacted ex-convict Herbert Dutton and offered him $5,000 to carry out the killing. Subsequently, Garcia and Dutton went to Estephan's house to inspect the area. They decided that Dutton would plant a bomb under Estephan's car.]

* * * Approximately three weeks after Sconce's initial conversation with Garcia, Sconce "just called it off. He said just forget about it, disregard doing it." Garcia did not see Dutton after the night they drove to Estephan's house. Although Garcia did not know it at the time Sconce told him not to kill Estephan, Dutton had been arrested on a parole violation. * * *

CONTENTIONS

The People contend the trial court erroneously set aside the information because Sconce's withdrawal from the conspiracy, although it might insulate him from liability for future conspiratorial acts, does not constitute a defense to liability for the conspiracy itself. * * *

DISCUSSION * * *

" 'Once the defendant's participation in the conspiracy is shown, it will be presumed to continue unless he is able to prove, as a matter of defense, that he effectively withdrew from the conspiracy. * * *' " (*People v. Lowery* (1988) 200 Cal.App.3d 1207, 1220, 246 Cal.Rptr. 443.)

Withdrawal from a conspiracy requires "an affirmative and bona fide rejection or repudiation of the conspiracy, communicated to the coconspirators." (*People v. Crosby,* [(1962) 58 Cal.2d 713], 730–731, 25 Cal.Rptr. 847, 375 P.2d 839.) * * *

Under California law withdrawal is a complete defense to conspiracy only if accomplished before the commission of an overt act * * *. * * *

"The requirement of an overt act before conspirators can be prosecuted and punished exists, * * * to provide a *locus p[o]enitentiae*—an opportunity for the conspirators to reconsider, terminate the agreement, and thereby avoid punishment for the conspiracy."

Obviously, the inverse of this rule is that once an overt act has been committed in furtherance of the conspiracy the crime of conspiracy has been completed and no subsequent action by the conspirator can change that.

Thus, even if it be assumed Sconce effectively withdrew from the conspiracy * * *, withdrawal merely precludes liability for subsequent acts committed by the members of the conspiracy. The withdrawal does not relate back to the criminal formation of the unlawful combination. In sum, conspiracy is complete upon the commission of an overt act. * * *

The rationale in favor of terminating liability is the one relied upon by the trial court, i.e., the reasons for allowing withdrawal as a defense to conspiracy—encouraging abandonment and thereby weakening the group—continue to apply after the commission of an overt act.

However, the rule remains that withdrawal avoids liability only for the target offense, or for any subsequent act committed by a coconspirator in pursuance of the common plan. "[I]n respect of the conspiracy itself, the individual's change of mind is ineffective; he cannot undo that which he has already done." (4 Wharton's Criminal Law, (14th ed. 1981) *Conspiracy,* § 734, pp. 555–557.)[4]

Even if this court were inclined to agree with the trial court, we are bound to follow the foregoing settled rule. Any change in the law is a matter for the Legislature.[5]

Because we conclude Sconce's withdrawal from the conspiracy is not a valid defense to the completed crime of conspiracy, we need not determine whether the evidence showed that Sconce, in fact, withdrew from the conspiracy and communicated that withdrawal to each coconspirator. * * *

---

4. The Model Penal Code recognizes a defense which it refers to as renunciation. The Model Penal Code states: "It is an affirmative defense that the actor, after conspiring to commit a crime, thwarted the success of the conspiracy, under circumstances manifesting a complete and voluntary renunciation of his [or her] criminal purpose." (Model Pen.Code, § 5.03, subd. (6).)

The defense of renunciation is not the same as withdrawal. "One difference is immediately apparent: In renunciation, the defendant must 'thwart the success' of the conspiracy. Another important difference is that renunciation is a complete defense, relieving liability for all prior involvement in the conspiracy." (Note, *Withdrawal from Conspiracy: A Constitutional Allocation of Evidentiary Burdens* (1982) 51 Fordham L.Rev. 438, 440, fn. 12.)

Renunciation is not available as a defense in California.

5. Although it is therefore unnecessary to wrestle with the policy concerns underlying the current rule, we note that avoidance of criminal liability for the target offense and for all future acts of the conspiracy continues to provide incentive for a conspirator to withdraw, assuming the legal fiction the conspirator is knowledgeable in the law of conspiracy.

NOTES AND QUESTIONS

1. *Problem.* During the winter of 2003 and the spring of 2004, *A, B, C,* and *D* concocted a plan to "blow up" the high school they attended. "The plan * * * involved a multifaceted assault on the school to take place the following school year on or near the anniversary of the murders at Columbine High School." Soon after the start of the school year, *B, C,* and *D* went to the police and told them that *A* was planning to blow up the school. At no time did *B, C,* or *D* indicate that they planned to participate in the attack. Did *D* renounce under Model Penal Code § 5.03(6)? Commonwealth v. Nee, 458 Mass. 174, 935 N.E.2d 1276 (2010).

2. *Impossibility: a defense to conspiracy?* *D1,* owner a company that makes adhesives, and *D2,* his daughter, wanted *X,* an employee of a competitor company, to provide them with trade secrets of the competitor. The FBI learned of these activities and convinced *X* to assist in a "sting" operation, in which *X* offered to provide *D1* and *D2* with documents, marked "confidential," which *X* claimed contained trade secrets. In fact, the documents were fake. *D1* and *D2* were charged with conspiracy to commit theft of a trade secret, a federal offense. *D1* and *D2* fought their conspiracy conviction on the ground of the defense of legal impossibility. United States v. Yang, 281 F.3d 534 (6th Cir.2002).

In a state that *retains* the common law defense of legal impossibility in *attempt* cases, is there a plausible argument for *rejecting* the defense in *conspiracy* prosecutions? Alternatively, might the case for recognizing the impossibility defense be *stronger* with conspiracies?

CHAPTER 11

LIABILITY FOR THE CONDUCT OF ANOTHER

■ ■ ■

A. ACCOMPLICE LIABILITY

1. GENERAL PRINCIPLES

a. Common Law Terminology and Its Significance

STATE v. WARD

Court of Appeals of Maryland, 1978.
284 Md. 189, 396 A.2d 1041.

ORTH, JUDGE.

With the common law of England * * * came the doctrine of accessoryship applicable to felonies. * * *

Accompanying the common law doctrine across the Atlantic were certain highly technical procedural rules, not altogether logical, which had developed from the distinction between principals and accessories before the fact. These rules operate to the advantage of the accused and the detriment of the prosecution, for they "tended to shield accessories from punishment notwithstanding overwhelming evidence of their criminal assistance." W. LaFave & A. Scott, Handbook on Criminal Law § 63, pp. 498–499. * * *

"In the field of felony the common law divided guilty parties into principals and accessories." Principals came to be classified as in the first degree (perpetrators) or in the second degree (abettors) and accessories as before the fact (inciters) or after the fact (criminal protectors).[1]

---

1. "According to the ancient analysis only the actual perpetrator of the felonious deed was a principal. Other guilty parties were called 'accessories', and to distinguish among these with reference to time and place they were divided into three classes: (1) accessories before the fact, (2) accessories at the fact, and (3) accessories after the fact. At a relatively early time the party who was originally considered an accessory at the fact ceased to be classed in the accessorial group and was labeled a principal. To distinguish him from the actual perpetrator of the crime he was called a principal in the second degree. Thereafter, in felony cases there were two kinds of principals, first degree and second degree, and two kinds of accessories, before the fact and after the fact." Perkins, Criminal Law 643 (2d ed. 1969).

A *principal in the first degree* is one who actually commits a crime, ~principal 1°~ either by his own hand, or by an inanimate agency, or by an innocent human agent. A *principal in the second degree* is one who is guilty of ~principal 2°~ felony by reason of having aided, counseled, commanded or encouraged the commission thereof in his presence, either actual or constructive. An ~accessory before the fact~ *accessory before the fact* is one who is guilty of felony by reason of having aided, counseled, commanded or encouraged the commission thereof, ~accessory after the fact~ without having been present either actually or constructively at the moment of perpetration. An *accessory after the fact* is one who, with knowledge of the other's guilt, renders assistance to a felon in the effort to hinder his detection, arrest, trial or punishment. * * *

At the common law the principal in the second degree may be tried and convicted prior to the trial of the principal in the first degree, or even after the latter has been tried and acquitted. Furthermore, a principal in the second degree may be convicted of a higher crime or a lower crime than the principal in the first degree. With respect to accessories, however, the common law took a different path. An accessory cannot be tried, without his consent, before the principal.[16] And an accessory could not be convicted of a higher crime than his principal. * * *

NOTES AND QUESTIONS

1. Two additional felony principal-accessory distinctions, besides those ~venue~ mentioned in *Ward,* developed in the common law era. First, an accessory could only be prosecuted in the jurisdiction in which the accessorial acts took place, rather than where the crime occurred. No similar rule applied to principals in the second degree. Second, strict rules of pleading and proof ~pleading & proof~ applied: a defendant charged as an accessory could not be convicted as a principal, and vice versa. These technicalities were avoided in misdemeanor and treason prosecutions, because all parties to such crimes were identified as principals.

Why did common law judges formulate and apply the technical rules described in *Ward* and this Note? According to Professor Perkins, the courts were satisfied with the relatively minor penalties imposed for misdemeanors,

---

"There is some authority for using the word 'accomplice' to include all principals and all accessories, but the preferred usage is to include all principals and accessories before the fact, but to exclude accessories after the fact." *Id.* at 648. * * *

16. Even when the accessory waives the right, and may be tried before the principal, if he is convicted it is necessary to respite judgment until the trial of the principal because a subsequent acquittal of the latter would annul this conviction.

The principal and the accessory may be tried jointly, unless the accessory is entitled to a severance, but if they are tried together the trier of fact must first inquire into the guilt of the principal, and, if it finds him not guilty, the accessory must be acquitted. Only upon finding the principal guilty may the trier of fact consider whether the accessory is guilty. An acquittal of the principal, of course, bars a subsequent trial of the accessory. Professor Perkins finds this aspect of the principal-accessory concept to be "quite absurd." He points out: "Anything which prevents conviction of the principal makes impossible the conviction of the accessory. Hence, if the principal is never apprehended, or if before the moment of conviction he should die or be pardoned, the accessory must go free although his guilt may be well known and easy to prove. Furthermore, if both are convicted in due course, but the conviction of the principal is thereafter reversed, the conviction of the accessory cannot stand." [Perkins] at 673.

~if principal acquitted, so must accessory~

and they considered death an appropriate punishment for all parties to treason, but they did not believe that all participants in other felonies should be executed, as then required. As a consequence, they devised intricate rules to shield some parties, primarily accessories, from conviction. Rollin M. Perkins, *Parties to Crime*, 89 U.Pa.L.Rev. 581, 607 (1941).

Nearly all states by legislation have abrogated the common law distinction between principals and accessories before the fact. More specifically, defendants who were characterized at common law as accessories before the fact typically may now be tried and punished without regard to the status of the principal's prosecution. E.g., Model Penal Code § 2.06(7).

In general, an accessory *after* the fact is no longer treated as a party to the crime committed by the principal in the first degree, but rather is subject to prosecution for a separate and lesser offense, such as misprision (see p. 141, Note 6) or "hindering apprehension or prosecution." Model Penal Code § 242.3.

b. Theoretical Foundation: Derivative Liability

"Accessorial liability is not a distinct crime, but only [a] * * * means by which a substantive crime may be committed." Robert Weisberg, *Reappraising Complicity*, 4 Buffalo Crim. L. Rev. 217, 225 (2000). Put differently, an accomplice (i.e., at common law, a principal in the second degree or accessory before the fact) is not guilty of the crime of "aiding and abetting," but instead is guilty of the substantive offense committed by the perpetrator (the principal in the first degree) because of the accomplice's complicity in the crime. Professor Kadish explains:

> [T]he doctrine of complicity (sometimes referred to as the law of aiding and abetting, or accessorial liability) emerges to define the circumstances in which one person (to whom I will refer as the secondary party or actor, accomplice, or accessory) becomes liable for the crime of another (the primary party or actor, or the principal). * * *

The nature of complicity liability follows from the considerations that called it forth. The secondary party's liability is derivative, which is to say, it is incurred by virtue of a violation of law by the primary party to which the secondary party contributed. It is not direct [liability] * * *. One who "aids and abets" [the primary party] to do those acts * * * can be liable for doing so, but not because he has thereby caused the actions of the principal or because the actions of the principal are his acts. His liability must rest on the violation of law by the principal, the legal consequences of which he incurs because of his own actions.

It is important not to misconstrue derivative liability as imparting vicarious liability. Accomplice liability does not involve imposing liability on one party for the wrongs of another solely because of the relationship between the parties. Liability requires action by the secondary actor * * * that makes it appropriate to blame him for what the primary actor does. The term "derivative" as used here merely means that his liability is dependent on the principal violating the law.

Sanford H. Kadish, *Complicity, Cause and Blame: A Study in the Interpretation of Doctrine*, 73 Cal.L.Rev. 323, 336–37 (1985).

Professor Kadish's explanation of accomplice liability raises three related questions: (1) What makes a person an accomplice, so as to justify holding her accountable for the actions of the primary party?; (2) In view of the fact accomplices derive their liability from the primary party, are there cases in which it is justifiable to convict a secondary party, although there is no liability to derive from the primary actor, or to convict the accomplice of a more serious offense than may be derived from the principal?; and (3) Under what circumstances, if any, may an accomplice avoid liability despite her participation in criminal activity? The materials in this chapter consider these questions.

2. "ELEMENTS" OF ACCOMPLICE #1 LIABILITY: IN GENERAL

STATE v. HOSELTON

Supreme Court of Appeals of West Virginia, 1988.
179 W.Va. 645, 371 S.E.2d 366.

PER CURIAM:

This case is before the Court upon the appeal of Kevin Wayne Hoselton from his conviction of entering without breaking a vessel, with intent to commit larceny, pursuant to *W.Va.Code*, 61–3–12 [1923].[1] * * *

The accused was charged * * * as a principal in the first degree for either breaking and entering or entering without breaking a storage unit on a docked barge with intent to commit larceny. He was eighteen years old at the time, and was with several friends, each of whom was separately indicted as a principal in the first degree. The accused was convicted of entering without breaking, as charged in the indictment.

The only evidence used to link the accused to the crime was his voluntary statement. The pertinent answers given by the accused in his voluntary statement were, as follows:

Q. Were you with some individuals that broke into the barge?

A. Yes, sir.

Q. Once you got to the barges, what happened?

A. We all walked up on that, and I was standing outside there. Mike, he tried to get the big door open, and he couldn't do it.

---

1. *W.Va.Code*, 61–3–12 [1923] reads, in pertinent part:

If any person shall, at any time, break and enter, or shall enter without breaking, any * * * steamboat or other boat or vessel, within the jurisdiction of any county in this State, with intent to commit a felony or any larceny, he shall be deemed guilty of a felony, and, upon conviction, shall be confined in the penitentiary not less than one nor more than ten years. * * *

Q.   M[...] A[...]?

A.   Yes, sir. And I heard a couple of other people back there—I don't know who it was—trying to get in.

Q.   Why couldn't you see them?

A.   Because I was standing at the end of the barge there.

Q.   Were you keeping a look-out?

A.   You could say that. I just didn't want to go down in there.

Q.   Do you know who actually gained entry to the barge[?]

A.   No, sir, I'm not sure.

Q.   Kevin, did you know at the time that you were down there that you all were committing a crime?

A.   Yes, I did know that, but—

The items stolen from the storage unit were tools, grease guns, grease and a battery charger. None of these items, or profits on their resale, were given to the accused. In both his statement and his trial testimony, the accused stated that he, standing at one end of the barge, with an obstructed view of the storage unit, was unaware of his friends' intent to steal the items until he heard the opening of the storage unit door. He then walked to the unit and saw his friends handling the goods. He then returned to the other end of the barge and went to an automobile, owned and operated by one of his friends, who remained in the storage facility. His friends returned to the automobile with the goods. The accused did not assist the others in placing the goods in the automobile. He was then immediately driven home.

The accused testified that he and his friends frequently trespassed upon the barge for fishing. * * *

On appeal, the accused contends that the evidence is insufficient to support a conviction for entering with intent to commit larceny. Therefore, the trial judge erred when he denied the accused's motions for acquittal and new trial. * * *

The State contends there was sufficient evidence to establish that the accused was a lookout, therefore, the conviction for breaking and entering as a principal in the first degree should stand.

A lookout is one who is "by prearrangement, keeping watch to avoid interception or detection or to provide warning during the perpetration of the crimes and thereby participating in the offenses charged ..."

This Court has consistently held that lookouts are aiders and abettors, principals in the second degree.

Principals in the second degree are punishable as principals in the first degree. *W.Va.Code,* 61–11–6 [1923].

An aider and abettor, or principal in the second degree must "in some sort associate himself with the venture, that he participate in it as something that he wishes to bring about, that he seek[s] by his action to make it succeed."

It is well established that in order for a defendant to be convicted as an aider and abettor, and thus a principal in the second degree, the prosecution must demonstrate that he or she shared the criminal intent of the principal in the first degree. * * *

State v. Harper, 365 S.E.2d 69, 74 (1987).[4]

Therefore, if the State establishes evidence that an accused acted as a lookout, it has necessarily established the requisite act and mental state to support a conviction of aiding and abetting. * * *

In this case, the only evidence that suggested the accused was a lookout was his response to the investigating officer's questioning: "Q. Were you a lookout? A. You could say that. I just didn't want to go down there."

In both his voluntary statement and during his testimony at trial, the accused stated that he had no prior knowledge of his friends' intentions to steal anything from the barge. When he heard the door open to the storage unit and saw his friends removing the goods, the accused left the barge and returned to the car. The accused never received any of the stolen property, which was later retrieved by the police from the other defendants. * * *

* * * [T]he accused's response that "[y]ou could say" he was a lookout, standing completely alone, does not establish that the accused was an aider and abettor by participating in, and wishing to bring about the entering with intent to commit larceny.

Viewed in the light most favorable to the prosecution, the State did not prove that the accused was a lookout. * * *

We therefore reverse and set aside the accused's conviction for entering without breaking.

NOTES AND QUESTIONS

1. Look again at footnote 4 in the opinion. In light of that footnote, why was Hoselton's conviction reversed? Is it that he did not assist in the crime? That he did not have the requisite intent? Or, both?

2. Although "aiding and abetting" is not itself a crime, courts and commentators frequently discuss accomplice liability in terms ordinarily reserved for criminal offenses. For example, the secondary party's assistance may be characterized as "the *actus reus*" of accomplice liability; the intent to

---

4. *See also* LaFave & Scott, *Substantive Criminal Law,* § 6 (1986) * * * Professor Scott writes:

> [i]t is useful to give separate consideration to whether a person has engaged in the requisite acts (or omissions) and to whether he had the requisite mental state. * * * It may generally be said that one is liable as an accomplice to the crime of another if he (a) gave assistance or encouragement or failed to perform a legal duty to prevent it (b) with the intent thereby to promote or facilitate commission of the crime. * * *

promote or facilitate the commission of the crime is "the *mens rea*" of accomplice liability.

Subject to important exceptions and clarifications considered in the next chapter subsection, the *mens rea* of an accomplice is sometimes described as a "dual intent," i.e., the intent to aid the primary party *and* the intent that such assistance result in the commission of the offense charged. The *actus reus* of accomplice liability can take the form of solicitation of the offense, active assistance in the commission of the crime, encouragement of the offense, or failure to prevent commission of the crime if the secondary party has the legal duty to make such an effort.

In this regard, look carefully at the structure of Model Penal Code § 2.06, the complicity provision. Subsection (1) provides that a person may be guilty of an offense by his own conduct (direct accountability) and/or "by the conduct of another person for which he is legally accountable" (indirect accountability). Subsection (2) sets out three ways in which indirect accountability may arise. One way—subsection (2)(c)—is to be an "accomplice of such other person in the commission of the offense."

Subsection (3) defines the term "accomplice." The required state of mind ("the purpose of promoting or facilitating the commission of the offense") is set out first in subsection (3)(a); the "*actus reus*" of accomplice liability is set out in three alternative subsection ((3)(a)(i)–(iii)).

3.   In *Hoselton,* would Kevin have been an accomplice in the commission of the charged offense in the following circumstances? Apply common law doctrine and Model Penal Code § 2.06 (as both are discussed in Note 2).

A.   Kevin's friends told him to wait in the car while they entered the barge. They falsely told Kevin (who believed their claims) that they were entering in order to pick up a television set the barge owner borrowed from them.

B.   Kevin's friends falsely told him that they had come to the barge "just to fool around." They asked him, and he agreed, to stay in the car and honk if he spotted the police. He spotted a police officer and honked. His friends hurried out of the barge, but were caught before they could escape.

C.   Same as (B), except that Kevin knew that his friends intended to steal property from the barge. His friends did not ask him to do anything, but he helped them by honking the horn when the police arrived.

D.   Same as (C), except that when he honked the horn, his friends did not hear him and were arrested by the police in the barge.

E.   Same as (B), except that his friends told him the truth, i.e., that they had come to steal items from the barge. No police officer arrived, so Kevin did not need to honk the horn.

F.   Same as (A), except that Kevin knew what his friends intended to do. While waiting in the car, he observed a telephone nearby, considered calling the police, but declined to do so.

3. MENS REA

a. Intent: "Purpose" or "Knowledge"?

PEOPLE v. LAURIA

California Court of Appeal, Second District, 1967.
251 Cal.App.2d 471, 59 Cal.Rptr. 628.

[For the opinion in this case, see p. 789 supra.]

NOTES AND QUESTIONS

1. *Complicity, "intention," agency, and "forfeited personal identity."* Assume that Lauria had been prosecuted as an accomplice, rather than as a co-conspirator, in the acts of prostitution committed by the women who used his answering service. Should guilt be assigned on the basis of knowing assistance, or should accountability as an accomplice require proof that the actor assisted with the *purpose* of facilitating the commission of the offense(s)?

As with conspiracy law, there has been vigorous debate on this issue. In United States v. Peoni, 100 F.2d 401 (2d Cir.1938), Circuit Judge Learned Hand came down on the side of requiring purposeful conduct:

> It will be observed that all [the] definitions [of the terms in the federal accomplice liability statute] have nothing whatever to do with the probability that the forbidden result would follow upon the accessory's conduct; and that they all demand that he in some sort associate himself with the venture, that he participate in it as in something that he wishes to bring about, that he seek by his action to make it succeed. All the words used—even the most colorless, "abet"—carry an implication of purposive attitude towards it.

[handwritten margin note: requires purpose]

Another federal court saw the matter differently:

> Guilt as an accessory depends, not on "having a stake" in the outcome of the crime * * * but on aiding and assisting the perpetrators; and those who make a profit by furnishing to criminals, whether by sale or otherwise, the means to carry on their nefarious undertakings aid them just as truly as if they were actual partners with them, having a stake in the fruits of their enterprise. * * * One who sells a gun to another knowing that he is buying it to commit murder, would hardly escape conviction as an accessory to the murder by showing that he received full price for the gun; and no difference in principle can be drawn between such a case and any other case of a seller who knows that the purchaser intends to use the goods which he is purchasing in the commission of felony.

[handwritten margin note: requires knowledge]

Backun v. United States, 112 F.2d 635, 637 (4th Cir.1940).

Whose view is preferable? Consider:

> The theory of the intentionality ["purpose"] requirement is not obvious. One possible explanation is social policy; namely, that it would

be undesirable to draw the circle of criminal liability any wider. A pall would be cast on ordinary activity if we had to fear criminal liability for what others might do simply because our actions made their acts more probable. This has been the dominant consideration in recent debates over proposals to extend liability to those who know their actions will assist another to commit a crime but who act for reasons other than to further those criminal actions—the supplier of materials, for example, who knows that a buyer plans to use them to commit a crime. The argument that people otherwise lawfully conducting their affairs should not be constrained by fear of liability for what their customers will do has tended to prevail over the argument that it is proper for the criminal law to prohibit conduct that knowingly facilitates the commission of crime. * * *

These policy considerations, however, may not be the whole story. * * *

The explanation for the intention requirement must be found elsewhere. It may reside in the notion of agreement as the paradigm mode by which a principal in agency law (the secondary party in the terminology of the criminal law) becomes liable for the acts of another person. The liability of the principal in civil law rests essentially on his consent to be bound by the actions of his agent, whom he vests with authority for this purpose. * * *

Insofar as manifesting consent to be bound by the acts of another is a general requirement for holding one person liable for the actions of another, the requirement of intention for complicity liability becomes more readily explicable. Obviously, in the context of the criminal law, literal consent to be criminally liable is irrelevant. But by intentionally acting to further the criminal actions of another, the secondary party voluntarily identifies himself with the principal party. The intention to further the acts of another, which creates liability under the criminal law, may be understood as equivalent to manifesting consent to liability under the civil law.

Sanford H. Kadish, *Complicity, Cause and Blame: A Study in the Interpretation of Doctrine*, 73 Cal.L.Rev. 323, 353–55 (1985).

Consider, as well, these observations regarding Professor Kadish's remarks:

[T]he concept of agency explains a great deal about why we feel justified in punishing an accomplice as if she were the perpetrator. Perhaps, however, our feelings may be described better in terms of "forfeited personal identity." Ordinarily a person is held criminally responsible for his own actions. However, when an accomplice chooses to become a part of the criminal activity of another, she says in essence, "your acts are my acts," and forfeits her personal identity. We euphemistically * * * impute the actions of the perpetrator to the accomplice by "agency" doctrine; in reality, we demand that she who chooses to aid in a crime [forfeit] her right to be treated as an individual. Thus, * * * distinctions between parties are rendered irrelevant. We pretend the accomplice is no more than an incorporeal shadow.

Joshua Dressler, *Reassessing the Theoretical Underpinnings of Accomplice Liability: New Solutions to an Old Problem*, 37 Hastings L.J. 91, 111 (1985); see People v. Prettyman, 14 Cal.4th 248, 58 Cal.Rptr.2d 827, 926 P.2d 1013 (1996) (invoking the "forfeited personal identity" concept).

2. *Problem.* Mark Manes, 22 years old, met Eric Harris, a 17–year–old youth, at a gun show. Manes purchased a semiautomatic handgun for the youth and accompanied Harris to a target-practice range where Harris shot at a tree trunk and exclaimed, "Imagine that is someone's [expletive] brain." A few months later, on April 19, 1999, Manes sold Harris one hundred rounds of 9 mm ammunition for $25. The following day, Harris and his friend Dylan Klebold entered Columbine High School in Littleton, Colorado and killed twelve fellow students and a teacher before killing themselves. (See Robert Weisberg, *Reappraising Complicity*, 4 Buffalo Crim. L. Rev. 217, 217–218 (2000) (quoting a Reuters news story).)

Assume that Harris (and Klebold) had not killed themselves and had been prosecuted and convicted of thirteen counts of murder. Assume further that Manes had been prosecuted as Harris's accomplice. Based on these assumptions, would Manes be guilty under *Lauria*? Under Model Penal Code § 2.06? *Should* he be convicted? Why, or why not?

In considering your answers to these questions, consider as well that the shooters thanked Manes (and another) on a tape recording. "You helped us do what we needed to do." But they also said that Manes had "no clue. So don't blame [him] and arrest [him] for what we did. Yeah, you know, it's not [his] fault. * * * We would have found someone else."

3. A post–9/11 federal statute makes it an offense to provide "material support or resources to a foreign terrorist organization." 18 U.S.C. § 2339B. Under this statute, "material support or resources" includes "any property, tangible or intangible, financial services, lodging, training, [or] expert advice or assistance" to a foreign terrorist organization. (This statute, unlike ordinary complicity law, renders such assistance an independent crime, even if no terrorist criminal activity occurs.) An indictment charged a Ph.D. student with being a Web master to various Internet Web sites that "recruit and raise funds for violent jihad." Assume the student knew of the purposes of the Web sites but was personally opposed to their goals. As a matter of public policy should he be convicted of this offense? If your answer is yes, would you also convict a person who fixes a fax machine owned by a terrorist group that advocates terrorism?

4. Suppose a person runs an anti-abortion Internet site, which provides the names and addresses of late-term abortion providers, and which site describes a particular doctor as a "mass murderer of defenseless children." Should he be convicted of murder, as an accomplice, if someone takes this information and kills the doctor? See generally Michael Vitiello, *The Nuremburg Files: Testing the Outer Limits of the First Amendment*, 61 Ohio St. L.J. 1175 (2000).

b.   When Is "Intent" Not Required?

i.   *Offenses Not Requiring Intent*

RILEY v. STATE

majority rule

Court of Appeals of Alaska, 2002.
60 P.3d 204.

MANNHEIMER, JUDGE.

Richard L. Riley and another man, Edward F. Portalla, opened fire on an unsuspecting crowd of young people who were socializing around a bonfire on the Tanana River near Fairbanks. Two of the young people were seriously wounded. Riley and Portalla were indicted on two counts of first-degree assault (recklessly causing serious physical injury by means of a dangerous instrument) * * *. * * * Riley challenges his two convictions * * *.

The State faced a problem in prosecuting Riley and Portalla for first-degree assault: the physical evidence (in particular, the ballistics analysis) did not reveal which of the defendants' weapons had fired the wounding shots. * * * Thus, with respect to each victim, the State could prove that the wound was inflicted by one of the two defendants, but the State could not easily prove which one.

At the close of Riley's trial, the jurors were instructed that, with regard to each count of first-degree assault, they should decide whether Riley acted as a "principal" (*i.e.,* by firing the wounding shot) or, if they could not decide beyond a reasonable doubt which man fired the shots, they should decide whether Riley acted as an "accomplice" (*i.e.,* by aiding or abetting Portalla to fire the wounding shot). The jurors found Riley guilty as an accomplice in the wounding of both victims.

Riley argues that his convictions for first-degree assault are flawed because the jurors were misinstructed regarding the elements of accomplice liability. The alleged flaw concerns the culpable mental state that must be proved when the State alleges a defendant's complicity in another person's crime.

In *Echols v. State,* 818 P.2d 691 (Alaska App.1991), this Court addressed a situation where a wife was charged as an accomplice to first-degree assault committed by her husband. The State's evidence showed that the defendant summoned her husband to discipline their child, then stood by and watched while the husband inflicted serious physical injury on the child by whipping her with an electric cord. The question was whether the wife's conduct was sufficient to establish her accountability as an accomplice to the assault.

The underlying crime of first-degree assault required proof that the principal (*i.e.,* the husband) acted recklessly with respect to the result (*i.e.,* the infliction of serious physical injury). The State argued that the wife could be convicted as an accomplice to the first-degree assault because (1) she solicited her husband to discipline the child and (2) she acted with the culpable mental state required for the crime—*i.e.,* she acted recklessly with respect to the possibility that the beating would result in serious physical injury to the child.

But this Court held that the wife's complicity could not be premised on recklessness. Rather, we held that the wife could be held accountable as an accomplice to the first-degree assault only if the State proved that she acted *intentionally* with respect to the prohibited result—*i.e.,* that her conscious objective was to have the child suffer serious physical injury.

In the present appeal, Riley relies on *Echols.* He contends that his jury instruction on accomplice liability was flawed because it failed to clearly inform the jurors that the State was obliged to prove that Riley intended to have Portalla inflict serious physical injury on the victims (and not simply that Riley acted recklessly with respect to the possibility that Portalla's conduct would cause this result). * * *

* * * [T]he State asks us to re-examine our holding in *Echols.* We have done so and, for the reasons explained here, we conclude that we misstated the law of complicity in *Echols.* * * *

Under the law of complicity codified in AS 11.16.110(2),[a] even though a defendant may have solicited, encouraged, or assisted another person's criminal conduct, the defendant can not be held criminally responsible for the other person's conduct unless the State proves that the defendant acted "with intent to promote or facilitate the commission of the offense." The question is: What did the legislature mean when they required proof that the accomplice acted with the intent to promote or facilitate "the offense"?

When the underlying offense requires proof of the defendant's intention to cause a particular result (for example, first-degree murder * * *, a crime that requires proof of an intent to cause death), the phrase "intent to promote or facilitate the commission of the offense" seems to offer little trouble. Because the principal must intend to cause death, any accomplice to first-degree murder must likewise intend to cause death.

But what if the underlying offense is defined in terms of an *unintended* result? For example, a person commits second-degree murder * * * by unintentionally causing a death while engaged in conduct "manifesting an extreme indifference to the value of human life." Similarly, a person commits manslaughter * * * by unintentionally causing a death while acting recklessly with respect to the possibility that their conduct would cause death. When the underlying crime is defined in terms of an unintended result, what does AS 11.16.110(2) mean by the phrase "intent to promote or facilitate the commission of *the offense*"?

---

a. Sec. 11.16.110 Legal accountability based upon the conduct of another.

A person is legally accountable for the conduct of another constituting an offense if * * *

   (2) with intent to promote or facilitate the commission of the offense, the person * * *

      (B) aids or abets the other in planning or committing the offense * * *.

In *Echols,* this Court * * * held that even though a person could be convicted of first-degree assault as a principal upon proof that they acted recklessly with respect to the prohibited result, a person could not be convicted as an accomplice unless the State proved a different, higher culpable mental state. Specifically, we held that whenever the underlying crime requires proof of a particular result, the statutory requirement that an accomplice "inten[d] to promote or facilitate the commission of the offense" means that the State must prove that the defendant acted "intentionally" with respect to this prohibited result.

* * * [T]his construction of the statute * * * leads to counterintuitive results in situations like the one presented in Riley's appeal.

For example, let us assume that Riley and Portalla engaged in the same conduct (jointly firing weapons into a crowd) but, through misfortune, one of their victims was killed. Let us further assume that the State believed that it was impossible to prove, beyond a reasonable doubt, that this death was intended, so the State charged both defendants with manslaughter. And finally, let us assume that the evidence linking the homicide to either Riley's or Portalla's personal conduct was so inconclusive that it was impossible to say, beyond a reasonable doubt, which of them was the principal and which the accomplice.

Under the rule of *Echols,* neither Riley nor Portalla can be convicted of manslaughter in this hypothetical situation. The State can prove that both defendants acted recklessly with respect to the possibility that their conduct would cause human death, and this culpable mental state would be sufficient to establish the *principal's* guilt of manslaughter. But the State can not prove (beyond a reasonable doubt) which of the defendants was the principal. This means that the State will have to prove both defendants' guilt under a complicity theory. And *Echols* holds that, to prove guilt under a complicity theory, the State has to prove that the defendants acted with the intent to kill. In effect, *Echols* says that, under these circumstances, the State has to prove the defendants guilty of first-degree murder (intentional taking of human life) or the defendants will escape criminal liability for the homicide. * * *

* * * *Echols* represents a distinctly minority view on this issue. * * *

Alaska's complicity statute is based on Model Penal Code § 2.06(3). This section reads:

A person is an accomplice of another person in the commission of an offense if:

(a) with the purpose of promoting or facilitating the commission of the offense, he

(i) solicits [the] other person to commit it, or

(ii) aids or agrees or attempts to aid [the] other person in planning or committing it, or

(iii) having a legal duty to prevent the commission of the offense, fails to make proper effort to do so[.]

In the Model Penal Code, this provision is immediately followed by § 2.06(4), a section which addresses the legal issue at the heart of this appeal * * *. Section 2.06(4) reads:

> When causing a particular result is an element of an offense, an accomplice in the conduct causing [that] result is an accomplice in the commission of that offense if he acts with the kind of culpability, if any, with respect to that result that is sufficient for the commission of the offense. * * *

§2.06(4)

The explanatory note to Model Penal Code § 2.06 states that subsection (4) "deals with a special case that arises when an actor is an accomplice in conduct within the meaning of [§ 2.06(3)], and when a criminal result—anticipated or unanticipated—flows from that conduct." In fact, the Model Penal Code commentary explains that §§ 2.06(3) and 2.06(4) were intended to be read together: § 2.06(3) defines the *conduct* for which an accomplice can be held accountable, while § 2.06(4) clarifies that, when that conduct produces a result prohibited by law, the accomplice's culpable mental state with respect to that result (and, thus, the accomplice's guilt or innocence, or the accomplice's degree of guilt) must be evaluated separately from anyone else's culpable mental state.[b] * * *

Alaska's complicity statute * * * specifies that a person can be held accountable for the conduct of another if the person (1) solicits that conduct, encourages the conduct, or assists in planning or performing the conduct, and (2) when doing so, the person acts "with intent to promote or facilitate the commission of the offense." The task facing this Court in *Echols* was to interpret what the drafters of Alaska's Criminal Code meant by "the offense." Do these words refer to the accomplice's intent to promote or facilitate the other person's conduct? Or do these words refer to the accomplice's intent to promote or facilitate the other person's conduct *and* ensuing result? We ultimately adopted the latter interpretation in *Echols*—concluding that whenever the elements of an offense include a particular result, a person can not be convicted as an accomplice

---

b. In discussing the liability of an accessory, when a particular result is an essential element to the commission of a crime, comment 7 of § 2.06, at page 321, states:

[S]ubsection (4) makes it clear that complicity in conduct causing a particular criminal result entails accountability for that result so long as the accomplice is personally culpable with respect to the result to the extent demanded by the definition of the crimes. * * *

The most common situation in which Subsection (4) will become relevant is where unanticipated results occur from conduct for which the actor is responsible under Subsection (3). His liability for unanticipated occurrences rests upon two factors: his complicity in the conduct that caused the result, and his culpability towards the result to the degree required by the law, that makes the result criminal. Accomplice liability in this event is thus assimilated to the liability for the principal actor; the principal actor's liability for unanticipated results, of course, would turn on the extent to which he was reckless or negligent, as required by the law defining the offense, toward the result in question. * * *

This formulation combines the policy that accomplices are equally accountable within the range of their complicity with the policies underlying those crimes defined according to results.

to that offense unless they consciously intended to achieve that result. * * *

But * * *, this suggestion is contradicted by the pertinent Model Penal Code commentary, and it has been rejected by most courts with Model Penal Code-based complicity statutes. The standard interpretation of the phrase "intent to promote or facilitate the commission of the offense" is that it requires proof of the accomplice's intent to promote or facilitate another person's *conduct* that constitutes the *actus reus* of the offense. With regard to the results of that conduct, the government must prove that the accomplice had whatever culpable mental state is required for the underlying crime. * * *

Thus, Riley could properly be convicted of first-degree assault under AS 11.41.200(a)(1) either upon proof that he personally shot a firearm into the crowd or (alternatively) upon proof that, acting with intent to promote or facilitate Portalla's act of shooting into the crowd, Riley solicited, encouraged, or assisted Portalla to do so. These are alternative ways of proving that Riley was accountable for the *conduct* that inflicted the injuries. The government was also obliged to prove that Riley acted with the culpable mental state specified by the first-degree assault statute. But regardless of whether Riley acted as a principal or an accomplice, the applicable culpable mental state remained the same: recklessness as to the possibility that this conduct would cause serious physical injury. * * *

For these reasons, we affirm Riley's two convictions for first-degree assault. * * *

NOTES AND QUESTIONS

1. The holding in *Echols,* discussed in *Riley* and overruled by it, was based on the following syllogism: accomplice liability only attaches where the defendant *intends* to facilitate or promote an underlying offense; the offense charged only required proof that the perpetrator *recklessly* caused the result; therefore, to convict the defendant as an accomplice in this offense would be to accept that the accused *intended* to aid an *unintentional* result, which is a logical impossibility.

How did *Riley* get around that argument? Which rule—*Echols* or *Riley*—is a better one as a matter of sensible public policy?

2. *A bit of a follow-up.* Co-defendant Edward Portalla, while on probation from his conviction in this case, was arrested for sexually assaulting a woman on a bike path. The first trial on *this* offense resulted in a hung jury, but he was acquitted on retrial. But, even that is not the end of the story. He was returned to prison for violation of the conditions of his probation (namely, committing the sexual assault for which he had been acquitted!), because probation can be revoked on the lesser standard of proof of "preponderance of the evidence." Portalla v. State, 2006 WL 3691697 (Alaska App.) He was later released, and apparently decided that Alaska was not a great place for him to stay. He moved to Oklahoma, where he was convicted in 2010

of multiple counts of obtaining (and attempting to obtain) money by false pretenses. He was due to be released from prison on March 30, 2013.

3. *Problem.* Alice informs Bob, a taxicab driver, that she is late for her airplane flight and that "you should drive as fast as necessary to get me to the airport on time. If I make it on time, you will get a very large tip." Is Alice an accomplice in the commission of negligent homicide by Bob, in the following two cases? Apply the Model Penal Code.

A. Bob exceeds the speed limit. As a consequence, he unintentionally strikes Carl's car from behind, causing it to strike a tree, killing Carl.

B. Bob exceeds the speed limit. At one intersection, while speeding, Bob runs through a red light, striking Carl's car, killing Carl.

4. *Problem.* State v. Foster, 202 Conn. 520, 522 A.2d 277 (1987):

> The jury could reasonably have found the following facts. In June, 1982, the defendant was living with his girlfriend and their child in an apartment near the Martin Luther King School in Hartford. At approximately 7:30 p.m. in the evening of June 16, 1982, while walking near the school, the defendant's girlfriend was robbed and raped by a young black male who held a straight-edged razor to her throat. During the one half hour encounter, she observed her attacker's features and later that night * * * described the assailant, with specific identifiable features, to the defendant.
>
> The defendant, who was "bitter" about the attack, purposely went looking for his girlfriend's attacker. On June 22, 1982, the defendant and a friend, Otha Cannon, * * * went walking in the vicinity where the rape and robbery had occurred. Near the Martin Luther King School, the defendant saw a man he thought matched the description of the assailant. After telling Cannon "[t]his is the guy who raped my lady," the defendant and Cannon confronted the suspected rapist, later identified as William Jack Middleton, in an alleyway next to the school. Upon being approached, Middleton became frightened and denied any involvement in the robbery or rape. * * * The defendant, desiring to bring his girlfriend to the scene to make an identification, told Middleton to "wait here" while he left to get her. Although Middleton agreed to wait, the defendant, suspecting that he might flee, gave a knife to Cannon and told him to stay with Middleton to prevent his escape. Thereafter, while waiting for the defendant to return, Middleton, as he was reaching for something in his pocket, apparently charged at Cannon. As Middleton ran toward him, Cannon held out the knife that the defendant had given him and fatally stabbed Middleton. The victim had a straight-edged razor in his pocket which was later identified by the defendant's girlfriend as the one wielded by her assailant during the rape incident.

Cannon (as principal) and Foster (as accomplice) were charged with negligent homicide. If Cannon is guilty as charged, what about Foster? Apply the Model Penal Code.

ii. Natural-and-Probable–Consequences Doctrine

STATE v. LINSCOTT
Supreme Judicial Court of Maine, 1987.
520 A.2d 1067.

SCOLNIK, JUSTICE.

William Linscott appeals from a judgment following a jury-waived trial * * *, convicting him of one count of murder, and one count of robbery. He contends that his conviction of intentional or knowing murder as an accomplice under the accomplice liability statute, 17–A M.R.S.A. § 57(3)(A) (1983), violated his constitutional right to due process of law in that he lacked the requisite intent to commit murder. * * *

The facts are not in dispute. On December 12, 1984, the defendant, then unemployed, and two other men—the defendant's step-brother, Phillip Willey, and Jeffrey Colby—drove * * * to the house of a friend, Joel Fuller. Fuller, with a sawed-off shotgun in his possession, joined the others. The defendant drove to the residence of Larry Ackley, where Fuller obtained 12–gauge shotgun shells.

Later that evening, Fuller suggested that the four men drive to the house of a reputed cocaine dealer, Norman Grenier * * *, take Grenier by surprise, and rob him. The defendant agreed to the plan, reasoning that Grenier, being a reputed drug dealer, would be extremely reluctant to call the police and request they conduct a robbery investigation that might result in the discovery of narcotics in his possession. Fuller stated that Grenier had purchased two kilograms of cocaine that day, and that Grenier had been seen with $50,000 in cash. Fuller guaranteed the defendant $10,000 as his share of the proceeds of the robbery.

The four drove up to Grenier's house, which was situated in a heavily wooded rural area on a dead-end road in Swanville. The defendant and Fuller left the car and approached the house. The defendant carried a hunting knife and switchblade, and Fuller was armed with the shotgun. * * *

The defendant and Fuller walked around to the back of Grenier's house. At that time, Grenier and his girlfriend were watching television in their living room. The defendant and Fuller intended to break in the back door in order to place themselves between Grenier and the bedroom, where they believed Grenier kept a loaded shotgun. Because the back door was blocked by snow, the two men walked around to the front of the house. Under their revised plan the defendant was to break the living room picture window whereupon Fuller would show his shotgun to Grenier, who presumably would be dissuaded from offering any resistance.

The defendant subsequently broke the living room window with his body without otherwise physically entering the house. Fuller immediately fired a shot through the broken window, hitting Grenier in the chest. Fuller left through the broken window after having removed about $1,300 from Grenier's pants pocket, later returning to the house to retrieve an empty shotgun casing. * * *

* * * At a jury-waived trial, * * * the defendant testified that he knew Fuller to be a hunter and that it was not unusual for Fuller to carry a firearm with him, even at night. He nevertheless stated that he had no knowledge of any reputation for violence that Fuller may have had. The defendant further testified that he had no intention of causing anyone's death in the course of the robbery.

At the completion of the trial * * * the trial justice found the defendant guilty of robbery and, on a theory of accomplice liability, found him guilty of murder. The court specifically found that the defendant possessed the intent to commit the crime of robbery, that Fuller intentionally or at least knowingly caused the death of Grenier, and that this murder was a reasonably foreseeable consequence of the defendant's participation in the robbery. However, the court also found that the defendant did not intend to kill Grenier, and that the defendant probably would not have participated in the robbery had he believed that Grenier would be killed in the course of the enterprise.

The sole issue raised on appeal is whether the defendant's conviction pursuant to the second sentence of subsection 3-A of the accomplice liability statute, 17-A M.R.S.A. § 57 (1983),[1] unconstitutionally violates his right to due process under Article I, section 6-A of the Maine Constitution and the Fourteenth Amendment of the United States Constitution. "[T]he Due Process Clause protects the accused against conviction except upon proof beyond a reasonable doubt of every fact necessary to constitute the crime with which he is charged." *In re Winship*, 397 U.S. 358, 364, 90 S.Ct. 1068, 1072, 25 L.Ed.2d 368 (1970). The defendant contends that the accomplice liability statute impermissibly allows the State to find him guilty of murder, which requires proof beyond a reasonable doubt that the murder was committed either intentionally or knowingly, without having to prove either of these two culpable mental states. Instead, the defendant argues, the accomplice liability statute permits the State to employ only a mere negligence standard in convicting him of murder in violation of his right to due process. We find the defendant's argument to be without merit.

The second sentence of section 57(3)(A) endorses the "foreseeable consequence" rule of accomplice liability. *See State v. Goodall*, 407 A.2d 268, 278 (Me.1979).[2] In that case we stated that

---

1. 17-A M.R.S.A. § 57(3)(A) (1983) provides:

   3. A person is an accomplice of another person in the commission of a crime if:

   A. With the intent of promoting or facilitating the commission of the crime, he solicits such other person to commit the crime, or aids or agrees to aid or attempts to aid such other person in planning or committing the crime. *A person is an accomplice under this subsection to any crime the commission of which was a reasonably foreseeable consequence of his conduct* . . .

   (Emphasis added).

2. The "foreseeable consequence" or "natural and probable consequence" rule in complicity law has been stated as follows: "an accessory is liable for any criminal act which in the ordinary

[t]he history of the statute demonstrates that the legislature indeed intended to impose liability upon accomplices for those crimes that were the reasonably foreseeable consequence of their criminal enterprise, *notwithstanding an absence on their part of the same culpability required for conviction as a principal to the crime.*

Id. (emphasis added). Accordingly, we have stated that section 57(3)(A) is to be interpreted as follows: Under the first sentence of that section, which is to be read independently of the second sentence,

liability for a "primary crime" * * * [here, robbery] is established by proof that the actor intended to promote or facilitate that crime. Under the second sentence, liability for any "secondary crime" * * * [here, murder] that may have been committed by the principal is established upon a two-fold showing: (a) that the actor intended to promote the *primary crime,* and (b) that the commission of the secondary crime was a "foreseeable consequence" of the actor's participation in the primary crime.

Id. at 277–278. We have consistently upheld this interpretation of section 57(3)(A). We discern no compelling reason to depart from this construction of the statute.

Furthermore, the foreseeable consequence rule as stated in Section 57(3)(A) merely carries over the objective standards of accomplice liability as used in the common law. Thus, a rule allowing for a murder conviction under a theory of accomplice liability based upon an *objective* standard, despite the absence of evidence that the defendant possessed the culpable *subjective* mental state that constitutes an element of the crime of murder, does not represent a departure from prior Maine law. * * *

We also do not find fundamentally unfair or disproportionate the grading scheme for sentencing purposes * * * [of] murder premised on a theory of accomplice liability * * *. The potential penalty of life imprisonment for murder under a theory of accomplice liability based on an objective standard "does not denote such punitive severity as to shock the conscience of the public, nor our own respective or collective sense of fairness." * * *

For the foregoing reasons, we find no constitutional defect in this statutory provision, nor any fundamental unfairness in its operation. * * *

NOTES AND QUESTIONS

1. Essentially, there is a four-step process the jury must use to decide whether the common law natural-and-probable-consequences doctrine applies in a particular case. First, it must decide if the primary party committed the target offense (or, at least, an inchoate version of the target offense). Second,

_____

course of things was the natural or probable consequence of the crime that he advised or commanded, although such consequence may not have been intended by him." 22 C.J.S. *Criminal Law* § 92 (1961) (footnote omitted). * * *

if she did, the jury must determine if the secondary party was an accomplice in the commission of the target offense. If the answer is yes at the second step, the jury must next determine if the primary party committed *another* crime or crimes, beyond the target offense. If so, then the fourth and final step is for the jury to decide whether the latter crimes, "although not necessarily contemplated at the outset, were reasonably foreseeable consequences of the original criminal acts encouraged or facilitated by the aider and abettor." People v. Woods, 8 Cal.App.4th 1570, 11 Cal.Rptr.2d 231 (1992).

2. Some states have rejected the natural-and-probable-consequences doctrine. E.g., Sharma v. State, 118 Nev. 648, 56 P.3d 868 (2002):

This doctrine has been harshly criticized by "most commentators * * * as both 'incongruous and unjust' because it imposes accomplice liability solely upon proof of foreseeability or negligence when typically a higher degree of mens rea is required of the principal." It permits criminal "liability to be predicated upon negligence even when the crime involved requires a different state of mind." Having reevaluated the wisdom of the doctrine, we have concluded that its general application in Nevada to specific intent crimes is unsound precisely for that reason: it permits conviction without proof that the accused possessed the state of mind required by the statutory definition of the crime. * * *

* * * Because the natural and probable consequences doctrine permits a defendant to be convicted of a specific intent crime where he or she did not possess the statutory intent required for the offense, we hereby disavow and abandon the doctrine. It is not only "inconsistent with more fundamental principles of our system of criminal law," but is also inconsistent with those * * * statutes that require proof of a specific intent to commit the crime alleged.

Reconsider Model Penal Code § 2.06, subsections (3) and (4), which were considered in *Riley* (p. 838). Does the Code apply the natural-and-probable-consequences doctrine?

3. In State v. Fitch, 600 A.2d 826 (Me.1991), the defendant was an accomplice in a robbery, during which a death ensued. The trial court instructed the jury with respect to the defendant's liability for murder in accordance with Maine's complicity statute (see footnote 1 in *Linscott*). During deliberations, the jury requested re-instruction on the subject. The trial judge, over the defendant's objection, explained to the jury that it could convict the defendant of murder if, "[d]uring the course of defendant's conduct in the participation of the offense of robbery, [it] was * * * a reasonably foreseeable consequence of that conduct that the murder of [the victim] could occur." Is the latter instruction correct?

iii. Attendant Circumstances

Suppose that Albert encourages Bob to have intercourse with Carla, an underage female. In most jurisdictions, Bob is guilty of statutory rape whether or not he knows Carla is underage, and even if he reasonably believes that she is old enough to consent, i.e., statutory rape is a strict liability offense.

What about Albert? Assuming that he, too, did not know that Carla was underage, is *he* guilty of statutory rape as an accomplice, or does the intent requirement of accomplice liability bar his conviction? Notice that on these facts Albert intends to promote or facilitate the conduct or result in question (sexual intercourse with Carla); what he lacks is the intent that the intercourse occur with an underage female. Thus, the issue is whether the intent requirement of accomplice liability applies to "attendant circumstance" elements of an offense, as it potentially does to "result" and "conduct" elements.

There is little case law on point. One approach to the issue is to require purpose or knowledge as to attendant circumstance elements, in which case Albert must be acquitted, even as Bob is convicted. Alternatively, an accomplice may be convicted if he acts with the kind of culpability, if any, with respect to the circumstance, that is sufficient to convict the primary party. Therefore, since Bob can be convicted in the absence of any culpability regarding Carla's age, the same standard would apply to Albert.

Unfortunately, the Model Penal Code provides no definitive solution:

> There is a deliberate ambiguity as to whether the purpose requirement extends to circumstance elements of the contemplated offense or whether, as in the case of attempts, the policy of the substantive offense on this point should control. * * * The result, therefore, is that the actor must have a purpose with respect to the proscribed conduct or the proscribed result, with his attitude towards the circumstances to be left to resolution by the courts.

American Law Institute, Model Penal Code and Commentaries, Comment to § 2.06 at 311 n.37 (1985).

Query: Should accomplice law here distinguish between a principal in the second degree and an accessory before the fact? See Commonwealth v. Harris, 74 Mass.App.Ct. 105, 904 N.E.2d 478 (2009) (holding that an accomplice who is present at the time of a statutory rape should be treated no differently than the perpetrator in terms of *mens rea*, but leaving open the question of whether, "avoidance of injustice may in some cases require proof that the [non-present accomplice] had more specific knowledge about the victim's age than would be required for conviction of the principal").

4. ACTUS REUS

In most, multi-party prosecutions, the *actus reus* component of accomplice liability is clear cut, e.g., the secondary party solicited the offense, furnished an instrumentality used in the commission of the crime, or provided other significant active aid in the perpetration of the offense. However, as the following cases demonstrate, difficult issues of fact and policy arise when the secondary party's participation is relatively slight or when the Government seeks to hold her accountable for her omissions, rather than for her conduct.

STATE v. V.T.

Court of Appeals of Utah, 2000.
2000 Utah Ct. App. 189, 5 P.3d 1234.

ORME, JUDGE: * * *

On June 12, 1998, V.T. and two friends, "Moose" and Joey, went to a relative's apartment to avoid being picked up by police for curfew violations. The boys ended up spending the entire night at the apartment.

The next morning, the relative briefly left to run an errand, while the boys remained in her apartment. She returned about fifteen minutes later to find the boys gone, the door to her apartment wide open, and two of her guns missing. She immediately went in search of the group and found them hanging out together near her apartment complex. She confronted the boys about the theft of her guns and demanded that they return them to her. When they failed to do so, she reported the theft to the police.

Two days after the theft of her guns, she discovered that her camcorder, which had been in the apartment when the boys visited, was also missing, and she immediately reported its theft to the police. The police found the camcorder at a local pawn shop, where it had been pawned on the same day the guns were stolen.

Still inside the camcorder was a videotape featuring footage of V.T., Moose, and Joey. The tape included a segment where Moose telephoned a friend, in V.T.'s presence, and discussed pawning the stolen camcorder. V.T. never spoke or gestured during any of this footage.

V.T. was * * * charged with two counts of theft of a firearm; [and] one count of theft, relating to the camcorder * * *.

* * * V.T. was tried [in juvenile court] under an accomplice theory on the three theft charges. The court found that V.T. had committed class A misdemeanor theft of the camcorder * * *. [The judge concluded that there was insufficient evidence to support a finding that V.T. was an accomplice in the gun thefts.]

The sole issue presented by V.T. is whether there was sufficient evidence to support the adjudication that he was an accomplice in the theft of the camcorder. * * *

Utah's accomplice liability statute, Utah Code Ann. § 76–2–202 (1999), provides:

> Every person, acting with the mental state required for the commission of an offense who directly commits the offense, who solicits, requests, commands, encourages, or intentionally aids another person to engage in conduct which constitutes an offense shall be criminally liable as a party for such conduct.

As with any other crime, the State must prove the elements of accomplice liability beyond a reasonable doubt.

The State argues that V.T.'s continued presence during the theft and subsequent phone conversation about selling the camcorder, coupled with his friendship with the other two boys, is enough evidence to support the inference that he had "encouraged" the other two in committing the theft and that he is therefore an accomplice to the crime. * * * Passive behavior, such as mere presence—even continuous presence—absent evidence that the defendant affirmatively did something to instigate, incite, embolden, or help others in committing a crime is not enough to qualify as "encouragement" as that term is commonly used.

The case law in Utah is consistent * * *: " 'Mere presence, or even prior knowledge, does not make one an accomplice' " to a crime absent evidence showing * * * that defendant "advised, instigated, encouraged, or assisted in perpetration of the crime." * * *

The juvenile court's conclusion that V.T. was an accomplice to the camcorder theft was not supported by the evidence in this case. No evidence whatsoever was produced indicating V.T. had encouraged—much less that he solicited, requested, commanded or intentionally aided—the other two boys in the theft of the camcorder.[7]

NOTES AND QUESTIONS

1. Bailey v. United States, 416 F.2d 1110 (D.C.Cir.1969): "Presence is * * * equated to aiding and abetting when * * * it designedly encourages the perpetrator, facilitates the unlawful deed—as when the accused acts as a lookout—or when it stimulates others to render assistance to the criminal act."

2. Hicks v. United States, 150 U.S. 442, 14 S.Ct. 144, 37 L.Ed. 1137 (1893):

We understand [the contested jury instruction] to mean that where an accomplice is present for the purpose of aiding and abetting in a murder, but refrains from so aiding and abetting * * *, he is equally guilty as if he had actively participated by words or acts of encouragement. Thus understood, the statement might, in some instances, be a correct instruction. Thus, if there had been evidence sufficient to show that there had been a previous conspiracy between Rowe [the perpetrator] and Hicks [the alleged accomplice] to waylay and kill [the victim], Hicks, if present at the time of the killing, would be guilty, even if it was found unnecessary for him to act. But the error of such an instruction, in the present case, is in the fact there was no evidence [of a prior conspiracy] on which to base it.

Why would Hicks be guilty of murder, *as an accomplice*, if he had previously conspired with Rowe, and he was present in order to assist in the killing, but found it unnecessary to act?

---

7. We would, of course, conclude otherwise had the evidence shown, for example, that V.T. had suggested to his two friends that they go rob the apartment, that he had pointed out where the camcorder was kept, that he had helped carry the stolen goods out, or that he helped select the pawn shop at which to sell the camcorder.

3. As the preceding materials demonstrate, the line between "*mere* presence" (which does not constitute aiding) and presence coupled with some other factor (which may constitute aiding), is a fine one, indeed. State v. Noriega, 187 Ariz. 282, 928 P.2d 706 (App. 1996), speaks to this issue:

> [S]uppose a pair of young people are lounging on a corner when one announces he is going to throw a rock at a passing vehicle. The companion, without comment, remains with the actor until that person chooses a vehicle and throws a rock at it, damaging that vehicle and injuring its occupant. The companion may have silently approved of the actor's deed and may even have remained at the scene with a private resolve to aid the actor if needed. He may also have demonstrated what would be considered a consciousness of guilt by immediately fleeing from the scene with the actor. Yet, under these facts, the companion is not criminally liable as an accomplice. * * * "An undisclosed intention to render aid if needed will not suffice. * * * Quite clearly, mere presence at the scene of the crime is not enough, nor is mental approval of the actor's conduct. * * * Mere presence plus flight has often been held insufficient."

When should an actor's failure to act, coupled with the requisite *mens rea*, constitute aiding and abetting? See Model Penal Code § 2.06(3)(a)(iii).

4. *Problem.* Francis is driving his car. His wife, their two infant children, and George, a friend, are passengers. With his wife's permission, Francis picks up a hitchhiker, who enters the backseat with George and one of the children. Subsequently, George pulls out a knife and takes the hitchhiker's wallet and watch. Francis says and does nothing during the episode and continues to drive. Is he an accomplice to the robbery? What about his wife? See Pace v. State, 248 Ind. 146, 224 N.E.2d 312 (1967). What would be the result under the Model Penal Code? What *should* be the result?

WILCOX v. JEFFERY

King's Bench Division, 1951.
1 All England Law Reports 464.

LORD GODDARD, C.J.: * * * Herbert William Wilcox, the proprietor of a periodical called "Jazz Illustrated," was charged on an information that "on Dec. 11, 1949, he did unlawfully aid and abet one Coleman Hawkins in contravening art. 1(4) of the Aliens Order, 1920, by failing to comply with a condition attached to a grant of leave to land, to wit, that the said Coleman Hawkins should take no employment paid or unpaid while in the United Kingdom, contrary to art. 18(2) of the Aliens Order, 1920." Under the Aliens Order, art. 1(1), it is provided that

> "* * * an alien coming * * * by sea to a place in the United Kingdom—(a) shall not land in the United Kingdom without the leave of an immigration officer * * *."

It is provided by art. 1(4) that:

> "An immigration officer, in accordance with general or special directions of the Secretary of State, may, by general order or notice or otherwise, attach such conditions as he may think fit to the grant of

leave to land, and the Secretary of State may at any time vary such conditions in such manner as he thinks fit, and the alien shall comply with the conditions so attached or varied * * *.''

If the alien fails to comply, he is to be in the same position as if he has landed without permission, *i.e.,* he commits an offence.

The case is concerned with the visit of a celebrated professor of the saxophone, a gentleman by the name of Hawkins who was a citizen of the United States. He came here at the invitation of two gentlemen of the name of Curtis and Hughes, connected with a jazz club which enlivens the neighbourhood of Willesden. They, apparently, had applied for permission for Mr. Hawkins to land and it was refused, but, nevertheless, this professor of the saxophone arrived with four French musicians. When they came to the airport, among the people who were there to greet them was the appellant. He had not arranged their visit, but he knew they were coming and he was there to report the arrival of these important musicians for his magazine. So, evidently, he was regarding the visit of Mr. Hawkins as a matter which would be of interest to himself and the magazine which he was editing and selling for profit. Messrs. Curtis and Hughes arranged a concert at the Princes Theatre, London. The appellant attended that concert as a spectator. He paid for his ticket. Mr. Hawkins went on stage and delighted the audience by playing the saxophone. The appellant did not get up and protest in the name of the musicians of England that Mr. Hawkins ought not to be here competing with them and taking the bread out of their mouths or the wind out of their instruments. It is not found that he actually applauded, but he was there having paid to go in, and, no doubt, enjoying the performance, and then, lo and behold, out comes his magazine with a most laudatory description, fully illustrated, of this concert. On those facts the magistrate has found that he aided and abetted. * * *

There was not accidental presence in this case. The appellant paid to go to the concert and he went there because he wanted to report it. He must, therefore, be held to have been present, taking part, concurring, or encouraging, whichever word you like to use for expressing this conception. It was an illegal act on the part of Hawkins to play the saxophone or any other instrument at this concert. The appellant clearly knew that it was an unlawful act for him to play. He had gone there to hear him, and his presence and his payment to go there was an encouragement. He went there to make use of the performance, because he went there, as the magistrate finds and was justified in finding, to get "copy" for his newspaper. It might have been entirely different, as I say, if he had gone there and protested, saying: "The musicians' union do not like you foreigners coming here and playing and you ought to get off the stage." If he had booed, it might have been some evidence that he was not aiding and abetting. If he had gone as a member of a *claque* to try to drown the noise of the saxophone, he might very likely be found not guilty of aiding and abetting. In this case it seems clear that he was there, not only to approve and encourage what was done, but to take advantage of it by getting "copy" for his paper. In those circumstances there was evidence on which the magistrate could find that the appellant aided and abetted, and for these reasons I am of opinion that the appeal fails. * * *

NOTES AND QUESTIONS

1. *Inquiring minds want to know.* Who is Jeffery in *Wilcox v. Jeffery*? He was the Magistrate of the Bow Street Magistrate's Court, from which this case originated.

2. Does this case stand for the proposition that everyone who applauded at the concert was an accomplice in the offense? What did Wilcox do that constituted assistance, since the court said it was not determined that he applauded? Was *every* person who paid for a ticket and attended an accomplice even if they did not applaud?

3. *Problem.* On March 6, 1983, a woman entered a tavern in New Bedford, Massachusetts to purchase cigarettes. Sixteen customers, fifteen of whom were male, and the male bartender were present. The victim spoke for a few moments to the other woman present. After the other female left, the victim started to leave. Two men approached her, knocked her to the ground, tore off her clothing, and over a 75–minute period forced her to commit various sexual acts on both of them, which she resisted. During this period, while the victim frequently cried out for help, she heard other customers yelling, laughing, and cheering. None of the customers, nor the bartender, came to her aid or called the police during the assaults. See Commonwealth v. Vieira, 401 Mass. 828, 519 N.E.2d 1320 (1988); Commonwealth v. Cordeiro, 401 Mass. 843, 519 N.E.2d 1328 (1988); Daniel B. Yeager, *A Radical Community of Aid: A Rejoinder to Opponents of Affirmative Duties to Help Strangers*, 71 Wash.U.L.Q. 1, 21 (1993).

Regarding the rapes, what is the liability, if any, of: (1) the cheering customers; (2) the bartender; (3) the non-cheering customers? Regarding the cheering customers, does their liability depend on whether the rapists heard the cheers? Would they be liable if the perpetrators heard the cheering, but would not have desisted even if the customers had remained silent or yelled at them to stop?

STATE v. HELMENSTEIN

Supreme Court of North Dakota, 1968.
163 N.W.2d 85.

STRUTZ, JUDGE.

* * * The defendant was [prosecuted] * * * on a charge of burglary of a grocery store in Hannover. * * * Trial by jury was waived * * *. After trial, the court found the defendant guilty of the offense as charged. This appeal is from the judgment of conviction and from an order denying the defendant's motion for new trial. * * *

The record discloses that, on the night of the alleged burglary, two groups of young people had been driving around in the vicinity of Center,

North Dakota. During the evening, these two groups met at the park in Center. Someone in one of the groups had obtained some beer, and this was passed around and all of them drank some of it. After a while, they all decided to get into one of the automobiles and ride around. They got into the defendant's car. A short time later, someone suggested that they drive to Hannover, about six miles west of Center, and break into the store at that place. When this suggestion was made, one person in the party said she wanted some bananas. Someone else expressed a desire for other articles which could be secured at the store. They drove over to Hannover and parked the car some distance from the store, and three of the party, including the defendant, went to the store, broke in, and returned with beer, cigarettes, candy, and bananas. They then drove back toward Center. On the way, the parties all agreed on what story they would tell the officers of the law if any of them should be questioned. At Center, they divided the loot and separated.

At the trial, five of the young people who had been in this party testified for the State against the defendant. The only witness other than those who were in the party on the night of the burglary was Harold Henke, the owner of the store that had been burglarized. His testimony established that he owned the store, that on the morning following the burglary he found that the store had been entered during the night, and that approximately $130 worth of merchandise had been taken. His testimony in no way connected the defendant with the offense, but merely established the fact that a crime had been committed.

The trial court found the defendant guilty. * * *

The first question for us to consider is whether there was competent evidence against the defendant sufficient to sustain the judgment of conviction. Our statute provides that a conviction may not be had upon the testimony of an accomplice unless his testimony is corroborated by such other evidence as tends to connect the defendant with the commission of the offense, and the corroboration is not sufficient if it merely shows the commission of the offense or the circumstances thereof. * * *

Now, in the light of these rules, let us examine the record before us to determine the status of the witnesses who testified for the State and who were members of the party of young people on the night of the burglary. Carol Weiss contends that she was against the burglary, but she kept her feelings to herself and did not express them. The record discloses that when the burglary was planned she expressed a desire for some bananas. * * * This clearly would make her an accomplice * * *.

Janice Zahn also was called as a witness by the State. She testified that when someone suggested that they break into the store at Hannover, everybody agreed. Thus she admitted that she herself agreed to the burglary when it was suggested, and we believe this makes her, as well as every other person in the party, an accomplice.

Another witness called by the State, who was in the party on the night of the burglary, was Kenneth Cahoon. He admitted that he took part in the actual burglary of the store with the defendant and with one Clem Rohrich. So his status clearly is that of an accomplice. * * *

* * * The only testimony, therefore, which could possibly have corroborated the testimony of the above-named persons—all of whom have clearly been shown to be accomplices—would be the testimony of the witness Glen Zahn. The decision in this case therefore depends entirely upon whether Glen Zahn was an accomplice. * * *

Let us therefore examine the testimony of Glen Zahn to see what he * * * said. He contends that he had secret objections to the burglary which he did not express to anyone. He further testified that he was asleep when the burglary was committed and that he did not take part in the actual burglary of the store. The trial court found that Glen had had too much to drink and that he was asleep during the time of the burglary and in no way aided or abetted or encouraged the crime. Zahn's own testimony, however, discloses that he does not claim to have fallen asleep until the three members of the party left the parked car for the store, for he remembers their leaving. After the burglary had been accomplished, all of them together made up a story to tell to investigating officers in case any of them should be questioned. Zahn admits that he helped make up the story to mislead the officers of the law, and he says, "Well, we all made a story together." Why would Zahn feel it necessary to make up a story to mislead the officers if he had no part in the offense? We believe that the record clearly shows that the burglary in this case was the result of a plan in which each of the parties had a part, and that each of these young people encouraged and countenanced the offense and that each of them thus was concerned in its commission. * * *

Since we hold Zahn to be an accomplice, there is no evidence in this case, other than that of persons who also are accomplices, connecting the defendant with the commission of the offense with which he is charged. Therefore, the evidence against him is insufficient to sustain the judgment of conviction. * * *

NOTES AND QUESTIONS

1. Many states have a corroboration rule as in *Helmenstein*, and/or require a jury instruction cautioning jurors to treat the testimony of an accomplice, or a witness who might be determined by the jury to be an accomplice, with caution.

2. Reconsider the Columbine school massacre (p. 837, Note 2) and Mark Manes's responsibility for the murders. You will remember that Harris said on the tape, "[I]t's not [Manes's] fault. *We would have found someone else.*" Assuming the italicized language is correct, does this matter? *Should* it matter?

In the same regard, do you believe that if "accomplice" Weiss had not asked for the bananas, the crime would not have occurred? In other cases, courts have stated that, with the requisite *mens rea*, a person is an accomplice if she: holds the perpetrator's baby while the latter steals cash, State v. Duran, 86 N.M. 594, 526 P.2d 188 (App. 1974); carries food to her husband for a midday meal "so that the work [of manufacturing bootleg liquor] might continue without interruption," Alexander v. State, 20 Ala.App. 432, 102 So. 597 (1925); or lends a smock to a person planning a murder to keep his clothes clean, George P. Fletcher, Rethinking Criminal Law 677–78 (1978) (reporting a German case).

Do these cases stand for the proposition that one can be an accomplice even if she is not a "but for" cause of the crime? Consider the following.

A. *Is causation required?* No, say most courts. Here is one example:

> We are therefore clear to the conclusion that, before [a defendant] can be found guilty of aiding and abetting the [perpetrator] to kill [the victim], it must appear that [the defendant's participation] * * * aided [the perpetrator] to kill [the victim], contributed to [the victim]'s death, in point of physical fact * * *. The assistance given, however, need not contribute to the criminal result in the sense that but for it the result would not have ensued. * * * It is quite enough if the aid merely rendered it easier for the principal actor to accomplish the end intended by him and the aider and abettor, though in all human probability the end would have been attained without it.[c]

Does Model Penal Code § 2.06 require a causal connection between the accomplice's assistance and the commission of the crime?

B. *Is the no-causation-requirement principle justifiable?* Reflect on the following observation:

> According to traditional complicity doctrine, the accomplice must in fact assist in the crime in the sense that her aid must contribute, at least trivially, to the outcome, but it is unnecessary for the government to prove beyond a reasonable doubt, or at all, that, in the absence of such assistance, the offense would not have occurred when it did.
>
> This absence of a causal requirement is significant. Causation serves a critical role in a just system of criminal laws. * * * [¶] * * * Causation serves as an essential (although not exclusive) tool in the accurate measurement of an actor's moral desert and proportional punishment for an outcome. * * * *But this critical just-deserts feature of criminal law is ignored in the law of complicity*. Because there is no causation requirement, an accomplice may be convicted of a crime only her principal caused, and she may be punished as severely as her cohort. It is this feature (or lack of feature, if you will) of complicity law that allows a prosecutor to obtain the conviction of a person who offers trivial encouragement by applauding the latter's illegality, or who holds a friend's baby so the friend can steal some money, or who responds "oh goody" to another person's stated intention to commit a crime, or who opens the bank door so that the other can enter to rob it; and it is this feature of complicity law that makes such a trivial accomplice subject to the same punishment as the mastermind or perpetrator of the crime.

c.   State ex rel. Martin v. Tally, 102 Ala. 25, 15 So. 722 (1894).

Joshua Dressler, *Reforming Complicity Law: Trivial Assistance as a Lesser Offense?*, 5 Ohio St. J. Crim. L. 427, 435–37 (2008).

3. As noted above, the criminal law generally treats accomplice alike: Each accomplice is guilty of the offense committed by the primary party, and each is subject to the same punishment as the primary actor, regardless of her degree of participation. Is there a better way to handle this? For example, should the law draw a distinction between a "causal accomplice"—one whose assistance is causally essential to the commission of the crime—and a "non-causal accomplice"? See Joshua Dressler, *Reassessing the Theoretical Underpinnings of Accomplice Liability: New Solutions to an Old Problem*, 37 Hastings L.J. 91 (1985) (supporting this distinction). Or, at least, should the law draw a distinction between those whose assistance is trivial and those whose aid is substantial, even if the line is not drawn on the basis of causation? See Paul H. Robinson & John M. Darley, Justice, Liability and Blame 41 (1995) (finding in their complicity study "what intuition would have led us to expect," namely, that "[t]he greater the degree of help provided by the accomplice, * * * the greater the liability assigned [by respondents] to the accomplice"); Dressler, Note 2, supra (suggesting this additional alternative).

4. *Accomplice liability by attempting to aid.* Suppose that Sadie unlocks the front door of Roger's house in order to facilitate Paul's later burglary. However, Paul enters through a window, unaware of Sadie's earlier action. Is Sadie an accomplice in the commission of Paul's burglary?

At common law, Sadie is not an accomplice. An actor is an accomplice in the commission of an offense if she intentionally aids—no matter how minimally—the primary party. Nonetheless, she must *in fact* assist. In Sadie's case, her efforts to help in both hypotheticals failed entirely.

So much for the common law. Would Sadie be guilty as an accomplice to the burglary in a Model Penal Code jurisdiction? Look at § 2.06(3).

Now consider this: Can "attempting to aid" itself constitute a crime? Read on.

PEOPLE v. GENOA

Court of Appeals of Michigan, 1991.
188 Mich.App. 461, 470 N.W.2d 447.

SHEPHERD, PRESIDING JUDGE.

The prosecution appeals * * * a lower court order dismissing a charge against defendant of attempted possession with intent to deliver 650 grams or more of cocaine. We affirm.

The charge against defendant stemmed from a June 6, 1988, transaction in which an undercover agent of the Michigan State Police met with defendant at a hotel and proposed that if defendant gave him $10,000 toward the purchase of a kilogram of cocaine, which the police agent claimed he would then sell, the agent would repay defendant the $10,000, plus $3,500 in profits and a client list. Defendant accepted the proposal and later returned with the $10,000. After defendant left, the police agent turned the money over to the Michigan State Police, and defendant was subsequently arrested.

The district court judge * * * dismissed the charge against defendant on the ground that because the police agent never intended to commit the contemplated crime and, indeed, never did commit it, defendant, though he believed he was giving money for an illegal enterprise, financed nothing. * * *

While the prosecution did not necessarily concede it below, it is readily apparent that the only theory by which it could prosecute defendant was that defendant attempted to aid and abet the crime of possession with intent to deliver cocaine. Defendant certainly could not be shown to have even attempted to constructively possess the cocaine himself, in that the evidence simply indicated that defendant was to help finance the proposed venture. And, while Michigan does not distinguish between principals and accessories for purposes of culpability, certain elements must be established to show someone aided and abetted the commission of a crime. Those elements are that: (1) the underlying crime was committed by either the defendant or some other person, (2) the defendant performed acts or gave encouragement which aided and assisted the commission of the crime, and (3) the defendant intended the commission of the crime or had knowledge that the principal intended its commission at the time of giving aid or encouragement.

Thus, while the conviction of the principal is not necessary to a conviction of an accessory, the prosecution must prove that the underlying crime was committed by someone, and that the defendant either committed or aided and abetted the commission of that crime. However, in the case at bar, it is clear that the underlying crime was never committed by anyone. The absence of this element made it legally impossible for defendant to have committed any offense.

It is apparent to us that the inability to charge or prosecute defendant results from a gap in legislation. * * *

NOTES AND QUESTIONS

1. How would *Genoa* be resolved under the Model Penal Code? See Sections 2.06 and 5.01(3).

2. *Problem.* Hayes proposed to Hill that Hill assist him in the burglary of a store. Unbeknownst to Hayes, Hill is a stepson of the store owner. Hill informed the owner of Hayes's intentions, and with the store owner's permission, feigned agreement. On the night of the planned burglary, Hayes opened a window and helped Hill inside. Hill picked up a side of bacon and handed it out to Hayes. Hayes assisted Hill out of the window, whereupon the two men took 15 to 20 steps (with Hayes holding the bacon) before the police arrived. State v. Hayes, 105 Mo. 76, 16 S.W. 514 (1891). At common law, what offenses (if any) did Hill and Hayes commit, and under what theory (as the perpetrator, or as an accomplice)? Specifically regarding Hayes, would your answer differ under the Model Penal Code?

3. In *Genoa*, the Michigan defendant was charged with attempted possession with intent to deliver cocaine, a prosecution that failed because the person he allegedly assisted was an undercover police officer who never proceeded with the "plan."

Before we leave this portion of the chapter, however, let's consider one more Michigan case, State v. Plunkett, 485 Mich. 50, 780 N.W.2d 280 (2010), although its raises a different "assistance" issue. Simplifying the facts, here is basically what happened: Defendant Plunkett (who, by the way, was an attorney!) gave his prostitute girlfriend, Corson, money and drove her to drug dealer, Spencer, so she could purchase illegal drugs, which she did. On *these* facts, Corson is uncontroversially guilty of *possession* of the drugs, and certainly Plunkett is guilty of *that* offense as an accomplice. But, would it be possible to properly charge attorney Plunkett as an accomplice in the much more serious (and, thus much more severely punished) offense of *delivery* (sale) of the drugs to Corson, committed by Spencer? And, if so, is Corson *herself* guilty of being an accomplice in Spencer's sale to her of the illegal drugs? (On the matter of *Corson*'s guilt as an accomplice in the sale, there is more to be said. See p. 870.)

5. DISTINGUISHING DIRECT FROM ACCOMPLICE LIABILITY

There cannot be a secondary party to a crime in the absence of a principal in the first degree; but an apparent secondary party may himself, on closer inspection, be the principal in the first degree.[d]

BAILEY v. COMMONWEALTH

Supreme Court of Virginia, 1985.
229 Va. 258, 329 S.E.2d 37.

CARRICO, CHIEF JUSTICE.

* * * The question on appeal is whether it was proper to convict Bailey of involuntary manslaughter when, in his absence, the victim was killed by police officers responding to reports from Bailey concerning the victim's conduct.

The death of the victim, Gordon E. Murdock, occurred during the late evening of May 21, 1983, in the aftermath of an extended and vituperative conversation between Bailey and Murdock over their citizens' band radios. During the conversation, which was to be the last in a series of such violent incidents, Bailey and Murdock cursed and threatened each other repeatedly.

Bailey and Murdock lived about two miles apart * * *. On the evening in question, each was intoxicated. Bailey had consumed a "twelve-pack" of beer and a "fifth of liquor" since mid-afternoon; a test of Murdock's blood made during an autopsy showed alcoholic content of ".271% * * * by weight." Murdock was also "legally blind," with vision of

---

d. Glanville Williams, Criminal Law: The General Part 350 (2d ed. 1961).

only 3/200 in the right eye and 2/200 in the left. Bailey knew that Murdock had "a problem with vision" and that he was intoxicated on the night in question.

Bailey also knew that Murdock owned a handgun and had boasted "about how he would use it and shoot it and scare people off with it." Bailey knew further that Murdock was easily agitated and that he became especially angry if anyone disparaged his war hero, General George S. Patton. During the conversation in question, Bailey implied that General Patton and Murdock himself were homosexuals.

Also during the conversation, Bailey persistently demanded that Murdock arm himself with his handgun and wait on his front porch for Bailey to come and injure or kill him. Murdock responded by saying he would be waiting on his front porch, and he told Bailey to "kiss [his] mother or [his] wife and children good-bye because [he would] never go back home."

Bailey then made two anonymous telephone calls to the Roanoke City Police Department. In the first, Bailey reported "a man * * * out on the porch [at Murdock's address] waving a gun around." A police car was dispatched to the address, but the officers reported they did not "see anything."

Bailey called Murdock back on the radio and chided him for not "going out on the porch." More epithets and threats were exchanged. Bailey told Murdock he was "going to come up there in a blue and white car"[1] and demanded that Murdock "step out there on the * * * porch" with his gun "in [his] hands" because he, Bailey, would "be there in just a minute."

Bailey telephoned the police again. This time, Bailey identified Murdock by name and told the dispatcher that Murdock had "a gun on the porch," had "threatened to shoot up the neighborhood," and was "talking about shooting anything that moves." Bailey insisted that the police "come out here and straighten this man out." Bailey refused to identify himself, explaining that he was "right next to [Murdock] out here" and feared revealing his identity.

Three uniformed police officers, Chambers, Beavers, and Turner, were dispatched to Murdock's home. None of the officers knew that Murdock was intoxicated or that he was in an agitated state of mind. Only Officer Beavers knew that Murdock's eyesight was bad, and he did not know "exactly how bad it was." Beavers also knew that Murdock would get "a little 10–96 (mental subject) occasionally" and would "curse and carry on" when he was drinking.

When the officers arrived on the scene, they found that Murdock's "porch light was on" but observed no one on the porch. After several minutes had elapsed, the officers observed Murdock come out of his house with "something shiny in his hand." Murdock sat down on the top step of the porch and placed the shiny object beside him.

---

1. Bailey owned a blue and white vehicle; the police vehicles were also blue and white.

Officer Chambers approached Murdock from the side of the porch and told him to "[l]eave the gun alone and walk down the stairs away from it." Murdock "just sat there." When Chambers repeated his command, Murdock cursed him. Murdock then reached for the gun, stood up, advanced in Chambers' direction, and opened fire. Chambers retreated and was not struck.

All three officers returned fire, and Murdock was struck. Lying wounded on the porch, he said several times, "I didn't know you was the police." He died from "a gunshot wound of the left side of the chest." * * *

In an instruction granted below and not questioned on appeal, the trial court told the jury it should convict Bailey if it found that his negligence or reckless conduct was so gross and culpable as to indicate a callous disregard for human life and that his actions were the proximate cause or a concurring cause of Murdock's death. Bailey concedes that the evidence at trial, viewed in the light most favorable to the Commonwealth, would support a finding that his actions constituted negligence so gross and culpable as to indicate a callous disregard for human life. He contends, however, that he "did not kill Murdock."

Bailey argues that his conviction can be sustained only if he was a principal in the first degree, a principal in the second degree, or an accessory before the fact to the killing of Murdock. The Attorney General concedes that Bailey was not a principal in the second degree or an accessory before the fact, but maintains that he was a principal in the first degree.

Countering, Bailey argues he was not a principal in the first degree because only the immediate perpetrators of crime occupy that status. Here, Bailey says, the immediate perpetrators of Murdock's killing were the police officers who returned Murdock's fire.[2] He was in his own home two miles away, Bailey asserts, and did not control the actors in the confrontation at Murdock's home or otherwise participate in the events that occurred there. Hence, Bailey concludes, he could not have been a principal in the first degree.

We have adopted the rule in this Commonwealth, however, that one who effects a criminal act through an innocent or unwitting agent is a principal in the first degree.

Bailey argues that the present case is distinguishable from *Collins*. There, Bailey says, the accused and the undercover policewoman were working in concert, pursuing a common goal of soliciting and collecting fees for sexual favors; although the policewoman was innocent of the crime of pandering because she had no intent to perform sexual acts, the accused was guilty nevertheless because the fees were collected on his behalf. Here, Bailey asserts, he and the police shared no common scheme

---

2. Bailey admits the officers acted in self-defense.

or goal. Neither, Bailey says, did he share a common goal with Murdock; indeed, "Murdock's intent was to kill Bailey."

The question is not, however, whether Murdock was Bailey's innocent or unwitting agent but whether the police officers who responded to Bailey's calls occupied that status. And, in resolving this question, we believe it is irrelevant whether Bailey and the police shared a common scheme or goal. What is relevant is whether Bailey undertook to cause Murdock harm and used the police to accomplish that purpose, a question which we believe must be answered affirmatively.

Knowing that Murdock was intoxicated, nearly blind, and in an agitated state of mind, Bailey orchestrated a scenario on the evening of May 21, 1983, whose finale was bound to include harmful consequences to Murdock, either in the form of his arrest or his injury or death. * * *

From a factual standpoint, it is clear from the sum total of Bailey's actions that his purpose in calling the police was to induce them to go to Murdock's home and unwittingly create the appearance that Bailey himself had arrived to carry out the threats he had made over the radio. And, from a legal standpoint, it is clear that, for Bailey's mischievous purpose, the police officers who went to Murdock's home and confronted him were acting as Bailey's innocent or unwitting agents.

But, Bailey argues, he cannot be held criminally liable in this case unless Murdock's death was the natural and probable result of Bailey's conduct. Bailey maintains that either Murdock's own reckless and criminal conduct in opening fire upon the police or the officers' return fire constituted an independent, intervening cause absolving Bailey of guilt.

We have held, however, that "[a]n intervening act which is reasonably foreseeable cannot be relied upon as breaking the chain of causal connection between an original act of negligence and subsequent injury." Here, under instructions not questioned on appeal, the jury determined that the fatal consequences of Bailey's reckless conduct could reasonably have been foreseen and, accordingly, that Murdock's death was not the result of an independent, intervening cause but of Bailey's misconduct. At the least, the evidence presented a jury question on these issues. * * *

NOTES AND QUESTIONS

1. Why is Bailey not an accessory before the fact? Would he be an accomplice under Model Penal Code § 2.06?

2. *Innocent agency doctrine.* Some applications of the "innocent agency" or "innocent instrumentality" doctrine, as applied in *Bailey,* are straightforward. For example, if *D,* intending to kill *V,* his infant son, hands *X,* his seven-year-old daughter, poisoned candy and instructs her to feed it to *V* (which she does, killing *V*), *D* is the principal in the first degree. *X,* who lacked the intent to kill and who, in any case, would be excused on the basis of infancy, is *D*'s innocent agent. *X* is no more the principal in the first degree than is a gun or a pit bull purposely used by one person to kill another. *D*'s

liability is predicated on *X*'s actions (as *D*'s putative agent), coupled with *D*'s own mental state. See Model Penal Code § 2.06(2)(a).

Was the court in *Bailey* correct in applying the innocent agency doctrine? Are there any problems in imputing the police officers' conduct to the defendant?

3. In *Bailey,* suppose that Murdock had killed one of the officers before being shot to death by the police. Would *Bailey* be guilty of criminal homicide of the *officer*? If so, would he be guilty as an accomplice or as the primary party?

4. *A case from very long ago . . . .* Consider this 1538 case, identified only as "Case 40," set out in Volume 1 of the Reports of Sir John Spelman: Father was charged with the murder of B. His son, under the age of twelve, testified that, indeed, Father killed B. Father was convicted and hanged. B then turned up alive. (Oops.) An investigation disclosed that the child was tricked or coerced to lie by a bailiff. The issue: Is bailiff guilty of murder? The justices "reported to the [King's] Council that [the bailiff was] not [guilty], for the death was by [process of] law * * *. And if the bailiff were to be [considered] a felon, he would have to be an accessory, but this cannot be [so] where he has no principal."

What did the justices mean by this? And, as we now understand the law, were they correct? (By the way, the opinion went on to state, "But it was advised that the bailiff should have perpetual imprisonment for this horrible act." The opinion fails to state the crime for which the bailiff should receive "perpetual imprisonment.")

5. *. . . And a case from not very long ago.* From Associated Press, March 31, 2007, dateline Arlington Texas:

> Darrell Roberson came home from a card game late one night to find his wife rolling around with another man in a pickup truck in the driveway. Caught in the act with her lover, Tracey Denise Roberson—thinking quickly, if not clearly—cried rape * * *. Her husband pulled a gun and killed the other man with a shot to the head.

The husband was arrested for murder, but the Grand Jury declined to charge the husband with murder or manslaughter. However, it did charge Denise Roberson with manslaughter. She was later convicted and sentenced to five years in prison. Debra Dennis, *Woman Who Falsely Cried Rape Sentenced to 5 Years in Prison*, Dallas Morning News, May 6, 1008.

Thoughts?

6. Harold, a visitor at a state prison, abducts Ira, an inmate, and coerces him to leave the prison. If Harold and Ira are prosecuted for escape, is Ira guilty? Is Harold? Apply Model Penal Code § 242.6(1) (escape).

If Harold *is* guilty, is he guilty as an accomplice or as the primary party? In this regard, look very carefully at Section 242.6(1): Why might it seem odd to say that Harold is the principal in the first degree of this offense? See Sanford H. Kadish, *Complicity, Cause and Blame: A Study in the Interpretation of Doctrine,* 73 Cal.L.Rev. 323, 373 (1985).

6. RELATIONSHIP OF THE LIABILITY OF THE ACCOMPLICE TO THE PRINCIPAL

a. If the Principal Is Acquitted

UNITED STATES v. LOPEZ

United States District Court, N.D. California, 1987.
662 F.Supp. 1083.

LYNCH, DISTRICT JUDGE.

[Ronald McIntosh landed a helicopter on the grounds of the Federal Correctional Institution in order to effect the escape of his girlfriend, Samantha Lopez, whose life allegedly was unlawfully threatened by prison authorities. The two were apprehended 10 days later and prosecuted for various offenses, including prison escape. Prior to their trial, McIntosh and Lopez indicated their intent to raise a "necessity/duress" defense based on the threats to Lopez's life. The following is an excerpt from the trial court's ruling on the government's motion *in limine* for an order barring the presentation of evidence on the defense of necessity or duress.]

* * * In response to the government's motion, each defendant has filed a written offer of proof *in camera*. By these offers of proof, defendants seek to establish the prima facie case required to be shown before defendants are entitled to an instruction on the defense of necessity/duress. The parties agree that if Lopez makes a prima facie showing of each element of the necessity/duress defense, she will be entitled to an instruction on that defense. * * *

McIntosh requests the following jury instruction: "If you find defendant Samantha Lopez not guilty of escape because she acted under necessity/duress, then you must also find defendant McIntosh not guilty of aiding and abetting her alleged escape." The government contends that McIntosh can be convicted of aiding and abetting Lopez' escape even if Lopez succeeds on her necessity/duress defense.

* * * The general rule is that a defendant can be convicted of aiding and abetting even if the principal is not identified or convicted; however, an aider and abettor may not be held liable absent proof that a criminal offense was committed by a principal. "The fact that the principal need not be identified or convicted has never been thought to obviate the need for proof showing that an underlying crime was committed by someone." *United States v. Powell,* 806 F.2d 1421, 1424 (9th Cir.1986).

This Court must therefore determine whether Lopez committed a criminal offense if her necessity/duress defense succeeds. This determination requires an examination of the theoretical distinctions between two categories of defenses: justification and excuse. Lopez' alleged defense of necessity/duress must then be classified as either a justification or an excuse.

Justification defenses are those providing that, although the act was committed, it is not wrongful. For example, a forest fire is burning toward a town of 10,000 residents. An actor burns a field of corn located between the fire and the town in order to set up a firebreak. By setting fire to the field with the intent to destroy it, the actor satisfies all the elements of the crime of arson; however, he most likely will have a complete defense because his conduct is justified. Burning the field avoided a greater societal harm; therefore, the act is not a crime.

When a defense is categorized as an excuse, however, the result is that, although the act is wrongful, the actor will not be held accountable. * * * Thus, an insane person who robs a bank will be excused from liability. * * *

The classification of a defense as a justification or an excuse has an important effect on the liability of one who aids and abets the act. A third party has the right to assist an actor in a justified act. Therefore, a third party could not be held liable for aiding and abetting the arson described in the hypothetical above. In contrast, a sane getaway driver could be convicted of aiding and abetting an insane person's bank robbery. Excuses are always personal to the actor.

The defense of duress or coercion traditionally arises when a person unlawfully commands another to do an unlawful act using the threat of death or serious bodily injury. * * *

The defense of necessity may be raised in a situation in which the pressure of natural physical forces compels an actor to choose between two evils. The actor may choose to violate the literal terms of the law in order to avoid a greater harm. The defense of necessity is categorized as a justification.

In the context of prison escapes, the distinction between duress/coercion and necessity has been hopelessly blurred. In fact, courts seem to use the two terms interchangeably. * * *

This Court believes, however, that the defense asserted by Lopez, under the facts of this case, most nearly resembles necessity, which is a justification to the alleged crime. In the present case, Lopez' claim is not that the alleged threats overwhelmed her will so that her inability to make the "correct" choice should be excused. Instead, Lopez claims that she, in fact, did make the correct choice. * * *

Accordingly, if the jury finds Lopez not guilty of escape by reason of her necessity defense, her criminal act will be justified. * * * No criminal offense will have been committed by a principal. McIntosh is therefore entitled to his requested jury instruction. * * *

NOTES AND QUESTIONS

1. *Follow-up*. Both Lopez and McIntosh were convicted of prison escape. Lopez was sentenced to imprisonment for five years. McIntosh received a similar sentence for assisting her, but received fifteen additional years on

additional charges, including air piracy. Their convictions were affirmed on appeal. 885 F.2d 1428 (9th Cir. 1989).

2. What if McIntosh had *not* known of Samantha Lopez's purported reason for wanting to escape. Assume he just wanted to help her escape because of their relationship. Should McIntosh be permitted to assert Lopez's necessity defense in these changed circumstances?

b. If the Principal Is Convicted

PEOPLE v. McCOY

Supreme Court of California, 2001.
25 Cal.4th 1111, 108 Cal.Rptr.2d 188, 24 P.3d 1210.

CHIN, J.

We granted review to decide whether an aider and abettor may be guilty of [a] greater homicide-related offense[] than * * * the actual perpetrator committed. Because defenses or extenuating circumstances may exist that are personal to the actual perpetrator and do not apply to the aider and abettor, the answer, sometimes, is yes. We reverse the judgment of the Court of Appeal, which concluded otherwise.

I. FACTUAL AND PROCEDURAL HISTORY

[Ejaan Dupree McCoy and Derrick Lakey were tried together and convicted of first-degree murder arising out of a drive-by shooting in Stockton in 1995. McCoy shot to death the victim, but he claimed self-defense. Although the jury rejected the defense, the Court of Appeal unanimously reversed McCoy's conviction on the ground that the trial judge misinstructed the jury on the theory of imperfect (unreasonable) self-defense. The appellate court stated that if the jury had accepted the imperfect self-defense claim, McCoy would have been guilty of voluntary manslaughter.

The Court of Appeal also reversed Lakey's murder conviction on the ground that, "under California law, a defendant who is tried as an aider and abettor cannot be convicted of an offense greater than that of which the actual perpetrator is convicted, where the aider and abettor and the perpetrator are tried in the same trial upon the same evidence."]

II. DISCUSSION

If a person kills or attempts to kill in the unreasonable but good faith belief in having to act in self-defense, the belief negates what would otherwise be malice, and that person is guilty of voluntary manslaughter or attempted voluntary manslaughter, not murder or attempted murder. McCoy's testimony provided evidence that he acted in unreasonable self-defense * * *. Thus, it is possible that on retrial McCoy will be found guilty of manslaughter * * * rather than murder * * *.

The question before us is whether reversal of McCoy's conviction[] also requires reversal of Lakey's. * * *

We have described the mental state required of an aider and abettor as "different from the mental state necessary for conviction as the actual perpetrator." The difference, however, does not mean that the mental state of an aider and abettor is less culpable than that of the actual perpetrator. On the contrary, outside of the natural and probable consequences doctrine, an aider and abettor's mental state must be at least that required of the direct perpetrator. * * *

As stated in [a] work by Professor [Joshua] Dressler, "many commentators have concluded that there is no conceptual obstacle to convicting a secondary party of a more serious offense than is proved against the primary party. As they reason, once it is proved that 'the principal has caused an *actus reus,* the liability of each of the secondary parties should be assessed according to his own *mens rea.*' That is, although joint participants in a crime are tied to a 'single and common *actus reus,*' 'the individual *mentes reae* or levels of guilt of the joint participants are permitted to float free and are not tied to each other in any way. If their *mentes reae* are different, their independent levels of guilt * * * will necessarily be different as well.' " (Dressler, Understanding Criminal Law (2d ed.1995) § 30.06[C], p. 450, fns. omitted.)

Professor Dressler explained how this concept operates with homicide. "An accomplice may be convicted of first-degree murder, even though the primary party is convicted of second-degree murder or of voluntary manslaughter. This outcome follows, for example, if the secondary party, premeditatedly, soberly and calmly, assists in a homicide, while the primary party kills unpremeditatedly, drunkenly, or in provocation. Likewise, it is possible for a primary party negligently to kill another (and, thus, be guilty of involuntary manslaughter), while the secondary party is guilty of murder, because he encouraged the primary actor's negligent conduct, with the intent that it result in the victim's death." * * *

As another example, assume someone, let us call him Iago, falsely tells another person, whom we will call Othello, that Othello's wife, Desdemona, was having an affair, hoping that Othello would kill her in a fit of jealousy. Othello does so without Iago's further involvement. In that case, depending on the exact circumstances of the killing, Othello might be guilty of manslaughter, rather than murder, on a heat of passion theory. Othello's guilt of manslaughter, however, should not limit Iago's guilt if his own culpability were greater. Iago should be liable for his own acts as well Othello's, which he induced and encouraged. But Iago's criminal liability, as Othello's, would be based on his own personal mens rea. If, as our hypothetical suggests, Iago acted with malice, he would be guilty of murder even if Othello, who did the actual killing, was not.

We thus conclude that when a person, with the mental state necessary for an aider and abettor, helps or induces another to kill, that person's guilt is determined by the combined acts of all the participants as well as that person's own mens rea. If that person's mens rea is more culpable than another's, that person's guilt may be greater even if the other might be deemed the actual perpetrator.[3]

NOTES AND QUESTIONS

1. *In regard to footnote 3.* In Regina v. Richards, [1974] Q.B. 776, Isabelle Richards solicited two men to grievously injure her husband. The men proceeded to wound the husband, but not grievously. She and the men were indicted for the offense of wounding with intent to do grievous bodily harm, under Section 18 of the Offenses against the Person Act (Count 1), and of the alternative and lesser charge of simple wounding, under Section 20 of the same Act (Count 2). The jury acquitted the men of Count 1, but convicted them of Count 2. Richards, however, was convicted of the greater offense (Count 1).

As in *McCoy*, appellant Richards argued that if the men who committed the crime were only guilty of wounding, her conviction of the greater offense of wounding with the intent to do grievous bodily harm could not stand. The Crown argued, as in *McCoy*, that Richards's level of guilt should depend on her own *mens rea*, which here was greater than that of the perpetrators. The Court of Appeal, Criminal Division ruled, however, that Richards's conviction for the greater offense could not stand.

Is there any way conceptually to justify this outcome without also rejecting the reasoning in *McCoy*? Consider Sanford H. Kadish, *Complicity, Cause and Blame: A Study in the Interpretation of Doctrine*, 73 Calif.L.Rev. 323, 388–89 (1985), who defended the Court of Appeal's ruling:

> Surely the strongest argument for [convicting Richards of the more serious offense] is that the culpability of her hirelings is irrelevant to *her* culpability. But that argument proves too much. If her hirelings committed no assault, but instead went to the police, it is incontrovertible that Mrs. Richards could not be found liable for any assault, let alone an aggravated assault. Yet whether her hirelings chose to do as she bade them or to go to the police is also irrelevant to her culpability. The point would be that however culpable her intentions she could not be blamed for an assault that did not take place. The same retort is applicable on the facts of the case: an actual assault took place (and Mrs. Richards is liable for it) but an aggravated assault did not take place. * * * She could properly be held liable for solicitation to commit an aggravated assault, not for aggravated assault.

Is Professor Kadish correct in defending the *Richard* result?

In Regina v. Howe, [1987] 1 App.Cas. 417, [1987] 1 All Eng.Rep. 771, the majority of the House of Lords agreed (albeit in dictum) that *Richards* should be overruled.

---

3. Because we cannot anticipate all possible nonhomicide crimes or circumstances, we express no view on whether or how these principles apply outside the homicide context.

7.   LIMITS TO ACCOMPLICE LIABILITY

IN RE MEAGAN R.

Court of Appeal, Fourth District, California, 1996.
42 Cal.App.4th 17, 49 Cal.Rptr.2d 325.

WORK, ACTING PRESIDING JUSTICE.

[Oscar Rodriguez broke into the home of Joani Rodriguez, his ex-girlfriend, with the assistance of 14–year–old Meagan R., in order for Oscar and Meagan to have sexual intercourse, in violation of California Penal Code § 261.5 (statutory rape).]

Meagan R. appeals a judgment entered on juvenile court true findings she had committed burglary * * *. She challenges the burglary finding predicated upon a finding she entered a residence with the intent to aid and abet her own statutory rape * * *. * * *

* * * The People acknowledge the English authority, The *Queen v. Tyrrell* (1893) 1 Q.B. 710, holding it was not criminal for a minor female to aid and abet a male in having unlawful sexual intercourse with her. The court reasoned the law was designed to protect women and girls against themselves and it would be nearly impossible to obtain convictions if women or girls were also brought within the scope of the law. The court further reasoned that by legislative design (the absence of any intent to treat the female as a criminal) young females were omitted from operation of the statute and potential criminal liability. The progeny of this English authority includes the U.S. Supreme Court's decision in *Gebardi v. United States* [see p. 823 supra], holding a woman who simply consents to be transported across the state line for the purpose of engaging in sexual intercourse is not a coconspirator to violate the Mann Act (18 U.S.C. § 2421 et seq.). The court rested its decision

> "upon the ground that we perceive in the failure of the Mann Act to condemn the woman's participation in those transportations which are effected with her mere consent, evidence of an affirmative legislative policy to leave her acquiescence unpunished. * * *"

Within the context of being an aider or abettor, the foregoing authority establishes a rule that where the Legislature has dealt with crimes which necessarily involve the joint action of two or more persons, and where no punishment at all is provided for the conduct, or misconduct, of one of the participants, the party whose participation is not denounced by statute cannot be charged with criminal conduct on either a conspiracy or aiding and abetting theory. So, although generally a defendant may be liable to prosecution * * * as an aider and abettor to commit a crime even though he or she is incapable of committing the crime itself,[e] the rule does not apply where the statute defining the substantive offense discloses an affirmative legislative policy the conduct of one of the parties shall go unpunished. Moreover, when the Legislature has imposed criminal penalties to protect a specific class of individuals, "it can hardly have meant

---

e. For example, at common law, a husband may be convicted as an accomplice in the rape of his wife, although he cannot be convicted as the perpetrator of the offense.

that a member of that very class should be punishable either as an aider or abettor or as a co-conspirator.''

* * * Meagan was the protected victim under section 261.5, a provision designed to criminalize the exploitation of children rather than to penalize the children themselves. * * * A ruling to the contrary that a child could be held responsible on a theory of aiding and abetting for violating such a statute would be contrary to express legislative intent. Consequently, Meagan, as the victim of the statutory rape, cannot be prosecuted on that charge, regardless whether her culpability be predicated upon being a coconspirator, an aider and abettor or an accomplice given her legislatively protected status.

Accordingly, given that Meagan under the circumstances of this case was the victim of statutory rape under section 261.5, the juvenile court cannot rely on that crime to serve as the predicate felony in a true finding she committed burglary. When she entered Joani's residence, she had no punishable intent, for she did not have the culpable state of mind required for burglary. * * *

The judgment is reversed * * * as to the true finding regarding the burglary. * * *

Notes and Questions

1. This case involves what is sometimes characterized as the "legislative exemption" defense to accomplice liability. How does the Model Penal Code deal with Meagan's situation? Look at MPC § 2.06(6).

2. Your answer to Note 1 should demonstrate that there is another limitation to accomplice liability besides the one raised in *Meagan R.* Reconsider the *Plunkett* case (p. 859, Note 3). If the prosecutor had chosen to charge Corson as an accomplice of Spencer in the sale of the drugs to her, would she have had a basis for avoiding conviction? Look again at the Model Penal Code.

STATE v. FORMELLA

Supreme Court of New Hampshire, 2008.
158 N.H. 114, 960 A.2d 722.

Galway, J.

The defendant, Paul Formella, appeals his conviction following a bench trial * * * for [a theft based on] criminal liability for the conduct of another. *See* RSA 626:8 (2007). We affirm.

The relevant facts are not in dispute. On the afternoon of Wednesday, June 13, 2007, the defendant, then a junior at Hanover High School, and two friends, were studying at the Howe Library near the school. Wednesdays were typically early release days at the school, and students had been dismissed at 2:00 p.m. After studying for approximately two hours, the defendant and his friends returned to the school to retrieve some books from their second-floor lockers. Upon entering the school, they encountered another group of students who said they intended to steal mathematics exams from the third floor. The defendant and his companions were asked to serve as lookouts during the theft, which they agreed to do. They were instructed to yell something like "did you get your math book?" up to the third floor as a code to alert the thieves if someone was coming.

The defendant and his friends then proceeded to their second-floor lockers. The defendant testified that on their way to their lockers they looked around to "confirm or dispel" whether anyone was there. Once the defendant and his friends had retrieved their books, they "were all feeling like this was the wrong thing to do," and decided to head back down to the first floor to wait for the other group. On their way down the stairs, they encountered some janitors who told them that they ought to leave the school. The defendant and his friends left the school building, but waited in the parking lot for approximately five to ten minutes for the other group. Eventually, the other students exited the school with the stolen examinations and all of the students shared the exam questions.

The next week, someone informed the dean of students that some students had stolen the exams. The police were called, and in connection with their investigation they interviewed the defendant, who admitted his involvement in the theft. He was later charged with [the theft based on] criminal liability for conduct of another. *See* RSA 626:8. Following his conviction, the defendant appealed to this court.

On appeal, the defendant * * * contends that the trial court erred in failing to make findings of fact relative to the timing of his withdrawal from the theft and the completion of the theft because, he argues, without such findings the trial court could not properly apply RSA 626:8. * * *

RSA 626:8 provides, in relevant part, that an individual is criminally liable for the conduct of another when he acts as an accomplice in the commission of an offense. A person is an accomplice when with the purpose of promoting or facilitating the commission of an offense, he aids or agrees or attempts to aid another person in planning or committing the offense. RSA 626:8 further provides, however, that a person is not an accomplice if he "terminates his complicity prior to the commission of the offense and wholly deprives it of effectiveness in the commission of the offense or gives timely warning to the law enforcement authorities or otherwise makes proper effort to prevent the commission of the offense."

The defendant does not dispute that he became an accomplice in the first instance when he agreed to act as a lookout. Accordingly, we are concerned only with whether the defendant's later acts terminated his liability as an accomplice. We note that the defendant does not contend that he gave timely warning to law enforcement or otherwise made "proper effort" to prevent the offense. Thus, under RSA 626:8, VI(c) the defendant was not an accomplice if: (1) he terminated his complicity in the crime; (2) his termination occurred prior to the commission of the offense;

and (3) he wholly deprived his complicity of effectiveness in the commission of the offense.

* * * As regards the third factor, * * * the statute does not define what is required for a person to "wholly deprive" his complicity of effectiveness in the commission of an offense. According to the State, an overt act aimed at undermining the prior complicity is required, while the defendant argues that, at least in this case, no such act is necessary. As the statute does not clarify whether such an act is necessary, we conclude that it is ambiguous, and we look to other sources to determine legislative intent.

RSA 626:8, like much of our criminal law, is based upon the Model Penal Code. Accordingly, we look to the Model Penal Code and its commentaries for guidance. RSA 626:8 tracks the provisions of section 2.06 of the Model Penal Code. Comment 9(c) to section 2.06 addresses situations where liability may be averted if the accomplice's complicity is terminated prior to the commission of the crime. The comment notes that the actions sufficient to deprive the prior complicity of effectiveness vary with the type of accessorial behavior. Relevant to the analysis here, the comment states that if "complicity inhered in request or encouragement, countermanding disapproval may suffice to nullify its influence, providing it is heard in time to allow reconsideration by those planning to commit the crime." The comments thus indicate that in order to deprive the prior complicity of effectiveness, one who has encouraged the commission of an offense may avoid liability by terminating his or her role in the commission of the crime *and* by making his or her disapproval known to the principals sufficiently in advance of the commission of the crime to allow them time to reconsider as well.

While there appears to be a paucity of authority on the issue, the view that an accomplice must make some affirmative act, such as an overt expression of disapproval to the principals, accords with that of other jurisdictions with statutes mirroring the provisions of the Model Penal Code. This is not to say that the terminating accomplice must actually prevent the crime from occurring. Instead, he need only make some act demonstrating to the principals of the crime that he has withdrawn, and he must do so in a manner, and at such a time, that the principals could do likewise. We agree with the rationale of these authorities.

With the above understanding, we turn to the defendant's specific claim[] of error. According to the defendant, the trial court erred in failing to make findings of fact regarding the time the defendant terminated his complicity, and the time the theft occurred because without such findings the trial court could not properly apply the statute. * * * [H]e contends, it was critical to know when he withdrew and when the crime was committed, so that it could be determined whether he withdrew at a time sufficient to satisfy the statute. We disagree.

The relevant portion of the statute is phrased in the conjunctive. For a person not to be an accomplice he must terminate his complicity prior to the commission of the offense *and* wholly deprive that complicity of its effectiveness. Even assuming the defendant terminated his complicity prior to the commission of the offense, he did not wholly deprive his complicity of its effectiveness.

As stated above, to extricate himself from accomplice liability, the defendant needed to make an affirmative act, such as communicating his withdrawal to the principals. Here, the defendant made no such act. * * * He did not communicate his withdrawal, discourage the principals from acting, inform the custodians, or do any other thing which would deprive his complicity of effectiveness. In fact, the principals remained unaware of his exit. Thus, the defendant did not do that which was necessary to undo his complicity.

The defendant contends that because he had been acting as a lookout, leaving the scene so as to no longer be "looking out" deprived his complicity of its effectiveness, and, therefore, findings regarding the timing of the offense were required. We disagree. While at the point he left the scene he was no longer an effective lookout, the defendant did nothing to counter his prior complicity. According to the defendant, the principals had requested aid in committing the offense, he agreed to provide it, and he agreed to warn the principals if anyone approached, thus encouraging the act. Further, upon reaching the second floor the defendant looked around to "confirm or dispel" whether anyone was around who might have apprehended the thieves or otherwise spoiled the crime. Thus, it was the complicity of agreeing to aid the primary actors and then actually aiding them that needed to be undone; silently withdrawing from the scene did not, in any way, undermine the encouragement the defendant had provided. As there was no evidence that the defendant had wholly deprived his complicity of its effectiveness, it was not error for the trial court to refuse to make findings on the timing of the offense because such findings would not have altered the result. * * *

B. CONSPIRACY LIABILITY

PINKERTON v. UNITED STATES

Supreme Court of the United States, 1946.
328 U.S. 640, 66 S.Ct. 1180, 90 L.Ed. 1489.

[For the opinion in this case, see p. 780, supra.]

NOTES AND QUESTIONS

1. Consider (again, if necessary) the Problem found at p. 782, Note 2. Now that you have learned about accomplice liability *and* conspiracy liability under *Pinkerton*, answer the Problem using *both* theories. Are the results the same? If not, why not?

C. VICARIOUS LIABILITY

COMMONWEALTH v. KOCZWARA

Supreme Court of Pennsylvania, 1959.
397 Pa. 575, 155 A.2d 825.

COHEN, JUSTICE.

This is an appeal from the judgment of the Court of Quarter Sessions of Lackawanna County sentencing the defendant to three months in the Lackawanna County Jail, a fine of five hundred dollars and the costs of prosecution, in a case involving violations of the Pennsylvania Liquor Code.

John Koczwara, the defendant, is the licensee and operator of an establishment on Jackson Street in the City of Scranton known as J.K.'s Tavern. At that place he had a restaurant liquor license issued by the Pennsylvania Liquor Control Board. The Lackawanna County Grand Jury indicted the defendant on [four] counts for violations of the Liquor Code. The first and second counts averred that the defendant permitted minors, unaccompanied by parents, guardians or other supervisors, to frequent the tavern on February 1st and 8th, 1958; the third count charged the defendant with selling beer to minors on February 8th, 1958; [and] the fourth charged the defendant with permitting beer to be sold to minors on February 8th, 1958 * * *. * * *

At the conclusion of the Commonwealth's evidence, count three of the indictment, charging the sale by the defendant personally to the minors, was removed from the jury's consideration by the trial judge on the ground that there was no evidence that the defendant had personally participated in the sale or was present in the tavern when sales to the minors took place. Defense counsel then demurred to the evidence as to the other three counts. The demurrer was overruled. Defendant thereupon rested without introducing any evidence and moved for a directed verdict of acquittal. The motion was denied, the case went to the jury and the jury returned a verdict of guilty as to each of the remaining three counts: two counts of permitting minors to frequent the licensed premises without parental or other supervision, and the count of permitting sales to minors. * * *

Defendant raises two contentions, both of which, in effect, question whether the undisputed facts of this case support the judgment and sentence imposed by the Quarter Sessions Court. Judge Hoban found as fact that "in every instance the purchase [by minors] was made from a bartender, not identified by name, and service to the boys was made by the bartender. There was no evidence that the defendant was present on any one of the occasions testified to by these witnesses, nor that he had any personal knowledge of the sales to them or to other persons on the premises." We, therefore, must determine the criminal responsibility of a licensee of the Liquor Control Board for acts committed by his employees upon his premises, without his personal knowledge, participation, or presence, which acts violate a valid regulatory statute passed under the Commonwealth's police power.

While an employer in almost all cases is not criminally responsible for the unlawful acts of his employees, unless he consents to, approves, or participates in such acts, courts all over the nation have struggled for years in applying this rule within the framework of "controlling the sale of intoxicating liquor." At common law, any attempt to invoke the doctrine of *respondeat superior* in a criminal case would have run afoul of our deeply ingrained notions of criminal jurisprudence that guilt must be personal and individual.[1] In recent decades, however, many states have enacted detailed regulatory provisions in fields which are essentially non-criminal, e.g., pure food and drug acts, speeding ordinances, building regulations, and child labor, minimum wage and maximum hour legislation. Such statutes are generally enforceable by light penalties, and although violations are labelled crimes, the considerations applicable to them are totally different from those applicable to true crimes, which involve moral delinquency and which are punishable by imprisonment or another serious penalty. Such so-called statutory crimes are in reality an attempt to utilize the machinery of criminal administration as an enforcing arm for social regulations of a purely civil nature, with the punishment totally unrelated to questions of moral wrongdoing or guilt. It is here that the social interest in the general well-being and security of the populace has been held to outweigh the individual interest of the particular defendant. The penalty is imposed despite the defendant's lack of a criminal intent or mens rea.

Not the least of the legitimate police power areas of the legislature is the control of intoxicating liquor. * * * It is abundantly clear that the conduct of the liquor business is lawful only to the extent and manner permitted by statute. Individuals who embark on such an enterprise do so with knowledge of considerable peril, since their actions are rigidly circumscribed by the Liquor Code.

Because of the peculiar nature of this business, one who applies for and receives permission from the Commonwealth to carry on the liquor trade assumes the highest degree of responsibility to his fellow citizens. As the licensee of the Board, he is under a duty not only to regulate his own personal conduct in a manner consistent with the permit he has received, but also to control the acts and conduct of any employee to whom he entrusts the sale of liquor. Such fealty is the *quid pro quo* which the Commonwealth demands in return for the privilege of entering the highly

---

1. The distinction between *respondeat superior* in tort law and its application to the criminal law is obvious. In tort law, the doctrine is employed for the purpose of settling the incidence of loss upon the party who can best bear such loss. But the criminal law is supported by totally different concepts. We impose penal treatment upon those who injure or menace social interests, partly in order to reform, partly to prevent the continuation of the anti-social activity and partly to deter others. If a defendant has personally lived up to the social standards of the criminal law and has not menaced or injured anyone, why impose penal treatment?

restricted and, what is more important, the highly dangerous business of selling intoxicating liquor.

In the instant case, the defendant has sought to surround himself with all the safeguards provided to those within the pale of criminal sanctions. He has argued that a statute imposing criminal responsibility should be construed strictly, with all doubts resolved in his favor. While the defendant's position is entirely correct, we must remember that we are dealing with a statutory crime within the state's plenary police power. In the field of liquor regulation, the legislature has enacted a comprehensive Code aimed at regulating and controlling the use and sale of alcoholic beverages. The question here raised is whether the legislature intended to impose vicarious criminal liability on the licensee-principal for acts committed on his premises without his presence, participation or knowledge.

This Court has stated, as long ago as Commonwealth v. Weiss, 139 Pa. 247, 251, 21 A. 10 (1891), that "whether a criminal intent, or a guilty knowledge, is a necessary ingredient of a statutory offense * * * is a matter of construction. It is for the legislature to determine whether the public injury, threatened in any particular matter, is such and so great as to justify an absolute and indiscriminate prohibition."

In the Liquor Code, Section 493, the legislature has set forth twenty-five specific acts which are condemned as unlawful, and for which penalties are provided in Section 494. Subsections (1) and (14) of Section 493 contain the two offenses charged here. In neither of these subsections is there any language which would require the prohibited acts to have been done either knowingly, wilfully or intentionally, there being a significant absence of such words as "knowingly, wilfully, etc." * * * The omission of any such word in the subsections of Section 494 is highly significant. It indicates a legislative intent to eliminate both knowledge and criminal intent as necessary ingredients of such offenses. * * *

As the defendant has pointed out, there is a distinction between the requirement of a mens rea and the imposition of vicarious absolute liability for the acts of another. It may be that the courts below, in relying on prior authority, have failed to make such a distinction.[5] In any case, we fully recognize it. Moreover, we find that the intent of the legislature in enacting this Code was not only to eliminate the common law requirement of a mens rea, but also to place a very high degree of responsibility upon the holder of a liquor license to make certain that neither he nor anyone in his employ commit any of the prohibited acts upon the licensed premises. Such a burden of care is imposed upon the licensee in order to protect the public from the potentially noxious effects of an inherently dangerous business. We, of course, express no opinion as to the *wisdom* of the legislature's imposing vicarious responsibility under certain sections of the Liquor Code. There may or may not be an economic-sociological justification for such liability on a theory of deterrence. Such determina-

---

5. We must also be extremely careful to distinguish the present situation from the question of *corporate* criminal liability. * * *

tion is for the legislature to make, so long as the constitutional requirements are met.

Can the legislature, consistent with the requirements of due process, thus establish absolute criminal liability? Were this the defendant's first violation of the Code, and the penalty solely a minor fine of from $100–$300, we would have no hesitation in upholding such a judgment. Defendant, by accepting a liquor license, must bear this financial risk. Because of a prior conviction for violations of the Code, however, the trial judge felt compelled under the mandatory language of the statute to impose not only an increased fine of five hundred dollars, but also a three month sentence of imprisonment. Such sentence of imprisonment in a case where liability is imposed vicariously cannot be sanctioned by this Court consistently with * * * Section 9, Article I of the Constitution of the Commonwealth of Pennsylvania.

The Courts of the Commonwealth have already strained to permit the legislature to carry over the civil doctrine of *respondeat superior* and to apply it as a means of enforcing the regulatory scheme that covers the liquor trade. We have done so on the theory that the Code established petty misdemeanors involving only light monetary fines. It would be unthinkable to impose vicarious criminal responsibility in cases involving true crimes. Although to hold a principal criminally liable might possibly be an effective means of enforcing law and order, it would do violence to our more sophisticated modern-day concepts of justice. Liability for all true crimes, wherein an offense carries with it a jail sentence, must be based exclusively upon personal causation. It can be readily imagined that even a licensee who is meticulously careful in the choice of his employees cannot supervise every single act of the subordinates. A man's liberty cannot rest on so frail a reed as whether his employee will commit a mistake in judgment. * * *

* * * [W]e are * * * holding that so much of the judgment as calls for imprisonment is invalid, and we are leaving intact the five hundred dollar fine imposed by Judge Hoban under the subsequent offense section. * * *

MUSMANNO, JUSTICE (dissenting).

The Court in this case is doing what it has absolutely no right to do. * * *

The Majority of this Court is doing something which can find no justification in all the law books which ornament the libraries and enlighten the judges and lawyers in this Commonwealth. It sustains the conviction of a person for acts admittedly not committed by him, not performed in his presence, not accomplished at his direction, and not even done within his knowledge. It is stigmatizing him with a conviction for an act which, in point of personal responsibility, is as far removed from him as if it took place across the seas. The Majority's decision is so novel, so unique, and so bizarre that one must put on his spectacles, remove them to wipe the lenses, and then put them on again in order to assure himself that what he reads is a judicial decision proclaimed in Philadelphia, the home of the Liberty Bell, * * * and the place where the fathers of our country met to draft the Constitution of the United States, the Magna Charta of the liberties of Americans and the beacon of hope of mankind seeking justice everywhere. * * *

The Majority builds its superstructure of rationalization on a spongy foundation of fallacy and misconception. The Majority Opinion says:

> "It is abundantly clear that the conduct of the liquor business is lawful only to the extent and manner permitted by statute."

This is only affirming what was said more fully by the Trial Court, namely:

> "The liquor business is an unlawful business and its conduct is only lawful to the extent and manner permitted by statute and the licensing of persons to sell liquor and other alcoholic beverages is an exercise of the police power."

The liquor business is *not* an unlawful business. If it is unlawful, then the Commonwealth of Pennsylvania is engaged in an illegal business. Obviously this cannot be so. The liquor business is as lawful as any other business conducted openly in the Commonwealth. The Majority does not save its broad statement that the liquor business is unlawful by adding that it "is lawful only to the extent and manner permitted by statute." In fact, this supposed modification only accentuates the absurdity of the major premise. What the Majority says about the liquor business can equally be said of the milk business because the milk business obviously is lawful only to the extent that those who engage in milking cows, filling milk bottles and distributing them for profit, abide by the laws and regulations of the Commonwealth controlling and regulating the milk business.

* * * That people abuse the consumption of liquor is evident by a glance into any tavern, cocktail lounge or convention, and this includes conventions of people dedicated to upholding the law. However, the imprudently over-abundant individual consumption of liquor has nothing to do with the legality of the business itself. * * *

The Majority introduces into its discussion a proposition which is shocking to contemplate. It speaks of "vicarious criminal liability." Such a concept is as alien to American soil as the upas tree. There was a time in China when a convicted felon sentenced to death could offer his brother or other close relative in his stead for decapitation. The Chinese law allowed such "vicarious criminal liability." I never thought that Pennsylvania would look with favor on anything approaching so revolting a barbarity.

The Majority Opinion attempts to give authority to its legislative usurpation by referring to twenty-five specific acts which are designated as unlawful in Section 494 of the Liquor Code. It is true that the General Assembly has enumerated certain proscribed situations, but nowhere has the Legislature said that a person may be tried and convicted for a personal act committed in the darkness of his absence and in the night of his utter lack of knowledge thereof. * * *

* * * The Majority Opinion finds the imprisonment part of the sentence contrary to law. Thus, in addition to the other things I have had to say about the Majority Opinion, I find myself compelled to pin on it the bouquet of inconsistency. * * * [I]f the Majority cannot sanction the incarceration of a person for acts of which he had no knowledge, how can it sanction the imposition of a fine? How can it sanction a conviction at all? * * *

* * * If it is wrong to send a person to jail for acts committed by another, is it not wrong to convict him at all? There are those who value their good names to the extent that they see as much harm in a degrading criminal conviction as in a jail sentence. The laceration of a man's reputation, the blemishing of his good name, the wrecking of his prestige by a criminal court conviction may blast a person's chances for honorable success in life to such an extent that a jail sentence can hardly add much to the ruin already wrought to him by the conviction alone. * * *

NOTES AND QUESTIONS

1. The court states that it recognizes the difference between strict liability and vicarious liability. What is the difference? Also, how does vicarious liability differ from accomplice liability?

2. *Model Penal Code.* Section 2.06(2)(b) of the Model Penal Code provides that a person is legally accountable for the conduct of another when "he is made accountable for the conduct of such other person by the Code or by the law defining the offense." This provision permits a legislative decision to impose vicarious liability. The Commentary to Section 2.06 warns that "[t]he latitude afforded by Subsection (2)(b) does not reflect a judgment that vicarious liability should be encouraged." American Law Institute, Model Penal Code and Commentaries, Comment to § 2.06 at 305–06 (1985). Any statute that imposes vicarious liability, however, is subject to the restrictive conditions of Section 2.05.

D. CORPORATE LIABILITY

STATE v. CHRISTY PONTIAC–GMC, INC.

Supreme Court of Minnesota, 1984.
354 N.W.2d 17.

SIMONETT, JUSTICE. * * *

In a bench trial, defendant-appellant Christy Pontiac–GMC, Inc., was found guilty of two counts of theft by swindle and two counts of aggravated forgery, and was sentenced to a $1,000 fine on each of the two forgery convictions. Defendant argues that as a corporation it cannot, under our state statutes, be prosecuted or convicted for theft or forgery and that, in any event, the evidence fails to establish that the acts complained of were the acts of the defendant corporation.

Christy Pontiac is a Minnesota corporation, doing business as a car dealership. It is owned by James Christy, a sole stockholder, who serves also as president and as director. In the spring of 1981, General Motors offered a cash rebate program for its dealers. A customer who purchased a new car delivered during the rebate period was entitled to a cash rebate, part paid by GM and part paid by the dealership. GM would pay the entire rebate initially and later charge back, against the dealer, the dealer's portion of the rebate. Apparently it was not uncommon for the dealer to give the customer the dealer's portion of the rebate in the form of a discount on the purchase price.

At this time Phil Hesli was employed by Christy Pontiac as a salesman and fleet manager. On March 27, 1981, James Linden took delivery of a new Grand Prix for his employer, Snyder Brothers. Although the rebate period on this car had expired on March 19, the salesman told Linden that he would still try to get the $700 rebate for Linden. Later, Linden was told by a Christy Pontiac employee that GM had denied the rebate. Subsequently, it was discovered that Hesli had forged Linden's signature twice on the rebate application form submitted by Christy Pontiac to GM, and that the transaction date had been altered and backdated to March 19 on the buyer's order form. Hesli signed the order form as "Sales Manager or Officer of the Company."

On April 6, 1981, Ronald Gores purchased a new Le Mans, taking delivery the next day. The rebate period for this model car had expired on April 4, and apparently Gores was told he would not be eligible for a rebate. Subsequently, it was discovered that Christy Pontiac had submitted a $500 cash rebate application to GM and that Gores' signature had been forged twice by Hesli on the application. It was also discovered that the purchase order form had been backdated to April 3. This order form was signed by Gary Swandy, an officer of Christy Pontiac.

Both purchasers learned of the forged rebate applications when they received a copy of the application in the mail from Christy Pontiac. Both purchasers complained to James Christy, and in both instances the conversations ended in angry mutual recriminations. Christy did tell Gores that the rebate on his car was "a mistake" and offered half the rebate to "call it even." After the Attorney General's office made an inquiry, Christy Pontiac contacted GM and arranged for cancellation of the Gores rebate that had been allowed to Christy Pontiac. Subsequent investigation disclosed that of 50 rebate transactions, only the Linden and Gores sales involved irregularities.

In a separate trial, Phil Hesli was acquitted of three felony charges but found guilty on the count of theft for the Gores transaction and was given a misdemeanor disposition. An indictment against James Christy for theft by swindle was dismissed, * * * for lack of probable cause. Christy Pontiac, the corporation, was also indicted, and the appeal here is from the four convictions on those indictments. * * *

I.

Christy Pontiac argues on several grounds that a corporation cannot be held criminally liable for a specific intent crime. Minn.Stat. § 609.52, subd. 2 (1982), says "whoever" swindles by artifice, trick or other means commits theft. Minn.Stat. § 609.625, subd. 1 (1982), says "whoever" falsely makes or alters a writing with intent to defraud, commits aggravated forgery. Christy Pontiac agrees that the term "whoever" refers to persons, and it agrees that the term "persons" *may* include corporations, *see* Minn.Stat. § 645.44, subd. 7 (1982), but it argues that when the word "persons" is used here, it should be construed to mean only natural persons. This should be so, argues defendant, because the legislature has defined a crime as "conduct which is prohibited by statute and for which the actor may be sentenced to imprisonment, with or without a fine," Minn.Stat. § 609.02, subd. 1 (1982), and a corporation cannot be imprisoned. Neither, argues defendant, can an artificial person entertain a mental state, let alone have the specific intent required for theft or forgery.

We are not persuaded by these arguments. The Criminal Code is to "be construed according to the fair import of its terms, to promote justice, and to effect its purposes." Minn.Stat. § 609.01, subd. 1 (1982). The legislature has not expressly excluded corporations from criminal liability and, therefore, we take its intent to be that corporations are to be considered persons within the meaning of the Code in the absence of any clear indication to the contrary. We do not think the statutory definition of a crime was meant to exclude corporate criminal liability; rather, we construe that definition to mean conduct which is prohibited and, if committed, *may* result in imprisonment. Interestingly, the specific statutes under which the defendant corporation was convicted, sections 609.52 (theft) and 609.625 (aggravated forgery), expressly state that the sentence may be either imprisonment *or* a fine.

Nor are we troubled by any anthropomorphic implications in assigning specific intent to a corporation for theft or forgery. There was a time when the law, in its logic, declared that a legal fiction could not be a person for purposes of criminal liability, at least with respect to offenses involving specific intent, but that time is gone. If a corporation can be liable in civil tort for both actual and punitive damages for libel, assault and battery, or fraud, it would seem it may also be criminally liable for conduct requiring specific intent. Most courts today recognize that corporations may be guilty of specific intent crimes. Particularly apt candidates for corporate criminality are types of crime, like theft by swindle and forgery, which often occur in a business setting.

We hold, therefore, that a corporation may be prosecuted and convicted for the crimes of theft and forgery.

II.

There remains, however, the evidentiary basis on which criminal responsibility of a corporation is to be determined. Criminal liability, especially for more serious crimes, is thought of as a matter of personal, not vicarious, guilt. One should not be convicted for something one does not do. In what sense, then, does a corporation "do" something for which it can be convicted of a crime? The case law, as illustrated by the authorities above cited, takes differing approaches. If a corporation is to be criminally liable, it is clear that the crime must not be a personal aberration of an employee acting on his own; the criminal activity must, in some sense, reflect corporate policy so that it is fair to say that the activity was the activity of the corporation. * * *

We believe, first of all, the jury should be told that it must be satisfied beyond a reasonable doubt that the acts of the individual agent constitute the acts of the corporation. Secondly, as to the kind of proof required, we hold that a corporation may be guilty of a specific intent crime committed by its agent if: (1) the agent was acting within the course and scope of his or her employment, having the authority to act for the corporation with respect to the particular corporate business which was conducted criminally; (2) the agent was acting, at least in part, in furtherance of the corporation's business interests; and (3) the criminal acts were authorized, tolerated, or ratified by corporate management.

This test is not quite the same as the test for corporate vicarious liability for a civil tort of an agent. The burden of proof is different, and, unlike civil liability, criminal guilt requires that the agent be acting at least in part in furtherance of the corporation's business interests. Moreover, it must be shown that corporate management authorized, tolerated, or ratified the criminal activity. Ordinarily, this will be shown by circumstantial evidence, for it is not to be expected that management authorization of illegality would be expressly or openly stated. Indeed, there may be instances where the corporation is criminally liable even though the criminal activity has been expressly forbidden. What must be shown is that from all the facts and circumstances, those in positions of managerial authority or responsibility acted or failed to act in such a manner that the criminal activity reflects corporate policy, and it can be said, therefore, that the criminal act was authorized or tolerated or ratified by the corporation. * * *

III.

This brings us, then, to the third issue, namely, whether under the proof requirements mentioned above, the evidence is sufficient to sustain the convictions. We hold that it is.

The evidence shows that Hesli, the forger, had authority and responsibility to handle new car sales and to process and sign cash rebate applications. Christy Pontiac, not Hesli, got the GM rebate money, so that Hesli was acting in furtherance of the corporation's business interests. Moreover, there was sufficient evidence of management authorization, toleration, and ratification. Hesli himself, though not an officer, had middle management responsibilities for cash rebate applications. When the customer Gores asked Mr. Benedict, a salesman, about the then discontinued rebate, Benedict referred Gores to Phil Hesli. Gary Swandy, a corporate officer, signed the backdated retail buyer's order form for the Linden sale. James Christy, the president, attempted to negotiate a settlement with Gores after Gores complained. Not until after the Attorney General's inquiry did Christy contact divisional GM headquarters. As the trial judge noted, the rebate money "was so obtained and accepted by Christy Pontiac and kept by Christy Pontiac until somebody blew the whistle * * *." We conclude the evidence establishes that the theft by swindle and the forgeries constituted the acts of the corporation.

We wish to comment further on two aspects of the proof. First, it seems that the state attempted to prosecute both Christy Pontiac and James Christy, but its prosecution of Mr. Christy failed for lack of evidence. We can imagine a different situation where the corporation is the alter ego of its owner and it is the owner who alone commits the crime, where a double prosecution might be deemed fundamentally unfair. Secondly, it may seem incongruous that Hesli, the forger, was acquitted of three of the four criminal counts for which the corporation was convicted. Still, this is not the first time different trials have had different results. * * *

PAMELA H. BUCY—CORPORATE ETHOS: A STANDARD FOR IMPOSING CORPORATE CRIMINAL LIABILITY

75 Minnesota Law Review 1095 (1991), 1102–1105

American jurisprudence has employed two major standards to determine when a corporation should be criminally liable. Both impose vicarious liability by imputing the criminal acts and intent of corporate agents to the corporation. The traditional or respondeat superior approach is a common law rule developed primarily in the federal courts and adopted by some state courts. Derived from agency principles in tort law, it provides that a corporation "may be held criminally liable for the acts of any of its agents [who] (1) commit a crime (2) within the scope of employment (3) with the intent to benefit the corporation." As construed by most courts, the latter two requirements are almost meaningless. Courts deem criminal conduct to be "within the scope of employment" even if the conduct was specifically forbidden by a corporate policy and the corporation made good faith efforts to prevent the crime. Similarly, courts deem criminal conduct by an agent to be "with the intent to benefit the corporation" even when the corporation received no actual benefit from the offense and no one within the corporation knew of the criminal conduct at the time it occurred. With these latter two requirements thus weakened, a corporation may be criminally liable whenever one of its agents (even an independent contractor in some circumstances) commits a crime related in almost any way to the agent's employment.

The American Law Institute's Model Penal Code (MPC) provides the major alternative standard for corporate criminal liability currently found in American jurisprudence. * * * The type of criminal offense charged determines which standard applies. The option that applies to the majority of criminal offenses[25] provides that a court may hold a corporation criminally liable if the criminal conduct was "authorized, requested, commanded, performed or recklessly tolerated by the board of directors or by a high managerial agent acting in behalf of the corporation within the scope of his office or employment." This standard still uses a respondeat superior model, but in a limited fashion: the corporation will be liable for conduct of only some agents (its directors, officers, or other higher echelon employees).

The critical weakness in both the traditional respondeat superior and MPC standards of liability is that they fail to sufficiently analyze corporate intent. Cases where a corporate employee acted contrary to express corporate policy and yet the court still held the corporation liable best exemplify this weakness. *United States v. Hilton Hotels Corp.*[27] provides an apt example. The purchasing agent at a Hilton Hotel in Portland, Oregon, threatened a supplier of goods with the loss of the hotel's business if the supplier did not contribute to an association that was formed to attract conventions to Portland. The corporate president testified that such action was contrary to corporate policy. Both the manager and assistant manager of the Portland Hilton Hotel also testified that they specifically told the purchasing agent not to threaten suppliers. Nevertheless, the court convicted the Hilton Hotel Corporation of antitrust violations under the respondeat superior standard of liability.

Because the respondeat superior standard focuses solely on an individual corporate agent's intent and automatically imputes that intent to the corporation, a corporation's efforts to prevent such conduct are irrelevant. Under this approach all corporations, honest or dishonest, good or bad, are convicted if the government can prove that even one maverick employee committed criminal conduct.

The MPC's requirement that a higher echelon employee commit, or recklessly supervise, the criminal conduct is an improvement over the traditional respondeat superior approach. Recognizing the unfairness of holding a corporation liable for the acts of all its agents, the MPC views the corporation as the embodiment of the acts and intent of only its "high managerial agent[s]." High managerial agents are those individuals "having duties of such responsibility that [their] conduct may fairly be assumed to represent the policy of the corporation or association."[33]

---

25. The MPC includes two additional standards of corporate liability. Section 2.07(1)(a) applies to minor infractions and non-Code penal offenses "in which a legislative purpose to impose liability on corporations plainly appears." The standard in § 2.07(1)(a) is broad respondeat superior, for the corporation is held liable whenever "the conduct is performed by an agent of the corporation acting in behalf of the corporation within the scope of his office or employment." Section 2.07(1)(b) applies to omissions and provides strict liability for the corporation that fails to "discharge a specific duty" imposed by law. * * *

27. 467 F.2d 1000 (9th Cir.1972), *cert. denied,* 409 U.S. 1125 (1973).

33. * * * § 2.07(4)(c).

The MPC's refinement of traditional respondeat superior suffers from three serious problems, however. The first problem, the maverick employee, still arises because the MPC uses the same conceptual paradigm as does respondeat superior—that is, the MPC automatically imputes the intent of individual corporate agents (albeit only the higher echelon agents) to the corporation. * * *

The second problem with the MPC standard is that even if a clear corporate policy caused a lower echelon employee to commit an offense, the corporation is liable only if there is evidence that a specific higher echelon official recklessly tolerated this conduct. Injustice also results from this problem but here the liability is too narrow: a corporation is not held criminally liable when it should be.

The third problem with the MPC standard is [that it] * * * encourages higher echelon officials to insulate themselves from knowledge of corporate employee activity. Under this standard, if higher echelon officials can maintain unawareness of illegal conduct by corporate employees, it is difficult to prove that they tolerated such conduct, and therefore nearly impossible to hold the corporation criminally liable. By encouraging such unawareness, the MPC discourages corporations from policing themselves.

NOTES AND QUESTIONS

1. Professor Bucy noted that the traditional common law approach to corporate liability is that a corporation is liable for the acts of any of its agents who commit a crime within the scope of employment and with the intent to benefit the corporation. But, as she also noted, states that apply this non-Model Penal Code approach seem to require little more than proof that one of the employees committed the crime in the broadest sense of being "within the scope" of the job.

Suppose no single employee is guilty of any crime. Should a prosecutor be able to aggregate the employees' knowledge and actions in order to charge a corporation with a crime? Consider Commonwealth v. Life Care Centers of America, Inc., 456 Mass. 826, 926 N.E.2d 206 (2010), in which the defendant nursing home was indicted for involuntary manslaughter (which, under state law, required proof of an act or omission that was "reckless" or "wanton") of a resident of the long-term care facility. The state was prepared to show widespread errors by individual employees in dealing with the victim, none of which, standing alone, constituted reckless or wanton acts or omissions, but which, when aggregated and then imputed to the defendant corporation, proved the requisite recklessness or wantonness. The state supreme court barred prosecution on this basis. Does this seem right? Can you defend your answer on the basis of either retributive or utilitarian theories of punishment?

The materials that follow consider what retributive and utilitarian theory may teach us about corporate criminal liability.

JOHN C. COFFEE, JR.—"NO SOUL TO DAMN: NO BODY TO KICK": AN UNSCANDALIZED INQUIRY INTO THE PROBLEM OF CORPORATE PUNISHMENT

79 Michigan Law Review 386 (1981), 386–397, 399–402

Did you ever expect a corporation to have a conscience, when it has no soul to be damned, and no body to be kicked?

Edward, First Baron Thurlow 1731–1806

The Lord Chancellor of England quoted above was neither the first nor the last judge to experience frustration when faced with a convicted corporation. * * * [T]he problem of corporate punishment seems perversely insoluble: moderate fines do not deter, while severe penalties flow through the corporate shell and fall on the relatively blameless. * * *

The literature on corporate sanctions sometimes seems to consist of little more than the repeated observation that the fines imposed on convicted corporations have historically been insignificant. True as this point undoubtedly is, it is also a short-sighted critique. It ignores both the judiciary's reasons for declining to impose more severe penalties and the possibility that a monetary penalty sufficiently high to deter the corporation may be infeasible or undesirable. Once these possibilities are considered, the problem of corporate criminal behavior becomes radically more complex. Three independent, but overlapping perspectives each suggest that monetary penalties directed at the corporation will often prove inadequate to deter illegal behavior. * * *

A. THE DETERRENCE TRAP

* * * Economists generally agree that an actor who contemplates committing a crime will be deterred only if the "expected punishment cost" of a proscribed action exceeds the expected gain. This concept of the expected punishment cost involves more than simply the amount of the penalty. Rather, the expected penalty must be discounted by the likelihood of apprehension and conviction in order to yield the expected punishment cost. For example, if the expected gain were $1 million and the risk of apprehension were 25%, the penalty would have to be raised to $4 million in order to make the expected punishment cost equal the expected gain. One may well question the adequacy of this simple formula when applied to individual defendants, because the stigmatization of a criminal conviction constitutes an additional and severe penalty for the white-collar defendant. But this loss of social status is a less significant consideration for the corporate entity, and we are thus forced to rely largely on monetary sanctions.

The crux of the dilemma arises from the fact that the maximum meaningful fine that can be levied against any corporate offender is necessarily bounded by its wealth. Logically, a small corporation is no more threatened by a $5 million fine than by a $500,000 fine if both are beyond its ability to pay. In the case of an individual offender, this wealth ceiling on the deterrent threat of fines causes no serious problem because we can still deter by threat of incarceration. But for the corporation, which has no body to incarcerate, this wealth boundary seems an absolute limit on the reach of deterrent threats directed at it. If the "expected punishment cost" necessary to deter a crime crosses this threshold, adequate deterrence cannot be achieved. For example, if a corporation having $10 million of wealth were faced with an opportunity to gain $1 million through some criminal act or omission, such conduct could not logically be deterred by monetary penalties directed at the corporation *if the risk of apprehension were below 10%.* That is, if the likelihood of apprehension were 8%, the necessary penalty would have to be $12.5 million (*i.e.,* $1 million times 12.5, the reciprocal of 8%). Yet such a fine exceeds the corporation's ability to pay. In short, our ability to deter the corporation may be confounded by our inability to set an adequate punishment cost which does not exceed the corporation's resources.

The importance of this barrier (* * * the "deterrence trap") depends on whether rates of apprehension for corporate crimes are typically low. Although there are exceptions, most corporate crimes seem highly concealable. This is so because, unlike victims of classically under-reported crimes (such as rape or child abuse), victims of many corporate crimes do not necessarily know of their injury. The victim of price-fixing may never learn that he has overpaid; the consumer of an unsafe, toxic, or carcinogenic product typically remains unaware of the hazards to which he has been exposed. Even the government or a fellow competitor may rarely discover the tax fraud or illegal bribe which has cost it a substantial loss in revenues. * * *

Beyond ease of concealment, legal and behavioral characteristics distinguish price-fixing from other corporate crimes: safety and environmental violations involve questions of judgment which the participants can rationalize without consciously (or at least explicitly) engaging in behavior they know to be illegal. In addition, many, if not most, forms of corporate crime require some element of intent (*i.e.,* "knowingly" or "willfully") which can be exceedingly difficult to prove in the context of prosecuting a white-collar worker for a "regulatory" offense. * * *

The final element in the deterrence equation requires little emphasis: corporate misbehavior involves high stakes. A $50,000 bribe may secure a $50 million defense contract, a failure to report a safety or design defect in a product may avert a multi-million dollar recall, and the suppression of evidence showing a newly discovered adverse side effect of a popular drug may save its manufacturer an entire product market. Thus, when all the elements of the equation are combined, it is not unrealistic to predict that cases will arise in which the expected gain may be $10 million or higher, while the likelihood of apprehension is under 10%. If so, a mechanical application of the economist's deterrence formula suggests that only penalties of $100 million or above could raise the "expected punishment cost" to a level in excess of the expected gain. Few corporations, if any, could pay such a fine * * *.

B. THE BEHAVIORAL PERSPECTIVE

An abstract quality surrounds the foregoing economic analysis. Lucid as its logic seems, it ignores the organizational dynamics within the firm and treats the corporation as a "black box" which responds in a wholly amoral fashion to any net difference between expected costs and benefits. Students of organizational decision-making have always rejected this "black box" model of the firm and have been quick to point out that a fundamental incongruence may exist between the aims of the manager and those of the firm. Indeed, this assertion is but a corollary of the famous Berle–Means thesis that control and ownership have been divorced in the modern public corporation.[23] Given this separation, it follows that the "real world" corporation manager may view corporate participation in criminal activities from the standpoint of how to maximize his own ends, rather than those of the firm.

Does the behavioral perspective indicate that corporate misbehavior may be easier to deter than the foregoing economic analysis suggests? Regrettably, the reverse may be the case: for several reasons, the behavioral perspective suggests that it may be extraordinarily difficult to prevent corporate misconduct by punishing only the firm. First, from such a perspective, it seems clear that the individual manager may perceive illegal conduct to be in his interest, even if the potential costs to which it exposes the firm far exceed the potential corporate benefits. For example, the executive vice president who is a candidate for promotion to president may be willing to run risks which are counterproductive to the firm as a whole because he is eager to make a record profit for his division or to hide a prior error of judgment. Correspondingly, the lower echelon executive with a lackluster record may deem it desirable to resort to illegal means to increase profits (or forestall losses) in order to prevent his dismissal or demotion. * * *

* * * [I]t is important to move from theoretical to empirical arguments. The theoreticians of deterrence tend to assume that the actor has perfect knowledge, or at least can calculate with reasonable accuracy the odds of apprehension. In reality, we lack even an approximate estimate of how much white-collar crime occurs or how often it results in conviction. Because an accurate calculation of the cost/benefit calculus which the microeconomic approach utilizes is thus improbable, the critical variable becomes the actor's attitude toward risk. Is he a risk averter or a risk preferrer? Other things being equal, the risk-averse manager tends to be deterred by high penalties even when they are associated with low rates of apprehension, while a risk-preferring manager would look at the same combination of penalties and probabilities and not be deterred. Knowing only that apprehension is a longshot, the risk preferrer will be likely to

---

23. A. Berle & G. Means, The Modern Corporation and Private Property (rev. ed. 1967). * * *

chance profitable illegal behavior, even though an apprehension would devastate his career.

Although some theorists have argued that the typical corporate manager is risk averse, some empirical evidence points in the opposite direction. Repeated studies have detected a phenomenon known as the "risky shift"; businessmen participating in role-playing experiments have shown a pronounced tendency to make "riskier" decisions when acting in a small group than when acting alone. That is, the degree of risk they are willing to accept increases dramatically when the decision is reached collectively within a small group—exactly the context in which most business decisions are made. * * *

Finally, the behavioral perspective highlights one of the most basic causes of misbehavior within organizations: individuals frequently act out of loyalty to a small group within the firm with which they identify. Thus, engineers working on the development of a particular project may develop an intense dedication to it which leads them to suppress negative safety findings. Similarly, a plant manager may falsify environmental data out of a fear that the prohibitive costs of bringing the plant into compliance might result in its closing. This pattern is consistent with a considerable body of social science data which suggests that the individual's primary loyalty within any organization is to his immediate work group. Within this group, he will engage in candid disclosure and debate, but he will predictably edit and screen data before submitting them to superiors in order to cast his sub-unit in a favorable light.

From this perspective, the following generalization becomes understandable: the locus of corporate crime is predominantly at the lower to middle management level. Although public interest groups are vocal in their denunciations of "crime in the suites," in truth the most shocking safety and environmental violations are almost exclusively the product of decisions at lower managerial levels. Senior executives may still bear some causal responsibility, but the chain of causation is remote, and their influence on decisions is only indirect. * * *

To sum up, in the modern public corporation it is not only ownership and control that are divorced (as Berle and Means recognized long ago), but also strategic decision-making and operational control. In an era of finance capitalism, the manager responsible for operational and production decisions is increasingly separated by organization, language, goals, and experience from the financial manager who today plans and directs the corporation's future. This tends both to insulate the upper echelon executive (who may well desire that the sordid details of "meeting the competition" or "coping with the regulators" not filter up to his attention) and to intensify the pressures on those below by denying them any forum in which to explain the crises they face. This generalization helps to explain both the infrequency with which corporate misconduct can be traced to senior levels and the limited effort made to date within many firms to develop a system of legal auditing which approaches the sophistication of financial auditing. * * *

C.   THE EXTERNALITY PROBLEM

The idea of externalities as applied to the actions of public bodies is probably best illustrated by the common practice of most highway departments in liberally dumping salt on frozen roads. This technique cures their problem of ice-coated roads at a relatively low cost, but it also imposes an "external cost" on landowners and drivers: plants die along the borders of such roadways, and cars rust and deteriorate more quickly because of the effect of the salt on their exteriors. This cost, however, is not borne by the highway department, and thus is externalized in the same sense that a manufacturer traditionally never bore the cost of his pollution that fell on the adjoining landowners downwind. * * *

The problem of external costs is present in the case of corporate punishment, and comes into focus when we consider the incidence of financial penalties imposed on the corporation. As a moment's reflection reveals, the costs of deterrence tend to spill over onto parties who cannot be characterized as culpable. Axiomatically, corporations do not bear the ultimate cost of the fine; put simply, when the corporation catches a cold, someone else sneezes. This overspill of the penalty initially imposed on the corporation has at least four distinct levels, each progressively more serious. First, stockholders bear the penalty in the reduced value of their securities. Second, bondholders and other creditors suffer a diminution in the value of their securities which reflects the increased riskiness of the enterprise. * * * The analysis, however, needs to be carried several steps further: the third level of incidence of a severe financial penalty involves parties even less culpable than the stockholders. As a class, the stockholders can at least sometimes be said to have received unjust enrichment from the benefits of the crime; this arguably justifies their indirectly bearing a compensating fine. However, if the fine is severe enough to threaten the solvency of the corporation, the predictable response will be a cost-cutting campaign, involving reductions in the work force through layoffs of lower echelon employees who received no benefit from the earlier crime. Severe financial penalties thus interfere with public goals of full employment and minority recruitment by restricting corporate expansion. * * * Finally, there is the fourth level of incidence of a financial penalty: it may be passed onto the consumer. * * * If this happens, the "wicked" corporation not only goes unpunished, but the intended beneficiary of the criminal statute (*i.e.,* the consumer) winds up bearing its penalty.

NOTES AND QUESTIONS

1.   Are there socially cheaper methods of punishing corporations? Among the strategies outlined in Professor Coffee's article are: implementation of "equity fines," whereby a corporation is ordered to authorize and issue shares

of the corporation to a State crime victim compensation fund in sufficient number that their expected market value is equivalent to the cash fine necessary to deter illegal activity; authorization of private law suits with treble damage penalties following Government prosecution; and increased plea bargaining by prosecutors, so that corporations would be required to provide restitution to injured victims in exchange for dismissal of criminal charges.

2. *The death penalty for corporate wrongdoing.* In considering whether vigorous criminal prosecution of businesses—or something less severe—is a good idea, the saga of Arthur Anderson, one of the so-called "Big Five" accounting firms, is worth noting. One of Arthur Anderson's clients was Enron Corporation, a business organization that ultimately filed for bankruptcy after investigation by the Securities and Exchange Commission suggested fraudulent conduct by its executives.

Arthur Anderson was itself indicted in 2002 for obstruction of justice because it launched a wholesale destruction of "literally tons of paperwork" relating to the Securities and Exchange Commission investigation into Enron's wrongdoing. (A partner of the accounting firm, aware of the Enron investigation, urged employees to comply with the firm's document retention policy, which policy conveniently called for destruction of non-work-paper documents and e-mails.) After a long trial and extensive deliberations, a jury convicted the firm. The United States Supreme Court unanimously overturned the conviction because of an improper jury instruction. Arthur Andersen LLP v. United States, 544 U.S. 696, 125 S.Ct. 2129, 161 L.Ed.2d 1008 (2005). That was small consolation to Arthur Anderson. By the time the case reached the Supreme Court, the firm that once employed 28,000 persons had itself been forced out of business.

3. *Are we punishing the innocent?* Professor Coffee described the "externality problem": "when the corporation catches a cold, someone else sneezes." Does this suggest that from both a deterrence and retributive perspective, corporate criminal liability is unjustifiable? Consider whether you are persuaded by these observations:

> The first necessary condition for criminal responsibility holds that the criminal sanction may be applied only when doing so advances a legitimate purpose of punishment. Imposing criminal sanctions on corporations for the offenses of their employees does not advance any legitimate purpose of punishment. * * *

> Who pays when a financial loss is imposed upon a corporation? To the extent that such a loss cannot be passed along to consumers, it is the * * * shareholders * * * who incur the penalty. The defining characteristic of the modern corporation is the separation of ownership and control. The shareholders, who own the corporation, have no direct control over or knowledge of the behavior of the corporate employees who commit criminal offenses. * * * How can punishing the innocent advance any of the legitimate purposes of punishment?

> It cannot.

John Hasnas, *The Centenary of a Mistake: One Hundred Years of Corporate Criminal Liability*, 46 Am. Crim. L. Rev. 1329, 1338–39 (2009).

Professor Hasnas defends his view that corporate criminal liability is a mistake by arguing, first, that punishing the innocent obviously violates retributive theory. As for deterrence, "[i]n the Anglo–American criminal justice system, deterrence refers to inflicting punishment on a *wrongdoer* to discourage others from committing similar offenses. It does not refer to punishing the innocent to pressure them into suppressing the criminal activity of their fellow citizen." Id. at 1339.

Professor Albert Alschuler, as well, casts doubt on corporate criminal liability:

> Of course criminal punishment cannot really be borne by a fictional entity. As Baron Thurlow, a Lord Chancellor of England, put it sometime before 1792, a corporation has "no soul to damn, no body to kick." This punishment is inflicted instead on human beings whose guilt remains unproven. Innocent shareholders pay the fines, and innocent employees, creditors, customers, and communities sometimes feel the pinch too. The embarrassment of corporate criminal liability is that it punishes the innocent along with the guilty.

> The Justice Department's *Manual for United States Attorneys* responds to this embarrassment with a shrug: "Virtually every conviction of a corporation, like virtually every conviction of an individual, will have an impact on innocent third parties." The Manual discusses the unjustified pain caused by the punishment of a corporation under the heading of "Collateral Consequences," listing it as one of many things a prosecutor "may consider" in deciding whether to file charges and enter deferred prosecution agreements.

Albert W. Alschuler, *Two Ways to Think About the Punishment of Corporations*, 46 Am. Crim. L. Rev. 1359, 1367–68 (2009).

Professor Alschuler rejects the Justice Department's "collateral consequences" analogy to convictions of individuals: "When an offender with children is sent to prison, his children may suffer, yet criminal justice officials may have no way to punish the offender appropriately without hurting other people. The human perpetrators of the crimes now attributed to corporations, however, can be convicted and incarcerated without punishing innocent shareholders and employees as well. Undeserved suffering that can be avoided should be avoided." Id. at 1369–70. How should the law deal, however, with a case in which no individual may properly be punished—no one person has the requisite *mens rea*—but in aggregation blame might be attached to a corporation, as in the *Life Care Centers* case (p. 885, Note 1)?

Or, is it silly to speak of attaching blame to a corporation? Alschuler contends that describing corporations as "blameworthy," and thus "deserving" of punishment, are reasons that "match those that once [long ago] might have been offered to justify the punishment of animals and inanimate objects that produced harm * * *. * * * [A]ttributing blame to a corporation is no more sensible than attributing blame to a dagger, a fountain pen, a Chevrolet, or any other instrumentality of crime." Id. at 1392.

CHAPTER 12

THEFT

■ ■ ■

INTRODUCTORY COMMENT

In the very early years of English legal history, theft of property was not a criminal offense. Only forcible appropriations of property, i.e., robberies, were punishable. During the middle ages, however, as economic conditions mandated a change in the law, the common law of crimes was expanded to include nonforcible, nonconsensual takings, i.e. larceny. As with all other common law felonies, grand larceny was a capital crime.

Larceny law did not develop in a simple or smooth manner. On the one hand, common law jurists did not consider death an appropriate penalty for many thefts, so they often construed the offense narrowly and developed technical rules that allowed some thieves to escape conviction and execution. On the other hand, the courts were sensitive to pressures from commercial interests to broaden the scope of the law, which they did over time.

The courts did not act fast enough to suit English lawmakers. Beginning in the eighteenth century, Parliament intervened and filled in various gaps in the law of theft. However, rather than redefine larceny, the legislators enacted new offenses, primarily the crimes of embezzlement and obtaining property by false pretenses.

For more than a century, English and American courts struggled to make sense of the larceny/embezzlement/false-pretenses trichotomy. Only partially successful in this effort, many states sought to simplify the law by combining these and other property crimes (e.g., receiving stolen property) into a single, consolidated theft statute. See, e.g., Model Penal Code § 223.1. Such consolidated statutes might simplify the law, but one recent study suggests that some of the common law's distinctions among various theft offenses may have reflected more than historical accident: they may have reflected morally relevant differences, with some common-law theft offenses believed by many to be more serious than others. See Stuart P. Green & Matthew B. Kugler, *Community Perceptions of Theft Seriousness: A Challenge to Model Penal Code and English Theft Act Consolidation*, 7 J. Empirical Legal Stud. 511 (2010). At any rate, even in states that have consolidated their property offenses, the simplification process has been incomplete, as courts frequently draw on the common law and its intricate distinctions to interpret the modern offense of theft. E.g., People v. Sanders, 67 Cal.App.4th 1403, 79 Cal.Rptr.2d 806 (1998) ("Combining several common law crimes under the statutory umbrella of 'theft' did not eliminate the need to prove the elements of the particular type of theft alleged.").

The following materials primarily focus on the historic theft offenses. Along the way, the Notes touch upon the aggravated property offenses of robbery and carjacking. The chapter concludes with a brief look at Congress's efforts to expand theft law beyond its original contours.

A. LARCENY

1. ACTUS REUS

a. "Trespassory Taking (Caption) and Carrying Away (Asportation) * * *"

LEE v. STATE

Court of Special Appeals of Maryland, 1984.
59 Md.App. 28, 474 A.2d 537.

BELL, J. * * *

Distinctions among larceny, embezzlement, obtaining by false pretenses, * * * and the other closely related theft offenses * * * can be explained by a brief exposition of the historical role criminal law played in protecting property. The history of these theft related offenses commenced with the common law courts' concern for crimes of violence (e.g. robbery) and for protecting society against breaches of peace; then expanded by means of the ancient quasi-criminal writ of trespass to cover all taking of another's property from his possession without his consent, even though no force was used. This latter misconduct was punished as larceny. Larceny at common law was defined as the trespassory taking and carrying away of personal property of another with intent to steal the same. The requirement of a trespassory taking made larceny an offense against possession;[1] and thus, a person such as a bailee who had rightfully obtained possession of property from its owner could not be guilty of larceny even if he used the property in a manner inconsistent with the owner's expectations.

Because of this narrow interpretation of larceny, the courts gradually broadened the offense by manipulating the concept of possession to

---

1. "Trespassory taking" under common law principles focused on the physical aspect of taking and obtaining possession. Under this traditional approach to larceny, the rule of "possessorial immunity" was fundamental in defining the contours of larceny. This rule provided that transferring possession of an object conferred immunity from the criminal law on the party receiving possession, for subsequent misuse or misappropriation of the entrusted object. This immunity terminated when the possessor (usually the bailee) returned possession to the owner or delivered the goods to another party.

embrace misappropriation by a person who with the consent of the owner already had physical control over the property. * * *

REX v. CHISSER

Court of King's Bench, 1678.
T. Raym. 275, 83 Eng.Rep. 142.

Upon a special verdict the jury find that on the day, and at the place in the indictment mentioned, Abraham Chisser came to the shop of Anne Charteris * * *, and asked for to see two crevats * * *, which she shewed to him, and delivered them into his hands, and thereupon he asked the price of them, to which she answered 7s, whereupon the said Abraham Chisser offered her 3s and immediately run out of the said shop, and took away the said goods openly in her sight, but whether this be felony, or not, is the question. * * *

And I am of opinion, that this act of Chisser is felony * * *.

* * * Although these goods were delivered to Chisser by the owner, yet they were not out of her possession by such delivery, till the property should be altered by the perfection of the contract, which was but inchoated and never perfected between the parties; and when Chisser run away with the goods, it was as if he had taken them up, lying in the shop, and run away with them. * * *

Notes and Questions

1. *"Physical" versus "constructive" possession.* With *Chisser's Case,* we see the common law at work, effectively broadening the law of larceny, by developing the distinction between physical possession of personal property—which Chisser certainly had—and constructive possession, which remained with shop owner Charteris. In the later language of the courts, Chisser had "custody" of the goods; Charteris retained "possession." Chisser trespassorily "took possession" of the goods from Charteris, however, when he fled with the shop owner's property: he now had custody *and* wrongful possession of the property.

In theory, this legal fiction could have been applied in the context of bailments, mentioned in *Lee.* That is, the English courts could have stated that a bailor retained constructive possession of her property even after she delivered it to a bailee, but the rule was clearly in place by the time of *Chisser* that full possession—physical and constructive—passed to the bailee by means of the bailment.

How were the courts going to deal with dishonest bailees? And, what about a dishonest employee (servant), who received property belonging to his employer (master) in the course of employment, and then converted it to his personal use? The courts came to the rescue of property owners and employers, as the next case demonstrates.

UNITED STATES v. MAFNAS

United States Court of Appeals, Ninth Circuit, 1983.
701 F.2d 83.

Per Curiam:

Appellant (Mafnas) was convicted in the U.S. District Court of Guam of stealing money from two federally insured banks in violation of 18 U.S.C. § 2113(b) which makes it a crime to "* * * take * * * with intent to steal * * * any money belonging to * * * any bank * * *."

Mafnas was employed by the Guam Armored Car Service (Service), which was hired by the Bank of Hawaii and the Bank of America to deliver bags of money.

On three occasions Mafnas opened the bags and removed money. As a result he was convicted of three counts of stealing money from the banks.

This Circuit has held that § 2113(b) applies only to common law larceny which requires a trespassory taking. Mafnas argues * * * he had lawful possession of the bags, with the consent of the banks, when he took the money.

This problem arose centuries ago, and common law has evolved to handle it. The law distinguishes between possession and custody. 3 Wharton's Criminal Law 346–57 (C. Torcia, 14th ed. 1980).

> Ordinarily, * * * if a person receives property for a limited or temporary purpose, he is only acquiring custody. Thus, if a person receives property from the owner with instructions to deliver it to the owner's house, he is only acquiring custody; therefore, his subsequent decision to keep the property for himself would constitute larceny.

3 Wharton's Criminal Law, at 353.

The District Court concluded that Mafnas was given temporary custody only, to deliver the money bags to their various destinations. The later decision to take the money was larceny, because it was beyond the consent of the owner, who retained constructive possession until the custodian's task was completed. This rationale was used in *United States v. Pruitt*, 446 F.2d 513, 515 (6th Cir.1971). There, Pruitt was employed by a bank as a messenger. He devised a plan with another person to stage a fake robbery and split the money which Pruitt was delivering for the bank. The Sixth Circuit found that Pruitt had mere custody for the purpose of delivering the money, and that his wrongful conversion constituted larceny.

Mafnas distinguishes *Pruitt* because the common law sometimes differentiates between employees, who generally obtain custody only, and others (agents), who acquire possession. Although not spelled out, Mafnas essentially claims that he was a bailee, and that the contract between the banks and Service resulted in Service having lawful possession, and not mere custody over the bags. *See Lionberger v. United States*, 371 F.2d 831, 840, 178 Ct.Cl. 151 (Ct.Cl.) *cert. denied*, 389 U.S. 844, 88 S.Ct. 91, 19

L.Ed.2d 110 (1967) ("A bailment situation is said to arise where an owner, while retaining title, delivers personalty to another for some particular purpose upon an express or implied contract.")

The common law also found an answer to this situation. A bailee who "breaks bulk" commits larceny.

> Under this doctrine, the bailee-carrier was given possession of a bale, but not its contents. Therefore, when the bailee pilfered the entire bale, he was not guilty of larceny; but when he broke open the bale and took a portion or all of the contents, he was guilty of larceny because his taking was trespassory and it was from the constructive possession of another.

3 Wharton's Criminal Law 353–54.

Either way, Mafnas has committed the common law crime of larceny, replete with trespassory taking.

Mafnas also cannot profit from an argument that any theft on his part was from Service and not from the banks. Case law is clear that since what was taken was property belonging to the banks, it was property or money "in the care, custody, control, management, or possession of any bank" within the meaning of 18 U.S.C. § 2113(b), notwithstanding the fact that it may have been in the possession of an armored car service serving as a bailee for hire.

Therefore, his conviction is Affirmed.

NOTES AND QUESTIONS

1. *Employers and employees.* Assume that *R*, an employer, asks *E*, her employee, to take the business's pickup truck to *X*, a mechanic, for brake repair. In which of the following cases is *E* guilty of larceny of *R*'s pickup truck, when he takes it out of town, with the intent to steal it?

A. Upon receiving the pickup truck from *R*, *E* drives it out of town.

B. As instructed by *R*, *E* drives the vehicle to *X* for repair. The next day, *E* returns, receives the vehicle from *X*, pays for the repairs, drives it toward *R*'s business, and then decides to steal it.

C. Suppose in B., *X* instructs *E* to remain at the repair shop while the brakes are fixed. An hour later, *E* receives the repaired vehicle, pays for it, drives it toward *R*'s business, and then decides to steal it.

2. *Bailees.* *A* purchases some drinking glasses from *X Company*. *X* hires *B*, a bailee, to deliver the glasses in their original box to *A*. In which of the following circumstances is *B* guilty of larceny?

A. *B* picks up the container from *X*, takes it to her own home, removes the glasses from the box, and keeps them.

B. *B* receives the container from *X*. On the way to *A*'s house, she decides to give the glasses to *C*, a friend of hers. She tells *C*, "Enjoy the drinking glasses, my gift to you." *B* leaves. Later, *C* opens the container and removes the contents.

C. *B* receives the container from *X* and delivers it to *A*, as instructed. At *A*'s request (*A* is on crutches and needs help), *B* removes the glasses and puts them on a shelf for *A*. *B* decides she wants to keep one glass as a keepsake, and surreptitiously takes one glass without *A* noticing.

3. *Asportation*. In *Mafnas*, the defendant opened the money bags and "removed" the money. Suppose Mafnas had been arrested immediately after the removal, but before he fled with the cash. Would he have been guilty of larceny or only of attempted larceny?

Notice that the offense of common law larceny is incomplete unless the property taken is "carried away." The slightest "carrying away" movement suffices: a shoplifter who takes property but is caught before he leaves the store is guilty of larceny, People v. Olivo, 52 N.Y.2d 309, 438 N.Y.S.2d 242, 420 N.E.2d 40 (1981); the requisite asportation is satisfied if a person yanks off an earring from the victim's pierced ear, and moves it only a few inches before it gets caught in the victim's hair, Rex v. Lapier, 1 Leach 320, 168 Eng.Rep. 263 (1784);[a] and larceny is proved if the thief, intending to steal a heavy leather bag containing various parcels, lifts the top of the bag from the floor, but drops it before he can get a full grasp of it, Rex v. Walsh, 1 Mood. 14, 168 Eng.Rep. 1166 (1824).

Although a culprit's movement need only be slight to constitute asportation, it must be a "carrying-away" movement. For example, in Cherry's Case, 1 Leach 236, 168 Eng.Rep. 221 (1871), twelve judges unanimously ruled that asportation (and, thus, larceny) was not proved when the defendant, intending to steal certain linen cloth, picked up a package containing the cloth, and stood it on its end in order to remove the cloth, but was apprehended before he could remove the cloth and carry it away.

How does the Model Penal Code deal with the asportation requirement? Consider Article 223 (Theft and Related Offenses) of the Code. In this regard, is *D* guilty of theft under the Model Penal Code if he breaks into your car, dismantles the steering column, manipulates the ignition switch turning on the radio and lighting the "check engine" light on the dashboard, but *not* engaging the engine? State v. Donaldson, 663 N.W.2d 882 (Iowa 2003).

4. *Problem: "taking," "carrying away," and the saga of the thwarted carjacker*. As Note 3 would suggest, the taking (caption) and carrying-away (asportation) elements of larceny are independent of each other. A person can take possession of property without carrying it away (as Cherry's Case suggests), and one can carry away property without taking *possession* (as distinguished from obtaining custody). One must do both to be guilty of larceny.

What about with other offenses? For example, in 1993 the California legislature added a new offense—carjacking—to its penal code. Carjacking was defined as:

the felonious taking of a motor vehicle in the possession of another, from his or her person or immediate presence, * * * against his or her will and with the intent to either permanently or temporarily deprive the person

---

a. Of what offense other than larceny might the culprit be guilty?

in possession of the motor vehicle of his or her possession, accomplished by means of force or fear. Cal. Penal Code § 215 (2006).

In light of this statute, consider these facts: *M* threatened *O* (who was sitting in his parked vehicle) with a knife, and ordered *O* out of the car. As *O* got out, however, he hit an ignition "kill" switch immobilizing the car. When *M* could not start the car, he ordered *O* to tell him how to start the vehicle. *O* refused. Then *M* discovered an unloaded gun in *O*'s car (*O* was a security guard), pointed it at *O* and, when *O* did not cooperate, twice pulled the trigger. *M* then demanded that *O* give him ammunition for the gun. *O* refused. Finally, *M* hit *O* in the face with the gun, knocking him down. *O* fled. Apparently, so did *M*, with *O*'s unloaded gun. The police discovered the car, unmoved and unoccupied, shortly thereafter. Is *M* guilty of carjacking? See People v. Montero, 56 Cal.Rptr.2d 303 (Ct. App. 1996), *vacated on other grounds*, 66 Cal.Rptr.2d 122, 940 P.2d 709 (1997).

5. *Robbery.* Generally speaking, common law robbery is, simply, larceny from a person by violence or intimidation. Rollin M. Perkins & Ronald N. Boyce, Criminal Law 343 (3d ed. 1982). That is, robbery is larceny coupled with the aggravating factor that the "thief" used or threatened to use force to obtain the property in question.

Do the facts in Note 4 support the claim that *M* was guilty of common law robbery? Was *M* guilty of robbery under the Model Penal Code? Consider § 222.1 of the Code.

D used a "shaved key" to open the door to *V*'s car, which was parked in an apartment complex carport. *D* started the car and waited for another car to open the carport gate so *D* could exit. The gate opened, another car entered, and *D* accelerated in order to leave before the gate closed. *D* accidentally struck and killed *V*, who had appeared on the scene. Robbery under the Model Penal Code? People v. Anderson, 51 Cal.4th 989, 125 Cal.Rptr.3d 408, 252 P.3d 968 (2011).

6. *Problem: the saga of the goose in the doughnut shop (or, crime Canada style).* A man entered a Toronto doughnut shop with a Canada goose in his arms, and yelled "give me some money or I'll wring the goose's neck." A female customer tried to convince him to release the bird, but when the man refused, she walked to a nearby bank machine, withdrew an undisclosed amount of money, returned to the stop, and handed it over to the man. He released the goose and fled. "The goose was not harmed." *Robber Uses Goose in Holdup*, Detroit Free Press, Apr. 26, 1996, at 6A. Is this robbery? Apply the Model Penal Code. Is he guilty of any Article 223 offense?

7. *Trespass.* Until now we have assumed that the caption and asportation elements of larceny occurred as the result of a trespass. But, what is a "trespass"? The next two cases provide an answer.

TOPOLEWSKI v. STATE

Supreme Court of Wisconsin, 1906.
130 Wis. 244, 109 N.W. 1037.

The accused was charged with having stolen three barrels of meat, the property of the Plankinton Packing Company, of the value of $55.20, and was found guilty. * * *

The evidence was to this effect: The Plankinton Packing Company suspected the accused of having by criminal means possessed himself of some of its property and of having a purpose to make further efforts to that end. A short time before the 14th day of October, 1905, one Mat Dolan, who was indebted to the accused in the sum of upwards of $100.00, was discharged from the company's employ. Shortly theretofore the accused pressed Dolan for payment of the aforesaid indebtedness and the latter, being unable to respond, the former conceived the idea of solving the difficulty by obtaining some of the company's meat products through Dolan's aid and by criminal means, Dolan to participate in the benefits of the transaction by having the value of the property credited upon his indebtedness. A plan was accordingly laid by the two to that end, which Dolan disclosed to the company. Such plan was abandoned. Thereafter various methods were discussed of carrying out the idea of the accused, Dolan participating with the knowledge and sanction of the company. Finally a meeting was arranged between Dolan and the accused to consider the subject, the packing company requesting the former to bring it about, and with knowledge of Dolan causing one of its employés to be in hiding where he could overhear whatever might be said, the arrangement being made on the part of the company by Mr. Layer[,] the person in charge of its wholesale department. At such interview the accused proposed that Dolan should procure some packages of the company's meat to be placed on their loading platform, as was customary in delivering meat to customers, and that he should drive to such platform, ostensibly as a customer, and remove such packages. Dolan agreed to the proposition and it was decided that the same should be consummated early the next morning, all of which was reported to Mr. Layer. He thereupon caused four barrels of meat to be packed and put in the accustomed condition for delivery to customers and placed on the platform in readiness for the accused to take them. He set a watch over the property and notified the person in charge of the platform, who was ignorant of the reason for so placing the barrels, upon his inquiring what they were placed there for, to let them go; that they were for a man who would call for them. About the time appointed for the accused to appear he drove to the platform and commenced putting the barrels in his wagon. The platform boss supposing, as the fact was, that the accused was the man Mr. Layer said was to come for the property, assumed the attitude of consenting to the taking. He did not actually help load the barrels on to the wagon, but he was by, consented by his manner and when the accused was ready to go, helped him arrange his wagon and inquired what was to be done with the fourth barrel. The accused replied that he wanted it marked and sent up to him with a bill. He told the platform boss that he ordered the stuff the night before through Dolan. He took full possession of the three barrels of meat with intent to deprive the owner permanently thereof and without compensating it therefor, wholly in ignorance, however, of the fact that Dolan had acted in the matter on behalf of such owner and that it had knowingly aided in carrying out the plan for obtaining the meat.

MARSHALL, J. (after stating the facts). * * *

* * * So in the circumstances characterizing the taking of the barrels of meat from the loading platform the case comes down to this: If a person procures another to arrange with a third person for the latter to consummate, as he supposes, larceny of the goods of such person and such third person in the course of negotiations so sanctioned by such person suggests the plan to be followed, which is agreed upon between the two, each to be an actor in the matter, and subsequently that is sanctioned secretly by such person, the purpose on the part of the latter being to entrap and bring to justice one thought to be disposed to commit the offense of larceny, and such person carries out a part of such plan necessary to its consummation assigned to such other in the agreement aforesaid, such third person not knowing that such person is advised of the impending offense, and at the finality causes one of its employés, to, tacitly at least, consent to the taking of the goods, not knowing of the real nature of the transaction, is such third person guilty of the crime of larceny, or does the conduct of such person take from the transaction the element of trespass or nonconsent essential to such crime?

It will be noted that the plan for depriving the packing company of its property originated with the accused, but that it was wholly impracticable of accomplishment without the property being placed on the loading platform and the accused not being interfered with when he attempted to take it. When Dolan agreed to procure such placing the packing company in legal effect agreed thereto. Dolan did not expressly consent nor did the agreement he had with the packing company authorize him to do so, to the misappropriation of the property. Did the agreement in legal effect with the accused to place the property of the packing company on the loading platform, where it could be appropriated by the accused * * * constitute consent to such appropriation?

The case is very near the border line, if not across it, between consent and nonconsent to the taking of the property. Reg. v. Lawrence, 4 Cox C.C. 438, it was held that if the property was delivered by a servant to the defendant by the master's direction the offense cannot be larceny, regardless of the purpose of the defendant. In this case the property was not only placed on the loading platform, as was usual in delivering such goods to customers, with knowledge that the accused would soon arrive, having a formed design to take it, but the packing company's employé in charge of the platform, Ernst Klotz, was instructed that the property was placed there for a man who would call for it. Klotz from such statement had every reason to infer, when the accused arrived and claimed the right to take the property, that he was the one referred to and that it was proper to make delivery to him and he acted accordingly. While he did not physically place the property, or assist in doing so, in the wagon, his standing by, witnessing such placing by the accused, and then assisting him in arranging the wagon, as the evidence shows he did, and taking the order, in the usual way, from the accused as to the disposition of the fourth barrel, and his conduct in respect thereto amounted, practically, to a delivery of the three barrels to the accused.

In Rex v. Egginton, 2 P. & P. 508, we have a very instructive case on the subject under discussion here. A servant informed his master that he had been solicited to aid in robbing the latter's house. By the master's discretion the servant opened the house, gave the would-be thieves access thereto and took them to the place where the intended subject of the larceny had been laid in order that they might take it. All this was done with a view to the apprehension of the guilty parties after the accomplishment of their purpose. The servant by direction of the master not only gave access to the house but afforded the would-be thieves every facility for taking the property, and yet the court held that the crime of larceny was complete, because there was no direction to the servant to deliver the property to the intruders or consent to their taking it. They were left free to commit the larceny, as they had proposed doing, and the way was made easy for them to do so, but they were neither induced to commit the crime, nor was any act essential to the offense done by any one but themselves. * * *

We cannot well escape the conclusion that this case falls under the condemnation of the rule that where the owner of property by himself or his agent, actually or constructively, aids in the commission of the offense, as intended by the wrongdoer, by performing or rendering unnecessary some act in the transaction essential to the offense, the would-be criminal is not guilty of all the elements of the offense. * * *

The logical basis for the doctrine above discussed is that there can be no larceny without a trespass. So if one procures his property to be taken by another intending to commit larceny, or delivers his property to such other, the latter proposing to commit such crime, the element of trespass is wanting and the crime not fully consummated however plain may be the guilty purpose of the one possessing himself of such property. That does not militate against a person's being free to set a trap to catch one whom he suspects of an intention to commit the crime of larceny, but the setting of such trap must not go further than to afford the would-be thief the amplest opportunity to carry out his purpose, formed without such inducement on the part of the owner of the property, as to put him in the position of having consented to the taking. * * *

If the accused had merely disclosed to Dolan, his ostensible accomplice, a purpose to improve the opportunity when one should present itself to steal barrels of meat from the packing company's loading platform, and that had been communicated by Dolan to the company and it had then merely furnished the accused the opportunity he was looking for to carry out such purpose, and he had improved it, the situation would be quite different. * * *

REX v. PEAR

Central Criminal Court, 1779.
1 Leach 212, 168 Eng.Rep. 208.

The prisoner was indicted for stealing a black horse, the property of Samuel Finch. It appeared in evidence that Samuel Finch was a Livery–Stable–keeper in the Borough; and that the prisoner, on the 2d of July 1779, hired the horse of him to go to Sutton, in the county of Surry, and back again, saying on being asked where he lived, that he lodged at No. 25 in King-street, and should return about eight o'clock the same evening. He did not return; and it was proved that he had sold the horse on the very day he had hired it, to one William Hollist, in Smithfield Market; and that he had no lodging at the place to which he had given the prosecutor directions.

The learned Judge said: There had been different opinions on the law of this class of cases; that the general doctrine then was that if a horse be let for a particular portion of time, and after that time is expired, the party hiring, instead of returning the horse to its owner, sell it and convert the money to his own use, it is felony, because there is then no privity of contract subsisting between the parties; that in the present case the horse was hired to take a journey into Surry, and the prisoner sold him the same day, without taking any such journey; that there were also other circumstances which imported that at the time of the hiring the prisoner had it in intention to sell the horse, as his saying that he lodged at a place where in fact he was not known. He therefore left it with the Jury to consider, Whether the prisoner meant at the time of the hiring to take such journey, but was afterwards tempted to sell the horse? for if so he must be acquitted; but that if they were of opinion that at the time of the hiring the journey was a mere pretence to get the horse into his possession, and he had no intention to take such journey but intended to sell the horse, they would find that fact specially for the opinion of the Judges.

The Jury found that the facts above stated were true; and also that the prisoner had hired the horse with a fraudulent view and intention of selling it immediately.

The question was referred to the Judges, Whether the delivery of the horse by the prosecutor to the prisoner, had so far changed the possession of the property, as to render the subsequent conversion of it a mere breach of trust, or whether the conversion was felonious?

The Judges differed greatly in opinion on this case; and delivered their opinions *seriatim* upon it at Lord Chief Justice De Gray's house on 4th February 1780 and on the 22nd of the same month Mr. Baron Perryn delivered their opinion on it. The majority of them thought, That the question, as to the original intention of the prisoner in hiring the horse, had been properly left to the jury; and as they had found, that his view in so doing was fraudulent, the parting with the property had not changed the nature of the possession, but that it remained unaltered at the time of the conversion; and that the prisoner was therefore guilty of felony.

NOTES AND QUESTIONS

1. Pear's offense has come to be known as "larceny by trick." When did the offense occur in *Pear?* Another way of asking the question is: When did the defendant trespassorily take possession of the horse? Assuming that Pear intended to steal the horse from the outset, did the larceny occur the moment he rode away on the animal, or only when he acted in violation of the real owner's interests, i.e., when he sold it? What are the practical implications of the latter interpretation?

BROOKS v. STATE

Supreme Court of Ohio, 1878.
35 Ohio St. 46.

The plaintiff in error, George Brooks, * * * was convicted of larceny in stealing $200 in bank bills, the property of Charles B. Newton. It appears from the evidence, that Newton * * *, on the 24th of October, 1878, * * * came to the city of Warren in a buggy to attend to some business. He fastened his horse to a hitching post on Market street. On his way home, in the forenoon of the same day, he discovered that he had lost the package of bank bills in question. He made search for it in various places where he had been, but failed to find it. He looked where he hitched his horse on Market street, but he states that he did not look there very carefully, as there was a team of horses hitched there at the time. Notice of the loss was published in the two newspapers printed in Warren, and in one printed in Leavittsburgh, which also had a circulation in Warren.

On Wednesday, the 20th of November following, the defendant, who resided in Warren, while working on Market street, near the post at which Newton hitched his horse, found the roll or package of bank bills. The package was found "five or six feet from the hitching post." He was, at the time, working in company with several other laborers. At the time he found the money one of these laborers was within ten feet and another within twenty feet of him, but he did not let any of them know that he had found the money. He states, in his testimony, that he put it in his pocket as soon as he found it. Just after finding the package, he picked up a one dollar bill, which he did show to them. This bill was wet and muddy, and he sold it to one of them for twenty-five cents, saying if none of them bought it he would keep it himself. He testifies the reason he sold it was that he did not want them to know at the time that he had found the other money. This bill was shown to several persons at the time, and was put on the hitching post to dry. Within a half hour after finding the money, at the time of stopping for dinner, he quit work, and, at his request, was paid off. He spent part of the money, the same day, for a pair of boots, and for other purposes, and let a Mrs. Lease have fifty dollars of it the same day, with which to purchase furniture for his wife, and for other purposes. * * *

Evidence was also given that the defendant, with his wife, shortly afterward left Warren, and that he attempted to secrete himself before he left. The evidence did not show that the defendant saw any of the notices of the loss of the money published in the newspapers, or that he had any notice of the loss by Newton at the time it was found. Much other evidence was given, but the foregoing is sufficient to show the character of the legal questions raised. * * *

WHITE, J. * * *

Larceny may be committed of property that is casually lost as well as of that which is not. The title to the property, and its constructive possession, still remains in the owner; and the finder, if he takes possession of it for his own use, and not for the benefit of the owner, would be guilty of trespass, unless the circumstances were such as to show that it had been abandoned by the owner.

The question is, under what circumstances does such property become the subject of larceny by the finder?

In Baker v. The State, 29 Ohio St. 184, the rule * * * was there laid down, that "when a person finds goods that have actually been lost, and takes possession with intent to appropriate them to his own use, really believing, at the time, or having good ground to believe, that the owner can be found, it is larceny."

It must not be understood from the rule, as thus stated, that the finder is bound to use diligence or to take pains in making search for the owner. His belief, or grounds of belief, in regard to finding the owner, is not to be determined by the degree of diligence that he might be able to use to accomplish that purpose, but by the circumstances apparent to him at the time of finding the property. If the property has not been abandoned by the owner, it is the subject of larceny by the finder, when, at the time he finds it, he has reasonable ground to believe, from the nature of the property, or the circumstances under which it is found, that if he does not conceal but deals honestly with it, the owner will appear or be ascertained. But before the finder can be guilty of larceny, the intent to steal the property must have existed at the time he took it into his possession. * * *

The case was fairly submitted to the jury; and from an examination of the evidence, we find no ground for interfering with the action of the court below in refusing a new trial.

OKEY, J., dissenting.

I do not think the plaintiff was properly convicted. * * * [The bills] had lain there several weeks, and the owner had ceased to make search for it. The evidence fails to show that the plaintiff had any information of a loss previous to the finding, and in his testimony he denied such notice. There was no mark on the money to indicate the owner, nor was there any thing in the attending circumstances pointing to one owner more than another. * * *

No doubt the plaintiff was morally bound to take steps to find the owner. An honest man would not thus appropriate money, before he had made the finding public, and endeavored to find the owner. But in violating the moral obligation, I do not think the plaintiff incurred criminal liability. * * *

The obligation * * * that the finder must deal "honestly" with the money, is too indefinite; and the opinion contains no satisfactory explanation of it. This leaves both law and fact to the jury, without any rule to guide them. What one jury might think was honest dealing, another jury might think was the reverse. * * *

NOTES AND QUESTIONS

1. Suppose that Brooks had turned in the package of bank bills to legal authorities, but (as he did here) sold the wet and muddy one-dollar-bill to a fellow worker. On these facts, is Brooks guilty of petty larceny? Suppose that it could be proved that the bill belonged to Newton, but that it had become separated from the original package.

2. Cliff, a wealthy man, discovers an extremely valuable watch on the road. He picks it up intending to keep it for a few days so that he can impress his even-richer friends, and then turn it over to the police. After impressing his friends, he decides to keep the watch. Is Cliff guilty of larceny?

b.   " * * * of the Personal Property of Another * * * "

LUND v. COMMONWEALTH

Supreme Court of Virginia, 1977.
217 Va. 688, 232 S.E.2d 745.

I'ANSON, CHIEF JUSTICE.

Defendant, Charles Walter Lund, was charged in an indictment with the theft of keys, computer cards, computer printouts and using "without authority computer operation time and services of Computer Center Personnel at Virginia Polytechnic Institute and State University [V.P.I. or University] * * * with intent to defraud, such property and services having a value of one hundred dollars or more." Code §§ 18.1–100 and 18.1–118 were referred to in the indictment as the applicable statutes. Defendant * * * was found guilty of grand larceny and sentenced to two years in the State penitentiary. * * *

Defendant was a graduate student in statistics and a candidate for a Ph.D. degree at V.P.I. The preparation of his dissertation on the subject assigned to him by his faculty advisor required the use of computer operation time and services of the computer center personnel at the University. His faculty advisor neglected to arrange for defendant's use of the computer, but defendant used it without obtaining the proper authorization.

The computer used by the defendant was leased on an annual basis by V.P.I. from the IBM Corporation. The rental was paid by V.P.I. which allocates the cost of the computer center to various departments within the University by charging it to the budget of that department. This is a bookkeeping entry, and no money actually changes hands. The departments are allocated "computer credits [in dollars] back for their use [on] a proportional basis of their [budgetary] allotments." Each department manager receives a monthly statement showing the allotments used and the running balance in each account of his department.

An account is established when a duly authorized administrator or "department head" fills out a form allocating funds to a department of the University and an individual. When such form is received, the computer center assigns an account number to this allocation and provides a key to a locked post office box which is also numbered to the authorized individual and department. The account number and the post office box number are the access code which must be provided with each request before the computer will process a "deck of cards" prepared by the user and delivered to computer center personnel. The computer print-outs are usually returned to the locked post office box. When the product is too large for the box, a "check" is placed in the box, and it is used to receive the print-outs at the "computer center main window."

Defendant came under surveillance on October 12, 1974, because of complaints from various departments that unauthorized charges were being made to one or more of their accounts. When confronted by the University's investigator, defendant initially denied that he had used the computer service, but later admitted that he had. He gave to the investigator seven keys for boxes assigned to other persons. One of these keys was secreted in his sock. He told the investigating officer he had been given the keys by another student. A large number of computer cards and print-outs were taken from defendant's apartment.

The director of the computer center testified that the unauthorized sum spent out of the accounts associated with the seven post office box keys, amounted to $5,065. He estimated that on the basis of the computer cards and print-outs obtained from the defendant, as much as $26,384.16 in unauthorized computer time had been used by the defendant. He said, however, that the value of the cards and print-outs obtained from the defendant was "whatever scrap paper is worth."

Defendant testified that he used the computer without specific authority. He stated that he knew he was a large computer user, but, because he was doing work on his doctoral dissertation, he did not consider this use excessive or that "he was doing anything wrong."

Four faculty members testified in defendant's behalf. They all agreed that computer time "probably would have been" or "would have been" assigned to defendant if properly requested. * * *

The defendant contends that his conviction of grand larceny of the keys, computer cards, and computer print-outs cannot be upheld under the provisions of Code § 18.1–100 because (1) there was no evidence that the articles were stolen, or that they had a value of $100 or more, and (2) computer time and services are not the subject of larceny under the provisions of Code §§ 18.1–100 or 18.1–118.

Code § 18.1–100 provides as follows:

"Any person who: (1) Commits larceny from the person of another of money or other thing of value of five dollars or more, or

(2) Commits simple larceny not from the person of another of goods and chattels of the value of one hundred dollars or more, shall be deemed guilty of grand larceny * * *."

Section 18.1–118 provides as follows:

"If any person obtain, by any false pretense or token, from any person, with intent to defraud, money or other property which may be the subject of larceny, he shall be deemed guilty of larceny thereof; * * *."

The Commonwealth concedes that the defendant could not be convicted of grand larceny of the keys and computer cards because there was no evidence that those articles were stolen and that they had a market value of $100 or more. The Commonwealth argues, however, that the evidence shows the defendant violated the provisions of § 18.1–118 when he obtained by false pretense or token, with intent to defraud, the computer print-outs which had a value of over $5,000.

Under the provisions of Code § 18.1–118, for one to be guilty of the crime of larceny by false pretense, he must make a false representation of an existing fact with knowledge of its falsity and, on that basis, obtain from another person money or other property which may be the subject of larceny, with the intent to defraud.

At common law, larceny is the taking and carrying away of the goods and chattels of another with intent to deprive the owner of the possession thereof permanently. Code § 18.1–100 defines grand larceny as a taking from the person of another money or other thing of value of five dollars or more, or the taking not from the person of another goods and chattels of the value of $100 or more. The phrase "goods and chattels" cannot be interpreted to include computer time and services in light of the often repeated mandate that criminal statutes must be strictly construed.

At common law, labor or services could not be the subject of the crime of false pretense because neither time nor services may be taken and carried away. * * * Some jurisdictions have amended their criminal codes specifically to make it a crime to obtain labor or services by means of false pretense. We have no such provision in our statutes.

Furthermore, the unauthorized use of the computer is not the subject of larceny. Nowhere in Code § 18.1–100 or § 18.1–118 do we find the word "use." The language of the statutes connotes more than just the unauthorized use of the property of another. It refers to a taking and carrying away of a certain concrete article of personal property. * * *

We hold that labor and services and the unauthorized use of the University's computer cannot be construed to be subjects of larceny under the provisions of Code §§ 18.1–100 and 18.1–118.

The Commonwealth argues that even though the computer print-outs had no market value, their value can be determined by the cost of the labor and services that produced them. We do not agree.

The cost of producing the print-outs is not the proper criterion of value for the purpose here. Where there is no market value of an article that has been stolen, the better rule is that its actual value should be proved. * * *

Here the evidence shows that the print-outs had no ascertainable monetary value to the University or the computer center. Indeed, the director of the computer center stated that the print-outs had no more value than scrap paper. * * * Hence, the evidence was insufficient to convict the defendant of grand larceny under either Code § 18.1–100 or § 18.1–118.

For the reasons stated, the judgment of the trial court is reversed, and the indictment is quashed.

NOTES AND QUESTIONS

1. As a result of *Lund*, the Virginia legislature in 1978 enacted Va. Code Ann. § 18.2–98.1, which provided that "[c]omputer time or services or data processing services or information or data stored in connection therewith is hereby defined to be property which may be the subject of larceny * * * or embezzlement * * * or false pretenses" under the state's applicable theft statutes.

That statute, in turn, was repealed in 1984, when the Virginia legislature enacted the Virginia Computer Crimes Act, which more fully deals with computer crimes, including one relating to theft of computer services. Va. Code. 18.2–152.6.

2. Was Lund guilty of any theft offense under the Model Penal Code?

3. At common law, one could not "steal" real property, because land is not capable of being carried away. The offense only encompasses tangible personal property. This does not mean that the line between real and personal property was always easy to draw. For example, assume that Roberta comes onto Samantha's land without permission, chops down a tree, and immediately carts off the timber for firewood. Is this common law larceny?

Suppose, instead, that after Roberta chops down the tree, she realizes that there is too much to take away at that time. She leaves and returns the next day with a pickup truck, at which time she carts off the timber. Larceny? See Rollin M. Perkins & Ronald N. Boyce, Criminal Law 293 (3d ed. 1982).

4. *"Of another."* It is not larceny to carry away one's own personal property; it must be the property "of another." But, what does "of another" mean? Think back to the "taking" requirement. What must a wrongdoer take in order for the offense to constitute larceny? In light of your answer, consider the following: Tom takes his car to a mechanic for repair. Later, he refuses to pay the repair bill and, late at night, comes to the garage and drives his automobile home. Assuming that he acted with the requisite *mens rea,* is Tom guilty of larceny?

5. *Problem.* A tourist in London was arrested for stealing a white teddy bear left outside St. James Palace by a little girl honoring Princess Diana after the latter's death in a car accident. The tourist said he wanted to give the bear—one of thousands of keepsakes, cards, and flowers left to honor the Princess—and an attached condolence card to his girlfriend as a gift. Larceny? Associated Press, Buffalo News, Sept. 10, 1997, at A2.

2. *MENS REA:* " * * * WITH THE INTENT TO STEAL THE PROPERTY"

PEOPLE v. BROWN

Supreme Court of California, 1894.
105 Cal. 66, 38 P. 518.

GAROUTTE, J. The appellant was convicted of the crime of burglary, alleged by the information to have been committed in entering a certain house with intent to commit grand larceny. The entry is conceded, and also it is conceded that appellant took therefrom a certain bicycle, the property of the party named in the information, and of such a value as to constitute grand larceny. The appellant is a boy of 17 years of age, and, for a few days immediately prior to the taking of the bicycle, was staying at the place from which the machine was taken, working for his board. He took the stand as a witness, and testified: "I took the wheel to get even with the boy, and, of course, I didn't intend to keep it. I just wanted to get even with him. The boy was throwing oranges at me in the evening, and he would not stop when I told him to, and it made me mad, and I left Yount's house Saturday morning. I thought I would go back and take the boy's wheel. He had a wheel, the one I had the fuss with. Instead of getting hold of his, I got Frank's, but I intended to take it back Sunday night; but, before I got back, they caught me. I took it down by the grove, and put it on the ground, and covered it with brush, and crawled in, and Frank came and hauled off the brush, and said: 'What are you doing here?' Then I told him * * * I covered myself up in the brush so that they could not find me until evening, until I could take it back. I did not want them to find me. I expected to remain there during the day, and not go back until evening." Upon the foregoing state of facts, the court gave the jury the following instruction: "I think it is not necessary to say very much to you in this case. I may say, generally, that I think counsel for the defense here stated to you in his argument very fairly the principles of law governing this case, except in one particular. In defining to you the crime of grand larceny, he says it is essential that the taking of it must be felonious. That is true; the taking with the intent to deprive the owner of it; but he adds the conclusion that you must find that the taker intended to deprive him of it permanently. I do not think that is the law. I think in this case, for example, if the defendant took this bicycle, we will say for the purpose of riding twenty-five miles, for the purpose of enabling him to get away, and then left it for another to get it, and intended to do nothing else except to help himself away for a certain distance, it would be larceny, just as much as though he intended to take it all the while. A man may take a horse, for instance, not with the intent to convert it wholly and permanently to his own use, but to ride it to a certain distance, for a certain purpose he may have, and then leave it. He converts it to that extent to his own use and purpose feloniously.'' This instruction is erroneous, and demands a reversal of the judgment. If the boy's story be true, he is not guilty of larceny in taking the machine; yet, under the instruction of the court, the words from his own mouth convicted him. The court told the jury that larceny may be committed, even though it was only the intent of the party taking the property to deprive the owner of it temporarily. We think the authorities form an unbroken line to the effect that the felonious intent must be to deprive the owner of the property permanently. The illustration contained in the instruction as to the man taking the horse is too broad in its terms as stating a correct principle of law. Under the circumstances depicted by the illustration, the man might, and again he might not, be guilty of larceny. It would be a pure question of fact for the jury, and dependent for its true solution upon all the circumstances surrounding the transaction. But the test of law to be applied to these circumstances for the purpose of determining the ultimate fact as to the man's guilt or innocence is, did he intend to permanently deprive the owner of his property? If he did not intend so to do, there is no felonious intent, and his acts constitute but a trespass. While the felonious intent of the party taking need not necessarily be an intention to convert the property to his own use, still it must in all cases be an intent to wholly and permanently deprive the owner thereof. * * *

NOTES AND QUESTIONS

1. *Continuing trespass.* Suppose that the youth in *Brown* had decided to keep the bicycle after he took it. Under ordinary principles of criminal law doctrine, he could not be convicted of larceny because the intent to steal (the *mens rea* of the offense) did not concur in time with the earlier trespassory taking and carrying away of the bicycle (the *actus reus* of the offense).

Common law jurists avoided this outcome by developing the legal fiction of "continuing trespass." Under this doctrine, the initial trespass continues as long as the wrongdoer remains in possession of the property that is the subject of the prosecution. State v. Somerville, 21 Me. 14 (1842). It is as if a new trespassory taking occurs at every moment in time. Thus, in *Brown*, if the youth, after wrongfully "borrowing" the bicycle (a trespassory taking), decided to deprive the owner of it permanently, the law would treat this new, felonious state of mind as concurring with the trespassory taking occurring at that instant.

In light of the continuing trespass doctrine, reconsider the liability of Cliff, the finder of the lost watch (Note 2, p. 906 supra).

2. *Claims of right.* The common law and Model Penal Code provide that a person is not guilty of theft if she takes and carries away another's property believing that it belongs to the actor or that she has some other legal right to take possession. See Model Code § 223.1(3). In such circumstances, the *animus furandi*—the intent to steal—is lacking. Historically, the same rule applies to robbery.

For example, *P* spotted what he incorrectly believed was his missing white German Shepard dog hooked to a post. He unhooked the dog and began to leave, when *V* (the dog's true owner) objected. *P* lifted his shirt, revealing a gun and knife, and then departed with the dog. *P* was charged with armed robbery. Phuong Ly, *Search for Pet May Land Man in Prison*, Detroit Free Press, June 27, 1995, at B1. Under common law principles, if *P* genuinely believed that the dog was his—no matter how unreasonable his belief might have been—he lacked the intent to steal *another's* property. To convict in such circumstances "would stand in patent conflict with both the common-sense notion that someone cannot steal his own property, and the corollary rule that 'theft,' the taking of 'the personal property of *another*' is a lesser included offense at the core of every robbery." People v. Tufunga, 21 Cal.4th 935, 90 Cal.Rptr.2d 143, 987 P.2d 168 (1999).

This "claim of right" rule of larceny law is breaking down, however, in the context of robbery, especially when the defendant claims a right to *another's* property as part of debt collection, as distinguished from a belief that the very property taken belongs to the defendant (as in the German Shepard case). Take, for example, People v. Barnett, 17 Cal.4th 1044, 74 Cal.Rptr.2d 121, 954 P.2d 384 (1998):

> Defendant's contentions are based principally upon this court's decision in *People v. Butler* (1967) 65 Cal.2d 569, 573, 55 Cal.Rptr. 511, 421 P.2d 703. In that case, the defendant was accused of felony murder based on the underlying crime of robbery. At trial, the defendant testified he had been employed by the victim, who had not paid him for some work. The defendant, armed with a gun, went to the victim's home one evening to collect payment. * * * During [a] * * * scuffle, the defendant shot and killed the victim * * *. After quickly searching the home for money and finding none, the defendant grabbed a wallet and ran from the house. In recounting the events, the defendant claimed he did not intend to commit robbery when he went to the house, but intended only to recover the money he was owed. Over the defendant's objection, the prosecutor was permitted to argue to the jury that a robbery had been committed even if the defendant honestly believed the victim owed him money. The jury convicted the defendant of first degree felony murder * * *.

A majority of this court reversed, concluding: "Although an intent to steal may ordinarily be inferred when one person takes the property of another, particularly if he takes it by force, proof of the existence of a state of mind incompatible with an intent to steal precludes a finding of either theft or robbery. It has long been the rule in this state and generally throughout the country that a bona fide belief, even though mistakenly held, that one has a right or claim to the property negates felonious intent. A belief that the property taken belongs to the taker, or that he had a right to retake goods sold is sufficient to preclude felonious intent. Felonious intent exists only if the actor intends to take the property of another without believing in good faith that he has a right or claim to it.''

In his dissent in *Butler*, Justice Mosk took a dim view of the majority's apparent authorization of armed robbery as a self-help measure. * * * [N]oting that the leading cases permitting forcible recapture of property were all decided before the turn of the century, Justice Mosk concluded that a six-shooter was no longer ''an acceptable device for do-it-yourself debt collection'' and that the ''might-makes-right'' doctrine of the previous century was of ''dubious adaptability'' to modern times.

Since *Butler* was decided, a number of other jurisdictions have rejected the claim-of-right defense for public policy reasons in cases where force, violence, or weapons are used for self-help debt collection. * * *

* * * [W]e have not been asked [today] to revisit *Butler*'s increasingly anachronistic authorization of the claim-of-right defense in the context of armed robbery. * * *

A year later, however, the California Supreme Court *was* asked to reconsider *Butler*:

We * * * conclude that *Butler* went well beyond the basic underlying notion that a thief or robber must intend to steal *another's* property when, on the facts before it, the court extended the availability of a claim-of-right defense to perpetrators who rob their victims assertedly to settle, satisfy, or otherwise collect on a debt. * * * [W]e find nothing * * * to suggest the Legislature intended to incorporate such a broad and expansive extension of the claim-of-right doctrine into the robbery statute. * * *

We therefore hold that to the extent *Butler* extended the claim-of-right defense to robberies perpetrated to satisfy, settle or otherwise collect on a debt, liquidated or unliquidated—as opposed to forcible takings intended to recover specific personal property to which the defendant in good faith believes he has a bona fide claim of ownership or title—it is * * * contrary to sound public policy, and in that regard is overruled.

People v. Tufunga, supra.

What is the Model Penal Code position in regard to such claims of right in robbery prosecutions?

PEOPLE v. DAVIS

Supreme Court of California, 1998.
19 Cal.4th 301, 79 Cal.Rptr.2d 295, 965 P.2d 1165.

MOSK, JUSTICE. * * *

Defendant entered a Mervyn's department store carrying a Mervyn's shopping bag. As he entered he was placed under camera surveillance by store security agent Carol German. While German both watched and filmed, defendant went to the men's department and took a shirt displayed for sale from its hanger; he then carried the shirt through the shoe department and into the women's department on the other side of the store. There he placed the shirt on a sales counter and told cashier Heather Smith that he had "bought it for his father" but it didn't fit and he wanted to "return" it. Smith asked him if he had the receipt, but he said he did not because "it was a gift." Smith informed him that if the value of a returned item is more than $20 and there is no receipt, the store policy is not to make a cash refund but to issue a Mervyn's credit voucher. At that point Smith was interrupted by a telephone call from German; German asked her if defendant was trying to "return" the shirt, and directed her to issue a credit voucher. Smith prepared the voucher and asked defendant to sign it; he did so, but used a false name. German detained him as he walked away from the counter with the voucher. * * *

Count 1 of the information charged defendant with the crime of petty theft * * *.[1] * * *

I * * *

The elements of theft by larceny are well settled: the offense is committed by every person who (1) takes possession (2) of personal property (3) owned or possessed by another, (4) by means of trespass and (5) with intent to steal the property, and (6) carries the property away. * * *

Applying these rules to the facts of the case at bar, we have no doubt that defendant (1) took possession (2) of personal property—the shirt—(3) owned by Mervyn's and (4) moved it sufficiently to satisfy the asportation requirement. Defendant does not contend otherwise.

Defendant does contend, however, that the elements of trespass and intent to steal are lacking. He predicates his argument on a distinction that he draws by dividing his course of conduct into two distinct "acts." According to defendant, his first "act" was to take the shirt from the display rack and carry it to Smith's cash register. He contends that act lacked the element of intent to steal because he had no intent to permanently deprive Mervyn's *of the shirt*; he intended to have the shirt in his possession only long enough to exchange it for a "refund." His second

---

1. * * * Penal Code section 484, subdivision (a), provides simply that "Every person who shall feloniously steal, take, carry, lead, or drive away the personal property of another * * * is guilty of theft." The statute is declaratory of the common law [of larceny].

"act," also according to defendant, was to misrepresent to Smith that he had bought the shirt at Mervyn's and to accept the credit voucher she issued. He contends that act lacked the element of trespass because the store, acting through its agent German, *consented* to the issuance of the voucher with full knowledge of how he came into possession of the shirt.

Defendant's argument misses the mark on two grounds: it focuses on the wrong issue of consent, and it views that issue in artificial isolation from the intertwined issue of intent to steal.

To begin with, the question is not whether Mervyn's consented to Smith's issuance of the voucher after defendant asked to "return" the shirt; rather, the question is whether Mervyn's consented to defendant's taking the shirt in the first instance. As the Court of Appeal correctly reasoned, a self-service store like Mervyn's impliedly consents to a customer's picking up and handling an item displayed for sale and carrying it from the display area to a sales counter with the intent of purchasing it; the store manifestly does not consent, however, to a customer's removing an item from a shelf or hanger if the customer's intent in taking possession of the item is to steal it. * * *

In these circumstances the issue of consent—and therefore trespass—depends on the issue of intent to steal. We turn to that issue.

* * * [T]he general rule is that the intent to steal required for conviction of larceny is an intent to deprive the owner *permanently* of possession of the property. * * * But the general rule is not inflexible: "The word 'permanently,' as used here is not to be taken literally." Our research discloses three relevant categories of cases holding that the requisite intent to steal may be found even though the defendant's primary purpose in taking the property is not to deprive the owner permanently of possession: i.e., (1) when the defendant intends to "sell" the property back to its owner, (2) when the defendant intends to claim a reward for "finding" the property, and (3) when, as here, the defendant intends to return the property to its owner for a "refund." There is thus ample authority for the *result* reached in the case at bar; the difficulty is in finding a rationale for so holding that is consistent with basic principles of the law of larceny. * * *

A. THE "SALE" CASES

The classic case of the first category is *Regina v. Hall* (1848) 169 Eng.Rep. 291. The defendant, an employee of a man named Atkin who made candles from tallow, took a quantity of tallow owned by Atkin and put it on Atkin's own scales, claiming it belonged to a butcher who was offering to sell it to Atkin. The jury were instructed that if they found the defendant took Atkin's property with the intent to sell it back to him as if it belonged to another and appropriate the proceeds, he was guilty of larceny. The jury so found, and the conviction was upheld on further review.

The defendant contended that his assertion of temporary ownership of the property for a particular purpose was not enough to constitute the required intent to permanently deprive. The justices expressed two rationales for holding to the contrary. First, one justice stressed that the deprivation would in fact have been permanent unless the owner had agreed to the condition imposed by the defendant, i.e., to "buy" the property: * * *

The second rationale was that the defendant's claim of the right to sell the property was an assertion of *a right of ownership* and therefore evidence of an intent to permanently deprive: Chief Justice Denman reasoned, "The only question attempted to be raised here is as to the *animus furandi*, the intent to deprive the owner of his property. What better proof can there be of such intent, than the assertion of such a right of ownership by the prisoner as to entitle him to sell it." * * *

Perkins offers yet another rationale for the rule that a defendant who takes property for the purpose of "selling" it back to its owner has the requisite intent to permanently deprive: by so doing the defendant creates a *substantial risk of permanent loss*, because if the owner does not buy back his property the defendant will have a powerful incentive to keep it in order to conceal the theft. As Perkins explains, "in the type of case suggested there is also a very considerable risk that [the owner] will not get back the property at all. If, for example, he should decide that his supply was ample and decline to pay the price, the trespasser would take away the property in order to conceal his own wrongdoing." (Perkins [& Boyce, Criminal Law (3d ed. 1982)], at p. 329.) * * *

B. THE "REWARD" CASES

The cases in the second category hold that a defendant who takes property for the purpose of claiming a reward for "finding" it has the requisite intent to permanently deprive. Again the courts invoke differing rationales for this holding. One line of these cases is exemplified by *Commonwealth v. Mason* (1870) 105 Mass. 163. The defendant took possession of a horse that had strayed onto his property, with the intent to conceal it until the owner offered a reward and then to return it and claim the reward, or until the owner was induced to sell it to him for less than its worth. The court affirmed a conviction of larceny on the theory that the requisite felonious intent was shown because the defendant intended to deprive the owner of "a portion of the value of the property." The court did not explain this theory further, but later cases suggested that the "portion of the value" in question was the right to claim a reward—ordinarily less than the property's full value—for its return. * * *

Another line of cases in this category also noted the taker's intent to appropriate "part of the value" of the property, but went on to emphasize a different rationale, i.e., that the taker had made the return of the property *contingent* on the offer of a satisfactory reward, and if the contingency did not materialize the taker would keep the property. * * *

Finally, Perkins again proposes the rationale of a substantial risk of permanent loss. He reasons that a taking with intent to hold for reward creates such a risk because "the intent will result in a permanent loss to the owner if he fails to offer or give a reward for the return of the property." Indeed, even the offer or payment of a reward may not eliminate the risk because the defendant still has an incentive to keep the property rather than expose himself to detection by returning it.

C. THE "REFUND" CASES

The third category comprises a substantial number of recent cases from our sister states affirming larceny convictions on facts identical or closely similar to those of the case at bar: in each, the defendant took an item of merchandise from a store display, carried it to a sales counter, claimed to own it, and asked for a "refund" of cash or credit. Although the cases are thus factually in point, the reasoning of their opinions is, ironically, of less assistance than the "sale" or "reward" cases in our search for a satisfactory rationale on the issue of the intent to permanently deprive. [The court explained that the cases either provided no rationale for affirming the larceny convictions, were statute-specific, or involved the alleged theft of the cash obtained as a refund, rather than theft of the property taken from the display counter.]

II

Several of the rationales articulated in the "sale" and "reward" cases * * * are also applicable to the "refund" cases. On close analysis, moreover, the relevant rationales may be reduced to a single line of reasoning that rests on both a principled and a practical basis.

First, as a matter of principle, a claim of the right to "return" an item taken from a store display is no less an assertion of a *right of ownership* than the claim of a right to "sell" stolen property back to its owner. And an intent to return such an item to the store only if the store pays a satisfactory "refund" is no less *conditional* than an intent to return stolen property to its owner only if the owner pays a satisfactory "reward." * * * It follows that a defendant who takes an item from a store display with the intent to claim its ownership and restore it only on condition that the store pays him a "refund" must be deemed to intend to permanently deprive the store of the item within the meaning of the law of larceny.

Second, as a practical matter, the risk that such a taking will be permanent is not a mere theoretical possibility; rather, by taking an item from a store display with the intent to demand a refund a defendant creates a substantial risk of permanent loss. This is so because if the defendant's attempt to obtain a refund for the item fails for any reason, he has a powerful incentive to keep the item in order to avoid drawing attention to the theft. A person who has taken an item from a store display and has claimed the right to "return" it at a sales counter, but has been rebuffed because, for example, he has no receipt, will not be inclined to run the risk of confirming the suspicions of the sales clerk or store security personnel by *putting the item back* in the display. Instead, just as in the case of a failed attempt to "sell" property back to its owner, "the trespasser would take away the property in order to conceal his own wrongdoing." * * *

III

Applying the foregoing reasoning to the facts of the case at bar, we conclude that defendant's intent to claim ownership of the shirt and to return it to Mervyn's only on condition that the store pay him a "refund" constitutes an intent to permanently deprive Mervyn's of the shirt within the meaning of the law of larceny, and hence an intent to "feloniously steal" that property within the meaning of Penal Code section 484, subdivision (a). Because Mervyn's cannot be deemed to have consented to defendant's taking possession of the shirt with the intent to steal it, defendant's conduct also constituted a trespassory taking within the meaning of the law of larceny. It follows that the evidence supports the final two elements of the offense of theft by larceny, and the Court of Appeal was correct to affirm the judgment of conviction. * * *

NOTES AND QUESTIONS

1. As the *Davis* court pointed out, the rule that theft requires the intent to deprive the owner of the property permanently "is not inflexible: 'The word "permanently," as used here is not to be taken literally.'" Subsequently the California supreme court held that "an intent to take * * * property for so extended a period as to deprive the owner of a major portion of its value or enjoyment satisfies the common law, and therefore California, intent requirement." People v. Avery, 27 Cal.4th 49, 115 Cal.Rptr.2d 403, 38 P.3d 1 (2002). Thus, it would follow that taking cut flowers from a florist without consent, albeit with the intent to return them in a week, would constitute "intent to steal."

B. EMBEZZLEMENT

REX v. BAZELEY

Central Criminal Court, 1799.
2 Leach 835, 168 Eng.Rep. 517.

[Bazeley, the prisoner, was the principal teller at a bank run by Esdaile and Hammett, the prosecutors of this action.[b] Bazeley's duty was to receive and pay money, notes and bills, at the counter. In January, 1799, he received bank-notes and cash for deposit from William Gilbert, through his servant, George Cock. Bazeley credited Gilbert's account, but placed a bank-note in his pocket, which he later appropriated to his own use.]

Const and Jackson, the prisoner's Counsel, * * * proceeded to argue the case upon the following points.

---

b. In England, private parties are permitted to prosecute some criminal actions.

First, That the prosecutors cannot, in contemplation of law, be said to have had a constructive possession of this Bank-note, at the time the prisoner is charged with having tortiously converted it to his own use.

Secondly, That supposing the prosecutors to have had the possession of this note, the prisoner, under the circumstances of this case, cannot be said to have tortiously taken it from that possession with a felonious intention to steal it.

Thirdly, That the relative situation of the prosecutors and the prisoner makes this transaction merely a breach of trust; and,

Fourthly, That this is not one of those breaches of trust which the Legislature has declared to be felony.

The first point, viz. That the prosecutor cannot, in contemplation of law, be said to have had a constructive possession of this Bank-note at the time the prisoner is charged with having tortiously converted it to his own use.—To constitute the crime of larceny, the property must be taken from the possession of the owner; this possession must be either actual or constructive; it is clear that the prosecutors had not, upon the present occasion, the actual possession of the Bank-note, and therefore the inquiry must be, whether they had the constructive possession of it? or, in other words, whether the possession of the servant was, under the circumstances of this case, the possession of the master? Property in possession is said by Sir William Blackstone to subsist only where a man hath both the right to, and also the occupation of, the property. The prosecutors in the present case had only a right or title to possess the note, and not the absolute or even qualified possession of it. It was never in their custody or under their controul. * * * Suppose the prisoner had not parted with the note, but had merely kept it in his own custody, and refused, on any pretence whatever, to deliver it over to his employers, they could only have recovered it by means of an action of trover or detinue, the first of which presupposes the person against whom it is brought, to have obtained possession of the property by lawful means, as by delivery, or finding; and the second, that the right of property only, and not the possession of it, either really or constructively, is in the person bringing it. The prisoner received this note by the permission and consent of the prosecutors, while it was passing from the possession of Mr. Gilbert to the possession of Messrs. Esdaile's and Hammett's; and not having reached its destined goal, but having been thus intercepted in its transitory state, it is clear that it never came to the possession of the prosecutors. It was delivered into the possession of the prisoner, upon an implied confidence on the part of the prosecutors, that he would deliver it over into their possession, but which, from the pressure of temporary circumstances, he neglected to do: at the time therefore of the supposed conversion of this note, it was in the legal possession of the prisoner. To divest the prisoner of this possession, it certainly was not necessary that he should have delivered this note into the hands of the prosecutors, or of any other of their servants personally; for if he had deposited it in the drawer kept for the reception of this species of property, it would have been a delivery of it into the possession of his masters; but he made no such deposit: and instead of determining in any way his own possession of it, he conveyed it immediately from the hand of Mr. Gilbert's clerk into his own pocket. Authorities are not wanting to support this position. * * *

Secondly, Supposing the prosecutor to have had the possession of this note, yet the prisoner, under the circumstances of this case, cannot be said to have tortiously taken it from that possession with a felonious intent to steal it. * * * In the present case there was no evidence whatever to shew that any such intention existed in his mind at the time the note came to his hands * * *. Besides, the prisoner had given a bond to account faithfully for the monies that should come to his hands: he was the agent of a trading company, and had the means of converting bills into cash, which would have enabled him, at the time, to repay to the prosecutor the £100, which he detained for his own use; but if, at the very time he received the note, he had no intent to steal it, it is no felony; for Sir Edward Coke and all the writers on Crown Law agree, that the intent to steal must be when the property comes to his hands or possession; and that if he have the possession of it once lawfully, though he hath the *animus furandi* afterwards, when he carrieth it away, it is no larceny.

But, thirdly, the situation which the prisoner held, and the capacity in which he acted in the banking-house of the prosecutors, make this transaction only a breach of trust. * * *

Fourthly, But a breach of trust is not, either by the Common Law or by Act of Parliament, in this case, felony. * * * [I]f there be such a consent of the owner of the property as argues a trust in the prisoner, and gives him a possession against all strangers, then his breaking that trust, or abusing that possession, though to the owner's utter deceit of all his interest in those goods, it will not be felony * * *. * * * Taking it, therefore, as a settled point, that a breach of trust cannot, by the rules of the common law, be converted into a felonious taking, the next and last inquiry will be, in what cases the Legislature has made this particular breach of trust felony? There are only four statutes upon this subject, viz. the 21 Hen. VIII. c. 7; the 15 Geo. II. c. 13, s. 12; the 5 Geo. III. c. 35, s. 17; and 7 Geo. III. c. 50. The two last Acts relate entirely and exclusively to breaches of trust committed by servants employed in the business of the Post–Offices; and the second to breaches of trust committed by servants employed in the business of the Bank of England, and of course, cannot affect, in any manner whatever, the present case. Nor can the case of the prisoner be construed within the statute 21 Hen. VIII. c. 7, * * * for it has been determined upon this statute, that it is strictly confined to such goods as are delivered by the master to the servant to keep. But this Bank-note, as has been already shewn, was not in the possession of the master, and therefore it cannot have been delivered by him; it being impossible for a man to deliver, either by himself or his agent, a thing of which he is neither actually nor constructively possessed; but, even admitting that it had been in the master's possession, and delivered by him to the prisoner, it would not have been delivered to him to keep, but for the purpose of entering it faithfully in the book, and handing it over to the Bank-note cashier. * * *

Fielding, for the Crown, argued the case entirely on the question, Whether the prosecutors, Esdaile and Hammett, had such a constructive possession of the Bank-note as to render the taking of it by the prisoner felony? He insisted, that in the case of personal chattels, the possession in law follows the right of property; and, that as Gilbert's clerk did not deposit the notes with Bazeley as a matter of trust to him; for they were paid at the counter, and in the banking-house of the prosecutors, of which Bazeley was merely one of the organs; and, therefore, the payment to him was in effect a payment to them, and his receipt of them vested the property *eo instanter* in their hands, and gave them the legal possession of it. * * *

The Judges, it is said, were of opinion * * * that this Bank-note never was in the legal custody or possession of the prosecutors, Messrs. Esdailes and Hammett; but no opinion was ever publicly delivered; and the prisoner was included in the Secretary of State's letter as a proper object for a pardon.

But in consequence of this case the statute 39 Geo. III. c. 85 was passed, entitled, "An Act to protect Masters and others against Embezzlement, by their Clerks or Servants"; and after reciting, that ["]whereas Bankers, Merchants, and others, are, in the course of their dealings and transactions, frequently obliged to entrust their servants, clerks, and persons employed by them in the like capacity, with receiving, paying, negotiating, exchanging, or transferring money, goods, bonds, bills, notes, bankers' drafts, and other valuable effects and securities; that doubts had been entertained, whether the embezzling the same by such servants, clerks, and others, so employed by their masters, amounts to felony by the laws of England; and that it is expedient that such offences should be punished in the same manner in both parts of the United Kingdom"; it enacts and declares, "That if any servant or clerk, or any person employed for the purpose in the capacity of a servant or clerk to any person or persons whomsoever, or to any body corporate or politic, shall, by virtue of such employment, receive or take into his possession any money, goods, bond, bill, note, banker's draft, or other valuable security or effects, for or in the name, or on the account of his master or masters, or employer or employers, and shall fraudulently embezzle, secrete, or make away with the same, or any part thereof; every such offender shall be deemed to have feloniously stolen the same from his master or masters, employer or employers, for whose use, or in whose name or names, or on whose account, the same was or were delivered to, or taken into the possession of, such servant, clerk, or other person so employed, although such money, & c. was or were no otherwise received into the possession of such master or masters, employer or employers, than by the actual possession of his or their servant, clerk, or other person so employed; and every such offender his adviser, procurer, aider or abettor, shall be liable to be transported for any term not exceeding fourteen years, in the discretion of the Court."

NOTES AND QUESTIONS

1. Embezzlement is a statutory offense, separate from larceny, that fills the gap left by *Bazeley*. Although embezzlement statutes vary by jurisdiction, in general they make criminal the conversion of property received by the wrongdoer in a nontrespassory manner. Usually, there must also be an element of entrustment, i.e., the actor must have received the property in trust for another, such that the embezzler's conversion of the property implicates a breach of that trust.

2. *Problem.* In Commonwealth v. Ryan, 155 Mass. 523, 30 N.E. 364 (1892), Justice Holmes described the events resulting in an embezzlement prosecution:

> The defendant was employed by one Sullivan to sell liquor for him in his store. Sullivan sent two detectives to the store, with marked money of Sullivan's, to make a feigned purchase from the defendant. One detective did so. The defendant dropped the money into the money-drawer of a cash-register, which happened to be open in connection with another sale made and registered by the defendant, but he did not register the sale, as was customary, and afterwards—it would seem within a minute or two— he took the money from the drawer. The question presented is whether it appears as matter of law that the defendant was not guilty of embezzlement, but was guilty of larceny, if of anything.

> How should the court answer the question?

3. Reconsider *Brooks* (p. 904 supra): Suppose that Brooks had picked up the lost money with the intention of turning it in, but then decided to keep it. Would he be guilty of embezzlement?

C. FALSE PRETENSES

PEOPLE v. INGRAM

California Court of Appeal, Fourth District, 1998.
76 Cal.Rptr.2d 553.c

HALLER, PRESIDING JUSTICE. * * *

At issue here are two forms of theft—larceny [by trick] and * * * false pretenses * * *. * * *

The common law crime of larceny was said to require a " 'trespass in the taking.' " If the owner of the property actually consents to the defendant's taking his property, there is no trespass in the taking and hence no larceny. * * * Larceny by trick or device occurs when the defendant obtains possession of (but not title to) another's property by

---

c. Petition for review was granted by the state supreme court, 964 P.2d 1276, 79 Cal.Rptr.2d 71 (1998), but review was later dismissed, 971 P.2d 985, 82 Cal.Rptr.2d 609 (1999).

fraud or trickery; fraud vitiates consent and takes the place of the trespass.

However, if one, through false representations and with the intent to steal, obtains both possession and *title* to property there cannot be common-law larceny. The statutory crime of theft by false pretenses was created to fill the gap.

Theft by false pretenses occurs where the defendant makes a false representation with the intent to defraud the owner of his or her property, and the owner is in fact defrauded. "In other words, as in any other case of fraud, the injured party must have been induced to part with his property in reliance on the false representation."

"The distinction between larceny and obtaining money or property by false pretenses turns on a question of title." The defendant who obtains property by larceny does not obtain title, while the defendant who obtains property by false pretenses does obtain title. As explained by our Supreme Court:

"Although the crimes of larceny by trick and device and obtaining property by false pretenses are much alike, they are aimed at different criminal acquisitive techniques. Larceny by trick and device is the appropriation of property, the *possession* of which was fraudulently acquired; obtaining property by false pretenses is the fraudulent or deceitful acquisition of *both title and possession*."

NOTES AND QUESTIONS

1. Rollin M. Perkins & Ronald N. Boyce, Criminal Law 364 (3d ed. 1982):

The statutes of the various states, while by no means uniform, * * * suggest the following definition: The crime of false pretenses is knowingly and designedly obtaining the property of another by means of untrue representations of fact with intent to defraud.

2. *Problem*. People v. Long, 409 Mich. 346, 294 N.W.2d 197 (1980):

Evidence introduced by the prosecution at trial indicated that the defendant was involved in a scheme whereby he short-changed two cashiers $10 each. He did so by creating confusion and impliedly representing that he was giving them an amount of money equal to that which he was receiving. By distracting them and asking for various amounts of change, he induced them to give him $10 more than they received from him.

This is a common scheme, sometimes described as "ringing the changes." As explained in *Long*, it is:

a trick frequently practiced on shopkeepers and salesmen, [and] is effected by tendering a large bill or coin in payment of a small purchase, and, after the correct change has been given, asking for other change and repeating the request until, in the confusion of mind created by so many operations, the thief obtains more money than he should.

Is this a case of larceny by trick or obtaining property under false pretenses?

3. *Problem.* Suppose that Brooks (p. 904 supra), attempting to return the lost money, had handed the bills over to Xavier, who had fraudulently claimed to have lost the money. Of what offense, if any, would *Xavier* have been guilty?

PEOPLE v. WHIGHT

California Court of Appeal, Third District, 1995.
36 Cal.App.4th 1143, 43 Cal.Rptr.2d 163.

SPARKS, ACTING PRESIDING JUSTICE.

Defendant Theodore Whight discovered that the automated teller machine (ATM) card connected to his defunct checking account could still be used to obtain cash at four local Safeway stores. For several weeks he availed himself freely of this happenstance to obtain thousands of dollars. This led to his conviction by a jury of four counts of * * * grand theft by false pretenses. * * *

Defendant opened a regular checking account at Tri Counties Bank (the bank) in Chico in January 1991. He was issued an ATM card which bore no expiration date. This card did not offer any overdraft protection and could be used only with the checking account. * * * Defendant originally deposited $3,750.99 into his checking account. By June 1991, defendant's account was overdrawn by $6.17. In accordance with the bank's normal practice, defendant was mailed a letter stating that his account was overdrawn, that his bank statement and canceled checks would be held at the bank and if no deposits were made to cover the shortage, the account would be closed. * * * On July 10, 1991, no deposit having been made, the bank closed the account because of the negative balance. From the bank's viewpoint, when defendant's checking account was closed, his ATM card was simultaneously canceled and revoked.

Despite the cancellation by the bank, defendant continued to use his ATM card, mainly at local Safeway markets. Safeway allows customers to make purchases and receive cash back by using ATM cards. Safeway's practice was to verify the cards through the use of a computer system operated by Wells Fargo Bank (Wells Fargo). Wells Fargo would report a code to Safeway which approved or disapproved of the proposed transaction. In some cases Wells Fargo would not be able to link up with the customer's bank or otherwise verify the card. If this lasted for more than about thirty seconds, Wells Fargo would report a "stand in" code to Safeway. Upon receipt of this code, Safeway would approve the transaction.

It appears that there was an error in the Wells Fargo computer, which repeatedly failed to notify Safeway that defendant's ATM card was invalid. In March and April 1992, defendant was able to use his ATM card at four different Safeway markets in Butte County. * * * He received a total of over $19,000. * * *

* * * At the time of his arrest, defendant admitted knowing his checking account was closed. * * *

Defendant * * * contends his convictions for grand theft by false pretense must be reversed because "Safeway relied on the code issued by Wells Fargo, rather than [defendant's] presentation of his ATM card, in approving [defendant's] request for money." This leaky contention cannot hold water. * * *

"To support a conviction of theft for obtaining property by false pretenses, it must be shown: (1) that the defendant made a false pretense or representation, (2) that the representation was made with intent to defraud the owner of his property, and (3) that the owner was in fact defrauded in that he parted with his property in reliance upon the representation." We are here concerned with causation or reliance.

The representation need not be in the form of an oral or written statement; it may also consist of conduct. "The false pretense may consist in any act, word, symbol, or token calculated and intended to deceive. It may be either express or implied from words or conduct." Thus, when defendant proffered his ATM card he impliedly represented, falsely, that it was valid. Reliance on a false representation may be, and in some cases must be, inferred from the evidence. However, if the evidence establishes that the victim did not rely on the false pretense, a conviction cannot stand. Defendant maintains that because the Safeway employees did not merely hand him cash upon presentation of the card, but instead verified the card through the computer system, Safeway did not actually rely on his implied representation and therefore he did not commit the crime of theft by false pretenses. In short, he urges there was no substantial evidence of the reliance element of the crime.

It is true that "[f]or false pretenses it is necessary that the swindler's misrepresentation *cause* the victim to pass title to his property or money to the swindler. Looking at the matter from the point of view of the victim, the same thought may be expressed thus: for false pretenses it is required that the victim pass title to his property *in reliance upon* the swindler's misrepresentation." * * *

* * * [T]he reliance or causation element of the crime may be found lacking in three typical situations: "(1) Where the complainant knew the representation was false, or did not believe it to be true. [¶] (2) Where, even if he believed it, he did not rely on it, but investigated for himself or sought and relied on other advice. [¶] (3) Where, although some false representations are proved, the complainant parted with his money or property for other reasons or in reliance on other representations not shown to be false."

But it is settled, as the Attorney General points out, that the false pretense need not be the sole reason for the victim to part with his money or property. "The false pretense or representation must have materially influenced the owner to part with his property, but the false pretense need not be the sole inducing cause." * * *

* * * [T]he causal chain of reliance is not broken merely because the victim undertakes some investigation. So long as the victim does not rely solely upon his own investigation, sufficient reliance is shown if the victim relied in part upon the defendant's representations. * * *

Defendant claims that Safeway relied upon the computer authorization rather than upon his implicit representation that his card was valid. Whether Safeway relied exclusively on the computer authorization would ordinarily pose a factual question to be resolved by the jury under proper instructions. But in this case the record conclusively established that Safeway did not rely upon any computer authorization from Wells Fargo.

The ATM terminals in the Safeway stores were connected to a computer system operated by Wells Fargo. When a customer uses his ATM card in the ATM terminal at a checkstand in a Safeway store by swiping it through the terminal, the magnetic stripe on the back of the card is read. This information is then sent by modem via telephone lines to computers at Wells Fargo. These computers then pass the information to a banking network. As a banking supervisor for Safeway described it, the information "goes from that network to the card holder's bank for an authorization. If the money's in the account, the bank approves it, comes back in through the network, through our bank and back to the store." For the most part, the system generates a code either approving or disapproving the transaction. If approved, the transaction is consummated. On the other hand, if the transaction is denied, the screen at checkstand states, "transaction declined" and sale and/or request for cash would be refused.

In addition to codes for approval and disapproval, the system generates what are called "stand-in" codes. Two types of "stand-in" codes were described by the banking supervisor. "First one being if any place along that network, that phone path that I have described may be down, the phone line may not be operational at any given point in time. That's one type. [¶] The other type where Safeway will stand in is if we don't get that authorization or that response through the system in a reasonable amount of time, then we will stand in for that transaction." Safeway would then automatically resubmit the transaction at a later time for approval. * * * This corporate decision was reiterated by Safeway's banking supervisor. "Again, it's for customer service. We feel that just because our system may not be available at a given point in time or that we don't get a response within a few seconds, that we will ultimately get an authorization and approval for those transactions, so we take the risk on stand-in transactions."

As it turned out, there was a glitch in Wells Fargo's system concerning defendant's account. Rather than transmitting a code declining the transaction because defendant's account had been closed, Wells Fargo kept returning a code to Safeway indicating that there was no response. This, in turn, caused Safeway to treat each transaction as a "stand-in" without a verification or approval from the computer banking system. Given these facts, it can hardly be said that Safeway relied upon the Well Fargo's computer system instead of defendant's representation that his card was valid. * * * [T]he computer system in fact never approved defendant's transactions. As a result, Safeway had nothing to rely upon except defendant's implicit representation that his ATM card was valid. It elected to take the risk and to rely solely on defendant's representation. On this record, the element of reliance or causation was indisputably established.

NOTES AND QUESTIONS

1. *Problems.* Alice goes to her bank and closes out her account, which contains ten dollars. Of what offense—larceny by trick, embezzlement, or false pretenses—if any, is she guilty in the following circumstances?

A. The teller mistakenly believes that Alice has twenty dollars in her account. He hands her two $10 bills. Alice is unaware of the teller's mistake until she leaves the bank. She decides to keep the extra money.

B. Same as A., except that Alice is aware of the teller's mistake as soon as the money is handed to her. She fails to disclose the error and leaves with the extra cash.

C. The teller, aware that Alice is entitled to only ten dollars, inadvertently delivers two $10 bills (the second bill was stuck to the first bill). Alice is unaware of the situation until she leaves the bank. She keeps the extra bill.

D. Same as C., except that Alice is aware of the teller's mistake as the cash is handed to her. She fails to disclose the error and leaves with the extra money.

D. FEDERAL MAIL, WIRE, AND COMPUTER FRAUD

UNITED STATES v. CZUBINSKI

United States Court of Appeals, First Circuit, 1997.
106 F.3d 1069.

TORRUELLA, CHIEF JUDGE.

Defendant-appellant Richard Czubinski ("Czubinski") appeals his jury conviction on nine counts of wire fraud, 18 U.S.C. §§ 1343, 1346, and four counts of computer fraud, 18 U.S.C. § 1030(a)(4). * * *

BACKGROUND * * *

For all periods relevant to the acts giving rise to his conviction, the defendant Czubinski was employed as a Contact Representative in the Boston office of the Taxpayer Services Division of the Internal Revenue Service ("IRS"). To perform his official duties, which mainly involved answering questions from taxpayers regarding their returns, Czubinski routinely accessed information from one of the IRS's computer systems known as the Integrated Data Retrieval System ("IDRS"). Using a valid password given to Contact Representatives, certain search codes, and taxpayer social security numbers, Czubinski was able to retrieve, to his terminal screen in Boston, income tax return information regarding virtually any taxpayer—information that is permanently stored in the IDRS "master file" located in Martinsburg, West Virginia. In the period of Czubinski's employ, IRS rules plainly stated that employees with passwords and access codes were not permitted to access files on IDRS outside of the course of their official duties.

In 1992, Czubinski carried out numerous unauthorized searches of IDRS files. He knowingly disregarded IRS rules by looking at confidential information obtained by performing computer searches that were outside of the scope of his duties as a Contact Representative, including, but not limited to, the searches listed in the indictment. Audit trails performed by internal IRS auditors establish that Czubinski frequently made unauthorized accesses on IDRS in 1992. For example, Czubinski accessed information regarding: the tax returns of two individuals involved in the David Duke presidential campaign; the joint tax return of an assistant district attorney (who had been prosecuting Czubinski's father on an unrelated felony offense) and his wife; the tax return of Boston City Counselor Jim Kelly's Campaign Committee (Kelly had defeated Czubinski in the previous election for the Counselor seat for District 2); the tax return of one of his brothers' instructors; the joint tax return of a Boston Housing Authority police officer, who was involved in a community organization with one of Czubinski's brothers, and the officer's wife; and the tax return of a woman Czubinski had dated a few times. Czubinski also accessed the files of various other social acquaintances by performing unauthorized searches.

Nothing in the record indicates that Czubinski did anything more than knowingly disregard IRS rules by observing the confidential information he accessed. No evidence suggests, nor does the government contend, that Czubinski disclosed the confidential information he accessed to any third parties. The government's only evidence demonstrating any intent to use the confidential information for nefarious ends was the trial testimony of William A. Murray, an acquaintance of Czubinski who briefly participated in Czubinski's local Invisible Knights of the Ku Klux Klan ("KKK") chapter and worked with him on the David Duke campaign. Murray testified that Czubinski had once stated at a social gathering in "early 1992" that "he intended to use some of that information to build dossiers on people" involved in "the white supremacist movement." There is, however, no evidence that Czubinski created dossiers, took steps toward making dossiers (such as by printing out or recording the information he browsed), or shared any of the information he accessed in the years following the single comment to Murray. No other witness testified to having any knowledge of Czubinski's alleged intent to create "dossiers" on KKK members.

The record shows that Czubinski did not perform any unauthorized searches after 1992. He continued to be employed as a Contact Representative until June 1995, when a grand jury returned an indictment against him * * *.

DISCUSSION

I. The Wire Fraud Counts

We turn first to Czubinski's conviction on the nine wire fraud counts.[4] To support a conviction for wire fraud, the government must prove two elements beyond a reasonable doubt: (1) the defendant's knowing and willing participation in a scheme or artifice to defraud with the specific intent to defraud, and (2) the use of interstate wire communications in furtherance of the scheme. *United States v. Sawyer*, 85 F.3d 713, 723 (1st Cir.1996). Although defendant's motion for judgment of acquittal places emphasis on shortcomings in proof with regard to the second element, by arguing that the wire transmissions at issue were not proved to be interstate, we find the first element dispositive and hold that the government failed to prove beyond a reasonable doubt that the defendant willfully participated in a scheme to defraud within the meaning of the wire fraud statute. * * *

The government pursued two theories of wire fraud in this prosecution: first, that Czubinski defrauded the IRS of its property, under section 1343, by acquiring confidential information for certain intended personal uses; second, that he defrauded the IRS and the public of their intangible right to his honest services, under sections 1343 and 1346. We consider the evidence with regard to each theory, in turn.

A. Scheme to Defraud IRS of Property

The government correctly notes that confidential information may constitute intangible "property" and that its unauthorized dissemination or other use may deprive the owner of its property rights. *See Carpenter v. United States*, 484 U.S. 19, 26, 108 S.Ct. 316, 320, 98 L.Ed.2d 275 (1987). Where such deprivation is effected through dishonest or deceitful means, a "scheme to defraud," within the meaning of the wire fraud statute, is shown. Thus, a necessary step toward satisfying the "scheme to defraud" element in this context is showing that the defendant intended to "deprive" another of their protected right.

The government, however, provides no case in support of its contention here that merely accessing confidential information, without doing, or clearly intending to do, more, is tantamount to a deprivation of IRS property under the wire fraud statute. In *Carpenter*, for example, the confidential information regarding the contents of a newspaper column

---

4. The federal wire fraud statute, 18 U.S.C. § 1343, provides in pertinent part:

Whoever, having devised or intending to devise any scheme or artifice to defraud, or for obtaining money or property by means of false or fraudulent pretenses, representations, or promises, transmits or causes to be transmitted by means of wire[, radio, or television] communication in interstate or foreign commerce, any writings, signs, signals, pictures, or sounds for the purpose of executing such scheme or artifice, shall be fined under this title or imprisoned not more than five years, or both.

was converted to the defendants's use to their substantial benefit.[d] We do not think that Czubinski's unauthorized browsing, even if done with the intent to deceive the IRS into thinking he was performing only authorized searches, constitutes a "deprivation" within the meaning of the federal fraud statutes.

Binding precedents, and good sense, support the conclusion that to "deprive" a person of their intangible property interest in confidential information under section 1343, either some articulable harm must befall the holder of the information as a result of the defendant's activities, or some gainful use must be intended by the person accessing the information, whether or not this use is profitable in the economic sense.[7] Here, neither the taking of the IRS' right to "exclusive use" of the confidential information, nor Czubinski's gain from access to the information, can be shown absent evidence of his "use" of the information. Accordingly, without evidence that Czubinski used or intended to use the taxpayer information (beyond mere browsing), an intent to deprive cannot be proven, and, *a fortiori*, a scheme to defraud is not shown. * * *

The resolution of the instant case is complex because it is well-established that to be convicted of mail or wire fraud, the defendant need not successfully carry out an intended scheme to defraud. The government does not contend either that Czubinski actually created dossiers or that he accomplished some other end through use of the information. It need not do so. All that the government was required to prove was the *intent* to follow through with a deprivation of the IRS's property and the use or foreseeable use of interstate wire transmissions pursuant to the accomplishment of the scheme to defraud. In the case at bar, the government failed to make even this showing.

The fatal flaw in the government's case is that it has not shown beyond a reasonable doubt that Czubinski intended to carry out a scheme to deprive the IRS of its property interest in confidential information. Had there been sufficient proof that Czubinski intended either to create dossiers for the sake of advancing personal causes or to disseminate confidential information to third parties, then his actions in searching files could arguably be said to be a step in furtherance of a scheme to deprive the IRS of its property interest in confidential information. The government's case regarding Czubinski's intent to make any use of the informa-

---

d. In *Carpenter*, a *Wall Street Journal* columnist interviewed corporate executives to provide interesting perspectives on the stocks he would highlight in upcoming columns. As a result of the perceived integrity of the column, comments in it often affected the price of the stocks that it examined. As a consequence, the official policy of the Journal was that, prior to publication, the contents of the column were the Journal's confidential information. Despite this rule, the reporter entered into a scheme with two stock brokers to give them advance information as to the contents and timing of his columns. As a result, they bought and sold stocks on the basis of the probable impact of the columns, and shared the considerable profits that ensued. The columnist and his cohorts were found guilty of violating the federal mail and wire fraud statutes, and for conspiracy to violate the statutes.

7. For example, had the government established that Czubinski disclosed or intended to disclose taxpayer information, then the deprivation or intended deprivation of property rights would have been shown.

tion he browsed rests on the testimony of one witness at trial who stated that Czubinski once remarked at a social gathering that he intended to build dossiers on potential KKK informants. We must assume, on this appeal, that Czubinski did indeed make such a comment. Nevertheless, the fact that during the months following this remark—that is, during the period in which Czubinski made his unauthorized searches—he did not create dossiers; given the fact that he did not even take steps toward creating dossiers, such as recording or printing out the information; given the fact that no other person testifying as to Czubinski's involvement in white supremacist organizations had any knowledge of Czubinski's alleged intent to create dossiers or use confidential information; and given the fact that not a single piece of evidence suggests that Czubinski ever shared taxpayer information with others, no rational jury could have found beyond a reasonable doubt that, when Czubinski was browsing taxpayer files, he was doing so in furtherance of a scheme to use the information he browsed for private purposes, be they nefarious or otherwise. In addition, there was no evidence that Czubinski disclosed, or used to his advantage, any information regarding political opponents or regarding the person prosecuting his father.

Mere browsing of the records of people about whom one might have a particular interest, although reprehensible, is not enough to sustain a wire fraud conviction on a "deprivation of intangible property" theory. Curiosity on the part of an IRS officer may lead to dismissal, but curiosity alone will not sustain a finding of participation in a felonious criminal scheme to deprive the IRS of its property.

B.   Honest Services Fraud (Section 1346)

In *McNally v. United States*, 483 U.S. 350, 107 S.Ct. 2875, 97 L.Ed.2d 292 (1987), the Supreme Court held that the mail and wire fraud statutes do not prohibit schemes to defraud individuals of their intangible, nonproperty right to honest government services. Congress responded to *McNally* in 1988 by enacting section 1346, the honest services amendment, which provides:

> For the purposes of this chapter, the term "scheme or artifice to defraud" includes a scheme or artifice to deprive another of the intangible right of honest services.

18 U.S.C. § 1346 (effective Nov. 11, 1988). We have held, after considering the relevant legislative history, that section 1346 effectively restores to the scope of the mail and wire fraud statutes[10] their pre-*McNally* applications to government officials' schemes to defraud individuals of their intangible right to honest services.

We recently had the opportunity to discuss, at some length, the proper application of the section 1346 honest services amendment to the wrongful acts of public officials. *See Sawyer*, 85 F.3d at 722–26. The discussion and holding in *Sawyer* directly guide our disposition of the

---

10.   Identical standards apply in determining the "scheme to defraud" element under the mail and wire fraud statutes.

instant appeal. First, as a general matter, we noted in *Sawyer* that although the right to honest services "eludes easy definition," honest services convictions of public officials typically involve serious corruption, such as embezzlement of public funds, bribery of public officials, or the failure of public decision-makers to disclose certain conflicts of interest. Second, we cautioned that "[t]he broad scope of the mail fraud statute, however, does not encompass every instance of official misconduct that results in the official's personal gain." Third, and most importantly, *Sawyer* holds that the government must not merely indicate wrongdoing by a public official, but must also demonstrate that the wrongdoing at issue is intended to prevent or call into question the proper or impartial performance of that public servant's official duties. In other words, "although a public official might engage in reprehensible misconduct related to an official position, the conviction of that official cannot stand where the conduct does not actually deprive the public of its right to her honest services, and it is not shown to intend that result."

Applying these principles to Czubinski's acts, it is clear that his conviction cannot stand. First, this case falls outside of the core of honest services fraud precedents. Czubinski was not bribed or otherwise influenced in any public decisionmaking capacity. Nor did he embezzle funds. He did not receive, nor can it be found that he intended to receive, any tangible benefit. His official duty was to respond to informational requests from taxpayers regarding their returns, a relatively straightforward task that simply does not raise the specter of secretive, self-interested action, as does a discretionary, decision-making role.

Second, we believe that the cautionary language of *Sawyer* is particularly appropriate here, given the evidence amassed by the defendant at trial indicating that during his span of employment at IRS, he received no indication from his employer that this workplace violation—the performance of unauthorized searches—would be punishable by anything more than dismissal. "To allow every transgression of state governmental obligations to amount to mail fraud would effectively turn every such violation into a federal felony; this cannot be countenanced." Here, the threat is one of transforming governmental workplace violations into felonies. We find no evidence that Congress intended to create what amounts to a draconian personnel regulation. We hesitate to imply such an unusual result in the absence of the clearest legislative mandate.

These general considerations, although serious, are not conclusive: they raise doubts as to the propriety of this conviction that can be outweighed by sufficient evidence of a scheme to defraud. The third principle identified in *Sawyer*, instructing us as to the basic requirements of a scheme to defraud in this context, settles any remaining doubts. The conclusive consideration is that the government simply did not prove that Czubinski deprived, or intended to deprive, the public or his employer of their right to his honest services. Although he clearly committed wrongdoing in searching confidential information, there is no suggestion that he failed to carry out his official tasks adequately, or intended to do so. * * *

II. The Computer Fraud Counts

Czubinski was convicted on all four of the computer fraud counts on which he was indicted; these counts arise out of unauthorized searches that also formed the basis of four of the ten wire fraud counts in the indictment. Specifically, he was convicted of violating 18 U.S.C. § 1030(a)(4), a provision enacted in the Computer Fraud and Abuse Act of 1986. Section 1030(a)(4) applies to:

> whoever * * * knowingly and with intent to defraud, accesses a Federal interest computer without authorization, or exceeds authorized access, and by means of such conduct furthers the intended fraud and obtains anything of value, unless the object of the fraud and the thing obtained consists only of the use of the computer.

We have never before addressed section 1030(a)(4). Czubinski unquestionably exceeded authorized access to a Federal interest computer. On appeal he argues that he did not obtain "anything of value." We agree, finding that his searches of taxpayer return information did not satisfy the statutory requirement that he obtain "anything of value." The value of information is relative to one's needs and objectives; here, the government had to show that the information was valuable to Czubinski in light of a fraudulent scheme. The government failed, however, to prove that Czubinski intended anything more than to satisfy idle curiosity.

The plain language of section 1030(a)(4) emphasizes that more than mere unauthorized use is required: the "thing obtained" may not merely be the unauthorized use. It is the showing of some additional end—to which the unauthorized access is a means—that is lacking here. The evidence did not show that Czubinski's end was anything more than to satisfy his curiosity by viewing information about friends, acquaintances, and political rivals. No evidence suggests that he printed out, recorded, or used the information he browsed. No rational jury could conclude beyond a reasonable doubt that Czubinski intended to use or disclose that information, and merely viewing information cannot be deemed the same as obtaining something of value for the purposes of this statute.

The legislative history further supports our reading of the term "anything of value." * * * Here, a Senate co-sponsor's comments suggest that Congress intended section 1030(a)(4) to punish attempts to steal valuable data, and did not wish to punish mere unauthorized access:

> The acts of fraud we are addressing in proposed section 1030(a)(4) are essentially thefts in which someone uses a federal interest computer to wrongly obtain something of value from another * * *. Proposed section 1030(a)(4) is intended to reflect the distinction between the theft of information, a felony, and mere unauthorized access, a misdemeanor. * * *

CONCLUSION

We add a cautionary note. The broad language of the mail and wire fraud statutes are both their blessing and their curse. They can address new forms of serious crime that fail to fall within more specific legislation. *See United States v. Maze*, 414 U.S. 395, 405–06, 94 S.Ct. 645, 651, 38 L.Ed.2d 603 (1974) (observing that the mail fraud statute serves "as a first line of defense" or "stopgap device" to tackle new types of frauds before particularized legislation is developed) (Burger, C.J., dissenting). On the other hand, they might be used to prosecute kinds of behavior that, albeit offensive to the morals or aesthetics of federal prosecutors, cannot reasonably be expected by the instigators to form the basis of a federal felony. The case at bar falls within the latter category. Also discomforting is the prosecution's insistence, before trial, on the admission of inflammatory evidence regarding the defendant's membership in white supremacist groups purportedly as a means to prove a scheme to defraud, when, on appeal, it argues that unauthorized access in itself is a sufficient ground for conviction on all counts. Finally, we caution that the wire fraud statute must not serve as a vehicle for prosecuting only those citizens whose views run against the tide, no matter how incorrect or uncivilized such views are. * * *

NOTES AND QUESTIONS

1. The federal mail fraud statute, 18 U.S.C. § 1341 (1989), is interpreted similarly to the wire fraud statute. It encompasses schemes to defraud involving the placement "in any post office or authorized depository for mail matter, any matter or thing whatever to be sent or delivered by the Postal Service * * *."

2. Although the prosecutions here failed, the federal mail and wire fraud statutes are used often and with considerable success by federal prosecutors to attack fraudulent schemes, even in a highly inchoate stage. And, because United States mails are often used in schemes to defraud, or telephone calls are made across state lines, or electronic mail is transmitted across state or international boundaries, federal prosecutions are now possible in many criminal enterprises that might otherwise fall exclusively within a state's (or more than one state's) jurisdiction. (The Constitution does not bar a state from prosecuting a defendant for violation of that jurisdiction's fraud laws, even if he is also prosecuted under federal law for the same conduct.)

3. Professor Francis Allen has written that the federal wire and mail fraud laws, and in particular their use to punish the theft of intangible rights to honest services, "assault[] the values of legality." Francis A. Allen, *The Erosion of Legality in American Criminal Justice: Some Latter–Day Adventures of the Nulla Poena Principle*, 29 Ariz. L. Rev. 385, 408–409 (1987). Can you figure out why he said this?

The Supreme Court recently decided that the mail and wire fraud statutes do not criminalize every theft of an actor's honest services from an entity to whom he owes such services. Instead, those statutes criminalize only thefts of honest services involving "bribery or kickback schemes," provided of course that the mail or wires were used in furtherance of the scheme. Such cases, said the Court, constituted the "solid core" of the honest-services doctrine. Skilling v. United States, 561 U.S. __, __, 130 S.Ct. 2896, 2930,

177 L.Ed.2d 619 (2010). Does this interpretation of the mail and wire fraud statutes address Professor Allen's concerns? Does it constitute a fair interpretation of 18 U.S.C. § 1346? What result in *Czubinski* after *Skilling*?

APPENDIX

AMERICAN LAW INSTITUTE MODEL PENAL CODE

■ ■ ■

TABLE OF CONTENTS

PART I. GENERAL PROVISIONS

ARTICLE 1. PRELIMINARY

Section

**PART II.   DEFINITION OF SPECIFIC CRIMES OFFENSES
INVOLVING DANGER TO THE PERSON**

ARTICLE 210.   CRIMINAL HOMICIDE

(Official Draft, 1962)

PART I. GENERAL PROVISIONS
Article 1. Preliminary

SECTION 1.01. [Omitted]

SECTION 1.02.* PURPOSES; PRINCIPLES OF CONSTRUCTION

(1) The general purposes of the provisions governing the definition of offenses are:

(a) to forbid and prevent conduct that unjustifiably and inexcusably inflicts or threatens substantial harm to individual or public interests;

---

* Subsection (2) was redrafted and approved by the American Law Institute in 2007.

(b) to subject to public control persons whose conduct indicates that they are disposed to commit crimes;

(c) to safeguard conduct that is without fault from condemnation as criminal;

(d) to give fair warning of the nature of the conduct declared to constitute an offense;

(e) to differentiate on reasonable grounds between serious and minor offenses.

(2) The general purposes of the provisions on sentencing, applicable to all official actors in the sentencing system, are:

(a) in decisions affecting the sentencing of individual offenders:

(i) to render sentences in all cases within a range of severity proportionate to the gravity of offenses, the harms done to crime victims, and the blameworthiness of offenders;

(ii) when reasonably feasible, to achieve offender rehabilitation, general deterrence, incapacitation of dangerous offenders, restoration of crime victims and communities, and reintegration of offenders into the law-abiding community, provided these goals are pursued within the boundaries of proportionality in subsection (a)(i); and

(iii) to render sentences no more severe than necessary to achieve the applicable purposes in subsections (a)(i) and (a)(ii);

(b) in matters affecting the administration of the sentencing system:

(i) to preserve judicial discretion to individualize sentences within a framework of law;

(ii) to produce sentences that are uniform in their reasoned pursuit of the purposes in subsection (a);

(iii) to eliminate inequities in sentencing across population groups;

(iv) to encourage the use of intermediate sanctions;

(v) to ensure that adequate resources are available for carrying out sentences imposed and that rational priorities are established for the use of those resources;

(vi) to ensure that all criminal sanctions are administered in a humane fashion and that incarcerated offenders are provided reasonable benefits of subsistence, personal safety, medical and mental-health care, and opportunities to rehabilitate themselves;

(vii) to promote research on sentencing policy and practices, including assessments of the effectiveness of criminal sanctions as measured against their purposes, and the effects of criminal sanctions upon families and communities; and

(viii) to increase the transparency of the sentencing and corrections system, its accountability to the public, and the legitimacy of its operations as perceived by all affected communities.

lenity principle

(3) The provisions of the Code shall be construed according to the fair import of their terms but when the language is susceptible of differing constructions it shall be interpreted to further the general purposes stated in this Section and the special purposes of the particular provision involved. The discretionary powers conferred by the Code shall be exercised in accordance with the criteria stated in the Code and, insofar as such criteria are not decisive, to further the general purposes stated in this Section.

SECTION 1.03. [*Omitted*]

SECTION 1.04. CLASSES OF CRIMES; VIOLATIONS

(1) An offense defined by this Code or by any other statute of this State, for which a sentence of [death or of] imprisonment is authorized, constitutes a crime. Crimes are classified as felonies, misdemeanors or petty misdemeanors.

(2) A crime is a felony if it is so designated in this Code or if persons convicted thereof may be sentenced [to death or] to imprisonment for a term that, apart from an extended term, is in excess of one year.

(3) A crime is a misdemeanor if it is so designated in the Code or in a statute other than this Code enacted subsequent thereto.

(4) A crime is a petty misdemeanor if it is so designated in this Code or in a statute other than this Code enacted subsequent thereto or if it is defined by a statute other than this Code that now provides that persons convicted thereof may be sentenced to imprisonment for a term of which the maximum is less than one year.

(5) An offense defined by this Code or by any other statute of this State constitutes a violation if it is so designated in this Code or in the law defining the offense or if no other sentence than a fine, or fine and forfeiture or other civil penalty is authorized upon conviction or if it is defined by a statute other than this Code that now provides that the offense shall not constitute a crime. A violation does not constitute a crime and conviction of a violation shall not give rise to any disability or legal disadvantage based on conviction of a criminal offense.

(6) Any offense declared by law to constitute a crime, without specification of the grade thereof or of the sentence authorized upon conviction, is a misdemeanor.

(7) An offense defined by any statute of this State other than this Code shall be classified as provided in this Section and the sentence that may be imposed upon conviction thereof shall hereafter be governed by the Code.

SECTION 1.05. ALL OFFENSES DEFINED BY STATUTE; APPLICATION OF GENERAL PROVISIONS OF THE CODE

(1) No conduct constitutes an offense unless it is a crime or violation under this Code or another statute of the State.

(2) The provisions of Part I of the Code are applicable to offenses defined by other statutes, unless the Code otherwise provides.

(3) This Section does not affect the power of a court to punish for contempt or to employ any sanction authorized by law for the enforcement of an order or a civil judgment or decree.

SECTION 1.06. [*Omitted*]

SECTION 1.07. METHOD OF PROSECUTION WHEN CONDUCT CONSTITUTES MORE THAN ONE OFFENSE

(1) *Prosecution for Multiple Offenses; Limitation on Convictions.* When the same conduct of a defendant may establish the commission of more than one offense, the defendant may be prosecuted for each such offense. He may not, however, be convicted of more than one offense if:

(a) one offense is included in the other, as defined in Subsection (4) of this Section; or

(b) one offense consists only of a conspiracy or other form of preparation to commit the other; or

(c) inconsistent findings of fact are required to establish the commission of the offenses; or

(d) the offenses differ only in that one is defined to prohibit a designated kind of conduct generally and the other to prohibit a specific instance of such conduct; or

(e) the offense is defined as a continuing course of conduct and the defendant's course of conduct was uninterrupted, unless the law provides that specific periods of such conduct constitute separate offenses.

(2) *Limitation on Separate Trials for Multiple Offenses.* Except as provided in Subsection (3) of this Section, a defendant shall not be subject to separate trials for multiple offenses based on the same conduct or arising from the same criminal episode, if such offenses are known to the appropriate prosecuting officer at the time of the commencement of the first trial and are within the jurisdiction of a single court.

(3) *Authority of Court to Order Separate Trials.* When a defendant is charged with two or more offenses based on the same conduct or arising from the same criminal episode, the Court, on application of the prosecuting attorney or of the defendant, may order any such charge to be tried separately, if it is satisfied that justice so requires.

(4) *Conviction of Included Offense Permitted.* A defendant may be convicted of an offense included in an offense charged in the indictment [or the information]. An offense is so included when:

(a) it is established by proof of the same or less than all the facts required to establish the commission of the offense charged; or

(b) it consists of an attempt or solicitation to commit the offense charged or to commit an offense otherwise included therein; or

(c) it differs from the offense charged only in the respect that a less serious injury or risk of injury to the same person, property or public interest or a lesser kind of culpability suffices to establish its commission.

(5) *Submission of Included Offense to Jury.* The Court shall not be obligated to charge the jury with respect to an included offense unless there is a rational basis for a verdict acquitting the defendant of the offense charged and convicting him of the included offense.

SECTIONS 1.08.–1.11. [*Omitted*]

SECTION 1.12. PROOF BEYOND A REASONABLE DOUBT; AFFIRMATIVE DEFENSES; BURDEN OF PROVING FACT WHEN NOT AN ELEMENT OF AN OFFENSE; PRESUMPTIONS

(1) No person may be convicted of an offense unless each element of such offense is proved beyond a reasonable doubt. In the absence of such proof, the innocence of the defendant is assumed.

(2) Subsection (1) of the Section does not:

(a) require the disproof of an affirmative defense unless and until there is evidence supporting such defense; or

(b) apply to any defense which the Code or another statute plainly requires the defendant to prove by a preponderance of evidence.

(3) A ground of defense is affirmative, within the meaning of Subsection (2)(a) of the Section, when:

(a) it arises under a section of the Code that so provides; or

(b) it relates to an offense defined by a statute other than the Code and such statute so provides; or

(c) it involves a matter of excuse or justification peculiarly within the knowledge of the defendant on which he can fairly be required to adduce supporting evidence.

(4) When the application of the Code depends upon the finding of a fact which is not an element of an offense, unless the Code otherwise provides:

(a) the burden of proving the fact is on the prosecution or defendant, depending on whose interest or contention will be furthered if the finding should be made; and

(b) the fact must be proved to the satisfaction of the Court or jury, as the case may be.

(5) When the Code establishes a presumption with respect to any fact that is an element of an offense, it has the following consequences:

(a) when there is evidence of the facts that give rise to the presumption, the issue of the existence of the presumed fact must be submitted to the jury, unless the Court is satisfied that the evidence as a whole clearly negatives the presumed fact; and

(b) when the issue of the existence of the presumed fact is submitted to the jury, the Court shall charge that while the presumed fact must, on all the evidence, be proved beyond a reasonable doubt, the law declares that the jury may regard the facts giving rise to the presumption as sufficient evidence of the presumed fact.

(6) A presumption not established by the Code or inconsistent with it has the consequences otherwise accorded it by law.

SECTION 1.13. GENERAL DEFINITIONS

In this Code, unless a different meaning plainly is required:

(1) "statute" includes the Constitution and a local law or ordinance of a political subdivision of the State;

(2) "act" or "action" means a bodily movement whether voluntary or involuntary;

(3) "voluntary" has the meaning specified in Section 2.01;

(4) "omission" means a failure to act;

(5) "conduct" means an action or omission and its accompanying state of mind, or, where relevant, a series of acts and omissions;

(6) "actor" includes, where relevant, a person guilty of an omission;

(7) "acted" includes, where relevant, "omitted to act";

(8) "person," "he" and "actor" include any natural person and, where relevant, a corporation or an unincorporated association;

(9) "element of an offense" means (i) such conduct or (ii) such attendant circumstance or (iii) such a result of conduct as

(a) is included in the description of the forbidden conduct in the definition of the offense; or

(b) establishes the required kind of culpability; or

(c) negatives an excuse or justification for such conduct; or

(d) negatives a defense under the statute of limitations; or

(e) establishes jurisdiction or venue;

(10) "material element of an offense" means an element that does not relate exclusively to the statute of limitations, jurisdiction, venue or to any other matter similarly unconnected with (i) the harm or evil, incident to conduct, sought to be prevented by the law defining the offense, or (ii) the existence of a justification or excuse for such conduct;

(11) "purposely" has the meaning specified in Section 2.02 and equivalent terms such as "with purpose," "designed" or "with design" have the same meaning;

(12) "intentionally" or "with intent" means purposely;

(13) "knowingly" has the meaning specified in Section 2.02 and equivalent terms such as "knowing" or "with knowledge" have the same meaning;

(14) "recklessly" has the meaning specified in Section 2.02 and equivalent terms such as "recklessness" or "with recklessness" have the same meaning;

(15) "negligently" has the meaning specified in Section 2.02 and equivalent terms such as "negligence" or "with negligence" have the same meaning;

(16) "reasonably believes" or "reasonable belief" designates a belief which the actor is not reckless or negligent in holding.

Article 2. General Principles of Liability

SECTION 2.01. REQUIREMENT OF VOLUNTARY ACT; OMISSION AS BASIS OF LIABILITY; POSSESSION AS AN ACT

(1) A person is not guilty of an offense unless his liability is based on conduct which includes a voluntary act or the omission to perform an act of which he is physically capable.

(2) The following are not voluntary acts within the meaning of this Section:

    (a) a reflex or convulsion;

    (b) a bodily movement during unconsciousness or sleep;

    (c) conduct during hypnosis or resulting from hypnotic suggestion;

    (d) a bodily movement that otherwise is not a product of the effort or determination of the actor, either conscious or habitual.

(3) Liability for the commission of an offense may not be based on an omission unaccompanied by action unless:

    (a) the omission is expressly made sufficient by the law defining the offense; or

    (b) a duty to perform the omitted act is otherwise imposed by law.

(4) Possession is an act, within the meaning of this Section, if the possessor knowingly procured or received the thing possessed or was aware of his control thereof for a sufficient period to have been able to terminate his possession.

SECTION 2.02. GENERAL REQUIREMENTS OF CULPABILITY

(1) *Minimum Requirements of Culpability.* Except as provided in Section 2.05, a person is not guilty of an offense unless he acted purposely, knowingly, recklessly or negligently, as the law may require, with respect to each material element of the offense.

(2) *Kinds of Culpability Defined.*

    (a) *Purposely.* A person acts purposely with respect to a material element of an offense when:

        (i) if the element involves the nature of his conduct or a result thereof, it is his conscious object to engage in conduct of that nature or to cause such a result; and

        (ii) if the element involves the attendant circumstances, he is aware of the existence of such circumstances or he believes or hopes that they exist.

    (b) *Knowingly.* A person acts knowingly with respect to a material element of an offense when:

(i) if the element involves the nature of his conduct or the attendant circumstances, he is aware that his conduct is of that nature or that such circumstances exist; and

(ii) if the element involves a result of his conduct, he is aware that it is practically certain that his conduct will cause such a result.

(c) *Recklessly.* A person acts recklessly with respect to a material element of an offense when he consciously disregards a substantial and unjustifiable risk that the material element exists or will result from his conduct. The risk must be of such a nature and degree that, considering the nature and purpose of the actor's conduct and the circumstances known to him, its disregard involves a gross deviation from the standard of conduct that a law-abiding person would observe in the actor's situation.

(d) *Negligently.* A person acts negligently with respect to a material element of an offense when he should be aware of a substantial and unjustifiable risk that the material element exists or will result from his conduct. The risk must be of such a nature and degree that the actor's failure to perceive it, considering the nature and purpose of his conduct and the circumstances known to him, involves a gross deviation from the standard of care that a reasonable person would observe in the actor's situation.

(3) *Culpability Required Unless Otherwise Provided.* When the culpability sufficient to establish a material element of an offense is not prescribed by law, such element is established if a person acts purposely, knowingly or recklessly with respect thereto.

(4) *Prescribed Culpability Requirement Applies to All Material Elements.* When the law defining an offense prescribes the kind of culpability that is sufficient for the commission of an offense, without distinguishing among the material elements thereof, such provision shall apply to all the material elements of the offense, unless a contrary purpose plainly appears.

(5) *Substitutes for Negligence, Recklessness and Knowledge.* When the law provides that negligence suffices to establish an element of an offense, such element also is established if a person acts purposely, knowingly or recklessly. When recklessness suffices to establish an element, such element also is established if a person acts purposely or knowingly. When acting knowingly suffices to establish an element, such element also is established if a person acts purposely.

(6) *Requirement of Purpose Satisfied if Purpose Is Conditional.* When a particular purpose is an element of an offense, the element is established although such purpose is conditional, unless the condition negatives the harm or evil sought to be prevented by the law defining the offense.

(7) *Requirement of Knowledge Satisfied by Knowledge of High Probability.* When knowledge of the existence of a particular fact is an element of an offense, such knowledge is established if a person is aware of a high probability of its existence, unless he actually believes that it does not exist.

(8) *Requirement of Wilfulness Satisfied by Acting Knowingly.* A requirement that an offense be committed wilfully is satisfied if a person acts

knowingly with respect to the material elements of the offense, unless a purpose to impose further requirements appears.

(9) *Culpability as to Illegality of Conduct.* Neither knowledge nor recklessness or negligence as to whether conduct constitutes an offense or as to the existence, meaning or application of the law determining the elements of an offense is an element of such offense, unless the definition of the offense or the Code so provides.

(10) *Culpability as Determinant of Grade of Offense.* When the grade or degree of an offense depends on whether the offense is committed purposely, knowingly, recklessly or negligently, its grade or degree shall be the lowest for which the determinative kind of culpability is established with respect to any material element of the offense.

SECTION 2.03.   CAUSAL RELATIONSHIP BETWEEN CONDUCT AND RESULT; DIVERGENCE BETWEEN RESULT DESIGNED OR CONTEMPLATED AND ACTUAL RESULT OR BETWEEN PROBABLE AND ACTUAL RESULT

(1) Conduct is the cause of a result when:

(a) it is an antecedent but for which the result in question would not have occurred; and

(b) the relationship between the conduct and result satisfies any additional causal requirements imposed by the Code or by the law defining the offense.

(2) When purposely or knowingly causing a particular result is an element of an offense, the element is not established if the actual result is not within the purpose or the contemplation of the actor unless:

(a) the actual result differs from that designed or contemplated, as the case may be, only in the respect that a different person or different property is injured or affected or that the injury or harm designed or contemplated would have been more serious or more extensive than that caused; or

(b) the actual result involves the same kind of injury or harm as that designed or contemplated and is not too remote or accidental in its occurrence to have a [just] bearing on the actor's liability or on the gravity of his offense.

(3) When recklessly or negligently causing a particular result is an element of an offense, the element is not established if the actual result is not within the risk of which the actor is aware or, in the case of negligence, of which he should be aware unless:

(a) the actual result differs from the probable result only in the respect that a different person or different property is injured or affected or that the probable injury or harm would have been more serious or more extensive than that caused; or

(b) the actual result involves the same kind of injury or harm as the probable result and is not too remote or accidental in its occurrence to have a [just] bearing on the actor's liability or on the gravity of his offense.

(4) When causing a particular result is a material element of an offense for which absolute liability is imposed by law, the element is not established unless the actual result is a probable consequence of the actor's conduct.

SECTION 2.04. IGNORANCE OR MISTAKE

(1) Ignorance or mistake as to a matter of fact or law is a defense if:

(a) the ignorance or mistake negatives the purpose, knowledge, belief, recklessness or negligence required to establish a material element of the offense; or

(b) the law provides that the state of mind established by such ignorance or mistake constitutes a defense.

(2) Although ignorance or mistake would otherwise afford a defense to the offense charged, the defense is not available if the defendant would be guilty of another offense had the situation been as he supposed. In such case, however, the ignorance or mistake of the defendant shall reduce the grade and degree of the offense of which he may be convicted to those of the offense of which he would be guilty had the situation been as he supposed.

(3) A belief that conduct does not legally constitute an offense is a defense to a prosecution for that offense based upon such conduct when:

(a) the statute or other enactment defining the offense is not known to the actor and has not been published or otherwise reasonably made available prior to the conduct alleged; or

(b) he acts in reasonable reliance upon an official statement of the law, afterward determined to be invalid or erroneous, contained in (i) a statute or other enactment; (ii) a judicial decision, opinion or judgment; (iii) an administrative order or grant of permission; or (iv) an official interpretation of the public officer or body charged by law with responsibility for the interpretation, administration or enforcement of the law defining the offense.

(4) The defendant must prove a defense arising under Subsection (3) of this Section by a preponderance of evidence.

SECTION 2.05. WHEN CULPABILITY REQUIREMENTS ARE INAPPLICABLE TO VIOLATIONS AND TO OFFENSES DEFINED BY OTHER STATUTES; EFFECT OF ABSOLUTE LIABILITY IN REDUCING GRADE OF OFFENSE TO VIOLATION

(1) The requirements of culpability prescribed by Sections 2.01 and 2.02 do not apply to:

(a) offenses which constitute violations, unless the requirement involved is included in the definition of the offense or the Court determines that its application is consistent with effective enforcement of the law defining the offense; or

(b) offenses defined by statutes other than the Code, insofar as a legislative purpose to impose absolute liability for such offenses or with respect to any material element thereof plainly appears.

(2) Notwithstanding any other provision of existing law and unless a subsequent statute otherwise provides:

(a) when absolute liability is imposed with respect to any material element of an offense defined by a statute other than the Code and a conviction is based upon such liability, the offense constitutes a violation; and

(b) although absolute liability is imposed by law with respect to one or more of the material elements of an offense defined by a statute other than the Code, the culpable commission of the offense may be charged and proved, in which event negligence with respect to such elements constitutes sufficient culpability and the classification of the offense and the sentence that may be imposed therefor upon conviction are determined by Section 1.04 and Article 6 of the Code.

SECTION 2.06.   LIABILITY FOR CONDUCT OF ANOTHER; COMPLICITY

(1) A person is guilty of an offense if it is committed by his own conduct or by the conduct of another person for which he is legally accountable, or both.

(2) A person is legally accountable for the conduct of another person when:

(a) acting with the kind of culpability that is sufficient for the commission of the offense, he causes an innocent or irresponsible person to engage in such conduct; or

(b) he is made accountable for the conduct of such other person by the Code or by the law defining the offense; or

(c) he is an accomplice of such other person in the commission of the offense.

(3) A person is an accomplice of another person in the commission of an offense if:

(a) with the purpose of promoting or facilitating the commission of the offense, he

(i) solicits such other person to commit it; or

(ii) aids or agrees or attempts to aid such other person in planning or committing it; or

(iii) having a legal duty to prevent the commission of the offense, fails to make proper effort so to do; or

(b) his conduct is expressly declared by law to establish his complicity.

(4) When causing a particular result is an element of an offense, an accomplice in the conduct causing such result is an accomplice in the commission of that offense, if he acts with the kind of culpability, if any, with respect to that result that is sufficient for the commission of the offense.

(5) A person who is legally incapable of committing a particular offense himself may be guilty thereof if it is committed by the conduct of another person for which he is legally accountable, unless such liability is inconsistent with the purpose of the provision establishing his incapacity.

(6) Unless otherwise provided by the Code or by the law defining the offense, a person is not an accomplice in an offense committed by another person if:

no
accomplice
liability

(a) he is a victim of that offense; or

(b) the offense is so defined that his conduct is inevitably incident to its commission; or

(c) he terminates his complicity prior to the commission of the offense and

(i) wholly deprives it of effectiveness in the commission of the offense; or

(ii) gives timely warning to the law enforcement authorities or otherwise makes proper effort to prevent the commission of the offense.

(7) An accomplice may be convicted on proof of the commission of the offense and of his complicity therein, though the person claimed to have committed the offense has not been prosecuted or convicted or has been convicted of a different offense or degree of offense or has an immunity to prosecution or conviction or has been acquitted.

SECTION 2.07.   LIABILITY OF CORPORATIONS, UNINCORPORATED ASSOCIATIONS AND PERSONS ACTING, OR UNDER A DUTY TO ACT, IN THEIR BEHALF

(1) A corporation may be convicted of the commission of an offense if:

(a) the offense is a violation or the offense is defined by a statute other than the Code in which a legislative purpose to impose liability on corporations plainly appears and the conduct is performed by an agent of the corporation acting in behalf of the corporation within the scope of his office or employment, except that if the law defining the offense designates the agents for whose conduct the corporation is accountable or the circumstance under which it is accountable, such provisions shall apply; or

(b) the offense consists of an omission to discharge a specific duty of affirmative performance imposed on corporations by law; or

(c) the commission of the offense was authorized, requested, commanded, performed or recklessly tolerated by the board of directors or by a high managerial agent acting in behalf of the corporation within the scope of his office or employment.

(2) When absolute liability is imposed for the commission of an offense, a legislative purpose to impose liability on a corporation shall be assumed, unless the contrary plainly appears.

(3) An unincorporated association may be convicted of the commission of an offense if:

(a) the offense is defined by a statute other than the Code which expressly provides for the liability of such an association and the conduct is performed by an agent of the association acting in behalf of the association within the scope of his office or employment, except that if the law defining the offense designates the agents for whose conduct the association is accountable or the circumstances under which it is accountable, such provisions shall apply; or

(b) the offense consists of an omission to discharge a specific duty of affirmative performance imposed on associations by law.

(4) As used in the Section:

(a) "corporation" does not include an entity organized as or by a governmental agency for the execution of a governmental program;

(b) "agent" means any director, officer, servant, employee or other person authorized to act in behalf of the corporation or association and, in the case of an unincorporated association, a member of such association;

(c) "high managerial agent" means an officer of a corporation or an unincorporated association, or, in the case of a partnership, a partner, or any other agent of a corporation or association having duties of such responsibilities that his conduct may fairly be assumed to represent the policy of the corporation or association.

(5) In any prosecution of a corporation or an unincorporated association for the commission of an offense included within the terms of Subsection (1)(a) or Subsection (3)(a) of this Section, other than an offense for which absolute liability has been imposed, it shall be a defense if the defendant proves by a preponderance of evidence that the high managerial agent having supervisory responsibility over the subject matter of the offense employed due diligence to prevent its commission. This paragraph shall not apply if it is plainly inconsistent with the legislative purpose in defining the particular offense.

(6)(a) A person is legally accountable for any conduct he performs or causes to be performed in the name of the corporation or an unincorporated association or in its behalf to the same extent as if it were performed in his own name or behalf.

(b) Whenever a duty to act is imposed by law upon a corporation or an unincorporated association, any agent of the corporation or association having responsibility for the discharge of the duty is legally accountable for a reckless omission to perform the required act to the same extent as if the duty were imposed by law directly upon himself.

(c) When a person is convicted of an offense by reason of his legal accountability for the conduct of a corporation or an unincorporated association, he is subject to the sentence authorized by law when a natural person is convicted of an offense of the grade and the degree involved.

SECTION 2.08.   INTOXICATION

(1) Except as provided in Subsection (4) of this Section, intoxication of the actor is not a defense unless it negatives an element of the offense.

(2) When recklessness establishes an element of the offense, if the actor, due to self-induced intoxication, is unaware of a risk of which he would have been aware had he been sober, such unawareness is immaterial.

(3) Intoxication does not, in itself, constitute mental disease within the meaning of Section 4.01.

(4) Intoxication that (a) is not self-induced or (b) is pathological is an affirmative defense if by reason of such intoxication the actor at the time of his conduct lacks substantial capacity either to appreciate its criminality [wrongfulness] or to conform his conduct to the requirements of law.

(5) *Definitions.* In this Section unless a different meaning plainly is required:

(a) "intoxication" means a disturbance of mental or physical capacities resulting from the introduction of substances into the body;

(b) "self-induced intoxication" means intoxication caused by substances which the actor knowingly introduces into his body, the tendency of which to cause intoxication he knows or ought to know, unless he introduces them pursuant to medical advice or under such circumstances as would afford a defense to a charge of crime;

(c) "pathological intoxication" means intoxication grossly excessive in degree, given the amount of the intoxicant, to which the actor does not know he is susceptible.

SECTION 2.09.   DURESS

(1) It is an affirmative defense that the actor engaged in the conduct charged to constitute an offense because he was coerced to do so by the use of, or a threat to use, unlawful force against his person or the person of another, that a person of reasonable firmness in his situation would have been unable to resist.

(2) The defense provided by this Section is unavailable if the actor recklessly placed himself in a situation in which it was probable that he would be subjected to duress. The defense is also unavailable if he was negligent in placing himself in such a situation, whenever negligence suffices to establish culpability for the offense charged.

(3) It is not a defense that a woman acted on the command of her husband, unless she acted under such coercion as would establish a defense under this Section. [The presumption that a woman acting in the presence of her husband is coerced is abolished.]

(4) When the conduct of the actor would otherwise be justifiable under Section 3.02, this Section does not preclude such defense.

SECTION 2.10.   MILITARY ORDERS

It is an affirmative defense that the actor, in engaging in the conduct charged to constitute an offense, does no more than execute an order of his superior in the armed services which he does not know to be unlawful.

SECTION 2.11. CONSENT

(1) *In General.* The consent of the victim to conduct charged to constitute an offense or to the result thereof is a defense if such consent negatives an element of the offense or precludes the infliction of the harm or evil sought to be prevented by the law defining the offense.

(2) *Consent to Bodily Harm.* When conduct is charged to constitute an offense because it causes or threatens bodily harm, consent to such conduct or to the infliction of such harm is a defense if:

(a) the bodily injury consented to or threatened by the conduct consented to is not serious; or

(b) the conduct and the injury are reasonably foreseeable hazards of joint participation in a lawful athletic contest or competitive sport or other concerted activity not forbidden by law; or

(c) the consent establishes a justification for the conduct under Article 3 of the Code.

(3) *Ineffective Consent.* Unless otherwise provided by the Code or by the law defining the offense, assent does not constitute consent if:

(a) it is given by a person who is legally incompetent to authorize the conduct charged to constitute the offense; or

(b) it is given by a person who by reason of youth, mental disease or defect or intoxication is manifestly unable or known by the actor to be unable to make a reasonable judgment as to the nature or harmfulness of the conduct charged to constitute the offense; or

(c) it is given by a person whose improvident consent is sought to be prevented by the law defining the offense; or

(d) it is induced by force, duress or deception of a kind sought to be prevented by the law defining the offense.

SECTION 2.12. DE MINIMIS INFRACTIONS

The Court shall dismiss a prosecution if, having regard to the nature of the conduct charged to constitute an offense and the nature of the attendant circumstances, it finds that the defendant's conduct:

(1) was within a customary license of tolerance, neither expressly negatived by the person whose interest was infringed nor inconsistent with the purpose of the law defining the offense; or

(2) did not actually cause or threaten the harm or evil sought to be prevented by the law defining the offense or did so only to an extent too trivial to warrant the condemnation of conviction; or

(3) presents such other extenuations that it cannot reasonably be regarded as envisaged by the legislature in forbidding the offense.

The Court shall not dismiss a prosecution under Subsection (3) of this Section without filing a written statement of its reasons.

SECTION 2.13.   ENTRAPMENT

(1) A public law enforcement official or a person acting in cooperation with such an official perpetrates an entrapment if for the purpose of obtaining evidence of the commission of an offense, he induces or encourages another person to engage in conduct constituting such offense by either:

(a) making knowingly false representations designed to induce the belief that such conduct is not prohibited; or

(b) employing methods of persuasion or inducement that create a substantial risk that such an offense will be committed by persons other than those who are ready to commit it.

(2) Except as provided in Subsection (3) of this Section, a person prosecuted for an offense shall be acquitted if he proves by a preponderance of evidence that his conduct occurred in response to an entrapment. The issue of entrapment shall be tried by the Court in the absence of the jury.

(3) The defense afforded by this Section is unavailable when causing or threatening bodily injury is an element of the offense charged and the prosecution is based on conduct causing or threatening such injury to a person other than the person perpetrating the entrapment.

Article 3. General Principles of Justification

SECTION 3.01.   JUSTIFICATION AN AFFIRMATIVE DEFENSE; CIVIL REMEDIES UNAF-
FECTED

(1) In any prosecution based on conduct that is justifiable under this Article, justification is an affirmative defense.

(2) The fact that conduct is justifiable under this Article does not abolish or impair any remedy for such conduct that is available in any civil action.

SECTION 3.02.   JUSTIFICATION GENERALLY: CHOICE OF EVILS

(1) Conduct that the actor believes to be necessary to avoid a harm or evil to himself or to another is justifiable, provided that:

(a) the harm or evil sought to be avoided by such conduct is greater than that sought to be prevented by the law defining the offense charged; and

(b) neither the Code nor other law defining the offense provides exceptions or defenses dealing with the specific situation involved; and

(c) a legislative purpose to exclude the justification claimed does not otherwise plainly appear.

(2) When the actor was reckless or negligent in bringing about the situation requiring a choice of harms or evils or in appraising the necessity for his conduct, the justification afforded by this Section is unavailable in a prosecution for any offense for which recklessness or negligence, as the case may be, suffices to establish culpability.

SECTION 3.03.   EXECUTION OF PUBLIC DUTY

(1) Except as provided in Subsection (2) of this Section, conduct is justifiable when it is required or authorized by:

(a) the law defining the duties or functions of a public officer or the assistance to be rendered to such officer in the performance of his duties; or

(b) the law governing the execution of legal process; or

(c) the judgment or order of a competent court or tribunal; or

(d) the law governing the armed services or the lawful conduct of war; or

(e) any other provision of law imposing a public duty.

(2) The other sections of this Article apply to:

(a) the use of force upon or toward the person of another for any of the purposes dealt with in such sections; and

(b) the use of deadly force for any purpose, unless the use of such force is otherwise expressly authorized by law or occurs in the lawful conduct of war.

(3) The justification afforded by Subsection (1) of this Section applies:

(a) when the actor believes his conduct to be required or authorized by the judgment or direction of a competent court or tribunal or in the lawful execution of legal process, notwithstanding lack of jurisdiction of the court or defect in the legal process; and

(b) when the actor believes his conduct to be required or authorized to assist a public officer in the performance of his duties, notwithstanding that the officer exceeded his legal authority.

SECTION 3.04.   USE OF FORCE IN SELF–PROTECTION

(1) *Use of Force Justifiable for Protection of the Person.* Subject to the provisions of this Section and of Section 3.09, the use of force upon or toward another person is justifiable when the actor believes that such force is immediately necessary for the purpose of protecting himself against the use of unlawful force by such other person on the present occasion.

(2) *Limitations on Justifying Necessity for Use of Force.*

(a) The use of force is not justifiable under this Section:

(i) to resist an arrest that the actor knows is being made by a peace officer, although the arrest is unlawful; or

(ii) to resist force used by the occupier or possessor of property or by another person on his behalf, where the actor knows that the person using the force is doing so under a claim of right to protect the property, except that this limitation shall not apply if:

(1) the actor is a public officer acting in the performance of his duties or a person lawfully assisting him therein or a person making or assisting in a lawful arrest; or

(2) the actor has been unlawfully dispossessed of the property and is making a re-entry or recaption justified by Section 3.06; or

(3) the actor believes that such force is necessary to protect himself against death or serious bodily harm.

(b) The use of deadly force is not justifiable under this Section unless the actor believes that such force is necessary to protect himself against death, serious bodily harm, kidnapping or sexual intercourse compelled by force or threat; nor is it justifiable if:

(i) the actor, with the purpose of causing death or serious bodily injury, provoked the use of force against himself in the same encounter; or

(ii) the actor knows that he can avoid the necessity of using such force with complete safety by retreating or by surrendering possession of a thing to a person asserting a claim of right thereto or by complying with a demand that he abstain from any action that he has no duty to take, except that:

(1) the actor is not obliged to retreat from his dwelling or place of work, unless he was the initial aggressor or is assailed in his place of work by another person whose place of work the actor knows it to be; and

(2) a public officer justified in using force in the performance of his duties or a person justified in using force in his assistance or a person justified in using force in making an arrest or preventing an escape is not obliged to desist from efforts to perform such duty, effect such arrest or prevent such escape because of resistance or threatened resistance by or on behalf of the person against whom such action is directed.

(c) Except as required by paragraphs (a) and (b) of this Subsection, a person employing protective force may estimate the necessity thereof under the circumstances as he believes them to be when the force is used, without retreating, surrendering possession, doing any other act which he has no legal duty to do or abstaining from any lawful action.

(3) *Use of Confinement as Protective Force.* The justification afforded by this Section extends to the use of confinement as protective force only if the actor takes all reasonable measures to terminate the confinement as soon as he knows that he safely can, unless the person confined has been arrested on a charge of crime.

SECTION 3.05. USE OF FORCE FOR THE PROTECTION OF OTHER PERSONS

(1) Subject to the provisions of this Section and of Section 3.09, the use of force upon or toward the person of another is justifiable to protect a third person when:

(a) the actor would be justified under Section 3.04 in using such force to protect himself against the injury he believes to be threatened to the person whom he seeks to protect; and

(b) under the circumstances as the actor believes them to be, the person whom he seeks to protect would be justified in using such protective force; and

(c) the actor believes that his intervention is necessary for the protection of such other person.

(2) Notwithstanding Subsection (1) of this Section:

(a) when the actor would be obliged under Section 3.04 to retreat, to surrender the possession of a thing or to comply with a demand before using force in self-protection, he is not obliged to do so before using force for the protection of another person, unless he knows that he can thereby secure the complete safety of such other person; and

(b) when the person whom the actor seeks to protect would be obliged under Section 3.04 to retreat, to surrender the possession of a thing or to comply with a demand if he knew that he could obtain complete safety by so doing, the actor is obliged to try to cause him to do so before using force in his protection if the actor knows that he can obtain complete safety in that way; and

(c) neither the actor nor the person whom he seeks to protect is obliged to retreat when in the other's dwelling or place of work to any greater extent than in his own.

SECTION 3.06.   USE OF FORCE FOR THE PROTECTION OF PROPERTY

(1) *Use of Force Justifiable for Protection of Property.* Subject to the provisions of this Section and of Section 3.09, the use of force upon or toward the person of another is justifiable when the actor believes that such force is immediately necessary:

(a) to prevent or terminate an unlawful entry or other trespass upon land or a trespass against or the unlawful carrying away of tangible, movable property, provided that such land or movable property is, or is believed by the actor to be, in his possession or in the possession of another person for whose protection he acts; or

(b) to effect an entry or re-entry upon land or to retake tangible movable property, provided that the actor believes that he or the person by whose authority he acts or a person from whom he or such other person derives title was unlawfully dispossessed of such land or movable property and is entitled to possession, and provided, further, that:

(i) the force is used immediately or on fresh pursuit after such dispossession; or

(ii) the actor believes that the person against whom he uses force has no claim of right to the possession of the property and, in the case of land, the circumstances, as the actor believes them to be, are of such urgency that it would be an exceptional hardship to postpone the entry or re-entry until a court order is obtained.

(2) *Meaning of Possession.* For the purposes of Subsection (1) of this Section:

(a) a person who has parted with the custody of property to another who refuses to restore it to him is no longer in possession, unless the property is movable and was and still is located on land in his possession;

(b) a person who has been dispossessed of land does not regain possession thereof merely by setting foot thereon;

(c) a person who has a license to use or occupy real property is deemed to be in possession thereof except against the licensor acting under claim of right.

(3) *Limitations on Justifiable Use of Force.*

(a) *Request to Desist.* The use of force is justifiable under this Section only if the actor first requests the person against whom such force is used to desist from his interference with the property, unless the actor believes that:

(i) such request would be useless; or

(ii) it would be dangerous to himself or another person to make the request; or

(iii) substantial harm will be done to the physical condition of the property which is sought to be protected before the request can effectively be made.

(b) *Exclusion of Trespasser.* The use of force to prevent or terminate a trespass is not justifiable under this Section if the actor knows that the exclusion of the trespasser will expose him to substantial danger of serious bodily harm.

(c) *Resistance of Lawful Re-entry or Recaption.* The use of force to prevent an entry or re-entry upon land or the recaption of movable property is not justifiable under this Section, although the actor believes that such re-entry or recaption is unlawful, if:

(i) the re-entry or recaption is made by or on behalf of a person who was actually dispossessed of the property; and

(ii) it is otherwise justifiable under paragraph (1)(b) of this Section.

(d) *Use of Deadly Force.* The use of deadly force is not justifiable under this Section unless the actor believes that:

(i) the person against whom the force is used is attempting to dispossess him of his dwelling otherwise than under a claim of right to its possession; or

(ii) the person against whom the force is used is attempting to commit or consummate arson, burglary, robbery or other felonious theft or property destruction and either:

(1) has employed or threatened deadly force against or in the presence of the actor; or

(2) the use of force other than deadly force to prevent the commission or the consummation of the crime would expose the actor or another in his presence to substantial danger of serious bodily harm.

(4) *Use of Confinement as Protective Force.* The justification afforded by this Section extends to the use of confinement as protective force only if the

actor takes all reasonable measures to terminate the confinement as soon as he knows that he can do so with safety to the property, unless the person confined has been arrested on a charge of crime.

(5) *Use of Device to Protect Property.* The justification afforded by this section extends to the use of a device for the purpose of protecting property only if:

(a) the device is not designed to cause or known to create a substantial risk of causing death or serious bodily injury; and

(b) the use of the particular device to protect the property from entry or trespass is reasonable under the circumstances, as the actor believes them to be; and

(c) the device is one customarily used for such a purpose or reasonable care is taken to make known to probable intruders the fact that it is used.

(6) *Use of Force to Pass Wrongful Obstructor.* The use of force to pass a person whom the actor believes to be purposely or knowingly and unjustifiably obstructing the actor from going to a place to which he may lawfully go is justifiable, provided that:

(a) the actor believes that the person against whom he uses force has no claim of right to obstruct the actor; and

(b) the actor is not being obstructed from entry or movement on land which he knows to be in the possession or custody of the person obstructing him, or in the possession or custody of another person by whose authority the obstructor acts, unless the circumstances, as the actor believes them to be, are of such urgency that it would not be reasonable to postpone the entry or movement on such land until a court order is obtained; and

(c) the force used is not greater than would be justifiable if the person obstructing the actor were using force against him to prevent his passage.

SECTION 3.07. USE OF FORCE IN LAW ENFORCEMENT

(1) *Use of Force Justifiable to Effect an Arrest.* Subject to the provisions of this Section and of Section 3.09, the use of force upon or toward the person of another is justifiable when the actor is making or assisting in making an arrest and the actor believes that such force is immediately necessary to effect a lawful arrest.

(2) *Limitations on the Use of Force.*

(a) The use of force is not justifiable under this Section unless:

(i) the actor makes known the purpose of the arrest or believes that it is otherwise known by or cannot reasonably be made known to the person to be arrested; and

(ii) when the arrest is made under a warrant, the warrant is valid or believed by the actor to be valid.

(b) The use of deadly force is not justifiable under this Section unless:

(i) the arrest is for a felony; and

(ii) the person effecting the arrest is authorized to act as a peace officer or is assisting a person whom he believes to be authorized to act as a peace officer; and

(iii) the actor believes that the force employed creates no substantial risk of injury to innocent persons; and

(iv) the actor believes that:

(1) the crime for which the arrest is made involved conduct including the use or threatened use of deadly force; or

(2) there is a substantial risk that the person to be arrested will cause death or serious bodily harm if his apprehension is delayed.

(3) *Use of Force to Prevent Escape From Custody.* The use of force to prevent the escape of an arrested person from custody is justifiable when the force could justifiably have been employed to effect the arrest under which the person is in custody, except that a guard or other person authorized to act as a peace officer is justified in using any force, including deadly force, that he believes to be immediately necessary to prevent the escape of a person from a jail, prison, or other institution for the detention of persons charged with or convicted of a crime.

(4) *Use of Force by Private Person Assisting an Unlawful Arrest.*

(a) A private person who is summoned by a peace officer to assist in effecting an unlawful arrest, is justified in using any force that he would be justified in using if the arrest were lawful, provided that he does not believe the arrest is unlawful.

(b) A private person who assists another private person in effecting an unlawful arrest, or who, not being summoned, assists a peace officer in effecting an unlawful arrest, is justified in using any force that he would be justified in using if the arrest were lawful, provided that (i) he believes the arrest is lawful, and (ii) the arrest would be lawful if the facts were as he believes them to be.

(5) *Use of Force to Prevent Suicide or the Commission of a Crime.*

(a) The use of force upon or toward the person of another is justifiable when the actor believes that such force is immediately necessary to prevent such other person from committing suicide, inflicting serious bodily injury upon himself, committing or consummating the commission of a crime involving or threatening bodily injury, damage to or loss of property or a breach of the peace, except that:

(i) any limitations imposed by the other provisions of this Article on the justifiable use of force in self-protection, for the protection of others, the protection of property, the effectuation of an arrest or the prevention of an escape from custody shall apply notwithstanding the criminality of the conduct against which such force is used; and

(ii) the use of deadly force is not in any event justifiable under this Subsection unless:

(1) the actor believes that there is a substantial risk that the person whom he seeks to prevent from committing a crime will cause death or serious bodily harm to another unless the commission or the consummation of the crime is prevented and that the use of such force presents no substantial risk of injury to innocent persons; or

(2) the actor believes that the use of such force is necessary to suppress a riot or mutiny after the rioters or mutineers have been ordered to disperse and warned, in any particular manner that the law may require, that such force will be used if they do not obey.

(b) The justification afforded by this Subsection extends to the use of confinement as preventive force only if the actor takes all reasonable measures to terminate the confinement as soon as he knows that he safely can, unless the person confined has been arrested on a charge of crime.

SECTION 3.08. USE OF FORCE BY PERSONS WITH SPECIAL RESPONSIBILITY FOR CARE, DISCIPLINE OR SAFETY OF OTHER

The use of force upon or toward the person of another is justifiable if:

(1) The actor is the parent or guardian or other person similarly responsible for the general care and supervision of a minor or a person acting at the request of such parent, guardian or other responsible person and:

(a) the force is used for the purpose of safeguarding or promoting the welfare of the minor, including the prevention or punishment of his misconduct; and

(b) the force used is not designed to cause or known to create a substantial risk of causing death, serious bodily injury, disfigurement, extreme pain or mental distress or gross degradation; or

(2) the actor is a teacher or a person otherwise entrusted with the care or supervision for a special purpose of a minor and:

(a) the actor believes that the force used is necessary to further such special purpose, including the maintenance of reasonable discipline in a school, class or other group, and that the use of such force is consistent with the welfare of the minor; and

(b) the degree of force, if it had been used by the parent or guardian of the minor, would not be unjustifiable under Subsection (1)(b) of this Section; or

(3) the actor is the guardian or other person similarly responsible for the general care and supervision of an incompetent person and:

(a) the force is used for the purpose of safeguarding or promoting the welfare of the incompetent person, including the prevention of his misconduct, or, when such incompetent person is in a hospital or other institution for his care and custody, for the maintenance of reasonable discipline in such institution; and

(b) the force used is not designed to cause or known to create a substantial risk of causing death, serious bodily harm, disfigurement, extreme or unnecessary pain, mental distress, or humiliation; or

(4) the actor is a doctor or other therapist or a person assisting him at his direction and:

(a) the force is used for the purpose of administering a recognized form of treatment which the actor believes to be adapted to promoting the physical or mental health of the patient; and

(b) the treatment is administered with the consent of the patient or, if the patient is a minor or an incompetent person, with the consent of his parent or guardian or other person legally competent to consent in his behalf, or the treatment is administered in an emergency when the actor believes that no one competent to consent can be consulted and that a reasonable person, wishing to safeguard the welfare of the patient, would consent; or

(5) the actor is a warden or other authorized official of a correctional institution and:

(a) he believes that the force used is necessary for the purpose of enforcing the lawful rules or procedures of the institution, unless his belief in the lawfulness of the rule or procedure sought to be enforced is erroneous and his error is due to ignorance or mistake as to the provisions of the Code, and other provision of the criminal law or the law governing the administration of the institution; and

(b) the nature or degree of force used is not forbidden by Article 303 or 304 of the Code; and

(c) if deadly force is used, its use is otherwise justifiable under this Article; or

(6) the actor is a person responsible for the safety of a vessel or an aircraft or a person acting at his direction and

(a) he believes that the force used is necessary to prevent interference with a lawful order, unless his belief in the lawfulness of the order is erroneous and his error is due to ignorance or mistake as to the law defining his authority; and

(b) if deadly force is used, its use is otherwise justifiable under this Article; or

(7) the actor is a person who is authorized or required by law to maintain order or decorum in a vehicle, train or other carrier or in a place where others are assembled, and:

(a) he believes that the force used is necessary for such purpose; and

(b) the force is not designed to cause or known to create a substantial risk of causing death, bodily harm, or extreme mental distress.

Section 3.09. Mistake of Law as to Unlawfulness of Force or Legality of Arrest; Reckless or Negligent Use of Otherwise Justifiable Force; Reckless or Negligent Injury or Risk of Injury to Innocent Persons

(1) The justification afforded by Sections 3.04 to 3.07, inclusive, is unavailable when:

(a) the actor's belief in the unlawfulness of the force or conduct against which he employs protective force or his belief in the lawfulness of an arrest which he endeavors to effect by force is erroneous; and

(b) his error is due to ignorance or mistake as to the provisions of the Code, any other provision of the criminal law or the law governing the legality of an arrest or search.

(2) When the actor believes that the use of force upon or toward the person of another is necessary for any of the purposes for which such belief would establish a justification under Sections 3.03 to 3.08 but the actor is reckless or negligent in having such belief or in acquiring or failing to acquire any knowledge or belief which is material to the justifiability of his use of force, the justification afforded by those Sections is unavailable in a prosecution for an offense for which recklessness or negligence, as the case may be, suffices to establish culpability.

(3) When the actor is justified under Sections 3.03 to 3.08 in using force upon or toward the person of another but he recklessly or negligently injures or creates a risk of injury to innocent persons, the justification afforded by those Sections is unavailable in a prosecution for such recklessness or negligence towards innocent persons.

Section 3.10. Justification in Property Crimes

Conduct involving the appropriation, seizure or destruction of, damage to, intrusion on or interference with property is justifiable under circumstances that would establish a defense of privilege in a civil action based thereon unless:

(1) the Code or the law defining the offense deals with the specific situation involved; or

(2) a legislative purpose to exclude the justification claimed otherwise plainly appears.

Section 3.11. Definitions

In this Article, unless a different meaning plainly is required:

(1) "unlawful force" means force, including confinement, which is employed without the consent of the person against whom it is directed and the employment of which constitutes an offense or actionable tort or would constitute such offense or tort except for a defense (such as the absence of intent, negligence, or mental capacity; duress; youth; or diplomatic status) not amounting to a privilege to use the force. Assent constitutes consent, within the meaning of this Section, whether or not it otherwise is legally effective, except assent to the infliction of death or serious bodily harm.

(2) "deadly force" means force which the actor uses with the purpose of causing or which he knows to create a substantial risk of causing death or serious bodily injury. Purposely firing a firearm in the direction of another person or at a vehicle in which another person is believed to be constitutes deadly force. A threat to cause death or serious bodily injury, by the production of a weapon or otherwise, so long as the actor's purpose is limited to creating an apprehension that he will use deadly force if necessary, does not constitute deadly force;

(3) "dwelling" means any building or structure, though movable or temporary, or a portion thereof, that is for the time being the actor's home or place of lodging.

Article 4. Responsibility

SECTION 4.01. MENTAL DISEASE OR DEFECT EXCLUDING RESPONSIBILITY

(1) A person is not responsible for criminal conduct if at the time of such conduct as a result of mental disease or defect he lacks substantial capacity either to appreciate the criminality [wrongfulness] of his conduct or to conform his conduct to the requirements of law.

(2) As used in this Article, the terms "mental disease or defect" do not include an abnormality manifested only by repeated criminal or otherwise antisocial conduct.

SECTION 4.02. EVIDENCE OF MENTAL DISEASE OR DEFECT ADMISSIBLE WHEN RELEVANT TO ELEMENT OF THE OFFENSE; [MENTAL DISEASE OR DEFECT IMPAIRING CAPACITY AS GROUND FOR MITIGATION OF PUNISHMENT IN CAPITAL CASES]

(1) Evidence that the defendant suffered from a mental disease or defect is admissible whenever it is relevant to prove that the defendant did or did not have a state of mind which is an element of the offense.

[(2) Whenever the jury or the Court is authorized to determine or to recommend whether or not the defendant shall be sentenced to death or imprisonment upon conviction, evidence that the capacity of the defendant to appreciate the criminality [wrongfulness] of his conduct or to conform his conduct to the requirements of law was impaired as a result of mental disease or defect is admissible in favor of sentence of imprisonment.]

SECTION 4.03. MENTAL DISEASE OR DEFECT EXCLUDING RESPONSIBILITY IS AFFIRMATIVE DEFENSE; REQUIREMENT OF NOTICE; FORM OF VERDICT AND JUDGMENT WHEN FINDING OF IRRESPONSIBILITY IS MADE

(1) Mental disease or defect excluding responsibility is an affirmative defense.

(2) Evidence of mental disease or defect excluding responsibility is not admissible unless the defendant, at the time of entering his plea of not guilty or within ten days thereafter or at such later time as the Court may for good cause permit, files a written notice of his purpose to rely on such defense.

(3) When the defendant is acquitted on the ground of mental disease or defect excluding responsibility, the verdict and the judgment shall so state.

SECTION 4.04.   MENTAL DISEASE OR DEFECT EXCLUDING FITNESS TO PROCEED

No person who as a result of mental disease or defect lacks capacity to understand the proceedings against him or to assist in his defense shall be tried, convicted or sentenced for the commission of an offense so long as such incapacity endures.

SECTION 4.05.   PSYCHIATRIC EXAMINATION OF DEFENDANT WITH RESPECT TO MENTAL DISEASE OR DEFECT

(1) Whenever the defendant has filed a notice of intention to rely on the defense of mental disease or defect excluding responsibility, or there is reason to doubt his fitness to proceed, or reason to believe that mental disease or defect of the defendant will otherwise become an issue in the cause, the Court shall appoint at least one qualified psychiatrist or shall request the Superintendent of the _____ Hospital to designate at least one qualified psychiatrist, which designation may be or include himself, to examine and report upon the mental condition of the defendant. The Court may order the defendant to be committed to a hospital or other suitable facility for the purpose of the examination for a period of not exceeding sixty days or such longer period as the Court determines to be necessary for the purpose and may direct that a qualified psychiatrist retained by the defendant be permitted to witness and participate in the examination.

(2) In such examination any method may be employed which is accepted by the medical profession for the examination of those alleged to be suffering from mental disease or defect.

(3) The report of the examination shall include the following: (a) a description of the nature of the examination; (b) a diagnosis of the mental condition of the defendant; (c) if the defendant suffers from a mental disease or defect, an opinion as to his capacity to understand the proceedings against him and to assist in his own defense; (d) when a notice of intention to rely on the defense of irresponsibility has been filed, an opinion as to the extent, if any, to which the capacity of the defendant to appreciate the criminality [wrongfulness] of his conduct or to conform his conduct to the requirements of law was impaired at the time of the criminal conduct charged; and (e) when directed by the Court, an opinion as to the capacity of the defendant to have a particular state of mind which is an element of the offense charged.

If the examination cannot be conducted by reason of the unwillingness of the defendant to participate therein, the report shall so state and shall include, if possible, an opinion as to whether such unwillingness of the defendant was the result of mental disease or defect.

The report of the examination shall be filed [in triplicate] with the clerk of the Court, who shall cause copies to be delivered to the district attorney and to counsel for the defendant.

SECTION 4.06. DETERMINATION OF FITNESS TO PROCEED; EFFECT OF FINDING OF UNFITNESS; PROCEEDINGS IF FITNESS IS REGAINED [; POST-COMMITMENT HEARING]

(1) When the defendant's fitness to proceed is drawn in question, the issue shall be determined by the Court. If neither the prosecuting attorney nor counsel for the defendant contests the finding of the report filed pursuant to Section 4.05, the Court may make the determination on the basis of such report. If the finding is contested, the Court shall hold a hearing on the issue. If the report is received in evidence upon such hearing, the party who contests the finding thereof shall have the right to summon and to cross-examine the psychiatrists who joined in the report and to offer evidence upon the issue.

(2) If the Court determines that the defendant lacks fitness to proceed, the proceeding against him shall be suspended, except as provided in Subsection (3) [Subsections (3) and (4)] of this Section, and the Court shall commit him to the custody of the Commissioner of Mental Hygiene [Public Health or Correction] to be placed in an appropriate institution of the Department of Mental Hygiene [Public Health or Correction] for so long as such unfitness shall endure. When the Court, on its own motion or upon the application of the Commissioner of Mental Hygiene [Public Health or Correction] or the prosecuting attorney, determines, after a hearing if a hearing is requested, that the defendant has regained fitness to proceed, the proceeding shall be resumed. If, however, the Court is of the view that so much time has elapsed since the commitment of the defendant that it would be unjust to resume the criminal proceeding, the Court may dismiss the charge and may order the defendant to be discharged or, subject to the law governing the civil commitment of persons suffering from mental disease or defect, order the defendant to be committed to an appropriate institution of the Department of Mental Hygiene [Public Health].

(3) The fact that the defendant is unfit to proceed does not preclude any legal objection to the prosecution that is susceptible of fair determination prior to trial and without the personal participation of the defendant.

[Alternative: (3) At any time within ninety days after commitment as provided in Subsection (2) of this Section, or at any later time with permission of the Court granted for good cause, the defendant or his counsel or the Commissioner of Mental Hygiene [Public Health or Correction] may apply for a special post-commitment hearing. If the application is made by or on behalf of a defendant not represented by counsel, he shall be afforded a reasonable opportunity to obtain counsel, and if he lacks funds to do so, counsel shall be assigned by the Court. The application shall be granted only if counsel for the defendant satisfies the Court by affidavit or otherwise that as an attorney he has reasonable grounds for a good faith belief that his client has, on the facts and the law, a defense to the charge other than mental disease or defect excluding responsibility.

[(4) If the motion for a special post-commitment hearing is granted, the hearing shall be by the Court without a jury. No evidence shall be offered at the hearing by either party on the issue of mental disease or defect as a defense to, or in mitigation of, the crime charged. After hearing, the Court may in an appropriate case quash the indictment or other charge, or find it to be defective or insufficient, or determine that it is not proved beyond a reasonable doubt by the evidence, or otherwise terminate the proceedings on the evidence or the law. In any such case, unless all defects in the proceedings are promptly cured, the Court shall terminate the commitment ordered under Subsection (2) of this Section and order the defendant to be discharged or, subject to the law governing the civil commitment of persons suffering from mental disease or defect, order the defendant to be committed to an appropriate institution of the Department of Mental Hygiene [Public Health].]

SECTION 4.07. DETERMINATION OF IRRESPONSIBILITY ON BASIS OF REPORT; ACCESS TO DEFENDANT BY PSYCHIATRIST OF HIS OWN CHOICE; FORM OF EXPERT TESTIMONY WHEN ISSUE OF RESPONSIBILITY IS TRIED

(1) If the report filed pursuant to Section 4.05 finds that the defendant at the time of the criminal conduct charged suffered from a mental disease or defect which substantially impaired his capacity to appreciate the criminality [wrongfulness] of the conduct or to conform his conduct to the requirements of law, and the Court, after a hearing if a hearing is requested by the prosecuting attorney or the defendant, is satisfied that such impairment was sufficient to exclude responsibility, the Court on motion of the defendant shall enter judgement of acquittal on the ground of mental disease or defect excluding responsibility.

(2) When, notwithstanding the report filed pursuant to Section 4.05, the defendant wishes to be examined by a qualified psychiatrist or other expert of his own choice, such examiner shall be permitted to have reasonable access to the defendant for the purposes of such examination.

(3) Upon the trial, the psychiatrists who reported pursuant to Section 4.05 may be called as witnesses by the prosecution, the defendant or the Court. If the issue is being tried before a jury, the jury may be informed that the psychiatrists were designated by the Court or by the Superintendent of the _____ Hospital at the request of the Court, as the case may be. If called by the Court, the witness shall be subject to cross-examination by the prosecution and by the defendant. Both the prosecution and the defendant may summon any other qualified psychiatrist or other expert to testify, but no one who has not examined the defendant shall be competent to testify to an expert opinion with respect to the mental condition or responsibility of the defendant, as distinguished from the validity of the procedure followed by, or the general scientific propositions stated by, another witness.

(4) When a psychiatrist or other expert who has examined the defendant testifies concerning his mental condition, he shall be permitted to make a statement as to the nature of his examination, his diagnosis of the mental condition of the defendant at the time of the commission of the offense charged and his opinion as to the extent, if any, to which the capacity of the defendant to appreciate the criminality [wrongfulness] of his conduct or to conform his conduct to the requirements of law or to have a particular state of mind that is an element of the offense charged was impaired as a result of mental disease or defect at that time. He shall be permitted to make any explanation reasonably serving to clarify his diagnosis and opinion and may

be cross-examined as to any matter bearing on his competency or credibility or the validity of his diagnosis or opinion.

SECTION 4.08. LEGAL EFFECT OF ACQUITTAL ON THE GROUND OF MENTAL DISEASE OR DEFECT EXCLUDING RESPONSIBILITY; COMMITMENT; RELEASE OR DISCHARGE

(1) When a defendant is acquitted on the ground of mental disease or defect excluding responsibility, the Court shall order him to be committed to the custody of the Commissioner of Mental Hygiene [Public Health] to be placed in an appropriate institution for custody, care and treatment.

(2) If the Commissioner of Mental Hygiene [Public Health] is of the view that a person committed to his custody, pursuant to paragraph (1) of this Section, may be discharged or released on condition without danger to himself or to others, he shall make application for the discharge or release of such person in a report to the Court by which such person was committed and shall transmit a copy of such application and report to the prosecuting attorney of the county [parish] from which the defendant was committed. The Court shall thereupon appoint at least two qualified psychiatrists to examine such person and to report within sixty days, or such longer period as the Court determines to be necessary for the purpose, their opinion as to his mental condition. To facilitate such examination and the proceedings thereon, the Court may cause such person to be confined in any institution located near the place where the Court sits, which may hereafter be designated by the Commissioner of Mental Hygiene [Public Health] as suitable for the temporary detention of irresponsible persons.

(3) If the Court is satisfied by the report filed pursuant to paragraph (2) of this Section and such testimony of the reporting psychiatrists as the Court deems necessary that the committed person may be discharged or released on condition without danger to himself or others, the Court shall order his discharge or his release on such conditions as the Court determines to be necessary. If the Court is not so satisfied, it shall promptly order a hearing to determine whether such person may safely be discharged or released. Any such hearing shall be deemed a civil proceeding and the burden shall be upon the committed person to prove that he may safely be discharged or released. According to the determination of the Court upon the hearing, the committed person shall thereupon be discharged or released on such conditions as the Court determines to be necessary, or shall be recommitted to the custody of the Commissioner of Mental Hygiene [Public Health], subject to discharge or release only in accordance with the procedure prescribed above for a first hearing.

(4) If, within [five] years after the conditional release of a committed person, the Court shall determine, after hearing evidence, that the conditions of release have not been fulfilled and that for the safety of such person or for the safety of others his conditional release should be revoked, the Court shall forthwith order him to be recommitted to the Commissioner of Mental Hygiene [Public Health], subject to discharge or release only in accordance with the procedure prescribed above for a first hearing.

(5) A committed person may make application for his discharge or release to the Court by which he was committed, and the procedure to be followed upon such application shall be the same as that prescribed above in the case of an application by the Commissioner of Mental Hygiene [Public Health]. However, no such application by a committed person need be considered until he has been confined for a period of not less than [six months] from the date of the order of commitment, and if the determination of the Court be adverse to the application, such person shall not be permitted to file a further application until [one year] has elapsed from the date of any preceding hearing on an application for his release or discharge.

SECTION 4.09.   [*Omitted*]

SECTION 4.10.   IMMATURITY EXCLUDING CRIMINAL CONVICTION; TRANSFER OF PROCEEDINGS TO JUVENILE COURT

(1) A person shall not be tried for or convicted of an offense if:

(a) at the time of the conduct charged to constitute the offense he was less than sixteen years of age[, in which case the Juvenile Court shall have exclusive jurisdiction*]; or

(b) at the time of the conduct charged to constitute the offense he was sixteen or seventeen years of age, unless:

(i) the Juvenile Court has no jurisdiction over him, or,

(ii) the Juvenile Court has entered an order waiving jurisdiction and consenting to the institution of criminal proceedings against him.

(2) No court shall have jurisdiction to try or convict a person of an offense if criminal proceedings against him are barred by Subsection (1) of this Section. When it appears that a person charged with the commission of an offense may be of such an age that criminal proceedings may be barred under Subsection (1) of this Section, the Court shall hold a hearing thereon, and the burden shall be on the prosecution to establish to the satisfaction of the Court that the criminal proceeding is not barred upon such grounds. If the Court determines that the proceeding is barred, custody of the person charged shall be surrendered to the Juvenile Court, and the case, including all papers and processes relating thereto, shall be transferred.

Article 5. Inchoate Crimes

SECTION 5.01.   CRIMINAL ATTEMPT

(1) *Definition of Attempt.* A person is guilty of an attempt to commit a crime if, acting with the kind of culpability otherwise required for commission of the crime, he:

(a) purposely engages in conduct that would constitute the crime if the attendant circumstances were as he believes them to be; or

(b) when causing a particular result is an element of the crime, does or omits to do anything with the purpose of causing or with the belief that it will cause such result without further conduct on his part; or

---

* The bracketed words are unnecessary if the Juvenile Court Act so provides or is amended accordingly.

(c) purposely does or omits to do anything which, [under the circumstances as he believes them to be,] is an act or omission constituting a substantial step in a course of conduct planned to culminate in his commission of the crime.

(2) *Conduct That May Be Held Substantial Step Under Subsection (1)(c).* Conduct shall not be held to constitute a substantial step under Subsection (1)(c) of this Section unless it is strongly corroborative of the actor's criminal purpose. Without negativing the sufficiency of other conduct, the following, if strongly corroborative of the actor's criminal purpose, shall not be held insufficient as a matter of law:

(a) lying in wait, searching for or following the contemplated victim of the crime;

(b) enticing or seeking to entice the contemplated victim of the crime to go to the place contemplated for its commission;

(c) reconnoitering the place contemplated for the commission of the crime;

(d) unlawful entry of a structure, vehicle or enclosure in which it is contemplated that the crime will be committed;

(e) possession of materials to be employed in the commission of the crime, that are specially designed for such unlawful use or which can serve no lawful purpose of the actor under the circumstances;

(f) possession, collection or fabrication of materials to be employed in the commission of the crime, at or near the place contemplated for its commission, where such possession, collection or fabrication serves no lawful purpose of the actor under the circumstances;

(g) soliciting an innocent agent to engage in conduct constituting an element of the crime.

(3) *Conduct Designed to Aid Another in Commission of a Crime.* A person who engages in conduct designed to aid another to commit a crime that would establish his complicity under Section 2.06 if the crime were committed by such other person, is guilty of an attempt to commit the crime, although the crime is not committed or attempted by such other person.

(4) *Renunciation of Criminal Purpose.* When the actor's conduct would otherwise constitute an attempt under Subsection (1)(b) or (1)(c) of this Section, it is an affirmative defense that he abandoned his effort to commit the crime or otherwise prevented its commission, under circumstances manifesting a complete and voluntary renunciation of his criminal purpose. The establishment of such defense does not, however, affect the liability of an accomplice who did not join in such abandonment or prevention.

Within the meaning of this Article, renunciation of criminal purpose is not voluntary if it is motivated, in whole or in part, by circumstances, not present or apparent at the inception of the actor's course of conduct, that increase the probability of detection or apprehension or which make more difficult the accomplishment of the criminal purpose. Renunciation is not complete if it is motivated by a decision to postpone the criminal conduct until a more advantageous time or to transfer the criminal effort to another but similar objective or victim.

SECTION 5.02. CRIMINAL SOLICITATION

(1) *Definition of Solicitation.* A person is guilty of solicitation to commit a crime if with the purpose of promoting or facilitating its commission he commands, encourages or requests another person to engage in specific conduct that would constitute such crime or an attempt to commit such crime or which would establish his complicity in its commission or attempted commission.

(2) *Uncommunicated Solicitation.* It is immaterial under Subsection (1) of this Section that the actor fails to communicate with the person he solicits to commit a crime if his conduct was designed to effect such communication.

(3) *Renunciation of Criminal Purpose.* It is an affirmative defense that the actor, after soliciting another person to commit a crime, persuaded him not to do so or otherwise prevented the commission of the crime, under circumstances manifesting a complete and voluntary renunciation of his criminal purpose.

SECTION 5.03. CRIMINAL CONSPIRACY

(1) *Definition of Conspiracy.* A person is guilty of conspiracy with another person or persons to commit a crime if with the purpose of promoting or facilitating its commission he: *must be a crime*

(a) agrees with such other person or persons that they or one or more of them will engage in conduct that constitutes such crime or an attempt or solicitation to commit such crime; or *impossibelety*

(b) agrees to aid such other person or persons in the planning or commission of such crime or of an attempt or solicitation to commit such crime. *impossibelety*

(2) *Scope of Conspiratorial Relationship.* If a person guilty of conspiracy, as defined by Subsection (1) of this Section, knows that a person with whom he conspires to commit a crime has conspired with another person or persons to commit the same crime, he is guilty of conspiring with such other person or persons, whether or not he knows their identity, to commit such crime.

(3) *Conspiracy With Multiple Criminal Objectives.* If a person conspires to commit a number of crimes, he is guilty of only one conspiracy so long as such multiple crimes are the object of the same agreement or continuous conspiratorial relationship.

(4) *Joinder and Venue in Conspiracy Prosecutions.*

(a) Subject to the provisions of paragraph (b) of this Subsection, two or more persons charged with criminal conspiracy may be prosecuted jointly if:

(i) they are charged with conspiring with one another; or

(ii) the conspiracies alleged, whether they have the same or different parties, are so related that they constitute different aspects of a scheme of organized criminal conduct.

(b) In any joint prosecution under paragraph (a) of this Subsection:

(i) no defendant shall be charged with a conspiracy in any county [parish or district] other than one in which he entered into such conspiracy or in which an overt act pursuant to such conspiracy was done by him or by a person with whom he conspired; and

(ii) neither the liability of any defendant nor the admissibility against him of evidence of acts or declarations of another shall be enlarged by such joinder; and

(iii) the Court shall order a severance or take a special verdict as to any defendant who so requests, if it deems it necessary or appropriate to promote the fair determination of his guilt or innocence, and shall take any other proper measures to protect the fairness of the trial.

(5) *Overt Act.* No person may be convicted of conspiracy to commit a crime other than a felony of the first or second degree, unless an overt act in pursuance of such conspiracy is alleged and proved to have been done by him or by a person with whom he conspired.

(6) *Renunciation of Criminal Purpose.* It is an affirmative defense that the actor, after conspiring to commit a crime, thwarted the success of the conspiracy, under circumstances manifesting a complete and voluntary renunciation of his criminal purpose.

(7) *Duration of Conspiracy.* For purposes of Section 1.06(4) [relating to periods of limitation for bringing prosecutions—ed.]:

(a) conspiracy is a continuing course of conduct that terminates when the crime or crimes that are its object are committed or the agreement that they be committed is abandoned by the defendant and by those with whom he conspired; and

(b) such abandonment is presumed if neither the defendant nor anyone with whom he conspired does any overt act in pursuance of the conspiracy during the applicable period of limitation; and

(c) if an individual abandons the agreement, the conspiracy is terminated as to him only if and when he advises those with whom he conspired of his abandonment or he informs the law enforcement authorities of the existence of the conspiracy and of his participation therein.

SECTION 5.04. INCAPACITY, IRRESPONSIBILITY OR IMMUNITY OF PARTY TO SOLICITATION OR CONSPIRACY

(1) Except as provided in Subsection (2) of this Section, it is immaterial to the liability of a person who solicits or conspires with another to commit a crime that:

(a) he or the person whom he solicits or with whom he conspires does not occupy a particular position or have a particular characteristic that is an element of such crime, if he believes that one of them does; or

(b) the person whom he solicits or with whom he conspires is irresponsible or has an immunity to prosecution or conviction for the commission of the crime.

(2) It is defense to a charge of solicitation or conspiracy to commit a crime that if the criminal object were achieved, the actor would not be guilty of a crime under the law defining the offense or as an accomplice under Section 2.06(5) or 2.06(6)(a) or (b).

SECTION 5.05.   GRADING OF CRIMINAL ATTEMPT, SOLICITATION AND CONSPIRACY; MITIGATION IN CASES OF LESSER DANGER; MULTIPLE CONVICTIONS BARRED

(1) *Grading.* Except as otherwise provided in this Section, attempt, solicitation and conspiracy are crimes of the same grade and degree as the most serious offense that is attempted or solicited or is an object of the conspiracy. An attempt, solicitation or conspiracy to commit a [capital crime or a] felony of the first degree is a felony of the second degree.

(2) *Mitigation.* If the particular conduct charged to constitute a criminal attempt, solicitation or conspiracy is so inherently unlikely to result or culminate in the commission of a crime that neither such conduct nor the actor presents a public danger warranting the grading of such offense under this Section, the Court shall exercise its power under Section 6.12 to enter judgment and impose sentence for a crime of lower grade or degree or, in extreme cases, may dismiss the prosecution.

(3) *Multiple Convictions.* A person may not be convicted of more than one offense defined by this Article for conduct designed to commit or to culminate in the commission of the same crime.

merger

SECTION 5.06.   POSSESSING INSTRUMENTS OF CRIME; WEAPONS

(1) *Criminal Instruments Generally.* A person commits a misdemeanor if he possesses any instrument of crime with purpose to employ it criminally. "Instrument of crime" means:

(a) anything specially made or specially adapted for criminal use; or

(b) anything commonly used for criminal purposes and possessed by the actor under circumstances that do not negative unlawful purpose.

(2) *Presumption of Criminal Purpose From Possession of Weapon.* If a person possesses a firearm or other weapon on or about his person, in a vehicle occupied by him, or otherwise readily available for use, it is presumed that he had the purpose to employ it criminally, unless:

(a) the weapon is possessed in the actor's home or place of business;

(b) the actor is licensed or otherwise authorized by law to possess such weapon; or

(c) the weapon is of a type commonly used in lawful sport.

"Weapon" means anything readily capable of lethal use and possessed under circumstances not manifestly appropriate for lawful uses it may have; the term includes a firearm that is not loaded or lacks a clip or other component to render it immediately operable, and components that can readily be assembled into a weapon.

(3) *Presumptions as to Possession of Criminal Instruments in Automobiles.* If a weapon or other instrument of crime is found in an automobile, it is

presumed to be in the possession of the occupant if there is but one. If there is more than one occupant, it shall be presumed to be in the possession of all, except under the following circumstances:

(a) it is found upon the person of one of the occupants;

(b) the automobile is not a stolen one and the weapon or instrument is found out of view in a glove compartment, car trunk, or other enclosed customary depository, in which case it is presumed to be in the possession of the occupant or occupants who own or have authority to operate the automobile;

(c) in the case of a taxicab, a weapon or instrument found in the passenger's portion of the vehicle shall be presumed to be in the possession of all the passengers, if there are any, and, if not, in the possession of the driver.

SECTION 5.07.   [*Omitted*]

Article 6. Authorized Disposition of Offenders*

SECTION 6.01.   DEGREES OF FELONIES

(1) Felonies defined by this Code are classified, for the purpose of sentence, into three degrees, as follows:

(a) felonies of the first degree;

(b) felonies of the second degree;

(c) felonies of the third degree.

A felony is of the first or second degree when it is so designated by the Code. A crime declared to be a felony, without specification of degree, is of the third degree.

(2) Notwithstanding any other provision of law, a felony defined by any statute of this State other than this Code shall constitute, for the purpose of sentence, a felony of the third degree.

SECTION 6.02.   [*Omitted*]

SECTION 6.03.   FINES

A person who has been convicted of an offense may be sentenced to pay a fine not exceeding:

(1) $10,000, when the conviction is of a felony of the first or second degree;

(2) $5,000, when the conviction is of a felony of the third degree;

(3) $1,000, when the conviction is of a misdemeanor;

(4) $500, when the conviction is of a petty misdemeanor or a violation;

(5) any higher amount equal to double the pecuniary gain derived from the offense by the offender;

(6) any higher amount specifically authorized by statute.

---

* This Article and Article 7 have undergone or are undergoing revision. See p. 58, Note 6.

SECTION 6.04.   PENALTIES AGAINST CORPORATIONS AND UNINCORPORATED ASSO-
CIATIONS; FORFEITURE OF CORPORATE CHARTER OR REVOCA-
TION OF CERTIFICATE AUTHORIZING FOREIGN CORPORATION
TO DO BUSINESS IN THE STATE

(1) The Court may suspend the sentence of a corporation or an unincorporated association that has been convicted of an offense or may sentence it to pay a fine authorized by Section 6.03.

(2)(a) The [prosecuting attorney] is authorized to institute civil proceedings in the appropriate court of general jurisdiction to forfeit the charter of a corporation organized under the laws of this State or to revoke the certificate authorizing a foreign corporation to conduct business in this State. The Court may order the charter forfeited or the certificate revoked upon finding (i) that the board of directors or a high managerial agent acting in behalf of the corporation has, in conducting the corporation's affairs, purposely engaged in a persistent course of criminal conduct and (ii) that for the prevention of future criminal conduct of the same character, the public interest requires the charter of the corporation to be forfeited and the corporation to be dissolved or the certificate to be revoked.

(b) When a corporation is convicted of a crime or a high managerial agent of a corporation, as defined in Section 2.07, is convicted of a crime committed in the conduct of the affairs of the corporation, the Court, in sentencing the corporation or the agent, may direct the [prosecuting attorney] to institute proceedings authorized by paragraph (a) of this Subsection.

(c) The proceedings authorized by paragraph (a) of this Subsection shall be conducted in accordance with the procedures authorized by law for the involuntary dissolution of a corporation or the revocation of the certificate authorizing a foreign corporation to conduct business in this State. Such proceedings shall be deemed additional to any other proceedings authorized by law for the purpose of forfeiting the charter of a corporation or revoking the certificate of a foreign corporation.

SECTION 6.05.   [*Omitted*]

SECTION 6.06.   SENTENCE OF IMPRISONMENT FOR FELONY; ORDINARY TERMS

A person who has been convicted of a felony may be sentenced to imprisonment, as follows:

(1) in the case of a felony of the first degree, for a term the minimum of which shall be fixed by the Court at not less than one year nor more than ten years, and the maximum of which shall be life imprisonment;

(2) in the case of a felony of the second degree, for a term the minimum of which shall be fixed by the Court at not less than one year nor more than three years, and the maximum of which shall be ten years;

(3) in the case of a felony of the third degree, for a term the minimum of which shall be fixed by the Court at not less than one year nor more than two years, and the maximum of which shall be five years.

ALTERNATE SECTION 6.06. SENTENCE OF IMPRISONMENT FOR FELONY; ORDINARY TERMS

A person who has been convicted of a felony may be sentenced to imprisonment, as follows:

(1) in the case of a felony of the first degree, for a term the minimum of which shall be fixed by the Court at not less than one year nor more than ten years, and the maximum at not more than twenty years or at life imprisonment;

(2) in the case of a felony of the second degree, for a term the minimum of which shall be fixed by the Court at not less than one year nor more than three years, and the maximum at not more than ten years;

(3) in the case of a felony of the third degree, for a term the minimum of which shall be fixed by the Court at not less than one year nor more than two years, and the maximum at not more than five years.

No sentence shall be imposed under this Section of which the minimum is longer than one-half the maximum, or, when the maximum is life imprisonment, longer than ten years.

SECTION 6.07. [*Omitted*]

SECTION 6.08. SENTENCE OF IMPRISONMENT FOR MISDEMEANORS AND PETTY MISDEMEANORS; ORDINARY TERMS

A person who has been convicted of a misdemeanor or a petty misdemeanor may be sentenced to imprisonment for a definite term which shall be fixed by the Court and shall not exceed one year in the case of a misdemeanor or thirty days in the case of a petty misdemeanor.

SECTIONS 6.09.–6.11. [*Omitted*]

SECTION 6.12. REDUCTION OF CONVICTION BY COURT TO LESSER DEGREE OF FELONY OR TO MISDEMEANOR

If, when a person has been convicted of a felony, the Court, having regard to the nature and circumstances of the crime and to the history and character of the defendant, is of the view that it would be unduly harsh to sentence the offender in accordance with the Code, the Court may enter judgment of conviction for a lesser degree of felony or for a misdemeanor and impose sentence accordingly.

SECTION 6.13. [*Omitted*]

Article 7. Authority of Court in Sentencing [*Omitted*]
PART II. DEFINITION OF SPECIFIC CRIMES
OFFENSES INVOLVING DANGER TO THE PERSON
Article 210. Criminal Homicide

SECTION 210.0. DEFINITIONS

In Articles 210–213, unless a different meaning plainly is required:

(1) "human being" means a person who has been born and is alive;

(2) "bodily injury" means physical pain, illness or any impairment of physical condition;

(3) "serious bodily injury" means bodily injury which creates a substantial risk of death or which causes serious, permanent disfigurement, or protracted loss or impairment of the function of any bodily member or organ;

(4) "deadly weapon" means any firearm or other weapon, device, instrument, material or substance, whether animate or inanimate, which in the manner it is used or is intended to be used is known to be capable of producing death or serious bodily injury.

SECTION 210.1.   CRIMINAL HOMICIDE

(1) A person is guilty of criminal homicide if he purposely, knowingly, recklessly or negligently causes the death of another human being.

(2) Criminal homicide is murder, manslaughter or negligent homicide.

SECTION 210.2.   MURDER

(1) Except as provided in Section 210.3(1)(b), criminal homicide constitutes murder when:

　　(a) it is committed purposely or knowingly; or

　　(b) it is committed recklessly under circumstances manifesting extreme indifference to the value of human life. Such recklessness and indifference are presumed if the actor is engaged or is an accomplice in the commission of, or an attempt to commit, or flight after committing or attempting to commit robbery, rape or deviate sexual intercourse by force or threat of force, arson, burglary, kidnapping or felonious escape.

felony murder rule

(2) Murder is a felony of the first degree [but a person convicted of murder may be sentenced to death, as provided in Section 210.6].

SECTION 210.3.   MANSLAUGHTER

(1) Criminal homicide constitutes manslaughter when:

　　(a) it is committed recklessly; or

　　(b) a homicide which would otherwise be murder is committed under the influence of extreme mental or emotional disturbance for which there is reasonable explanation or excuse. The reasonableness of such explanation or excuse shall be determined from the viewpoint of a person in the actor's situation under the circumstances as he believes them to be.

EMED

(2) Manslaughter is a felony of the second degree.

SECTION 210.4.   NEGLIGENT HOMICIDE

(1) Criminal homicide constitutes negligent homicide when it is committed negligently.

(2) Negligent homicide is a felony of the third degree.

Section 210.5.   Causing or Aiding Suicide

(1) *Causing Suicide as Criminal Homicide.* A person may be convicted of criminal homicide for causing another to commit suicide only if he purposely causes such suicide by force, duress or deception.

(2) *Aiding or Soliciting Suicide as an Independent Offense.* A person who purposely aids or solicits another to commit suicide is guilty of a felony of the second degree if his conduct causes such suicide or an attempted suicide, and otherwise of a misdemeanor.

[Section 210.6.   Sentence of Death for Murder; Further Proceedings to Determine Sentence*

(1) *Death Sentence Excluded.* When a defendant is found guilty of murder, the Court shall impose sentence for a felony of the first degree if it is satisfied that:

(a) none of the aggravating circumstances enumerated in Subsection (3) of this Section was established by the evidence at the trial or will be established if further proceedings are initiated under Subsection (2) of this Section; or

(b) substantial mitigating circumstances, established by the evidence at the trial, call for leniency; or

(c) the defendant, with the consent of the prosecuting attorney and the approval of the Court, pleaded guilty to murder as a felony of the first degree; or

(d) the defendant was under 18 years of age at the time of the commission of the crime; or

(e) the defendant's physical or mental condition calls for leniency; or

(f) although the evidence suffices to sustain the verdict, it does not foreclose all doubt respecting the defendant's guilt.

(2) *Determination by Court or by Court and Jury.* Unless the Court imposes sentence under Subsection (1) of this Section, it shall conduct a separate proceeding to determine whether the defendant should be sentenced for a felony of the first degree or sentenced to death. The proceeding shall be conducted before the Court alone if the defendant was convicted by a Court sitting without a jury or upon his plea of guilty or if the prosecuting attorney and the defendant waive a jury with respect to sentence. In other cases it shall be conducted before the Court sitting with the jury which determined the defendant's guilt or, if the Court for good cause shown discharges that jury, with a new jury empanelled for the purpose.

In the proceeding, evidence may be presented as to any matter that the Court deems relevant to sentence, including but not limited to the nature and circumstances of the crime, the defendant's character, background, history, mental and physical condition and any of the aggravating or mitigating circumstances enumerated in Subsections (3) and (4) of this Section. Any such evidence, not legally privileged, which the Court deems to have probative

---

* The American Law Institute in 2009 withdrew this section of the Code. See p. 339, footnote *i*.

force, may be received, regardless of its admissibility under the exclusionary rules of evidence, provided that the defendant's counsel is accorded a fair opportunity to rebut such evidence. The prosecuting attorney and the defendant or his counsel shall be permitted to present argument for or against sentence of death.

The determination whether sentence of death shall be imposed shall be in the discretion of the Court, except that when the proceeding is conducted before the Court sitting with a jury, the Court shall not impose sentence of death unless it submits to the jury the issue whether the defendant should be sentenced to death or to imprisonment and the jury returns a verdict that the sentence should be death. If the jury is unable to reach a unanimous verdict, the Court shall dismiss the jury and impose sentence for a felony of the first degree.

The Court, in exercising its discretion as to sentence, and the jury, in determining upon its verdict, shall take into account the aggravating and mitigating circumstances enumerated in Subsections (3) and (4) and any other facts that it deems relevant, but it shall not impose or recommend sentence of death unless it finds one of the aggravating circumstances enumerated in Subsection (3) and further finds that there are no mitigating circumstances sufficiently substantial to call for leniency. When the issue is submitted to the jury, the Court shall so instruct and also shall inform the jury of the nature of the sentence of imprisonment that may be imposed, including its implication with respect to possible release upon parole, if the jury verdict is against sentence of death.

Alternative formulation of Subsection (2):

(2) *Determination by Court.* Unless the Court imposes sentence under Subsection (1) of this Section, it shall conduct a separate proceeding to determine whether the defendant should be sentenced for a felony of the first degree or sentenced to death. In the proceeding, the Court, in accordance with Section 7.07 [relating to procedures on sentence], shall consider the report of the presentence investigation and, if a psychiatric examination has been ordered, the report of such examination. In addition, evidence may be presented as to any matter that the Court deems relevant to sentence, including but not limited to the nature and circumstances of the crime, the defendant's character, background, history, mental and physical condition and any of the aggravating or mitigating circumstances enumerated in Subsections (3) and (4) of this Section. Any such evidence, not legally privileged, which the Court deems to have probative force, may be received, regardless of its admissibility under the exclusionary rules of evidence, provided that the defendant's counsel is accorded a fair opportunity to rebut such evidence. The prosecuting attorney and the defendant or his counsel shall be permitted to present argument for or against sentence of death.

The determination whether sentence of death shall be imposed shall be in the discretion of the Court. In exercising such discretion, the Court shall take into account the aggravating and mitigating circumstances enumerated in Subsections (3) and (4) and any other facts that it deems relevant but shall not impose sentence of death unless it finds one of the aggravating circumstances enumerated in Subsection (3) and further finds that there are no mitigating circumstances sufficiently substantial to call for leniency.

(3) *Aggravating Circumstances.*

(a) The murder was committed by a convict under sentence of imprisonment.

(b) The defendant was previously convicted of another murder or of a felony involving the use or threat of violence to the person.

(c) At the time the murder was committed the defendant also committed another murder.

(d) The defendant knowingly created a great risk of death to many persons.

(e) The murder was committed while the defendant was engaged or was an accomplice in the commission of, or an attempt to commit, or flight after committing or attempting to commit robbery, rape or deviate sexual intercourse by force or threat of force, arson, burglary or kidnapping.

(f) The murder was committed for the purpose of avoiding or preventing a lawful arrest or effecting an escape from lawful custody.

(g) The murder was committed for pecuniary gain.

(h) The murder was especially heinous, atrocious or cruel, manifesting exceptional depravity.

(4) *Mitigating Circumstances.*

(a) The defendant has no significant history of prior criminal activity.

(b) The murder was committed while the defendant was under the influence of extreme mental or emotional disturbance.

(c) The victim was a participant in the defendant's homicidal conduct or consented to the homicidal act.

(d) The murder was committed under circumstances which the defendant believed to provide a moral justification or extenuation for his conduct.

(e) The defendant was an accomplice in a murder committed by another person and his participation in the homicidal act was relatively minor.

(f) The defendant acted under duress or under the domination of another person.

(g) At the time of the murder, the capacity of the defendant to appreciate the criminality [wrongfulness] of his conduct or to conform his conduct to the requirements of law was impaired as a result of mental disease or defect or intoxication.

(h) The youth of the defendant at the time of the crime.]

Article 211. Assault; Reckless Endangering; Threats

SECTION 211.0. DEFINITIONS

In this Article, the definitions given in Section 210.0 apply unless a different meaning plainly is required.

SECTION 211.1. ASSAULT

(1) *Simple Assault.* A person is guilty of assault if he:

(a) attempts to cause or purposely, knowingly or recklessly causes bodily injury to another; or

(b) negligently causes bodily injury to another with a deadly weapon; or

(c) attempts by physical menace to put another in fear of imminent serious bodily injury.

Simple assault is a misdemeanor unless committed in a fight or scuffle entered into by mutual consent, in which case it is a petty misdemeanor.

(2) *Aggravated Assault.* A person is guilty of aggravated assault if he:

(a) attempts to cause serious bodily injury to another, or causes such injury purposely, knowingly or recklessly under circumstances manifesting extreme indifference to the value of human life; or

(b) attempts to cause or purposely or knowingly causes bodily injury to another with a deadly weapon.

Aggravated assault under paragraph (a) is a felony of the second degree; aggravated assault under paragraph (b) is a felony of the third degree.

SECTION 211.2. RECKLESSLY ENDANGERING ANOTHER PERSON

A person commits a misdemeanor if he recklessly engages in conduct which places or may place another person in danger of death or serious bodily injury. Recklessness and danger shall be presumed where a person knowingly points a firearm at or in the direction of another, whether or not the actor believed the firearm to be loaded.

SECTION 211.3. TERRORISTIC THREATS

A person is guilty of a felony of the third degree if he threatens to commit any crime of violence with purpose to terrorize another or to cause evacuation of a building, place of assembly, or facility of public transportation, or otherwise to cause serious public inconvenience, or in reckless disregard of the risk of causing such terror or inconvenience.

Article 212. Kidnapping and Related Offenses; Coercion

SECTION 212.0. DEFINITIONS

In this Article, the definitions given in section 210.0 apply unless a different meaning plainly is required.

SECTION 212.1. KIDNAPPING

A person is guilty of kidnapping if he unlawfully removes another from his place of residence or business, or a substantial distance from the vicinity where he is found, or if he unlawfully confines another for a substantial period in a place of isolation, with any of the following purposes:

(a) to hold for ransom or reward, or as a shield or hostage; or

(b) to facilitate commission of any felony or flight thereafter; or

(c) to inflict bodily injury on or to terrorize the victim or another; or

(d) to interfere with the performance of any governmental or political function.

Kidnapping is a felony of the first degree unless the actor voluntarily releases the victim alive and in a safe place prior to trial, in which case it is a felony of the second degree. A removal or confinement is unlawful within the meaning of this Section if it is accomplished by force, threat or deception, or, in the case of a person who is under the age of 14 or incompetent, if it is accomplished without the consent of a parent, guardian or other person responsible for general supervision of his welfare.

SECTION 212.2. FELONIOUS RESTRAINT

A person commits a felony of the third degree if he knowingly:

(a) restrains another unlawfully in circumstances exposing him to risk of serious bodily injury; or

(b) holds another in a condition of involuntary servitude.

SECTION 212.3. FALSE IMPRISONMENT

A person commits a misdemeanor if he knowingly restrains another unlawfully so as to interfere substantially with his liberty.

SECTION 212.4. INTERFERENCE WITH CUSTODY

(1) *Custody of Children.* A person commits an offense if he knowingly or recklessly takes or entices any child under the age of 18 from the custody of its parent, guardian or other lawful custodian, when he has no privilege to do so. It is an affirmative defense that:

(a) the actor believed that his action was necessary to preserve the child from danger to its welfare; or

(b) the child, being at the time not less than 14 years old, was taken away at its own instigation without enticement and without purpose to commit a criminal offense with or against the child.

Proof that the child was below the critical age gives rise to a presumption that the actor knew the child's age or acted in reckless disregard thereof. The offense is a misdemeanor unless the actor, not being a parent or person in equivalent relation to the child, acted with knowledge that his conduct would cause serious alarm for the child's safety, or in reckless disregard of a likelihood of causing such alarm, in which case the offense is a felony of the third degree.

(2) *Custody of Committed Persons.* A person is guilty of a misdemeanor if he knowingly or recklessly takes or entices any committed person away from lawful custody when he is not privileged to do so. "Committed person" means,

in addition to anyone committed under judicial warrant, any orphan, neglected or delinquent child, mentally defective or insane person, or other dependent or incompetent person entrusted to another's custody by or through a recognized social agency or otherwise by authority of law.

SECTION 212.5. CRIMINAL COERCION

(1) *Offense Defined.* A person is guilty of criminal coercion if, with purpose unlawfully to restrict another's freedom of action to his detriment, he threatens to:

(a) commit any criminal offense; or

(b) accuse anyone of a criminal offense; or

(c) expose any secret tending to subject any person to hatred, contempt or ridicule, or to impair his credit or business repute; or

(d) take or withhold action as an official, or cause an official to take or withhold action.

It is an affirmative defense to prosecution based on paragraphs (b), (c) or (d) that the actor believed the accusation or secret to be true or the proposed official action justified and that his purpose was limited to compelling the other to behave in a way reasonably related to the circumstances which were the subject of the accusation, exposure or proposed official action, as by desisting from further misbehavior, making good a wrong done, refraining from taking any action or responsibility for which the actor believes the other disqualified.

(2) *Grading.* Criminal coercion is a misdemeanor unless the threat is to commit a felony or the actor's purpose is felonious, in which cases the offense is a felony of the third degree.

Article 213. Sexual Offenses

SECTION 213.0. DEFINITIONS

In this Article, unless a different meaning plainly is required:

(1) the definitions given in Section 210.0 apply;

(2) "Sexual intercourse" includes intercourse per os or per anum, with some penetration however slight; emission is not required;

(3) "Deviate sexual intercourse" means sexual intercourse per os or per anum between human beings who are not husband and wife, and any form of sexual intercourse with an animal.

SECTION 213.1. RAPE AND RELATED OFFENSES

(1) *Rape.* A male who has sexual intercourse with a female not his wife is guilty of rape if:

(a) he compels her to submit by force or by threat of imminent death, serious bodily injury, extreme pain or kidnapping, to be inflicted on anyone; or

(b) he has substantially impaired her power to appraise or control her conduct by administering or employing without her knowledge drugs, intoxicants or other means for the purpose of preventing resistance; or

(c) the female is unconscious; or

(d) the female is less than 10 years old.

Rape is a felony of the second degree unless (i) in the course thereof the actor inflicts serious bodily injury upon anyone, or (ii) the victim was not a voluntary social companion of the actor upon the occasion of the crime and had not previously permitted him sexual liberties, in which cases the offense is a felony of the first degree.

(2) *Gross Sexual Imposition.* A male who has sexual intercourse with a female not his wife commits a felony of the third degree if:

(a) he compels her to submit by any threat that would prevent resistance by a woman of ordinary resolution; or

(b) he knows that she suffers from a mental disease or defect which renders her incapable of appraising the nature of her conduct; or

(c) he knows that she is unaware that a sexual act is being committed upon her or that she submits because she mistakenly supposes that he is her husband.

SECTION 213.2.　DEVIATE SEXUAL INTERCOURSE BY FORCE OR IMPOSITION

(1) *By Force or Its Equivalent.* A person who engages in deviate sexual intercourse with another person, or who causes another to engage in deviate sexual intercourse, commits a felony of the second degree if:

(a) he compels the other person to participate by force or by threat of imminent death, serious bodily injury, extreme pain or kidnapping, to be inflicted on anyone; or

(b) he has substantially impaired the other person's power to appraise or control his conduct, by administering or employing without the knowledge of the other person drugs, intoxicants or other means for the purpose of preventing resistance; or

(c) the other person is unconscious; or

(d) the other person is less than 10 years old.

(2) *By Other Imposition.* A person who engages in deviate sexual intercourse with another person, or who causes another to engage in deviate sexual intercourse, commits a felony of the third degree if:

(a) he compels the other person to participate by any threat that would prevent resistance by a person of ordinary resolution; or

(b) he knows that the other person suffers from a mental disease or defect which renders him incapable of appraising the nature of his conduct; or

(c) he knows that the other person submits because he is unaware that a sexual act is being committed upon him.

SECTION 213.3.　CORRUPTION OF MINORS AND SEDUCTION

(1) *Offense Defined.* A male who has sexual intercourse with a female not his wife, or any person who engages in deviate sexual intercourse or causes another to engage in deviate sexual intercourse, is guilty of an offense if:

(a) the other person is less than [16] years old and the actor is at least [four] years older than the other person; or

(b) the other person is less than 21 years old and the actor is his guardian or otherwise responsible for general supervision of his welfare; or

(c) the other person is in custody of law or detained in a hospital or other institution and the actor has supervisory or disciplinary authority over him; or

(d) the other person is a female who is induced to participate by a promise of marriage which the actor does not mean to perform.

(2) *Grading.* An offense under paragraph (a) of Subsection (1) is a felony of the third degree. Otherwise an offense under this section is a misdemeanor.

SECTION 213.4. SEXUAL ASSAULT

A person who has sexual contact with another not his spouse, or causes such other to have sexual conduct with him, is guilty of sexual assault, a misdemeanor, if:

(1) he knows that the contact is offensive to the other person; or

(2) he knows that the other person suffers from a mental disease or defect which renders him or her incapable of appraising the nature of his or her conduct; or

(3) he knows that the other person is unaware that a sexual act is being committed; or

(4) the other person is less than 10 years old; or

(5) he has substantially impaired the other person's power to appraise or control his or her conduct, by administering or employing without the other's knowledge drugs, intoxicants or other means for the purpose of preventing resistance; or

(6) the other person is less than [16] years old and the actor is at least [four] years older than the other person; or

(7) the other person is less than 21 years old and the actor is his guardian or otherwise responsible for general supervision of his welfare; or

(8) the other person is in custody of law or detained in a hospital or other institution and the actor has supervisory or disciplinary authority over him.

Sexual contact is any touching of the sexual or other intimate parts of the person for the purpose of arousing or gratifying sexual desire.

SECTION 213.5. INDECENT EXPOSURE

A person commits a misdemeanor if, for the purpose of arousing or gratifying sexual desire of himself or of any person other than his spouse, he exposes his genitals under circumstances in which he knows his conduct is likely to cause affront or alarm.

SECTION 213.6.   PROVISIONS GENERALLY APPLICABLE TO ARTICLE 213

(1) *Mistake as to Age.* Whenever in this Article the criminality of conduct depends on a child's being below the age of 10, it is no defense that the actor did not know the child's age, or reasonably believed the child to be older than 10. When criminality depends on the child's being below a critical age other than 10, it is a defense for the actor to prove by a preponderance of the evidence that he reasonably believed the child to be above the critical age.

(2) *Spouse Relationships.* Whenever in this Article the definition of an offense excludes conduct with a spouse, the exclusion shall be deemed to extend to persons living as man and wife, regardless of the legal status of their relationship. The exclusion shall be inoperative as respects spouses living apart under a decree of judicial separation. Where the definition of an offense excludes conduct with a spouse or conduct by a woman, this shall not preclude conviction of a spouse or woman as accomplice in a sexual act which he or she causes another person, not within the exclusion, to perform.

(3) *Sexually Promiscuous Complainants.* It is a defense to prosecution under Section 213.3, and paragraphs (6), (7) and (8) of Section 213.4 for the actor to prove by a preponderance of the evidence that the alleged victim had, prior to the time of the offense charged, engaged promiscuously in sexual relations with others.

(4) *Prompt Complaint.* No prosecution may be instituted or maintained under this Article unless the alleged offense was brought to the notice of public authority within [3] months of its occurrence or, where the alleged victim was less than [16] years old or otherwise incompetent to make complaint, within [3] months after a parent, guardian or other competent person specially interested in the victim learns of the offense.

(5) *Testimony of Complainants.* No person shall be convicted of any felony under this Article upon the uncorroborated testimony of the alleged victim. Corroboration may be circumstantial. In any prosecution before a jury for an offense under this Article, the jury shall be instructed to evaluate the testimony of a victim or complaining witness with special care in view of the emotional involvement of the witness and the difficulty of determining the truth with respect to alleged sexual activities carried out in private.

OFFENSES AGAINST PROPERTY

Article 220. Arson, Criminal Mischief, and Other Property Destruction

SECTION 220.1.   ARSON AND RELATED OFFENSES

(1) *Arson.* A person is guilty of arson, a felony of the second degree, if he starts a fire or causes an explosion with the purpose of:

(a) destroying a building or occupied structure of another; or

(b) destroying or damaging any property, whether his own or another's, to collect insurance for such loss. It shall be an affirmative defense to prosecution under this paragraph that the actor's conduct did not recklessly endanger any building or occupied structure of another or place any other person in danger of death or bodily injury.

(2) *Reckless Burning or Exploding.* A person commits a felony of the third degree if he purposely starts a fire or causes an explosion, whether on his own property or another's, and thereby recklessly:

(a) places another person in danger of death or bodily injury; or

(b) places a building or occupied structure of another in danger of damage or destruction.

(3) *Failure to Control or Report Dangerous Fire.* A person who knows that a fire is endangering life or a substantial amount of property of another and fails to take reasonable measures to put out or control the fire, when he can do so without substantial risk to himself, or to give a prompt fire alarm, commits a misdemeanor if:

(a) he knows that he is under an official, contractual, or other legal duty to prevent or combat the fire; or

(b) the fire was started, albeit lawfully, by him or with his assent, or on property in his custody or control.

(4) *Definitions.* "Occupied structure" means any structure, vehicle or place adapted for overnight accommodation of persons, or for carrying on business therein, whether or not a person is actually present. Property is that of another, for the purposes of this section, if anyone other than the actor has a possessory or proprietary interest therein. If a building or structure is divided into separately occupied units, any unit not occupied by the actor is an occupied structure of another.

SECTION 220.2. CAUSING OR RISKING CATASTROPHE

(1) *Causing Catastrophe.* A person who causes a catastrophe by explosion, fire, flood, avalanche, collapse of building, release of poison gas, radioactive material or other harmful or destructive force or substance, or by any other means of causing potentially widespread injury or damage, commits a felony of the second degree if he does so purposely or knowingly, or a felony of the third degree if he does so recklessly.

(2) *Risking Catastrophe.* A person is guilty of a misdemeanor if he recklessly creates a risk of catastrophe in the employment of fire, explosives or other dangerous means listed in Subsection (1).

(3) *Failure to Prevent Catastrophe.* A person who knowingly or recklessly fails to take reasonable measures to prevent or mitigate a catastrophe commits a misdemeanor if:

(a) he knows that he is under an official, contractual or other legal duty to take such measures; or

(b) he did or assented to the act causing or threatening the catastrophe.

SECTION 220.3. CRIMINAL MISCHIEF

(1) *Offense Defined.* A person is guilty of criminal mischief if he:

(a) damages tangible property of another purposely, recklessly, or by negligence in the employment of fire, explosives, or other dangerous means listed in Section 220.2(1); or

(b) purposely or recklessly tampers with tangible property of another so as to endanger persons or property; or

(c) purposely or recklessly causes another to suffer pecuniary loss by deception or threat.

(2) *Grading.* Criminal mischief is a felony of the third degree if the actor purposely causes pecuniary loss in excess of $5,000 or a substantial interruption or impairment of public communication, transportation, supply of water, gas or power, or other public service. It is a misdemeanor if the actor purposely causes pecuniary loss in excess of $100, or a petty misdemeanor if he purposely or recklessly causes pecuniary loss in excess of $25. Otherwise criminal mischief is a violation.

Article 221. Burglary and Other Criminal Intrusion

SECTION 221.0. DEFINITIONS

In this Article, unless a different meaning plainly is required:

(1) "occupied structure" means any structure, vehicle or place adapted for overnight accommodation of persons, or for carrying on business therein, whether or not a person is actually present.

(2) "night" means the period between thirty minutes past sunset and thirty minutes before sunrise.

SECTION 221.1. BURGLARY

(1) *Burglary Defined.* A person is guilty of burglary if he enters a building or occupied structure, or separately secured or occupied portion thereof, with purpose to commit a crime therein, unless the premises are at the time open to the public or the actor is licensed or privileged to enter. It is an affirmative defense to prosecution for burglary that the building or structure was abandoned.

(2) *Grading.* Burglary is a felony of the second degree if it is perpetrated in the dwelling of another at night, or if, in the course of committing the offense, the actor:

(a) purposely, knowingly or recklessly inflicts or attempts to inflict bodily injury on anyone; or

(b) is armed with explosives or a deadly weapon.

Otherwise, burglary is a felony of the third degree. An act shall be deemed "in the course of committing" an offense if it occurs in an attempt to commit the offense or in flight after the attempt or commission.

(3) *Multiple Convictions.* A person may not be convicted both for burglary and for the offense which it was his purpose to commit after the burglarious entry or for an attempt to commit that offense, unless the additional offense constitutes a felony of the first or second degree.

SECTION 221.2. CRIMINAL TRESPASS

(1) *Buildings and Occupied Structures.* A person commits an offense if, knowing that he is not licensed or privileged to do so, he enters or surreptitiously remains in any building or occupied structure, or separately secured or

occupied portion thereof. An offense under this Subsection is a misdemeanor if it is committed in a dwelling at night. Otherwise it is a petty misdemeanor.

(2) *Defiant Trespasser.* A person commits an offense if, knowing that he is not licensed or privileged to do so, he enters or remains in any place as to which notice against trespass is given by:

(a) actual communication to the actor; or

(b) posting in a manner prescribed by law or reasonably likely to come to the attention of intruders; or

(c) fencing or other enclosure manifestly designed to exclude intruders.

An offense under this Subsection constitutes a petty misdemeanor if the offender defies an order to leave personally communicated to him by the owner of the premises or other authorized person. Otherwise it is a violation.

(3) *Defenses.* It is an affirmative defense to prosecution under this Section that:

(a) a building or occupied structure involved in an offense under Subsection (1) was abandoned; or

(b) the premises were at the time open to members of the public and the actor complied with all lawful conditions imposed on access to or remaining in the premises; or

(c) the actor reasonably believed that the owner of the premises, or other person empowered to license access thereto, would have licensed him to enter or remain.

Article 222. Robbery

SECTION 222.1. ROBBERY

(1) *Robbery Defined.* A person is guilty of robbery if, in the course of committing a theft, he:

(a) inflicts serious bodily injury upon another; or

(b) threatens another with or purposely puts him in fear of immediate serious bodily injury; or

(c) commits or threatens immediately to commit any felony of the first or second degree.

An act shall be deemed "in the course of committing a theft" if it occurs in an attempt to commit theft or in flight after the attempt or commission.

(2) *Grading.* Robbery is a felony of the second degree, except that it is a felony of the first degree if in the course of committing the theft the actor attempts to kill anyone, or purposely inflicts or attempts to inflict serious bodily injury.

Article 223. Theft and Related Offenses

SECTION 223.0. DEFINITIONS

In this Article, unless a different meaning plainly is required:

(1) "deprive" means: (a) to withhold property of another permanently or for so extended a period as to appropriate a major portion of its economic

value, or with intent to restore only upon payment of reward or other compensation; or (b) to dispose of the property so as to make it unlikely that the owner will recover it.

(2) "financial institution" means a bank, insurance company, credit union, building and loan association, investment trust or other organization held out to the public as a place of deposit of funds or medium of savings or collective investment.

(3) "government" means the United States, any State, county, municipality, or other political unit, or any department, agency or subdivision of any of the foregoing, or any corporation or other association carrying out the functions of government.

(4) "movable property" means property the location of which can be changed, including things growing on, affixed to, or found in land, and documents although the rights represented thereby have no physical location. "Immovable property" is all other property.

(5) "obtain" means: (a) in relation to property, to bring about a transfer or purported transfer of a legal interest in the property, whether to the obtainer or another; or (b) in relation to labor or service, to secure performance thereof.

(6) "property" means anything of value, including real estate, tangible and intangible personal property, contract rights, choses-in-action and other interests in or claims to wealth, admission or transportation tickets, captured or domestic animals, food and drink, electric or other power.

(7) "property of another" includes property in which any person other than the actor has an interest which the actor is not privileged to infringe, regardless of the fact that the actor also has an interest in the property and regardless of the fact that the other person might be precluded from civil recovery because the property was used in an unlawful transaction or was subject to forfeiture as contraband. Property in possession of the actor shall not be deemed property of another who has only a security interest therein, even if legal title is in the creditor pursuant to a conditional sales contract or other security agreement.

SECTION 223.1. CONSOLIDATION OF THEFT OFFENSES; GRADING; PROVISIONS APPLICABLE TO THEFT GENERALLY

(1) *Consolidation of Theft Offenses.* Conduct denominated theft in this Article constitutes a single offense. An accusation of theft may be supported by evidence that it was committed in any manner that would be theft under this Article, notwithstanding the specification of a different manner in the indictment or information, subject only to the power of the Court to ensure fair trial by granting a continuance or other appropriate relief where the conduct of the defense would be prejudiced by lack of fair notice or by surprise.

(2) *Grading of Theft Offenses.*

(a) Theft constitutes a felony of the third degree if the amount involved exceeds $500, or if the property stolen is a firearm, automobile, airplane, motorcycle, motorboat or other motor-propelled vehicle, or in the case of theft by receiving stolen property, if the receiver is in the business of buying or selling stolen property.

(b) Theft not within the preceding paragraph constitutes a misdemeanor, except that if the property was not taken from the person or by threat, or in breach of a fiduciary obligation, and the actor proves by a preponderance of the evidence that the amount involved was less than $50, the offense constitutes a petty misdemeanor.

(c) The amount involved in a theft shall be deemed to be the highest value, by any reasonable standard, of the property or services which the actor stole or attempted to steal. Amounts involved in thefts committed pursuant to one scheme or course of conduct, whether from the same person or several persons, may be aggregated in determining the grade of the offense.

(3) *Claim of Right.* It is an affirmative defense to prosecution for theft that the actor:

(a) was unaware that the property or service was that of another; or

(b) acted under an honest claim of right to the property or service involved or that he had a right to acquire or dispose of it as he did; or

(c) took property exposed for sale, intending to purchase and pay for it promptly, or reasonably believing that the owner, if present, would have consented.

(4) *Theft from Spouse.* It is no defense that theft was from the actor's spouse, except that misappropriation of household and personal effects, or other property normally accessible to both spouses, is theft only if it occurs after the parties have ceased living together.

SECTION 223.2.   THEFT BY UNLAWFUL TAKING OR DISPOSITION

(1) *Movable Property.* A person is guilty of theft if he unlawfully takes, or exercises unlawful control over, movable property of another with purpose to deprive him thereof.

(2) *Immovable property.* A person is guilty of theft if he unlawfully transfers immovable property of another or any interest therein with purpose to benefit himself or another not entitled thereto.

SECTION 223.3.   THEFT BY DECEPTION

A person is guilty of theft if he purposely obtains property of another by deception. A person deceives if he purposely:

(1) creates or reinforces a false impression, including false impressions as to law, value, intention or other state of mind; but deception as to a person's intention to perform a promise shall not be inferred from the fact alone that he did not subsequently perform the promise; or

(2) prevents another from acquiring information which would affect his judgment of a transaction; or

(3) fails to correct a false impression which the deceiver previously created or reinforced, or which the deceiver knows to be influencing another to whom he stands in a fiduciary or confidential relationship; or

(4) fails to disclose a known lien, adverse claim or other legal impediment to the enjoyment of property which he transfers or encumbers in consideration for the property obtained, whether such impediment is or is not valid, or is or is not a matter of official record.

The term "deceive" does not, however, include falsity as to matters having no pecuniary significance, or puffing by statements unlikely to deceive ordinary persons in the group addressed.

SECTION 223.4. THEFT BY EXTORTION

A person is guilty of theft if he obtains property of another by threatening to:

(1) inflict bodily injury on anyone or commit any other criminal offense; or

(2) accuse anyone of a criminal offense; or

(3) expose any secret tending to subject any person to hatred, contempt or ridicule, or to impair his credit or business repute; or

(4) take or withhold action as an official, or cause an official to take or withhold action; or

(5) bring about or continue a strike, boycott or other collective unofficial action, if the property is not demanded or received for the benefit of the group in whose interest the actor purports to act; or

(6) testify or provide information or withhold testimony or information with respect to another's legal claim or defense; or

(7) inflict any other harm which would not benefit the actor.

It is an affirmative defense to prosecution based on paragraphs (2), (3) or (4) that the property obtained by threat of accusation, exposure, lawsuit or other invocation of official action was honestly claimed as restitution or indemnification for harm done in the circumstances to which such accusation, exposure, lawsuit or other official action relates, or as compensation for property or lawful services.

SECTION 223.5. THEFT OF PROPERTY LOST, MISLAID, OR DELIVERED BY MISTAKE

A person who comes into control of property of another that he knows to have been lost, mislaid, or delivered under a mistake as to the nature or amount of the property or the identity of the recipient is guilty of theft if, with purpose to deprive the owner thereof, he fails to take reasonable measures to restore the property to a person entitled to have it.

SECTION 223.6. RECEIVING STOLEN PROPERTY

(1) *Receiving.* A person is guilty of theft if he purposely receives, retains, or disposes of movable property of another knowing that it has been stolen, or believing that it has probably been stolen, unless the property is received, retained, or disposed with purpose to restore it to the owner. "Receiving" means acquiring possession, control or title, or lending on the security of the property.

(2) *Presumption of Knowledge.* The requisite knowledge or belief is presumed in the case of a dealer who:

(a) is found in possession or control of property stolen from two or more persons on separate occasions; or

(b) has received stolen property in another transaction within the year preceding the transaction charged; or

(c) being a dealer in property of the sort received, acquires it for a consideration which he knows is far below its reasonable value.

"Dealer" means a person in the business of buying or selling goods including a pawnbroker.

SECTION 223.7.   THEFT OF SERVICES

(1) A person is guilty of theft if he purposely obtains services which he knows are available only for compensation, by deception or threat, or by false token or other means to avoid payment for the service. "Services" includes labor, professional services, transportation, telephone or other public service, accommodation in hotels, restaurants or elsewhere, admission to exhibitions, use of vehicles or other movable property. Where compensation for service is ordinarily paid immediately upon the rendering for such service, as is the case of hotels and restaurants, refusal to pay or absconding without payment or offer to pay gives rise to a presumption that the service was obtained by deception as to intention to pay.

(2) A person commits theft if, having control over the disposition of services of others, to which he is not entitled, he knowingly diverts such services to his own benefit or to the benefit of another not entitled thereto.

SECTION 223.8.   [*Omitted*]

SECTION 223.9.   UNAUTHORIZED USE OF AUTOMOBILES AND OTHER VEHICLES

A person commits a misdemeanor if he operates another's automobile, airplane, motorcycle, motorboat, or other motor propelled vehicle without consent of the owner. It is an affirmative defense to prosecution under this Section that the actor reasonably believed that the owner would have consented to the operation had he known of it.

Article 224. Forgery and Fraudulent Practices

SECTION 224.0.   DEFINITIONS

In this Article, the definitions given in Section 223.0 apply unless a different meaning plainly is required.

SECTION 224.1. FORGERY

(1) *Definition.* A person is guilty of forgery if, with purpose to defraud or injure anyone, or with knowledge that he is facilitating a fraud or injury to be perpetrated by anyone, the actor:

(a) alters any writing of another without his authority; or

(b) makes, completes, executes, authenticates, issues or transfers any writing so that it purports to be the act of another who did not authorize that act, or to have been executed at a time or place or in a numbered sequence other than was in fact the case, or to be a copy of an original when no such original existed; or

(c) utters any writing which he knows to be forged in a manner specified in paragraphs (a) or (b).

"Writing" includes printing or any other method of recording information, money, coins, tokens, stamps, seals, credit cards, badges, trade-marks, and other symbols of value, right, privilege, or identification.

(2) *Grading.* Forgery is a felony of the second degree if the writing is or purports to be part of an issue of money, securities, postage or revenue stamps, or other instruments issued by the government, or part of an issue of stock, bonds or other instruments representing interests in or claims against any property or enterprise. Forgery is a felony of the third degree if the writing is or purports to be a will, deed, contract, release, commercial instrument, or other document evidencing, creating, transferring, altering, terminating, or otherwise affecting legal relations. Otherwise forgery is a misdemeanor.

Sections 224.2.–224.4. [*Omitted*]

Section 224.5. Bad Checks

A person who issues or passes a check or similar sight order for the payment of money, knowing that it will not be honored by the drawee, commits a misdemeanor. For the purposes of this Section as well as in any prosecutions for theft committed by means of a bad check, an issuer is presumed to know that the check or order (other than a postdated check or order) would not be paid if:

(1) the issuer had no account with the drawee at the time the check or order was issued; or

(2) payment was refused by the drawee for lack of funds, upon presentation within 30 days after issue, and the issuer failed to make good within 10 days after receiving notice of that refusal.

Section 224.6. Credit Cards

A person commits an offense if he uses a credit card for the purpose of obtaining property or services with knowledge that:

(1) the card is stolen or forged;

(2) the card has been revoked or cancelled; or

(3) for any other reason his use of the card is unauthorized by the issuer.

It is an affirmative defense to prosecution under paragraph (3) if the actor proves by a preponderance of the evidence that he had the purpose and ability to meet all obligations to the issuer arising out of his use of the card. "Credit card" means a writing, or other evidence of an undertaking to pay for property or services delivered or rendered to or upon the order of a designated person or bearer. An offense under this Section is a felony of the third degree if the value of the property or services secured or sought to be secured by means of the credit card exceeds $500; otherwise it is a misdemeanor.

SECTIONS 224.7.–224.14.   [Omitted]

OFFENSES AGAINST THE FAMILY

Article 230. Offenses Against the Family

SECTION 230.1.   BIGAMY AND POLYGAMY

(1) *Bigamy.* A married person is guilty of bigamy, a misdemeanor, if he contracts or purports to contract another marriage, unless at the time of the subsequent marriage:

   (a) the actor believes that the prior spouse is dead; or

   (b) the actor and the prior spouse have been living apart for five consecutive years throughout which the prior spouse was not known by the actor to be alive; or

   (c) a Court has entered a judgment purporting to terminate or annul any prior disqualifying marriage, and the actor does not know that judgment to be invalid; or

   (d) the actor reasonably believes that he is legally eligible to remarry.

(2) *Polygamy.* A person is guilty of polygamy, a felony of the third degree, if he marries or cohabits with more than one spouse at a time in purported exercise of the right of plural marriage. The offense is a continuing one until all cohabitation and claim of marriage with more than one spouse terminates. This section does not apply to parties to a polygamous marriage, lawful in the country of which they are residents or nationals, while they are in transit through or temporarily visiting this State.

(3) *Other Party to Bigamous or Polygamous Marriage.* A person is guilty of bigamy or polygamy, as the case may be, if he contracts or purports to contract marriage with another knowing that the other is thereby committing bigamy or polygamy.

SECTION 230.2.   INCEST

A person is guilty of incest, a felony of the third degree, if he knowingly marries or cohabits or has sexual intercourse with an ancestor or descendant, a brother or sister of the whole or half blood [or an uncle, aunt, nephew or niece of the whole blood]. "Cohabit" means to live together under the representation or appearance of being married. The relationships referred to herein include blood relationships without regard to legitimacy, and relationship of parent and child by adoption.

SECTION 230.3.   [Omitted]

SECTION 230.4.   ENDANGERING WELFARE OF CHILDREN

A parent, guardian, or other person supervising the welfare of a child under 18 commits a misdemeanor if he knowingly endangers the child's welfare by violating a duty of care, protection or support.

SECTION 230.5.   PERSISTENT NON-SUPPORT

A person commits a misdemeanor if he persistently fails to provide support which he can provide and which he knows he is legally obliged to provide to a spouse, child or other dependent.

OFFENSES AGAINST PUBLIC ADMINISTRATION

Article 240. Bribery and Corrupt Influence

SECTION 240.0. DEFINITIONS

In Articles 240–243, unless a different meaning plainly is required:

(1) "benefit" means gain or advantage, or anything regarded by the beneficiary as gain or advantage, including benefit to any other person or entity in whose welfare he is interested, but not an advantage promised generally to a group or class of voters as a consequence of public measures which a candidate engages to support or oppose;

(2) "government" includes any branch, subdivision or agency of the government of the State or any locality within it;

(3) "harm" means loss, disadvantage or injury, or anything so regarded by the person affected, including loss, disadvantage or injury to any other person or entity in whose welfare he is interested;

(4) "official proceeding" means a proceeding heard or which may be heard before any legislative, judicial, administrative or other governmental agency or official authorized to take evidence under oath, including any referee, hearing examiner, commissioner, notary or other person taking testimony or deposition in connection with any such proceeding;

(5) "party official" means a person who holds an elective or appointive post in a political party in the United States by virtue of which he directs or conducts, or participates in directing or conducting party affairs at any level of responsibility;

(6) "pecuniary benefit" is benefit in the form of money, property, commercial interests or anything else the primary significance of which is economic gain;

(7) "public servant" means any officer or employee of government, including legislators and judges, and any person participating as juror, advisor, consultant or otherwise, in performing a governmental function; but the term does not include witnesses;

(8) "administrative proceeding" means any proceeding, other than a judicial proceeding, the outcome of which is required to be based on a record or documentation prescribed by law, or in which law or regulation is particularized in application to individuals.

SECTION 240.1. BRIBERY IN OFFICIAL AND POLITICAL MATTERS

A person is guilty of bribery, a felony of the third degree, if he offers, confers or agrees to confer upon another, or solicits, accepts or agrees to accept from another:

(1) any pecuniary benefit as consideration for the recipient's decision, opinion, recommendation, vote or other exercise of discretion as a public servant, party official or voter; or

(2) any benefit as consideration for the recipient's decision, vote, recommendation or other exercise of official discretion in a judicial or administrative proceeding; or

(3) any benefit as consideration for a violation of a known legal duty as public servant or party official.

It is no defense to prosecution under this Section that a person whom the actor sought to influence was not qualified to act in the desired way whether because he had not yet assumed office, or lacked jurisdiction, or for any other reason.

SECTIONS 240.2.–240.7. *[Omitted]*

Article 241. Perjury and Other Falsification in Official Matters

SECTION 241.0. DEFINITIONS

In this Article, unless a different meaning plainly is required:

(1) the definitions give in Section 240.0 apply; and

(2) "statement" means any representation, but includes a representation of opinion, belief or other state of mind only if the representation clearly relates to state of mind apart from or in addition to any facts which are the subject of the representation.

SECTION 241.1. PERJURY

(1) *Offense Defined.* A person is guilty of perjury, a felony of the third degree, if in any official proceeding he makes a false statement under oath or equivalent affirmation, or swears or affirms the truth of a statement previously made, when the statement is material and he does not believe it to be true.

(2) *Materiality.* Falsification is material, regardless of the admissibility of the statement under rules of evidence, if it could have affected the course or outcome of the proceeding. It is no defense that the declarant mistakenly believed the falsification to be immaterial. Whether a falsification is material in a given factual situation is a question of law.

(3) *Irregularities No Defense.* It is not a defense to prosecution under this Section that the oath or affirmation was administered or taken in an irregular manner or that the declarant was not competent to make the statement. A document purporting to be made upon oath or affirmation at any time when the actor presents it as being so verified shall be deemed to have been duly sworn or affirmed.

(4) *Retraction.* No person shall be guilty of an offense under this Section if he retracted the falsification in the course of the proceeding in which it was made before it became manifest that the falsification was or would be exposed and before the falsification substantially affected the proceeding.

(5) *Inconsistent Statements.* When the defendant made inconsistent statements under oath or equivalent affirmation, both having been made within the period of the statute of limitations, the prosecution may proceed by setting forth the inconsistent statements in a single count alleging in the alternative that one or the other was false and not believed by the defendant. In such case it shall not be necessary for the prosecution to prove which statement was false but only that one or the other was false and not believed by the defendant to be true.

(6) *Corroboration.* No person shall be convicted of an offense under this Section where proof of falsity rests solely upon contradiction by testimony of a single person other than the defendant.

SECTIONS 241.2.–241.9. [*Omitted*]

Article 242.   Obstructing Governmental Operations; Escapes

SECTIONS 242.0.–242.1. [*Omitted*]

SECTION 242.2.   RESISTING ARREST OR OTHER LAW ENFORCEMENT

A person commits a misdemeanor if, for the purpose of preventing a public servant from effecting a lawful arrest or discharging any other duty, the person creates a substantial risk of bodily injury to the public servant or anyone else, or employs means justifying or requiring substantial force to overcome the resistance.

SECTION 242.3.   HINDERING APPREHENSION OR PROSECUTION

A person commits an offense if, with purpose to hinder the apprehension, prosecution, conviction or punishment of another for crime, he:

(1) harbors or conceals the other; or

(2) provides or aids in providing a weapon, transportation, disguise or other means of avoiding apprehension or effecting escape; or

(3) conceals or destroys evidence of the crime, or tampers with a witness, informant, document or other source of information, regardless of its admissibility in evidence; or

(4) warns the other of impending discovery or apprehension, except that this paragraph does not apply to a warning given in connection with an effort to bring another into compliance with law; or

(5) volunteers false information to a law enforcement officer.

The offense is a felony of the third degree if the conduct which the actor knows has been charged or is liable to be charged against the person aided would constitute a felony of the first or second degree. Otherwise it is a misdemeanor.

SECTIONS 242.4.–242.5. [*Omitted*]

SECTION 242.6.   ESCAPE

(1) *Escape.* A person commits an offense if he unlawfully removes himself from official detention or fails to return to official detention following temporary leave granted for a specific purpose or limited period. "Official detention" means arrest, detention in any facility for custody of persons under charge or conviction of crime or alleged or found to be delinquent, detention for extradition or deportation, or any other detention for law enforcement purposes; but "official detention" does not include supervision of probation or parole, or constraint incidental to release on bail.

(2) *Permitting or Facilitating Escape.* A public servant concerned in detention commits an offense if he knowingly or recklessly permits an escape. Any person who knowingly causes or facilitates an escape commits an offense.

(3) *Effect of Legal Irregularity in Detention.* Irregularity in bringing about or maintaining detention, or lack of jurisdiction of the committing or detaining authority, shall not be a defense to prosecution under this Section if the escape is from a prison or other custodial facility or from detention pursuant to commitment by official proceedings. In the case of other detention, irregularity or lack of jurisdiction shall be a defense only if:

(a) the escape involved no substantial risk of harm to the person or property of anyone other than the detainee; or

(b) the detaining authority did not act in good faith under color of law.

(4) *Grading of Offenses.* An offense under this Section is a felony of the third degree where:

(a) the actor was under arrest for or detained on a charge of felony or following conviction of crime; or

(b) the actor employs force, threat, deadly weapon or other dangerous instrumentality to effect the escape; or

(c) a public servant concerned in detention of persons convicted of crime purposely facilitates or permits an escape from a detention facility.

Otherwise an offense under this section is a misdemeanor.

SECTIONS 242.7.–242.8. [*Omitted*]

Article 243. Abuse of Office [*Omitted*]

OFFENSES AGAINST PUBLIC ORDER AND DECENCY

Article 250. Riot, Disorderly Conduct, and Related Offenses

SECTION 250.1. Riot; Failure to Disperse

(1) *Riot.* A person is guilty of riot, a felony of the third degree, if he participates with [two] or more others in a course of disorderly conduct:

(a) with the purpose to commit or facilitate the commission of a felony or misdemeanor;

(b) with purpose to prevent or coerce official action; or

(c) when the actor or any other participant to the knowledge of the actor uses or plans to use a firearm or other deadly weapon.

(2) *Failure of Disorderly Persons to Disperse upon Official Order.* Where [three] or more persons are participating in a course of disorderly conduct likely to cause substantial harm or serious inconvenience, annoyance or alarm, a peace officer or other public servant engaged in executing or enforcing the law may order the participants and others in the immediate vicinity to disperse. A person who refuses or knowingly fails to obey such order commits a misdemeanor.

SECTION 250.2. DISORDERLY CONDUCT

(1) *Offense Defined.* A person is guilty of disorderly conduct if, with purpose to cause public inconvenience, annoyance or alarm, or recklessly creating a risk thereof, he:

    (a) engages in fighting or threatening, or in violent or tumultuous behavior; or

    (b) makes unreasonable noise or offensively coarse utterance, gesture or display, or addresses abusive language to any person present; or

    (c) creates a hazardous or physically offensive condition by any act which serves no legitimate purpose of the actor.

"Public" means affecting or likely to affect persons in a place to which the public or a substantial group has access; among the places included are highways, transport facilities, schools, prisons, apartment houses, places of business or amusement, or any neighborhood.

(2) *Grading.* An offense under this section is a petty misdemeanor if the actor's purpose is to cause substantial harm or serious inconvenience, or if he persists in disorderly conduct after reasonable warning or request to desist. Otherwise disorderly conduct is a violation.

SECTIONS 250.3.–250.4. [*Omitted*]

SECTION 250.5. PUBLIC DRUNKENNESS; DRUG INCAPACITATION

A person is guilty of an offense if he appears in any public place manifestly under the influence of alcohol, narcotics or other drug, not therapeutically administered, to the degree that he may endanger himself or other persons or property, or annoy persons in his vicinity. An offense under this Section constitutes a petty misdemeanor if the actor has been convicted hereunder twice before within a period of one year. Otherwise the offense constitutes a violation.

SECTION 250.6. LOITERING OR PROWLING

A person commits a violation if he loiters or prowls in a place, at a time, or in a manner not usual for law-abiding individuals under circumstances that warrant alarm for the safety of persons or property in the vicinity. Among the circumstances which may be considered in determining whether such alarm is warranted is the fact that the actor takes flight upon appearance of a peace officer, refuses to identify himself, or manifestly endeavors to conceal himself or any object. Unless flight by the actor or other circumstance makes it impracticable, a peace officer shall prior to any arrest for an offense under this Section afford the actor an opportunity to dispel any alarm which would otherwise be warranted, by requesting him to identify himself and explain his presence and conduct. No person shall be convicted of an offense under this Section if the peace officer did not comply with the preceding sentence, or if it appears at trial that the explanation given by the actor was true and, if believed by the peace officer at the time, would have dispelled the alarm.

SECTIONS 250.7.–250.12. [*Omitted*]

Article 251. Public Indecency

SECTION 251.1. OPEN LEWDNESS

A person commits a petty misdemeanor if he does any lewd act which he knows is likely to be observed by others who would be affronted or alarmed.

SECTION 251.2. PROSTITUTION AND RELATED OFFENSES

(1) *Prostitution.* A person is guilty of prostitution, a petty misdemeanor, if he or she:

(a) is an inmate of a house of prostitution or otherwise engages in sexual activity as a business; or

(b) loiters in or within view of any public place for the purpose of being hired to engage in sexual activity.

"Sexual activity" includes homosexual and other deviate sexual relations. A "house of prostitution" is any place where prostitution or promotion of prostitution is regularly carried on by one person under the control, management or supervision of another. An "inmate" is a person who engages in prostitution in or through the agency of a house of prostitution. "Public place" means any place to which the public or any substantial group thereof has access.

(2) *Promoting Prostitution.* A person who knowingly promotes prostitution of another commits a misdemeanor or felony as provided in Subsection (3). The following acts shall, without limitation of the foregoing, constitute promoting prostitution:

(a) owning, controlling, managing, supervising or otherwise keeping, alone or in association with others, a house of prostitution or a prostitution business; or

(b) procuring an inmate for a house of prostitution or a place in a house of prostitution for one who would be an inmate; or

(c) encouraging, inducing, or otherwise purposely causing another to become or remain a prostitute; or

(d) soliciting a person to patronize a prostitute; or

(e) procuring a prostitute for a patron; or

(f) transporting a person into or within this state with purpose to promote that person's engaging in prostitution, or procuring or paying for transportation with that purpose; or

(g) leasing or otherwise permitting a place controlled by the actor, alone or in association with others, to be regularly used for prostitution or the promotion of prostitution, or failure to make reasonable effort to abate such use by ejecting the tenant, notifying law enforcement authorities, or other legally available means; or

(h) soliciting, receiving, or agreeing to receive any benefit for doing or agreeing to do anything forbidden by this Subsection.

(3) *Grading of Offenses Under Subsection (2).* An offense under Subsection (2) constitutes a felony of the third degree if:

> (a) the offense falls within paragraph (a), (b) or (c) of Subsection (2); or

> (b) the actor compels another to engage in or promote prostitution; or

> (c) the actor promotes prostitution of a child under 16, whether or not he is aware of the child's age; or

> (d) the actor promotes prostitution of his wife, child, ward or any person for whose care, protection or support he is responsible.

Otherwise the offense is a misdemeanor.

(4) *Presumption From Living off Prostitutes.* A person, other than the prostitute or the prostitute's minor child or other legal dependent incapable of self-support, who is supported in whole or substantial part by the proceeds of prostitution is presumed to be knowingly promoting prostitution in violation of Subsection (2).

(5) *Patronizing Prostitutes.* A person commits a violation if he hires a prostitute to engage in sexual activity with him, or if he enters or remains in a house of prostitution for the purpose of engaging in sexual activity.

(6) *Evidence.* On the issue whether a place is a house of prostitution the following shall be admissible evidence: its general repute; the repute of the persons who reside in or frequent the place; the frequency, timing and duration of visits by non-residents. Testimony of a person against his spouse shall be admissible to prove offenses under this Section.

SECTION 251.3.–251.4.   *[Omitted]*

PART III.   TREATMENT AND CORRECTION *[Omitted]*

PART IV.   ORGANIZATION OF CORRECTION *[Omitted]*

INDEX

References are to Pages

†